Y0-BZT-090

MORRIS AUTOMATED INFORMATION NETWORK

0 1021 0145515 6

ON LINE

Twentieth-Century Literary Criticism

Guide to Gale Literary Criticism Series

For criticism on	Consult these Gale series
Authors now living or who died after December 31, 1999	*CONTEMPORARY LITERARY CRITICISM (CLC)*
Authors who died between 1900 and 1999	*TWENTIETH-CENTURY LITERARY CRITICISM (TCLC)*
Authors who died between 1800 and 1899	*NINETEENTH-CENTURY LITERATURE CRITICISM (NCLC)*
Authors who died between 1400 and 1799	*LITERATURE CRITICISM FROM 1400 TO 1800 (LC)* *SHAKESPEAREAN CRITICISM (SC)*
Authors who died before 1400	*CLASSICAL AND MEDIEVAL LITERATURE CRITICISM (CMLC)*
Authors of books for children and young adults	*CHILDREN'S LITERATURE REVIEW (CLR)*
Dramatists	*DRAMA CRITICISM (DC)*
Poets	*POETRY CRITICISM (PC)*
Short story writers	*SHORT STORY CRITICISM (SSC)*
Black writers of the past two hundred years	*BLACK LITERATURE CRITICISM (BLC)* *BLACK LITERATURE CRITICISM SUPPLEMENT (BLCS)*
Hispanic writers of the late nineteenth and twentieth centuries	*HISPANIC LITERATURE CRITICISM (HLC)* *HISPANIC LITERATURE CRITICISM SUPPLEMENT (HLCS)*
Native North American writers and orators of the eighteenth, nineteenth, and twentieth centuries	*NATIVE NORTH AMERICAN LITERATURE (NNAL)*
Major authors from the Renaissance to the present	*WORLD LITERATURE CRITICISM, 1500 TO THE PRESENT (WLC)* *WORLD LITERATURE CRITICISM SUPPLEMENT (WLCS)*

ISSN 0276-8178

Volume 111

Twentieth-Century Literary Criticism

**Criticism of the
Works of Novelists, Poets, Playwrights,
Short Story Writers, and Other Creative Writers
Who Lived between 1900 and 1999,
from the First Published Critical
Appraisals to Current Evaluations**

Linda Pavlovski
Editor

Scott Darga
Assistant Editor

GALE GROUP

THOMSON LEARNING

*Detroit • New York • San Diego • San Francisco
Boston • New Haven, Conn. • Waterville, Maine
London • Munich*

STAFF

Lynn M. Spampinato, Janet Witalec, *Managing Editors, Literature Product*
Kathy D. Darrow, Ellen McGeagh, *Content-Product Liaisons*
Linda Pavlovski, *Editor*
Mark W. Scott, *Publisher, Literature Product*

Scott Darga, Ron Morelli, *Assistant Editors*
Jenny Cromie, Mary Ruby, *Technical Training Specialists*
Deborah J. Morad, Joyce Nakamura, Kathleen Lopez Nolan, *Managing Editors, Literature Content*
Susan M. Trosky, *Director, Literature Content*

Maria L. Franklin, *Permissions Manager*
Kim Davis, Debra Freitas, *Permissions Associates*

Victoria B. Cariappa, *Research Manager*
Sarah Genik, *Project Coordinator*
Tamara C. Nott, Tracie A. Richardson, *Research Associates*
Nicodemus Ford, *Research Assistant*

Dorothy Maki, *Manufacturing Manager*
Stacy L. Melson, *Buyer*

Mary Beth Trimper, *Manager, Composition and Electronic Prepress*
Gary Leach, *Composition Specialist*

Michael Logusz, *Graphic Artist*
Randy Bassett, *Imaging Supervisor*
Robert Duncan, Dan Newell, Luke Rademacher, *Imaging Specialists*
Pamela A. Reed, *Imaging Coordinator*
Kelly A. Quin, *Editor, Imaging and Multimedia Content*

Library of Congress Catalog Card Number 76-46132
ISBN 0-7876-5227-X
ISSN 0276-8178
Printed in the United States of America

10 9 8 7 6 5 4 3 2 1

Contents

Preface vii

Acknowledgments xi

Literary Criticism Series Advisory Board xiii

Preface

Since its inception more than fifteen years ago, *Twentieth-Century Literary Criticism* (*TCLC*) has been purchased and used by nearly 10,000 school, public, and college or university libraries. *TCLC* has covered more than 500 authors, representing 58 nationalities and over 25,000 titles. No other reference source has surveyed the critical response to twentieth-century authors and literature as thoroughly as *TCLC*. In the words of one reviewer, "there is nothing comparable available." *TCLC* "is a gold mine of information—dates, pseudonyms, biographical information, and criticism from books and periodicals—which many librarians would have difficulty assembling on their own."

Scope of the Series

TCLC is designed to serve as an introduction to authors who died between 1900 and 1999 and to the most significant interpretations of these author's works. Volumes published from 1978 through 1999 included authors who died between 1900 and 1960. The great poets, novelists, short story writers, playwrights, and philosophers of the period are frequently studied in high school and college literature courses. In organizing and reprinting the vast amount of critical material written on these authors, *TCLC* helps students develop valuable insight into literary history, promotes a better understanding of the texts, and sparks ideas for papers and assignments. Each entry in *TCLC* presents a comprehensive survey on an author's career or an individual work of literature and provides the user with a multiplicity of interpretations and assessments. Such variety allows students to pursue their own interests; furthermore, it fosters an awareness that literature is dynamic and responsive to many different opinions.

Every fourth volume of *TCLC* is devoted to literary topics. These topics widen the focus of the series from the individual authors to such broader subjects as literary movements, prominent themes in twentieth-century literature, literary reaction to political and historical events, significant eras in literary history, prominent literary anniversaries, and the literatures of cultures that are often overlooked by English-speaking readers.

TCLC is designed as a companion series to Gale's *Contemporary Literary Criticism,* (*CLC*) which reprints commentary on authors who died after 1999. Because of the different time periods under consideration, there is no duplication of material between *CLC* and *TCLC*.

Organization of the Book

A *TCLC* entry consists of the following elements:

- The **Author Heading** cites the name under which the author most commonly wrote, followed by birth and death dates. Also located here are any name variations under which an author wrote, including transliterated forms for authors whose native languages use nonroman alphabets. If the author wrote consistently under a pseudonym, the pseudonym will be listed in the author heading and the author's actual name given in parenthesis on the first line of the biographical and critical information. Uncertain birth or death dates are indicated by question marks. Single-work entries are preceded by a heading that consists of the most common form of the title in English translation (if applicable) and the original date of composition.

- A **Portrait of the Author** is included when available.

- The **Introduction** contains background information that introduces the reader to the author, work, or topic that is the subject of the entry.

- The list of **Principal Works** is ordered chronologically by date of first publication and lists the most important works by the author. The genre and publication date of each work is given. In the case of foreign authors whose works have been translated into English, the English-language version of the title follows in brackets. Unless otherwise indicated, dramas are dated by first performance, not first publication.

- Reprinted **Criticism** is arranged chronologically in each entry to provide a useful perspective on changes in critical evaluation over time. The critic's name and the date of composition or publication of the critical work are given at the beginning of each piece of criticism. Unsigned criticism is preceded by the title of the source in which it appeared. All titles by the author featured in the text are printed in boldface type. Footnotes are reprinted at the end of each essay or excerpt. In the case of excerpted criticism, only those footnotes that pertain to the excerpted texts are included.

- A complete **Bibliographical Citation** of the original essay or book precedes each piece of criticism.

- Critical essays are prefaced by brief **Annotations** explicating each piece.

- An annotated bibliography of **Further Reading** appears at the end of each entry and suggests resources for additional study. In some cases, significant essays for which the editors could not obtain reprint rights are included here. Boxed material following the further reading list provides references to other biographical and critical sources on the author in series published by Gale.

Indexes

A **Cumulative Author Index** lists all of the authors that appear in a wide variety of reference sources published by the Gale Group, including *TCLC*. A complete list of these sources is found facing the first page of the Author Index. The index also includes birth and death dates and cross references between pseudonyms and actual names.

A **Cumulative Nationality Index** lists all authors featured in *TCLC* by nationality, followed by the number of the *TCLC* volume in which their entry appears.

A **Cumulative Topic Index** lists the literary themes and topics treated in the series as well as in *Classical and Medieval Literature Criticism, Literature Criticism from 1400 to 1800, Nineteenth-Century Literature Criticism,* and the *Contemporary Literary Criticism* Yearbook, which was discontinued in 1998.

An alphabetical **Title Index** accompanies each volume of *TCLC*. Listings of titles by authors covered in the given volume are followed by the author's name and the corresponding page numbers where the titles are discussed. English translations of foreign titles and variations of titles are cross-referenced to the title under which a work was originally published. Titles of novels, dramas, nonfiction books, and poetry, short story, or essay collections are printed in italics, while individual poems, short stories, and essays are printed in roman type within quotation marks.

In response to numerous suggestions from librarians, Gale also produces an annual paperbound edition of the *TCLC* cumulative title index. This annual cumulation, which alphabetically lists all titles reviewed in the series, is available to all customers. Additional copies of this index are available upon request. Librarians and patrons will welcome this separate index; it saves shelf space, is easy to use, and is recyclable upon receipt of the next edition.

Citing *Twentieth-Century Literary Criticism*

When writing papers, students who quote directly from any volume in the Literary Criticism Series may use the following general format to footnote reprinted criticism. The first example pertains to material drawn from periodicals, the second to material reprinted from books.

George Orwell, "Reflections on Gandhi," *Partisan Review* 6 (Winter 1949): 85-92; reprinted in *Twentieth-Century Literary Criticism*, vol. 59, ed. Jennifer Gariepy (Detroit: The Gale Group, 1995), 40-3.

William H. Slavick, "Going to School to DuBose Heyward," *The Harlem Renaissance Re-examined,* ed. Victor A. Kramer (AMS, 1987), 65- 91; reprinted in *Twentieth-Century Literary Criticism,* vol. 59, ed. Jennifer Gariepy (Detroit: The Gale Group, 1995), 94-105.

Suggestions are Welcome

Readers who wish to suggest new features, topics, or authors to appear in future volumes, or who have other suggestions or comments are cordially invited to call, write, or fax the Managing Editor:

Managing Editor, Literary Criticism Series
The Gale Group
27500 Drake Road
Farmington Hills, MI 48331-3535
1-800-347-4253 (GALE)
Fax: 248-699-8054

Acknowledgments

The editors wish to thank the copyright holders of the excerpted criticism included in this volume and the permissions managers of many book and magazine publishing companies for assisting us in securing reproduction rights. We are also grateful to the staffs of the Detroit Public Library, the Library of Congress, the University of Detroit Mercy Library, Wayne State University Purdy/Kresge Library Complex, and the University of Michigan Libraries for making their resources available to us. Following is a list of the copyright holders who have granted us permission to reproduce material in this volume of *TCLC*. Every effort has been made to trace copyright, but if omissions have been made, please let us know.

COPYRIGHTED EXCERPTS IN *TCLC*, VOLUME 111, WERE REPRODUCED FROM THE FOLLOWING PERIODICALS:

The Atlantic Monthly, v. 274, September, 1994 for "The Great American Studies Novel" by Charles Trueheart. Reproduced by permission of the author.—*Best Sellers,* v. 38, August, 1978. Copyright 1978, by the University of Scranton. Reproduced by permission. —*Clues,* v. 4, Spring-Summer, 1983. Copyright © 1983 by Bowling Green State University Popular Press. All rights reserved. Reproduced by permission. —*Commonweal,* v. XXXXVII, February 13, 1948. Reproduced by permission. —*Critique,* v. 20, 1978. Copyright © 1978 Helen Dwight Reid Educational Foundation. Reproduced with permission of the Helen Dwight Reid Educational Foundation, published by Heldref Publications, 1319 18th Street, NW, Washington, DC 20036-1802. —*Cultural Critique,* v. 31, Fall, 1995 for "Adorno, Ellison and the Critique of Jazz" by James Harding. © 1995 by *Cultural Critique*. Reproduced by permission of the University of Minnesota Press and the author. —*Encounter,* v. XXXVII, October, 1976 for "Dr. Adorno's Bag of Tricks" by David Martin. © 1976 by David Martin. Reproduced by permission of Curtis Brown Pty Ltd. on behalf of the author. —*Essays in Literature,* v. 23, Fall, 1996. Reproduced by permission of Western Illinois University. —*Forum and Century,* v. 93, April, 1935. Copyright, © 1935, by Current History, Inc. Reproduced by permission from Current History, Inc. —*German Quarterly,* v. 54, March, 1981. Reproduced by permission. —*The Gettysburg Review* volume 9, number 1, for "A Return to *Raintree County*" by Gerald Weales first appeared in, and is reprinted here with the acknowledgment of the editors. —*The Journal of Aesthetics and Art Criticism,* v. 50, Summer, 1992. Reproduced by permission of Blackwell Publishers. —*Kliatt Young Adult Paperback Book Guide,* v. XIII, September, 1979. Copyright © 1979 by KLIATT Paperback Book Guide. Reproduced by permission. —*Lingua Franca,* v. 8, November, 1998. Reproduced by permission. —*The Markham Review,* v. 8, Winter, 1979. Reproduced by permission. —*Midamerica,* v. II, 1975 for "Ross Lockridge, *Raintree County*, and the Epic of Irony" by Gerald C. Nemanic; v. IV, 1977 for "The Presence of the Past in the Heartland: *Raintree County* Revisited," by Joel M. Jones. Copyright 1977, 1975 by the Society for the Study of Midwestern Literature. All rights reserved. Reproduced by permission of the publisher and the respective authors. —*MLN,* v. 109, December, 1994. © 1994 by The Johns Hopkins University Press. Reproduced by permission. —*The Nation,* New York, v. 140, May 22, 1935. Reproduced by permission. —*New German Critique,* v. 29, Spring-Summer, 1983; v. 31, Winter, 1984; v. 72, Fall, 1997. Reproduced by permission of Telos Press Ltd. —*The New Republic,* v. 82, April 10, 1935. © 1935 *The New Republic,* Inc. Reproduced by permission of *The New Republic*. —*New York Herald Tribune Books,* February 24, 1935. Copyright © 1935 by The New York Times Company. Reproduced by permission. —*The New York Times Book Review,* February 24, 1935. Copyright 1935, renewed 1963 by The New York Times Company. Reproduced by permission. —*Perspectives of New Music,* vol 27, Summer, 1989 for "Language for One, Language for All: Adorno and Modernism," by Rainer Rochlitz, translated by Roberta Brown. © 1989 by Perspectives of New Music, Inc. Reproduced by permission of the publisher and the author. —*Popular Music and Society,* v. 12, Winter, 1988; v. 15, Fall, 1991. Reproduced by permission of The Bowling Green State University Popular Press. —*Punch,* v. 170, 1926. Reproduced by permission. —*Saturday Review of Literature,* v. 11, March 2, 1935. © 1935 *Saturday Review Magazine,* © 1979 General Media International, Inc. Reproduced by permission. —*South Atlantic Quarterly,* v. 92, Winter, 1993. Copyright © 1993 by Duke University Press. Reproduced by permission. —*Studies in the Novel,* v. 27, Winter, 1995. Copyright 1995 by North Texas State University. Reproduced by permission. —*Tennessee Studies in Literature,* v. 27, 1984. Copyright © 1984 by The University of Tennessee Press. Reproduced by permission of The University of Tennessee Press. —*Times Literary Supplement,* n. 3977, June 23, 1978. © The Times Supplements Limited 1978. Reproduced from *The Times Literary Supplement* by permission. —*Tulsa Studies in Women's Literature,* v. 7, Spring, 1988 for "Feminine Sensationalism, Eroticism, and Self-Assertion: M.E. Braddon and Ouida," by Natalie Schroeder. © 1988 by The University of Tulsa. Reproduced by permission of the publisher and author. —*University of Hartford Studies in Literature,* v. 10, 1978. Copyright © 1978 by the University of Hartford. Reproduced by permission. —*University of Toronto Qarterly,* v. 62, Spring, 1993 for "Disclosure as 'Cover-Up': The Disclosure of Madness in *Lady Audley's Secret*" by Jill L. Matus. © University of Toronto Press 1993. Reproduced by permission of University of Toronto

Literary Criticism Series Advisory Board

The members of the Gale Group Literary Criticism Series Advisory Board—reference librarians and subject specialists from public, academic, and school library systems—represent a cross-section of our customer base and offer a variety of informed perspectives on both the presentation and content of our literature criticism products. Advisory board members assess and define such quality issues as the relevance, currency, and usefulness of the author coverage, critical content, and literary topics included in our series; evaluate the layout, presentation, and general quality of our printed volumes; provide feedback on the criteria used for selecting authors and topics covered in our series; provide suggestions for potential enhancements to our series; identify any gaps in our coverage of authors or literary topics, recommending authors or topics for inclusion; analyze the appropriateness of our content and presentation for various user audiences, such as high school students, undergraduates, graduate students, librarians, and educators; and offer feedback on any proposed changes/enhancements to our series. We wish to thank the following advisors for their advice throughout the year.

Theodor Adorno
1903-1969

(Full name Theodor Wiesengrund Adorno) German philosopher, sociologist, musicologist, and critic.

INTRODUCTION

Adorno is widely considered to have been the most brilliant member of the Frankfurt School, a group of sociologists and psychologists organized formally as the Frankfurt Institute for Social Research, a privately endowed center for Marxist studies that was founded after the rise of fascism in Europe in the 1920s.

BIOGRAPHICAL INFORMATION

Adorno was born in Frankfurt, Germany, in 1903. His father, Oscar Wiesengrund, was a wealthy wine merchant of Jewish descent, and his mother, Maria Calvelli-Adorno, was a well-known professional singer of German-French-Genoese parentage. As a child Adorno was quiet and intensely intellectual. He was strongly influenced by the many singers and musicians who frequented his parents' house and hoped to become a composer. At the University of Frankfurt, however, Adorno studied philosophy, psychology, and sociology as well as musicology. After earning his doctorate in philosophy in 1925, he moved to Vienna to study musical composition, but he was bitterly disappointed to find that he lacked the talent to succeed. However, while in Vienna, Adorno began to contribute essays and reviews to various Viennese journals, and he soon established himself as a knowledgeable, original, and perceptive critic and philosopher of music, as well as a champion of avant-garde composers. The range of his critical writings soon widened to include literature, aesthetics, and culture in general, while his approach to the arts, under the influence of his friend Walter Benjamin, became increasingly sociological and political. In 1928 Adorno returned to Frankfurt and the University. A few years later he began his long friendship with Max Horkheimer, who was director of the Frankfurt Institute for Social Research from 1930 to 1958. Adorno did not at first become a member of the Institute, which moved first to Geneva and then to the United States after Adolf Hitler's rise to power in 1933. Instead, Adorno went to Merton College, Oxford, to study philosophy and then to Princeton University in the United States. In 1938 he became head of music studies at the Institute's Office of Radio Research at Princeton. In 1941, when Horkheimer moved to California because of ill health, Adorno followed, becoming part of a brilliant expatriate community that included

Thomas and Heinrich Mann, Bertolt Brecht, and Alfred Doeblin. Adorno served as co-director and theoretician of the most famous of the Institute's American projects, the Research Project on Social Discrimination, from 1944 to 1949. That year the Institute moved back to Frankfurt, and nine years later Adorno succeeded Horkheimer as director. At the same time he became professor of philosophy and sociology at the University of Frankfurt, into which the Institute was incorporated. The Frankfurt School had by that time ended its connections with orthodox Marxism, and was disillusioned with both the Soviet Union and the industrial working class. In the postwar years it functioned primarily as a center of academic sociology, where Adorno and Horkheimer passed on to their students what they had learned of empirical social science in the United States. Through the 1950s and 1960s Adorno published widely on a variety of topics, including music, philosophy, literature, and popular culture. In the late 1960s the Institute's offices were frequently invaded by students protesting its misperceived conservatism. In April of that year three politically radical female students entered Adorno's classroom, bared their breasts, mocked him with flowers and kisses, and finally declared him dead as an institution. Adorno was horrified by the outburst and, according to some, never recovered. He died of a heart attack later that year.

MAJOR WORKS

Adorno's writings strongly reflect his Marxist, anti-fascist, beliefs. From 1942 to 1944 Adorno collaborated with Horkheimer on writing *Philosophische Fragmente* (*Philosophical Fragments*; 1944), later translated as *Dialectic of Enlightenment*. In this work Adorno and Horkheimer argued that the European masses had allowed themselves to be exploited by their leaders, who had substituted the pursuit of power for the pursuit of happiness during the period of fascist power in Europe. In 1950 Adorno published the results of the Institute's Research Project on Social Discrimination under the title *The Authoritarian Personality*. In the study, about two thousand American citizens were interviewed to establish personality traits and family backgrounds that characterize people who develop racist and anti-democratic views. Adorno also published extensively on music, both books and essays, generally focusing on the social aspects of the art form. In *The Philosophy of Modern Music* (1949) Adorno contrasted Arnold Schoenberg and Igor Stravinsky as the positive and negative poles of the new music. In *Versuch über Wagner* (1952) Adorno argued that the music of Richard Wagner helped to inspire the beginnings of National Socialism, which developed into Nazism in Germany. Many of Adorno's essays on music demonstrate his hostility to jazz and other forms of popular music as being a drug employed by the establishment to pacify the exploited masses. *Minima Moralia: Reflections from Damaged Life* (1951) is a more personal collection of aphorisms criticizing fascist tendencies in the twentieth century and the materialism of modern industrial civilization. Two major philosophical works of Adorno's later career stand out. In *Negative Dialectics* (1966) Adorno discussed Kant, Hegel, and Heidegger and their textual reproductions of reality. In his *Ästhetische Theorie* (1970), which was left unfinished at his death, Adorno argued in favor of a theory of the autonomy of artistic works and explored the connection between art and society.

CRITICAL RECEPTION

While Adorno's writing is considered difficult and at times almost abstract, his ideas on aesthetics, sociology, music, and popular culture have been both admired and excoriated. Many music critics, for example, admit the brilliance of Adorno's observations on classical music but find his work on popular music—in particular jazz—unenlightened and ignorant. Other critics, however, believe that Adorno's writings on jazz and other popular music have been long misinterpreted. Despite his lifelong stance as a vigorous anti-fascist and his strong influence on modern European democratic thought, Adorno came under fire later in his life because of his refusal to take radical political action and because some of his writings on aesthetics and culture were interpreted as overly conservative. European university students frequently protested and stormed the offices of the Frankfort Institute. More recently, Adorno has been restored to his respected place in modern philosophy and sociology, with some critics maintaining that his works are some of the most important of the twentieth century.

PRINCIPAL WORKS

Kierkegaard: Konstruktion des ästhetischen [*Kierkegaard: Construction of the Aesthetic*] (philosophy) 1933

Memorandum: Music in Radio (musicology) 1938

Philosophische Fragmente [with Max Horkheimer] (philosophy) 1944; revised edition published as *Dialektik der Aufklärung: Philosophische Fragmente* 1947; published as *Dialectic of Enlightenment* 1972

Philosophie der neuen Musik [*Philosophy of Modern Music*] (philosophy) 1949

The Authoritarian Personality (sociology) 1950

Minima Moralia: Reflexionen aus dem beschädigten Leben [*Minima Moralia: Reflections from Damaged Life*] (philosophy) 1951

Versuch über Wagner [*In Search of Wagner*] (philosophy) 1952

Die gegängelte Musik: Bemerkungen über die Musikpolitik der Ostblockstaaten (musicology) 1954

Dissonanzen: Musik in der verwalteten Welt (musicology) 1956

Zur Metakritik der Erkenntnistheorie: Studien über Husserl und die phänomenologischen Antinomien [*Against Epistemology: A Metacritique*] (philosophy) 1956

Aspekte der Hegelschen Philosophie (philosophy) 1957

Die Funktion des Kontrapunkts in der neuen Musik (musicology) 1957

Prismen: Kulturkritik und Geselschaft [*Prisms*] (philosophy) 1957

Noten zur Literatur 4 vols. (criticism) 1958-74

Einleitung in die Musiksoziologie [*Introduction to the Sociology of Music*] (sociology) 1962

Drei Studien zu Hegel (philosophy) 1963

Jargon der Eigentlichkeit: Zur deutschen Ideologie [*The Jargon of Authenticity*] (philosophy) 1965

Negative Dialektik [*Negative Dialectics*] (philosophy) 1966

Komposition für den Film [*Composing for the Films;* with Hanns Eisler] (musicology) 1969

Ästhetische Theorie (philosophy) 1970

Aufsätze zur Gesellschaftstheorie und Methodology (essays) 1970

Gesammelte Werke 23 vols. (collected writings) 1970

Der Positivismusstreit in der Deutschen Soziologie [*The Positivist Dispute in German Sociology*] (essays) 1976

CRITICISM

Ben Agger (essay date 1976)

SOURCE: "On Happiness and the Damaged Life," in *On Critical Theory,* edited by John O'Neill, The Seabury Press, 1976, pp. 12-33.

[*In the following essay, Agger explains Adorno's place in critical theory.*]

Critical theory chances to be either a museum-piece in the hands of its modern inheritors or a living medium of political self-expression. My argument is that critical theory can only be renewed—as Marx would have hoped—by refusing to concentrate on its philosophical inheritance and instead by writing the theory in a direct and unmediated way. The old saw that to be a Marxist is to surpass Marx is just as true for critical theory: Adorno, Horkheimer, and Marcuse blazed the trail for a theory of late capitalism, yet now they can only be suitably remembered by new formulations of theory responsive to the altered nature of the socio-cultural world.

The central motif in this task of reinvigoration is that of language. Critical theory employs a vocabulary of hope and defeat. Marx's great contribution was his notion of theory as a stimulant to political action, if not as action's mere reflection. The rhetoric of critical theory emerges from the theorist's sense of the possibility of social change and itself contributes to fostering or deflecting emancipatory activity.

In this sense, Adorno's nearly unmitigated pessimism contrasts with Marcuse's guarded and sophisticated optimism about cracking the one-dimensional totality. Although *Eros and Civilization* states definitely that only the "surplus" of ego-constitutive repression can be purposefully eliminated, Marcuse remains hopeful about the prospect of lessening this surplus. Similarly, O'Neill's "wild sociology" defends the commonplaces of everyday life as the inalienable basis of any community, from which all radicalism must inevitably proceed. For Adorno, there was an *equivalency* between basic and surplus repression, and thus few opportunities for social change.

The language of critical theory is its own meta-language. Objective description of things contains a vision of an *Aufgehoben,* a transcended-reconstructed world. The dialectic is captured in the capacity of objective knowledge for political enlightenment. Critique in Marx meant the imagination and analysis of a world without exploitation, a human world. This must be embodied in the forms of critical expression such as social thought, art, music, and philosophy. A dialectical language both describes the dissonant world and bespeaks the possibility of redemption.

> The new sensibility and the new consciousness which are to project and guide such reconstruction demand a new *language* to define and communicate the new "values" (language in the wider sense which includes words, images, gestures, tones). It has been said that the degree to which a revolution is developing *qualitatively* different social conditions and relationships may perhaps be indicated by the development of a different language: the rupture with the continuum of domination must also be a rupture with the vocabulary of domination.[1]

Adorno employed a negative language and favoured negative culture. Marcuse was less negative because he glimpsed the point at which evil could be redeemed. Concretely, Adorno believed that the demise of a politically organized working class sealed the fate of Marxism, whereas Marcuse and O'Neill have responded to the libidinal rebellion of American youth as a potentially revolutionary phenomenon. However, O'Neill goes even beyond Marcuse's ingrained prejudice for high-culture in siding with Norman O. Brown against Marcuse in terms of what he calls "the Left version of the generation gap."[2] Whereas Marcuse flirts with turned-on youth, uncertain of their revolutionary potential, O'Neill celebrates them. Adorno saw negative theory captured in the mind-boggling rows of twelve-tone music where Marcuse and O'Neill hear the crash and flight of rock music as a new promise of freedom, providing a vision of the preverbal harmony of socialist life: the *carnal* grounds of socialism.

For too long, Marxism has been under the sway of a taboo prohibiting the depiction of the image of socialism. In Adorno's later work, there is barely a hint of the promised land. Critical theory, transplanted from Germany to North America, has become a crabbed style of philosophical analysis, replete with a scholastic structure of authority. My thesis is that this taboo must be lifted and Adorno's dismal reluctance to sing about socialism opposed. Marxism under the influence of its great founder has always assumed that history consisted in radical interruptions; Marx's eschatology revealed a temporal gap between the alienating present and *future* socialism. The taboo on graven images was erected because it was thought that the socialist future was too far off to admit of sensible description in the here and now. Yet in my opinion the "moment" of abstract negation—out of which Adorno's theory is built—must be superseded, and the temporal model of a long road to a redeemed future scrapped.

Marcuse explicitly rejects the model of critical theory as abstract negation; since his work on Freud he has concerned himself with depicting the *body politic* of the new society, its politics, sexuality, art, and philosophy. Freud enabled him to translate Marx's rationalism into naturalistic terms, into the body-language of a new version of critical theory. At the same time, Marcuse also rejected the notion of the long road to socialism and suggested instead that "revolutionary" forces could be perceived as emerging in the present society. Adorno's impatience with jazz and rock as culture-forms is rejected by Marcuse and O'Neill who search for oppositional impulses *anywhere,* even in *apparently* non-proletarian and non-political forms.

This potential for transfiguration is not at all obvious amidst the vulgarity and garbage of Woodstock or the May revolution. But this is the way of wild sociology into the world; it can enter only through self-mockery, nihilistic flirtations and the very self-violence which it seeks to avoid. Its way is profane because its resources are nothing else than the world and its people struggling for improvement. It is easy to be cynical about the organizational and promotional features of "rock-ins" and "maybe's," to dissolve them in a phrase, to empty their *logos* into the waste-bin of fashion. Indeed, the spontaneity, festivity and refusals which constitute these events make it inevitable that the participants will "blow it," will be unable to sustain their enthusiasm and disintegrate as at Altamont, in Paris and elsewhere. The critics will observe failure and speak wisely of what is to be done within the limits of an untransfigured world which lives without fancy and avoids enthusiasm in favour of the pigeonholes of politics, history and sociology.[3]

Modern critical theory in Marcuse and O'Neill has therefore abandoned the traditional model of the politically organized working class. Opposition can come from any quarter; the nature of modern opposition consists in rejecting the division of labour and in the actual creation of a new political body. Dialectical thought today rejects the thesis of a long road and indeed all crisis-theory rooted in the classical Marxian terms of a proletarian revolution. Instead, critical theory must—as Marx taught time and again—sensitize itself to *all* on-going oppositional movements in attempting to channel them in palpably political directions. Critical theory cannot afford to remain in the 1920s and 1930s when—perhaps—the old working class model did apply.

My thesis about O'Neill's and Marcuse's sensitivity to non-traditional forms of opposition, in contrast to Adorno, turns on their approach to certain cultural forms like language and music. They have tried to conceive how modes of expression like music and theory *themselves* constitute a new body politic and socialist relations. Theory is a praxis which concretizes and communicates the image of socialism. It contains within itself, as does music, a sense of the future which is emerging *from* the present. I want to read Marcuse, O'Neill, and Adorno as singing the world in different ways, as engaging in different styles of cultural opposition. The way of O'Neill and Marcuse is a direct attempt to create a socialist body politic through the medium of musical and theoretic harmony. Adorno's way is a form of abstract negation through dissonance.

Both body-politics and abstract negation must be moments of oppositional practice today. Marx's famous notion of the dialectic between theory and practice really bespeaks the practical potential of theory itself as a form of cultural politics. O'Neill's and Marcuse's "critical theory" is the cultural practice of a *new sensibility*; it is not a form of life separable from political practice. Adorno's "theory" is an abject resignation before a seemingly intractable world. Marcuse and Adorno cannot be compared according to the lifeless epistemological standard of bourgeois social science but only in terms of their varying styles of cultural opposition. My view is that Adorno is unjustified in resigning from the effort to build a socialist society in the actual here and now of everyday politics.

One-dimensional society swallows up deviance but leaves the traces of idealism in theory, art, and music through which opposition can find its voice. Inasmuch as the thought of freedom remains conscious, there is a chance to create a society grounded in active and reciprocal expression. Once the thought of freedom is buried in the unconscious, hope withers along with the subject of hope. I want to restore the self-consciousness of action and vision to critical theory in turning it towards its own potential for speech and conviction, thereby combatting its ossification as another differentiated form of academic thought.

O'Neill and Marcuse remain hopeful that theory can transcend itself as a new science and technology, whereas Adorno wrote of his own irreparably "damaged life." Adorno's view was that theory remains imprisoned on the level of thought, that truth does not inhere in a collectivity or class. Theory in this vein is but a tragic expression of will, a theme reminiscent of Nietzsche and Schopenhauer. In a way, Nietzsche's *The Birth of Tragedy* represents one of the options of language and style open to critical theory today. Nietzsche writes of the sublation of tragedy by "Socratism" and its destruction of music as a pure expression of the unencumbered will. Socratic optimism in its modern genre employs the techniques of opera, romantic classical music, and rock, while the tragic version of critical theory takes refuge in the dissonance of twelve-tone music.

Adorno is the theorist of atonality, while Marcuse is the opera buff wavering between romantic high-culture and the youth-culture of rock and acid. Their difference is the split between tragedy and epiphany, the one humbly owning up to its essential impotence, the other committing the sin of pride and challenging the world to change. Critical theory has two broad cultural styles, the one tragic or Nietzschean, the other more optimistic or Hegelian-Marxian.

The "negative totality" of modern capitalism has produced one-dimensionality and reduced criticism to imitation and private language. Marcuse believes in the possibility of a concrete harmony between subject and object, while Adorno rejected all identity-theory found in Hegel and Marx. The alternative to the Hegelian optimism of Marcuse is a Nietzschean perspective of tragedy and eternal recurrence for which things either remain the same or get worse. *Dialectic of Enlightenment* by Horkheimer and Adorno is an echo of *The Birth of Tragedy*. Nietzsche believed that Aeschylus had been eternally wronged by Euripides and Socrates, whereas Horkheimer and Adorno thought that western civilization began to die with Odysseus' rationalism.

Marcuse has not been overly reluctant to hypostatize a worker-student-Third World coalition as the new collective subject. This has been largely an argumentative device, the alliteration of critical theory, in that Marcuse, like Marx and Lenin, never failed to reduce praxis to individuating acts. Hegel's phenomenology of mind underwrote Marx and Marcuse by offering them an image of the political nature of reflection and cognition. Marcuse's debt to Hegel is revealed in the second preface to *Reason and Revolution* where he writes that Hegel has restored the "power of negative thinking" in a time when the "second dimension" of transcendent critique has been assimilated to the positive affirmation of the given. But Hegel was not a tragic thinker in the same sense as Nietzsche. Hegel was a dialectical theorist who tried to comprehend how history was animated by its thought of itself, its essentially progressive reflexivity.

Critical theory mediates between the thought of freedom and the actuality of a free world. Mortal Marxism embodies in the struggling but hopeful subject the mediations which can let theory become a practice. The Nietzschean conception of the mortally self-limited subject differs radically from the Hegelian-Marxian idea of the potentially universal subject of world history. For Adorno, everything we do in the way of subjectively mediating present and future will end in disappointing failure; rebellion only strengthens the system. For Marcuse and O'Neill, we cannot avoid the attempt to translate emancipatory ideals into the concrete particulars of place, time and emotion.

> To think sociologically is to dwell upon a question we have answered long ago: How it is that men belong to one another despite all differences? This is the task of a *wild sociology,* namely, to dwell upon the platitudes of convention, prejudice, place, and love; to make of them a history of the world's labor and to root sociology in the care of the circumstance and particulars that shape the divine predicaments of ordinary men. The work of sociology, then, is to confront the passionless world of science with the epiphany of family, of habit, and of human folly, outside of which there is no remedy. This is not to deny scientific sociology. It is simply to treat it as a possibility that has yet to convince the world.[4]

Critical theory either translates the universal of Freedom into sensible dimensions of experience and language or it acts as a fatalistic expression of the heteronomous will. I think it can be argued that Adorno hoped that music itself could express a theory too abstruse for words. Nietzsche heard the sound of tragedy in the choral music of Aeschylus. Tragedy and a certain mortal finity were expressed through the song. Adorno considered Schoenberg to be a prophet of tragedy—a tragedy essentially beyond the reach of the discursive voice. The negative dialectic must be base enough to bespeak an evil world.

Marcuse speaks about human tragedy without ascending to Aeschylean heights in forgetting the potential of the positive. He searches for a language with which to express the Good contained within the shape of the present. Art and theory prepare us for the time when social relations will not scar the human face. Yet criticism will also preserve the distance between vital lived experience and the recon-

structed experience of language. That is to say, each society needs critics and artists to idealize a higher order of freedom than that which has been actually attained. Whereas Adorno felt that the jargon of authenticity rendered language impossible, O'Neill and Marcuse want to reserve the most revealing languages for the time when a socialist order is itself in need of pretheoretical invigoration.

> Wild sociology will encourage radicalism. Yet it will be hard on its own radicalism, suspecting further evils from its own activity should it presume upon its relation to the lay community. It may well be that the daily practice of sociology encourages arrogance upon the part of its members, undermining the very resources of humanism with a numb professionalism or the shrill cry of ideology. If this is not to happen wild sociology must make a place for itself, and to accomplish this it must engage hope and utopia. Hope is the time it takes to make the place in which men think and talk and work together. Thus wild sociology is essentially engaged in the education of the oppressed.[5]

Praxis thus is anything we can do to remain critically alive, sensitive to pervasive dissonance *and* transcendent harmony. As its own metalanguage, critical theory is a praxis. It talks about the world as it assesses the social potential for freedom. My point is that for Adorno, O'Neill, and Marcuse theory is not always discursively set out but can assume prelinguistic forms. O'Neill draws from Vico's argument that poetry is the originary substratum of language and that critical theory must return to poetry in resurrecting the natural rationality of human expression. Vico implies that humanity can be redeemed *because* we are the original authors of our own humanity; we can hear the *sound* of our own humanity in non-discursive forms of expression like poetry and music.

> Language fractures in the modern world because our speech is no longer the reflection of anything that is ordered either inside or outside of us. Every historical order ultimately collapses the literary, artistic, and philosophical languages that for a time allowed an age to speak of itself and to gather its particular goods and evils. It is an axiom of Vico's wild sociology that if history is at all saved it is saved by language. For it is in the history of our language that we recover our humanity. It is in language that we discover the gradual making of the institutions that have made us human.[6]

Music like poetry is a *form* of critical theory in that it stimulates and solicits resignation or rebellion. Adorno felt that twelve-tone music captured the negative dialectic of an insufferable society, whereas O'Neill's patience with rock and drug culture emerges from his contention that there is something elementally *political* in the ecstasy of turned-on youth. In a sense, Marcuse is located somewhere between Adorno's gloom and O'Neill's song of the inalienable commonplaces of humanity, less willing than O'Neill to relinquish the Greek ideal of Reason in favour of the mundane rationality of the body and voice.

Ultimately, critical theory develops an aesthetics of the good life. Marx resisted writing such an aesthetics, although he gave ample hints in the Paris manuscripts about the *sense* of socialism. Today, this aesthetics must depict the form and feel of socialism, not merely discursively, but through the *body* and *voice* of the new man, his art, music, architecture, sexuality. Marcuse was the only Frankfurt theorist to take the development of this aesthetics seriously, relying heavily on Freud for the sexual underpinning of a new body politic. O'Neill's concept of the "body politic" also renders this aesthetics as a possible sociological artifact, an aesthetics produced by all the forms of human expression. O'Neill's vision of a wild sociology is a version of critical theory which sings of commonplace pain and hope and thus constitutes itself *as* a form of music. The bittersweet harmony of Beethoven or Dylan is joined with the pretheoretical affirmation of common humanity which wild sociology provides. The organon of Marcuse's "new science" and of O'Neill's "wild sociology" is the *body politic*.[7]

In this sense, critical theory must *build* a body politic which has three dimensions. Theory sings, paints, writes, makes love. In so doing, it evaluates modern society against concrete criteria of socialist possibility. Marx's ideal of dis-alienation is rendered phenomenological in the translation of socialism into an actual political body. The taboo on graven images is explicitly rescinded, for the taboo robs us of an organizational device with which to redirect youthful opposition into political channels. Superficially, the Rolling Stones are not revolutionary for they are a product of late bourgeois society and the modern culture industry. Yet the libidinal responsiveness of the young to the sights and sounds of their music is a *potentially* political phenomenon, an essential component of the aesthetics of socialism.

The concept of praxis thus has a more allusive and negative formulation in Adorno; Marcuse and O'Neill locate the realm of praxis in the "infrastructure" of the psyche and body. The tragic form of theory has its roots in the philosophy of Nietzsche. I want to focus on the function of art in Adorno's view, a perspective which is not dissimilar to Nietzsche's own theory of music expressed in *The Birth of Tragedy.* Adorno says of music:

> Its truth appears guaranteed more by its denial of any meaning in organized society, of which it will have no part—accomplished by its own organized vacuity—than by any capability of positive meaning within itself. Under the present circumstances it is restricted to definitive negation.[8]

Negation of what? Of social forms of domination? Certainly not. "Aesthetic authenticity is a socially necessary illusion: no work of art can thrive in a society founded upon power, without insisting upon its own power."[9] Art negates only as it promises a different, better world and thereby breaks through the one-dimensional totality by the example of its own abrasive contingency. Yet Adorno unlike Marcuse does not sanction Brecht's concept of the estrangement-effect, an art which shocks and educates. Atonal music was not to contain anything but the experience of pain; it was not a pedagogy of the oppressed. Marcuse's fondness for romanticism contrasts with Adorno's utter lack of sentimentality, issuing from his tragic concept of the negative subject. Marcuse's subject, rooted in Schiller's "play-impulse," suffers greatly at the hands of the world yet can express his suffering in the hope of romantic redemption.

Aesthetic dissonance refuses to be sentimentally hopeful by giving in to harmony. Art mimetically mirrors the insane world. Rigour characterizes Schoenberg's music whereas sentimentality hiding only affirmative neo-objectivism taints the music of Stravinsky. Rigour can show us the evils of the world, but only subliminally through the preconceptual and precoherent effects of sound.

As Adorno and Horkheimer wrote in **Dialectic of Enlightenment,** "the triumph of advertising in the culture industry is that consumers feel compelled to buy and use its products even though they see through them."[10] Dissonant music serves as revolutionary advertising since it never falls on deaf ears. It insinuates its way into consciousness and tries to gain a foothold in the buried critical spirit of the subject. The clash of symbols reminds us however remotely of the din of the bourgeois city. Twelve-tone rows recall for us the seriality of our lives.

Music for Adorno is a social form because it is an element in a comprehensive social whole, almost a reflex of a noisy society. Music is not simply sold as use-value but gains its allure from its bourgeois purposive-purposelessness. Art is thought to have *no* use-value. The art-object delights because it represents the affluence of a culture which can afford to employ artists to do nothing in particular.

Theory itself for Adorno does not consist in a form of life exuding the positive character and need of its subject. Like dissonant music, it is socially useful noise. Its language cannot fail to be the language of the dominant society, extended to its limit of rationality. Adorno once believed that the social whole contained its own principle of contradiction to be revealed by a theory which comprehends the untruth of the whole. Theory is the critique of an ideology which does not penetrate its own veneer of half-truths and glosses. Theory opposes the premature harmony of liberal capitalism by denouncing the tragedy of liberalism, its ultimately cheerful seriality. Both Adorno and Nietzsche situated the originary mythologization of enlightenment in Socrates who first hoped rationally to eliminate tragedy. **Dialectic of Enlightenment** resonated the sentiment that Marxism had failed by breaking insufficiently with the ethos of the domination of nature and society. **Negative Dialectics** charts the self-consciousness of enlightened dominion which has produced a thoughtless world. Adorno has rephrased Hegel's cunning of reason as the cunning of unreason: the inexorable "progress" of enlightenment which can be depicted only in an enlightened, disenchanted music. Adorno ultimately abandoned Marx's hope that contradictions within society could be resolved and harmony created.

Like Marx, Adorno was concerned to reveal by reproducing the contradictions of the negative totality through ideology-critique. Schoenberg's music became the ultimate critique of ideology in its abrasive reproduction of social dissonance. "The penetrating eye of consciousness" is an art which bespeaks the world as it has come to be and apparently serves us as the critique of political economy served Marx. Hegelian rationality reveals the essential *telos* of things by peering behind their common-sense appearances. Adorno believed that a discursive philosophy would fail in this effort; that only art and music could truly disclose the negative inauthenticity of the bourgeois world.

"Modern music sees absolute oblivion as its goal. It is the surviving message of despair from the shipwrecked."[11] Theory is the bottle in which the shipwrecked deposit their plea for help. But no bottle is ever found except when it survives long after the shipwrecked have perished. Negative or radical music evokes only the negative. It provides a mood for the "penetrating eye of consciousness" and enables it to comprehend the depravity of things. The whole is the untruth and critical theory fails to change the world.

The subject is so deformed by his presence in a brutalizing, privatizing world that he can *never* resurrect himself with the aid of discursive theory, precoherent art, or concerted activity. The sin of Socratism which tried to comprehend all mysteries has plagued every subsequent generation. The sin of pride scars the subject by forcing him outside himself in the externalizations of technology. Realism overwhelms the subject with the things themselves. Adorno contrasts the music of Schoenberg to that of Stravinsky which expresses the ideal of an unradical neo-objectivism.

> Stravinsky does justice to reality. The primacy of specialty over intention, the cult of the clever feat, the joy in agile manipulations such as those of the percussion in *L'Histoire du Soldat*—all these play off the means against the end. The means in the most literal sense— namely, the instrument—is hypostatized: it takes precedence over the music. The composition expresses only one fundamental concern: to find the sounds which will best suit its particular nature and result in the most overwhelming effect.[12]

Adorno felt that critical theory could restore the value of intention by asserting the primacy of music over against techniques to express sound. Radical music cuts to the heart of instrumentality by following out the logic of musical instrumentality to its ultimate conclusion. The "ideal of authenticity" for which Stravinsky's music strives is similar to the authenticity pursued by Heidegger's philosophy. Both forms of expression are jargons inasmuch as each sublates the objective subject by hypostatizing the abstract importance of technique and of care. Heidegger's *Dasein* is as inhuman as the subject of Stravinsky's composition—if indeed music has any conception of the subject, as Adorno would probably have claimed for it.

The annihilation of the ego is the residue of late bourgeois society which has collapsed the realms of ideology and re-

ality. One-dimensional society contains no sensible criterion of unfulfilled actuality because reality contains every illusion and promise made by the ideology of limitless liberalism. Adorno's particular genius was to have recognized the phenomenology of one-dimensionality in its most insidious and abstracted socio-cultural forms.

Culture is the jutting tip of the iceberg of bourgeois society. But culture "progressively" penetrates downwards to affect the base by transforming the sensibilities and expectations of workers and their received ideology of the work-ethic and erotic renunciation. A phenomenology of advanced capitalism reveals the ground of the forms we invoke when we speak about a "one-dimensional" society.

Yet theory in Adorno's terms does not enlighten in the hortatory way in which Marx-the-rationalist conceived of theory doing. Theory merely acts as a bell-weather of domination by reflecting the deformations of subjectivity. The more insane is the object of critical theory, namely, late bourgeois society, the more allusive critical theory must be. The more that culture is disenchanted, the more theory will have to be mythological. Just here, dialectical theory in Marx's sense becomes frozen. Allusive theory responds reflexively to the deformations of culture. The dialectic of the real and the possible has been defused by the social totality and its metamorphosis into a universe which can liberally encompass deviance. Adorno understood that theory had become undialectical because the world had been totalized in its total evil to a degree which denied the critical immanence and transcendent quality of *thought*. Marx's conception of a critical theory which could reveal the *telos* of deformed things has been transformed in times when the negative totality of society has lost its principle of dynamic contradiction. Thus the falling rate of profit projected by Marx has not materialized in a final crisis as capitalism has "temporarily" curbed the disruptive principle of its own self-negation.

Adorno characterizes the damaged subject as a casualty of "social progress." The "fallen nature of man" is the existential reality to be treated and hopefully resurrected by theorists. Music and theory can only express the tragedy of a world which through liberal enlightenment has lost sight of tragedy. There can be no guarantees that the music or theory composed by damaged, neurotic subjects can be anything but damaged expressions. Dissonant music bespeaks the dissonance of community and man. Likewise, allusive and gloomy theory stands witness to the seemingly eternal fall of enlightenment into myth.

The Nietzschean root of Adorno's thought is revealed in Adorno's affinity for Nietzsche's *amor fati*, the love of fate. Eternal recurrence of tragedy occasions a love of fate which can be broken through only by total redemption, fallen from the stars, a product of the unpredictable cunning of insanity. The Baconian root of modernity is the manipulative scientism which purges doubt and uncertainty from human experience. What Nietzsche disparagingly called "Socratism" in *The Birth of Tragedy* was Socrates' belief in the purposive reduction of uncertainty through technical rationality *(epistemé).*

Music in its non-tragic form sings the positive love of the earth and the eternal recurrence of existential mortality. We succeed only because we comprehend that success will not render the person transparent. Redemption is our atonement for the sin of pride. Critical theory sings the world because it is disenchanted with Marxist and bourgeois system-builders. In the profound despair of Adorno there is a kernel of mortal love for all men and for nature. The kernel will burst out of its shell only if we banish the Socratic and Baconian notions of the reduction of uncertainty through the objectifying control of society and nature. Adorno's critical theory sings the falleness of the world only because it cannot truthfully engage in the superficial and insidiously affirmative dialogue of enlightenment.

Marcuse always believed that the "power of negative thinking" contained within it a rational kernel of positive hope. In fact, the theory of liberation offered by Marcuse treats the subject as a relatively undamaged agent of revolutionary praxis. The Hegelian power of reason, its determinate negation of the apparent world, informs Marcuse's hopeful conception of the objectively natural subject. Nowhere does Marcuse allude to the permanently fallen hopelessness of critical praxis. Even his notorious *One-Dimensional Man* holds out the possibility of redemption. "It is only for the sake of those without hope that hope is given to us."

Marcuse's "new sensibility," like O'Neill's "wild sociology," is an amalgam of bodily and mental senses, of libidinal and symbolic rationality. The bourgeois idealist concept of reason ignores the rationality of the body by concentrating solely on an abstract intellectual rationality, thus denying Freud's profound naturalism and his conception of the *objective subject.*[13]

> Beyond the limits (and beyond the power) of repressive reason now appears the prospect for a new relationship between sensibility and reason, namely, the harmony between sensibility and a radical consciousness: rational faculties capable of projecting and defining the objective (material) conditions of freedom, its real limits and chances. But instead of being shaped and permeated by the rationality of domination, the sensibility would be guided by the imagination, mediating between the rational faculties and the sensuous needs. The great conception which animates Kant's critical philosophy shatters the philosophical framework in which he kept it. The imagination, unifying sensibility and reason, becomes "productive" as it becomes practical: a guiding force in the reconstruction of reality—reconstruction with the help of a *gaya scienza,* a science and technology released from their service to destruction and exploitation, and thus free for the liberating exigencies of the imagination. The rational transformation of the world could then lead to a reality formed by the aesthetic sensibility of man. Such a world could (in a literal sense!) embody, incorporate, the human faculties and desires to such an extent that

they appear as part of the objective determinism of nature—coincidence of causality through nature and causality through freedom.[14]

In *An Essay on Liberation* Marcuse suggests that any future revolution will have to emerge through a new infrastructure of undistorted human needs and instincts. *Counterrevolution and Revolt* elaborates this in terms of Marcuse's critique of the American New Left which has regrettably eschewed the critical function of rationality. He also discusses the political aesthetic of a future society and a new nonantagonistic alliance between man and nature. New science can reconstruct the exchange between humanity and nature. The object-world is but a proving-ground for liberated subjectivity which has an ineluctably objective component in the body and instincts. Marxian scientism has contributed to the decomposition of Marx's original notion of the sensuous nature of man. The person has been falsely and narrowly treated as a socio-economic cipher devoid of libidinal, emotional faculties. Mechanical Marxism ultimately has no conception of the objective naturalness of the subject, a conception derived by Marcuse from the great works of psychoanalysis.

> Behind these familiar traits of a socialism yet to come is the idea of socialism itself as a qualitatively different *totality.* The socialist universe is also a moral and aesthetic universe: dialectical materialism contains idealism as an element of theory and practice. The prevalent material needs and satisfactions are shaped—and controlled—by the requirements of exploitation. Socialism must augment the quantity of goods and services in order to abolish all poverty, but at the same time, socialist production must change the quality of existence—change the needs and satisfactions themselves. Moral, psychological, aesthetic, intellectual faculties, which today, if developed at all, are relegated to a realm of culture separate from and above the material existence, would then become factors in the material production itself.[15]

The historical nature of the subject itself stands at the ideological crossroads between the critical theorists. What is the nature of the subject? Can we even speak about the subject, except by very indirect analogy in our music or our science? Adorno supposed that the subject was an effete residual of bourgeois philosophy which perished in the Nazi death-camps. Marcuse and O'Neill by contrast argue that the kernel of positive opposition lies in the "libidinal rationality" beginning to emerge from the embodied subject. They have tried to harness the prepolitical reaction of subjectivity against surplus repression in building a new body politic.

Whereas Adorno read Freud as the prescient prophet of the completely eradicated subject, Marcuse employs the allegedly "gloomy" Freud to postulate a buried libidinal substratum capable of healthy creativity and socialist relations. The initial revolt of 1960s youth against an oppressive superego was not dismissed by Marcuse or O'Neill as merely another version of Oedipal reaction, but as indicating that the instinctual substratum was beginning to emerge. Marcuse's Freudianism enabled him to harness the natural subject as the new agent of body politics.

Marcuse and O'Neill want to restore the experience of the embodied subject to Marxism. Ideology-critique opposes the scientization of Marx in arguing that the fate and potential of the subject is important for oppositional activity. Although Hegel spiritualized the subject in terms of a world-historical Spirit, Marx re-objectivized and re-naturalized the concept of the subject through his labour-theory. Marx saw that contemplation was itself a kind of production, akin to work and possessing the same permanent objective residue. *The German Ideology* relentlessly criticizes the spiritualization of the subject in German philosophy and argues that the so-called objective spirit is a product of nineteenth-century ideology.

Restoring the bodily and libidinal health of the subject is for Marcuse and O'Neill tantamount to resuscitating the power of critical rationality. Adorno never believed that Hegel's concept of thought as negation was an adequate form of political activity; but negative thought was better than no thought at all. Marcuse believes that negative reason can actually be a form of praxis: the Great Refusal of what is. Hegel's concept of negation was revised by Marcuse to become a self-sufficient form of critical praxis: negation pregnant with the hidden positive. Marcuse's notion of the political character of sensibility turned the moment of thought into a directly political moment. Surplus repression was the libidinal counterpart of the extraction of surplus value.

Adorno's conception of the frozen quality of the social totality denied even the critical power of thought. The subject was so damaged—with no libidinal prepolitical potential—that his thought and speech were but determinations of the society's material and ideological forms. Total domination could *not* occasion total opposition unless opposition mirrored the form of domination.

Adorno's dialectic was defused and bent away from the social totality. Dialectic no longer reveals the unfulfilled purpose of things, but instead simply mirrors a "negative dialectic" of society which successfully reconciles all social contradictions. Dissonant music apes the prematurely de-structured dialectic which becomes sedimented in eternally contradictory social institutions. For example, increasing private leisure-time occasions a more thorough-going domination of the subject by corporate prerogatives. Indeed, leisure itself is captured by the culture industry as needs are turned into commodities. Critique has no field for its expression in that it would fall upon deaf ears. Everything can be made to seem affirmative, even Marxism.

The aesthetic theories of O'Neill, Marcuse, and Adorno all respond to the premature reconciliation of contradictions in late bourgeois society. O'Neill's turn towards a political aesthetic responds to the deformation of the subject and yet remains sensitive to nascent opposition on the level of body politics. Marcuse's hope of re-sensitizing the subject

lies in an active conception of libidinal rationality and preservation of the transcendent function of art. Adorno argued that the dialectical method was stagnant, archaic; the only possible form of negation remained on the mimetic level of dissonant thought. Praxis, the self-externalization of the labouring subject, always fails to achieve its purpose, namely, the liberation of other men. Thought alone could conceivably remain undamaged by the pernicious totality.

In *Negative Dialectics,* Adorno argues that the conception of the subject itself is a remnant of bourgeois idealism. The subject could not be thought without thinking the object which dominated it. To subjectivize social theory was falsely to represent the actual powers of the nearly impotent, voiceless person. Theory was circumscribed by its own inability to theorize about a separate entity called the human being. In reality, the subject was almost perfectly synonymous with the objects to which it was politically subordinated. Thus, the subject is a trivial and forgotten moment in a dialectical method which charts the progress of the object's preponderance.

It is clear that Adorno does not completely banish a concept of the subject from his musicology, for music needs an audience. The culture-critique of Adorno deals with culture as an objectified domain of spirit which has somehow gone wrong. *Minima Moralia* is characteristically embellished with the sub-title "Reflections of a Damaged Life." In *Philosophy of Modern Music* Adorno says that the avant-garde's rejection of Schoenberg's music which hides behind the apology of incomprehension masks their real hatred of the abrasive atonality of the music. Each sentence in Adorno's work likewise resonates a harshly dissonant quality through which he tries to capture the frozen quality of the dialectic.

Marcuse's theorizing makes thought practical by embedding thinking in the totality of the sensuous person. In O'Neill, "sensibility" is a combination of good sense and of good senses, intellectual and libidinal rationality. The ego itself is a dialectic between unfulfilled hopes and concrete possibilities. Thought thinks of the future and grapples with the "chance of the alternatives" which springs from the present circumstance. There can be no dialectical movement without the complicity of the self-conscious subject, a subject not as damaged as Adorno supposed. Whereas for Adorno culture was merely a domain for the system's ugly self-reflection, culture for O'Neill and Marcuse is a potential launching-pad for oppositional projects.

Negative theory for Marcuse works to create the aesthetic of socialist forms; it contains the positive within the negative. In O'Neill the Great Refusal breaks into song. In Adorno, the Refusal peters out in a vague imitation of social insanity by the crazy composer. There is a tendency both on the part of Adorno and his modern inheritors to reject youth culture as a superficial spin-off of the affirmative culture industry. Marcuse by contrast recognizes the *ambivalent* nature of the 1960s youth phenomenon. Events like Woodstock are obviously corporate rip-offs, yet they *also* represent a real attempt to create a new order of political togetherness, the beginning of a new class consciousness. Woodstock was an ambivalent phenomenon because American youth lacked the political structures—like an organized Left—within which to situate their erotic-aesthetic rejection of inner-worldly asceticism. Marcuse and O'Neill, unlike Adorno, see the positive within the negative, the real concretization of socialist experience within an otherwise disorganized, pre-ideological youth movement.

Rock music and drugs are sources of prepolitical ecstasy which in their ecstatic moments free the person from the spacetime of serial bourgeois life. Atonal music merely mocks seriality. Marcuse and O'Neill both attempt to force the moment of prepolitical ecstasy into the mold of a new body politic. The ecstasy of habitual, free and easy togetherness experienced at rock concerts can be recollected as an authentic mode of socialist co-existence. Ultimately, the ecstatic forms of youth culture constitute aspects of the everyday life of a socialist body politic. The naive, pre-ideological honesty of gentle folk can thus be preserved as a vital archetype of the post-ideological socialist personality. Marx's icon of the Paris Commune as the epitome of communism is replaced today by the icon of the "be-in."

It is insufficient merely to reject these moments of cathartic subjectivity as fodder for the culture industry. Social change is effected between the moments of subjective abandon and objective sobriety; Marx roughly distinguished cultural from economic modes in accepting this motif. Yet nowhere did he rule out the *objective potential* of initially subjective rebellion. The "counter" culture is not actually against culture; it is against cultural forms which are serially divorced from political forms. The archetypal hippie, for all his apparent prepolitical innocence, actually rejected the bourgeois segregation of culture from economics and politics, and in this was engaged in a quintessentially political form of opposition. The "counter" culture opposed the categorial boundaries *between* bourgeois culture and politics. Indeed, Marcuse's new science and O'Neill's wild sociology are forms of cultural opposition against this very fragmentation of the modern lifeworld. Wild sociology attempts to reunite fractured humanity in rejecting the vulgar Marxist dichotomy between "superstructure" and "base." It is a dialectical sociology because it digs beneath the apparently unpolitical surface of phenomena like Woodstock and the Rolling Stones and turns them towards the political light of day: towards the new dawn of a truly socialist world.

Adorno accepted a very deterministic model of the relation between economics and culture. Marcuse imputed less determinative force to the structure of capital and more to a relatively autonomous cultural sphere. I would argue that Marcuse's model is closer to that of Marx in that Marx also tried to discover prepolitical modes of opposition before they entered the schema of class-conflict. Today it is

imperative to move *further* away from Adorno's model of a frozen, totally managed world in reassessing certain non-proletarian cultural forms for their contribution to the creation of a new body politic. It is also imperative that we reject Marx's model of the politically organized working class and the theory of crisis which supports it. In Marx's *spirit,* but not slavishly imitating him, we must become sensitive to untraditional modes of political opposition.

> For Marxian theory, the location (or rather contraction) of the opposition in certain middle-class strata and in the ghetto population appears as an intolerable deviation—as does the emphasis on biological and aesthetic needs: regression to bourgeois or, even worse, aristocratic, ideologies. But, in the advanced monopoly-capitalist countries, the displacement of the opposition (from the organized industrial working classes to militant minorities) is caused by the internal development of the society; and the theoretical "deviation" only reflects this development. What appears as a surface phenomenon is indicative of basic tendencies which suggest not only different prospects of change but also a depth and extent of change far beyond the expectations of traditional socialist theory.[16]

We have contrasted Adorno, Marcuse, and O'Neill better to comprehend the alternative of critical theory as music and critical theory as the activist sin of pride, as praxis itself. Adorno thought that everything we do in the way of praxis is wrong, or at best insufficient; theory contemplates freedom which can only be expressed atonally: there is no collective subject anymore. The primacy of the object forces the subject into a meek and abstract compliance with the interdictions of the object. In late bourgeois society, Schoenberg sings the truth, although it is a dismal, negative truth. The dialectical blockage of dynamic forces issues in the death of opposition. We can only sing the tragedy of a world which has forgotten tragedy.

Adorno thinks that science has no song but that of mathematics. Nietzschean tragedy has been banished from memory by the instrumental success of scientism. Culture has been made an industry by those who attempt to harmonize the fundamentally tragic universe; culture is a painless ideology, another great myth.

Marcuse is less Nietzschean than Hegelian in that he does not accept the inherent tragedy of human existence. In fact, his conception of the mortal subject is based on Freud's essentially constructive matrix of instincts: natural man. His own theorizing presupposes Marx's optimism about eliminating domination. Critical theory can perhaps even serve as an expressive medium for the recreation of sensibility. The Great Refusal is a form of praxis, but dissonant music is not. Music is merely negative theory, resigned to its heteronomous quality. Marcuse's theory transcends itself in becoming a form of embodied sensibility, a political structure of needs and feelings. A dialectical theory must herald the *negation* of contradiction, couched in historically comprehensible terms and forms, which is to say that it must be a theory of *hope*.

Adorno's negative theory does not negate dissonance because it cannot rise above the terms of discourse of a dissonant world. O'Neill transcends pain through an optimism rooted in the *natural* or *wild objectivity* of the instinctual body. Without this source of naturalism critical theory will fail to rise above tragedy. Critical theory has become scholastic because its second generation could not come to terms with psychoanalysis and its theory of the objective character of subjectivity. Marcuse's *Eros and Civilization* failed to convince enough Marxists that the objectivity of subjectivity was a wellspring of hope, not despair. Therefore, in failing to assimilate Freud, critical theory runs the risk of neglecting vital cultural forms of opposition which kick surplus repression in the teeth.

Freud provides what Marx neglected: a transmission-belt between economic structure and cultural forms, the objective subject. Ultimately, Marx did not understand *why* the collapse of capital *could* emerge in a new order of society; he did not theorize the political sensibility which stands between the moments of structure and consciousness. Capitalism survived because workers could not translate the pain of hard labour and their fundamental insecurity as wage-labourers into a sensible language which pointed towards a new order. Marx himself did not tell them what the future could be like; he did not tell them what socialism would *feel* like.

Critical theory today must do so, even if it uses a crude, sensory language like that of freaked-out youth. The one-dimensional totality denies the experiences of imagination and union, experiences which are essential to the non-linear spacetime of rock and drugs. It is in this sense that the language of a critical theory which transcends its own scholasticism must portray the raw feeling of ecstasy through media which somehow escape the levelling influence of the culture industry.

We are not faced with a discrete choice between culture-forms like symphony, opera, jazz, or rock. Atonal music recollects the painful disassociation of meaning under alienating society; rock recollects the libidinal rationality of good times, the promise of living ecstatically beyond instrumental rationality. If critical theory is a discourse, it must talk even when ordinary language has been exhausted. Between Adorno, O'Neill, and Marcuse there lies the distance between disappointment and the cautious re-awakening of hope, a distance vital for a practice with eyes wide open to a history which occasionally delights as well as disappoints.

Critical theory itself is a culture-form, a product of history and place. In singing the world, this theory chooses either to deny or affirm the possibility of a resurrected humanity arising from *this* earth. Atonal music evokes the scream of tortured Jews, appropriate to its time. Rock sings of sexual rationality and the transcendence of functional differentiation. Between Auschwitz and Haight-Ashbury critical theory has changed its tune, first Adorno, then Marcuse. As I said initially, critical theory must surpass *itself* in remaining within the dialectic of the real and the possible. New science recovers grounds for positive rebellion in the carnal body, the body politic. "Critical theory" is not a school but rather the way we choose to oppose inhumanity in different songs of joy.

Notes

1. Herbert Marcuse, *An Essay on Liberation* (Boston: Beacon Press, 1969), pp. 39-40.

2. John O'Neill, *Sociology as a Skin Trade* (New York: Harper & Row/London: Heinemann, 1972), p. 53.

3. John O'Neill, "Gay Technology and the Body Politic," in *The Body as a Medium of Expression*, eds. Jonathan Benthall and Ted Polhemus (London: Allen Lane, 1975), p. 299.

4. John O'Neill, *Making Sense Together* (New York: Harper & Row/London: Heinemann, 1974), p. 10.

5. Ibid., p. 80.

6. Ibid., p. 34.

7. See John O'Neill, "Gay Technology and the Body Politic," pp. 291-302.

8. Theodor W. Adorno, *Philosophy of Modern Music* (New York: Seabury Press, 1973), p. 20.

9. Ibid., p. 216

10. Max Horkheimer and Theodor W. Adorno, *Dialectic of Enlightenment* (New York: Herder and Herder, 1972), p. 167.

11. Adorno, *Philosophy of Modern Music,* p. 133.

12. Ibid., p. 172.

13. See Russell Jacoby, *Social Amnesia* (Boston: Beacon Press, 1975).

14. Herbert Marcuse, *An Essay on Liberation* (Boston: Beacon Press, 1969), pp. 37-38.

15. Herbert Marcuse, *Counterrevolution and Revolt* (Boston: Beacon Press, 1972), p. 3.

16. Marcuse, *An Essay on Liberation,* pp. 58-59.

David Martin (essay date 1976)

SOURCE: "Dr. Adorno's Bag of Tricks," in *Encounter,* Vol. 47, No. 4, October, 1976, pp. 67-76.

[*In the following essay, Martin reviews* Minima Moralia, *finding the book intriguing even though he disagrees with many of Adorno's assertions.*]

> Our society distributes itself into Barbarians, Philistines and Populace.
>
> —Matthew Arnold

Those qualified to judge are inclined to regard T. W. Adorno's **Minima Moralia**[1] as the masterwork of the Frankfurt

School. Certainly it illustrates one of that School's cardinal tenets: a rejection of over-arching system. An author who claims that "the whole is the untrue" probably represents his position best by collections of fragments. The *Minima Moralia* is fragmented in the way Pascal's *Pensées* is fragmented; and, as with Pascal, one suspects that a work which brought all the bits and pieces into a rounded system would result in distortion. Adorno's work is about multiple distortion, and you can only attack multiple distortion by continually criticising it from different angles and moving in from different starting points. If distortion of nature and man, science and culture is protean, then its negation must acquire a complementary variety of form. If the situation is as deeply distorting and pervasive as you claim, then any rounded system is both impossible and untrue to its object and objective. The rounded-off has no cutting edges to do the job it sets itself. "These fragments have I shored against my ruins."

The fragmented mode is related more precisely to his view of the role of the individual and of the concept of the individual within a context of deepening cultural and social twilight. After the Twilight of the Gods, the twilight of man. Horkheimer and Adorno, in a sense joint authors of the *Minima Moralia,* came to see the notion of the individual as containing resistances which the onward march of the collective in its right- and its left-wing formations made doubly precious. After all, in one's social philosophy and political allegiance it is not merely a question of what is right, but where to lay one's weight when the worst tendencies of one or other alternative seem to be dominant. The problem for Adorno was compounded, however, by his belief that the individual was ceasing to have any weight to lay, or for that matter to experience; but that hardly made him less precious. Indeed even such strength as lay in archaic forms of the individual should be salvaged for the unequal battle.

This is his very first point in his dedication to Max Horkheimer, and this the text that informs this work right up to the final reflections on redemption. It is worth quoting:

> What the philosophers once knew as life has become the sphere of private existence and now of mere consumption, dragged along as an appendage of the process of material production, without autonomy or substance of its own.

So the plight of the intellectual is precisely how he may preach autonomy when the objective preconditions of the autonomous sermon are not genuinely present. No valid sermon can come from those who are representatives of what they condemn; and insofar as preachers are exempted from the general plight the exemption is almost too shameful to be exploited. Yet the paradox is that the exemption *must* be exploited, and all the historically outdated resources of the individual drawn upon in order to preserve a memory which can be carried forward into a new realization of individuality whenever that may become possible.

To know the alienation of one's power and experience is to be less than totally alienated. (After all it has been the malign achievement of Marxist régimes to use a vocabulary—in which alienation is central—in order to repress consciousness of its existence.) It is, therefore, possible as well as necessary to protest against the domination of productive forces; against technicism; against the measurement of the incommensurate; against a psychoanalytic cure of souls eliminating the soul in an ideology of adjustment; against the conception of science as a mere accumulation of instrumentalities; and against the ubiquitous character of the exchange relationship. This last is crucial for Adorno. He has a nostalgia for *noblesse oblige* and a hatred of precisely those aspects of contemporary life which use a parody of *noblesse oblige* to hide the reality of exchange. His *obiter dicta* on American hotels and trains are minor outworkings of this point. So strong is this feeling that even degenerations associated with the onset of the bourgeois era appear in retrospect to retain a precious possibility. His remarks on the humane protection afforded by "distance" could have been written by Professor Mary Douglas, and his treatment of "tact" can be taken as a precise illustration of his essential concern. It is worth some consideration.

For Adorno, tact is based on a convention which remains intact yet has lost its binding force. Tact both expresses alienation and represents a saving accommodation between human beings. Though inseparable from renunciation and the loss of the possibility of total contact, tact protects because it discriminates between different persons and situations. Without convention there emerges a demand that each individual shall be met in precisely the manner which befits him, and this replaces the careful modulations of manners by naked power. To be direct "places" a man. The abolition of convention heralds the advent of domination. Freedom dissolves in rib-digging camaraderie.

But why does this last point follow? On the surface it might seem that rib-digging is simply a convention of a pseudo-egalitarian kind supplanting another older type of convention. The answer is found in a typical Adorno paradox. In his view egalitarianism unveils a latent brutality lying behind the façade of affability. This is because condescension and thinking oneself no better are two sides of the same coin. If you adapt to the weakness, style, language, even the music, of the oppressed, you consent to deprivation and so to what makes deprivation possible. And simultaneously you develop in yourself the coarseness and the violence required to be an oppressor. In the end it may be that only the egalitarian adaptation remains visible, and such an adaptation is the perfect mask for power. To share men's pleasures in such a fashion is to collude in their pains. All the intellectual can do under such circumstances is to demonstrate solidarity by remaining inviolable. Hence Adorno's "snobbery" can be reinterpreted as closer to revolutionary solidarity than self-conscious slumming and the inversion of taste.

The excursus on tact, like the fragmentary mode in general, does justice to his main point: the intimate substance is gnawed at by the logic of the productive process. But in dealing with the problem Adorno was faced by a further paradox. He confronted two possibilities. The first was to lay bare with the utmost brutality the ruthless penetration of even sublime relationships by material interests and exchange. The second was to recognise that to assist in the brutal destruction of even the chimeras which impotently point to better things is to collude yet again with barbarism.

It is in the face of all these quite genuine paradoxes that one sees how Adorno could be regarded as a defender, not only of the best in bourgeois culture, but even of those elements that had fallen away from the best. Basically this is because he knows that there is no "good end" mysteriously waiting to be born as the beast of time shuffles towards the last antithesis. He says so precisely. Marxists who are

> cured of the Social Democratic belief in cultural progress and confronted by growing barbarism are under constant temptation to advocate the latter in the interests of the "objective tendency" and in an act of desperation to await salvation from their mortal enemy, who, as the antithesis, is supposed in blind and mysterious fashion to help prepare the good end.

That should make everything clear. He does not believe in the long-term beneficence of the objective tendency or therefore in colluding with it to hasten the birth pangs of a better future. However, the passages on tact show that he *does* believe in an ideal of total contact and of pleasure in the thing itself which has never yet been realised except in constricted mediating forms like tact. As things are today, even the constricting mediations represent archaic sources of strength; and once this weak strength has ebbed away there is only naked confrontation and power. So here we have both his utopia and his nostalgia; and a man is known by his utopias and his nostalgias. What he does not quite admit is that an ancient partial good will never be reabsorbed in a surpassing future good, but that the partial and the constricting elements express certain ineluctable limits and conditions. His utopia is only realizable in love and music; hence perhaps his love of music. To use a phrase of Walter Benjamin, Adorno's angel "flew forward with face turned back."

The implications of all this go beyond the posing of paradox against paradox and fragment over fragment. They need to be set in the context of Hegel (who stands behind the *Minima Moralia*) and especially in the context of Hegel and the individual. Hegel, says Adorno, argued against individual "being-for-itself"; and aphoristic fragments are directly drawn from individual selfhood. This tells against Adorno; but if the individual is vanishing, then the self can only fasten on the evanescent. Only by dwelling on what has almost ceased to be has it power to be. At precisely the moment of decay the experience of the individual contributes again to knowledge. What was once obscurantist in viewing itself as dominant now partakes in its weakness of the possibility of liberation. In Adorno's view,

Hegel knew nothing of this because his conception of a whole harmonious throughout all its antagonisms assigned inferior status to individuation, whatever its importance as a dynamic force. Just as the social principle of individuation has concluded in the triumph of fatality so philosophy has hitched itself (understandably) to the triumphal car of objective tendencies. Yet in fact the whole is the untrue. Subjective experience, fragmented and without theoretical cohesion, has its contribution to make to truth.

There is one final reason for fragmentation. What Adorno writes is neither philosophy nor sociology but belongs to a class of philosophical reflection on society and on social fact rejecting both reflection and fact conceived in themselves. Merely to reflect on the given is simply to reflect the given, just as merely to reflect (*i.e.* mirror) the given is to leave everything as it is and claims to be. Philosophy conceived as pure reflection may achieve a systematic, rounded exposition, and science as the mirror of the given may also achieve systematisation. But the complicated reflexives of the critical dialectic have to work backwards, forwards, and across themselves, making every partial truth less partially true in the light of its negation and in the further light of a negation of that negation. Adorno writes in the double or triple negative, and this prevents an elegant, rounded mode of writing. The light has to be dark enough to be light. Nothing is as it seems, and truth is paradoxically layered. You can only break through to truth by exposing the paradoxes and masquerades at each layer and setting them against other masquerades and paradoxes. The first act of unmasking is not enough. The cunning of social reality is to delude you with the pleasure of thinking that you have got somewhere with the first act of unmasking. Indeed, it may even be that the cunning of social reality is to delude you with the pleasure of unmasking right down to that last layer which looks like hiding the truth. It is of the nature of critical reflection always to be discontented, even with a philosophy which insists on the last layer being the true. Maybe there was a truth as well as a lie at each point in the process of unmasking. I do not mean that Adorno held such a view; but that the complexity and constant attempt at self-correction and renewed suspicion of the correction always forces him to move from layer to layer sceptically suspicious and yet also suspicious of mere scepticism.

This makes him very difficult to attack. When you advance on him you have to ask which corner he has just turned around. There are some thinkers who are basically committed to doing the same disappearing trick around the same corner. Once you spot the nature of the disappearing trick you have them by the coat-tails and can haul them over the coals. But Adorno's trick is to look as if disappearing around the first corner when he is really round corner three or corner five, and to go round the corner in such a way as to prevent you supposing that corners one, three, and five can really be categorised over against two, four, and six. He is very tricky, and tempts you to declare you have him in order to laugh triumphantly and say you are illustrating just the point he is making, though not of course realizing it in the sense in which *he* realises it. He is a specialist in evasive affirmation and does so not only by covering himself at every point but by declaring his exposed parts more virtuous than obscene. The points at which he seems exposed *are* his virtues. For example, in a world where facts are disguises is it not virtue to be exposed to the charge of indifference to fact? There is a lower and higher form of indifference and to take the measure of the inordinate, incommensurable, is to defeat measurement even more truly than mere refusal to measure.

If one had to invent one of his own aphorisms one would say "the unmeasured is the true." He *is* unmeasured and, as he says of psychoanalysis, only the exaggerations are true. Certainly the exaggerations enable one to *see*. Not that even this is the whole truth: there must be another aphorism posed against that aphorism. The result, as Anthony Quinton has remarked,[2] resembles a highbrow party very late at night. The clever paradoxes cap each other tipping more and more tipsily towards complementary profundities until the final gross statement, made against all mundane commonsensical likelihood, appears as the only possible stand-in for the enigmatic truth. Be drunk enough on dialectic and the sibylline even becomes the obvious, and vice versa. If *you* see what I mean. It all depends on how much you have had. A simple man and proud of it can only find Adorno disgusting.

I want to move from approach and style to substance, which is a difficult move with a writer in whom the two are joined together. Basically I want to criticise his uncriticizability, and what bothers me at this juncture is that he evades criticism by never saying anything of substance. He certainly asserts and affirms, but he never says anything is "just so" because he rejects the category of the "just so." Paul Lazarsfeld parted from him both in anger and in admiration partly because he found that Adorno was indifferent to criteria of more or less "just so", since if things are not so you cannot have more or less of them. Lazarsfeld found that Adorno's notions just could not be operationalised. I am not surprised. Adorno preferred accentuating the negative to accentuating the positive, and above all he disliked positive science. His own assertions were subject not to the criteria of positive science but interpretative criteria. They constitute a category of statement *between* the metaphysical and evaluative categories on the one hand and the category of positive science. They make empirical connections, but they are not subject to criteria of test or to falsifiability or verifiability.

It is the fact that Adorno works in this intermediate mode which uses facts but does not allow them to constitute the court of final appeal which makes him ultimately elusive. I want to illustrate this category from his analysis of astrology, because this is relatively well-developed and illustrates very well his style of analysis and the difficulty of subjecting it to tests which might carry much intersubjective conviction. He is, in short, beyond the verifiability principle. Perhaps I might say, parenthetically, that I do not accept his view that positive science, by paying attention to the given, is thereby committed to defending the given. This is just not true. I am, however, interested in a class of interpretative statement which appears to be beyond the normal criteria of science. As a sociologist I ask myself how such statements are justified and how they may be integrated with that other class of statements which is subject to the normal scientific criteria of justification. How can you *use* sociology and not be in the sociological mode?

Adorno's whole method is exposed *in nuce* by his treatment of astrology. I chose astrology because it relates to Adorno's favorite theme of genuine individual subjectivity confronting technology, in that astrology is a pseudo-technology utilised for individual ends. You could regard astrology as the randy grandsire of positive science and as its contemporary parody. The persistence of superstition is necessarily an important issue because it challenges so many assumptions about the unique authority of the scientific world view precisely in those sectors of the population where that authority is supposed to be best established. For Adorno, however, the emphasis of criticism must lie on the notion of a social fate transferred to the individual level. Men are haunted by their own spirits dispossessed of a home in their own concrete existences. Deprived of the Holy Spirit they have lost the instinct for the unconditional set over against the conditional and have confused the two, treating spirit as a form of factuality. (The parody of positivism is here very clear.) At the same time Judicious Reason has become ensnared in the demise of the Spirit. Ratio has become implicated in the fall of Sophia. The fall is a premonition of social disaster. If I may rephrase Adorno: it is an omen, an augury of what lies veiled in the future. The horoscope corresponds to official directives, and number mysticism to the mystique of administrative statistics and cartel prices, the break in the life-line to terminal cancer in the body politic. Official progress mocks the blocked hope of human beings and forces the absent—experience—to make its presence felt elsewhere in phantasmagoria and dreams from which there seems no awakening. The actual content of the dream reflects social nullity. The secondary, projected reality runs parallel to the prosaic emptiness of the primary reality and reinforces it: the spirits have nothing much or interesting to say.

The spirits are also falsely spiritual. In Occultism the Spirit does not vivify matter as in the resurrection of the body but floats above it in permanent schizoid disjunction. Spirit cannot say "This is my body", demonstrating its reality, but becomes a thing "out there", demonstrating its unreality. The usual parody of "fact" is conjoined to the self-inflated pomposity of the experimental routine. After the positivist ritual of experiment expels the ghosts and materializations they return to haunt the world with an appeal to experiment. By a parallel progression the idealist exaltation of Mind (rooted in and expressing the social supremacy of the mental over the manual) achieves reabsorption through Occultism in determinate, deterministic categories of Nature. It is the last bankruptcy of Hegel's original investment in the spirit.

I hope I have not given Adorno's views a false Anglo-Saxon clarity, but in any case there are certain things anyone in an Anglo-Saxon tradition can and must say. The first concerns the status of such interpretations. Some of them are simply the working-out of this or that internal logic. What he says, for example, about the relation of body and spirit in Christianity is an exposition, and a correct one at the abstract level, of the inner logic of that religion. Again, the transformations he proposes, such as the "degenerating" shifts in the logic of idealism, are just logical possibilities. So far no difficulty. The trouble comes with such a notion as "correspondence." By what criteria can we show that there is a correspondence between the break in the life-line and the terminal illness of sick society? Adorno is not merely employing an illustrative image but asserting a link between the palmist practice and social praxis.

So far as I can see "correspondences" of this kind are partly in the hands of intelligent manipulators. There are always *some* phenomena at the level of everyday practice and *some* pathic elements in the body politic which permit the determined scryer to see the "correspondence" he wishes to see. The crystal ball is large enough. Fragments of evidence and degrees of similarity are not hard to come by, and even when the similarity is not clear one can always argue it is paradoxically imaged back to front in the mirror, or is "hidden", or has undergone a "significant" process of distortion. And so you simply manipulate certain notions and make them play crystal ball for your analysis. You determine what shall be *truly* significant and what not, where *real* accident begins and genuine essence ends, what is to count under the rubric "It is no accident that. . . ." It is no accident, implies Adorno, that one man said he believed in the Occult *because* he did not believe in God. The isolated empirical fragment fits neatly into the logic of part of Adorno's case, but it really remains a question how many empirical swallows are necessary to make a dialectician's summer.

The above is concerned with the technique of picking out the single swallow to validate your hint of summer, but there are certain assertions of a different kind embedded in the dialectical framework. If you choose to take certain phenomena or statements and let the weight of your significance and of meta-interpretation rest on them, no man can say you nay. But if you declare that the secondary projected reality reinforces the primary reality and its conformism, you make what looks like a straight empirical statement. I have said that Lazarsfeld complained during his collaboration with Adorno that he could not derive testable empirical propositions out of his work, and one can indeed see the difficulty, just as one can also understand Adorno's violent rejection of the pomposities attached to the routine of experimental verification. Yet Adorno says something here about conformism which can be construed as an empirical statement about a linkage and about a state of affairs. (As a matter of fact, recent research, such as that of Patricia Hartmann, does indeed suggest the practitioners and devotees of the Occult are very conformist and conventional, which is consistent with Adorno's contention without precisely proving it.)

I mean it is relevant to Adorno's contention without constituting quite direct verification. But if the dialectical, critical mode permits of reference to relevant empirical material, by what criteria can it dismiss other material, or ignore the whole universe of comparative materials over time and social space? Researches also show, to give but one other instance, that Occultists are only marginally less believing in God than their age and status equals. Would this fact disrupt the analysis in terms of the posited transition from the Holy Spirit to the spirits? In other words does the statement of one possible logical transformation which probably exists in a few historical instances carry any weight in terms of an overall balanced interpretation of data? One can see why Adorno thought that in psychoanalysis only the exaggerations were true. I am not saying that all data have the same rights to significance, since there is I believe a class (or classes) of statement which are not open even in principle to empirical proof and yet which do assert empirical connections. At the same time such assertions are often open to some *limitation* on the ranges of interpretation which are consistent with the data. A clever dialectician may manipulate his framework to achieve an accommodation of the awkward and even make awkward empirical devils sing the dialectical Creator's praise. But the point is that he has to manipulate and can be seen to manipulate.

In Adorno's case he does not manipulate because he is indifferent, and this is exactly the substance of Lazarsfeld's charge against him. Adorno defended a reference to the specificities of history; but by ignoring data as a control on his imagination, he easily converted his assertions into free-floating ahistorical abstract possibilities. He could have looked at the enormous increase for astrology coincident with the *rise* of the bourgeois world-view, and he could have shuffled his dialectical frame around until he accommodated the fatality of both early bourgeois society and of late bourgeois society. And today he might have looked at the manner in which, under Communism, superstition has in some ways shown more resilience even than religion. Anybody can play the dialectical game and accommodate a vast range of seemingly contradictory evidence. But the act of accommodation in essence acknowledges the existence of a problem: Adorno made no such acknowledgment. His pessimistic dialectics required nothing beyond incidental illustration, which is not to say, of course, that he was not often right. And, in addition, he had the priceless advantage of the pessimist: in the last analysis you are bound to appear right some time. Doomsters cannot in the nature of things be wrong *hic ubique et semper.* When you are borne out by events, you can then say that the real revelations are now emerging from the veiled. But even religious revelations can utilise that privilege. Men carrying placards announcing that the last day is at hand are only wrong about the date. Adorno saved himself by ignoring both dates and data.

I want now to move on to another interesting analysis by Adorno because it illustrates another facet of his ability to do the disappearing trick. In this instance he not only makes doubtful connections but also refuses to acknowledge an ineluctable contradiction. The issue I select does not arise in the front arena of social debate, yet it presents a sociological and ethical problem of primary importance. It is the question of "first come, first served."

Adorno argues that, where the intimate affections are concerned, temporal priority excludes genuine preference; the accidental precludes freedom of choice. A man and a woman meet each other at a particular point in time and mutually offer the unrepeatable. Their possession of each other is the very antithesis of the idea of property. Once this process has occurred objective moral right lies with whoever arrived first: priority has priority. But this principle leads to the antagonism of siblings, to age sets, to exclusive rights in a given national inheritance, and to the persecution of minorities. In short, it leads to Fascism.

The crucial reason, says Adorno, lies in the exclusiveness of what comes first. Possession is meaningful in relation to loss, and the fear of loss converts a genuine possession into mere property. The claim "my own, my very own" contains an implicit forfeit of that claim. What is a possession becomes an object in the universe of exchangeable objects and thereby changes the unique into the general and abstract. Yet—he says—truly to love is to speak *specifically* to the other, and it involves attachment to beloved *features,* not to some "idol of personality" which merely reflects the notion of possession and abstraction. At this point Adorno has arrived at a happy reprieve from all his difficulties. What is specific, *i.e.* features and immediate experiences of affection, is by definition unrepeatable. Ergo, infidelity is impossible. The cheat here is that Adorno defines specific features and experiences as concrete, unique, and incapable of distortion into the abstract and exchangeable. Yet, in fact, reaction to features (as distinct from reaction to that unique constellation of features which is a person) precisely converts the specific into the abstract.

Features are repeatable commodities capable of being made up into innumerable supermarket packages. Being loyal to this-or-that feature or experience merely means being loyal when you feel like it. By fragmenting people into features and experiences, Adorno achieves a worse objectification than exists in the idea of exclusive possession. He sidesteps the ineluctable dilemmas of morality and experience by sleight-of-hand. And all the sidestepping by partial analogy through sibling rivalry to Fascism is to throw back on to a genuine dilemma of personal relations the irrelevant odium of Fascism. Loyalty, by virtue of logical tricks and contagious analogy, is somehow tangled up with Fascism and the doctrine of an all-white Australia. Adorno is the kind of intellectual cheat who knows how to look sympathetic and be irresponsibly clever and superior at the same time. It is a capacity few of us lack entirely, but he had it in highly developed form.

Finally, there are two topics which can be used to back up the theme of what Adorno meant by the decomposition of the individual. One is his analysis of the Culture Industry, the other his negative assessment of Existentialist philosophy and theology. They can, and indeed should, be linked together.

The first is bound up with his critique of Positivism, the distortion of technology, social manipulation, technical and conformist concepts of health; and it is of a richness and complexity which summarization is bound to misrepresent. Again, there is the relationship of exchange, and the façade behind which that relationship lies omnipresent. Both can be combined in his image of the Hotel Manager. He outdoes aristocrats with his glossy, hygienic, elegant façade, but he lives by the tip. The Culture Industry, in apparently waiting on the customer, argues that its victims are its judges. It anticipates the spectator's imitation of itself like a parent talking baby language. Even its bad conscience is carefully put on public view. It indulges in a form of knowing self-criticism intended only to quieten the consumer. It admits to the propagation of an ideology of escape, and justifies it by distinguishing escapism from social realism, which is itself a supremely practical distinction because the escapist's dream is no more subversive than a pale reflection of the ordinary and because it carries the message: flee from flight. In all this, the objective character of manipulation, rooted in economic calculation and technical criteria, requires no censorship. In the older folk art, the lament against domination still remained audible, whereas the voice of the Culture Industry is alienation posing as togetherness, human closeness proclaimed through loudspeakers and the psychology of advertising. The confidential touch on the shoulder of Everyman is the consummate act of betrayal. The manufactured immediacy is a mediation reducing men so completely to things that real humanity becomes unimaginable. Men are made objects: decomposed consequences of exchange.

To lament this decay of the individual in the Existential manner is merely to describe a condition and to blame the weakness of individuals on to individuals without paying attention to the social principle lying behind individuation. To see the problem as an individual one is to give way to the social reality in the very act of criticism. Similarly the individual's freedom *from* society deprives that freedom of any genuine strength. Indeed, direct absolute individuation, beyond the restraint exercised by specific interests, leads to a situation where the weakest individual goes to the wall. The naked individual is easily captured and put in a cage or else himself becomes a keeper. When nothing can be required of the naked individual in terms of content, then all that can be asked for is genuineness and authenticity. From this arises the jargon of authenticity both in a religious form and usurping the place of religion.[3]

Yet in fact the self is *not* an absolute but an imitative playful consequence, and without society just a void. The claim of the self to be absolute is itself the consequence of a particular social process and amounts to a glorification of the void. God is the only possible ontological root of self-hood, just as Society is the source of all its richness and content. In a society dominated by exchange and inter-changeability the claim to be genuine and unique is the first primal lie. The theological version celebrates faith for its own sake, and thereby breeds a vocabulary of pure in-wardness which lives by verbal inflation. Such verbal in-flation may be either radical or conformist, since it has no specific content; but either way the tortured wrestling of Jacob always ends up with the self in the right position. It is, perhaps, though Adorno does not say so, the analogue within the intellectual stratum of the colourful original personality, Star of Stage and Screen.

So much Adorno has to say about pure individuality and the naked self. So far I agree with him. In general, how-ever, I am bound to disagree. He generalises far beyond the evidence and even glories in the maltreatment of evi-dence. He ignores the critical potential in positive knowl-edge, and he makes a facile link between everything he dislikes and "Fascism." He mistakes the nostalgia of the *haut bourgeois* for the reality of general cultural decline. He constantly slides away from real ineluctable alterna-tives and those general limits on human possibility with-out which there is no potential at all. Total contact and pure pleasure cannot be socially embodied without disas-ter. Above all, he puts his criticism beyond criticism, and what is beyond criticism is often just not worth criticising.

Yet his text, fragmented and partial, is richly layered, imaginative, paradoxical. It represents an anti-holistic unity, an anti-individualistic defence of the individual, a critical Marxist attack on the *haute bourgeoisie* which could be an *apologia pro vita sua*, a non-believing affir-mation that only theology is possible in the world as it now is and is likely to be.

> The only philosophy which can be responsibly prac-tised in face of despair is the attempt to contemplate all things as they would present themselves from the stand-point of redemption. Knowledge has no light but that shed on the world by redemption: all else is reconstruc-tion, mere technique. Perspectives must be fashioned that displace and estrange the world, reveal it to be, with its rifts and crevices, as indigent and distorted as it will appear one day in the messianic light. To gain such perspectives without velleity or violence, entirely from felt contact with its objects—this alone is the task of thought. It is the simplest of all things, because the situation calls imperatively for such knowledge, indeed because consummate negativity, once squarely faced, delineates the mirror-image of its opposite. But it is also the utterly impossible thing, because it presup-poses a stand-point removed, even though by a hair's breadth from the scope of existence, whereas we well know that any possible knowledge must not only be first wrested from what is, if it shall hold good, but is also marked, for this very reason, by the same distor-tion and indigence which it seeks to escape. The more passionately thought denies its conditionality for the sake of the unconditional, the more unconsciously, and so calamitously, it is delivered up to the world. Even its own impossibility it must at last comprehend for the

sake of the possible. But beside the demand thus placed on thought, the question of the reality or unreality of redemption itself hardly matters.

Notes

1. T. W. Adorno, *Minima Moralia: Reflections from Damaged Life.* Translated by E. F. N. Jephcott. New Left Books, £4.25.

2. Anthony Quinton, "Critical Theory", *Encounter* (October 1974).

3. See my essay "The Naked Person", *Encounter* (June 1973).

Philip Rosen (essay date 1980)

SOURCE: "Adorno and Film Music: Theoretical Notes on *Composing for the Films,*" in *Yale French Studies,* Vol. 60, 1980, pp. 157-82.

[*In the following essay, Rosen discusses Adorno's little-known volume* Composing for the Films.]

Important recent work on the ideological operations of cinema bases itself on a view of the history of the graphic arts deriving from studies by Francastel and a more or less Althusserian view of ideology.[1] But cinema incorporates non-graphic elements which have their own histories and social roles "outside of" and "before" cinema, and ideo-logical analysis must account for the integration into cin-ema of such elements. One such component of film is mu-sic. An important study of film music based on a distinctive view of music as an autonomous art form and with a con-cern for the ideological operations of film already exists in the often noted but rarely discussed 1947 book *Compos-ing for the Films.*

At first signed only by the composer Hanns Eisler, this book was actually co-authored by the eminent social phi-losopher and aesthetician Theodor W. Adorno.[2] What fol-lows is no more than notations from a reading of *Compos-ing for the Films* in the context of Adorno's theories of society, music, and culture. The purpose is not to become involved in a dispute over authorship or to downgrade the significance of Eisler's views and contributions. It is rather to underline certain aspects of the book which may be of use now, given the current interests in the ideological functioning of film and in so-called Western Marxism.

Like Eisler's, Adorno's musical education included an as-sociation with the Vienna School of composition (for some time he studied under Berg), but by the 1930's Adorno was concentrating most of his efforts on philosophy and social theory.[3] He had already developed a viewpoint en-abling him to cross back and forth among philosophical analysis, knowledgeable commentary on music and litera-ture, criticism of mass culture, and his distinctive view of culture in general in advanced capitalist societies. The fate of human subjectivity in such societies always held his special attention, and it is from his account of that fate that one must read *Composing for the Films* as part of his *corpus.*

1. SOME ELEMENTS OF ADORNO'S THOUGHT

Limitations of space make a detailed explication of Adorno's theories impossible here, but a brief list of certain motifs in his thought with regard to questions of knowledge, art, music, and the culture industry will help to contextualize *Composing for the Films.* The theoretical groundwork for it as well as for his analysis of music in *Philosophy of New Music* (1948) is provided by the contemporaneous *Dialectic of Enlightenment* (1947), written with Max Horkheimer. All of these are in debt to the Hegelian Marxist approach formulated by Lukács in *History and Class Consciousness.* It is well known that by modeling the victory of the proletariat on the realization of Hegel's *Geist,* Lukács elevated the epistemological problem of subject and object to centrality in Marxist theory, made the problem of knowledge a crucial historical and political question, and by means of concepts such as reification and alienation focussed attention on the limitations of the realization of the rational imposed by the social structure on humanity.

In a sense, Adorno assumed the position of a radical critic of capitalist society by developing Lukács's work to account for the persistence of capitalist society. A Lukácsian problematic provided conceptual tools of great use for explicating the increasingly total social control Adorno saw at work throughout the bourgeois administrative-cultural order. Unlike his elder Lukács, however, Adorno was never transfixed by the image of an immediate, totalizing transformation of society; rather, he believed that contemporary refinements in mechanisms of alienation and reification render impossible any vision of an immediate reconciliation of subject and object, humanity and existence. Chief among these mechanisms is an omnipresent pretense to such immediacy, a pretense which pervades life thanks to the universalization of the principles of positivist science as the ultimate standard of knowledge. It is his theory of knowledge which is a primary aspect of Adorno's famous "pessimism."

Adorno's thought is thus to a large extent based on an attack on an ideal of reason he finds to have dominated in the West since the Enlightenment. The Enlightenment ideal conceives of the realization of human rationality in objectifying, hypostatizing terms of calculation and repeatable categories that serve as instruments to conquer nature and hence displace myth with science. Knowing would thus require an immediate abstraction from the particular qualities of objects of knowledge in order that given factuality can become quantifiable, hence commensurable, therefore exchangeable. As capitalism becomes entrenched, this narrow view of rationality is fetishized and applied to all areas of human existence through the growth in administration and bureaucratic methods associated in part with

industry. The ideal of human rationality dominating nature for the benefit of humanity becomes the rationalization of life, which in fact dominates the human and becomes a means of social control.

To Enlightenment rationalization Adorno opposes his "negative dialectics." For him, knowing requires not an immediate translation from part to universal through the automatic application of abstract categories, but rather conceiving of the object of knowledge as a totality of mediations which are its linkage to the social whole. The immediate givens of existence must be grasped "as the superficies, as mediated conceptual moments which come to fulfillment only in the development of their social, historical, and human significance." Adorno thus places himself in a Hegelian line for which any whole must be known as a mediated totality which is the synthesis of many determinations. Knowing is founded on the "determinate negation of each im-mediacy."[4]

Dialectic of Enlightenment, which outlines the consequences of the universal legitimation of non-dialectical conceptions of knowledge, is still the story of *Geist,* but of a *Geist* gone bad. Supposedly triumphant human subjectivity is now judged by the categories it attributes to objectivity, and the principles of rationalization assume the irrational function of myth in their universalization. The dialectic of Enlightenment is the subjection of human subjectivity to the irrational components of its own advance. The idea that subjectivity participates in its own subjection explains the importance of psychoanalysis for Adorno, but his analysis of the universal immediacy of abstract equivalence is intended primarily as a totalizing social critique which engages the totalization of social control at its own level of comprehensiveness. As the following passage indicates, Adorno retains many elements of the classic Marxist view:

> To the individual, domination appears to be the universal: reason in actuality. Through the division of labor imposed on them, the power of all members of society—for whom as such there is no other course—amounts over and over again to the realization of the whole, whose rationality is reproduced in this way. What is done to all by the few always occurs as the subjection of individuals by the many.[5]

It is his view of knowledge which grounds the ambivalent position Adorno assigns to the work of art under advanced capitalism. The art work in bourgeois society is defined by a negative social role: it is useless, cut off from the practical by a kind of sacred "magic circle." Even the most serious art work is inserted into the area of acknowledged superstition and cannot be taken seriously.

On the other hand, this regressive position means that the work can be constructed as a mediated totality and hence embody a progressive negation of the abstract rationalization characteristic of advanced capitalism. Adorno is sometimes attracted by Benjamin's notion of *aura*[6] to help describe the art work. By its insistence on its own unique presence, its specific here-and-now, the traditional art work maintains a distinctive connection with the particular time and space of its own origin and existence. The work becomes unexchangeable; there is no abstract equivalent by which it can be measured.

Thus, the regressive social situation of the art work, evinced in its aura, (often a regressive phenomenon for Benjamin) may permit the art work to achieve an epistemologically progressive protest against or negation of the given. If it avoids succumbing to the irrationalist and/or reifying temptations offered by its social role, the work can attain the traditional aesthetic goal of being a structure of particulars defined uniquely by their relationships to one another through the whole—in sort, a mediated totality. The price good art pays for the achievement of such monadic totality is often social isolation and misunderstanding on the part of the general population.

Crucially, the art work as a totality can be read as a working through of the relation of subject and object in a given social formation. The aesthetic subject (not identical to the biological human who assumes the social place of "artist") constructs a totality—a network of relations of parts and whole—by manipulation of the material of the art form (often historically limited, then hypostatized as its "nature") within a definite artistic tradition and social situation. The subject-object relation thereby established is a stance toward the epistemological possibilities of a given society. This is why as early as 1932 Adorno could equate autonomous (concert hall) music with social theory.[7]

In *Philosophy of New Music* Schoenberg's greatness is thus explicated from an account of the specific involvement of music in the dialectic of Enlightenment. Music is the rationalization of sounds, so the history of music can be measured as the use of various compositional logics that organize sound. In traditional bourgeois music, that organization constitutes the position of the subject in relation to the musical objectivity of the harmonic system of tonality, which is taken as musical "nature" itself. For example, in Beethoven's method of thematic-motivic development, there is an unprecedented total organization of the musical work; he constructs a musical totality which drives toward the final coda to reconfirm tonality (the natural, the universal), but in a forcefully unique way, for every individual element attains musical meaning only as it is mediated through the whole. But the impulse toward subjective expression in the later bourgeois era—related to the impulse to dominate nature—leads to the Romantic attack on tonality in the name of subjective spontaneity and uniqueness. After Wagner there is no longer a musical "nature" or objectivity through which the subject can express itself, and the construction of a mediated totality becomes difficult as music succumbs to irrationality by assuming the function of presenting a subjective immediacy. This reflects the impossible situation of genuine humanity and rationality under advanced capitalism.

The question for modern music, then, becomes how to construct a musical objectivity which will once again per-

mit genuinely rational subjective expression. Schoenberg's great virtue is that, unlike Stravinsky, he does not pretend to the illogical and impossible accomplishment of simply bypassing the subjective moment hypostatized by Romanticism. Rather, with the method of the twelve-tone row Schoenberg introduces a new musical objectivity. But this new objectivity is unique to each individual work. The result is an even more totally organized music than that of Beethoven, for every element of the work—melody, counterpoint, harmony, timbre, etc.—is determined by the tone row unique to the individual work. A musical totality is again the goal of compositional technique, but the totalizing, honest expression of subjectivity that results inevitably alienates the audience—which still exists in the musical "nature" of tonality—from the music which most truthfully expresses that audience's situation.

The danger of this project is a temptation to succumb to the new musical nature in a dialectic of Enlightenment by stifling the spontaneity of subjective expression sought by Schoenberg with a mere mathematical calculation of necessities engendered by the row. Adorno defines Schoenberg's ultimate virtue with the peculiar compliment that, unlike Webern, Schoenberg ultimately learned to compose "twelve-tone music as though there were no such thing as twelve-tone technique."[8] A work by Schoenberg could thus attain the most exalted role Adorno was able to attribute to a serious art work in the bourgeois era: as a useless, isolated monadic totality, it refuses the immediacies of existence and hence exposes the truth about subjectivity in the age of advanced capitalism, when genuine individuality is suppressed under a banner of reified individualism.

Now, it might superficially seem that autonomous music and film play drastically opposed roles in Adorno's analysis of culture. The culture industry—with film as its most characteristic branch—incessantly produces affirmation of the immediate as universal. In their classic essay on the culture industry in *Dialectic of Enlightenment* Adorno and Horkheimer argue that the culture industry works by instant linkage of a detail within a work to the cultural system as a whole, instead of mediating the significance of the detail through the structure of the individual work. Films, radio programs, advertisements, etc. are composed of details instantly recognizable, exchangeable in their givenness, and hence affirmations of the existing order.

Nevertheless, it is a mistake to read "The Culture Industry" as absolutizing the opposition between high culture and mass culture with all virtue on the side of the former. The essay contains a critique of high art which partially collapses that opposition to explain the ease with which so many apparent art works assume the position of commodity. The critique proceeds by a comparison of the ideals of various schools of bourgeois aesthetics as they are to be realized in individual *works* (e.g. catharsis, purposefulness without purpose, *Gesamkunstwerk*) with the accomplishments of the *system* of the culture industry as a whole. This produces a series of ironic inversions intended to show that the culture industry accomplishes the goals of bourgeois aesthetics through the system of incessant repetitions of interchangeable effects. But the resulting repression of genuine frustration in consumers reveals the regressive social implications of those ideals. From this perspective, the lighter arts are simply "the bad social conscience" of the serious arts, and the explicit capitulation of the culture industry to the commodity structure is socially truer than the implicit claim of the serious arts to genuine autonomy.[9]

One can also note that, despite the unceasingly condemnatory tone of the essay, such dialectical continuities can point to a potential not there emphasized. If the dialectic of Enlightenment means that art as an attempt to envision a realized human subjectivity always threatens to turn into its opposite, might it not be that an industry which clearly bases itself on the objectification of human subjectivity contains elements that could generate its own antithesis? Cultural production rejecting the sacredness on which the best bourgeois art depends to establish its seriousness might be able to escape magic, to foresee the integration of the spiritual and the practical in a more progressive way. Desite the fact that Adorno himself attacked Benjamin's versions of this argument,[10] elements of it surface at points in *Composing for the Films.*

2. FILM AND IMMEDIACY

Composing for the Films is a work of description and prescription. What is described are the methods and products of what some now call classical cinema—the kind of film-making dominated economically, technologically, and aesthetically by Hollywood during the period of the studio system. The book thus takes narrative as a given and treats film as a major branch of the "cultural industry." Perhaps most interesting is the fact that the book is one of the rare full-scale Hegelian Marxist discussions of any aspect of film; hence, despite the totalizing view of the culture industry usually imputed to Adorno, Adorno and Eisler base their analysis on the delineation of contradictions. For example, filmic narrative as a problem for the composer is discussed in terms of an opposition beloved by Hegelian aestheticians, i.e. as an alternation between dramatic and novelistic (epic) methods.

Certain of these contradictions are of special interest for questions of film and ideology. One is a contradiction between the technological nature of film, which gives it an inherent appeal as the direct transmission of everyday life, and the historical origins of cinema in the melodrama and the fair, which has resulted in film's penchant for the surprising or sensationalistic effect evident in the abrupt shifts in mood and tone with which film music must deal. Adorno and Eisler explicitly suggest the progressive potential in this contradiction: not only does the persistence of melodrama hold films "below" the artistic ideals of middle-class aesthetics, but also the sensationalism may be able to lift a film above the mere affirmation of the drudgery of everyday life recorded as the natural with moving photography (pp. 35-36).[11]

For Adorno and Eisler the most fundamental contradiction of film is perhaps a more general one between film as the record of an event with its own unique "here and now" and film as mass reproduction. Their discussion of this contradiction is in inverted congruence with the arguments of Benjamin, to whom reference is made in ***Composing for the Films.*** A shot records a unique here-and-now, implicitly insisting on its own singularity. But socially and technically film is a mass medium; that is, it multiplies the unique. This paradox leads Benjamin to situate film on the leading edge of a progressive revolt against the very idea of art, the concept of which is inseparable from the notion of uniqueness. But Adorno (who finds a subversive moment precisely in the presumption of uniqueness by traditional art works) with Eisler gives more weight to the totalization of administrative control which the mass reproduction side of the contradiction entails. Their general argument, which is in line with ***Dialectic of Enlightenment*** is that administrative rationalization of culture defuses the emancipatory potential inherent in a genuinely rational development of the technology.

The stunting of art by the administration of culture is a general phenomenon which surfaces most explicitly in organs of the culture industry. Adorno and Eisler find that in the film industry the fundamental "artistic" method consists in a calculation of audience reactions to the individual details of a film, so that the detail is used only for its immediate effect, which derives from an affirmative identification with the commodity cultural system as a whole. The problem of mediated totalities is thus eliminated. The success of the operation is measured by box office receipts—sheer exchange value, hence a reified standard—which are anyway subject to certain controls. Thus, the contradiction between technological progress and administration can be seen from the subjective side as one between the apparent directness of the appeal of film to its audience as literal immediacy and the "unbridgeable remoteness" from its audience which is the actuality of film production processes and techniques. Ultimately, the methods and products operate to deny real contact in production or consumption between a film and the actual needs of its public. (pp. 53, 58-59)

The establishing of the immediate identity of the detail in relation to the sociocultural system serves to universalize that system as the only rational one. It thereby obscures such contradictions, awareness of which could lead to a consciousness of the detail as a mediated element of the system. A progressive practice, then, would question the immediacy of the detail to the end of exposing and using contradictions.

In this general prescription for a less acquiescent filmic practice, Adorno and Eisler are near the famous Russian Formalist notion of defamiliarization. The culture industry operates by means of an associative automatism which gives the detail instant significance as an element in the system. It is this automatism whose vehicle is the apparently literal immediacy of the moving photographic image, which must be the first line of attack. This premise, for example, is the basis for the proposition that the melodramatic components of filmic practice have a progressive function.

The difference between the combat against "literal immediacy" recommended by Adorno and Eisler and the Formalist conception of defamiliarization is that the former have as their standard of knowledge the grasp of a concrete, mediated totality and partly as a result stress contradiction as a social phenomenon. This makes the appeal of Adorno and Eisler to the principle of montage in its broadest sense unsurprising. Despite the severe (and largely irrefutable) critique of Eisenstein on the relation of image and music which pervades *Composing for the Films,* the book makes montage as cognition the basis for a proper practice of film making.[12]

3. Automatism in Film Music

In Adorno's *corpus* there is a good deal of discussion of the mechanical reproduction of Western high art music as a component of cultural degeneration. His general thesis is that the newer means of reproduction participate in a trivialization of musical listening which obstructs understanding of the connection between musical technique and the totality of a work.[13] Musical Romanticism and Tin Pan Alley are also parts of this process. The result is that a composer like Beethoven, who worked towards a genuine totality within the "natural" idiom of tonality, is generally heard incorrectly in terms of musical meaning; and a composer like Schoenberg, who did not work within the "natural" musical framework, is heard even by experienced concert-goers as being incomprehensible and unbearable.

Adorno and Eisler argue that the dominant practices of film music are fully implicated in this general cultural phenomenon. It is not just that the industry embraces the cultural norm of tonality as musical "nature," but that normal film music exists as a group of standardized devices which are rooted in a relatively short period of the history of Western music. And these devices are employed in a way that robs them even of their original musical significance.

Composing for the Films begins with a listing of some of the most common of such devices: the use of leitmotifs—a compositional technique which degenerates quickly into quotation as opposed to invention—without any organic link to the huge musical totality presupposed by Wagner; the fetish for melody, which usually consists of completely predictable tunes dominated by small diatonic intervals; use of only the most widely familiar kinds of harmony to insure easy intelligibility; the unobtrusiveness of the music, which serves to avoid any musical interruption of the drama and enforces the supposedly complete identification of music with image; the childish devices of immediate visual justification for music, and the related use of music to illustrate what is already occurring on screen, as in the musical imitation of a storm; the use of inauthentic "local"

music for film with exotic settings; and stock music which "trade-marks" well-known excerpts from concert hall music, sometimes even by basing the resulting clichéd associations on titles rather than the music itself (for example, a night scene accompanied by the "Moonlight Sonata" pp. 4-15).

This kind of musical standardization participates not only in the trivialization of musical listening, but also in the processes by which instant comprehension of the detail through the system displaces the more difficult comprehension of the detail in relation to the individual work. Furthermore, such standardization results from the assimilation of all activities to the socioeconomic sphere and therefore is part of the suppression of the human (in this case, musical) subject. Composing for a film becomes simply the selection of a musical device which will result in a specific audience effect already indicated in the dramatic scene. This grounds composition on a pre-existing categorization of musical devices as audience effects, which in turn lends itself to the departmental regulation of musical production common in Hollywood studios. In the studio rationalization of musical production, the dominant tendency is for composers to assume the roles of mere hired employees who are specialists in selecting the correct devices from the storehouse of musical effects. The audience will automatically read the individual musical devices as instant "meanings," regardless of their precise position within the film. Methods of industrial organization and production turn out a false yet automatic identity of music and image.

One might wish for more theoretical attention to the whole notion of musical codification, but anyone familiar with films of the 1930's and 1940's will recognize the practices here condemned. So far the description of those practices accounts for the adoption of certain production techniques, but does not explain why cinema as such attracts music in the first place. Adorno and Eisler do provide such an explanation.

4. The Eye Versus the Ear

Adorno and Eisler base their explanations of the need for music in cinema on the proposition that in contemporary society there is a contradiction between visual and aural perception. The eye "has become accustomed to conceiving reality as made up of separate things, commodities, objects that can be modified by practical activity" and is thus selective and active; the eye is associated with the definite, be it the singular object or the rational concept. The ear, on the other hand, has not adapted as readily to bourgeois rationalization, finding it more difficult to perceive separate things as such; hence, the ear of the musical layman "is indefinite and passive." Perception through the ear involves a regression toward the primitive, the pre-individualistic collectivity in its resistance to the practical rationalization procedures that are the mark of bourgeois civilization (pp. 20-23).

This leads to the associated position that music is the most immediate of all the arts. As the art of the ear *par excel-*

lence, music is aimed at a perceptual-mental apparatus which resists the rationalization of sounds music embodies. This resistance can draw musical technique towards forms which promote an understanding of the organization of sounds as an indistinct impression of collectivity and/or unmediated subjective spontaneity. This helps explain how the most standardized music can be so widely regarded as an expression of "subjective inwardness" (p. 71). Music can make an apparently direct appeal both as a manifestation of the divine or supra-individual and of the essentially human—or better, of the divine, sacred, unrationalizable aspects of the human.

We are thus back to the notion that, like all the arts, music currently has its regressive aspects. In other contexts Adorno emphasizes the opportunities of this situation, but **Composing for the Films** highlights the dangers, on the one hand of slipping into pure epistemological regression and on the other hand of succumbing to the reified but secure social position offered by Enlightenment rationalization. Both dangers distort music as cognition. In effect, the basic charge Adorno and Eisler make against normal film music is that it is an extreme condensation of both these poles.

As the rationalization procedures discussed above indicate, film music clearly accepts its social role as commodity and its epistemological function as instant affirmation. More specifically, Adorno and Eisler argue that film requires magical, irrational aspects of music for consumption to proceed smoothly, and the film industry therefore develops the irrational aspects of musical listening. Having assigned music to the realm of what cannot be rationalized, bourgeois culture finds ways to use this "irrationality" in a planned way. Elements lacking in the world of bourgeois rationalization and individualization can be supplied by the rationalization of musical effects. With film music, which must confront the contradiction between eye and ear, film's literal immediacy incorporates a required irrational component.

5. SPECTATOR, CONTRADICTION, AND MUSIC

The specification of this last point begins from the proposition that film, shot through with contradictions as it is, generates a certain subjective "uneasiness" in the spectator, an uneasiness which threatens the film's coherent, immediate image of the world. Normal film music functions to overcome such contradictions and hence to suppress the potential for subversion inherent in this legitimate uneasiness. Adorno and Eisler offer accounts of some ways that music responds to contradictions.

One example is the contradiction discussed above between film's supposed function and effect (direct appeal to the spectator) and the remoteness of its administrative organization and technical character. A conscious comprehension of this contradiction would result in the spectator's understanding that the film is *to* him or her but not *for* him or her. Film music, according to Adorno and Eisler, helps

suppress the uneasiness potential in this contradiction by supplying an apparently immediate humanity to the product. The music

> attempts to interpose a human coating between the reeled-off pictures and the spectators. Its social function is that of a cement, which holds together elements that otherwise would oppose each other unrelated—the mechanical product and the spectators, and also the spectators themselves. . . . It is the systematic fabrication of the atmosphere for the events of which it is itself part and parcel. It seeks to breathe into the pictures some of the life that photography has taken away from them.

This account helps explain the limitations on dominant compositional practices for cinema. The music of a film must act as a kind of universal advertisement for the images, always expressing enthusiasm for the effects supposedly attained on the screen and thus "ensnaring the customer." By giving the image a veneer of humanity, music obscures the film's lack of humanity. The most serious modern music, composed as a response to the real position of humanity under advanced capitalism, could not be suitable for this purpose, for its truth content alienates it from the middle-class civilization it reflects (pp. 56-61).

This position can be described in a slightly different way by an attention to the incorporation of music as an "auratic" art into film. The performance and reception of concert-hall music marks it off as an art which insists on the "concrete uniqueness" of the occasion of its performance. Film music uses a number of techniques drawn from this tradition to signify the existence of its own sacred here-and-now, its own unique being. However, the result is mechanically produced; therefore, cues that the music is "authentic" in the traditional sense are lies. The persistence of such musical cues, in combination with other falsely auratic tactics such as the star system, bestows on films a kind of "degenerate aura" that operates to suppress the fact of film as the result of a technified administrative process. Such "pseudo-individualization" is a strategy for displacing the truth of the rationalization of film production and purposes, and that truth is precisely the irrelevance of the human individual (pp. 129-131).

In one of their most interesting discussions of the contradictions of cinema Adorno and Eisler find a legitimate uneasiness on the part of the spectator stemming from the material heterogeneity of the medium. They explore this contradiction as a problem for aesthetics with consequences for the subjective position of the spectator. Aesthetically, they argue from Hegelian premises, the fusion of sound and image in cinema is an accident due to economic and technological factors rather than the result of inherent tendencies in the arts of sound-making and image-making. Were an aesthetics of the cinema possible (which is doubtful), it would therefore begin from the proposition that sound and image are inherently contradictory. The fetishization of direct identity or duplication of image by music, promoted both in Hollywood practices and in Eisenstein's fascination with synaesthesia, is therefore mistaken (pp. 63-78).

At one point Adorno and Eisler analyze the subjective position of the spectator as a response to this contradiction, concentrating on an opposition between pictorial representation and one element of the sound track, the spoken word. They begin by suggesting that spectators of a purely silent cinema must have been subject to a certain unpleasantness and even shock, for the moving two-dimensional figures of humans seen on screen are *ghostly,* in that they exist on the borderline between the living and non-living. The point is not that spectators of early cinema experienced a literal fear of ghosts, but that they experienced a subconscious shock because of their own socially imposed likeness to the half-live effigies on the screen. Under advanced capitalism individuals are "threatened by muteness" thanks to the decay of spoken language explored by Karl Kraus. This helps explain why music was so quickly added to film. Its cultural role as magic and immediate subjective inwardness helped "exorcise" the ghostliness of the images by supplying an indication of genuine, spontaneous life. This helped the spectator to overcome the shock and accept the literal immediacy of the image.

This speculation leads to an extremely significant hypothesis about the synchronized sound film. Adorno and Eisler do not treat this innovation as a break with silent film, but rather as its continuation. The image, which is dominant in cinema, is self-evidently, "pictorial" in that it lacks spatial depth. But reproduced sound, even in synchronization with moving photographic representation, is not an "image" in the same sense. Here Adorno and Eisler use terminology similar to that of Béla Balázs, but their conclusion is not the crude one Balázs draws, namely that there is no difference "in dimension and reality" between the original sound and its reproduction.[14] Adorno and Eisler seem to be arguing only that representation of sound is of a different quality than visual representation in that reproduced sound resonates and thus representation of sound occurs in three dimensions. There is, then, always a large gap in the reception of a dialogue film between spoken word and image, no matter what the visual and aural cues that link the two. Psychologically this gap is virtually as great as that between intertitle and picture in the silent cinema: *"the talking picture, too, is mute.";* The cinema is governed by gesture (photographed movement), and speech remains a kind of disjunctive label attached to moving effigies. This explains the commonly felt uneasiness at films which seem to depend on a large amount of dialogue: "speech, which presupposes man as a self, rather than the primacy of the gesture, ultimately is only loosely superimposed upon the characters."

Thus, the unity of word and picture which is a fundamental "aesthetic" principle of the sound film's normal illusion of reality is "unconsciously registered" by the spectator as "fraudulent and fragile." The muteness of the characters is still a threat to the spectator, even in the sound film. The sound film therefore still requires the impression of immediate life supplied by music (and possibly non-verbal sound). Music gives the picture "a sense of corporeity, as it were" to overcome the muteness of the image as spoken

language cannot, and thereby helps the film bypass the contradiction between word and image (pp. 75-78).

The implications of this argument can be summarized to correspond to the previous account of film music as social cement. In terms of the subjective position of the cinema spectator, *music is on the side of the image.* It supplies a perceptual-psychological human "depth" which augments the literal immediacy of the pictorial illusion of reality. The primary relation for the music is to the gesture, which, in a sense, requires music as motivation and justification for its claim to being like life. The apparently artificial musical score is a psychological condition for the existence of the "naturalness" of the film image. This analysis has important implications, for if the analysis has correct elements, current studies of the suturing of the spectating subject "into" the film may require greater attention to the musical track.

6. TOWARDS AN OPPOSITIONAL PRACTICE

Composing for the Films offers a description of the dominant practices of producing film music first of all as those practices correspond to the administrative organization of the film industry, which assures their economic legitimacy within the cultural system of advanced capitalism. It also offers a description of the ways that film music works to suppress the contradictions of the eye-ear conjunction as subjective immediacy, mystic spontaneity, and/or aesthetic empathy to the ultimate end of affirming the existing order. This suppression assures the ideological legitimacy of the dominant practices in conjunction with (in current terms) the positioning of the spectating subject as an untroubled entity.

Given these interlocked sociohistoric, ideological, and aesthetic descriptions, Adorno and Eisler can propose a number of prescriptions for the composition of film music that might constitute an oppositional practice. Instead of leading the spectator toward easy identity and false comfort, such a practice would attempt to stimulate genuine cognition through a more troubled kind of entertainment. It may be tempting to see this loosely "Brechtian" attitude as Eisler's contribution to the book, especially in view of the compositional examples he supplies in an appendix; however, this attitude is not at variance with the book's general argument.

The prescriptive sections of *Composing for the Films* are based on the need for defamiliarizing strategies which would displace the automatizing musical devices that promote instant comprehension of the film as literal immediacy and hence as an advertisement for the unmediated universality of the sociocultural system as a whole. The relevance of a mediated totality for the spectator can be established by exploitation of contradictions. Ultimately this implies a labor on the spectator's identification, which is subject to social controls. For music specifically, this entails techniques designed to refuse a direct identity between image and music.

The point is not that image and music should simply be unrelated. At any rate, according to Adorno and Eisler, this is an impossible goal, because the two are always related in some mediated way through the social whole. (This mediation through the social whole explains the dominant fetishism for identity of image and music.) Adorno and Eisler even agree with what they define as current prejudice that the image must always in some sense determine the music; however, this determination should not result in the immediate duplication of sight by sound through naturalized, automatizing musical conventions or through some farfetched attempt at *Gesamkunstwerk.*

Adorno's insistence on the significance of the individual work comes into play here. *Composing for the Films* argues that no positive general rules are available on the relation of music to image: each film must establish its own unique relations. The principle of montage should govern not only the image track, but also the musical track and the relation between the two. The structure of each work is to be a unique labor on the socially determined contradictions of the medium, in opposition to the system of the culture industry and hence the existing social formation as automatic universal. A genuine musical and filmic rationality can then displace the rationalization of culture.

7. MUSICAL PLANNING IN CINEMA

The call for a genuinely rational film music in *Composing for the Films* has much in common with the outlook of *Philosophy of New Music.* In general, Adorno and Eisler prescribe the displacement of the fetishization of a certain, extremely limited musical "nature" prevalent in film music (and general musical culture) with strategies of composition made possible by the most advanced developments in twentieth-century music. It should be stressed that, despite their own educational allegiances, they do not end up prescribing the automatic use of twelve-tone technique as a universal solution to the problems of film music. They are concerned with the construction of each film (and therefore its music) as a unique work, in line with Adorno's promotion of the aesthetic monad.

The key term used by Adorno and Eisler to indicate the compositional approach they advocate is *planning,* which retains some of its connotations of scientific management but goes beyond the latter. The score of a film must be planned in advance as a whole in the construction of a mediated unity of music, image, word, narrative, and recorded noise. Identification between detail and system is to be eliminated in favor of a *relation* between part and the individual film as a whole. All of this will make the eye-ear contradiction into an element of the film's construction rather than lead to its obfuscation.

The displacement of identification by planned relation demands of the composer a much more precise control of musical resources than that supplied by the Hollywood storehouse of musical effects. A new film music will require a greater quantity of expressive possibilities than is provided by the harmonically safe techniques of a limited period of music history. Adorno and Eisler therefore demand opening up practices of film music so that the composer, working with the production team on the whole film from the beginning, can choose and/or invent any musical resources her or his imagination may deem necessary to the individual film.

The primary question for compositional technique now becomes one of structure: how can musical sense be made from such a potentially disparate collection of musical means? The answer lies in modern autonomous music. Given Adorno's argument elsewhere that Schoenberg is the latest in a compositional line which progressively establishes control over a greater and greater amount of sonic resources, it is unsurprising that Adorno and Eisler argue that modern music can supply the methods and models which would enable the film composer to organize the necessarily wide variety of musical material he or she may have to use. But the organizational virtues exemplified for Adorno by Schoenberg's music are now said to be attributes of all the best modern music, including the very different practices of Bartok and even Stravinsky (who is elsewhere treated as reactionary by both Adorno and Eisler). Autonomous music can teach film composers how to *plan* a unique musical structure engaging a wide variety of musical devices—atonal and tonal—instead of restricting themselves to the usual musical tricks, which do not depend on musical meaning (pp. 32-35, 79-84).

Adorno and Eisler also make another argument for the use of new musical resources, one which is based on their conception of film as a medium of extreme tensions (of montage and drama), abruptly shifting scenes, moods, and tones, and instantaneous, irregular visual progressions. They argue that most of the forms developed in serious music in the tradition of tonality are not flexible enough to be useful in establishing precise relationships between music and image. For example, traditional tonal forms move toward the resolution of musical tensions, as opposed to forms using modern harmony, which is founded on extreme suspense and knows no "natural" tendency toward its relief; with some danger of self-contradiction, Adorno and Eisler conclude from this that modern music is more appropriate for the tension-filled film than traditional music. Also, they point out that the abrupt changes in scene and tone in cinema require a music capable of abrupt changes, but that traditional harmony tends to presuppose a certain temporal expansion necessary for the formal developments, repetitions, etc. which give the final reconfirmation of the tonal center its force; the new music, on the other hand, allows for formal structures of extremely brief duration, which makes it more appropriate for film.

A genuine film music, then, will be based on neither the universalization of a certain compositional technique nor an indiscriminate incorporation of all the forms and devices of the tradition of serious Western music. Rather, the film composer needs at his or her disposal precise, condensed forms which will have special use for rapid changes available, say, from variational techniques or coloristic effects. The new music widens the possibilities of expression and provides the means of organizing the musical structure as a whole. But models can range from classical fantasias to the work of Webern and Bartok (pp. 38-42, 95-100, 113).

Although the word as such is not emphasized in *Composing for the Films,* it is clear that the desired music-image relation is there conceptualized as a dialectical one. The implicit model for the structure of the sound film is a mediated totality, and the only general requirement consistently mentioned is that the relation retain some contradictory aspects: "From the aesthetic point of view, this relation is not one of similarity but as a rule, one of question and answer, affirmation and negation, appearance and essence. This is dictated by the divergence of the media in question and the specific nature of each." (p. 70)

8. THE MUSICAL SUBJECT AND CINEMA

There is a contradiction in the structure of *Composing for the Films* itself, namely between description and prescription. Despite all of the practical hints for the composer, ranging from tips about the importance of the head of the studio music department all the way to exemplary scores composed by Eisler, the economic and ideological power attributed to the rationalization procedures of the culture industry at the least must obstruct a genuinely rational musical practice in cinema. This contradiction is confronted most squarely by Adorno and Eisler in their consideration of the aesthetic subject in film music.

Adorno holds that autonomous music in advanced capitalist society is able to grapple with real problems of subjectivity and cognition only because of its social isolation, its "uselessness," which allows it to establish a self-sufficient totality. But film music, by definition, not only retains a relation with something outside its musical structure, namely the drama conveyed through the images; it must even subordinate itself to something external, although still avoiding a simple duplication of that something. Film music is therefore denied the self-contained isolation which enables serious music to construct a more genuine position of musical subjectivity. Film music must still refuse to identify itself with the external (visual and, more distantly, social), yet it is denied the solution of blocking all relations with the external.

This is reflected in the situation of the musical subject. Even in the most organized autonomous music, there is an arbitrary starting point that Romanticism fetishizes as inspiration. For example, the most reified twelve-tone music still requires a spark of compositional spontaneity in the initial construction of the row, which only then determines every compositional parameter. Even the privileged model for complete planning of the score thus presupposes the existence of an arbitrary (in terms of absolute organization) subjectivity. In autonomous music the arbitrary is supplied by the musical subject expressed in the work, and so is still in some sense internal to the music.

In film music, however, the composer must integrate an already existing starting point which governs the music and yet produce a meaningful musical structure. The ideal kind of composing for films therefore requires a genuine musical subjectivity of the traditional kind, that is, a composer completely involved in the construction of a musical totality. But at the same time such a composer is denied the traditional function of the involvement, to be the one source of the arbitrary element. The ideal composer for films, then, "must, so to speak, both be and not be the subject of his music." Adorno and Eisler remark that it is impossible to predict where such a contradiction will lead (p. 85).

But there are some indications in *Composing for the Films* as to the direction in which such a contradiction might take us. As necessities and dangers in composition, questions of organization, planning, and rationalization are crucial in the evolution of music. But it is in film music that style (the specific strategy of constructing an organic unity out of the tension between form and content) becomes totally outmoded. Thus, the contradiction between the need for a musical subject and a music without a function for the subject could lead towards a new kind of art. A genuine film music would give up style for planning, yet still would have to include a certain compositional spontaneity; it would give up the esoteric isolation of autonomous music, yet include a real musical subjectivity. That is, Adorno and Eisler envision a music in which the aesthetic subject need not be expressed only in its isolation, for the music will not be isolated. The musical expression of such a subject would in fact be the achievement of a reconciliation of freedom and necessity, of subject and object, which Adorno had previously found accomplished only temporarily by Beethoven and which Lukács foresaw as the triumph of the proletariat. In such genuine film music is to be found the realization of music itself and simultaneously its self-transcendence as bourgeois art.

Adorno and Eisler are even willing to venture a tentative characterization of such music. Current practices of film music degenerate into uniform affirmation but pretend to the seriousness of the best autonomous music through procedures of pseudo-individualization. The final prescription in *Composing for the Films* is that since film music cannot assume the internal self-sufficiency of genuine negation achieved by the best serious music, it should abandon that music's comprehensive seriousness. This is not to argue for musical humor, since film requires alternations between the most varied kinds of musical expression. But it is to argue for what Adorno and Eisler call a certain "discretion" in film music. Film music cannot pretend to organicism, being constituted as it is by contradictions (e.g. music as unique immediacy vs. its reproducibility in film, the impossibility of a completely free musical subjectivity in cinema vs. the necessity for a spontaneous musical subject, etc). Therefore, contradiction must be incorporated into the music. The musical subject must assume a less serious formal relation between itself and its object than is found in autonomous music. This requires a "formal self-negation of music that plays with itself" and hence attains a distance from the position of immediacy exploited by autonomous music in its expression of subjectivity. In a *formal, relational* (not expressive or associative) sense, film music must begin to approach the structure of the joke. Such a structure will be "nothing but the awareness of music that it is mediated, technically produced and reproduced" (pp. 128-132).

This helps explain why Adorno and Eisler, despite their insistence on the importance of the technical compositional procedures of autonomous music, intermittently make reference to certain types of already existing film music, such as music of animated cartoons and musical revues. Such music can serve a "Brechtian" strategy of narrative and dramatic interruption, and it accomplishes this by means of a certain reflexivity which, in its more or less comic function, distances itself from a purely musical immediacy, helps block pseudo-individualization, and therefore provides hints for a progressive practice of film music.

Such discretion, if achieved successfully for films with a serious content, again implicitly points towards a reconciliation of subject and object. In the context of Adorno's *corpus,* the abandonment of the requirement for seriousness while the music is still totally planned through the agency of a genuine musical subject constitutes a prescription for a music which surpasses that of Schoenberg. It makes the technified, industrially administered medium of film the basis for subjective expression, and that possibility suggests a way out of the isolation imposed on Schoenberg precisely by the administration of culture.

Ultimately, as the authors point out in a footnote which cites Hegel on the elimination of art, their vision of film music presages the development of art into something qualitatively different. The reconciliation of technification with subjective expression would be the end of the aura of music. Such a new kind of music "abandons itself to its concrete occasion as 'unique' . . . but at the same time takes care not to seek its fulfillment in the triumph of intruding upon something unique." This is a vision of a freely expressed human subjectivity which does not require the realm of the sacred or magic to conceive of itself, yet does not submit to the processes of rationalization described in ***Dialectic of Enlightenment.*** An ideal film music implies a humanity which finds its specificity in something other than a magic immediacy. Hence, the concluding prescription in ***Composing for the Films***: "By displaying a tendency to vanish as soon as it appears, motion picture music renounces its claim that it is *there,* which is today its cardinal sin" (pp. 129, 133).

For Adorno's Hegelian Marxism, this kind of formulation only makes sense in an industrial and cultural order other than those we know. As in all of Adorno's work, the description of the present situation is founded on a comparison with an impossibility. Yet it is that impossibility which is the concept of a genuine film music. The gap between concept and object is a condemnation of the society in which we live.

Notes

1. See, for example, Jean-Louis Baudry, "Ideological Effects of the Basic Cinematographic Apparatus," trans. Alan Williams, *Film Quarterly,* 28 (Winter, 1974-75), 39-47; Jean-Louis Comolli, "Technique et idéologie: caméra, perspective, profondeur du champ," a series which appeared intermittently in *Cahiers du cinéma,* nos. 229 (May, 1971) through 241 (Sep.-Oct., 1972); and Stephen Heath, "Narrative Space," *Screen,* 17 (Autumn, 1976), 68-112.

2. Subsequent references are to the original edition: Hanns Eisler, *Composing for the Films* (New York: Oxford University Press, 1947). For a note on Eisler's aesthetics as a vacillation between positions of Adorno and of Brecht, see Hans Mayer, "An Aesthetic Debate of 1951: Comment on a Text by Hanns Eisler," trans. Jack Zipes, *New German Critique,* no. 2 (Spring, 1974), pp. 58-62.

External evidence regarding authorship is murky. After Eisler went to East Germany, a translation was published there which contained some changes to which Adorno did not consent. A 1969 translation into German authorized by Adorno included no changes from the 1947 editions. See Susan Buck-Morss, *The Origins of Negative Dialectics: Theodor W. Adorno, Walter Benjamin and the Frankfurt Institute* (New York: The Free Press, 1977), p. 296, n. 32. On the other hand, before he went to East Germany Eisler claimed *Composing for the Films* as his artistic credo in testimony before the House Committee on Un-American Activities. See Hanns Eisler, *A Rebel in Music: Selected Writings,* ed. Manfred Grabs and trans. Marjorie Meyer (New York: International Publishers, 1978), p. 151.

3. See Buck-Morss, pp. 11-17, for Adorno's musical activities in the 1920's.

4. Max Horkeimer and Theodor W. Adorno, *Dialectic of Enlightenment,* trans. John Cumming (New York: Herder and Herder, 1972), pp. 26-27. The concrete totality was a basic concept for Lukács. The seminal formulation of the concept in classical Marxist literature is in Karl Marx, *Grundrisse: Foundations of the Critique of Political Economy,* trans. Martin Nicolaus (New York: Vintage Books, 1973), pp. 100-108.

5. *Dialectic of Enlightenment,* p. 22.

6. See Walter Benjamin, "The Work of Art in the Age of Mechanical Reproduction" in *Illuminations,* ed. Hannah Arendt and trans. Harry Zohn (New York: Schocken, 1976), pp. 217-251.

7. Theodor W. Adorno, "On the Social Situation of Music," trans. Wes Blomster, *Telos,* no. 35 (Spring, 1978), p. 130.

8. Theodor W. Adorno, *Philosophy of New Music,* trans. Anne G. Mitchell and Wesley V. Blomster (New

York: Seabury Press, 1973), p. 77. On *Philosophy of New Music,* cf. Frederic Jameson, *Marxism and Form: Twentieth-Century Dialectical Theories of Literature* (Princeton: Princeton University, 1974) for the essay on Adorno. Also helpful is T. W. Adorno, "The Radio Symphony: An experiment in Theory," in *Radio Research 1941,* eds. Paul Lazersfeld and Frank N. Stanton (New York: Duell, Sloane and Pearce, 1941), pp. 110-139.

On the relation of melody and tonality in Western music as a problem of the rationalization of music, cf. Max Weber's 1921 essay, *The Rational and Social Foundations of Music,* ed. and trans. Don Martindale, Johannes Riedel, and Gertrude Neuwirth (Carbondale: Southern Illinois University, 1969). Weber there outlines the case for the necessity of an irreducible subjective component of music, given the ultimately unrationalizable character of the well-tempered scale. Weber, of course, was a touchstone for both Lukács and Adorno on rationalization, administration, and bureaucracy.

9. See, for example, *Dialectic of Enlightenment,* pp. 135, 124, 144, 158.

10. A classic exchange between Adorno and Benjamin on this point is in Ernst Bloch, *et al., Aesthetics and Politics,* ed. Ronald Taylor (London: New Left Books, 1977), pp. 110-141.

11. References to *Composing for the Films* are in parentheses in the text.

12. For a discussion of German leftist notions of montage and the relation of the Russian Formalist concept of defamiliarization and Brecht's alienation-effect, see Ben Brewster, "From Shklovsky to Brecht: A Reply," *Screen,* 15 (Summer, 1974), 82-102.

13. See Adorno, "The Radio Symphony."

14. Béla Baláazs, *Theory of the Film: Character and Growth of a New Art,* trans. Edith Bone (New York: Dover, 1970), p. 216.

Peter Uwe Hohendahl (essay date 1981)

SOURCE: "Autonomy of Art: Looking Back at Adorno's *Ästhetische Theorie,*"[1] in *German Quarterly,* Vol. 54, No. 2, March, 1981, pp. 133-48.

[In the following essay, Hohendahl examines critical response to the publication of Adorno's Ästhetische Theorie.*]*

Theodor Adorno's major contribution to the philosophy of art, his *Ästhetische Theorie,* appeared in 1970.[2] The work was almost completed when the author died in 1969. Adorno meant to rewrite the introduction, but otherwise the text needed only formal revisions, which were carried out by Rolf Tiedemann, Adorno's faithful disciple and editor. Tiedemann rightly felt that *Ästhetische Theorie* deserved immediate publication since it was the legacy of Critical Theory. Yet it was precisely this aspect which marred the reception of the book. Except for a few voices in the liberal and conservative camp, the response was surprisingly negative. One might have expected that the East German critics would denounce Adorno's theory as a typical example of Western ideology—which they did; more alarming was the unfriendly or at least cool reception among the West German Left. If the members of the Frankfurt Institute considered *Ästhetische Theorie* as Adorno's legacy, it turned out to be an *Erbe* which was clearly unwelcome. The charges varied, but there was almost a consensus among the critics of the left camp that Adorno's last book did not offer the materialist theory of art that everybody was looking for. It was particularly Adorno's insistence on the autonomy of the art work and his well known indictment of *Tendenz* and political art which angered the Left. Adorno evidently had not changed his position. In his last work he reiterated his critique of unmediated *Engagement* and once more presented modernism and the avant-garde as the only viable responses to the increasing brutality of advanced capitalism. His renewed claim that, in the final analysis, only the authentic work of art overcomes the stultifying atmosphere of the cultural industry met with disbelief and outspoken disapproval. The hostility was so strong that the German Left dismissed the book out of hand and left the appropriation to the conservatives who at this point were inclined to use some of Adorno's arguments for the defense of their aesthetic and moral beliefs.

What were the reasons for this bizarre development? After all, the left movement in Germany owed most of its theoretical insights to the Frankfurt School and especially to Theodor W. Adorno who taught the younger generation the critical approach to literature and music. When *Ästhetische Theorie* came out, the West German student movement had reached the climax of its public influence. At the same time, however, it faced its first major crisis. The remarkable public recognition did not translate into a lasting, serious impact on the social system which they critiqued and attacked. Unlike the American students, the West German students tried to solve this problem by forming more structured political organizations or moving closer to established political parties (DKP). In 1970 the student movement, entering its second phase, turned against its initial belief in spontaneous political expression and rallied around more orthodox leader figures like Lenin, Trotsky, or Mao-Tze-Tong. As much as these various groups fought among themselves and disagreed about strategy, they had one thing in common: their dislike of the Frankfurt School and its interpretation of Marxism.[3] They redefined their goals in terms of immediate political action and tried to establish a closer connection with the working class. Critical Theory became the victim of this reorientation. Since the New Left had been under the influence of the Frankfurt School at least until 1969, this critique was more than anything else a self-critique and therefore carried out with uncommon harshness. The members of the

Frankfurt School were openly condemned as bourgeois and their theory denounced as liberal middle class ideology. The liberal element in Adorno's writing—not only his concept of genuine culture, which clearly owed much to the eighteenth and nineteenth century and showed the *Bildungsbürger* in Adorno, but also his defense of individual freedom against the demands of the state and political parties, made Adorno definitely unpopular with a movement that struggled to transform the social structure of West Germany. Using the yardstick of orthodox Marxism, Adorno's left critics found it easy to dismiss his late work, especially *Ästhetische Theorie,* as irrelevant for the Marxist project. It was either Lukács or Brecht and Benjamin who became the new cultural heroes, and their theoretical work was appropriated to develop an alternative position. Ever since the famous Benjamin-issue of *alternative* in 1967 (no. 56/57), the extremely complicated personal relationship between Walter Benjamin and the younger Adorno, who became Benjamin's disciple, critic and editor, was presented as a clear-cut opposition: on the one hand the smug Adorno who tried to suppress certain parts of Benjamin'soeuvre because they did not agree with his understanding of Benjamin's essential philosophy (which cannot be denied); on the other hand Walter Benjamin who moved closer to Brecht, transcended idealism and developed a truly materialist theory of art. We have to understand this emotionally charged debate as a political rather than philological discourse. The heart of the matter for the New Left was a defense of Benjamin's oeuvre against the authority of Adorno and its integration into the dogma of the Frankfurt School.[4]

The interest in Benjamin, particularly in his essays of the thirties, which support the Communist party, reflects the yearning of the New Left to grasp and to revive the element of political praxis in aesthetic theory. Since the Left placed the emphasis primarily on those elements in Benjamin's work which agreed with Brecht and overlooked other traditions, Adorno's critique of these essays, which he advanced already in letters during the thirties, could only fuel the aversion against the devious influence of Adorno's aesthetic elitism.

Although this debate has not yet come to an end—the question of Benjamin's Marxism seems to be as undecided as ever—there is a growing consensus among the Left and its various factions, that the initial approach and the way it shaped the discourse has lost its usefulness and its critical edge. While Benjamin scholars have realized that we have to get out of the old mold, if we want to appropriate Benjamin's writings for the eighties,[5] the discussion about Adorno's theory seems to linger without any direction.[6] It is time to take another look at *Ästhetische Theorie* and Adorno's essays on literature. This is not to make Adorno less controversial and thereby more acceptable to the established forces of the academy. The perspective which guided the interpretation and critique of Adorno in the early seventies was rooted, as I have tried to show, in a singular historical situation—the struggle between the student movement and the West German establishment. The

historical distance from these events, which only the nostalgic observer can overlook, calls for a reappreciation. This rereading cannot simply dismiss the arguments of the early seventies and pretend to face the text for the first time, but it must be conscious of the limitations which were imposed on the interpretation at that time.

According to the Left, Adorno refused to apply his own theory to the political realm. He indulged in pessimism. Indeed the social theory of the Frankfurt School which started out in the thirties as a Marxist project became increasingly pessimistic with respect to Marx' prognosis that capitalism would ultimately self-destruct and give way to a socialist society.[7] Faced with fascism in Germany and Italy on the one hand and monopoly capitalism in the USA on the other, Horkheimer and Adorno concluded in the forties that the Enlightenment, which was supposed to bring freedom and emancipation, had resulted in barbarism and slavery, not as an accidental relapse, as the liberal mind preferred to see this development, but rather as the logical outcome of the historical process. In their *Dialektik der Aufklärung* Horkheimer and Adorno argued that the historical unfolding of *ratio* would lead to the increasing domination of nature by man who then would become the victim of his own structure of domination. Since Horkheimer and Adorno, unlike Lukács, had given up the belief that the proletariat would revolutionize the given social structure, their analysis of advanced capitalism did not include the revolutionary perspective of traditional Marxism. The Frankfurt School reached a position where man can analyze the logic of history but not organize political opposition. As late as 1969, shortly before his death, Adorno defended this stance against the demands of the students. The unity of theory and praxis, he argued, tends to privilege action.[8] And this emphasis becomes irrational when imposed on philosophy. Adorno denounced the call for praxis as dogmatic and insisted that the uncompromising rigor of theory which defends its realm against the onslaught of positivism offers the truly critical opposition. This last effort to preserve the priority of theory came close to the very position that the Frankfurt School castigated as traditional in the thirties. Adorno's use of the category of negation became abstract and thereby lost its critical edge.

Although Adorno refused to view his attitude as pessimistic, we cannot overlook that the gap between theory and praxis is widening in his later writings. His late work tends to dwell on the importance of art. It is not accidental that Adorno's last book deals with aesthetic rather than social problems. His concern with social questions leads to aesthetic rather than political theory. Adorno's philosophy of art is his final answer to the dilemma of social praxis. Adorno offers the authentic work of art as that emphatic opposition which can no longer materialize in political organizations. This perspective might look more attractive today than ten years ago when there appeared to be hope that the age of capitalism might come to an end. But is this kind of relevance a good reason for us to return to Adorno's criticism? Is Adorno perhaps becoming fashionable again because his aestheticism and his pessimism appeal to the readers of the troubled eighties? By asking these questions I do not want to discredit the legitimacy of our present interests and simply restore the authority of Adorno and the Frankfurt School. Still, the question: what does *Ästhetische Theorie* offer to us today? should be coupled with the complementary question: what do we offer to Adorno's theory, from where do we look at it?

Let me begin with a broad description of Adorno's philosophy. His oeuvre is clearly grounded in the tradition of German Idealism, particularly in Hegel. The same can be said about Georg Lukács, but the results are strikingly different. When Lukács moved from an idealist to a Marxist position and attempted to work out a materialist basis for his criticism, he adopted Lenin's reflection theory which is supposed to support Lukács' concept of the organic work of art as the only authentic form of art. Adorno rejects this more traditional part of Hegel's aesthetics and insists that the rigorous historical approach should be extended to basic aesthetic norms and rules. Lukács also historicizes art and literature. However, coming from reflection theory and a general concept of realism he favors those forms of literature which express the interest and concerns of the proletariat—in other words social realism. Adorno, who admired the early Lukács, refused to accept this argument. In his essay **"Erpresste Versöhnung"**[9] he distanced himself from Lukács' theory of realism and at the same time harshly critiqued Lukács' concept of the organic work of art. Adorno denounces Lukács' struggle against modernism, i.e., writers like Kafka and Joyce, as the regressive part of Hegel's influence—a reduction of the work of art to considerations of content. Adorno on the other hand defends modernism precisely because he shares the historical approach with the Hegelian tradition. To put it more concretely: he rejects the attack on modernism because it is rooted in an ontological, ahistorical understanding of the organic work of art. Modern writers are not decadent and therefore unable to synthesize content and form; rather they try to work out the dialectic of social change and aesthetic innovation. What we call the history of literature, changes of style and genres, is not just a sequence of facts and events, it consists of a dialectical process in which the individual work is seen against the background of conventions and norms. Authenticity is reached only through the negation of the affirmative tradition. This stress on novelty should not be mistaken for an apology of the fashionable, it rather indicates that the aesthetic material itself is drawn into the historical process.

Adorno follows the idealist tradition of Kant, Schiller, and Hegel and emphasizes the autonomy of the art work. Unlike the aesthetic theory of the later nineteenth century in Germany, which tends to view aesthetic principles as metahistorical, Adorno is much closer to Hegel's intention when he applies the historical critique also to the basic aesthetic categories—including the concept of autonomy. The legitimacy of this category is limited to the period between the eighteenth and the twentieth centuries, although Adorno is never quite clear whether this period has come

to an end or not. In his famous lecture on poetry and society of 1957[10] Adorno referred to the collective *Grundstrom* in the poems of Brecht and Lorca without indicating however whether this grounding in a collective spirit marks the beginning of a new progressive era or the decline of poetry as a medium of philosophical truth. I shall come back to this ambiguity later. First I would like to develop another important aspect of Adorno's theory: the correlation between the aesthetic and the social sphere.

When literary theory in the late eighteenth century developed the notion that art is autonomous, the intention was to free the art work from the demand of social praxis. The result is an abstract opposition between the social and the aesthetic sphere. By historicizing the major categories of aesthetic theory Adorno brings these realms closer together again. Ultimately art and society belong to the same stream of history. This insight is certainly not new. The left Hegelians, beginning with Heine, used Hegel's model of history to understand the evolution of literature as representative for the development of social and political history. Adorno's approach stands in this tradition, but he is very much aware of its dangers. While he insists on the dialectic of art and society (the art work is also a social fact), he does not, unlike Lukács, conceive of it in terms of reflection. Adorno's *Ästhetische Theorie* is his final effort to grasp and theoretically refine the dialectic of the social and the aesthetic sphere.

Adorno's theory not only defends and legitimizes modernism and the avant-garde, it may well be called a theory of the avant-garde. Its author is clearly on the side of those historical forces which undermine the rule of European classicism. Adorno is a distant and skeptical observer of Winckelmann's ideas. Looking back at Greek classicism Adorno points out the material conditions of Greek history which were anything but ideal: brutal warfare, slavery and oppression are the reality which have to be suppressed before we can enjoy the notion of perennial beauty and harmony in Greek art. "Die vom Klassizismus veranstaltete Einheit des Allgemeinen und Besonderen war schon in attischen Zeiten nicht erreicht, geschweige denn später. Daher blicken die klassischen Bildwerke mit jenen leeren Augen, die eher—archaisch—erschrecken, als daß sie jene edle Einfalt und stille Größe ausstrahlten, welche das empfindsame Zeitalter auf sie projizierte. Was heute an der Antike sich aufdrängt, ist grundverschieden von der Korrespondenz mit dem europäischen Klassizismus in der Ära der Französischen Revolution und Napoleons, und noch der Baudelaireschen" (p. 241). The object of this critique is the neo-humanism of Weimar and its glorification of Greek art. This seemingly historical polemic, however, has a methodological aspect which I want to bring to the foreground: Adorno, at least implicitly, speaks here against the model that was used by the early Lukács to situate the novel form. Adorno undercuts the fundamental assumption of Lukács' *Theorie des Romans* that early Greek literature was grounded in social conditions which were free of alienation.

This critique of classicism becomes important because it is at the same time a critique of a model which was further developed by Lucien Goldmann. For Goldmann the task of the critic and sociologist of literature is to establish a homology between the social and the literary structure.[11] Adorno's theory looks similar, yet this similarity is deceptive. While Adorno shares with Goldmann the interest in formal structures and rejects any kind of *Inhaltssoziologie* as vulgar materialism, he is careful not to press the correlation into the homology model. The difference becomes apparent when Adorno defines his approach as *immanent*. The critic is starting out from the text rather than beginning with an analysis of the social structure. It is the explication of the work of art which offers the insight into the social conditions that defined the production of the work of art. In his essay, **"Rede über Lyrik und Gesellschaft"** he unfolds the notion that the social meaning of the poem is expressed through its language. The poem relates to social history only indirectly. Adorno calls the poem a philosophical and historical sundial: by deciphering the structure of the poem the critic decodes the meaning of social history. Again, this sounds like Goldmann's theory, but we have to note the distinction: the interpretation of the poem refers to the *meaning* of history, not to the facts or the objective structures. The two realms are mediated by philosophy—more specifically the philosophy of the early Marx. Unlike Goldmann, Adorno would never identify the work of art with an individual social group or class. This procedure which is typical of Goldmann's criticism, is unacceptable to Adorno on grounds of principle. The correspondence between art and society, the aesthetic and the social meaning, *transcends* the particular group or class. Authentic are only those works which are representative of the whole. The choice of the sundial as the key metaphor signals that for Adorno the important element in the text is its expressive force and much less the author and his/her intentions to build up a coherent vision of the world. The individual author enters the sphere of criticism only as the human voice, the historical subjectivity that objectifies the expression through the work. Thus the emphasis is placed on the objective side: The authentic work of art is given the status of a permanent testament of human history—it embodies the hopes and the sufferings, the expectations and the contradictions of the human race.

In *Ästhetische Theorie* Adorno tries to unfold this argument. He notes: "Opponiert sie der Empirie durchs Moment der Form—und die Vermittlung von Form und Inhalt ist nicht zu fassen ohne deren Unterscheidung—, so ist die Vermittlung einigermaßen allgemein darin zu suchen, daß ästhetische Form sedimentierter Inhalt sei" (p. 15). Or another definition: "Nur vermöge der Trennung von der empirischen Realität, die der Kunst gestattet, nach ihrem Bedürfnis das Verhältnis von Ganzem und Teilen zu modeln, wird das Kunstwerk zum Sein zweiter Potenz" (p. 14). Here Adorno, following Walter Benjamin, introduces the concept of the *monad*. By comparing art works with monads Adorno tries to explore the dialectic of art and reality. Monads are closed, they have, so to speak, no windows and therefore offer no immediate access to reality.

This, as it turns out, is quite unnecessary, since the outside world is already contained in the monad. Adorno then applies this idea to the understanding of aesthetic forms: "Die ungelösten Antagonismen der Realität kehren wieder in den Kunstwerken als die immanenten Probleme ihrer Form. Das, nicht der Einschuß gegenständlicher Momente, definiert das Verhältnis der Kunst zur Gesellschaft" (p. 16). These unanswered questions provide literary and art history with their dynamic force. The increasing contradictions of reality show up as dissonances of form, they propel the evolution of art to the point where the avant-garde artist negates the very principle of the art work itself. Thus only those works deserve to be called authentic which question their own formal structure.

By stressing the formal aspect of literary history Adorno arrives at a position which is close to that of Russian Formalism. He also argues that aesthetic criticism should primarily be concerned with questions of *technique*. The detailed analysis of seemingly technical points, in other words close reading, throws light on the social meaning. The comparison with Russian Formalism is fruitful with respect to considerations of form. There are also important differences. Adorno would have rejected the formalist notion that literary history can be fully understood in terms of its intrinsic evolution. As we shall see, Adorno insists on the totality of history no less than Hegel or Lukács. Therefore the approach of Tynyanov[12] that the critic has to look first at the literary sequence, then at the political or economic evolution, and finally try to relate these sequences would be shunned as undialectical and positivistic. While Adorno shares the concern of the Russian Formalists with technique, his interpretation of history follows a model which is quite different.

In spite of his outspoken critique of the traditional dialectic which moves from thesis to antithesis and finally ends with a synthesis, Adorno's philosophy is still grounded in Hegel's philosophy of history. The concept of history which the formalists propose, although analytically sound, is unacceptable to Adorno, because it deprives the work of art of its emphatic truth value (*Wahrheitsgehalt*). Adorno's interest in literary evolution is not that of the historians who are satisfied when they have demonstrated how a genre changes or a motif is expressed in different ways. Adorno's theory puts a high premium on aesthetic innovation. Patterns, forms, genres are not fixed entities, but historical categories. However, the notion of change and innovation must not be fetishized. Its meaning can be understood only as a part of a larger historical context. Close reading is for Adorno, strange as this may sound, a contextual reading. When Adorno postulates that the sociologist of art must begin with the text, he presupposes a model of history in which the various spheres—the social, the political, the philosophical, the aesthetic—are part of a unified process. Thus Adorno's claim to *Immanenz* should not be interpreted as a German version of New Criticism, the equivalent of Emil Staiger for instance. Stressing the intrinsic approach means the opposite: it is the attempt to overcome the reification of traditional interpretation. Formalized professional scholarship insists on the rigorous definition of its object, the separation of the researcher and his/her material, without paying attention to their dialectical relationship in which the subject is very much part of the object and, on the other hand, the seemingly objective material the result of the subject's activities. When we talk about Adorno's approach we have to realize that he refuses to offer an objectified scientific method which can be abstracted from the individual act of understanding and then applied to various works.

Among the three approaches to the work of art, the interest in the origin and production of art, the interest in its structure, and the interest in its impact and reception, Adorno privileges, as we have seen, the structural procedure. He is less sympathetic to studies which try to understand art in terms of communication. Adorno argues: "Die Objektivation der Kunst, von der Gesellschaft draußen her ihr Fetischismus, ist ihrerseits gesellschaftlich als Produkt der Arbeitsteilung. Darum ist das Verhältnis der Kunst zur Gesellschaft nicht vorwiegend in der Sphäre der Rezeption aufzusuchen. Es ist dieser vorgängig: in der Produktion. Das Interesse an der gesellschaftlichen Dechiffrierung der Kunst muβ dieser sich zukehren, anstatt mit der Ermittlung und Klassifizierung von Wirkungen sich abspeisen zu lassen, die vielfach aus gesellschaftlichem Grunde von den Kunstwerken und ihrem objektiven gesellschaftlichen Gehalt gänzlich divergieren" (p. 338f). This hostile remark against reception studies is primarily directed against positivism in musicology which tried to develop a quantitative method in order to demonstrate the success and significance of music.[13] Adorno himself was clearly interested in reception and wrote a number of important essays on the sociology of hearing.[14]

Adorno's emphasis on production as the key to the understanding of the art work deserves closer scrutiny. What does he mean? Certainly not the kind of studies which were popular in the late nineteenth century, when the critic explained the work of art by documenting its sources and demonstrated the roots in the biography of the author. The individual author and his/her intentions receive rarely more than fleeting attention. Biography is in most cases treated on the anecdotal level. Adorno would agree with Lukács' argument that Balzac's intentions and the meaning of his novels were not identical. He carefully refrains from praising the *genius,* knowing well that this category is part of the liberal ideology: the self-promotion of the artist who has to deal with the market place. Adorno defines production of art in terms of the general economic and social conditions under which the artist has to work—feudal patronage, the competition of the capitalist market or the situation of culture industry in advanced capitalist societies. Secondly, Adorno wants to emphasize artistic labor: the concrete struggle of the artists with the techniques which are available at a certain time. By focusing attention on the process of production the critic at the same time reveals its meaning and truth value.

I want to give an example from **Ästhetische Theorie** to demonstrate what Adorno has in mind. There is no doubt that Adalbert Stifter was a conservative author. Both his critical prose and his works of fiction express a moderate and cautious stance. It is not accidental therefore that Stifter's reading public consisted to a large extent of educated conservative German *Bürger,* while the left camp remained indifferent or hostile. Typically enough, Lukács denied Stifter the status of a major German writer. Adorno agrees with neither side. His interpretation wants to rescue Stifter's work from his conservative admirers who find their own ideology confirmed in the message of the novels. Adorno is fully aware that this effort is problematical when he notes: "Die Schichten, die ihm seine halb esoterische Popularität verschafften, blättern ab. Damit jedoch ist nicht das letzte Wort über ihn gesagt, Versöhntheit und Versöhnlichkeit zumal seiner Spätphase sind outriert. Objektivität erstarrt zur Maske, beschworenes Leben wird zum abweisenden Ritual. Durch die Exzentrizität des Mittleren schimmert das verschwiegene und verleugnete Leid des entfremdeten Subjekts hindurch und die Unversöhntheit des Zustands" (p. 346). This statement, however, is followed by another one which demonstrates Adorno's understanding of the authentic value within the conservative ideology. "Ideologische Überspannung verleiht dem Werk mittelbar seinen unideologischen Wahrheitsgehalt, seine Überlegenheit über alle Literatur tröstenden Zuspruchs und beflissen landschaftlicher Geborgenheit und erwirbt ihm die authentische Qualität, die Nietzsche bewunderte" (p. 346). Adorno clearly differentiates between the meaning that Stifter wanted to express in his writings and the *Gehalt* which is hidden in the structure of the work. In the case of Stifter Adorno sets the utopian element apart from the conservative ideology of the author. This is a significant move. The sociologist who concentrates on the plot and the characters of, let us say, *Nachsommer* can read this novel as a typical example of the conservative mood of the eighteen-fifties.[15] The overriding themes offer plenty of evidence for this thesis. Adorno, to be sure, does not deny the validity of this aspect, yet ultimately the thematic conservatism of Stifter's novels is seen as part of a large context. Adorno's reading links the conservative component to the industrial revolution of the fifties. The legitimacy of *Nachsommer* is its negation of the new industrial society.

The category of negativity is crucial for Adorno's philosophy. Through its negativity the work of art secures its authenticity and sets itself apart from the convention of its time and genre. Indeed, Adorno deemphasizes conventions because, as socially accepted modes of artistic expression, they indirectly also affirm the social status quo. This is the reason why Adorno never feels quite comfortable with older literature or music. The works of the sixteenth and seventeenth centuries rely heavily on conventional devices and moreover fulfill immediate social functions. They are still embedded in social and cultural traditions of individual social groups and classes. For Adorno they are less valuable because they belong to a specific social setting and are not fully autonomous. Their truth value appears to be more limited. This bias shows that Adorno's criticism is not just another form of ideology critique. In this respect Goldmann's theory is certainly closer to Marxist orthodoxy. Goldmann's procedure focuses on a specific social and historical situation, for instance the situation of the *noblesse de robe* in France, and then relates his findings to the structure of individual works of literature, for example Racine's tragedies. In the final analysis he maintains a base/superstructure model. Adorno on the other hand, makes use of ideology critique in order to undermine ossified structures and reified thought patterns. He firmly holds that those works of art which deserve to be called *gelungen,* i.e., genuine and excellent, cannot be reduced to the status of documents which reflect the ideas of a particular class. Although the authentic work of art is grounded in its historical moment, its truth value (*Wahrheitsgehalt*) transcends this historical moment. This truth value, Adorno argues in a key passage of *Ästhetische Theorie,* on which their rank ultimately rests is historical through and through. "Er [i.e., truth value] verhält sich nicht relativ zur Geschichte derart, daß er, und damit der Rang der Kunstwerke, einfach mit der Zeit variierte. Wohl hat eine solche Variation statt: und Kunstwerke von Qualität etwa vermögen durch Geschichte sich zu entblättern. Dadurch indessen fallen Wahrheitsgehalt, Qualität nicht dem Historismus anheim" (p. 285). Against any relativistic notion Adorno maintains that there is an objectively correct historical consciousness. I quote once more from the same passage: "Vielmehr heißt richtiges Bewußtsein, seitdem das Potential von Freiheit aufging, das fortgeschrittenste Bewußtsein der Widersprüche im Horizont ihrer möglichen Versöhnung" (p. 285). The aesthetic analogy of this advanced consciousness are the forces of production within the art work, i.e., the craftsmanship of the artist, mastering the material, struggling against the general trend towards conformity. Artistic innovation, in other words, is the equivalence of the advanced historical consciousness.

It should be obvious by now that Adorno's theory summarizes the development of the last century. Its examples are the composition of Schönberg and his disciples and the evolution of modern poetry since Baudelaire. Whether this philosophy can be applied to medieval art seems doubtful to me, since the category of autonomy is central to the basic argument. This brings us back to my initial question. After I have outlined what Adorno has "to offer," we have to ask ourselves where we stand and how we relate to this theory today. If we mean to take Adorno's philosophy of art seriously, we cannot evade this question, because theory itself is no less historical than literature and music. And Adorno was quite aware of this problem. In the introduction to *Ästhetische Theorie* he states: "Vom Begriff der philosophischen Ästhetik geht ein Ausdruck des Veralteten aus, ähnlich wie von dem des Systems oder der Moral" (p. 493). Then the question arises: How can we develop a systematic aesthetic theory when most of the traditional categories on which this theory was built have become obsolete? The fact that recent history has liquidated basic concepts like the beautiful makes any attempt to systematize aesthetics highly problematical.

Baumeister and Kulenkampff have argued that Adorno could no longer follow Hegel's philosophy of art which places the emphasis on content rather than form, because it privileges rational discourse and therefore imposes its concepts on art in such a way that art loses its status as an independent mode of expression.[16] Those elements of the work of art which cannot be grasped by theoretical concepts are indeed the most meaningful ones for Adorno who is distrustful of rational discourse. By the same token Adorno cannot hark back to a more traditional genre theory which rests on metahistorical norms. Nor can he return to Kant's aesthetic theory which is concerned with aesthetic experience. Still Adorno is convinced that modern art and literature are in need of aesthetic theory. Appreciation as a mode of criticism is not enough. Since philosophical criticism aims at the truth value of art, the critics must not confine themselves to subjective experience. The task is to decipher objective meaning and this can be accomplished only with the help of a theoretical framework. Especially the complexity of modern art calls for a theoretical approach. Adorno notes: "Gerade die aufs Subjekt nicht zu reduzierenden, nicht in blanker Unmittelbarkeit zu besitzenden Momente der Kunst bedürfen des Bewußtseins und damit der Philosophie. Sie wohnt aller ästhetischen Erfahrung inne, wofern sie nicht kunstfremd, barbarisch ist. Kunst erwartet die eigene Explikation" (p. 524). So Adorno, in spite of his skepticism against rational discourse, clearly relates back to the tradition of philosophical aesthetics and turns explicitly against the concept of experience offered by positivism and pragmatism. He defines the goal of aesthetic theory in the following way: "Ästhetik heute müßte über der Kontroverse zwischen Kant und Hegel sein, ohne sie durch Synthese zu glätten" (p. 528). This reference to Kant and Hegel, Adorno's shorthand for two types of aesthetic theory, locates the realm in which Adorno tries to work out the tension between theory and history. He suggests that the categories of idealism still help us capture the emphatic meaning of modern art and literature, although modernism and the avant-garde are no longer grounded in idealism. Adorno is fully aware of the dilemma. The philosophical concepts of criticism are at the same time indispensable and inadequate. Because of this ambiguity the late work of Adorno tends to identify philosophy and art, since the process of deciphering and preserving, in other words criticism, is the only way in which truth in an emphatic sense can be revealed. Genuine art, for Adorno the last bastion that has not yet capitulated, is the sphere where the deception of instrumental reason is without consequence. This vision owes its force to Hegel, although it does not share Hegel's negative attitude toward postclassical art. For Adorno art and philosophy are inseparable but not identical. This position allows Adorno to cling to the concepts of the work of art (*Kunstwerk*) and truth value (*Wahrheitsgehalt*) as his categories. When philosophy, as Adorno claims, in the phase of late capitalism, has lost most of its emancipatory functions, it becomes the task of the authentic art work to stand in and defend the tower of truth.

I started this essay with some remarks about the hostile reception of *Ästhetische Theorie* in the early seventies. This animosity was partly caused by the frustration of the student movement. The students were looking for a leader in their political struggle and had to realize that Adorno was unwilling and also unprepared to step into this role. This explanation, however, is not sufficient. The lack of appreciation which the younger generation showed in 1970 must be related to a broader phenomenon. Between 1967 and 1970 West Germany witnessed an almost unparalleled breakdown of the literary system. The radicals called for the end of literature and criticism, since the capitalist system had turned them into meaningless toys of the establishment. This crisis undermined the belief in the autonomy of art which Adorno defended against *Tendenz.* This debate in my opinion is only the foreground for a deeper problem which had been lingering after World War II. I mean the fate of the avant-garde. Adorno's philosophy of art is closely related to the avant-garde of the early 20th century. He takes most of his examples from works that were written or composed between 1890 and 1930. Seldom does he refer to later works. His literary criticism favors authors of the nineteenth and early twentieth centuries, such as Heine, Balzac, Eichendorff, George, Wedekind, Kraus, and Benjamin. The notable exception is his interpretation of Beckett's *Endgame* (1957)—a play which speaks very much to the mood of Adorno's late years.[17] Occasionally Adorno would play with the idea that the concept of autonomy of art might not be fully appropriate for the period that followed World War II. Here and there he cautiously alludes to the end of the avant-garde, yet he fails to pursue this perspective in any rigorous manner.

Today, however, it would be futile to suppress this question: did the neo-avant-garde still have the same critical edge which Adorno saw in the works of the previous generation? The New Left answered this question in the negative. They appropriated the arguments of Horkheimer's and Adorno's ***Dialektik der Aufklärung*** that there is no room for genuine culture in advanced industrial societies and therefore rejected the notion of aesthetic opposition. As I mentioned earlier, they discovered Benjamin's writings and followed his thesis that the autonomy of art, which was grounded in its ritual function, faded away with the advent of mechanical mass reproduction. Benjamin had argued: "In dem Augenblick aber, da der Maßstab der Echtheit an der Kunstproduktion versagt, hat sich auch die gesamte Funktion der Kunst umgewälzt. An die Stelle ihrer Fundierung aufs Ritual tritt ihre Fundierung auf eine andere Praxis: nämlich ihre Fundierung auf Politik."[18] This thesis guided the theoretical efforts of the student movement. They wanted to tear down the walls of the aesthetic ghetto and apply the arts to the political realm. By 1975 it was clear that this movement had failed to reach its goal. The literary system slowly but surely returned to the status quo ante. I cannot go into the political and philosophical reasons for this failure.[19] My argument is exclusively concerned with the critique of Adorno's ***Ästhetische Theorie,*** as it emerged from the crisis of the literary system.

As soon as we focus on this question we begin to realize what separates our situation from that of Adorno in the sixties. We notice that Adorno's philosophy of art has become historical. Adorno stresses the precarious state of modern art and emphasizes the negative impact of capitalism on culture, yet he maintains that the function of art has basically not changed since the advent of modernism. To put it differently: Adorno's theory takes the institution of art for granted. Peter Bürger advanced the argument in his *Theorie der Avantgarde* (1974) that Adorno failed to critique the concept of autonomy.[20] It was the aim of the avant-garde movement, according to Bürger, to overcome the gap between the aesthetic and the practical sphere and to regain the political impact by destructing the traditional aesthetic autonomy. Bürger convincingly demonstrates that Adorno, in spite of his hostility towards Lukács, shares basic philosophical assumptions with him. Their disagreement about realism and modernism is based on a common notion of the autonomous work of art. While Lukács tilted towards a model of organic works of art, Adorno placed the emphasis on the raison d'être of tensions and contradictions. In Bürger's analysis the sharp edge of the historical dialectic finally turns against Adorno himself. Following Benjamin, Bürger describes the avant-garde movement in terms of a self-critique which denounces the complacency of modern aestheticism. Compared with this radical stance where art moves towards its own destruction, Adorno's aesthetic theory reads like a somewhat belated summary of modernism—a recapitulation which is not quite ready to accept the extreme conclusions of the avant-garde of the twentieth century.

Not all critics and theorists have consented to Bürger's thesis. W. Martin Lüdke for instance, in a response to Bürger, has questioned whether *Theorie der Avantgarde* does justice to Adorno's category of modernism (Moderne).[21] He takes issue with Bürger's presentation of Adorno's theory of aesthetic innovation, and finally tries to show that Bürger's critique is not really intrinsic, but rather inspired by the social theory of Jürgen Habermas. I find Lüdke's rejoinder persuasive as an interpretation of ***Ästhetische Theorie,*** but it is ultimately beside the point. Adopting a Habermasian position, i.e., looking at the Frankfurt School from a stance which has modified some of the basic tenets, enables Bürger to situate Adorno's aesthetic theory *historically.* Precisely because he stands outside of Adorno's theory he can point out that the logic of this theory is limited to a specific period of European art.

Although it may not be obvious at first sight, this argument has far-reaching consequences. It undercuts Adorno's key metaphor: the art work is no longer the sundial of history. The period after 1945, according to Bürger, is marked by a legitimate coexistence of different styles and tendencies. There is no stringent correlation between social and art history.

On the whole I find Bürger's critique and its strategy sound and convincing. Yet I would like to go one step further. To some extent Bürger himself still operates within the confines of Adorno's model. His major thesis, i.e., that the production and reception of literature between 1780 and

1910 is basically determined by the concept of autonomous art, is obviously derived from Adorno. Looking back at this period today and viewing it within the broader context of preceding and following literary history, we realize that Adorno's idea of autonomy, which was then historicized by Bürger, never covered more than a part of the actual literary production of the nineteenth century. Much of the Restoration period (1815-1848), with Heinrich Heine as the prime example, would not fit.[22] Aesthetic autonomy as an episode of history: this perspective looks more familiar to us than to Adorno. He was not prepared to accept this interpretation, because it would have deprived him of any meaningful approach to history. In his essay **"Das Altern der Neuen Musik"** Adorno is ready to concede that modern music was more radical in its beginnings than in its later phases. Still he refuses to unfold the implications of this argument. He laments this development as a loss. His remark about Bartok's later work is quite typical of this attitude: "Die Naivetät des Fachmusikers, der sein Metier besorgt, ohne an der Bewegung des objektiven Geistes recht teilzuhaben, ist dafür mitverantwortlich."[23] This reference to the objective spirit indicates that Adorno, in the final analysis, relies on a Hegelian model of history in which all strands relate to one single center. The application of this model, however cautiously Adorno proceeded, seems to blind him with respect to the divergence of artistic trends and movements. While Adorno certainly rejected a reductive reading of history and was also skeptical of historical laws, his thinking is deeply rooted in the concept of a unified historical process. This idea then, since the project of the Enlightenment has failed, leads him to the notion that the evolution of modern music is regressive because there is less personal freedom and an increasing amount of alienating bureaucracy in our society.[24] In a way, this argument puts the blame on history for not following the course that the philosopher has mapped out for it.

What is problematical in Adorno's philosophy of art, in other words, comes from the historical determinism which he inherited from the Hegelian and Marxian tradition. The link between this tradition and the Frankfurt School is the work of Georg Lukács, especially *History and Class Consciousness.* Those orthodox Marxists who denounced Adorno's theory as liberal ideology, failed to notice that they did not share his concept of the work of art and his approach to criticism, but based their aesthetic theories on the same understanding of history: history as a dialectical process in which the concrete is by definition part of the whole. For Adorno there is no philosophy without *Universalgeschichte.* As Russell Berman puts it in a recent article: "This historical scheme, an attempt to retain the universal history of Hegel and Marx, evidently precludes the possibility of perceiving the qualitatively new, for the new is only more of the old."[25] Although Berman in my opinion underestimates the difference between Adorno and orthodox Marxism, he has a valid point.

What are we to learn from this critique? Does it mean that any project of defining aesthetic theory in historical-philosophical terms has become impossible, as Bubner[26] claims? Or are we to take the advice of H. R. Jauss and turn to a system of aesthetic experience? Both Bubner and Jauss, in his *Kleine Apologie der ästhetischen Erfahrung,*[27] are prepared to eliminate history. This way they hope to regain a less problematical theory of art. I would not be willing to pay this price, for the loss of history would imply a fragmentation of experience which would decrease its meaning.

Notes

1. This essay was first presented as a lecture at Dartmouth College and Smith College in February 1980.

2. For a full account of the genesis of *Ästhetische Theorie* see Rolf Tiedemann's "Editorisches Nachwort" in: Theodor W. Adorno, *Ästhetische Theorie, Gesammelte Schriften,* vol. 7 (Frankfurt: Suhrkamp Verlag, 1970), pp. 537-44. The following quotations from *Ästhetische Theorie* are from this edition.

3. For the development of the West German student movement and its impact on literature see *Literatur und Studentenbewegung,* ed. W. Martin Lüdke (Opladen, 1977); *Nach dem Protest. Literatur in Umbruch,* ed. W. Martin Lüdke (Frankfurt, 1979).

4. Cf. Jürgen Habermas, "Bewußtmachende oder rettende Kritik-Die Aktualität Walter Benjamins," in *Zur Aktualität Walter Benjamins* (Frankfurt, 1972), pp. 175-223; also Philip Brewster and Carl Howard Buchner, "Language and Critique: Jürgen Habermas on Walter Benjamin," *New German Critique,* 17 (1979), pp. 15-29.

5. Cf. Anson Rabinbach, "Critique and Commentary/Alchemy and Chemistry: Some Remarks on Walter Benjamin and this Special Issue," *New German Critique,* 17 (1979), pp. 3-14.

6. Among the recent contributions to Adorno see Richard Wolin, "The De-Aesthetization of Art: On Adorno's *Ästhetische Theorie,*" *Telos,* 41 (Fall 1979), pp. 105-27.

7. For a precise account of the development of the political theory of the Frankfurt School see *The Essential Frankfurt School Reader,* ed. Andrew Arato and Eike Gebhardt (New York, 1978), pp. 3-25.

8. Adorno, "Resignation," in Adorno, *Kritik. Kleine Schriften zur Gesellschaft* (Frankfurt, 1971), pp. 145-50.

9. *Gesammelte Schriften,* vol. 11, pp. 251-80.

10. "Rede über Lyrik und Gesellschaft," *Gesammelte Schriften,* vol. 11, pp. 48-68.

11. Lucien Goldmann, *Pour une sociologie du roman* (Paris, 1964); *Recherches dialectiques* (Paris, 1959).

12. Jurij Tynjanov, "Über die literarische Evolution" in *Texte der russischen Formalisten,* Bd. 1, ed. Jurij Striedter, (München, 1969), pp. 393-431.

13. Adorno, "Thesen zur Kunstsoziologie," in Adorno, *Ohne Leitbild* (Frankfurt, 1970), pp. 94-103.

14. Adorno, *Einleitung in die Musiksozologie* (Frankfurt, 1962).

15. For example Uwe-K. Ketelsen, "Adalbert Stifter: Der Nachsommer (1857). Die Vernichtung der historischen Realität in der Ästhetisierung des bürgerlichen Alltags" in *Romane und Erzählungen des bürgerlichen Realismus* ed. Horst Denkler (Stuttgart, 1980), pp. 188-202.

16. Thomas Baumeister und Jens Kulenkampff, "Geschichtsphilosophie und philosophische Ästhetik. Zu Adornos Ästhetischer Theorie," *Neue Hefte für Philosophie,* 5 (1973), pp. 74-104.

17. Adorno, "Versuch, das Endspiel zu verstehen" in *Gesammelte Schriften,* vol. 11, pp. 281-331.

18. Walter Benjamin, *Illuminationen* (Frankfurt, 1961), p. 156.

19. See my forthcoming essay "Politisierung der Kunsttheorie: Zur ästhetischen Diskussion nach 1967" in *Literatur in der Bundesrepublik Deutschland seit 1965,* ed. Paul Michael Lützeler und Egon Schwarz (Königstein, 1980).

20. *Theorie der Avantgarde* (Frankfurt, 1974), pp. 117-27.

21. Lüdke, "Die Aporien der materialistischen Ästhetik—kein Ausweg? Zur kategorialen Begründung von P. Bürgers *Theorie der Avantgarde*" in: *Theorie der Avantgarde. Antworten auf Peter Bürgers Bestimmung von Kunst und bürgerlicher Gesellschaft,* ed. W. Martin Lüdke, (Frankfurt, 1976), pp. 27-71.

22. Cf. Friedrich Sengle, *Biedermeierzeit,* vol. 1, (Stuttgart, 1971), pp. 83-109.

23. Adorno, *Dissonanzen* (Göttingen, 1972), p. 140.

24. *Dissonanzen,* p. 157.

25. Berman, "Adorno, Marxism and Art," *Telos,* 34 (Winter 1977-78), p. 165.

26. Rüdiger Bubner, "Über einige Bedingungen gegenwärtiger Ästhetik," *Neue Hefte für Philosophie,* 5 (1973), pp. 38-73.

27. Konstanz, 1972.

Andreas Huyssen (essay date 1983)

SOURCE: "Adorno in Reverse: From Hollywood to Richard Wagner," in *After the Great Divide: Modernism, Mass Culture, Postmodernism,* Indiana University Press, 1986, pp. 16-43.

[*In the following essay, originally published in 1983, Huyssen discusses the influence of Adorno's theory of the "culture industry."*]

Ever since the failure of the 1848 revolution, the culture of modernity has been characterized by the contentious relationship between high art and mass culture. The conflict first emerged in its typical modern form in the Second Empire under Napoleon III and in Bismarck's new German Reich. More often than not it has appeared in the guise of an irreconcilable opposition. At the same time, however, there has been a succession of attempts launched from either side to bridge the gap or at least to appropriate elements of the other. From Courbet's appropriation of popular iconography to Brecht's immersion in the vernacular of popular culture, from Madison Avenue's conscious exploitation of avantgardist pictorial strategies to postmodernism's uninhibited learning from Las Vegas there has been a plethora of strategic moves tending to destabilize the high/low opposition from within. Yet this opposition—usually described in terms of modernism vs. mass culture or avantgarde vs. culture industry—has proven to be amazingly resilient. Such resilience may lead one to conclude that perhaps neither of the two combatants can do without the other, that their much heralded mutual exclusiveness is really a sign of their secret interdependence. Seen in this light, mass culture indeed seems to be the repressed other of modernism, the family ghost rumbling in the cellar. Modernism, on the other hand, often chided by the left as the elitist, arrogant and mystifying master-code of bourgeois culture while demonized by the right as the Agent Orange of natural social cohesion, is the strawman desperately needed by the system to provide an aura of popular legitimation for the blessings of the culture industry. Or, to put it differently, as modernism hides its envy for the broad appeal of mass culture behind a screen of condescension and contempt, mass culture, saddled as it is with pangs of guilt, yearns for the dignity of serious culture which forever eludes it.

Of course, questions raised by this persistent complicity of modernism and mass culture cannot be solved by textual analysis alone or by recourse to categories such as taste or quality. A broader framework is needed. Social scientists in the Marx-Weber tradition such as Jürgen Habermas have argued that with the emergence of civil society the sphere of culture came uncoupled from the political and economic systems. Such a differentiation of spheres (*Ausdifferenzierung*) may have lost some of its explanatory power for contemporary developments, but it is certainly characteristic of an earlier stage of capitalist modernization. It was actually the historical prerequisite for the twin establishment of a sphere of high autonomous art and a sphere of mass culture, both considered to lie outside the economic and political spheres. The irony of course is that art's aspirations to autonomy, its uncoupling from church and state, became possible only when literature, painting and music were first organized according to the principles of a market economy. From its beginnings the autonomy of art has been related dialectically to the commodity form. The rapid growth of the reading public and the increasing capitalization of the book market in the later 18th century, the commercialization of music culture and the development of a modern art market mark the beginnings of the high/low dichotomy in its specifically modern form. This dichotomy then became politically charged in decisive ways when new class conflicts erupted in the mid-19th century and the quickening pace of the industrial revolution required new cultural orientations for a mass populace. Habermas himself has analyzed this process in his *Strukturwandel der Öffentlichkeit* where he argues convincingly that the period of the Second Reich occupies a central place in the emergence of a modern mass culture and in the disintegration of an older bourgeois public sphere.[1] What Habermas has attempted to do, of course, is to insert a historical dimension into what Adorno and Horkheimer, some twenty years earlier, had postulated as the closed and seemingly timeless system of the culture industry. The force of Habermas' account was not lost on John Brenkman who, in an important article, fully agrees with Habermas' periodization: "This public sphere, like all the institutions and ideologies of the bourgeoisie in the 19th century, underwent extreme contortions as soon as its repressive functions showed through its initial transforming effects. The ethical-political principle of the public sphere—freedom of discussion, the sovereignty of the public will, etc.—proved to be a mask for its economic-political reality, namely, that the private interest of the capitalist class determines all social and institutional authority."[2] Indeed there can be little doubt that—just as the beginnings of modernism—the origins of modern mass culture date back to the decades around 1848, when, as Brenkman sums up, "The European bourgeoisie, still fighting to secure its triumph over aristocracy and monarchy, suddenly faced the counterrevolutionary task of suppressing the workers and preventing them from openly articulating *their* interests."[3]

While the emphasis on revolution and counterrevolution in the mid-19th century is important to a discussion of the origins of mass culture, it certainly does not tell the whole story. The salient fact is that with the universalization of commodity production mass culture begins to cut across classes in heretofore unknown ways. Many of its forms attract cross-class audiences, others remain class-bound. Traditional popular culture enters into a fierce struggle with commodified culture producing a variety of hybrid forms. Such resistances to the reign of the commodity were often recognized by the modernists who eagerly incorporated themes and forms of popular culture into the modernist vocabulary.[4] When we locate the origins of modern mass culture in the mid-19th century, the point is therefore not to claim that the culture of late capitalism "began" in 1848. But the *commodification of culture* did indeed emerge in the mid-19th century as a powerful force, and we need to ask what its specific forms were at that time and how precisely they were related to the industrialization of the human body and to the commodification of labor power. A lot of recent work in social history, history of technology, urban history and philosophy of time has converged on what Anthony Giddens calls the "commodification of time-space" during the formative decades of industrial capitalism.[5] We only need to think of the well-documented changes in the perception and articulation of

time and space brought about by railroad travelling,[6] the expansion of the visual field by news photography, the restructuring of city space with the Haussmannization of Paris, and last but not least the increasing imposition of industrial time and space on the human body in schools, factories, and the family. We may take the periodic spectacles of the World Expositions, those major mass-cultural phenomena of the times, as well as the elaborate staging of the commodity in the first giant department stores as salient symptoms of a changing relationship between the human body and the object world that surrounds it and of which it is itself a major part. What, then, are the traces of this commodification of time and space, of objects and the human body, in the arts? Of course, Baudelaire's poetry, Manet's and Monet's painting, Zola's or Fontane's novels and Schnitzler's plays, to name but a few examples, provide us with powerful visions of modern life, as it used to be called, and critics have focused on a number of social types symptomatic for the age, such as the prostitute and the dandy, the flaneur, the bohemian and the collector. But while the triumph of the modern in "high art" has been amply documented, we are only beginning to explore the place of mass culture vis-à-vis the modernization of the life-world in the 19th century.[7]

Clearly, Adorno and Horkheimer's concept of the culture industry does not yield much with regard to specific historical and textual analyses of 19th-century mass culture. Politically, adherence today to the classical culture industry thesis can only lead to resignation or moralizing about universal manipulation and domination. Blaming the culture industry for capitalism's longevity, however, is metaphysics, not politics. Theoretically, adherence to Adorno's aesthetics may blind us to the ways in which contemporary art, since the demise of classical modernism and the historical avantgarde, represents a new conjuncture which can no longer be grasped in Adornean or other modernist categories. Just as we would want to avoid elevating Adorno's **Aesthetic Theory** to the status of dogma, the last thing we want to start with is a simple projection of the culture industry theory back into the 19th century.

Yet, a discussion of Adorno in the context of the early stage of the mass culture/modernism dichotomy may still make sense for a number of simple reasons. First, Adorno is one of a very few critics guided by the conviction that a theory of modern culture must address both mass culture and high art. The same cannot be said for most literary and art criticism in this country. Nor can it be said of mass communication research which takes place totally apart from literary and art historical studies. Adorno actually undermines this very separation. The fact that he himself insists on fundamental separation between the culture industry and modernist art is to be understood not as a normative proposition but rather as a reflection of a series of historical experiences and theoretical assumptions which are open to debate.

Secondly, the theory of the culture industry has exerted a tremendous influence on mass culture research in Germany and, to a somewhat lesser extent, also in the United States.[8] Recalling the ways in which Adorno theorized about modern mass culture may not be the worst place to start. After all, a critical, yet sympathetic discussion may be quite fruitful in countering two current trends: one toward a theoretically decapitated and mostly affirmative description of "popular" culture, the other toward a moralizing condemnation of imperial mind management by a media apparatus allegedly totally in the grip of capital and profit interests.

Any discussion of Adorno, however, will have to begin by pointing out the theoretical limitations inherent in his thought which, contrary to what one often hears, cannot be reduced simply to a notion of brainwashing or manipulation. Adorno's blindnesses have to be interpreted as simultaneously theoretical and historical ones. Indeed, his theory may appear to us today as a ruin of history, mutilated and damaged by the very conditions of its articulation and genesis: defeat of the German working class, triumph and subsequent exile of modernism from central Europe, fascism, Stalinism and the Cold War. I do not feel the need to either resurrect or bury Adorno, as the saying goes. Both gestures ultimately fail to place Adorno in the ever shifting context of our attempts to understand the culture of modernity. Both attitudes tend to sap the energy from a body of texts which maintain their provocation for us precisely because they recede from a present which increasingly seems to indulge in a self-defeating narcissism of theory or in the hopeless return of jolly good old humanism.

I will begin, then, by briefly recapitulating some of the basic propositions of the culture industry concept and by pointing to some of the problems inherent in it. In a second section, I will show that Adorno can be read against the grain, that his theory is by no means as closed as it may appear at first sight. The task of this reading is precisely to open Adorno's account to its own hesitations and resistances and to allow it to function in slightly different frames. In the two final sections I will discuss how both Adorno's theory of modernism and the theory of the culture industry are shaped not only by fascism, exile and Hollywood, but also quite significantly by cultural phenomena of the late 19th century, phenomena in which modernism and culture industry seem to converge in curious ways rather than being diametrically opposed to each other. Locating elements of the culture industry, with Adorno, in l'art pour l'art, Jugendstil and Richard Wagner may serve two purposes. It may help sustain the claim that Adorno's view of the culture industry and modernism is not quite as binary and closed as it appears. And, on a much broader level, it may point us—in a reversal of Adorno's strategy—toward a desirable and overdue exploration of how modernism itself appropriates and transforms elements of popular culture, trying like Antaeus to gain strength and vitality from such contacts.[9]

CULTURE INDUSTRY

I will organize this brief outline in four clusters of observations:

1. Culture industry is the result of a fundamental transformation in the "superstructure" of capitalist societies. This transformation, completed with the stage of monopoly capitalism, reaches so deep that the Marxian separation of economy and culture as base and superstructure is itself called into question. While Marx's account reflected the realities of 19th-century liberal capitalism, its free market ideology and its belief in the autonomy of culture, 20th-century capitalism has "reunified" economy and culture by subsuming the cultural under the economic, by reorganizing the body of cultural meanings and symbolic significations to fit the logic of the commodity. Especially with the help of the new technological media of reproduction and dissemination monopoly capitalism has succeeded in swallowing up all forms of older popular cultures, in homogenizing all and any local or regional discourses, and in stifling by co-option any emerging resistances to the rule of the commodity. All culture is standardized, organized and administered for the sole purpose of serving as an instrument of social control. Social control can become total since in "the circle of manipulation and retroactive need . . . the unity of the system grows ever stronger."[10] Beyond that, culture industry even succeeds in abolishing the dialectic of affirmation and critique which characterized high bourgeois art of the liberal age.[11] "Cultural entities typical of the style of the culture industry are no longer *also* commodities, they are commodities through and through."[12] Or, in a more precise Marxian version which plays out Marx's distinction of use value and exchange value thus making the culture industry all-encompassing and totalitarian: "The more inexorably the principle of exchange value cheats human beings out of use values, the more successfully it manages to disguise itself as the ultimate object of enjoyment."[13] Just as art works become commodities and are enjoyed as such, the commodity itself in consumer society has become image, representation, spectacle. Use value has been replaced by packaging and advertising. The commodification of art ends up in the aestheticization of the commodity. The siren song of the commodity has displaced the *promesse de bonheur* once held by bourgeois art, and consumer Odysseus blissfully plunges into the sea of commodities, hoping to find gratification but finding none.[14] More than the museum or the academy even, department store and supermarket have become the cemeteries of culture. Culture and commodification have been collapsed in this theory to the extent that the gravitational pull of the culture industry leaves no meaning, no signification unscathed. For Adorno, modernist art is precisely the result of this conjuncture. But such a black-hole theory of capitalist culture is both too Marxist and not Marxist enough. It is too Marxist in that it rigorously applies a narrow reading of Marx's theory of commodity fetishism (the fetish as mere phantasmagoria) to the products of culture. It is not Marxist enough in that it ignores praxis, bypassing the struggles for meaning, symbols, and images which constitute cultural and social life even when the mass-media try to contain them. I am not denying that the increasing commodification of culture and its effects *in* all cultural products are pervasive. What I would deny is the implied notion that function and use are

totally determined by corporate intentions, and that exchange value has totally supplanted use value. The double danger of Adorno's theory is that the specificity of cultural products is wiped out and that the consumer is imagined in a state of passive regression. If cultural products were commodities through and through and had only exchange value, they would no longer even be able to fulfill their function in the processes of ideological reproduction. Since they do preserve this use value for capital, however, they also provide a locus for struggle and subversion. Culture industry, after all, does fulfill public functions; it satisfies and legitimizes cultural needs which are not all *per se* false or only retroactive; it articulates social contradictions in order to homogenize them. Precisely this process of articulation can become the field of contest and struggle.

2. The postulated integration and manipulation of the mass of individual consumers from above into the false totality of the authoritarian state or of the culture industry has its psychoanalytic correlate in the theory of the decay of the ego. Löwenthal once put it this way: culture industry is psychoanalysis in reverse, referring of course to Freud's famous statement: "Where Id is, Ego shall be." In a more serious vein, the Institute's *Studies on Authority and the Family* elaborated a theory postulating the objective decline of paternal authority in the bourgeois family. This decline of paternal authority in turn has led to a change in personality type based on conformity to external standards rather than, as in the liberal age, on the internalization of authority. Internalization of authority, however, is held to be a necessary prerequisite for the later (mature) rejection of authority by a strong ego. The culture industry is seen as one of the major factors preventing such "healthy" internalization and replacing it by those external standards of behavior which inevitably lead to conformism. Of course, this analysis was intimately bound up with the Institute's analysis of fascism. Thus in Germany, Hitler could become the substitute father, and fascist culture and propaganda provided the external guidance for the weak, gullible ego. The decay of ego formation in the family, according to Adorno, is complemented by the ontogenetically subsequent invasion of the psyche by the laws of capitalist production: "The organic composition of man is growing. That which determines subjects as means of production and not as living purposes, increases with the proportion of machines to variable capital."[15] And further: "In this reorganization the ego as business manager delegates so much of itself to the ego as business-mechanism, that it becomes quite abstract, a mere reference-point: self-preservation forfeits the self."[16]

A lot could be said about this theory of the shrinking ego from the viewpoint of psychoanalysis and gender as well as from that of recent changes in family structure and child rearing. I will limit myself to one observation. While the question of the historical constitution of the subject remains important (against essentialist notions of an autonomous subject as well as against ahistorical notions of a decentered subject), the theory of the decay of the ego seems to imply a nostalgia for the strong bourgeois ego and fur-

thermore remains locked into patriarchal patterns of thought. The culture industry as substitute father—Jessica Benjamin has eloquently criticized this view as "patriarchy without father."[17] Critical Theory also remains tied here to a traditional subject philosophy, and one does not need to resort to a critique of the whole trajectory of Western metaphysics in order to see that the notion of a stable "self" is historically datable and dated with the bourgeois age. Just as in their interpretation of culture Adorno and Horkheimer collapse the structure of art with that of the commodity, here they collapse the economic structure of society with the psychic dismantling of the individual, and again a form of closure prevails. Emptied subject and totality immobilize each other. The world appears frozen into nightmare.

3. The analysis of the culture industry draws out and applies to culture the premises of the Hegelian-Weberian Marx reception which had first been articulated in Lukács' *History and Class Consciousness,* the founding text, if there ever was one, of Western Marxism. Indeed, the culture industry chapter of the ***Dialectic of Enlightenment*** can be read as a political, theoretical and historical reply to Lukács' reworking of Marx's commodity fetishism and Weber's rationalization theory into a philosophy of social praxis. Adorno and Horkheimer's text gains its political cutting edge from its rejection of Lukács' belief in the proletariat as the identical subject-object of history, and the theory of the culture industry becomes the classical locus where its authors show how and why commodity fetishism and reification have forever lost their emancipatory function in the dialectic of history. To a large degree, it is this implied political and theoretical debate with Lukács which led to Adorno's excessive privileging of the pivotal critical categories of reification, totality, identity and commodity fetishism and to his presentation of the culture industry as a frozen system. Combined with the fearfully observed decay of the ego, this cluster of categories, however, can only prevent a differentiated analysis of social and cultural practices. It has to block out any insight into the functional autonomy of the various subsystems within the total system of production and reproduction. One is almost tempted to speak of an implosion of categories which translates into the incredible density of Adorno's writing, but which ultimately also makes the individual and serial phenomena of which culture industry consists vanish from sight as a field of concrete historical analysis. Even though Adorno recognizes quite frequently that there are limits to the reification of the human subject, he never asks himself whether perhaps there are also limits to the reification of the cultural commodities themselves, limits which become evident when one begins to analyze in detail the signifying strategies of those cultural commodities and the mesh of repression and wish fulfillment, of the gratification, displacement and production of desire which are invariably involved in them and in their reception. On the other hand, we have to acknowledge that Adorno's contribution to the mass culture debate lies in his struggle against another kind of invisibility. His analysis of mass culture as a means of social control ripped to shreds that mystifying veil cast

over the culture industry by those who sell it as "mere entertainment," or, even worse, as a genuinely popular culture.

4. Contrary to what Fred Jameson has recently argued, Adorno never lost sight of the fact that, ever since their simultaneous emergence in the mid-19th century, modernism and mass culture have been engaged in a compulsive *pas de deux.* It indeed never occurred to Adorno to see modernism as anything other than a reaction formation to mass culture and commodification, as my later discussion of Adorno's views of Wagner and Schönberg will show. In a famous letter to Benjamin, in which he criticized Benjamin's reproduction essay, he wrote: "Both [modernist art and mass culture] bear the scars of capitalism, both contain elements of change. Both are torn halves of freedom, to which however they do not add up."[18] Adorno sees the dichotomy as historically produced, and he clearly interprets modernism as a "symptom and a result of cultural crisis rather than as a new 'solution' in its own right."[19] Adorno could not agree more with Jameson's claim that the commodity is "the prior form in terms of which alone modernism can be structurally grasped."[20] Even though Adorno's dialectical view of the relationship between modernism and mass culture may ultimately not be dialectical enough, it warrants repeating—in face of the often voiced mandarin reproach—that he is miles apart from the evaluative schemes of conservative mass culture critics and does not have much in common with the happy-go-lucky apologists of the triumph of modernism. Nevertheless, as I will argue in more detail later on, the problematic nature of Adorno's culture industry theory results precisely from the fact that it functioned, in the Derridean sense, as a *supplément* to his theory of modernism. Thus the lack of breadth and generosity which is so striking in Adorno's canon of modernism is not simply the result of personal, "elitist" taste, but it flows from his rigorous and relentless analysis of the cultural effects of commodification. The validity of that analysis has to be questioned if one wants to deal critically with Adorno's modernist canon. In this context, I think it is significant to point out that Adorno's modernism theory relies on certain strategies of exclusion which relegate realism, naturalism, reportage literature and political art to an inferior realm. All forms of representation fall under the verdict of reification which had been pronounced over the culture industry: *Verdoppelung* and *Reklame,* duplication and advertising. Just as the products of the culture industry, representational modern art is dismissed as a reified reproduction of a false reality. It is certainly strange to see one of the most perceptive critics of realism affirm, if only negatively, the power of language and image to represent reality, to reproduce the referent. Without pursuing this problem any further I am taking the status of realism in Adorno's modernism theory as support for my claim that any critique of the culture industry theory must be grounded to Adorno's modernist aesthetic. And I would even make the stronger, more general claim that to speak of modernism without mentioning capitalist mass culture is like praising the free market while ignoring the multinationals.

MARGINAL REVISIONS: READING ADORNO
AGAINST THE GRAIN

No account of the culture industry theory can be considered adequate unless it also locates Adorno's hesitations, resistances, and displacements within the texts themselves. In a close reading of Adorno's **"Transparencies on Film"** Miriam Hansen has recently made a convincing case for reading Adorno against the grain.[21] Such a reading can indeed show that Adorno himself frequently cast doubt in the positions taken in *Dialectic of Enlightenment.* One of the most salient examples, quoted by Hansen, can be found in the posthumously published draft **"Schema der Massenkultur,"** which was originally meant to be part of the culture industry chapter in *Dialectic of Enlightenment.* In capsule form Adorno and Horkheimer give the central thesis of the work: "Human beings, as they conform to the technological forces of production which are imposed on them in the name of progress, are transformed into objects which willingly allow themselves to be manipulated and thus fall behind the actual potential of these productive forces."[22] But then, in a dialectical move, the authors place their hope in the very repetitiveness of reification: "Because human beings, as subjects, still constitute the limit of reification, mass culture has to renew its hold over them in an endless series of repetitions; the hopeless effort of repetition is the only trace of hope that the repetition may be futile, that human beings cannot be totally controlled."[23] Examples such as this one could easily be multiplied. But while reading the classical texts on the culture industry against the grain may testify to Adorno's insight into the potential limitations of his theory, I doubt whether such insights should compel us to fundamentally revise our interpretation of these texts. The difficulty may only have been displaced to another area. The same move in which the monolithic closure of the culture industry theory comes undone in the margins seems to reaffirm another closure at the level of the subject. In the quoted passage any potential resistance to the culture industry is ascribed to the subject, however contingent and hallowed out it may be, rather than, say, to intersubjectivity, social action, and the collective organization of cultural experience in what Negt and Kluge have called counter-public spheres (*Gegenöffentlichkeiten*). It is not enough to reproach Adorno for holding on to a monadic or "bourgeois" notion of the subject. Isolation and privatization of the subject are after all the very real effects of much of capitalist mass culture, and the resulting subjectivity is, in Adorno's own terms, quite different from that of the ascendant earlier bourgeois class. The question rather has to be how Adorno defines that subjectivity which would elude manipulation and control.

Jochen Schulte-Sasse has recently argued that Adorno relies on an ahistorical hypostatization of the subject as a self-identical ego equipped with analytical power.[24] If this reading is correct, the subject resisting reification through mass culture is none other than the critical theorist's younger brother, less stable perhaps and less forceful in his resistance, but the hope for resistance would indeed have to place its trust in the residues of that ego-formation which the culture industry tends to destroy. But here, too, one can read Adorno against the grain and point to passages in his work in which the stable and armored ego is seen as the problem rather than the solution. In his critique of Kant's subject of epistemology Adorno attacks the notion of the self-identical subject as a historically produced construct bound up with social experiences of objectification and reification: "It is obvious that the hardness of the epistemological subject, the identity of self-consciousness mimics the unreflected experience of the consistent, identical object."[25] Adorno's critique of the deeply problematic nature of such fortifications of the subject, which is reminiscent of the Jena romantics is summed up poignantly when he writes: "The subject is all the more a subject the less it is so; and the more it imagines itself to *be* and to be an objective entity for itself, the less it is a subject."[26]

Similarly, in a critical discussion of Freud and the bourgeois privileging of genital sexuality, Adorno recognized the principle of ego-identity as socially constituted: "Not to be oneself is a piece of sexual utopia . . . : negation of the ego principle. It shakes up that invariant of bourgeois society understood in its broadest sense: the demand of identity. First identity had to be constructed, ultimately it will have to be overcome (*aufzuheben*). That which is only identical with itself is without happiness."[27] Such passages point to Adorno's fragile utopian vision of a reconciliation with nature which, as always in Adorno and Horkheimer, is understood as both outer and inner nature in a way that calls their very separation into question: "The dawning sense of freedom feeds upon the memory of the archaic impulse not yet steered by any solid I. The more the I curbs that impulse, the more chaotic and thus questionable will it find that pre-historic freedom. Without an anamnesis of the untamed impulse that precedes the ego—an impulse later banished to the zone of unfree bondage to nature—it would be impossible to derive the idea of freedom, although that idea in turn ends up in reinforcing the ego."[28] As against the previous quote from *Eingriffe* where the *Aufhebung* of bourgeois ego-formation seemed to hold out a promise, here the dialectic ends in aporia. Surely, one problem is that Adorno, like Freud in *Civilization and Its Discontents*, metaphorically collapses the phylogenetic with the ontogenetic level. He permits his historical and philosophical speculations about the dialectic of self-preservation and enlightenment to get in the way of pursuing the question, in relation to mass culture, to what extent and for what purposes the products of the culture industry might precisely speak to and activate such pre-ego impulses in a non-regressive way. His focus on how the commodification of culture dissolves ego-formation and produces mere regression blinds him to that possibility. He founders on the aporia that in his philosophy of civilization these impulses preceding the ego simultaneously contain a sign of freedom and the hope for a reconciliation with nature on the one hand while on the other hand they represent the archaic domination of nature over man which had to be fought in the interest of self-preservation.

Any further discussion of such pre-ego impulses (e.g., partial instincts) in relation to mass culture would lead to the central question of identification, that ultimate bogeyman of Adorno's—and not only Adorno's—modernist aesthetic. Adorno never took that step. The suspension of critical distance which is at stake in any identification with the particular leads inexorably to a legitimation of the false totality. While Adorno recognized that there were limitations to the reification of human subjects through the culture industry which made resistance thinkable at the level of the subject, he never asked himself whether perhaps such limitations could be located in the mass cultural commodities themselves. Such limits do indeed become evident when one begins to analyze in detail the signifying strategies of specific cultural commodities and the mesh of gratification, displacement and production of desires which are invariably put in play in their production and consumption. How precisely identification works in the reception of mass culture, what spaces it opens and what possibilities it closes off, how it can be differentiated according to gender, class and race—these are questions to which the theory of the culture industry might have led had it not been conceived, in the spirit of the negative dialectic, as the threatening other of modernism. And yet, reading Adorno against the grain opens up precisely some of these spaces inside his texts where we might want to begin rewriting his account for a post-modern age.

PREHISTORY AND CULTURE INDUSTRY

To write a prehistory of the modern was the stated goal of Benjamin's never completed arcades project on 19th-century Paris. The dispute between Benjamin and Adorno revolving around their different readings of cultural commodification and of the relationship between prehistory and modernity is well-documented and researched. Given Adorno's trenchant critique of Benjamin's 1935 exposé of the arcades project it is somewhat baffling to find that he never wrote about mass culture in the 19th century. Doing so would have allowed him to refute Benjamin on his own ground, but the closest he ever came to such an undertaking is probably the book on Wagner written in London and New York in 1937 and 1938. Instead he chose to battle Benjamin, especially the Benjamin of "The Work of Art in the Age of Mechanical Reproduction," in his analysis of the 20th-century culture industry. Politically, this choice made perfect sense in the late 1930s and early 1940s, but the price he paid for it was great. Drawing on the experience of mass culture in fascism and developed consumer capitalism, the theory of the culture industry was itself affected by the reification it decried since it left no room for historical development. Culture industry represented for Adorno the completed return to prehistory under the sign of the eternal recurrence of the same. While Adorno seemed to deny mass culture its own history, his critique of Benjamin's arcades exposé shows clearly that he saw the later 19th century as prefiguring that cultural commodification which reached its fully organized state in the culture industry of the 20th century. If the late 19th century, then, already lives under the threat of cultural barbarism and regression, one might want to take Adorno another step further back. After all, throughout his work he interpreted the culture of modernity with its twin formation of modernism and culture industry as tied to high or monopoly capitalism which in turn is distinguished from the preceding phase of liberal capitalism. The decline of the culture of liberal capitalism, never very strong in Germany in the first place, was by and large complete with the foundation of the Second Reich, most certainly by the 1890s. The history of that crucial transition from the culture of liberal capitalism to that of monopoly capitalism never receives much explicit attention in Adorno's writing, certainly not as much as the artistic developments in the later 19th century which led to the emergence of Adorno's modernism. But even here Adorno writes about the major artists of the period only (the late Wagner, Hofmannsthal, George) while ignoring the popular literature of the times (Karl May, Ganghofer, Marlitt) as well as working-class culture. For naturalism he only reserves some flippant remarks and the early developments of technological media such as photography and film are all but absent from his accounts of the late 19th century. Only with Wagner does Adorno reach back to that earlier stage; and it is no coincidence that Wagner is indeed the pivotal figure in Adorno's prehistory of the modern.

Another point needs to be raised pertaining to this curious absence of 19th-century mass culture in Adorno's writing. Already in the 1930s Adorno must have been aware of historical research on mass culture. He only had to look at the work of one of his fellow researchers at the Institute, Leo Löwenthal, who did much of his work on 18th- and 19th-century German culture, high and low, and who never tired of drawing the connections that existed between 20th-century critiques of mass culture and earlier discussions of the problem in the work of Schiller and Goethe, Tocqueville, Marx and Nietzsche, to name only the most salient figures. Again the question presses itself upon us: why does Adorno ignore the mass culture of the Second Reich? He could have made much of the observation that many of the late 19th-century popular classics were still common fare in the Third Reich. Interpreting such continuities could have contributed significantly to the understanding of the prehistory of fascist culture[29] and the rise of authoritarianism, the process George Mosse has described as the nationalization of the masses. But that was just not Adorno's primary interest. His first and foremost goal was to establish a theory of *die Kunst der Moderne,* not as a historian, but as a participant and critic reflecting upon a specific stage in the development of capitalist culture and privileging certain trends within that stage. Adorno's prime example for the emergence of a genuinely modernist art was the turn to atonality in the music of Arnold Schönberg rather than, as for Benjamin and many historians of modernism, the poetry of Baudelaire. For my argument here the difference in choice of examples is less important than the difference in treatment. Where Benjamin juxtaposes Baudelaire's poetry with the texture and experience of modern life showing how modern life invades the poetic text, Adorno focuses more narrowly on the development of the musical material itself which he nevertheless interprets as *fait social,* as an aesthetic texturing and constructing of the experience of modernity, however mediated and removed from *subjective* experience that construction may ultimately turn out to be. Given Adorno's belief that the late 19th-century commodification of culture prefigures that of the culture industry and sets the stage for the successful modernist resistance to commodification in the works of Schönberg, Kafka and Kandinsky, it seems only logical that Adorno should attempt to locate the germs of the culture industry in the high art of the late 19th century which precedes modernism—in Wagner, Jugendstil and l'art pour l'art. We are faced, then, with the paradox of having to read Adorno on the high art of the times if we want to find traces of the mass culture problematic in his writings on 19th-century culture. Here I anticipate the habitual battlecry of "elitism" which usually serves to end all discussion. Certainly, the bias is there in Adorno. But it is not as if the questions he raises had ever been convincingly answered. If modernism is a response to the long march of the commodity through culture, then the effects of cultural commodification and all it entails *also* need to be located *in* the development of the artistic material itself rather than only in the department store or in the dictates of fashion. Adorno may be wrong in his answers—and his rigorously atrophied account of modernism simply leaves too much out—but he is most certainly right in his questions. Which, again, is not to say that his questions are the only ones we should ask.

How, then, does Adorno deal with the late 19th century? On the face of it his history of modernism seems to coincide with that of Anglo-American criticism which sees modernism evolving continuously from the mid-19th century to the 1950s, if not to the present. Despite occasional shifts in the evaluation of certain authors (e.g., George and Hofmannsthal) Adorno privileges a certain trend of modernist literature—to take but one medium—from Baudelaire and Flaubert via Mallarmé, Hofmannsthal and George to Valéry and Proust, Kafka and Joyce, Celan and Beckett. The notion of a politically committed art and literature is anathema for Adorno as it is for the dominant account of modernism in Anglo-American criticism. Major movements of the historical avantgarde such as Italian futurism, Dada, Russian constructivism and productivism as well as surrealism are blatantly absent from the canon, an absence which is highly significant and which bears directly on Adorno's account of the late 19th century.

A closer look at Adorno's aesthetic theory will indeed dispel the notion of unilinear evolutionary development of modernism since the mid-19th century. It will show on the contrary that Adorno locates a major rupture in the development of modern art after the turn of the century, i.e., with the emergence of the historical avantgarde movements. Of course, Adorno has often been described as a theorist of the avantgarde, a use of terminology based on the problematic collapsing of the notion of the avantgarde with that of modernism. Since Peter Bürger's *Theory of the Avantgarde,* however, it seems no longer permissible to use the terms interchangeably, even though Bürger himself, at least in his earlier work, still talks about Adorno as a theorist of the avantgarde.[30] But if it is true, as Bürger argues, that the main goal of the historical avantgarde was the reintegration of art into life, a heroic attempt that failed, then Adorno is not a theorist of the avantgarde, but a theorist of modernism. More than that, he is a theorist of a construct "modernism" which has already digested the failure of the historical avantgarde. It has not gone unnoticed that Adorno frequently scorned avantgarde movements such as futurism, Dada, and surrealism, and that he acidly rejected the avantgardes' various attempts to reintegrate art and life as a dangerous regression from the aesthetic to the barbaric. This insight, however, has often prevented critics from appreciating the fact that Adorno's theory of modernism owes as much to the historical avantgarde's onslaught against notions of the work of art as organism *or* as artificial paradise as it owes to late 19th-century aestheticism and to the autonomy aesthetic. Only if one understands this double heritage will statements such as the following in the ***Philosophy of Modern Music*** be fully comprehensible: "Today the only works which really count are those which are no longer works at all."[31] As far as I can see, only Peter Bürger has located this historical core of Adorno's aesthetic theory when he wrote in a more recent essay: "Both the radical separation of art from life completed by aestheticism *and* the reintegration of art and life intended by the historical avantgarde movements are premises for a view which sees art in total opposition to any rationally organized life-praxis and which at the same time attributes to art a revolutionary force challenging the basic organization of society. The hopes which the most radical members of the avantgarde movements, especially the dadaists and early surrealists, invested in this possibility of changing society through art, these hopes live on residually in Adorno's aesthetic theory, even though in a resigned and mutilated form. Art is that 'other' which cannot be realized in the world."[32] Adorno indeed holds in charged tension two diverging tendencies: on the one hand aestheticism's insistence on the autonomy of the art work and its double-layered separateness from everyday life (separate *as* work of art *and* separate in its refusal of realistic representation) and, on the other, the avantgarde's radical break with precisely that tradition of art's autonomy. In doing so he delivers the work's autonomy to the social while preserving it at the same time: "Art's double character, its being autonomous and fait social, relentlessly pervades the zone of its autonomy."[33] Simultaneously he radicalizes modernity's break with the past and with tradition in the spirit of avantgardism: "Contrary to past styles, it [the concept of modernity] does not negate earlier art forms; it negates tradition per se."[34] We need to remember here that the radical break with tradition, first articulated by artists such as Baudelaire and Manet, becomes dominant in German culture much later than in France: in Schönberg rather than Wagner, Kafka rather than George, i.e., after the turn of the century. From the perspective of German developments Baudelaire could then be seen as Adorno sees Poe in relation to Baudelaire: as a lighthouse of modernity.[35]

Adorno's fundamental indebtedness to the project of the post-1900 historical avantgarde can be gleaned from the ways in which he discusses l'art pour l'art, Jugendstil and the music of Richard Wagner. In each case, the emergence of "genuine" modernism is seen as resulting from a deterioration *within* forms of high art, a deterioration which bears witness to the increasing commodification of culture.

Adorno's work bristles with critiques of aestheticism and the l'art pour l'art movements of the 19th century. In his essay **"Standort des Erzählers im zeitgenössischen Roman"** (1954) we read: "The products [of modernist art] are above the controversy between politically committed art and l'art pour l'art. They stand beyond the alternative which pits the philistinism of *Tendenzkunst* against the philistinism of art as pleasure."[36] In ***Dialectic of Enlightenment*** Adorno relates l'art pour l'art polemically to political advertising: "Advertising becomes art and nothing else, just as Goebbels—with foresight—combines them: l'art pour l'art, advertising for its own sake, a pure representation of social power."[37] L'art pour l'art, advertising and the fascist aesthetization of politics can only be thought together under the sign of that false universal of modernity which is the commodity. In a more historical vein, to give a third example, Adorno writes in ***Ästhetische Theorie***: "L'art pour l'art's concept of beauty is strangely hollow, and yet it is obsessed with matter. It resembles an art nouveau event as revealed in Ibsen's charms of hair entwined with vine leaves and of a beautiful death. Beauty seems paralyzed, incapable of determining itself which it could only do by relating to its 'other.' It is like a root in the air and becomes entangled with the destiny of the invented ornament."[38] And somewhat later: "In their innermost constitution the products of l'art pour l'art stand condemned by their latent commodity form which makes them live on as Kitsch, subject to ridicule."[39] Adorno's critique here is actually reminiscent of Nietzsche's, that most trenchant and yet dubious critic of mass culture in Imperial Germany, whose influence on Critical Theory has recently been the subject of much debate. But while Nietzsche criticizes l'art pour l'art, for instance in *Beyond Good and Evil,* as a form of decadence and relates it metaphorically to the culture of deluded scientific objectivity and of positivism, Adorno succeeds in grounding the critique systematically with the help of Marx's notion of the commodity form. It is this emphasis on the commodity form (to which Nietzsche was totally oblivious) which permits Critical Theory to articulate a consistent critique of the objectivistic social sciences and of a reified aestheticism. And it furthermore connects Adorno's critique of l'art pour l'art with his discussion of Jugendstil, a style which in a certain sense aimed at reversing l'art pour l'art's separation from life.

The Jugendstil of the turn of the century is indeed pivotal to Adorno's historical account of the emergence of modernist art. Although he highly values certain individual works that were part of Jugendstil culture (e.g., works by the early Stefan George and the young Schönberg), he argues that the commodity character of art which had been an integral, though somewhat hidden part of all emancipated bourgeois art becomes external in Jugendstil, tumbling, as it were, out of the art works for all to see. A longer quote from *Ästhetische Theorie* is appropriate here: "Jugendstil has contributed greatly to this development, with its ideology of sending art back into life as well as with the sensations created by Wilde, d'Annunzio and Maeterlinck, all of them preludes to the culture industry. Increasing subjective differentiation and the heightened dissemination of the realm of aesthetic stimuli made these stimuli manipulable. They could now be produced for the cultural market. The tuning of art to the most fleeting individual reactions allied itself with art's reification. Art's increasing likeness to a subjectively perceived physical world made all art abandon its objectivity thus recommending it to the public. The slogan l'art pour l'art was but the veil of its opposite. This much is true about the hysterical attacks on decadence: subjective differentiation reveals an element of ego weakness which corresponds to the spiritual make-up of the clients of the culture industry. The culture industry learned how to profit from it."[40] Three brief observations: Adorno's aversion against later avant-gardist attempts to reintegrate art and life may have been as strong as it was because he held those attempts, however one-sidedly, to be similar to that of Jugendstil. Secondly, the avantgarde's attempts to dissolve the boundaries between art and life—whether those of Dada and surrealism or those of Russian productivism and constructivism—had ended in failure by the 1930s, a fact which makes Adorno's skepticism toward sending art back into life quite understandable. In a sense never intended by the avantgarde, life had indeed become art—in the fascist aesthetization of politics as mass spectacle as well as in the fictionalizations of reality dictated by the socialist realism of Zhdanov and by the dream world of capitalist realism promoted by Hollywood. Most importantly, however, Adorno criticizes Jugendstil as a prelude to the culture industry because it was the first style of high art to fully reveal the commodification and reification of art in capitalist culture. And it would not be Adorno if this account of Jugendstil did not precisely thrive on the paradox that the culture industry's antecedents are traced to a style and an art which is highly individualistic and which was never meant for mass reproduction. Jugendstil, nevertheless, marks that moment of history in which the commodity form has pervaded high art to the extent that—as in Schopenhauer's famous example of the bird hypnotized by the snake—it throws itself blissfully into the abyss and is swallowed up. That stage, however, is the prerequisite for Adorno's negative aesthetic of modernism that first took shape in the work of Schönberg. Schönberg's turn to atonality is interpreted as the crucial strategy to evade commodification and reification while articulating it in its very technique of composition.

RICHARD WAGNER: PHANTASMAGORIA AND MODERN MYTH

Schönberg's "precursor" in the medium of music of course is Richard Wagner. Adorno argues that the turn toward atonality, that supreme achievement of musical modernism, is already latent in certain composition techniques of Richard Wagner. Wagner's use of dissonance and chromatic movement, his multiple subversions of classical harmony, the emergence of tonal indeterminacy and his innovations in color and orchestration are seen as setting the stage for Schönberg and the Vienna School. And yet, Schönberg's relation to Wagner, which is central to Adorno's account of the birth of modernism in the arts, is described as one of continuation *and* resistance, most succinctly perhaps in the **"Selbstanzeige des Essaybuches 'Versuch über Wagner'"**: "All of modern music has developed in resistance to his [Wagner's] predominance— and yet, all of its elements are latently present in him."[41] The purpose of Adorno's long essay on Wagner, written in 1937/38, was not to write music history or to glorify the modernist breakthrough. Its purpose was rather to analyze the social and cultural roots of German fascism in the 19th century. Given the pressures of the times—Hitler's affiliation with Bayreuth and the incorporation of Wagner into the fascist culture machine—Wagner's work turned out to be the logical place for such an investigation. We need to remember here that whenever Adorno says fascism, he is also saying culture industry. The book on Wagner can therefore be read not only as an account of the birth of fascism out of the spirit of the *Gesamtkunstwerk,* but also as an account of the birth of the culture industry *in* the most ambitious high art of the 19th century. On the face of it such an account would seem patently absurd since it appears to ignore the existence of a well developed industrial mass culture in Wagner's own time. But then Adorno's essay does not claim to give us a comprehensive historical description of the origins of mass culture as such, nor does he suggest that the place to develop a theory of the culture industry is high art alone. What he does suggest, however, is something largely lost in the dominant accounts of modernism which emphasize the triumphal march of abstraction and surface in painting, textual self-referentiality in literature, atonality in music and irreconcilable hostility to mass culture and Kitsch in all forms of modernist art. Adorno suggests that the social processes that give shape to mass culture cannot be kept out of art works of the highest ambition and that any analysis of modernist or, for that matter, premodernist art will have to trace these processes in the trajectory of the aesthetic materials themselves. The ideology of the art work's autonomy is thus undermined by the claim that no work of art is ever untouched by the social. But Adorno makes the even stronger claim that in capitalist society high art is always already permeated by the textures of that mass culture from which it seeks autonomy. As a model analysis of the entanglements of high art with mass cultural commodification the Wagner essay is actually more stimulating than, say, the ***Philosophy of Modern Music*** which in many ways represents the negative version of modernist triumphalism. Preceding Jugendstil and l'art pour l'art which are blamed for simply capitulating to the commodity, it is the body of Wagner's oeuvre, towering as it does at the threshold of modernity, which becomes the privileged locus of that fierce struggle between tradition and modernity, autonomy and commodity, revolution and reaction, and, ultimately, myth and enlightenment.

As I cannot possibly do justice here to Adorno's various writings on Wagner, I will only outline those elements which connect Wagner's aesthetic innovations to features of the modern culture industry. The other half of Adorno's Wagner—Wagner as premodernist—will have to remain under-exposed.

To begin with, Adorno concedes throughout his essay that in his time Wagner represented the most advanced stage in the development of music and opera. However, he consistently emphasizes both progressive *and* reactionary elements in Wagner's music making the point that the one cannot be had without the other. He credits Wagner for heroically attempting to elude the market demands for "easy" opera and for trying to avoid its banality. But this flight, according to Adorno, leads Wagner even more deeply into the commodity. In his later essay **"Wagner's Aktualität"** (1965) Adorno finds a powerful image for this dilemma: "Everything in Wagner has its historical core. Like a spider, his spirit sits in the gigantic web of 19th-century exchange relations."[42] No matter how far Wagner would spin out his music, spider and web will always remain one. How, then, do these exchange relations manifest themselves in Wagner's music? How does the music get caught in the web of cultural commodification? After a discussion of Wagner as social character, which I will skip here, Adorno turns to an analysis of Wagner's role as composer-conductor. He argues that Wagner disguises the growing estrangement of the composer from the audience by conceiving his music "in terms of the gesture of striking a blow" and by incorporating the audience into the work through calculated "effects": "As the striker of blows . . . the composer-conductor gives the claims of the public a terrorist emphasis. Democratic considerateness towards the listener is transformed into connivance with the powers of discipline: in the name of the listener, anyone whose feelings accord with any measure other than the beat of the music is silenced."[43] In this interpretation of Wagner's "gesture" Adorno shows how the audience becomes "the reified object of calculation by the artist."[44] And it is here that the parallels with the culture industry emerge. The composer-conductor's attempt to beat his audience into submission is structurally isomorphic to the way in which the culture industry treats the consumer. But the terms of the isomorphism are reversed. In Wagner's theater the composer-conductor is still visible and present as an individual—a residue of the liberal age, as it were—and the spectators are assembled as a public in the dark behind the conductor's baton. The industrial organization of culture, however, replaces the individual conductor with an invisible corporate management and it dissolves the public into the shapeless mass of isolated consumers. The culture industry thus reverses the relations typical of the liberal age by de-individualizing cultural production and privatizing reception. Given Adorno's description of Wagner's audience as the reified object of aesthetic calculations it comes as no surprise that he would claim that Wagner's music is

already predicated on that ego-weakness which would later become the operational basis of the culture industry: "The audience of these giant works lasting many hours is thought of as unable to concentrate—something not unconnected with the fatigue of the citizen in his leisure time. And while he allows himself to drift with the current, the music, acting as its own impresario, thunders at him in endless repetitions to hammer its message home."[45] Such endless repetitions manifest themselves most obviously in Wagner's leitmotiv technique which Adorno relates to Berlioz's *idée fixe* and to the Baudelairian spleen. Adorno interprets the leitmotiv's double character as allegory and advertising. As allegory the leitmotiv articulates a progressive critique of traditional totalizing musical forms and of the "symbolic" tradition of German idealism. At the same time, however, it functions like advertising in that it is designed to be easily remembered by the forgetful. This advertising aspect of the leitmotiv is not something projected back onto it from hindsight. Adorno already locates it in the reactions of Wagner's contemporaries who tended to make crude links between leitmotivs and the persons they characterized. The commercial decay of the leitmotiv, latent in Wagner, becomes full-blown in Hollywood film music "where the sole function of the leitmotiv is to announce heroes or situations so as to help the audience to orientate itself more easily."[46]

Reification emerges as the conceptual core of Adorno's account. "Allegorical rigidity" has not only infected the motiv like a disease, it has infected Wagner's oeuvre as a whole—its music and its characters, its images and myths, and last but not least its institutionalization in Bayreuth as one of the major spectacles of the times. Adorno goes on to discuss reification, which can be regarded as the effect of commodification *in* the musical material, on the levels of melody, color, and orchestration. The overriding concern here is the question of what happens to musical time in Wagner's oeuvre. Adorno argues that time becomes abstract and as such defies musical and dramatic development on the level of melody as well as on that of character. The musical material is pulverized, characters are frozen and static. The construction of motiv as temporal sequence is replaced by impressionistic association: "For the composer the use of the beat is a fallacious method of mastering the empty time with which he begins, since the measure to which he subjects time does not derive from the musical content, but from the reified order of time itself."[47] The predominance of "sound" in Wagner also dissolves the temporal pressures of harmony. It spatializes musical time, depriving it, as it were, of its historical determinations.[48]

These observations about the leitmotiv, the reified order of time and the atomization of musical material lead Adorno to a central point where he affiliates Wagner's composition technique with the mode of production: "It is difficult to avoid the parallel with the quantification of the industrial labor process, its fragmentation into the smallest possible units. . . . Broken down into the smallest units, the totality is supposed to become controllable, and it must submit to the will of the subject who has liberated himself from all pre-existing forms."[49] The parallel with the culture industry becomes fully obvious when we read a little further on: "In Wagner's case what predominates is already the totalitarian and seigneurial aspect of atomization; that devaluation of the individual vis-à-vis the totality, which excludes all authentic dialectical interaction."[50]

What Adorno describes here, of course, is the reflection of the 19th-century industrialization of time and space in Wagner's oeuvre. The devaluation of the individual vis-à-vis the totality appears in Wagner's orchestration as the tendency to drown out the voice of the individual instrument in favor of a continuum of timbres and large-scale melodic complexes. The "progress" of such orchestration techniques is as suspect to Adorno as the progress of the industrial upsurge of the Bismarck era to which it is compared.

If reification of musical and dramatic time is one major element of Adorno's account, then subjectivistic association and ambiguity of musical meaning is the other side of the same coin. What is at stake here is that which Wagner's contemporaries described as nervousness and hypersensitivity, what Nietzsche called decadence, and what we might call Wagner's modernity. It is interesting to take notice of Adorno's scattered references to the relationship of Wagner's modernity to that of Baudelaire and Monet: "Like Baudelaire's, his reading of bourgeois high capitalism discerned an anti-bourgeois, heroic message in the destruction of *Biedermeier.*"[51] In the essay **"Wagner's Aktualität"** the discussion of the composer's handling of color unmistakably conjures up the art of Monet: "Wagner's achievement of a differentiation of color by dissolution into minute detail is supplemented by his technique of combining the most minute elements constructively in such a way that something like integral color emerges."[52] Yet Wagner only approaches that threshold which Baudelaire and Monet had already crossed: "No comparison of Wagner with the impressionists will be adequate unless it is remembered that the credo of universal symbolism to which all his technical achievements subscribe is that of Puvis de Chavannes and not Monet's."[53] Therefore Adorno calls Wagner an "impressionist *malgré lui*" and relates his backwardness to the backwardness of economic and aesthetic developments in mid-19th-century Germany. The key point that emerges from this comparison is the paradox that Wagner's anticipation of the culture industry is proportionate to his aesthetic backwardness in his own time. His music conjures up a distant future because it has not yet succeeded in shedding a past rendered obsolete by modern life. To put it differently, the modernity of allegory and dissonance in Wagner's work is consistently compromised by that "universal symbolism" which simulates a false totality and forges an equally false monumentality, that of the Gesamtkunstwerk.

Wagner's affinity to the culture industry is worked out most explicitly by Adorno in the chapters on phantasmagoria, Gesamtkunstwerk, and myth. Adorno's characteriza-

tion of Wagner's opera as phantasmagoria is an attempt to analyze what happens to aesthetic appearance (*ästhetischer Schein*) in the age of the commodity and as such it is the attempt to come to terms with the pressure commodity fetishism puts on works of art. As phantasmagorias Wagner's operas have veiled all traces of the labor that went into their production. Blocking out traces of production in the work of art is of course one of the major tenets of an earlier idealist aesthetic and as such nothing new in Wagner. But that is precisely the problem. As the commodity form begins to invade all aspects of modern life, all aesthetic appearance is in danger of being transformed into phantasmagoria, into the "illusion of the absolute reality of the unreal."[54] According to Adorno, Wagner yields to the pressures of the commodity form. With some minor changes the following passage taken from the chapter on phantasmagoria could easily be imagined as part of the mass culture chapter in *Dialectic of Enlightenment*: "It [the illusion of the absolute reality of the unreal] sums up the unromantic side of the phantasmagoria: phantasmagoria as the point at which aesthetic appearance becomes a function of the character of the commodity. As a commodity it purveys illusions. The absolute reality of the unreal is nothing but the reality of a phenomenon that not only strives unceasingly to spirit away its own origins in human labor, but also, inseparably from this process and in thrall to exchange value, assiduously emphasizes its use value, stressing that this is its authentic reality, that it is 'no imitation'—and all this in order to further the cause of exchange value. In Wagner's day the consumer goods on display turned their phenomenal side seductively towards the mass of consumers while diverting attention from their merely phenomenal character, from the fact that they were beyond reach. Similarly, in the phantasmagoria, Wagner's operas tend to become commodities. Their tableaux assume the character of wares on display (*Ausstellungscharakter*)."[55] At this point myth enters the stage as the embodiment of illusion and as regression to prehistory: "Phantasmagoria comes into being when, under the constraints of its own limitations, modernity's latest products come close to the archaic. Every step forward is at the same time a step into the remote past. As bourgeois society advances it finds that it needs its own camouflage of illusion simply in order to subsist."[56] As phantasmagoria Wagner's opera reproduces the dream world of the commodity in the form of myth: "He [Wagner] belongs to the first generation to realize that in a world that has been socialized through and through it is not possible for an individual to alter something that is determined over the heads of men. Nevertheless, it was not given to him to call the overarching totality by its real name. In consequence it is transformed for him into myth."[57] Myth becomes the problematic solution to Wagner's struggle against the genre music of the Biedermeier period, and his gods and heroes are to guarantee the success of his simultaneous flight from the banality of the commodity age. But as the present and the mythical merge in the Gesamtkunstwerk, Wagner's divine realm of ideas, gods, and heroes is nothing but a deluded transcription of the banal world of the present. In a number of scattered observations Adorno juxtaposes, in a quite Benjaminean way, moments of Wagner's oeuvre to the culture of everyday life in late 19th-century Germany. Thus the *Mastersingers* are said to conjure up—like the images on the box containing the famous *Nürnberger Lebkuchen*—the bliss of an unsullied, premodern German past, which later fed seamlessly into völkisch ideology. Elsa's relationship to Lohengrin ("My lord, never shall this question come from me") celebrates the subjugation of women in marriage. Wotan is interpreted as the phantasmagoria of the buried revolution, Siegfried as the "natural" rebel who accelerates rather than prevents the catastrophic destruction of civilization. The thunder motiv from the *Ring* becomes the signal sounded by the horn of the Emperor's motor car. Adorno gets to the historical core of Wagner's modern mythology when he writes: "It is impossible to overlook the relationship between Wagnerian mythology and the iconic world of the Empire, with its eclectic architecture, fake Gothic castles, and the aggressive dream symbols of the New-German boom, ranging from the Bavarian castles of Ludwig to the Berlin restaurant that called itself 'Rheingold.' But the question of authenticity is as fruitless here as elsewhere. Just as the overwhelming power of high capitalism forms myths that tower above the collective conscious, in the same way the mythic region in which the modern consciousness seeks refuge bears the marks of that capitalism: what subjectively was the dream of dreams is objectively a nightmare."[58] Thus the drama of the future, as Wagner called his Gesamtkunstwerk, prefigures that nightmarish regression into an archaic past which completes its trajectory in fascism. The Gesamtkunstwerk is intended as a powerful protest against the fragmentation and atomization of art and life in capitalist society. But since it chooses the wrong means it can only end in failure: "Like Nietzsche and subsequently Art Nouveau, which he [Wagner] anticipates in many respects, he would like, singlehanded, to will an aesthetic totality into being, casting a magic spell and with defiant unconcern about the absence of the social conditions necessary for its survival."[59] While the mythic dimension of Wagner's opera conjures up fascism, its homogenization of music, word, and image is said to anticipate the essential features of Hollywood film: "Thus we see that the evolution of the opera, and in particular the emergence of the autonomous sovereignty of the artist, is intertwined with the origins of the culture industry. Nietzsche, in his youthful enthusiasm, failed to recognize the art work of the future in which we witness the birth of film out of the spirit of music."[60] The totality of Wagner's music drama, however, is a false totality subject to disintegration from within: "Even in Wagner's lifetime, and in flagrant contradiction to his programme, star numbers like the Fire Music and Wotan's farewell, the Ride of the Valkyries, the Liebestod and the Good Friday music had been torn out of their context, re-arranged and become popular. This fact is not irrelevant to the music dramas, which had cleverly calculated the place of these passages within the economy of the whole. The disintegration of the fragments sheds light on the fragmentariness of the whole."[61] The logic of this disintegration leads to Schönberg's modernism on the one hand and to the Best of

Wagner album on the other. Where high art itself is sucked into the maelstrom of commodification, modernism is born as a reaction and a defense. The point is made bluntly in *Philosophy of Modern Music*: "The liberation of modern painting from representation (*Gegenständlichkeit*), which was to art the break that atonality was to music, was determined by the defensive against the mechanized art commodity—above all photography. Radical music, from its inception, reacted similarly to the commercial depravity of the traditional idiom. It formulated an antithesis against the extension of the culture industry into its own domain."[62] While this statement seems quite schematic, especially in its mechanical derivation of abstraction in painting, it serves to remind us again that modernism itself is held hostage by the culture industry and that theories of modernism neglecting this conjuncture are seriously deficient. Adorno's bleak description of modern mass culture as dream turned nightmare has perhaps outlived its usefulness and can now take its place as a historically contingent and theoretically powerful reflection on fascism. What has not outlived its usefulness, however, is Adorno's suggestion that mass culture was not imposed on art only from the "outside," but that art was transformed into its opposite thanks precisely to its emancipation from traditional forms of bourgeois art. In the vortex of commodification there was never an outside. Wagner is the case in point.

CODA

Reading Adorno in reverse, from *Dialectic of Enlightenment* backwards to the Wagner essay of 1937/38, from fascism and the capitalist culture industry back to Imperial Germany, leads to the conclusion that the framework for his theory of the culture industry was already in place *before* his encounter with American mass culture in the United States. In the Wagner book the pivotal categories of fetishism and reification, ego-weakness, regression, and myth are already fully developed, waiting, as it were, to be articulated in terms of the American culture industry. At the same time, reading Adorno's brilliant tour de force on Wagner—and a tour de force it is—produces a strange sense of déjà vu in which the temporal terms are once more displaced. It is as if accompanying Adorno on his travels into the 19th century we were simultaneously travelling into yet another time-space Adorno himself did not live to experience: that of the postmodern. Large segments of the book on Wagner could be read as a modernist polemic against postmodernism. It is indeed easy to imagine how Adorno would have panned those facile citations of the historical idiom in postmodern architecture and music, how he would have poured scorn over the decay of allegory into the "anything goes" of the art "scene," how he would have resisted the new mythology of aesthetic experience, the cult of performance, of self-help and of other forms of narcissistic indulgence. Adorno would not have hesitated one moment to see the disintegration of modernism as a return to its prehistory and to collapse the prehistory of the modern with its posthistory.

After all, the art work is still in the grip of the commodity form, more so, if anything, than in the 19th century. The giant spider web of exchange relations Adorno spoke of has certainly expanded since that time. The late 19th century still had resistant popular cultures and it left more uncolonized spaces for possible evasions and challenges than today's thoroughly administered culture. If such a reading is by and large correct we will have to ask what the chances are for a genuine contemporary art after the demise of classical modernism. One conclusion would be to see the only possibility for contemporary art in a further elaboration of the modernist project. Possibly, Adorno would have advocated this route even though he was perfectly aware of the dangers of alexandrian sterility, of a dogmatic ossification of modernism itself. Another conclusion, however, would be to try and relocate contemporary artistic production and practices in the interstices between modernism and mass culture. Commodification invaded Wagner's oeuvre without completely debilitating it. On the contrary, it actually gave rise to great works of art. But then one must be permitted to ask why it should not be possible today to produce ambitious and successful works of art which would draw both on the tradition of modernism and on mass culture, including various subcultures. Some of the most interesting art of our time seems to pursue precisely this project. Of course Adorno would argue that the conjuncture that produced Wagner's oeuvre is irretrievably past. True enough, but I am not suggesting simply to revive Wagner's art as a model for the present. Where something like that is being done, e.g., in the films of Syberberg, the results are often less than convincing. The point is rather to take heart from Adorno's account of Wagner's contradictions and dilemmas and to abandon that set of purist stances which would either lock all art in the laboratory of ever more involuted modernist experimentation or reject, uncompromisingly, any attempt to create a contemporary art precisely out of the tensions between modernism and mass culture. Who, after all, would want to be the Lukács of the postmodern. . . .

Notes

1. Jürgen Habermas, *Strukturwandel der Öffentlichkeit* (Neuwied/Berlin: Luchterhand, 1962). See also Habermas, "The Public Sphere," *New German Critique,* 3 (Fall, 1974), 49-55.

2. John Brenkman, "Mass Media: From Collective Experience to the Culture of Privatization," *Social Text,* 1 (Winter 1979), 101.

3. Ibid.

4. For a recent discussion of the interface between modernism and popular culture in Germany see Peter Jelavich, "Popular Dimensions of Modernist Elite Culture: The Case of Theatre in Fin-de-Siècle Munich," in Dominick LaCapra and Steven L. Kaplan, eds., *Modern European Intellectual History* (Ithaca and London: Cornell University Press, 1982), pp. 220-250.

5. Anthony Giddens, "Modernism and Postmodernism," *New German Critique,* 22 (Winter, 1981), 15. For a different approach to the problem of changes in per-

ception in the 19th century see Anson G. Rabinbach, "The Body without Fatigue: A 19th-Century Utopia," in Seymour Drescher, David Sabean and Allan Sharlin, eds., *Political Symbolism in Modern Europe* (New Brunswick, N.J.: Transaction Books, 1982), pp. 42-62.

6. Wolfgang Schivelbusch, *Geschichte der Eisenbahnreise. Zur Industrialisierung von Raum und Zeit im 19. Jahrhundert* (Munich and Vienna: Hanser, 1977). Translated into English as *The Railway Journey* (New York: Urizen, 1979).

7. At the same time it should be noted that the major accounts of modernism in literature and art rarely if ever try to discuss the relationship of the modernist work of art to the social and cultural process of modernization at large.

8. I do not know of any specific study which traces the pervasive impact of the culture industry thesis on mass culture research in Germany. For the impact of Adorno and Horkheimer in the United States see Douglas Kellner, "Kulturindustrie und Massenkommunikation. Die kritische Theorie und ihre Folgen," in *Sozialforschung als Kritik,* ed. by Wolfgang Bonss and Axel Honneth (Frankfurt am Main: Suhrkamp, 1982), pp. 482-515.

9. For an excellent discussion of the theoretical and historical issues involved in an analysis of the modernism/mass culture/popular culture nexus see Thomas Crow, "Modernism and Mass Culture in the Visual Arts," in S. Guilbaut and D. Solkin, eds., *Modernism and Modernity* (Halifax, Nova Scotia: The Press of the Nova Scotia College of Art and Design, 1983).

10. Horkheimer/Adorno, *Dialectic of Enlightenment,* trans. John Cumming (New York: Herder & Herder, 1972), p. 121.

11. On the notion of affirmative culture see Herbert Marcuse, "The Affirmative Character of Culture," in *Negations* (Boston: Beacon Press, 1968).

12. Adorno, "Culture Industry Reconsidered," *New German Critique,* 6 (Fall 1975), 13.

13. Adorno, *Dissonanzen,* in *Gesammelte Schriften,* vol. 14 (Frankfurt am Main: Suhrkamp, 1973), p. 20.

14. On the usage of ship and ocean metaphors in the history of department stores see Klaus Strohmeyer, *Warenhäuser. Geschichte, Blüte und Untergang im Warenmeer* (Berlin: Wagenbach, 1980). For a recent study of commodity culture in late 19th-century France see Rosalind H. Williams, *Dream Worlds: Mass Consumption in Late 19th-Century France* (Berkeley/Los Angeles/London: University of California Press, 1982).

15. Adorno, *Minima Moralia: Reflections from a Damaged Life,* trans. E. F. N. Jephcott (London: New Left Books, 1974), p. 229.

16. Ibid., p. 230.

17. Jessica Benjamin, "Authority and the Family Revisited: Or, World Without Fathers?," *New German Critique,* 13 (Winter 1978), 35-58.

18. Printed in Walter Benjamin, *Gesammelte Schriften,* I:3 (Frankfurt am Main: Suhrkamp, 1974), p. 1003.

19. Fred Jameson, "Reification and Utopia in Mass Culture," *Social Text,* 1 (Winter 1979), 135.

20. Ibid.

21. Miriam Hansen, "Introduction to Adorno's 'Transparencies on Film'," *New German Critique,* 24-25 (Fall/Winter 1981-82), 186-198.

22. Horkheimer/Adorno, "Das Schema der Massenkultur," in Adorno, *Gesammelte Schriften,* 3 (Frankfurt am Main: Suhrkamp, 1981), p. 331.

23. Ibid.

24. Jochen Schulte-Sasse, "Gebrauchswerte der Literatur," in Christa Bürger, Peter Bürger and Jochen Schulte-Sasse, eds., *Zur Dichotomisierung von hoher und niederer Literatur* (Frankfurt am Main: Suhrkamp, 1982), pp. 62-107.

25. Adorno, "Zu Subjekt und Objekt," in *Stichworte* (Frankfurt am Main: Suhrkamp, 1969), p. 165.

26. Ibid. On Adorno's relationship to early German romanticism see Jochen Hörisch, "Herrscherwort, Geld und geltende Sätze: Adornos Aktualisierung der Frühromantik und ihre Affinität zur poststrukturalistischen Kritik des Subjekts," in B. Lindner/W. M. Lüdke, *Materialien zur ästhetischen Theorie Th. W. Adornos* (Frankfurt am Main: Suhrkamp, 1980), pp. 397-414.

27. Adorno, "Sexualtabus und Rechte heute," in *Eingriffe* (Frankfurt am Main: Suhrkamp, 1963), p. 104 f.

28. Adorno, *Negative Dialectics,* trans. E. B. Ashton (London: Seabury Press, 1973), p. 221 f. (trans. modified).

29. See for instance Bertold Hinz, *Die Malerei im deutschen Faschismus* (Munich: Hanser, 1974).

30. Peter Bürger, *Theory of the Avant-Garde* (Minneapolis: University of Minnesota Press, 1984).

31. Adorno, *Philosophy of Modern Music* (New York: Seabury Press, 1973), p. 30.

32. Peter Bürger, *Vermittlung-Rezeption-Funktion* (Frankfurt am Main: Suhrkamp, 1979), p. 130 f. Eugene Lunn, in his valuable study *Marxism and Modernism* (Berkeley, Los Angeles and London: University of California, 1982), has emphasized Adorno's indebtedness to the "aesthetic of objectified expression" prevalent in Trakl, Heym, Barlach, Kafka and Schönberg.

33. Adorno, *Ästhetische Theorie* (Frankfurt am Main: Suhrkamp, 1970), p. 16.

34. Ibid., p. 38.

35. Ibid.—The problem here is a historical one, namely that of non-simultaneous developments in different countries and different art forms. Explaining such *Ungleichzeitigkeiten* is no easy task, but it certainly requires a theory of modernism able to relate artistic developments more cogently to social, political and economic context than Adorno's (theoretically grounded) *Berührungsangst* would permit him to do. This is not to say that Adorno misunderstood the genuine modernity of Baudelaire or Manet. On the contrary, it is precisely in the way in which Adorno distinguishes Wagner from the early French modernists that we can glimpse his recognition of such *Ungleichzeitigkeiten.* More on this later.

36. Adorno, *Noten zur Literatur,* I (Frankfurt am Main: Suhrkamp, 1958), p. 72.

37. Horkheimer/Adorno, *Dialectic of Enlightenment,* p. 163.

38. Adorno, *Ästhetische Theorie,* p. 352.

39. Ibid.

40. Ibid., p. 355.

41. Adorno, *Gesammelte Schriften,* 13 (Frankfurt am Main: Suhrkamp, 1971), p. 504. For a good discussion of Adorno's Schönberg interpretation see Lunn, *Marxism and Modernism,* pp. 256-266. The question of whether Adorno is right about Wagner from a musicological standpoint cannot be addressed here. For a musicological critique of Adorno's Wagner see Carl Dahlhaus, "Soziologische Dechiffrierung von Musik: Zu Theodor W. Adornos Wagner Kritik," *International Review of the Aesthetics and Sociology of Music,* 1:2 (1970), 137-146.

42. Adorno, *Gesammelte Schriften,* 16 (Frankfurt am Main: Suhrkamp, 1978), p. 562.

43. Adorno, *In Search of Wagner,* trans. Rodney Livingstone (London: New Left Books, 1981), p. 31 (transl. modified).

44. Ibid. Cf. also Michael Hays, "Theater and Mass Culture: The Case of the Director," *New German Critique,* 29 (Spring/Summer 1983), 133-146.

45. Ibid., p. 32.

46. Ibid., p. 46.

47. Ibid., p. 33.

48. Adorno, *Gesammelte Schriften,* 13, p. 499.

49. Adorno, *In Search of Wagner,* p. 49.

50. Ibid., p. 50.

51. Ibid., p. 101.

52. Adorno, "Wagners Aktualität," in *Gesammelte Schriften,* 16, p. 555.

53. Adorno, *In Search of Wagner,* p. 50.

54. Ibid., p. 90.

55. Ibid.

56. Ibid., p. 95.

57. Ibid., p. 119.

58. Ibid., p. 123.

59. Ibid., p. 101.

60. Ibid., p. 107.

61. Ibid., p. 106.

62. Adorno, *Philosophy of Modern Music,* p. 5 (transl. modified).

Martin Jay (essay date 1985)

SOURCE: "Adorno in America," in *Permanent Exiles: Essays on the Intellectual Migration from Germany to America,* Columbia University Press, 1985, pp. 120-37.

[*In the following essay, Jay analyzes the theoretical, sociological, and aesthetic work Adorno did while living and working in the United States.*]

The exemplary anecdotes are known to us all. Adorno arrives in America in 1938 to work on Paul Lazarsfeld's Princeton Radio Research Project. Lazarsfeld writes of his new acquaintance: "He looks as you would image a very absent-minded German professor, and he behaves so foreign that I feel like a member of the Mayflower society."[1] Adorno travels to the Project's offices in an abandoned brewery in Newark, New Jersey, through a tunnel under the Hudson River and admits "I felt a little as if I were in Kafka's Nature Theater of Oklahoma."[2] The attempt to adapt his ideas to the needs of the Project soon proves, not surprisingly, a failure, as Adorno's concept of fetishization resists all efforts to operationalize it. Lazarsfeld's hope to achieve what he later called "a convergence of European theory and American empiricism"[3] is quickly abandoned with no small amount of embarrassment and bitter feelings on both sides.

A decade later, the *Institute für Sozialforschung* is invited back to Frankfurt, and Adorno, with no hesitation, joins Max Horkheimer and Friedrich Pollock in its reconstruction. Having noted in *Minima Moralia* that "every intellectual in emigration is, without exception, mutilated," in particular because "his language has been expropriated, and the historical dimension that nourished his knowledge, sapped,"[4] he leaves his exile home for good in 1953 and never looks back. Twelve years later, he tells his German audience in a radio talk entitled "Auf die Frage: Was ist Deutsch?"[5] that both subjective and objective reasons de-

termined his return. The former include the slight to his self-esteem dealt him by an American publisher who criticized *Philosophie der neuen Musik* for being "badly organized."[6] The latter, which he claims are more substantial, center around his desire to write in his native tongue, whose "elective affinity" for philosophy, in particular its speculative and dialectical moment, he claims is superior to that of English.

When Adorno dies in 1969, *The New York Times* carries a short obituary, which soon gains modest notoriety for its remarkable garbling of Adorno's life and work.[7] Focusing for mysterious reasons on an obscure piece he once wrote on jitterbugging, it fails to record any of the important theoretical dimensions of his thought. At the time of his death, Adorno is known in America almost entirely as the first name on the title page of *The Authoritarian Personality,* a study whose uneasy mixture of empirical methods and Critical Theory was very atypical of his work as a whole. The only translation of his writings on cultural themes then available is *Prisms,* which a small British publisher had brought out in 1967 and failed to distribute in America. Not a single philosophical work is accessible to readers unable to take on the challenge of Adorno's formidable German.

The image of Adorno's relation to America conveyed by these anecdotes is not difficult to discern. The sensitive European mandarin is shocked and bewildered by the commercialism, vulgarity, and theoretical backwardness of his temporary home. Belittling the assimilationist tendencies of other emigrés as a form of craven accommodation to economic necessity, he hustles back to Germany as soon as the opportunity avails itself. America in return finds him arrogant, snobbish, and incomprehensible. His departure is little noted and even less mourned.

That this image is more than just impressionistically anecdotal is confirmed by a sample of the critical literature on Adorno's relation to America. The linguistic barrier, for example, is widely remarked even after translations are attempted. The musicologist and Stravinsky confidante Robert Craft speaks for many when he complains that "a more convoluted, abstruse, and floridly unintelligible style is scarcely conceivable. It can have been designed for one purpose only, that of maintaining the highest standards of obfuscation throughout."[8] No less disconcerting to many is Adorno's merciless critique of mass culture, which offends the populist pieties of progressive American thought. Edward Shils, Leon Bramson, and Herbert Gans lead a phalanx of critics who point to the apparent paradox of a self-proclaimed leftist so contemptuous of democratic tastes and values.[9] Adorno is called a covert Puritan and ascetic for his hostility to the simple pleasures of the common man.[10] Behind the facade of a modernist, one critic spies "a yearning for European liberal-bourgeois society and the life-style of its cultured upper-middle-class members."[11] According to another, Adorno's debts to figures like Spengler and Nietzsche make it "far more useful and evocative to regard" him and his colleagues in the Frankfurt School "as men of the Right than of the Left."[12] To still a third, Adorno can "be described, not *altogether* unfairly, as a materialist *dandy* . . . a stranded spiritual aristocrat doomed to extinction by the 'rising tide of democracy.'"[13]

These examples are all taken from American responses to Adorno, but the image they convey has not been confined to our shores. In 1976, a very hostile essay entitled "'Beute der Pragmatisierung': Adorno und Amerika" was published in a collection on *Die USA und Deutschland* edited by Wolfgang Paulsen.[14] Its author, Dagmar Barnouw, compared Adorno with the French aristocrats who emigrated during the French Revolution. Criticizing his "autocratic snobbism" and paranoiac *ressentiment,* she concluded that works like **Dialectic of Enlightenment** were little more than "poetic performances in total reaction against a social reality"[15] that Adorno neither understood nor appreciated.

The grain of truth in these contentions, however exaggerated and one-sided they may be, must be acknowledged. The Adorno who could complain that "it is made unmistakably clear to the intellectual from abroad that he will have to eradicate himself as an autonomous being if he hopes to achieve anything"[16] was clearly not an eager convert to the "American way of life." There can be no question that the linguistic uprootedness that Adorno felt with a keenness more typical of literary than scholarly emigrés[17] was a genuine trauma, as his frequent quarrels with Siegfried Kracauer over the use of English abundantly demonstrate.[18] Nor is it disputable, as Adorno's notoriously unsympathetic treatment of jazz illustrates, that he tended to flatten out the dynamic contradictions of the popular culture he knew only from afar. It is equally clear that many of the analyses he made of his emigré home were colored by the aftereffects of his forced departure from Europe. As one commentator has recently noted, the major works he completed in exile all "contained many passages which assimilated American society to that of Nazi Germany"[19] with an insensitivity obvious in hindsight. And it would be no less difficult to detail the ways in which the American reception of Adorno mirrors this image of hostility and incomprehension.

But it would nonetheless be a travesty of the truth to remain content with so one-dimensional an account of the impact of America on Adorno and the impact of Adorno on us. To make better sense of this dual relationship, it would be useful to borrow the celebrated image of a constellation which Adorno himself borrowed from Benjamin. It is, in fact, helpful to conceptualize Adorno's general place in the intellectual life of the twentieth century by understanding the multiple impulses contained in his work as forming a figure of juxtaposed elements irreducible to any one dominant star. For rather than turning Adorno into essentially an elitist mandarin merely pretending to be a Marxist or an aesthetic modernist with only residual nostalgia for the world he left behind, it is better to acknowledge the countervailing energies of each of these forces in his field. If we add to them several others, most notably his ambiguous identification with the Jews, which appears in his dark ruminations on the meaning of the Holocaust, and what might be called his proto-deconstructionist impulse, to which I will return later, a more fully nuanced understanding of the irreconcilable tensions in Adorno's formation can be grasped. Rather than reduce Adorno to any one star in his constellation, be it Western Marxist, elitist mandarin, aesthetic modernist, or whatever, we must credit all of them with the often contradictory power they had in shaping his idiosyncratic variant of Critical Theory. For what made Adorno so remarkable a figure was the fact that the negative dialectics he so steadfastly defended, with its valorization of nonidentity and heterogeneity, was concretely exemplified in his own intellectual composition, which never produced any harmoniously totalized world view.

The same approach, I want to argue, will allow us to make sense as well of his uneasy relationship to America, which was far more complicated than the conventional image expressed in the anecdotes and scholarship mentioned a few moments ago. For although there can be little doubt that the European star in Adorno's constellation shone brighter than the American, the gravitational pull of the latter was by no means negligible. If the aphorisms of **Minima Moralia** were reflections on an emigré's damaged life, it is, after all, important to recognize that the original source of the damage was not the culture industry in America, but rather the crisis of European culture and society that forced him into exile in the first place. Although it would be foolish to claim that the damage was somehow healed during his stay, it is also not entirely correct to see his experience as merely deepening his pessimism about the universality and irreversibility of the crisis. For when Adorno returned to Frankfurt, he was a changed man. "It is scarcely an exaggeration to say," Adorno would ultimately acknowledge, "that any contemporary consciousness that has not appropriated the American experience, even if in opposition, has something reactionary about it."[20] Although Adorno's appropriation was largely in opposition, it nonetheless did include two positive elements.

First, the doubts he had already entertained about the redemptive power of high culture, doubts instilled in him in part by his Marxist and aesthetic modernist inclinations, were immeasurably strengthened by his contact with a society in which no such faith could be found. "In America," he later wrote, "I was liberated from a certain naive belief in culture and attained the capacity to see culture from the outside. To clarify the point: in spite of all social criticism and all consciousness of the primacy of economic factors, the fundamental importance of the mind—'Geist'—was quasi a dogma self-evident to me from the very beginning. The fact that this was not a foregone conclusion, I learned in America."[21] Adorno put this knowledge to good use in the essay he wrote in 1949 entitled **"Cultural Criticism and Society,"** which was first published two years later in a *Festschrift* for Leopold von Wiese and then served as the opening essay of **Prisms.**[22] His American-induced critique of the fetishism of high culture, which expanded on the earlier analysis of "affirmative culture"[23] made by Horkheimer and Marcuse in the years shortly after their own arrivals in New York, might, in fact, be seen as evidence of the radicalizing effect of Adorno's emigration. One commentator has gone so far as to claim that this change shows that "in certain ways Adorno now moved closer toward a Marxian analytical framework."[24]

In more directly political terms, however, the emigration seems to have had the opposite effect. For the second lesson Adorno appropriated from his years in the United States was derived from what he called his "more fundamental, and more gratifying . . . experience of the substance of democratic forms: that in America they have penetrated the whole of life, whereas in Germany at least they were never more than formal rules of the game."[25] Here Adorno seems to exemplify the deradicalization familiar in the histories of many leftist intellectuals who came to America, much to the chagrin of some later observers like Joachim Radkau.[26] But interpreted more generously, these remarks can be seen as indicating a cautiously realistic optimism about the value of trying to contribute "something toward political enlightenment"[27] in his native land, as he was to put it many years hence. For by his actions after his return, it is clear that Adorno, like the other members of the repatriated *Institut* staff, had hopes that the substance of democratic forms might also be introduced to a Germany which had never known them in the past. Rather than bemoaning the penetration of American commercialism and vulgarity, which to be sure he did in other contexts, Adorno came back to Europe with the belief that something of genuine political value might be brought with him across the Atlantic.

It was in this spirit that Adorno, obviously fighting his earlier inclinations, cautiously defended the usefulness of public opinion research in Germany in the 1951 conference on empirical social research in Frankfurt.[28] Pointing to the disparagement of such techniques during the era that had just ended, he noted that the Nazis had understood all too well the democratic potential of a method that treats every voice as having equal weight. With belated recognition of the original aim of Lazarsfeld's Radio Research Project, he contended that the unmediated opposition posited by some between "administrative" and "critical" social research was a fallacious oversimplification. His positive experience working on *The Authoritarian Personality* project clearly left its mark on Adorno, as it did other members of the *Institut.*[29] Although in later years he would reconsider some of his enthusiasm for empirical techniques, because of their threat to replace Critical Theory entirely, he never lost his respect for their potential as tools of enlightenment.

In a country where most of the basic "facts" of social and political life had been systematically distorted for a dozen years, it is not difficult to see why Adorno would have modified his earlier hostility to empiricism or even have begun talking positively about the possibility of enlightenment. It was, of course, with the hope of reeducating his countrymen about those facts that Adorno would later contribute to the debate about Germany's "unmastered past" in such essays as **"Was bedeutet: Aufarbeitung der Vergangenheit"** in 1959 and **"Erziehung nach Auschwitz"** in 1966.[30] That Adorno could speak positively about pedagogy rather than revolution shows how deeply impressed by his American experience he was. So too does his emphasis on the importance of psychoanalysis in the process of reeducation, for it was one of the cardinal lessons of *The Authoritarian Personality* that the traditional progressive faith in reason alone was inadequate. As the concluding sentences of the study assert, "we need not suppose that appeal to emotion belongs to those who strive in the direction of fascism, while democratic propaganda must limit itself to reason and restraint. If fear and destructiveness are the major emotional sources of fascism, *eros* belongs mainly to democracy."[31] It was in the hope of harnessing the insights of psychoanalysis for emancipatory purposes that Adorno and his *Institut* colleagues organized the influential conference on "Freud in die Gegenwart" in Frankfurt in 1956[32] and were supportive of the work of Alexander Mitscherlich and the Sigmund Freud Institute.

In his essay on **"Aufarbeitung der Vergangenheit,"** Adorno explicitly tied the absence of a lively psychoanalytic culture in Germany to the effects of anti-semitism, whose central importance seems only to have become gradually apparent to Adorno and his colleagues during their American exile. When they returned to Germany, the glib Marxist formulas that had characterized their work at least as late as Horkheimer's "Die Juden und Europe" of 1939 were now things of the past.[33] In the "Elements of Anti-Semitism" section of *Dialectic of Enlightenment* in particular, Adorno had come to understand the intimate relationship between hatred of the Jews and the extirpation of non-identity that was the dominant bugbear of his negative dialectics. It was not merely the supposed guilt of the survivor that made him sensitive to the implications of Auschwitz for Western culture, but also the experience he had in America of a nonreductive reaction to anti-Semitism that avoided the trivializations of the European left.

In summary, although it might be said that while in America Adorno tended to interpret his new surroundings through the lens of his earlier experience, once back home he saw Germany with the eyes of someone who had been deeply affected by his years in exile. Negatively, this meant an increased watchfulness for the signs of an American-style culture industry in Europe.[34] Positively, it meant a wariness of elitist defenses of high culture for its own sake, a new respect for the value of democratic politics, a grudging recognition of the emancipatory potential in certain empirical techniques, and a keen appreciation of the need for a psychological dimension in pedagogy. To put it in capsule form, only an Adorno who had spent time in the United States could have written a sentence like the following from his *Introduction to the Sociology of Music*: "In general, outrage at the alleged mass era has become an article for mass consumption, fit for inciting the masses against politically democratic forms" (p. 132).

If it is misleading, then, to discount the effects of Adorno's American experience as a subtle counterweight to his European origins and thus miss the dynamic tensions in his intellectual force-field, it would be no less so to characterize the American response to his work as entirely uncomprehending and hostile. For here too the relation between Adorno and America is far more complex and ambivalent than the anecdotal impressions mentioned earlier would suggest. As early as 1954 and C. Wright Mills' acknowledgment in *The Saturday Review* that the return of Horkheimer and Adorno to Germany was "to the great loss of American social studies,"[35] a positive awareness of his work has been evident among growing circles of American intellectuals. Benefiting from the popularity of their former colleague Herbert Marcuse in the 1960s, the Frankfurt School as a whole gained widespread attention in the United States only a few years after its explosive rise to prominence in West Germany. Critical Theory seemed the most appropriate form of heterodox Marxism for a society without a large-scale militant working-class movement and with a growing counterculture distrustful of technological rationality. Unlike in Britain, where Althusser's brand of scientist scholasticism and political orthodoxy attracted extensive admiration, in America, the New Left found Marcuse's version of the Frankfurt School's ideas especially congenial. Some of its members, like Donald Kuspit,[36] Samuel and Shierry Weber, Jeremy Shapiro, and Angela Davis, were stimulated enough to go to the source and study in Frankfurt.

Adorno, of course, was initially far less well known back in America and was thus spared the type of controversy over the practical implications of his ideas that swirled around him in Germany shortly before his death. Although I can recall a heated conversation in 1968 with the leader of the Columbia University SDS and later member of the Weatherman underground, Mark Rudd, who dismissed Adorno as a betrayer of the revolution, this attitude rarely surfaced in the American New Left's reception of his work, such as it was. Far more typical was the joint dedication of a book edited by Paul Breines called *Critical Interruptions: New Left Perspectives on Herbert Marcuse,* published in 1970,[37] which, with no apparent irony, was addressed to Adorno and another recently deceased hero of the movement, Ho Chi Minh. Although by the mid-1970s, some of the same complaints against Adorno's politics that had appeared in Germany were repeated in America, it was in the less volatile context of the postpolitical academization of Marxism.[38]

If the moment when Adorno's work became more than merely an enticing rumor for the American New Left could be dated, it would probably be 1967 with the publication of an essay entitled "Adorno: or, Historical Tropes" by the Marxist literary critic Fredric Jameson in the journal *Salmagundi.*[39] Four years later, it served as the opening chapter in his widely influential *Marxism and Form,* which presented the first substantive survey of Western Marxism to an English-speaking audience. Although concluding that **Negative Dialectics** was "in the long run a massive fail-

ure," Jameson nonetheless praised Adorno's concrete studies as "incomparable models of the dialectical process, essays at once both systematic and occasional, in which pretext and consciousness meet to form the most luminous, if transitory, of figures or tropes of historical intelligibility."[40] In the same year as Jameson's essay first appeared, George Steiner's highly lauded collection *Language and Silence* introduced Adorno's lament about the impossibility of writing poetry after Auschwitz to American readers.[41] Scattered remarks throughout the rest of the book indicated that Steiner saw Adorno and other continental Marxists like Benjamin and Lukács as major cultural critics, whose absence from the Anglo-American scene was a scandalous indication of its sterility. No less powerful an endorsement came from the other leading guide to recent European theory of those years, George Lichtheim, whose interest lay more in political and philosophical matters than aesthetic or cultural ones. Although many of his best pieces appeared in British journals like the *Times Literary Supplement,* in 1968 Northwestern University's *Triquarterly* published his sympathetic overview of Western Marxism entitled "From Marx to Hegel," which treated Adorno as the "spiritual antipode"[42] to Lukács in that tradition. Three years later, Lichtheim republished the piece in a collection with the same name that included an admiring essay solely on Adorno, which had first appeared anonymously in the *TLS* in 1967, as well as several other essays on Critical Theory. Although somewhat journalistic in tone, Lichtheim's sympathetic appreciations of the Frankfurt School, with whose general position he explicitly identified,[43] played a constructive role in the early years of Adorno's American reception.

Although Adorno's death in 1969 was, as we have seen, an event of little importance in the popular media, it was followed by a more serious appraisal of his significance in academic circles. In December 1969, the Jewish review *Midstream* published my essay on "The Permanent Exile of Theodor W. Adorno,"[44] which tried to provide a broad overview of his career, including its last, unhappy episodes. In the following year, the newly founded radical philosophy journal *Telos* brought out the first of its many considerations of Adorno's work, Russell Jacoby's ecstatically favorable review of *Aufsätze zur Gesellschaftstheorie.*[45] Jacoby, whose admiration for Adorno went so far that he emulated many of his stylistic mannerisms, soon became his major American defender against all attacks from the right or left. Intransigently insisting that negative dialectics was completely compatible with Marxism at its most radical, he quickly became notorious for his sharply worded critiques of all attempts to make sense of the Frankfurt School's work in less glowing terms.[46]

Telos was also the journal where other very positive assessments of Adorno's work by Dick Howard and Susan Buck-Morss first appeared.[47] Although far from the center of American intellectual life during these years—in its Spring 1970 issue it proudly described itself as "a philosophical journal *definitely outside* the mainstream of American philosophical thought"[48]—it soon established itself as the major interpreter of Western Marxist ideas for the English-speaking world. Its only rival was the *New Left Review* in England, which was much more favorably inclined towards Althusserian and other allegedly scientific Marxisms than towards Critical Theory.[49] Other journals like *Social Research, New German Critique, Theory and Society,* and *Cultural Hermeneutics* also opened their pages to articles about Adorno and his colleagues, but none was as tenacious as *Telos* in promoting his work in America, not only through articles about him, but also by translating many of his more important essays.

The difficult task of rendering Adorno's longer works into English began in earnest in the early 1970s: *Dialectic of Enlightenment* and *Aspects of Sociology* in 1972, *Philosophy of Modern Music, Negative Dialectics,* and *Jargon of Authenticity* in 1973, *Minima Moralia* in 1974, *Introduction to the Sociology of Music* and *The Positivist Dispute in German Sociology* in 1976, *In Search of Wagner* in 1981, and *Against Epistemology* and the republication of *Prisms* in 1982. Further translations of the *Notes on Literature* and the *Aesthetic Theory* have been announced. Although of very mixed quality—Edmund Jephcott's rendition of *Minima Moralia* is often said to be the most successful, while several others vie for the honor of being the least—the English translations of Adorno's major works in the past decade did make it possible for a much wider audience to confront his work. Against the backdrop of several accounts of the Frankfurt School as a whole, which began with my *The Dialectical Imagination* in 1973 and continued with the surveys and collections of Slater, Tar, O'Neill, Held, Friedman, Connerton, and Arato and Gebhardt,[50] they provided the basis for an increasingly sophisticated American reception of his work, which is by no means at its end.

One of the clearest indications of that sophistication is the progressive refinement of the American perception of Adorno's unique place in the Western Marxist tradition, which is now no longer understood in the simplified terms of a return "from Marx to Hegel." In 1977, Susan Buck-Morss published her penetrating study of *The Origin of Negative Dialectics,*[51] which used previously untapped primary sources to demonstrate Adorno's indebtedness to Benjamin and subtle differences with Horkheimer. Moving beyond my emphasis on the relative coherence of a unified Frankfurt School in *The Dialectical Imagination,* she persuasively showed the ways in which Adorno was always an idiosyncratic member of the *Institut*'s inner circle. Other scholars have scrutinized the complexities of Adorno's relationships with his friends Siegfried Kracauer and Leo Lowenthal, as well as exploring the implications of Lichtheim's remark that he was the "spiritual antipode" of Lukács within Western Marxism.[52] More recently still, the full ramifications of his complicated interaction with Benjamin have been reexamined, most probingly in excellent new books by Richard Wolin and Eugene Lunn.[53] Lunn, in fact, has succeeded in modifying still further Buck-Morss's modification of my argument about the collective coherence of the Frankfurt School by demonstrating the differ-

ences between Adorno and Benjamin even in the 1920s, before their celebrated dispute over mass culture, technology, and political engagement. Stressing Adorno's roots in an Expressionism that was moving beyond its subjective phase toward the objectification of its anguish, he contrasted Adorno's version of aesthetic modernism with Benjamin's, which was more deeply indebted to Surrealism and Symbolism with their relative indifference to the fate of subjectivity.

Adorno's differences with Habermas, most extensively spelled out in an article by Axel Honneth translated in *Telos* in 1979,[54] have also attracted widespread comment in recent years. Those like the ecologically minded anarchist Murray Bookchin use Adorno's analysis of the domination of nature against Habermas, whom they accuse of complicity with the instrumental rationality the older Frankfurt School found so oppressive.[55] Others like Joel Whitebook invoke the ambiguities of the dialectic of enlightenment against what they see as Habermas' "compulsively modernistic"[56] project. Still others, like the English sociologist Gillian Rose, the author of a major study of Adorno entitled *The Melancholy Science,* chastise Habermas for violating Adorno's injunction against identity theory through his positing of an ideal speech situation.[57] Those, on the other hand, who find Habermas' position more politically promising, often contrast his stress on intersubjectivity with Adorno's retreat into the wreckage of the bourgeois subject.[58] Admiring Habermas' attempt to break the logjam of classical Critical Theory and develop new ways of conceptualizing the still unresolved contradictions of contemporary society, they also applaud his search for a more viable normative ground than the immanent critique whose power Adorno himself often came to question.

Although these debates cannot be pursued in greater detail now, I hope the general point has been made. The American reception of Adorno's work has been immeasurably improved by the increasing precision of our understanding of his place in the general context of Western Marxism. Not only are we increasingly aware of the differences as well as similarities between Adorno and the other members of the Frankfurt School, we are also far more sensitive than we were to the unexpected convergences between his position and that of other Western Marxists in the anti-Hegelian camp, like Althusser and Colletti.[59] Although there are still some defenders of the absolute distinction between critical and scientific Marxisms,[60] the second thoughts many American leftists have had about the virtues of neo-Hegelianism have led them to seek new ways to conceptualize the legacy of Western Marxism and Adorno's place in it.

If we turn now to the ways that specific dimensions of Adorno's work have been treated in America, the implications of this shift will become apparent. As might be expected, certain aspects of Adorno's work have been more readily accepted than others. In large measure because of the absence of translations, his writings on literature and aesthetics have been less widely discussed than his cultural criticism and philosophy. Aside from still unpublished dissertations by Michael Jones on the literary essays and Lambert Zuidervaart on the *Aesthetic Theory,*[61] there have been no full-length treatments of these themes. Although scholars who teach European literatures, like Jameson, Russell Berman, and Peter Uwe Hohendahl,[62] have incorporated and debated Adorno's ideas, those who concentrate on English and American literature have not. As Frank Lentricchia concedes in his magisterial survey, *After the New Criticism,* Adorno and other Western Marxist aestheticians "have a great deal to say to American critics, but . . . they have not been shaping influences."[63]

Adorno's musical writings, which are somewhat more readily available in English, have fared marginally better. But scattered essays by Ronald Weitzmann (who is English), Donald Kuspit, Wesley Blomster, Rose Rosengard Subotnik, and James L. Marsh cannot really compare with the very extensive reception of Adorno's musicological works in Germany.[64] In Charles Rosen's widely admired book on Schoenberg, for example, there is no mention of Adorno, nor is he widely cited in the American literature on Wagner.[65] And if Adorno has had little impact on musicological circles, it is even less likely, although I cannot be absolutely certain, that he has influenced actual American composers, as Carl Dalhaus claims was the case in Germany during the 1950s and 1960s.[66] Perhaps Robert Craft's remark in his critical review of the translation of *Philosophy of Modern Music* suggests the reason: it "comes twenty-five years too late to exert any active influence. Not that Adorno's interpretation has been proved or disproved. It simply has been passed by, relegated to academe when the music finally escaped the custody of theoretical critiques and entered the live performing repertory."[67]

Adorno's thoughts on culture in general, however, have been far more influential in the still lively debate over the implications of mass culture. The model of the "culture industry" was, after all, first developed with America in mind and several of Adorno's former colleagues who remained in the United States, especially Lowenthal and Marcuse, were notable contributors to the discussion which followed. In the 1950s, many respected American intellectuals, including Dwight MacDonald and David Riesman, drew on Adorno's work, even if indirectly. By the 1960s and 1970s, many younger commentators, such as Diane Waldman, Andreas Huyssen, Stanley Aronowitz, Douglas Kellner, Philip Rosen, Miriam Hansen, Mattel Calinescu, John Brenkman, and Thomas Andrae, found Adorno a source of even greater inspiration.[68] Interestingly, one of the keenest areas of interest has been Adorno's scattered remarks on film, which have attracted attention in part because of the increased American awareness of the new German cinema. The impact of Adorno's criticisms of traditional Hollywood films on directors like Alexander Kluge has not gone unnoticed by American critics. The translations of Adorno's essays **"Culture Industry Reconsidered"** and **"Transparencies on Film"**[69] have also led to an appreciation of the ways in which he came to nuance

the remittingly bleak prognosis of the original analysis in *Dialectic of Enlightenment* His reconsiderations in this area have allowed his critique of film to be taken more sympathetically than his less forgiving attack on jazz, which is probably the least successful aspect of his work in America.

Adorno's powerful critique of mass culture has been especially influential because of its roots in his social psychology. Although the dust raised by the controversy over *The Authoritarian Personality* settled long ago in the 1950s, other aspects of Adorno's appropriation of Freud have continued to attract attention. In works like Bruce Brown's *Marx, Freud, and the Critique of Everyday Life* and Russell Jacoby's *Social Amnesia,*[70] Adorno's defense of the radical potential of Freud's early work and his critique of the premature harmony of sociology and psychology, a critique elaborated by Marcuse in his attack on Fromm in *Eros and Civilization,* have been endorsed with enthusiasm. In the even more influential studies of Christopher Lasch, *Haven in a Heartless World* and *The Culture of Narcissism,*[71] many of the Frankfurt School's arguments about the decline of the family and its invasion by the professional bureaucracies of the administered world have been given still greater currency. Joel Kovel's probing dissections of contemporary analytic practice, *A Complete Guide to Therapy* and *The Age of Desire: Reflections of a Radical Psychoanalyst,*[72] are also indebted to Critical Theory's earlier considerations of this issue. Thus, although the general Frankfurt School use of Freud has not been spared criticism from a variety of perspectives,[73] it has nonetheless been and continues to be an enormous stimulus to the American attempt to harness Freudianism for emancipatory ends.

If, however, we really want to understand the implications of the shift I mentioned a few moments ago in the perception of Adorno's place in the Western Marxist tradition, it is to the reception of his philosophy that we must turn. For it is here that the most movement has occurred in the past ten years in the American understanding of Adorno's work. In fact, just as Adorno's differences from more mainstream Western Marxists like Lukács were becoming increasingly appreciated, so too were his similarities with non-Marxist continental philosophers. Adorno's complicated relationship with phenomenology, for example, has been the source of considerable interest, in part because of the translations of his critiques of Heidegger and Husserl and in part because of a prior awareness of Marcuse's debt to these same thinkers. In the early 1970s, *Telos,* in particular its editor Paul Piccone, was hopeful of finding a common ground between Critical Theory and phenomenology. Bemoaning the overt hostility of Adorno toward Husserl and Heidegger, Piccone and the Italians he translated in *Telos* like Pier Aldo Rovatti,[74] refused to take their apparent incompatability as the final word on this issue. To reach the opposite conclusion, their strategy was to emphasize the importance of Husserl's late work, in particular *The Crisis of European Sciences,* which appeared after the Frankfurt School's position against Husserl had hardened. Finding common ground in their critical attitudes towards technology and hoping to integrate the phenomenological investigation of the *Lebenswelt* with negative dialectics, Piccone and his allies contended that the results would offer a better basis for a more genuinely materialist Marxism than that provided by Lukács' neo-Hegelianism. By the end of the decade, however, Piccone's faith in Marxism of any kind had waned so far that any thoughts of a creative synthesis had vanished, although he continued to rely on the traditional Critical Theory idea of an administered world in his notion of "artificial negativity."[75]

At about the same time, a parallel effort was being made by Fred Dallmayr to find fruitful links between Adorno and Heidegger. Once again the strategy was to claim that Adorno's hostility was directed more against his target's early than late works. In an essay he published in 1976 and a book entitled *Twilight of Subjectivity: Contributions to a Post-Individualist Theory of Politics* that appeared five years later,[76] Dallmayr argued that despite the outward signs of animosity, a close kinship existed between the two thinkers:

> Adorno's strictures against individualism and the philosophy of consciousness correspond closely to Heidegger's critique of "subjectivism" and of the tradition of Western "metaphysics" with its accent on subjective reflection. Likewise, Adorno's comments on the ambivalence of Enlightenment thought and modern rationalism find a parallel in the existentialist posture toward logical calculation and the conception of man as "rational animal"; in particular, the argument that the growing sway of "instrumental" rationality reflects ultimately man's "will to power"—the desire to subjugate and control nature—is reminiscent of Heidegger's treatment of modern technology as an anthropocentric stratagem. A further affinity . . . can be found in the common stress of the two thinkers on historical exegesis and on the importance of "pre-understanding" or tradition in human cognition.[77]

Thus, like Hermann Mörchen,[78] Dallmayr called into question Adorno's own self-understanding in order to find convergences where previously only antagonism had been recognized. What made Dallmayr's rapprochement plausible was his emphasis on Heidegger's late works with their critique of identity and defense of difference. Insisting as well on the parallels between both of their positions and Merleau-Ponty's philosophy of ambiguity, Dallmayr sought to forge a postsubjectivist and posthumanist philosophy that would avoid the domination of nature and "egological" individualism present in so many traditional Western philosophies.

To establish his point, Dallmayr also drew on the work of a fourth figure, whose surprising resemblance to Adorno has received increasing notice in America, Jacques Derrida. Indeed, as I mentioned earlier, it is arguable that one of the stars in Adorno's intellectual constellation can be identified with the poststructuralism of Heidegger's heterodox French disciples. This is not to say, however, that Adorno should be construed as a deconstructionist *avant*

la lettre or that we can ignore the very important differences between his position, with its still Hegelian and Marxist dimensions, and theirs. Indeed, as one of the poststructuralists, Jean-François Lyotard, has recognized,[79] a very nondeconstructionist nostalgia for a lost totality still permeates even a negative dialectics. And yet, it makes even less sense to build impermeable walls between two of the most significant theoretical movements of our time.

The most compelling historical reason for the similarity is, of course, the common respect for Nietzsche found in both Adorno and the poststructuralists. Virtually all of the literature on Adorno in English recognizes his remarkable debt to a philosopher for whom most other Marxists, Western or otherwise, had only contempt.[80] It is partly for this reason that writers like the English critic Terry Eagleton have contended that

> the parallels between deconstruction and Adorno are particularly striking. Long before the current fashion, Adorno was insisting on the power of those heterogeneous fragments that slip through the conceptual net, rejecting all philosophy of identity, refusing class consciousness as objectionably "positive," and denying the intentionality of signification. Indeed there is hardly a theme in contemporary deconstruction that is not richly elaborated in his work—a pointer, perhaps, to the mutual insularity of French and German culture, which now, ironically, converge more and more only in the Anglo-Saxon world.[81]

An even more extensive attempt to defend the comparison has been made by Michael Ryan in his 1982 *Marxism and Deconstruction*.[82] Although acknowledging that Adorno's emphasis is on society and Derrida's on language, he nonetheless argues that both share a hatred of logocentric hierarchies, both attack "the idealist privilege of identity over nonidentity, universality over particularity, subject over object, spontaneous presence over secondary rhetoric, timeless transcendence over empirical history, content over mode of expression, self-reassuring proximity over threatening alterity, ontology over the ontic, and so on."[83] In fact, in his zeal to assimilate Adorno and Derrida, Ryan goes so far as to make them common enemies of the domination of reason, without acknowledging that Adorno's more discriminating wrath was directed against only certain forms of rationality rather than rationality *tout court*.

If the parallels between Adorno and Derrida have been noted in America, so too have those between Adorno and Foucault.[84] In particular, the striking similarity between the arguments of *Dialectic of Enlightenment* and *Discipline and Punish* about the pervasiveness of disciplinary power in our administered world has been remarked.[85] Although it would be misleading to ignore their different evaluations of psychoanalysis, both Adorno and Foucault share a common skepticism about the sexual utopianism of certain Freudo-Marxists, including Marcuse. And both are at one in their sensitivity to what in *Dialectic of Enlightenment* he and Horkheimer called the "underground history"[86] of the European body, which Foucault's investigations of "bio-power" have helped bring to the surface. One final parallel might be mentioned, which concerns Adorno's regretful insistence in "The Actuality of Philosophy" that it was no longer possible for thought "to grasp the totality of the real" and Foucault's contention in *Power/Knowledge* that "the role for theory today seems to me to be just this: not to formulate global systematic theory which holds everything in place, but to analyze the specificity of mechanisms of power, to locate the connections and extensions, to build little by little a strategic knowledge."[87] In both cases, a micrological analysis takes the place of the grand syntheses that were so much a trademark of Hegelian Marxism at its most ambitious. Or more precisely, for both Adorno and Foucault, totality is retained only as a term of opprobrium to indicate the pervasive domination of power relations that can only be challenged on the local and particular level.

One way, to be sure, in which Adorno and the poststructuralists part company is in their differing attitudes towards aesthetic modernism. Whereas Adorno seems to have had little faith in an art that would follow the classical modernism of Schoenberg and Beckett, many poststructuralists such as Lyotard eagerly defend the postmodernism that apparently has. Interestingly, leftist American students of Critical Theory who have struggled with the elitism inherent in Adorno's position have found this alternative a promising one. Thus, for example, the same Fredric Jameson who did so much to introduce Adorno to American audiences now complains that his later work in particular fails to register the inevitable historicity of modernism.[88] Rather than eternally contrasting avant-garde modernism and the culture industry, postmodernism, so Jameson suggests, calls into question the very dichotomy. Against Adorno, Jameson now argues for "some sense of the ineradicable drive towards collectivity that can be detected, no matter how faintly and feebly, in the most degraded works of mass culture just as surely as in the classics of modernism."[89]

Whether or not postmodernism can be harnessed for radical purposes is, of course, not yet clear, as Habermas has frequently warned.[90] It may therefore be healthy to contrast Adorno in some respects with those recent philosophical currents that support it, rather than assimilate him too quickly to them. Moreover, as Habermas has also recently cautioned,[91] there are important distinctions that ought not to be forgotten in their different appropriations of the Nietzschean critique of the Enlightenment, which prevented Adorno, contrary to the hasty reading of Ryan, from attacking all forms of rationality as oppressive.

And yet, despite the dangers of turning Adorno into a deconstructionist with a German accent, it would be equally misguided to ignore the undeniable parallels that allow us with hindsight to see the implication of Adorno's thought as more complicated than would have been foreseen during his own lifetime. And if Eagleton is correct in claiming that this recognition has happened primarily in the Anglo-Saxon world because of the "mutual insularity of French and German culture," then we must take seriously the impact of his American reception. For if Adorno had to leave home to learn the lessons about democratic politics and the fetishization of high culture described earlier, the emigration of his thought may also have been necessary to bring out all of its potential implications. It has sometimes been argued that the first detached and analytical overviews of the Frankfurt School's history could only have been written by outsiders with no stake in the polemical wars within Germany that surrounded Critical Theory.[92] No less perhaps might be said of the reception of Adorno's work, some of whose implications may be more apparent on foreign shores than at home. Although, as I mentioned earlier, Adorno never returned to America after 1953, it is thus perhaps symbolically just that when his heart gave out in Switzerland sixteen years later, he was in fact preparing to do so in order to give the Christian Gauss lectures at Princeton University. The lectures were never delivered, but Adorno's thought did return nonetheless.[93]

We might therefore in conclusion adopt the trope of chiasmus, so frequently used by Adorno himself, to describe his complicated relationship to America.[94] As in such sentences as "history is nature; nature is history," Adorno employed chiasmus to indicate the unreconciled and unsublated relationship between two elements that nonetheless are inextricably intertwined. It is appropriate to call his peculiar status as a thinker tensely suspended between his native land and his emigré home a form of chiasmus. For as an American, he was obviously a displaced European, while as a European, he was deeply affected by his years in America. As a result he was able to remain in permanent exile from both contexts, and still does after his death. Although surely a source of pain, this condition, as Adorno doubtless knew, was also a stimulus to his creativity and originality. It also paradoxically made him into something of an exemplary figure for contemporary man. For as he argued in his essay in ***Noten zur Literatur*** entitled **"Die Wunde Heine,"** "today, the fate Heine suffered has literally become the common fate: homelessness has been inflicted on everyone. All, in language and being, have been damaged as the exile himself was."[95]

It is perhaps especially fitting that I borrow this citation from the opening remarks made by the American literary critic Harvey Gross at the earlier symposium honoring Adorno that was held in Los Angeles on the tenth anniversary of his death.[96] For not the least of Adorno's gifts to his emigré asylum, a country known for receiving rather than generating refugees, was the knowledge that in some sense we too are still suffering from Heine's wound, we too are still leading the damaged lives of men unable to find their way home.

Notes

1. Paul Lazarsfeld, "An Episode in the History of Social Research: A Memoir," *The Intellectual Migration: Europe and America, 1930-1960,* Donald Fleming and Bernard Bailyn (Cambridge, 1969), p. 301.

2. Theodor W. Adorno, "Scientific Experiences of a European Scholar in America," *The Intellectual Migration,* p. 342.

3. Lazarsfeld, p. 313. For an account of the failure written from Lazarsfeld's perspective, see David E. Morrison, "Kultur and Culture: The Case of Theodor W. Adorno and Paul F. Lazarsfeld," *Social Research* (Summer 1978), 45(2):331-55.

4. Adorno, *Minima Moralia: Reflections from Damaged Life,* trans. E. F. N. Jephcott (London, 1974), p. 22.

5. Adorno, *Gesammelte Schriften,* (Frankfurt, 1977).

6. *Ibid.,* p. 698.

7. *The New York Times,* August 7, 1969. It is held up to ridicule in Hans Mayer, *Der Repräsentant und der Martyrer: Konstellationen der Literatur* (Frankfurt, 1971), p. 145; Martin Jay, "The Frankfurt School in Exile," *Perspectives in American History* (1972), 6:356; and Zoltan Tar, *The Frankfurt School: The Critical Theories of Max Horkheimer and Theodor W. Adorno* (New York, 1977), p. 11.

8. Robert Craft, "A Bell for Adorno," *Prejudices in Disguise* (New York, 1974), p. 94.

9. Edward Shils, "Daydreams and Nightmares: Reflections on the Criticism of Mass Culture," *Sewanee Review* (Autumn 1957), 65(4):587-608; Leon Bramson, *The Political Context of Sociology* (Princeton, 1961); Herbert J. Gans, "Popular Culture in America: Social Problem in a Mass Society or Social Asset in a Pluralist Society?" in *Social Problems, A Modern Approach,* ed. Herbert S. Becker (New York, 1966).

10. This in particular was Shils' argument, which paid no attention to the hedonist dimension of Critical Theory.

11. Tar, p. 118.

12. George Friedman, *The Political Philosophy of the Frankfurt School* (Ithaca, 1981), p. 32.

13. Irving Wohlfahrt, "Hibernation: On the Tenth Anniversary of Adorno's Death," *Modern Language Notes* (December 1979), 94(6):980-81. Wohlfahrt, who studied with Adorno in the 1960s and wrote one of the first introductions to him in English (the short "Presentation of Adorno" in *New Left Review* [January 1968], no. 46), is a far more sensitive analyst of his work, and that of Benjamin, than either of the two previously cited authors. He ends this compact but very insightful piece by reversing its generally critical direction and warning against "blaming the messenger [Adorno] for the news" (p. 982).

14. Dagmar Barnouw, "'Beute der Pragmatisierung': Adorno und Amerika," in *Die USA und Deutschland: Wechselseitige Spieglungen in der Literatur der Gegenwart,* ed. Wolfgang Paulsen (Bern, 1976). The author teaches in the German Department of Brown University in America, so perhaps the essay can be taken as another example of the American response to Adorno rather than a German reading of it.

15. *Ibid.,* p. 76.

16. Adorno, *Prisms: Culture Criticism and Society,* trans. Samuel and Shierry Weber (London, 1967), p. 98.

17. For a good discussion of this issue, see Egbert Krispyn, *Anti-Nazi Writers in Exile* (Athens, Ga., 1978).

18. The correspondence between them, which can be found in the Kracauer Nachlass in the Schiller National Museum in Marbach am Neckar, contains many examples of their differing views of English.

19. Eugene Lunn, *Marxism and Modernism: An Historical Study of Lukács, Brecht, Benjamin, and Adorno* (Berkeley, 1982), p. 209.

20. Adorno, "Scientific Experiences of a European Scholar in America," pp. 369-70. H. Stuart Hughes is one of the few observers who has noted the validity of Adorno's remarks about his debt to America. See his *The Sea Change: The Migration of Social Thought, 1930-1965* (New York, 1975), pp. 150f. He points out how frequently American terms enter his vocabulary in the writings done after his return, terms like "healthy sex life," "some fun," "go-getters," "social research," "team," "middle range theory," "trial and error," "administrative research," "common sense," "fact finding," "statement of fact," "case studies," "facts and figures," "nose counting," and "likes and dislikes" (p. 166).

21. Adorno, "Scientific Experiences of a European Scholar in America," p. 367.

22. See, for example, his remarks that "the greatest fetish of cultural criticism is the notion of culture as such. . . . Only when neutralized and reified, does Culture allow itself to be idolized. Fetishism gravitates towards mythology." *Prisms,* pp. 23-24.

23. See, in particular, Marcuse, "The Affirmative Character of Culture," *Negations: Essays in Critical Theory,* trans. Jeremy J. Shapiro (Boston, 1968); the first use of the term came in Horkheimer's "Egoismus und Freiheitsbewegung," *Zeitschrift für Sozialforschung* (1936), 5(2):161-231.

24. Lunn, p. 208.

25. Adorno, "Scientific Experiences of a European Scholar in America," p. 367.

26. Joachim Radkau, *Die deutsche Emigration in den USA: Ihr Einfluss auf die amerikanische Europapolitik 1933-1934* (Düsseldorf, 1974). Radkau includes the *Institut für Sozialforschung* in his general indictment because of their psychologization of social problems. But he notes that Adorno's "Scientific Experiences" essay has a "skeptical and pessimistic undertone" that sets it apart from other emigré memoirs (p. 13).

27. Adorno, "Scientific Experiences of a European Scholar in America," p. 370. The desire of the returning *Institut* members to contribute to political enlightenment is expressed in a letter Horkheimer sent to Lowenthal on April 13, 1951, in which he wrote:

> We stand here for the good things: for individual independence, the idea of the Enlightenment, science freed from blinders. When Fred [Pollock] reports to me that you and other friends see the type of empirical social science we are conducting here as in many ways conventional, I am convinced that you would be of another opinion could you see the thing with your own eyes. . . . As much as I yearn for pure philosophical work again, as much as I am determined to take it up again under the right conditions and devote myself solely to it, so much do I also know that effectiveness here, either for the education of students or for ourselves, is not lost.

(Lowenthal archive).

28. Adorno, "Zur gegenwärtigen Stellung der empirischen Sozialforschung in Deutschland," in *Empirische Sozialforschung: Meinungs- und Marktforschung Methoden und Probleme: Schriftenreihe des Instituts zur Förderung öffentlicher Anglegenheiten e.V.* (Frankfurt, 1952).

29. See for example, Friedrich Pollock, ed. *Gruppenexperiment: Ein Studienbericht: Frankfurter Beiträge zur Soziologie,* vol. 2 (Frankfurt, 1955).

30. Adorno, *Gesammelte Schriften,* 10.2.

31. Adorno et al., *The Authoritarian Personality* (New York: 1950), 2:976.

32. The proceedings of the conference were collected as *Freud in der Gegenwart: Frankfurter Beiträge zur Soziologie,* (Frankfurt, 1957), vol. 6. The Institute's purpose in sponsoring this conference were expressed in a letter Horkheimer sent to Lowenthal on January 20, 1956:

> I participate in the affair—on the urgent request of Mitscherlich—because such an event in Germany means a restrengthening of enlightened cultural forces, because young people in general no longer know of these things, but should be led through them, because the jurists in regard to the new formation of the penal code, the ministers and pedagogues in regard to the new teaching code should be reminded of these things, because psychiatry to a great extent is a scandal. I am very aware of the risks brought by such an undertaking, but it belongs to the things that justify my being here.

(Lowenthal archive).

33. For an overview of the Frankfurt School's changing attitude toward this issue, see chapter 6.

34. See, for example, his remark in *Introduction to the Sociology of Music,* trans. E. B. Ashton (New York,

1976), that "it is different in America, where one meets scientists who must strain even to imagine experiencing music otherwise than by radio. The culture industry has become much more of a second nature than thus far on the old continent" (p. 231).

35. C. Wright Mills, "I.B.M. Plus Reality Plus Humanism-Sociology," *Saturday Review* (May 1954), p. 54.

36. Kuspit actually went earlier, from 1957 to 1960. See his "Theodor W. Adorno: A Memoir," *Chateau Review* (1983), 6(1):20-24.

37. Paul Breines, ed., *Critical Interruptions: New Left Perspectives on Herbert Marcuse* (New York, 1970). In 1968, Breines had written an essay on "Marcuse and the New Left in America," in Jürgen Habermas, ed., *Antworten auf Herbert Marcuse* (Frankfurt, 1968), in which he noted that "Horkheimer, Adorno, Benjamin and the perspectives developed in the *Institut für Sozialforschung* remain all but unknown" in America (p. 137).

38. See, for example, the work of Ben Agger, "On Happiness and Damaged Life," in John O'Neill, ed., *On Critical Theory* (New York, 1976); and "Dialectical Sensibility I: Critical Theory, Scientism and Empiricism," *Canadian Journal of Political and Social Theory* (Winter 1977) 1(1):1-30; "Dialectical Sensibility II: Towards a New Intellectuality," *Canadian Journal of Political and Social Theory* (Spring-Summer 1977) 1(2):47-57.

39. Fredric Jameson, "Adorno: or, Historical Tropes," *Salmagundi* (Spring 1967), 5:3-43.

40. Jameson, *Marxism and Form: Twentieth-Century Dialectical Theories of Literature* (Princeton, 1967), pp. 58-59.

41. George Steiner, *Language and Silence: Essays on Language, Literature, and the Inhuman* (New York, 1967).

42. George Lichtheim, "From Marx to Hegel," *Triquarterly* (Spring 1978) 12:5-42; republished in *From Marx to Hegel* (New York, 1971), where the citation appears on p. 21.

43. Lichtheim, *From Marx to Hegel,* p. viii. For an overview of Lichtheim's career, which discusses his links with Critical Theory, see chapter 10.

44. Martin Jay, "The Permanent Exile of Theodor W. Adorno," *Midstream* (December 1969), 15(10):62-69.

45. Russell Jacoby, review of Adorno, *Aufsätze zur Gesellschaftstheorie,* in *Telos* (Fall 1970), 6:343-48. For a general account of *Telos* and its debt to Critical Theory, see John Fekete, "Telos at 50," *Telos* (Winter 1981-1982), 50:161-71.

46. Russell Jacoby, "Marcuse and the New Academics: A Note on Style," *Telos* (Spring, 1970) 5:188-190;

"Marxism and the Critical School," *Theory and Society* (1974), 1:231-38; "Marxism and Critical Theory: Martin Jay and Russell Jacoby," *Theory and Society* (1975), 2:257-63; review of Phil Slater, *Origin and Significance of the Frankfurt School* in *Telos* (Spring 1977), 31:198-202; review of Zoltan Tar, *The Frankfurt School* in *Sociology and Social Research* (1978), 63:168-71; review of George Friedman, *The Political Philosophy of the Frankfurt School* in *Telos* (Fall 1981), 49:203-15.

47. Dick Howard, review of *Jargon der Eigentlichkeit*, in *Telos* (Summer 1971), 8:146-49; Susan Buck-Morss, "The Dialectic of T. W. Adorno," *Telos* (Winter 1972), 14:137-44.

48. *Telos* (Spring 1970), no. 5, table of contents.

49. *The New Left Review* did publish a two-part translation of Adorno's "Sociology and Psychology" in numbers 46 (November-December 1967) and 47 (January-February 1968), but its first extended analysis of *Critical Theory* was the Althusserian attack of Göran Therborn, "Frankfurt Marxism: A Critique," in number 63 (September-October, 1970), pp. 65-89. My essay, "The Frankfurt School's Critique of Marxist Humanism," *Social Research* (Summer 1972), 34(2):285-305 was in part a rebuttal to Therborn.

50. Martin Jay, *The Dialectical Imagination: A History of the Frankfurt School and the Institute of Social Research, 1923-1950* (Boston, 1973); Phil Slater, *Origin and Significance of the Frankfurt School: A Marxist Perspective* (London, 1977); Tar, *The Frankfurt School*; O'Neill, ed., *On Critical Theory*; David Held, *Introduction to Critical Theory: Horkheimer to Habermas* (Berkeley, 1980); Friedman, *The Political Philosophy of the Frankfurt School*; Paul Connerton, *The Tragedy of Enlightenment: An Essay on the Frankfurt School* (Cambridge, 1980); Andrew Arato and Eike Gebhardt, eds., *The Essential Frankfurt School Reader* (New York, 1977); and *The New Left Review*, ed., *Aesthetics and Politics: Debates Between Bloch, Lukács, Brecht, Benjamin, Adorno* (London, 1977). For an overview of the American reception of Critical Theory, see Douglas Kellner and Rick Roderick, "Recent Literature on Critical Theory," *New German Critique* (Spring-Summer 1981), 23:141-70.

51. Susan Buck-Morss, *The Origin of Negative Dialectics: Theodor W. Adorno, Walter Benjamin and the Frankfurt Institute* (New York, 1977). See also her "Piaget, Adorno, and the Possibilities of Dialectical Operations," in Hugh J. Silverman, ed. *Piaget, Philosophy and the Human Sciences* (Atlantic Highlands, N.J., 1980).

52. David Gross, "Lowenthal, Adorno, Barthes: Three Perspectives on Popular Culture," *Telos* (Fall 1980), 50:122-40; Martin Jay, "The Concept of Totality in Lukács and Adorno," *Telos* (Summer 1977), 30:117-37; and in Shlomo Avineri, ed., *Varieties of Marxism*

(The Hague, 1977); Martin Jay, "Adorno and Kracauer: Notes on a Troubled Friendship," *Salmagundi* (Winter 1978) 40:42-66; reprinted below as chapter XIII.

53. Richard Wolin, *Walter Benjamin: An Aesthetic of Redemption* (New York, 1982); Lunn, *Marxism and Modernism.*

54. Axel Honneth, "Adorno and Habermas," *Telos* (Spring 1979), 39:45-61. See the response in the same issue by James Schmidt, "Offensive Critical Theory? Reply to Honneth," pp. 62-70.

55. Murray Bookchin, *The Ecology of Freedom* (Palo Alto, Ca., 1982); "Finding the Subject: Notes on Whitebook and 'Habermas Ltd.,'" *Telos* (Summer 1982), 52:78-98.

56. Joel Whitebook, "Saving the Subject: Modernity and the Problem of the Autonomous Individual," *Telos* (Winter 1981-1982), 50:94.

57. Gillian Rose, *The Melancholy Science: An Introduction to the Thought of Theodor W. Adorno* (London, 1978), pp. 146f. She continues the attack on Habermas in *Hegel Contra Sociology* (London: Athlone, 1981), pp. 33f, but now her perspective is closer to Hegel than to Adorno, whom she also accuses of regressing back to a form of neo-Kantianism.

58. See, for example, Jean Cohen, "Why More Political Theory?," *Telos* (Summer 1979), 40:70-94, and Seyla Benhabib, "Modernity and the Aporias of Critical Theory," *Telos* (Fall 1981), 49:39-59. Although these writers are by no means uncritical supporters of Habermas, they clearly find his version of Critical Theory an advance over Adorno's.

59. See, for example, the review of Colletti's *Marxism and Hegel* by Ben Agger in *Telos* (Summer 1975), 24:191. See also the chapter on Della Volpe and Colletti in my *Marxism and Totality: The Adventures of a Concept from Lukács to Habermas* (Berkeley, 1984).

60. See, for example, Russell Jacoby, *Dialectic of Defeat: Contours of Western Marxism* (Cambridge, 1981).

61. Michael T. Jones, "Constellations of Modernity: The Literary Essays of Theodor W. Adorno" (Ph.D. diss., Yale University, 1978); Lambert Zuidervaart, "Refractions: Truth in Adorno's Aesthetic Theory" (Ph.D. diss., University of Amsterdam, 1981 (Zuidervaart is a Canadian); the best essay in English on Adorno's aesthetic theory is Richard Wolin, "The De-Aestheticization of Art: On Adorno's *Aesthetische Theorie*," *Telos* (Fall 1979) 41:105-127. See also Robert Lane Kauffmann, "The Theory of the Essay: Lukács, Adorno, and Benjamin," (Ph.D. diss., University of California, San Diego, 1981), and J. N. Mohanty, "The Concept of Intuition in Aesthetics Apropos a Critique by Adorno," *The Journal of Aesthetics and Art Criticism* (1980), 39:39-45.

62. Russell Berman, "Adorno, Marxism and Art," *Telos* (Winter 1977-1978, 34:157-66; Peter Uwe Hohendahl, "Autonomy of Art: Looking Back at Adorno's *Aesthetische Theorie*," *German Quarterly* (1981), 54:133-148, and *The Institution of Criticism* (Ithaca, 1982).

63. Frank Lentricchia, *After the New Criticism* (Chicago, 1980), p. xii.

64. Ronald Weitzman, "An Introduction to Adorno's Music and Social Criticism," *Music and Letters* (July 1971), 102(3):287-98; Donald B. Kuspit, "Critical Notes on Adorno's Sociology of Music and Art," *Journal of Aesthetics and Art Criticism* (1975), 33:321-77; Wesley Blomster, "Sociology of Music: Adorno and Beyond," *Telos* (Summer 1976), 28:81-112; Rose Rosengard Subotnik, "Adorno's Diagnosis of Beethoven's Late Style: Early Symptoms of a Fatal Condition," *Journal of the American Musicological Society* (Summer 1976), 29(2):242-75; "Why is Adorno's Music Criticism the Way It Is?," *Musical Newsletter,* (Fall 1977) 7(4):3-12,; "The Historical Structure: Adorno's 'French Model' for Nineteenth-Century Music," *Nineteenth-Century Music* (July 1978), 2(1):36-60; "Kant, Adorno, and the Self-Critique of Reason: Toward a Model for Music Criticism," *Humanities in Society* (Fall 1979), 2(4):353-86, and James L. Marsh, "Adorno's Critique of Stravinsky," *New German Critique* (Winter 1983), 28:147-69. One might also add two articles by the Hungarian-born sociologist, now living in Australia, Ferenc Fehér, because they were written for American journals: "Negative Philosophy of Music—Positive Results," *New German Critique* (Winter 1975), 4:99-111, and "Rationalized Music and its Vicissitudes (Adorno's Philosophy of Music)," *Philosophy and Social Criticism* (1982), 9(1):42-65. Compare this rather paltry collection of essays with the German reception of Adorno's musicological works, a bibliography of which can be found in Burkhardt Lindner and W. Martin Lüdke, eds. *Materielien zur ästhetische Theorie Th. W. Adornos Konstruktion der Moderne* (Frankfurt, 1979, pp. 543f. For the reception in several other European countries, see the essays in *Adorno und die Musik*, ed. Otto Kolleritsch (Graz, 1977). See also Anne G. Mitchell Culver, "Theodor W. Adorno's Philosophy of Modern Music, Evaluation and Commentary," (Ph.D. diss., University of Colorado, 1973).

65. Charles Rosen, *Arnold Schoenberg* (Princeton, 1975), which does not even list anything by Adorno in the bibliography. Rosen gave a hostile paper on "Adorno and Stravinsky" at the Adorno conference at the University of Southern California in 1979, but it was not included in the proceedings published in *Humanities in Society* (Fall 1979), 2(4). Adorno's influence can, however, be seen in Gary Schmidgall, *Literature as Opera* (New York, 1977), especially in the chapter on Berg's *Wozzeck.*

66. Carl Dalhaus, *Esthetics of Music,* trans. William Austin (Cambridge, 1982), p. 101.

67. Craft, p. 92.

68. Andreas Huyssen, "Introduction to Adorno," *New German Critique* (Fall 1975), 6:3-11; Diane Waldman, "Critical Theory and Film: Adorno and 'The Culture Industry' Revisited," *New German Critique* (Fall 1977), 12:39-60; Stanley Aronowitz, *The Crisis in Historical Materialism: Class, Politics and Culture in Marxist Theory* (South Hadley, Mass., 1981); Douglas Kellner, "TV, Ideology, and Emancipatory Popular Culture," *Socialist Review* (1979), 45:13-53; "Network Television and American Society: Introduction to a Critical Theory of Television," *Theory and Society* (January 1981) 10(1):31-62; "Kulturindustrie und Massenkommunikation. Die Kritische Theorie und ihre Folgen," in Wolfgang Bonss and Axel Honneth, eds. *Sozialforschung als Kritik: Zum Sozialwissenschaftlichen Potential der Kritischen Theorie* (Frankfurt 1982); Philip Rosen, "Adorno and Film Music: Theoretical Notes on *Composing for the Films*," *Yale French Studies* (1980), 60:157-182; Miriam Hansen, "Introduction to Adorno, 'Transparencies on Film' (1966)" *New German Critique* (Fall/Winter, 1981-82) 24/25:186-98; Matei Calinescu, *Faces of Modernity: Avant-Garde, Decadence, Kitsch* (Bloomington, 1977); Jon Brenkman, "Mass Media: From Collective Experience to the Culture of Privatization," *Social Text* (Winter 1979), 1:94-109; Thomas Andrae, "Adorno on Film and Mass Culture," *Jump Cut* (May 1979) vol. 20: For still more recent considerations, see J. Frow, "Mediation and Metaphor Adorno and the Sociology of Art." *Clio* (1982), 12:57-66, and Patrick Brantlinger, *Bread and Circuses: Theories of Mass Culture and Social Decay* (Ithaca: 1983), chap. 7.

69. Adorno, "Culture Industry Reconsidered," *New German Critique* (Fall 1975) 6:12-19; "Transparencies on Film," *New German Critique* (Fall/Winter 1981-82), 24/25:199-205.

70. Bruce Brown, *Marx, Freud, and the Critique of Everyday Life: Toward A Permanent Cultural Revolution* (New York, 1973); Russell Jacoby, *Social Amnesia* (Boston, 1975).

71. Christopher Lasch, *Haven in a Heartless World* (New York, 1977); *The Culture of Narcissism* (New York, 1979).

72. Joel Kovel, *A Complete Guide to Therapy* (New York, 1977); *The Age of Desire: Reflections of a Radical Psychoanalyst* (New York, 1981).

73. See, for example, Jessica Benjamin, "The End of Internalization: Adorno's Social Psychology," *Telos* (Summer 1977), 32:42-64; "Authority and the Family Revisited: or, a World Without Fathers," *New German Critique* (Winter 1978), 13:35-57; "Die Antinomien des patriarchalischen Denkens: Kritische

Theorie und Psychoanalyse," in Bonss and Honneth; Mark Poster, *Critical Theory of the Family* (New York, 1978).

74. Pier Aldo Rovatti, "Critical Theory and Phenomenology," *Telos* (Spring 1973), 15:25-40. Rovatti is an editor of *Aut Aut* and heavily influenced by the phenomenological Marxism of Enzo Paci, which also had a strong impact on Piccone. See, for example, his "Beyond Identity Theory" in O'Neill, in which he attacks the Frankfurt School for its lack of appreciation for Husserl.

75. Paul Piccone, "The Crisis of One-Dimensionality," *Telos* (Spring 1978), 35:43-54; "The Changing Function of Critical Theory," *New German Critique* (Fall 1977), 12:29-37. Piccone's point is that the system is so well-established now that it can tolerate, indeed even generate, pockets of "artificial" negativity that nonetheless function to stabilize it.

76. Fred R. Dallmayr, "Phenomenology and Critical Theory: Adorno," *Cultural Hermeneutics,* 3:367-405; *Twilight of Subjectivity: Contributions to a Post-Individualist Theory* (Amherst, 1981). It might also be noted that another philosophical target of Adorno's, Wittgenstein, has been defended in precisely the same way. According to H. Stuart Hughes, "in Adorno's failure to come to grips with the *Philosophical Investigations,* an enormous intellectual opportunity was missed—the chance to associate two of the finest intelligences of the century in the enterprise of bridging the philosophical traditions which Wittgenstein's death had cut off in midcourse" (*The Sea Change,* p. 167).

77. Dallmayr, "Phenomenology and Critical Theory: Adorno," p. 395.

78. Herman Mörchen, *Adorno und Heidegger—Untersuchung einer philosophischen Kommunikationsverweigerung* (Stuttgart, 1981).

79. Jean-Francois Lyotard, "Adorno as the Devil," *Telos* (Spring 1974), 19:128-37.

80. See, for example, James Miller, "Some Implication of Nietzsche's Thought for Marxism," *Telos* (Fall 1978), 37:22-41 and Rose, pp. 18f. Another common theme that some commentators have claimed links Adorno and Derrida is the importance of Husserl as a target of their work. It would, in fact, be very interesting to compare Adorno's *Metakritik der Erkenntnistheorie* with Derrida's *Speech and Phenomena: and Other Essays on Husserl's Theory of Signs,* trans. David B. Allison (Evanston, 1973).

81. Terry Eagleton, *Walter Benjamin: Or Towards a Revolutionary Criticism* (London, 1981), p. 141.

82. Michael Ryan, *Marxism and Deconstruction: A Critical Articulation* (Baltimore, 1982).

83. *Ibid.,* p. 75.

84. Hubert L. Dreyfus and Paul Rabinow, *Michel Foucault: Beyond Structuralism and Hermeneutics* (Chicago, 1982), p. xii.

85. Tom Long, "Marx and Western Marxism in the 1970's," *The Berkeley Journal of Sociology* (1980), 25:36.

86. Horkheimer and Adorno, *Dialectic of Enlightenment,* trans. John Cumming (New York, 1972), p. 231.

87. Foucault, *Power/Knowledge: Selected Interviews and Other Writings 1972-1977,* ed. Colin Gordon, trans. Colin Gordon et al. (New York, 1980), p. 145.

88. Jameson, "Reification and Utopia in Mass Culture," *Social Text* (Winter 1979), 1:130-48. See also his further reflections on these issues in *The Political Unconscious: Narrative as a Socially Symbolic Act* (Ithaca, 1981); and his "Reflections in Conclusion" to *Aesthetics and Politics.*

89. Jameson, "Reification and Utopia in Mass Culture," p. 148.

90. Habermas, "Modernity versus Postmodernity," *New German Critique* (Winter 1981), 22:3-14.

91. Habermas, "The Entwinement of Myth and Enlightenment," *New German Critique* (Spring/Summer 1982), 26:13-30.

92. See, for example, Peter Uwe Hohendahl, review of Buck-Morss in *Telos* (Winter 1977-78), 34:185.

93. As the examples cited above demonstrate, his American reception has been confined almost entirely to academic circles. But a glimmer of a slightly more popular appreciation may perhaps be discerned in the fact that a play entitled "The Dialectic of Enlightenment" by Daryl Chin was produced off-Broadway in New York in 1982. The play seems to have borrowed only the title from Horkheimer and Adorno's work. But surely there is some significance in the fact that the reviewer for *The Village Voice,* Roderick Mason Faber, could assume enough recognition of the authors to pun on one of their names in his negative review, which was called "Adore? No."

94. See Rose, p. 13.

95. Adorno, "Die Wunde Heine," in *Noten zur Literatur, Gesammelte Schriften* 2 (Frankfurt, 1974), p. 100.

96. Harvey Gross, "Adorno in Los Angeles: The Intellectual in Emigration," *Humanities in Society* (Fall 1979), 2:350.

William P. Nye (essay date 1988)

SOURCE: "Theodor Adorno on Jazz: A Critique of Critical Theory," in *Popular Music and Society,* Vol. 12, No. 4, Winter, 1988, pp. 69-73.

[In the following essay, Nye examines the ways in which Adorno's opinions about American culture affected his criticism of jazz.]

The school of social thought called critical theory has two major branches. The younger is associated with the work of Jurgen Habermas and colleagues and has little relevance to the concerns of this paper. The focus here is on the other variety of critical theory which often goes by the name of the Frankfurt School, for it officially began with the establishment of the Institute of Social Research, in Frankfurt, in 1923. The Institute sought to synthesize aspects of the work of Kant, Hegel, Marx, Weber, Lukacs and Freud, among others, and attracted a diverse and discontented group of intellectuals. Erich Fromm, Friedrich Pollock, Franz Neumann, Leo Lowenthal, and Walter Benjamin were among those associated with the Frankfurt School at one time or another.

However, the primary architects of the emergent perspective of critical theory were Max Horkheimer, Herbert Marcuse and Theodor Adorno (Held, 1980: 14-16). All three were interested in the nature and function of the arts in modern societies but Adorno and Horkheimer collaborated on a systematic approach to the arts in their ***Dialectic of Enlightenment*** (1947). According to Held (1980: 77) Horkheimer and Adorno's approach to the arts was to seek "to understand given works in terms of their social origins, form, content and function—in terms of the social totality. The conditions of labour, production and distribution must be examined, for society expresses itself through its cultural life and cultural phenomena contain within themselves reference to the socio-economic whole."

Adorno's interest in a critical theory of the arts was particularly strong in regard to music, for over half of his published writings are devoted to the topic (Held, 1980: 78). His early formal training as a musician probably accounts for much of his interest in this field, but in his later years, or after his forced emigration from Hitler's Germany and subsequent involvement in American radio research, Adorno fastened his critical ears on the nature, production and social implications of American popular music.

One view of what happened is given by Held (1980: 78):

> The emergence of an entertainment industry, the growth of the mass media, the blatant manipulation of culture by the Nazis and other totalitarian regimes, the shock of immigration to the U.S., the inevitable discovery of the glamour and glitter of the film and record industries: together all made imperative the task of assessing the changing patterns of culture.

A much different, and from the perspective of this essay more accurate, view of Adorno's critical and often contemptuous stance toward American popular music is suggested in this biographical assessment:

> The thought and attitudes of Adorno were decisively shaped by his bourgeois social background and its con-

comitant life style, his training in music in Vienna, and the sociohistoric experiences of his encounter with American civilization . . .

> Adorno encountered every aspect of American civilization with shock. Being suddenly transplanted from *'baroque'*; and *gemutlich* Vienna with its nineteenth century atmosphere, via Oxford, England, to the slums of Newark, New Jersey, necessarily brought forth shock and panic

(Tar, 1977: 171-72).

The raw, rough and raucous undercurrents of American culture seem to have repelled Adorno's refined artistic sensibilities beyond the usual limits of scholarly restraint, for he scathingly lambasted American popular music in its every form and guise. When stripped of invidious labels many of his comments on popular music appear both accurate and insightful, but only when applied to certain kinds of songs and performances. Yet, his analyses are demonstrably excessive when it is noted that Adorno intended his criticisms to apply to all music that fits under the Germanic rubric of *Leichte Musik* (Adorno, 1973, 1941). He approved the translation of this phrase as popular music and offered a rambling definition that covered virtually all music with any entertainment value. Examining the matter historically, Adorno applied the label of popular music to everything from *The Magic Flute* to *My Fair Lady*, not to mention Rachmaninoff, Offenbach, Gershwin, film scores, jazz and Tin Pan Alley (Adorno 1973: 23-25).

The concern here, however, is not in Adorno's criticisms of everything he called popular music. It is to examine Adorno's critique of jazz to demonstrate how his general approach is one of ethnocentric cultural elitism; an approach which led him to make value-ladened, prejudicial and poorly documented assertions about a primary source of virtually all American popular music.[1] In order to be brief, primarily one source of supporting counter-evidence will be used, the readily available and eminently authoritative, "The Smithsonian Collection of Classic Jazz" (Columbia Special Products, P611891; hereafter referred to as SCCJ).

Generally, Adorno's criticisms of popular music are couched in terms of comparison with what he calls "serious" music and such comparisons serve to give definition to both types of music in his work. For example, Adorno writes that in serious music, themes and details are highly interwoven with the whole, whereas in popular music, the structure of the whole does not depend upon details, the whole is not altered by individual detail.

If one considers jazz a soloist's music wherein the soloist composes the music on the spot, then it is easy to find many recorded and musicologically analyzed examples of jazz solos that are perfectly conceived from start to finish in the sense that the original theme (or motive) is stated, developed and concluded in a manner lending it the status of a "mini" musical masterpiece. SCCJ examples would be Louis Armstrong's "West End Blues," Charlie Parker's first take of "Embraceable You" and Sonny Rollins' "Blue 7."

Adorno also says that themes are carefully developed in serious music, whereas popular music exhibits a melodic structure which is highly rigid and is frequently repeated. In jazz, again considered as our concrete example of popular music, the melodic structure is anything but rigid. Only the chord sequences are repeated and frequently with new variations on each repeat. In fact, a hallmark of an accomplished jazz musician is the ability to create melodies in a spontaneous fashion which are musicologically superior to that given in the opening and frequently borrowed theme of a typical jazz performance. SCCJ examples of the wondrous things the best jazz performers can do to melodies are Louis Armstrong's version of "Sweethearts on Parade," Coleman Hawkins' famous rendition of "Body and Soul," Charlie Parker's remarkably different but equally brilliant back-to-back takes of "Embraceable You" and Art Tatum's wizardry on "Willow Weep for Me" and "Too Marvelous for Words." Furthermore, a jazz singer of the calibre of Billie Holiday can appear to sing and repeat the melody of a song on one level, yet inflect each round of interpretation with subtle but powerful tonal, dynamic and rhythmic nuances which tend to transform the song into a unique personal possession of the performer. SCCJ performances by Billie Holiday, Sarah Vaughan and Ella Fitzgerald are all noteworthy in this regard.

Elsewhere, Adorno observes that in serious music consistency is maintained between formal structure and content (themes), but in popular music, stress is on the combination of individual "effects," or on sound, color, tone, beat and rhythm. What has already been said about the employment and development of themes in jazz applies here as well, but perhaps more importantly, Adorno's belief that popular music stresses the wrong elements reflects a general ignorance of what jazz in particular is all about. The importance of rhythm in jazz is undeniable and underscores the music's historical indebtedness to African music where rhythm was and remains the paramount consideration. Is Adorno suggesting that music which emphasizes rhythm cannot be serious? It sounds like it, which suggests that Adorno's critical stance may be biased in favor of European classical music which places great emphasis on harmonic sophistication often at the expense of rhythmic, tonal or even melodic complexity.

Adorno likewise misunderstands the historical origins and musical implications of popular music's concern with sound and color. European music at least since the time of J.S. Bach, has established strict tonal criteria for virtually all instruments normally found in a symphony orchestra, including the human voice. In a relative sense, musicians trained in the European manner achieve a standardization of tone production which is both historically and geographically rare. Jazz musicians, on the other hand, draw from the African musical tradition in which the development of a distinctly individual and widely expressive voice

is a common goal of all who would seek to rise to the top of the profession.

For example, Jean Pierre Rampal and James Galway are two acknowledged masters of the European flute tradition. An experienced ear can discern differences in their respective tones and each would interpret the same piece a little differently. Yet, they still sound more alike than different when it comes to elements of vibrato, attack, intonation, and the like. To understand how different this is from the jazz tradition, one merely has to listen to the masters of jazz trumpet included in the SCCJ. It does not take an experienced ear to hear the obvious differences in sound produced by Louis Armstrong, Bix Beiderbeck, Dizzy Gillespie and Miles Davis. Each produces a sound as personal, unique and as instantly recognizable as John Hancock's signature, and this is exactly what each sought to achieve through years of practice and experimentation. Adorno's critical deprecation of this aspect of popular music reflects a myopic ethnocentrism toward non-European music in general, and perhaps a disguised racism when applied to jazz.

Comment on one more of Adorno's criticisms of popular music should be enough to intellectually discredit his theoretical perspective. According to him, if standard themes are employed in serious music, say for a dance section, they still maintain a key role in the whole. He contrasts this to popular music in which, to use Held's (1980: 101) interpretation, "improvisations become normalized (the boys can only 'swing it' in a narrow framework)" and "details are substitutable ('they serve their functions as cogs in machines')." Putting this in a jazz context, Adorno is saying that jazz musicians do not really improvise and jazz compositions and performances are no more than tired musical cliches thrown together in new and perhaps even random combinations. Suffice it to say that good jazz musicians improvise in the fullest sense of the word and the truth of this is given in the sense of awe with which many accomplished "serious" or classically trained musicians regard the best and even the better jazz musicians. In response to Adorno's claim that jazz is mechanically produced, consider the SCCJ selections by Duke Ellington. Today it is widely conceded that Mr. Ellington is among the very best of America's composers. Yet he composed jazz. Therefore, if what Adorno says about jazz is true, then a logical conclusion is that thus far, America has produced little, if any, serious music of significance.

On the other hand, a more appropriate and justifiable conclusion would be to agree with Zoltan Tar (1977: 207), who had this to say about Theodor Adorno and the Frankfurt School: "Indeed, Critical Theory is the document of the disintegration of old Central European bourgeois society and the tragic fate of a group of intellectuals of that society."

Note

1. The criticisms of popular music credited to Adorno are drawn from Held's (1980: 101, 103 and passim)

summary. The original sources are scattered in English and German publications listed under Adorno's name in the bibliography.

Bibliography

Adorno, Theodor W. 1936. Uber jazz (published under pseudonym Hektor Rottweiler). Zeitschrift fur Sozialforshung 5 (No. 3).

Adorno, Theodor W. 1941. (With the assistance of George Simpson). On popular music. Studies in Philosophy and Social Science 9.

Adorno, Theodor W. 1964. Moments Musicaux: Neugedruckte Aufsatze, 1928 bis 1962. Frankfurt: Suhrkamp.

Adorno, Theodor W. 1973. Introduction to the Sociology of Music. Tr. E. B. Ashton, New York: Seabury Press.

Held, David. 1980. Introduction to Critical Theory: Horkheimer to Habermas. Berkeley and Los Angeles: University of California Press.

Horkheimer, Max and Theodor W. Adorno. 1947. Dialektik der Aufklarung. Amsterdam: Querido Verlag, N.V.

Schroyer, Trent. 1973. The Critique of Domination. Boston: Beacon Press.

Tar, Zoltan. 1977. The Frankfurt School: The Critical Theories of Max Horkheimer and Theodor W. Adorno. New York: John Wiley and Sons.

Rainer Rochlitz (essay date 1988)

SOURCE: "Language for One, Language for All: Adorno and Modernism," in *Perspectives on Musical Aesthetics,* edited by John Rahn, W. W. Norton & Company, 1994, pp. 21-39.

[*In the following essay, originally published in French in 1988, Rochlitz locates Adorno's place in aesthetic modernity.*]

Modernity can be assigned a minimalist as well as a maximalist definition. In the first case, one would go back to the birth of modern subjectivity, to the Renaissance, the Reformation, the French Revolution, and modernity would be understood as the perpetual re-questioning of the normative criteria on which a posttraditional society is founded, as a chronic tension between the demands of profitability, of efficaciousness, of maintenance, and the demands of validity, of the autonomous logics in the sciences, of norms, and of arts.[1] From this perspective, the historical catastrophes of the nineteenth century do not justify the verdict which denounces modern reason as such. In the second case, modernity can be seen as the absolute radicality of the political and artistic avant-gardes and of their continuous bid for change, especially since the middle of the nineteenth century, a radicality which opposes to the apocalyptic negativity of modern societies a demand for rational reconciliation without compromise. In this latter case, after the successive defeats of the radical movements, there appears a deceived and bitter, cynical or desperate "postmodernity," and a sceptical realism which ends up denouncing as utopian the perspectives of minimalist modernity.[2]

Adorno's thought is situated midway between these two definitions, and leans strongly toward the second. What separates Adorno from postmodernity is his paradoxical effort to save normativity and the emancipating potential of reason, whose totalitarian drift he nevertheless denounces. As for his successors, the principle of all essential change is resolutely confined to a force which is exterior to reason, and notably to the imagination without which it would be sterile and repressive.

Historically, Adorno's thought stems from a triple failure: the failure of Western humanism at Auschwitz, a catastrophe which the culture of Bach and Beethoven, of Goethe and Hölderlin, of Kant and Hegel, did not know how to prevent; the failure, in Stalinism, of the political movement which had claimed "to realize philosophy";[3] the failure, finally, of Western culture in a cultural industry dominated by the American model. In all three cases, Adorno (and Horkheimer, with whom he wrote *La Dialectique de la raison,* completed in 1944) sees the triumph of instrumental or practical reason in the modern subject, a subject which ends up by abolishing itself as subject.

However—and it is this which links Adorno to the first definition of modernity—philosophy "keeps itself alive" by virtue of its practical failures. It strives to save that which instrumental reason can only miss or destroy: the nonidentical, the individual, and the particular.[4] What permits thinking, in opposition to the spontaneous tendency of thought—"to think means to identify"[5]—is the very failure of an identification which misses its object; by a sort of return of the repressed, that which is nonidentical forces thought into a "dialectic," that is to say, into a critical reflection on itself, and into a mimetic relation with its object, much like the processes which are expressed in art. Instead of identifying its object, dialectical thought identifies itself with it, while at the same time retaining its identity as critical thought.

As Habermas has shown, this conclusion is inevitable within the framework of a philosophy of the subject, such as Adorno's philosophy remains. It can apprehend only by objectification—and thus by "reification"—that which arises from an essentially intersubjective "identity" of persons and of relations of reciprocity on which, in a final analysis, the social fabric relies. That is why it attempts to offer a remedy by a mimetic approach and a conceptuality founded on "affinity." The recent theory which grounds society, language, and personal identity on the activity of communication, anterior to any reifying objectification, can avoid this stumbling block and more accurately assign a place to the pathologies of modernity. It escapes the aporias of maximalism and its postmodern consequences, because it is not compelled to attribute to the catastrophes of the twentieth century a meaning tied to the totalitarian essence of the modern subject.

I

Among the theories of modern art, the aspiration of the Adornian project is unique; it is comparable only to the three or four great syntheses of German philosophy, to the aesthetics of Kant and Schelling, of Hegel and the young Lukács, and to the collection of essays by Walter Benjamin which served as a model for the musical and literary studies of Adorno himself. Of all these theories, that of Adorno is the only one which was able to take into account, not only romanticism and postromanticism, but also the avant-gardes, their decline, and their influence up to the threshold of postmodernism.

In spite of the pessimistic tone which he consciously adopts, Adorno still speaks of an artistic modernity of the future. For him in 1969, not only is this adventure, menaced by cultural industry, yet to be concluded, but he places in it his hope for the survival of the critical spirit, since, according to him, dialectical thought itself relies on a conceptual equivalent of the mimetic attitude. Right up to its negation by a radically demystified art, aesthetic appearance is for him the basis of hope. It is this and this alone which maintains the perspective of a reconciled world, a view which philosophic thought is incapable of preserving without the aid of art.[6] Demystified and reconciled myth, rational mimesis, art, and especially the disenchanted art of the avant-garde constitute the normative base of Adornian philosophy; this is the base which authorizes its critique of society.

The ultimate and incomplete synthesis of all Adorno's essays, his *Aesthetic Theory,* attempts to reconstruct all of artistic modernity as a function of the same historical situation. All modern works should be understood as responses to one and the same problem, that of myth, of disenchantment which is the process of an Enlightenment ongoing for thousands of years, and finally of reconciliation. It is a reflection on art seen from the interior, from the point of view of creation and of the work, with all the complexity and all the reflexive character that this implies for a modern artist. This is why the *Aesthetic Theory*—with its concentric structure and its aphoristic writing—draws close to being a work of art in itself, playing with the concepts to render them more permeable to their objects, and denying itself the transparency of a linear reading. No aesthetic connects art and modernity as closely; art is only realized by liberating itself from all heteronomy; it is the art of the avant-garde which reveals the essence of all art, but also its aporias.

Adorno's thought is paradoxical. Dedicated entirely to modernity, at the same time it gnaws away at its very foundations. In spite of the disastrous balance sheet which he draws up, Adorno nevertheless refuses to abandon the project of modernity. It is this which constitutes his inter-

mediate position between the two definitions of modernity. There is no *other* root of reason for him; if the dialectical concept tends to be mimetic, the mimesis of modern art is rational and—contrary to Nietzsche and Heidegger—does not thrust its roots into a past which is anterior to Reason. It is this which saves Adorno from irrationalism, without however permitting him to differentiate art and philosophy as much as he would like to do.

One can say—in reflecting on Albrecht Wellmer's analysis[7]—that the paradox of Adornian thought is due to his fusion of two types of criticism, that of a rational philosophy of history and that of a critique of reason in the name of its other. The appeal to reason's other becomes inevitable once Adorno and Horkheimer begin to interpret the rationality of the historical process according to the Hegelian and Marxist dialectic of progress as well as to the Weberian analysis of bureaucratic rationality.[8] Instrumental reason, which governs the development of the Mind (or of the productive forces), thus escapes all rational control, to the extent that *all* reason is instrumental, is the objectification of a reality by a subject. From this perspective, the critique of reason can only be carried forth in the name of reason's other, in the name of the nonidentical (nature, urges, poetry, the oppressed). Adorno's originality with regard to Nietsche lies in the fact that for him the nonidentical is not irrational, but rather a deformed element of integral reason. The dynamic which connects the two sides of reason, the "dialectic of reason," is fundamentally a dialectic of mimesis: domination mimes the violence of natural forces in order to master them by work and by conceptual thought—it is a mimesis of death in the name of the conservation of self—whereas aesthetic affinity mimes that which is dominated.

As with Heidegger, the development of the modern subject coincides with the progress of reification, of the objectifying and dominating relation to nature, both external and internal; but analogously, the development of the subject is accompanied for Adorno by an internal differentiation whose effects are beneficial. Dominating reason gives rise to the birth of mimetic reason in the arts and in dialectical thought. To the extent that it is contrasted with magic, art is a rationalized mimesis, an appearance conscious of its unreality. Alone, it cannot reconcile a reality which has been oppressed and destroyed by instrumental reason; it can only testify to a possible reconciliation, evoked by aesthetic appearance, while representing nonreconciled reality.[9] Modern works—those of Schönberg, of Kafka, or of Beckett—thus call forth reconciliation and at the same time deny it by their use of dissonance; to present dissonance as resolved in creating a harmonious work of art would deprive art of its critical force.

According to Adorno, humanity will escape its self-destruction by instrumental reason only to the extent that the two sides of mimesis reach a reconciliation. Now, the imbalance of modernity results from the fact that avant-garde art is already a synthesis of mimesis and of rationality—of the most advanced techniques and principles of organization—whereas positivist philosophy, sciences, technology, economic administration, and management have eliminated every mimetic element. As a successful synthesis of the human endeavor, art thus once again becomes the model for philosophy.[10]

If modern art is obscure and refuses itself to immediate comprehension, this is because its apparent irrationality is the inverse of instrumental reason. In exploring the repressed domain of the nonidentical which it is in the business of saving, this art incarnates a form of reason which would no longer be instrumental. It is thus that in speaking of artistic modernity Adorno does not cease to consider current problems in philosophy.

The dialectic of mimesis appears especially in connection with concepts of innovation and experimentation; it culminates in that which Adorno calls the "subjective point," a sort of point of no return for artistic radicality.

Designed on the model of a commodity which must affirm its competitive uniqueness, the novelty of the modern work is at the same time a mortal parody of itself, to the point of the self-destruction of art. Contrary to appearances, a new work shows reality as it is, increasingly damaged under its polished surface, disfigured by the universal reign of merchandise, a final avatar of classical domination. The novelty of avant-garde art is its incessant transcendence of negativity. At the same time, the work nonetheless remains an artistic appearance, and in this manner a promise of happiness, thanks to a form, in itself new, which projects a distanced light on the reality which it reveals. This entanglement of disillusion and of utopian promise constitutes the dialectic of artistic modernity according to Adorno; it associates the content of truth with a quasi-messianic function of appearance in general.

If the new is "irresistible,"[11] that is because each work which is truly new forces itself as a conquest upon other artists, analogous to a scientific discovery, henceforth not to be dismissed. It is this which connects the development of art both to the history of truth and to the development of productive forces, including the knowledge of artistic techniques. A work of art is intimately linked to a commodity in a capitalist society and can only affirm its autonomy by pulling itself away from the circulation of exchange by dint of its uselessness, in the manner of a "ready-made" by Duchamp.[12] The truth of an avant-garde work consists in revealing all the violence, all the inhumanity, all the reification which crystallizes in a commodity produced by modern society.[13] It remains to be known if art can be associated this closely to truth and to a philosophy of history univocally reduced to a course toward the catastrophe, whose Benjaminian image seems to have profoundly impressed Adorno.[14]

Dominating reason being irrational—the destruction of nature and of humankind—apparent irrationality in modern art is according to Adorno a form of rational reaction which denounces false instrumental logic. More precisely—and in this Adorno undoubtedly intends to take into account the Kantian systematic—art opposes to instrumental rationality the very finality of reason. In its continual reaction to the development of productive forces, art follows their logic by anticipating the diversion of technical potentials to human ends.[15] It is to this intimate relation with the movement of history that aesthetic novelty owes its "irresistible" character.

By establishing such a close relation between art and historic reality, Adorno denies himself the concept of a logic proper to the artistic creation itself, founded on the emancipation and the differentiation of subjectivity, in the sense of a minimalist theory of modernity. This, moreover, is why he relativizes the autonomy of art from the very start of his *Aesthetic Theory.*[16] The seductive force of the Adornian aesthetic is tied to the fact that a great number of modern artists were themselves involved with a logic of transcendence, devolving from the motion of the historic process toward the worst, even if they did not adhere to the dialectic of reason and of its mimetic inverse. The debate on the "end of the avant-gardes," ongoing since the 1970s, has revealed a break with this logic of transcendence. In this context, the renunciation of the maximalist model could open out into two opposing perspectives: a pure and simple inversion of radical logic, or the elaboration of another logic, compatible with the minimalist model. Discussions on postmodernism fall within the first hypothesis; rather than a pursuit of radicalization, there is a provocative acceptance of all that which former reasoning had banished from modernism: a taste for the eccentric, for kitsch, for luxuriant excess rather than ascetic rigor; rather than a critical conscience going against the stream, a complacent adherence to what is in vogue. This inversion remains attached in a negative sense to avant-gardist dogmatism: "one must be absolutely postmodern." In the second hypothesis, it is a question of reconstructing a logic of artistic modernity which is not simply the obverse of economic and social history, but which reacts in its own way, according to its own proper logic. The first path follows, in spite of itself, the logic of maximalism through a new global turning point and a new sectarianism which this time is eclectic; the second separates out the elements of a subjective singularization of language, even as in the apocalyptic logic of the avant-gardes.

If the dialectic of modernism tries to establish a relation between art and historic truth, the analysis of experimentation is concerned with the status of the subject in modernity; it defines the procedure which a subject impaired by identifying reason must follow—to bring about that which is modern. Originally, the concept of experimentation "simply meant that a self-conscious will set out to explore unknown and illicit ways of doing things;"[17] at a later time—a time that was current for Adorno—this concept designated "the fact that the artistic subject uses methods the results of which it cannot foresee."[18] By abandoning itself to heteronomy—in aleatory music, in action painting, and in automatic writing—the subject exposes itself to regression while trying to remain master of itself at the point of contact with that which is the most alien to it.[19] Artistic modernity is thus a test for the sovereignty of the aesthetic subject before the insignificant and the nonaesthetic; but for Adorno, the irrational element which thus imposes itself upon the subject has the characteristics of truth repressed by reason.

The theory of the "subjective point" relates to the same problematic of the subject: "If modern art as a whole can be understood as a continual intervention of the subject, which is no longer at all disposed to let the traditional game of forms of works of art play in a nonreflective way, then to the continual interventions of the self, there corresponds a tendency to give up in powerlessness."[20] For when everything is a construction of the subject, "there remains only abstract unity, freed from the antithetical moment by which alone it became united."[21] Art is at the same stroke "rejected at the point of pure subjectivity,"[22] by the cry of expressionism, by cubist construction, by the gesture of Dada, by the intervention of Duchamp. After having reached this extreme point, the artist—as Picasso and Schönberg themselves illustrate—can only come back to a more traditional order. In this, Adorno sees signs of the end of an art which renounces itself rather than compromise; truth content risks destroying aesthetic appearance. Beckett alone succeeds at this *tour de force*: "The space assigned to works of art, between discursive barbarism and poetic prettification, is hardly more vast than the point of indifference in which Beckett has set up shop."[23]

This restrictive concept of subjectivity as an integrative force—which, once having lost the aid of tradition, could only choose between sterile domination and abandonment of self—is due to the limits of the philosophy of the subject, the domain within which Adorno's thought remains.[24] According to this philosophy, the subject is essentially an objectifying activity, even when it examines itself; it would thus not be able to constitute any meaning, since meaning is always intersubjective. According to Adorno, the growing weight of the absurd in modern art is due to the increasing force of a subject which dismantles all valid meaning. One might thus believe that Adorno expresses a regret vis-à-vis the objectivity of meaning in traditional societies, but this is not at all so. In truth, the stakes of art are for him foreign to the signification; art is a kind of "nonsignifying language,"[25] as he characterizes both natural beauty and a modern art which—as does music—moves away from all narration. The progressive intellectualization of art contributes to this just as does its primitivism, the taste for fauvism. But in spite of this refusal of signification, Adorno attributes a very precise message to the language of art: it is the "language of suffering"; it evokes the negativity of reality and exorcises it through form. All "authentic" works convey this same message, which converges with the ultimate goal of philosophy.

II

Recent attempts to liberate aesthetics from this metaphysical heritage which—for Adorno, but also for Heidegger—

makes of art the preserver of a precise truth, generally have the flaw of remaining negatively dependent on these concepts. Thinking to return to Kant or to Nietzsche, they substitute something for truth, be it the play of subjective faculties, authenticity, or a relativization of the concept of truth.

Albrecht Wellmer and Martin Seel,[26] who endeavor to reinterpret Adorno in light of the thought of Habermas, are drawn to aesthetics as a means of completing a theory of the forms of rationality. Their analysis concentrates on the contribution of art and of aesthetic reception to the collective process of communication. Thus, Wellmer opens aesthetics to art, an aesthetics which is posterior to the *Aesthetic Theory,* by attributing to modern subjectivity the same power of regeneration and integration that Adorno had reserved for the open forms of art. This allows him to reformulate the Adornian aesthetic utopia as a salvation for the socially excluded and repressed, not only in an aesthetic testimony of truth, but in a communication constantly enlarged through the action of art.

As for Martin Seel, he renounces such a utopia to conceive a social game of rationalities in which art serves as invitation to make experiences—experiments—for their own sake. The work of art presents a "way of seeing" which cannot be objectivized (p. 272) but which, if it succeeds, can be actualized and made the object of a discourse showing others the mode of perception which leads to such a comprehension.

In the history of aesthetics, Martin Seel distinguishes two great, erroneous tendencies: the "privative," which considers a work of art as inexpressible, radically foreign to a discursive apprehension of the real (Seel cites Nietzsche, Valéry, Bataille, Bubner); and the "superlative," which sees in the aesthetic phenomenon the manifestation of a truth superior to that which discursive reason can attain; the first tendency is purist, the second fundamentalist (pp. 46-47). Now, Seel's endeavor consists in defining a more rational relation with art, that of attention to a content of experience presented in the form of a nonpropositional articulation. The criterion for the aesthetic value is not truth but rather aesthetic "success" (pp. 126ff.). Those works or artistic manifestations are successful which express the contents of lived attitudes to which they alone give us access; of which they reveal to us a new sense; and which appear to us as adequate and essential for a "just" life in the present time (pp. 210-11). Aesthetic rationality appears initially in an argumentative form highlighting that which shows itself to be expression in the artistic phenomenon (p. 214). Such an emphasis is both interpretation (commentary) and actualization (confrontation, immediate emotion), and becomes criticism by combining these two aspects. Criticism specifies the mode of perception which reveals the signification of the aesthetic phenomenon (p. 296); the artists themselves do not communicate any signification but make something which is significant in itself (p. 291).

For Seel, art does not aim for anything other than to acquaint us with the experiences that are possible on the horizon of the historic present—and first to draw our distancing attention to the experience which is ours; it does not convey any other utopia (p. 330). That of a widening message, integrating what up until then was inexpressible, is not specifically aesthetic, but rather political. Those who make the experience aesthetic live the fragile presence of liberty, not its ever-vanishing future (p. 332). Seel thus rejects all aesthetics of "preappearance" or of the anticipation of a real utopia, where he sees nothing but illusion.

His book is an important attempt to articulate a domain which is difficult to grasp, that of an expression which is neither idiosyncratic nor conceptual. He represents the most recent example of a paradoxical effort characteristic of German thought since Kant: to make sense of art through philosophy, while at the same time making art a privileged object of reflection, and keeping guard against its philosophic overevaluation. Reason has need of an art which clarifies, but art is not the totality of reason (p. 326).

Wellmer and Seel react against the privilege Adorno assigns to the creative process and to the work of art. As does H. R. Jauss (and Paul Ricoeur, who develops in *Time and Narrative* a theory of mimesis as refiguration of reality through the configuration of the artwork itself), they endeavor to reintroduce the receptive subject that the **Aesthetic Theory** had dismissed. This option actually recommends itself when one perceives the limits of the philosophy of the subject, which lead Adorno to admit of no social impact on the part of modern works, and to conceive only the evocation of a utopian reconciliation with nature, one which balks at all practical realization.

It remains that aesthetics—unlike ethics—is concerned with historically dated and completed objects which have the particularity of being able to influence well beyond the time of their creation.[27] If aesthetic judgment renders "present" an experience crystallized in the work, one must admit that the work itself is not devoid of that rationality that criticism realizes; "a moment of reason is affirmed in the autonomy of the radically differentiated domain of avant-garde art."[28] Before analyzing the activity which consists in appropriating and making available the experience contained in the work, it is thus necessary to examine the rationality inherent in the aesthetic object, without which there is neither aesthetic nor critical experience. Without it, the work of art remains reason's irrational other and gains access to rationality only in critical discourse.

Traditional art—narrative, coherent, significant by itself—often seems to be rational in that it is composed of elements arising from a cognitive or moral rationality; on the other hand, modern art distinguishes itself precisely—and Adorno stresses this—by its apparent irrationality. It is this which led Nietzsche to see in the work of Wagner a resurgence of "presocratic" Dionysianism, radically foreign to the modern *logos*. The problem thus consists in identifying, precisely in this modern art which is reduced to that

which is unique to it, the element which constitutes aesthetic validity—that in the name of which a work is considered a success—and which allows it to be judged. This brings us back to associating the rationality of the work of art with its validity as a work.

Aesthetics always comes up against the difficulty of reconciling the virtually universal validity of the successful work, the equivocal or polysemous character of this universality, and the singular character of the experience to which it gives form (often even of the material in which it is realized). Kant thus speaks of a universality without the intervention of a concept, Adorno of a nonsignificant eloquence. In both cases, one of the terms has a particular connotation: for Kant, the nonconceptual aspect expresses both a deficiency which turns art into the "symbol of morality," and a path which leads to a moral life; for Adorno, eloquence is paradoxically univocal: it tells of the suffering that knowledge cannot express, and thus the difference between works becomes secondary in relation to the "nonrepresentable" which is the content of truth.

Art—especially modern art—is thus a language, but a language charged with intense energy and which denies communication.[29] Aesthetic eloquence establishes itself in two ways: by a break with the established significations of ordinary language and by the creation of a singularized and intensified language, a language "for one." The elaboration of this language "for one" transforms it into a language "for all," made virtually universal by dint of its intelligibility, which necessitates a deciphering.[30] Aesthetic comprehension—and criticism—is thus an art of translation which causes the apparent singularity of the work (and of the experience which constitutes it) to attain a virtually universal signification, but which is for its own part a function of a particular actualization. The unity of aesthetic "validity" does not in any way reduce the diversity of the "nonsignificant eloquence" particular to each work, nor the plurality of interpretations of which each can become the object, precisely to the extent that it is successful.

For Adorno, the particular nature of modern art was a function of reality—of absolute suffering under the reign of totalitarian identity—about which artworks unfurled their eloquence. According to the concept which has just been sketched, modern art is essentially a function of an internal necessity of decentralized subjectivity; a language "for one" charged with individual energy, which becomes "language for all" when the work is successful, is a proposal of meaning[31] in the form of contingent figures and ordered materials.

The intensified proposals of meaning do not form a continuous tradition, according to the concept of hermeneutics; nor do they reveal a hidden essence along the line of the truth of being, but rather, a fragile construction whose internal coherence is always a little strained. That which saves the meaning—that rare commodity of postmetaphysical modernity—from contingency and total arbitrariness, is the fact that its elaboration is subterraneanly a collective work, constantly nourished by the social exchange of experiences, which is the foundation of artistic configurations; no singularity deprived of all supra-individual signification can crystallize into a work.

Proposals of meaning reflect an interpretation and an arrangement of sensitive perception for which the accuracy of tone and the original character of the experience (and of the language found to express it) count more than the conformity to facts and to norms. Art is not in the order of the everyday, even though it seeks its epiphanies in the most ordinary life; it can take the liberty—and this is in fact what one expects from it—of ignoring the intersubjective demands which constitute daily life in society. Only in this way does the stylization of the proposal of meaning become possible. For the receiving subjects, impressed by this ordering of meaning acquired at the price of a certain number of abstractions, the proposal will be confronted with suitable experiences, but also with quotidian demands, and its pertinence will be tested against the true and the just.

From here onwards, one can attempt to explain—without premature reference to historical reality—certain characteristics of modern art, notably the status of negativity and its avatars. According to our hypothesis, the proposal for a coherence of meaning based upon an absolutely singular experience brings into play the demand for a radical expression of self which—from Baudelaire to Beckett—comes up against rigid and intolerant social structures. It is this which gives to aesthetic singularity the appearance of the destructive, satanic, revolted negative. It breaks with the everyday and the constraints of rational subjectivity to bring to life an instant of absolute presence. The sudden shock of ecstasy or of sacred horror snatches it away from all habit and from all familiarity and plunges it into a lucid rapture. Extreme singularity wounds hopes for inviolable personal integrity, whose pathological deformations it denounces while at the same time becoming attached to them in as much as they are images of singularity. So long as the singularity of the subject is not established, it appears demoniac, and art is inhabited by a spirit of revolt; once it is recognized—and it is this which seems today to be the case—art loses its role of representing the "accursed part." Initially subversive, artists tend to become public characters, proposing each of their singularities as a model across the schemas of their experience. Contrary to that which maximalist modernity dreads, it is not the absolute singularity whose existence is menaced, that will be mutilated, leveled, or abolished by social normalization. What risks generalization is a singularity that is without universal bearing, a pluralism of "differences," empty and flatulent.[32] At the extreme, current culture tends to multiply voiceless narcissisms one upon another, and to confuse the fugitive attention that they arouse with aesthetic or intellectual expression. Hence also, during a certain time, the cult of madness, of perversions and of abnormalities of all sorts, which themselves have no aesthetic value, but only documentary interest. The demand for aesthetic validity

which characterizes an intensified proposal of meaning calls for a symmetry between the "voice" emanating from the work and that of the receiving subject; so long as it is a "proposal of meaning," the work is not a psychoanalytical "case" which one studies, and this symmetry is the basis of aesthetic rationality.

In accordance with its subversive side, aesthetic singularity thus questions the forms of social normativity which uselessly limit the expression of self. Inversely, coherence of meaning, placed under the demand for originality, is ceaselessly confronted with the resistance of the nonmeaningful and the untenable. From Manet and Baudelaire to Beckett and Bacon, the sovereignty of art affirms itself in the face of the negative and the insignificant. The work is a "proposal" of meaning at the risk of failure: of a meaning which can remain private or of limited interest. In the course of this process, the means employed to affirm the sovereignty of the artist are continually reduced to the "essential": to the expression of an invincible singularity, inexpressible in existing artistic languages. Basic geometric shapes, primitive strokes, pure or elementary colors, bidimensionality, distanced daily objects, raw materials, displayed in the context of a show, can play this role, and arouse the shock of the inartistic annexed by the sovereignty of the artistic sphere.

"Proposal of meaning" signifies finally that the language "for one"—the singularity of the work which seeks to be recognized as singular universal[33]—must be presented to an audience, in order to put to the test its virtually universal intelligibility, its effect of aesthetic coherence as a singularized language, and its power to make the singularity of its experience resonate in the historical experience of the receiving subjects. It is thus necessary that the work overcome at least the three stumbling blocks of absolute singularity: being nonintelligible or stripped of interest; the obstacle of aesthetic incoherence, or that of a break in tone incompletely mastered; and of inadequacy to historical expectations of originality, or of the nontopicality of the dissonance to which it responds.

Contrary to dramaturgical activity in daily life, which aims at influencing others to attain a precise goal, the presentation of works before an anonymous audience—a sort of generalized Other—establishes a contract between the work and its viewers.[34] Nothing, in fact, obliges them to subject themselves to the discipline of the work, but once they have freely abandoned themselves to it, they will experience—or not—the internal necessity, and will recognize it by their aesthetic emotion and their critical judgment. It is this logic which makes of art (and of the aesthetic experience) a sphere of a demand for validity analogous to those which define science and ethics, but of a weaker demand, incapable of assuring the cohesion of society; it is a demand without an immediate "illocutory force," without necessary consequence for daily life. That which could have welded together the audience of certain works in the past—recited epics, tragedies presented before the entire city on special occasions—was due to values other than aesthetic. The modern novel and painting, or recorded music, address themselves to an isolated individual; and the collective experience of the concert, of the theater, and of the cinema, even if it can mobilize shared values, does not create any real tie capable of uniting individuals outside of the aesthetic space.

The demand for truth always comes back to a necessity inherent in the arguments, and only in the second place to facts and events (which cannot of themselves assert their truth). The demand for moral justice is already inherent in the norms themselves, whose legitimacy is presupposed in every modern society, and only secondly in the arguments which justify them.[35] As for the aesthetic demand, it is expressed by each singular, historically situated work which offers itself to the public, and only secondly by the criticism which justifies it, which recommends it or contests its value. But unlike truth and justice, no subject is obliged to accept the proposal of aesthetic meaning. If truth and justice are fallible, their demand is peremptory once one is obliged to admit its pertinence; the universality of a work of art, and more recently, of certain films evoking solidarity, remains on the contrary precarious and tied to the possibility of actualizing singular experience. That is why there exists a mortal rivalry among the works for the conquest of a universality of meaning; in this rivalry, the contingency of the subject's situation—which gives the subject access to a privileged experience—escapes the will of the artist. It is the "natural" part of the "genius"; only the capacity to exploit it, to confer upon it the form of a language "for all," is within the province of the artist.

The cognitive and moral dimensions of language tend to parenthesize the particular meaning of the historic situation; the existence or the nonexistence of the facts and events, the normative adequation or inadequation of maxims of action and of institutions do not imply in themselves any relation of these demands either to the plans of the subjects or to the ultimate goals that they are pursuing. Intensified proposals of meaning schematize in pregnant materials the historical interpretations of the desires and the situations of the world; they thus reduce the metaphysical projects of the past to horizons of meaning that subjectivity assigns to itself in the aesthetic space.[36] In modern society, this meaning must prove itself in the process of artistic reception, where it interacts with other demands for validity and with rival proposals. Postmodern "aestheto-centrism," inspired by the Nietzschean theory of the "artist philosopher," can thus be understood as a refusal of this reduction of metaphysics to a hypothetical status, to simple proposals of meaning; it is through loyalty to the lost absolute that everything is reduced to a game of appearances.

. . . . .

What makes Adorno correct in his analysis of radical modernity is that, until recently, most artists themselves admitted the logic of the worst and of apocalyptic anticipation. From Baudelaire to Beckett, including Kafka and Schönberg, modernity constantly repeated an apocalyptic

blackmail which aimed to force the course of history. It is this implicit theology which collapses along with maximalist modernity. But just as the moral catastrophes of the twentieth century prohibit, in ethics, a simple "return to" a classical doctrine, and necessitate instead a redefinition of moral theory, neither can aesthetics go back in time. To reformulate the conditions of recognition of an action or a work does not mean to dissolve all criteria in "contextuality."

Writers like Thomas Bernhard illustrate the passage from the apocalyptic vision (e.g., *Corrections*) to a proposal of meaning of the minimalist type (*Le neveu de Wittgenstein*). One may regret the passing of the fascinating beauty of the apocalyptic works, animated as they are by a certainty which transcends singularity, for even the nonmeaningful in them is more powerful than the risk of triviality that lies in wait for the atheological creator; but the decline of this type of creation has seemed inevitable since the banalization of singular difference. At the same time, the proposal of meaning that was apocalyptic blackmail— "going beyond real negativity by the despair of the imagination," according to Adorno's formula—becomes an option among others, somewhat historically dated, and one would seek in these works that which connects with the stylization of a singularity. In this sense, postmodern "sensibility" is a proposal of meaning that is legitimate in itself.

Such an aesthetics—and it is still this which distinguishes it from that of Adorno—is not the principal support of a critical theory of society; it is complementary to an ethics inscribed in the ordinary language of modern societies. This ethics constitutes the normative expectations of reciprocity which allow for evaluation of the legitimacy of the social order and of equity in interpersonal relations. In a society which plays against the universality of egalitarian commerce the card of singularity and of the "difference" of each one—including anarchist and ultraconservative impulses—aesthetics cannot of itself represent the normative base of criticism. Tolerance for the expression of singularities serves often as a safety valve for persistent injustices. As for works of post-avant-gardist modernity which content themselves with seeking a "secular illumination" in the frame of a world which is neither the worst nor the best, their critical force will be all the greater as their normative reference is no longer an inverse image of redemption, but rather a meaning which is conceivable here below, here and now.

Notes

1. Cf. Jürgen Habermas, "La Modernité: un projet inachevé," translated by G. Raulet, *Critique,* no. 413 (October 1981): 950-69.

2. Jean-François Lyotard, *La Condition postmoderne* (Paris: Éditions de Minuit, 1979) and A. Wellmer, *Zur Dialektik von Moderne und Postmoderne* (Frankfurt: Suhrkamp Verlag, 1985) converge in this way up to a certain point in their criticism of Haber-

mas. [Jean-François Lyotard, *The Postmodern Condition: A Report on Knowledge,* translated by Geoff Bennington and Brian Massumi, foreword by Frederic Jameson (Manchester: Manchester University Press; Minneapolis: University of Minnesota Press, 1984).]

3. Theodor W. Adorno, *Dialectique négative* (Paris: Éditions Payot, 1978), 11. [Originally published in German as *Negative Dialektik* (Frankfurt: Suhrkamp Verlag, 1966). English edition, *Negative Dialectics,* translated by E. B. Ashton (London: Routledge & Kegan Paul; New York: Seabury Press, 1973).]

4. *Dialectique négative,* 15.

5. *Dialectique négative,* 12.

6. The *Aesthetic Theory* defines the content of the verities in works of art as "the act of freeing oneself from myth and bringing about a reconciliation with it" [trans. C. Lenhardt (London: Routledge & Kegan Paul, 1983), 266]. This definition is borrowed from Walter Benjamin's essay on Goethe. The schema is invariably applied in all the concrete interpretations of Adorno, whether it is a matter of Goethe or Balzac, of Schönberg, of Kafka, or of Beckett. [This and subsequent references to the English translation of *Aesthetic Theory* are for the convenience of the reader. In most cases, we have translated directly from the French translation by Marc Jimenez (Paris: Éditions Klincksieck, 1974), as cited in the original form of the article.]

7. Albrecht Wellmer, "Wahrheit, Schein, Versöhnung. Adornos ästhetische Rettung der Modernität," in *Zur Dialektik,* 9-47 (cf. note 2).

8. Cf. Jürgen Habermas, *Théorie de l'agir communicationnel,* translated by Jean-Marc Ferry and Jean-Louis Schlegel (Paris: Éditions Arthème Fayard, 1987), vol. 1, 371ff. [Originally published in German as *Theorie des kommunikativen Handelns,* 2 vols. (Frankfurt: Suhrkamp Verlag, 1981-85). English translation, *The Theory of Communicative Action,* 2 vols., translated by Thomas McCarthy (London: Heinemann; Boston: Beacon Press, 1984-87).]

9. This is what Wellmer calls the "dialectic of aesthetic appearance," *Zur Dialektik,* 15ff. Cf. Horkheimer and Adorno, *La dialectique de la raison,* trans. E. Kaufholz (Paris: Éditions Gallimard, 1974), 35-36. [Originally published in German as *Philosophische Fragmente* (New York: Institute of Social Research, 1944). English edition, *Dialectic of Enlightenment,* translated by John Cumming (London: Allen Lane; New York: Seabury Press, 1972).]

10. *Dialectique de la raison,* 36: "In so far as an expression of totality, art claims the dignity of the absolute. It is this which has at times prompted philosophy to concede the primacy over knowledge to art. According to Schelling, art begins at the point where knowledge fails; art is 'the model of science and is already found where science has yet to penetrate.' According to his theory, the separation of the image and the sign is 'completely abolished each time that there is an artistic representation.' The bourgeois world was only rarely inclined to show such trust in art."

11. *Aesthetic Theory,* 31.

12. In connection with the young Marx, it was often observed that his criticism of alienated work was based upon a creativist model close to the human ideal of the Renaissance and of German idealism. If this model disappears in *Das Kapital, Aesthetic Theory* goes back to a normative basis founded on the model of artistic creation.

13. This is why Adorno's aesthetics remain in a sense an aesthetics of "reflection" (cf. Wellmer, *Zur Dialektik,* 29).

14. With the exception of Peter Bürger, the German critics of Adorno question the predominance of the concept of truth in his aesthetics. They propose either a theory of aesthetic pleasure, indifferent to truth (Karl Heinz Bohrer, Rüdiger Bubner), or a relativization of the concept of truth (authenticity with Franz Koppe; "potential for truth" with Albrecht Wellmer).

15. Art is truly modern, according to Adorno, "when it has the capacity to absorb the results of industrialization under capitalist relations of production, while following its own experiential mode and at the same time giving expression to the crisis of experience." *Aesthetic Theory,* 50.

16. "To be sure, autonomy remains irrevocable. . . . Today, however, autonomous art begins to manifest an aspect of blindness. . . . It is not certain that after its total emancipation, art would not have undermined and lost those presuppositions which made it possible." *Aesthetic Theory,* 1-2.

17. *Aesthetic Theory,* 35.

18. *Aesthetic Theory,* 35.

19. *Aesthetic Theory,* 36.

20. *Aesthetic Theory,* 43.

21. *Aesthetic Theory,* 43.

22. *Aesthetic Theory,* 44.

23. *Aesthetic Theory,* 47.

24. It is this which Jürgen Habermas (*Théorie de l'agir communicationnel,* and Albrecht Wellmer (*Zur Dialektik*) demonstrate.

25. "The total subjective elaboration of art, in so far as it is a nonconceptual language, is, at the stage of rationality, the only figure in which something is reflected which resembles the language of Creation. . . . Art tries to imitate an expression that would not contain human intention." *Aesthetic Theory,* 115.

26. Wellmer, *Zur Dialektik*; Martin Seel, *Die Kunst der Entzweiung: Zum Begriff der ästhetischen Rationalität* (Frankfurt: Suhrkamp Verlag, 1985).

27. Cf. György Lukács, *Philosophie de l'art (1912-1914): premiers écrits sur l'esthétique,* translated by Rainer Rochlitz and Alain Pernet (Paris: Éditions Klincksieck, 1981), 159ff. [Originally published in German as *Heidelberger Philosophie der Kunst (1912-1914),* edited by György Márkus and Frank Benseler (Darmstadt: Luchterhand, 1975).]

28. Jürgen Habermas, *Der philosophische Diskurs der Moderne* (Frankfurt: Suhrkamp Verlag, 1985), 117. [English edition as *The Philosophical Discourse of Modernity: Twelve Lectures,* translated by Frederick Lawrence (Cambridge: Polity, in association with Basil Blackwell; Cambridge, Mass.: MIT Press, 1987).]

29. Wellmer (*Zur Dialektik,* 62ff.) emphasizes the equal importance of signifying and energetic aspects in the aesthetic object.

30. It is this process which is dealt with by the phenomenology of the creative process developed by Lukács in his *Philosophie de l'art,* 41ff.

31. "The power to create meaning, presently confined for the most part to aesthetic domains, remains contingent as does any truly innovative force." Habermas, *Der philosophische Diskurs der Moderne,* 373. According to Lukács's *Philosophie de l'art,* a work of art is the utopia of a world which can satisfy our expectations of integral self-realization. Such a definition excludes negative works from art, whereas the "proposition of meaning" accepts the affirmation of an experience of nonmeaning.

32. Michel Foucault had observed this phenomenon of a deceptive individuation in contemporary society, attributing it unilaterally to a result of power; cf. *Surveiller et punir* (Paris: Éditions Gallimard, 1975) [English edition as *Discipline and Punish: The Birth of the Prison,* translated by Alan Sheridan (London: Allen Lane; New York: Pantheon Books, 1978)] and *Volonté de savoir* (Paris: Éditions Gallimard, 1976) [English translation as *The History of Sexuality,* vol. 1, *An Introduction,* translated by Robert Hurley (London: Allen Lane; New York: Pantheon Books, 1978).]

33. Cf. Jean-Paul Sartre, *L'Idiot de la famille: Gustave Flaubert de 1821 à 1857,* 3 vols., Bibliothèque de philosophie (Paris: Éditions Gallimard, 1971-83), vol. 1, 7. [English translation as *The Family Idiot: Gustave Flaubert, 1821-1857,* translated by Carol Cosman (Chicago: University of Chicago Press, 1981-).]

34. Cf. *Aesthetic Theory,* 108: "The viewer unknowingly and unintentionally signs a contract with the art work, as it were, pledging to subordinate himself to the work on condition that it speak to him."

35. Cf. Jürgen Habermas, *Morale et communication,* translated by Chr. Bouchindhomme (Paris: Édition du Cerf, 1986), 80ff. [Originally in German as *Moralbewuβtsein und kommunikatives Handeln* (Frankfurt: Suhrkamp Verlag, 1983).]

36. Cf. Lukács, *Philosophie de l'art,* 213-26.

Rüdiger Bubner (essay date 1989)

SOURCE: "Concerning the Central Idea of Adorno's Philosophy," in *The Semblance of Subjectivity: Essays in Adorno's Aesthetic Theory,* edited by Tom Huhn and Lambert Zuidervaart, The MIT Press, 1997, pp. 147–75.

[*In the following essay, originally published in German in 1989, Bubner interprets the major points of Adorno's philosophical system.*]

"I do not want to decide whether my theory is grounded in a particular understanding of humanity and human existence. I deny, however, that it is necessary to have recourse to such an understanding." This lapidary statement occurs at the end of the *Aktualität der Philosophie,* the inaugural lecture with which Theodor W. Adorno began his academic career in 1931.[1] The lecture is important because it foreshadows many of the main ideas of his later philosophy. The statement itself reflects an orientation toward philosophy Adorno would maintain throughout his life.

Adorno's philosophical theses arise from certain fundamental assumptions, as do all meaningful propositions and especially those expressing pure theoretical insights. His intentional and emphatic refusal, however, to give an account of his premises is responsible for the form these assumptions take in the course of their theoretical development. Most assumptions that inform our everyday thinking and discussions about the world are so self-evident we pay no attention to them whatsoever. It is, however, theory's unique task to provide the most exhaustive and airtight account possible of just such tacit assumptions. Since its inception, philosophical theory has embraced an ethos urging the establishment of rational grounds. Adorno's startling statement, of which there are many others like it, does not deny that theories are constructed in this way. Instead, it calls into question our received ideas about theory in order to challenge their claims. For Adorno, the point is not to discover a different type of theory or to jettison theory tout court and replace it with a new, irrational mode of expression. Adorno remains firmly oriented toward an understanding of theory that "refuses to abandon philosophy."[2] Only against the backdrop of this explicitly philosophical orientation does Adorno's refusal to account for first principles, in the traditional sense, have any meaning at all. Nothing else, however, pervades Adorno's philosophy so thoroughly as his unremitting refusal to meet theory's traditional demands.

In the inaugural lecture, Adorno goes on to appeal to the essay as the appropriate form for philosophical discourse.[3]

Later on, this approach, from which Adorno's mature theory will emerge, is formulated in various ways. For example, "critical theory" characterizes his entire undertaking. "Negative dialectic" describes the leading intention behind the polemics he wages against Hegel. An important catchphrase is the "dialectic of enlightenment." Adorno's thought, however, finds its definitive expression in the title *Aesthetic Theory.* This posthumously published work has proven to be his true philosophical testament. As is well known, the title is equivocal. "Aesthetic theory" does not only mean that theoretical aesthetics is one subdivision of an extensive, theoretical edifice. More important, it means that the text's main concern is the process by which theory itself becomes aesthetic—the convergence of knowledge and art. "Aesthetics is not a form of applied philosophy, rather it is in itself philosophical."[4] What does this mean?

HISTORICAL DIAGNOSIS

The question I pursue here aims at discovering the reasons that, for Adorno, theory must give way to aesthetics. Even to raise this question is tantamount to dismissing out of hand both Adorno's refusal to reveal what his premises are and the verdict that the question itself is petty and lacks refinement. Such a purely stylistic concern, which makes it taboo to tamper with an argument's finely wrought unity, is usually a manifestation of sophistry and of little philosophical value. Adorno would have certainly fended off questions like the one I just raised by saying that there is no place within the structure of his work where they can gain a foothold. This objection is to be rejected. To maintain a stony silence when confronted with a call for the reasons that ground the type of theory Adorno advocates does not make the theory in any way more plausible.

Adorno, however, does give a thorough explanation of his motivation for encouraging silence. He argues *historically.* The demand to specify the foundations presupposed by theory is a relic of idealism's overestimation of philosophy's importance and continues to foster the illusion that thought contains an absolute beginning.

> "Philosophy, however, that no longer presumes to be autonomous, that no longer believes reality to be grounded in the *ratio,* but time and again assumes the transgression of an autonomous, rational legislation by a Being that is not adequate to such legislation and cannot be rationally construed as a totality, will not pursue to the end the path leading back to rational premises but will come to a standstill wherever irreducible reality intrudes. . . . The intrusion of irreducible reality occurs concretely and historically, and this is why history keeps the movement of thought from returning to presuppositions."[5]

To begin with, it is not at all convincing to denounce every theory's search for grounds as being tainted with idealistic presumption. Ever since the Socratic challenge of the *logon didonai,* it has been one of philosophy's most basic tenets to give an account of why we say what we say. In addition, rationalism's various systems have claimed to provide proof that their respective principles

were absolute and could not be surpassed by any other. That was true for Spinoza and especially for Fichte and Schelling, who both, not by chance, returned to Spinoza. In contrast, Hegel, whom Adorno quotes with particular relish when it comes to idealistic hubris, showed much more caution than his contemporaries, who were always too quick to assert that they had surpassed each other in building unsurpassable systems. The absoluteness Hegel's philosophy in fact lays claim to did not arise out of historical myopia or the arbitrary positing of abstract principles. Rather, it was acquired on the basis of consistently confronting the one immutable idea of philosophy with the experience of the historically contingent forms the idea must assume if there is to be philosophy at all. All of this, however, does not directly concern us.[6] What is at issue here is Adorno's reluctance to give an account of his own underlying philosophical premises.

Adorno's reference to an *irreducible Being,* which intrudes on philosophy through the backdoor of history, is either a surreptitious way of establishing grounds or nothing more than an empty incantation. The first alternative gives rise to difficulties that I will consider below. Understood as an example of the polemics Adorno continually wages against Heidegger, the second alternative is pointless to pursue. The surprising parallels between Adorno's early works and Heidegger's *Seinsphilosophie,* do, however, bear closer examination.[7] From early on, Adorno never tired of pillorying the "new ontology" as the form par excellence of ahistorical hypostasis.[8] With the publication of *Being and Time* (1927), which immediately received wide recognition, Adorno must have clearly sensed his unsettling philosophical proximity to Heidegger. The way Heidegger sometimes expresses his hope for a Being that will directly reveal itself at the end of traditional metaphysics' long history of decline, a Being that only makes itself known within the dimension of concrete existence, beyond the reach of philosophical insight, comes very close indeed to mirroring many of Adorno's theses. In order to undermine the outward impression that he might have shared similar insights with Heidegger, Adorno emphasized, in the strongest possible terms, the substantial differences between their two philosophical standpoints.

Adorno thus pursues throughout his *Habilitationsschrift* on Kierkegaard the ulterior motive of contesting existentialism's appropriation of this church father of the protest against Hegel's brand of idealism.[9] Adorno also takes Heidegger to task for his dubious and, in terms of style, not exactly surefooted attempts to take refuge in poetic metaphor in order to avoid the atrophy that, according to Heidegger, had overtaken the expressive power of the language traditionally used by philosophers.[10] Only later, however, did Adorno succeed in delivering the decisive blow that contributed to removing Heidegger from the center of public influence. As Heidegger's star began to fade during the period of Germany's restoration after the Second World War, Adorno's essay called *The Jargon of Authenticity,* intended as a pamphlet, certainly came at precisely the right moment. Since then, the laconic expression *Sein* has been taken out of circulation and replaced by the more complicated sounding *das Nichtidentische*. What is meant in both cases is that reality eludes or, in Adorno's words, is not absorbed by the philosophical concept. Only insofar as the concept recognizes reality can the dimension of truth really be disclosed to it. As Adorno writes, "[C]oncepts for their part are moments of the reality that requires their formation."[11]

Those who are not satisfied with bare, emphatic assertions can interpret the reference to historical experience, which forbids recourse to rational premises, as itself an unacknowledged premise for the type of theory Adorno has in mind. The grounding of theory must be carried out in a way which shows that precisely today, under the prevailing conditions of the here and now, and after society has reached its present level of historical development, it has become impossible to return to the old naive way of pursuing philosophy. Adorno's work resonates from many sides with similar formulations. But why should an account of the historical hour be sufficient to bid "traditional theory" a final farewell and to put in its place a form of theory whose sole function is "critique," a theory "which holds that the core of truth is historical, rather than an unchanging constant to be set against the movement of history"?[12] The blanket answer to this question is *mystification* [*Verblendungszusammenhang*], that is, the profound and all-pervasive blindness to sociohistorical truth that sets in once society has fallen under the sway of ideology.

According to this thesis, in all societies in the grip of late capitalism, ideology has become so total and totalizing that there is no way to escape its influence. Even the simple act of stating what is falls prey to mystification, for it necessarily fails to add that everything that is should not have been in the first place. Thus, every statement made in the interests of serving truth must simultaneously recant the insight it was meant to express. Such a paradoxical use of language immediately exhausts theory's already-limited possibilities. All hope must now be directed toward another type of language, toward art. "The true is revealed to discursive knowledge, but for all that, not attained; the knowledge that is art has the true, but as something incommensurable."[13]

DRIVE TOWARD TOTALITY

Before it is possible to understand how art can function as a substitute for theory in the context of the above considerations, we must discuss the difficulties implicit in Adorno's historical diagnosis that underlies the transition from theory to art. The controversy surrounding historical diagnosis has nothing at all to do with actual assessments of the current political situation or with occasional ad hoc attempts to improve it. Nor does it have anything to do with a strategy of moral intimidation that all too easily silences naive doubt, by holding up examples of cataclysmic historical events. Rather, what is problematic is the paralysis the diagnosis brings on itself by assuming that everything is exactly as it makes it out to be. The belief in the totaliz-

ing power of ideology to mystify all aspects of modern life, including our own individual powers of judgment, thoroughly deprives theory of the freedom to move within its own sphere of operation. Under the distorting lens of historical diagnosis, everything, without exception, appears reified. As a result, theory completely succumbs to the very same coercive ideology it was, in fact, enlisted to describe.

Trading in hypotheses, tedious to-and-fro argumentation, ponderous deliberations, proofs, objections, questions raised about other theories and about itself—all this drops away as soon as the diagnosis calls the universal spell by its proper name. Thereafter, it would be an example of systematic self-delusion if theory carried on as if nothing at all had happened. The moment at which historical truth is revealed simultaneously ushers in the moment at which historical truth slips forever beyond theory's grasp, a negative *kairos*. Because it now senses that all of its knowledge is unavoidably false, theory also realizes that truth by means of theory is no longer possible. With this insight, its concepts are subjected to an entirely heteronomous determination.

The paralysis that has overtaken theory now sets in on its object and affects the process by which theory determines what its appropriate field of inquiry should be. This, however, fundamentally contradicts the avowed intentions of *critique* and *dialectic*. The very same totality, with which theory has invested the *bruta facta* of ideology, consistently ties the hands of critique. Confronted with the opponent's superior strength, theory has only one viable recourse—to strike back with the most stringent, thoroughgoing form of negativity. Because, as theory itself has shown, there can no longer be any exceptions to the global rule of ideology, it is forced to denounce everything under the sun as being a product of ideology. The bogus ideal of totality, which theory in its newly won role of critique attributes to traditional systems, insidiously turns back on theory with the same intensity with which it afflicts everything else.

In order to preserve its critical edge over against a world dominated by the totalizing effects of ideology, theory must target the objects of its inquiries before it has direct knowledge of them. It must maintain a critical attitude toward these objects to ensure that it deals with them impartially and remains immune to whatever charms they may hold for it. Theory must keep itself at a safe distance from the flux of phenomena and reestablish this distance whenever they threaten to lead it astray. To sustain its opposition toward what is immediately given, theory is forced endlessly to redefine itself by successive acts of reflection. This means, however, that theory winds up being driven by an inner necessity to validate itself and thus replicates the dogmatic self-certainty displayed by the philosophical concept—the object of Adorno's unmitigated contempt.[14]

As much as Adorno would like to claim that the emergence of Critical Theory is historical and concrete, the truth of the matter lies elsewhere. In fact, it is based on sweeping, a priori assumptions. These assumptions, guiding the course of Adorno's earlier thinking, remain just as much in force later on. Adorno himself confirms this in a chance observation: "Actually, there is one ontology maintained throughout history, the ontology of despair. If, however, ontology is what is perennial, then thought experiences every historical period as the worst and, most of all, its own which it knows directly."[15] To be secure in the belief that from its very beginning the world has always been thoroughly degenerate makes every present historical moment appear in the most dismal light. Because historical diagnosis is guided by such foreknowledge, it necessarily cuts off all discussion.

As we have just seen, Critical Theory does, in fact, rest on a *full-fledged theory of history that claims ontological status.* If such a theoretical foundation did not exist, Adorno would not have proposed so vehemently that we renounce traditional theories in favor of one whose sole function is to unmask the workings of ideology. Of course, to avoid the penalty of transgressing all that Critical Theory stands for, the actual underlying ontology must remain out of the discussion. The validity of such a foundation, however, can be tested only when it is openly defended in discussion. This would allow for an undogmatic assessment of Critical Theory's soundness. Adorno, however, deliberately formulates all his arguments to preclude such a possibility. We thus have no other choice but to follow the clues implicit in his silence. This will lead us into the terrain of aesthetics.

Adorno bans discussion not out of a desire to surround his argument in an aura of mystery. On the contrary, the strategy of keeping silent acquires an overt and novel function within the architectonic that underpins a highly intricate thought progression. Adorno's position, that theory is no longer viable in a world dominated by ideology, must be construed as his attempt to demonstrate the necessity of the transition from philosophy to aesthetics. Yet in order to continue to give expression to theory's departure from its traditional function of establishing grounds, Adorno offers a special form of discourse. Instead of following Wittgenstein's famous maxim to keep silent on that about which there is nothing to say, Adorno transforms aesthetics into the one legitimate way to speak about the ban on speaking about theory per se.

DIALECTIC OF ENLIGHTENMENT

It has been often observed that the *Dialectic of Enlightenment* holds the keys to understanding Adorno's *Aesthetic Theory.*[16] The studies or "philosophical fragments" that constitute the *Dialectic of Enlightenment* were written while Horkheimer and Adorno lived in exile in the United States. The text is characterized by the authors' own political and existential concerns, translated into general philosophical terms. It occupies a central place in their thought because it does not, as is usually the case with their other work, subject external issues to critique but turns critique back on itself so that it becomes its own object: "the point is . . . that the Enlightenment *must consider itself.*"[17] Against the backdrop of their historical experience of fascism, as well as Stalin's perversion of Marxist theory, they felt it had become imperative to embark on a critique of ideology, which, since Marx, had remained nothing more than a desideratum.

If the critique of ideology is not based on a "socially detached intelligentsia," as Karl Mannheim's sociology of knowledge would have us believe, what then is the special form of objectivity the critics are so deeply rooted in that they are not blinded by the universal mystification caused by ideology?[18] Or is the critique of ideology secretly just as prone to ideological appropriation as all those theories it relentlessly takes to task? Lukács was one of the first to be struck by the problem of how enlightenment becomes stymied once orthodoxy sets in. His remedy is to introduce Hegel's concept of reflection into Marx's concept of class consciousness. One should not underestimate the role Lukács's important book *History and Class Consciousness* played in inspiring the Frankfurt School. Nevertheless, Lukács's attempt to identify the one revolutionary class, the proletariat, as the sole bearer of historically correct consciousness could not, in the final analysis, prevent the decline in political relevance of a theory that had once been the source of so much hope.

The idea of a "dialectic of enlightenment" deals with the paradox that a dialectic plays with enlightenment instead of explicitly working in its interests. In contrast to Marx, whose dialectical method coincided with the possibility of real historical progress, Horkheimer and Adorno conceive the process of enlightenment itself as succumbing to a dialectical reversal into its opposite, a reversal that takes place behind the back of enlightened reflection.[19] This, however, should not be confused with Hegel's critique of enlightenment, which was meant to overcome the biased nature of enlightened reflection in order to open the way for a truly speculative movement of ideas. Adorno and Horkheimer specifically intend that their dialectic of enlightenment should not culminate in absolute knowing. Indeed, for them, idealism's final configuration continually serves as an ominous reminder of how philosophy is brought to a standstill. How is it possible to make use of Hegel's dialectic and, at the same time, be dead set against its logical and historical consequences?

To prevent theory from being absorbed by idealist speculation, it is necessary to check the automatic, dialectical progression from reason's critique of enlightenment, as carried out in the realm of the understanding, to the autonomy that theory achieves in Hegel's system. This requires, in defiance of enlightened thinking, that a natural prerogative be granted to all those deep-seated prejudices and superstitions from which enlightenment promises to emancipate humankind. The privileged position these irrational beliefs have in our thinking, however, is obvious from the fact that, despite all its efforts, enlightenment always fails to dislodge them. All the exertion expended in good faith to raise this intractably irrational substance to the level of the concept comes to absolutely nothing. The more enlightenment is convinced of itself and the correctness of what it does, the more it risks being dominated by the same irrational principle it struggles to supplant. Thus, in the end, reason's omnipotence turns out to be just as irrational as nature's despotism, against which all the first cultural revolutions were fought. In this way, the dialectic of enlightenment is made to atone for the Fall that, before all recorded time, drove humankind out of paradise and into history.

In order to describe this hard-to-grasp dialectical reversal of enlightenment into its opposite, Adorno and Horkheimer introduce a concept of myth that, however much it may have been inspired by Judeo-Christian tradition, is at odds with all usual meanings of the word. We might consider Rousseau's ambivalence toward modernity in general and the Enlightenment in particular to help see how a projection back through history to an original state of nature is solely a consequence of the Enlightenment's having reached the zenith of its historical development and yet, at the same time, is the standard by which the Enlightenment measures reason's historical progress. Understood in this way, Rousseau's fictional reconstruction of the state of nature serves as a mirror in which the hopes of the Enlightenment are reflected from afar, and the sins, inherent in cultural progress, seem to be completely wiped away. Myth is not a word for a primordial state out of which human reason slowly and successfully evolved. On the contrary, reason is already present in the earliest myths; conversely, the mythical maintains its presence throughout the Enlightenment's entire historical development. The culmination of the Enlightenment in scientific knowledge is, in fact, a reversion to earliest times, which shows, contrary to the expectations of philosophers and other enlightened thinkers, that nothing at all has changed.

Precisely understood, the word "myth" maps out a dimension that is not affected by the dialectic of history, because it forms the basis of this dialectic.[20] This reveals the limits and futility of believing in open-ended historical progress; in whatever direction history may happen to push forward, it cannot escape this pregiven situation.[21] Of course, corresponding to this understanding of history is a vaguely defined ideal of an *eschatological reconciliation* in which all differences are eliminated, all errors are avoided, and historical change is brought to an absolute standstill. Knowledge of this reconciliation lies beyond the finite capacity of our rational faculties and, therefore, also avoids being compromised by our ideological thinking. As mere mortals, however, we can experience such a reconciliation only in the limited way afforded to us by the pseudoreality created by art.[22]

Philosophy has a concept available that, as a product of reason, marks out, in the most subtle way, reason's own limits—the concept of *illusion*. Although, in the first place, illusion is something other than the philosophical concept, nevertheless, it is illusion only because the concept recog-

nizes it as such. Philosophy has always seen the true nature of art mirrored in the concept of illusion.[23] It is one of the terms in which the problem of the *Dialectic of Enlightenment* is articulated. To designate illusion as the locus where this problem can be adequately addressed means to obscure the line of division that separates art from philosophy.[24]

THE DOGMA OF CONTRADICTION

Schelling's philosophy of art is the appropriate court of appeal for a type of philosophy whose most deep-seated intentions are to be transposed into the medium of art.[25] Schelling thought that the absolute indifference of subject and object could be brought to the level of intuition by means of art. Philosophy cannot achieve this identity without transcending itself and ceasing to be philosophy. The last point reached by reflection, where it abandons its own claims for the sake of absolute, seamless unity, simultaneously reveals the limits of discursive philosophy. In contrast to philosophy, art realizes this unity on its own accord and without distortion. In order, however, for art to succeed in this undertaking of speaking for philosophy, both sides of the relation between art and philosophy must be adequately determined.

The younger Schelling drew on the idea of an *organon*[26] to conceptualize the relationship in which philosophy establishes a close proximity to art. This allowed Schelling to use art as an antidote to philosophy's shortcomings without art's merely substituting for philosophy. On the one hand, this lets art remain autonomous and prevents the intentional and unintentional transformation of art into a philosophical hybrid that solely serves the interests of philosophical proof. Art must not be defined as an *ancilla philosophiae*; it is precisely art's autonomy that enables it to serve the function philosophy requires of it. On the other hand, the function art assumes on behalf of philosophy must lend itself to characterization so that art remains accessible to philosophy. Nothing is to be gained either by an intoxicated feeling of identity that blurs all distinctions between art and philosophy or by a neutral coexistence in which philosophy and art have nothing to say to each other. Considering the extreme nature of the opposing demands philosophy makes on art, the Aristotelian model of an organon is only, at best, a makeshift solution. Art is not, at any price, to be instrumentalized by philosophy, the way, for example, tools are subordinated to the ends they serve. Art is able to express philosophy's most difficult paradoxes only when it has parity with philosophy and, therefore, like philosophy, is not a means to an end but is an end in itself. This is the reason Schelling later abandoned the organon model and relied less heavily on the problematic relationship between philosophy and art.[27]

Critical Theory's general program is informed by a tension whose extremes are characterized by Kant's doctrine of the *Ding an sich* and Hegel's absolute concept, whereas the arena in which these two extremes are battled out was prepared by Marx and the Young Hegelians. Adorno's aesthetics, which emerged from these conditions, is best understood, however, in connection with Schelling, a connection almost all interpreters of Adorno and modern aesthetics have failed to take into consideration. If, for once, this suggestion is taken to heart, then the question of defining the relation between philosophy and art can be posed more clearly than Adorno would have been willing to admit. Adorno himself always stressed that philosophy and art converge in knowledge. It will be more difficult, however, to understand what the terms of this convergence are.

To begin with, not all forms of art entail knowledge per se. As opposed to idealist naiveté, the critic of ideology makes a strict distinction between liberal or "enlightened" art and art that, as part of the "culture industry," is complicit in furthering the general deception produced by ideology. This distinction does not automatically coincide with qualitative distinctions based on pure aesthetic categories. Rather, it presupposes a highly attuned awareness of prevailing historical conditions. The art critic's aesthetic sense becomes more finely honed through knowledge that is extraneous to aesthetic considerations, that is, philosophical and sociological insights into the factors determining the present state of society and possible prospects for the future. By emphasizing that artworks of true aesthetic import are also ones that boast a *progressive* outlook, Adorno forces aesthetic and political judgments to overlap. This echoes Walter Benjamin's tenuous attempt to understand the "artist as producer" in such a radical way that the mastery of the technical side of art production and "the correct political tendency" are predicated on each other.[28] Increase in technical skill and keeping in step with the course of history amount to the same thing—progressive art.[29]

In referring, on the one hand, to the expertise involved in discerning art's purely formal aspects and, on the other, to the knowledge involved in evaluating its content according to the degree it furthers the cause of humanity, the term "progressive art" brings aesthetic and political concerns under one roof. Sometimes the language Adorno uses to reconcile the universal with the particular is reminiscent of *classical poetics,* for example, Goethe's concept of symbol.[30] At the same time, however, the critic must rein in the writer of poetic theory in order to prevent the deception from insinuating itself should it be forgotten that the reconciliation achieved by art is fictive, that it is not present in reality but lies forever in a distant, utopian future. Art must simultaneously present things in two different ways. On the one hand, it must present the concrete particular as something that is not eclipsed by abstract universality but exercises its own right in harmonizing with the universal; on the other hand, art must make manifest the irreality of such a reconciliation.[31] The status of important artworks is established by the contradiction that takes shape between harmony and its disillusionment. What constitutes the historical meaning of works of art must find expression in their artificial construction.

Adorno's theory thus presupposes that the extra-aesthetic categories that form the basis of the critic's interpretations are directly embodied in the artworks themselves. Strictly speaking, then, art expresses only what someone who already has knowledge of historical processes can possibly understand. In fact, this remarkable type of art, with just such an interiorized awareness of its own historical position, is modern art. Complete rejection of the traditional canon, which we have come to expect of modern art, seems to provide the paradigm for Adorno's theory. Obviously, here, the contradiction has become real between art's immanent, self-contained harmony and the sudden shattering of this longed-for harmony. The critic's task is to bring out what is already embedded in the structure of art, and consequently the critic is reduced to a mere recipient to whom art provides whatever he or she might require. The critic's role would be completely redundant, were it not for the complication that not all of the art produced in the last hundred years can be counted as progressive, even when some works seem to look or sound "modern." In the updated *musée imaginaire,* it is once again a question of separating the sheep from the goats. The critic's function, which seemed to have entirely merged with the structure of artworks, is given a new and apparently independent lease on life. The critic's task, however, is no longer to distinguish between good and bad art. Rather, the critic must now distinguish between progressive and reactionary art, a distinction that obviously is no longer based solely on aesthetic criteria.

In relation to modern art, the rehabilitation of the critic's function shows that in truth the formal laws supposedly governing modern art production are merely invoked to divert attention away from criteria introduced by critical aesthetics. Untutored perception alone can never disclose the meaning of art. In order to penetrate art's structure, it is necessary to have command over the history of philosophy and its categories. "To be sure, an immanent method of this type always presupposes, as its opposite pole, philosophical knowledge that transcends the object. The method cannot, as Hegel believed, rely on 'simply looking-on.'"[32] This is the difference between progressive art and all other forms of art production, which only seem to be comparable to it. Without such philosophical and historical categories, the controversy Adorno stages, for example, between Schönberg, the standard bearer of "true" modernity, and Stravinsky, the incarnation of "false" modernity, would be nothing more than an academic debate between two opposing schools of musical composition.[33] Philosophy thus adds what is not already contained in innocent artworks, indeed what can never be contained in them: the interpretation of their meaning as *the negation of existing reality.*

With this, the cornerstone of Adorno's aesthetic theory is in place. It will be obvious now why it is necessary to compare art and social reality from an *external* vantage point in order to discover the moment of contradiction in certain works—by no means art in general. If all art were to stand opposed to reality, then the distinction between art shot through with ideology and progressive art would be totally meaningless. By the same token, if the pseudoreality created by art represented the complete negation of existing reality, then art would lose its oppositional stance toward the external world and would forfeit its function as critique. In the guise of uncompromising protest, art would then be guilty of passing off its illusion of harmony for the real thing. Thus Adorno is perfectly consistent in rejecting all forms of "engaged" art;[34] only art that is entirely itself, and does not attempt to have an effect outside of itself, is able to confront reality's most dominant features with sufficient autonomy to allow the contradictions to force themselves on the spectator. The universal mystification of social reality and art's complete autonomy stand radically opposed to each other. But only from a *third position,* totally removed from ideology, which affects all aspects of everyday life and art production, can mystification be exposed in all its ramifications. This position can be assumed only by the critic.

I needed to pursue the analysis to this point in order to arrive at an approximate answer to the question raised above. In connection with the discussion concerning transformation of philosophy into aesthetics, the question was posed as to the possibility of *determining both sides of the relationship between art and philosophy.* A confused mirroring of philosophical concepts in artworks and vice versa will not yield the knowledge of social reality for whose sake art was introduced into the consideration in the first place. It turns out, however, that two corresponding, fundamental assumptions are presupposed that work in tandem to support the thesis that art and philosophy converge in knowledge. By insisting, on the one hand, on reality's completely ideological character and, on the other, on the complete autonomy of art production, philosophy and art are forced to act on each other in such a way as to make the truth of social reality totally transparent. Adorno's conclusions can be made to appear persuasive only if a strict separation is dogmatically presupposed between art and reality, both of which, with equal right, follow their own internal laws and remain directly opposed to each other.

The unique relationship art and philosophy share with regard to knowledge can only be established once it has already been accepted on good faith that art stands diametrically opposed to reality. According to this ungrounded dogma, art is the adversary of fetishized reality that, by carrying out its own form of negation, is capable of breaking ideology's spell. Thus, as if by an act of providence, art comes to the aid of philosophy as it struggles to break free from the dialectic of enlightenment. Only the critic's powers of interpretation, however, can make us aware of this feat of negation, accomplished in and by art.

MIMESIS AND WORKS OF ART

Things become more complicated when we turn to aesthetic experience. According to Adorno, to view paintings or to listen to symphonies does not automatically give us access to their truth content. If we want art to perform the additional service of ideology critique, then we must relinquish the classical idea that beauty imparts its truth unaided. All aesthetic experiences require theory in advance. "The demand of artworks to be understood by taking hold of their content [*Gehalt*] is tied to a specific experience of them. This, however, can only be completely fulfilled by a theory that reflects upon experience."[35] If only theory is able to complete what is laid out in experience, then art's critical *function of enlightenment* depends, once again, on its undiminished *autonomy.* As we have seen, autonomy means in this case that art remains independent of philosophy and is not used for the purposes of supporting or validating philosophical insights. What art has to say will come to the fore against the backdrop of philosophy, so long as philosophy does not impose its interests on art.

By means of the oldest concept known to the philosophy of art, Adorno's aesthetic theory attempts to find a way out of this self-imposed impasse. *Mimesis,* which has certainly undergone a remarkable change in meaning and importance, was understood by the tradition as an imitative mode of representation, parasitic on an independently given and higher-order reality. Plato thought that mimesis was inimical to truth, because it produced likenesses "three removes" from reality,[36] and Aristotle classed mimesis among those most fundamental attributes that make humans "the most mimetic of all animals."[37] For Adorno, mimesis is a virtue, because it resists being defined by reason, and because it is so firmly rooted in human behavior. He also places a high value on the necessarily derivative nature of all mimetic forms of representation, something that was anathema to the tradition. Philosophy's recourse to mimetic behavior is intended to repair the damage mimesis suffered at the hands of the philosophical concept. "There is no way for the concept to plead the case of mimesis, without losing itself in mimesis, which it itself supplanted, other than by incorporating something of mimesis in its own conduct. In this respect, the aesthetic moment is not accidental to philosophy, though for reasons quite different from the ones Schelling proposed."[38]

By way of mimesis, Spirit is restored to a quasi-prehistorical attitude toward the phenomenal world. Spirit adapts itself to experience as its other without offering any resistance and abandons its need to dominate the concrete. Blind imitation, which philosophy has held in contempt since the advances made in perfecting conceptual representation, is now seen as a corrective to what has become philosophy's idling machinery of empty categories. Philosophy comes into closer proximity to art, for which it had so little respect, the more theory's sovereignty is called into question. Mimesis in art acquires an altogether new meaning once theory's monopoly on appropriating reality has been challenged.

Adorno's new assessment of mimesis, as a corrective to theory, was fated to run against the grain of the *traditional copy theory of art.* Above all, Adorno objected to reviving axioms of traditional mimetic art theory in a neo-Marxist principle requiring that art produce mirror images of reality. Starting out from Marxist premises, Lukács, in his later writings, adhered to a thoroughly orthodox theory of art that called for faithful reproductions of a pregiven reality. Considering Adorno's understanding of the relation of art to reality, it is not surprising that he vehemently opposed such a misuse of mimesis, which substitutes images for knowledge and prefers concealment to disclosure. "The most fundamental weakness of Lukács's position may be that he . . . applies categories that refer to the relationship between consciousness and reality to art as though they simply meant the same thing here. Art exists within reality, has its function in it. . . . But nevertheless, as art, by its very concept it stands in an antithetical relationship to the status quo."[39]

Adorno's newly accentuated concept of mimesis can be defended against entrenched traditional views only by dint of ingenious argumentation. Understood as a basic form of assimilation, capable of overcoming the concept's rigidity, mimesis is not a remnant of another age that has come down to us intact so that the worn-out concept can revert to it at any time. It would be an illusion for philosophy to believe that mimesis can, with the touch of a magic wand, restore a more direct relation to reality. Without the help of well-reasoned explanations, the concept of mimesis has no meaning whatsoever. This becomes all too obvious in the dispute between Adorno and Lukács, in which bare assertions are traded back and forth and the continually cited crown witnesses, Adorno's Samuel Beckett and Lukács's Thomas Mann, are given permission to speak only when they can give testimony on behalf of the respective positions.[40] Seen in this way, Adorno's recourse to mimesis, as a form of "mimicry" of spirit, fails to persuade.

One last consequence remains to be considered. For the sake of the coherence of his own insights into modern art, Adorno cannot get around reinstating an *unqualified work category* in his aesthetic theory, even if the theory itself constantly maintains the opposite. Where else can the concrete and the universal be reconciled in a way that is far removed from all conceptual schematizations, if not within the autonomous sphere created by artworks? What else is to serve as a mirror for exposing "bad" reality, if not an objective example? What else can reflection cling to as it founders in the vortex created by the dialectic of enlightenment, if not a tangible product of mimetic behavior? In spite of whatever statements Adorno may have made to the contrary, it is beyond all doubt that the work category plays a central role in his undertaking. The theory as well as the actual writings on art criticism bear witness on every page that Adorno systematically presupposes the given fact of artworks.

Just as little can it be doubted, however, that modern art, the basis of Adorno's aesthetic theory, represents one continuous process, *the demise of the work category*.[41] If the diverse forms of art production crudely classified as "modern" permit being reduced to one common denominator, then the main trend embodied by modern art is the steady subversion of the traditional work category. In the absence of the work category, modern art has resorted to a number of strategies, ranging from playful skepticism to ironic distortion and surrealistic shock, from the systematic destruction of unity and the radical reduction of planned construction to the increased, constitutive function assigned to chance; readymades, found objects, happenings, and performance pieces are the most obvious examples. Modern art denies the ontological status of a second reality that, although derivative, would be equal to the first. *Ergon,* as an independent bearer of meaning, has disappeared from art altogether. Where modern art does not aim to disappoint the traditionally passive spectator, who usually expects to find a full-fledged work, it often serves to inspire the spectator's imagination and active participation, at least to some degree. What used to be attributed to the creative process of actual art production has been transformed by modern art into a process that is automatically set in motion after the work has been completed.[42] In this way, the entire notion of the autonomous artwork has been overtaken by aesthetic experience, which, according to Adorno, is always a "reciprocal" experience between the work of art and the spectator.

This understanding is not new. Nor, to be reminded of it, do we need to turn to Adorno, who, with considerable insight, describes how modern art eroded the central role the traditional work category formerly played in art production and aesthetic theory. All the same, it is worth mentioning two arguments that are often raised and profess to jeopardize this thesis. It is often said that the demise of the traditional work category, in fact, only makes room for *new kinds of artworks.* If this is true, then the entire modern art movement is by no means as revolutionary as it is made out to be. Modern art would represent only a further phase in a long series of style changes and historical shifts to be indifferently classified by the art historian. Above all, those analyses that are of vital importance to Adorno's aesthetic theory would prove to be invalid. For Adorno, what is truly innovative about modern art and specifically distinguishes it from art of all other periods is precisely its protest character; therefore, it should be interpreted in this way. If we subscribe to critical aesthetics, then we can hardly take seriously the argument just mentioned.[43]

The second argument is based on the conviction that modern art simply makes explicit what is implicit to art in general. Fragility is art's true abiding essence, whereas substantiality is make-believe. This argument takes two forms. First, current ideas about art are simply projected back on the entire past, so that modern art is not seen as modern but merely as a new expression of what we understand art to have always been. To draw conclusions about the past on the basis of the present and to level all historical differences results in a distorted foreshortening of historical perspectives. Second, similar to Marx's famous dictum that the anatomy of man is the key to the anatomy of the ape, this argument often reverts to a teleological model that presupposes the most recent stage of art's historical development to be the culmination of art's entire history, and thus allows all the preliminary stages leading up to a completed process of historical development to be taken in at a glance. Apart from the dubious nature of the method involved in historical teleology—which even in Marx's case, despite his materialist examples, had strong roots in idealism—such a belief in progress, together with the claim of rendering ever more transparent the origins of the current historical moment, once again robs aesthetics of its potential as critique. As Adorno saw, rational capacity does not develop according to the dictates of an inner telos. Art that opposes the advance of rationality and, like Faust's return to the mothers,[44] reverts to fundamental, mimetic levels of human existence is the last place of refuge from where it is possible to expose the new and ever-deeper inroads deception continues to make into history.

To conclude, we cannot avoid *synthesizing the following two irreconcilable sides of modern art.* On the one hand, modern art undermines the traditional work category, and it is thanks to this that it acquires its protest character. On the other hand, modern art has no means of expression other than individual concrete works; aside from their autonomous structure, no place remains where they can carry out their mission of critique. Adorno resolutely engages both sides of this paradox. Theory cannot provide us with any solution. The paradox can be defused only by means of casuistry. On the basis of case-by-case analyses of literary texts and musical scores, the two sides of the paradox can be set off against each other, that is, modern art's need to destroy unity for the sake of preserving its critical function and its need to maintain unity for the sake of giving expression to its critical function.

Merely providing examples, however, can in no way substitute for establishing the grounds for a theory. As plausibly as Adorno may have sometimes demonstrated his general insights with regard to particular literary and musical works, he provides little in the way of evidence to ground the application of these insights. Every one of his interpretations hinges far too much on his hermeneutical starting point and rhetorical skill to serve as evidence for the conclusions he draws. If the same works are considered from a different perspective and with different intentions, then, to a certain extent, the resulting interpretations would also make sense. The ultimate ploy, which Adorno all too gladly uses to give his interpretations an authoritative tone, is to insinuate that all possible alternative interpretations are to be suspected of being ideologically biased or, worse still, philistine. This, however, only camouflages the shaky foundations on which his own interpretations are built. To shift the burden of fundamental aesthetic issues intentionally onto the shoulders of interpretation underhandedly obscures the difference between aesthetic theory and aesthetic experience.

AESTHETIC EXPERIENCE

The role aesthetic experience plays in Adorno's aesthetic theory is particularly puzzling. In fact, the tautological character of his analysis of how art affects us renders his theory incapable of shedding light on the structure of aesthetic experience; it presupposes a definite effect, which it then uses to account for its findings. The possibility of analysis slips away when theory is fashioned after an aesthetic paradigm, which should, in fact, form the object of analysis. Since art is at theory's beck and call to produce exactly the kind of knowledge theory wants, the outcome of actual encounters with concrete artworks is always determined in advance. Theory knows art has a critical effect, because it knows art's autonomy is the last bastion of resistance in a world blinded by ideology. Theory, therefore, also knows how to distinguish between truly avant-garde art that looks ahead and art that, despite its modern trappings, is reactionary.

Because art always reconfirms the structural insights theory brings to bear on the wealth of aesthetic phenomena, there is no longer, to put it bluntly, a need for individual aesthetic experience. The undeniable attraction of the concrete interpretations Adorno offers us in his numerous essays lies in his versatility and in the keenness for detail with which he makes aesthetic experience meet the conditions laid down by aesthetic theory, rather than in the freedom and range of understanding with which he is prepared to confront the unexpected in aesthetic experience.

Because it makes all actual experience superfluous, the absolute certainty that art is the source of a type of knowledge is the weakest aspect of Adorno's theory. This is why Adorno's aesthetic theory tends toward dogmatic self-validation,[45] shutting itself off in narcissistic reflection from doubt and from anything else that might disturb its conception of itself. If we use Adorno's theory as a guide to aesthetic experience, nothing out of the ordinary will ever happen to us; we will see, hear, feel nothing new, because the theory has already accounted for every possible reaction we might have. True aesthetic experience is predicated on the willingness to remain open to what is unexpected. An ironclad theory can never be a substitute for this openness, which allows art to provoke us into seeing the world in new, unchanneled ways.

The true antidote to traditional theory's dogmatic self-certainty, which Adorno's aesthetics was meant to provide, consists in giving precedence to the possibility of engaging art in a way not already thoroughly determined by theory. *Aesthetic experience must be made the basis for aesthetic theory* and not the other way around. The entrenched illusions generated by ideology can be dispelled only when there is freedom to confront the official face of reality with alternatives. This freedom is first and foremost acquired by an *unfettered play of reflection,* which can be set in motion only by genuine aesthetic experience. Let us consider this a bit more closely.

In contrast to our everyday experiences of the world as we find it, encounters with aesthetic phenomena are unique in that they do not require organization by the understanding; nor, strictly speaking, do artworks prescribe how these encounters will turn out. Aesthetic experience encourages consciousness to engage in a form of reflection that does not restrict it in any way. This highly unusual experience opens up for consciousness new and previously unrealized possibilities. The age-old solution to the problem of how to reawaken deadened forms of perception lies entirely in the possibility of being moved by art. The extreme nature of modern art production, however, makes openness and breadth of vision especially necessary to have such experiences.

I have deliberately introduced this description of aesthetic experience in order to bring Kant to mind. It is time to rediscover his analysis of how aesthetic phenomena affect consciousness, an analysis that Schelling and Hegel thought they had consigned to history.[46] Kant's insights into the structure of reflective judgment, applied to modern art, not only dispense with a fixed, traditional work canon but also make it imperative that we reconsider aesthetic experience, not in terms of confirming what we already think or know about the world but as the way art enhances our powers of perception and understanding. To account for the basis of aesthetic experience in terms of what Kant called our disinterested pleasure in objects allows us to define art without directly identifying it with knowledge. The true nature of art thus consists in its capacity to stimulate thought without restricting it and to bring reflection to a level of independence where it is no longer bound to concepts. Because it loosens reflection's ties to specifically determined cognitive functions, only the type of art that is capable of initiating the free play of reflection can do without the services of thought.

In contrast, art whose entire function is critique is in fact not conducive to critique, as Adorno would have it. Rather, just the opposite is true. Instead of freeing knowledge, it succeeds only in trammeling knowledge. Art that takes on meaning only in opposition to reality is the reverse side of art that merely copies reality. In both cases, consciousness is condemned to fixed, predetermined, almost mechanical reactions in its apprehension of art. Neither of these concepts of art is capable of bringing about the freedom of reflection necessary for true aesthetic experience.

Dialectic of Limits or Philosophy and Art

Hegel's dialectical method, which Adorno unabashedly employs at strategically crucial moments, may help us understand why the latter places so little value on true aesthetic experience. Hegel's objection to Kant's concept of the *Ding an sich,* resurrected in Adorno's concept of the *Nichtidentische,* involves the *dialectic of limits.* Hegel's argument maintains that in order to define the limit of something, a position must already be assumed outside of that limit. Limits can never be drawn from only one side. To recognize a limit thus implies the possibility of overcoming it. Within the context of his debate with Hegel there is no way, other than blind obstinacy, that Adorno can circumvent the consequences this insight has on his own "negative dialectic." Adorno must first explicitly complete the dialectic of limits in order then to sublate it again.[47] *Theory's transformation into aesthetics* rests squarely on this step.

Insight into theoretical knowledge's limitations cannot lead to theory's consummation by transcending its limits. According to what I have identified as Adorno's a priori principle, which accounts for the convergence of art and philosophy in terms of their shared orientation toward knowledge, this insight into theory's limits would seem to fall within the purview of art. By locating the point of convergence in art, however, the mediation is cut short, which prevents the dialectic from culminating in an absolute system. If this mediation were to be completed, then theory would be able to draw its own limits, which would make art's limiting role superfluous. That theory's limits are determined by art, however, is by no means a self-evident truth. In fact, theory imposes its limits on itself and thus determines what its proper domain should be. Aesthetics, as the limit of theory, can be determined only by theory. This, however, sets the dialectic of limits in motion again.

This relationship can be understood as the *inversion of the relationship* in which Hegel ranks art with respect to philosophy. According to Hegel, art is historically prior to philosophy, but because art represents absolute Spirit only in its immediacy, art is subordinate to philosophy. Spirit's unmediated presence in art gives rise to a mediation by which Spirit comes into its own as philosophy. Philosophy, in spelling out what is spiritual in art, necessarily destroys art's autonomous sphere. To raise art to the level of the concept means to put an end to how aesthetic illusion creates its unrestricted effect, which depends on immediacy. Illusion recognized as illusion is robbed of its power and magic. The advent of the philosophy of art thus rings out the age of art.

> Neither with respect to its content nor its form is art the highest and most absolute way for Spirit to bring its true interests to consciousness. The type of creation and works peculiar to art no longer fulfill our highest needs. . . . For this reason, in our age, the *science* of art is much more of a prerequisite than for those times in which art pure and simple really did offer complete satisfaction. Art invites us to consider things in a thinking way; not for the purpose of creating new works of art, but rather to know, in a scientific way, what art is.[48]

In a certain sense, it can be said that Adorno's aesthetics reverses the process by which Hegel's philosophy destroys art's independent sphere. Although Adorno discovers in art philosophy's most fundamental interests, he does not subject art to a philosophical concept of truth, as Hegel does. To do so would deprive art of its power to impose limits on philosophy. In order to save art from sinking back to the level of one of Spirit's irrelevant, preliminary stages, Adorno would rather dispense with reflection. This would reveal, of course, that it was philosophy, in the first place, that had conferred the status of knowledge on art. Adorno thus conceals from himself that it is only by way of philosophical interpretation that art can be put on an equal footing with philosophy. The fact that he does not admit philosophy's constitutive role gives art the aura of independence. The truth of the matter, however, is that

Adorno uses art as a deus ex machina, which he hauls in to save the day for philosophy. Perhaps, in spite of all its self-effacing gestures, it is Adorno's aesthetic theory that treats art with the most extreme condescension, the condescension of an anonymous sovereign power.

All these complications could have been avoided if Adorno had once and for all given up the dream that it is possible for philosophy to remain itself and at the same time be different from itself. *The aestheticizing of theory impoverishes a theory of the aesthetic.* Although Adorno professes to promote art's autonomy, he always has theory's interests at heart. In this way, aesthetics is rendered thoroughly heteronomous. The line of argumentation that begins with the insight into universal mystification and extends through the dogma that art and reality are diametrically opposed to each other, in the end, transforms art into an agent of critical theory's interests. Because these interests cannot be openly articulated, they are imputed to the artworks themselves, thus determining in advance how we will experience them. In this way, theory prevails in the very act of denying that it plays a constitutive role in aesthetics.

Notes

1. Theodor W. Adorno, *Gesammelte Schriften* (GS),vol. 1 ("Die Aktualität der Philosophie"), pp. 325-44, 343. See also the preface to Theodor W. Adorno, *Negative Dialektik* (ND) (1966), GS 6:9; trans. E. B. Ashton (New York: Continuum, 1973), p. xix.

2. Max Horkheimer and Theodor W. Adorno, *Dialektik der Aufklärung. Philosophische Fragmente* (DA) (1944/1947 and 1969), GS 3:10; trans. J. Cumming (New York: Seabury Press, 1972), p. x.

3. See also Theodor W. Adorno, "Der Essay als Form" (1958), in *Noten zur Literatur,* vol. 1, GS 11:9-33; trans. as "The Essay as Form," *Notes to Literature,* vol. 1, trans. Shierry Weber Nichelsen (New York: Columbia University Press, 1991), pp. 3-23.

4. Theodor W. Adorno, *Ästhetische Theorie* (AT) (1970), GS 7:140, trans. C. Lenhardt (London: Routledge & Kegan Paul, 1984), p. 134 (translation modified).

5. GS 1 ("Die Aktualität der Philosophie"), p. 343.

6. For a detailed account, see my essay "Problemgeschichte und systematischer Sinn der 'Phänomenologie' Hegels," in *Dialektik und Wissenschaft* (Frankfurt: Suhrkamp, 1973). This essay has been translated as "Hegel's Concept of Phenomenology" for a book on Hegel's *Phenomenology of Spirit,* ed. Gary K. Browning (Netherlands: Kluwer Academic Publishers, 1997).

7. For an extensive treatment of the philosophical similarities, see Hermann Mörchen, *Adorno und Heidegger. Untersuchung einer philosophischen Kommunikationsverweigerung* (Stuttgart: Klett-Cotta, 1981).

8. See GS 1 ("Die Idee der Naturgeschichte" [1932]), pp. 345-65.

9. *Kierkegaard, Konstruktion des Ästhetischen* (1933); GS 2; *Kierkegaard: Construction of the Aesthetic,* trans. R. Hullot-Kentor (Minneapolis: University of Minnesota Press, 1989).

10. Theodor W. Adorno, "Parataxis. Zur späten Lyrik Hölderlins" (1963/1964), in *Noten zur Literatur,* vol. 3, GS 11:447-91.

11. ND, GS 6:23; trans., p. 11.

12. DA, GS 3:9; trans., p. ix.

13. AT, GS 7:191; trans., p. 183 (translation modified).

14. These are sketches of analyses I have dealt with in more detail in my essay "What Is Critical Theory?" in R. Bubner, *Essays in Hermeneutics and Critical Theory,* trans. E. Matthews (New York: Columbia University Press, 1988), pp. 1-35.

15. Theodor W. Adorno, "Offener Brief an Rolf Hochhuth" (1967), in *Noten zur Literatur,* vol. 4, GS 11:591-98, 598.

16. For example, see T. Baumeister and J. Kulenkampff, "Geschichtsphilosophie und philosophische Asthetik," in *Neue Hefte für Philosophie,* no. 5 (1973): pp. 74-104.

17. DA, GS 3:15; trans., p. xv.

18. Karl Mannheim, *Ideology and Utopia: Introduction to the Sociology of Knowledge,* trans. L. Wirth and E. Shils (London: Routledge & Kegan Paul, 1948). See M. Horkheimer, "Ein neuer Ideologiebegriff?" (1930), in *Gesammelte Schriften,* vol. 2 (Frankfurt: Fischer, 1987), pp. 271ff.; "A New Concept of Ideology?" in *Between Philosophy and Social Science: Selected Early Writings,* trans. G. F. Hunter, M. S. Kramer, and J. Torpey (Cambridge, Mass.: MIT Press, 1993), pp. 129-49. This essay is similar to Adorno's "Das Bewußtsein der Wissenssoziologie" (1937, first published 1953), in *Prismen. Kulturkritik und Gesellschaft* (1955), GS 10/1:31-46; "The Sociology of Knowledge and Its Consciousness," in *Prisms,* trans. Samuel and Shierry Weber (Cambridge, Mass.: MIT Press, 1981), pp. 35-49.

19. In his essay on Samuel Beckett's *Endgame,* Adorno refers to this reversal as follows: "The irrationality of bourgeois society in its late phase rebels at letting itself be understood; those were the good old days, when a critique of the political economy of this society could be written that judged it in terms of its own *ratio.*" ("Versuch, das Endspiel zu verstehen" (1961), in *Noten zur Literatur,* vol. 2, GS 11:281-321, 284); "Trying to Understand *Endgame,*" *Notes to Literature,* vol. 1, p. 244.

20. See Adorno's essay "Zum Klassizismus von Goethes Iphigenie" (1967), in *Noten zur Literatur,* vol. 4 GS 11:495-514, 512ff.

21. "As far back as we can trace it, the history of thought has been a dialectic of enlightenment." ND, GS 6:124; trans., p. 118.

22. Compare AT, GS 7:16, 67, 114; trans., pp. 78, 60, 108.

23. For example, consider Plato's *Republic X.*

24. DA, GS 3:36-37; trans., pp. 18-19. Cf. also T. Adorno, *Philosophie der neuen Musik* (1949) (Berlin, 1972), pp. 20ff., 189.

25. DA, GS 3:36-37; trans., pp. 18-19; AT, GS 7:120, 197, 511; trans., pp. 113-14, 189, 457; ND, GS 6:26-27; trans., p. 15.

26. Friedrich Schelling, *System des transzendentalen Idealismus* (1800).

27. Friedrich Schelling, *Philosophie der Kunst* (1802/1804) (Darmstadt, 1959), pp. 8ff.; *Vorlesungen über die Methode des akademischen Studiums* (1803), lecture 14.

28. W. Benjamin, "Der Autor als Produzent," in *Versuche über Brecht* (Frankfurt: Suhrkamp, 1968), pp. 96ff.; "The Author as Producer," in *Reflections,* trans. E. Jephcott (New York: Harcourt Brace Jovanovich, 1978), pp. 220-38.

29. For example, T. W. Adorno, *Ohne Leitbild. Parva Aesthetica* (1967/1968), GS 10/1:289-453, 299ff.

30. Theodor W. Adorno, "Zum Klassizismus von Goethes Iphigenie," in *Noten zur Literatur,* vol. 4, GS 11:502ff. (Cf. Goethe, *Maximen und Reflexionen,* no. 751.) For a pertinent observation about Adorno's essay, see Gerhard Kaiser, "Adornos Ästhetische Theorie," in *Antithesen* (Frankfurt: Athenäum, 1973), pp. 309ff.

31. Citing "historico-philosophical reasons" and referring to his favorite example, Samuel Beckett, Adorno demonstrates the following "change in the a priori of drama: the fact that there is no longer any substantive, affirmative metaphysical meaning that could provide dramatic form with its law and its epiphany. That, however, disrupts the dramatic form down to its linguistic infrastructure. Drama cannot simply take negative meaning, or the absence of meaning, as its content without everything peculiar to it being affected to the point of turning into its opposite." "Versuch, das Endspiel zu verstehen," *Noten zur Literatur,* vol. 2, GS 11:282; "Trying to Understand Endgame," in *Notes to Literature,* vol. 1, p. 242.

32. Theodor W. Adorno, *Philosophie der neuen Musik,* p. 31. Adorno's reference to Hegel is completely misleading. What Hegel describes as "simply looking on" [*das reine Zusehen*] refers specifically to the method appropriate to a "phenomenology of Spirit." It does not apply to his philosophy in general, nor does phenomenological *Zusehen* mean that systematic premises are lacking. See *Phänomenologie des Geistes,* in *Werke,* vol. 3 (Frankfurt: Suhrkamp, 1986), p. 77; *Phenomenology of Spirit,* trans. A. V. Miller (Oxford: Oxford University Press, 1977), p.

54. In this connection, see my essay "Hegel's Concept of Phenomenology."

33. Such an innocuous observation, as F. Busoni made in his *Entwurf einer neuen Ästhetik der Tonkunst* (1916; new ed., Frankfurt: Suhrkamp, 1974), does not at all come to grips with the problem: "Ephemeral qualities constitute what is 'modern' about a work of art; the immutable qualities save it from becoming 'old-fashioned.' For 'modern times,' just as much for 'former times,' there is good and bad, authentic and inauthentic. The absolutely modern does not exist. There is only what comes into existence earlier or later, what flourishes longer or fades away more rapidly. There have always been things which are modern and things which are old" (p. 8).

34. AT, GS 7:134; trans., p. 128. In his essay "Engagement" (1962), Adorno chooses to make Sartre and Brecht into opponents (*Noten zur Literatur,* vol. 3, GS 11:409-30).

35. AT, GS 7:185; also 189, 193ff., 391; trans., p. 179; also pp. 181-82, 186ff., 370-71 (translation modified).

36. Plato, *Republic* 595c ff.

37. Aristotle, *Poetics* 1448b.

38. ND, GS 6:26; trans., pp. 14-15 (translation modified). See also AT, GS 7:86ff., 180ff.; trans., pp. 79ff., 174ff.

39. Theodor W. Adorno, "Erpreßte Versöhnung" (1958), in *Noten zur Literatur,* vol. 2, GS 11:251-80, 260; "Extorted Reconciliation," *Notes to Literature,* vol. 1, pp. 216-40, 224.

40. On the background and orientation of this debate about materialistic aesthetics, see my essay, "Über einige Bedingungen gegenwärtiger Ästhetik," in R. Bubner, *Ästhetische Erfahrung* (Frankfurt: Suhrkamp, 1989), pp. 23ff.

41. Ibid., esp. pp. 30ff.

42. For a good standard work on *Rezeptionsästhetik,* see Wolfgang Iser, *Der implizite Leser. Kommunikationsformen des Romans von Bunyan bis Beckett* (Munich: Fink, 1972); *The Implied Reader: Patterns of Communication in Prose Fiction from Bunyan to Beckett* (Baltimore: Johns Hopkins University Press, 1974).

43. That holds for Peter Bürger, *Theorie der Avantgarde* (Frankfurt: Suhrkamp, 1974). See my essay, "Moderne Ersatzfunktion des Ä;sthetischen," in *Ästhetische Erfahrung,* pp. 76ff.

44. Johann W. v. Goethe, *Faust. Der Tragödie zweiter Teil,* 6216ff.

45. From an external standpoint, this consequence is particularly striking, as Marc Jimenez has shown in his insightful analysis in *Theodor W. Adorno: Art, idéologie et théorie de l'art* (Paris: Union générale d'éditions, 1973), pp. 270ff.

46. See, R. Bubner, *Ästhetische Erfahrung,* pp. 34ff.

47. Compare, ND, GS 6:9, 397ff; trans., pp. xix, 405ff; *Philosophie der neuen Musik,* pp. 20ff., 189.

48. G. W. F. Hegel, *Vorlesungen über die Ästhetik,* ed. H. G. Hotho (1842), *Werke* 10.1:13ff., 16.

Carol V. Hamilton (essay date 1991)

SOURCE: "All That Jazz Again: Adorno's Sociology of Music," in *Popular Music and Society,* Vol. 15, No. 3, Fall, 1991, pp. 31-40.

[*In the following essay, Hamilton argues that Adorno's ideas about jazz, understood in their proper context, do have relevance as a part of his larger aesthetic theory.*]

Theodor Adorno's **"On Jazz"** is as infamous in academic circles as it is misunderstood. In the Winter, 1988, issue of *Popular Music and Society,* William P. Nye renewed the attack on Adorno, dismissing not only his analysis of jazz, but his work in general, that of other Frankfurt School members, and the claims of critical theory to be a scholarly, oppositional means of understanding popular culture. The subtitle of Nye's article is "A Critique of Critical Theory," and he quotes Zoltan Tar's damning one-sentence summary of the Frankfurt School: "Critical theory is the document of the disintegration of old Central European bourgeois society and the tragic fate of a group of intellectuals of that society." While many of their positions have been absorbed, modified, and revised by the current generation of theorists, the ideas of Adorno, Walter Benjamin, Herbert Marcuse and other Frankfurt School members are still influential in current debates about aesthetics and politics.[1] A 1990 book on Adorno, Fredric Jameson's *Late Marxism: Adorno, or the Persistence of the Dialectic,* argues for "the special relevance of Adorno's Marxism, and of its unique capacities within our own equally unique 'late' or third stage of capitalism" (12). In this far briefer response to William Nye's article, I want to challenge some of Nye's claims and suggest why readers of *Popular Music and Society* might give Adorno's work a second look. My aim is not to renew Adorno's critique of jazz but to contextualize it.

One can criticize Adorno's understanding of jazz without, as Nye puts it, "intellectually discrediting his theoretical perspective." Like other Frankfurt School theorists, Adorno's premise is that all cultural products, including those of so-called "high art," participate in a larger social logic, one which, under capitalism, is subservient to "exchange value." Just as one worker can be replaced by another, so can, and must, one popular song or style of dress replace another. Written when the bourgeoisie was still a progressive class, the production aesthetic of "serious music"—its formal structure—escaped subjection to commodification, only to be threatened by capitalist modes of distribution and reception. Unlike Walter Benjamin, author of "The

Work of Art in the Age of Mechanical Reproduction," Adorno was pessimistic about the effects of twentieth-century technology (the cinema, radio, phonograph album), fearing the standardization of culture. The ten-inch 78 rpm record, for example, restricted recording time to three minutes, with obvious formal constraints on the complexity and duration of the music (Harrison 574). Adorno and his colleague Horkheimer wrote a long essay called "The Culture Industry," in which they articulated their critique in detail.

It was the culture industry against which the critical fury of the Frankfurt School was directed, not popular culture forms *per se.* Indeed, the term "culture industry" was chosen to refute the very idea of an authentic, potentially counter-hegemonic popular culture. Adorno understands twentieth-century American and European popular music as written for consumption, not for aesthetic contemplation; unlike the uncompromising music of Schoenberg, pop music refuses to acknowledge either the horrors or the routine of an era of assembly lines, world wars, and concentration camps. It is "affirmative," in contrast to the "negative aesthetic" that Adorno considered truly oppositional and the only strategy for art in a society in which everything is up for sale. (In non-Marxist parlance, Adorno is talking about commercialism—as in recent explanations of *New Kids on the Block* as an example of an artificial, prefab, marketing success.) In his *Aesthetic Theory,* Adorno speaks of "the ability of art to incorporate into its formal language those phenomena that bourgeois society outlaws, revealing in them a natural other, the suppression of which is truly evil" (137).

The reference to a "formal language" is important for the subject of jazz, which Adorno understands in terms of both its musical structure and the construction of the subject/listener. But what does Adorno mean by "jazz"? The term has to be historicized; clearly, since **"On Jazz"** was published in 1936, it does not mean the improvisations of Keith Jarrett or even some of the later, extended compositions of Duke Ellington, like the 1943 work *Black, Brown and Beige.* The entry on jazz written by Max Harrison in the *New Grove Dictionary of Music and Musicians* (1980) begins as follows: "Attempts at a concise—even a coherent—definition of jazz have invariably failed. Initial efforts to separate it from related forms of music resulted in a false primacy of certain aspects such as improvisation, which is neither unique nor essential to jazz, or swing . . . which is absent from much authentic jazz, early and late" (561). Harrison then states: "the conventional view that jazz emerged from a balanced meeting of African and European musical characteristics is an oversimplification" (561). In other words, "jazz," like "the novel," presents a genre problem: what are its origins, what belongs to it, what lies outside? The *Grove* goes on to describe "the slowly assembled mixture of mutually influential folk and popular styles" as indigenously American and neither predominantly black nor white: "the diverse elements making up this idiom—in effect a broad and composite 'matrix'— gave it a potential for development . . . whose fullest realization is found in jazz." The prehistory that the *Grove* describes does imply a partial refutation of Adorno's critique: namely that if jazz has origins that predate the culture industry, then its structure may not be totally dominated by commodity logic. The *Grove* states: "There has indeed been an evolutionary succession of styles, and this has maintained the continuity, logic, and inner necessity that characterizes real art" (562).

If jazz cannot be formally defined, and if Adorno himself does not define his use of the term, to what music was Adorno referring? He does not engage in attacks on specific albums or musicians. One good guess is that **"On Jazz"** is really about swing, the dominant form of popular music in the 1930s and a form dominated by white musicians—not, of course, because they were more gifted but because they were more saleable to a predominantly white society. Attali points out that the first jazz recording was that of a white band, the Original Dixieland Jazz Band, and that in the early days of jazz recording, the best-known musicians, such as Benny Goodman, Paul Whiteman, and Stan Kenton, were white (Attali 104). And Jameson writes that Paul Whiteman is "the proper referent for what Adorno calls 'jazz,' which has little to do with the richness of a Black culture we have only long since then discovered" (*Late Marxism* 141).

This is significant because the lurking suspicion about **"On Jazz"** is that it is racist. That Adorno was Eurocentric in his attitudes is not in doubt. According to the *Grove*, however, jazz was for decades taken more seriously as an art form in Europe than in America, and "Europe became a haven for American jazz musicians" (577). If Max Harrison is correct in his claim that jazz is a melting pot of white and black folk idioms and is indigenously American, not African, in origins, then the equation of jazz with black music becomes problematic. Adorno himself did not make this equation, remarking, "It is difficult to isolate the authentic Negro elements in jazz" (Adorno "Perennial" 146). Consequently, the assumption that Adorno is a white European snob lashing out at African-American music ignores three issues: the mixed racial prehistory of jazz, its commercialization by white Americans, and its positive reception by many Europeans.

Despite his generally critical stance, some of Adorno's observations in the later essay **"Popular Music"** would surprise William Nye. Adorno remarks, for example, that "the minuets of lesser seventeenth-century composers were as fatally alike as our pop songs" and "within pop music, jazz has its unquestioned merits. Against the idiotic derivatives from the Johann Strauss type operetta it taught technique, presence of mind, and the concentration which pop music had discarded, and it developed the faculties of tonal and rhythmical differentiation" (Adorno, ***Introduction*** 32-33).

Admirers of Adorno's work point out his weaknesses as well as his strengths. In *Understanding Toscanini*, Joseph Horowitz devotes considerable attention to Adorno's ac-

count of the commodification of Western art music; he observes that "the strength of Adorno's ideological grounding is its heuristic breadth. Working from a general base, he is attuned to issues, even musical issues, that other writers on music overlooked or could not take seriously" (Horowitz 242). On the other hand, Horowitz admits, "Adorno's shortcomings of tone are unignorable. More often than not, his anger at commodity society seems mainly directed at its victims, whom he holds in contempt" (Horowitz 239). An authority on the Frankfurt School, Martin Jay describes Adorno as follows:

> Adorno's relentless animus towards mass culture was among his most controversial characteristics, often leading to the charge that he was an elitist snob, an arrogant mandarin, and even (because of his hatred for jazz) a covert racist. These glibly defensive epithets fail to acknowledge the extent to which the very same criticisms he levelled against mass culture were often directed as well against most elite culture, which he refused to fetishize as inherently superior . . . although he may have been overly eager to demonstrate the sadomasochistic core of jazz, he was no less willing to discern the same pathology in the music of Stravinksy
>
> (Jay 119).

It is the discussion of sadomasochism and castration that is the most offensive part of **"On Jazz."** Contemporary critics would probably understand some of the same issues in terms of gender rather than psychopathology and would substitute rock music for jazz. The datedness of Adorno's 1936 essay is evident in its references to jazz as a "mass phenomenon"; in fact, much of **"On Jazz"** is simply out of date, given the different strains of jazz produced since it was written and the revisions of Freudian psychology that have appeared in the past decade. But Western art music is still, as Adorno implied then, culturally coded as feminine or effeminate in opposition to a supposedly robust and masculine popular music. Such gendered cultural codings have nothing to do with the intrinsic qualities of the music or its performers but spring rather from perceptions of class (the social class above, in its relative refinement, perceived as feminine) and cultural stereotypes (Europe gendered as feminine, America as masculine). Adorno argues, in effect, that this cultural coding intimidates younger American male listeners from expressing an interest in art music.

Adorno is not alone, however, in some of his formalist criticisms of jazz. Carl Dahlhaus, the late German musicologist, makes similar observations in an essay entitled "Composition and Improvisation." His argument, unlike Adorno's, is not only about jazz, is almost purely formal (Dahlhaus doubts the very project of a sociology of music), and lacks the harshness that sometimes mars Adorno's work.[2] For these reasons Dahlhaus can be helpful in elucidating Adorno's formalist analysis.

Improvisation is not, as William Nye's article implies, foreign to Western art music.[3] If you look up the term in a reference work like the *New College Encyclopedia of Mu-*

sic you will read that "the fame of J. S. Bach in his life-time rested chiefly on the powers of improvisation which he showed in well-known instances," that "Handel used improvisation freely in playing his organ concertos," and that "Mozart and Beethoven were renowned for their improvising of cadenzas and of complete movements" (Westrup and Harrison 332). Improvisation is thus something that jazz and art music have in common historically, even though the emphasis in the latter has shifted to aleatory techniques and electronic music. In both cases it has functioned as a sign of the performer's virtuosity.

Dahlhaus describes the emotional content of improvisation as "the hope that musical improvisation is the expression of, and a means of achieving, an emancipation of consciousness and of feeling" (Dahlhaus 265). The word "emancipation" implies, as Adorno would quickly point out, a pre-existing state of oppression or slavery; freedom depends upon its absence in a dialectical relationship. The longing for utter freedom in improvisation suggests that more is at stake than music; the belief that such freedom is possible implies a denial of social as well as musical constraints. Like Adorno, Dahlhaus is doubtful about the degree of freedom in improvisation, whether in jazz or in other kinds of music:

> Analyzed soberly, improvisation almost always relies to a large extent on formulas, tricks of the trade, and models. . . . The improviser must be able to fall back at a moment's notice on a repertoire of cliches, on a store of prefabricated parts, which he may indeed modify or combine differently, but which he does not invent on the spur of the moment if he does not wish to get into difficulties or grind to a halt. The idea that he can commit himself entirely to the vagaries of chance is a fiction
>
> (Dahlhaus 268).

Dahlhaus understands improvisation as opposed to composition, which "tends to balance the various aspects of compositional technique . . . melody, rhythm, and harmony"; in contrast:

> Improvisation is almost always one-sided. It almost always concentrates on a single, isolated feature of the music, be it rhythm, harmony or tone color. And the real object of the improvisation stands out from its surroundings on account of its novelty, its differentiation or surprise effects, whereas everything else, being a mere foil, remains conventional and formalized
>
> (Dahlhaus 269).

In the course of this article, the binary oppositions African/American, American/European, and masculine/feminine have emerged and broken down. The opposition improvisation/composition suggests another, that between orality and literacy. Jacques Derrida has treated a version of this opposition—speech and writing, presence and absence—at length in *Of Grammatology*. Ever since Plato, according to Derrida, Western philosophy has privileged speech and presence over writing and absence: "Speech is

seen as in direct contact with meaning: words issue from the speaker as the spontaneous and nearly transparent signs of his present thought, which the attendant listener hopes to grasp" (Culler 100). It is obvious how this description would apply to a live concert. William Nye's critique of Adorno is oddly full of terms which Derrida, Roland Barthes, and other poststructuralist thinkers have successfully put into theoretical disrepute. "Voice," "mastery," "signature," and "possession," language which Nye uses to defend jazz, are now recognizable as crucial terms in Western metaphysics, a philosophical tradition constructed upon binary oppositions—male/female, self/other, white/black, etc.—in which one term is privileged over the other with oppressive socio-cultural implications. "Voice" belongs to the logocentric discourse that Derrida finds in Plato and throughout Western thought. "Mastery" implicitly excludes women from the achievement it describes; "possession" belongs to the discourse of private property that Barthes exposed in "The Death of the Author." "Signature," which Nye uses as a variant of "possession," is the subject of an amusing debate between Derrida and another philosopher, John Searle, in which Derrida deconstructs the concept to reveal its internal contradictions.

In rejecting Adorno's formal analysis of jazz, William Nye does not offer another formal analysis of his own but retreats instead to value judgments like "wizardry," "mastery," and "wondrous things." Such terms stand in contrast to Adorno's elaborate musical analyses, his exegesis of a musical text to expose its governing logic, and his recognition of the social implications of musical logic. Adorno was himself a student of the composer Alban Berg and possessed a musician's sophisticated understanding of theoretical issues. It is the combination of musical and philosophical erudition that makes his work impressive; those readers who dismiss it are most likely offended by its Western Marxist premises, its assumption that art, psychology, politics, and economics cannot be cleanly separated from each other but are instead intermeshed. Adorno's analysis of jazz should be refuted by someone who uses Adorno's own weapons; the *Grove* entry, which addresses both the formal strengths and weaknesses of jazz and which is far more specific than Adorno in its references to musicians and composers, is a better potential critique.

In defending jazz improvisation, Nye writes, "good jazz musicians improvise in the fullest sense of the word and the truth of this is given in the sense of awe with which many accomplished 'serious' or classically trained musicians regard the best and even the better jazz musicians." There are at least two problems with this defense. One is that the value judgment "the fullest sense of the word" begs the question of what, technically, improvisation is; secondly, by appealing to classical musicians' "sense of awe" (another emotional claim substituting for an analytical one), Nye reinscribes the superiority of "classical training" that he sets out to refute.

Nye's characterization of classically trained musicians—that they "sound more alike than different"—is also misconceived in several respects. It is true that listeners expect to recognize a Mozart piece when they hear one, not to be misled by an unduly whimsical or self-aggrandizing interpreter; there is thus the same emphasis on a distinctive, although theoretically problematic, individuality in Western art music as there is, according to Nye, in African music, but the primary emphasis is on the composer, not the interpreter. A Mozart concerto, for example, is not only an opportunity for a performer to showcase her own abilities; it involves complex textual and interpretive decisions. Nonetheless, Nye underestimates the differences between classically trained musicians, the more accomplished of whom are almost instantly distinguishable. I remember once standing in a record store while a symphony was being played on the store stereo system; a young man walked in the door and remarked, "It's the BPO (Berlin Philharmonic Orchestra)!" Similarly, I once surprised a musician friend when I walked into a room where the radio was playing Bach and said, "It's Glenn Gould." In both cases, recognition of the performers was virtually simultaneous with recognition of the composers.

Ultimately, what's wrong with Nye's strategy is that he attempts to rescue one musical tradition from attack by attacking another, thus replicating Adorno's own fault. If Adorno misrepresented jazz, misrepresenting "classical" music will not repair the damage. Jazz and "classical" music are not inherently oppositional; not only do many listeners enjoy both, but performers and composers in the one have been influenced by or performed the other. Modernist composers like Milhaud, Ravel and Stravinsky drew enthusiastically upon jazz idioms, and Charlie Parker asked avant-garde composer Edgar Varese to tutor him in composition.[4] In 1938 Benny Goodman recorded the Mozart clarinet quintet with the Budapest String Quartet and commissioned Bartok's *Contrasts* (*Grove* 577). In 1990 the Kronos String Quartet and the Modern Jazz Quartet appeared in concert together in Berkeley, California. If the musicians themselves take such an interest in each other's music, why should listeners be hostile? Indeed, there has probably been more cross-fertilization between jazz and "classical" than between any other major forms of music in the West. The antagonism is not musical but social. The privileged position Western art music has maintained, its associations with wealth and class, have also marginalized it; in the United States, with its ambivalent attitudes toward Europe, "classical" music is often regarded with a kind of xenophobic animosity, sometimes tainted with homophobia. We need to understand how social and institutional contexts situate musical discourses, not to essentialize those discourses. One-sided attacks on either jazz or "classical" music tend to contain within them the kind of binary oppositions that privilege the "civilized" over the "primitive," or else merely invert the opposition, as Nye does, without deconstructing it. This while is ultimately an appeal for openness, in the hope that music may provide, on occasion, a utopian moment in which social tensions are sublated.

Notes

1. A 1989 book edited by Christopher Norris, *Music and the Politics of Culture,* cites Adorno often; particularly interesting in this context is Ken Hirschkop's contribution, "The Classical and the Popular."

2. Dahlhaus's *Schoenberg and the New Music* contains his critique of the sociology of music.

3. William Nye objects to Adorno's use of the term "serious music"; this is not unique to Adorno but is fairly common in music criticism. A more recent but also problematic version is "art music." "Classica" is a period term; Adorno called its wider usage "vulgar."

4. Parker wrote Varese the following: "Take me as you would a baby and teach me music. I speak in only one voice. I want to have structure. I want to write orchestral scores" (quoted in the *Grove,* 576).

Works Cited

Adorno, Theodor W. "Perennial Fashion—Jazz." *Prisms.* Trans. Samuel and Sherry Weber. Cambridge: MIT Press, 1981. 119-132.

———. *Introduction to the Sociology of Music.* New York: Continuum, 1988.

Attali, Jacques. *Noise: The Political Economy of Music.* Minneapolis: University of Minnesota Press, 1985.

Culler, Jonathan. *On Deconstruction: Theory and Criticism After Structuralism.* Ithaca: Cornell University Press, 1985.

Dahlhaus, Carl. "Composition and Improvisation." *Schoenberg and the New Music.* Trans. Derrick Puffett and Alfred Clayton. Cambridge: Cambridge University Press, 1988. 265-73.

Harrison, Max. "Jazz." *The New Grove Dictionary of Music and Musicians.* Stanley Sadie, ed. London: Macmillan, 1980.

Horowitz, Joseph. *Understanding Toscanini.* Minneapolis: University of Minnesota Press, 1987.

Jameson, Fredric. *Late Marxism: Adorno, or the Persistence of the Dialectic.* Minneapolis: University of Minnesota Press, 1990.

Jay, Martin. *Adorno.* Cambridge, Mass: Harvard University Press, 1984.

Westrup, J. A. and F. Harrison, ed. *The New College Encyclopedia of Music.* New York: Norton & Company, 1960.

James M. Harding (essay date 1992)

SOURCE: "Historical Dialectics and the Autonomy of Art in Adorno's *Ästhetische Theorie*," in *Journal of Aesthetics and Art Criticism,* Vol. 50, No. 3, Summer, 1992, pp. 183-95.

[In the following essay, Harding argues that Adorno's thesis in Ästhetische Theorie *is based on a notion of historical dialectics.]*

As Peter Hohendahl has noted, the posthumous publication of Adorno's ***Ästhetische Theorie*** in 1970 disappointed many who expected that it would provide a materialist aesthetic which would cultivate praxis.[1] The Left, who dismissed the work "out of hand," maintained that, though anti-capitalist, the text advocated an anachronistic cultural elitism.[2] After Hohendahl (re)constructs the historical context in which Adorno's text was so negatively received, he suggests that the time has come (1981; 1991) to reassess the ***Ästhetische Theorie.*** Interestingly, while implying that the apparent flexibility of German society in the 1970s produced an inadequate analysis of Adorno's final work, Hohendahl's reappraisal still embraces the cornerstone of that analysis: like Peter Bürger, he posits the autonomy of art as the central thesis of the ***Ästhetische Theorie*** and then places the work squarely in the historical tradition of German idealism.

The brash rejection of the ***Ästhetische Theorie*** does call for a reassessment, but that reassessment ought not neglect questioning the role the autonomy of art has in the work's overall project. At stake is whether the initial reception cited by Hohendahl centered on a problem of secondary importance to the more subtle and comprehensive analysis occurring in Adorno's text. The dismissal of the ***Ästhetische Theorie*** on the grounds that it advocates an autonomy of art preconceived the meaning of aesthetic autonomy rather than deriving it from the text, i.e., from Adorno's usage. Consequently, the dismissal sidestepped a confrontation with the work's greater concerns: an analysis which explores how historical dialectics are erratic and lack uniformity and stability.[3] As the following arguments will demonstrate, the autonomy of art in the ***Ästhetische Theorie*** is not—as Bürger maintains—merely an historical category describing the detachment of art from practical life. It results from an historical dialectic whose mechanics, Adorno argues, are faltering and unable to enact supersession *(Aufhebung)*. In the ***Ästhetische Theorie,*** art is autonomous because of the unique formulation of dialectics posited by Adorno: art manifests itself in dialectical tensions with its own historical moment—in this respect art and life are indelibly intertwined—but these tensions remain unresolved; though art receives its identity from its negative critical relation with society, it does not have the ability to sublate the social dimensions that it negates. As society inevitably changes, an art work's non-identity becomes increasingly encapsulated—and therein lies the autonomy. For Adorno, the autonomy of art refers to the unresolved dialectical tensions of a work that respond to socio-historical conditions that have subsequently changed. Autonomy denotes the aesthetic tension's lack of resolution, a resolution that only supersession at a specific historical moment could have brought.

When Bürger argues that the autonomy of art is a category that describes art's detachment from practical contexts, he isolates only one aspect of (and thereby impairs) the dynamic at play in Adorno's discussions.[4] For Adorno, the autonomy of art is double-edged, and although he appears to hold to a philosophy of *l'art pour l'art,* Adorno has a radical theoretical adherence to the relation between art and society. On the one hand, he affirms that socio-historical change makes the separation of art and practical life unavoidable. But on the other, the separation does not denote the irrelevance of art to life. The relevance, however, can only be stated in negative terms. Adorno uses the autonomy of art to sustain art's negative value, i.e., to sustain the integrity of the unresolved negative tensions (the non-identity) a work has with a specific historic moment.

Aesthetic autonomy occurs with the inevitable movement of history, and Adorno uses autonomy to defend art against the reification that results from elevating a work's aesthetic non-identity to a status of validity beyond its historic moment. On its most immediate level, the ***Ästhetische Theorie*** uses the autonomy of art as the foundation for an emphatic plea *not* to turn previous aesthetic *non-identity* into subsequent *positive values.* The plea is the natural heir to Adorno's reservations about supersession. Without supersession, the movement from negation to positive value falters, and a work's non-identity remains intact, i.e., autonomous. The point is this: for Adorno, historicizing a work does not solely relegate its negative (aesthetic) value to the past; historicization revitalizes a work's non-identity in the sense that historicization enacts its own brand of negation.

A criticism that historicizes art in order to counteract reification initiates a negation ancillary to the negation implicit in an art work's original non-identity. Like the art it discusses, the criticism has a negative function: the negation of reification. A criticism that underscores a work's unresolved tensions results in an unresolved tension of its own. Like the art it discusses, the criticism generates an unresolvable tension in the positive value it derives from maintaining what it heralds as essentially negative, art's non-identity. Thus, Adorno revitalizes art in an act of mimicry—a mimicry which his idiosyncratic conception of the autonomy of art to a great extent facilitates. Yet in terms of importance, the autonomy of art is subordinate to the (negating) mimicry that marks the whole of Adorno's ***Ästhetische Theorie***; both are only possible as by-products of the revision of dialectics that precede them. In the ***Ästhetische Theorie,*** the autonomy of art has to be understood in the context of this revision. This is not to say that the mimicry in Adorno's criticism is without its problems—they will be explored in this work—but it seems to me that an adequate reassessment of Adorno's final work has to look at the dynamic Adorno constructs between his revision of dialectics and his mimicry of art.

The early reception of the ***Ästhetische Theorie*** mistook Adorno's defense of the autonomy of art as an exchange of praxis for an aesthetics of retreat—in fact, the defense of the autonomy of art serves as the premier example for de-reified critical activity. In answer to the calls for an aesthetic that cultivates political praxis, Adorno offered an aesthetic that, by using the autonomy of art as its primary example, challenged the ossified presumptions underlying praxis. Not only did it preclude art as a tool for social change, it argued that art exposed the delusory presuppositions of *engagement*.[5] The specific rigor that the *Ästhetische Theorie* applies to the concept of art—to proving that as a concept, art itself lacks continuity—is the central strategy of its larger enterprise: that of fostering critical attitudes resilient to reification. More importantly, the critique of aesthetics, the argument that the concept of art lacked continuity, offered a subtle critique of presumed continuity in the goals guiding political activism, certainly during the sixties and seventies if not in general.

The sub-text on history that structures the autonomy of art in the *Ästhetische Theorie* employs an historical-materialist dialectic in which neither universals nor particulars are precluded from change.[6] Rather than appealing to immutable, transcendent (e.g., Kantian) aesthetic criteria, Adorno posits an autonomy of art bound to society by its non-identity with a specific socio-historical moment.[7] The elements of this dialectic can be seen in the following statement which, interestingly enough, also indicates that Adorno's defense of art's autonomy is not positivist, as Hohendahl suggests Adorno's early reception implies. For Adorno, the autonomy of art makes assumptions about the structure of dialectics, not an assertion that art is independent from practical life or society. He writes:

> Works of art are after-images of the empirically living, inasmuch as they offer to the latter what outside is denied them, and thus liberate from their objective-external experience which shapes them.[8]

The key terms here are "after-images" (*Nachbilder*) and "the empirically living" (*das empirisch Lebendige*), the former not being a mere replica of the latter, but rather a dynamic counter-image to what the "empirically living" denies. Of equal importance to this counter-image is the peculiar formulation *das empirisch Lebendige,* what Adorno also calls *die empirische Realität* or simply *die Empirie*. From the section's subheading, "On the Relation Between Art and Society," we can gather that these obscure references to living, to experience and to the senses make broad allusions to society while trying not to succumb to its reified categories. In other words, Adorno echoes the art works he describes: he employs these peculiar terms to circumvent the denials inherent in the dominant discursive patterns of society. Like art, Adorno's terms "should assist the non-identical, which the coerced identity in reality represses."[9]

Whether the circumvention succeeds is debatable. Adorno's elocutions possess an amazing flexibility which is offset by an equally amazing vagueness. (One need only consider that they accommodate aesthetic discussions as diverse as adultery in *Madame Bovary* and absurdity in Beckett.) But the negative import of the terms *das Nichtidentische* and *Nachbild* allow Adorno to undercut the fixed criteria normally associated with the autonomy of art—

that is, once he supplements the terms with assertions about the ephemeral nature of every work of art. He argues *not* that each work has its place in history but that important works of art "age, go cold and die."[10] Each individual work dies as the conditions of empirical reality change. Rather than contributing to the evolution of a concept, a work's characteristic counter-image or non-identity survives only as long as do the historical conditions from which it emerged. "What was once true in a work of art . . . [was] dismantled in the course of history."[11] This death necessitates a new form of aesthetic criticism, but more importantly, death precludes *Aufhebung*.

Instead of a movement of negation that resolves itself into subsequent moments (as in Hegel), historical passage is, for Adorno, the steady accumulation of unresolved tensions, repressed beneath the appearance of resolution. By questioning *Aufhebung*, Adorno can argue that the dialectical tensions between an art work and its origins remain intact and unresolved, buried beneath the passage of time. The autonomy of art is premised upon this lack of resolution, upon temporal movement without a reconciliatory absorption into a greater whole, i.e., upon the persistence of tension between an art work and *die empirische Realität* from which it emerges. What Adorno's aesthetics seek, then, is to bring these unresolved tensions back into focus and thereby subvert the appearance of their resolution, the appearance which contributes to their reification.

In the absence of transcendent and inalterable aesthetic criteria, this refocus is for each work of art, a new project following new criteria—and in the absence of sublation, this refocus is especially in need of persistent revision because the unfolding continuity implied by *Aufhebung* obscures and even reifies the tensions upon which the autonomy of art is premised.[12]

The disparity and lack of resolution in historical movements, which Adorno posits, allow art to occupy a watershed-position within historical passage. Yet the former is inextricably bound to the latter: "Directly as artefacts, however, as products of social work, they [art works] also communicate with the empirical experience that they reject and out of which they draw their content."[13] Art is always in response to the social empirical reality, and the social empirical reality always provides the substance or "origins" from which art emerges. The restructuring of historical dialectics which procures the autonomy of art also binds it: the socio-historical context, "the empirically living," structures art and its autonomy.

The structural relation between the socio-historical and the autonomy of art is most evident in the foundational dynamic Adorno argues exists between the two. The dynamic is itself dialectical. What remains constant in Adorno's aesthetic is that, though neither universal nor particular is exempt from the consequences of historical passage, art always emerges from a negative dialectical or non-identical relation to its corresponding *Empirie*. But inasmuch as the instability of historic sublation procures the autonomy of art, the negative dialectical movement of art out of its socio-historic context is subject to a corresponding instability. Adorno's contention about the instability of sublation in the socio-historical process, the very instability that allows for the autonomy of art, brings the stability of aesthetic negation into question as well.

While art may in fact owe its existence to a negative dialectical relation with its socio-historical context, art reflects this context foremost in its own inability to prompt sublation with the "origins" or context to which it is bound in antithetical (negative) dialectical opposition, i.e., in its own inability to enact a comprehensive and nonetheless de-reified transformation of the social whole (whether politically oriented or otherwise).[14] The instability of aesthetic negation, its inability to sublate—in the material social environment—the "origins" it negates, procures their autonomy while confirming art's own. Both are contingent upon the instability of sublation. The continued autonomy of an art work's origins, despite their aesthetic negation, is the logical consequence of the law (*Bewegungsgesetz*) creating the autonomy of art itself.[15] What results is not a bifurcation of art and society into separate, autonomous realms, but a bilateral staggering of tensions straining against one another.

While the initial reception of Adorno's study in aesthetics latched on to the prominent position he gives to the autonomy of art, Adorno's questioning of sublation itself, not art's autonomy, is the central focus of the *Ästhetische Theorie.* But this clarification would not have been enough to re-ingratiate Adorno with the Left, from whom he was estranged in his last years. Using aesthetics as the catalyst for a rigorous inquiry into *Aufhebung* did little to meet the Left's demands. While the Left sought an aesthetics for activists, Adorno developed Leftist cultural thought. In this respect, Hohendahl is correct in his assessment: the *Ästhetische Theorie* is consistent with Adorno's general resistance to the dogmatic privileging that an emphasis on praxis gives to action.[16] If, for Adorno, art and philosophical thought were not the last bastions of critical opposition to society, he at least prescribed them as a seemingly interminable prerequisite to *engagement.*

Hohendahl is cautious not to dismiss the initial reception of Adorno's final work, like the work itself was dismissed. Nor do I want to dismiss this reception "out of hand." Although my coming remarks argue that to interpret the autonomy of art as the central thesis of the *Ästhetische Theorie* is to mistake effect for thesis, the prevalence of this interpretation cannot be explained solely on the basis of the political climate of the 1970s. It is the result of Adorno's rhetorical stance, his articulating his theory from the perspective of art itself, i.e., of his adopting the voice of the aesthetic position he purports to describe.

By positing the autonomy of art as the *Ästhetische Theorie*'s central thesis, Hohendahl and the initial reception of Adorno's last work missed a crucial link in the chain of Adorno's reasoning: an argued discontinuity in the concept of art is part of Adorno's project to revise historical dialectics, and, once Adorno pinpoints this discontinuity, he can challenge traditional dialectics because as a system they provide an insufficient account of art. As his revision unfolds, the autonomy of art comes to signify how art functions in the absence of conceptual continuity. But if the excessive attention Adorno devotes to the autonomy of art while restructuring historical dialectics did not in itself explain why the student and academic Left thought his central thesis was art's autonomy, then Adorno's rhetorical stance gave them what seems to be understandable cause.

In the sections which follow, I argue that Adorno creates the illusion that one can reside (indefinitely) in the autonomy figured by works of art. He does this by rhetorically adopting the voice of art looking in retrospect on what he describes as its negated origins. This rhetorical strategy is arguably an attempt by Adorno to distance himself from the reified social structures negated by art. But in his efforts to avoid succumbing to reification, Adorno side-steps the crucial question of origins itself. He side-steps the socio-historical particularity upon which aesthetic autonomy is based. It seems to me that this strategy displays a preference which obscures a most problematic and unwritten chapter in Adorno's last work. Rhetorically, the *Ästhetische Theorie* occupies the same position that Adorno repeatedly asserts must find new and discontinuous forms in a non-identical relation to specific socio-historical origins.

II. Articulating the Already Autonomous

Early in the *Ästhetische Theorie* Adorno clarifies that the autonomy attributed to art is sustained only in movement, and that this movement, in contrast to immutable criteria, depends not upon what art is, but on art's differentiating itself from what it is not. In other words, art defines itself through a process of negation or a continuous non-identity. Adorno writes:

> It is through its dynamic laws, not through some invariable principle, that art can be understood. It is defined by its relation to what is different from art. This other makes it possible for us to arrive at a substantive understanding of the specifically artistic in art. It is this approach to art that alone meets the criteria of a materialist and dialectical aesthetic, which evolves by segregating itself from its own matrix.[17]

In this general statement, Adorno provides the structure, indeed the modus operandi, underlying his subsequent claim that art works are "counter-images" to the "empirically living." In these and similar passages in **"On the Relation Between Art and Society,"** Adorno constructs a definition of the autonomy of art based on an ever-changing socio-historical context. Art obtains autonomy in opposition—this is the cornerstone of negation—while its socio-historical context, the object of its opposition, structures (*bestimmt*) both the nature of that opposition and the character of art's autonomy.

When socio-historical context provides the substance "out of which . . . [art draws its] content," and out of which art determines itself in negating recoil, each work of art constitutes a definitive instance of autonomy.[18] Aesthetic autonomy is indelibly defined by the non-identical tensions it possesses with its historical context. Aesthetic negation, the emergence of the artistic out of its Other, is neither a more accurate articulation nor a progressive unfolding of autonomy. Individual instances of autonomy have only the movement of non-identity in common. Each instance is connected to other instances not in any reciprocal confirmation of having taken different paths to the same destination, nor in having assisted one another in a greater realization of potential autonomy, but in a dynamic, mutually-negating interaction that challenges the universal position of autonomy as a concept. The interaction of heterogenous autonomies occupied by or articulated through different works of art dispels the reified illusion of autonomy as a realm unto itself. The autonomy of art pivots on the negation of autonomy as a reified ideal. Each work of art is singularly exemplary, its non-identity not being an example of a greater universal, but a singular instance of itself. For Adorno, any conception of the autonomy of art, other than the position a given work occupies in negative relation to its Other, regresses into reification and a repressive positivism.

This last point—which it seems to me does much to vindicate Adorno from his critics—is not immediately apparent in Adorno's writing. On the contrary, Adorno gives the appearance of adherence to a fixed conception of autonomy because he attempts to avoid reification by speaking from the general position or perspective of art that is already autonomous, i.e., from the perspective that has already negated its socio-historical context. For example, in the claim that the artistic (*das Kunsthafte*) specifies itself out of its Other (*das Andere*), the movement of aesthetic negation is an event spoken of in retrospect, when the socio-historical is already positioned as an object of hindsight, signified here by the term "the Other." By speaking from the position of art, Adorno eliminates the necessity for exploring the vast complexities underlying the socio-historical, choosing instead to dismiss them as the single collectivity, "the Other." As previously stated, this strategy of adopting the voice of art as a means of avoiding a reified concept of autonomy gave his initial readers the impression that Adorno had traded the goals of political activism for the consolations of aesthetic pleasure.

Yet for Adorno, aesthetic negation could never meet the demands of activists: aesthetic negation is not the direct articulation of criticism nor is it the positing of formulated goals or hypothetical alternatives—all of which sustain prevailing, delimiting discourse by appealing to tolerated and defusing avenues of dissent. Negation would be neutralized if subordinated to protest or if constricted to preconceived reified concepts of autonomy. Aesthetic negation, according to Adorno's argument, occurs when art resists the temptation to oppose the portrayed "unredeemed" state with formulated or implicit ideals. He specifies this in his *Ästhetische Theorie*:

> By cathecting the repressed, art internalizes the repressing principle, i.e., the unredeemed condition of the

world (Unheil), instead of merely airing futile protests against it. Art identifies and expresses that condition, thus anticipating its overcoming. It is this and not the photographic rendition of the unredeemed state or a false sense of beatitude, that defines the position of authentic modern art towards a gloomy objectivity.[19]

Adorno's distinction between an anticipatory, cathected internalization of the repressing principle (*Lust am Verdrängten*) and mere protests against the principle arguably respond to the demand for an aesthetic which instigates political activism. While politically *engaged* art like Brecht's—which often serves as a whipping-boy for Adorno—attempts to adjust the social whole by protesting society's aberration from preconceived guidelines or values, such art fails to recognize that these same values are intrinsically structured by the dominant discourses which they ostensibly oppose.[20] In the place of such limited aesthetic approaches, Adorno suggests the need for art works which incorporate the preconceived notions of autonomy into themselves and thereby expose how the dominant social discourses permeate current ideals. He posits an aesthetic whose autonomy resides in its negative dialectic or non-identity with prevalent conceptions of autonomy.

The futility of protest, its false sense of beatitude, lies in the mistaken presumption that subjects can detach themselves enough from the mediations of repression so as to offer an alternative that does not subscribe to the same repressive forces. Instead of offering protests that attempt to redirect within the status quo, art seeks to deadlock repression and thereby violate its limits. The deadlock generates a crisis in meaning, whereas protest only simulates crisis while still perpetuating prevalent constricting delusions. The crisis occurs through an exposure of stultification and reification in perception, thus exposing the ways accepted interpretations of reality dictate experience. Art is anticipatory in that it upsets or obstructs habitual, unexamined principles of conduct. Adorno argues that "Willfulness amid spontaneity—this is the vital element of art," a willfulness that facilitates spontaneity by negating repression.[21] Art demands a willfulness, a courage, which allows new meaning. This meaning is a departure from reification into spontaneity and the unknown.

Art's incorporation of the repressive principle into itself objectifies the dynamic of negation. When an art work objectifies repression, it becomes the progenitor of aesthetic reflection, and its non-identical movement subverts the repression. According to Adorno, objectification alters the social environment of those who come in contact with the work. More than a mere reflection of the social milieu, an art work that objectifies its origins alters the socio-historical context, offering in its "counter-image" to "the empirically living" what the "empirically living" denies.[22] The non-identical generates tension between itself and its origins that endures beneath the appearance of resolution. The work becomes a limited part of the social environment, but nonetheless an object to which an individual potentially can respond. Adorno argues:

> Aesthetic expression is objectification of the nonobjective. Put more precisely, through its objectifica-

tion expression becomes a second non-objective substance, one that speaks out of the artefact [sic] rather than out of the subject.[23]

The aesthetic voice emerging from the artifact anticipates a new-found autonomy in the contemplation it facilitates. Anticipation would seem the correct term here because aesthetic expression is only potentially autonomous. Negation is not cancellation, i.e., final. It denotes a dynamic impasse in a continuing struggle for dominance. Here we are speaking of two distinct autonomies: one ephemeral and terminal, and the other resulting from historical passage. The former resides in what an art work potentially offers to an individual in the counter-image it provides to a specific socio-historical context. The latter is the autonomy addressed earlier in this paper, the autonomy that results from the unresolved tensions an art work has with a specific historic moment.

III. The Question of Origins

The autonomy of art depends upon such an elaborate conception of historical dialectics that Adorno's writing from the perspective of the non-identical is arguably a subtle method for talking about the autonomy of art without becoming entangled in the complexities leading to it. But the method also has the tendency to presume that the origins with which an artwork is non-identical are non-problematic. Thus Adorno dismisses the question of origins in an early section of the **Ästhetische Theorie** entitled "Gegen Ursprunsfrage." The dismissal might not be so problematic were it not for two points: First of all, art owes its non-identical existence to the origins which Adorno dismisses. Immediately after dismissing the question of origins, Adorno specifies that aesthetic negation and the subsequent autonomy of art are meaningless without the origins from which they emerge: "Works of art became what they are by negating their origins."[24] Secondly, Adorno keeps the question open at the margins of his discussions by pushing it into an appendix.[25]

When he finally does return to the question of origins in the appendix, the reasons for his discomfort quickly become evident; the excursus is a documented explication of his earlier rejection.[26] The rejection of origins as a topic worthy of consideration is based upon its association with debates concerning the origin of art itself. For Adorno, the origin of art is irrelevant to the origins an art work negates, and he dismisses the question of art's origin because the question presupposes a continuity in art which, according to Adorno, is at odds with art itself. This is ostensibly why he begins with, in the excursus, the claim that the endeavor to understand the essence of art by looking to its origins is "necessarily disappointing."[27]

While the distinction between the origin of art and the origins an art work negates is important to the subordination of universals to the influence of historical dialectics, Adorno also overplays the distinction. The excursus rigorously dismantles and obstructs a view of art as a continuous and unfolding concept, but does so at the expense of

an adequate explanation of what constitutes the origins an art work negates. Like his structurally binding "autonomy" to socio-historical specifics, his rejection of the "Ursprungsfrage" emphasizes historical distinction or particularity over historical evolution or continuity. Adorno's views on the autonomy of art and on the origins negated by art bear the additional similarity that, in both instances, the socio-historical occupies the position of the unarticulated. But the point is that regardless of whether Adorno rejects the term "origin(s)" in its common usage, he still employs a structural conception of it whose explanation he neglects.

Although the excursus refuses to provide an adequate explanation of what is meant by the "origins" an art work negates, the methodology of the excursus lends itself to an inferential construction of the underlying structures governing Adorno's use of the term. Adorno's use of "origins" rests at the center of a dynamic tension between a radical historicization and an equally radical questioning of what comprises historicity. Like the art works whose negative basis they form, the origins to which art works owe their existence are historical.[28] But while historicity joins an art work to its origins, one must also understand what constitutes the substance of history to understand origins. Unfortunately, it is not enough to say that the material and the social are the substance of the historical.

The vagueness of the term "origins" hedges between a catch-all phrase and a critical expression that calls into question the material and the social realms to which it refers. It alludes not only to socio-historical context but also questions the fixity and stability of such a concept. By saying that art negates its origins rather than its socio-historical context, and by adopting the position of art looking in retrospect on the "Other" it has left behind, Adorno concedes that art responds to social reality, but leaves open the question as to what constitutes that reality.

The scope of the origins to which art responds extends beyond the specifically "material" life men and women lead. As Peter Hohendahl has noted:

> [Adorno] . . . used Hegel's model of history to understand the evolution of literature as representative for the development of social and political history. . . . While he insists on the dialectic of art and society (the art work is also a social fact), he does not, unlike Lukács, conceive of it in terms of reflection.[29]

Adorno's opposition to the arguments that art is a reflection of social reality stem from his assumption that consciousness is not merely a reflection of the material. The lives men and women lead respond to a social milieu comprised of ideas as well as materiality. Rather than thought mirroring the material-social environment, art actively contributes to it. The origins negated by an art work denote a socio-historical context that includes art and philosophy—not as reflection but as substance. As Hohendahl notes: "Ultimately, art and society belong to the same stream of history."[30] "Origins" denotes them both.

Once art and philosophy become part of the socio-historical context that a work of art negates, it is not difficult to understand why Adorno is so opposed to studies tracing art back to its prehistoric origins. Such studies presuppose a separate qualitative continuity in art that Adorno claims each work must negate in order to be art at all: "It must turn against that which determines its own concept and thereby becomes uncertain within its deepest fibers."[31] His combining the intellectual with the material in a single milieu subordinates abstractions and concepts—which try to stand "above" or "outside"—to the qualitative substance, i.e., the origins that a work must negate to become art. The consequences of this subordination occur at numerous levels. First of all, it radically alters the notion of "an unfolding concept," by leaving each work of art disjointed and severed from the next. At the same time that Adorno places art amidst specific socio-historical parameters, he expands the width of these parameters by replacing reflection theory with a conception of the socio-historical as an admixture of the intellectual and the material.[32] Combined, these two maneuvers suggest a revision of dialectics that distinguishes Adorno from Hegel. They make up a dynamic that pulls at its own seams: once the historical becomes an admixture of intellectual and material, the elements of history, which include the disjointed concept of art, lose their qualitative continuity.

Adorno's emphatic rejection of a qualitative continuity in the concept of art has implications for the movements of history in general. A discontinuity in concepts implies a corresponding discontinuity in history—especially within the Hegelian model where concepts are traditionally the movers of history itself. Even if the concept of art were a special case—which here it is not, despite other privileges Adorno gives to art—its being an exception among concepts would have ramifications that demand a conceptual restructuring of history. The qualitative discontinuity of the concept of art suggests that, rather than evolving, concepts expire once outside of their socio-historical context. They have a bounded, contextual vitality. This is the essence of their autonomy. Like an individual work of art, concepts in general sustain a dialectical tension which thrives within their socio-historical context, but which reifies once beyond this context.

While reification in place of a dialectical synthesis brings into question the conception of history as a unified process, it has specific consequences for aesthetics as well. Socio-historical change de-stabilizes the referents of the terms and ideals with which previous works of art formulated their non-identity. Historical passage slips these terms into the origins with which later works are qualitatively at odds. Once de-stabilized, previous aesthetic ideals or discourse lend themselves to appropriation and ultimately to the opposite of their earlier non-identical opposition, viz. repression and reification.[33]

With the contextual, qualitative specificity of the concept of art, an additional element vies for position within the dynamic tension of its negated origins: Adorno's radical

historicization is not only offset by a rigorous questioning of what comprises history; this historicization is offset by a questioning of supersession as well. Art's non-identical origins are a socio-historical context in which the content of the social and the historical are brought into question, and in which reification prevails beneath the appearance of supersession.

The "origins" of Adorno's *Ästhetische Theorie* presuppose a model of history in which even the basic oppositions of Hegelian dialectics are brought into question, a model in distinct contrast to Hohendahl's Hegelian reading of Adorno and to the reading of Eugene Lunn, who defends a similar position. Lunn notes Adorno's frequent juxtaposition of "seeming opposites . . . so as to mediate them by developing each of the apparent antinomies out of the other in mutual critique." This strategy is according to Lunn "a dialectic procedure which . . . [Adorno] owed to Hegel."[34] With origins, however, the mediation quickly extends beyond the mutual critique of antinomies. It escalates instead into a constellation of mediations: at one level, there is the socio-historical that brings its very substance into question, and the socio-historical is in dynamic tension with a rigorous inquiry into the presumptions underlying supersession, the continuity thought to gauge temporal passage. While one can single out specific elements—as, for example, the apparent antinomy that the continuity of a concept becomes a litmus test for its reification—the question of socio-historical substance is no less a mediating factor to a concept (*ein Begriff,* in the Hegelian sense) than is the question of its continuity. The complex mediation within "origins," indeed, mediation in general, occurs at a level where the antinomies are never quite clear because opposites are themselves never stable enough to polarize and ossify into the Hegelian categories of thesis and antithesis.

The diverse and dynamic mediation occurring beneath Adorno's own use of the term "origins" helps to pinpoint the referent in the sentence with which he opens "Gegen Ursprungsfrage": "Art has its concept in the historically changing constellation of moments."[35] The weight of this sentence rests on the definite article, on the specificity that it connotes. The constellation to which he refers is the "origins" that he says an art work must negate. But the concept of art is not that which is changing or evolving, at least not evolving beyond the constellation itself, within which, it continues to unfold because its dialectical tensions remain unresolved. It is the constellation of moments that changes and the constellation from which art receives its concept, each new constellation necessitating a new non-identical concept of art and of autonomy. The dialectical evolution continues within the constellation itself, but the concept has no continuity outside of the contextual origins structuring it.

While Adorno's polemic against the so-called origin of art does emphasize a discontinuity that is presupposed in the autonomous, non-identical movement of aesthetic negation, and while the description of origins as a constellation or dynamic of tensions does much to highlight the presumptions functioning beneath Adorno's own application of the term "origins," these characterizations still describe the consequences of aesthetic negation and not really origins per se. The characterizations are part of Adorno's rhetorical stance. They still come from the perspective of art looking in retrospect on the origins or "the Other" it has negated. Aesthetic negation uncovers the discontinuity of concepts—i.e., the breakdown in sublation—and it illuminates the unresolved, thriving dialectical tensions obscured beneath the appearance of supersession. To say that art has its concept in the historically changing constellation of moments is to describe origins in their negated relation to an artwork, to describe origins after the appearance of continuity and stability has given way to an aesthetic force capable of reinscribing the constellation which appearance obscures. But it makes sense, at least according to the dictates of Adorno's argument, that the origins as Adorno presents them must already be in their negated state: if the origins were already obviously discontinuous and unresolved, an art work could not find the stable basis—however illusory that basis proves to be—against which to build its non-identical relation without positing continuity so as later to dispel it.

The origins negated by art remain unarticulated in Adorno's theories, more so than the non-identity of art itself. One might think that this is as it should be, given that the *Ästhetische Theorie* is after all a work on aesthetics, and given that the theory itself emphasizes the socio-historical specificity of origins, a specificity articulation might dilute. Yet for all its non-identity, art presupposes a corresponding specificity as well, the structure and not merely the details of which Adorno neglects by addressing the consequences of negation instead of clarifying his own use of the term "origins." As a result, both the non-identity of art and its negated origins remain cryptic and formulaic. Crucial structural aspects of the dynamics between art and society persist in the form of mostly unexplored terms—e.g., "non-identity," "what it is not," "the Other" and above all "origins"—although their exploration would foster a clarity rather than dilution. In part, this lacuna results from and is even obscured by Adorno's having selected the concept of art to illustrate the discontinuity of concepts in general, the discontinuity that aesthetic negation exposes. This unexplored territory results, in part, from Adorno's mesmerizing account of the consequences of negation—an account that is in itself suspect because, by articulating the consequences of negation rather than the structural conditions leading to it, the account comes dangerously close to the formulation of immutable criteria which artifacts must meet in order to be art. At the very least, the account of the consequences of negation cultivates registers with which a critic/reader can search for that which appears to correspond to preconceived results. It borders on begging the question. While these last possibilities are at odds with more dominant tendencies in Adorno's text, their emergence in the theory's central dynamic raises questions that cannot be ignored. For the present suffice it to say that, though the terms may remain unexplored, their function is to provide the means with which to discuss the aesthetic exposure of the heterogeneity which society obscures.

IV. HETEROGENEITY AND THE CRISIS IN DIALECTICS

Rainer Nägele argues that "if Hegel's dialectic is the attempt to master the heterogeneous in philosophical concepts, negative dialectics is the attempt to reinscribe the heterogeneous as heterogeneous also in thought."[36] In Adorno's *Ästhetische Theorie,* art's non-identity is this re-inscription. This means that the non-identity of art, because it *re*-inscribes heterogeneity, presupposes the homogeneity, i.e., a continuity in concepts, which negation dispels. More than a mere reversal of Hegel, reinscribing the heterogeneous articulates a crisis in the basic mechanics of Hegelian dialectics. Without continuity in concepts, sublation comes to a standstill—in this respect there is a brilliance in Adorno's having focused on the discontinuity or disunity of the concept of art.[37] Art's own heterogeneity gives it the conceptual basis from which to question and negate the appearance of continuity in concepts; its heterogeneity is its non-identity with its origins; and it is at the avant-garde of the heterogeneity it uncovers.

Adorno's rejection of theories on "the origin of art" and this rejection's connection with his reworking of historical dialectics are but two aspects within a larger critical constellation. While the discontinuity of art suggests that sublation forces or creates the illusion of unity "where none in fact exist[s]," Adorno's rejection of continuity also initiates a reworking of the idea of reification—which here signifies the glossing over or repression of heterogeneities beneath the appearance of unity.[38] The appearance of a resolution (*Aufhebung*) that leads from one historical constellation into another robs art of the dialectical vitality it has within its specific socio-historical context.

In contrast to the continuity of origins implied by supersession, Adorno posits layers of constellations whose essential tensions have not resolved, but are buried beneath a reified rhetorically imposed supersession which accompanies temporal passage. This same lack of resolution is, for example, what allows Adorno to make the claim with which he opens *Negative Dialektik:* "Philosophy, which once seemed obsolete, lives on because the moment to realize it was missed."[39] Philosophy is not a floating potential waiting for realization—its moment has passed. It is rather the premier example of unresolved tension surviving within its specific moment or constellation and providing a point of focus from which to scrutinize fabricated resolution. In the unity and stability presupposed by the origins art negates, Adorno finds a false and reified history—just as the question of the origin of art is a false question based upon a reified concept of art. While origins presuppose historical continuity, negation reinscribes historical heterogeneity. Art's negation of its origins is twofold: it uncovers unresolved dialectical tensions that the apparent unity within origins obscures; and its non-identity with these origins generates a dialectical tension that also knows no resolution.

In *Negative Dialektik* Adorno argues that unity was fraudulently posited at the expense of plurality, and that whatever the initial source of this fraudulence might have been, the end result was that as "unity" gained in prominence, it also gained the power to repress those resisting it.[40] He argues:

> The universal by which every individual is determined at all, as one of his particular kind, that universal is borrowed from what is extraneous and therefore as heteronomous to the individual as anything once said to have been ordained for him by demons.[41]

Adorno's resort to the image of demons in his description is not gratuitous. The image forms a negative or contrast to the Hegelian Spirit, specifically a contrast to the continuity so central to the movements of Hegelian dialectics: a contrast between the singularity of an all-superseding and unifying Spirit and the diverse plurality of demons reinscribing heterogeneity. The image of demons admonishes against concepts of unity because these concepts erase the history they purport to trace. Art negates these posited origins with the reinscription of particularity, the cornerstone of heterogeneity. The contrast in imagery extends even into the structural morphology of Adorno's descriptions: while "origins" retroproject an evolution through sublation, art recalls "an objectivity removed [enthoben] from categorical frameworks."[42] The contrast between the subsuming supersession of Spirit and the heterogeneous reinscriptions of demons resides in the distinction between an *auf-* and *ent- (ge)hobene Objektivität*. The polarities of demons and Spirit, the *Enthobene* and the *Aufgehobene,* are the opposing elements in art's non-identity with its origins. The reinscription of heterogeneity is the recovery of the *Enthobene* vis-à-vis the overwhelming appearance of the *Aufgehobene*.

Yet despite the forcefulness of this contrast, it still remains within descriptions of consequences at the expense of an explanation of the structural conditions leading to it. By articulating the discussion from the perspective of art looking in retrospect on the origins or "the Other" it has negated, Adorno posits his (art's) oppositions rather than allowing art to formulate them on its own. In this case, the necessary opposite is Hegel whose dialectics foster the appearances with which art is non-identical, but which persist in each instance of art's non-identity to them. Inasmuch as art persists in the lack of resolution of its dialectical tensions, so too do the counter-elements of these tensions. Though Adorno attempts to circumvent Hegel by arguing that art recalls a reality before the Hegelian system, *eine dem kategorialen Gefüge enthobene Objektivität,* his having built aesthetic negation in opposition to Hegel reflects Adorno's own irresolute and unresolved tension with his origins.

Notes

1. For a brief definition of the term "materialist," I would recommend Lambert Zuidervaart's discussion of Marxist aesthetics in his recent book *Adorno's Aesthetic Theory* (MIT Press, 1991)—in particular, his statement: "Marx's historical materialism implies that conflicts within art must be examined in terms of conflicts within the technological and economic base" (p. 69). For the whole of Zuidervaart's argument see pages 68-77. This section substantially revises arguments first formulated in his "The Social Significance of Autonomous Art: Adorno and Bürger," *Journal of Aesthetics and Art Criticism* 48 (1990): 61-77. Insofar as the term "materialist" is associated with the disappointment that marked the reception of the *Ästhetische Theorie,* it is worth tracing the term back to Marx's "Thesen über Feuerbach," in which "materialism" is "sinnlich menschliche Tätigkeit" and in which "materialism" is concerned with changing the world. See Marx-Engels *Werke,* vol. 3 (Berlin: Dietz Verlag, 1956), pp. 5-7. For a more thorough discussion of the Left's disappointment with Adorno's *Ästhetische Theorie* see Peter Uwe Hohendahl, *Reappraisals* (Cornell University Press, 1991), pp. 1-21 and especially pp. 75-98. The latter section is a reprint of his "Looking Back at Adorno's *Ästhetische Theorie,*" *German Quarterly* 54 (1981): 133-148.

2. Hohendahl maintains that with the formation of the Brandt government "radical [political] reform seemed to be possible" (*Reappraisals* p. 9), and the Left abandoned what they interpreted as Adorno's pessimistic aesthetics of hibernation—what Peter Bürger describes as Adorno's succumbing to the historical bourgeois separation of art from the context of practical life. See *Theorie der Avant-Garde* (Frankfurt am Main: Suhrkamp, 1974), p. 63; trans. Michael Shaw (University of Minnesota Press, 1984), p. 46. Bürger maintains this same position in his more recent article "Adorno's Anti-Avant-Gardism," *Telos* 86 (1990-91): 49-60.

3. Adorno's revision of dialectics preceded *Ästhetische Theorie,* having already occurred in *Negative Dialektik,* where, as Martin Jay has pointed out, drawing upon the ideas of Benjamin, Adorno replaced the Hegelian conception of synthesis with that of the constellation of ideas. See *Negative Dialektik* (Frankfurt: Suhrkamp, 1973), pp. 158-168; trans. E. B. Ashton (New York: Continuum, 1973), pp. 156-166. For Martin Jay's account see *Marxism and Totality* (University of California Press, 1984), pp. 241-275, especially pp. 246-252. These revisions and their relation to Adorno's aesthetics will be discussed later in this work.

4. Bürger, *Theorie,* Suhrkamp, p. 63; University of Minnesota, p. 46.

5. For further discussion of this last issue see Jochen Schulte-Sasse, "Theory of Modernism versus Theory of the Avant-Garde," Foreword, *Theory of the Avant-Garde,* pp. xviii; see also Elizabeth Wright, *Postmodern Brecht* (New York: Routledge, 1989), pp. 68-89. For a specific discussion of the effect of Adorno's

negativism on his reception see "Introduction to Adorno," *Telos* 7 (1974): 2-3.

6. The most recent assessment of this unique form of dialectics can be found in Fredric Jameson's discussion of Adorno's aversion to positivism: see *Late Marxism* (New York: Verso, 1990), pp. 89-90.

7. For an analysis of the aesthetics of Kant and Adorno see Lambert Zuidervaart, "The Artefactuality of Autonomous Art: Kant and Adorno," *The Reasons of Art,* ed. Peter McCormick (University of Ottawa Press, 1986), pp. 256-263.

8. "Kunstwerke sind Nachbilder des empirisch Lebendigen, soweit sie diesem zukommen lassen, was ihnen draußen verweigert wird, und dadurch vom dem befreien, wozu ihre dinghaft-auswendige Erfahrung sie zurichtet." [translation corrected] Theodor Adorno, *Ästhetische Theorie* (Frankfurt am Main: Suhrkamp, 1973), p. 14; trans. C. Lenhardt (Boston: Routledge & Kegan Paul, 1984), p. 4.

9. "soll dem Nichtidentischen beistehen, das der Identitätszwang in der Realität unterdrückt." [translation corrected] Adorno *AT* Suhrkamp, p. 14; Routledge, p. 6.

10. "altern, erkalten und sterben" [translation corrected] Adorno *AT* Suhrkamp, p. 14; Routledge, p. 6.

11. "Was einmal in einem Kunstwerk wahr gewesen ist . . . [ward] durch den Gang der Geschichte demontiert." [translation corrected] Adorno *AT* Suhrkamp, pp. 67-68; Routledge, p. 60.

12. The controversy regarding Adorno's seemingly contradictory application of the term "reification," a controversy pursued by Gillian Rose and picked up by Martin Jay, is explained by Adorno's argument on the inadequacy of synthesis as a means of accounting for historical passage. As later discussion will show, Adorno replaces sublation with the idea of constellations. While "constellations" maintain the dimension of the socio-historical, they avoid the illusion of resolution that Adorno argues is inherent to the notion of sublation. It is this illusory resolution that Adorno combats and that constitutes what he deems as reification. See Gillian Rose, *The Melancholy Science* (London: Macmillan, 1978), pp. 40-47 and Martin Jay, *Marxism and Totality,* pp. 266-272.

13. "Gerade als Artefakte aber. Produkte gesellschaftlicher Arbeit kommunizieren sie auch mit der Empirie, der sie absagen, und aus ihr ziehen sie ihren Inhalt." [translation corrected] Adorno *AT* Suhrkamp, p. 15; Routledge, pp. 6-7.

14. Bruce Baugh uses this lack of comprehensiveness for a convincing revision of Adorno's aesthetics. Baugh argues that an artwork's non-identity is addressed to specific groups and is much more contextualized than Adorno allows. See "Left-Wing Elitism: Adorno on Popular Culture" *Philosophy and Literature* 14 (1990): 65-78.

15. The term "Bewegungsgesetz" will be explored in the sections that follow.

16. Hohendahl *Reappraisals,* p. 80.

17. "Deutbar ist Kunst nur an ihrem Bewegungsgesetz, nicht durch Invarianten. Sie bestimmt sich im Verhältnis zu dem, was sie nicht ist. Das spezifisch Kunsthafte an ihr ist aus ihrem Anderen: inhaltlich abzuleiten; das allein genügte irgend der Forderung einer materialistisch-dialektischen Ästhetik. Sie spezifiziert sich an dem, wodurch sie von dem sich scheidet, woraus sie wurde." Adorno *AT* Suhrkamp, p. 12; Routledge, p. 4.

18. Adorno *AT* Suhrkamp, p. 15; Routledge, pp. 6-7.

19. "In der Lust am Verdrängten rezipiert Kunst zugleich das Unheil, das verdrängende Prinzip, anstatt bloß vergeblich dagegen zu protestieren. Daß sie das Unheil durch Identifikation ausspricht, antezipiert seine Entmächtigung; das, weder die Photographie des Unheils noch falsche Seligkeit, umschreibt die Stellung authentischer gegenwärtiger Kunst zur verfinsterten Objektivität." Adorno *AT* Suhrkamp, pp. 35-36; Routledge, pp. 27-28.

20. In his recent article "Karl Popper and the Frankfurt School," Robert D'Amico observes the emergence of similar arguments in Horkheimer's late writings. D'Amico maintains that for Horkheimer and the Frankfurt School, moral commitments and theoretical agendas "followed different logics of analysis" (p. 41). See *Telos* 86 (1990-91): 33-48.

21. "Willkür im Unwillkürlichen ist das Lebenselement der Kunst." Adorno *AT* Suhrkamp, p. 174; Routledge, p. 167.

22. Ibid., p. 14; Ibid., p. 4.

23. "Ästhetischer Ausdruck ist Vergegenständlichung des Ungegenständlichen, und zwar derart, daß es durch seine Vergegenständlichung zum zweiten Ungegenständlichen wird, zu dem, was aus dem Artefakt spricht, nicht als Imitation des Subjekts." Ibid., p. 170; Ibid., p. 163. (A small note on the translation is in order because in the original it is not the expression that becomes "a second non-objective substance," but the objectified "non-objective." The "artefact" is the aesthetic expression, and it consists of more than the objectification of the non-objective. Otherwise negation would not occur, and the "artefact" would remain an "imitation of the subject." That the objectified non-objective becomes a "second non-objective" acknowledges its role in the dynamic or dialectic of aesthetic negation.)

24. "Fraglos . . . sind die Kunstwerken nur, indem sie ihren Ursprung negierten, zu Kunstwerke zu werden." Ibid., p. 12; Ibid., p. 4.

25. The placement of these arguments in an appendix may be the consequence of editorial decisions made

after Adorno's death. But this is not explicit in the afterword to the *Ästhetische Theorie* written by Gretel Adorno and Rolf Tiedemann. Indeed, the editors mention the paralipomena (appendix I) that Adorno wished to incorporate into the final draft of the text and the introduction (appendix III) that Adorno had planned to revise. No mention is made of the excursus "Theorien über den Ursprung der Kunst," the only appendix to which Adorno gave a separate title and which he called an "Exkurs," i.e., a digression from the main issues of his concern.

26. Ibid., p. 480-490; Ibid., p. 447-455.

27. "Enttäuschen notwendig." Ibid., p. 480; Ibid., p. 447.

28. Ibid., p. 480; Ibid., p. 447.

29. Hohendahl *Reappraisals*, p. 82.

30. Ibid.

31. "Sie muβ gegen das sich wenden, was ihren eigenen Begriff ausmacht, und wird dadurch ungewiβ bis in die innerste Fiber hinein." [translation corrected] Adorno *AT* Suhrkamp, p. 10; Routledge 2.

32. While Hohendahl is correct in distinguishing Adorno from this position, his associating Lukács with it is somewhat sweeping and obscures the diversity of positions Lukács defended during his life.

33. In a recent essay entitled "Adorno and the Metaphysics of Modernism: The Problem of a 'Postmodern' Art," Peter Osborne has pointed out that this destabilization is not a phenomena unique to works of art. He argues that aesthetics itself experiences this crisis and that the attempts to circumvent the exhaustion of aesthetics is at the center of Adorno's project. He writes:

> If art had reached a point at which it must 'revolt against its essential concepts' in order to survive, it none the less remains inconceivable without them. All modern art, according to Adorno, is inscribed within the terms of the contradiction. Under such conditions, aesthetics can have only one goal: 'to foster the rational and concrete dissolution of conventional aesthetic categories' in such a way as to 'release new truth content into these categories' by confronting them with the most recent forms of artistic experience
>
> (p. 24).

See *The Problems of Modernity,* ed. Andrew Benjamin (New York: Routledge, 1989), pp. 23-48.

34. *Eugene Lunn, Marxism and Modernism* (University of California Press, 1982), p. 230.

35. "Kunst hat ihren Begriff in der geschichtlich sich verändernden Konstellation von Momenten." [translation corrected] Adorno *AT* Suhrkamp, p. 11; Routledge, p. 3.

36. Rainer Nägele, "The Scene of the Other: Theodor W. Adorno's *Negative Dialectic* in the Context of Poststructuralism," *Boundary 2* 11 (1982-83), p. 68.

37. In *Marxism and Totality,* Martin Jay attributes Adorno's questioning of sublation to the influence of Benjamin, for whom also "dialectical mediation with its goal of *Aufhebung* (sublation) too quickly forced a unity where none in fact existed." Jay argues that Adorno drew heavily on Benjamin's *Der Ursprung des Deutschen Trauerspiels* in this instance and with regard to "constellations" as well. See *Marxism and Totality,* p. 248.

38. Martin Jay, *Adorno* (Harvard University Press), p. 248.

39. "Philosophie, die einmal überholt scheint, erhält sich am Leben, weil der Augenblick ihrer Verwirklichung versäumt ward." Theodor W. Adorno *ND* Suhrkamp, p. 15; Continuum, p. 3.

40. Ibid., p. 309; Ibid., p. 315.

41. "Das Allegemeine, durch welches jeder Einzelnen sich überhaupt als Einheit seiner Besonderung bestimmt, ist dem ihm Auswendigen entlehnt und darum dem Einzelnen auch so heteronom, wie nur, was einst Dämonen über ihn sollten verhängt haben." Ibid., p. 310; Ibid., p. 315.

42. "eine dem kategorialen Gefüge enthobene Objektivität." [translation corrected] Adorno *AT* Suhrkamp, p. 488; Routledge, p. 453.

Richard Wolin (essay date 1992)

SOURCE: "Mimesis, Utopia, and Reconciliation: A Redemptive Critique of Adorno's *Aesthetic Theory*," in *The Terms of Cultural Criticism: The Frankfurt School, Existentialism, Poststructuralism,* Columbia University Press, pp. 62-79.

[*In the following essay, Wolin examines the utopian elements of Adorno's aesthetics.*]

In 1980, Leo Lowenthal formulated a set of prescient insights about the future of Critical Theory in an interview entitled "The Utopian Motif is Suspended."[1] By "utopian motif," Lowenthal was referring to the eschatological hopes for a better life in the here and now that inspired not only the enterprise of Critical Theory, but an entire generation of Central European Jewish thinkers who, like himself, came of age around the time of World War I and drew on utopian aspects of the Jewish tradition as a source of messianic inspiration.[2] Among this generation, a decisive influence on the "inner circle" of Critical Theorists was exercised by the thought of Ernst Bloch, Georg Lukács, and Walter Benjamin.[3]

Prima facie, the claim epitomized in the title of the Lowenthal interview cannot help but seem a startling admission. For if we try to imagine the work of Horkheimer, Adorno, and Marcuse stripped of this dimension of utopian longing, it seems divested of its most fundamental impulses. Moreover, Lowenthal's contention seems a striking concession in the direction of Jürgen Habermas, who has made a point of trying to integrate Critical Theory with contemporary developments in social science and philosophy of language at the expense of its speculative-utopian tendencies. "Maybe [Habermas] is right," Lowenthal observes. "Perhaps [the speculative-utopian moment] is ballast. When I speak of such things, I feel a bit old and obsolete. After all, one cannot just live from utopian hopes based in never-never land, whose realization seems scarcely in the realm of the possible. Maybe this is a cause of the sadness I spoke of at the outset. But perhaps the theoretical realism I sense in Habermas is the only means of salvaging the motifs present in Critical Theory and thereby of protecting them from a complete disintegration into an empty, melancholy pessimism."[4]

Of course, Lowenthal's comments must in no way be construed as an abandonment of the critical intellectual legacy he helped found. Instead, in keeping with the nobler aspects of the dialectical tradition, they represent a constructive modification of what seem to be, from the vantage point of the current historical hour, extraneous preoccupations. As Lowenthal explains, Critical Theory's own revolutionary ardor was decisively cooled in the aftermath of the twin catastrophes of Nazism and Stalinism. For him, however, the loss of concrete utopian prospects in fact signifies the need for a redoubling of original critical energies. "It would be criminal to bury ideology critique now," Lowenthal remarks. "What has not been lost is, of course, the critical approach: the process of analysis, retaining the good and rejecting the bad, the need to accuse, the indictment of all that exists, . . . but without explicit hopes. What has occurred is not a retreat into skepticism or cynicism but sadness. The utopian motif has been suspended."

Lowenthal's sober appraisal of the utopian side of Critical Theory represents a valuable point of departure for examining Adorno's *Aesthetic Theory.* For it is in *Aesthetic Theory* that we find Adorno at his most utopian. In the later Adorno, philosophy is assigned the "negative" role of ruthlessly criticizing itself in order, against all odds, to undo its manifold past failings. This is the message of *Negative Dialectics,* a work which, in eminently quixotic fashion, fights against the domination of the concept through the use of concepts. Only as aesthetics does philosophy for the first time truly come into its own. It thus relinquishes its traditional position of privilege as *prima philosophia* and instead becomes a handmaiden to the arts as their faithful interpreter. Its new mission is to give voice to the speechless particularity of aesthetic objectivations, which, as "art," are nonconceptual, and thus devoid of the capacity for theoretical expression. It is precisely at this intersection of art and philosophy, that the utopian dimension of Adorno's work manifests itself. For this intersection is also the locus of *aesthetic theory.*

The stakes in this debate over the continued relevance of the utopian dimension of Critical Theory are high: an answer to this question will go far toward determining one's

receptivity to the "linguistic turn" in Critical Theory spurred by the work of Habermas. To be sure, Habermas' oeuvre is far from devoid of utopian potential: the theory of communicative competence sets forth an ideal speech situation in which generalized and unconstrained participation in decisionmaking becomes the counterfactual normative touchstone. Yet, unlike his predecessors, Habermas is someone who is fully at home with the ethical presuppositions of the modern world. He is for the most part interested in bringing these preconditions to consummation; or, as he once phrased it, the project of the modern age must be brought to completion. It is in this spirit that he has felicitously characterized the political implications of his theories as a "radical reformism." Absent from his perspective is the "romantic anti-capitalist" impulse that pervaded the worldview of the first generation of Frankfurt theorists. It was precisely this impulse that impelled their program of a "ruthless critique of everything existing" (Marx), which took the form of an unmitigated existential antipathy toward capitalist modernity as a whole. In eminently dialectical fashion, it was precisely this existential antipathy that spurred the profound utopian longings of Adorno, Horkheimer, Lowenthal, Marcuse, etc.

While Habermas has not hesitated to criticize vigorously the various "social pathologies" engendered by late capitalism, the sentiment of anticapitalist, "existential antipathy" is fundamentally foreign to his way of thinking. Correspondingly, he has often attacked the romantic anticapitalist utopianism of Critical Theory as one of its weakest aspects. The Critical Theorists' rejection of the notion of "immanent critique" is seen as essentially Nietzschean: they accept Nietzsche's *Zeitdiagnose* of bourgeois modernity by concurring with him that its cultural ideals are wholly bankrupt; and this conclusion forces them, like Nietzsche, to abandon the concept of immanent critique for that of "total critique." In both cases, the equation of modernity with a prosaic logic of "rationalization" ("instrumental reason"), where the unexalted mentality of the Weberian "Fachmensch" reigns triumphant, leads to a search for *aestheticist* alternatives. For Habermas, conversely, the ideals of bourgeois modernity (embodied in the differentiated spheres of science, morality, and art) remain serviceable as a basis for the immanent criticism of its various "social pathologies." The authors of *Dialectic of Enlightenment* have abandoned too much by succumbing to Nietzsche's heady, totalizing critique of the bourgeois world—for example, the potentials for communicative reason embodied in modern bourgeois law and morality.

We may summarize Habermas' objections by saying that as a result of a totalistic and undialectical understanding of the significance of modernity, Horkheimer and Adorno remained incapable of comprehending future sources of social change: from a "totally administered world" no good can conceivably emerge. And in consequence of this diagnostic incapacity, emancipatory prognoses of necessity took on an unrealistic, utopian hue. Unable to locate progressive emancipatory tendencies in the concrete historical present, the Critical Theorists were constrained to identify ersatz repositories of negation deriving from the aesthetic sphere. But in the last analysis, art was unable to bear the heavy burden accorded it in their framework. Instead, one is left with the conceptual aporia of a "totally administered world" side by side with historically unrealizable utopian projections. Both Lowenthal's observations and Habermas' critique, therefore, cast serious doubt on the utopian aspirations of Adorno's aesthetics.

One cannot help but be struck by the indebtedness of Adorno's aesthetic theory to insights first expressed by Max Weber in the famous "Zwischenbetrachtung" to his great work on the *Sociology of World Religions.*[5] Certainly, Adorno the musicologist learned much from Weber's essay on the *Rational and Social Foundations of Music.* The fundamental concept of that work—the "rationalization" of musical techniques in the modern West—plays a major role in Adorno's analysis of aesthetic modernity *tout court.* As Adorno emphasizes repeatedly, the imperatives of aesthetic modernity dictate that only those works of art which rely on the most advanced techniques historically available become worthy of serious consideration. In this context, he approvingly quotes Rimbaud's dictum, "Il faut être absolument moderne."

But it is Weber the theorist of the "Aesthetic Sphere" in modern life who establishes the parameters for Adorno's theory of aesthetic modernism. Following Kant's discussion of art in the third *Critique* as "purposiveness without purpose," Weber points out that in traditional or premodern art, art's inner logic remained stultified, insofar as *form* was always subordinated to *content*: the independent development of artistic technique was perennially subservient to the ends of salvation. In fact, these two aspects, form and content, stood in grave conflict, since aesthetic means inherently threatened to outstrip the demands of the religious message per se. (The annals of art history are replete with such tensions. For the sake of illustration, I mention three: Augustine's concern about the enticement to pleasure for pleasure's sake in musical liturgy; Tarkovsky's conflicted icon painter in *Andrei Rublov*; and the threat posed to the worldview of the Church by the "new realism" of Renaissance painting.)

All this changes, according to Weber, with the differentiation of the spheres of science, morality, and art that follows from the thoroughgoing rationalization of life in the modern age. For the first time, art (and the same claims can also be made for the spheres of morality and science) need no longer legitimate itself in terms of a logically prior, all-encompassing worldview. Instead, it is free to develop its own intrinsic formal potentialities to an unprecedented extent. The result, for Weber, is the creation of the "Aesthetic Sphere" in the modern sense, a historically unique network of artists and persons of taste, whose interactions are mediated by a new series of public institutions: theaters, galleries, feuilletons, critics, public libraries, museums, and so forth. Weber encapsulates this development—with characteristic pith and discernment—as follows: "[Under] the development of intellectualism and the rationalization of life . . . art becomes a cosmos of more and more consciously grasped independent values, which exist in their own right. Art takes over the function of this-worldly salvation, no matter how this may be interpreted. It provides *salvation* from the routines of everyday life, and especially form the pressures of theoretical and practical rationalism."[6]

I think there could be no better lead-in to the basic intentions of Adorno's aesthetic theory than the remarks of Weber just cited; above all, his characterization of aesthetic modernism as a type of inner-worldly salvation. To be sure, Adorno, following the lead of Walter Benjamin, is primarily concerned with de-auraticized (or postauratic) art; that is, with forms of modernism that have relinquished the immediacy of the Stendhalian *promesse de bonheur,* the "beautiful illusion" that happiness might be attainable in the here and now. Nevertheless, Weber attributes a special *redemptory function* to art in the modern world, which, for men and women of culture, surpasses religion to become a unique locus of ultimate meaning and value in life.

Art performs an analogous *redemptory* function in Adorno's aesthetics. For him, too, art represents a form of salvation vis-à-vis the pressures of "theoretical and practical rationalism" that predominate in daily life. Moreover, in Adorno's aesthetics, art becomes a vehicle of salvation in an even stronger sense. It takes on a compelling utopian function as a *prefiguration of reconciled life.* If Adorno stands Hegel on his head by claiming that "the whole is the untrue," it is art alone that offers the prospect of reversing this condition, of redirecting a lacerated social totality along the path of reconciliation (*Versöhnung*).

It is important to recognize that *Aesthetic Theory,* Adorno's magnum opus, fulfills an important systematic function in his oeuvre as a whole, addressing a concern originally posed jointly with Max Horkheimer in ***Dialectic of Enlightenment.***[7] There, social evolution is comprehended, in a manner reminiscent of both Nietzsche and Freud, in terms of the progressive mastery of unsublimated impulse. The latter must be perpetually subordinated to the "organizational imperatives" of civilization. *Individuation* thus means *domination*: increasing control of human drives on the part of the superego, the internalized agent of social authority. Ultimately, this dual process of self-renunciation and the extirpation of "otherness"—of those spheres of life that remain nonidentical with the subject qua *res cogitans*—leads to the horror of Auschwitz: the Jew, with his pre-Christian rites and physiognomy, represents the ultimate incarnation of otherness at the heart of European modernity. So pervasive is this dilemma that *conceptualization itself*—the very process of making the nonidentical intellectually comprehensible to the subject—is fully implicated in this world-historical march of unreason. As Horkheimer and Adorno observe, "The universality of ideas, as developed by discursive logic, domination in the conceptual sphere, is raised up on the actual basis of domination. The dissolution of the old magical heritage, of the old diffuse ideas, by conceptual unity, expresses the hierarchical constitution of life by those who are free. The individuality that learned order and subordination in the subjection of the world, soon wholly equated truth with the regulative thought without whose fixed distinctions truth cannot exist." And further: "Enlightenment behaves toward things as a dictator behaves toward men. He knows them insofar as he can manipulate them."[8] *Dialectic of Enlightenment* may thus be read as a type of cautionary tale concerning the fate of civilization once it has succumbed to the identitarian spell of formal logic.

In the context at hand, it is not so much the accuracy of the *Zeitdiagnose* set forth by Horkheimer and Adorno that concerns us, as the fact that an analogous preoccupation with "domination in the conceptual sphere" pervades Adorno's epistemological musings some years later in *Negative Dialectics.* To be sure, the historico-philosophical framework of the latter work is very much of a piece with *Dialectic of Enlightenment.* As Adorno remarks at one point: "No universal history leads from savagery to humanitarianism, but there is one that leads from the slingshot to the megaton bomb."[9] But of greater relevance for our purposes is the fact that the theme of the "domination of the concept" occupies pride of place in the work, which may thus be understood as an elaborate meditation on a specific *epistemological* problem that had been inherited from the philosophy of history of the 1940s. For Adorno, "the original sin of all philosophy is that it tries to grasp the nonconceptual through conceptual means." It is the tacit alliance between society and ratiocination, which manifests itself in their mutual hostility to the nonidentical, that Adorno seeks to undo via negative dialectics—which, paradoxically, "strives by way of the concept, to transcend the concept."[10] Adorno has drunk deeply from Nietzschean waters: his critique of conceptualization derives from the latter's characterization of philosophy as a manifestation of the "will to power."

Adorno offers a succinct rendering of his philosophical program—an intransigent defense of nonidentity—in the following statement: "To change [the] direction of conceptualization, to give it a turn toward the non-identical, is the linchpin of negative dialectics. Insight into the constitutive character of the nonconceptual in the concept would end the compulsive identification which the concept brings unless halted by such reflection. Reflection on its own meaning is the way out of the concept's seeming being-in-itself as a unit of meaning. . . . Disenchantment of the concept is the antidote of philosophy. It keeps it from growing rampant and becoming an absolute unto itself."[11]

A prior account of Adorno's stance on the philosophy of history and theory of knowledge is crucial for an informed appreciation of the stakes of his *Aesthetic Theory,* which is the direct philosophical heir of these earlier works. More importantly, in *Aesthetic Theory,* Adorno explicitly attempts to posit "solutions" to the dilemmas of abstract conceptualization—"domination in the conceptual sphere"—targeted in his previous work. And these solu-

tions are integrally related to the redemptory or utopian function he assigns to works of art as ciphers of reconciled life.

Adorno fully accepts the Hegelian turn in aesthetics whereby art is deemed a serious vehicle of knowledge and truth. Thus, for Adorno, like Hegel, art remains an embodiment of Spirit; however, in opposition to Hegel, art is no longer deemed a subaltern manifestation of the latter insofar as it represents the Idea merely in the realm of sensuous appearance. Instead, he in effect reverses the terms on his idealist predecessor. The truth claims of the aesthetic sphere are potentially superior to those of philosophical truth precisely because of their greater affinities with the realm of sensuous appearance.

Philosophical truth is by definition disembodied. Whereas for Hegel, this high degree of "spiritualization" accounted for its distinct superiority vis-à-vis, for example, the pictorial representation of the absolute in religious lore, for Adorno, the reverse is true: the sensuous nature of works of art means that they display a greater affinity with objectivity as such. In his eyes, therefore, philosophical thought, which seeks to represent the nature of things by use of abstract concepts, operates at a more distant remove from the reality it seeks to grasp.

The greater concretion of works of art, their inherent affinities with the realm of "sensuous externality," is not, however, an unequivocal gain. Instead, the increase in material concretion simultaneously signifies a diminution in intelligibility. For unlike philosophy, the language of art is sensuous. Its mode of articulation relies on images, sounds, and colors rather than the clarity of discursive argument. Consequently, as vehicles of truth, works of art are inherently enigmatic, *rätselhaft.* And it is precisely this enigmatic quality that beseeches, implores, and requires the *philosophical interpretation* of art. This dynamic alone mandates the necessity of *aesthetic theory.*

Similarly, it is only in light of the epistemological problematic inherited from *Dialectic of Enlightenment* and *Negative Dialectics* that one of Adorno's more controversial theoretical strategies in *Aesthetic Theory* becomes comprehensible: a rehabilitation of the category of natural beauty. Here, too, a comparison with Hegelian aesthetics is instructive. For Hegel, natural beauty was indisputably inferior to the humanmade variety, insofar as nature is inherently de-spiritualized. At best, it represents spirit in the mode of "otherness." There is no mistaking the fact that *Aesthetic Theory* is in the main a theory of aesthetic modernism. But this fact only makes the elaborate justification of natural beauty contained therein all the more surprising. To be sure, if various artistic movements throughout history have emphasized "naturalism" as a paramount criterion of aesthetic value, such a mind-set is completely foreign to the sensibility of modernism, for which all residues of naturalist sentiment must be ruthlessly expulsed (otherwise one ceases to be "absolument moderne"). Adorno's concerted efforts to rehabilitate this category from the legacy of pre-Hegelian aesthetics can only be understood in light of the ulterior epistemological agenda of his aesthetics.

Thus, just as Adorno criticizes the pan-logism of Hegelian metaphysics for its perpetual willingness to sacrifice the nonidentical to the imperatives of systematic unity, he similarly attempts to overturn Hegel's dismissal of natural beauty as part and parcel of a process of "spiritualization" (*Vergeistigung*) that must be combated. "Spiritualization" bespeaks an imperious anthropocentrism, in which all that is alien to and other than the subject must be rendered equivalent to the latter at the expense of its own intrinsic contents. Consequently, in the framework of Adorno's nonidentitarian theory of knowledge—a theory that takes issue with the main epistemological desideratum of German idealism: the *identity of subject and object*—the category of natural beauty is endowed with immense metaphorical significance: it represents the irreducible Other, a pristine condition beyond the reach of subjective self-assertion that is for this reason to be cherished and emulated. Adorno expresses this view forcefully when he opines, "The beautiful in nature is *the residue of non-identity in things* in an age in which they are spellbound by universal identity." As a "residue of non-identity," natural beauty is at the same time a utopian cipher of "reconciliation": utopia would be a state of "reconciliation," i.e., a condition in which the nonidentical could freely articulate itself, rather than function—as is the case at present—solely under the aegis of the concept. "The beautiful in nature," observes Adorno, "is different from both the notion of a ruling principle and the denial of any principle whatsoever. It is like a state of reconciliation."[12]

It is the conceptual triad nonidentity-reconciliation-utopia that assumes central significance in *Aesthetic Theory*; though for Adorno, unlike Hegel, in the *Aufhebung* of reconciliation, nonidentity is not effaced but first truly comes into its own. For Hegel, it is the very existence of nonidentity that accounts for an antagonistic (or unreconciled) state; and this condition must be overcome via the moment of synthesis. Conversely, for Adorno, it is the *suppression* of nonidentity by its other, the concept, that is the root of all injustice in the theoretical sphere; thus, reconciliation signifies the elimination of the identitarian urge, rather than, as with Hegel, its consummation.

But on the whole, the utopian potential of natural beauty is of minor moment in *Aesthetic Theory* in comparison to that of works of art—and especially modern works. Works of art are utopian constructs of necessity, according to Adorno. Social life exists in an unredeemed, "fallen" state. Its elements are subject to the rule of heteronomous and alien principles such as the law of universal equivalence characteristic of a commodity economy. Amid the omnipresent degradation of the phenomenal world, works of art possess a unique *saving power*: they incorporate these phenomena within the context of a freely articulated, non-coercive totality, thereby redeeming them from their deficient everyday state. According to Adorno, in a capitalist

society dominated by considerations of utility, phenomena are allowed to subsist only in an inferior state of universal Being-for-Other, which militates against the prospects of authentic Being-for-Self. In a flash, works of art dramatically reverse this state of affairs: "Whereas in the real world all particulars are fungible, art protests against fungibility by holding up images of what reality might be like if it were emancipated from the patterns of identification that are imposed on it."[13] Works of art for the first time allow the Being-in-Itself of things to emerge by virtue of the redeeming capacities of aesthetic form: "The utopia anticipated by artistic form is the idea that things at long last ought to come into their own. Another way of putting this is to call for the abolition of the spell of selfhood hitherto promoted by the subject."[14]

For Adorno, art is intrinsically utopian by virtue of the nonutilitarian principle of construction that is peculiar to it. Art emancipates by virtue of its formal principle, which is that of "free articulation" rather than "instrumental reason." And this emancipatory aesthetic practice is actually *enhanced* in the case of *modern* works of art, in which the principle of montage becomes predominant, such that the individual parts attain independence, and are thereby no longer mechanically subjugated to the whole. Art redeems the material elements of everyday life by absorbing them within the liberating contours of an aesthetic constellation. This inherently emancipatory effect of aesthetic form contrasts starkly with the coercive nature of contemporary social organization. According to Adorno, at the present stage of historical development, aesthetic form signifies a unique refuge in which things are temporarily freed of the constraints of Being-for-Other and their Being-for-Self is allowed to flourish. In this way alone can one break the "spell" of the subject as well as the principle of social organization that follows therefrom—instrumental reason.

In the discussion of the utopian function of art in *Aesthetic Theory,* Adorno comes close to violating the Judeo-Marxian *Bilderverbot* (the taboo against graven images), insofar as utopia is well-nigh concretely depicted. He explicitly recommends aesthetic form as a positive alternative to the reigning principle of social organization. His aestheticist solution to the dominant pressures of "theoretical and practical rationalism" is wholly consistent with Weber's discussion of the aesthetic sphere. In this respect, Adorno's approach is at one with a tradition beginning with romanticism and continuing through *l'art pour l'art,* whereby the nonutilitarian logic of the aesthetic realm is viewed as the only alternative to an increasingly rationalized and prosaic bourgeois social order. In accord with both the romantics as well as the proponents of art for art's sake, Adorno seeks to redeem the vaunted *promesse de bonheur* that art counterposes to an antagonistic social totality. Art comes to represent a world of happiness and fulfillment that is denied in the workaday world of bourgeois material life. It embodies claims to sensuousness and affective solidarity that are repulsed in a social world in which formal rationality is the dominant principle. For Adorno, "Art is a refuge of mimetic behavior" and thus signifies a "response to the evils and irrationality of a rational bureaucratic world. . . . The memory trace of mimesis unearthed by works of art . . . anticipates a condition of reconciliation between the individual and the collectivity." As such, art becomes a form of "remembrance," joining "the present to the past." As Adorno phrases it, "Remembrance alone is able to give flesh and blood to the notion of utopia, without betraying it to empirical life." That Adorno interprets works of art as *concrete utopian projections* in more than a metaphorical sense is indicated by his contention that one must "reverse the copy theory of realist aesthetics: in a sublimated sense, reality ought to imitate works of art, rather than the other way around."[15]

That Adorno makes a concerted effort to emphasize the relation between mimesis, reconciliation, and utopia in the passages just cited is far from accidental. For the utopian program of *Aesthetic Theory*—and the link between "mimesis" and "remembrance" which is its linchpin—bears a profound resemblance to the one adumbrated jointly with Horkheimer some twenty-five years earlier in *Dialectic of Enlightenment*. There, too, ruthless domination over external nature becomes the central theoretical problematic. What has been lost in the species' inexorable drive toward rational self-assertion is the capacity to view nature *mimetically* or *fraternally*. The solution to this dilemma hinges upon the capacity for remembrance of nature in the subject: "By virtue of the remembrance of nature in the subject, in whose fulfillment the unacknowledged truth of all culture lies hidden, enlightenment is universally opposed to domination."[16] The subject must remember that it, too, is part of nature; and that consequently all violence perpetrated against the latter will in the last analysis redound implacably against subjectivity itself. The program of enlightenment is thus fulfilled only in a distorted and one-sided sense when it is equated simply with the advance of the rational concept. Equally important is the "natural" or "sensuous" substratum of subjectivity—the subject as a medium of desires, drives, and somatic impulses—which comes into its own only via a conscious act of remembrance: an act that recaptures the "natural" dimension of subjectivity which remains ever-present, though dormant, in our mimetic faculty.[17]

The mimesis-reconciliation-utopia triad plays a key role in Adorno's response to the epistemological problem of the "domination of the concept." For in his eyes, works of art possess the singular advantage of greater immediacy over against the abstract mediations of the conceptual sphere. It is this enhanced immediacy that accounts for their greater affinities with the sensuous dimension of objectivity as such, unlike pure concepts, which exist at a studied remove from the objective world they seek to grasp intellectually.

Art, therefore, may be said to possess a certain epistemological superiority vis-à-vis philosophical truth. Philosophical cognition is suspect insofar as it is inherently implicated in the dialectic of enlightenment: since concepts know phenomena only insofar as they can manipulate them, they are a priori part and parcel of the historical unfolding of domination. As Adorno remarks: "The derivation of thought from logic ratifies in the lecture room the reification of man in the factory and office."[18]

Since theoretical reason is untrustworthy, the aestheticist solution Adorno posits in response is far from surprising. It is of a piece with the standard critique of a rationalized, bourgeois cosmos by the elevated *Kulturmensch*. It is precisely because of this inordinate distrust of formal rationality that the wager on the aesthetic dimension in Critical Theory is so pronounced: art alone, it would seem, can undo the damage wrought by a logic of unrestrained subjective rationality gone awry.

Adorno emphasizes the superior representational capacities of the aesthetic faculty, as opposed to philosophy, when the depiction of truth is at issue. In art the mimetic faculty, long repressed, is emancipated: one no longer need suppress the desire to be like the Other. The realm of aesthetic illusion or *Schein* thus frees the subject from his or her otherwise natural compulsion to objectify the Other for purposes of enhanced control. "Works of art represent selfsameness that has been freed of the compulsion to identify," remarks Adorno.[19] Only works of art are exempt from the Kantian proscription against depicting the "intelligible realm"—a ban that must be upheld in the case of theoretical reason. They alone possess the capacity to express the ineffable, to represent the unrepresentable, by virtue of the magical, transformative capacities of aesthetic *Schein*. Works of art represent a secular redemption of myth: they alone are capable of depicting a superior, transcendent world order in which—unlike the world at present—good, evil, and beauty are assigned their rightful niches. Yet, unlike traditional myth, aesthetic cosmologies no longer stand in the service of alien powers, but in that of a potentially redeemed humanity. At the same time works of art, in contrast to philosophy, never attempt to serve up the absolute as something immediately accessible. Instead, it always appears enigmatically, via the embellishment and indirection of aesthetic form. As Adorno himself expresses this point: "Works of art speak like fairies in tales: if you want the absolute, you shall have it, but only in disguise." They are enigmatic "images of Being-in-itself."[20] Art restores the element of wonder or *thaumazein* to the everyday phenomenal world; a power, according to Aristotle, once possessed by philosophy, but which the latter has surrendered in recent times in favor of protocol statements and analytical truths. Art is the utopian reenchantment of radically disenchanted social totality. It serves as irrefutable proof of the fact that the existing universe of facts is not all there is. It is a constant reminder of a state of not-yet-Being (Bloch) that eludes our concrete grasp at the moment, but which for that reason remains nonetheless "real." As Adorno remarks, "Aesthetic experience is the experience of something which spirit per se does not provide, either in the world or in itself. It is the possible, as promised by its impossibility. Art is the promise of happiness, a promise that is constantly being broken."[21]

. . . . .

Can the utopian potential of Adorno's aesthetics be redeemed? This is only another way of responding to the Lowenthal query with which we began: to what extent has the utopian motif in Critical Theory been suspended? The case of Adorno's aesthetics is paradigmatic, since the utopian wager of Critical Theory was so often couched in aesthetic terms.

In order to be redeemed, Adorno's aesthetics must be refunctioned. To be sure, few theorists have probed the fundamental parameters of aesthetic experience in the modern world more deeply than Adorno. Yet it seems that the true import of Adorno's aesthetic utopianism remains limited by certain fundamental shortcomings of his metatheoretical framework. Adorno's aesthetics are therefore in need of a redemptive critique so that they may be freed from the prejudicial constraints of his own theoretical presuppositions.

The conceptual deficiencies alluded to emanate primarily from two quarters: Adorno's theory of knowledge and his philosophy of history. Both components of his theoretical framework were originally articulated in ***Dialectic of Enlightenment.***[22] It is these two aspects of the Adornian worldview that prevent his aesthetic doctrines from receiving the fully exoteric redemption they merit.

We turn first to his theory of knowledge, having already indicated that ***Aesthetic Theory*** is very much concerned with resolving certain epistemological problems inherited from German Idealism.

In this respect, it is in no way accidental that one of the book's central categories is the eminently Hegelian concept of the "truth-content" or *Wahrheitsgehalt* of art. It was unquestionably an advance on the part of Hegel over the aesthetic doctrines of the eighteenth century to have valorized the cognitive dimension of aesthetic objectivations, to have viewed them as legitimate incarnations of the "Idea" or truth. And in this regard, Adorno's aesthetics are eminently Hegelian, even if he values the sensuous side of works of art to an incomparably greater extent.

Nevertheless, once works of art are viewed primarily as "epistemological vehicles" (and in this fundamental respect there is really very little difference between Hegel and Adorno), another crucial component of aesthetic experience tends to fall out of account: the *pragmatic dimension,* on which the essence of aesthetic experience depends. Because Adorno tries to conceive of works of art primarily as vehicles of philosophical truth, in his approach the entire pragmatic side of works of art—their role in shaping, informing, and transforming the lives of historically existing individuals—falls by the wayside.

That Adorno succumbs to this error in judgment is due to an eminently Hegelian preconception: a belief in an "emphatic concept of truth," whereby truth is viewed as something transcendent and noncontingent, which escapes the fallibility of the human condition. Adorno's thought—despite the conceptual pyrotechnics of negative dialectics—still very much moves within the horizon of traditional metaphysical theories of truth. One might go so far as to say that his entire philosophical program is motivated by a nostalgia for the lost prelapsarian unity of subject and object, concept and thing. It is this nostalgia that accounts for the prominence of *mimesis* in his thinking—the importance of a fraternal, nonobjectivating relationship to the external world—as well as the category of *reconciliation,* the explicit hope for a future condition *beyond* the subject-object split.

As a result of this tendentious preoccupation with works of art as vehicles of truth, the richness of aesthetic experience—i.e., art's status as a pragmatic phenomenon capable of altering the existential parameters of human life—is significantly downplayed. Interpreting art becomes primarily an *esoteric philosophical exercise* in deciphering the work's "enigmatic character" (*Rätselcharakter*); with the result that Walter Benjamin's question concerning the exoteric value of aesthetic experience—the capacity of art to produce "profane illuminations"—is lost sight of.

This deficiency of Adorno's framework is, moreover, systematic rather than accidental in nature. Since his debate with Benjamin in the 1930s over the status of mechanically reproduced works of art, Adorno—who was very likely correct in terms of the particulars of the debate itself—remained undialectically wedded to the concept of an esotericized, autonomous art as an absolute model of aesthetic value. In the debate with Benjamin, he pointed out, in the cases of both film and surrealism, that the act of bursting the vessels of aesthetic autonomy does not automatically produce an emancipatory effect. Instead, one runs the risk of a false sublation of autonomous art, whereby a crucial refuge of negativity and critique would be prematurely integrated with facticity as such. Adorno's cautionary remarks concerning the dangers of a premature integration of art in life-praxis remain valuable to this day. The problem, however, is that his own stance in this debate became rigidified, and thus possible countervailing tendencies in the postwar period were ruled out a priori. The "culture industry" thesis from ***Dialectic of Enlightenment*** ossified into a monolithic, self-fulfilling prophecy—a mere mirror image of that undifferentiated continuum of the always-the-same that Adorno himself had projected onto social life under advanced capitalism.

In the present context, we can only fleetingly touch on the second systematic deficiency of Adorno's approach: a philosophy of history that was formulated during one of the darkest hours of recent memory: the era of Nazism, Stalinism, and the ensuing Cold War period, when international politics was reduced to the avoidance of successive, imminent catastrophes. However, his theory of a *"totale Verblendungszusammenhang"*—a context of total delusion—formulated during these years cannot withstand transposition to very different historical conditions without undergoing extensive modification. Consequently, Adorno's historico-philosophical thinking became similarly ossified, reinforcing his unreceptiveness to oppositional cultural forms with genuinely exoteric, generalizable potential.

The utopian moment of Critical Theory is redeemable; but one must specify very carefully what type of utopia one intends to redeem. What is *not* meant by utopia in the present context is the variety of utopianism criticized by Marx throughout his writings of the 1840s: a utopian future which is in essence a secularized version of eschatological religious longing. This strong version of utopianism resurfaces in the secular messianism of Bloch, Benjamin, the early Lukács, and Marcuse. In Adorno's work, it appears in the guise of a "negative theology": utopia would be the obverse of the present state of things.[23] This *strong version of utopianism,* whose *telos* is a state of reconciliation—of humanity with nature, existence and essence, thought and being—beyond the split between subject and object, is the type that Lowenthal has rightly consigned to an outmoded theoretical paradigm.

The weak version of utopianism that is recuperable from Adorno's **Aesthetic Theory** pertains to his advocacy of "aesthetic alienation": art presents the familiar and everyday to us in a new and unexpected light, such that we are impelled to modify our habitual modes of thought and perception. Authentic works of art are the archfoes of all intellectual complacency and positivist affirmation. Adorno is essentially correct in his claim that works of art exist in a state of constant polemical tension vis-à-vis the given universe of facts. Genuine works of art are intrinsically utopian insofar as they both highlight the indigent state of reality at present and seek to illuminate a path toward what has never-yet-been. The profane illuminations of aesthetic experience seek to unseat the predominant tendencies toward "theoretical and practical rationalism"; and as such they give expression to an affective dimension of life that is routinely tabooed by bourgeois subjectivity and its unceasing will toward rational self-preservation: they are powerful repositories of a mimetic, noninstrumental relation to nature, of human fraternity, of nonutilitarian playfulness.

Habermas has expressed a similar insight: aesthetic experiences "are possible only to the extent that the categories of the patterned expectations of organized daily experience collapse, that the routines of daily action and conventions of ordinary life are destroyed, and the normality of foreseeable and unaccountable certainties are suspended." By being "incorporated into the context of individual life-histories" art "belongs to everyday communicative practice. It then . . . reaches into our cognitive interpretations and normative expectations and transforms the totality in which these moments are related to each another. In this respect, modern art harbors a utopia that becomes a reality to the degree that the mimetic powers sublimated in the

work of art find resonance in the mimetic relations of a balanced and undistorted intersubjectivity of everyday life."[24]

A precondition for redeeming Adorno's theory of aesthetic modernity would be its transposition to an exoteric context: aesthetic illumination is not just the province of critics, aesthetes, artists, and experts, but a general phenomenon of daily life that concretely alters the life-histories of individuals. The "truth-content" of art is in principle accessible to a plurality of recipients.

There are, moreover, several structural features of contemporary aesthetic experience that suggest that Adorno's argument for the esoteric redemption of artistic truth-content is being undercut from below. For example, in an essay on "The Decline of the Modern Age," Peter Bürger points to the obsolescence of modernist high art in favor of a new series of hybrid genres and forms that are loosely identified as "postmodern."[25] Bürger correctly questions the descriptive cogency of the latter term, observing that many so-called postmodern art forms (e.g., neo-dada, neo-expressionism, etc.) are in fact continuous with the modern. The important point is that the conception of modernism on which Adorno's aesthetic theory was predicated—the idea of a select canon of hermetic, self-referential, autonomous works—has burst asunder. Any attempt to preserve the contemporary relevance of his theories must of necessity incorporate this manifestly new "state of the arts" into the total picture.

The changed configuration of contemporary aesthetic experience, the dissolution of traditional genre distinctions that has been described by Bürger and others, suggests the prospect of redeeming Adorno's aesthetics on a truly generalizable scale. And although this new aesthetic constellation is fraught with contradictions and tensions whose ultimate outcome remains difficult to foresee, it seems to indicate a potentially new sphere of operation for an aesthetics of negativity such as Adorno's. For the contemporary fusion of genres and levels of aesthetic experience suggests the real possibility that the profane illuminations Adorno sought to cull from esoteric art may now be *exoterically available*—in a way Adorno himself may have been incapable of anticipating. The apparent dissolution of the traditional European "aesthetics of autonomy" seems to indicate that the types of critical aesthetic experiences Adorno confined to hermetic works have now taken root in the life-world of late capitalism in general. That the aesthetic sensibility of modernism seems to have been *democratized*—and this is certainly one prominent aspect of the various strands of cultural experience commonly referred to as "postmodern"—is a phenomenon to be welcomed. For it means that an aesthetics of rupture, discontinuity, de-familiarization, and disenchantment—in sum, the "ideology-critical" function Adorno attributes to authentic works of art—has shifted to the plane of everyday artistic endeavor. An entire series of "popular" genres and cultural forms that as a rule fell beneath the threshold of Adorno's theoretical purview—popular music, cinema, even television in certain respects—have over the course of the last two decades displayed a new pluralism and inventiveness. To subsume them immediately under the "culture industry" thesis as originally formulated in the 1940s would be rash. It is, moreover, hardly surprising that this assault on the tenets of high modernism originated in the U.S., where (European) cultural elitism has always been at odds with a fundamentally democratic cultural self-understanding.

Nevertheless, the tendencies we have just described are far from unambiguous. The two most salient features of the much vaunted postmodern turn in the arts are 1) random historical borrowing of artistic styles; and 2) a collapse of the distinction between high and low culture, art and entertainment. The first trend poses the specter of a historicist loss of historical consciousness; if "all ages are equally close to God" (Ranke), then the course of history itself is trivialized, and all epochs are simultaneously equally meaningful and equally meaningless. And an absolute effacement of the distinction between high and low culture would be a far from untroubling development: for it harbors the prospect of a false sublation of art in the domain of life praxis, whereby art would to all intents and purposes become *fused* with the phenomenal sphere of daily life. The last-named tendency represents a real danger for the various artistic currents commonly referred to as postmodern. And thus, from the bursting of the vessels of aesthetic autonomy, an emancipatory effect does not necessarily follow. Here, the main risk is a slackening of the critical tension between art and life that proved the linchpin of modernist aesthetics. Consequently, the danger arises that once the boundaries between art and life become blurred, the critical potentials of art decay, and art itself is transformed into a *vehicle of affirmation*: i.e., the uncritical mirror-image of the "happy consciousness" of late capitalism. Adorno's "aesthetics of determinate negation" provide an important safeguard against this eventuality.

Notes

1. Leo Lowenthal, "The Utopian Motif is Suspended" (interview conducted with Martin Lüdke), *New German Critique* 38 (Spring-Summer 1986): 105-111. It has also appeared in Lowenthal's autobiography, *An Unmastered Past,* edited by Martin Jay (Berkeley: University of California Press, 1987), pp. 237-246.

2. For the best account of this generation and its various programs, see Michael Löwy, *Rédemption et Utopie* (Paris: PUF, 1988).

3. In a private conversation, Lowenthal identified Bloch's *Geist der Utopie* and Lukács' *Theorie des Romans* as the two works that most influenced his own early development.

4. Lowenthal, "The Utopian Motif," p. 111.

5. Translated in English as "Religious Rejections of the World and Their Directions," in *From Max Weber,* pp. 323-359.

6. Ibid., p. 342.

7. It may seem paradoxical to attribute "systematic intentions" to the author of *Negative Dialectics.* However, it should be kept in mind that despite his pronounced aversion to *l'esprit de system, l'esprit systematique* was not a concept entirely alien to his way of thinking: from Rolf Tiedemann's "Nachwort" to *Aesthetic Theory,* we learn that Adorno intended to compose a major treatise on moral philosophy upon completion of the latter work. Had this intention not been cut short by his death in 1969, Adorno's three major works would have corresponded to the subject matter of Kant's three *Critiques.*

8. Horkheimer and Adorno, *Dialectic of Enlightenment,* pp. 14, 9.

9. Adorno, *Negative Dialectics,* p. 321.

10. Ibid., p. 15.

11. Ibid., pp. 12-13.

12. Adorno, *Aesthetic Theory,* pp. 122, 124.

13. Ibid., pp. 122-123.

14. Ibid.

15. Ibid., pp. 190, 192; emphasis added.

16. Horkheimer and Adorno, *Dialectic of Enlightenment,* p. 40.

17. Cf. Walter Benjamin, "The Mimetic Faculty," in *Reflections,* edited by Peter Demetz (New York: Harcourt Brace, 1978), pp. 333-336.

18. Horkheimer and Adorno, *Dialectic of Enlightenment,* p. 30.

19. Adorno, *Aesthetic Theory,* p. 183.

20. Ibid., pp. 183, 184.

21. Ibid., p. 196.

22. Although the true intellectual historical origins of his outlook on philosophy and history go back to two profoundly Benjaminian essays from the early 1930s. See "Die Aktualität der Philosophie" and "Die Idee der Naturgeschichte," both in Theodor Adorno, *Gesammelte Schriften* I (Frankfurt: Suhrkamp, 1974), pp. 325-344, 345-365.

23. On the relation between Adorno and negative theology, see F. Grenz, *Adornos Philosophie in Grundbegriffen* (Frankfurt: Suhrkamp, 1974).

24. Jürgen Habermas, "Questions and Counterquestions," in *Habermas and Modernity,* edited by Richard J. Bernstein (Cambridge: Polity Press, 1985), pp. 200-202.

25. Peter Bürger, "The Decline of the Modern Age," *Telos* 62 (Winter 1984-1985): 117-130.

Miriam Hansen (essay date 1993)

SOURCE: "Of Mice and Ducks: Benjamin and Adorno on Disney," in *South Atlantic Quarterly,* Vol. 92, No. 1, Winter, 1993, pp. 27-61.

[*In the following essay, Hansen discusses differences in the way Disney was viewed by Adorno and Walter Benjamin, finding in their respective analyses important keys to their opinions on twentieth-century American mass culture.*]

Walter Benjamin's reflections on film and mass culture repeatedly revolved around Disney, in particular early Mickey Mouse cartoons and Silly Symphonies.[1] Theodor W. Adorno took issue with Benjamin's investment in Disney, both in direct correspondence and implicitly, in his writings on jazz and, after his friend's death, in the analysis of the culture industry in his and Max Horkheimer's **Dialectic of Enlightenment.** These scattered references to Disney encoded central questions concerning the politics of mass culture, the historical relations with technology and nature, the body and sexuality. They demonstrate, in an exemplary way, a mode of thinking that transformed observations on mass-cultural phenomena into a critical theory of culture and history.

In this essay, I reconstruct Benjamin's and Adorno's arguments on Disney as a debate on these larger questions. By doing so I do not intend to reiterate the familiar pattern of adjudicating between the two writers—dismissing one as mandarin and pessimistic while claiming the other for a radical, Brechtian or Cultural Studies canon of mass culture theory. For one thing, Adorno's reservations about Disney highlight ambivalences in Benjamin's own thoughts. For another, maintaining these conflicting perspectives in a stereoscopic view seems to me a more productive way of engaging problems and possibilities of mass culture and modernity in general and, for that matter, the media culture of postmodernity.

Nor is the point of this essay to measure Benjamin and Adorno's remarks on Mickey Mouse and Donald Duck in terms of their critical adequacy or inadequacy toward Disney as a textual and historical phenomenon. Rather, I am interested in the way the Disney films became emblematic of the juncture of art, politics, and technology debated at the time. The key question for critical theory in the interwar years was which role the technical media were playing in the historical demolition and restructuring of subjectivity: whether they were giving rise to new forms of imagination, expression, and collectivity, or whether they were merely perfecting techniques of total subjection and domination. This was not just an abstract question of power as discourse; in the face of fascism, Stalinism, and American Fordism, theorizing mass culture was a highly political effort to come to terms with new, bewildering, and contradictory forces, to map possibilities of change and prospects of survival. In this situation, the Disney films catalyzed discussions on the psycho-politics of mass-cultural reception, specifically the linkage of laughter and violence and the sadomasochistic slant of spectatorial pleasure. But they also rehearsed, especially for Benjamin, alternative visions of technology and the body, prefiguring the mobilization of a "collective physis" and a different organization of the relations between humanity and nature.

The questions that Benjamin and Adorno raised in connection with Disney point not only beyond the textual occasion, but also beyond the specific historical context of critical theory. In the age of global integration and postmodern diversification, the imbrication of technology with violence still prevails, confronting us as the unresolved legacy of modernity or, if you will, hegemonic modernism. Now as then, the industrial-technical media are as much part of the problem as they constitute the horizon through which solutions can be envisioned and fought for. Now as then, the issue is the organization and politics of sensory perception, of "aesthetics" in the etymological sense which Benjamin, as Susan Buck-Morss reminds us, significantly resumes.[2]

Focusing on Benjamin, and interweaving Adorno's comments intermittently, I will proceed from a key passage on Mickey Mouse in the 1935/36 essay "The Work of Art in the Age of Technical Reproducibility." I will then trace the appearances of the Disney mascot through various constellations in Benjamin's writings of the 1930s, which means complicating the modernist and psychoanalytic concerns of the more familiar Benjamin with the lesser-known historical-anthropological perspective of his work on the Paris Arcades.

Over the past two decades, Benjamin's Artwork essay may have been invoked more often than any other single source (with Jacques Lacan's paper on the mirror stage and Laura Mulvey's on visual pleasure as runners up), whether in film theory, cultural history, or the post-modern art scene. In the course of these ritualistic invocations, the essay has not necessarily acquired new meanings nor has it become any less problematic. Perhaps there should be a moratorium on quoting it or, as Peter Wollen has recently suggested, it should be shelved altogether in favor of those of Benjamin's texts that are not marred by the rhetoric of left Fordism, such as his essays on surrealism and the Arcades project.[3]

But which Artwork essay are we talking about? The vast majority of references in English are to the translation published in *Illuminations* in 1969, a translation that is not altogether reliable. This translation in turn is based on a German version of the essay first published in 1955, edited by Adorno and Friedrich Podszus. As the editors of Benjamin's *Collected Works* have established, moreover, that version is probably the most compromised among the four versions we now have. The first typed, and for Benjamin definitive, version, did not turn up until 1989: this is the text that Benjamin submitted to the *Journal of Social Research* in February 1936 and to which Adorno responded in his famous letter from London of 18 March 1936.[4] The first version to be published was the French, translated by Pierre Klossowski, which roughly corresponds to the essay in its well-known shape but still contains some passages from the earlier versions. The French, along with the first, handwritten version, has been generally accessible since 1974, when it was reprinted in volume I of the *Collected Works.*

In this handwritten, first draft of the essay, the entire section devoted to the notion of an "optical unconscious" is entitled "Micky-Maus." Where the third, familiar version meanders through a reference to Freud's *Psychopathology of Everyday Life,* the earlier versions (including the French) open with an epigrammatic thesis: "The most important among the social functions of film is to create a balance [*Gleichgewicht*] between the human being and technology [*Apparatur*]." To that effect, Benjamin stresses the importance of film, not only for the manner in which human beings present themselves to the apparatus, but also for their effort to represent, "to themselves," their industrially changed environment. This implies an aesthetics of film that utilizes the camera's exploratory, cognitive, and liberating possibilities. To recall the beautiful passage that appears in all versions of the essay:

> Our taverns and city streets, our offices and furnished rooms, our train stations and factories appeared to have us locked up beyond hope. Then came film and exploded this prison-world with the dynamite of one-tenth seconds, so that now, in the midst of its far-flung ruins and debris, we calmly embark on adventurous travels. With the close-up, space expands; with slow motion, movement is extended. Thus it becomes evident that it is a different nature that speaks to the camera than speaks to the naked eye. Different above all, because an unconsciously permeated space substitutes for a space consciously explored by human beings. . . . [The camera] introduces us to the optical unconscious as does psychoanalysis to unconscious impulses.[5]

The psychoanalytic metaphor here serves to underscore the discontinuity between consciously perceived and unconsciously permeated spaces, and the ability of film to *reveal* this "other" space. The object of such revelation is at once redemptive—in enscripting the "trivial milieus" of everyday life—and critical—in destroying the fixed perspectives that have naturalized social and economic arrangements.

In the passage that follows in the earlier versions of the Artwork essay, however, Benjamin gives the analogy between film and psychoanalysis a slightly different twist. Film not only makes visible formations hitherto invisible to the human eye, but registers aspects of psycho-perceptual reality that only emerged, historically, with modern technology; as Benjamin put it elsewhere, film gives rise to *"a new region of consciousness."*[6] But these new aspects of reality are not necessarily all liberating. On the contrary, Benjamin locates them largely "outside the *normal* spectrum of sense perceptions," in the region of "psychoses, hallucinations and dreams." Thus, "the deformations and stereotypes, transformations and catastrophes that may occur in the perceptual world of film" provide an unconscious optics for the borderline experience that comes with the pressures of urban-industrial modernity.[7]

The point of the psychoanalytic analogy here is not merely the revelation or "prismatic" analysis of latent structures. Rather, Benjamin is concerned with film's *therapeutic* function, based on its ability to translate individually experienced borderline states, such as the psychoses and nightmares engendered by industrial and military technology, into *collective* perception. These coordinates mark the cue for the entrance of Mickey Mouse.

> Film has launched an attack against the old Heraclitean truth that in waking we share a world while sleeping we are each in separate worlds. It has done so, less with representations of dreams, than with the creation of figures of the collective dream such as the globe-orbiting Mickey Mouse.

As an antidote to the violent return of modern civilization's repressed, effecting "a therapeutic detonation of the unconscious," the image of the frantic Mouse is brought to a standstill at the crossroads between fascism and the possibility of its prevention:

> *If one takes into account the dangerous tensions which technification and its consequences have engendered in the vast masses—tensions which, at critical stages, take on a psychotic character—then one cannot but recognize that this same technification has created as protection against such mass psychosis the possibility of psychic inoculation by means of certain films in which a forced articulation of sadistic fantasies or masochistic delusions can prevent their natural and dangerous ripening in the masses. The collective laughter signifies a premature and therapeutic eruption of such mass psychoses.*[8]

Like American slapstick comedy (*Groteskfilme*) and the figure of the "eccentric," notably Chaplin, Benjamin concludes, the Disney films pioneer ways of inhabiting the new space or margin (*Spielraum*) that historically emerged with film, by disarming the destructive effects of technology through technologically mediated laughter.

In his response to Benjamin's Artwork essay, Adorno was clearly troubled by this passage: "Your dig at Werfel gave me great pleasure; but if you take the Mickey Mouse instead, things are far more complicated, and the serious question arises as to whether the reproduction of every person really constitutes that *a priori* of film which you claim it to be, or whether this reproduction is not part of precisely that 'naive realism' whose bourgeois nature we so thoroughly agreed upon in Paris."[9] In light of the passage cited above, we can understand why Adorno had problems with Benjamin's Mickey Mouse: not because of the Mouse's relation to representational realism but because of Benjamin's endorsement of the collective laughter that the films provoked in the mass audience.

Adorno's objections to Benjamin's political investment in collectivity (such as the concept of the "dreaming collective" in the Arcades project) are well-known: besides straying into the vicinity of C. G. Jung's "collective unconscious," Benjamin, according to Adorno, seriously underrated the extent to which any existing collective today was imbricated with the commodity character. The more specific point of dissension, in this case, was the sadistic—and, for Adorno, effectively masochistic—slant of the collective laughter. In the letter quoted above, Adorno cautions Benjamin emphatically against romanticizing the barbarism manifested in mass-cultural reception: "The laughter of the cinema audience is . . . anything but good and revolutionary; instead, it is full of the worst bourgeois sadism." He extends this verdict even to Chaplin, who had been a politically good object, after all, not just for Siegfried Kracauer, but generally in leftist-intellectual and avant-garde circles of the time. Instead of elaborating the point, Adorno refers Benjamin to his soon-to-be completed essay on jazz, which contains remarks on the figure of the eccentric.

Like the essay **"The Fetish Character of Music and the Regression of Listening,"** Adorno's writings on jazz represent a running argument with Benjamin's work on mass culture. In a postscript written in Oxford in 1937, Adorno delineates the "jazz subject," the listener's position in the musical text, in terms of sadomasochistic pleasures shortcircuited in the service of social integration. Like its precursor, the eccentric, the jazz subject is marked by a pseudo-individuality which Adorno pinpoints as the root of the jazz ritual's "curiously affirmative character." Instead of real autonomy, the "individual traits [of the jazz subject] by which it protests against social authority are in truth the very stigmata of mutilation inflicted upon him by society." This makes for a form of identification in which the subject takes pleasure in his or her own mutilation, yet without consciousness, identifying with the sadistic principle, internalizing the threat of castration. In the dancers' relation to the music, this submission corresponds to a stubborn refusal to really dance the "break" (English in the original), the syncope which is jazz's futile assertion of difference. This is the place where Adorno ambiguously situates the Disney mascot: "[I]t is key to the success of Mickey Mouse that he/she/it alone translates all the breaks into precise visual equivalents."[10]

The association of Mickey Mouse and jazz was a commonplace in Weimar and Nazi Germany, perhaps more so than in the United States. The connection was not only the literal one, suggested by a synchronization of the figure's movements with the rhythms of the music (which was, in fact, rarely, properly speaking, jazz); but both Mickey and jazz figured prominently in the German discourse of Americanism, that is, a modernism predicated on industrial-capitalist rationalization, on Taylorized labor and a Fordist organization of production and consumption. Like Chaplin and American slapstick comedy, jazz and cartoons represented, as it were, the "other" side of Americanism, a branch of consumer culture that seemed to subvert the economically imposed discipline through orgies of destruction, magic, and parody.[11] Disney's relation to Fordism was anything but critical, to be sure, and he espoused Fordist principles both in his aesthetics and business strategies.[12] Still, Mickey's enormous success in Germany from the late 1920s through the 1930s no doubt owed much to the figure's anarchic, ecstatic appeal which was, in a more exoticized vein, what people expected from jazz.

It is not surprising that the National Socialists early on included Mickey Mouse in their campaign against the "Ver-niggerung" (negroization) of German popular culture.[13] The ideological conflation of Mickey and jazz throws into relief the question of the figure's blackness and thus inserts it into the long history of white projections of African-American culture. In a recent exhibit on the reception of Disney in Germany, 1927-1945, a number of vernacular depictions (caricatures, mugs, figurines) show Mickey with protruding white teeth and Africanized features, while others make him look like an inversion of black face, that is, a black figure wearing a white face and white gloves.[14] Whether Benjamin and Adorno were aware of this racialized subtext is unclear; that Adorno, by placing Mickey Mouse in the context of white projection—for which he (mis)took jazz—came close to spelling out the figure's racial and racist connotations might also account for his greater ambivalence.

For Mickey, in Adorno's reading, is not simply an embodiment of the jazz subject (as Lawrence Rickels would have it), but rather one element in a configuration of desire: the bait of difference, the fantasy of a break.[15] It is no coincidence that Adorno later, in a kind of substitution trick, switched his polemic against Disney from Mickey to Donald Duck, a cartoon character who fits the authoritarian profile much more smoothly. Thus we read in Adorno and Horkheimer's chapter on the culture industry in ***Dialectic of Enlightenment***: "Donald Duck in the cartoons, like the unfortunate in real life, gets his beating so that the viewers can get used to the same treatment." Sadistic pleasures are mobilized, not to challenge the regime of heterosexual genitality, but to rehearse the internalization of terror. The "iron bath of fun" administered by the culture industry does not inspire a conciliatory laughter that would "echo the escape from power," but a *Schadenfreude,* a terrible laughter that "overcomes fear by capitulating to the forces which are to be feared."[16] Humor provides the glue that prevents the subject from recognizing him/herself as the object of mutilation. These ideological effects of the Disney humor are at once revealed and sanctioned in the *locus classicus* of "laughter betrayed" (Kracauer): the climax of Preston Sturges's *Sullivan's Travels* (1942), in which the screening of an old, rather violent, Mickey Mouse cartoon to an audience of chain-gang prisoners persuades the eponymous director-in-disguise that cathartic laughter is a better gift to humanity than any realist critique of social conditions.[17]

Benjamin, writing in the mid-1930s, was no less aware of the direction in which the Disney films were heading. In a footnote to the section cited above, following the therapeutic reclamation of the collective laughter inspired by these films, he concedes that their comic aspects are often indistinguishable from horror. In particular the most recent Mickey Mouse films, he observes, manifest a tendency already latent in the earlier films "to put up comfortably [*gemütlich*] with bestiality and cruelty as corollaries of existence." By doing so, they resume an "old and nothing less than confidence-inspiring tradition" that is led by the "dancing hooligans" in "medieval depictions of pogroms" and vaguely reverberates in the "riff-raff" of Grimm's fairy tales.[18]

The affinity of comedy and cruelty is an old story, though it clearly assumed an acute meaning in the face of the more systematic, totalizing manifestations of anti-Semitic terror after 1933. But Benjamin actually comes closer to describing a psycho-perceptual structure similar to that observed by Adorno in another part of the Artwork essay, the epilogue, where he castigates the aestheticization of politics that culminates in fascism and war. "Mankind, which in Homer's time was an object of spectacle for the Olympian gods, has now become one for itself. Its self-alienation has reached such a degree that it can experience its own destruction as an aesthetic pleasure of the first order."[19] This configuration seems only the most extreme instance of the *miscognition* Adorno sees operating in mass-cultural reception, the identification with the aggressor by which the consumers assent to their own mutilation and subjection.

Susan Buck-Morss reads Benjamin's analysis of fascism in the larger context of the fate of human sense perception under the impact of modern technology, which she sees defined by a "tripartite splitting of experience" into agency, object, and observer. This splitting is graphically illustrated by a remarkable quote from Edmund Husserl: "If I cut my finger with a knife, then a physical body is split by the driving into it of a wedge, the fluid contained in it trickles out, etc."[20] The separation of cognitive and bodily experience, and of both in turn from agency, is a decisive moment in the process Buck-Morss characterizes as a dialectics of "anaesthetics" and "aestheticization," a defensive numbing of the human senses in response to technologically created "shock" and the concomitant, ever-more-relentless stimulation of the senses through technologically generated "phantasmagoria." In the media mise-en-scène of fascist rallies and parades, epitomized by Leni Riefenstahl's *Triumph of the Will,* the tripartite splitting of experience takes on monumental, collective, and national dimensions: spectatorial pleasure is divorced from both political agency and its object, the purpose of the display: the militarization of society and the telos of mass destruction. In Buck-Morss's words, this kind of aesthetics promotes an "*an*aesthetization of reception."

Obviously, there is a difference between the fascist aestheticization of politics and the ideological mechanisms that Adorno imputes to Hollywood cartoons and jazz. But the structural similarity between the forms of miscognition that Benjamin and Adorno see at work in the respective syndromes is nonetheless striking. In each case, there is a complicity between historical subjects and their particular mode of subjection; in each case, this complicity hinges on a numbing of (self-) perception, an inability to recognize one's own vital interests and one's mortal enemies; in each case, there is a denial of the gaps between the sundered positions of experience. The disagreement between Adorno and Benjamin lies less in the diagnosis than in the assessment of whether and by whom this complicity could be undone, how the integrity of the human senses could be restored.

There is no doubt also a convergence with another analysis of miscognition, elaborated around the same time and probably in view of some of the same historical developments—Lacan's theory of the mirror stage.[21] Like Benjamin and Adorno, Lacan confronted the problem of the infinitely amplified power of imaginary relations in the structuring of psychic, sexual, social, and political realities. While Lacan focused primarily on the narcissistic register in the process of identification which, if the imaginary unity of the ego is threatened, results in aggressivity, Adorno stressed the sadomasochistic logic that governed, unrecognized, processes of mass-cultural identification. For Benjamin, the miscognition operative in the fascist mass ornament falls under the heading of humanity's "self-alienation," a concept that is likewise indebted to psychoanalysis but interweaves Freudian motives with Gnostic-Messianic and anthropological-materialist ones. The concept of self-alienation leads Benjamin—via the question of technology—to the opposing concept of "innervation," and it is in this constellation that Mickey Mouse assumes an alternative, even utopian significance.

In Benjamin's analysis of the fascist mass spectacle, two distinct strands of human self-alienation come to a head: one turning on the consumer's "identification" (*Einfühlung*) with the commodity, the other on the failed and fatal reception of technology. The first is related to Benjamin's discussion of exchange-value as a "phantasmagoria," as a sensuous transfiguration of the commodity, an illusion that is at once mental drug and utopian wish-image. The nineteenth-century world exhibitions, for instance, beckon their visitors with a phantasmagoria that makes the use-value recede, ostensibly for the purpose of distraction. Prepared by the entertainment industry which has been raising them to the level of the commodity all along, human beings easily "yield to the manipulation, by enjoying their alienation from themselves and from others."[22] However, since the consumerist phantasmagoria simultaneously represents a displaced form of human desire, commercially promoted distraction also contains the antidote to such self-alienation: the practice of collective reception, which for Benjamin provides a matrix for the political self-organization of the masses. The life-and-death alternative of "giving the masses an aesthetic expression" (the fascist imaginary) vs. giving them "their rights" is thus already implicit in the ambivalent structure of a collective, if still individualized, identification with the commodity.

The second trajectory of self-alienation is the legacy of the nineteenth-century dream of technology which first exploded in the inferno of World War I. Fettered by capitalist relations of production and Imperialist politics, advanced technology has turned against human beings with a vengeance. Reduced to a mere instrument for the human domination of nature, technology confronts human beings as a second nature, insufficiently understood in its moral dimensions, as a human, social activity, and hence infinitely more destructive. For the human species to survive, Benjamin insists, technology has to be transformed from a means of mastering nature into a medium for "mastering the interplay between human beings and nature."[23] Yet for this to happen, technology would have to become an "organ of the collective," an object of collective "innervation."[24]

The notion of a "collective innervation" of technology first appears at the end of Benjamin's essay on surrealism (1929), linked to the idea of an integral "body and image space" to which I will return. The central arenas for such innervation, as Benjamin increasingly came to realize, were the technical media—photography, film, radio, the gramophone—that is, the very technologies that participate in the historical proliferation of the shock experience and thus escalate the spiral of sensory alienation, phantasmagoria, and violence. The expropriation of the human senses that culminates in Imperialist warfare and fascism can be countered only on the terrain of technology itself, by means of perceptual technologies that allow for a figurative, mimetic engagement with technology at large, as a productive force and social reality. In other words, the technical media would have to set into play their metonymic relationship with other technologies, so as to function as a supplement or pharmakon to the latter, to provide a discourse of experience that would allow for a collective adaptation of and to technology. This is why film assumes such political importance for Benjamin, not as a medium of realistic representation, but as a perceptual training ground for an industrially transformed physis: "To make the vast technical apparatus of our time an object of human innervation—this is the historical task in whose service film has its true meaning."[25]

But how do we distinguish between a film practice that "breaks through the numbing shield of consciousness" and one that "merely provides a 'drill' for the strength of its defenses?"[26] Where do we draw the line between a defensive adaptation to technology and a mimetic, cognitive one? On one level, Benjamin indeed envisioned the process of innervation, like the notion of shock, in rather neurological, electrodynamic terms. In that sense, the paralyzing and destructive effects of technology are only the flip side of tensions, currents, and forces which, under different relations of production and reception, could have a mobilizing and empowering effect. To return to Mickey Mouse, the therapeutic diffusion of violent mass psychoses that Benjamin attributes to the films is accomplished through a process of transference by which individual alienation can leap into collective, public recognition. Such transference is brought about by a series of staged shocks or, if you will, countershocks—in this case, the precise rhythmic matching of acoustic and visual movement (which Adorno and Eisenstein understood more clearly than Benjamin as Disney's particular aesthetic innovation). In the stimulation of involuntary and collective laughter, the Mickey Mouse films affect their viewers in a manner at once physiological and cognitive.[27]

Notwithstanding this neuro-energetic model, Benjamin assigns Mickey Mouse a rather specific historical, cultural, and political place. For the currents that electrified Mick-

ey's German audience have one pole in the cataclysm of World War I and another, as Benjamin foresaw as early as 1933, in "the coming war," implicit in the fascist rise to power. As it did for many Weimar intellectuals, World War I had an emblematic, epistemic function for Benjamin, not only because it exploded the nineteenth-century dream of technology and progress, but because it catalyzed an unprecedented crisis of "experience" (*Erfahrung*). Technologically facilitated mass destruction changed all the familiar coordinates of experience; and it expelled the private individual from the shell of the bourgeois interior. In "Erfahrung und Armut" ("Experience and Poverty"), a programmatic essay of 1933, Benjamin writes: "A generation that still drove to school in a horse-drawn streetcar now stood under the open sky in a landscape in which nothing remained unchanged but the clouds, and, in the center, in a forcefield of destructive torrents and explosions, the tiny, fragile human body."[28]

The monstrous fruition of technology has not only muted the faculty of experience, the capability of individuals to narrate and communicate their experience; it has also revealed the bankruptcy of existing discourses of experience, in particular those predicated on a classical humanist notion of the subject. The inadequacy of the latter, and its myriad sectarian offshoots, for dealing with the psychosocial consequences of the war and the subsequent economic catastrophe only compounds the "poverty of experience" that Benjamin observes on an anthropological scale, "a new kind of barbarism." Instead of condemning this barbarism on moral grounds, however, he advocates a "new, positive concept of barbarism," an attitude he sees exemplified in constructivist painting (Paul Klee), modern architecture (the Bauhaus, Adolf Loos, Le Corbusier), and the work of writers such as Brecht and Paul Scheerbart. This new culture—or anti-culture—is a "culture of glas," a phrase Benjamin borrows from Scheerbart: a culture that rejects the privacy of the bourgeois interior, the *Etui* (case) and the overstuffed armchair, the personal trace, anthropomorphism, symbolism, the mystery of the "aura." The popular cousin of these "new barbarians" is Mickey Mouse, herald of an imagination that does not rely on experience, citizen of a "world in which it does not pay to have experiences." In the Disney films, Benjamin says in a fragment of 1931, "humanity prepares itself to survive civilization."[29]

The concept of *Erfahrung* is one of the most central, difficult, and ambivalent in Benjamin's work, linked to the equally elusive notion of the "aura."[30] Throughout his life, Benjamin was concerned with the problem of how to conceptualize a cognitive discourse vis-à-vis the transformations of modernity when those same transformations had eroded the very capacities that would enable such a discourse on a collective and public scale—capacities of being open to and reflecting upon experience, of seeing relations and making connections (for instance, between the split positions of observer, object, and agency), of remembering the past and imagining a different future. The problem was compounded with the more acute insight that these capacities, indeed the very concept of experience, were being held hostage by a bourgeois-humanist culture that had tied them to the perpetuation of social privilege, to aestheticism, escapism, and hypocrisy. In view of this dilemma, revealed in the aftershock of World War I, Benjamin opts for a desperate leap forward, into the "purgatory of New Objectivity [*Neue Sachlichkeit*]."[31] The decline of experience is troped into an opportunity to abolish it altogether; the "new barbarism" of experiential poverty appears as the proletarian alternative to a moribund bourgeois culture. We find this position elaborated in, among other things, Benjamin's work on Brecht, his essays on Karl Kraus and "The Destructive Character."

At the same time, Benjamin never abandoned his effort to reconceptualize, rather than simply abolish, experience. As he remarked in 1929 regarding a critical essay on "experience" written in his youth: "[M]y attack only punctured the word without annihilating it."[32] The contours of a new theory of experience can be found, for instance, in his essays on surrealism, Proust, and Kafka and his speculations on the "mimetic faculty" (1933/35), that is, in writings *concurrent* with his Brechtian, leftist-Fordist phase. If the essay "The Storyteller" (1936) appears to revert to nostalgic lamentation, the work on Baudelaire and respective sections in the Arcades project attempt more systematically to keep both irrevocable disintegration and the need for a refiguration of experience in view—as does, as I have argued elsewhere, the Artwork essay. For by this time, fascism had brought home the vulnerability of a collective lacking a discourse on technological modernization, lacking a public horizon that would enable human beings to recognize and negotiate the effects of historical fragmentation, rupture and loss, of collective yet privatized self-alienation. Without the self-reflective, anamnestic, and figurative dimension of experience, Benjamin knew, collective innervation would mean nothing but a behaviorist adaptation to the present.

Even in the programmatic endorsement of a "poverty of experience," Mickey Mouse does not fully merge with the "destructive character," but retains some of the fairy-tale appeal that Benjamin had noted in 1931 ("the motif of one who set out to learn fear").[33] To people "tired" of experience, "fed up" with *Kultur* and "the human being," the existence of Mickey Mouse is "a dream that compensates for the sadness and discouragement of the day" and shows them that "simple and quite magnificent existence which waking they lack the energy to realize." But unlike the aesthetics of *Neue Sachlichkeit,* this dream does not imitate the forms and functions of technology. On the contrary, it seems much closer to a surrealist fantasy than to the functionalist sobriety of the Bauhaus or the didactic rationalism of a Brecht. The existence projected by the Mickey Mouse films

> is full of miracles that not only surpass those of technology but make fun of them. For the most curious thing about them is that they all emanate, without machinery and improvised, from the body of the Mickey Mouse, her/his/its partisans and pursuers, from the most

quotidian furniture just as from trees, clouds or a lake. Nature and technology, primitivism and comfort have completely become one, and before the eyes of people who have grown tired of the endless complications of the everyday and to whom the purpose of life appears as nothing more than a distant vanishing point in an endless perspective of means, there appears as a redemption an existence which at every turn is self-sufficient in the most simple and simultaneously most comfortable way, in which a car does not weigh more than a straw-hat and the fruit on the tree grows round as fast as a hot-air balloon.[34]

Like Eisenstein, Benjamin was impressed with the metamorphoses staged by the Disney films, with what Eisenstein called their "plasmatic" tendency: "[A] displacement, an upheaval, a unique protest against the metaphysical immobility of the once-and-forever given."[35] But where Eisenstein, writing at the height of World War II, curiously elides the role of technology in these metamorphic games, Benjamin reads them as figures of innervation, anticipating an emancipatory incorporation of technology. As he had stressed in the 1931 fragment, the Mickey Mouse films engage technology not as an external force, in a literal or formal rendering of "mechanization," but as a "hidden figure": they hyperbolize the historical imbrication of nature and technology through humor and parody. While mechanically produced, the miracles of the animated cartoon seem improvised out of the bodies and objects on the screen, in a freewheeling exchange between animate and inanimate world.[36] This aesthetic self-sublation of technology not only condenses the supplementary, homeopathic relation between the technical media and other technologies; it also prefigures the utopian potential of technology for reorganizing the relations between human beings and nature.

The notion of an aesthetically sublated technology points toward Benjamin's cryptic remarks, in the Artwork essay, concerning film's ability to make its own technology disappear. There he refers to the "equipment-free aspect of reality" created through editing as "the height of artifice," "the 'blue flower' in the land of technology."[37] The invocation of this highly auratic emblem of the Romantic imagination remains puzzling, especially in light of more recent film theory's pinpointing of the "equipment-free aspect of reality" as a guiding principle of the Hollywood continuity system, the ideological masking of the apparatus that subtends the diegetic effect of classical narrative. Rather than dismissing it for perpetuating the illusion of reality, Benjamin sees the cinematic crossing of supreme artificiality with physiological immediacy as a chance—to rehearse technological innervation in the medium of the optical unconscious.

The parallel between Mickey Mouse and the cinematic Blue Flower effect throws into relief the relationship between animation and live-action film which is of some importance here. In the ideological division of labor between the two—rather unequal—genres, animation traditionally served the role of exemplifying the "mechanical magic" of the cinematic apparatus as a whole so as to complement and uphold mainstream narrative films' claim to "realism." To be sure, cartoons also imitated live-action films, not necessarily all in a parodic spirit, and Disney in particular began to develop a naturalistic look patterned on the Hollywood continuity style; while the pulsating rhythm of the Disney cartoons prior to the mid-1930s destabilizes just about everything within the frame, most of the subsequent productions, especially the features, show an increased concern for a stable animated diegesis.[38] But, if verisimilitude in animation was debated as a matter of stylistic choice, comparable options for live-action film were restricted in advance due to the institutional investment in the medium's photographic iconicity. In our context, this is particularly relevant for conventions of representing the human body, that is, in classical cinema, the illusory self-identity of the human figure as embodied by the star.

As a prototype of innervation, Benjamin's Mickey Mouse competes with the figure of the screen actor. In the earlier versions of the Artwork essay, Benjamin elaborates at much greater length on the profound changes that the mediation through the apparatus has visited upon the phenomenology of performance. In a significant respect he takes a position diametrically opposed to the later version: in the screen actor's confrontation of the apparatus, the audience is constructed as identifying, not with the testing, critical, impersonal attitude of the camera (as in the later version), but with the actor as their stand-in, as a representative of their own daily battle with an alienating technology who takes "revenge in their place." The actor's forced self-alienation in front of the camera, microphones, and klieg lights, the extreme presence of mind required in the absence of the aura of live performance, shows the masses how "[one's] humanity (or whatever may appear to them as such) can assert itself in the face of the apparatus." This is to say that humanity, what being human means in the twentieth century, can be redefined through the performance of self-alienation: "In the representation of human beings through the apparatus human self-alienation has found a most productive realization."[39]

In the historical task of making self-alienation productive, Mickey Mouse has certain advantages over the screen actor. While the actor remains tied to a realistic imaging of the human shape and thus can be naturalized and fetishized in the capitalist cult of the star, the cartoon figure does not lend itself to such false restoration of the aura—or so it seems, at least, in theory.[40] The appeal of the animated creature, and this goes beyond Mickey, owes much to its hybrid status, its blurring of human and animal, two-dimensional and three-dimensional, corporeal and neuro-energetic qualities. This hybrid status brings Mickey Mouse into the purview of Benjamin's reflections on the body: the problematic of the psycho-physiological boundaries that are supposed not only to contain the subject within but also to distinguish the human species from the rest of creation.

The vast transformations of second nature could not have left human beings' primary nature untouched: they have changed the meaning of sexuality and death; they have pervaded the boundaries of the human body and endowed it with prosthetic extensions; they have initiated, as Kracauer put it in his essay on the "mass ornament," the human figure's exodus from luscious organic splendor and individual form into anonymity. Indeed, the technically induced mutations of "our historical metabolism" have called into question the very distinction between first and second nature.[41]

The figure of Mickey Mouse answers to the historical experience of mutilation and fragmentation in technological warfare and industrial production. In 1931 Benjamin notes that the Mickey Mouse film upsets "relations of property": it visualizes, "for the first time, that one's own arm, even one's own body can be stolen."[42] This bodily fragmentation, actually quite rare in Mickey Mouse, is more typical of "radical" animation in general: think of figures such as Felix the Cat, Koko the Clown, or even Disney's own Oswald the Lucky Rabbit.[43] In the context of the German 1920s, moreover, the playful fragmentation of bodies in the cartoons forms a constellation with Dadaist depictions of the body as a dysfunctional automation or a dismembered mannequin. As Hal Foster has persuasively argued with respect to works by Max Ernst and Hans Bellmer, such depictions do not just respond to physical violations of the human shape but, more specifically, to the psycho-social reconfiguration of the body as whole: they deconstruct the defensive transmutation of military-industrial trauma into the prosthetic fantasy of the male body as armor.[44]

In Benjamin's work, the antithesis to the phantasmic wholeness of the "metallized" male body is the embodiment of the alien in the writings of Kafka. In his great essay on Kafka, he delineates a third etiology of self-alienation in the human relationship with the body, "one's own body," which he calls the "most forgotten alien land [*Fremde*]."[45] The strangeness or distortion that characterizes the inhabitants of Kafka's world is the result of a primal "forgetting," a forgetting in which psychic repression mingles with prehistoric forces, reverberations from a Gnostic abyss. The forgotten alien that is part of oneself extends beyond the human body to the strange and simultaneously familiar creatures that populate Kafka's tales, hybrid or imaginary creatures like the Cat Lamb or Odradek that challenge the taxonomies of an anthropocentric creation.

This psychoanalytic-Gnostic perspective makes it sufficiently clear that Benjamin's concept of self-alienation does not imply an alienation from an ostensibly prior, authentic, identical self. Rather, Kafka's figurations of the forgotten alien point to a constitutive split, an anthropological condition which only culminates, historically, in the effects of modern technology and commodification. The answer is therefore not a return to an unalienated, undivided, natural state but, as we already saw in the case of the screen actor, a productive transformation of self-alienation in the medium of representation. Benjamin compares Kafka's situation with that of experimental subjects who, watching themselves on film or hearing themselves speak on a gramophone, do not recognize their own walk or their own voice. But this moment of trompe l'oeil (and its acoustic equivalent), this salutary miscognition prompts an inquiry into "the fragments of one's own existence."[46]

In an early Messianically inflected text, Benjamin elaborates on a similar, species-specific form of alienation when he reflects on the basic discrepancy between human physis and the human senses, the inaccessibility of the body to sensory perception: "We cannot see our face, our back, not even our whole head, that is, the most noble part of our body." But this dilemma, like human perception itself, is historically variable, given the transformations of nature and the human physis.[47] If one traces out this line of thought, the task of the technical media vis-à-vis human self-alienation is actually two-fold: *allegorical,* in the sense of making the dilemma visible, readable in materialist terms (which includes the way technology perpetuates, instead of overcoming, sensory alienation); and *utopian,* in the sense of compensating for the anthropological lack (without denying it) by rehearsing a collective innervation of technology. In the latter, the Messianic motif of an integral presence converges with the revolutionary motif of technology as a liberated and liberating productive force.

If Chaplin is exemplary of the allegorical function of film, the embodiment of self-alienation in the spirit of Kafka, Mickey Mouse prefigures the utopian interpenetration of body and image space which Benjamin delineates at the end of his essay on surrealism.[48] What the surrealists, according to Benjamin, have understood on an individual basis, Mickey accomplishes in the arena of mass reception: by generating in the sphere of the image, through techniques of "profane illumination," the reality of a "collective physis" (*Kollektivleib*). Where image space and physis coincide, there is no place for armored bodies. The leap into the apparatus opens up the dimension of the optical unconscious, makes it public and redemptive; hence Benjamin's initial choice of the title "Micky-Maus" for the entire section devoted to the optical unconscious in the Artwork essay.

As an animated, artificial subjectivity, Mickey Mouse not only unfetters the human sensorium from its imaginary confinement to the human shape, but also projects the demise of the human species in an anthropomorphic, anthropocentric sense. "The Mickey Mouse demonstrates that the creature [*Kreatur*] continues to exist even when it has shed all similarity with humans. He/she/it ruptures the hierarchy of creatures predicated on the human being." In the context of the *Passagen-Werk,* the deliberate blurring of boundaries between human and nonhuman nature joins Mickey Mouse in a constellation with Charles Fourier, with the utopian project of "cracking the teleology of nature." Like Fourier's extravagances, Mickey Mouse represents a "moral mobilization of nature," and as in Fourier, the vector of this mobilization is humor: "The cracking of natural teleology proceeds according to the plan of humor."[49]

Benjamin, like the surrealists, was fascinated with Fourier's fantastic visions in which technology found a playful use in the cosmic reorganization of nature. When the ocean turns to lemonade; when human beings will be able to live like fish in the water and fly like birds in the air; when they can turn themselves into amphibians at will by closing the hole in the cardiac chamber; when oranges will blossom in Siberia and the most dangerous beasts will be configured into their opposites—anti-lions will deliver the mail and anti-whales will help human beings tug boats; when new stars come into existence that replace the old which, as we speak, are rotting anyway. . . . It is evident why Benjamin perceived an afterglow of the Fourierist imagination when he saw films in which trees court and marry, cars turn into dangerous monsters, pigs into accordions, fish into tigers, and octopuses into elephants.[50]

Benjamin's peculiar form of negative anthropology, which links his reading of Kafka with his interest in Fourier, superimposes the historical-political trajectory of modernity—from the Second Empire to fascism—with a different temporality, closer to the Messianic speculations of the "Theses on the Philosophy of History."[51] Even in the context of the Artwork essay, he sees the problem of revolution defined by the disjunction between "the utopia of the second nature," concerned with society and technology (the Soviet experiment) and "the utopia of the first," concerned with the human body, with "love and death" (Fourier, de Sade). If the utopia of second nature takes on the legacy of one or more centuries, the utopia of a changed physis refers itself to the grand scheme of "natural history"; like Kafka, it thinks "in terms of cosmic epochs" (*in Weltaltern*).[52] Inasmuch as the concept of collective innervation bridges first and second nature, it also telescopes anthropological, global-ecological and Messianic perspectives into the politics of perception mandated by the contemporary crisis. Mickey Mouse becomes a dialectical image for Benjamin because he/she/it embodies the disjunctive temporalities of human and natural history.

As is well-known, Benjamin was not the only writer who perceived Mickey as an instance of the utopian imagination.[53] And the earliest Mickey Mouse films (such as *Steamboat Willie* and *Plane Crazy* [1928]), like some of the Silly Symphonies of the early 1930s, indeed contain glimpses of a playfully transformed nature, nature liberated from anthropocentric, phallocentric oppositions and hierarchies, a nature in which the boundaries between humans and animals, mechanical and organic, living and inanimate objects, master and slave, labor and play become fluid. Is Mickey a mouse? Or an android? Is the creature woman, man, or child?

If such blurring of boundaries had a utopian appeal, it also involved an encounter with the uncanny. For Mickey's otherness was not that of an easily recognizable difference (like his "blackness"), but his/her/its very hybridity, the peculiar, syncretistic blend of strange and familiar elements that the genre of the animated cartoon permits. Contemporary responses to Mickey, including Disney's own, tend to register the creature's uncanny fallout, but only to domesticate it in various ways.

Fritz Moellenhoff, for instance, in the first major psychoanalytic attempt to come to terms with Mickey Mouse, relates the figure to "doubts and anxieties" caused by the "overpoweringly rapid development" of technology. Drawing on an important essay by Hanns Sachs, "The Delay of the Machine Age" (1933), Moellenhoff sees Mickey as a "playful inversion of the machine age," inasmuch as the Mouse "ridicules" the "goddess" which technology has become. If the division between organic and mechanical, "living and lifeless," breeds anxiety under conditions of reality, Mickey's animated, artificial, dreamlike existence allays those fears by appealing to our narcissism and fantasies of omnipotence. In a similar gesture, Moellenhoff enumerates other aspects that combine at once transgressive and reassuring appeals: Mickey's inversion of the mouse character, the fearless pluckiness of the tiny, weak creature; Mickey's hybrid gender (especially after Disney gave the creature the voice of a eunuch or prepubescent child, which was, coincidentally, his own); Mickey's acting out of polymorphous perversions, in particular sadism and orality, without guilt or punishment; and the absence of castration symbolism and of Oedipal conflicts and confrontations. Moellenhoff concludes by venturing that the key to Mickey Mouse's success is his symbolic significance of "a phallus but a desexualized one." Lacking genital interest—and thus refusing heterosexual reproduction—"he does not stir up wishes which have to be suppressed and consequently he does not arouse anxiety."[54]

The psychoanalytic discourse on Mickey Mouse evokes, once more, Adorno's association of the Disney figure with the "jazz subject." If jazz has a socially nonconforming, resistant element, Adorno grants, it may lie in its gender hybridity. For even as the sound approximates the human voice, the timbre of the jazz instruments refuses to be characterized in terms of sexual difference: it is "impossible to diagnose the muted trumpet as masculine-heroic; or to define the anthropoid sound of the saxophone as the voice of a noble virgin in the manner in which Berlioz still used the related clarinet." To be sure, the partial drives released in the moment of regression are as soon repressed, falsely integrated, and become detrimental in their particular social configuration which turns "sadism into terror," "homosexuality into a conspiratorial collective." Nonetheless, Adorno discerns in jazz's momentary rebellion "against patriarchal genitality" an affinity with the most advanced esoteric music (Berg, Schönberg) in which "the partial drives are called up one by one." The timbres in which this naming takes place are the same ones that in jazz appear as "parodistic."[55]

The radical edge the first Disney cartoons might have had, critics tend to agree, disappeared sometime during the early 1930s. Perhaps Disney had his own or, rather, his corporation's, second thoughts on the uncanny hybrid that some of his viewers discovered in his creation. Mickey's perverse streaks were sanitized, his rodent features domes-

ticated into neotenic cuteness; the playful, anarchic engagement with machinery was functionalized to comply with the work ethic; and outlandish fantasy gave way to an idealized, sentimentalized world. And despite—and, perhaps, through—this process of normalization, violence and terror became a staple of the Disney films, including the features.[56]

Benjamin's investment in Mickey Mouse no doubt corresponded to certain traits present in the films that were also perceived by his contemporaries. But there is a moment of excess in this investment (an excess comparable to Eisenstein's obsession with Disney's fire imagery in *The Moth and the Flame*) that has at least as much to do with the writer's unconscious as with that of the spectating collective whose reactions are claimed as evidence. Compared with Benjamin's Gnostic science fiction fantasy of the Disney Mouse, the psychoanalytic efforts at explanation or critique (including Adorno's) invariably sound tame and normalizing. Benjamin's own effort to rationalize Mickey as part of a presentist "culture of glas" suggests that the utopian overvaluation of the figure is a reaction formation against a formidable fear, unleashed by thinking the destruction of the subject. The fear that Mickey "sets out to learn" in Benjamin's technological fairy tale is that of the reactions that it might catalyze in the mass audience, the "inhuman laughter" that may be therapeutic discharge or prelude to a pogrom.

Today, Benjamin's image of Mickey Mouse enters a constellation with the cyborg, as an emblem of a similar confusion of boundaries—between organism and machine, animal and human, male and female, Oedipal and social, public and private. The cyborg, in Donna Haraway's famous manifesto, is the prototype of "a kind of disassembled and reassembled, postmodern collective and personal self."[57] Benjamin's Mickey Mouse has an affinity with Haraway's cyborg not only in the (post)-anthropological, cosmic perspective but also in the assessment of the political stakes, the insistence on holding both infinite destructive power and new possibilities with a double, stereoscopic vision:

> From one perspective, a cyborg world is about the final imposition of a grid of control on the planet, about the final abstraction embodied in a Star Wars apocalypse waged in the name of defense, about the final appropriation of women's bodies in a masculinist orgy of war. . . . From another perspective, a cyborg world might be about lived social and bodily realities in which people are not afraid of their joint kinship with animals and machines, not afraid of permanently partial identities and contradictory standpoints. The political struggle is to see from both perspectives at once because each reveals both dominations and possibilities unimaginable from the other vantage point.[58]

Like Haraway, Benjamin could not envision a transformed relationship between technology, human beings, and nature without a different organization of the social, economic, and sexual order—a postnational, postcolonial, and non-Oedipal order of humanity:

Human beings as a species may have completed their development tens of thousands of years ago; humanity as a species, however, is only at its beginning. For that species, technology organizes a physis in which the exchange with the cosmos takes on new and different forms from those of peoples and families.[59]

With somewhat less pathos, Benjamin makes a similar point in his Kafka essay, when he recounts Max Brod's anecdote of Kafka referring to contemporary humankind as "nihilistic thoughts, suicidal thoughts that come into God's head" when he is in a bad mood, has a "bad day." Asked if that means that there is "hope outside this manifestation of the world that we know," Kafka is supposed to have responded: "Oh, plenty of hope, an infinite amount of hope—but not for us." Which leads Benjamin to single out a particular group of "extremely strange figures" in Kafka who may be exempt from this verdict: "the assistants" (*Gehilfen*), unfinished and awkward creatures who alone "have escaped from the bosom of the family and for whom there may be hope," that is, *because* they have escaped from the family circle.[60]

"To see from both perspectives at once" even as they seem to rule each other out: this program is not without danger. For it involves going further along with the powers of destruction than any humanist critique would dare to permit. Benjamin's own rhetoric is characterized by a fascination with technological violence and simultaneous attempts to check the vehemence of the destructive imagination. Thus the utopian passage from *One-Way Street* cited above is preceded by an organicist-sexist fantasy that can compete with anything Ernst Jünger or Oswald Spengler wrote about technology. Warning against a failure to theorize humanity's need for an ecstatic and communal contact with the cosmos, Benjamin points to the terrible realization of this need in the "last war, which was an attempt at a new and unprecedented mating with the cosmic powers."

> Human multitudes, gases, electrical forces were hurled into the open country, high-voltage currents coursed through the landscape, new constellations rose in the sky, aerial space and ocean depths thundered with propellers, and everywhere sacrificial shafts were dug into Mother Earth. This immense wooing of the cosmos was enacted for the first time on a planetary scale, that is, in the spirit of technology.

Benjamin's style mimics the phallic, heterosexist, irrational thrust of the military imaginary even as he goes on to pull the anti-capitalist emergency brake: "But because the lust for profit of the ruling class sought penitence for its own will technology betrayed humanity and turned the bridal bed into a bloodbath."[61]

A similar pattern seems to be at work in Benjamin's inscription of Mickey Mouse with the utopian idea of a collective innervation of technology, revealing this idea as the site of an intense ambivalence. By the time he was writing the Artwork essay, he was well aware of how close the Disney subject could come to the spirit of fascism. In a note accompanying the first version, he considers the "us-ability of the Disney method for Fascism," a remark he elaborates in the already cited footnote to the second version.[62] "The somber fireworks [of the more recent Mickey Mouse films] manifest an already present but latent trait that suggests how comfortably fascism, in this area too, appropriates 'revolutionary' innovations."[63] Recent research on the German reception of Disney confirms Benjamin's suspicions. Contrary to Disney publicity, Hitler was a great fan of Mickey Mouse, and Disney films and comics continued to be circulated even after and against the official prohibition; Mickey appeared as a mascot on German fighter planes well into the war.[64]

For Benjamin, the fine line that separated the Fourier/Disney dream of a transformed nature from the nightmare of fascism was that of humor: only in a playful, parodistic form can the revolution counter the "beastly seriousness" of fascism, its retrenchment of the dialectic of second nature into the literalist, essentialist myth of blood and soil.[65] This is no doubt an important point. But in the context of the reception of the Disney films, Benjamin's insistence on the therapeutic, redemptive role of humor suggests a rhetorical emergency break similar to the anti-capitalist afterthought in his war-as-mating fantasy. For one thing, not all cartoons—and certainly not all Disney cartoons—are funny; as Kristin Thompson points out, the view of cartoons as comic was part of the ideological construction of animation, a way to rationalize departures from standards of verisimilitude.[66] For another, making humor the answer to the question of a non-fascist innervation of technology sends us back to an issue that had been in question all along: the politics of the collective laughter.

It may well be that Benjamin had maneuvered himself into a genuine aporia, and his squirming (in the footnote to the second version) over the legitimacy of raising the question of the relative humanity or inhumanity of this laughter suggests as much. Adorno may have had a more acute assessment of the sadomasochistic mechanisms operating in mass-cultural reception; and his individual-humanist critique put him at a safe distance from fascism. Unlike Adorno, Benjamin took both technology and mass-cultural reception seriously as productive forces, and came close to getting caught in the rhetoric of their destructive reality. Yet even in these aporetic and ambivalent moments, the price of a tendency to think through extremes, he understood something about the success of fascism that Adorno did not.

Benjamin's ambivalence (of which Adorno's critique is an important part) holds important implications for our own unresolved relations with technology. To be sure, the catastrophe unleashed by fascism has changed the world to which Benjamin and Adorno responded, and subsequent transformations on a global scale have given their theories a historical and local patina. The use of technology in the service of domination can no longer be distinguished by the criterion of monumentality, and "play versions of second nature" (Benjamin)—such as video games—have become a major site for naturalizing violence, destruction, and oppression. In the postmodern age, technology has become infinitely smaller, miniaturized like Mickey Mouse, while power has expanded into totalities that defy representation. The global and cosmic dimensions that Benjamin superimposed upon the present through his figurative telescope have become an electronic reality.

Still, even as the stakes have multiplied, the evasions, gaps, and contradictions in our public—and, for that matter, also academic—discourses on technology remain. The confusion of death and play in contemporary entertainment culture is as symptomatic in this regard as is the unshaken belief in technology's subservience to the cause of American democracy/hegemony, to say nothing of the optimistic narratives of current media theory sailing under the flag of Cultural Studies. The perceptual splitting of agency, object, and spectacle that Benjamin and Adorno observed in different contexts is as strong as ever, and jeremiads about the media's complicity with violence tend to perpetuate that split rather than lead to a different media practice. Now as then, a politicized aesthetics of technology is key to the project of social and sexual transformation. As Benjamin insisted vis-à-vis Adorno, the very media that exacerbate human self-alienation have to be mobilized if humanity is to take charge of its own fate and ensure not only the survival but, for the first time in history, the conscious innervation of a collective physis.

For both Benjamin and Adorno, the Disney syndrome was perched on the threshold to fascism: for Benjamin, a dialectical image of the utopian possibilities of technology in an age of technological warfare; for Adorno, a sociogram of the psychic deformations that linked the liberal-capitalist culture industry to its *völkisch* counterpart. Half a century later, in an age of cyborgs, global integration, and more sophisticated technological warfare, the questions posed by Benjamin and Adorno's debate on Disney are still with us, suggesting a line of inquiry that can help us defamiliarize the all-too-familiar opposition of high-modernist critique and postmodernist affirmation.

Notes

1. This essay is based on a lecture written for the centennial symposium on Walter Benjamin, "The Visual Arts in a Technological Age," Wayne State University, Detroit, April 1992. For discussions and readings that have helped shape this essay I wish to thank Lauren Berlant, Bill Brown, Susan Buck-Morss, Donald Crafton, Hank Sartin, and, especially, Michael Geyer. Unless otherwise indicated, translations are my own.

2. Susan Buck-Morss, "Aesthetics and Anaesthetics: Walter Benjamin's Artwork Essay Reconsidered," *October* 62 (Fall 1992): 3-41.

3. Peter Wollen, "Detroit: Capital of the Twentieth Century," lecture presented at the Detroit Benjamin symposium; for an earlier version, see Peter Wollen, "Cinema/Americanism/the Robot," in *Modernity and Mass Culture,* ed. James Naremore and Patrick

Brantlinger (Bloomington, 1991). Wollen's suggestion assumes a reading of the Artwork essay that I have contested in "Benjamin, Cinema and Experience: The Blue Flower in the Land of Technology," *New German Critique* 40 (Winter 1987): 179-224.

4. Theodor W. Adorno, letter to Walter Benjamin, 18 March 1936, trans. Harry Zohn, in *Aesthetics and Politics,* ed. Fredric Jameson (London, 1977), 120-26; a number of points in Adorno's letter, such as the remarks concerning Mickey Mouse and Benjamin's distinction between a "first" and a "second technology" (*Technik*), do not make sense unless one refers to this version of the essay. The textual vicissitudes of the Artwork essay are described in the editorial apparatus accompanying the eventual publication of the second version in volume 7 of *Gesammelte Schriften* (hereinafter cited as *GS*), ed. Rolf Tiedemann and Hermann Schweppenhäuser (Frankfurt, 1989).

5. Walter Benjamin, "The Work of Art in the Age of Mechanical Reproduction," in *Illuminations,* trans. Harry Zohn (New York, 1969) 236f.: translation modified. For an earlier elaboration of the "optical unconscious," see Walter Benjamin, "Short History of Photography" (1931), in *One-Way Street and Other Writings,* trans. Edmund Jephcott and Kingsley Shorter (London, 1979); *GS* 2:371; and draft notes in *GS* 2:1140.

6. Walter Benjamin, "Erwiderung an Oscar A. H. Schmitz" (1927; reply to an anticollectivist review of *Battleship Potemkin*), in *GS* 2:752. The subsequent elaboration of this point reads like a draft for the passage from the Artwork essay cited above.

7. Benjamin, *GS* 7:376ff.

8. Ibid., 7:377.

9. Adorno, letter to Benjamin, 18 March 1936, in Jameson, ed., *Aesthetics and Politics,* 124; translation modified. I am aware that the literal translation of the definite article (*die* Micky-Maus) is unidiomatic, but I wish to convey the vernacular, more concrete and physical sense of the creature in Benjamin and Adorno's style. Likewise, in the following text, I will preserve the sexual ambiguity of the figure resulting from the "naturally" feminine gender of the German "Maus."

10. Theodor W. Adorno, "Oxforder Nachträge," in *Gesammelte Schriften,* ed. Rolf Tiedemann (Frankfurt, 1982), 17:101, 105. Also see Theodor W. Adorno, "On Jazz" (1936), trans. Jamie Owen Daniel, *Discourse* 12.1 (Fall-Winter 1989-90): 45-69; and "Perennial Fashion: Jazz," in *Prisms,* trans. Samuel and Shierry Weber (Cambridge, Mass., 1981).

11. On the concept of "Americanism" in general, see Victoria de Grazia, "Americanism for Export," *Wedge* 7-8 (Winter-Spring 1985): 74-81; on German Americanism between the wars, see O. Basler, "Amerikan-

ismus: Geschichte eines Schlagwortes," *Deutsche Rundschau* 224 (August 1930); and John Willett, *Art and Politics in the Weimar Republic: The New Sobriety, 1917-1933* (New York, 1978). Siegfried Kracauer captures the two sides of Americanism in a review of 1926: "One has to hand this to the Americans: with slapstick films they have created a form that offers a counterweight to their reality: if in that reality they subject the world to an often unbearable discipline, the film in turn dismantles this self-imposed order quite forcefully (*Frankfurter Zeitung,* 29 January 1936). Sergei Eisenstein makes a similar point about Disney in *Eisenstein on Disney,* ed. Jay Leyda, trans. Alan Upchurch (New York, 1988) 3f., 21-22, 42.

12. Richard Schickel, *The Disney Version* (New York, 1971), 208f., 107, and passim. Also see *Noah's Ark* (1959), Disney's paean to Fordist-Taylorist methods of production.

13. J. P. Storm and M. Dressler, *Im Reiche der Micky Maus: Walt Disney in Deutschland, 1927-1945* (Berlin, 1991), 61. An article in the party paper of the Gau Pommern of 1931 calls Mickey Mouse "the most miserable ideal ever revealed," a "dirty and filth-covered vermin, the greatest bacteria carrier in the animal kingdom," another instance of the "Jewish brutalization of the people" (ibid.). Art Spiegelman uses this quotation as an epigraph in the second volume of *Maus: A Survivor's Tale* (New York, 1991).

14. Storm and Dressler, *Im Reiche der Micky Maus,* 55-56, 156, and passim.

15. Lawrence A. Rickels, *The Case of California* (Baltimore, 1991), 59.

16. Max Horkheimer and Theodor W. Adorno, *Dialectic of Enlightenment* (1944), trans. John Cumming (New York, 1969), 138; translation modified. The sadomasochistic structure described here is actually not limited to Disney; it can be found as well in some of the stylistically more radical Warner Brothers cartoons of the period, such as *You Ought to Be in Pictures* (Porky Pig/Freleng, 1940) or *Hiawatha's Rabbit Hunt* (Bugs Bunny/Freleng, 1941).

17. Siegfried Kracauer, "Sturges or Laughter Betrayed," *Films in Review* 1.1 (February 1950): 11-13, 43-47.

18. Benjamin, *GS* 7:377.

19. Ibid., 1:508; and *Illuminations,* 242 (translation modified). Adorno invokes this passage in his analysis of mass-cultural forms of alienation in "On Jazz," 49. Also see Benjamin's review of Ernst Jünger's collection, *Krieg und Krieger,* "Theories of German Fascism" (1930), trans. Jerolf Wikoff, *New German Critique* 17 (Spring 1979): 120-28; and "Pariser Brief [I]" (1936), in *GS* 3:482-95.

20. Edmund Husserl, *Ideas Pertaining to a Pure Phenomenology and to a Phenomenological Philosophy,* vol. I, trans. R. Rojcewicz and A. Schuwer (Boston, 1989), quoted and discussed in Buck-Morss, "Aesthetics and Anaesthetics," 30. A key text for Benjamin's notion of "shock" and the historical crisis of perception is his well-known essay, "On Some Motifs in Baudelaire" (1939).

21. Jacques Lacan, "The Mirror Stage as Formative of the Function of the I" (1936/49), in *Ecrits,* trans. Alan Sheridan (New York, 1977). As Buck-Morss points out ("Aesthetics and Anaesthetics," 37), the first version of Lacan's paper was presented the same year as Benjamin's Artwork essay, at a meeting of the International Psychoanalytic Association at Marienbad in 1936; during that conference, Lacan traveled to Berlin in order to watch the fascist imaginary in action at the Olympics which were being held there. See David Macey, *Lacan in Contexts* (New York, 1988).

22. Walter Benjamin, "Paris—the Capital of the Nineteenth Century," in *Charles Baudelaire: A Lyric Poet in the Era of High Capitalism,* trans. Harry Zohn and Quintin Hoare (London, 1983), 165; and *GS* 5:50f. On the concept of "phantasmagoria" in Benjamin's *Passagen-Werk,* see Susan Buck-Morss, *The Dialectics of Seeing: Walter Benjamin and the Arcades Project* (Cambridge, Mass., 1989), chaps. 4, 5, and passim.

23. Walter Benjamin, "Planetarium," in *GS* 4:147; and *One-Way Street* (selection), in *Reflections,* trans. Edmund Jephcott (New York, 1979), 93; translation modified. Benjamin elaborates on this distinction by resorting to the analogy of education: "Is not [the purpose of] education above all the indispensable ordering of the relationship between the generations and therefore mastery, if we are to use this term, of that relationship and not of children?" Also relevant here is Benjamin's distinction between a "first" and a "second technology," relating to the historical distancing of human agency from its effects, in the second version of the Artwork essay, in *GS* 7:359f. For a detailed account of Benjamin's philosophy of technology see Norbert Bolz, *Theorie der neuen Medien* (Munich, 1990), pt. 2; and *Auszug aus der entzauberten Welt: Philosophischer Extremismus zwischen den Weltkriegen* (Munich, 1989), pt. 3.

24. As Jean Laplanche and J. B. Pontalis point out, Freud used the term "innervation" to describe a "physiological process: the transmission, generally in an efferent direction, of energy along a nerve-pathway," possibly produced by the "conversion of psychical into nervous energy" (*The Language of Psychoanalysis,* trans. D. Nicholson-Smith [New York, 1973], 213). Whether Benjamin took the term directly from Freud or from French psychoanalytic discourse of the period, he must have found it useful for conceptualizing historical transformation as a process of converting images into somatic and collective reality. Thus, he speaks of the idea of "the revolution as an

innervation of the technical organs of the collective," comparing the at once utopian and practical aspects of this process with the development of "the child who learns how to grasp by trying to catch the moon" (*GS* 5:777; Artwork essay, second version, in *GS* 7:360 n. 4).

25. Benjamin, Artwork essay, first version, in *GS* 1:445. The corresponding passage in the second version spells out more clearly the physiological and cognitive components of that task: *"Film serves to train human beings in apperceptions and reactions caused by the interaction with technology* [Apparatur] *whose importance in their lives grows almost daily.* The interaction with technology teaches them at the same time that the enslavement in its service will not give way to a liberation by this same technology until the constitution of humanity has adapted itself to the new productive forces opened up by the second technology" (*GS* 7:359f.).

26. Buck-Morss, "Aesthetics and Anaesthetics," 18 n. 62.

27. "A Mickey Mouse film may still be incomprehensible today to [this or that] individual, but not to an entire audience [*Publikum*]. And a Mickey Mouse film can govern an entire audience through rhythm" (Benjamin, *GS* 2:962). Eisenstein was particularly interested in Disney's synaesthetic matching of sound and image tracks in conjunction with his own collaboration with Prokofiev on *Alexander Nevsky* (1938): see *The Film Sense*, ed. and trans. Jay Leyda (New York, 1947), 161f.; and *Non-Indifferent Nature*, cited in *Eisenstein on Disney*, 98-100, 65f. On the ambiguity of Benjamin's notion of "shock," see Hansen, "Benjamin," 210-11.

28. Walter Benjamin, "Erfahrung und Armut" (December 1933), in *GS* 2:214. The same passage reappears five years later, in Benjamin's essay on Nikolai Leskov, "The Storyteller," in *Illuminations,* 84, where it serves to set up a position that by and large reverses that of the earlier essay.

29. Benjamin, "Erfahrung und Armut," 215-18; "Zu Micky-Maus" (1931), in *GS* 6:144.

30. The German word *Erfahrung*, more than the English word "experience," preserves an etymological connection with both "*fahren*" (to ride) and *Gefahr* (danger) and thus conveys a sense of mobility, of journeying, wandering, or cruising, that is, temporal dimensions of duration, habit, repetition, and return, as well as a sense of risk to the experiencing subject—connotations that distinguish *Erfahrung* from the more neutral, singular occurrence of *Erlebnis* (event, adventure), a meaning contained in "experience." On the centrality of "aura" for Benjamin's theory of experience, see Marleen Stoessel, *Aura, das vergessene Menschliche: Zu Sprache und Erfahrung bei Walter Benjamin* (Munich, 1983).

31. Bolz, *Auszug,* 95. See also Burkhardt Lindner, "Technische Reproduzierbarkeit und Kulturindustrie: Benjamin's 'Positives Barbarentum' im Kontext," in *"Links hatte noch alles sich zu enträtseln . . ."*: *Walter Benjamin im Kontext,* ed. Burkhardt Lindner (Frankfurt, 1978).

32. Benjamin, *GS* 2:902; "Erfahrung" (1913), in *GS* 2:54-56.

33. Siegfried Kracauer saw the fairy-tale motif of "the weak creature who asserts himself in the struggle against the evil forces of this world" as a distinctive characteristic of both animated cartoon and slapstick comedy, but criticizes Disney for abandoning this line, the revelation of the everyday as a fairy tale, in his longer films by merely assimilating stereotypical fairy-tale figures to a more and more conventional depiction of the everyday ("*Dumbo*," *The Nation*, 8 November 1941, 463).

34. Benjamin, *GS* 2:218f.

35. *Eisenstein on Disney,* 33.

36. For a discussion of animation's specific relation to technology, see Michael Wassenaar, "Strong to the Finich: Machines, Metaphor, and Popeye the Saylor," *Velvet Lighttrap* 24 (1989): 20-32.

37. Benjamin, *GS* 1:495; and *Illuminations,* 233, where the proverbial Blue Flower is demoted to a generic "orchid."

38. Kristin Thompson, "Implications of the Cel Animation Technique," in *The Cinematic Apparatus,* ed. Teresa de Lauretis and Stephen Heath (New York, 1980), 106-20; Richard Schickel, *Disney Version,* chap. 21 and passim; and Kracauer, "*Dumbo.*" See also Eisenstein's critical remarks about "the crude naturalism" of the landscapes in *Bambi* (*Eisenstein on Disney,* 99). Hank Sartin confirms my suspicion that, contrary to received opinion, Disney's move toward "realism" already began prior to the features, with the stabilization and standardization of the background drawings that were thus distinguished from the throbbing, rhythmic movement of the figures.

39. Benjamin, *GS* 1:450-51; 7:365, 369. See also my "Benjamin," 205-7, 219-21; and Bolz, *Auszug,* 129.

40. Cartoon figures, Mickey Mouse in particular, did of course assume star status, with the attendant phenomena of fan mail, fan clubs, and copyright exploitation; in the measure that the name Disney increasingly referred to a giant corporation of anonymous employees, the star aura was transferred to Walt the inventor, artist, American genius. A considerable number of Warner Brothers cartoons, by contrast, present parodies of the star cult and of particular stars.

41. Siegfried Kracauer, "The Mass Ornament" (1927), trans. Barbara Correll and Jack Zipes, *New German Critique* 5 (Spring 1975): 67-77; and Fredric Jameson, *Late Marxism: Adorno, or, The Persistence of the Dialectic* (New York, 1990), 95.

42. Benjamin, *GS* 6:144.

43. I am indebted to Hank Sartin for this observation.

44. Hal Foster, "Armor Fou," *October* 56 (Spring 1991): 65-97; the by now classical argument on this fantasy is Klaus Theweleit, *Male Fantasies* (1977/78), 2 vols., trans. S. Conway, E. Carter, and C. Turner (Minneapolis, 1987/89).

45. Walter Benjamin, "Franz Kafka," in *GS* 2:431; *Illuminations,* 132, 126. On the body in Benjamin, see Sigrid Weigel, "Passagen und Spuren des 'Leib- und Bildraums' in Benjamins Schriften," in *Leib- und Bildraum: Lektüren nach Benjamin,* ed. Sigrid Weigel (Cologne, 1992), 49-64; for a different position, see Stoessel, *Aura,* 61f., 72-77, and chap. 5.

46. Benjamin, *GS* 2:436; and *Illuminations,* 137. I am using the term "trompe l'oeil" here in the sense developed by Mary Ann Doane, "'When the Direction of the Force Acting on the Body Is Changed': The Moving Image," *Wide Angle* 7.1-2 (1985): 45-49.

47. Walter Benjamin, "Wahrnehmung und Leib," in *GS* 6:67; for a more extensive comment on this fragment, see Gertrud Koch, "Cosmos in Film: On the Concept of Space in Walter Benjamin's 'Work of Art' Essay," trans. Nancy Nenno, *Qui Parle* 5.2 (Spring/Summer 1992): 61-73.

48. In the draft notes to the Kafka essay, Benjamin repeatedly aligns Kafka and Chaplin and both in turn with the medium of silent film, a "reprieve" in the historical process to which Kafka furnishes the "last intermediary texts" (*Verbindungstexte*) (*GS* 2:1256-57); on Chaplin, see also Benjamin, *GS* 1:1040, 1047. Kracauer had made an explicit linkage between Kafka and silent film in his essay "Photography" (1927) and an implied one in his review of *The Castle* (*Frankfurter Zeitung,* 28 November 1926), both of which Benjamin had read. See my "Decentric Perspectives: Kracauer's Early Writings on Film and Mass Culture," *New German Critique* 54 (Fall 1991): 47-76.

49. Benjamin, *GS* 6:144, 5:777, 781.

50. The last example is actually from one of Eisenstein's favorite Silly Symphonies, *Merbabies* (1938), in which he perceived a similar play with evolutionist teleology; see *Eisenstein on Disney,* 4, 10, 33.

51. See, in particular, Benjamin's thesis 18, in *GS* 1:703, in which he cites a biologist on the minute fracture that human history represents in relation to organic life on earth and equates this disproportion to the "time of the now" which, as a model of Messianic time, represents, in an "enormous abbreviation," the history of all humanity (Benjamin, *Illuminations,* 263; translation modified).

52. Draft notes on the second version of the Artwork essay, *GS* 7:665f.; "Kafka," in *GS* 2:410; *Illuminations,*

113. On the concept of "natural history" (*Naturgeschichte*) in Benjamin and Adorno, see Susan Buck-Morss, *The Origin of Negative Dialectics* (New York, 1977), 52-57; and *Dialectics of Seeing* chaps. 3 and 6. Jameson, *Late Marxism,* 95, ironically notes the scandal, "worse than old-fashioned . . . a kind of social blunder," involved in Critical Theory's evocation of "the larger, more abstract thoughts" of natural history, that is, from the perspective of Althusserian Marxism, and goes on to link the notion of natural history to the discourse of contemporary science fiction.

53. *Eisenstein on Disney*; Kracauer, *"Dumbo"*; also see Gregory A. Waller, "Mickey, Walt, and Film Criticism from *Steamboat Willie* to *Bambi,*" in *The American Animated Cartoon,* ed. Gerald Peary and Danny Peary (New York, 1980), 49-57; Timothy R. White, "From Disney to Warner Bros.: The Critical Shift," *Film Criticism* 16.3 (1992): 3-16; and Jonathan Rosenbaum, "Dream Masters I: Walt Disney," *Film Comment* (January-February 1975): 64-69.

54. Fritz Moellenhoff, "Remarks on the Popularity of Mickey Mouse," *American Imago* (June 1940), rpt. *American Imago* 46.2-3 (Summer/Fall 1989): 105-19. Hanns Sachs's essay first appeared in *Psychoanalytic Quarterly* 2 (1933): 404-24. Ariel Dorfman and Armand Mattelart take the Disney characters' refusal to reproduce—and thus evade 'natural' motherhood—as part of the comics' authoritarian structure; see their *How to Read Donald Duck: Imperialist Ideology in the Disney Comic,* trans. David Kunzle (New York, 1975).

55. Adorno, "Oxforder Nachträge," 106f.

56. Robert Sklar, "The Making of Cultural Myths: Walt Disney," in Peary and Peary, eds., *American Animated Cartoon,* 58-65; David I. Berland, M.D., "Disney and Freud: Walt Meets the Id," *Journal of Popular Culture* 15.4 (1982): 93-104; Elizabeth A. Lawrence, "In the Mick of Time: Reflections on Disney's Ageless Mouse," *Journal of Popular Culture* 20.2 (1986): 65-72; and Leonard Maltin, *Of Mice and Magic* (New York, 1987), 37. Also see Schickel, *Disney Version,* on the films' reputation of terrifying children (most impressively, Dr. Benjamin Spock's allegation that Nelson Rockefeller told his wife "that they had to reupholster the seats in Radio City Music Hall because they were wet so often by frightened children" [185]).

57. Donna J. Haraway, *Simians, Cyborgs, and Women: The Reinvention of Nature* (New York, 1991), 163.

58. Ibid., 154.

59. Benjamin, *GS* 4:147; *Reflections,* 93; translation modified.

60. Benjamin, *GS* 2:414f.; *Illuminations,* 116f.

61. Benjamin, *GS* 4:147; *Reflections,* 93; translation modified.

62. Benjamin, *GS* 1:1045.

63. Ibid., 7:377.

64. Storm and Dressler, *Im Reiche der Micky Maus,* for instance, cite the following entry from Goebbels's diary, 20 December 1937: "I present the Führer with thirty of the last years' top films and eighteen Mickey Mouse films . . . for Christmas. He is very pleased and quite happy over this treasure which will hopefully bring him much joy and recreation" (11). When Leni Riefenstahl visited the United States in the winter of 1938-39, she was boycotted by the industry; the only producer who gave her a warm welcome was Walt Disney (128f.); see also 64ff., 142-46, and Carsten Laqua, *Wie Micky unter die Nazis fiel: Walt Disney und Deutschland* (Reinbek bei Hamburg, 1992).

65. Benjamin, *GS* 1:1045.

66. Thompson, "Cel Animation," 110.

Thomas Pepper (essay date 1994)

SOURCE: "Guilt by (Un)Free Association: Adorno on Romance *et al*," in *MLN,* Vol. 109, No. 5, December, 1994, pp. 913-37.

[*In the following essay, Pepper analyzes the aphorisms in* Minima Moralia.]

> It follows from this that anybody who attempts to come out alive—and survival itself has something nonsensical about it, like dreams in which, having experienced the end of the world, one afterwards crawls from a basement—ought also to be prepared at each moment to end his life.[1]

> But this is to condemn and to love in an abusive way.[2]

Minima Moralia is a hard book to read all at once, both because it is simply too delicious and at the same time because it is highly repetitious—I, for one, cannot eat chocolate all day—also because it is not quite repetitious enough, but demands a considerable amount of energy to keep alert so as to be able to follow the dialectical pattern of Adorno's sentences to their often startling and unexpected conclusions, thus to admit that his scorn and his despair are not necessarily one's own. Reading this book must be an experience that never spares the reader the constant need to examine his or her specific difference. Identification as a readerly strategy belongs to the New Old Right, which is why we don't have to throw out Adorno because he rejects, for example, jazz: it is only the uncritical desire to seek a Master, thus to be a Slave, that would demand of a great thinker that his taste always be right. It is silly enough, but the mistake is so often made that an error of such serious proportions could force an absolute reader-text estrangement or divorce. But this would be to miss the point of the notion of a, or of the, critical reader

Adorno promulgates, which notion refuses to allow the reader off the hook, and refuses as well to allow the reader simply to indulge in the (naively construed) aesthetic pleasures of turning our author into just another example of an irate parent on the other side of the generation gap.

The theoretical justification behind these apparent *obiter dicta,* however much these may find echoes—or not—in the arena of the politically correct, is not to be found in some recent polemic in the debates surrounding cultural studies, but in a place apparently far removed from them. While the point I am making can be found more or less everywhere in Hegel—for Adorno, His Master's Text—a passage from the *Aesthetics* will serve as well as any to make the point. When Hegel defines allegory as representing the separation of subject from predicate, of individual singularity from the universal conceptuality that is being predicated of it, he thinks that he can reproach allegorical intention as being inferior to that, say, of the symbolic. But the moment of this separation reveals itself to be structural and incapable of being eliminated, despite whatever derogations or tonal regrets. This form of non-identification of universal and particular, and our understanding in some way of the nonidentity they maintain over the copula, is, in fact, the very possibility of our being able to make meaningful sentences in which singular terms are related to universals at all (SS, 774-75).

It is also, of course, the very possibility of criticism itself that is at issue here, that is to say of the ethical necessity of owning up to *not* identifying with what one reads. For a critic to identify with what he reads is not merely silly—the equivalent of the character played by Woody Allen in his *Zelig*—it is, epistemologically speaking, a massive error, a blatant stupidity. A sentence as simple as 'the sky is blue' is dependent, for its interpretation, on this ability to recognize, even without being able necessarily to explain, the kind of relation that is meant, even if what is also *said* is the inability of any universal term to link up with or cover any particular. The structural predicament of allegory, which thus infects all discourse, will not be gotten rid of by demoting it as an aesthetically inferior mode.

And where the particular is of the highest importance, the most important is what is tendency, *Tendenz,* and inclination, *Neigung.* At the moment one thinks oneself to be engaged in the spirit of conspiratorial identification between author and reader (precisely the sort of theatrical conspiracy which constitutes the central irony of Kierkegaard's *oeuvre,* with which Adorno was passionately involved from his adolescence and which was the subject of his first book) something intervenes, and one is very likely to miss a beat in this nothing-but-syncopated book if one isn't careful not to adopt Adorno's or anyone else's scorn entirely as one's own.

The tightness of the aphorisms that make up Adorno's Minimabilia is Pascalian.[3] The regression toward the particular of the essay, itself the denial of system, cannot be tolerated in a work that makes a claim to totality, even though it can only exist in a silent relation to the assertion of that totality, as Adorno remarks in the little preface—actually not a preface, but a dedication to Max Horkheimer on Valentine's Day, Horkheimer's birthday—to *Minima Moralia.* The difference between a preface—to a book such as *The Phenomenology of Spirit*—and a dedication—to a book such as *Minima Moralia*—is the formal symptom of the full-scale critique of Hegel's conception of Science that Adorno is mounting, not merely a literary device to be philosophically dismissed. It is a matter of where one chooses to put one's emphasis, and thus it is a question of what I will call, in the extremely precise but unfashionable language of the New Critics, *tone.*

Adorno, who would have disdained any attempt to justify work by recourse to mere humor, makes a logical argument for this most abstractly confessional of books by reproaching Hegel for his neglect of the particular, in what is itself one of Adorno's most stunningly ironic coups:

> Thus Hegel, whose method schooled that of *Minima Moralia,* argued against the mere being-for-itself of subjectivity on many levels. Dialectical theory, abhorring anything isolated, cannot admit aphorisms as such. In the most lenient instance they might, to use a term from the *Preface* to the *Phenomenology of Mind,* be tolerated as 'conversation.' But the time for that is past. Nevertheless, this book forgets neither the system's claim to totality, which would suffer nothing to remain outside it, nor that it remonstrates against this claim.

Up to this point in the paragraph, Adorno is merely asserting the fact that he knows well enough where *his* present is falling out of the System, but has not yet hit bottom. He has no illusions, he is nobody's—least of all Hegel's—fool. But the truly philosophical moment of critique begins when the baldness of a temporal scheme of later-is-less-naive (the equivalent of *post hoc propter hoc* in the history of ideas) is left behind for an argument based on grounds internal to Hegel's text itself:

> In his relation to the subject Hegel does not respect the demand that he otherwise passionately upholds: to be in the matter and not 'always beyond it,' to 'penetrate into the immanent content of the matter.' If today the subject is vanishing, aphorisms take upon themselves the duty 'to consider the evanescent itself as essential.' They insist, in opposition to Hegel's practice and yet in accordance with his thought, on negativity: 'The life of the mind only attains its truth when discovering itself in absolute desolation. The mind is not this power as a positive which turns away from the negative, as when we say of something that it is null, or false, so much for that and now for something else; it is this power only when looking the negative in the face, dwelling upon it.'
>
> (*Minima Moralia* [hereafter abbreviated as *MM*], Dedication, 8-9/16-17)

Minima Moralia is announced, then, as an attack on the soft underbelly of the Hegelian System. But this attack does not come from outside the system, it is simply the re-

sult of attending to the details, the matter, *die Sache,* of Hegel's own system. This is a critical argument. But, on the other hand, it may now be necessary to take Adorno's assertion of his later-therefore-wiser quite seriously. For, given the prodosis of the rebuke, with its temporalizing *Setzung,* even if hypothetically stated ("If today the subject is vanishing. . . ."), Adorno is marking something else, his being on the other side of a watershed, attempting an *almost* post-phenomenological investigation from the perspective of the moment of the subject's matutinal evanescence.

It is crucial for his argument, for his attack, that the subject has not entirely vanished yet, else one would hardly be able to write in reference to the System at all. The aphorism will be used to rebuke the System, which, *qua* system, had to throw itself in with the matter of the universal element, precisely in order to be able to enunciate itself as the arrival of Science on the world stage. Hegel is reproached for being at odds with his own intention: to attend to the matter itself is always the claim of the person who announces himself as the phenomenologist.

The dialectics of this paragraph are, as is fitting for a dedication or an exoteric paratext, clear enough. But what is disturbing, in its very obviousness, are these very *moments,* these *puncta*: "The time for that is past," "if today the subject is vanishing. . . ." The only way for Adorno entirely to avoid being eaten alive by the Pantagruelian—or perhaps better, phagocytotically vacuolizing or macrophagic—dialectic of the Master, even at the very moment when he is admitting where he himself was "schooled," is to inscribe the entirety of the Hegelian lesson into a history as a moment now over.

This, then, is the work of a mature poet, who has swerved successfully from his father and the father of all of us moderns, in addition to being perhaps the first post-Auschwitz classic. It laments modernity's passing and fully evil flowering on the very eve of what some have hailed as its dissolution. Adorno's dedication cites *The* Preface, the only one, in order to *get past* the moment of Hegel's Preface (Hegel as preface to Adorno), that is to say the emergence of Science, that is, Hegel, on the world scene. What Adorno the son wants to bring as his gift to the Father (Grandfather?) is the message of the first son who got it, Søren Kierkegaard, who wrote, in his *Repetition*:

> The exception explains the general and itself. And if one wants to study the general correctly, one only needs to look around for a true exception. It reveals everything more clearly than does the general. Endless talk about the general becomes boring; there are exceptions. If they cannot be explained, then the general also cannot be explained. The difficulty is usually not noticed because the general is not thought about with passion but with a comfortable superficiality. The exception, on the other hand, thinks the general with intense passion.[4]

One might repeat with insistence and with Kierkegaard, in order to gloss Adorno's strategy in respect of Hegel, from a different moment in the dialectic of *Fear and Trembling,* published on the same day as *Repetition*: "the one who will work gives birth to his own father."[5] Adorno continues in his reproaches:

> The dismissive gesture which Hegel, in contradiction to his own insight, constantly accords the individual, derives paradoxically enough from his entanglement in liberalistic thinking. The conception of a totality harmonious through all its antagonisms compels him to assign to individuation, however much he may designate it as a driving moment in the process, an inferior status in the construction of the whole. The knowledge that in pre-history the objective tendency asserts itself over the heads of human beings, indeed by virtue of annihilating individual qualities, without the reconciliation of general and particular—constructed in thought—ever yet being accomplished in history, is distorted in Hegel: with serene indifference he opts once again for liquidation of the particular. Nowhere in his work is the primacy of the whole doubted. The more questionable the transition from reflective isolation to glorified totality becomes in history as in Hegelian logic, the more eagerly philosophy, as the justification of what exists, attaches itself to the triumphal car of objective tendencies. The culmination of the social principle of individuation in the triumph of fatality gives philosophy occasion enough to do so. Hegel, in hypostasizing both bourgeois society and its fundamental category, the individual, did not truly carry through the dialectic between the two. Certainly he perceives, with classical economics, that the totality produces and reproduces itself precisely from the interconnection of the antagonistic interests of its members. But the individual as such he for the most part considers, naively, as an irreducible datum—just what in his theory of knowledge he decomposes. Nevertheless, in an individualistic society, the general not only realizes itself through the interplay of particulars, but society is essentially the substance of the individual.
>
> (*MM,* Dedication, 9-10/16-17)

There you have it. The Master has now been rather magisterially treated as a moment in the preface of the son. Exit Daddy, Teddie arrives. But the sweetness of revenge is tempered by a terrible melancholy: these "reflections from the damaged life" attach themselves to the triumphal car of the silly optimism of bourgeois liberalism, but in doing so are not one, but at least two steps behind the objective tendencies, which perhaps no longer exist. We are all in the cortège at the end of Sirk's *Imitation of Life.* Hegel's dismissive gesture toward the individual becomes here Adorno's chastising gesture toward one very specific individual—Hegel—at the same time that he is addressing this book of aphorisms to one very specific individual, Max Horkheimer, "in thanks and promise."

The final blow of the lesson is contained in the last sentence of the paragraph, in which Adorno tells us what the objective tendencies of this time of writing are, in a corrective gesture, a tribute that Hegel *qua* Hegel cannot take. And, in a move of truly Adornian irony, we find the opposite of what we have, thus far, expected him to say: It is not Hegel's romantic yearning for totality or totalization or any other such history of ideas claptrap which forced him toward utter contempt for the individual. Rather it is his engagement precisely with the Protestant and bourgeois ideology of individualism which, rather than pushing him toward giving a stronger valence to the individual in his philosophy, robs, on the contrary, the individual of his weight by making it—the individual—into yet another bloodless form of universality, even if, according to Hegel the bourgeois, it is the very form of our being and of our social being.[6] It is the very form of our existence which Adorno reproaches Hegel for ignoring. In a sense it is, if you will, Adorno's ultimate condescension to Hegel's naïveté to be able to broach or to inflict such an ironic blow, to be able to strike a blow at a prejudice that emanates from the level of the axiomatic form of the System itself: the form of the thinking subject is I (SS, 767-79).

All of this being said, the most striking aspect of this passage is the fact that it is a reading of Hegel on the Terror. The Terror is the moment in which the pure universality of the law-without-law, the nakedness of the symbolic order, reigns and strips every subject of his or her individuality and right to persist in living. "With serene indifference he opts for the liquidation of the particular": how can we hear this, from Santa Monica, Grand Hotel Abyss, in 1944-45, as anything other than what we will be dealing with presently in our chosen singularity, our exemplary aphorism, as yet indicated but untouched, as "the Fascist eradication of the racial minority itself"? *This* is the objective tendency of *our* hearing. It is not a matter of Freedom, Equality, Brotherhood as the truth of the Universal Revolution that produced the Universal Declaration of the Rights of Man. It is a matter of Jew, Gypsy, Homosexual, Asocial, Mentally Ill: it is a matter of the reduction of humanity to types, absorbing the absolute singularity of individuals into the global and levelling universality of predicates, concepts, which reveals the truth of Reason in the Terror.

But in order to deal with the sweating out of these foreign bodies reduced to types and thus to concepts and thus to ashes at Auschwitz, I want to talk about the structure of the French Terror. Let us turn for a moment to what Adorno's contemporary, Maurice Blanchot, is saying about similar motifs and about some of the same passages in Hegel, reviewing Kojève, shortly after Adorno writes up the damaged life in California:

> Let us acknowledge that in a writer there is a movement which proceeds without pause, and almost without transition, from nothing to everything. Let us see in him that negation that is not satisfied with the unreality in which it exists, because it wishes to realize itself and can only do so by negating something real, more real than words, more true than the isolated individual in control: it therefore keeps urging him towards a worldly life and a public existence in order to induce him to conceive how, even as he writes, he can become that very existence. It is at this point that he encounters those decisive moments in history when everything seems put in question, when law, faith, the State, the world above, the world of the past—everything sinks

effortlessly, without work, into nothingness. The man knows he has not stepped out of history, but history is now the void, the void in the process of realization; it is *absolute* freedom which has become an event. Such periods are given the name Revolution. At this moment, freedom aspires to be realized in the *immediate* form of *everything* is possible, everything can be done. A fabulous moment—and no one who has experienced it can completely recover from it, since he has experienced history as his own history and his own freedom as universal freedom. These moments are, in fact, fabulous moments: in them, fable speaks; in them, the speech of fable becomes action. That the writer should be tempted by them is completely appropriate. Revolutionary action is in every respect analogous to action as embodied in literature: the passage from nothing to everything, the affirmation of the absolute event and of every event as absolute. Revolutionary action explodes with the same force and the same facility as the writer who has only to set down a few words side by side in order to change the world. Revolutionary action also has the same demand for purity, and the certainty that everything it does has absolute value, that it is not just any action performed to bring about some desirable and respectable goal, but that it is itself the ultimate goal, the Last Act. This last act is freedom, and the only choice left is between freedom and nothing. This is why, at that point, the only tolerable slogan is: *freedom or death.* Thus the Reign of Terror comes into being. People cease to be individuals working at specific tasks, acting here and only now: each person is universal freedom, and universal freedom knows nothing about elsewhere or tomorrow, or work or a work accomplished. At such times there is nothing left for anyone to do, because everything has been done. No one has a right to private life any longer, everything is public, and the most guilty person is the suspect—the person who has a secret, who keeps a thought, an intimacy to himself. And in the end no one has a right to his life any longer, to his actually separate and physically distinct existence. This is the meaning of the Reign of Terror.[7]

Revolution is the flower absent from all bouquets, that is to say, it is the moment of purest negation, when there are no compromises. The compromises always come afterwards. It is in this sense that revolution is fabular or allegorical: as soon as it happens—and since it is, by definition, an extralegal situation, it is hard to speak of agency and to say anything other than it happens, *es ereignet sich,* like the true, it occurs—a certain number of names take on the form of blank subjects that are then filled in during the temporal economy thus opened up and which follows: terrors, reactions, decapitations, consulates, Final Solutions, liquidations, Exterminations.

As far as the nationalist moment here is concerned, the distinction between the Revolutions American and French can be registered by comparing the mottos: if the French have "Freedom or Death," where both words should be capitalized as allegorical, fabular entities, we in the United States have something like "your money or your life," in which both substantives as well as the possessives are written in the lower case.[8] French absolutism here is capi-

tal and crucial, providing as it does the motive for the very Hegelian text both Adorno and Blanchot-via-Kojève are commenting upon: the Preface to the *Phenomenology,* written, proverbially, that is to say fabularly enough, as Napoleon was sidling up to the gates of Jena, home of the German Romantics (who were busy working on the theory of irony inside).

Now it is time to zero in on the text we have been slouching towards since the beginning, the aphorism from *Minima Moralia* entitled "Morals and the Order of Time":

> —While literature has treated all psychological modes of erotic conflicts, the most simple, mechanical matter of conflict has remained unattended by virtue of its self-evidence. It is the phenomenon of being possessed: that a beloved person refuses himself [*sich uns versagt*] to us not because of inner antagonisms or inhibitions, because of too much coldness or too much repressed warmth, but rather because a relationship already exists that excludes another. In truth abstract temporal sequence plays the role one would like to ascribe to the hierarchy of feelings. In being previously taken there lies—apart from freedom of choice and of decision—also something of the wholly accidental that seems entirely to contradict the claim of freedom. Especially in a society cured of the anarchy of commodity production, rules would hardly [*schwerlich*] keep watch over the sequence [*Reihenfolge*] in which one gets to know people. Were it otherwise, such an arrangement would have to amount to the most unbearable intrusion upon freedom. From this comes the fact that even the priority of the accidental has powerful grounds on its side: if a newcomer is preferred to some person, one does to this person inevitably an evil thing—in that the past of a shared life is annulled [*annulliert*], experience itself likewise crossed out. The irreversibility of time delivers an objective moral criterion. But it, the criterion, is a sibling of myth, like abstract time itself. The exclusionary character posited in time unfolds according to its own concept towards the exclusionary dominance of hermetically sealed groups, in the end those of big business. Nothing is more touching than the anxiety of the loving woman, lest the newcomer be able to draw love and tenderness—her best possessions, precisely because they do not allow themselves to be possessed— toward herself, precisely because of that newness, which itself is produced by the privilege of the older. But from this stirring up, through which all warmth and everything sheltering immediately dissolve, begins an irresistible way upon which the stations are the disinclination of the little brother for the one later born[9] and the contempt of the fraternity student for his pledge to the immigration laws that keep all non-Caucasians out of Social-Democratic Australia, and unto the Fascist extermination of the racial minority, in which in fact warmth and shelter explode into nothing. As Nietzsche knew, not only were all good things once evil; but the most tender, left to their own momentum [*Schwerkraft*], have the tendency to end up in unimaginable brutality.

> It would be superfluous to try to indicate a way out of this entanglement. But the disastrous moment that brings the entire dialectic into play most probably allows itself to be named. It lies in the exclusionary char-

acter of the first. The originary relation, in its mere immediacy, already requires [*voraussetzt*] abstract temporal order. Historically, the concept of time is itself modeled on the basis [*Grund*] of the order of ownership. But the wish to possess reflects time as fear of losing, of the irretrievable. What is, is experienced in relation to its possible non-being. Only thus does it really get made into a possession and, thus fixed, into a functional thing that allows for its being exchanged for other, equivalent possessions. Once become entirely a possession, the beloved person is simply no longer looked at. Abstractness in love is the complement of exclusionariness, which deceptively makes its appearance as the opposite, as a clinging to this very one being. But exactly this holding on loses its hold on its object, in that it makes it into an object, and thus misses the person whom it denigrates to "my person." Were people no longer possessions, they could no longer be exchanged. True affection [*Neigung,* preference, inclination] would be one that speaks specifically to the other, that attaches itself to beloved traits [*Züge*] and not to the idol of personhood, the reflection of possession. The specific is not exclusionary: it lacks the drive [*Zug*] toward totality. But in another sense it is nonetheless exclusionary, in the sense that it does not forbid, but by means of its pure concept does not even allow substitution of the experience indissolubly bound up with it to occur. The protection of the entirely determined is that it cannot be repeated, and thus it tolerates the other. To the property relation to the person, to the exclusionary law of priority, belongs exactly this wisdom: God, they are all only people, whichever one it is is not so important after all. Affection that would know nothing of such wisdom would not need fear infidelity, because it would be guarded against faithlessness.

(*MM* I, 96-99/78-80)[10]

One might well ask, rather: But without such "wisdom," how can there be any *true* affection? And this in so many senses: Time, experienced by the subject as anxiety before death and other endings—and this by lovers most of all—or rather, the demand to spend time, to do time, the demand on a beloved that we do time together, etc., cannot be tempered, pragmatically speaking, without the irony, this time of consciousness, necessary to shrugging the shoulders and simply waiting for the other to come, if ever. I take this as both psychologically and phenomenologically true, and therefore, linguistically, almost certainly uninteresting. To demand of the would-be conquering lover that he simply give the love object space out of infinite love for that love object is to ask too much from anyone who has not acquired enough wisdom to know not to be impatient enough to fall in love in the first place. As Kierkegaard knows, every love is the first love, and following from this, in and as its inevitable disappointment (as Bataille knows, for it is the experience he shares with us as the experience motivating his *L'expérience intérieure*), is the realization that to love and not to do so in an abusive manner it is counterproductive or even destructive to desire to be everything.

Down to brass tacks. Literature is a collection of particulars, of singularities, and, as such, it is a set that forms the totality that treats all the psychological species of erotic conflict. This is not what Adorno says, but it is worthy of being thought, as a definition of literature. But the simplest has escaped being included in this baroque catalogue. What is the simplest? It is what the logicians call material implication, cause and effect, what Kant himself knew to be unanalyzable at the conceptual level.[11]

But the fact of the simplest having escaped notice is not insignificant. As atom, the simplest itself has no epistemic valence until it combines, until it is sequenced into a series of moments in which it will receive its value as *first.* The potential love object refuses *himself* to us out of a monogamous prior commitment. The assumption here, at least at this point, is that every monad has a valence of one: monogamy is the presumed atomic fact, *Sachverhalt,* to use Wittgenstein's Tractarian term with rigid precision.

But at this point the dialectic has already come into play, for the monad is only seen to be (a) monad(ic)—remember the monad is a mirror and a window—in relation to its complement. Abstract temporal sequence is abstract here because it applies structurally to all subjects *qua* subjects. It is not as though there might be any way to sidestep this predicament, which is why the references to prehistory and to history, both in the passage from the Dedication cited above as well as here, are so interesting. The reference to prehistory [*Vorgeschichte*] is Adorno's way of denouncing the idyll of a mythic time before time in which such relations would not have obtained.

We are limited to analyzing the structure of the events in question, but that proves to be quite a lot. For what we are up against is the very birth of consciousness in the Oedipal triangle, the primal repression of the Father's No. The parental pair is, after all, the first dyad. Teddie will, after all, marry into Mommy's name, contracting Daddy's land holdings into that celebrated W.[12] Not might makes right, but time makes right: (The) I got (t)here first. Or at least that is the story it tells after getting there. In psychoanalytic terms, the law of priority, of temporal relations is called the Oedipus Complex, which can be summarized for our purposes here in Lacan's lapidary "if you do that again, I'll cut it off."[13]

In the matter of constraint, or, as Adorno puts it here, of freedom of choice and decision, there is more than a hint of the F. W. Schlegelian language of irony as unrelieved arbitrariness, *unbedingte Willkür.* The accidental fact of time makes right not only seems, but is in flat contradiction to the claims of freedom. Lest we be mistaken for speaking only of things as they are in that fallen state of commodity fetishism (Adorno's supposedly secular equivalent for Pascal's state of Man's Fallenness), Adorno spells it out: even in a society cured of such human relations as object relations, it would not be possible to predict or to plan better, to regulate the order in which one met people. One would have to say, precisely in such a "cured" society, that the arbitrariness of quickies would be even more manifest, because even more purely related to some kind of myth of spontaneous desire.

But the fact is, Adorno has just explained to us not only why such a society is not possible, but, in fact, unimaginable. In fact, it is the matter of this already announced abstract sequencing operation itself, structurally unavoidable, that is precisely the explanation for why commodity production is inevitable, at least in a society based on the not-yet-vanished atom of the subject. What we are dealing with here is a metaphorical catastrophe of the first order. We thought that the false, inauthentic relations among people were going to be at least partially accounted for by the evil contingencies of our production system, and now what we have discovered to be the case is the opposite, namely that the fetishism of the production system is determined by the abstract element that imposes itself in and as sequence in human relationships.

The sentence "historically, the concept of time is itself modelled on the basis of the order of ownership" in the second paragraph of our aphorism is not to be read as a statement of the historical truth or falsehood of the twinned origin of these concepts. Rather this generalization at this moment in the narrative of this fable repeats what has already been said: reification, making the person into "my person," thus implying possession, must bring a before and a potential after along with it. Thus we might want to say not that these two concepts are historically linked, but rather that history *is* precisely what we call that which is constituted in this linkage. The only time or place within which such relations would not obtain would neither be in history nor in pre-history, but in no history at all. For time to be time, such relations must exist.

Hence pre-history, as well as the post-history toward which more vulgar readings of Kojève yearn, are both delusions. Only myth can name the idyllic non-time when such relations did not obtain. Myth is thus both more and less than pre- or post-history: it is the name here for the negation of history. The tendential inevitability of the obtaining of the situation Adorno is describing (as opposed to the one for which he erases all hope) is evidence enough that neither such pre-history nor its after-the-fact mirror image have anything to do with actual or potentially existing states of affairs. Rather these names with unreal referents can only serve as structural moments in the unfolding of the story in their being denounced as the impossible.

This is why the "objective moral criterion" delivered by "the irreversibility of time"—irreversibility and time being, for all intents and purposes, the same here—is a sibling of myth: the myth in question is that of an "abstract time" that would exist without being filled by the kinds of events that occur in and as historical time. The myth here *is* the myth of a pre- or a post-history that would not be historical, i.e., a time which would not be defined as time is defined by the commodified relations that obtain for us. On the other hand, "if today the subject is vanishing," this would also imply that time, as part of the form of the subject, is vanishing too.

But the question is, isn't the subject always vanishing?, hasn't the subject always been vanishing? If the structural

faults to which Adorno points in the constitution of the System in fact are there, then the answer is yes. But vanishing may not imply the perfection of its activity, so that time and the subject in fact never vanish absolutely into the mythic, abstract time-without-the-subject that the subject projects into the past as pre-history or a different future, the possibility of deliverance into which is given the lie by the contrary-to-fact subjunctive verbs in which this time after time is described.

And when time is troubled, so is experience. Why is experience deleted, why are things misused, annulled? Because what is happening here is that relations are being dictated by rhetorical figures. Substitutions are taking place at the level of entities because the chiastic, hypallagous rhetorical structure demands it. The structure always wants a matched, mathed, mathematized crossing. And so the eraser or cursor moves over one term, deletes it, and fills in the blank with another individual, whose substitutability occurs by virtue of that person's being the bearer of a name to which, for the purposes of this very operation, he or she may be reduced, has to be reduced.[14] And a name can also, in this context, be reduced to a number.

There is the name and the thing. But discourse, like and as the Terror, is capable of taking the name of the thing and combining it with other thingly and abstract-thingly (it does not matter if the referent exists materially or not) names, which are then read and used as a template for mixing and matching the phenomenal entities. The annulment, the effacement of previous experience, is the very operation of the verb *tilgen* Hegel assigns to the function of the name when he says, in the *Encyclopedia,* it is in names that we think, and when he proclaims that the sign must be declared to be something great because it allows us to subject the material world to the powers of mind in exchanging qualities in discourse that cannot be exchanged in so-called reality, which has, by now, fully earned its scare quotes, those linguistico-phenomenological brackets (SS, 766-77). The priority of the fortuitous assigns to chance the power of unrelieved arbitrariness, what Merleau-Ponty will call, shortly before his death, the irony of things. It has powerful arguments on its side because it assigns to fate the ultimate power of the subject, that of defacing-refacing the world according to its wishes.

But now we enter a new dimension, with the bringing into play of the question of irreversibility. For it is the irreversibility of sequence—the revenge, to speak metaleptically, of the young on the old—that dictates the entire schema. Property is irreversibility: this in the sense of property as in "life, liberty and . . .", as well as in the sense of *Merkmale,* that which a subject acquires in taking on predicates. The fact that we can go from A to B but not back again sets things up so that what is done is done. It is related to myth in the sense that it is, *qua* abstract, part of that allegorico-fabular dimension of template structures we use to negotiate our stories about ourselves, one of the stories we tell ourselves in order to live.

And now comes that conspiracy-theory laden moment when we explode into the discourse labelled "Marxist":

the exclusivity in time takes us to inherently hermetic groups, big business. That is just to say, the combines, the constellations that come together to keep ahold of what they have by having more are the material instantiations of the steady accretion disks of these figures. Pull back from the totalization: the little woman appears, defenseless Olive Oyl, waiting for Popeye to come rescue her from the evil usurper.

What happens here is that the initial couple of stable, heterosexual nature and origin (they always must needs be the same, in this context, at this moment), the man and woman, who can move "naturally"—but, remember, we are in a post-Pascalian universe, where nature has been effaced—over the copula, have drifted into being the couple of the first partner and her youthful or new replacement.[15] What we are dealing with now is catty bitchery. And it is her or their own—structural—fault, because if she didn't have her arms around him in public, the character ready to rob her of her prize wouldn't know to take her cue.

We are approaching the moral of the end of this paragraph, in which a series of parallel totalizations are presented. And here is where the moral of the story gets complicated and therefore interesting, *qua* fable. Perspective has been collapsed: we have moved back from big business to the innocence of the atom. And now it is a matter of showing how this telescopic manoeuvre has been accomplished. The motif that gets globalized is not necessarily a heterosexual partner's fear of replacement, but rather the fear before the evident structure of replaceability in general. For the next link in the chain is the little boy's fear of being replaced by his younger brother, or the fraternity student's contempt for his "fag,"—as Jephcott translates it, his pledge, "Fuchs" in German, "fox," his younger cadet.

There is an important twist on the Oedipal cliché here: Usually, what one is referring to when one makes reference to oedipal anxiety is the anxiety of the infant. But what of the anxiety of the Father, what of *his* anxiety at the arrival of a possible replacement in the child? One might call this the neglected, countertransferential dimension of the Oedipus Complex. But it helps to make the link between the intergenerational aggression implied in the all-too-familiar idea of Oedipal conflict and the sibling aggression, the intragenerational competition Freud discusses, for example, in "Eine Kindheitserinnerung aus *Dichtung und Wahrheit.*"[16] Only now can we move on to the racism of so-called democratic societies, and thence to Fascism, the negative-theological name for ultimate horror in our almost exhausted if not yet ended century. And the appearance of Nietzche's name here has as much to do with his talents as an aphorist as with his being the author of *The Genealogy of Morals.*

It is time to comment on the famous line from the aphorism "Tough Baby,"[17] where Adorno tells us that "Homosexuality and Totality belong together." The sublimated homosexual urges to which Freud often pointed as the ho-

mosocial glue of society are, Adorno is saying, not very far off from the paranoia (with its foreclosive trait of lack of connection to any other) that Freud also ascribes to the same repressed, homosexual urges. In both cases, however, it is the repression of homosexual drives that is at issue. But it is the violence of the latter, of paranoia, that needs to designate an object as foreign in order to call itself whole, to constitute itself as a totality. So the older brother, who is supposed to identify with Daddy, must neutralize the threat of the newcomer, the younger brother, in passing on the threat of castration, thus of feminization, which is how the feminized-castrated male becomes the object of fear: if it can happen to him, it can happen to me. This is the fear that must be kept at bay in the designation of this figure as foreign, other. In between the first loving couple and the various constitutions of social bodies around a figure to be excluded, then, come the situations in which the persecution of the newcomer presents itself as the strategic excuse by means of which the hyperbological extension towards totality will be made.[18] But Adorno, for whom the distinction between male homosociality and male homosexuality is no distinction at all, himself does not seem to see, in "Tough Baby," that it is the matter of priority he is discussing in "Morals and the Order of Time" that is even more primordial than the gender relations it conditions or engenders.

After this piece of writing, which dates from the end of the War, I think it would be preposterous to blame the French defenders of reading Heidegger for being Fascist thinkers, or at least of being tainted. Their point, rather, is that it is Heidegger who, in producing an integral reading of the tradition—even if this reading leaves much out and does great violence—has given us the tools to think Fascism as the monstrosity of Western culture, not as something that flew in, on a given day, from the outside. It is clear that this is no excuse for not reading the French, nor for not reading Heidegger either, given that it is now clear that one would have to call Adorno thus tainted as well.

And the fact is, he is, we all are, and should be. For it is this very desire for purity itself, this desire not to be involved, not to be tainted, because the subject *qua* subject knows precisely that if it is involved, it risks losing what it 'has,' being replaced,—it is this desire for purity that, pursued to the end, led to Auschwitz, the marginal place in the light of the East where Germany sweated out its hysterical fantasm of the Jews as a foreign body.[19] The literalization of the figure of the atopic Jew through mass carbonization, so that there not be a trace, is, in this sense, the horrible realization of the psychotic-foreclosive fantasy of cleaning up one's territory so that it be absolutely immaculate, pure, *rein.*

Nietzsche told us this fable: How one gets from the bad to the good through dilution and legitimation, also how, moving in the direction in which Adorno is rigorously drifting, how one gets from the good to the ugly. Now that the fatal sequence has been sequenced, and the unquestionable but dreaded truth has been uttered, it is a matter of asking, what now? Since we cannot get out of this trap (what Paul de Man might call a predicament, something predicated, spoken before and after, prejudiced, demanded by [*vorausgesetzt*] by sequence) what is left?

The structure of this *pensée* cuts it almost exactly in two.[20] The first part gives us the figure, and itself consists of two parts, that is to say, the delivery of the figure as the mechanism of replaceability, and the explosive movement towards totalization that is generated as soon as one realizes that the chain of substitutability or replaceability can be hyperbolically extended to cover the entire social field[21] conceived of as a text, that is to say, the entire tropological field.[22] In seeing this we see as well that the reason why this one of the aphorisms singles itself out as exceptional, as requiring special handling, is because it is a rather pure version of a tropological model, that is to say, of substitution or substitutability as such. "Abstract temporal sequence" is precisely what Paul de Man will call the story of the figure in the course of its undoing, decomposition in and as the text, that is to say, narrative, that is to say, allegory.[23] Temporality, for us, is not, then, as it was for Kant, the form of inner experience, therefore the first form, but the form of textual procedure, of the way in which argument and storytelling inextricably commingle in and as precisely what we call text.

The second part of Adorno's now disfigured maxim, then, plays the part of the moral of this fable, what we might call, in its belated phase, its consolation:

> It would be superfluous to try to indicate a way out of this entanglement. But the disastrous moment that brings the entire dialectic into play most probably allows itself to be named. It lies in the exclusionary character of the first. The originary relation, in its mere immediacy, already requires [*voraussetzt*] abstract temporal order.

I say *consolation* advisedly, for what we are dealing with should be called the consolation of critique in that very Kantian sense of mapping out and knowing the scope and limits of the region one is in. The knowing of the structure has to serve—has to because it is the only thing that can serve—as the consolation for a machine for unstoppable, inevitable, rigorous, impersonal and therefore brutal ubiquity. At least we can *name* it, and, in naming it, we can, among other things, inscribe it as one punctum in the scansion of moments that is this book of mourning, **Minima Moralia.** We can inscribe it as one moment cleverly hidden to look like just one moment among others, even if it perhaps, figurally speaking, brings all the other moments into play, prefigures them, if it doesn't contain them outright, absolutely.

The original relationship, in its mere immediacy—*blosse Unmittelbarkeit* (let not the sense of lack of mediation in the technical sense be lost from that mere immediacy) already establishes the conditions for (*voraussetzt*) abstract temporal sequence. Triumph of the dialectic as cortège. The *already* of this sentence conditions the abstract temporal sequence. Immediacy is an after-effect, a *Nachtrag*, in Freudian terms, of the mediations that follow immediately upon this wavering dyad of the first loving duo. Wanting to possess makes for fear of loss, of that which cannot be brought back, *Unwiederbringlichkeit*. This sentence gives the logical explanation for the purported historical explanation of the last. What is, is experienced in relation to its not only potential but in fact inevitable non-being. This sentence brings (whether Adorno wishes it or not) an entire Heideggerian register into play, and with a very interesting twist.

For if Heidegger's Dasein is the being for which Being is an issue, the being for which Being is an issue precisely because it, Dasein, is continually exposed, held out over the possibility of its non-Being, then Adorno's commentary takes Heidegger's topos out of a certain kind of self-interested deep-structure narcissism into the realm of care about others, while at the same time exposing the presumed charity of that care for others or the significant other as self-interest about and for one's own property. Christian charity is revealed as the theologically sanitized version of private property—what we knew all along. Only thus is the other truly a possession, when it is transfixed into some functional form as a commodity, which form allows it to be exchanged for other equivalent possessions.

Time for the subject is time for a transaction. Once become a property—not *Merkmal* here, but *Besitz*, a possession, but a prop to be moved around also—the beloved is in fact no longer seen. Its first figure has been effaced. Abstraction in love, this turning the beloved into a bloodless placeholder, is the complement, that which completes exclusionariness, which manifests itself deceptively as the opposite, as this holding fast to this one being, the one that is *thus, dies eine so Seiende*. The object is lost to the degree to which it is objectified, and misses, wrongs (*verfehlt*) the person whom it reduces to mine.

It might appear to be a reduction of this lofty melancholy to say so, but we are still in the thick of the Hegelian topos of the relation between universals, concepts, and particulars here. But the crucial difference between Adorno and Hegel is the melancholy tone of the former as opposed to the scientific optimism of the latter. It is much like the night before the morning after.[24] And Adorno is writing, in 1944, at dawn on the day after. Dawn on the first postmodern day: the discourse of the concept is *over*. The bringing of the other under a concept led to the extermination, *Vernichtung*, in which all otherly qualities were effaced to zero. This is the inversion, the logical end of Blanchot's fable of the fable of the French Revolution, of the allegorical dance of Reason, Progress, Enlightenment: *fabula rasa*. This is the sad dance of the realization, not of the impossibility of bringing all particulars under the concept—to say that would be fatuous—but of realizing what happens when this is done. This is mass murder, extermination, holocaust. This is the very moment of our realization that the key to allegory is its failure, its ability, not to teach a stable lesson, but only to tell the story of the disjunction between subject and predicate, universal and particular. Totalitarian Hegelian optimism about the march of the dialectic has to be read against the young Hegel's own warnings, against his "Who Thinks Abstractly?" for example, which dates from the same year as the *Phenomenology* and to which Adorno's diction points here.

"If people were no longer possessions, they could no longer be exchanged" is this paragraph's complement to the last's "even, and precisely, in a society cured of the anarchy of commodity production, it would hardly be possible for rules to surveil the order in which one met people." But this time, the need for Adorno to struggle against the hopelessness, which he himself is in the process of teaching in this after of the last paragraph's before, forces him to make this instantaneous idyll of a hypothesis out of what he has already shown to be impossible: the shimmering phantasm of post-commodity romance. True affection would be—but *is* not—one that speaks specifically to the other, and becomes attached to beloved features—predicates—and not to the idol of personality, the Idol that is the mirror image of personality. But in the realm of the imaginary that is the realm—and the only one—in which human relations are constructed, there is only the *méconnaissance* of the idols. To speak, as Hegel did not cease to remind us, is to speak in the realm of the general. The particular is lost as soon as one begins to speak. There is only one option: love and be silent. There are no words for this one love. The specific is not exclusive, it does not close out other things. The beloved in one port is different, after all, from each one in every other. Or I might say, every beloved not has, but *is* its own harbor. In this sense, each love *is* exclusive or exclusionary: because, having gone through this allegorical regression to the particular, we realize that our moral vision is precluded from the vulgarity of impossible, hence inappropriate comparisons—even though this is all that our language, which is a language of particular and universal terms, can do.

Adorno's language either helps him or trips him up: he says, the specific lacks the trait, pull, almost the drive—*Zug*—to totality. But the last sentence has told us that true affection attaches itself to the traits, *Züge,* of the other, not to their harmonized image, itself always, as Lacan tells us, a totality *qua* image. The attention to the beloved traits, *Züge,* of the specific love non-object keep that object from being reduced to being prey to the holocaust of totality or of totalization, the train, *Zug,* on the way to totality, into the all. The singular and plural of this word cannot be reconciled with each other, for the singular, *Zug,* in its sense of 'drive,' connotes a unity of direction, a single motion in the direction of the all—an idol to be sure—that the plural, *Züge,* in its senses of 'traits,' thus of plurality and disparity—but not of the idol of totality—would oppose. It is the lower gods, the idols, that are praised with the promise of the All. They listen for praise like children, infants learning to speak by collecting together their traits into a false image, Man, in the mirror.

The specific precludes replacement in this exclusivity of a higher power, radicalized—as they said in the Seventies and early Eighties—its essence precludes it. But its essence precludes it because, in a manner of speaking, its essence is to have no essence.[25] Thus: "But in another sense nonetheless it *is* exclusionary, in that the substitution [Adorno uses the Latin *Substitution,* not the German *Ersetzung*] the substitution of the experience indissolubly bound up with it [*ihm*, the specific] doesn't forbid, but through its pure concept [*reinen Begriff*] doesn't allow it even to come up."

Now, with the entrance of the language of the concept, that is to say, of language, what can be said in the realm of the general, not merely meant, opined, *gemeint,* onto the scene, we see that what Adorno is dreaming is the idyll of the world in which to each object, or subject, there is a concept. Or better yet: for each object, there is one aphorism. But this is, then, the end of the concept, the end of philosophy. The protection of the completely determined, determined through all its properties, is that it cannot be repeated, and therefore that it tolerates the other, allows for, makes room for, is patient for the other. Let there not be only or dead repetition.

Kierkegaard's entrance here, of whose book of this title Adorno is writing the canniest abstract, should confuse and disorient, if not simply terrify. For from Kierkegaard's narrative, it is not really possible to figure out if repetition in his sense, as opposed to melancholy recollection (which is what Adorno paraphrases and condemns here) exists or is possible. The question is not (only) "Will I go back to Berlin?," but "can I go back to Berlin?," to love, true love, to Hegel, to the System, to philosophy. And the fact that Adorno says repetition when he is paraphrasing what Kierkegaard, in the book *Repetition,* calls recollection, would tend to indicate that Adorno does not put much faith in the possibility of repeating, let alone understanding, what Kierkegaard meant by repetition.

To the property relation to human beings, to the exclusive right of priority, this kind of *ius primae noctis* valid for all nights before the morning after, belongs exactly this wisdom: God, it's only people, and it's no big thing which one. Inclination which would know nothing of such wisdom—the published translator misses the contrary-to-fact subjective—would not need fear infidelity, for it would be fast protected from faithlessness. But it is precisely the contrary-to-fact mood of every verb in his last sentence that tells us that we have all drunk of this wisdom, and that all we can do, to continue with that old Cole Porter song, is sigh a little. No matter how present, *this* song is an *ars amatoria* in the pluperfect tense. This is why, though the time be long, the true will indeed come to pass. But what about love?

—True love was always in another.

Notes

1. All references to T. W. Adorno, *Minima Moralia. Reflexionen aus dem beschädigten Leben* (Frankfurt/M:

Suhrkamp, 1951), and to its translation by E. F. N. Jephcott, *Minima Moralia: Reflections from Damaged Life* (London: NLB, 1974) will be given by the abbreviation MM, followed by the number of the part of the book given in Roman numbers, the section number in Arabic numbers, and the relevant page numbers from these editions separated by a slash. Hence this citation MM I/17, 39/38. In the course of this essay I also refer to Paul de Man, "Sign and Symbol in Hegel's *Aesthetics*" (*Critical Inquiry* 8:4 [Summer 1982]), by the abbreviation SS, followed by page number. De Man's essay is itself a very complex piece of work, to which I do not pretend to do justice here.

2. Maurice Blanchot, "Literature and the Right to Death" in his *The Gaze of Orpheus and Other Literary Essays,* ed. George Quasha, trans. Lydia Davis (Barrytown, NY: Station Hill Press, 1981), 33.

3. De Man remarks that each of the *Pensées* can only be sustained over a very brief period of time because the rigor of their chiastic pattern of attribute-crossing (hypallage) does not lend itself to longer narrative exposition. See his "Pascal's Allegory of Persuasion," in Stephen Greenblatt, ed., *Allegory and Representation* (Baltimore: The Johns Hopkins University Press, 1981). The same observation can be applied to de Man himself, in order to explain why the essay, and not the treatise, was his form. Oddly enough, reflection on the tension between essay and treatise produced much of the great work of Adorno and Benjamin both. To see this one need only think of the Epistemo-Critical Preface to Benjamin's *The Origin of German Tragic Drama,* and its valorization of the treatise as method in and as digression, in relation to what Adorno says about the form of the essay. I would call this development, in Adorno's "The Essay as Form," regression toward the particular. Adorno quite simply predicates of the essay what Benjamin had said of the treatise fifty years earlier. Both with right: the difference is in the 'before' and the 'after,' pre- and post-1945. Adorno might just as well have written, in the *Negative Dialektik,* "After Auschwitz, no more treatises." The fact that both of these signal and crucial *essays* are written as paratexts should be reflected upon.

4. Cited from the end of the first chapter, "Definition of Sovereignty," of Carl Schmitt, *Political Theology: Four Lectures on the Concept of Sovereignty,* George Schwab, trans. (Cambridge, MA: MIT Press, 1985), 15. It is hardly an accident that the person in our century who cites this maxim from Kierkegaard is Carl Schmitt, the man whose critique of parliamentary democracy during the Weimar Republic, whose formulation of the idea of the "State of Emergency" as the moment at which democratic decision making fails, whose attempt to formulate a theory of sovereignty under the maxim "He who is sovereign is the one who decides the exception," and whose revival of the idea of political theology in our time all coexist within the same text.

5. I cite from the translation of Howard and Edna Hong, in Søren Kierkegaard, *Fear and Trembling/Repetition* (Princeton: Princeton University Press, 1983), 27. This translation is in agreement with at least two German translations and with the French translation published in the *Oeuvres complètes,* as well as with significant and learned commentaries, such as that of Gregor Malantschuk (see his *Søren Kierkegaard's Frygt og Bæven* [Copenhagen: Reitzel, 1980]). What is at issue is the occurrence in the same sentence of two uses of the same verb, which can mean both 'to bear' and 'to nourish': "[d]en, der ikke vil arbeide, ham passer det paa, hvad der staaer skrevet om Israels Jomfruer, han føder Vind, men den, der vil arbeide, han føder sin egen Fader." (Søren Kierkegaard, *Samlede Værker,* vol. 5 (Copenhagen: Gyldendal, 1963), 27. Several contemporary Kierkegaard scholars would prefer to render this sentence as "he who will work hard nourishes [*føder*] his own father." I thank Henrik Blicher, Niels Jørgen Cappelørn, and Kim Ravn for a discussion of this matter, which I shall pursue elsewhere.

6. Heiner Müller comments on the same theme in respect not of Hegel, but of the continuation of the Prussian state in what Müller sees as its avatar, East German Socialism reified into a state apparatus. See his *Jenseits der Nation* (Berlin: Rotbuch, 1991). Müller describes the East German State as being defined by its lack of relation to femininity, a theme familiar from his *Hamlet Machine* and from the sections of *The Civil Wars* he wrote with Robert Wilson. In these works the primal scene of Frederick the Great's absolute monarchy is represented as his being forced to watch the execution of his male lover for desertion from the army, a crime the young Prince committed as well but which punishment he was spared because of his royal station. As in Adorno, we are in the topos of the relationship between the repression of male homosexuality and absolute power.

7. Maurice Blanchot, "Literature and the Right to Death," in Blanchot, *op. cit.,* 37-38.

8. I am thinking of the different inflections Lacan gives to these two expressions, the latter in *Les Quatre concepts fondamentaux de la psychanalyse* (Paris: Seuil, 1972), and the former in "La Science et la vérité," in *Ecrits* (Paris: Seuil, 1966).

9. Think, with Avital Ronell, of Freud's "Eine Kindheitserinnerung aus *Dichtung und Wahrheit.*" See her *Dictations: On Haunted Writing* (Bloomington: Indiana University Press, 1986).

10. Because Jephcott's translation is so inaccurate, I have resorted to what is no doubt an even worse one of my own, although I still offer his pagination for the purposes of easy comparison. If my own translation has anything at all to offer it is no doubt due to the dialectical impatience of Jan Keppler.

11. The reference to the *Critique of Pure Reason* here is overwhelming, and culminates in the use of the word *Reihenfolge,* sequence, which I have inserted into my translation in brackets. Sequence, in Kant's Transcendental Aesthetic, is the form of inner perception as time itself, and hence logically precedes that other logical form, space, which can only be treated once the inner form of time has been established. Likewise causality, also a form, is not analyzable in the way that objects given to experience within these forms are. The forms of subjectivity are not part of the experience of the subject. They are the conditions of its possibility. All of which makes Adorno's aphorism out to be playing for the highest stakes indeed, since what is at issue is this miming of the founding text of modern transcendental-critical discourse. Jacques Lacan has a fascinating and not unrelated commentary on this Kantian moment in his *Four Fundamental Concepts of Psychoanalysis,* which, since it begins with the notion of the discovery of the unconscious through the discourse of hysterics and their symptoms, has to ask—parallel to its asking how psychoanalysis is a science and what would that mean, for psychoanalysis, for science—how the unconscious can be said to *cause* all the phenomena (dreams, parapraxes, symptoms) that lead us to the hypothesis of its existence. Lacan's discussion has capital implications for the post-Kantian theory of the subject, for if the unconscious is pre-subjective and timeless—pre-ontological, as Lacan asserts, not yet of the order of Being—it is not so easy to speak of things such as cause in respect of it, because cause is part of the formal structure of subjective experience and belongs thus, in Freudian terms, to secondary and not to primary process.

12. See Peter Sloterdijk, *Critique of Cynical Reason,* trans. Michael Eldred (Minneapolis: University of Minnesota Press, 1987), xxxv: "With Adorno, the denial of the masculine went so far that he retained only one letter from his father's name, *W.* The path to the meadow (*Wiesengrund*), however, does not exactly have to be the wrong one (*Holzweg*)."

13. See his *Télévision* (Paris: Seuil).

14. This is the very meaning of ideology as the mistaking of linguistic for phenomenal structures, such as Paul de Man defines it in "The Resistance to Theory" in the book of the same title (Minneapolis: University of Minnesota Press, 1986). The pre-history of this moment in this essay would seem to be the essay "Roland Barthes and the Limits of Structuralism," now in Paul de Man, *Romanticism and Contemporary Criticism* (Baltimore: The Johns Hopkins University Press, 1993).

15. For all those who blame the contemporary French and their minions for having invented the sex-gender distinction: Go back and read Pascal.

16. In Sigmund Freud, *Studienausgabe,* Band X, Mitscherlich, Richards, Strachey, Grubrich-Simitis,

eds. (Frankfurt/M: Fischer, 1969). I made the link between the Father's anxiety in the Oedipus Complex and sibling anxiety in a conversation with Gene Ray during which we were discussing Lacan's reading of the Dream of the Burning Child. For this occasion, as for so many other thoughtful ones, a word of thanks.

17. This title is in English in the original.

18. Lacan is in the same register when he proclaims television and racism to be the same (see his *Télévision, op. cit.*). Racism is the name for the same psychotic-foreclosive manoeuvre by which one's own object is thrown out into the field of the real in order to return as a hallucination. Television presents or materializes this very fact: the far comes back into the near as a framed, inscribed object presented to the unity of a single—in this case collective—gaze. Reason and race come from the same etymon, which is a figural way of relating the unity of the logos to its exclusion of other *types.*

19. This is what Michel Foucault is talking about in the preface to the English-language edition of *Anti-Oedipus,* when he refers to the Fascism inside all of us.

20. If this is not exactly unique within the covers of this book, it is still interesting, as Adorno's next unit of form above the sentence is the paragraph—or, in the other direction, the one-liner. I thank Jack Cameron for having called this matter of disposition to my attention.

21. Lacan has a similar insight toward the end of his 1948 "Le temps logique et l'assertion de la certitude anticipée: un nouveau sophisme," in his *Ecrits* (Paris: Seuil, 1966), when he is attempting to make the structure of subjectivation triadic, and then to extend his cellular-triadic model toward a field that could always add one more subject, hence be globalized to account for social structures. The potential for false idealization inherent in the essay on "The Mirror Stage," which postdates the essay on logical time, makes the dyadic structure of the Mirror Stage essay an anachronic regression from the rigor of the triadic one on logical time. The crucial character of this essay for the entire unfolding of Lacan's thought is evinced by the overwhelming reference he himself continues to make to it, for example in *The Four Fundamental Concepts of Psycho-Analysis,* where the story told about it is also and simultaneously the story of the temporal beating or pulsation of the atemporal unconscious in and as the production of consciousness and of time.

22. The notion of *the* tropological field, like the notion of *the* language game, is in fact generated by this tropological urge towards totalization. The totality of the world does not exist as totality except in language. *This* is the truth of the always-already of the abstract.

23. The typescript of de Man's essay on *Julie,* now printed as "Allegory (*Julie*)" in *Allegories of Reading,* bears the title "Narrative." The textual model of the figure in the course of its undoing-decomposition is the paradigm for all texts de Man offers early in that essay. See Paul de Man, *Allegories of Reading* (New Haven: Yale UP, 1979), 205-77, also the critique of Genette in "Reading (Proust)" within the same covers.

24. Thomas Bernhard puts these words in the mouth of Paul Wittgenstein the younger as a description of Karl Boehm conducting *Die Frau ohne Schatten.* See Bernhard's *Wittgenstein's Nephew: A Friendship* for many more such manically delectable lines. The melancholy of Bernhard's writing is in the fact that one can only enjoy it once, the first time. After that, it is forever the morning after, recollection in the Kierkegaardian sense. Its energy is that of all of our philosophical adolescence. Except, perhaps, for *Old Masters,* and the prosaic horror of the autobiographies, which have a certain real ecstasy to their hammering.

25. This is what the other is, in Levinasian ethics, as it is mapped out in its greatest statement, *Otherwise Than Being or Beyond Essence,* which began as an essay, now the book's central core, called "Substitution."

James M. Harding (essay date 1995)

SOURCE: "Adorno, Ellison, and the Critique of Jazz," in *Cultural Critique,* Vol. 31, Fall, 1995, pp. 129-58.

[*In the following essay, Harding finds similarities between Adorno's ideas about jazz and those of Ralph Ellison's narrator in* Invisible Man.]

All totaled, Theodor Adorno wrote seven essays on jazz: three in the thirties, two in the forties, and two in the early fifties. His portrait of jazz was never flattering and was highly idiosyncratic. In the thirties, Adorno's criticisms of jazz functioned as the negative critical movement in what can be described as his dialectical embrace of Walter Benjamin's classic essay "The Work of Art in the Age of Mechanical Reproduction" (Arato and Gebhardt 270; Daniel 41-42). For while a polemic against technology endures throughout Adorno's subsequent writing on jazz, extending well into the sixties and framing his discussion of jazz in *Dissonanzen* (1962), Thomas Levin has recently noted that even as far back as the thirties, Adorno was simultaneously calling for a reading of popular music that was "sensitive to both its reified and its utopian dimensions," and he began to acknowledge the didactic and "decidedly progressive" advantages offered by phonographs and radio programs (Schönherr 85; Adorno, *Dissonanzen* 6; Levin 28, 47). Despite this call, Adorno lingered on the "reified" and never ventured into the "utopian dimensions" of jazz. Even Adorno's defenders concede that his criticisms are

marked by an almost fanatical rigidity and that the criticisms tend to "flatten out the dynamic contradictions of popular culture" (Jay, "America" 122). Two comparable tendencies to "flatten out" surface in Adorno scholarship on jazz: those who criticize Adorno the strongest examine neither all of his essays on jazz nor the historical context of his arguments, and those who sympathize with Adorno ignore the vast amount of research on jazz that is at their disposal.[1] In both cases, jazz is handled as a homogeneous collective entity, which thus obscures the internal dynamics of jazz and attributes to it a privileged ahistorical status.

To understand Adorno's criticisms of jazz requires situating them in a social history that considers the internal (dynamic) tensions within the jazz tradition. One means of highlighting the socio-historical complexities of this tradition is to juxtapose Adorno's criticisms with the representations of jazz in Ralph Ellison's *Invisible Man* (1952). In his essays, Ellison has proven himself to be a formidable jazz critic in his own right. Bringing the two writers into the same discussion not only confronts Adorno's arguments with those of a critic who had first-hand experience of the formative years of jazz, but also, because of the important role that African-American musical traditions have in Ellison's novel, discussion of it side-by-side with discussion of Adorno places Adorno's criticisms within a context of the social complexities of the jazz tradition.[2] My goal in pursuing such considerations is to demonstrate Adorno's place in the history of jazz criticism and to give a much needed historical grounding to the debate on Adorno, jazz, and popular music. In particular, I want to focus on the pivotal position that Louis Armstrong plays in *Invisible Man*'s prologue and epilogue. What emerges from this focus is a surprising correlation between the attitudes of the narrator in Ellison's novel and of Adorno in his criticisms of jazz.

During the thirty years that span Adorno's writings on jazz, his only major discursive shift resulted from his encounter with two books which, save for numerous earlier discussions in Frankfurt with the jazz critic Mátyás Seiber, were to become the intellectual sources of all his subsequent writing on jazz: Winthrop Sargeant's *Jazz: Hot and Hybrid* (1938) and Wilder Hobson's *American Jazz Music* (1938). In one respect, the review which Adorno wrote of these books in 1941, and which is marred by misquotations and misrepresentations of Sargeant's and Hobson's arguments, only widens Adorno's frame of reference for opinions he already had about classical music and about jazz. Written roughly two years after Adorno's arrival in America, the review, interestingly enough, criticizes the defenders of jazz not because they equate jazz with classical music, but rather because in doing so—to invert Jay's phrase—they "flatten out the dynamic contradictions of" classical music. By reaffirming the internal disparities of classical music, Adorno begins in his review to dismantle what two years earlier he argued was an obsolete distinction between classical and popular music. Adorno believed that the culture industry had long since appropriated the distinction and thus undermined the presumptions of both Sargeant's and Hobson's arguments.

Jazz: Hot and Hybrid and *American Jazz Music* became fixed diametrical points of reference for Adorno, and the arguments Adorno formulated for his review resurface in his last three essays. Though critical of Sargeant's "naive" defense of jazz, Adorno admired him as a fellow musician and critic. Sargeant was a Viennese trained violinist with the New York Philharmonic, and his book was, according to Adorno, of "much more serious scientific intentions and . . . much more adequate to the subject matter" than Hobson's (Adorno, "Review" 168). The fact that Adorno twists many of Sargeant's arguments against him did not stop Adorno from later frequently appealing to Sargeant as a "scientific" authority to substantiate his own arguments. The appeals span twenty years: from Adorno's short contribution to Runes' and Schrickel's *Encyclopedia of the Arts* (1946), to his article "Perennial Fashion" (1953) and his little-known published polemic with Joachim-Ernst Berendt (1953), to his *Introduction to the Sociology of Music* (1962).

Adorno's handling of Hobson, on the other hand, was curt if not abusive. He attacked Hobson's attempt to define jazz as America's classical music, reacted negatively to Hobson's understanding of how jazz had found its way into modern classical composition, and challenged Hobson's uncritical conception of modern classical music. In his equation of jazz and classical music, Hobson fails to distinguish between Viennese schools which understood themselves in terms of rivalry and opposition, and Adorno's disapproval derives in large part from the strong personal investment that he had in maintaining the clarity of these oppositions. By citing both Alban Berg's "Wozzeck" and Krenek's "Jonny Spielt Auf" (in the same sentence) as examples of jazz-influenced concert music, Hobson merges the avant-garde atonal school of Schönberg with the *Gebrauchsmusik* of composers like Hindemith, Krenek, and Weill (Hobson 82-83; Craig 475). Adorno associated Hindemith's circle with *Neue Sachlichkeit,* which was the subject of much of his aesthetic criticism and which was, temperamentally at least, incompatible with Schönberg's atonal philosophy.

It is safe to say that as far as Adorno was concerned, if jazz was associated with *Neue Sachlichkeit* or *Gebrauchsmusik,* so much the worse for jazz. Indeed, as early as his 1936 essay **"On Jazz,"** Adorno had rejected jazz because of its association with *Neue Sachlichkeit* and the movement's ideological undertones (49). It is no small coincidence then that after his review of *American Jazz Music,* Adorno subtly revises Hobson's argument in his contribution to Runes' and Schrickel's *Encyclopedia of the Arts* (1946). He cites all the examples given by Hobson, but replaces the reference to Berg with one to Stravinsky, who, in *The Philosophy of Modern Music* (1949), was to become the central figure of contrast which Adorno used in his praise of Schönberg. Four years later, in Adorno's published polemic with the German jazz critic Joachim-Ernst

Berendt, **"Für und Wider den Jazz"** (1953), Adorno turns the tables on Berendt, who in defense of jazz notes the similarities it bears to the compositions of Stravinsky and Hindemith. Adorno responds that whoever believes Stravinsky and Hindemith to be the vanguard of the new and modern clearly is unfamiliar with Viennese atonality (Adorno and Berendt, **"Wider"** 892).

Aside from how the two books summon Adorno's investment in the rivalries of twentieth-century European music, Hobson's and Sargeant's books are important to an understanding of Adorno's views on jazz because, while both books trace the migration of jazz musicians from New Orleans to Chicago, they were published prior to the advent of bebop. This is a source of enlightening irony in "Perennial Fashion" and also in *Introduction to the Sociology of Music,* since in both instances Adorno appeals to the authority of Sargeant when he rejects both swing and bebop ("Perennial" 121; *Sociology* 33-34). Published when they were, Hobson's and Sargeant's books could provide no account of the period of musical innovation and philosophical redefinition that occurred in jazz during the forties. Hobson's and Sargeant's arguments precede the period which Adorno used them to reject, and Adorno's appeal to Sargeant in his rejection of bebop suggests that Adorno's opinions about jazz were already solidified before the rise of the movement he slights in passing reference. With the exception of his categorical rejections in 1953 and 1962, Adorno displays no knowledge of bebop whatsoever.

There is little question about the inexcusable disservice that Adorno did to jazz and to his own arguments by relying so heavily in the forties, fifties, and sixties on jazz histories published in the thirties. But what this disservice means for Adorno's critique is another question. His arguments precede what has often been called the second half of jazz history. If we can accept Miles Davis's claim that the history of jazz is summed up in four words, "Louis Armstrong Charlie Parker," then it is worth considering the place and the significance that Adorno's opinions have in relation to the first half of that history. Despite his condemnation of bebop, Adorno's criticism focuses primarily on the early history of jazz, and philosophically, his criticism coincides frequently with the underpinnings of the first major movement in jazz history after Louis Armstrong's migration to Chicago.

Inasmuch as Adorno maintains that, in the aftermath of the culture industry's rise, a serious distinction can still be made in classical music between *Gebrauchsmusik* and Schönberg's avant-garde atonality, he concedes the possibility that other musical forms may sustain comparable critical disparities within the discourse of their own cultural traditions. Bebop's relation to swing, for example, can be understood in these terms, despite Adorno's having categorically rejected this interpretation. On this point, which is the logical baggage carried by Adorno's own arguments, it is helpful to apply to jazz Adorno's claim that works of art represent the last vestiges of critical resistance to social repression. Acknowledging the internal dynamics of the jazz tradition thus offers the possibility to heed Adorno's social and cultural critiques without succumbing to his penchant for totalizing concepts. Such an acknowledgment salvages Adorno's cultural theories by circumventing his monolithic conception of society and culture and by giving it a critical diversification and flexibility. To consider the dynamics of the jazz tradition facilitates an evaluation of jazz in terms of the "rigor," to follow Adorno, with which it established itself within a vast diversity of cultural contexts which Adorno passes over. The question thus arises concerning the extent to which jazz too is marked by dynamic disparities comparable to those whose integrity Adorno so vociferously defended with regard to modern European music. Pursuing this question provides a clear avenue into the workings of *Invisible Man* because Ellison draws heavily upon the disparities of jazz when constructing the essential tensions of his novel.

When Ellison's novel begins, the story has already ended, and the invisible man has retreated into hibernation, which he defines as "a covert preparation for a more overt action" (13). As a source of solace and inspiration, the invisible man listens to records by Louis Armstrong, who he says has "made poetry out of being invisible" and who has already moved into a realm of "overt action" comparable to that for which the invisible man is preparing and which takes form in the poetic structure of the story he narrates (8). For the invisible man, Armstrong's significance derives from an ability to create poetic meaning out of a situation with which the invisible man is only beginning to come to terms. Of central importance is the invisible man's distinction between the "covert" and "overt," because it is here that through literature he imitates Armstrong and develops what Deleuze and Guattari call a "minor literature" within the major cultural tradition which can afford him no visible recognition. In short, he begins to understand the revitalizing power of the vernacular amidst the dominant discourse which excludes him.

Briefly, Deleuze and Guattari argue that minorities (like the Czech/German Jews of Kafka's Prague) often construct a minor literature within a major language. Minor literatures emerge as a source of identity within an immediate political/cultural context. With regard to Adorno and the question of jazz, it is possible to modify Deleuze's and Guattari's arguments to accommodate a notion of a "minor culture" and to use this modification to examine two concurrent but disparate forms of cultural experience, what the invisible man calls the "overt" and "covert." The first instance falls under the scrutiny of Adorno's claim that resistance to uniformity demands the most rigorous critical activity. But the second becomes the minor cultural locus of identity and resistance which Deleuze and Guattari describe. A sense for the "covert" and "overt," or the "minor" and the "major," is implicit in the invisible man's act of self-naming, i.e., in the identity that he assumes while in hibernation.

"Jack-the-Bear," the name which the invisible man assumes for himself in his secluded basement room, be-

longed to an actual jazz musician and in the context of the invisible man's hibernation alludes to what in criticism has been acclaimed as the most vital element of jazz culture. Ostendorf recounts that Louis Armstrong learned his art in private sessions where jazz musicians gathered, competed with one another, and forged musical innovations in improvised "cutting contests" (Ostendorf 166). Jack-the-Bear was an avid participant in these sessions in Harlem during the thirties (Sales 74). In his own essays on jazz, Ellison describes the sessions as "a retreat, a homogeneous community where a collectivity of common experience could find continuity and meaningful expression" (*Shadow* 209). Even Sargeant notes in his revised edition of *Jazz: Hot and Hybrid* that jazz historians have frequently discussed the double life of jazz, that a covert or sub-cultural form of jazz existed "for the enjoyment of the players themselves" beneath the popular commercialized version criticized by Adorno (18). This duplicity in jazz culture is reflected in the name which the invisible man assumes for himself. Not only was Jack-the-Bear a legendary (covert) cutter, but his name later served as the title for one of Duke Ellington's greatest popular (overt) successes (Collier, *Making* 247).

The duplicity is also reflected in the structure of jazz music itself, and a momentary consideration of this structure suggests that the "covert" life of jazz is not merely a transitory respite to be discarded once the musician has prepared for "overt" action. The "covert" and "overt" exist concurrently, forming a social cultural parallel to the multilayered rhythms of jazz that are traceable to African influences and that are part of the religious cultural heritage of African Americans (Kofsky, "Folk Tradition" 3). In jazz a major beat in one line may simultaneously be a twelfth in another line, and thus jazz rhythm incorporates a notion of multiple meanings (Brown 117, 125-26).

Likewise, Amiri Baraka argues that in jazz improvisation the notes are not merely a departure from the score, but have multiple mediations and hence multiple meanings (*Black Music* 15). What in one setting constitutes the type of commercial exploitation for which Armstrong was later criticized by beboppers and Adorno alike, in another setting makes up the virtuosity upon which the legend of Armstrong firmly rests. Certainly, "the improvisatory skills of jazz musicians reflect the . . . flexibility and immediacy of response" which have been necessary for black American survival (Cowley 196). Later in the novel, this same type of flexibility enables the blues singer Trueblood, as Pancho Savery, Houston Baker, Jr., and Berndt Ostendorf have noted, to reaffirm "his [folk] identity" despite catastrophe, "translate his personal disaster into a code of blues," and resist the "centralized [cultural] monologue" which would condemn him (Savery 69; Baker, *Blues* 190; Ostendorf 151). The covert thus functions as a strategy for dealing with the deficiencies of overt social experience. More importantly, however, in jazz a double cultural life emerges, and in its parallels to the multilayered rhythms of African music, the duplicity of the jazz social experience is a distinctly African contribution to

American culture. The duplicity is as much a part of the structures of the music itself as it is reflective of the lives of jazz musicians.

Given that Hitler's stigmatization of jazz as non-Aryan belonged to the same ideology that forced Adorno, a German Jew, to flee Nazi Germany, one would think that Adorno might have developed a sensibility for the struggles for freedom within African American folk culture—or, to follow Deleuze and Guattari, that, as a member of one minor culture, Adorno might have felt strong affinities for the articulated struggles of another. In fact, Adorno claimed to have precisely such an affinity for black experience when, shortly after he published "Perennial Fashion," Joachim-Ernst Berendt accused him of implicit racism and suggested that Langston Hughes would be a more appropriate spokesperson than Adorno on behalf of black struggles for civil and cultural equality. The tag of racism has plagued Adorno since his earliest writings on jazz. Adorno reminds Berendt quite accurately that he (Adorno) co-authored the most significant study of racism in America in recent times, *The Authoritarian Personality* (1950). Adorno explains to Berendt that he desires merely to point out where blacks are being exploited as "eccentric clowns" and where jazz subtly makes entertainment out of what has been done to African Americans (Adorno and Berendt, **"Wider"** 892-93). In this respect, Adorno's response to Berendt corresponds with criticisms voiced in the African American community itself. In fact, Adorno's argument coincides almost verbatim with Ellison's argument in "Change the Joke and Slip the Yoke," where he claims that "the entertainment industry . . . [debases] all folk materials" and reduces blacks to grotesque comedy (*Shadow* 48). For Adorno, however, understanding of debasement and racism is inseparable from the forced experiential lessons he learned amidst the fascist rise to power in Weimar Germany. The seemingly racist undertones of his criticisms of jazz are a combination of abhorrence to both the culture or entertainment industry and the implementation of Nazi ideology.

Given the historical context of Nazi cultural politics, one can read, for example, the oft criticized grounds that Adorno uses for rejecting jazz in his first article on the subject, **"Abschied vom Jazz"** (1933), as a subtle defense of it. Adorno wrote this first article shortly after the Nazis outlawed the broadcasting of jazz on the radio. When one places Adorno's claims that jazz is "not Black, not powerful, not dangerous . . . [nor] emancipatory" in the context of fascist Germany, Adorno's arguments refute point by point the hysteria to which the Nazis appealed when they banned jazz music. As Marc Weiner has argued, it is thus "possible that [Adorno] intended . . . [his claims] to be read as a strategic response to the conservativism discernible in his contemporaries' reaction to the music" (Weiner 484).

The problem with Weiner's reading of **"Abschied vom Jazz"** is that, unless the article is placed within the general schema of Adorno's critique of fascist cultural ideol-

ogy, it is equally possible to read **"Abschied vom Jazz"** as a defense of high culture, a reading which is encouraged by Adorno's scathing review of Wilder Hobson's book. This is the most frequent criticism of Adorno, typified by critics like Lorenzo Thomas, William Nye, or Peter Townsend who argue that, as a Eurocentric cultural elitist, Adorno had a deaf ear when it came to vernacular cultural expressions. Fredric Jameson subscribes to a similar position, although with a more apologetic tone, by simply redefining Adorno's writing on jazz as a critique not of "serious jazz" but of "Paul Whiteman" and by comparing Adorno's criticism with a rejection of a "standard Hollywood Grade-B genre film" (141). In Adorno's defense, Martin Jay, Ulrich Schönherr, and Jamie Owen Daniel have noted that Adorno's controversial opinions on jazz employ the identical dialectical methodology that, a year after he published **"On Jazz,"** Adorno used when criticizing Wagner in *In Search of Wagner* (Jay, *Adorno* 119; Schönherr 86; Daniel 40).[3] Two years later in **"On the Fetish-Character in Music and the Regression of Listening"** (1938) Adorno suggested that the Nazis' banning of jazz was as disgusting as their subsequent programmatic attempt to "cultivate" the masses by broadcasting the greatest achievements of German classical music.

The importance of **"On the Fetish-Character in Music and the Regression of Listening"** to any understanding of Adorno's concerns in his criticism of jazz cannot be underestimated. It undercuts the charges that Adorno was defending a high cultural elitism, because in it he asserts that "the differences in the reception of official 'classical' music and light music no longer have any real significance" (276). For Adorno "the real dichotomy . . . was not between 'light' and 'serious' music—he was never a defender of traditional cultural standards for their own sake— but rather between music that was market-oriented and music that was not" (Jay, *Imagination* 182). According to Adorno, the culture industry (and fascism is implicated here as well) had gained control of both classical and folk or popular music and employed similar mechanisms in both cases to manipulate the market. Although Adorno's favorable comments on music always refer to European music, to argue that Adorno's criticisms of jazz are a defense of high culture is to ignore his focus on the socio-historical tendencies which have rendered "the organization of culture into 'levels' . . . patterned after low, middle and highbrow," not only obsolete but also "reprehensible" (Adorno, **"Perennial"** 127).[4] Adorno's general critique of the commodity character of music as it has evolved under late capitalism challenges the survival of both classical music and jazz as forms of entertainment.

In *Adorno's Aesthetic Theory* Lambert Zuidervaart argues that in the early stages of capitalism "music was produced to be purchased, and it was purchased to be enjoyed." Adorno's objection was not against enjoyment, but rather that at the hands of the late-capitalist culture industry the use value of enjoyment had been supplanted and exchange value was now presented as "as an enjoyable use value" (Zuidervaart 77-78). When Adorno speaks about the necessity of jazz's constantly promising "its listeners something different [to] excite their attention," Adorno is not so much talking about jazz itself as the industry that props it up (**"Perennial"** 126). But as a consequence, this industry seriously compromises the possibility for critical assessments of the quality of the entertainment provided by the music, whether jazz or classical. On this point Adorno is no voice in the wilderness. In *Black Nationalism and the Revolution in Music* (1970), Frank Kofsky notes the conflict of interest resulting from the fact that the critics of jazz are by and large "dependent on the recording industry for their livelihood" (75). They cannot afford to be critical because they are the same people who earn their living by writing record jackets. More recently, John Gennari has explained that early jazz critics would have had trouble avoiding these conflicts, that anyone "trying to make a living as a jazz critic in the 1930s . . . would have had a hard time *not* looking for the most remunerative possibilities available in the practice of his craft" (475). To say that "Jazz, like everything else in the culture industry, gratifies desires only to frustrate them at the same time" refers to the advertising hype which redirects "enjoyment" to the actual purchase and the often misleading thought that one is getting something "new" and "innovative" (Adorno, **"Perennial"** 126).[5]

Although Adorno's criticisms of modern music hinge on a dichotomy between market orientation and resistance to commodification, his reservations about jazz folk culture as a locus of struggle and liberation cannot entirely be linked to the abuses of the entertainment or culture industry. They are also "tied . . . to his revulsion with Nazi pseudo-folk culture" (Jay, *Adorno* 120). Martin Jay has noted that for Adorno:

> Folk music was no longer alive, because the spontaneous *Volk* had been consumed in a process that left popular music, like all popular culture, the creature of manipulation and imposition from above.

> *(Imagination* 185)

Inasmuch as the manipulations "from above" can be associated with the entertainment industry, so too are Adorno's criticisms of jazz inseparable from an intellectual opposition to the conditions which he believes led to the election of Hitler (Daniel 40). Adorno's apprehensions about jazz culture stem from his having observed the Nazis manipulate folklore to their own propagandistic ends.

Adorno's concern that jazz culture lends itself to appropriation does not appear to have been groundless. Scott DeVeaux observes in "Constructing the Jazz Tradition" that the history of jazz is a "struggle for possession of that history and the legitimacy that it confers" (DeVeaux 528-29). The struggle is often waged through definition by exclusion. Jazz has so frequently been coopted by groups with contradictory agendas that Amiri Baraka complained that white critics who seek to define "jazz as an art (or folk art)" often do so without giving consideration to the intelligent "sociocultural philosophy" from which it stems

(*Black Music* 14). During different periods, jazz has been embraced across the political spectrum. Cold Warriors and the State Department have used it as an avatar of American cultural values (Kofsky, *Revolution* 31, 111; DeVeaux 526; Gennari 478). In the twenties and thirties, the left too vied for possession of the jazz tradition in accordance with Lenin's general wishes that all branches of the party render "direct aid to all the revolutionary movements among the dependent and underprivileged nations (for example, Ireland, the American Negroes, etc.) and in the colonies" (Berry and Blassingame 416). Citing S. Frederick Starr's *Red and Hot,* James Lincoln Collier has noted that in 1928 "the Comintern decided . . . to treat American blacks as a 'colonized nation'" and that consequently critics like John Hammond, Otis Ferguson, Charles Edward Smith and B. H. Haggin represented jazz in left-oriented presses "as the 'folk music' of . . . [a] colonized race" ("Faking" 37; *Reception* 70-71). Incidentally, Collier himself has been the subject of much deserved criticism for his own selective revision of the jazz tradition.[6] But his argument on the subtleties of the left's interest in jazz offers some provocative insights into how *Invisible Man* questions the substantial theoretical support that black nationalists historically received from the Communist party. Lenin's insistence on "the right of subjugated peoples to self-determination" takes the ironic form of the Brotherhood's concern that the invisible man might not be black enough to represent their interests in Harlem and in the invisible man's being given "freedom of action" while remaining "under strict discipline to the committee" (Berry and Blassingame 416; Ellison, *IM* 351). Here, the irony emerges as it becomes increasingly evident to the invisible man that the Brotherhood will tolerate only its own limited preconception of what is black and what constitutes legitimate ethnic expression.

In his recent article "The Signifying Modernist," William Lyne observes that when the invisible man is asked by another member of the Brotherhood to sing a "Negro work song," the invisible man's mentor Jack rifles his ability to respond, subsumes it beneath the monologic interests of the Brotherhood, and thus disarms the "double-voiced tools [in jazz] that are supposed to undermine and transform . . . official hierarchies." In short, Jack, whose own expressions occasionally regress into a European tongue, appropriates "one of the most important parts of African American expressive culture" (Ellison, *IM* 304; Lyne 328). He can only understand enjoyment of African American musical traditions as degrading and as a remnant of racist attitudes. Collier's arguments suggest that a similar procedure marks the left's manipulation of jazz for its own political ends. On this point, he is in agreement with other historians, except that it is euphemistic to describe their view of jazz merely "as the 'folk music' of . . . [a] colonized race." Jack's disapproving retort, "the brother *does not sing!*," differs from the left's provisional embrace of jazz only in its frank rejection of the value of jazz traditions.

Scott DeVeaux has argued that Starr and Collier misperceive jazz and see it as a crippled articulation of a repressed people. Yet the same can be said of the left whose appreciation of jazz in the thirties was as often scurrilous as it was supportive (534). Examples abound. John Hammond was subjected to severe criticism in the *Daily Worker* when, after his "Spirituals to Swing" concert (1939), he claimed that "jazz music is uniquely American, the most important cultural exhibit we have given to the world" (Naison 22). Following the benefit given the next year for the Spaniards who were fighting against fascism, Hammond was so infuriated with the party's patronizing response to Fats Waller and Cab Calloway that "he demanded and received an apology from the *Daily Worker*" (Naison 3-4, 15). The source of the left's criticism of Hammond and of their patronizing attitudes toward jazz musicians lies in their assessment of jazz itself, an assessment which treated black folklore and jazz not as "important cultural exhibits" but rather as Eugene Gordon depicted them at the American Writers' Congress in 1935: "as a 'national psychosis' resulting from repression" (Strout 82). In this respect, Jack's blunt rejection of the request that the invisible man sing "a Negro work song" parallels the left's view of jazz: that it needed to be overcome.

At first glance Adorno's own position on jazz would appear to coincide with that expressed by Eugene Gordon and by the character Jack in Ellison's novel. In **"Perennial Fashion,"** he argued that a "real unadulterated jazz" could not be distinguished from "the abuse of jazz" because abuse was an innate dimension of jazz itself. Negro spirituals, he argued, "were slave songs and as such combined the lament of unfreedom with its oppressed confirmation" (**"Perennial"** 122). To celebrate "Negro spirituals" now was also to celebrate the unfreedom that they confirm. However, Adorno's position differs from the left's provisional support of jazz specifically with regard to the question of abuse. Gordon's reservations about the aesthetic virtue of jazz did not hinder the left's appropriation of it as a tool for its own agenda.

Of particular interest to the left was the desire to dampen rivalries with black nationalists who had described themselves "as a nation within a nation" some seventy years prior to the Comintern's decision to adopt a similar line (Berry and Blassingame 397). In terms of improving the living standards of the African American community, the gains brought about by the left's activism in the 1930s had weakened support for black nationalist ideologies of Garveyism. Ellison portrays this competition in the Brotherhood's rivalry with the black nationalist Ras the Exhorter (Naison 2; Strout 82). Jazz fell within the scope of this agenda, in part, because the Nazi denunciation of it as degenerate galvanized black civil rights activists and the left in a common fight against the racist attitudes of fascism (Naison 3). But Jazz was not supported for jazz's sake. Rather the left's embrace of jazz further undermined black nationalism by coopting what Mary Berry and John Blassingame have called its cultural nationalistic program (388).

Ellison's novel parallels the left's use of jazz when, on the advice of the invisible man, the Brotherhood attempts to gain a consensus for its overall agenda by forging one on a specific community issue, the resistance to evictions. The strategy is to force Ras and his black nationalist followers into a position where the only way for them to keep from contradicting their own rhetoric is to give their support to the Brotherhood. Having gained community support for this specific goal, Jack then shifts focus from local issues to international ones (*IM* 355, 418). Likewise, specific support by the left for jazz music in the thirties was an attempt to gain consensus for a larger political agenda. Insofar as the left capitalized on the opportunity presented by the Nazi denunciation of jazz, their interest in jazz was as "unadulterated" as the Brotherhood's interest in pushing the issue of unjust evictions in Harlem; both serve to divert support from black nationalism and build consensus for their own program; both are part diversion and ploy.

In contrast to such political stratagems, Adorno's criticisms evince an unwillingness to pay disingenuous lip service, i.e., to abuse jazz, as a political strategy for forging consensus. Having witnessed how easy it was for the Nazis to manipulate folklore in a similar manner, Adorno approached jazz with apprehension and caution, recognizing that out of their element the artifacts of folk culture can become powerfully dangerous rhetorical tools. In this regard, Adorno's apprehensions have a subtle correspondence with the arguments of those whose defense of jazz emphasizes a cultural nationalism over the celebrated double life of jazz. Like Adorno, jazz critics who tend toward cultural separatism are most vehemently critical of the degrading abuse that jazz and jazz musicians have suffered and are skeptical of programmatic attempts to integrate them into a larger communal system.

Unlike Adorno, however, separatist critics attempt to circumvent the abusable dimensions of jazz by asserting its purity and value vis-à-vis environments that are prone toward abuse. Jazz becomes a music of "doing," whose vitality is lost in the recordings that document it (Williams 251). Or the vitality of jazz diminishes "the further jazz move[s] away from the stark blue reality of the blues continuum and the collective realities of Afro-American and American life" (Baraka, *Daggers* 271). In a new context, jazz becomes recoded, vitiated, reified. The vital literally becomes an object, manipulable and marketable. The separatist project, then, is to shelter jazz from abusive environments—except the problem with blaming abuse entirely on socio-historical mediations (i.e., the social context), exempting jazz itself, is that the two cannot be neatly separated. The fact that jazz readily glides from one context to next would suggest that it is fundamentally not as separatist as those who would "protect" it.

In reply to the unsympathetic analyses of black cultural nationalism that have dominated scholarship, Mary Berry and John Blassingame counter that, given the abysmal failures of integration, black separatism is no more "pathological," fantastic, or "unrealistic" as an idea than is integration (396). Yet neither is it any less problematic. If it were possible for jazz to thrive within a social vacuum, then perhaps apprehension would not have dominated Adorno's critique—and it is here that he parts ways with the majority of separatists. Whereas separatist critics often attack the abusers of jazz, Adorno pursues a radical critique aimed at eliminating the potential for abuse within cultural artifacts. His arguments presume that the potential for abuse (not just of jazz but of any cultural artifact) is one of the few areas of potential whose realization is virtually inevitable. This is no less true of jazz in the hands of the white jazz establishment than it is of communism in the hands of Stalin. The same is true of the Enlightenment philosophies which underlie the Brotherhood's ideology in Ellison's novel and which Adorno and Horkheimer subjected to a rigorous critique in *Dialectic of Enlightenment* precisely because, like jazz, the potential for abuse was part of their structure. For Adorno, the project of cultural criticism—however dubious its prospects might be—is to develop a discourse at whatever cultural level (high or low, aesthetic or philosophical) that cannot be appropriated, that cannot be abused. Not only does Adorno use the same dialectical method in his criticisms of Wagner and of jazz; but, insofar as jazz purports to be a voice of liberation (separatist or otherwise), it also falls within the scope of Adorno's dialectical critique of Enlightenment philosophy. In both cases the issue for Adorno is to point out where discourses of liberation perpetuate the domination that they ostensibly eliminate, to show where they generate the abuse they are supposed to prevent. To criticize jazz is simultaneously to criticize the social structures from which it seeks (or purports) to disentangle itself, structures which inevitably absorb, appropriate, and alter jazz almost as quickly as it appears.

Unlike those paying lip service, the invisible man's interest in jazz is not a strategy for building consensus. He turns to jazz and the recordings of Armstrong in disillusionment with the Brotherhood, once he realizes that their "words [can] no longer teach him anything" (de Romanet 113). At first one might argue that the turn coincides with sentiments of many jazzmen who, "unable to convey . . . [their] deepest emotions in the received idiom . . . , invented terms of . . . [their] own" (Leonard 152). The correspondence between Armstrong's voice and his horn would suggest that in Armstrong's musical riffs the invisible man seeks what the "Brotherhood's" idiom precludes (Schuller 100). Or along these same lines, the invisible man's shift from the Brotherhood to Armstrong coincides with Larry Neal's classic argument that Ellison is a counter-Marxian black nationalist, who develops, as Baker has added, "a theory of culture able to lend clarity to the quest for Afro-American liberation" (Baker, *Afro-American Poets* 153). But in Ellison's novel the recordings of Louis Armstrong are not merely a reinstatement of the "double-voiced" tools repressed by those whose interest in the black community was never more than a calculated ploy in a larger struggle for power. The invisible man's relation to Armstrong is far more ambivalent and coincides with

Adorno's own apprehensions about jazz—particularly with regard to the critique of jazz as a discourse of liberation.

Kimberly Benston argues that in his plight for recognition the invisible man "is drawn into . . . the Marxian (or more accurately, Hegelian) historical myth of progress through linear, spiralling development," in short, progress toward a teleological goal ("Historicism" 91). According to Benston, the invisible man's movement toward freedom necessitates a recognition that teleological history is a myth ("Historicism" 91; "Performing" 170). Yet this myth is precisely what the invisible man finds repeated in Armstrong's music. In "The Poetics of Jazz," Ajay Heble explores how early jazz musicians, like Armstrong, relied on a diatonic scale. Structurally, the music resembles the "linear, spiralling development" cited by Benston. Armstrong's music drives toward resolution. Always evolving toward a goal, viz. the tonic, the music "begs for completion," fosters the illusion of *telos* and "produce[s] a semblance of [the] sociality" that has been denied the invisible man in his own experiences (Heble 53; Hullot-Kentor 100).

The *telos* reflected in Armstrong's music may explain why the invisible man listens to "What Did I Do To Be So Black And Blue," rather than to Armstrong's legendary "West End Blues" or "Weather Bird." Like Adorno himself, the invisible man recognizes that "in music, the concept of representation or imitation as a way of correlating art and reality is not particularly fruitful" (Hohendahl 66). Adorno is as apprehensive about jazz culture as he is about Enlightenment philosophy—so too is the invisible man as ambivalent with Armstrong's teleological diatonic music as he is with the Brotherhood's teleological, dialectical ideology.

The myth of progress has beaten and excluded the invisible man. In the novel's epilogue, he says he is uncertain whether his disillusionment "has placed him in the rear or in the avant-garde" (*IM* 599). This question of historical position, whether he is behind or ahead, reiterates the invisible man's relation to Armstrong. The position that he develops in relation to Armstrong not only resembles the ambivalence to jazz that Adorno expresses in his rejection of folk culture. It also expresses an attitude that only in retrospect has been called part of jazz history.

As is the case with Charlie Parker and bebop, the invisible man's personal history begins with his ambivalent relation to the diatonic music of Armstrong. When the invisible man says that he likes Louis Armstrong because "he's made poetry out of being invisible," his subsequent explanation of his "own grasp of invisibility" is a paraphrase of Charlie Parker. The invisible man explains: "Invisibility . . . gives one a slightly different sense of time, you're never quite on the beat. Sometimes you're ahead and sometimes behind" (*IM* 8). This is an explanation of the musical structure that Parker developed and that became the signature of bebop (Collier, *Making* 350, 353-54). Upon its arrival, bebop was called everything but jazz. The musical dimension of bebop responded to a long history of repression and the rejection of bebop by contemporary jazz critics fueled its momentum as a sub-cultural phenomenon. The subsequent placement of bebop in the jazz tradition was possible only by an improvised concept of history which, like the music of bebop itself, "denies system, closure, purity, abstract design" (Ostendorf 154). Like Schönberg's own rejection of late romanticism's organic development, continuity, and closure, bebop marks a departure from the organic musical structures that Adorno observed in the early forms of jazz. Insofar as the invisible man aligns himself with bebop's temporal and rhythmic revisions of Armstrong's music, he is also shifting conceptual modes of history. He shifts from a repressive systematic teleology to the unsystematic and also to un-totalizing historical improvisation.

Critics have argued that, viewed from its social aspect, bebop was a "manifesto of rebellious black musicians unwilling to submit to further exploitation" and "was a deliberate attempt to avoid playing the role of the flamboyant black entertainer, which whites had come to expect" (Kofsky, *Revolution* 57; Collier, *Jazz* 360). In this regard, Adorno's most vociferous attacks on the commercial jazz industry are contemporaneously as well as philosophically in harmony with the temperament of bebop. His criticisms coincided with a growing self-consciousness that occurred within African American communities as bebop was on the rise. Baraka argues that during the forties African Americans began to "consciously analyze and evaluate American society in many of that society's own terms." The crucial realization was that being black was not the only liability but rather that the society itself was also lacking. As the African American community grew increasingly self-conscious and confident, the general deficiencies of American society became more apparent (Baraka, *Blues People* 184-85). Like Adorno during his exile in the United States, black artists began to recognize the presence of these deficiencies specifically in entertainment, and they sought art forms in which they could distance themselves "from a cultural tradition that . . . [had] been integrated into the culture industry" (Hohendahl 65). Bebop was actively engaged in this search. So was Ellison.

For all its emphasis on racial identity and on resistance to exploitation, bebop still succumbed to the debasement which it tried to avoid. The reasons for this are complex; bebop succumbs not, as Frank Kofsky has argued, solely because whites controlled the "jazz establishment," and forced jazz musicians to conform because they found bebop's black nationalist undertones incompatible with their business interests ("Forerunners" 2). Rather the debasement resulted from dialectical tendencies in American society which were able to blunt "the sharp, ugly lines of . . . [the bebop] rebellion" (Ellison, *Shadow* 204). In short, black nationalist or anti-capitalist sentiment has proven to be a lucrative product in the marketplace. "The culture industry can diffuse . . . rebellious sentiment . . . by repeating the same ideas and themes, even if they speak to the deepest contradictions of capitalism, until they lack all

meaning" (Koval 2-3). Just as the invisible man turns to jazz when the Brotherhood's words of liberation and freedom prove to be the contrary, so too does the revolutionary promise of the jazz idiom accommodate, indeed contain, its opposite.

The presence of this opposite is most immediately apparent in bebop's point of departure, i.e., its attempted break from the traditions that Armstrong was said to embody. Through the figure of Armstrong in his novel, Ellison exposes the delusory, even contradictory, idealism that seethed beneath the beboppers' "rejection of the traditional entertainer's role" (Ellison, *Shadow* 225). In his essays Ellison expresses understanding for the desire of Parker's contemporaries to move beyond the "heritage from the minstrel tradition," viz. the tradition carried on by Armstrong, but at the same time he notes that the beboppers were caught up in the contradiction of trying to get "rid of the role they demanded, [striving] in the name of their racial identity . . . [for] a purity of status which by definition is impossible for the performing artist" (*Shadow* 225). Against the backdrop of "the thrust toward respectability exhibited by the Negro jazzmen of Parker's generation," the invisible man points out that Armstrong has not been superseded (Ellison, *Shadow* 225). The breakup of a linear teleological history has preserved him. Armstrong, the invisible man says, "is still around with his music and his dancing and his diversity, and I'll be up and around with mine" (Ellison, *Shadow* 225; *IM* 568). Though clearly not Armstrong's, neither is the invisible man's diversity that of the beboppers.

An awareness of these contradictory tendencies—or deficiencies—pervades the writings of both Adorno and Ellison, and it is the search for a form in which to critically articulate the awareness of them that finally places the two writers dialectically at odds with both the deficiencies in American society to which bebop responded and to bebop itself. While Ellison's novel alludes sympathetically to bebop, the novel is no mere apology for it—any more than the unflattering portrayal of the Brotherhood is merely a criticism of the deficiencies of the communist party. First of all, inasmuch as bebop carries either a revolutionary or black nationalist agenda, it too falls within the scope of Ellison's critical presentation of the Brotherhood and of Ras. The invisible man does after all spear the black nationalist in the jaw. Secondly, to argue that bebop has superseded the pitfalls into which Armstrong fell is to grant to jazz the teleological history with which the invisible man is at odds. Correspondingly, the more one examines where and how Adorno's arguments diverge from the general similarities that they bear to bebop, the more Adorno's arguments converge with the attitude that Ellison develops toward jazz and bebop in his novel.

In particular, the beboppers were "resentful of Louis Armstrong," as Ellison was later to argue, "confusing the spirit of his music with his clowning" (*Shadow* 211). If Ellison's depiction of the beboppers is accurate, then Adorno's association of jazz with the antics of an "eccentric clown" at first appears to have fallen into the same trap (Adorno, **"Jazz"** 512). In terms of general disposition, Adorno certainly had more in common with beboppers than he either realized or was willing to admit. How far this convergence extends beyond general disposition is another matter. Recently, Ulrich Schönherr has suggested implicitly that the convergence extends a great deal. Although Schönherr does not pursue the historical similarities between Adorno's arguments and those of bebop, he does argue that the contributions of musicians who followed in the wake of bebop have "largely fulfilled what Adorno had not seen realized in jazz" (93). But Schönherr has not gone unchallenged.

In the introduction to the volume in which Schönherr's article appears, Russell Berman and Robert D'Amico challenge Schönherr on the grounds that "to continue to defend jazz . . . through its later exponents and more 'artsy' performances vastly underestimates the force of Adorno's suspicion of emancipatory appearances" (73). Although it sounds as if Berman and D'Amico are addressing one issue and Schönherr another (i.e., as if Berman and D'Amico are reaffirming Adorno's dismissal of the notion that jazz is a source of liberation and Schönherr is merely concerned with musical innovations), the two are in fact intimately related, because the area in which jazz's most significant innovations have occurred is also the area in which jazz has traditionally expressed its emancipation: improvisation.

Schönherr's claim presupposes the position of critics like Bruce Baugh, who argues that Adorno relies too heavily on musical notation and thus fails to recognize the significance of the unscorable subtleties of jazz and blues improvisation (73-74). Yet, such assertions, which are standard criticism of Adorno, are premised upon a fundamental mis-perception about musical scores. Adorno points out that rather than producing mechanical acts, classical score establishes a sophisticated context for interpretation, the subtleties of which scoreless improvisations cannot provide and which are not part of notation anyway. Indeed, Adorno argues that "a performance of a Beethoven quartet that conveyed exclusively what was prescribed in the music would not make sense" (**"Review"** 168). "Inner transfiguration" and "paraphrases," traits which André Hodeir cites as hallmarks of improvisation, occur in every act of playing from the score (158-81). The point is this: reading a musical score is already an improvisatory act, just as reading a text is an act of construction. The inevitable improvisatory movements within the context established by the score may in fact be the only prospects of liberation which music offers. For Adorno, the exploitative, abusive wherewithal of the culture industry is so pervasive that only the most concerted effort can circumvent it (in this case only the musician's interpretative response to an already orchestrated context of resistance).

Adorno's defense of scored music coincides with his general views on the critical function of art and culture as a whole. Each genuine cultural artifact facilitates an interaction that in turn cultivates critical resistance. This is not to say that, collectively, cultural artifacts lead to a unified concept of resistance or even of liberation. Rather they comprise a diverse array of critical contexts, the individual mastery of which impedes abuse and appropriation in specific repressive situations. Nor is this to say that jazz music has never achieved the level of critical sophistication to which Adorno refers; it is merely the false dichotomy of "free" improvisation and "constrictive" musical notation that is reductive.

Adorno's position on context, resistance, and cultural artifacts helps to explain the disparate cultural repertoire that the invisible man employs in order to break the rhetorical bind that Jack places him in with the contradictory statement: "You will have freedom of action—and you will be under strict discipline to the committee" (Ellison, *IM* 351). The diverse field of reference in Ellison's novel provides "the resources of consciousness and imagination . . . [which the invisible man] brings to bear against the pressures of a changing environment" (Tanner 49). For the invisible man, the "changing environment" is reflected in the evolution of Jack's sentence, in the casual (almost unobservable) glide from "freedom" to "strictness." Perhaps the invisible man's single most significant accomplishment lies in marshaling his diverse interaction with cultural artifacts in a grand unmasking of the latent "strict" repression in each of the discourses of liberation in the novel.

Armstrong belongs to the invisible man's cultural repertoire and to his process of unmasking repressive "strictness" masquerading as liberation. Insofar as the invisible man is able to use Armstrong in this regard, Ellison provides a positive dialectical compliment to Adorno's claim in **"Perennial Fashion"** that "the organization of culture" in levels of high, middle, and lowbrow is anachronistic and "reprehensible." Most importantly, Ellison uses Armstrong to read bebop against the grain. He uses what Adorno describes as the obsolescence of high and lowbrow distinctions in order to undercut bebop's attempt to obtain liberation through a recognition by "high" culture. To undercut this appeal to high culture, Ellison embraces Armstrong and places improvisation in the most debasing light (*Shadow* 225). The most explicit example of this is to be found in the factory hospital attendants who, while trying to give the invisible man an electronic lobotomy, tell him—like fans encouraging a jazz player to improvise—to "Get hot, boy! Get hot!" (*IM* 232). The hotter he gets the more effect the lobotomy will have. Ellison thereby creates a position sensitive to the criticisms Parker and his contemporaries levied against Armstrong while at the same time subjecting bebop to critical scrutiny. In this respect, the invisible man is able to transform his original ambivalence for Armstrong into a critical negative dialectic.

This dialectic is manifest in the hospital scene as well because the scene can also be read as an allusion to the degrading side of the jazz tradition that Parker and his contemporaries were trying to circumvent. They sought to avoid not merely the entertainer's role but also the association of this role with the tradition of minstrelsy. Adorno shared this sentiment, repeatedly drawing attention to the continued presence of minstrelsy in modern jazz. In 1938 he echoed the stock leftist interpretation of jazz and argued that "the European-American entertainment business" had such control over jazz that its "triumph[s]" were "merely a confusing parody of colonial imperialism" (**"On Jazz"** 53). Nowhere was this colonial attitude more played out than in minstrelsy. Baker has noted that in minstrelsy white Americans "conceptualized a degraded, subhuman animal as a substitute for the actual African" (*Blues* 193).

The only way out of this degrading role is for Baker, like Ellison, to maintain that the private session of jazz and blues singers—when the white oppressor is absent—is where the real playing occurs (Baker, *Blues* 193-94). Baker's argument is compelling so long as one is of the opinion that there are adequate opportunities for the mask to be cast aside and so long as earlier role playing does not impair or constrain the player when he or she is alone. In these presumptions, Baker follows the arguments previously articulated by Robert B. Stepto in *From Behind the Veil* (1979). Both critics rely on an idealistic conception of the self whose integrity is immune from impairment despite the repeated "self-humiliation" and the "symbolic self-maiming," which according to Ellison is enacted by the minstrel (*Shadow* 49). Stepto, for example, claims that one of the great achievements of *Invisible Man* is "its brave assertion that there is a self and form to be discovered beyond the lockstep of linear movement within imposed definitions of reality" (168). Not merely the advent of poststructural theories of the self challenges Stepto's and Baker's claims. So too does the invisible man's relation to minstrelsy. His "improvisation" at the factory hospital questions the extent to which the formation of a vernacular theory compensates for the "maiming."

In **"On the Fetish-Character in Music . . . ,"** Adorno begins his critique with an argument on the dissolution of the subject, a dissolution which arguably takes "humiliation" and "symbolic self-maiming" seriously and interprets such tendencies as having lasting debilitating consequences (276). According to these arguments, vernacular theory is purchased at great cost. More recently, Eric Lott has explored how Blackface Minstrelsy enacted a complex symbolic castration of black males (33-37). An allusion to this disturbing aspect of the jazz tradition occurs in the invisible man's dream when he is in the coal pit at the novel's end. Not only does he dream of castration, but he does so sleeping atop the material used to blacken faces in minstrelsy (*IM* 557). While Lott's exploration provides historical documentation for Adorno's infamous assertion that jazz has a "eunuchlike sound," the invisible man's dream graphically depicts what for Adorno were the most disturbing aspects of the blackfaced minstrelsy out of which jazz emerged. Indeed, Adorno was never able to see a function of jazz beyond the minstrelsy which he criticized in 1936 and 1938.

That the legacy of minstrelsy lies at the foundation of the jazz tradition is hardly subject to debate, but whether one can equate the colonialistic prejudices embodied in the figure of the minstrel with the late-capitalist enterprise embodied in the jazz musician is another question. What Adorno does in his reading of jazz is to presume that the interest of capital in culture is tantamount to the gross subhuman parodies of African Americans in minstrelsy. While the two are historically related, they are not the same, and to imply that they are succumbs to a blinding ahistoricism—with regard to minstrelsy but more significantly with regard to the historical consequences of late industrial capitalism. To undo this conflation is simultaneously to place Adorno in historical context and to uncover the dialectic at play in Ellison's novel. It is to apply the invisible man's break with the teleological historicism of the Brotherhood, his break with Armstrong's diatonic music, and his break with bebop's supposed evolution beyond swing; it is to apply all of these ruptures to the supposed continuity between minstrelsy and jazz. The question that jazz raises with regard to Adorno is whether the interest of the culture industry can really be reduced to a kiss of death for *all* cultural expression.

Scott DeVeaux has argued that jazz implicitly challenges traditional *agoraphobia*, the fear of the marketplace, which in cultural issues has manifested itself within an inflexible dialectic between "commercial" versus "artistic." Jazz challenges this dialectic because it "developed largely within the framework of modern mass market capitalism" (DeVeaux 530). Insofar as jazz has maintained a double life, this is perhaps where it is most readily to be found: in the forging of a space which is simultaneously commercial and aesthetically interesting. In fact, Adorno provides the basis for this argument in the peripheries of **"On Jazz,"** where he concedes the need for quality jazz in order to promote mass consumption and to "allow the upper class to maintain a clear conscience about its taste" (51). In his novel, Ellison moves Adorno's argument from periphery to center and explores the history of jazz as a securing and expanding of the parameters of the limited space for the quality (jazz or hibernation) that Adorno allows for marketing purposes.

Instead of merely dismissing Adorno as a cultural elitist, it is far more fruitful to address the evolution of his own terms—in other words, to consider whether the encroachment of technology and the culture industry is a process which halts once uniformity is supposedly reached. Florindo Volpacchio has argued that technical advances in market machinery were in direct response to the need to accommodate an increasingly diverse and fragmented consumer public. For its own survival the entertainment industry has had to accommodate heterogeneity (Volpacchio 120). Given Adorno's own pessimistic concerns regarding the momentum behind the culture industry, it is difficult to imagine how it would come to a standstill or avoid diversification in its own interest. There is an inkling of this awareness in a peripheral reference to jazz late in *Aesthetic Theory*, but whether the covert spaces of jazz would have attained visibility in the final version of Adorno's unfinished manuscript is a matter of speculation.

Notes

1. The reasons for this neglect derive in part from the fact that until 1991 there had been no adequate critical examination of the socio-historical and ideological dimensions of jazz criticisms. This lack led Gary Carner, in the introduction to the special issue on jazz that *Black American Literature Forum* (25.3) published in 1991, to argue that after seventy years of jazz literature, it is finally time for some serious attempt to examine it (443). As an illustration of the state of scholarship on the question of Adorno and jazz, it is worth noting that in the same year *Telos* published a special issue on Adorno, jazz, and popular music (87.1). While Adorno receives only a passing swipe in *Black American Literature Forum, Telos* examines Adorno's views without a single reference to the array of scholarship *Black American Literature Forum* was exploring at the same time.

2. The importance of African American music to this novel has often been cited, most notably by Houston Baker, Jr., Kimberly Benston, and Berndt Ostendorf. Their work will be discussed later in this essay.

3. The foundations for these arguments were first provided in Andreas Huyssen's "Adorno in Reverse: From Hollywood to Richard Wagner," which was first published in *New German Critique* 29.2-3 (1983): 3-38, and then later included in *After the Great Divide*. For Huyssen's entire argument, see *After the Great Divide* 16-43. It is important, however, to note that while, with regard to the effects of the culture industry, there are similarities between Adorno's critique of Wagner and of jazz, Adorno's association of Wagner with the beginning of the culture industry is in large part a rhetorical counter to Wagner's anti-Semitism. By locating the beginning of the culture industry with Wagner, Adorno subtly rebuts Wagner's claim that Jewish financial interests are corrupting German culture. Thus a simple association of the two critiques is highly problematic. Unlike his discussion of the culture industry and jazz, Adorno's discussion of the culture industry and Wagner is inseparable from his critique of Wagner's anti-Semitism. I examine the problematic nature of this comparison in the chapter of the book manuscript to which this article belongs.

4. Despite these general statements by Adorno, which challenge high-low cultural dichotomies, his fixation on European music demonstrates that he only made cultural concessions on a theoretical level and was unable to finally turn his recognition that high-low distinctions were "obsolete" into a serious consideration of the critical dimensions of "light" music. In his discussion of what he calls the "incestuous choice" of the German intellectual exiles who fled from Nazi Germany to Los Angeles, Mike Davis has implicitly provided a partial explanation for this tendency in Adorno's writings. Davis notes that "segregated from native Angelenos, the exiles composed a miniature society in a self-imposed ghetto, clinging to their old-world prejudices like cultural life-preservers" (*City of Quartz* 47). While Davis' metaphor of the "life-preserver" highlights the personal investment in Adorno's, Horkheimer's, Schönberg's, and Mann's German cultural predilections, they also saw themselves as contributing to the preservation of the culture that the Nazis were destroying.

5. Adorno began to develop this critique of jazz as far back as 1936 in his essay "On Jazz," in which he claimed that use value of jazz intensifies rather than supersedes alienation because its innovations are produced "in terms none other than its marketability" (48). He repeats the same argument in "Fetish Character of Music and the Regression of Hearing" and again in 1941 in his review of Sargeant and Wilder: jazz "cheats the masses as soon as it holds them in its grip" ("Review" 170).

6. See, in particular, John Gennari, "Jazz Criticism: Its Development and Ideologies" 496-504.

Works Cited

Adorno, Theodor W. "Abschied vom Jazz." 1933. *Gesammelte Schriften*. Vol. 18. Frankfurt am Main: Suhrkamp, 1984. 795-99.

———. *Aesthetic Theory*. 1970. Trans. C. Lenhardt. New York: Routledge, 1984.

———. *Dissonanzen*. Göttingen: Vandenhoeck und Ruprecht, 1962.

———. "On the Fetish-Character in Music and the Regression of Listening." 1938. *The Essential Frankfurt School Reader*. Ed. Andrew Arato and Erike Gebhardt. New York: Urizen, 1978. 270-99.

———. *Introduction to the Sociology of Music*. 1962. Trans. E. B. Ashton. New York: Continuum, 1989.

———. "Jazz." *Encyclopedia of the Arts*. Ed. Dagobert D. Runes and Harry G. Schrickel. New York: Philosophical Library, 1946. 511-13.

———. "On Jazz." 1936. Trans. Jamie Owen Daniel. *Discourse* 12.1 (1989-90): 45-69.

———. "Perennial Fashion—Jazz." 1953. *Prisms*. Trans. Samuel Weber and Shierry Weber. Cambridge: MIT P, 1981. 119-32.

———. *The Philosophy of Modern Music*. 1949. New York: Continuum, 1985.

———. Review of *American Jazz Music* by Wilder Hobson and of *Jazz: Hot and Hybrid* by Winthrop Sargeant. *Studies in Philosophy and Social Science* 7.9 (1941): 167-78.

———. *In Search of Wagner.* 1952. Trans. Rodney Livingstone. New York: Verso, 1981.

Adorno, Theodor W., and Joachim-Ernst Berendt. "Für und Wider Jazz." *Merkur: Deutsche Zeitschrift für Europäisches Denken* 7.9 (1953): 887-93.

Adorno, Theodor W., Else Frenkel-Brunswik, Daniel J. Levison, and R. Nevitt Sanford. *The Authoritarian Personality.* New York: Harper, 1950.

Adorno, Theodor W., and Max Horkheimer. *Dialectic of Enlightenment.* 1944. Trans. John Cumming. New York: Continuum, 1991.

Arato, Andrew, and Erike Gebhardt. *The Essential Frankfurt School Reader.* New York: Urizen, 1978.

Baker, Houston A., Jr. *Afro-American Poets.* Madison: U of Wisconsin P, 1988.

———. *Blues, Ideology, and Afro-American Literature: A Vernacular Theory.* Chicago: U of Chicago P, 1984.

Baraka, Imamu Amiri. [LeRoi Jones.] *Black Music.* 1967. Westport: Greenwood P, 1980.

———. *Blues People.* New York: William Morrow, 1963.

———. *Daggers and Javelins.* New York: William Morrow, 1984.

Baugh, Bruce. "Left-Wing Elitism: Adorno on Popular Culture." *Philosophy and Literature* 14.1 (1990): 65-78.

Benjamin, Walter. "The Work of Art in the Age of Mechanical Reproduction." *Illuminations.* Trans. Harry Zohn. New York: Schocken, 1968. 217-51.

Benston, Kimberly W. "Controlling the Dialectical Deacon: The Critique of Historicism in *Invisible Man.*" *Delta* 18 (1984): 89-103.

———. "Performing Blackness: Re/Placing Afro-American Poetry" *Afro-American Literary Study in the 1990's.* Ed. Houston A. Baker, Jr. and Patricia Redmond. Chicago: U of Chicago P, 1989. 164-85.

Berman, Russell A., and Robert D'Amico. "Introduction: Popular Music from Adorno to Zappa." *Telos* 87.1: 71-77.

Berry, Mary Frances, and John W. Blassingame. *Long Memory: The Black Experience in America.* New York: Oxford UP, 1982.

Brown, Lee B. "The Theory of Jazz Music: 'It Don't Mean a Thing.'" *Journal of Aesthetics and Art Criticism* 49.2 (1991): 115-27.

Carner, Gary. "Introduction [to Special Volume on Jazz]." *Black American Literature Forum* 25.3 (1991): 441-48.

Collier, James Lincoln. "The Faking of Jazz." *New Republic* 18 Nov. 1985: 33-40.

———. *The Making of Jazz.* Boston: Houghton Mifflin, 1978.

———. *The Reception of Jazz in America.* New York: Institute for Studies in American Music, 1988.

Cowley, Julian. "The Art of Improvisers: Jazz and Fiction in Post-Bebop America." *New Comparison* 6 (1988): 194-204.

Craig, Gordon. *Germany 1866-1945.* New York: Oxford UP, 1978.

Daniel, Jamie Owen. "Introduction to Adorno's 'On Jazz.'" *Discourse* 12.1 (1989-90): 39-44.

Davis, Mike. *City of Quartz: Excavating the Future in Los Angeles.* New York: Vintage, 1992.

Deleuze, Gilles, and Félix Guattari. *Kafka: Toward a Minor Literature.* Trans. Dana Polan. Minneapolis: U of Minnesota P, 1986.

DeVeaux, Scott. "Constructing the Jazz Tradition: Jazz Historiography." *Black Literature Forum* 25.3 (1991): 525-60.

Ellison, Ralph. *Invisible Man.* 1952. New York: Vintage, 1972.

———. *Shadow and Act.* New York: Random House, 1964.

Gennari, John. "Jazz Criticism: Its Development and Ideologies." *Black American Literature Forum* 25.3 (1991): 449-523.

Heble, Ajay. "The Poetics of Jazz: From Symbolic to Semiotic." *Textual Practice* 2.1 (1988): 51-68.

Hobson, Wilder. *American Jazz Music.* New York: Norton, 1938.

Hodeir, André. *Jazz: Its Evolution and Essence.* Trans. David Noakes. New York: Grove P, 1956.

Hohendahl, Peter. *Reappraisals: The Shifting Alignments in Postwar Critical Theory.* Ithaca: Cornell UP, 1991.

Hullot-Kentor, Robert. "The Impossibility of Music: Adorno, Popular and Other Music." *Telos* 87.1 (1991): 97-117.

Huyssen, Andreas. "Adorno in Reverse: From Hollywood to Richard Wagner." *New German Critique.* 29.3-4 (1983): 8-38.

———. *After the Great Divide.* Bloomington: Indiana UP, 1986.

Jameson, Fredric. *Late Marxism: Adorno, or, the Persistence of the Dialectic.* New York: Verso, 1990.

Jay, Martin. *Adorno.* Cambridge: Harvard UP, 1984.

———. "Adorno in America." *Permanent Exiles.* New York: Columbia UP, 1985. 120-37.

———. *Dialectical Imagination.* Boston: Little, Brown, 1973.

Kofsky, Frank. "Afro-American Innovation and the Folk Tradition in Jazz: Their Historical Significance." *Journal of Ethnic Studies* 7.1 (1979): 1-12.

———. "Black Nationalism in Jazz: The Forerunners Resist Establishment Repression, 1958-1963." *Journal of Ethnic Studies* 10.2 (1982): 1-27.

———. *Black Nationalism and the Revolution in Music.* New York: Pathfinder P, 1970.

Koval, Howard. "Homogenization of Culture in Capitalist Society." *Popular Music and Society* 12.4 (1988): 1-16.

Leonard, Neil. "The Jazzman's Verbal Usage." *Black American Literature Forum* 20.1-2 (1986): 150-60.

Levin, Thomas. "For the Record: Adorno on Music in the Age of Its Technological Reproducibility." *October* 55.4 (1990): 23-47.

Lott, Eric. "Love and Theft: The Racial Unconscious of Blackface Minstrelsy." *Representations* 39.2 (1992): 23-50.

Lyne, William. "The Signifying Modernist: Ralph Ellison and the Limits of the Double Consciousness." *PMLA* 107.2 (1992): 319-30.

Naison, Mark. "Communism and Harlem Intellectuals in the Popular Front: Anti-Fascism and the Politics of Black Culture." *Journal of Ethnic Studies* 9.1 (1981): 1-25.

Neal, Larry. "Ellison's Zoot Suit." *Ralph Ellison: A Collection of Critical Essays.* Ed. John Hersey. Englewood Cliffs: Prentice Hall, 1974. 58-79.

Nye, William P. "Theodor Adorno on Jazz: A Critique of Critical Theory." *Popular Music and Society* 12.4 (1988): 69-73.

Ostendorf, Berndt. "Anthropology, Modernism, and Jazz." *Ralph Ellison.* Ed. Harold Bloom. New York: Chelsea House, 1986. 145-72.

de Romanet, Jerome. "Musical Elements in *Invisible Man* with Special Reference to the Blues." *Delta* 18 (1984): 105-18.

Sales, Grover. *Jazz: America's Classical Music.* New York: De Capo, 1992.

Sargeant, Winthrop. *Jazz: A History.* New York: McGraw-Hill, 1964. Rpt. of *Jazz: Hot and Hybrid.* 1938.

Savery, Pancho. "Ellison's Existential Blues." *Approaches to Teaching Ellison's Invisible Man.* New York: MLA, 1989. 65-74.

Schönherr, Ulrich. "Adorno and Jazz: Reflections on a Failed Encounter." *Telos* 87.1: 85-96.

Schuller, Gunther. *Early Jazz: Its Roots and Musical Development.* New York: Oxford UP, 1968.

Starr, S. Frederick. *Red and Hot: The Fate of Jazz in the Soviet Union.* New York: Oxford UP, 1983.

Stepto, Robert B. *From Behind the Veil: A Study of Afro-American Narrative.* Urbana: U of Illinois P, 1979.

Strout, Cushing. "'An American Negro Idiom': *Invisible Man* and the Politics of Culture." *Approaches to Teaching Ellison's Invisible Man.* New York: MLA, 1989. 79-85.

Tanner, Tony. "The Music of Invisibility." *Ralph Ellison.* Ed. Harold Bloom. New York: Chelsea House, 1986. 37-50.

Thomas, Lorenzo. "'Communicating by Horns': Jazz and Redemption in the Poetry of the Beats and the Black Arts Movement." *African American Review* 26.2 (1992): 291-98.

Townsend, Peter. "Adorno on Jazz: Vienna versus the Vernacular." *Prose Studies: History, Theory, Criticism* 11.1 (1988): 69-88.

Volpacchio, Florindo. "The Unhappy Marriage of Music and Emancipation." *Telos* 87.1 (1991): 118-23.

Weiner, Marc A. "*Urwaldmusik* and the Borders of German Identity: Jazz in Literature of the Weimar Republic." *German Quarterly* 64.4 (1991): 475-87.

Williams, Martin. *The Jazz Tradition.* Rev. ed. New York: Oxford UP, 1983.

Zuidervaart, Lambert. *Adorno's Aesthetic Theory.* Cambridge: MIT P, 1991.

Peter Uwe Hohendahl (essay date 1995)

SOURCE: "The Philosopher in Exile," in *Prismatic Thought: Theodor W. Adorno,* University of Nebraska Press, 1995, pp. 21-44.

[*In the following essay, Hohendahl discusses works from Adorno's period living in the United States as well as Adorno's traumatic experience as an exile from his native Germany.*]

It would be difficult to describe Theodor W. Adorno's connection to America—which for him meant the United States—as a happy or successful relationship. In fact, most commentators have rightly stressed its highly problematic nature, either by pointing out how unable and unwilling Adorno was to adjust to the American way of life or by emphasizing how the United States failed to receive and integrate the persona and work of the German-Jewish philosopher. Charges of cultural elitism and arrogance, common among American as well as foreign contemporary observers, were later reiterated by critics of Adorno or intellectual historians dealing with the generation of German intellectuals exiled from Germany after 1933.[1] His defenders tend to foreground the incongruity between his European outlook and the intellectual atmosphere in the United States during the 1940s and early 1950s. By and large, foes and friends seem to agree that Adorno's complex and ambiguous attitude to America was rooted in his European and German *Weltanschauung* and his critical humanism, which motivated him to reject modern America: its political order, its economic system, and particularly its culture. Because of his education and his commitment to an (elitist) humanist tradition (steeped in classical literature), so the argument goes, he formulated a largely negative account of the United States. He even failed to acknowledge American democracy as the true antagonist of German fascism.

There is no denying that Adorno shared some of the typical prejudices of the cultured European against America, which not only influenced his behavior but also manifested themselves in his writings: his 1938 essay on jazz ([*Gesammelte Schriften*] *GS* 14:14-50) for instance, and his numerous remarks on the United States in **Minima Moralia.** There is no doubt that he never felt at home in America; he always remained—and self-consciously so—the exile waiting to be allowed to return home.

Although Adorno could never quite overcome the gulf between America and his German social and cultural formation, he was keenly aware of the potential dangers of his position. A dogmatic defense of high culture, so common among European émigrés of the 1930s and 1940s, would not do justice to the historical nature of the problems at hand. As Andreas Huyssen has persuasively argued, Adorno already understood in the 1930s, when he wrote his essay on Wagner ([**"Fur und Wider den Jazz"**] FW), that in the age of industrial capitalism high culture and mass culture are entwined and ultimately inseparable, because they are rooted in the same social conditions.[2] In other words, Adorno was aware of the problematic position of official high culture (as in the case of Richard Wagner) before he came to the United States and was therefore critical of a position that would identify 'bad' mass culture exclusively with America and 'good' high culture with Europe. This point has to be made; otherwise, an isolated reading of the famous chapter on the culture industry in **Dialectic of Enlightenment** may reinforce the image of Adorno as European elitist.

In the essay **'Cultural Criticism and Society,'** written just before his return to Germany, Adorno once more clarified his understanding of *critique* by stressing that cultural criticism must not accept without suspicion the notion of culture (*Kultur*) as an unquestionable value ([**Prisms**] **PR** 17-34; *GS* 10 [1]: 11-30). What did distinguish America from Western Europe in his eyes was the more systematic transformation of literature and the arts under the impact of monopoly capitalism. As we will see, Adorno's writings tended to insist on the advanced character of American society—especially compared with that of prewar Germany. The fact that he spent his American years first in New York City and then in California, without ever seeing much of middle America, may have contributed to this conception.

Evidence for his negative view can be found in Adorno's letters as well as in **Minima Moralia,** where the New World seems to be portrayed in terms that recall Aldous Huxley's *Brave New World*. This conventional reconstruction of Adorno's view is not without problems, however. It fails to contextualize his American years, looking at them too exclusively from Adorno's point of view (or that of the Frankfurt School) without seriously interrogating the American experience of the 1940s. Although it is certainly true that Adorno's personal experience was limited in scope, his connections with the intellectual climate of the 1940s were, I believe, more complex than is commonly presumed. In many ways Adorno and Horkheimer, although hardly on close terms with the leading intellectual figures of that time, developed positions in their own work that were not as far removed from contemporary American thought as has typically been assumed. Their retreat from a Marxist-socialist position, for example, which occurred during the early 1940s, was paralleled by a significant shift within the American left from a socialist to a liberal position with strong nationalist overtones. When Horkheimer and Adorno returned to Germany after the war, they shared an explicitly anti-Communist bias with American intellectuals such as Sidney Hook and Irving Kristol, who, however, went much further to the right than the members of Frankfurt's Institut für Sozialforschung ever considered. In a curious way, they came back to Germany with an 'American' agenda, even though they clearly distanced themselves from American civilization as they had experienced it in California.

When Adorno entered the United States in 1938, the country had not yet fully overcome the economic depression, but its threat to the fabric of the American society was becoming less acute. By the same token, the enthusiasm for radical social reforms among American intellectuals was decreasing. There was a growing resistance to Communist solutions that would fundamentally change the American way of life and its legitimizing values. The suspicion of such solutions, which was not limited to one particular faction, was linked to major European events: on the one hand the Stalin trials, and on the other the rise of fascism in Germany. Especially after the outbreak of war in 1939 and Hitler's extraordinary military successes, the imminent threat of another world war forced all camps to reconsider their goals and allegiances. Indirectly, this situation helped Franklin Delano Roosevelt's nonsocialist New Deal to achieve a specifically democratic American response to the same economic and social problems that had led to fascism in Germany. The Moscow show trials had a similar effect on the American left: Stalin's ruthless annihilation of his former comrades discredited Communism as a radical answer to social problems in the United States.[3] In the light of the impending war, the hostilities between progressive liberals and the radical left as well as the rivalries between the competing factions of the radical left were losing their former significance. As Richard Pells points out, the intellectual climate of the late 1930s can no longer be adequately described in terms of the socialist agenda that had defined the years following the crash of the stock market. In particular, the militancy of intellectuals' social commitment either weakened or shifted toward a new goal: the defense of American democracy.[4]

This assessment, strangely enough, applies equally to the Frankfurt School. By 1938, as Helmut Dubiel has shown, the core members of the Institute were beginning to distance themselves from the program of the early 1930s.[5] The rise of Stalin and the purges in the Soviet Union increasingly discouraged support of a Communist position. In other areas, however, this increasing distance vis-à-vis traditional Marxist positions did not coincide with the American configuration. Unlike Bertholt Brecht, the Frankfurt School did not give much support to the Popular Front, which became so important for the self-reflection of the American left. While the alliance of the Popular Front moved closer to Roosevelt's New Deal, thereby diminishing radical opposition, the Institute and Adorno began to work from a position that would implicitly critique the administration of the New Deal.

The fascist expansion in Europe after 1939 and the potential American involvement in the war transformed not only the agenda of the radical left but also the political position of the liberals. A common national concern became more important than the social issues that had dominated the debates of the 1930s, and the willingness of intellectuals to rally around Roosevelt certainly grew. Liberal intellectuals in particular began to emphasize the need for strong national leadership in a time of international crisis. During the 1940s Roosevelt's administration could count on considerably more support from both the moderate left and the liberals. Clearly, the fascist threat from the outside shifted the focus of the liberal project as much as that of the radicals.[6]

The *New Republic* in particular, with a growing circulation (28,000 in 1930; 41,000 in 1946), voiced the new political commitment of the liberals by affirming Roosevelt's representation of American democracy. The call for decisive action based on sober planning and management downplayed the role of the House of Representatives and the Senate. Both houses of Congress came in for scorn and anger because they failed to acknowledge the need for FDR's unrestricted leadership. 'By the early 1940s, the *New Republic* had come to speak within the intellectual community for a form of administrative liberalism that relied increasingly on the White House, the Cabinet, and government agencies staffed with ideologically sympathetic appointees for social reform at home and victory abroad.'[7] In other words, liberal intellectuals moved away from traditional liberal concerns with civil rights and individual freedom, toward a social democracy dependent on government agencies. In this respect they were not far removed from moderate socialist reformers, who accepted the existing economic system as the platform for social intervention.

Radicals such as C. Wright Mills and Dwight Macdonald, by contrast, warned against this potentially totalitarian combination of state power and corporate capitalism; Macdonald especially still relied on the notion that a revolutionary working class would ultimately overthrow the hegemonic bourgeoisie.[8] Indeed, one crucial issue of the debates of the 1940s was the question, could one assume that the American working class wanted a socialist economy and was prepared to fight for it? When Sidney Hook cautioned liberals and radicals against an alliance with the New Deal administration, arguing that the centralized power of the state would ultimately not benefit the working class,[9] he was more or less in agreement with the analysis of state capitalism articulated by the Frankfurt School. As we will see, however, Friedrich Pollock, Horkheimer, and Adorno were prepared to draw more radical conclusions than those of Hook or Macdonald.

Despite general agreement on the task of defeating fascist Germany and imperialist Japan, then, there was no consensus on the solution of America's internal social problems. Liberals such as Bruce Brevan, George Soule, and Max Lerner argued in favor of a well-designed welfare state in which the working class would find a secure home; the radicals focused their attention on the political organizations of the working class.[10] A simultaneous critique of both positions would lead to the point of view articulated by Adorno and Horkheimer during the 1940s. The culture industry chapter of their ***Dialectics of Enlightenment*** presupposes the disintegration of the working class and its reconstitution as a mass, as well as the failure of a progressive conception of history in which the state can function as the primary agent of reason.

By 1944 Adorno and Horkheimer had come to the conclusion that the Second World War would probably result in the defeat of fascism but would not prepare a social revolution. Similarly, both American liberals and Marxists, who had perceived the war as 'revolutionary' and had predicted profound changes in Europe, began to realize that these expectations might not come true.[11] To American observers it became quite clear how much the war effort had helped to rebuild the American economy. Under Roosevelt's leadership the United States was expected to come out of the war not as a socialist but as a strong capitalist democracy facing the territorial expansion of the Soviet Union. The growing disappointment among liberal and radical intellectuals with the Democratic administration (especially after FDR's death) was increasingly overshadowed by the changes in the Soviet Union. Whereas the American left had perceived the Soviet Union as a socialist experiment during the 1930s, the emphasis of the war years was more on the national strength of Russia and the American-Russian alliance, which was praised by the liberal *New Republic* as well. By 1945, however, the notion of a common American-Russian agenda was no longer clear in the minds of the *New Republic*'s editors. The friction between those allies as soon as the enemy was defeated forced the left camp to reassess its own values and political priorities.

In this process (which began around 1944 and was more or less completed by 1948), the political discourse separated the concepts of democracy and socialism (Communism), turning them ultimately against each other. The defense of American democracy against the Eastern threat redefined the Soviet Union in such terms that it became similar to, if not identical with, Nazi Germany. It was Hannah Arendt, of course, who articulated this critical view, in her theory of the totalitarian state,[12] but it was by no means limited to her work; rather, the emergence of the Cold War was paralleled by a slow and sometimes painful realignment of the American left. The radical anti-Stalinist faction that gathered around such journals as *Commentary* and *Partisan Review,* disappointed in particular with Harry Truman's administration, had to struggle on two fronts: with the critiques of capitalism on the one hand, and the polemic against Stalinism on the other. As much as the contributors of *Partisan Review* attacked the former liberal supporters of the New Deal, their position on foreign politics after 1945 was primarily anti-Communist. The former distinction between anti-Stalinist and anti-Communist or anti-Marxist, which had defined the position of the radical left during the early 1940s, collapsed. Increasingly, the socialist project was conflated with the Soviet Union and thereby judged in terms of Stalin's oppressive use of the Party as well as his foreign politics, especially his expansionist moves during and after the war. In the context of the Cold War it became possible for the New York intellectuals to refer to Communism as 'Red Fascism.'[13] As Pells observed, 'For all their intellectual acrobatics, and their feelings of being newcomers dependent more on their wit than on their familial roots in America, the contributors to *Commentary* and *Partisan Review* evolved during the postwar years into articulate exponents of the new orthodoxy on foreign affairs.'[14]

This formulation would be equally appropriate for Horkheimer and Adorno. When they returned to Germany in 1949 and reopened the Institute, the spirit of the Cold War was part of their baggage. Furthermore, they shared with the younger generation of radical American intellectuals a skeptical, if not negative, attitude toward the socialist project of the 1930s. Their commitment to democracy no longer included an allegiance to a socialist revolution. Instead, they stressed the Western democratic tradition and focused their polemic on East European Communism. The parallel can be traced back to the early 1940s, when Adorno and Horkheimer had worked out the dialectic of instrumental reason that left no room for a socialist revolution.[15] It is important to remember that during the later 1940s the agenda of the *Partisan Review* radicals and Adorno's position were not far apart.

Adorno and Horkheimer took part also in the shift from an outright political critique to cultural criticism, a shift with significant political implications.[16] In fact, Adorno's work of the 1940s anticipated this change, since he was less involved in the American political discourse. Furthermore, since he did not participate in the war effort, his critique of America took the form of cultural criticism, beginning with his early essay on jazz, followed by *Minima Moralia* and *Dialectic of Enlightenment.* The concept of the culture industry was, at least in part, Adorno's critique of FDR's New Deal. Unlike American intellectuals of the 1930s and early 1940s, Adorno had no memory of the Great Depression in the United States; for him, as a refugee from Nazi Germany, the workers were not poor but docile. The position of Adorno and the Frankfurt School became viable in America only after the memory of the Depression had receded—that is, during the late 1940s and early 1950s. Looking back, the former radical Trotskyist

Seymour Lipset summarized the new situation: 'Since domestic politics, even liberal and socialist politics, can no longer serve as the arena for serious criticism from the left, many intellectuals have turned from a basic concern with the political and economic systems to criticism of other sections of the basic culture of American society.'[17]

The new Pax Americana, the combination of democracy and advanced capitalism, called for a different approach. In the writings of Macdonald, Daniel Boorstin, Mary McCarthy, and David Riesman, the focus of criticism shifted from the political to the social and cultural. For the affluent society with its new suburban middle class, the traditional tools of liberal and Marxist theory appeared to be less effective than formerly. In particular, the impact of the new media (radio, film, television) resisted traditional analysis.[18] Radical left cultural criticism of the 1950s, articulated in the writings of Macdonald, Bell, Clement Greenberg, and Paul Goodman, paralleled the work of Adorno, particularly in its concern about traditional high culture and literature. As a result of this critique, their commitment to mass democracy became more ambivalent, since the undeniable greater political equality of the citizen was subverted by the emergence of 'mass man,' the consumer of cultural goods.

As we have seen, Adorno's intellectual position in the United States during the 1940s was less isolated than some scholars have assumed. In several respects his own development (within the Frankfurt School) and that of intellectuals of the American left show similarities—despite the fact that Adorno probably knew little about the United States when he arrived in 1938. He was unfamiliar with its history and not well informed about its political system. Initially, as a result, he found it difficult to follow and assess the ongoing political and social debates. The transformation of the presidency under FDR, for example, and the increased power of the central bureaucracy during the war years were not immediately visible to an observer for whom the fascist state was the immediate threat. Furthermore, we must keep in mind that Adorno, like fellow German émigrés such as Thomas Mann, Bertholt Brecht, and Lion Feuchtwanger, came with a Eurocentric view of a world in which North America was expected to play a supplementary role. What, then, did Adorno see of the United States? How could he incorporate his experience into his own philosophical 'system'? And how did he respond to this unfamiliar civilization for which numerous European stereotypes were available? Perhaps even more important, what did he *not* see? What remained beyond his horizon?

All the accounts we have of Adorno's experience in America, including his own testimony, point to a traumatic experience. He was, perhaps, psychologically even less prepared for exile than other members of the Frankfurt School. In his own account, written after his return to Germany, a sense of alienation is unmistakable. It ranges from the structure of research institutes to the formation of the American landscape, from greeting rituals to cultural entertainment. Adorno's own sense of not belonging clearly reinforced his perception of the reified nature of American society and the isolated status of the individual. To this marginalized observer, America appeared to be a country without tradition, a modern, completely rationalized society that aggressively celebrated its own modernity by rejecting its European past. Since Adorno spent most of his American years in southern California and never visited New England or the South, a notion of an older, *premodern* American tradition was not part of his personal experience. Moreover, his professional contacts in the East, where he was involved in a radio research project, and his links to Hollywood could only reinforce the image of a radically modern society dominated by the new mass media. For this reason, his analysis of the culture industry emphasized the 'American' nature of those phenomena, making Hollywood the center of the new cultural configuration. What mattered for Adorno was the contrast with traditional European high culture and the European avant-garde. In other words, his view of North America was strongly informed by a set of oppositions aligned in such a way that American mass culture, advanced capitalism, and technology stood against European high culture, a premodern social structure, and a traditional life-world. At least, this is the first impression one gets from Adorno's observations; a closer analysis will reveal how much more complex and involved his argument actually is.

What is striking in Adorno's writings of the 1940s, however, is his distance from the contemporary political configuration and American history. The numerous observations about North America in **Minima Moralia** [hereafter abbreviated as **MM**] do not examine the development of the United States or touch on political problems. From Adorno's writings it would be difficult to get a clear sense of racial problems or the social tensions of the 1930s to which Roosevelt's New Deal responded. Rural and small-town America too is almost invisible in Adorno's account; where it occasionally appears, it is represented as a strange and alienating landscape:

> The shortcoming of the American landscape is not so much, as romantic illusion would have it, the absence of historical memories, as that it bears no traces of the human hand. This applies not only to the lack of arable land, the uncultivated woods often no higher than scrub, but above all to the roads. These are always inserted directly in the landscape, and the more impressively smooth and broad they are, the more unrelated and violent their gleaming track appears against its wild, overgrown surroundings. They are expressionless. Just as they know no marks of foot or wheel, no soft paths along their edges as a transition to the vegetation, no trails leading off into the valley, so they are without the mild, soothing, unangular quality of things that have felt the touch of hands or their immediate implements. It is as if no-one had ever passed their hand over the landscape's hair. It is uncomforted and comfortless. And it is perceived in a corresponding way. For what the hurrying eye has seen merely from the car it cannot retain, and the vanishing landscape leaves no more traces behind than it bears upon itself.

> (**MM** 48; GS 4:53-54)

Yet this negative verdict is contrasted with another comment that reveals Adorno's awe: 'Beauty of the American landscape: that even the smallest of its segments is inscribed, as its expression, with the immensity of the whole country' (**MM** 49; GS 4:54). In either case, the formulation articulates impressions and reflections. It is precisely this highly subjective element, the self-reflexive nature of the text, that gives Adorno's observations significance. The writer sees himself as an uprooted European intellectual who had to surrender his past when he was admitted to the United States. Not only are his observations fragmentary; his own subjectivity is fragmented, damaged. Accordingly, the force of his assessment of America in **Minima Moralia** results precisely from its lack of contextualization, its lack of 'understanding' the American way of life.

This comes out most clearly in Adorno's commentary on social situations and customs. His remarks tend to focus on particular moments, on incidents that the native American would treat as 'natural' and self-evident—rituals such as greeting another person, or the memo format instead of the formal letter in interoffice correspondence (**MM** 41; GS 4:45). Under Adorno's gaze the life-world of California crystallizes in the shape of allegories, strange habits and conventions that the outsider must learn to decipher. In the following example he remarks about the rules of the cocktail party that

> the taboo on talking shop and the inability to talk to each other are in reality the same thing. Because everything is business, the latter is unmentionable like rope in a hanged man's home. Behind the pseudo-democratic dismantling of ceremony, of old-fashioned courtesy, of the useless conversation suspected, not even unjustly, of being idle gossip, behind the seeming clarification and transparency of human relations that no longer admit anything undefined, naked brutality is ushered in.

> (**MM** 41-42; **GS** 4:46)

To this he adds:

> The direct statement without divagations, hesitations or reflections, that gives the other the facts full in the face, already has the form and timbre of the command issued under Fascism by the dumb to the silent. Matter-of-factness between people, doing away with all ideological ornamentation between them, has already itself become an ideology for treating people as things.

> (**MM** 42; **GS** 4:46)

In this reading, Adorno connects a seemingly harmless social convention in America with a general trend toward an 'objectivication' that ultimately results in fascism. Similarly, his observations about American hotels and motels, their cold but proper functionalism, quickly turns into a sharp critique of modern civilization—far beyond the immediate American context (**MM** 116-18; **GS** 4:130-31).

Whenever Adorno touches a detail, it becomes a frozen image, an emblem to be interrogated by the pondering mind. He sees an uninhabitable life-world where human beings have lost their individuality and derive their transitory happiness from filling out the role that society has assigned to them. Typical in this respect is his commentary on IQ tests as a quintessential reification of the mind: 'The socialization of mind keeps it boxed in, isolated in a glass case, as long as society is itself imprisoned. As thought earlier internalized the duties exacted from without, today it has assimilated to itself its integration into the surrounding apparatus, and is thus condemned even before the economic and political verdicts on it come fully into force' (*MM* 197; *GS* 4:222). Adorno's gaze focuses on the modern character of America, its preference for technical solutions and its flair for social engineering. This perspective blends out history: for Adorno, even the American landscape lacks history; as unmediated nature it remains alien to the observing critic.

One would expect this uncomfortable distance to reinforce his European allegiance, provoke a positive stress on European high culture. Although there are nostalgic moments in *Minima Moralia,* Adorno resists this attitude for the most part, emphasizing instead the growing similarities between the continents. German high culture, he argues, was not destroyed by the National Socialists in 1933; rather, its demise had occurred already during the 1920s. Consequently, he does not share the hope of many émigrés that German culture can simply be rebuilt after the war. What he expects is a configuration much closer to American mass culture than to nineteenth-century European high culture, and these anticipated similarities distress him more than the life-style of Hollywood. The growing similarities frighten him even more in another respect: the warfare in Europe increasingly diminishes the difference between the fighting parties. The mass destruction of German cities caused by Allied air raids repeats the German air raids on Rotterdam and Coventry. Again, Adorno's reflection takes its cues from the isolated document, the newsreel, rather than the contextualized, ideological version in the print media. During the early 1940s he felt that the American defense of democracy did not coincide with an improvement of democracy; hence, he was less inclined than Leo Lowenthal or Herbert Marcuse to support the war effort.

The representation of the United States in *Minima Moralia* consists of many small, heterogeneous fragments that occasionally contradict one another; Adorno refrains from a synthetic definition. Still, the particular details selected reflect a bias: they are signifiers for the most advanced capitalist society. Adorno's interest in North America, one might argue, was limited to what he perceived as relentless modernity bordering on self-destruction. It is important to note that like the other members of the Frankfurt School, he insisted on the link between capitalism, modernity, and the avant-garde. Hence, the more analytical approach to American society that we find in *Dialectic of Enlightenment* foregrounds this connection more than does *Minima Moralia.* The chapter on the culture industry, in particular, forcefully argues that American mass culture owes its existence as well as its function to organized capitalism. Adorno and Horkheimer were convinced that the transition from liberal to organized capitalism would result in a systematic reorganization of the cultural system, based on the principles of mass production. Just as Karl Marx had focused on England as the most economically advanced society of the nineteenth century, Adorno and Horkheimer decided to concentrate on the United States as the most advanced Western society of this century. Clearly, in *Dialectic of Enlightenment,* they are more concerned with structures than with particular moments, more with a general process (the dialectical history of reason) than with contrasts between Europe and America. When they do stress the contrast, it is usually within a temporal frame in which the United States marks the most advanced capitalist society. Yet even this scheme does not do justice to the complex configuration because, as we will see, fascist Germany appears in this context as the alternative version of modernity. For Adorno and Horkheimer, an analysis of the American society included, explicitly or implicitly, an analysis of modern Germany, since they saw both the political system of the National Socialists and the organization of culture in North America as aspects of the same historical dialectic of reason.

In fact, it was the rise of fascism in Germany that forced the members of the Frankfurt School to rethink received ideas about the development of modern industrial capitalism. Their early work during the 1930s remained more closely linked to the orthodox paradigm of Marxism, in which fascism had its place as the ultimate response of monopoly capitalism to severe economic crises, but during the early 1940s Franz Neumann, Otto Kirchheimer, Pollock, and Horkheimer advanced revised theories that could better account for the actual relationship between the fascist state and the capitalist economy. For Adorno, Pollock's theory of state capitalism was more important than Neumann's analysis in *Behemoth* or Kirchheimer's essays.[19] Adorno and Horkheimer followed Pollock's interpretation that state capitalism in Nazi Germany reversed the traditional causal connection between the political system and the economy. The priority of the economy vanishes. This means that the state has taken over the basic functions of capitalist enterprise. As Dubiel writes: 'The market, as an indirect instrument coordinating supply and demand, is replaced by a system of direct planning. This planning system rests in the hands of a powerful bureaucracy, itself the product of a fusion of state bureaucracy and top industrial management. The total economic process takes place within the framework of a general plan with guidelines for production, distribution, consumption, savings, and investments.'[20]

What made Pollock's theory significant for Adorno and Horkheimer was its drive toward a more general theory of advanced Western societies and its political applicability to, among other countries, the United States.[21] In *Dialectic of Enlightenment* Pollock has an unacknowledged presence, at least in the sense that his theory replaces more traditional Marxist notions about the structure of Nazi Germany, as well as that of the United States under the

New Deal. The potentially common ground is the priority of politics over economics in the form of a governmental apparatus designed to centralize all efforts. Under the impact of Pollock's theory, traditional economic analysis becomes unnecessary.

The vantage point of Adorno and Horkheimer's analysis—namely, the concern with German fascism—explains the contrast between their understanding of the American society and the accounts of contemporary American historians and sociologists who tended to view their own society in terms of its internal development. This is not to say, however, that the Americans never came to similar conclusions. C. Wright Mills's assessment of the contemporary American middle class in *White Collar,* for example, describes the transition from the nineteenth-century middle class to the new society of the 1930s and 1940s in terms that are compatible with Adorno's critique. Yet his argument focuses almost exclusively on the United States, with no more than occasional references to the work of Arcadius Gurland, Kirchheimer, and Neumann. The parallels are not worked out in detail.[22]

Mills's emphasis was not motivated by patriotism; rather, it was determined by his focus on the political economy. The pioneering work of Robert and Helen Lynd has a different focus. In *Middletown* (1929) and *Middletown in Transition* (1937), they provide a detailed social map of a midwestern town from the 1890s to the 1930s. Their mostly descriptive approach avoids open political criticism, foregrounding instead the cultural matrix of the town. The Lynds share with Mills a preference for concrete details (basic empirical research) and a narrow focus, but the result is a picture with a different emphasis. Moreover, the American society of the 1920s, which the Lynds contrast with that of the late nineteenth century, seems far removed from the American society of the 1940s as it is represented in **Minima Moralia.** Even in *Middletown in Transition,* which deals with the Depression years, traditional social institutions appear to be in place. The reader hardly gets the impression of a radical qualitative change that would fundamentally question democracy in America.

Robert and Helen Lynd describe a modern, differentiated society but clearly not a mass society where the individual has become faceless and open to far-reaching manipulation. What the Lynds report is an attempt of the people in Middletown to cope with the problems of the Depression by reinforcing their traditional value system rather than by addressing the problems in a radical manner. Neither is the Lynds' own methodology radical; their 'thick description' affirms the self-understanding of the American society. It is noteworthy that for them the uprooting of American society, which Adorno took for granted in 1944, had hardly begun. The 1930s appear as a period of severe economic and social problems, but not as a period completely determined by alienation.

It is C. Wright Mills who, in *White Collar* (1951), redefines American modernity in Adornian terms: 'Estranged from community and society in a context of distrust and manipulation; alienated from work and, on the personality market, from self; expropriated of individual rationality, and politically apathetic—these are the new little people, the unwilling vanguard of modern society.'[23] By 1951, radical American sociology, using a model of class conflict, was reaching conclusions similar to those of Adorno and Horkheimer. For Mills the world of the small entrepreneur was a thing of the past, superseded by economic concentration and major transformation in property. His own narrative of American social history remains more concrete than Adorno's, though it is certainly less detailed than the Lynds' account. The difference is not just a matter of method and style; rather, particularly between Adorno and Mills, it is a difference in perception. Under Adorno's gaze the phenomena lose their particular context. The American society of the 1930s and 1940s appears to be decades ahead of itself. Rather than an analysis of the 1940s, Adorno's writings read more like a commentary on the 1960s and 1970s: that is, on the strains and the contradictions of the Pax Americana during the Vietnam War, when the convergence of organized capitalism and state power became much more problematic for American citizens. These were also, of course, the years of Critical Theory's greatest impact in the United States, although that impact occurred more through the work of Herbert Marcuse than through that of Adorno, who had become a rather marginal figure in America after his return to Germany.

Still, Critical Theory maintained a limited visibility in the United States during the 1950s. For anyone who had developed a highly critical assessment of contemporary America, as Mills had done, for instance, the question of mass culture could not be answered by celebrating the general access to culture as a democratic force. In the American debate on the politics of culture during the late 1940s and 1950s, Adorno had a (frequently unacknowledged) presence. In a prosperous postwar America, where traditional class struggles had become almost invisible, Adorno's analysis of mass-produced culture became more important than in 1944. As Richard Pells has argued, a significant shift in focus after the 1948 election brought the political implications of cultural issues into the foreground: 'In a wealthy society, overt ideological and social quarrels rarely erupted; class antagonism remained muted; the real differences of life were minimized or ignored in the electoral campaigns.'[24] Frustrations and unresolved conflicts had to be addressed in a different way by writers such as Dwight Macdonald, Daniel Bell, Paul Goodman, Mary McCarthy, and David Riesman.[25] Now intellectuals dissatisfied with the status quo tended to articulate their opposition in terms of subversion rather than overt radicalism. The focus became the American dream that failed precisely because it had come true. In this context the image of American society underwent an important change. Clearly, the position of Bell and Mills and Macdonald and Boorstin was much closer to Adorno's conception than to that of Robert and Helen Lynd. For American critics the 'culture industry' became real, even if the term was not used.

Macdonald's influential essay 'Masscult & Midcult' (first published in *Politics* in 1944 under the title 'A Theory of Popular Culture,' then rewritten and republished in 1953) explicitly refers to Adorno's essay **'On Popular Music'** without necessarily sharing Adorno's theoretical foundations. What Macdonald did share with Adorno was a strong sense of the danger of mass culture, a threat not limited to artistic and aesthetic considerations. For Macdonald, mass culture is defined by its impersonality and its lack of standards.[26] Its products are the result of literary mass production based on strictly regulated conventions. He answers the obvious question as to why it exists in the first place by referring to David Riesman's 'lonely crowd' and the concept of 'mass man,' the atomized individual. The parallel with Frankfurt School thought is hard to overlook, yet by no means are either the emphases or the theoretical positions identical. For one thing, Macdonald maintains a much more positive view of traditional high culture than Adorno ever did. When he offers a scathing critique of mass culture, he does not question the legitimacy of high culture, which appears to have transhistorical value. Hence, his sharp attack on Edward Shils, the social scientist who defended popular culture, concerns only the function of mass culture, leaving the function of high culture untouched. Macdonald's disagreement with the defenders of popular culture comes out in his insistence on the manipulative character of mass culture, which, as a debased form of high culture, he sees as 'becoming an instrument of domination.'[27]

It was precisely this point that separated *Dialectic of Enlightenment* from traditional *Kulturkritik* (cultural criticism) and its emphasis on the literary canon. Macdonald extends his criticism to middlebrow culture—the slick but decent and polished version of high culture—without, however, working out the connection between 'mass cult' and 'midcult' systematically. As a result, he tends to revert to cultural criticism, showing a preference for a stable high culture, although he admits that this solution is less than democratic.[28] Looking at the wasteland of postwar American culture, he feels, as he states in the preface to *Against the American Grain,* 'that a people which loses contact with its past becomes culturally psychotic.'[29] In his view, the American cultural tradition rooted in the New England of the seventeenth and eighteenth centuries had been compromised by waves of immigrants from non-English-speaking countries who wanted easy access to the culture of their new homeland.[30]

In the heated debate of the 1950s over the value of modern mass culture in America, Adorno and the Frankfurt School did not play a central role; still, their arguments were picked up and utilized by the 'cultural' camp, while their opponents—mostly social scientists—branded the defense of high culture elitist and ultimately undemocratic. Both Edward Shils—whom Macdonald singled out as the

Pangloss of the new enlightenment—and Seymour Lipset argued that mass culture was an inevitable and ultimately desirable feature of modern democracies, an important part of enlightenment and modernization. In their view, the expanded cultural market would not only proliferate 'bad' culture but also bring serious literature and music to a large segment of the population. Even Clement Greenberg, not known for his admiration of mass culture, felt that the media provided 'some sort of enlightenment' for the masses.'[31] From this perspective, the critique of mass culture smacked of conservatism, since it defended a cultural formation that excluded the majority of the population. Accordingly, intellectuals such as Paul Goodman, Daniel Boorstin, and Greenberg, who decried the corruption of high culture and the rise of the new media, seemed to misread the logic of modern history.

One aspect of Adorno's assessment of North America has to be stressed: his view that the tendency of modern mass societies is toward authoritarian and ultimately totalitarian structures. The definition of the mass as a passive body of manipulable people allows him to connect the fascist society in Germany and the consumer society in America. This link becomes especially apparent when he discusses American mass culture in *Dialectic of Enlightenment.* The chapter on the culture industry presents a two-pronged argument for Adorno's thesis that under advanced capitalism, mass democracies reorganize culture in such a way that older traditions of high culture and entertainment become completely integrated. On the one hand, he develops a psychoanalytical theory of reception, focusing on the moment of regression in the mass reception of art. On the other hand, he advances economic and institutional arguments to demonstrate the determination of mass culture by basic economic factors, such as its dependence on certain segments of the industry.

In *Dialectic of Enlightenment* this argument becomes part of the larger thesis that advanced monopoly capitalism has not only reorganized the workplace but also restructured leisure time in order to extend its grip over the working masses. In other words, for Adorno, mass culture in America is not simply a new phase of culture—for example, a more democratic version of culture—but, specifically, the result of a thorough restructuring of the cultural sphere by the industry that controls the newest media: radio and film. These media cannot have a liberating function, he argues, because their structure assumes complete control by the owner and a passive audience. Thus they are perfect instruments for fascist propaganda but, in Adorno's mind, unsuitable for democracy. For this reason, he disagrees with Walter Benjamin's position that the cinema might have a liberating function for the modern masses.

On the basis of the culture industry chapter, one might come to the conclusion that Adorno's response to America can be defined only in negative terms. It is important to note, however, that he does not regard the culture industry by any means as an exclusively American phenomenon. He attempts to explore the organization of culture in advanced industrial societies generally; for this reason, the

German example is as significant for him as the American one. The transition from Weimar culture to fascist mass culture provides the focal point for his analysis. His concern is the defeat of the individual (of liberal societies) under the impact of monopoly capitalism: 'One has only to become aware of one's own nothingness, only to recognize defeat and one is one with it all. Society is full of desperate people and therefore a prey to rackets' (*DE* 153; *GS* 3:176). This insight applies not only to the Weimar entertainment industry but also to the highbrow novels of Alfred Döblin and Hans Fallada. For Adorno, Weimar culture was on the road to the fascist leader long before he actually entered the political arena; consequently, Adorno does not expect a restoration of German high culture after the defeat of the Nazis, since its existence before 1933 was largely an ideological construct. Adorno realizes that the opposition of Germany (as part of Europe) versus America is problematic, yet the analysis of the culture industry invokes this opposition as a means of contrasting the conception of culture in the nineteenth century with its reorganization under advanced capitalism. His cultural map is meant to signify the transition from the bourgeois individual to the fascist personality *or* the pseudo-individuality of the Hollywood star.

During the 1940s Adorno's perception of the United States emphasized the modern nature of its society, a social structure characterized by urban concentration and human alienation. Of course, he recognized the democratic nature of the political system, but, as can be gleaned from *Minima Moralia,* this knowledge did not play a major role in his evaluation of the country. Although he and Horkheimer certainly wished for the defeat of Nazi Germany, Adorno was not inclined to identify with the aims and strategies of the Allies. In this respect he was more isolated during the war years than those members of the Frankfurt School (Marcuse, Lowenthal) who served the American government. It was only after his return to Germany in 1949 that the matter of the political system became more central to Adorno's view of America. His involvement with the project of German reeducation as a professor of philosophy at the University of Frankfurt significantly changed his evaluation of American democracy. To a certain degree this reorientation is reflected in the 1968 essay **'Scientific Experiences of a European Scholar in America,'** which stresses, much more than one would expect from previous statements, his positive response to American civilization. Although he leaves no doubt about his European cultural allegiance and his unwillingness to develop an 'American' personality, he does point to a strand of American history with which he could identify—the Enlightenment tradition: 'The spirit of enlightenment also in relation to cultural problems, in the American intellectual climate a matter of course, had the greatest attraction for me.'[32] For Adorno, the American Enlightenment (unlike German culture) could manifest itself either as reified modern positivism (the strand that he critiqued in *Dialectic of Enlightenment*) or as a will to human emancipation through democratic forms—for example, through research projects involving groups of social scientists.

In this respect, the project on the 'authoritarian personality' in which Adorno participated during the 1940s, figures as a prominent example of politically committed social research within the American academy.[33] Confronting and analyzing racial prejudice, especially anti-Semitism, remained a crucial task for Adorno after he returned home. When he addressed this question in Germany, he frequently drew on the authoritarian personality project as a model of theory-oriented empirical research coming out of a specifically American cultural and intellectual climate. In 1968 he remarked: 'This kind of cooperation in a democratic spirit that does not get bogged down in formal political procedures and extends into all details of planning and execution, I found to be not only extremely enjoyable but also the most fruitful thing that I became acquainted with in America, in contrast to the academic tradition in Europe.'[34] A comparison with *Minima Moralia* makes it quite apparent that this statement articulates Adorno's reorientation during the 1950s and 1960s rather than his attitude during the 1940s. Looking at postwar Germany, where authoritarian and fascist patterns of thought had by no means automatically vanished in 1945, he now stresses the need for democratic reorganization of research and therefore favors an 'American' model.

The pro-American reorientation of Adorno and Horkheimer was, as we have seen, motivated by the confrontation with postwar Germany. There were both institutional and ideological reasons for this attitude. Horkheimer's desire to move the Institute back to Germany could be carried out only with the help of sympathetic forces in Frankfurt, especially at the university. But the university administration, as Rolf Wiggershaus has shown, was not particularly eager to reinstate the émigrés.[35] Under these circumstances, Horkheimer and Adorno decided to play the 'American' card, to use their United States citizenship along with their American connections. In particular, they shared the American assessment of the power relation between the two countries, an assessment in which the new Federal Republic was viewed as a 'colony' with little separate cultural and political identity. The power of the United States over West Germany, they thought, would help the Frankfurt School to reestablish itself in Frankfurt.

The American connection became important for Adorno's ideological position as well. The political division of Germany in 1949, resulting from the Cold War, raised the latent anti-Communist bias of the Western zones to the level of a state ideology. Under these circumstances, a pro-socialist position, not to mention a pro-Marxist point of view, could become a political liability. Hence, Adorno was very concerned about an essay by Max Bense in which the Frankfurt School was mentioned together with the work of Georg Lukács and Ernst Bloch; he tried to prevent its publication, arguing that the position of the Institute was clearly opposed to that of Lukács and Bloch, who were seen as ideologues of the East.[36] In 1949 this opposition was apparently more important for Adorno than the common theoretical heritage.[37] His 1958 polemical essay **'Reconciliation under Duress'** (*GS* 11:251-80) extended his anti-Communist bias to the field of literary theory by attacking Lukácsian reflection theory.

This stance was probably motivated by two concerns: first, Adorno and Horkheimer had already distanced themselves from their own orthodox socialist position of the early 1940s; second, the new West German society made anti-Communism almost a requirement for its citizens. The postwar definition of democracy included the stance against Communism; hence, a differentiated response to the 'threat' of Communism became difficult, to say the least. Although Adorno and Horkheimer continued to make use of core elements of Marxist theory, they now tended to avoid the rhetoric of dialectical materialism.[38] Needless to say, anti-Communism was also one of the effective ideological links between the United States and the Federal Republic of Germany. Although Adorno could not possibly support the presence of older right-wing ideologies in the Federal Republic, he and Horkheimer could and did participate in the new consensus. Their own theoretical development during the 1940s, which incidentally paralleled the development of many American intellectuals on the left, had prepared them for this position and moved them more to the center in the new West German system than they ever had been in the Weimar Republic. Still, although they shared certain political assumptions of the Konrad Adenauer era, they remained highly critical observers of the postwar years.

Notes

1. The most complete account of Adorno's life and reception in the United States is to be found in Jay, 'Adorno in America,' 120-40.

2. Andreas Huyssen, 'Adorno in Reverse: From Hollywood to Richard Wagner,' in *After the Great Divide*, 16-43.

3. For the reaction of Trotsky and his group, see Alan M. Wald, *The New York Intellectuals: The Rise and Decline of the Anti-Stalinist Left from the 1930s to the 1980s* (Chapel Hill: University of North Carolina Press, 1987), 128-38.

4. Richard H. Pells, *The Liberal Mind in a Conservative Age* (New York: Harper & Row, 1985), 76f. Though Pells's assessment is generally correct, he tends to downplay the resistance of the radical anti-Stalinist left to mainstream liberalism and the Democrats. During the early 1940s it was not only James P. Cannon, Max Schachtman, and the Trotskyist radicals who defended a strictly revolutionary Marxist position, attacking the Stalinists from the left, but also intellectuals such as Sidney Hook, Irving Howe, and Dwight Macdonald, who later distanced themselves from their revolutionary past and insisted on a Marxist, antiliberal position during World War II. See Wald, *The New York Intellectuals*, 193-96, 199-210.

5. Helmut Dubiel, *Theory and Politics: Studies in the Development of Critical Theory*, trans. Benjamin

Gregg (Cambridge: MIT Press, 1985). The exception was Herbert Marcuse, who, it seems, remained more faithful to the earlier program. See Douglas Kellner, *Herbert Marcuse and the Crisis of Marxism* (Berkeley: University of California Press, 1984).

6. Although Sidney Hook, stressing the imperialist character of the impending war, argued during the 1930s that it should not be defended in terms of an opposition between democratic and fascist regimes, during the 1940s the New York intellectuals came out in favor of the war against fascism. See Wald, *The New York Intellectuals*, 193-99.

7. Pells, *The Liberal Mind*, 18.

8. For this reason Macdonald, together with the editors of *Partisan Review*, originally opposed the war. After the Hitler-Stalin Pact he joined the Socialist Workers Party and defended its pro-war stance, but he continued to define himself as an anti-Stalinist revolutionary struggling for socialism within the United States. See Wald, *The New York Intellectuals*, 199-207.

9. See Pells, *The Liberal Mind*, 21-23.

10. During the 1930s the position of Sidney Hook in *Towards the Understanding of Karl Marx* (1933) and of Max Eastman paralleled that of the early Lukács in *History and Class-Consciousness*; they used Lukácsian arguments to attack the Stalinist orthodoxy. See Wald, *The New York Intellectuals*, 118-27. The issue of the proletariat as the revolutionary agent was still alive during the early 1940s.

11. By and large, the editors of the liberal *New Republic* were pleased by developments in 1944-45. The journal gave public support to FDR's position in Yalta and Potsdam. The journal *Common Sense*, on the other hand, with its anti-Stalinist agenda, was disappointed to see a development in Europe that did not encourage radical democracy. See William O'Neill, *A Better World: Stalinism and the American Intellectuals* (New Brunswick NJ: Transaction, 1990), 110-15.

12. Hannah Arendt, *The Origins of Totalitarianism* (1951; New York: World, 1958).

13. See Wald, *The New York Intellectuals*, 268.

14. Pells, *The Liberal Mind*, 75. As Irving Howe points out in his memoirs, *Partisan Review* shifted its position after the war by moving away from Marxism altogether, becoming fascinated instead by French writers such as Sartre and Camus. Kafka replaced Trotsky. See Irving Howe, *A Margin of Hope: An Intellectual Autobiography* (San Diego: Harcourt Brace Jovanovich, 1982), 130-31, 143. The Waldorf Conference of 1949 was, in Howe's words, 'perhaps the last major effort of American Stalinism to reestablish itself as a cultural force in this country' (156). The anti-Stalinist intellectuals, though not effective in their opposition at that conference, had a much greater impact in later years. Also see O'Neill, *A Better World*, 143-68.

15. At the same time, James Burnham, in *The Managerial Revolution* (1941) and *The Machiavellians* (1943), undercut the conventional distinction between democratic and fascist states, insisting on the similarities between the New Deal in America, Nazi Germany, and the Soviet Union. After 1945 Burnham joined the left revisionists and focused his attack on Stalinist Russia as the embodiment of an anti-democratic system. It should be noted that Burnham's position was rather eccentric during the earlier 1940s, as Macdonald's and William Phillips's critiques make clear; Phillips, especially, denied the contention that Stalinism was the logical extension of Marxism. See Wald, *The New York Intellectuals,* 280-82.

16. Another important line of criticism in the work of Adorno concerned psychological patterns and mental structures; see, e.g., the collective project of Theodor Adorno with Else Frenkel-Brunswick, Daniel J. Levinson, and R. Nevitt Sanford *The Authoritarian Personality* (New York: Harper & Row, 1950).

17. Seymour Martin Lipset, *Political Man: The Social Bases of Politics* (Garden City NY: Doubleday, 1960), 445. Under these conditions the work of the Frankfurt School could find a better reception among American left intellectuals. Thus Adorno claimed that Riesman failed to acknowledge the impact of Critical Theory in his work.

18. American critics such as Lewis Mumford, Gordon Allport, and Harold Lasswell had begun to examine the effects of the mass media during the 1930s. Pells allows that the Frankfurt School contributed to this effort but overlooks the difference in attitude. Adorno clearly rejected the neutral empirical method of the new radio research; he was closer to such critics as Macdonald and Clement Greenberg, who foregrounded the broader cultural and social ramifications of a culture based on mass media.

19. For the theory of state capitalism, see Friedrich Pollock, 'State Capitalism: Its Possibilities and Limitations,' in Arato and Gebhardt, *The Essential Frankfurt School Reader,* 71-94.

20. Dubiel, *Theory and Politics,* 79.

21. See also Moishe Postone and Barbara Brick, 'Critical Theory and Political Economy,' in *On Max Horkheimer: New Perspectives,* ed. Seyla Benhabib et al. (Cambridge: MIT Press, 1993), 215-96.

22. For an analysis of Mills's relationship to the Institute, see Martin Jay, 'The Jews and the Frankfurt School: Critical Theory's Analysis of Anti-Semitism,' in *Permanent Exiles,* 46.

23. C. Wright Mills, Introduction to *White Collar* (New York: Oxford University Press, 1956), xviii.

24. Pells, *The Liberal Mind,* 185. Also see O'Neill, *A Better World,* on the importance of the Henry Wallace campaign for the cause of the progressionists (142-60) and the Korean War as the final turning-point for the majority of American radicals (202-11).

25. For a more detailed account of this transition, see Wald, *The New York Intellectuals,* 226-63. Wald defines the transformation in terms of an ideological shift from an openly political understanding of literature to a more individual 'neoliberalist position' in writers such as Mary McCarthy and Edmund Wilson.

26. Dwight Macdonald, *Against the American Grain* (New York: Random House, 1962), 7; Adorno, 'On Popular Music,' *Studies in Philosophy and Social Sciences* 9 (1941): 17-48.

27. Macdonald, *Against the American Grain,* 14; David Riesman, *The Lonely Crowd: A Study of the Changing American Character* (New Haven: Yale University Press, 1950).

28. Macdonald, *Against the American Grain,* 73.

29. Macdonald, *Against the American Grain,* xii.

30. In certain respects the position of Clement Greenberg, the influential modernist art critic, is even closer to Adorno's, since he does acknowledge the historical significance of the avant-garde for the evaluation of art. In 'Avant-Garde and Kitsch' (first published in *Partisan Review* 1946: rpt. in *Mass Culture,* ed. Bernard Rosenberg and David Manning White [New York: Free Press, 1957], 98-107). Greenberg uses a formalist and historical model to demonstrate the need for artistic change. The avant-garde appears as the historically needed opposition to bourgeois culture. Emphasizing the formal aspect of modern art, Greenberg insists, like Adorno, on the evolution of the aesthetic material: the absolute poem or painting is (historically) moving. Also, his definition of kitsch—i.e., mass culture—and its relationship to modern art is fairly close to Adorno's understanding of the culture industry: 'Kitsch is mechanical and operates by formulas. . . . Kitsch changes according to style, but remains always the same' (102). Greenberg argues that kitsch is part of a modern production system and relies on an already established cultural system whose traditions it exploits. Given the industrial character of kitsch, it is international and thereby inauthentic. Unlike Adorno and more in agreement with Macdonald, Greenberg assumes a stable cultural and artistic tradition that can serve as a foil to frame mass culture, but, more than Adorno does, he points to the close connection between high culture and political power when he discusses premodern art.

31. Clement Greenberg, 'The Plight of our Culture,' *Commentary* 15 (June 1953): 566.

32. Adorno, 'Scientific Experiences of a European Scholar in America,' in *The Intellectual Migration: Europe and America, 1930-1960,* ed. Donald Fleming and Bernard Bailyn (Cambridge: Harvard University Press, 1969), 339; GS 10 (2): 702-38.

33. Adorno et al., *The Authoritarian Personality.*

34. Adorno, 'Scientific Experiences of a European Scholar in America,' 358.

35. Wiggershaus, *Die Frankfurter Schule,* 452 f.

36. Wiggershaus, *Die Frankfurter Schule,* 450-51.

37. In this context it is crucial to distinguish an anti-Stalinist from an anti-Communist stance. Whereas the former position allows for a variety of approaches to the issue of Marxist theory (one could agree with Marx against Stalin, or be critical of Stalinism as a strand of Marxist orthodoxy), the latter is predicated on a rigid opposition of two belief systems: Marxist theory as Communism takes on the role of a negative religion that has to be eradicated by the democratic forces in the name of Christian or at least humanist values. Although the Frankfurt School by and large was quite conscious of this distinction, its members did not always clarify their disagreement with vulgar forms of anti-Communism. Yet after its return to Germany the Frankfurt School, like the group around *Partisan Review,* could not sustain its belief in a third position and thus ended up in the liberal establishment of postwar West Germany. Unlike the editors of *Commentary,* however, Adorno did not tolerate the witch-hunts of Senator Joseph McCarthy. See Alexander Bloom, *Prodigal Sons: The New York Intellectuals and Their World* (New York: Oxford University Press, 1986), 209-15.

38. For this reason they disagreed with Herbert Marcuse's 1947 unpublished working paper in which he described the postwar situation in terms of two hostile camps: a neofascist camp led by the United States, and a Communist camp dominated by the Soviet Union. For Marcuse, both camps were antirevolutionary and therefore problematic. What Adorno and Horkheimer objected to was Marcuse's belief that one could rely on classical Marxist theory for an analysis of the postwar configuration. See Wiggershaus, *Die Frankfurter Schule,* 431-33. This disagreement parallels the split within the American left between the Trotskyist progressionists and the revisionists.

Kaspar Maase (essay date 1996)

SOURCE: "A Taste of Honey: Adorno's Reading of American Mass Culture," in *European Readings of American Popular Culture,* edited by John Dean and Jean-Paul Gabilliet, Greenwood Press, 1996, pp. 201-11.

[In the following essay, Maase examines what he sees as misreadings of Adorno's theories on mass culture in America.]

During the 1950s, Max Horkheimer and Theodor Adorno, together with other European emigrants to the United States such as Hannah Arendt, Günter Anders, and Leo Löwenthal, became protagonists of the theoretical critique of contemporary mass culture.[1] Their philosophical study on the "Dialectic of Enlightenment" was first published in German in the United States in a mimeographed version in 1944; slightly revised, it came out as a book in Amsterdam in 1947. Without a doubt, this essay has proved to be one of the most influential intellectual works in the second half of our century. The broad reception, however, inevitably implied that much of the complexity of thought was lost in favor of stereotyped judgments.

The book's chapter on the culture industry has shared the fate of being misread quite often. The authors, so it was perceived, absolutely condemned all manifestations of mass culture by applying the standards of autonomous art and of the good life in the decidedly moral sense of the term. "There can be no good life in the wrong"—Adorno's aphorism of 1944[2] was cited frequently; it served to foster a fairly shallow reading of a highly dialectical critique. In the end, the antifascists' essay on the aporias of progress and enlightenment was adapted to the mainstream of predominantly conservative theories of mass society.[3]

In this discussion I want to recall that Horkheimer and Adorno had a much more differentiated understanding of mass culture, especially of its material and sensuous satisfactions. In a hitherto unpublished lecture, Adorno sketched what he regarded as positive aspects of American culture; his argument culminated in the thesis that the affluence on which mass consumption is based contained an element of realized utopia. The importance of this idea for the necessary reshaping of our way of life will be the topic of a short final consideration.

The Right To Happiness and the Misreadings of Critical Theory

Dialectic of Enlightenment is a very complex text, and it is hard work to reconstruct its intellectual architecture. The book's effect is not in the least due to a pervasive rhetoric leaving the underlying argument in some ambiguity and hermetic darkness. Much could be said about the authors' motives for this style of presenting their critique of the spiritual foundations of modern society,[4] but this discussion is not the place to do so. It is beyond doubt, however, that Horkheimer and Adorno's work in itself contained some starting points for the conservative reading that dominated its reception in the 1950s and 1960s, and that in some regard is still influential today.[5]

Above all, two lines of historical experience can be traced in the *Dialectic of Enlightenment.* First, Horkheimer and Adorno tried to understand how the rise to power and the barbaric crimes of fascism had been possible. Second, their fate as Jewish expatriates made them highly sensitive to any sign of marginalization of autonomous thinking and autonomous individuality—and they perceived an alarmingly high number of such signs in contemporary American society. This was why they took up de Tocqueville's argument that democracy (in America) would facilitate a new kind of dictatorship by means of a most powerful social pressure toward conformism. Their essay pointed out two concrete historical preconditions for such a development. One was a monopolized culture industry subjugating intellectual and artistic production to the laws of making profit, of mass markets and of mass consumption. The other prerequisite was a relatively high standard of living that had made traditional conceptions of impoverishment and class struggle baseless.

The core argument of *Dialectic of Enlightenment* is political and humanist, not cultural. "What matters is not culture as a value . . . a critical self-reflection of enlightenment is necessary, rather, if man shall not be betrayed altogether."[6] Horkheimer and Adorno never intended to denounce the betterment of living conditions of the working class as generating a threat to culture. They violently attacked the total transformation of intellectual creativity into a branch of industry catering to the most comfortable consumption of cultural commodities. They deeply despised the mainstream of slick entertainment, and they joined the critics judging that popular music, pulp literature, and Hollywood movies only served to make people forget about their social situation and to make light of human suffering by the stereotyped way of showing it.[7] But the dark side of mass culture became a cause for being alarmed only within the social and political trend to barbarization. The problem was an absurd state of conditions "turning even the good things in life into elements of disaster" (Horkheimer and Adorno, 1971: 4f). It is only within this very distinct context that we find critical commentary on mass consumption, for instance, the remark that "the powerlessness and tractability of the masses are increasing with the amount of goods apportioned" (4).

Reading a text means adapting it by framing it with the reader's view of life. The intellectual elites on both sides of the Atlantic were no exception to the rule. They perceived the dialectical critique of the Frankfurt School as a well-formulated variation on the traditional theme of "the uneducated masses wasting their time and money on the vulgar satisfactions of the body instead of lifting themselves up to enjoy the longlasting pleasures of the spirit." Pointed catchwords such as that of "the people's wicked love for what is done for them" (Horkheimer and Adorno, 1971: 120) were grist on the mills of those who cynically defended their cultural privilege. By isolating such remarks, Horkheimer and Adorno's critique was watered down and misinterpreted along the lines of the "bread and circuses" stereotype of mass culture and mass society (Brantlinger, 1983).

In their preface to the *Dialectic of Enlightenment,* Horkheimer and Adorno dissociated themselves unmistakably from the contemporary criticism of culture (*Kulturkritik*). Authors such as Huxley, Ortega y Gasset, Jaspers, and others worried that culture as a value in itself was being threatened. Horkheimer and Adorno, however, started from the conviction that it was humankind that had to be safe-

guarded and that to this end it was not the past that had to be conserved but the hopes of the past that had to be redeemed. In their view, outstanding among these hopes was the idea of a state of fulfilled human existence integrating all sensuous joy.[8]

Martin Jay has pointed out that "the claim to happiness has always been a relevant and basic element of Critical Theory" (Jay, 1981: 217; Wiggershaus, 1986: 205-208). Horkheimer's outstanding essay entitled "Egoism and Emancipation Movement" pleaded emphatically for "unrationalized free pleasure aspired without any justifications" and for the legitimacy of an "absolute desire for happiness" (Horkheimer, 1936: 170, 171). According to the author, modern bourgeois thinking, religious or not, was grounded on an ascetic anthropology and had effectively informed people's attitudes with the "disapproval of 'vulgar' lust" (Horkheimer, 1936: 172). The denouncement of natural drives and basic human desires conflicted most sharply with the materialistic and hedonistic traditions to which Horkheimer and Adorno referred.

From this point of view, an incessant dialectic pervaded all forms of individual consumption. Criticizing Veblen's concept of conspicuous consumption as one-dimensional, Adorno stated that there was a presentiment of real happiness even in such a highly alienated activity. Adorno spoke of the "dialectic of luxury"; it meant that the satisfaction drawn from the idea of gaining status was spoiled through and through by barbaric social relations, but even this experience of joy inevitably transcended the status quo by the promise of some other, different happiness (Adorno, 1977: 86f).

Public as well as academic reception tends to understimate or even ignore the fundamental role of the idea of uncurtailed happiness in Critical Theory. This fact is partly due to the specific method of argumentation preferred by the authors. Especially in the *Dialectic of Enlightenment,* Horkheimer and Adorno strictly refrained from positively developing their concept of a free and humane society. They attempted to apply the method of "particular negation" (*bestimmte Negation*) to analyze the mechanisms responsible for the self-destructive and barbaric dynamics of bourgeois society up to the point where a possibility of sudden change (*Umschlag*) appeared.

"MORE ICE CREAM, LESS FEAR"

I must admit that for quite some time I had adhered to the opinion that with respect to mass culture, Horkheimer and Adorno shared many judgments put forward by conservative cultural criticism—and in my view this meant no recommendation. So I was most surprised when I came across a newspaper report of a lecture held by Adorno in 1957; the journalist summarized Adorno's assessment of American culture with the headline: "More ice cream, less fear."[9] What made me extremely curious to know more about this lecture were the reported views on the utopian dimension of American mass culture. My own studies on the image of America among the German working class had led to the assumption that the popular perception of the American way of life bore distinct connotations of the land where milk and honey flow[10]—and here it seemed as if Adorno could be a most unexpected representative of such a view.

Adorno held his lecture on German and American culture at least 13 times between 1956 and 1966. The only printed version is from a tape recording slightly revised by the author (Adorno, 1959);[11] the text has not been included in his **Collected Works (*Gesammelte Schriften*)**. Adorno's foreword stresses that the small brochure was just meant to support his listeners' memory and that he was not taking any responsibility for the text. Nevertheless, the lecture contains a unique sketch of what might have been the content of an essay on the "positive aspects of mass culture," which Horkheimer and Adorno had announced in their preface to the 1944 version of *Dialectic of Enlightenment* (Wiggershaus, 1986: 360). Thus, reconstructing Adorno's argument does not mean paying tribute to an academic cult of personality. Treating mass consumption as a materialization (although deeply perverted) of the pursuit of happiness means intervening into a highly topical contemporary debate.

Adorno's starting point was the decisive difference between the European and the American notions of culture. On the Old Continent, and most prominently in Germany, "culture" fixed on a canon of excellent intellectual works and implied an ideal of spiritual self-development. In America, the idea of culture was related to the practice of shaping reality: forming social relations as well as taming nature and mastering natural resources by means of technology. Both of these dimensions were rooted in the meaning that the notion of culture gained in early modern Europe. "Culture" derives from the Latin verb "colere," which means to cultivate, to care for something. One interpretation of this basic meaning was man taking control over nature in the sense of governing the resisting forces of nature outside as well as controlling the natural urges within himself—the human drives and the unconscious. But cultivation is not tantamount to ruling. Cultivation of nature also included maintaining the essence of all that is appropriated and molded for human use. This kind of relationship with nature demanded contemplation and self-reflection of human praxis; it demanded a kind of spiritualization in order to civilize the power exercized on external and internal nature.

According to Adorno, the different accentuation of culture in America and Germany was due to the different historical experience of the middle classes in the two countries. American society was based on a purely bourgeois foundation, and here the principles of middle-class culture were realized in the most consequent way. Germany, in contrast, had never experienced a successful bourgeois revolution, and in 1918 the foundation of a democratic civil society was distorted by the paramount middle-class fear of socialism. Under these circumstances, culture assumed a highly spiritualized character, thus compensating

for the lack of opportunities to shape German society according to middle-class ideals. This concentration on intellectual and spiritual refinement facilitated the achievements of German music and philosophy; but the price for setting free the absolute powers of the human mind was a significant deficit of contact with reality.

As a result, most German intellectuals have tended to denounce the alleged rule of "materialism" in the United States. Adorno confronted them with his dialectical view of mass production and mass consumption:

> Probably one of the most intense experiences for a person coming to America is the overwhelming wealth of goods presented there. Sometimes I feel suspicion against the idea that a world capable of producing so many goods should be solely materialist. I hear the well-known overtones of the grapes hanging too high. For this reason we should judge extremely cautiously and delicately. This amount of goods has got a certain feeling to it . . . which you can hardly explain to anyone who has not himself had the experience; but we should not deny this impression, and, above all, we should not value it too lowly. There is a touch of the land of Cockaigne in it. Just pass through one of the so-called American supermarkets only once, and somehow you will feel—however deceitful and superficial this feeling may be—: there is no more deprivation, it is fulfilment, boundless and perfect fulfilment of all material needs.

(Adorno, 1959: 7)

Of course, Adorno added, nothing was free in monopoly capitalism. In America, as in any other country, the aim of the most rationalized and reckless methods of production was profit, not human well-being. But then we find a statement that may sound very simple and commonsensical from a liberal point of view; but—as far as I can see—it is unique in the context of Critical Theory and it means a kind of break with the principles of the postwar Frankfurt School. Adorno noted that the production system in the United States was so enormously effective that despite the profit orientation, each single person got an overwhelming amount of consumer goods. By taking the perspective of the common people's individual experience, Adorno not only contradicted traditional Marxism but opposed the entire discourse of conservative cultural criticism that dominated in West Germany until the mid-1960s. He connected individual material well-being with the fact that in America the principle of bourgeois culture—which he saw as closely interwoven with the principle of humanity—not only had been radically thought but had been realized with final consequence.

Adorno gave an example. In America, the mass media successfully popularized some ideas of modern psychology and so-called progressive education. Not all results were pleasant:

> But the fact that each American child may actually eat a so-called ice-cone incessantly . . . thus finding a kind of fulfilment of children's happiness at any mo-

ment, that happiness for which our children once craned their necks in vain—this is really a part of utopia come true.

> It has got something of that peacefulness, that absence of fear and threat which we would imagine to prevail in a chiliastic kingdom. The abundance of goods, the fact that deprivation diminishes . . .—this brings into everyday experience a trait of that peacefulness and un-aggressive behaviour which we have lost nearly totally in Europe. It is a kind of friendliness that you may observe especially with so-called common people . . . , pervading the whole society with humanity in behavior itself. This makes up very well for the fact that the people in question may perhaps not pronounce the names of Bach and Beethoven in the correct fashion which we believe to be indispensable for real refinement.

> (Adorno, 1959: 71)

Today, the image of American society is generally associated with the omnipresence of violence in the media as well as in the streets. Against this background, it is most enticing to brush aside Adorno's observations: a German philosopher, incurably romantic, confusing a Norman Rockwell painting with reality. But, strange as it may seem to an American public, you will find similar impressions in the reports of Germans who have traveled through the small towns of present-day urban America. In fact, the frightening increase of aggression and violence in everyday life is much more apt to corroborate Adorno's notions on the correlation between the satisfaction of material needs and a peaceful social climate than to refute it. And, apart from this empirical problem, the point of Adorno's theoretical argument is as keen today as it was in the 1950s: humanity in behavior is a social value ranking high above the knowledge of even the greatest works of art; and peacefulness is not tied to the European concept of cultural refinement.

In exploring the utopian potential of mass culture, Adorno had not deserted his critical point of view. In the United States, so he told his audience, the bourgeois principle of a society solely based on market exchange had been realized with utmost consistency. This resulted in cutting off all institutions that might reach beyond the exchange principle and beyond the closed circle of pragmatic activity. Thus nowhere in society could a critical spirit be rooted, and the expanding apparatuses of mass production, mass consumption, and mass communication exercized a most effectful pressure toward intellectual conformity.

But as a dialectical thinker Adorno insisted on his thesis that the American way of life had to be understood as a "universal victory of enlightenment in the sense of the all-European process of enlightenment" (Adorno, 1959: 10). American preoccupation with the practical dimensions and consequences of intellectual work and philosophical ideas made it possible to transfer the demands of "culture" from the spiritual realm to the outside world.

Adorno sharply distinguished between two dimensions of mass culture, which the common discourse on the topic united indiscriminately. The sphere of material reproduction of human beings and the patterns of everyday behavior connected therewith were following a logic quite different from that inherent in mass communication and mass entertainment. The argument is in some way related to the Marxist view of material basis and ideological superstructures. Mass consumption—by fulfilling the needs of human beings as natural, sensuous beings—was always related to the basic dimensions of human happiness. This truth could by no means excuse or even justify a type of rationalized, monopolized production subduing its objects as well as its agents to a logic of domination. Defending the human right to freedom of material privation could never legitimize destroying external nature, human nature, and the large majority of people outside the highly industrialized countries. On the other hand, Critical Theory had to delimit its radical negation of capitalist economy from the religious struggle against earthly satisfaction and sensual joy and from the conservatives' contempt for the striving of the masses for a life of modest abundance. For Adorno, returning to a standard of living typical of the early twentieth century was out of the question. The barbarism inherent in the spiral of mass production, the shaping of needs, and mass consumption was obvious. But the philosophical bias for dealing with these flagrant contradictions from a progressive point of view was to stick to the material, sensuous foundations of any ideal of human happiness.

According to Adorno, the same way of looking at things was to be applied to the cultural relevance of another founding element of American culture. The exchange principle had penetrated the farthest corner of American society informing even the most sublime interpersonal relations. The entire range of intellectual production was evaluated by its capacity for bringing profit or becoming a success on the market. This is why autonomous philosophy and arts in the European sense of culture remained marginalized in the United States, surviving only in the niches of nonconformism. Children were socialized toward an ego-ideal of success, thus preparing them to accept the pressures of social adjustment and conformism. But for Adorno there was yet another side to the domination of the exchange principle: it supported the social rooting of democracy and a certain openness in social behavior: "The omnipresence of exchange activity means at the same time that all people are there for all other people. No one will harden himself in the limitations of his individual interest in the way you find in . . . Europe" (Adorno, 1959: 8). In Germany, the ideal of self-identity often produced a type of character with a grim, chilly appearance, indicating to all other people from the start that they actually did not matter for him and that they should not interfere with his precious and precarious inwardness (*Innerlichkeit*). This attitude was responsible for an internal distance from democracy, especially among the intellectuals. However, the American accent on adjusting to a social standard of "being there for other people" generated a further positive trait in American culture if compared to German *Kultur.* Adorno supposed "that a person educated with some social pressure to behave in a friendly fashion is yet more likely to practice a certain humanity in his relations with other people" (Adorno, 1959: 10).

Here, Adorno probably by far overshot the mark. If things only were so easy! Nevertheless, we have to ask why the critical philosopher got carried away enough to praise American mass culture in such a manner. There are two answers, one more global and one concretely historical. From about the middle of the 1950s, tendencies of pragmatism grew in Adorno's attitude. During those years he prepared his most radical book, *Negative Dialectic,* in which he worked out that the only authentic way of referring to society was to negate it. As a social science professor, however, he became involved in discussions about practical measures of cultural betterment, for instance, media pedagogics (Kausch, 1988: 197-214).

However, the decisive motive for touring the country with such a provocative lecture was Adorno's conviction that "the global historical trend will boil down to an Americanization of Europe" (Adorno, 1959: 14). He did not hide his criticism of this development, but he was above all worried that in response, the strong attitude of cultural anti-Americanism among German intellectuals would be radicalized.[12] This, he was afraid, could only strengthen the disastrous anti-democratic undercurrent of German thinking that had always expressed its hostility to Modernity by hateful attacks on Western civilization (Adorno, 1971: 137). In order to shatter his listeners' stereotyped convictions that *Kultur* was so much superior to American culture, Adorno answered rudeness with rudeness. He presented American supermarkets and ice cream for children as the realization of the innermost motives of spiritual creation. "Does not any culture in our European sense of spiritual culture contain something like a reference to this utopia of fulfilment?" he asked. Taking *Romeo and Juliet* as an example, Adorno insisted that all great works of art drew their power from the dream that "there shall be happiness, people shall give themselves to each other, there shall be fulfilment, not prohibition" (Adorno, 1959: 7).[13]

By praising the utopian elements in American mass culture, Adorno tried to shake the self-righteousness of his German contemporaries. I think it is to this historical and presumably also emotional confrontation that we owe the disclosure of some motives that Adorno used to cut down nearly to invisibility in his writings.

CONCLUSION

With the omnipresence of the culture industry and with the spreading of prosperity in West Germany, anti-sensual, ascetical critique of mass culture lost ground. But since the late 1970s, the tradition of German cultural criticism has made an impressive comeback. Today, cultural and pedagogical elites draw on irrefutable ecological arguments to prove that the standars of material convenience and the al-

leged hedonistic way of living of the "masses" in the highly industrialized countries are immoral and self-destructive. Undoubtedly the habits of private everyday life in the so-called affluent societies do waste limited resources, pollute the environment, and deepen the gap between the inhabitants of the "First World" and the expanding dominions of misery and starvation on earth. But among those who are calling for a radically new design of our way of life, I hear a lot of voices asking directly or indirectly: "Haven't we always told you that unlimited mass consumption and the hedonistic chasing after ever new thrills are the cause of evil, that you should turn to the immaterial riches of life?"

Actually, those voices are sounding much more often and much louder in Europe than in America—as they have always done throughout the nineteenth and twentieth centuries. But the general question remains: Where do intellectuals and scholars rank the material conveniences and sensual satisfactions of mass culture when debating the necessity to reshape our way of life? Do the pleasures of the body and of the senses just make up the lowland of contemporary culture, prominent only because of the dubious influence of uneducated masses and without any substantial value? Or should we stick to the hedonistic tradition that goes back to ancient philosophers such as Aristippus and Epicurus? Critical Theory insisted that any disrespect for the natural needs in man would inevitably damage human culture as a whole and could only result in a deformation of our spiritual heritage. In my view, this remains a very serious contribution to the debate on the future of mass culture.

Notes

1. Since the late 1930s, the attitude among radical American intellectuals toward modern mass media and its aesthetics had turned from hope to fear. The convergence of this criticism with the theoretical framework of the European scholars becomes evident in the classical readers: Rosenberg and White, 1957; Jacobs, 1961; another example is Dwight MacDonald's 1960 text "Masscult and Midcult" reprinted in MacDonald, 1982: 3-75. For an outline of the intellectual development, cf. Richard Pells, "Die Moderne und die Massen. Die Reaktion amerikanischer Intellektueller auf die populare Kultur in den dreißiger Jahren und in der Nachkriegszeit," in Krenzlin, 1992: 102-117.

2. "Es gibt kein richtiges Leben im falschen." *Minima Moralia. Reflexionen aus dem beschadigten Leben* (Frankfurt: Suhrkamp, 1987) 42.

3. Cf. Giner, 1976: 166-182.

4. Cf. Wiggershaus, 1986: 338-390; Jay, 1981: 253-259, 297-326.

5. Cf. Kausch, 1988; Kellner, 1982: 508-515.

6. Horkheimer and Adorno, 1971: 4 (preface).

7. Cf. the chapter "Culture Industry: Enlightenment as Mass Deception" in Horkheimer and Adorno, 1971.

8. Translating German philosophers into English is itself quite presumptuous, and with the writings of Horkheimer and Adorno one feels doomed to failure. A central notion for this discussion is that of *Glück,* generally translated here as "happiness." In the discourse of the Frankfurt School, *Glück* is a concept of highest philosophical dignity; it is a kind of short formula for the quality of existence in a free and humane society. *Glück* includes the sensations of the body from sexual lust to the pleasures of eating and drinking, the satisfactions derived from any intense activity, as well as the spiritual joy of art and thinking. Depending on the context I am using terms such as "joy," "pleasure," or "fulfilment," but I ask the reader to be aware of the overtone of *Glück,* of happiness in the full philosophical sense.

9. "Mehr Eiscreme, weniger Angst. Professor Adorno zur deutschen und amerikanischen Kultur," *Frankfurter Rundschau,* 16 May 1957.

10. Cf. Maase, 1992: 42-46, 186-190.

11. Newspaper reports on 12 additional public lectures are collected at the Theodor W. Adorno Archives, Frankfurt; I am very grateful especially to Henri Lonitz for supplying these materials.

12. For European anti-Americanism, see Henningsen, 1974; Kroes and van Rossem, 1986. For Germany, see Fraenkel, 1959; Berg, 1963; Schwabe, 1976; Maase, 1992.

13. This corresponds surprisingly to the tenor of Jean Baudrillard's account of his travels through the United States in *America.* In his view, American culture is the carefree materialization of ideals that had been articulated in Europe; on the Old Continent, in contrast, justice, affluence, equality, and freedom were regarded as final goals of history, and the realization of this utopia was postponed to a distant future.

References

Adorno, Theodor W. (1959). "Kultur und Culture." Vortrag, gehalten am 9. Juli 1958 bei den Hochschulwochen für staatswissenschaftliche Fortbildung in Bad Wildungen, Sonderdruck, Bad Homburg u. a.: Gehlen, no date.

———. (1971). "Was bedeutet: Aufarbeitung der Vergangenheit." *Eingriffe: Neun kritische Modelle,* 7th ed. Frankfurt: Suhrkamp.

———. (1977). "Veblens Angriff auf die Kultur." *Gesammelte Schriften,* vol. 10.1. Frankfurt: Suhrkamp.

Berg, Peter (1963). *Deutschland und Amerika 1918-1929. Über das deutsche Amerikabild der zwanziger Jahre.* Lübeck: Matthiesen.

Brantlinger, Patrick (1983). *Bread and Circuses: Theories of Mass Culture as Social Decay.* Ithaca: Cornell University Press.

Diner, Dan (1993). *Verkehrte Welten. Antiamerikanismus in Deutschland.* Frankfurt: Eichborn.

Fraenkel, Ernst (1959). *Amerika im Spiegel des deutschen politischen Denkens.* Köln: Westdeutscher Verlag.

Giner, Salvador (1976). *Mass Society.* London: Robertson.

Henningsen, Manfred (1974). *Der Fall Amerika. Zur Sozial- und Bewuβtseingeschichte einer Verdrängung.* München: List.

Horkheimer, Max, and Theodor W. Adorno (1971). *Dialektik der Aufklärung: Philosophische Fragmente.* Frankfurt: Fischer. Translated as *Dialectic of Enlightenment* (New York: Herder & Herder, 1972).

Horkheimer, Max (1936). "Egoismus und Freiheitsbewegung. Zur Anthropologie des bürgerlichen Zeitalters." *Zeitschrift für Sozialforschung* 5.2.

Jacobs, Norman (ed.) (1961). *Culture for the Millions?* Princeton: Van Nostrand.

Jay, Martin (1981). *Dialektische Phantasie: Die Geschichte der Frankfurter Schule und des Instituts für Sozialforschung 1923-1950.* Frankfurt: Fischer. First published as *The Dialectical Imagination: A History of the Frankfurt School and the Institute of Social Research, 1923-1950* (Boston: Little, Brown, 1973).

Kausch, Michael (1988). *Kulturindustrie und Populärkultur. Kritische Theorie der Massenmedien.* Frankfurt: Fischer.

Kellner, Douglas (1982). "Kulturindustrie und Massenkommunikation. Die Kritische Theorie und ihre Folgen." *Sozialforschung als Kritik. Zum sozialwissenschaftlischen Potential der Kritischen Theorie,* eds. Wolfgang Bonβ and Axel Honneth. Frankfurt: Suhrkamp, 482-515.

Krenzlin, Norbert (ed.) (1992). *Zwischen Angstmetapher und Terminus: Theorien der Massenkultur seit Nietzsche.* Berlin: Akademie-Verlag.

Kroes, Rob, and M. van Rossem (eds.) (1986). *Anti-Americanism in Europe.* Amsterdam: Free University Press.

Maase, Kaspar (1992). *BRAVO Amerika. Erkundungen zur Jugendkultur der Bundesrepublik in den fünfziger Jahren.* Hamburg: Junius.

MacDonald, Dwight (1982). *Against the American Grain.* New York: Da Capo Press.

Rosenberg, Bernard, and David M. White (eds.) (1957). *Mass Culture.* Glencoe, IL: Free Press.

Schwabe, Klaus (1976). "Anti-Americanism within the German Right 1917-1933." *Amerikastudien* 21.2: 89-107.

Wiggershaus, Rolf (1986). *Die Frankfurter Schule: Geschichte—Theoretische Entwicklung—Politische Bedeutung.* München/Wien: Hanser.

Nico Israel (essay date 1997)

SOURCE: "Damage Control: Adorno, Los Angeles, and the Dislocation of Culture," in the *Yale Journal of Criticism,* Vol. 10, No. 1, Spring, 1997, pp. 85-113.

[*In the following essay, Israel examines* Minima Moralia *for insights into Adorno's character and personality and the impact his exile in the United States had on his critical thought.*]

1. FLYING T.W.A . . .

To begin with an ending of sorts: at the conclusion to his 1967 Foreword to the English edition of **Prisms,** Theodor Wiesengrund Adorno suggests, rather formally, that

> [f]inally, the author could wish for nothing better than that the English version of **Prisms** might express something of the gratitude that he cherishes for England and for the United States—the countries which enabled him to survive the era of persecution and to which he has ever since felt himself deeply bound.[1]

"Gratitude," "cherish," and "deeply bound" are scarcely words that one would generally expect from, or associate with, Adorno, much less with his impressions of the United States, where he resided from 1938 until 1949, first in New York and then in Los Angeles, before returning to Frankfurt to help rebuild the Institute for Social Research. Yet they appear in this fashion in **Prisms,** and again shortly afterward, in slightly altered form, in a longer meditation on his stay in the U.S., a 1968 essay somewhat curiously titled **"Scientific Experiences of a European Scholar in America."** Here he similarly concludes with an expression of "gratitude, including intellectual gratitude, toward America," and, switching to the first person, with a declaration that "I [n]ever expect to forget as a scholar what I learned there."[2]

The following year, while vacationing in Switzerland, four months after having been humiliated publicly by a militant student group and its demands for active political engagement to match a revolutionary political theory, Adorno died of a sudden heart attack.[3] And his death consequently lends an eerie sense of epitaphic finality to these "grateful" expressions. Are they to be viewed as a sober revaluation, as mere politesse, or, rather, as a brief instance of retrospective illusion over a particularly difficult period of his life?

More familiar to us, of course, is another, less overtly grateful Adorno, who rails against an array of manifestations of American cultural production, from jazz to Hollywood movies, from astrology journalism to suburban tract housing, from Americans' use of nicknames to their propensity to smile. In an anecdote contained in the **"Scientific Experiences"** essay mentioned above, for example, he vents his spleen with more characteristically cantankerous wit. Writing of the Princeton Radio Project, in which he participated from 1938 to 1940, he claims that

> [a]mong the frequently changing colleagues who came in contact with me in the Princeton Project was a young lady. After a few days she came to confide in me and asked in a completely charming way, "Dr. Adorno, would you mind a personal question?" I said, "It depends on the question, but just go ahead." And she

continued, "Please tell me: are you an extrovert or an introvert?" It was as if she was already thinking, as a living being, according to the pattern of the so-called "cafeteria" questions on questionnaires, by which she had been conditioned. [. . .] Reified minds are in no way limited to America, but are fostered by the general tendency of society. But I first became aware of this in America.[4]

Although any contemporary American critic confronting the depth, rigor, and elusiveness of Adorno's thought runs the risk of misunderstanding the latter's project—of continually posing, much like the "young lady" scholar he describes above, the wrong questions—the aim of this paper is, among other things, to "just go ahead and ask" "personal" questions of **Minima Moralia,** a particularly "introverted" text that Adorno wrote while in Los Angeles, about America, about himself, and about what exile might mean for philosophy. Taking exception to long-standing claims that the core of Adorno's thought remains constant over the course of his long and extraordinarily productive career,[5] I shall be examining what is distinct about Adorno's writing from, and understanding of, the U.S.—and how the experience of emigration in "the era of persecution" changed the course of his thinking. For, as Adorno himself comments, "[i]t is scarcely an exaggeration to say that any contemporary consciousness that has not appropriated the American experience, even if in opposition, has something reactionary about it."[6] Determining the extent to which Adorno "appropriated" America in **Minima Moralia**—indeed the relationship between exile, appropriation, and "opposition"—will be the central focus of this study.

In negotiating this rough theoretical terrain between philosophy, autobiography, and cultural critique, I shall be paying particular attention to the role played by the physical and psychical space of Adorno's Los Angeles; as it is in Los Angeles that he developed some of the central theses of Frankfurt School thought. But I also will demonstrate how Adorno's more specific or "local" observations, written of and in exile, are extended, often uneasily, to the realm of the more general and global. Just how genuinely global Adorno's world view might be is, of course, open to contention; I shall argue that, although clearly subject to their own highly problematic blind spots, Adorno's trenchant analyses of cultural politics, national identity and the (shifting and shifty) place of the intellectual can perhaps help to re-orient and refine contemporary academic debates concerning disciplinarity, social space, and the politics of difference.

My aim, it must be stressed at the outset, is not to defend or "recuperate" Adorno's (often mistaken) analyses of American cultural phenomena, but instead to complicate those hasty and often reductive readings that seem to have sedimented into the present "take" on Adorno in the American academy, in which his and Horkheimer's culture industry argument is often taken as a metonym for Adornian thinking on America, indeed for Adornian thinking in general.[7] The following; however, as it engages largely with one text, can neither attain the systematicity of broader treatments of Adorno's *oeuvre*,[8] nor address the wide variety of Adornian texts written in America, or even in Los Angeles[9]; rather, in its attention to Adorno's nervous self-exiles into and from the architecture of his own writing, and in its exploration of the cultural geography of his philosophy, it ought to be viewed as a kind of intellectual provocation, or, in Adorno's own peculiar definition of the term, an "essay." For if, according to Adorno, "the essay's innermost formal law is heresy,"[10] then at issue here is heresy against one of the century's foremost intellectual heretics, a transgression for which I hope I might be forgiven.

2. BLUE NOTE

Written in 1944-47 and importantly subtitled "Reflections from Damaged Life,"[11] *Minima Moralia* [hereafter abbreviated as *MM*] could perhaps best be described as a kind of philosophical memoir in a period in which writing autobiography, much like writing poetry after Auschwitz in Adorno's best-known and most frequently misunderstood maxim, had, owing to certain historical and psychological "mutilations," become virtually impossible. "Subjective reflection, even if critically alerted to itself," he points out in his introduction to the text, "has something sentimental and anachronistic about it."[12] To combat such sentimentality and anachronicity, Adorno employs an aphoristic style—evanescent and deliberately self-contradictory, "dialectical" but by no means especially methodical.[13] The text, whose title draws on, and ironically reverses, that of *Magna Moralia*, Aristotle's ethical treatise, consists of one hundred and fifty-three entries of varying length (none longer than a few pages, most shorter), organized into three parts, or, borrowing a musical metaphor, "movements." Each part, corresponding to the three phases of the text's composition, is designed to begin with reflections on the "narrowest private sphere" (*MM* Intro., 18, [11]), the dilemma of the individual thinker or artist in exile, proceeding to engage with issues of "broader social and anthropological scope" (*MM* Intro., 18, [11]), and ending with philosophical and world-historical declarations; but the pattern is not consistent, the trajectory not particularly "progressive." Moreover, as Gillian Rose points out, individual entries—or, as Adorno calls them, "points of attack" (*MM* Intro., 18, [11])—often stand in marked contradistinction to the ones that precede them, so that no aphorism offers the "final word" on a particular issue: instead, a contrapuntal signification system is set up, in which the entries accrue meaning through their "negation."[14]

It is helpful to recognize that the aphoristic mode of *Minima Moralia* is largely an outgrowth of the fragmentary "Notes and Drafts" section that concludes Adorno and Horkheimer's *Dialectic of Enlightenment,* completed in 1944. In fact, the entire work, Adorno suggests, "bears witness" to a "*dialogue intérieur*" with Horkheimer, to whom the book is dedicated and who, like Adorno, was also living in Los Angeles at the time (although because Horkheimer was very ill during much of the time of

Minima Moralia's composition, he was not an active interlocutor).[15] As many critics have suggested, Horkheimer was always the more "empirically" inclined of the two thinkers; and here, disencumbered of the demands of a scientistic sociology with which he was arguably always uncomfortable, Adorno gives freer rein to his critical methods as well as to his cultural idiosyncrasies and predilections. It is in this sense that this "*dialogue intérieur*" is Adorno's most introspective work; but it is (as even his use of the French term possibly indicates) a profoundly unsettled "personal" mode, committed to locating—and standing—its own philosophical and discursive ground, while simultaneously aware of the precariousness, and pitfalls, of writing of and from exile.

The initial entry of *Minima Moralia*'s first part, for example, is entitled "For Marcel Proust," and it presents a reflection on this paragon of twentieth-century introspection, his class status, and the "departmentalization of Spirit" (*Departamentalisierung des Geistes*) that threatens to obliterate such introspection. Adorno's "image" of Proust, it should be mentioned at the outset, owes a great deal to Walter Benjamin's; in fact, the latter's brilliant and succinct assertion that the texts which comprise Proust's *Recherche* "are the result of an unconstruable synthesis in which the absorption of a mystic, the art of a prose writer, the verve of a satirist, the erudition of a scholar, and the self-consciousness of a monomaniac have combined in an autobiographical work," could perhaps also apply to much of Benjamin's own work, or indeed to *Minima Moralia,* which at times seems particularly indebted to Benjamin's *One Way Street* and *A Berlin Childhood.*[16]

"The son of well-to-do parents," begins Adorno, "who, whether from talent or weakness, engages in a so-called intellectual profession, as an artist or a scholar,"

> will have a particularly difficult time with those bearing the distasteful title of colleagues. It is not merely that his independence is envied, the seriousness of his intentions mistrusted, or that he is suspected of being a secret envoy of the established powers. Such suspicions, though betraying a deep-seated resentment, would usually prove well-founded. But the real resistances lie elsewhere.
>
> (*MM* 1, 21 [15])

These "real resistances" (*Widerstände*—literally, oppositions), it turns out, as one works through the labyrinthine logic of the entry, emerge from contradictions inherent in the division of labor itself, and, more especially, from the societally endorsed cordoning off of intellectual labor (art and scholarship) from the productive ethos with which, for Adorno, intellectual labor putatively does battle. "The [financially] independent intellectual," even one who "take[s] pleasure in his work," can never entirely repudiate this work ethos, which remains the source of the very economic value that enables his "independence." "Thus," he concludes contentiously, "is order ensured":

> Some have to play along [*müssen mitmachen*] because they cannot otherwise live, and those who could live

otherwise are kept out because they do not want to play along [*nicht mitmachen wollen*].[17] It is as if the class from which independent intellectuals have defected takes its revenge, by pressing its demands home in the very domain where the deserter takes refuge.

(*MM* 1, 21 [15])

This "domain"—art, or critical thought, for in *Minima Moralia* the terms are, as above, often intertwined—offers no such "refuge" (*Zuflucht*—literally, place to "flee" to), because a realm outside of productive logic is foreclosed. Whether it emerges from Proust's Paris bedroom or his own writing desk in Southern California—and indeed Adorno's comparison is necessarily an ironic one, because of the radical incommensurability between the living conditions, and objects of critique, of the two men, and moreover because Adorno in 1944 could hardly be considered an "independent intellectual"[18]—writing itself cannot help "playing along," its will not to do so notwithstanding. Furthermore, despite the fact that financially independent intellectuals are ostracized, or rendered "beside the point"—not only by those who actually "work for a living" (Adorno later contentiously calls them "They, the People" in a rare English entry title) but also by those intellectual "colleagues" attached more obviously to cultural institutions[19]—this does not exempt them from succumbing to the reproduction of the ideology that benefits the status quo.

That Adorno's shifting rhetoric of open and closed—or, to borrow from his lexicon, "refuge" and its opposite ("subsumption," "liquidation")—here seems to offer, and then withdraw, a space for critique, is, of course, an essential element of that critique: its very evanescence and apparent self-canceling mirror the broader process of "groping" for a philosophy that would wrench the "good life" from the jaws of the very bad.[20] How the predicament of exile at once informs and prohibits this process—a contradiction which Adorno treats alternately with hyperbole and lament from this very first entry—becomes clearer as one proceeds into the sinews of the text.

"Every intellectual in emigration," he writes in an early aphorism ironically called "Protection, Help, and Counsel" (*Schutz, Hilfe und Rat*—a title that in German carries the charge of a police-force motto), "is, without exception, mutilated" (*beschädigt*) (*MM* 13, 33 [32]). "His language," Adorno continues, "has been expropriated, and the historical dimension that nourished his knowledge, sapped" (*MM* 13, 33 [32]). The situation is exacerbated by the presence of factions within the emigré community; because "[a]ll emphases are wrong, perspectives disrupted," their attempts to organize politically seem futile. "All this," he suggests, [. . .] "leaves no individual unmarked" ([*a*]*ll das hinterläßt Male in jedem Einzelnen*—it leaves "stains" or "bruises" on people), affecting every aspect of their existence. The public sphere demands absolute conformity (an "unspoken oath of allegiance to the platform"), while "[p]rivate life asserts itself unduly, hectically, vampire-like, trying convulsively, because it really no longer exists, to prove it is alive" (*MM* 13, 33 [33]).

In the face of this bloodsucking exilic double-bind—to feel utterly alone, but to have no genuine private life—the "damage" mounts, and the emigré intellectual begins to show symptoms. "The eyes," writes Adorno, "take on a manic yet cold look of grasping, devouring, commandeering" (*MM* 13, 33 [33]), and, in the "hopeless second struggle" of those alienated from an already alienated population, mutual suspicion reigns. For this intolerable situation, there is no readily apparent solution, and the only course of action is, Adorno suggests, yet more rigorous analysis: "There is no remedy but steadfast diagnosis of oneself and others, the attempt, through awareness, if not to escape doom, at least to rob it of its dreadful violence, that of blindness" (*MM* 13, 33 [33]).

It is noteworthy how often Adorno, in *Minima Moralia* and elsewhere, returns to metaphors of vision. Here, a sort of thankless critical insight ("awareness") opposes the "violence" of "blindness" (ideology and reification); above, the eyes respond to the "hopeless second struggle" within the exilic community. And later, in the same aphorism, he refers to "the blindest self-interest" that was often masked by what he calls "esoteric" philosophy.[21] The "sight" that would counteract such "blindness," however, is neither lasting nor easily transmissible to others. Moreover, the "truth" it reveals (Adorno sometimes calls it "reality") tends, almost immediately, to recede from view.

Along with this recurrent metaphor of vision, another, related, frequently deployed and equally multivalent Adornian figure in *Minima Moralia* is that of the home and its various architecturally-inclined subdivisions, including domicile, dwelling, and, as we have seen, "shelter." Where, Adorno repeatedly asks, is "home"? What does it mean to be "at home"? When is a house a home? Of course, such apparently homely questions also bear on nationhood and nationality as well. Indeed, throughout *Minima Moralia,* Adorno employs the terms *Heim* (home) and *Heimat* (homeland, native place) interchangeably, and, given his nuanced awareness of the Nazi appropriation of the terms, almost always ironically. Yet for Adorno, of course, the *Heimat* could never consist of *Blut und Boden,* nor even of mother-tongue, however much the loss of the latter emerges as a theme in the pages of *Minima Moralia.* Nor, for that matter, could it involve the "house of being" associated with an existential "Jargon of Authenticity" of the type of which he accuses Heidegger, whose thought, in *Minima Moralia,* he links with that of Ludwig Klages. For Heidegger, homelessness or *Heimatlosigkeit* referred to the state of *Dasein*'s thrownness, which Adorno immediately relates to the idea of racial community (*MM* 41, 67 [81]). In "dialectical" contrast, Adorno posits dwellinglessness or *Obdachlosigkeit* as a putatively more specifically socio-historical phenomenon, which is to say a more "materialist" phenomenon, to be disentangled via the "work of the negative."[22]

Consequently, when Adorno inveighs against the ready-made quality of modern homes, calling them, as in entry 18 ("Refuge for the Homeless"[23]), "living-cases manufactured by experts for philistines," or "factory sites that have strayed into the consumption sphere, devoid of all relation to the occupant" (*MM* 18, 38 [40]), these invectives should not be mistaken for a simple-minded nostalgia for old bourgeois manors; in fact, the latter incite an even greater degree of ridicule, associated, as they are in Adorno, with the bourgeois nuclear family and its manifold social and psychological repressions.[24] What Adorno rather seeks to resist is the prefabricated, ready-made thought that could produce the concentration and death camps along with the single-family suburban house with garden. This kind of modern home is, indeed, uninhabitable.

For Adorno, the development of thought had reached an historical juncture in which "*Das Haus ist vergangen*"—an enigmatic and hyperbolic sentence which signifies "the house is gone," but also "the house is [in the] past" (*MM* 18, 39 [41]); that is, the era of the house is no longer. Under these circumstances, Adorno declares with a morose irony, "it is part of morality not to be at home in one's own house" (*Es gehört zur Moral nicht bei sich selber zu Hause zu sein*[25]). In this text, whose title implies a search for the most minuscule degree of morality in the face of unprecedented historical mass suffering, such a prescription must be taken seriously. What could it mean to see homelessness as a moral imperative, or even a moral virtue? If indeed, as Adorno suggests at the end of the entry, "wrong life cannot be lived rightly" [*Es gibt kein richtiges Leben im falschen*—literally, "there is no right life in the false one" (*MM* 18, 39 [41])], where *can* one live a "right life"? Is there really to be no "refuge" for the "homeless"?

In various entries in **Minima Moralia,** Adorno seems to hold out the possibility that the act of writing itself provides a kind of asylum for the exiled thinker. In the series of aphorisms that constitute "Memento" (entry 51), for example, Adorno considers what he calls "properly written texts"—those that have a "purity of expression," avoid clichés, and have been vigorously honed down by self-editing and deletion. Such texts, he suggests, are "like spiders' webs: tight, concentric, transparent, well-spun and firm" (*MM* 51, 87 [108]). As if to demonstrate this proposition, Adorno proceeds with an arachnoid exploration of the "home-in-writing" (itself perhaps a modernist cliché):

> In his text, the writer sets up house. Just as he trundles papers, books, pencils, documents untidily from room to room, he creates the same disorder in his thoughts. They become pieces of furniture that he sinks into, content or irritable [. . .]. For a man who no longer has a homeland, writing becomes a place to live. In it he inevitably produces, as his family once did, refuse and junk [*Abfall und Bodenramsch*]. But now he lacks a store-room, and [. . .] it is not easy to part with garbage [*es ist . . . nicht leicht vom Abhub sich zu trennen*]. So he pushes it along in front of him, in danger finally of filling his pages with it. The demand that one harden oneself against self-pity [means that the writer must counter . . .] any slackening of intellectual tension with the utmost alertness, and . . . eliminate anything that has begun to encrust the work. [This encrustation . . .] may at an earlier stage have served [. . .]

> to generate the warm atmosphere conducive to growth, but [it] is now left behind, flat and stale. In the end, the writer is not even allowed to live in his writing.

> (*MM* 51, 87 [108])

To comprehend this enigmatic passage, with its melancholic finale, one must unpack the metaphors of refuse and excrement associated with the house of writing. The man who no longer has a homeland produces biodegradable "junk" which it is not easy to get rid of; but the need to "harden" oneself against self-pity requires that the "encrustation" of thought, which, like a kind of intellectual manure, might once have been "conducive to growth," must itself be "eliminated"; ultimately, because the house is left with only "flat and stale" remains, it becomes uninhabitable. Adorno thus "builds" a house out of writing, replete with intellectual "furniture," then, in effect, evicts himself, or, rather, is evicted by the—stinking—process of writing. The exile is not allowed to live in his prose, because if exilic writing is indeed a "place to live," it is a house suffering severe dilapidation.

These examples amply illustrate the difficulty of writing criticism-in-exile, of "taking place" in the negative, of finding a "home" outside of the logic of the administered world. But what of the more "local" observations of the geographical place that Adorno in exile by necessity called home? How is it that Adorno moves cognitively from those specific sites to the broader sight of the universal? Already we have witnessed the comparison of the type of tract housing Adorno must have come across in Southern California to the concentration camps of Europe. But what are we to make of his problematic assertion that "in Anglo-Saxon countries the prostitutes look as if they purveyed, along with sin, the attendant pains of hell" (*MM* 29, 49 [55]), or of his comments on the burgeoning California physical-exercise culture, in which "all the movements of health resemble the reflex-movements of beings whose hearts have stopped beating" (*MM* 36, 59 [70])? **Minima Moralia** is laden with such "site-specific" reflections, cultural details that all somehow flow into the bad totality that must be opposed by critical thinking. To begin to consider Adorno physically and psychically "experiencing" the Hollywood that he loathed—but that he nevertheless recognized as "today's prototypical culture" (*MM* 36, 58 [68])[26]—requires that a broader investigation of his exilic situation be undertaken, one particularly attentive to the pitfalls of writing culture.

3. AC-CEN-TU-ATE The Negative

It is strange, indeed, almost perverse to imagine Adorno strolling along Malibu beach, a light cotton sweater draped around his neck; or heading over to the supermarket to pick up food for a Sunday brunch; or being driven to nearby Schwab's drugstore for bacon and eggs or a root beer float. Published biographical information from this period of Adorno's life is surprisingly scarce, but, according to the Adorno Institute in Frankfurt, during his years in Southern California, Adorno lived in a large, two-story

"Monterey style" duplex at 316 South Kenter Avenue, in the Brentwood Heights section of West Los Angeles.[27] This would place him about two or three miles east of Horkheimer's Pacific Palisades "bungalow"—in which meetings of the West Coast Institute for Social Research took place.[28] Horkheimer's immediate neighbors were Thomas Mann and Lion Feuchtwanger; while by 1942 Bertolt Brecht, Hanns Eisler, and Herbert Marcuse all lived in the vicinity.[29] Slightly to the east of them but west of Adorno (and north of Sunset Boulevard) lived Arnold Schoenberg, on Rockingham Avenue, the street recently made famous by the Simpson murder trial. And, further east but still nearby were the homes of Ernst Lubitsch and Otto Preminger (in Bel Air) and Billy Wilder (in Westwood, near the present site of UCLA).[30]

In addition to attending the Institute's meetings, Adorno, as is well known, collaborated with Mann on parts of the novel *Doctor Faustus,* providing the author with a copy of his manuscript version of **On the Philosophy of Modern Music** as well as regularly discussing the intricacies of Schoenberg's twelve-tone method with him.[31] This was much to the eventual dismay of Schoenberg[32]; but Mann's "gratitude" to Adorno is encoded in the novel's newly-added lyrics to a Beethoven piano sonata, in which Mann inserts the word "meadowground" (*Wiesengrund*), ostensibly as a token of his appreciation.[33] Less well known is the story, recounted in an only-recently-translated Adorno essay, **"Zweimal Chaplin,"** of a bizarre occurrence at a party in Malibu that both Adorno and Charlie Chaplin attended. Adorno tells how, at the party, he was introduced to the actor who played a troubled World War II veteran in the film *The Best Years of Our Lives* (an aptly ironic title for Adorno's Los Angeles experience).[34] Out of instinct or politesse, Adorno reached up and sought to shake hands in greeting, only to shudder when he realized that the man, who had actually been badly injured in the war, had a prosthetic iron right hand that Adorno claims looked like a "claw." Then, to make matters worse, in order to cover up his initial shock, Adorno grimaced in an "obliging" way that must, he notes, have seemed far more horrible, as the actor left the party. Chaplin, who was standing nearby, witnessed the incident, and, to the cathartic laughter of the partygoers but to the apparent embarrassment of Adorno, mimicked the entire scene.[35]

From these two anecdotes we can discern that Adorno was thus no hermit but inevitably part of a (largely Jewish) community of Southern California German (and German speaking) exiles—a group in which he was, however, not particularly integrated, and about which, as we have already seen, he felt a great deal of anxiety and suspicion. There is a black and white photograph, reproduced in Wiggerhaus's book on Adorno, that succinctly conveys the logic of Adorno's "private" working space. Adorno sits on a heavy wooden chair at his enormous, ornate and certainly European desk of dark wood (probably oak), his bald head craning back toward the camera, a quizzical and impatient expression on his face, as if he has been caught in the middle of working, although there are no papers on the desk. He is wearing a sports jacket and a pair of glasses, and his right hand leans on the writing surface. On the top part of the desk stand little sculptures of African animals—giraffes, a small zebra, and, a little lower, a tiny monkey—that seem to be peering down on him; to his left (and out of focus) is an Asian carved wooden chair representing two long-necked birds. To his right is a rectangular-shaped mirror, beneath which stands a small bureau with a metal "in"-type box on top of it. Further to his right, and behind him, is a sash-window typical of Los Angeles 1940s architecture (with half-closed Venetian blinds) that is actually lower than the top of the very tall desk.

The layout of the room is such that it is tempting if somewhat unrigorous to relate it to Adorno's thinking process in **Minima Moralia**: the window facing outside (toward the city) is furthest away from him; the mirror closer; and the transplanted European writing desk (with its African and Asian curios[36]) closest of all. And it is as if this "dialectical" process of observing (through windows, in this case covered by blinds), self-consciously reflecting upon (through the mirror), and writing in the European (and putatively universal) grain inflects all of his impressions of Los Angeles, and of America in general.

And what Adorno "sees" is tawdry, fallen, phony to its core, or strangely pathetic. Consider, for example, his impressions of Californian roads and the surrounding landscape in the sardonically titled "Paysage" (entry 28):

> [Roads] are always inserted directly in the landscape, and the more impressively smooth and broad they are, the more unrelated and violent their gleaming track appears to be against the all-too-wild, overgrown surroundings. They are expressionless [. . .]. It is as if no one had ever passed his hand over the landscape's hair. [The landscape] is uncomforted and comfortless.
>
> (*MM* 28, 48 [54])

The violence of the implementation of (sub)urban planning—these roads are, according to Adorno, "always" inserted into or blasted from (*gesprengt*) the landscape—is thus akin to a rape, in which the victim (the landscape), coded as female, undergoes a kind of trauma. The smooth, broad and "gleaming" roads, however, cover over the traces (*Spuren*—which also means lanes on the road) of this act, while the landscape is left to recover alone, for the viewer of the scene, stuck in a moving vehicle, is powerless to help. The conclusion to the aphorism makes this clear:

> It is uncomforted and comfortless. And it is perceived in a corresponding way. For what the hurrying eye has seen merely from the car it cannot retain, and the vanishing landscape leaves no more traces behind than it bears upon itself.
>
> (*MM* 28, 48 [55])

These images of things "hurrying," "vanishing" and leaving no "traces" or "tracks," are symptomatic of Adorno's "perception" of America, a perception that is itself uncomforted and comfortless. No matter how "impressive" the surroundings may be, there is something of the sublime in every disappearing particle: "Beauty of the American landscape: that even the smallest of its segments is inscribed, as its expression, with the immensity of the whole country" (*MM* 29, 49 [55]). In the face of this "immensity"—a rubric that is strangely reminiscent of Conrad's *Heart of Darkness*—the perceiver of these inscriptions is, like Marlow, unutterably overwhelmed.[37]

Dotted alongside these roads are motels and restaurants, which serve only to remind Adorno of the old, once-*Grands Hôtels*. Probably, he notes ironically, "the decline of the hotel dates back to the dissolution of the ancient unity of inn and brothel" (*MM* 75, 117 [151]). But in its current phase of development, the temporary dwelling place, though separated from bodily pleasure, is all too linked to the "intercourse" of business, itself thoroughly compartmentalized.

> That the "Restaurant" is divided by gulfs of antagonism from the Hotel, an empty husk of rooms, is a matter of course, as are the time-limits on eating and on insufferable "room service," from which one flees to the drugstore, blatantly a shop, behind whose inhospitable counter a juggler with fried-eggs, crispy bacon and ice cubes proves himself the last solicitous host.
>
> (*MM* 75, 117 [151])

The word "snob" flies off of the page in passages like these, replete with sarcastic quotation marks which themselves indicate a kind of displacement, but each fragment of the observation is in fact thoroughly theorized: Adorno's preference for old hotels is (or so he claims) not so much for their luxury as for their reminder, with their failing central heating and bathroom across the landing, that the human body and hence human subject physically exist, and that a narrative of "progress," which for Adorno represents the potential annihilation of that humanness, might thereby somehow be resisted. Thus when he calls the modern restaurant "hostess" a "synthetic landlady" whose "true function" is "to see to it that the incoming guest does not even choose for himself the table at which he is to be processed," and concludes that "her graciousness is the reverse side of the dignity of the bouncer" (*MM* 75, 117-18 [152]), it is not so much the West-coast diner culture itself but its barely camouflaged link to a lurking violence that is at issue. However, it takes several levels of intellectual "processing" to move from the particular instance to the universal symptom.

In this (bright) light, it is surely significant that one of the nicknames for the Frankfurt School's Southern California meeting place (in Horkheimer's house) was "*Grand Hôtel Abgrund,*" or Grand Hotel Abyss—a name which seems to pun on Adorno's deleted (or curtailed) patronymic, *Wiesengrund*.[38] The idea of the abyss, perceived as a kind of giant drain of thought and language, irretrievably distanced from any sort of political practice, has, of course, become a familiar critique of poststructuralist writing

(think for example of Mark Tansey's painting, "Derrida Queries De Man" which pictures the two dancing on the dangerous edge of a Romantic cliff). A similar critique was applied to Adorno in the 1940s: his detailed analysis of cultural fragments was perceived, by Brecht for example, as dangerously removed from, if not antagonistic to, the realm of praxis: Wiesengrund's "Grand Hotel" of thought was situated too close to the *Abgrund*.

Yet it is imperative to recognize the political and by no means merely "post-Marxist" impulse in all of Adorno's criticism, even at its most apparently "abysmal." For, in addition to these sights, or sites, of California—the road, the house, the hotel, the restaurant—Adorno addresses more apparently significant intellectual and political movements in the American grain. One of the more immediately noticeable objects of Adorno's critique in **Minima Moralia** is the translation of psychoanalysis into "therapy"—an early symptom of that which would only later (in the 1960s and '70s) become a Californian cultural trademark. The Frankfurt School's work is often reductively called Freudo-Marxian (a rubric that, as Jameson points out, is better reserved for Marcuse[39]); but, in **Minima Moralia,** Adorno lashes out against the failure of psychoanalysis to resist, or even account for, social forces of domination.

He locates part of the problem in Freud's project itself. In an entry called "This Side of the Pleasure Principle," for example, Adorno suggests, contentiously, that Freud's "unenlightened enlightenment plays into the hands of bourgeois disillusion" (*MM* 37, 60 [72])[40]: "As a late opponent of hypocrisy," Adorno continues, Freud "stands ambivalently between desire for the open emancipation of the oppressed, and apology for open oppression" (*MM* 37, 60-61 [72]). This "ambivalence" or ambiguity in Freud's thinking leads to a depressing paradox: psychoanalysis, Adorno suggests, "gives us the means for discovering" the "common root" of "mind [or Spirit] and pleasure" (*Geist und Lust*), but "unintentionally" reproduces a "hostility towards both" (*MM* 37, 61 [72]).[41]

In its North American setting, the "reproduction" of this "hostility" is made manifest by the wide influence of the so-called Horney school. Karen Horney, herself a refugee from Nazi Germany (who incidentally, like Adorno, also taught at the New School for Social Research in the late 1930s), asserted that personal-environmental conditions, as opposed to biological drives, largely determine personality traits and disorders. In **Minima Moralia,** Adorno considers these theories to be a banalization of psychoanalytic insight; and consequently places American psychoanalysis firmly within the bounds of mass culture, which is itself, and not unproblematically, portrayed as a kind of invading bacterium: "Now that depth psychology, with the help of films, soap operas and Horney, has delved into the deepest recesses, people's last possibility of experiencing themselves has been cut off by organized culture" (*MM* 40, 65 [78]). That which Adorno derisively calls "ready-made enlightenment" transforms all thought into "mass-produced articles"; and "the painful secrets of the individual history, which the orthodox method [i.e. Freudianism] is already inclined to reduce to formulae, [become] commonplace conventions." Consequently,

> instead of working to gain self-awareness, the initiates become adept at subsuming all instinctual conflicts [. . .]. Terror before the abyss of the self is removed by the consciousness of being concerned with nothing so very different from arthritis or sinus trouble. Thus conflicts lose their menace. They are accepted, but by no means cured, being merely fitted as an unavoidable component into the surface of standardized life.
>
> (*MM* 40, 65 [78])

At issue here is not merely the fact that psychoanalysis has been "exiled" from its "proper" European setting into the land where people "speak of it but never think of it"[42]—although that does indeed seem to be part of the problem for Adorno. Rather, the bracketing of social-historical truth and the pursuit of an individually discoverable and reparable set of "symptoms" create a scenario in which the "Real" past—one of collective suffering—is forgotten, and the possible future foreclosed. Or, as Adorno concludes the entry:

> Thus psychoanalysis falls victim to the very replacement of the appropriate super-ego by a stubbornly adopted, unrelated, external one, that it taught us itself to understand. The last grandly-conceived theorem of bourgeois self-criticism has become a means of making bourgeois self-alienation, in its final phase, absolute, and of rendering ineffectual the lingering awareness of the ancient wound, in which lies hope of a better future.
>
> (*MM* 40, 66 [79-80])

The "awareness" of the "ancient wound" (*uralten Wunde*)—what this "wound" or "sore" might be, and what caused it, are, significantly, left unstated[43]—is numbed by a therapy that, through use of mind-measurement techniques such as Rorschach, personality, and intelligence-quotient standardized tests, focuses on hygiene and "self-fulfillment." All of these forms of psychical "understanding" result in the subsumption of the sick self into the status quo, as opposed to a recognition that standardized society itself is "sick" and must be radically overturned.

The entry called "Health unto Death," a titular reversal of Kierkegaard's *Die Krankheit zum Tode,* expands upon this critique of American "soundness" (*Gesundheit*). Here Adorno lambastes the exuberant normality of those individuals whom he calls "*Der regular guy*" and "*Das popular girl,*" and the psychical processes that engendered their behavior. "No science," he writes, "has yet explored the inferno in which were forged the deformations that later emerge to daylight as cheerfulness, openness, sociability, successful adaptation to the inevitable, an equable, practical frame of mind" (*MM* 36, 59 [69]). This infernal list of American behavioral idiosyncrasies amounts to a cata-

logue of neuroses, if not psychoses—symptoms that only reveal themselves through barely legible somatic "traces" or "tracks" (again Adorno uses the German term *Spur*[*en*]). "[T]he traces of illness," claims Adorno, "give them away[.] [T]heir skin seems covered by a rash printed in regular patterns, like a camouflage of the inorganic" (*MM* 36, 58-9 [69]). The smiling faces of the putatively healthy-and-happy are thus, in essence, masks—as it were, mass-produced masks—a camouflage unable completely to cover over (as in the gleaming roads above) the tracks of sickness, tracks subject to disappearance.

Even such "healthy" Californian homes as his own—lots of airy rooms filled with sunshine—are viewed as symptomatic by the appropriately cranky Adorno:

> Just as the old injustice[44] is not changed by a lavish display of light, air and hygiene, but is in fact concealed by the gleaming transparency of rationalized big business, the inner health of our time has been secured by blocking flight [or escape—*Flucht*] into illness without in the slightest altering its aetiology. The dark closets have been abolished as a troublesome waste of space, and incorporated into the bathroom. [. . .] The brightest rooms are the secret domain of faeces.
>
> (*MM* 36, 58-9 [69])

Here the trope of the virtually invisible mask (the "gleaming transparency" of "rationalized big business") combines with the excrement metaphor: the brightest rooms, in effect, cover up or over the dirtiest of spaces. Houses are like bodies: no matter how "clean" they appear to be, they inevitably contain, and produce, filth. Yet, as "inner health" has been forced on the individual, any genuine way out for or purging of this filth—i.e. escape through mental illness—is blocked, unable to pass.

Adorno's culturally descriptive metaphors thus initially seem to conform to a "classically" architectural Marxian base/superstructure model; only here, the superstructure (*der Überbau*) infuses virtually all aspects of thought and feeling—so that the super-ego (*das Über-ich*) is itself viewed as a kind of societal policing device. The spatialization of ideology—it is, virtually, all over and over all (*über Alles*)—makes ostensibly "sound" people unable to recognize "the possible course their lives might be given by reason" (*MM* 36, 59 [70]). But how best to listen to "reason" when one can never, with the pace of things moving so quickly, locate its source?

Throughout **Minima Moralia,** Adorno addresses the *speed* of contemporary American existence—the speed, if you will, of "sound" life—and laments the (for him) coterminous diminution of individuals' ability to think rationally. There are thus frequent, almost always derisive, references to express trains, rocket ships, and especially, automobiles (particularly to General Motors' cars[45]), all of which vehicles are symptomatic of what he calls "the runaway tempo of things" (. . . *Tempo der losgelassenen Sachen*—literally, the tempo of unleashed things) (*MM* 92, 141 [185]). At issue in this critique of speed is neither a wholesale rejection of technology *per se* nor merely a quest for intellectual quietude. (Indeed, little seems to annoy Adorno more than those "cultivated philistines"—a derisive term he borrows from Nietzsche—who recommend that he "relax and take it easy."[46]) Rather, it is the immediacy, and, hence, unintelligibility, of the speeding object that threatens to overwhelm rationality for the benefit of the total system, and which must be opposed.

Significantly, Adorno illustrates "the runaway tempo of things" by referring to "the mad race at the end of a film cartoon," and it is precisely this sense of unleashed, irrepressible power that constitutes what is perhaps his essential objection to the cinematic form. Cinema demands attentiveness just as it dissolves attention: like a rocket bomb, it apparently "career(s) without a subject," and with equally disastrous results. Adorno's well-known disagreement with Benjamin's optimistic view of the potentialities of radical cinema—absorbed in Benjamin's hesitant postscript to the "Work of Art in the Age of Mechanical Reproducibility"[47]—pivots around this question of *acceleration.* In Adorno's view, capitalist modern technology, which offers up ever-newer, ever-faster means of "transport" (conceived in the broadest sense), moves the subject of technology (viewer, reader, rider) further towards subjection, and more quickly too.

Our concern here, however, is neither Adorno's objection to the filmic medium per se, nor the so-called "culture industry" debate which has (reductively) come to define Adorno's position on America, but rather the emerging society of speeding, disciplinary spectacularity, and his exilic relation to it. This rhetoric allows him to describe, more than thirty years before Baudrillard's *Simulations,* how "men are reduced to walk-on parts in a monster documentary film which has no spectators, since the least of them has his bit to do on the screen" (*MM* 33, 55 [64]), and yet to portray his thinking self as somehow, at least temporarily, on the "other side" of this screen, in the role of spectator. To be sure, Adorno does not view his own position as exilically elect, beyond the sway of market forces—this much was made clear in the first entry of *Minima Moralia,* explored above. But the rigorously "uncommitted, suspended [. . .] mode of conduct" that he recommends (*MM* 18, 39 [41])—in his view, the only position under which "genuine" art and thought can viably function—must strive to occupy this negative, non-identical "other side." Consequently, it is the very slowness and difficulty of art and thought (the critical interrelatedness of the latter two bears emphasizing), that resists *Verdinglichung* and refuses to be subsumed into the faster, monstrous side of the screen. The vast majority of what passes for "American culture" cannot achieve such exalted negative status, and thereby becomes subsumed by the administered world, where things speed along, virtually unrecognizably and illegibly, like a single frame of a cartoon on a reel of moving film.

Perhaps no single social space more clearly exemplifies this dual tendency of late capitalism toward technological acceleration and subjective subsumption than the modern American office. Drawing on nigh-Kafkaesque caricatures, but adjusting and updating them to fit the context, Adorno frequently ridicules the bureau-mentality and its products. Here, bosses call each other by their nicknames (a genuine pet peeve of Adorno's—albeit again a theorized one[48]), while secretaries attend to the phone, which itself becomes a kind of icon of the circulation of invisible capital among the "sound." Yet it is not merely technocratic, alienated office labor that is the object of his critique, but also the very idea of the official work day as a discrete unit separated from leisure time. "Work while you work, play while you play—this is a basic rule of repressive self-discipline," writes Adorno in the entry called "Timetable" (*MM* 84, 130 [169][49]). "But one could no more imagine Nietzsche sitting in an office, with a secretary minding the telephone in an anteroom, at his desk until five o'clock, than playing golf after the day's work was done" (*MM* 84, 130 [170]). The workaday world has no time for genuine thought or pleasure, while "no spark of reflection is allowed to fall into leisure time, since it might otherwise leap across to the workaday world and set it on fire" (*MM* 84, 130 [170]). Labor and amusement are, from this potentially pyrotechnic perspective, becoming dangerously alike, even though "they are at the same time being divided ever more rigorously by invisible demarcation lines" (*MM* 84, 130 [170]).

4. SAYING "I"

It is arguably the diminishing visibility and legibility of these "demarcation lines," and their incursion into the realm of thought and subjectivity itself, that provides the central theme of *Minima Moralia.* Adorno's rhetoric of exile, as we have been exploring, relies upon similar imagined cultural demarcation lines—between inside and outside, national and extranational, selfhood and otherness—and for Adorno, the latter, weaker terms of these binaries must, in a sense, be defended, even though the effects of such divisions must be opposed. Thus while Part One of *Minima Moralia* begins with a recognition of the difficulty of authentically "independent" thinking—a motif that in Part Two leads to a consideration of how the "ego" has itself become a kind of "business manager"—Part Three, in contrast, chronically assumes a more "intimate" tone, in which the irreducible specificity of the individual *qua* individual is asserted. The word "intimate" belongs within quotation marks, because it is not clear how genuine these autobiographical sentiments are, or whether they are to be taken seriously as documents of personal memories. But they are startling, nonetheless, particularly as they represent some of the few such assertions in Adorno's philosophical *oeuvre.*

The entry called "The Bad Comrade" ("*Der böse Kamerad*"[50]), for example, commences with the claim that, "In a real sense, I ought to be able to deduce Fascism from the memories of my childhood," and proceeds with an analysis of one such set of recollections, deploying a colonial, martial simile: "As a conqueror dispatches envoys to the remotest provinces, Fascism had sent its advance guard there long before it marched in: my schoolfellows." After a brief excursus on the proper names of these peers,[51] which, to Adorno, themselves anticipate properties of fascism, he continues:

> The outbreak of the Third Reich did, it is true, surprise my political judgement, but not my unconscious fear. So closely had all the motifs of permanent catastrophe brushed me, so deeply were the warning signs of the German awakening burned into me, that I recognized them all in the features of Hitler's dictatorship: and it often seemed to my foolish terror as if the total State had been invented expressly against me, to inflict on me after all those things from which, in my childhood, its primeval form, I had been temporarily dispensed.

> (*MM* 123, 192 [255])

This striking passage, with its unexpectedly frank admission of personal psychical harm, contains, in distilled form, some of Adorno's essential theses on the philosophy of history. First, it exhibits the relation between rational judgment and the individual unconscious, expressed here in terms of its negative dispensation of "fear" (*Angstbereitschaft*—literally, "readiness for anxiety"). Second, it posits the idea of "permanent catastrophe," which characterizes Adorno's entirely Benjaminian view of historical "development." Third, the historical "inscription"—discrete memory—is conceived as brushed against ("*gestreif[t]*") or burnt into ("*eingebrannt*") each subject, data that can potentially be read forward or backward into time, as advance symptom or deferred action.

Although Adorno goes on to adumbrate why these particular memory-scenes conspired to form a legitimately suspicious, even paranoid view of the world—the entry chillingly describes the brutal and proleptically Nazi behavior of conformity-minded children who despise, and ridicule, their different or creative peers[52]—what is perhaps most salient in the present context is that these moments are viewed as a kind of nightmarish precursor to his own inevitable exile. Writing of these obnoxious classmates, who became "officials and recruits," Adorno concludes the entry:

> Now that they [. . .] have stepped visibly out of my dream and dispossessed me of my past life and my language, I no longer need to dream of them. In Fascism the nightmare of childhood has come true. [*Im Faschismus ist der Alp der Kindheit zu sich selber gekommen*—it has come into its own.]

> (*MM* 123, 193 [256-57])

Not unlike Stephen Dedalus in *Ulysses,* Adorno (who would himself eventually experience a rather unlikely Nostos in Frankfurt) here laments the inexorable, nightmarish course of history. But for Adorno (who is, in any case, perhaps as reminiscent of the Jewish outcast Bloom as of the philosophizing Dedalus), fascism represents a *realization* or malignant outgrowth of childhood memories, which themselves contained the seeds of impending disaster.

There is, in fact (to shift back to a text to which Adorno himself refers—Proust's *Recherche*), a kind of negative or anti-madeleine memory-structure in place in the latter part of the text. Whereas the bedridden Marcel was, upon tasting a biscuit, flooded with "positive" mnemonic sensations, Adorno's exilic memory is here triggered by almost "opposite" physical stimuli. Indeed, it is curiously incongruous that, while residing in mid-1940s Southern California, he reflects, in one of his fragmentary "monograms," upon how "[i]n early childhood [he] saw the first snow-shovellers in thin shabby clothes" (*MM* 122, 190 [253]). It is moreover a rather unlikely place for a "Regression" (his titular term) to music he heard as a child—Brahms's "Cradle Song" or Taubert's lullabies, for example. (Incidentally, Adorno and his wife, Margarethe "Gretel" Karplus—who served as his secretary and chauffeur and whose deep influence on his thinking remains almost entirely unexplored—themselves had no children.) Of course, personal memories are by no means determined by social space alone, but the way Los Angeles becomes a kind of filter for Adorno's impressions (secondary elaborations?) of Nazism and the holocaust is remarkable: he sees barbaric traces (*Spuren*) of "home" everywhere in the new world, the result being that while Germany and the U.S. are by no means identical, they are, through his lens, converging, like lanes on a highway.[53]

And yet, it is imperative to recognize that Adorno's conception of the bad totality is no Orwellian global dystopia, just as *Minima Moralia* is no mere justification for "the existence of the distanced, lonely critic of society."[54] To lodge Adorno in either of these philosophical "ruts"—representing, respectively, the universal and the particular—would be to misread how the concept of non-identity (or "freedom") relates and responds to the sameness of massified society. In the celebrated "Finale" of *Minima Moralia,* Adorno, returning to a motif sounded throughout the text, writes that

> [t]he only philosophy which can be justified [*verantworten*] in face of despair is the attempt to contemplate all things as they would present themselves from the standpoint of redemption. Knowledge has no light but that shed on the world by redemption: everything else exhausts itself in its reconstruction and remains mere technique [*alles andere erschöpft sich in der Nachkonstruktion und bleibt ein Stück Technik*]. Perspectives must be fashioned that displace and estrange the world, reveal it to be, with its rifts and crevices, as indigent and distorted as it will appear one day in the messianic light. To gain such perspectives without velleity or violence, entirely from felt contact with its objects—this alone is the task of thought [*Darauf allein kommt es dem Denken an*—this alone is what thought wants to know].

> (*MM* 153, 247 [334])

This dual "task," locating the standpoint of liberation and fashioning a displaced perspective out of objects themselves, is, for Adorno, both the "absolute simplest" and most utterly impossible thing: simplest because "consummate negativity, once squarely faced, delineates the mirror image of its opposite," but impossible because negativity presupposes a position (ein "*Standort*") removed or set apart from the sphere of existence ("*Bannkreis des Daseins*"), even if only by the most minuscule degree ("*um ein Winziges*").

Thus we revisit the double bind of "placement" in Adorno: that which allows philosophy to "take place," to ground itself, also threatens to undermine it and render it ineffectual. The standing place (*Standort*) from which to discern the imaginary standing point (*Standpunkt*) of redemption is highly unstable—indeed, on the verge of collapse. And Adorno, of course, recognizes the negative's shaky ground[55]: "the more passionately thought denies its conditionality for the sake of the unconditional," he writes, "the more unconsciously, and so calamitously, it is delivered up to the world. Even its own impossibility it must at last comprehend for the sake of the possible." And yet, he concludes, in comparison with all of these demands placed on a self-conscious, socially-responsible philosophy,

> the question of the reality or unreality of redemption itself is almost trivial [*die Frage nach der Wirklichkeit oder Unwirklichkeit der Erlösung [ist] selber fast gleichgültig*].
>
> (*MM* 153, 247 [354])

The final word of **Minima Moralia** is, therefore, a repudiation of the very idea of a final word. The space of deliverance (*Erlösung*)—a Benjaminian, weak messianic inflection of Utopia[56]—which he had just held out as the only viable point from which to view things-as-they-are, is revealed to be no "place" at all. The release promised by *Erlösung* may be real or unreal, but it is the tireless process of searching for its flickering light in the darkness of "despair" that, according to Adorno, itself constitutes philosophy's moral minimum.

5. CODA

My aim thus far has been to explore the "exilic" properties of Adorno's most despairingly exilic text, by asking both how exile takes place—which it does delicately and often self-contradictorily—and how Adorno fashions a critical (non) identity out of (a) place: the Los Angeles that would, initially at least, seem to represent a kind of literalization of his demand for an "estranged" philosophy. The question of exile in Adorno, as we have seen, can never be entirely divorced from that of (Marxian) alienation—in which the subject under capitalism is viewed as irretrievably separated from the products of his or her labor—but neither should exile be reduced to mere equivalency with *Entfremdung*. Indeed, by reading the broader question of the various positionalities and oppositionalities of exile in Adorno's critical thought against his personal, historically specific cultural relation to a place in time (or time in place), I have sought to work up and through the relation between criticism and labor, and thereby to expose aspects of Adorno's cultural and aesthetic theory that have received insufficient attention. For nothing could be further

from Adorno's stand on exile than the smug European touristic notion, often mistakenly associated with him, that America (unlike yogurt, as the joke would have it) has no culture, or, conversely, that German exiles themselves "embody" culture.[57] To view Adorno as merely an apologist for European "high culture," and hence enemy of the "popular," would be to banalize his anything-but-implacable philosophy, which aims above all to account and make room for cultural difference, amid what he perceives to be the increasing sameness of disciplinary technological society.

Written in the shadow of a genocidal war that was, in Adorno's view, the inexorable, logical outgrowth of material, technological "progress" and techniques of ideological manipulation, both of which entailed the further reification, and nullification, of individuals, **Minima Moralia** seeks to expose the relationship between an increasingly global system and the diminishing power of the thinking, resistant subject. "For many people," Adorno writes, "it is already an impertinence to say I" (*Bei vielen Menschen ist es bereits eine Unverschämtheit, wenn sie Ich sagen*) (**MM** 29, 50 [57]). In such a "climate," and despite the evident complicity between "bourgeois subjectivity" and Auschwitz, it becomes all the more imperative for Adorno "to say" a certain kind of "I." **Minima Moralia** presents Adorno saying it in the only way available to him: crankily, woefully, but in an exceedingly rigorous fashion.

Such was the nature of Adorno's "present" to Horkheimer. What that present has to offer the present climate of thought is open to question. Although one would hesitate to call Adorno, as Jameson has, somewhat contentiously, the philosopher of the 1990s,[58] the idea that Adorno could perhaps be perceived as "in vogue" or at least pertinent again is intriguing. It is a curious irony that one of the many complicated reasons that Adorno, who had become an internationally celebrated academic figure in the late 1960s, fell out of favor in the '70s involved, on the one hand, an enthusiasm for interrogations of identity, *logos,* and power (many of which he could be said to have anticipated), and, on the other, a short-lived optimism over liberation struggles in the developing world. If Adorno's fragmented, "subjective," highly particular portrayal of a total system seems somehow more apt in this age of a "New World Order" in which the idea of a "non-aligned" third world seems to be disappearing along with the "socialist" second—while poverty remains, even spreads—if his thinking appears "fresher" (far fresher than that of, say, Sartre or Marcuse), this may have more to do with the durability of his pessimism than with the viability of his philosophical system.

In any case, while Adorno would almost certainly have no truck with contemporary theorizations of difference—say, postcoloniality[59] or queer theory,[60] both of which he addresses, negatively, in what might be called their nascent discursive forms—there may be reason to believe that his gnomic, autobiographical, untimely meditations have something decidedly "current" about them. And if the once nearly bereft Adorno, who always insisted on the temporary, interventionist role of critical theory, can regain his currency, it is perhaps because he poignantly articulates, from the often desperate site/non-site of exile, the necessity for philosophy to address and resist a shocking current: the one we, perhaps mistakenly, call culture.[61]

Notes

1. Theodor W. Adorno, *Prisms,* trans. Samuel and Shierry Weber (Cambridge, Mass.: MIT Press, 1992), 8.

2. Adorno, "Scientific Experiences of a European Scholar in America," trans. Donald Fleming, *Perspectives in American History* 2 (1968): 370. Reprinted in Fleming and Bernard Bailyn, eds., *The Intellectual Migration: Europe and America, 1930-1960* (Cambridge, Mass.: Harvard UP, 1969), 370.

3. Martin Jay, in the concise biographical chapter in his book *Adorno,* notes the relation between the "symbolic patricide"—in which three female members of the student group "bared their breasts and 'attacked' [Adorno] with flowers and erotic caresses, [. . .] mockingly proclaiming that 'as an institution, Adorno is dead'"—and his actual death (Cambridge, Mass.: Harvard UP, 1984), 55. For a broader biographical picture, outlining Adorno's relation to other members of the Frankfurt School, see Jay's *The Dialectical Imagination: A History of the Frankfurt School and the Institute of Social Research 1923-1950* (Boston: Little, Brown and Company, 1973). See also Rolf Wiggershaus's thorough *The Frankfurt School,* trans. Michael Robertson (Cambridge, England: Polity Press, 1994).

4. "Scientific Experiences," 347.

5. Susan Buck-Morss has in particular noted the concordance of Adorno's earliest work (the "inaugural lecture" of 1931) with that of *Negative Dialectics,* his last major complete work and most programmatic text. See her *The Origin of Negative Dialectics: Theodor W. Adorno, Walter Benjamin, and the Frankfurt Institute* (New York: Free Press, 1977).

6. "Scientific Experiences," 369-70.

7. Recent efforts by, among others, Andreas Huyssen, Shierry Weber Nicholsen, Thomas Levin, Peter Uwe Hohendahl, and Harry Cooper have begun this important revaluation.

8. This is the avowed aim of Jameson's *Late Marxism: Adorno, or, The Persistence of the Dialectic* (London and New York: Verso, 1990), and the implicit project of Lambert Zuidervaart's *Adorno's Aesthetic Theory: the Redemption of Illusion* (Cambridge, Mass. and London: MIT Press, 1991).

9. These latter include not only *Dialectic of Enlightenment, Philosophy of Modern Music* and the work on Wagner, but also a book on film music (written with Hanns Eisler), a study of the *Los Angeles Times*'; as-

10. *Notes to Literature,* vol. 1, ed. Rolf Tiedemann, trans. Shierry Weber Nicholsen (New York, Columbia UP, 1991), 23.

11. The question of the difficulty of translating Adorno's notoriously sinuous German emerges at the very outset of any extended treatment of his work: even the titular adjective *"beschädigten"* could signify both "damaged" (as in "damaged goods") and "mutilated," as Jephcott later translates the word. Fredric Jameson has noted the wide range of quality of Adorno translations in the introduction to his *Late Marxism.* Jephcott's *Minima Moralia* is rightly regarded as one of the better renderings; nevertheless, I shall be reading Adorno's German "alongside" Jephcott's English, and adjusting the translations when appropriate. This may occasionally result in some obtrusive "bracketings"; but I feel that an elaboration of the multivalency of Adorno's prose is, for the purposes of this study, preferable to the brevity (and relative grace) of Jephcott's translation.

12. *Minima Moralia: Reflections from Damaged Life,* trans. E. F. N. Jephcott (New York and London: Verso, 1991), 16. *Minima Moralia: Reflexionen aus dem beschädigten Leben* (Frankfurt a.M., Suhrkamp, 1991 [1951]). Further references to the work will appear in the body of the text, preceded by the initials *MM,* followed by entry number, and page numbers in the English, then, in brackets, German editions. For a deeply thoughtful consideration of problems of translating Adorno, see Samuel Weber's introduction to *Prisms.*

13. While dialectics—especially "negative" dialectics—is obviously the cornerstone to Adorno's thinking, and while *Minima Moralia* may indeed demonstrate that which Jameson calls the "persistence" of the dialectic, my aim here is not so much to read the dialectical text "dialectically" as to explore the rhetorical figures that undergird Adorno's "exilic" relation to the object of his critique. For a comparison of French post-structuralism and the German philosophical tradition see Peter Dews, *Logics of Disintegration.* For a provocative treatment of Derrida and Adorno, see Rainer Nägele, "The Scene of the Other," in *Boundary 2* 11.1-2 (1982-3): 59-79.

14. See Rose's *Melancholy Science,* esp. 16-26, for a more detailed discussion of Adorno's essay technique. See also Tom Pepper's "Guilt By (Un) Free Association: Adorno on Romance et al," *Modern Language Notes* 109.5 (1994): 913-37, for a discussion of Adorno's anxious appropriation of Hegelian dialectical analysis.

15. The first part of what was to become *Minima Moralia* was given as a fiftieth birthday present (and

Valentine) to Horkheimer on February 14, 1945. Very little has been written about the Adorno-Horkheimer collaboration. Wiggershaus, in his *The Frankfurt School,* discusses some of the tensions (financial, emotional) between members of the Institute, but mentions friction in the Adorno-Horkheimer relationship only in passing. It must be remembered that Horkheimer was some nine years older than Adorno, and more academically established when they left Europe. While he certainly looked after Adorno's interests, he also took credit for much of the latter's work. On the title page of *Dialectic of Enlightenment,* for example, Horkheimer's name, alphabetically second, appears first.

16. Benjamin's profound influence on Adorno remains to be studied. Susan Buck-Morss, in her *Origin of Negative Dialectics,* and Richard Wolin, in *Walter Benjamin: An Aesthetic of Redemption,* have opened, but by no means exhausted, this area of inquiry. The passage above is from "The Image of Proust," *Illuminations,* 203. *Minima Moralia*'s aphoristic style also clearly draws on the work of Nietzsche, Karl Krauss, Ernst Bloch, and Horkheimer (especially the latter's *Dämmerung*), among others.

17. The verb *mitmachen* (literally "to do-with" or "to make-with"), which signifies to join in, take part in, follow, "play the game" or, as I prefer, owing to its musical significance, "play along"—is a recurrent expression in Adorno. In this sentence, it is juxtaposed with its opposite, "*nicht mitmachen,*" in an excellent example of the chiasmatic structure that characterizes Adorno's technique in *Minima Moralia.*

18. In fact, Adorno had drawn a stipend from the Rockefeller Foundation during the first few years of his American stay. As Rolf Wiggershaus puts it, in relation to Horkheimer's drawing of a similar stipend, it came from "the very institution which, by his own standards, was investing the merest fraction of the surplus from the oldest and largest capitalist conglomerates in the USA in the corruption of intellectual activity and culture." Doubtless Adorno and Horkheimer recognized this double-bind. Wiggershaus, *The Frankfurt School,* 281.

19. Adorno's tenuous relation to the Southern California German emigré community has received scant attention. I discuss this relation more fully below.

20. An avowed intention of *Minima Moralia* is to return to the "true field of philosophy[: . . .] the teaching of the good [or right] life (*[des] richtige[s] Leben*)" (*MM* Intro., 15 [7]).

21. Adorno combines the figure of vision with an elaborate nautical metaphor, in order to juxtapose the "esoteric gesture" with "the concept of austerity," which he deems more proper to life in emigration. "If in Europe the esoteric gesture was often only a pretext for the blindest self-interest, the concept of austerity, though hardly ship-shape or watertight, still seems,

in emigration, the most acceptable lifeboat." He follows this, however, with a sober assessment of the viability of "austerity": "Only a few, admittedly, have a seaworthy example at their disposal. To most boarders, it threatens starvation or madness" (*MM* 13, 34 [33-4]).

22. Since Heidegger also uses the term "dwell" (*wohnen*) in the famous 1951 essay "Building Dwelling Thinking" (*Bauen Wohnen Denken*)—an essay that he ends by addressing the then-current "housing shortage" in Germany—any easy distinction between Adorno's "materialist" view of houses and Heidegger's "existential" one might seem suspect. Nevertheless, while Adorno and Heidegger both indeed do attack modern homes and homelessness, they approach the idea of "housing" from entirely opposite positions: Heidegger's concluding question "What if man's homelessness consisted in this, that man still does not even think of the *real* plight of dwelling as *the* plight?" and his response that "As soon as man gives thought to his homelessness, it is a misery no longer" could not in fact be more "alien" to Adorno's thinking. *Basic Writings,* ed. David F. Krell (San Francisco: Harper, 1977), 339, italics in text. This is not to suggest that a broader analysis of Adorno's and Heidegger's positions on housing, dwelling, and thinking might not prove fruitful. For an important study of Heidegger's position on the house, the home, and violence, see Mark Wigley, "Heidegger's House: The Violence of the Domestic," *D: Columbia Documents in Architecture and Theory* 1 (1992), 91-121. For an interesting attempt to explore the interface between the thought of Adorno and Heidegger, see Fred Dallmayr's *Life World, Modernity and Critique* (Cambridge, U.K.: Polity Press, 1991), 44-71. Dallmayr's analysis itself draws heavily upon Hermann Mörchen's appropriately subtitled *Adorno und Heidegger: Untersuchung einer philosophischen Kommunikationsverweigerung* (Examination of a Refused Philosophical Communication) (Stuttgart: Klett-Cotta, 1981).

23. Other entry titles reflecting these concerns include "Pro Domo Nostra," "Addressee Unknown," "Inside and Outside," "Grassy Seat," and "Hothouse Plant."

24. Of these, he writes: "The traditional residences we grew up in have grown intolerable: each trait of comfort in them is paid for with a betrayal of knowledge, each vestige of shelter with the musty pact of family interests" (*MM* 18, 38 [40]).

25. This phrase represents a melancholic addendum to the "Gay" or "Joyful" Science of Nietzsche, who writes "*Es gehört selbst zu meinen Glücke, kein Hausbesitzer zu sein*" (I consider myself lucky not to be a homeowner).

26. As Marx studied England as it represented, in the nineteenth century, the most advanced capitalist society of his age, so did Adorno consider the U.S.

economy and culture to be most "advanced," and, indeed, the wave of the future. As Peter Uwe Hohendahl points out, Adorno never visited New England or the Southern states; but this did not detract from Adorno's conviction that what he was witnessing in Los Angeles was a cultural dominant. See Hohendahl's *Prismatic Thought: Theodor W. Adorno* (Lincoln, Nebraska and London: Univ. of Nebraska Press, 1995), esp. 21-44, which offers a useful comparison of Adorno's work to that of American scholars of the late 1940s. For a consideration of the "idea" of California in German philosophical thought, see Laurence A. Rickels, *The Case of California* (Baltimore and London: Johns Hopkins UP, 1991).

27. Cornelius Schnauber's guidebook for intellectually-inclined German-speaking tourists, *Spaziergänge durch das Hollywood der Emigranten* (Walking through the Hollywood of the Emigrants) incorrectly places Adorno at 316 North Kenter (Zürich: Arche, 1992), 103, and implies that Adorno possessed the entire house, whereas he had only half.

28. Wiggershaus's *The Frankfurt School* offers the most detailed biographical treatment of how the intellectual community began to coalesce around Horkheimer in 1941, but it is not particularly thorough on the links between the Horkheimer circle and the Hollywood community. Other published treatments of the emigré community include Anthony Heilbut's well researched *Exiled in Paradise: German Refugee Artists and Intellectuals in America, from 1930 to the Present* (New York, Viking, 1983), which treats Adorno's writing quite sympathetically, and Mike Davis's rather superficial *City of Quartz: Excavating the Future in Los Angeles* (New York: Vintage, 1992), which does not. Davis, who derisively calls the Institute's meetings "soirées," accuses "the exiles" of not being able to link their critique to such political actions as a local munitions factory strike in the mid-1940s. Other accounts that offer biographical information about Adorno during this period include Wiggerhaus's still-untranslated *Theodor W. Adorno* (Munich: C. H. Beck, 1987); Harvey Gross's "Adorno in Los Angeles: the Intellectual in Emigration," *Humanities in Society* 2.3 (1979): 339-351; and Martin Jay's "Adorno in America," *New German Critique* 31 (1984): 285-305. The latter focuses more on Adorno's reception in the North American academy than on the biography.

29. Schnauber, *Spaziergänge,* 92-112. See also Wiggershaus, *The Frankfurt School,* 265 ff.

30. Though the mythical one thus surrounded them, the real, geographically correct Hollywood was in fact several miles to the east.

31. See Mann's *Story of a Novel: The Genesis of Doctor Faustus,* trans. Richard and Clara Winston (New York: Knopf, 1961). Playing on the title of Mann's novel, Jean-François Lyotard, in his (pre-*Postmodern*

Condition) "Adorno as the Devil," seeks to critique the idea of the negative (and, implicitly, of totality) in Adorno, and to substitute his concept of libidinal economy as a means of understanding "objectivity" in capital. *Telos* 19 (1974): 127-137. My reading of Adorno in these pages has been influenced by this short but provocative essay.

32. See the *Saturday Review* article of Nov. 13, 1948, in which Schoenberg adamantly distanced himself from the theories, and personality, of Leverkühn, the novel's protagonist. Excerpts of the letter are cited in Schnauber, *Spaziergänge,* 103.

33. The episode is recounted in Otto Friedrich, *City of Nets: Hollywood in the 1940s* (New York: Harper and Row, 1986). Friedrich notes that the tune is Beethoven's last piano sonata, Opus 111, and that the words or "poetic little illustrative phrases," as Mann called them, are rendered in English as "Heaven's blue, lover's pain . . . meadow-land [*Wiesengrund*]," but does not question Mann's claim about having slipped the word into his novel as a way of "showing [his] gratitude" to his "teacher." See 274 and 274 note. As I suggest below, however, others in the Los Angeles circle seemed in fact to ridicule this (deleted) name.

34. Adorno gets some of the details wrong, curiously calling the movie *The Best Years of Our Life,* and calling the actor—who must have been Harold Russell—the "leading man" (*Hauptdarsteller*) when in fact Fredric March was the lead. Moreover, Russell, who played a character ironically named "Homer" (resonating with Adorno's own treatment of the long-exiled figure in *Dialectic of Enlightenment,* here suffering a kind of symbolic castration before "coming home") had lost not one but both of his hands. Russell won two Academy Awards: one for Best Supporting Actor and another for being an inspiration to handicapped veterans. In fact, the film itself involves several such "handshake" scenes. The Chaplin essay appears in Adorno's *Gesammelte Schriften* Bd 10.1 (Frankfurt a.M.: Suhrkamp, 1977), 365 ff, and the incident is alluded to in Gunzelin Schmid Noerr, "Adornos Erschaudern: Variationen über den Händedruck," in *Vierzig Jahre Flaschenpost: Dialektik der Aufklärung, 1947-1987,* ed. Willem van Reijen and Gunzelin Schmid Noerr (Frankfurt a.M: Fischer, 1987), 235-36. It has recently been translated, by John MacKay, as "Chaplin Times Two" in *The Yale Journal of Criticism* 9.1 (1996): 58-61. See also MacKay's brief but insightful introduction, 57-58.

35. In "Adornos Erschaudern: Variationen über den Händedruck," Noerr points out the strangeness of Adorno's theory of handshakes, and links the Chaplin incident correctly but only briefly to Adorno's broader theses on mimesis. He also productively gauges Habermas's quite different memory of the story, which Adorno had recounted verbally to him. The question is particularly interesting because Hab-

ermas himself, slightly physically challenged, has a speech impediment, and may well be sensitive to such encounters. I thank Eva Geulen for mentioning the Chaplin anecdote to me.

36. Significantly, Adorno writes of the translation and domestication of the formerly "exotic" in the entry entitled "Mammoth": "The fact that animals really suffer more in cages than in the open range [. . .] reflects on the inescapability of imprisonment. It is a consequence of history. The zoological gardens in their authentic form are products of nineteenth century colonial imperialism. They flourished since the opening-up of wild regions of Africa and Central Asia, which paid symbolic tribute in the shape of animals. The value of tributes was measured by their exoticism, their inaccessibility. The development of technology has put an end to this and abolished the exotic" (*MM* 74, 116 [149-150]).

37. It is also surely significant that Adorno is in the position of "passenger" here, as he himself, according to information provided by the Adorno Archive in Frankfurt, was not able to drive.

38. Lukács reserves this nickname (*Grand Hôtel Abgrund*) explicitly for Adorno in the 1962 Preface to *Theory of the Novel,* but then-contemporary critics applied the term to Frankfurt School thought more generally. See the Introduction to Gunzelin Schmid Noerr and Willem van Reijen, eds., *Grand Hotel Abgrund, Eine Photobiographie der Frankfurter Schule* (Hamburg, Junius, 1988), 10-12, for a brief discussion of Lukács's deployment of the term "*Abgrund.*" Adorno's use, beginning in the mid-1930s, of his mother's Corsican maiden name (and shortening of the Jewish-sounding *nom du père* to "W") may have provoked some ridicule among his colleagues. However professionally or politically viable the name change may have been, Adorno's disavowal of "Jewishness" is surely significant, especially in relation to his treatment, throughout the 1940s, of questions of anti-Semitism. I view these texts (namely the "Elements of Anti-Semitism" chapter of *Dialectic of Enlightenment* and the *Authoritarian Personality* study also written in Los Angeles) as also curiously if tenuously "autobiographical." In a forthcoming longer version of the present essay (a book project I am completing with Stanford University Press), I plan to pursue these questions in greater detail.

39. *Late Marxism,* 254, n. 4.

40. Like "regressive progress," the expression "unenlightened enlightenment" (*unaufgeklärte Aufklärung*) expresses through simple negation the contradictions latent in a concept.

41. And he concludes, vituperatively: "The therapeutically much-lauded transference, the breaking of which is not for nothing the crux of analytic treatment, the artificially contrived situation where the subject performs, voluntarily and calamitously, the annulment of the self which was once brought about involuntarily and beneficially by erotic self-abandonment, is already the pattern of the reflex-dominated, follow-my-leader behavior which liquidates, together with all intellect, the analysts who have betrayed it" (*MM* 37, 61 [73]). Curiously, Adorno, who had studied in Vienna in the early 1920s, was, along with Frederick Pollock and Herbert Marcuse, one of the three members of the *Institut für Sozialforschung* who had not been analyzed. (Fromm, Löwenthal, and Horkheimer all had.) See Wiggershaus, *The Frankfurt School,* 267.

42. The title of the entry, as translator Jephcott notes, is an inversion of *"Nie davon reden, immer daran denken,"* a pro-*Anschluβ*; slogan in pre-war Austria: in the American context, the "it" in question is sex.

43. The word *Wunde* takes on different resonances—in relation to lyric poetry, to anti-Semitism, and to language—in Adorno's later essay, "Heine the Wound," *Notes to Literature* I, 80-85. The conclusion to the essay, in particular, bears witness to Adorno's own exile, and to his thoughts about its "universality": "Now that the destiny which Heine sensed [i.e. homelessness] has been fulfilled literally [. . .], the homelessness has become everyone's homelessness; all human beings have been as badly injured in their beings and their language as Heine the outcast was. His words stand in for their words: there is no longer any homeland other than a world in which no one would be cast out any more, the world of a genuinely emancipated humanity. The wound that is Heine will heal only in a society that has achieved reconciliation" (85).

44. *"Das alte Unrecht."* Notice the similarity between this phrase and *"die uralten Wunde,"* above.

45. Despite his seemingly sarcastic comments about "knowledge of trade-union organizations or the automobile industry" in the entry called "Protection, Help and Counsel" (Entry 13), by Entry 77 ("Auction"), Adorno demonstrates a familiarity with fundamentals of Fordist production: "While a Cadillac undoubtedly excels a Chevrolet by the amount that it costs more, this superiority, unlike that of the old Rolls Royce, nevertheless proceeds from an overall plan which artfully equips the former with better, the latter with worse cylinders, bolts, accessories, without anything being altered in the basic pattern of the mass-produced article: only minor rearrangements in production would be needed to turn the Chevrolet into a Cadillac" (*MM* 77, 119-20 [154-55]). . . . For an elaboration on this idea of "interchangeable parts" as it applies to the realm of popular music, see Bernard Gendron, "Theodor Adorno Meets the Cadillacs," in Tania Modleski, ed., *Studies in Entertainment: Critical Approaches to Mass Culture* (Bloomington and Indianapolis: Indiana UP, 1986), 18-36. Adorno, it ought to be noted somewhere, seems to be uncomfortable with the very word "automobile," which, on

the first page of the essay "Cultural Criticism and Society," he compares to the similarly Greek-Latin blended term "Kulturkritik," a word which, according to Adorno, has "an offensive ring." See *Prisms*, 19.

46. Adorno scathingly refers to this "watchword" of the cultivated philistines as "a formula borrowed from the language of the nursing home" (*MM* 139, 217 [290]). Adorno often turns to the English original when deriding a specifically Anglo-Saxon concept; hence here the German text reads "*Da muß es nach den englischen Formeln relax und take it easy hergehen, die aus der Sprache der Krankenschwestern kommen*" (291).

47. For a broader discussion of this context of this "debate," see the essays collected in *Aesthetics and Politics: Theodor Adorno, Walter Benjamin, Ernst Bloch, Bertolt Brecht, Georg Lukács*, trans., ed. Ronald Taylor (London and New York: Verso, 1990). See also Thomas Levin's trenchant critique of reductive accounts of Adorno's position on technology, in Levin's "For the Record: Adorno on Music in the Age of Its Technological Reproducibility," *October* 55 (1990): 23-47.

48. Adorno's objection to nicknames inheres in the false sense of proximity that they seem to provide. In the "Culture Industry" chapter of *Dialectic of Enlightenment*, he writes that "the bourgeois family name [. . .] seems antiquated. It arouses a strange embarrassment in Americans. In order to hide the awkward distance between individuals, they call one another 'Bob' and 'Harry,' as interchangeable team members. This practice reduces relations between human beings to the good fellowship of the sporting community and is a defense against the true kind of relationship." *Dialectic of Enlightenment*, trans. John Cumming (New York: Continuum, 1991), 165. *Dialektik der Aufklärung: Philosophische Fragmente* (Frankfurt a.M., S. Fischer, 1991), 174. Elsewhere, he suggests that "perhaps names are no more than frozen laughter, as is evidenced nowadays in nicknames" (77 [85]).

49. The phrase is rendered in English within the German text ("Work while you work, play while you play—*das zählt zu den Grundregeln der repressiven Selbstdisziplin*" [169]), again suggesting the distinct "Americanness" of the concept.

50. As translator Jephcott notes, this title reverses that of a song, "*Der gute Kamerad*," popular during the Nazi period.

51. "Children already equipped with Christian names like Horst and Jürgen and surnames like Bergenroth, Bojunga and Eckhardt enacted the dream [of a brutal national community] before the adults were historically ripe for its realization" (*MM* 123, 192 [255]). (One wonders what Habermas thinks of this passage!)

52. Adorno pointedly highlights how these fellow students criticized his youthful writing style: "They who could not put together a correct sentence but found all of mine too long—did they not abolish German literature and replace it by their 'writ'?" (*MM* 123, 193 [256-57]). It is as if Adorno's "mature" writing style were thus itself a kind of "regression," a maintenance of a link with a (lost) pre-war world.

53. Jameson delves into Adorno's position on so-called "convergence theory" in greater detail than I can offer here. See his *Late Marxism*, esp. 123-154. Lest the conflation of the U.S., Nazi Germany, and the "State Capitalist" USSR seem, in retrospect, strained or ludicrous, it is worth remembering that the U.S. would, within months of Adorno's completion of *Minima Moralia*, begin the House Un-American Activities Commission hearings on "the communist infiltration of the motion picture industry," before which Eisler and Brecht would be called. Eisler was eventually *de facto* deported, while Brecht left for Switzerland the day after his testimony. On Adorno and Horkheimer's extreme (some would say inexcusable) caution in regards to HUAC—Adorno did not attach his name to a text on film music he wrote with Eisler until 1969—see Wiggershaus, 389-390 (Wiggershaus incorrectly refers to the hearings as performed by the "HCUA").

54. Rolf Wiggershaus further views Adorno, in *Minima Moralia*, as an "advocate for the non-conformist intellectual." *The Frankfurt School*, 394.

55. The metaphor is, in fact, consistent with Adornian terminology. In the epigraph to Part Three, quoting from Baudelaire, he asks "*Avalanche, veux-tu m'emporter dans ta chute?*"

56. Of theories of Utopia, generally associated in the Marxian tradition with Ernst Bloch (and, later, Marcuse), Adorno writes, in the entry called "Baby with the Bath Water": "Since Utopia was set aside and the unity of theory and practice demanded, we have become all too practical" (*MM* 22, 44 [49]). Strangely enough, in one of the *Authoritarian Personality* essays he authored, Adorno castigates Americans for not being able to imagine Utopia, calling this tendency "an anti-Utopia complex." See especially the section "There Will Be No Utopia," in Adorno et al., *The Authoritarian Personality* (New York: Harper Brothers, 1950), 695-698.

57. See the entry "Back to Culture," where Adorno writes of the romanticization of pre-Nazi German culture: "This has led to fatal confusion. Hitler eradicated culture, Hitler drove Mr. X [in German: "*Herr Ludwig*"] into exile, therefore Mr. X is culture. He is indeed. A glance at the literary output of those emigrés who, by discipline and a sharp separation of spheres of influence, performed the feat of representing the German mind, shows what is to be expected of a happy reconstruction: the introduction of Broadway methods on the *Kurfürstendamm* [Berlin's theater

district], which differed from the former in the Twenties only through its lesser means, not its better intentions" (*MM* 35, 56-57 [68]). Visitors to contemporary Berlin would, indeed, confirm the validity of this prediction.

58. *Late Marxism,* 251. See also Jameson's more general comments on Adorno and "post-modernism" on 246-252.

59. Although anti-colonial independence struggles were chronologically imminent—India and Pakistan would become nation-states in 1947, while China would declare itself a "people's republic" in 1949—Adorno did not look to "outer-realm" victims of European imperialism; indeed, his conception of liberation seems far removed from actual liberation struggles. About these he had, throughout his career, very little to say—save some rather scathing comments in *Minima Moralia* about the romanticization of "African students of political economy" and "Siamese at Oxford." Under the heading "Savages are not more Noble," he writes, quite presciently, that "There is some reason to fear that the involvement of non-Western peoples in the conflicts of industrial society, long overdue in itself, will be less to the benefit of the liberated peoples than to that of rationally improved production and communications, and a modestly raised standard of living. Instead of expecting miracles of the pre-capitalist peoples, older nations should be on their guard against their unimaginative, indolent taste for everything proven, and for the successes of the West" (*MM* 32, 52-3 [60-1]). Rather, his concern, along with that of Horkheimer and other members of the Frankfurt School, was clearly that repository of difference *within* the logic of the same. And the figure that most embodied that sense of difference—in Europe and America at least—was "the Jew."

60. Throughout his work, Adorno points—problematically—to connections between fascism and latent homosexuality. See for example, the "Elements of Anti-Semitism" chapter of *Dialectic of Enlightenment,* or the entry in *Minima Moralia* called "Tough Baby." See also his comments about the conversion of Proust's work—which Adorno views as revolutionary—into that of a "prize winning homosexual" (*MM* 132, 207 [276]).

61. The author would like to thank the following people for their insight, advice, and/or editorial prowess: Jennifer Wicke, Samuel Weber, Sara Suleri-Goodyear, Thad Ziolkowski, Adam Green, Eric Schwab, Martin Harries, Joanna Spiro, and Jessica Morgan.

Leonard Olschner (essay date 1997)

SOURCE: "Chapter 100: 1951," in *Yale Companion to Jewish Writing and Thought in German Culture 1096-1996,* edited by Sander. L. Gilman and Jack Zipes, Yale University Press, 1997, pp. 691-96.

[*In the following essay, Olschner examines the relevance of Adorno's assertion that lyric poetry could not be written after the events of the Holocaust.*]

A tenaciously recurring leitmotif accompanying, at least implicitly, much West German discourse and criticism on lyric poetry after about 1960 has been the veritable possibility or impossibility of writing poetry after Auschwitz. Why lyric poetry should be singled out rather than, say, prose fiction or drama, has partially to do with the aporetic problem of representing the Shoah at all, but perhaps more with traditional German understanding of this particular genre. The question is fundamental, not merely academic; whether it is in fact relevant requires explication.

In 1949, the same year he returned to West Germany to teach temporarily at the University of Frankfurt after having lived in exile in the United States since 1938, Adorno wrote his essay **"Kulturkritik und Gesellschaft" ("Cultural criticism and society")**. The essay first appeared in print in 1951 and then again, more visibly, in 1955 in *Prismen* (*Prisms*). Drawing on a Central European notion of *Kultur* with its various repertoires of articulation, while at the same time pessimistically reaffirming the ossification of bourgeois understanding of what culture is and can mean, Adorno attempted to interpret the transformed meaning of the term and phenomenon in society after fascism and after the Shoah. This task became all the more complicated with the realization that culture had had no appreciably moderating effect on the conception and execution of the Final Solution. To the contrary, Adorno appears to suspect a moment of complicity in cultural criticism itself: "Such critical consciousness remains servile toward culture in that it distracts from the horrors, but it also determines culture as a complement of the horrors" (22). In its closing argument, this essay contained a provocative pronouncement that would occupy West German—and evidently only West German—literary critics throughout and beyond the 1960s, especially since a long overdue counterposition to conservative criticism had found articulation, and this articulation had reached a responsive critical awareness among increasingly influential younger critics. The statement in question reads: "By being neutralized and processed, traditional culture in its entirety today becomes insignificant. . . . Even the most extreme consciousness of the catastrophe threatens to degenerate into drivel. Cultural criticism exists in confrontation with the final level of the dialectic of culture and barbarism: to write a poem after Auschwitz is barbaric, and that also gnaws at the knowledge which states why it has become impossible to write poems today" (30).

In virtually every reference made to Adorno's postulate, critics confined themselves to what they understood to be its pithy essence: "to write a poem after Auschwitz is barbaric." The aphoristic reduction would seem to preclude interpretation, and thus critics irresponsibly or at least misleadingly abbreviated Adorno's thought to assert the impossibility of poetry at all after Auschwitz. This reduction, however, always occurred in reviews and discussions of poetry—often remarkable poetry, often sympathetic reviews—that had found their way to publication. The patent contradiction critics evoked here only to leave unresolved seemed strangely unworthy of further attention, as did a closer examination of what Adorno might have intended by such an absolute claim. Even recently Günter Grass has skeptically asked whether speaking about Adorno's sentence might have only satisfied a ritual of dismay, and whether the self-interrogations of writers in the 1950s and early 1960s only served as rhetorical exercises (Grass 1990, 10).

Certainly part of the responsibility for the limited understanding and the later superficial readings and resultant misunderstanding lies in Adorno's strained articulation of the problem of comprehending and representing or treating the Shoah in poetry. He does not indicate what he holds "poetry" to be, as if, even in cultural circles, a consensus existed. One may not assume that Adorno found the very genre of lyric poetry had become culturally insignificant or superfluous, given his major essays and the passages within other works written after 1949 and devoted to the poetry of George, Hofmannsthal, Borchardt, Eichendorff, Mörike, Heine, and others. Indeed, most of these names provide a key to aspects of poetry that Adorno held dear: with the exception of Heine, these poets belonged to a conservative poetic tradition in nineteenth- and twentieth-century Germany that helped define the poetic canon and formative mainstream bourgeois *Bildung* and mentality. Of great significance is the fact that the same year his essay **"Kulturkritik und Gesellschaft"** appeared—and not in 1957, as is commonly assumed—Adorno also published for the first time his later radio essay **"Rede über Lyrik und Gesellschaft"** (**"Talk on poetry and society"**). In constituting a retrospective analysis of earlier poetry and of the function of society in poetic utterance, this essay does not contradict Adorno's radical pronouncement, but it does open other and more differentiated vistas for a reading of poetry that went far beyond the non-historicizing intrinsic readings that were the norm at this time. In the essay, Adorno demonstrates how individual poetic expression becomes artistic expression only when it participates in more general or more universally shared experience, and that implies society, social influence, and societal developments; the poetic subject represents, according to Adorno, a more general, collective subject (Adorno 1958, 74-75, 91).

In his dictum on poetry after Auschwitz, Adorno had himself inadvertently become distracted by the very phenomenon he feared—namely, the not unfounded expectation of a conservative continuation of pre-1933 poetic forms and themes that dominated poetic writing throughout the fascist years, both in Germany itself and even among prominent exile writers. By affirming traditional poetics, such writing would be unable to overcome impotence in reacting to the devastations of fascism. Poetry had been primarily thought of as originating in feeling, and, since Goet-

he's poetry of experience and Hegel's lectures on aesthetics, as the most subjective of literary genres. Adorno without doubt assumed such a non-response to the catastrophe to be severely inadequate, historically displaced and inappropriate, and potentially dangerous, not to mention a brutal disregard for the suffering and death of fascism's victims. He can only have based his verdict that writing poetry after Auschwitz is barbaric on his own previous understanding of what poetry was, rather than what its function and potential might be, both aesthetically and sociologically. Some consistency in his position remained, however. His defense of Stefan George in the **"Rede über Lyrik und Gesellschaft"** and the later essay **"George"** (1967), as well as his introduction to and selection of poems by Rudolf Borchardt (1968), document Adorno's effort to redeem these conservative poets critically—at a time that, remarkably, coincided with the beginnings of the student movement in the Federal Republic.

Beginning in 1945-46 and continuing into the early 1950s, a veritable deluge of new poetry flooded the journals and, in the form of individual volumes and anthologies, the bookstores. The bulk of this poetry, largely forgotten today, exhibited traditional themes from personal experience and nature in rhymed strophic forms, indicated no awareness of the avant-garde, and showed little interest in exploring the limitations of language even (or especially) where it occasionally thematized postwar realities. It corresponded to a deeply felt need among both poets and readers in the ruins after the war to seek out metaphysical havens of interiority and timelessness, rather than constructive introspection and a sense of the historicity of their own time. The designation "pure poetry" (*reine Dichtung* or *reine Lyrik*) became, not surprisingly, the supreme recognition of poetic accomplishment.

In intuiting this development and formulating his premise, Adorno failed to anticipate a counterdevelopment, to postulate or envision a poetic writing possible after Auschwitz. At present one can only speculate about the actual texts Adorno might have read during the fascist years and immediately thereafter by poets within and outside of Germany and how these texts might have affected his thinking. The few names he briefly mentions in his ***Minima Moralia*** (written 1944-47)—Hölderlin, Goethe, Verlaine, Liliencron, Trakl, Däubler, Stramm, George, and Rilke—only confirm his adherence to the canon and betray a characteristic reception of poets he and his educated contemporaries would have read in younger years. Brecht, the outstanding non-Jewish representative of poetic response to fascism, albeit not to the Shoah, did not become a paradigm of poetic voice for Adorno, even in view of such Brecht poems as "Schlechte Zeit für Lyrik" (Bad times for poetry, 1939), which, by lamenting the inopportuneness of writing poetry as usual, implicitly calls for a (political) poetry suited to defy fascism. Nonetheless, Adorno must have become aware of important Jewish writing by the early 1950s, primarily that by Nelly Sachs, whose collection *In den Wohnungen des Todes* (In the dwellings of death) appeared in Berlin (East) in 1947, and by Paul

Celan, whose work he had read at least by the late 1950s, whom he planned (but failed) to meet in 1959 in Engadin, and to whom he dedicated the second publication of his essay **"Valérys Abweichungen"** (**"Valéry's divergences"** 1961).

Hans Magnus Enzensberger appears to have become the first to challenge Adorno's pronouncement in eulogizing Nelly Sachs, who had lived in exile in Sweden since 1940 and whose work before 1961 had moved from publisher to publisher and received only irregular, if indeed favorable, attention by critics. In 1959 Enzensberger published in *Merkur* his essay on Sachs's poetry, "Die Steine der Freiheit" ("The stones of freedom"), which appeared again in an homage to Nelly Sachs in 1961. Here he counters Adorno: "Adorno has written a sentence which belongs to the most severe judgments that can be made about the time in which we live: after Auschwitz it is no longer possible to write a poem. If we want to continue living, we have to disprove this proposition. Only few [writers] are able to do so. Nelly Sachs belongs to these few. A moment of redemption is inherent in her language. In speaking, she gives back to us, sentence by sentence, what we have been in danger of losing: language" (Enzensberger 1961, 47).

Sachs, who saw herself as a quasi-depersonalized voice or mediator speaking for the remembered and mourned dead, attempted to place her work outside the confines of subjective expression. As early as 1948 Sachs had written to a friend that she had tried "to capture the apocalyptic time" in her most recent poems, while at the same letting "the eternal mysteries shine through." "Just as times past," she continued, "our time, as horrible as it is, does have to find its expression in art; it must be attempted with all new means, for the old means are no longer sufficient" (Sachs 1985, 98).

In his essay **"Engagement"** (**"Commitment"** 1962), Adorno concurred with Enzensberger's rebuttal in principle by saying that a refutation of the verdict through poetry was necessary, lest the very existence of poetry commit itself to cynicism: "I am not inclined to mitigate the sentence that says it is barbaric still to write poetry after Auschwitz; in this statement the impulse is expressed that inspires *littérature engagée*. . . . But Enzensberger's rejoinder remains true that poetry has to stand up to precisely this verdict and hence has to be such that it does not surrender to cynicism through its very existence after Auschwitz. Poetry's own situation is paradoxical, not the manner in which one chooses to view poetry. The excesses of real suffering do not permit forgetting" (Adorno 1965, 125-26).

In his **"Meditationen zur Metaphysik"** (**"Meditations on metaphysics"**), first published in *Negative Dialektik* (*Negative dialectics*; 1966), Adorno contextualizes his pronouncement anew. The opening section, entitled "After Auschwitz," contains his final statement on poetry after Auschwitz: "Perennial suffering has just as much a right to receive expression as the tortured victim has to scream; hence it may have been wrong to say that poetry could not be written after Auschwitz. Not wrong, however, is the less cultural question as to whether living is at all possible after Auschwitz, as to whether whoever by chance escaped death and legitimately [*rechtens*] should have been killed has a right to live at all" (Adorno 1980, 355).

Adorno retracts his original statement, but even more he revises its radical gesture and places it in the more encompassing context of what culture and education, survival and life itself, could possibly mean after Auschwitz. At this point it is important to recall those Jewish poets such as Gertrud Kolmar and Selma Meerbaum-Eisinger who wrote anticipating the Shoah (and who perished in its wrath) and the poetry written in the ghettos and camps by many nameless and some remembered authors. Ruth Klüger (1992, 122-27) has written an eloquent personal testimony about the meaning of poetry for her as a young girl in the camps, poetry she recited to herself to pass the time and assuage fear, as well as poetry she herself wrote. Three pioneering lyric anthologies have collected verse by camp inmates and others: *Jüdisches Schicksal in deutschen Gedichten: Ein abschließende Anthologie* (Jewish fate in German poems: A final anthology, 1959), *An den Wind geschrieben: Lyrik der Freiheit. Gedichte der Jahre, 1933-1945* (Written in the wind: Poetry of freedom. Poems, 1933-1945; 1960), and *Welch Wort in die Kälte gerufen: Die Judenverfolgung des Dritten Reiches im deutschen Gedicht* (What a word called into the cold: The persecution of the Jews by the Third Reich in German poetry; 1968). Of these collections, the first evidently received little or no attention, and the last, an East German publication, disappeared from the bookstores and even certain libraries. Only the second, after the editor's initial difficulty in locating a willing publisher, found readers and is again in print today. Yet other poets such as Else Lasker-Schüler and Nelly Sachs, in exile, turned to poetic expression in German as the only vehicle remaining to them to explore the contemporary horrors they had suffered. In a poem written in 1944 in a work camp, "Nähe der Gräber" (Nearness of the graves), Paul Celan apostrophizes his murdered mother, seeking dispensation to continue writing in his mother-tongue: "Und duldest du, Mutter, wie einst, ach, daheim, / den leisen, den deutschen, den schmerzlichen Reim?" ("And can you bear, Mother, as you did back home, / the quiet, the German, the painful rhyme?") (Celan 1983, v., 20). The young Celan was aware of the same dilemma as Adorno; he questioned not the possibility of poetry, however, but the possibly of using the German language. This perhaps was the blind spot in Adorno's original argument, because he can hardly have proposed that poetry in any language was impossible.

Lyric poetry existed not in a time-eternity dichotomy, but on borrowed time; it had to discontinue now questionable traditions and become the direct product of historical experience (and perforce of redefined poetics). Adorno, who at the time of his death had planned an essay on Celan, recognized that this poet was one of the few capable of addressing the Shoah and indicated as much in his *Aesthetic Theory*: "This poetry is permeated by the shame of art in view of the suffering that evades both experience and sublimation. Celan's poems want to express extreme horror by maintaining silence [*Verschweigen*]" (Adorno 1973, 477). The silence to which Adorno perhaps misleadingly refers is not congruent with that of those who would silence the horror, but rather with the frequently hermetic language of poetry that cautiously moves toward the ineffable. Of German-language lyric poetry, Celan observed in 1958: "With dismal gloom in its memory and dubiousness surrounding it, it can, despite the presence of the tradition in which it stands, no longer speak the language which some sympathetic ears still appear to expect from it. Its language is more austere, more factual; it distrusts the "Beautiful"; it attempts to be true. . . . This language does not transfigure, does not "poeticize"; it names and constructs meaning; it attempts to measure the space of the given and the possible. To be sure, language itself, language per se is never at work here, but always only a voice speaking under the angle of its existential inclination, interested in contour and orientation. Reality does not exist as such; reality needs to be sought and attained" (Celan 1983, 3:167-68).

Celan did not claim to speak for all of his contemporaries, although he felt he could speak for many. Speaking from the periphery as a Romanian-born, German-speaking Jew living in Paris, whose works were published (with a few minor exceptions) exclusively in the Federal Republic and whose literary reception in the 1950s and 1960s was strongest in that country, he experienced reactions to his work ranging from perplexity to praise and from scandalous charges of plagiarism to misreadings destined to neutralize the poetry's efficacy. But part of this reception would seem to fulfill the foreboding Adorno had had in 1949. In an essay of 1960 in a pedagogical journal, a German teacher wrote about interpreting Celan's "Todesfuge" (Death fugue; 1944-45) in the school classroom: "One may not expect the pupils to have precise knowledge of the fate of the Jews under the Hitler regime. The pupil first has to learn as historical material what the teacher consciously experienced as a contemporary. Hence a discussion of 'Death Fugue' could easily lapse into an explanation of the persecution of the Jews, whereby the poem would then only be a pretext, not the constant focus of the discussion" (Butzlaff 1960, 42).

In this essay, a remarkable combination of didactic myopia, historical naïveté, and impudence sees the poem as a purely literary, historically irrelevant utterance that warns the reader not to politicize the text; in a tastelessly didactic gesture the author proceeds to compare the "fugal" technique in "Todesfuge" with that of a poem by Ernst Bertram, a poet and Germanist who lost his chair at the University of Cologne in 1945 because of his fascist activity. The mentality betrayed in this essay is not appreciably distant from the discussion of the mid-1960s concerning the aestheticization of the Shoah by precisely such poems as "Todesfuge." Using the negatively charged category of

aestheticizing the catastrophe thus becomes a further strategy for silencing a victim's expression of having been terrorized.

The author of this didactic essay saw in Celan's "Death Fugue" a thematization of Auschwitz that would stand in the way of literary interpretation. But Auschwitz, a reality and incessant presence in his life (Grass 1990, 30), nowhere became a theme in Celan's writing, as Peter Szondi unequivocally pointed out. Celan's lyrical writing, Szondi wrote in 1964 in refuting a critique by Hans Egon Holthusen, disproves Adorno's dictum by recalling Auschwitz and the Shoah in virtually every text he wrote without merely "thematizing" it (Szondi 1993, 165-67). In a hermeneutically intense reading of Celan's "Engführung" (Stretto; 1958), Szondi sees this poem as the precise refutation of Adorno's earlier position: "No poem is possible after Auschwitz, unless it be conceived by reason of Auschwitz" (Szondi 1972, 102-3).

Without advocating an aesthetics of suffering, we can view poems after and about a metonymically understood Auschwitz as attempts to work through unspeakable personal and collective trauma, as long as their means break new ground and do not merely utilize worn forms, images, and gestures. Thus understood, poetry after Auschwitz is not only not barbaric by its very existence, but in certain of its manifestations vitally necessary. It may be significant that the correspondence between Celan and Sachs contains no mention of Adorno or of the controversy, presumably because these poets saw no reason to theorize about the ethical feasibility of texts they wrote as a necessity for survival. Even in the verse of a number of postwar poets who are not Jewish and who do not treat Auschwitz explicitly (for example, Ingeborg Bachmann, Enzensberger, and Günter Eich), one senses not only an intangible awareness of traditions and poetry's responsibility toward history, but also a distrust of blithe indifference.

Bibliography

Theodor W. Adorno, *Ästhetische Theorie,* ed. Gretel Adorno and Rolf Tiedemann (Frankfurt a. M.: Suhrkamp, 1973); Adorno, "Engagement," *Noten zur Literatur III* (Frankfurt a. M.: Suhrkamp, 1965), 109-35; Adorno, "Kulturkritik und Gesellschaft," *Kulturkritik und Gesellschaft I: Prismen. Obne Leitbild* (Frankfurt a. M.: Suhrkamp, 1977), 11-30; Adorno, "Meditationen zur Metaphysik," *Negative Dialektik* (Frankfurt a. M.: Suhrkamp, 1980), 354-61; Adorno, "On the Question: 'What Is German?'" *New German Critique* 36 (fall 1985): 121-31; Adorno, "Rede über Lyrik und Gesellschaft," *Noten zur Literatur I* (Frankfurt a. M.: Suhrkamp, 1958), 73-104; Wolfgang Butzlaff, "Paul Celan: 'Todesfuge,'" *Der Deutschunterricht* 12 (1960): 42-51; Paul Celan, *Gesammelte Werke in fünf Bänden,* ed. Beda Allemann and Stefan Reichert with Rolf Bücher, 5 vols. (Frankfurt a. M.: Suhrkamp, 1983); Hans Magnus Enzensberger, "Die Steine der Freiheit," *Nelly Sachs zu Ehren* (Frankfurt a. M.: Suhrkamp, 1961), 45-51; Günter Grass, *Schreiben nach Auschwitz: Frank-*

furter Poetik-Vorlesung (Frankfurt a. M.: Luchterhand, 1990); Ruth Klüger, *Weiter leben: Eine Jugend* (Göttingen: Wallstein, 1992); Nelly Sachs, *Briefe der Nelly Sachs,* ed. Ruth Dinesen and Helmut Müssener (Frankfurt a. M.: Suhrkamp, 1985); Peter Szondi, *Briefe,* ed. Christoph König and Thomas Sparr (Frankfurt a. M.: Suhrkamp, 1993); and Szondi, "Durch die Enge geführt: Versuch über die Verständlichkeit des modernen Gedichts," *Celan-Studien,* ed. Jean Bollack with Henriette Beese et al (Frankfurt a. M.: Suhrkamp, 1972), 47-111.

Michael Rothberg (essay date 1997)

SOURCE: "After Adorno: Culture in the Wake of Catastrophe," in *New German Critique,* Vol. 72, Fall, 1997, pp. 45-81.

[*In the following essay, Rothberg discusses the legacy and frequent misinterpretations of Adorno's assertion that "to write poetry after Auschwitz is barbaric."*]

I. INTRODUCTION: THE POLITICS OF COMMEMORATION

In January 1995 a controversy erupted in connection with the fiftieth anniversary commemoration of the liberation of the Auschwitz concentration camp. Upset that the Polish government seemed to be slighting the specifically Jewish elements of the Nazi extermination at Auschwitz, Jewish leaders and spokespeople, including Elie Wiesel, threatened to boycott the ceremonies. In the end, many Jewish groups attended, but they also organized an alternative ceremony that took place while Polish President Lech Walesa was opening the official Government commemoration with a speech that made no specific mention of Jewish victims.[1] This controversy constitutes one more episode in a half-century history of struggle over the meaning and memory of Auschwitz (and the Nazi genocide for which it has come to stand). From debates over the number of victims who died there, to the barely veiled anti-Semitism of Holocaust deniers who claim that no genocide took place, to the conflicts over the national, religious, or moral "ownership" of the site, Auschwitz has been contested ground since the first Soviet soldiers arrived at the end of January 1945. The recent international focus on the so-called liberation has revived the memory wars, which can serve as tools of education, but such a focus also limits an understanding of Auschwitz by framing the narration of the events by the point of view of the victors. When the Soviets entered the camp, they found 7,000 prisoners—all who remained of the almost one and a half million (90% of whom were Jewish) who had passed through the Auschwitz complex. Many of those survivors died *after* liberation. Several days before the Soviets arrived, the Nazis had taken the majority of the surviving 65,000 prisoners on a death march in a perverse effort to maintain control and hide the evidence of atrocity as the war slipped away. Placing these events under the sign of liberation says less about the events of the Holocaust than it does about the

desire of contemporary cultures to master an elusive past whose echoes still resonate in the present.

While recent events highlight the ethnic and national politics of memory and identity, Auschwitz has also long been a locus for intellectual debate about what German-Jewish philosopher Theodor Adorno called in 1959, "coming to terms with the past" [*Vergangenheitsbewältigung*]. Adorno is very much responsible for the centrality that Auschwitz has had in academic and popular discourses. His proposition that "[t]o write poetry after Auschwitz is barbaric" amounts—along with Walter Benjamin's related insight that "[t]here is no document of civilization which is not at the same time a document of barbarism"—to the most famous and probably most frequently cited statement about modern culture in the twentieth century. Adorno's phrase (not even a full sentence in the original German) has been quoted, and just as often misquoted,[2] by writers working in a variety of contexts and disciplines, including philosophy, theology, aesthetics, and literary criticism.[3] Besides the conscious rewritings of Adorno's thought which extend it to fields never mentioned by Adorno and the unconscious distortions of his words—"No poetry after Auschwitz," "After Auschwitz, it is no longer possible to write poems"[4]—the phrase has also circulated with even greater ease in the reduced, ever-malleable form: "after Auschwitz." As a two-word sound bite, "after Auschwitz" has become the intellectual equivalent of the political poster slogan "Never Again!"

Without a doubt, Adorno would be horrified to see his own words on the Nazi genocide turned into an academic truism; he would probably also be unsurprised, finding in the commodification of Holocaust discourse one more proof of the power of the late capitalist totality to reproduce itself and to colonize even the seemingly most resistant areas of social life. Yet, Adorno's self-citations and his use of the sound-bite version "nach Auschwitz"—which, translated into the English "after Auschwitz," has an ironically poetic effect—have facilitated the frequency with which the concept has circulated.[5] In this case, it is the repetitions, and not the original, which have attracted the most attention. The most frequent allusions to the "after Auschwitz" proposition which actually cite Adorno refer to works in which Adorno was commenting on his earlier statement. Given this pattern, as well as the infamous difficulty of Adorno's thought, it is not surprising that most commentary on this theme has de- and re-contextualized the words, often taking them far from Adorno's intended meaning.

The interdisciplinary nature of Adorno's writing has, somewhat ironically, left a fragmentary intellectual legacy, reaching diverse groups of readers, both hostile and friendly, in isolated institutional locations. Few of Adorno's commentators who have picked up on his Auschwitz hypothesis have been interested in his system of thinking as a whole; rather, they have been concerned with the implications of the proposition for the study of some aspect of culture in the light of the Nazi genocide. Inversely, those who *have* been concerned with Adorno's philosophical system have tended *not* to assign a central position to Auschwitz, relating it, at most, to the larger issues of his sociological theory, his relation to other members of the Frankfurt School, his unorthodox Marxism, or his particular version of dialectics. This split in critical approaches makes a more bifocal reading of the significance of the Holocaust in Adorno's thought all the more attractive, if no less daunting.

After briefly tracking the way Adorno's proposition has entered the writings of two very different critics (George Steiner and Eric Santner), I will offer a close reading of Adorno's Auschwitz texts and of related works. One purpose of such an exercise is to bring to view the production of an important cultural category, one which has migrated from the heights of philosophy into the currents of popular intellectual culture. More crucially, I want to demonstrate, through an analysis based on Bakhtin's category of the chronotope, how critical and philosophical approaches to the Shoah, even ones which declare its uniqueness, always project a theory of history. According to Bakhtin, the chronotope captures the simultaneity of spatial and temporal articulations in cultural practices: in the production of chronotopes, "[t]ime, as it were, thickens, takes on flesh, becomes artistically visible; likewise, space becomes charged and responsive to the movements of time, plot, and history."[6] As Hayden White remarks, the "socially structured domain" of the chronotope "defines the horizon of possible events, actions, agents, agencies, social roles, and so forth of all imaginative fictions—and all real stories too."[7] While Adorno himself does not use the term "chronotope," his account of culture "after Auschwitz" both constructs a complex philosophical chronotope and serves as a stunning example of the kind of analysis envisioned by Bakhtin.

After Auschwitz, Adorno implies, philosophical categories must themselves become chronotopes—time-places that serve as imperfect embodiments of historical events and tendencies. Adorno's meditations on Auschwitz ultimately transform his own thinking from within and lead him to reformulate the philosophy of history that had buttressed his writings of the 1940s. One of the later Adorno's most important insights is that the Holocaust forces a confrontation between thought and the event from which neither philosophy nor history can emerge unscathed. In place of the negative teleology of modernity found in Adorno's earlier works, *Negative Dialectics* represents modern history as a traumatic shock, a shock which leads to a critical reformulation of enlightenment. But Adorno's focus on Auschwitz is not just turned toward the past; rather, it creates a constellation between the past and a series of postwar developments in Germany and to a lesser extent in the United States and the Soviet Union. These developments include the persistence of the very modes of thinking and social organization that made the Holocaust possible. The becoming-historical of thought in Adorno thus corresponds to an ethical and political imperative to prevent the recurrence of "Auschwitz," an imperative which entails a critical program of public pedagogy and an ongoing engagement with modernity and democracy.[8]

II. REWRITING ADORNO

Among the rewritings of Adorno, two strategies of interpretation have emerged, one which reads him *à la lettre* and one which takes his words as a jumping off point for even grander claims. Both strategies have produced conflicting evaluations of those interpretations, although the great majority of the literalist critics have rejected Adorno's claim. After all, the production of poetry continues apace with no immediately obvious barbaric side effects. Adorno has found more sympathetic readers in those who choose to stretch his insights beyond the restricted realm of poetry, as he himself ultimately did. Many, of course, have read Adorno in both ways, combining a particular attention to poetry or language with considerations of other areas of culture which readily come to mind as vulnerable to the catastrophe of genocide. I have chosen to discuss two particular adaptations here, not because they are necessarily typical of either tendency, but because, even in misreading Adorno, they produce significant variants of his Auschwitz chronotope.

Careful attention to the literal realm of Adorno's proposal (that is, poetry) does not necessarily result in an Adornian analysis, as the case of George Steiner demonstrates. Adorno's claim has produced sustained reflection by Steiner on the status of poetry and language after Auschwitz. Steiner, who is probably responsible for the initial impact of the phrase on an English-speaking audience, is one of the few who have taken seriously the effect of Nazi brutality on the writing of poetry. In 1959, and without mentioning Adorno, he diagnosed the German language as not yet free of the contamination produced by years of service to the Third Reich. Steiner impugns not just the human agents of Nazism, but their instruments as well: "the German language was not innocent of the horrors of Nazism. . . . Nazism found in the language precisely what it needed to give voice to its savagery." What it needed, Steiner implies, was precisely the opposite of the language's rich poetic tradition: Hitler "sensed in German another music than that of Goethe, Heine, and Mann; a rasping cadence, half nebulous jargon, half obscenity" (*LS* 99). Even fifteen years after the fall of the Reich, Germany's reconstruction was, as the essay's title maintains, a "Hollow Miracle," because the nation's "language is no longer lived," but propagates "a profound deadness of spirit" (*LS* 96).

Despite some reconsiderations about the status of contemporary German literature, Steiner reprinted the already controversial essay in his 1967 collection, *Language and Silence.* Although possessing an extremely wide range of reference, this work on "language, literature, and the inhuman" is premised on the Adornian proposition and seems to reflect a reading especially of Adorno's *Notes To Literature,* which contains his second, better known pronouncement on Auschwitz. In the preface, Steiner declares, "We come after. We know now that a man can read Goethe or Rilke in the evening, that he can play Bach and Schubert, and go to his day's work at Auschwitz in the morning" (*LS* ix). This paradoxical relation of poetry and culture to barbarism stimulates some of the book's fine insights into the spatial and temporal frameworks in which genocide takes place and in which we who come after approach it. In an essay aptly titled, "Postscript," Steiner defines his project as an attempt "to discover the relations between those done to death and those alive then, and the relations of both to us; to locate, as exactly as record and imagination are able, the measure of unknowing, indifference, complicity, commission which relates the contemporary or survivor to the slain" (*LS* 157). Steiner draws (imprecisely) on Adorno's chronotope in a macabre illustration of such a relationship between past and present: "'No poetry after Auschwitz,' said Adorno, and Sylvia Plath enacted the underlying meaning of his statement in a manner both histrionic and profoundly sincere" (*LS* 53).

As these formulations indicate, Steiner considers language not just a transparent, instrumental medium—although "The Hollow Miracle" demonstrates how it can be *instrumentalized*—but part of the historical metabolism of the social. Yet Steiner's view of history is profoundly different from Adorno's. Steiner's conception of "after" imports an ideology foreign to Adorno, for, unlike Adorno, Steiner presupposes the existence of what he calls "humane literacy": "We come *after*, and that is the nerve of our condition. After the unprecedented ruin of humane values and hopes by the political bestiality of our age" (*LS* 4). Such a story of decline is far from Adorno's dialectical evaluation of the legacy of the Enlightenment, as I will argue in the next section. Instead of marking the intimate connection between bourgeois culture and modern terror—explicit in Benjamin and in Adorno's appropriation of him—Steiner laments the latter's emergence at the expense of the former: "The possibility that the political inhumanity of the twentieth century and certain elements of the technological, mass society which has followed on the erosion of European bourgeois values have done injury to language is the underlying theme of this book" (*LS* 49). Such an idealist understanding of historical change, which places values before material and political determinants, inverts Adorno's thinking. Since at least ***Dialectic of Enlightenment***'s reading of *The Odyssey*, Adorno has demonstrated the brutality inherent in the tendential hegemony of "bourgeois values." The message of "after Auschwitz" is not one of nostalgia for a glorious culture where language approximated light or music, but of the necessity of a new relationship to the future.[9]

If Steiner's account stands or falls on its conception of what comes *before* Auschwitz (which one could contrast, for example, to Adorno's discussion of lyric poetry), other approaches have attempted to move Adorno into a new era after Auschwitz. In a fascinating study of postwar German film and culture, Eric Santner provides a strong and expansive misreading of the poetry proposition. Santner frames his study, which deals primarily with the mourning and working through of the recent German past, by pro-

posing to investigate the symmetries and asymmetries of the "postwar," "post-Holocaust," and "postmodern" periods. He critically aligns himself with postmodern theory, arguing that it "represent[s] a kind of translation into more global terms of Adorno's famous dictum that there could be no poetry after Auschwitz. After Auschwitz—after this trauma to European modernity—critical theory becomes in large part an ongoing elaboration of a seemingly endless series of 'no longer possibles.'" Santner considers aesthetic, political, cognitive, and social practices as part of that iterative chain of what has becomes impossible: "an inability to tolerate difference, heterogeneity, nonmastery."[10] He thus understands the phrase "after Auschwitz" as signifying a fundamental transformation in culture which *displaces* the conditions of, and leading up to, Auschwitz.

Santner follows Alice Jardine in giving an affirmative reading of the "no longer possibles." Jardine writes, "I have preferred to speak of our epoch as one of impossibility, and to call for an *ethics* of impossibility: im-possi-bility, the antithesis of *posse/potis/pàtis*, the antithesis of that which relies on power, potency, possessors, despots, husbands, masters."[11] Santner's (and Jardine's) vision of the post-Holocaust future appears as a kind of mirror of Steiner's nostalgic humanism. If the postmodernists emphasize difference as opposed to some mythical common culture, they nevertheless both posit a positive vision of an alternative that has existed or does exist. In this they are equally far from Adorno, who despite the ambiguous formulations of his texts, allows no direct formulation of culture after Auschwitz and proposes no such absolute break in modernity (whether or not it has in fact taken place).

While Santner distances himself from some postmodern tendencies to erase historical specificity, his appropriation of Adorno leaves it unclear whether the "no longer possibles" which he and Jardine enumerate are sketches of an ethical imperative or the actually existing condition of our epoch. Santner's translation of Adorno's "poetry after Auschwitz" dictum into the postmodern ethical demand "to tolerate difference, heterogeneity, nonmastery" elides the materialist and radically negative dimensions of Adorno's thought and replaces them with a liberal pluralist discourse. Adorno's comments are not so much a call for opposition to power, as are Jardine's, but a questioning of the possibility of such resistance. In bringing these two very different discourses together, Santner risks reversing the significance of Adorno's thought without remarking on it. At the least, such a translation would need to specify the relation between ideological/theoretical formulations of difference and the material conditions in which they take place. If this problem remains unresolved in Santner's text, Santner nevertheless poses the important question of how to "[undo] a certain repetition compulsion of modern European history" that "found its ultimate staging in Auschwitz."[12] In turning to Adorno's *oeuvre* the question becomes: in what ways does Adorno's philosophical restaging of Auschwitz entail (or not entail) a break with the condition of modernity which constitutes the matrix of the Nazi genocide?

III. Adorno on Auschwitz

Adorno's philosophizing takes place in a complicated tension with the modernist chronotope of progress—the belief in a constant movement forward through a homogenous space/time that continuously breaks with the past.[13] From his *Dialectic of Enlightenment,* co-written with Max Horkheimer in 1944 but not published until 1947, to his *Negative Dialectics,* Adorno simultaneously reveals the lacunae in the progressive vision of history and holds out for more enlightenment, as opposed to an impossible return to the pre-modern.[14] Viewing Adorno's work through the very particular lens of Auschwitz cannot give the complete picture of his, in any case, incredibly diverse work. But, given the status of the Holocaust within debates about modernity, the view opened up by a close, contextual reading of the pertinent texts is not insignificant. Adorno's Auschwitz chronotope is, in fact, a constellation of concepts which reconfigures itself over the course of two decades. It combines elements of aesthetics ("To write poetry"), temporality ("after"), and place ("Auschwitz") with a morally or politically evaluative predicate ("is barbaric"). My reading of Adorno will mobilize all of those categories in an attempt to reconstruct and examine his successive conceptual constellations. Despite the simplistic symmetry implied by the copula ("is"), neither the phrase as a whole nor its individual particles is transparent, and they all demand interpretation.

A brief consideration of the status of "Auschwitz" serves to unsettle whatever literalist suspicions underlie one's reading of the phrase. As architectural historian Robert-Jan van Pelt has demonstrated, Auschwitz was initially to be the site of a National Socialist "design for utopia": "Himmler insisted that all Poles and Jews would be removed from the area, and that Auschwitz itself would become a 'paradigm of the settlement in the East.'" Only over the course of time, and relatively late in the camp's existence, did Auschwitz become the "dystopia" which we know it as today—although certainly, I would argue, this second moment was already contained in the "utopian" vision of the first.[15] As a Germanization by the occupying power of the Polish town of Oswiecim, the name Auschwitz already reveals colonial violence. But it is almost immediately clear that Auschwitz, a place name, is intended to refer not so much to a place as to an event or events. How else could something come after it? We know today that the event to which it refers is the slaughter by Nazi Germany of an estimated 1.6 million people (of whom 90 percent were Jewish) during the course of four years (1940-1944). The extermination which created Auschwitz's infamy was, for the most part, carried out at Auschwitz II, known as Birkenau, itself the sight of a razed Polish village, Brzezinka.[16] At the time that Adorno wrote, however, an accurate account of events at Auschwitz was not yet available, nor was Auschwitz even the camp best known to the European and American publics, which were more familiar with the camps liberated by Britain and the United States, such as Belsen, Dachau, and Buchenwald. In disseminating such a formula, it seems unlikely, then, that Adorno

meant to refer only to the effects of the events at Auschwitz, since that particular camp was part of a much larger system created and run by the Nazis. Auschwitz takes on both metonymic and synecdochic significance in Adorno's phrase: the place-name refers both to events proximate to it and to a totality of events of which it is one part.[17]

Pierre Nora's work on "sites of memory" and James Young's crucial consideration of Holocaust memorials as such sites in *The Texture of Memory* remind us that memory is not indigenous to a (rhetorical or literal) place, but must be created through the ongoing intervention of human agents.[18] In the case of Auschwitz, the process of memorialization had already begun by the time of Adorno's first mention of it: "[i]n 1947, the Polish parliament declared that the [remains] of the camp would be 'forever preserved as a memorial to the martyrdom of the Polish nation and other peoples'." This incipient nationalization of memory contrasted with another tendency, that of the International Committee of Auschwitz, founded in 1952, to put a socialist spin on the memory preserved there.[19] Unlike the efforts of the Polish and Soviet states, the International Committee, other groups of survivors, or variously interested parties, Adorno does not seek to alter the physical topography of Auschwitz. Nevertheless, through his mobilization of the proper name Auschwitz, he has intervened in Holocaust memory work and has powerfully contributed to the negotiated significance of Auschwitz as a literal and rhetorical site of remembrance.

Much of Adorno's writing during his exile from Nazi Germany in the 1940s concerns the links between modernity, fascism, capitalism, and culture. This is true for the grand theorizing of *Dialectic of Enlightenment* as for the fragmentary, more personal insights of *Minima Moralia* (written 1944-47; published 1951).[20] These works set the stage for the Auschwitz comments, which appear first in the essay **"Cultural Criticism and Society"** (written 1949; published 1951). This essay does not primarily concern the effects of World War II or the implications of genocide. Adorno dedicates the majority of the essay to a kind of sublation of cultural criticism. In good Hegelian Marxist fashion, he first demonstrates the implication of such criticism in "sinister, integrated society" ([*Prisms*; hereafter *P*] 34) and in the culture which "shares the guilt of society" (*P* 26); he then argues that cultural criticism can be surpassed by the dialectical critic:

> To accept culture as a whole is to deprive it of the ferment which is its very truth—negation. The joyous appropriation of culture harmonizes with a climate of military music and paintings of battle-scenes. What distinguishes dialectical from cultural criticism is that it heightens cultural criticism until the notion of culture is itself negated, fulfilled, and surmounted in one.
>
> (*P* 28)

The dialectical method, for Adorno, entails a double movement back and forth between "the knowledge of society as a totality" and "the specific content of the object" (*P* 33).

Cultural criticism, on the other hand, either reduces the object to a simplified notion of the social or exalts culture as a source of humane values. Against these tendencies, Adorno respectively castigates vulgar class analysis and insists that, "only insofar as it withdraws from Man, can culture be faithful to man" (*P* 20, 23).

If Adorno's stated goal as dialectical critic is "to shed light on an object in itself hermetic by casting a glance at society [and] to present society with the bill which the object does not redeem" (*P* 33), what can we make of the intrusion of Auschwitz in the essay's final paragraph? This last passage exemplifies Adorno's characteristic absolutism and puts the Auschwitz phrase in a context not usually considered by cultural critiques of Adorno:

> The more total society becomes, the greater the reification of the mind and the more paradoxical its effort to escape reification on its own. Even the most extreme consciousness of doom threatens to degenerate into idle chatter. Cultural criticism finds itself faced with the final stage of the dialectic of culture and barbarism. To write poetry after Auschwitz is barbaric. And this corrodes even the knowledge of why it has become impossible to write poetry today. Absolute reification, which presupposed intellectual progress as one of its elements, is now preparing to absorb the mind entirely. Critical intelligence cannot be equal to this challenge as long as it confines itself to self-satisfied contemplation.
>
> (*P* 34)

As the movement of this passage (and the essay from which it is taken) demonstrates, Auschwitz does not stand alone, but is part of a historical process. Adorno assigns Auschwitz a critical position in this history, but less as an autonomous entity than as a *moment*: Auschwitz is "the final stage of the dialectic of culture and barbarism." This does not necessarily entail a position on the uniqueness of the event, but it does demonstrate what is missing from critics of Adorno who ignore the place of genocide in "society as a totality."

The complicated and ambiguous structure of Adorno's German (as well as the tendency to decontextualize the Auschwitz phrase—a tendency facilitated by its English translation into a separate sentence) reveals the source of the mistaken interpretation that Adorno is declaring Auschwitz the source of poetry's impossibility. The context reveals that the agent of the impossibility is "absolute reification," the process which "absorb[s] the mind entirely." In this essay at least, Adorno places Auschwitz within his larger critique of capitalist modernity and the Enlightenment, which stand behind the movement of reification. Adorno assigns Auschwitz a particular position as the apotheosis of barbarism, but the significance of barbarism emerges from its place in what he sees as its Enlightenment dialectic with culture. The specificity of Nazi barbarism does not rupture, but continues, the strange blend of instrumentally rational means and irrational ends that the Frankfurt School understands as the primary legacy of modernity.

The barbarism or irrationality of poetry after Auschwitz is that, against its implicit intentions, it cannot produce knowledge of its own impossible social status. This impossibility is neither technical nor even moral, for Adorno clearly does not see barbarism as the result of individual abilities, actions, or attitudes; it results instead from an objective and objectifying social process which tends toward the liquidation of the individual. As a form of ostensibly free individual expression, the writing of poetry would contribute to that "semblance of freedom [which] makes reflection upon one's own unfreedom incomparably more difficult" (*P* 21). That semblance is false since the tendential expansion of capitalist society integrates the individual as well as relatively autonomous spheres such as culture, and unifies them according to the identificatory logic of exchange. In Adorno's reading even Marxist theory must change to keep up with the logic of capital since the latter "no longer tolerates even those relatively independent, distinct moments to which the theory of causal dependence of superstructure on base once referred. In the open-air prison which the world is becoming, it is no longer so important to know what depends on what, such is the extent to which everything is one" (*P* 34). The dark vision of this passage is self-evident, but it also leaves open possibilities for a less absolutist position. The emphasis on "becoming" is a crucial qualifier to Adorno's totalizing critique, implying that domination has not yet eliminated all possible resistance. Secondly, the change in relation between base and superstructure signals an increased role for cultural politics since the cultural realm appears no longer derivative of economics. Yet, however other critics or a later Adorno might exploit these openings, in **"Cultural Criticism"** no such optimism is to be found.

In this essay, experience and expectation collapse into each other, as the mind is absorbed, creating a surface on which domination plays itself out with deadeningly repetitive blows. Time is reduced to a series of stages whose difference is one of degree but not kind. Meanwhile space suffers a similar iterative demise as the concentration camp replicates itself in the places of public life: the world becomes an "open-air prison." If the citizens of the world do not recognize Auschwitz as the reflection of their lives, that is only, according to Adorno, because terror functions more abstractly outside of the camps through the logic of identity that laid the groundwork for genocide and which has not disappeared. The triumph of exchange value, another name for identity in Adorno's work, prepared the way for mass murder by rendering human life indifferent and therefore expendable. The two words of the phrase "after Auschwitz" are thus equivocal: they mark the limits of an era, but one which was already on its way and which remains today; and they locate a crisis, but only in order to extend its effects well beyond its original space of experience.

The form that Adorno's reflections take here seems as much a product of Adorno's long exile in the United States during the 1930s and 1940s as it does of the situation in Europe. Adorno's experience of what he called "late capitalism" in the United States did not initially leave him with much belief in the existence of alternatives to the logic of fascism.[21] To the contrary, Horkheimer and Adorno's analysis in *Dialectic of Enlightenment*—with its adjacent chapters on the culture industry and anti-Semitism—suggests a parallel between American-style monopoly capitalism and Hitlerian National Socialism. Passages in the "Culture Industry" chapter make those similarities explicit:

> "No one must go hungry or thirsty; if anyone does, he's for the concentration camp!" This joke from Hitler's Germany might shine forth as a maxim from above all the portals of the culture industry. . . . Under liberalism the poor were thought to be lazy; now they are automatically objects of suspicion. Anybody who is not provided for outside should be in a concentration camp, or at any rate in the hell of the most degrading work and the slums.[22]

Whatever its truth-value (and who can deny its grain of truth in an era of homeless "shelters" and welfare "reform"), Adorno's argument demonstrates the spatio-temporal situatedness of the production of chronotopes (the latter are always produced from within other chronotopes). First, Adorno's writing bears obvious traces of his American location, as his later writings will intervene in a more strictly German context. Secondly, I think it is arguable that such a "comic" comparison could only take place at a moment *before* the camps had been sacralized as sites of ultimate and unspeakable terror—before Auschwitz was "Auschwitz." This is not to say that there was not already consciousness of the camps which Adorno cites in creating this phrase, for indeed there were already memoirs, films, and other accounts. But it is to suggest that the temporal break which we retroactively infer in the phrase "after Auschwitz" had not yet taken place in the 1940s' public consciousness. The response to, and the form of, some of the texts of the late 1940s (including Adorno's) confirm that the afterlife of an event needs to be periodized as carefully as the event itself. An event alone does not always rupture history; rather, the constellation which that event forms with later events creates the conditions in which epochal discontinuity can be thought.

The tenuous, if not imaginary, quality of the individual and of non-reified production in "administered society" is certainly one of Adorno's great themes, one which he expressed most emphatically in the "Culture Industry" chapter of *Dialectic of Enlightenment.* But poetry, to which Adorno refers in this context, presents a particular aesthetic case which should not be immediately subsumed under the general view of culture under late capitalism. In reflecting on the specificity of poetry in Adorno's system we observe the emergence of inconsistencies. In his 1957 essay **"On Lyric Poetry and Society,"** Adorno shows the limits of lyric poetry—"the most fragile thing that exists"—in the attempt "to attain universality through unrestrained individuation."[23] The process of individuation fails, and the lyric cannot remain aloof from the "bustle and commotion" of society, because "the demand that the lyric world be virginal, is itself social in nature. It implies a protest against a social situation that every individual experiences as hostile, alien, cold, oppressive" ([**Notes on Literature**; hereafter *NL*] 37, 39). Poetry cannot actualize its own ideal and stand outside the forces of the rationalized social totality. However, the essay on lyric poetry does not entirely endorse the pessimism about culture evident in the cultural criticism essay, because it shows poetry as registering an element of protest. Poetry is not simply an ideological attempt "to falsely present some particular values as general ones," Adorno warns in 1957. The essence of poems, and other works of art, "consists in giving form to the crucial contradictions in real existence": in direct contradiction to the ideas of ideology critique, "the greatness of works of art . . . consists solely in the fact that they give voice to what ideology hides" (*NL* 39). For Adorno in the late 1950s, poetry has an important mimetic function, one that consists not in reproducing the harmonious narrative of traditional realist forms, but rather in expressing the rifts that realist mimesis represses. The distinction between this revelatory notion of art as expression and the earlier idea that poetry after Auschwitz mystifies knowledge of the social points to the existence of a dual theory of poetry in Adorno. When, in a later discussion, Adorno switches from "poetry after Auschwitz" to "lyric poetry after Auschwitz," he also shifts his conception of the aesthetic from that in **"Cultural Criticism and Society"** to that in **"On Lyric Poetry in Society."**

Thirteen years after first measuring the possibility of post-Auschwitz culture and after much intervening public debate, Adorno returned to the theme in his essay **"Commitment"** [hereafter abbreviated as **"C"**]. This work, better known than **"Cultural Criticism and Society,"** criticizes Sartre's then fashionable notion of engaged literature. The Auschwitz section, entitled in one of its English translations as "The Problem of Suffering," serves as a hinge between a critique of Sartre's and, especially, Brecht's politicized aesthetic and a defense of the "autonomous" art of Kafka and Beckett. Adorno devastatingly reveals the contradictions of Sartre's conception of art, demonstrating that his plays are "bad models of his own existentialism": "they display in their respect for truth the whole administered universe which his philosophy ignores; the lesson we learn from them is one of unfreedom."[24] Adorno similarly exposes the lack of fit between form and content in Brecht's satire of fascism. Brecht trivializes fascism, making it appear "mere hazard, like an accident or crime," so that its "true horror . . . is conjured away" (**"C"** 308). Adorno is not immune to Brecht's political claims, but he remains unimpressed by the political level of the work: "If we take Brecht at his word and make politics the criterion by which to judge his committed theatre, by the same token it proves untrue" (**"C"** 309). Thus far then, Adorno seems to confirm the aesthetic pessimism we saw in the earlier essay, now extending it beyond bourgeois individualist production into the engaged art of the people.

The example of Auschwitz reveals a third possibility beyond the antinomy of political/apolitical art. Adorno begins by self-consciously reiterating his earlier claim, now specified as a citational "saying" about *lyric* poetry, and then goes on to complicate (if not contradict) it:

> I have no wish to soften the saying [*Satz*] that to write lyric poetry after Auschwitz is barbaric; it expresses in negative form the impulse which inspires committed literature. . . . But [Hans Magnus] Enzensberger's retort also remains true, that literature must resist this verdict, in other words, be such that its mere existence after Auschwitz is not a surrender to cynicism.[25]

The paradoxical situation of art is that this cynicism can be avoided only when kept at bay by a full recognition and remembrance of the horrors of the age. The purpose of art is neither to represent the interests of the proletariat or the individual, nor to grant meaning to abstract humanity, but to remain true to suffering: "The abundance of real suffering tolerates no forgetting. . . . Yet this suffering, what Hegel called consciousness of adversity, also demands the continued existence of art while it prohibits it; it is now virtually in art alone that suffering can still find its own voice, consolation, without immediately being betrayed by it" ("C" 312). The impossible demand put on art more closely resembles the status of lyric poetry in the 1957 essay—the anguished individual expression of social contradictions—than it does the notion of poetry as that which prevents the comprehension of its own impossibility. But, although lyric poetry is mentioned by Adorno, it does not serve as the primary example of post-Auschwitz aesthetics.

The **"Commitment"** essay mobilizes a different aesthetic in the wake of the catastrophe from that dismissed in **"Cultural Criticism and Society"** or partially rescued in **"Lyric Poetry and Society"**—its name is Beckett. For Adorno, Beckett's writings (as well as Kafka's) enact what others only proclaim: "Kafka and Beckett arouse the fear which existentialism merely talks about. By dismantling appearance, they explode from within the art which committed proclamation subjugates from without, and hence only in appearance" ("C" 314-15). In these writers—one who proleptically internalized the disaster, the other who retrospectively maintains its absent presence—the notion of art's barbarity is not refuted but enacted in order to present the barbarity of the age. This allows them to avoid the more chilling paradox present in "the so-called artistic representation" of historical terror: "When genocide becomes part of the cultural heritage in the themes of committed literature, it becomes easier to continue to play along with the culture which gave birth to murder" ("C" 312-13). Representational art creates the possibility for sadistic identification in members of the audience because it contains a surplus of pleasure: "The so-called artistic representation of the sheer physical pain of people beaten to the ground by rifle butts contains, however remotely, the power to elicit enjoyment out of it" ("C" 312). The problem of pleasure is intrinsic to the non-synchronicity of representation—in retrospect, it seems, any historical situation can be mobilized for the enjoyment of the spectator who consumes history at a spatial and temporal distance. Beckett's art, Adorno claims, evades this problem through its refusal of realist figuration, but one is justified in asking why it too cannot be appropriated by the culture industry. This is precisely what happens, according to Frederic Jameson, during the transition to postmodernism. Calling Adorno's essay an "anti-political revival of the ideology of modernism," Jameson draws attention to the way that "what was once an oppositional and anti-social phenomenon in the early years of the century, has today become the dominant style of commodity production."[26] Adorno's defense of high modernism need not be understood uniquely, however, as a transcendental defense of a particular ideology of style. Reading Adorno in context demonstrates the specificity of his intervention in a post-Auschwitz culture, even as it inevitably illustrates the contextual limitations of his political and aesthetic vision.

Adorno makes clear that "autonomous" art's apparent avoidance of social realism should not be confused with ahistoricism. In **"Trying to Understand *Endgame*,"** written contemporaneously with **"Commitment,"** he gives a more complete analysis of Beckett and uses this play to add to the "after Auschwitz" chronotope already under construction in his other essays. Adorno once again contrasts Beckett to existentialism, claiming that "French existentialism had tackled the problem of history. In Beckett, history swallows up existentialism" (*NL* 244). In its refusal to find any figment of humanity within the post-catastrophic landscape, *Endgame* figures forth "the historical horror of anonymity" (*NL* 245). The subject, and the subject's historical sense, may have atrophied, but, for Adorno, this is itself a historical process for which Beckett's play serves as a registration of the real. If existentialism "negat[es] precisely the particularity, individuation in time and space, that makes existence existence and not the mere concept of existence," "Beckett poses the decisive antithesis. . . . Instead of omitting what is temporal in existence—which can be existence only in time—he subtracts from existence what time, the historical tendency, is in reality preparing to get rid of" (*NL* 246). Beckett's chronotope is thus one of space and time's tendential erasure—not an abstract negation of particularity, but a concrete process affecting "consciousness' power to conceive [history], the power to remember" (*NL* 247).

This chronotope, while certainly incorporating the temporality of the atomic age, among other factors, has intimate ties with the post-Holocaust era. Hiroshima and Auschwitz combine to transform living into halflife, or better, *after*-life: "After the Second World War, everything, including a resurrected culture, has been destroyed without realizing it; humankind continues to vegetate, creeping along after events that even the survivors cannot really survive, on a rubbish heap that has made even reflection on one's damaged state useless" (*NL* 244). The emphasis in **"Cultural Criticism and Society"** was on the extermination camp as the "final stage" of reification owing its existence to the triumph of an instrumental reason unleashed by the Enlightenment and capitalism. This tendential reading of history—itself a kind of inverted reflection of the concept of progress—is certainly still present, but Adorno's reflections on Beckett put more emphasis on what comes after the "Final Solution," on the survival of the ultimate barbarism into an era premised on reparation [*Wiedergutmachung*].

Adorno was writing in the wake of a period of postwar reconstruction during which there was an ongoing attempt to normalize and legitimate West German democracy and its "economic miracle"; this could only work through a selective forgetting of the recent past and an instrumentalization of the state's financial reparations to individual Jews and to Israel. According to Johannes von Moltke, West Germany's official "politics of memory" *vis-à-vis* the Holocaust and Jews served (and, to a certain extent, continue to serve) as "the Federal Republic's entry-ticket into the Western alliance."[27] Adorno was dubious about the break with the past that this instrumentalization of memory implied. He went so far as to suggest in 1959 that he "consider[ed] the continued existence of National Socialism *within* democracy potentially more threatening than the continued existence of fascist tendencies *against* democracy."[28] Bearing the message that all cannot be made good again, Beckett's plays and Adorno's essays intervene in the affirmative postwar cultural politics of Western, and particularly German, society. Adorno finds evidence of the underside of the postwar European "rebirth" in the fate of the characters Nagg and Nell, which represents the hypocrisy of the "welfare system": "*Endgame* prepares us for a state of affairs in which everyone who lifts the lid of the nearest trash-can can expect to find his own parents in it. . . . The Nazis have irrevocably overthrown the taboo on old age. Beckett's trashcans are emblems of the culture rebuilt after Auschwitz" (*NL* 266-67). The "state of affairs" uncovered by Adorno recalls George Steiner's controversial denunciation of what he termed Germany's "hollow miracle." Steiner, who would a few years later bring Adorno's ideas about Auschwitz to an English-language readership, argued in 1959 that the German language itself was tainted by the afterlife of the Shoah.[29] Adorno attempts to expose that hollowness from a strategic position within the Federal Republic, but his account of the cultural devastation extends beyond national boundaries, as ultimately does Steiner's.[30]

Both of the essays that privilege Beckett's autonomous art—finding in them that to which "has fallen the burden of wordlessly expressing what is barred to politics"—end, unsurprisingly, with a paradox. **"Commitment"** evokes Paul Klee's painting *Angelus Novus* (the model for Benjamin's Angel of History) in order to capture the ambiguity of the chronotope of "after Auschwitz": "The machine angel's enigmatic eyes force the onlooker to try to decide whether he is announcing the culmination of disaster or salvation hidden within it" (**"C"** 318). In the *Endgame* essay, Adorno claims that in Beckett's "imageless image of death . . . the distinction between absolute domination—the hell in which time is completely confined within space, in which absolutely nothing changes any more—and the

messianic state in which everything would be in its right place, disappears" (*NL* 274). Although Adorno's writing often seems to find in this "last absurdity" confirmation for what he calls in *Minima Moralia* his "melancholy science," we might also find in these later essays that science's "standpoint of redemption."[31]

Perhaps because of the melancholic's refusal to break with a traumatic event, some historical sense is preserved, even if only in the form of the "imageless image" or the "wordless expression." The essay, **"Trying to Understand *Endgame*,"** is dedicated, after all, "To S. B., *in memory* of Paris, Fall 1958" (*NL* 244; emphasis added—MR). The patently Benjaminian language and themes of these passages raise interesting questions about the relation between Adorno and the author of the "Theses on the Philosophy of History."[32] Most significantly for this project would be the impetus that Adorno takes from the Theses for the construction of a chronotopic constellation between the *Hitlerzeit* and the postwar era which Benjamin never knew. Differentiating historical materialism from historicism, Benjamin claims that the former understands historicity as a retrospective quality of events: facts "[become] historical posthumously." The historical materialist

> grasps the constellation which his own era has formed with a definite earlier one. Thus he establishes a conception of the present as the 'time of the now' [*Jetztzeit*] which is shot through with chips of Messianic time.[33]

The kind of memory Adorno produces in Beckett's texts is the effect of a constellation connecting Europe and the Federal Republic with its recent past. But while Benjamin is primarily concerned with "blast[ing] open the continuum of history,"[34] Adorno's rather different concern here is to exhibit the continuity which underlies a superficially discontinuous German history.

In a famous study from the late 1960s, Alexander and Margarete Mitscherlich argued that the vast majority of German people had never come to terms with their relationship to the crimes of the Nazi era, but had, instead, repetitively and unconsciously attempted to break entirely with the past: "That so few signs of melancholia or even of mourning are to be seen among the great masses of the population can be attributed only to a collective denial of the past."[35] Adorno anticipated this diagnosis of Germany's "inability to mourn" in his 1959 discussion of working through the past [*Aufarbeitung der Vergangenheit*]. He reads what the Mitscherlichs term "rupture" with the past as a surface phenomenon which indicates a deeper continuity: "This collective narcissism [whereby powerless individuals were gratified through identification with the whole] was grievously damaged by the collapse of the Hitler regime; a damage which, however, occurred in the realm of simple fact, without each individual becoming conscious of it and thereby getting over it."[36]

In his writings from the late 1950s and early 1960s, we see Adorno refining and reshaping the conception of Auschwitz first mentioned in **"Cultural Criticism."** Here he is concerned with the production and reception of culture in a context where rupture and continuity coexist—where, in other words, layers of different conceptions of space and time can cluster around a single name, Auschwitz. He writes from *within* a situation in which the historicity of Auschwitz has not yet settled into a fact. Rather, it floats within certain institutionally determined parameters, as a fact in the making and thus as one of the means and the stakes of various political negotiations. His concern is obviously not with the individual psychology of Germans but with objective "conditions over which [the majority of people] have no control, thereby keeping this majority in a condition of political immaturity [*Unmündigkeit*]."[37] To combat such immaturity he recognizes the need to wage a battle over the construction of chronotopes, hence his championing of forms of cultural production, such as that of Beckett, which represent contemporary history as the persistence of dark forces from the recent past. Adorno considers such a historical vision necessary to the opening of alternative futures and not a retreat into defeatism. In his late writings, Adorno will continue this discussion in the realm of metaphilosophical discourse, emphasizing the austere pedagogical and theoretical praxis necessary for truly activating what Benjamin called the Messianic potential of the present.

While I have pointed to a break or shift in Adorno's thinking between the first two moments of his continuing "after Auschwitz" discourse, the historical period which encompasses those two moments does not so much witness a break as mark the development of Germany's postwar reconstruction. Adorno's second reiteration of "poetry after Auschwitz," on the other hand, not only shifts the tenor of his thinking, but was also published in a cultural context where the meaning of the events of World War II was in the process of transforming itself significantly. Because of the different emotional and historical forces unleashed by the Eichmann trial in Israel in 1961, the Auschwitz trials in the mid-1960s, the 1967 Arab-Israeli War, and the 1968 international student revolts, the 1960s saw a rapid and uneven development of "Holocaust consciousness."[38] The belated emergence of this historical consciousness varied according to national context, as well as more local and psychological factors, but it remains a social fact that, somewhere in that decade, Auschwitz took on a new significance. The repetition of "after Auschwitz" by Adorno and his followers such as George Steiner both reflects this emergence and helped to shape it.

Adorno's testimony to the persistence of historical memory in unlikely cultural locations (i.e., the writings of Beckett) makes clear that the near-silence and imagelessness of art after Auschwitz should not be confused with actual silence or with a ban on representation *tout court*. "Not even silence gets us out of the circle" of culture and barbarism after Auschwitz, Adorno writes in *Negative Dialectics*. "In silence we simply use the state of objective truth to rationalize our subjective incapacity, once more degrading truth into a lie."[39] Here, Adorno preempts the reading of his

proposition that implies that because the horror of the annihilation of the Jews cannot be perfectly imitated or reproduced according to the ideals of a naive realism (as if anything could be), all artistic representation should cease. Adorno disallows evidence of the subject's incapacity to represent total horror as grounds for the abdication of art. Such a negative aesthetic of silence, he argues, would only be functionally motivated by the desire "to rationalize" its own predestined failure. But this would be no refusal of the administered society which made Auschwitz possible, since "to instrumentalize art is to undercut the opposition art mounts against instrumentalism."[40] Art's role is its "afunctionality," and thus its success lies in its very failure (although not *any* failure). Hence Adorno values the *proximity* of the art to silence. This proximity is not an abdication but an articulation of suffering. Adorno finds this quality in the poetry of Paul Celan, whom he compares to Beckett on the basis of a common "anorganic" writing practice: "[Celan's] poetry is permeated by a sense of shame stemming from the fact that art is unable either to experience or to sublimate suffering. Celan's poems articulate unspeakable horror by being silent, thus turning their truth content into a negative quality."[41] Such an assessment of Celan in Adorno's final work takes on added significance, given that the original statement about poetry after Auschwitz is considered in popular mythology a pointed rejoinder to the former's "Todesfuge."[42]

After the disavowal in postmodernism of the "great divide," as Andreas Huyssen calls it, between high and mass culture, Adorno has frequently been criticized for his conception of an aesthetic realm autonomous from the social.[43] Yet Adorno's comments about art after Auschwitz demonstrate his understanding of the social content of the "silent" aesthetic. In *Negative Dialectics,* Adorno echoes his comments in **"Commitment"** and goes on to suggest links between art and historical understanding: "Perennial suffering has as much right to expression as a tortured man has to scream; hence it may have been wrong to say that after Auschwitz you could no longer write poems." He then immediately renders this recantation ambiguous: "But it is not wrong to raise the less cultural question whether after Auschwitz you can go on living."[44] This last thought brings Adorno's philosophy to the edge of the abyss, but it is only in this position that he finds the resources for a thoroughgoing negation of *what is*.

The guilt of living after the so-called Final Solution, Adorno suggests in this emotionally charged passage, "is irreconcilable with living": "And the guilt does not cease to reproduce itself, because not for an instant can it be made fully present to consciousness. This, nothing else, is what compels us to philosophize. And in philosophy we experience a shock: the deeper, the more vigorous its penetration, the great our suspicion that philosophy removes us from things as they are."[45] This passage anticipates psychological insights about what has come to be known as "survivor's guilt," but, more importantly, recognizes the implications of those insights for culture at large and points us toward the social framework in which this condition's symptoms should be read. The surprising *personal* quality exhibited by Adorno's writing testifies to a *social* context in which, during and after the Eichmann trial, survivors were beginning to be recognized as a group that had been silently haunted by a particular set of experiences and expectations about life "after Auschwitz."[46]

In this light, it is interesting to compare the reflections in *Negative Dialectics* with the famous Eichmann testimony of Holocaust novelist Yehiel De-Nur (whose pen-name, Ka-Tzetnik, is derived from the German acronym for concentration camp). Before literally collapsing on the stand, in "one of the most dramatic moments in the country's history," according to an Israeli journalist,[47] De-Nur described his experience of the camps in words which Adorno's formulation echoes: "Time there was different from what is here on earth. . . . And the inhabitants of that planet had no names. . . . They were not born there nor did anyone give birth. Even their breathing was regulated by the laws of another nature. They did not live, nor did they die, in accordance with the laws of this world."[48] These words could come from Adorno's description of the universe of a Beckett play. This public enunciation of an "Auschwitz" chronotope, from someone who, unlike Adorno, had been at its center, contributed to the climate in which an "after Auschwitz" chronotope could also be spoken. Only beginning in the 1960s could survivors and others who come after begin to bring their respective experiences and expectations to bear on each other in the public sphere. Such a delayed "event" (or the doubling of the event in its working through) also necessitates reflection on the preexisting modes of reflection; Adorno's late work attempts to bring theory into line with the cultural confrontation with trauma and the attempts at the work of mourning happening all around him.

The passage from *Negative Dialectics* [hereafter abbreviated as *ND*] in which Adorno assesses the "guilt" of the post-Holocaust world, also marks the limits of philosophy itself, as Sigrid Weigel has recently argued. What compels philosophy is not only guilt, but the non-synchronicity of guilt and consciousness, those moments that consciousness cannot fully grasp and which therefore return ceaselessly. But if consciousness of "the other of consciousness," i.e., genocide and its aftermath, grounds philosophy after Auschwitz, it also strips away its ground, since it produces the traumatic "shock" that these non-integratable moments of guilt cannot be reconciled with any already existing philosophy of history.[49] Thinking modern history under the sign of trauma does not, however, lead Adorno to abandon his engagement with modernity, but rather to reformulate it.

The "after Auschwitz" context forces a recognition that philosophy itself has been transformed by the material forces of history which led to the Shoah; in fact, it forces that very materialism of history "upon metaphysics." Such a process makes for some rather ironic philosophical actors: "a new categorical imperative has been imposed by Hitler upon unfree mankind: to arrange their thoughts and

actions so that Auschwitz will not repeat itself" (*ND* 365). This mutation of philosophy, however, should not be seen simplistically as the symptom of a complete historical break which would install a radically new stage in Western culture, although much of the rhetoric of "after Auschwitz" would seem to imply this. As Adorno makes clear in a radio broadcast from the same year as *Negative Dialectics,* the categorical imperative not to repeat Auschwitz—here considered as the primary goal of education—is necessary precisely because such a break has *not* taken place. In **"Erziehung nach Auschwitz"** ["Education after Auschwitz"], Adorno encourages the attempt to build consciousness of the links between civilization and barbarism for the very reason that "the fundamental structure of society and its members, which brought it on, are today the same." Adorno locates the roots of genocide in the development of modern nationalism and inscribes its potential in a "societal tendency" which cannot be separated from the "great tendencies of progress, of Enlightenment."[50]

While in **"Cultural Criticism and Society,"** Adorno seemed to subscribe to a notion of history as the inverse of progress—a theoretical position which appeared to leave no room for the possible redirection of social tendencies—in his later work he mobilizes a more complex view of history, but one which at first glance seems even gloomier. In *Negative Dialectics* he at once negates and affirms different notions of the kind of universal history implicit in the notion of Auschwitz as a stage in a process of reification: "No universal history leads from savagery to humanitarianism, but there is one leading from the slingshot to the megaton bomb." The domination of nature and humanity—epitomized in the Nazi genocide and the threat of nuclear annihilation—"is the unity that cements the discontinuous, chaotically splintered moments and phases of history. . . . History is the unity of continuity and discontinuity" (*ND* 320). In order to provoke a liberating discontinuity which would not be irrational chaos, it will not do to locate a parallel or parasitic progress alongside or within the universal history of barbarism. For Adorno, thought's resistance to universality comes not from a celebration of difference (what he would call the non-identical) as in much poststructuralism, but rather from a refusal to rationalize or grant meaning to that which already exists. Thus, while the desirability of universality is denied, its stranglehold on history is not. Adorno replaces the affirmation of difference in the present with an appeal to a version of "the theological ban on images" [*Bilderverbot*] that defers the emergence of difference to a post-totalitarian world which has not yet arrived.[51] Echoing his assessment of Celan and Beckett, Adorno holds that "[m]aterialism brought that ban into secular form by not permitting Utopia to be positively pictured; this is the substance of its negativity" (*ND* 207). Here the aesthetic and the political are shown to possess a similar critical engagement with the present. There are clear links between the ban on articulating utopia and on Celan's imageless image and Beckett's wordless expression. The latter are the artistic and discursive correlates of utopia in a theory that doubles historical time, asserting the coexistence of a linear regression and a discontinuous hope which can only be voiced through determined and determinate negation.

Adorno does not propose this theory *as* "universal history," but as the product, once again, *of* history. Philosophy becomes materialist because "after Auschwitz there is no word tinged from on high, not even a theological one, that has any right to exist unless it underwent a transformation" (*ND* 367). The philosophy of history responds to material forces, as well. If Adorno ascribes the overarching lines of force to the tendential history of capitalism, he reserves a particular place for Auschwitz:

> [T]he capitalist system's increasingly integrative trend, the fact that its elements entwine into a more and more total context of functions, is precisely what makes the old question about the cause—as opposed to the constellation—more and more precarious. We need no epistemological critique to make us pursue constellations; the search for them is forced upon us by the real course of history.
>
> (*ND* 166)

Drawing attention to the chronotopic dimensions of the Benjaminian constellation in this passage, Fredric Jameson observes "the way in which Adorno here uses the spatiality of the figure of the constellation to argue explicitly against 'linear causality,' but in the name of history itself."[52] The paradox is that this spatialization of historical understanding is, in some way, the product of the movements of a more progressive, linear history: the "increasingly integrative trend" of capitalism and Enlightenment. The Nazis were, Adorno sometimes implies, the agents of the qualitative transformation whereby history reached a new spatialized stage. The exemplary space of this stage is the concentration, or more accurately, extermination camp: "Genocide is the absolute integration. It is on its way wherever men are leveled off—'polished off,' as the German military called it—until one exterminates them literally, as deviations from the concept of their total nullity. Auschwitz confirmed the philosopheme of pure identity as death" (*ND* 362). In Adorno, the language of "identity," of "levelling," is directly connected with the domination of exchange value which capitalism sets in place. Thus Auschwitz is at once an effect of reification and the ultimate fulfillment of its tendency to eliminate particularity, in this case the particularity of those human beings not integrated into the Aryan "race."

The name that Adorno gives in *Negative Dialectics* for this relationship that Auschwitz has with the social totality is the "model." The third part of that work is divided into three sections, which Adorno names "models of negative dialectics," and the last, **"Meditations on Metaphysics,"** includes his most extensive reflections on Auschwitz. Adorno's explanation of what he means by "models" is crucial to understanding how the Holocaust intersects with his thought:

> They are not examples; they do not simply elucidate general reflections. Guiding into the substantive realm,

they seek simultaneously to do justice to the topical intention of what has initially, of necessity, been generally treated—as opposed to the use of examples which Plato introduced and philosophy repeated ever since: as matters of indifference in themselves. The models are to make plain what negative dialectics is and to bring it into the realm of reality, in line with its own concept.

> (*ND* xx)

The prominence given to Auschwitz in Adorno's critique of metaphysics makes it almost a model among models. In *The Differend,* Jean-François Lyotard chooses the "after Auschwitz" model as his designation for "an 'experience' of language that brings speculative discourse to a halt." Such a view of the stakes of Adorno's text derives from an understanding of the model as "the name for a kind of experience where dialectics would encounter a non-negatable negative, and would abide in the impossibility of redoubling that negative into a 'result.'"[53] Lyotard quite correctly reads Adorno's meditations as a critique of Hegelian dialectics in which the negation of the negation produces an affirmative result. When this experience or encounter with that which cannot be raised up into a positive term takes the form of the Auschwitz event, it results in a shift in the horizon of expectation. The Holocaust leaves a permanent wound in the self-conception of humanity that cannot be overcome, but can at best be prevented from recurring.[54] Hence Lyotard insists that what results from this event is a lack of result, and Adorno emphasizes the meaninglessness of the event, and thus seeks to shelter it from "committed" or sentimental works of art.

Despite its lack of affirmative result or meaning, the form of the "model" event must henceforth be factored into philosophical discourse as the becoming-temporal of thought. In opening his **"Meditations on Metaphysics,"** Adorno declared, "We cannot say any more that the immutable is truth, and that the mobile, transitory is appearance. The mutual indifference of temporality and eternal ideas is no longer tenable" (*ND* 361). After Auschwitz, culture—the avowed realm of "eternal ideas"—is folded back into barbarism and the corrosive passage of time. The production of the model is an attempt to think from a place no longer determined by anti-materialist idealism. As the ultimate instance of modern culture's definitive subordination to barbarism, as the rationalized production of death, Auschwitz not only models the model, it casts a retroactive judgment on the ideology of Enlightenment with its trust in reason and the sanctity of culture. This rejection of an optimistic account of progressive reason does not entail that Adorno abandon reason for the delirium of the irrational since he does not place his hopes in the progressive narrative. Here, Adorno diverges from Lyotard, whose postmodern disavowal of the "grand narratives" of Enlightenment reason is much more thoroughgoing.[55] Lyotard rejects enlightened modernity even as he remains, like Adorno, faithful to aesthetic modernism.[56] Adorno, on the other hand, attempts—through a reworking of philosophical form in the light of the catastrophe—to wrench reason free from its instrumental determinations.

Thus, the concept of the model necessitates a new form of philosophical representation. Adorno borrows the concept of the model, Jameson suggests, from music, and specifically from Schönberg's serialism. In twelve-tone composition the model is "the raw material of a specific composition . . . the particular order and configuration of the twelve notes of the scale which, chosen and arranged in advance, *becomes* the composition, in so far as this last is 'nothing more' than an elaborate series of variations and permutations . . . of that starting point."[57] The significance of Jameson's understanding of the model, and that which opposes it to the tenor of Lyotard's post-Marxist argument, is that in this musical reading the model is revealed as that fragment which already contains the totality within it. Jameson's wording, however, is somewhat ambiguous, and seems to imply that the relationship between the model and the totality (the composition) is one of what Althusser termed "expressive causality."[58] The relationship between part and whole in Jameson's musical metaphor seems too simple, a combinatorial logic where the part immediately generates the whole.

Jameson's Hegelian reading does not properly account for the process of "structural causality," which Adorno's account of the model seems to suggest. In this case, we do not simply derive Auschwitz from a history which moves externally to it (as we would in a mechanistic deduction); we grasp that history through the necessary mediation of Auschwitz. But the process is not mere induction either, since Auschwitz does not generate or reflect the totality of the history of modernity. Yet had it not "taken place," the history to be grasped would clearly not be the same. After Auschwitz, modernity and Shoah need to be read in light of each other; our understanding of each is mediated by the other.[59] The model is not a matter of indifference, as is the example in speculative thought, nor is it simply an element in a permutational series. The manner in which thought can arrive at some understanding of that which the model models is less direct. As Adorno wrote in **"The Essay as Form,"** "the essay has to cause the totality to be illuminated in a *partial* feature, whether the feature be chosen or merely happened upon, without asserting the presence of the totality" (emphasis added—MR). From his account of the essay, we can presume that Adorno's use of the model is not an attempt to be "systematic," as Jameson's metaphor suggests, but rather has the "characteristic of an intention groping its way" (*NL* 16). The non-assertive, almost blind illumination of essayistic thought is once again the "imageless image," and *its* model is autonomous art. With the selection of "poetry after Auschwitz" as the partial feature through which to illuminate the Holocaust and its relation to modernity, Adorno preserves a tension between part and whole that maintains both the power of the modern totality and the truth content of its various local expressions.

We can now grasp something of the temporality and location of "after Auschwitz" as Adorno employs it in his late works. In fact, the famous opening line of *Negative Dialectics*—"Philosophy, which once seemed obsolete, lives on because the moment to realize it was missed" (*ND* 3)—expresses the defunct temporality of lifeless survival which the "experience" of Auschwitz inaugurates, according to the text's final **"Meditations on Metaphysics."** And the place of this thought is revealed as that constricted zone of nearly annihilated expectation, the death camp: "Beckett has given us the only fitting reaction to the situation of the concentration camps—a situation he never calls by name, as if it were subject to an image ban. What is, he says, is like a concentration camp. At one time he speaks of a lifelong death penalty" (*ND* 380-81). If, in Beckett, the concentration camp is the "unnamable," in Adorno the camp (Auschwitz) is the repetitively invoked name for something else which must be grasped in a situation of indirect illumination.

That something else is, strangely enough, the yearning for utopia, that which has no-place. Faced with the "lifelong death penalty," Beckett's writing

> seems stoical but is full of inaudible cries that things should be different. Such nihilism implies the contrary of identification with nothingness. To Beckett, as to the Gnostics, the created world is radically evil, and its negation is the chance of another world that is not yet. As long as the world is as it is, all pictures of reconciliation, peace, and quiet resemble the picture of death.
>
> (*ND* 381)

The significance of positing "another world that is not yet" derives not from any positive qualities of that world (which fall under the image ban), but from the coexistence of an alternative chronotope—the *concept* of another space and time—in a field where the replacement of experience with integrated, administered consciousness obliterates expectation and hope. Elsewhere, Adorno formulates this concept in terms of the indexicality of thought: "utopia is essentially in the determined negation . . . of that which merely is, and by concretizing itself as something false, it always points at the same time to what should be."[60] In Bakhtin's formulation, the indexical function of the chronotope points backwards toward the event—thus underlining representation's belatedness in relation to that event. In Adorno the necessity of coming after the catastrophe coexists with an anticipatory temporality. The construction of the chronotope blocks the event itself but in so doing casts a shadow whose outline registers utopia. For even if we always come *after* the event in Adorno's thought (both historically and epistemologically), we are also always *too early* to grasp it. We live in a world where reconciliation has not yet taken place and thus has not yet provided the standpoint from which to view the event from outside the flow of "damaged life." The repeated citation of Auschwitz is an attempt to make one's way through that flux, to provide a temporary map of the historical present as the means to a future that would install a break with the conditions which nurtured fascism.

In a sense we return to Adorno's initial phrasing of "after Auschwitz" where he castigated poetry for blocking knowledge of the "radically evil" social totality. Now, however, we see that some poetic practices (that is, Celan's, Beckett's) and Adorno's writings on poetry seek, through their direct or indirect invocation of Auschwitz, to block a positive comprehension of what, after Auschwitz, can only be known negatively. Only by avoiding "faded positivities" can writing avoid "conspiring with all extant malice, and eventually with the destructive principle itself" (***ND*** 381). The repeated performance of the terrifying chronotope, "after Auschwitz," holds a place for a time not yet emergent.

IV. CONCLUSION: AFTER ADORNO

If the space and time "after Auschwitz" occupies some middle zone between past and future events that defy representation, its own substance remains conceptual, which is not to say imaginary. After Adorno one cannot conceive of genocide in quite the same fashion. But when or what is "after Adorno"? Irving Howe remarked, quite correctly, that it is difficult "to think of another area of literary discourse in which a single writer has exerted so strong, if diffused, an influence as Theodor Adorno has on discussions of literature and the Holocaust."[61] Yet Howe also realized, as did Adorno, that the "speculation that human consciousness could no longer be what it had previously been" after Auschwitz was unfortunately not true.[62] We can certainly explain this latter fact in Marxist terms, arguing that a change of consciousness could only follow a change in the material organization of society—this is precisely Adorno's critique of postwar European culture. But the former remark on Adorno's influence reasserts the question of consciousness and intellectual intervention, while it suggests that that intervention should lie elsewhere than in "speculations" on consciousness.

If Adorno is correct in ***Negative Dialectics,*** speculation must give way to a new form of dialectical materialist analysis in the wake of Auschwitz. One consequence of this proposition would be the need to take into account the material effects of philosophizing. Instead of seeking in Adorno the reflection of a historical break called "Auschwitz," we might understand him as producing a series of concepts (in the form of chronotopes) which retroactively pose the possibility of a break, at the same time that they illuminate the eternal return of the same in those places which have not yet worked through the Auschwitz model. Thought "alone" cannot alter history but, in citing and re-signifying a discursive chain (such as that connecting Auschwitz to "Auschwitz"), it can keep the past present and the future open. The production of concepts also helps structure the field out of which the agency to alter the spatio-temporal parameters of the present must emerge.

As Howe implies, the major influence of Adorno's Auschwitz chronotope has taken place in aesthetic realms. This must be taken for its negative as well as its positive implications. Adorno provides complex, contradictory, and frequently misunderstood concepts for evaluating "Holocaust art." Despite those discouraging adjectives, various interpretations of Adorno continue to structure critical re-

sponse to such art in the present, and even when Adorno's name is not mentioned (or even known). One potentially positive effect of my reading of Adorno would be to shift this terrain from what remains a primarily *moralizing* discourse to a *materialist* and *ethical* critique. Instead of evaluating a work's "decorum" according to principles assumed to adhere in the event itself, we can recognize our ambiguous distance from the event, and inquire into the relationship a work establishes between the past it mobilizes and its contemporary context. Reading Adorno's works as interventions in concrete situations meant to produce effects deprives them of their oracular quality, but also increases their relevance and their usefulness in the present.

It is equally true, however, that the particular way in which Adorno's thought structures the field of possibilities limits the kinds of interventions that he would promote. Adorno's aesthetics remain, as Jameson points out, strictly modernist.[63] Since modernism no longer represents a challenge to quiescent ideologies, a more properly postmodernist critique would offer a crucial reconsideration of mass culture.[64] In particular, a full-blown consumer society demands an acknowledgment of the status of the Holocaust commodity. In the midst of postmodernism's proliferation of aesthetic techniques new kinds of historical art are taking shape.[65] Some postmodern works, such as Art Spiegelman's *Maus,* challenge the assumptions about the necessary "autonomy" of art after Auschwitz which have emerged from Adorno's (albeit critical) reception, even as they recognize the risks of commodification.[66]

Equally limiting to the project of confronting the historical legacy of genocide is the way in which Adorno focuses primarily on aesthetic objects, even as he refers them back to the conditions of their production. This is of course ironic since his initial statement of the problematic seems deliberately anti-aesthetic. Adorno's subsequent reformulations, and most of his writings, refine the status of the aesthetic, granting authentic or autonomous art a role of absolute importance in articulating a critique of capitalist society. But the wholesale substitution of reflective and aesthetic practice for other forms of praxis hardly seems justifiable on political or theoretical grounds.

This is not all there is, however, in late Adorno. If the ethico-political call to arms after Auschwitz derives from the necessity of preventing its recurrence, then the pedagogical moment that sometimes surfaces in Adorno's writings and, especially, speeches and radio talks ought to be kept in mind. In those more obviously conjunctural interventions, Adorno stresses the concept of education to maturity [*Erziehung zur Mündigkeit*]. In sketching this notion of "democratic" or "mature political pedagogy," Adorno not only leaves the autonomy of the aesthetic realm but suggests a project of "public enlightenment" whose formulation and actualization remain today as critical as they do unfinished.[67] Ultimately, this relocation of the confrontation with Auschwitz in the public sphere of democratic education may be as great a contribution to the process of coming to terms with the past as the more famous reflections on representation. In fact, the lively debates surrounding many recent films, literary and historical texts, memorials, and museums seem to indicate a renewed interest in historical understanding that has been spurred precisely by controversies about representation. Viewed retrospectively from the vantage point of such debates, Adorno's contribution is all the more impressive; he brought together the questions of Holocaust representation and education at a moment when they had not yet been fully articulated.

Notes

1. This controversy was reported in the *New York Times* 27 Jan. 1995: A3.

2. For misquotations, see note 4. Among the many citations, see, for example, in philosophy: Jean-François Lyotard, *The Differend,* trans. George Van Den Abbeele (Minneapolis: U of Minnesota P, 1988); Detlev Claussen, "Nach Auschwitz," *Zivilisationsbruch: Denken nach Auschwitz,* ed. Dan Diner (Frankfurt/Main: Fischer, 1988). In theology, see Richard Rubenstein, *After Auschwitz: Radical Theology and Contemporary Judaism* (New York: Bobbs-Merrill, 1966); Johann Baptist Metz, "Suffering Unto God," *Critical Inquiry* 20.4 (1994): 611-22; Emil Fackenheim, *To Mend the World: Foundations of Post-Holocaust Jewish Thought* (New York: Schocken, 1982). In aesthetics, see Lambert Zuidervaart, *Adorno's Aesthetic Theory: The Redemption of Illusion* (Cambridge: MIT, 1991); Terry Eagleton, *The Ideology of the Aesthetic* (Cambridge: Blackwell, 1990). In literary and cultural criticism, see Lawrence Langer, *The Holocaust and the Literary Imagination* (New Haven: Yale UP, 1975); Irving Howe, "Writing and the Holocaust," *Writing and the Holocaust,* ed. Berel Lang (New York: Holmes and Meier, 1988); George Steiner, *Language and Silence: Essays on Language, Literature, and the Inhuman* (New York: Atheneum, 1967); Eric Santner, *Stranded Objects: Mourning, Memory, and Film in Postwar Germany* (Ithaca: Cornell UP, 1990). See also Maurice Blanchot's reflections in *Après Coup* (Paris: Minuit, 1983). Lastly, Charlotte Delbo's memoirs, entitled *Auschwitz et Après,* were recently translated. See Charlotte Delbo, *Auschwitz and After,* trans. Rosette Lamont (New Haven: Yale UP, 1995).

3. As testimony to the continued interest in Adorno and Auschwitz in the German context, two volumes have recently appeared. Manuel Köppen's edited volume *Kunst und Literatur nach Auschwitz* (Berlin: Erich Schmidt, 1993) is an interdisciplinary set of interventions growing out of a recent conference. Reclam has just issued an important source book entitled *Lyrik nach Auschwitz?* ed. Petra Kiedaisch, (Stuttgart: Reclam, 1995) that collects excerpts from Adorno's work in which the status of Auschwitz is in question and responses by poets and critics to his dictum. The editor's introduction is the only essay that I know other

than the present one and the one by Claussen cited above which draws attention to the variety of Adorno's articulations and to the frequent partial or miscitations of Adorno's critics. However, while Kiedaisch and Claussen are at pains to emphasize the continuity of Adorno's thought, I argue here for discontinuities in his articulations of Auschwitz. In this sense I am closer to Sigrid Weigel, who, while not providing a systematic reading of Adorno's *oeuvre,* does emphasize the differences between the writings of the 1940s and those of the 1960s. See Weigel, "'Kein philosophisches Staunen'—'Schreiben im Staunen': Zum Verhältnis von Philosophie und Literatur nach 1945: Benjamin, Adorno, Bachmann." *Deutsche Vierteljahresschrift* 70.1 (1996): 120-37.

4. The first phrase (or paraphrase) is from Steiner, *Language and Silence* 53; hereafter referred to parenthetically within the text as *LS.* The second case is slightly stranger. Shoshana Felman subtly, but significantly, misquotes Adorno's *Negative Dialectics*—"it may have been wrong to say that after Auschwitz you could no longer write poems"—thus detracting from the tentativeness of Adorno's sentence, and adding the question of "possibility," which, as we will see, is a complex one. Nevertheless, on the back cover of *Testimony,* the quotation is the standard, correct one from Adorno's original statement, nowhere cited by Felman or Steiner. (There, however, Adorno is referred to as an "Austrian musicologist"!) See Shoshana Felman and Dori Laub, *Testimony: Crises of Witnessing in Literature, Psychoanalysis and History* (New York: Routledge, 1992) 33. Cf. Adorno's *Negative Dialectics,* trans. E. B. Ashton (New York: Continuum, 1973) 362.

5. Gary Weissman pointed out to me the possible poetic seductiveness of the near assonance in "after Auschwitz."

6. M. M. Bakhtin, *The Dialogic Imagination,* trans. C. Emerson and M. Holquist (Austin: U of Texas P, 1981) 84.

7. Hayden White, "Historical Emplotment and the Problem of Truth," *Probing the Limits of Representation: Nazism and the "Final Solution,"*; ed. Saul Friedländer (Cambridge: Harvard UP, 1992) 341n.

8. For an extended discussion of Adorno's interventions in democratic pedagogical practice and theory, see Peter Uwe Hohendahl, "Education After the Holocaust," *Prismatic Thought: Theodor W. Adorno* (Lincoln: U of Nebraska P, 1995) 45-72.

9. See Steiner, *Language and Silence* 41-46. With *In Bluebeard's Castle* (New York: Atheneum, 1971), Steiner appears to be making a somewhat different, perhaps more Adornian, argument. Here he wants to read the inhuman events of the twentieth century, now referred to as the "Thirty Years' War" of 1915-1945, as anticipated by the *"ennui"* of nineteenth-century culture. However, even in negating the pas-

toral view of the last century and the more general nostalgia for past "Golden Ages," his writing still preserves the sentiment of decline. Implicit in such phrases as "undermining European stability," "the dissolution of civilized norms," and "the breakdown of the European order" (22, 25, 29) is the same investment in the greatness of European culture found in *Language and Silence,* even at the same time that that culture's impotence before barbarism is exposed. To get out of this bind, Steiner constructs a "religious" theory of culture, which is particularly un-Adornian in its anachronistic idealism.

10. Santner 8-9.

11. Cited in Santner 165n. See Alice Jardine, "Copyright 2000," *Copyright* 1 (Fall 1987): 6.

12. Santner 9.

13. The spatio-temporal articulation of modernity as consisting of a constant break between the "space of experience" and the "horizon of expectation" can be found in Reinhart Koselleck, *Futures Past: On the Semantics of Historical Time,* trans. Keith Tribe (Cambridge: MIT, 1985).

14. In "Cultural Criticism and Society," Adorno writes: "The cultural critic is barred from the insight that the reification of life results not from too much enlightenment but from too little." See Adorno, *Prisms,* trans. Samuel and Shierry Weber (Cambridge: MIT, 1981) 24. Hereafter referred to parenthetically as *P* in the text. Considering Adorno's ideas in the light of debates over modernity and postmodernity, Albrecht Wellmer argues for a notion of postmodernity as a "second" or "postmetaphysical modernity": "a modernity without the dream of ultimate reconciliations, but [which] would still preserve the rational, subversive, and experimental spirit of modern democracy, modern art, modern science and modern individualism." See Albrecht Wellmer, *The Persistence of Modernity: Essays on Aesthetics, Ethics, and Postmodernism* (Cambridge: MIT, 1991) viii.

15. Robert-Jan Van Pelt, "A Site in Search of a Mission," *Anatomy of the Auschwitz Death Camp,* eds. Yisrael Gutman and Michael Berenbaum (Bloomington: Indiana UP, 1994) 94, 106.

16. James Young, *The Texture of Memory* (New Haven: Yale UP, 1993) 128.

17. While we in the United States have, since the 1960s, conventionally called that totality of events the Holocaust, it is unlikely that Adorno, at least in his earliest writings, had the same object in mind when he referred to Auschwitz. More likely, he was referring to the totality of Nazi barbarism, and not necessarily its specifically Jewish component. It is important to keep in mind that the general significance of Auschwitz changed along with Adorno's conceptualization of it—although Adorno's prophetic reference to what would become the best known of the camps

also makes clear how influential his thought was in this very history.

18. Pierre Nora, "Between Memory and History: *Les Lieux de Mémoire,*" *Representations* 26 (Spring 1989): 7-25.

19. Young 130.

20. Adorno, *Minima Moralia,* trans. E. F. N. Jephcott (New York: Verso, 1974).

21. For some of Adorno's reflections on his U.S. exile, see Adorno, "On the Question: 'What is German?'" *New German Critique* 36 (Fall 1985): 121-31; and Adorno, "Scientific Experiences of a European Scholar in America," *The Intellectual Migration: Europe and America, 1930-1960,* eds. Donald Fleming and Bernard Bailyn (Cambridge: Harvard UP, 1969) 338-70. The latter account, in particular, represents a more positive take on his experiences in America than the wartime and immediate postwar writings do. In *Prismatic Thought,* Hohendahl argues convincingly that this "pro-American reorientation" was "motivated by the confrontation with postwar Germany" (43).

22. Max Horkheimer and Theodor Adorno, *Dialectic of Enlightenment,* trans. John Cumming (New York: Continuum, 1972) 149-50.

23. Adorno, *Notes to Literature* vol. 1, trans. Shierry Weber Nicholsen (New York: Columbia UP, 1991) 37, 38. Hereafter referred to parenthetically in the text as *NL.*

24. Adorno, "Commitment," *The Essential Frankfurt School Reader,* eds. Andrew Arato and Eike Gebhardt (New York: Continuum, 1982) 304. Hereafter primarily referred to parenthetically in the text as "C."

25. Adorno, "Commitment" 312. In German, "Satz" is more neutral than "saying," meaning "sentence" or "phrase," but the sense of self-citation is still present.

26. Fredric Jameson, "Reflections in Conclusion," *Aesthetics and Politics,* eds. Ernst Bloch et al. (London: New Left, 1977) 209.

27. Johannes von Moltke, "Exhibiting Jewish Lifeworlds," *Found Object* 3 (Spring 1994): 15. For an important consideration of the "Jewish question" in postwar Germany, see Anson Rabinbach, "The Jewish Question in the German Question," *New German Critique* 44 (1988): 159-92. For an Israeli perspective on the politics of *Wiedergutmachung,* see Tom Segev, *The Seventh Million,* trans. Haim Watzman (New York: Hill and Wang, 1993) 189-252.

28. Adorno, "What Does Coming to Terms with the Past Mean?" *Bitburg in Moral and Political Perspective,* ed. Geoffrey Hartman (Bloomington: Indiana UP, 1986) 115.

29. Steiner, *Language and Silence* 95-109.

30. See the other essays in Steiner's *Language and Silence,* written in the early and mid-1960s and clearly influenced by Adorno.

31. Adorno, *Minima Moralia* 15, 247.

32. For consideration of Benjamin's influence on Adorno's *Negative Dialectics,* see Susan Buck-Morss, *The Origins of Negative Dialectics* (Hassocks: Harvester P, 1977) and Fredric Jameson, *Late Marxism: Adorno, or, the Persistence of the Dialectic* (London and New York: Verso, 1990) 49-58.

33. Walter Benjamin, *Illuminations,* trans. Harry Zohn (New York: Schocken, 1969) 263.

34. Benjamin 262.

35. Cited in Santner 4.

36. Adorno, "What Does Coming To Terms With the Past Mean?" 122; cited in Santner 5.

37. Adorno, "What Does Coming To Terms With the Past Mean?" 124.

38. See the essays collected in Saul Friedländer, *Memory, History, and the Extermination of the Jews of Europe* (Bloomington and Indianapolis: Indiana UP, 1993) for insights into the growth of Holocaust memory in different national contexts. For the United States context in particular, see Peter Novick, "Holocaust Memory in America," *The Art of Memory: Holocaust Memorials in History,* ed. James Young (New York: Prestel, 1994) 159-65.

39. Adorno, *Negative Dialectics* 367.

40. Adorno, *Aesthetic Theory,* trans. C. Lenhardt (New York: Routledge and Keegan Paul, 1984) 442.

41. Adorno, *Aesthetic Theory* 311, 444.

42. For an example of this error, see Alvin Rosenfeld, *A Double Dying: Reflections on Holocaust Literature* (Bloomington: Indiana UP, 1980) 13.

43. Andreas Huyssen, "Mapping the Postmodern," *Feminism/Postmodernism,* ed. Linda Nicholson (New York: Routledge, 1990) 249.

44. Adorno, *Negative Dialectics* 362-63. The German makes it clear that the "could" and the "can" of these sentences refers not to an ability, but an ethical principle: "nach Auschwitz ließe kein Gedicht mehr sich schreiben . . . ob nach Auschwitz noch sich leben lasse, ob vollends es dürfe. . . ." The original verbs *lassen* and *dürfen* used here denote "allowance" and "permission."

45. Adorno, *Negative Dialectics* 364; translation modified—MR. Hereafter referred to parenthetically in the text as *ND.*

46. Miriam Hansen has made a similar point about Adorno's notion of experience in the context of her brilliant foreword to Oskar Negt and Alexander Kluge, *Public Sphere and Experience,* trans. Peter Labanyi, Jamie Owen Daniel, and Assenka Oksiloff (Minneapolis: U of Minnesota P, 1993): "the 'structure' of Adorno's experience was not merely a generalized perception of 'horror'; it was the insistence on a fundamental *Zusammenhang* [relation, connection, context], the persistence of the past in the present that maintained the imperative to engage the legacy of mass annihilation across generational boundaries" (xix).

47. Segev 4.

48. Cited in Segev 3.

49. Weigel 129f.

50. Adorno, "Erziehung nach Auschwitz," *Gesammelte Schriften* 10.2:675. My translation—MR.

51. For a critique of the version of the *Bilderverbot* implicit in Adorno's approach to Auschwitz, see Klaus Laermann, "'Nach Auschwitz ein Gedicht zu schreiben, ist barbarisch': Uberlegungen zu einem Darstellungsverbot," *Kunst und Literatur nach Auschwitz* 11-15.

52. Jameson, *Late Marxism* 59.

53. Lyotard 88.

54. In a famous passage from one of his historian's debate [*Historikerstreit*] interventions, Habermas wrote: "There [in Auschwitz] something happened, that up to now nobody considered as even possible. There one touched on something which represents the deep layer of solidarity among all that wears a human face; notwithstanding all the usual acts of beastliness of human history, the integrity of this common layer had been taken for granted. . . . Auschwitz has changed the basis for the continuity of the conditions of life within history." Cited in Saul Friedländer, "Introduction," *Probing the Limits of Representation: Nazism and the "Final Solution";* (Cambridge: Harvard UP, 1992) 3.

55. See, especially, Jean-François Lyotard, *The Postmodern Condition: A Report on Knowledge,* trans. Geoff Bennington and Brian Massumi (Minneapolis: U of Minnesota P, 1984).

56. Huyssen, "Mapping the Postmodern" 266.

57. Jameson, *Late Marxism* 61.

58. Jameson's wording here is ironic given that he popularized Althusser's critique of "expressive causality," and championing of "structural causality." See Jameson, *The Political Unconscious* (Ithaca: Cornell UP, 1981) 23-58. For Althusser's development of these ideas, see Althusser, "Contradiction and Overdetermination," *For Marx,* trans. Ben Brewster (New York: Pantheon, 1969) 87-128; and Althusser and Etienne Balibar, *Reading Capital,* trans. Ben Brewster (London: Verso, 1979).

59. This account of the Holocaust as a possibility within modernity which forever modifies our notion of the latter is close to Zygmunt Bauman's: "From the fact that the Holocaust is modern, it does not follow that modernity is a Holocaust." See Zygmunt Bauman, *Modernity and the Holocaust* (Ithaca: Cornell UP, 1989) 93.

60. Adorno in conversation with Ernst Bloch in Bloch, *The Utopian Function of Art and Literature: Selected Essays,* trans. Jack Zipes and Frank Mecklenburg (Cambridge: MIT, 1988) 12.

61. Howe 178.

62. Howe 198.

63. Jameson, "Reflections in Conclusion." See also Zuidervaart's extensive critique of Adorno's aesthetics for a useful discussion of its strengths and weaknesses. Zuidervaart is also quite critical of Jameson's theory of postmodernism, although this section of his book is less convincing to me.

64. For a defense of the possibilities of mass cultural representation of the Nazi genocide that pays particular attention to one important mass cultural text, the television mini-series, *Holocaust,* see Andreas Huyssen, "The Politics of Identification," *New German Critique* 19 (1981): 117-36.

65. For the articulation of a "popular modernist" position on the representability of the Holocaust that seeks to elude the outmoded antinomies of modernist art, see Miriam Hansen, "*Schindler's List* Is Not *Shoah*: The Second Commandment, Popular Modernism, and Public Memory," *Critical Inquiry* 22 (Winter 1996): 292-312.

66. Art Spiegelman, *Maus,* vols. 1 and 2 (New York: Pantheon, 1986, 1991). On Spiegelman, see Michael Rothberg, "'We Were Talking Jewish': Art Spiegelman's *Maus* as 'Holocaust' Production," *Contemporary Literature* 35.4 (1994): 661-87.

67. Adorno, "What Does Coming To Terms With the Past Mean?" 124-29.

Noah Isenberg (essay date 1998)

SOURCE: "Critical Theory at the Barricades," in *Lingua Franca: The Review of Academic Life,* Vol. 8, No. 8, November, 1998, pp. 19-22.

[*In the following essay, Isenberg examines the student backlash against Adorno and other members of the Frankfurt School in Germany in the 1960s.*]

On April 22, 1969, shortly after beginning a lecture in his course on dialectical thought before an audience of nearly one thousand students at the University of Frankfurt, the eminent Frankfurt School sociologist and Marxist cultural critic Theodor W. Adorno found himself in an unusual situation. A student in one of the back rows interrupted him, demanding that he engage in "self-criticism." Another student silently walked up to the blackboard and wrote the following words: "He who only allows dear Adorno to rule will uphold capitalism his entire life." After Adorno told the class that they would have five minutes to decide if his lecture should continue, three female students dressed in leather jackets rushed the podium. They showered him with roses and tulips, exposed their breasts, and tried repeatedly to kiss him. Incensed and humiliated, Adorno stormed out of the lecture hall.

This incident, which came to be known as the *Busenaktion* ("breast action"), has never figured with much prominence in American studies of the Frankfurt School. Americans are far more apt to think of the leading figures of Critical Theory—Adorno, Max Horkheimer, Herbert Marcuse, and others—languishing in exile in New York and southern California during the Nazi period, or of the eclectic blend of Marxism, psychoanalysis, and sociology that characterized their thought. Their work is famous for its mandarinism, its abstraction, and—especially in the case of Adorno—its uncompromising commitment to the independence of critical thought and high art. Yet in Germany, on the thirtieth anniversary of the student revolts of 1968, the Frankfurt School is also remembered for its vexed role in the volatile, sometimes violent political upheavals of the 1960s.

The *Busenaktion* was just one of many confrontations between the increasingly "praxis"-oriented German New Left and the theoreticians who had been its mentors. The turbulent evolution of this relationship is the subject of Wolfgang Kraushaar's elaborate three-volume work, *Frankfurter Schule und Studentenbewegung: Von der Flaschenpost zum Molotowcocktail, 1946-1995* (The Frankfurt School and the Student Movement: From the Message in the Bottle to the Molotov Cocktail, 1946-1995), published in Germany this past spring by Rogner & Bernhard. A political scientist at Hamburg's Institute of Social Research and a bona fide '68er, Kraushaar has produced a painstaking and lavish collection. It consists of a meticulously detailed historical overview, an extensive compendium of documents and photographs, and a collection of retrospective essays with titles like "Dialogues on Theory and Praxis" and "The Oedipal Complex of the '68ers."

The story that these volumes tell ends on a sorry note. Adorno and Horkheimer, the grand old men of the German intellectual left, saw their lectures heckled, their institute occupied, and their own students, notably Adorno's protégé Hans-Jürgen Krahl, turn against them. In a moment of despair during the student occupation of the institute in January 1969, Adorno called the police. Students were outraged at his betrayal. "Adorno as institution is dead," declared a flyer distributed by a radical group of sociology students in April of that year.

Adorno himself would survive just another few months. He died of a heart attack in Switzerland on August 6,

1969, at the age of sixty-five. Six weeks earlier, he had written to Marcuse of his "extreme depression" and of his revulsion at the fascist overtones he sensed in the tactics and demands of the students.

Yet relations between leftist German students and their mentors had not always been so antagonistic. Kraushaar begins in the late 1940s, when Horkheimer and Adorno, the two central figures from the prewar incarnation of the Frankfurt-based Institut für Sozialforschung, returned to Germany from their American exile. Their "critical sociology," which fused the insights of Weber with those of Marx and Hegel, along with their trenchant critique of fascism, attracted students looking for alternatives to the positivism and conservatism that dominated German intellectual life.

When Horkheimer first returned to Germany, originally as a guest professor at the University of Frankfurt in 1948 and then as the chair of sociology and philosophy in 1949, his students received him warmly. From the outset, he and Adorno assumed the role of spokesmen for "the reeducation of German youth." Because they were left-wing intellectuals and returned Jewish refugees who had been personally affected by the horrors of National Socialism, the two were less suspect to radical students than instructors who had remained in Germany under Hitler. Both found that German students took to their ideas, and both recognized promising signs of intellectual advancement among their disciples. "They are learning to express themselves and to have the freedom to say what they believe," announced Horkheimer in a Frankfurt-based student newspaper in 1960. Several of their early students and associates, Jürgen Habermas among them, would go on to become leading intellectuals.

As the political climate shifted in the mid-1960s, however, the very students who had been vocal and independent just a few years earlier became disenchanted with the Olympian detachment of their mentors. In 1964, under the charismatic leadership of Rudi Dutschke, the radical organization Subversive Aktion undertook a series of confrontations with the elder spiritual leaders. Dutschke was also largely responsible for the spread of anti-Establishment activism within the growing Sozialistischer Deutscher Studentenbund (Union of German Socialist Students, or SDS), which demanded the total transformation of German society. His group challenged the conservatism of the Adenauer administration and declared that the denazification of West German society and its institutions had been halfhearted and ineffectual. The rise of the civil rights and anti-Vietnam movements on the other side of the Atlantic further inspired the radicalism of these students. In a 1967 debate, Dutschke dismissed Habermas's thought as outdated; Habermas responded by calling Dutschke's unbridled activism "left-wing fascism."

At the same time that Adorno was working on such rarefied theoretical works as *Negative Dialectics* (1966) and *Aesthetic Theory* (1970), the SDS was operating under the

banner "Enlightenment through Action," and engaging in demonstrations: against the Vietnam War, against repressive university reforms, and against the right-wing German media monopoly. The elder professors were not amused. Like such American Old Guard leftists as Irving Howe, who expressed distaste for Tom Hayden and the American Students for a Democratic Society, the Frankfurt School veterans were disturbed by the youthful disrespect of liberal institutions and disgusted by what they saw as a dogmatic faith in the primacy of action. "I established a theoretical model of thought," Adorno remarked. "How could I have suspected that people would want to implement it with Molotov cocktails?"

But members of the student movement did not abandon the work of their elders altogether. They circulated pirated copies of *Dialectic of Enlightenment* (1947); they rediscovered Georg Lukács and the Marxist texts of Walter Benjamin; and above all they turned their attention to the writings of Marcuse. His *One-Dimensional Man* (1964), already influential in America, appeared in German translation in 1967. The year before, Marcuse, who had remained in American exile, visited Germany. At the University of Frankfurt, he gave the keynote lecture at a student-sponsored conference on Vietnam, an event at which more than two thousand students were present and which led to mass antiwar demonstrations. Already known for his support of the American student movement, and for his mentorship of Angela Davis, Marcuse drew instant sympathy from the German students and formed a lasting friendship with Dutschke. In his celebrated essay "Repressive Tolerance" (published in German in 1966), Marcuse declared that in the case of insurrections among the oppressed, "no third party, and least of all the educator and intellectual, has the right to preach them abstention."

Unsurprisingly, Horkheimer and Adorno were suspicious of Marcuse's engagement with the student rebels. A firm believer that science (*Wissenschaft*) and culture (*Kultur*) should be autonomous spheres, free of any direct involvement with politics, Adorno declared that he would remain a "theoretical human being," unwilling to draw practical consequences from his ideas. "If I were to give practical advice in the way that Herbert Marcuse has to a certain extent done," Adorno remarked in a 1969 interview in *Der Spiegel*, "it would be at the cost of my own productivity."

Although the students vilified him for such quietism, Adorno's view of them was more ambivalent. On his deathbed he dictated a final letter to Marcuse, hoping to prevent the gulf between them from growing any wider. His words struck a remarkably conciliatory note: "I am the last to underestimate the merits of the student movement," he insisted. "It has disrupted the smooth transition to a totally administered world"—the world whose coming his own work so passionately decried.

In 1959, in his lecture **"What Does Coming to Terms With the Past Mean?"**—a key text for Germany's postwar confrontations with its National Socialist legacy—

Adorno had argued that the most urgent task facing post-war Germany was the eradication of those aspects of German culture and society that had enabled fascism to take root. In a different way, the German '68ers saw themselves as carrying out that very task. Of course, the wounds of the past, inflamed by the rise of terrorism (led by guerrilla groups like the Red Army Faction), in the 1970s, may not yet be healed. But now, thanks to Kraushaar, participants in this generational conflict can begin to come to terms with their own past.

FURTHER READING

Criticism

Dallmayr, Fred R. "Phenomenology and Critique: Adorno." In *Critical Encounters: Between Philosophy and Politics,* pp. 39-72. Notre Dame, Ind.: University of Notre Dame Press, 1987.
> Examines Adorno's place in the phenomenological movement.

Frow, John. "Mediation and Metaphor: Adorno and the Sociology of Art." *Clio* 12, No. 1 (Fall 1982): 57-65.
> Discusses Adorno's ideas about art and mass culture.

Gendron, Bernard. "Theodor Adorno Meets the Cadillacs." In *Studies in Entertainment: Critical Approaches to Mass Culture,* edited by Tania Modleski, pp. 18-36. Bloomington and Indianapolis: Indiana University Press, 1986.
> Explores Adorno's thoughts on popular music.

Jarvis, Simon. *Adorno: A Critical Introduction.* New York: Routledge, 1998, 283 p.
> Provides an overview of Adorno's writings.

Krukowski, Lucian. "Form and Protest in Atonal Music: A Meditation on Adorno." In *The Arts, Society, and Literature,* edited by Harry R. Garvin, pp. 105-24. London and Toronto: Associated University Presses, 1984.
> Discusses Adorno's response to atonal, "radical" music.

Paddison, Max. "The Critique Criticised: Adorno and Popular Music." *Popular Music* 2 (1982): 201-18.
> Analyzes Adorno's writings on popular music, suggesting ways in which his theories have been misinterpreted.

Pickford, Henry W. "Critical Models: Adorno's Theory and Practice of Cultural Criticism." *Yale Journal of Criticism* 10, No. 2 (1997): 247-70.
> Examines Adorno's essays on culture and politics.

Wellmer, Albrecht. "Truth, Semblance, Reconciliation: Adorno's Aesthetic Redemption of Modernity." In *The Persistence of Modernity: Essays on Aesthetics, Ethics and Postmodernism,* translated by David Midgley, pp. 1-35. Frankfurt am Main: Polity Press, 1991.
> Discusses the lasting influence of Adorno's aesthetics.

Additional coverage of Adorno's life and career is contained in the following sources published by the Gale Group: *Contemporary Authors,* Vols. 25-28R, 89-92; *Contemporary Authors New Revision,* Vol. 89.

Thomas Boyd
1898-1935

American novelist, biographer, and short story writer.

INTRODUCTION

In his short writing career, spanning only twelve years, Boyd was known for his vivid, unromanticized depictions of war in the twentieth century, as well as for his biographies of American figures. Admired by F. Scott Fitzgerald and often compared to the works of Ernest Hemingway, Boyd's writings were considered to be some of the most accurate and evocative portraits of wartime experience.

BIOGRAPHICAL INFORMATION

Born in Defiance, Ohio, in 1898, Boyd dropped out of high school before graduating to join the marines. During World War I he served with the Sixth Regiment at Verdun-sur-Meuse, Belleau Wood, Soissons, and Saint-Mihiel—all in France—before effects from a gas-shell explosion at Blanc Mont in October of 1918 ended his military career. Living in St. Paul, Minnesota, in the early 1920s, Boyd worked as literary editor of the *St. Paul Daily News* and was part owner of Kilmarnock Bookshop, where he established close friendships with visiting writers, including F. Scott Fitzgerald. In 1922 Boyd sent a manuscript copy of his novel *Through the Wheat* (1923) to Fitzgerald, who interceded on Boyd's behalf with Scribner's, which had previously rejected the book. Shortly thereafter Boyd received a cable from the publisher accepting his book for publication. The success of *Through the Wheat* and the rapid acceptance and publication of subsequent fictional works convinced Boyd to devote himself to writing fulltime, moving with his family to the Connecticut countryside. Over the next four years he published several highly acclaimed biographies, adding to the critical respect he had already earned. In 1934 Boyd, disillusioned with capitalism and convinced that greed and ambition were the causes of all wars, joined the Communist Party and in the fall of that year ran for governor of Connecticut on the Communist platform. He lost the election but remained faithful to his social and political ideals. Boyd was an active member of the League of American Writers and was in strong support of the creation of the first American Writers' Congress in 1935. That year Boyd suffered a mild stroke. He died of a cerebral hemorrhage two weeks later.

MAJOR WORKS

Boyd's first novel, *Through the Wheat*, is a portrait of twentieth-century war stripped of the romance and glamour that had previously been associated with military service. Boyd's own service in World War I gave him an insider's view of the death, filth, and despair of service on the front lines. The protagonist of the novel, William Hicks, is stationed in France during World War I. Despite his disgust and exhaustion, he remains with his regiment and continues fighting. Hicks is depicted as a typical American soldier of the era, willing to fight for survival but completely without delusions of glory or honor. Boyd's second book, *The Dark Cloud* (1924), tells the story of a British scout in Indian territory during the American Revolution. In *Samuel Drummond* (1925) Boyd returned to the historical genre, depicting the dramatic changes in the life of an American farmer from the mid-1800s to the 1920s. Boyd's next publication, *Points of Honor* (1925) is a collection of short stories dealing again with the experiences of soldiers during World War I that cemented Boyd's reputation as a great chronicler of twentieth-century warfare. The most lauded story, "The Long Shot," was adapted for the screen as *Blaze O' Glory* in 1929. In 1928 Boyd began publishing a series of biographies that reflected his changing social and political beliefs. Chronicling the lives of American figures, Boyd's biographies established him as a respected nonfiction writer. Boyd's last two books, the novel *In Time of Peace* (1935) and the biography *Poor John Fitch, Inventor of the Steamboat* (1935), were both published posthumously.

CRITICAL RECEPTION

While Boyd's work is today generally overshadowed by the works of more well-known writers of the World War I era, his fiction at the time of publication was highly respected and often compared favorably with the war writings of Ernest Hemingway and E. E. Cummings. Boyd is remembered as a writer who captured the American experience in clear, unadorned language and narration.

PRINCIPAL WORKS

Through the Wheat (novel) 1923
The Dark Cloud (novel) 1924
Points of Honor (short stories) 1925
Samuel Drummond (novel) 1925
Shadow of the Long Knives (novel) 1928
Simon Girty, the White Savage (biography) 1928
Mad Anthony Wayne (biography) 1929

Light-Horse Harry Lee (biography) 1931
In Time of Peace (novel) 1935
Poor John Fitch, Inventor of the Steamboat (biography) 1935

CRITICISM

John W. Crawford (review date 1923)

SOURCE: "A Malicious Panorama," in *The Nation,* Vol. 117, No. 3028, 1923, p. 66.

[*In the following review, Crawford calls* Through the Wheat *"a remarkable first novel" despite a disappointing ending.*]

War is a panorama of "grim comic imbecility" to the eyes of Mr. Boyd's character Hicks. Toplofty idealism is brought into the picture, only to be shattered by a barrage of deftest malice. A pompous captain, with a Napoleonic vision, or a zealous top sergeant, actuated by a crusading delusion, becomes helplessly ridiculous in the face of a platoon of unimpressed and "kidding" soldiers. The antithesis is given a more sharply ironic twist in the spectacle of men under fire becoming vocal in photographically trivial conversation about mail, food, and cigarettes. The popular sentimentalism of a bitter and personal hatred for the Germans is dismissed with a hilarious gesture:

> Possibly for an hour during his whole life he [Hicks] had hated the German army. Now he only disliked them. And for one reason: because they marched in a goose-step. He felt that for any people to march in that manner was embarrassing to the rest of humanity.

The author permits himself a broader view than would be provided through the personality of Hicks. Mr. Boyd takes a dive into the mental processes of a subordinate character to heighten the absurdity of his self-importance and his ponderously grave acceptance of war hokum. What these excursions over a wide field cost him in immediacy in terms of Hicks he recovers in his total effect of a tragic buffoonery.

Mr. Boyd further contrasts the recruiting-poster with actualities in a cumulative series of episodes. He begins with the grumbling of the soldiers at menial tasks. A night raiding party loses a man to the clumsy artillery attack of its own trenches and is thrown into a panic by a false gas-alarm. The commanding officer responsible for these blunders is touched off with a slight sneer as "a former professor of English at a Texas college." In the same casual tone, instance after instance is given of unprotected, meaningless advances in the midst of machine-gun nests. Hicks thinks it would save time and ammunition simply to offer all their necks to the kaiser's ax.

All the while, the pallid boyish witticisms and the endless succession of rumors of their destination are interrupted only by the dead silence of physical exhaustion. Hicks is paralyzed with fear while he is slowly advancing; he feels his "spine bare with scorpions parading along the flesh" when he is forced to wait upon orders from headquarters. At other times Hicks walks among dangers with the same irreverent unconcern that marks his offhand dubbing of President Wilson "old horse-face."

Without having the attention jerked toward them, the reader becomes aware of fields of yellow wheat as background to marching men, fighting men, hiding men, and dead men. The wheat lends an impersonal indifference and a serene sense of growth to a pageant of unrelated waste of life and energy. Hicks in the wheat-fields sees his friends shot away, gassed, shell-shocked. He is strung to an unbearable nervous tension, waiting, hungry, deafened, not knowing why he is there or where he is going. His mind patters off in childish games with words. He talks to dead men with a mock solemnity born of fatigue-drunkenness. Hicks is left with a foolish smile on his face and his stumbling, undirected feet guiding him away from an approaching line of German soldiers.

Mr. Boyd falters at the end. Hicks is a little undefined and his spiritual disintegration is thereby rendered less poignant. The author seems to hesitate between a finality and a progression and achieves neither. *Through the Wheat* is nevertheless a remarkable first novel.

Edmund Wilson (review date 1923)

SOURCE: "The Anatomy of War," in *The Dial,* Vol. 75, July, 1923, pp. 93-5.

[*In the following review, Wilson deems* Through the Wheat *an important war novel.*]

Mr Thomas Boyd's *Through the Wheat* is much less brilliant than *Three Soldiers,* but I believe that it is nearly as important. Mr Dos Passos rendered one thing admirably: the nightmare oppression of the army, the ruin by war of certain characters which might under normal conditions have proved decent and useful. But Mr Boyd's theme is something different: the adventures of the man who does not break down. His Sergeant Hicks is a hero: he endures, he accepts authority, he fights boldly. But he is a hero *tout autrement intéressant* than that other hero Sergeant Empey. His endurance is half helpless exhaustion, his obedience is deeply tinctured with bitterness, and his bravery becomes finally an utter numbness beyond horror and beyond pain. This is probably the only candid account on record of what it meant to be a hero in the Marines, and a valuable document on the ordinary human virtues in reaction to the conditions of modern warfare.

Yet in tone **Through the Wheat** resembles *Three Soldiers* and most other sincere pictures of modern war. It is a tone which, I should think, if persisted in, should ultimately discourage humanity with war altogether. One finds it first in its characteristic coolness after the Napoleonic wars. Not that there had ever been lacking in European literature a realistic attitude toward war: Homer describes its ignominies as well as its glories; Aristophanes never tired of making fun of it, and Pindar writes, "Γλυκύ ἀπείροισι πόλεμος," (war is sweet to those who have never tried it); The Roman Empire, to be sure, dignified its conquests with a noble ideal (*parcere subjectis et debellare superbos*); but by the chaos of the Middle Ages common sense was revolted again and great men from Dante to Kant devoted much thought to European peace: the religious wars provoked the satire of Erasmus and Grotius' foundations of international law, and as comment on the War of the Spanish Succession you had Swift's pamphlet on *The Conduct of the Allies* and Southey's poem about little Peterkin finding the skull from the Battle of Blenheim; then where Swift had applied irony to the economics of war Voltaire turned the same livid light on its cruelty and the whole civilized Europe of the Enlightenment was in general agreement against it. At last the tremendous boom in war under Napoleon brought the formula of our present detachment.

For the stagy and hectic glories of Napoleon had their counterbalance in a scientific dryness. Goya in his engravings gave frank expression to the scorn which had apparently been implicit in Callot's *Misères de la Guerre* of two hundred years before, and even the noble stoicism of de Vigny could not cloak the littleness of the military life; but it was Stendhal, who had ridden the tidal wave of the Napoleonic romance, who, outliving the romantic age, put warfare to its cruellest scrutiny. Not that he held any brief against war in general: he had merely a passion for ironic analysis. For him the Battle of Waterloo becomes a chaos of trivial or hectic incidents; as we go through it with young Fabrice del Dongo in La Chartreuse de Parme there is nothing glorious or romantic about it: first a *vivandière*, then a corpse, then a general swearing at getting splashed. And when Stendhal had described the first great battle of the century the foundation of modern war fiction had been laid. Tolstoy and Hugo acknowledged their debt to him and most of their successors have debts to acknowledge. Flaubert adds venom to Stendhal's coldness in his steel engraving of the shootings of '48 in *L'Education Sentimentale*; and in Michelet the attitude of mockery has invaded even military history so that the heroisms of Agincourt or Pavia wear a new and disconcerting aspect. Then the Franco-Prussian War drenched dryness in despair with Zola and his disciples: you find the same formula applied with more or less bitterness in any number of books—in the *Soirées de Médan,* in Maupassant, in the early novels of Mirbeau. In the United States Stephen Crane wrote *The Red Badge of Courage,* which, whether or not inspired by Stendhal, represents precisely the same approach to the subject.

With the World War Barbusse burst his bombshell of naturalism compounded with humanitarianism and Dos Passos drew on Barbusse and Stendhal for a more local bombshell of his own. Finally Mr Boyd has rewritten *The Red Badge of Courage,* which I am told he had never read, as Crane had rewritten *La Chartreuse de Parme,* which I dare say he had never read either. It is not merely a literary trick which they have all learnt, but a common way of thinking which they have arrived at. And it is a way of thinking which in the future may make the melodramatization of war more and more difficult. What books on war are likely to be read by the educated young people of the next generation? Not the movie-poster propaganda of the press bureaus, but the books I have mentioned above. There are scarcely any other literary works which can be conceived as having a chance of survival; the well-written books of the war, if they are not detached and prosaic like Mr Boyd's, are in general either the saddened reflections of noncombatant older writers—like Masefield's history of Gallipoli or Kipling's epitaphs for dead soldiers; or, like the poems of Siegfried Sassoon, they are the expression of madness and despair.

The Dial (essay date 1925)

SOURCE: A review of *The Dark Cloud,* in *The Dial,* Vol. 79, July, 1925, p. 77.

[*In the following review, the critic finds* The Dark Cloud *to be an interesting and picturesque "prose panorama."*]

The Dark Cloud, by Thomas Boyd, projects a picture of life with camera sharpness, and yet the outlines of it have been so softened by tones of understanding that the effect is in no sense photographic. Mr Boyd has sought and successfully recaptured the picturesque background of early steamboat days along the Mississippi; he has written a narrative of incident rather than of sustained plot, done in flexible and vigorous prose. It is chiefly interesting as a prose panorama, sweeping from Quebec to Detroit, across to Cincinnati, and down the great waterway as it was in the enthralling fifties of the last century.

Punch (review date 1926)

SOURCE: A review of *Samuel Drummond,* in *Punch, or the London Charivari,* Vol 170. June 16, 1926, p. 647-48.

[*In the following review, the critic praises Boyd's realism in* Samuel Drummond.]

If Mr. Thomas Boyd has already written other books I do not know them. If he should write others in the future I shall certainly read them. For **Samuel Drummond** is a satisfying book, unexciting, but as nourishing to the mind as the kindly fruits of the earth are to the body. Its scene is Ohio before, during and after the Civil War; its theme the simple annals of a farmer's life. When we first meet Samuel he is a boy working on his father's farm. But soon Marthy Jane, a poor relation of his mother's, golden of hair and blue of eye, comes on the scene, and after a brief rivalry with his brother, who is as gay and voluble as Samuel is solid and tongue-tied, Samuel marries her. He takes a farm of his own, builds a house and later a larger one, clears his land, sells his timber, sows his corn and rears his stock. He drives to market, occasionally drinks a little more than he should, once is nearly drowned in a flood. He loves, and has little differences with, his wife. Four children are born to him—all girls, though he badly wants a boy. The war breaks out and he enlists, late and reluctantly, for he cares little for politics and his father's sympathies are with the South. He returns from the front and goes on with his farming. His parents die and one of his daughters elopes with a German neighbour, but comes home and is forgiven. He grows less prosperous than of old, raises a mortgage and sells his farm to his son-in-law. We leave him driving with Marthy Jane to the little holding he has bought in its stead. That is all, but it is enough for a sane man's pleasure. Thus, one feels, must life have been in the time and place. Mr. Boyd is a realist who makes no fuss about his realism. His character-building is four-square. His story moves with the grave and beautiful deliberation of a horse at the plough, and has a savour of earth which is refreshing to nostrils cloyed with the heady scents of our town romancers.

H. W. Boynton (essay date 1935)

SOURCE: A review of *In Time of Peace,* in *The Saturday Review of Literature,* Vol. 11, No. 33, March 2, 1935, p. 517.

[*In the following review, Boynton admires Boyd's storytelling in* In Time of Peace *despite sections of moralizing.*]

The success of **Through the Wheat** (was it really a dozen years ago?) did not tempt the late Thomas Boyd to repeat himself. So far as the form of the novel was concerned, he had said his say about the world in wartime. The book established him as a writing man, and he continued to write. But his later novels dealt with a safer and remoter past, to be recalled, if with qualified approval, at least without anguish. In biography too he found the ease and release of contact with men and issues too far off, too thoroughly done for, to call for indignation or resentment. Meanwhile the person behind the author was experiencing the business of peace with the same exacting ardor he had brought to the business of war; and the author was taking notes. We were bound to get the record of it all, soon or late, and here it is. **In Time of Peace** sums up the post-war decade as clearly and vigorously and as bitterly as the earlier narrative summed up the war itself.

To assure a sense of continuity, the story centres in the same person whose physical and spiritual adventures we

followed through the wheat. Now we carry on the tale of Bill Hicks from the end of the war to the low point of the depression as represented by the end of the Coolidge-Hoover régime, a natural full stop for the contemporary historian.

Bill Hicks, we recall, was saved for democracy by a whiff of gas that reached him just before the rest of his platoon were wiped out in action. He returns to his native town after demobilization to find his name on the local honor roll and himself stranded in "an indifferent and even hostile world." Within six months he is committed to the service of a monster lathe in a Chicago machine shop, through a twelve-hour shift that uses up every ounce of his strength and courage, night by night. It is too much: he escapes from the slavery of the industrial machine to the less exhausting servitude of a white-collar job. Chance rather than ability lands him in a newspaper office in a small midland city. His distrust of things as they are welcomes the idea of *The Farmer-Labor Beacon* as a champion of the working man. He becomes a reporter on general assignment. His salary is average, he likes the life well enough, but he is promptly disillusioned as to the real reason for The Beacon's existence. It is the tool of a politician who cares nothing for the working class.

In revulsion Hicks changes to *The News-Dispatch,* a sheet for the white-collar constituency. It ignores the existence of a class struggle, relying on a vague gospel of "progress." Hicks finds a sort of refuge in the cynicism of his tribe, supremely expressed in Fitzmaurice, the crack police reporter. To be hard-boiled, Hicks discovers, is the great virtue for reporters as for soldiers. Soon, too, his stirring idealism is smothered by petty expediency. For even before he was sure of a job he had taken the lonely man's chance of marriage. His wife is plenty good enough for him, with equal brains and more business ability. But now, far too soon, a child arrives and the hapless struggle to run a city household on a reporter's wage begins. It can't be done by these two, and before long their worrying about money matters has taken all the joy out of their life together.

At last the child is old enough for the clever mother to take a job of her own. Soon she earns as much as Hicks. Their joint four hundred a month looks big to them, but real and fancied needs more than keep pace with it. Things are booming, everybody is spending money. A car, a house, meaningless hospitality, leave them always in the red at the end of the month, no matter how much they take in by regular and extra work.

Then comes the crash. Hicks is out of the market, but his house, not yet wholly paid for, goes downstream. Then his pay is cut and cut again, and finally *The News-Dispatch* goes broke and he is out of a job. His wife keeps hers, they can live. But he is not willing to be the man at home. So arrives the hour when he finds himself in a line of job-seekers at the gates of a great automobile plant. After a long wait all but a handful of the half-frozen applicants are roughly dismissed and ordered off the company property by company guards. There is an outcry of "Jobs!" and a rush toward the gates, and Hicks is promptly felled by a machine gun bullet in the leg.

And now suddenly all is clear to him. His mistake, he has known for some time, was "in thinking war and peace were two different animals." Now peace has struck him down with the hand of war. And a strong will to live surges up in him. Suddenly he sees what a feeble thing his life has been, with its half-faiths, its time-serving, its entanglement with a daughter of Mammon, its legal bondage to a handmaid of "success":

> Pain rushed with the air into his wound—hot, exquisite stabs of violence. His chin dropped, waggling from self-pity. But no, by God! Back of the guards stood the police, back of the police the politicians, back of the politicians the Libbys, and behind them all the sacred name of Property. In the name of property men could be starved to death, and if they even so much as raised their heads, there was war. Hicks gritted his teeth. If it was war again, he was glad to know it. He at least had something to fight for now.

It is an honest if a bitter book. Hicks of course is not Hicks's maker, but they evidently share their distrust of things as they are. Special "cases" are presented with acrid realism, examples of official clumsiness or double-dealing, of police brutality, of studied injustice to workers and the selfishness and intellectual cowardice of hereditary wealth; of the skullduggery of employers, banks, loan associations. There are moments when the storyteller frankly leaves his booth in the bazaar to mount his earnest neighbor's soap box. But through all the story survives, moves on, unfailingly holds the listener's ear and mind.

Ramon Guthrie (review date 1935)

SOURCE: "Blood of the Pioneers," in *The New Republic*, Vol. 82, No. 1062, April 10, 1935, p. 252.

[*In the following review, Guthrie admires the documentary nature of both* In Time of Peace *and* Through the Wheat.]

In Time of Peace is a posthumous novel. Thomas Boyd died suddenly a few days before its publication. He was thirty-six years old. His literary output consisted of a dozen books about evenly divided between novels and biographies. His first book and the one for which he is best known is *Through the Wheat,* a novel which, a dozen years after it appeared, still deserves to be rated as the most authentic picture of the World War as the average American soldier saw and felt it. If he had written no other book than this, Boyd could still claim the honor of being the only American writer to show the War as it was, without retouched high-lights and shadows, empty of even the glamor of sordidness and disillusion, a dull, cruel mummery that even death and suffering could not raise to the plane of tragedy.

It is noteworthy that most of the outstanding American war books were written by men who had served with foreign armies. Dos Passos and Cummings, who served with the French, and Hemingway, who chose the Italians, are examples. Like their heroes, they came in contact with foreign cultures and were reasonably at home in at least one foreign language. Boyd's experience, like himself, was as American as pumpkin pie. He left a small-town high school in Ohio to enlist in the Marine Corps, learned to dig holes, salute officers and bayonet dummies, won a Croix de Guerre in Belleau Wood, was gassed, hospitalized and returned to a land where his ancestors, whose physique and mentality must have been much like his own, had toted squirrel guns with Lewis and Clark and poled flatboats down to the Mississippi.

In the post-war period when most writers of his generation were fleeing to boulevards and ivory towers to escape from their American backgrounds and traditions, Boyd's effort was to sink his roots more deeply into his native soil. He had a strong sense of the continuity of American culture. His knowledge of the literature, history and arts of colonial and pioneer days seemed almost instinctive. It was natural that as subjects for his biographies he should choose figures from his own background, Light Horse Harry Lee, the renegade Simon Girty, Mad Anthony Wayne, who built Fort Defiance on the site of the town where Boyd was born. A few days before his death he had finished the manuscript of a biography of another pioneer in the Ohio Valley, John Fitch, the inventor of the steamboat. In his novels, Boyd stuck equally close to home. "James Drummond" centers about the author's grandfather; and Hicks, the hero of *Through the Wheat,* is an objective double of Thomas Boyd himself.

In Time of Peace carries on the story of William Hicks from his return from France, through the era of postwar prosperity and into the depression. In his characters Boyd has achieved accurate composite portraits of average Americans living in circumstances and through events that every adult American will recognize for their resemblance to his own experience.

It is difficult to pass on the merits of the book as a novel, not because of any deficiencies of structure or of style, but because it seems apparent that Boyd's aim was not essentially that of a novelist at all. Felicities of invention and expression were of secondary interest. Distortion for artistic effects would have thwarted his purpose. Like his first book, *In Time of Peace* is less a narrative than an honest, clear-sighted document, valuable to the understanding of another great and cruel phenomenon of our times.

Although Boyd himself was an ardent Communist, his book is propaganda only to the extent that any faithful picture of America in the present day must contain an inherent indictment of the system under which we live. Neither Karl Marx nor Communism is mentioned, and none of the characters is made a mouthpiece for the author's convictions. If Hicks arrives finally at a vague comprehension that the force set on crushing out his life is the capitalist system rather than some blind malignant chance, the wonder is less that one man should come to this belief than that millions of other workers should not have traveled the same path.

Boyd did not join the Communist Party until less than a year before his death; but judging from the tendencies of his thought and writings for the past dozen years, there is every reason to accept his statement that he was "always a Communist without knowing it." In Communism he saw—and this was a thesis that he hoped to develop in a book to be entitled "The Aftermath of the American Revolution"—a culmination of the revolutionary spirit and the faith in collective endeavor that he believed to be the dominant characteristics of Americans as a people.

In 1934 Boyd consented to run as Communist candidate for the governorship of Vermont. His was the only name on the slate. It was a tribute to his personality and an evidence of the confidence inspired by his obvious integrity that, despite the difficulty of canvassing a sparsely settled and mountainous region, he did obtain the fifteen hundred signatures required to place the Communist ticket for the first time on the official ballot of the most conservative state in the Union.

Granville Hicks (essay date 1935)

SOURCE: "Last Spree of the Middle Class," in *New York Herald Tribune Books,* Sunday, February 24, 1935, p. 6.

[*In the following essay, Hicks praises the scope and depth of* In Time of Peace.]

Thomas Boyd's last novel, *In Time of Peace,* continues the story of the hero of his first, *Through the Wheat,* William Hicks, six months after he got out of the Army, was working a twelve-hour night shift in a Chicago machine shop. He threw up his job to go to another city to visit his girl. The girl, Patsy Hughes, wanted to see him wearing a white collar, and he succeeded in getting work on *The Farmer-Labor Beacon.*

A wife, a child, and mounting bills, to say nothing of increasing disillusionment with pseud-radicalism, sent Hicks from *The Beacon* to the more respectable *News-Dispatch.* The golden day dawned; prosperity came. Patsy got a job; Hicks had raises and picked up additional work. A car, a fine house, drinking parties, and an affair with the wife of the town's leading business man balanced a growing burden of debt, harder and harder work, boredom, irritability and headaches.

Then, as the stock market crumbled and the banks closed, the extra jobs vanished, and finally *The News-Dispatch* failed. The new house went to the mortgage-holder. Patsy held her job, by doing another person's as well, and Hicks looked for work. Despite Patsy's protest, he was willing to

forego the white collar, and, hearing that Victory Motors was hiring men, joined the long line of job hunters. Though the guards told them that no one would be taken on, the men waited, and, when demonstrators appeared, shouting "Work or Relief," Hicks joined them. The answer came from machine guns behind the factory gates. With a bullet through his leg, Hicks makes up his mind: "If it was war again, he was glad to know it. He at least had something to fight for now."

There used to be a good many novels about the excesses and emptiness of life in the twenties, and of late we have had novels about the crisis and the growth of revolutionary sentiment. *In Time of Peace* gives us the whole decade, from the minor depression at the outset, through the boom, to the major depression at the end.

The central character, though almost unique in American fiction, is nontheless representative of American life. A manual laborer at the outset, he also is—or would be if he could get a job—a manual laborer at the end. In the meantime he has tasted the life of the middle class, has even strutted a little at country clubs and been invited to the best homes. Through all this he keeps a certain feeling for the working class; he class-angles his stories when he can; he hates the cheap superiority of the country-club people. But the almost unconscious growth of upper-class habits obscures the lesson of capitalist corruption and exploitation that his daily job teaches him, and the cynicism of the journalist cushions his self-contempt. The depression not only thrusts him back among the workers, it makes him see for the first time the full meaning of their fight.

In Time of Peace is likely to have a wider appeal to the middle class than any revolutionary novel that has yet appeared. The younger revolutionary writers have broken almost completely with the traditions of the twenties. They start from new assumptions, and many of them practice new techniques. This is necessary and right, but the result is that many readers find their work unaccountable and strange. Boyd has a different point of view from the Lewises and Fitzgeralds, but the theme and method of *In Time of Peace* are not drastically unlike the themes and methods of *Babbitt* and *The Great Gatsby.*

This is obviously an advantage in so far as a large section of the reading public is concerned, but certain weaknesses result from the carrying over of some of the equipment of the disillusioned writers of the twenties. Boyd would most certainly have wanted to be judged as a revolutionary novelist. After all, he was the candidate of the Communist party for Governor of Vermont last fall. And as a revolutionary novel, *In Time of Peace* is open to fairly sharp criticism.

The objections are not political. They can be most simply stated by saying that, from a revolutionary point of view, *In Time of Peace* is superficial. There are moments of insight, moments when Boyd probes, with true Marxist precision, into the rotten sores of capitalism, but much of the time he is writing, as Lewis or Fitzgerald might have written, merely of symptoms. One feels this superficiality in all the characters except William Hicks. Hicks is sound and true, and the reader knows him as he is, but Patsy and Carlotta and Fitzmaurice and Vaughan are figures hastily glimpsed as they whirl by in the prancings of the middle class on its last spree.

One regrets this superficiality because it is so clear that Boyd was not merely capable of better work but would surely have done it had he lived. His communism was not an accident nor a fad nor yet a matter of logic; it was, like his hero's union with the working class, self-discovery. While he was still very young, he wrote, out of his deep hatred of war, *Through the Wheat,* the most genuine and realistic of American war novels. Thereafter he wrote historical novels and biographies, good enough in their way but not basically related to his own problems and preoccupations. Only when he had become a Communist could he understand and master the grotesque confusion of which he had been part. In the ordinary course of events *In Time of Peace* might have been a transition to more fully integrated novels, based on a sharper and more sustained awareness of the contemporary world.

But let it be understood that the novel, whatever its weaknesses, is by no means to be disregarded. It will have thousands of readers, who will be stirred and shaken by its simple account of American life in the twenties. And they will realize how much American literature has lost by the death of Thomas Boyd.

The Nation (review date 1935)

SOURCE: A review of *In Time of Peace,* Vol. 140, No. 36, May 22, 1935, p. 609.

[*In the following review, the critic dismisses* In Time of Peace *as "plodding" and forgettable.*]

It is unusual to find a proletarian novel which is not violent enough for the most sensational taste. Yet it must be confessed that *In Time of Peace,* Thomas Boyd's last work, is too placid to realize the revolutionary intent. It continues the story of Hicks, the protagonist of the war novel *Through the Wheat,* carrying him through boom times, through marriage and a successful, moneyed career as a newspaperman, down to the crisis, the depression, and ultimate personal failure. It is the tale of a man's brief apostasy to the working class, his surrender to capitalist interests, and their inevitable betrayal of him. To the execution of this theme Thomas Boyd brought honesty and care and fidelity of observation, but these are not enough. Such a theme demands harshness, bitterness, intensity of feeling; even a display of pyrotechnics would not have been unseemly. Lacking these things, Mr. Boyd's novel for all its seriousness of purpose falls into the large and useless class of plodding, studiously lifelike novels, which are read to pass the time away, and whose scenes and characters are so well padded with comfortable verbal realism that they are easily forgotten.

Saturday Review of Literature (essay date 1935)

SOURCE: A review of *In Time of Peace,* in *The Saturday Review of Literature,* Vol. 11, No. 33, March 2, 1935, p. 517.

[*In the following review, the critic finds* In Time of Peace *unoriginal and didactic.*]

This last and posthumously published novel, by the author who scored so brilliant a success with *Through the Wheat,* charts a straight course through the post-war social history of the United States and elaborates a pattern that has been made thoroughly familiar to us by many novels and short stories, and by a great mass of factual reporting. During the past sixteen years we have heard much of the hero's return, of the difficulty of the soldier's readjustment to peace-time conditions. We have also read many tales of young married couples who were lifted up on the flood of Coolidge prosperity, cast down with paralyzing force by the 1929 collapse, and then swept along, battered and bewildered and embittered, in the trough of the subsequent depression. And we have been eloquently assured, by many victims and observers, that the one way of preventing a recurrence of our recent disasters is to abolish the capitalistic system, and to replace it by a society in which there will be neither exploiters nor exploited, but only honest workmen, all of whom will be conscientiously concerned with giving one another a helping hand and an even break. Thomas Boyd's novel, then, is triply familiar; for it is the story of the soldier's return (a return haunted by war memories); the story of the young married couple; and the story of the man who comes to see no salvation for society save in class war, and in the final defeat of those who have by those who have not.

We last saw William Hicks as the protagonist of *Through the Wheat.* We meet him again, in this new novel, clad in his old army shirt, sweating at a lathe in a Chicago mill. But factory work holds no future for the young man who is in love with Patsy Hughes, who has recently lost her job on a Chicago paper, and who has returned to the parental roof in a nameless mid-Western city. He will leave the mill, follow Patsy, and marry her; and this he does according to schedule. By a happy accident, rather than according to schedule, he lands a newspaper job himself, and he and Patsy settle down to matrimonial bliss in a tiny flat. And then? There is little that the reader will not anticipate until house is gone, job is gone, and Patsy, the breadwinner, is filled with bitter resentment against "the system" responsible for it all. Last scene: William Hicks downed by a bullet in his leg, fired by a guard "defending" the property of Victory Motors against a crowd of unemployed and unarmed men.

Were this narrative animated by unusual emotional force, or made interesting by fully realized characters, it might even now seem fresh and stirring. But there is no such animation, and there are no such characters. Hicks moves as a stock figure along a well-grooved path. Patsy is little more than a name, so Hicks's relations with her can never be made vital or engrossing; and the affair with Carlotta remains curiously unreal. What we have here is merely the competent presentation, in fiction form, of an economic argument; and we have heard the same argument often, expressed in the same terms, but expressed sometimes with greater power, and sometimes with surer art.

Edith H. Walton (review date 1935)

SOURCE: A review of *In Time of Peace,* in *Forum and Century,* Vol. 93, No. 4, April, 1935, p. iv.

[*In the following review, Walton finds* In Time of Peace *an unsatisfactory sequel to Boyd's* Through the Wheat.]

Written just before his recent death, the title of Mr. Boyd's novel is astringently ironical. Hicks, the hero of that excellent war book, *Through the Wheat,* finds, after passing through a typical experience of the 'twenties, that peace can be as cruel and murderous as ever the war was and that for the underdog everywhere the fight is not over. A stubborn, honest-minded, rather inarticulate man, Hicks marries during the early postwar depression days, finds an ill-paying newspaper job, and has a desperate struggle to stretch out his meager budget. With the boom, however, he and Patsy strike solid ground, and, though Hicks remains a little skeptical of their comparative affluence, he is swept up into the feverish currents of the jazz age. Then comes the depression, destroying all their precarious gains, and Hicks' latent sympathies are finally crystallized in the direction of radicalism. *In Time of Peace* has some excellent material in it, as well as some shoddy and poorly executed sections, but it is by no means so good a book as *Through the Wheat* and as a revolutionary novel it is a little fumbling and unsatisfactory.

Paul Fussell (review date 1978)

SOURCE: Shrapnel and Solecisms, in *Times Literary Supplement,* No. 3977, June 23, 1978, p. 694.

[*In the following review, Fussell asserts that* Through the Wheat *has been overvalued as both literature and as a document of war-time experience.*]

Thomas Boyd's novel of 1923 about his experiences with the United States Marines in France during the First World War was said by Boyd's friend F. Scott Fitzgerald to be "not only the best combatant story of the great war, but also the best war book since *The Red Badge of Courage.*" It is neither, nor does it provide, as James Dickey asserts

in an afterword, "a vision of war that is as profound as any vision of any war has ever been." But it is a serious, if awkward, autobiographical first novel in the American 1920s tradition of that genre and worth revival for historical if not for artistic reasons.

Like Fitzgerald and Hemingway, Boyd was a Midwesterner and thus initially a little more vulnerable to shock and disillusion than most. After the war, in which he was gassed, he entered literary journalism as editor of the book section of the *St Paul Daily News.* With *Through the Wheat* he began a copious production of novels, stories, and popular biographies. He died, aged thirty-six, in 1935, and it would be interesting to be told what he died of. The editors' silence suggests not gas poisoning but suicide or cancer. Why not assist literary history by telling us?

Boyd's fictional projection and victim-hero is Private William Hicks, a former Ohio office worker, now an automatic rifleman in the Fourth Brigade of the United States Marine Corps. It is spring 1913, and although Hicks's platoon undergoes several tours in the trenches, it mainly exhausts itself in the mobile tactical warfare possible for the first time since 1914. Hicks begins as a standard, unindividualized Marine, objectively and impersonally viewed by his author. But as he proceeds through the standard front-line experiences—sleeping on guard and being reprimanded, participating in a night raid, enduring cruel shellings and ridiculous inspections, getting lost, witnessing self-inflicted wounds and a suicide and the extermination of prisoners—he begins to manifest a sort of personality and grows fond of a not very subtle irony directed never at the announced enemy but at President Wilson and such nearer targets as the company officers and the effete YMCA chocolate vendors well behind the lines. (Every American war must have these or their equivalents: in the Second World War they were the hospital ladies of the American Red Cross whose charity extended to selling toothbrushes and razors to the naked and cashless wounded.)

The climax of Hicks's experience and the one impressive part of the novel is a prolonged attack over hills and through woods and across wheatfields, an attack which only one-fifth of the battalion survives. This is really a separable short story about the murky psychological springs of "heroic" behaviour set as a long episode into an episodic novel. It is in this ending only that the novel distantly approaches the Stendhalian and Tolstoyan merits Mr Dickey finds for it.

Pinned under vicious machine-gun fire with his friends dying everywhere around, Hicks reacts to unreason with an impulsive gesture of unreason. Terrified, dead-tired, and thoroughly browned-off, he simply gets up and, seeking any relief, walks numbly toward the enemy. Sheeplike, others do the same. "Their cowardice," Boyd observes, "made them brave men, heroes." But Hicks has been scarred inside, and soon he is hysterically addressing corpses and shaking them soundly when they decline to answer. The novel ends before the battle does with Hicks so beaten down that nothing, literally nothing, matters. "The soul of Hicks was numb" is the final sentence.

Boyd's novel, one of the earliest in the Anglo-Saxon world to "tell the truth about the war"—it is full of brains in helmets and limbs flying "foolishly" into the air—would be comparable to Manning's *The Middle Parts of Fortune* if it were not so badly written. The text here is a facsimile of Scribner's first edition, and the sainted Max Perkins must have been dozing when as editor he passed a sentence like "The drivers of the camions were Japanese, which, as purveyors of information, made them as useful as do many 'professional' silent men of the President's cabinet." Or: "They observed the sun, which was slowly climbing over the horizon and shedding the earth with a silvery light." There are very un-Tolstoyan grammatical blunders and some danglers ("A distance of two miles, the platoon crawled along like an attenuated turtle") fit for the *New Statesman*'s "This English" whimsy. But Boyd's clumsy-genteel style, padded with unnecessary relative pronouns and wordy passive evasions, has for the critic the value of clearly displaying the context of Hemingway's early originality in economy and excision. The creator of Jake Barnes and Frederic Henry developed his own style by resolutely not writing like this: "Being rather reckless, probably the first time that Major Adams's remark that he might get a general court martial was fully realized by him was at the moment when he and Bullis had been sent back to their dugout."

The reason for the bizarre over-valuation of *Through the Wheat* then and now is hinted at in Edmund Wilson's remark that it is "probably the most authentic novel yet written by an American about war," where "authentic" registers the critic's satisfaction with Boyd as a muckraker—that is, with his exposure of President Wilson's high-mindedness and his documentary success in showing that soldiers prosecuting even an idealist cause are led inevitably to cruelty and madness. In the 1920s, that was news.

Frank Wilson (review date 1978)

SOURCE: A review of *Through the Wheat*, in *Best Sellers*, Vol. 38, No. 5, August, 1978, p. 140.

[*In the following review, Wilson laments Boyd's early death, asserting that* Through the Wheat *is a well-wrought novel.*]

There is a certain kind of novel that is simply a straightforward chronicle of events. It is a kind usually written in a manner equally straightforward and precise. Such is Thomas Boyd's *Through the Wheat,* a novel of World War I first published in 1923—when it was glowingly reviewed by F. Scott Fitzgerald—and now reissued by University of Southern Illinois Press as part of its Lost American Fiction series.

Like his protagonist, Private Hicks, Boyd left high school to join the Marines, doubtless inspired by all the hogwash current at the time about waging a war to end war and making the world safe for democracy. His novel, however, is more the story of Hicks's platoon than of Hicks himself. If the focus eventually centers upon Hicks exclusively, it is simply because Hicks is the one who happens to survive.

Boyd writes well, and his book is easy to read—too easy, in fact. There being no stylistic capers, one turns the pages at a clip, hardly noticing how sharp the author's observations are and how subtle his phrasing. So, for maybe two-thirds of the book, one seems to be reading just a slick factual account of a platoon's progress into war.

Then, there is left of the original platoon only Private Hicks, who undergoes the brutal satori of the seasoned warrior, his routine heroism merely a gesture of exhaustion waved in the face of despair:

> Now he had entered the fringe of the forest. Dimly he recognized a face before him to be that of a German. There was the oddly shaped helmet covering the head, the utilitarian gray of the German uniform. The face did not at all appear barbaric. It was quite youthful, the chin covered with a white down. He veered the muzzle of his rifle toward the face, and, without raising his rifle to his shoulder, pulled the trigger. The face disappeared.

Thomas Boyd died in 1935, age thirty-six. It's too bad. I think we lost a damn good writer too damn soon.

Kliatt (review date 1979)

SOURCE: A review of *Through the Wheat*, in *Kliatt*, Vol. 13, No. 6, Fall, 1979, p. 5.

[*In the following review, the critic recommends* Through the Wheat *to young readers because of the book's unsentimental presentation of the experience of war.*]

[In ***Through the Wheat***] we follow Private William Hicks's days in the trench warfare of World War I, along a slow hard-fought front in which each field, each wood is taken with enormous losses of men. From Hicks's viewpoint, the strategy and the purpose of the war are not visible; the war is made up of exhaustion, monotony, hunger, hot coffee, dirt, interrupted by sudden attacks and deaths. Over everything hangs the stench of the decaying dead and surrounding them are fields of yellow unharvested wheat.

There is no story line but there are episodes, of fetching water and rations, of marching and getting lost, of burying the dead. There is, however, a kind of progression, for in the end numbness settles on Hicks; he is moving but not alive. The author is not making an ideological point about

World War I, and perhaps not even about war, but he presents, in detail, the sensations of being in a war.

It is very effective; for young people, the details are an antidote to abstract ideas of what war is like.

A postscript by the editor of this series tells us that Boyd fought in World War I and died in 1935, aged 36. It also quotes a long appreciative review by F. Scott Fitzgerald, written when the novel appeared in 1923.

Additional coverage of Boyd's life and career is contained in the following sources published by the Gale Group: *Contemporary Authors,* Vols. 111, 183; *Dictionary of Literary Biography,* Vol. 9; *Dictionary of Literary Biography Documentary Series,* Vol. 16.

M. E. Braddon
1835-1915

(Full name Mary Elizabeth Braddon; also wrote under the pseudonym Babington White) English novelist, playwright, editor, and short story writer.

INTRODUCTION

A prolific writer in many genres, as well as the editor of several popular London periodicals, Braddon was one of the best known and most innovative writers of the sensation novel from the 1860s until her death in 1915. Virtually ignored by critics for decades, Braddon's works gained the attention of feminist scholars in the 1970s, when women's issues moved to the forefront of literary study. Today Braddon is credited with revolutionizing the Victorian female protagonist and introducing elements of darkness and criminality into literary portrayals of middle- and upper-class households.

BIOGRAPHICAL INFORMATION

Braddon's personal life was nearly as scandalous as those of her fictional heroines. Born in London in 1835, she was the daughter of Henry Braddon and Fanny White Braddon. Early in their marriage, her parents wrote articles together for Pitman's *Sporting Magazine* under pseudonyms. Braddon herself wrote unpublished fairy tales and domestic and historical fiction as a teenager. But the family struggled with money, and Braddon's father abandoned them when she was in her early twenties. Hoping to achieve financial independence, Braddon sought a career as a stage actress, a decision considered highly questionable at the time. While she did not find much success as an actress, Braddon wrote her first comedy for the stage, which was produced in 1860. She was soon commissioned to write a long narrative poem on Garibaldi's campaign, and she published her first novel, a detective thriller called *Three Times Dead* (1860), which was reissued in 1861 by a larger publisher under the title *The Trail of the Serpent*. Braddon's writing found immediate success with the readers of inexpensive periodicals of the time, known as penny dreadfuls, which featured stories of crime and sex. At the same time, Braddon met John Maxwell, a magazine publisher married to a woman in a mental institution. Braddon spent the next fourteen years living out of wedlock with Maxwell and the couple's five children. Braddon wrote prolifically during this period to support Maxwell and their children, publishing nineteen books and plays between 1861 and 1868, as well as editing journals. In 1868, however, she had a severe nervous breakdown in response to her

mother's death and was unable to write for the next two years. She returned to writing in 1870 and published her first social novel, *The Lovels of Arden,* in 1871. Until then, Braddon had concentrated mostly on the sensation novels for which she was most famous. But later in her career she experimented with a variety of narrative styles, finding popular success with each. In 1874 Maxwell's wife died, allowing Braddon and Maxwell to legally marry. They lived together happily until Maxwell's death in 1895. Braddon continued to support herself by writing, and she had a loyal readership, which included such eminent literary figures as Charles Dickens, Alfred Lord Tennyson, Thomas Hardy, Henry James, and Oscar Wilde, despite critics who had excoriated her works and her lifestyle for years. Braddon died in 1915.

MAJOR WORKS

Braddon's first two novels earned the notice of readers, but it was with her third novel, *Lady Audley's Secret* (1862), that she achieved the wild popularity that would last throughout her career. With *Lady Audley's Secret* Braddon helped to create the Victorian sensational novel, which typically featured an innocent-looking but deceitful female protagonist, bigamy, murder, and madness. Braddon's major innovation in plot was to place these elements in respectable middle- and upper-class households. Lady Audley, for example, appears to be the perfect Victorian angel of the house, married to an elderly baronet. But when her first husband suddenly enters her new life, she attempts to kill him by pushing him down a well to hide the fact that she is a bigamist who falsified her own death. Lady Audley then tries to burn down the inn where two men who know her secret are staying. When her first husband reappears alive, Lady Audley is sent to a Belgian madhouse for the rest of her life. Braddon experienced similar success with *Aurora Floyd* (1863), *John Marchmont's Legacy* (1863), *Birds of Prey* (1867), and *Charlotte's Inheritance* (1868) all of which were again sensational novels. In 1864 Braddon published *The Doctor's Wife,* an adaptation of Gustave Flaubert's infamous *Madame Bovary,* but Braddon was much more sympathetic to the unhappily married heroine and had her devote herself to philanthropy in her later years rather than commit suicide. While her novels were always known for their sharp wit, Braddon made social satire the focus of *Vixen* in 1879, the story of a wild young woman testing the restraints of her middle-class upbringing. In the twentieth century Braddon continued to feature strong women of dubious character in her novels. She is also remembered for her short stories, many of which helped to popularize fictional elements of the supernatural.

CRITICAL RECEPTION

In her lifetime Braddon's works were largely condemned by critics as being lewd and trashy. Yet many illustrious writers of the time, including Henry James and Robert Louis Stevenson, not only supported her work but wrote articles and reviews announcing their admiration. After her death, Braddon's were ignored by critics until feminist literary study moved to the forefront in the late 1970s. At that point critics recognized in Braddon's fiction a strong subversive bent against traditional women's social roles. That her female characters are largely unlikeable as human beings—Aurora Floyd, for example, beats a dog, and Lady Audley is a fraudulent, murderous arsonist—does not prevent them from being viewed as heroines trying to live on their own terms, as well as complex psychological studies of women at the time. Additionally, Braddon was one of the first fiction writers to place criminality and perversion in middle and upper-class settings, thus using her writing as a vehicle for social commentary on the moral corruption of the wealthy. Critics also consider Braddon's short stories to be an important step in the development of the mystery and detective genres. Indicating the magnitude of her popularity and success, Robert Louis Stevenson wrote to Braddon from Samoa, "It is something to be out and away greater than Scott, Shakespeare, Homer, in the South Seas, and to that you have attained."

PRINCIPAL WORKS

The Loves of Arcadia (drama) 1860
Three Times Dead; or, The Secret of the Heath (novel) 1860; revised edition, as *The Trail of the Serpent,* 1861
Garibaldi and Other Poems (poetry) 1861
The Captain of the Vulture (novel) 1862
Lady Audley's Secret (novel) 1862
The Lady Lisle (novel) 1862
Ralph the Bailiff and Other Tales (short stories) 1862
Aurora Floyd (novel) 1863
Eleanor's Victory (novel) 1863
John Marchmont's Legacy (novel) 1863
The Doctor's Wife (novel) 1864
Henry Dunbar: The Story of an Outcast (novel) 1864
Only a Clod (novel) 1865
Sir Jasper's Tenant (novel) 1865
The Lady's Mile (novel) 1866
Birds of Prey (novel) 1867
Circe (novel) 1867
Rupert Godwin (novel) 1867
Charlotte's Inheritance (novel) 1868
Dead Sea Fruit (novel) 1868
The Model Husband (drama) 1868
Run to Earth (novel) 1868
Fenton's Quest (novel) 1871
The Lovels of Arden (novel) 1871
Robert Ainsleigh (novel) 1871
The Summer Tourist: A Book for Long and Short Journeys on Rail, Road, or River [editor] (travel) 1871
To the Bitter End (novel) 1872
Griselda; or, The Patient Wife (drama) 1873
Lucius Davoren; or, Publicans and Sinners (novel) 1873
Milly Darrell and Other Tales (short stories) 1873
Strangers and Pilgrims (novel) 1873
Lost for Love (novel) 1874
Taken at the Flood (novel) 1874
Hostages to Fortune (novel) 1875
A Strange World (novel) 1875
Dead Men's Shoes (novel) 1876
Joshua Haggard's Daughter (novel) 1876
The Black Band; or, The Mysteries of Midnight (novel) 1877
Weavers and Weft and Other Tales (short stories) 1877
An Open Verdict (novel) 1878
The Cloven Foot (novel) 1879
Vixen (novel) 1879
Just as I Am (novel) 1880
The Missing Witness (novel) 1880
The Story of Barbara (novel) 1880
Asphodel (novel) 1881
Boscastle, Cornwall: An English Engadine (travel) 1881
Dross; or, The Root of Evil (drama) 1882
Flower and Weed (novella) 1882
Marjorie Daw: A Household Idyl (drama) 1882
Married beneath Him (drama) 1882
Mount Royal (novel) 1882
The Golden Calf (novel) 1883
Phantom Fortune (novel) 1883
Under the Red Flag (novella) 1883

Flower and Weed and Other Tales (short stories) 1884
Ishmael (novel) 1884
Wyllard's Weird (novel) 1885
The Good Hermione: A Story for the Jubilee Year (novel) 1886
Mohawks (novel) 1886
One Thing Needful, and Cut by the County (novel) 1886
Under the Red Flag and Other Tales (short stories) 1886
Like and Unlike (novel) 1887
The Fatal Three (novel) 1888
The Day Will Come (novel) 1889
For Better, For Worse (drama) 1890
One Life, One Love (novel) 1890
Gerard; or, the World, the Flesh, and the Devil (novel) 1891
The Venetians (novel) 1892
All Along the River (short stories) 1893
The Christmas Hirelings (novel) 1894
Thou Art the Man (novel) 1894
Sons of Fire (novel) 1895
London Pride; or, When the World Was Younger (novel) 1896
Under Love's Rule (novel) 1897
In High Places (novel) 1898
Rough Justice (novel) 1898
His Darling Sin (novel) 1899
The Infidel: A Story of the Great Revival (novel) 1900
The Conflict (novel) 1903
A Lost Eden (novel) 1904
The Rose of Life (novel) 1905
The White House (novel) 1906
Dead Love Has Chains (novel) 1907
Her Convict (novel) 1907
During Her Majesty's Pleasure (novel) 1908
Our Adversary (novel) 1909
Beyond These Voices (novel) 1910
The Green Curtain (novel) 1911
Miranda (novel) 1913
Mary (novel) 1916

CRITICISM

Henry James (review date 1865)

SOURCE: A review of *Aurora Floyd*, in *Notes and Reviews*, Dunster House, 1865, pp. 108-116.

[*In the following review, James praises* Aurora Floyd *as an important development in Braddon's literary career.*]

Miss Aurora Floyd, as half the world knows, was a young lady who got into no end of trouble by marrying her father's groom. We had supposed that this adventure had long ago become an old story; but here is a new edition of her memoirs to prove that the public has not done with her

yet. We would assure those individuals who look with regret upon this assumption by a "sensation" novel of the honors of legitimate fiction, that the author of **Aurora Floyd** is an uncommonly clever person. Her works are distinguished by a quality for which we can find no better name than "pluck"; and should not pluck have its reward wherever found? If common report is correct, Miss Braddon had for many years beguiled the leisure moments of an arduous profession—the dramatic profession—by the composition of fictitious narrative. But until the publication of **Lady Audley's Secret** she failed to make her mark. To what secret impulse or inspiration we owe this sudden reversal of fortune it is difficult to say; but the grim determination to succeed is so apparent in every line of **Lady Audley's Secret,** that the critic is warranted in conjecturing that she had at last become desperate. People talk of novels with a purpose; and from this class of works, both by her patrons and her enemies, Miss Braddon's tales are excluded. But what novel ever betrayed a more resolute purpose than the production of what we may call Miss Braddon's second manner? Her purpose was at any hazard to make a hit, to catch the public ear. It was a difficult task, but audacity could accomplish it. Miss Braddon accordingly resorted to extreme measures, and created the sensation novel. It is to this audacity, this courage of despair, as manifested in her later works, that we have given the name of pluck. In these works it has settled down into a quiet determination not to let her public get ahead of her. A writer who has suddenly leaped into a popularity greatly disproportionate to his merit, can only retain his popularity by observing a strictly respectful attitude to his readers. This has been Miss Braddon's attitude, and she has maintained it with unwearied patience. She has been in her way a disciple as well as a teacher. She has kept up with the subtle innovations to which her art, like all others, is subject, as well as with the equally delicate fluctuations of the public taste. The result has been a very obvious improvement in her style.

She had been preceded in the same path by Mr. Wilkie Collins, whose *Woman in White,* with its diaries and letters and its general ponderosity, was a kind of nineteenth century version of *Clarissa Harlowe.* Mind, we say a nineteenth century version. To Mr. Collins belongs the credit of having introduced into fiction those most mysterious of mysteries, the mysteries which are at our own doors. This innovation gave a new impetus to the literature of horrors. It was fatal to the authority of Mrs. Radcliffe and her everlasting castle in the Apennines. What are the Apennines to us, or we to the Apennines? Instead of the terrors of *Udolpho,* we were treated to the terrors of the cheerful country-house and the busy London lodgings. And there is no doubt that these were infinitely the more terrible. Mrs. Radcliffe's mysteries were romances pure and simple; while those of Mr. Wilkie Collins were stern reality. The supernatural, which Mrs. Radcliffe constantly implies, though she generally saves her conscience, at the eleventh hour, by explaining it away, requires a powerful imagination in order to be as exciting as the natural, as Mr. Collins and Miss Braddon, without any imagination at all, know how to manage it. A good ghost-story, to be half as terrible as a good murder-story, must be connected at a hundred points with the common objects of life. The best ghost-story probably ever written—a tale published some years ago in *Blackwood's Magazine*—was constructed with an admirable understanding of this principle. Half of its force was derived from its prosaic, commonplace, daylight accessories. Less delicately terrible, perhaps, than the vagaries of departed spirits, but to the full as *interesting,* as the modern novel reader understands the word, are the numberless possible forms of human malignity. Crime, indeed, has always been a theme for dramatic poets; but with the old poets its dramatic interest lay in the fact that it compromised the criminal's moral repose. Whence else is the interest of *Orestes* and *Macbeth*? With Mr. Collins and Miss Braddon (our modern Euripides and Shakespeare) the interest of crime is in the fact that it compromises the criminal's personal safety. The play is a tragedy, not in virtue of an avenging deity, but in virtue of a preventive system of law; not through the presence of a company of fairies, but through that of an admirable organization of police detectives. Of course, the nearer the criminal and the detective are brought home to the reader, the more lively his "sensation." They are brought home to the reader by a happy choice of probable circumstances; and it is through their skill in the choice of these circumstances— their thorough-going realism—that Mr. Collins and Miss Braddon have become famous. In like manner, it is by the thoroughgoing realism of modern actors that the works of the most poetic of poets have been made to furnish precedent for sensational writers. There are no *circumstances* in *Macbeth,* as you read it; but as you see it played by Mr. Charles Kean or Mr. Booth it is nothing but circumstances. And we may here remark, in parentheses, that if the actors of a past generation—Garrick and Mrs. Siddons—left with their contemporaries so profound a conviction of their *greatness,* it is probably because, like the great dramatists they interpreted, they were ideal and poetic; because their effort was not to impress but to express.

We have said that although Mr. Collins anticipated Miss Braddon in the work of devising domestic mysteries adapted to the wants of a sternly prosaic age, she was yet the founder of the sensation novel. Mr. Collins's productions deserve a more respectable name. They are massive and elaborate constructions—monuments of mosaic work, for the proper mastery of which it would seem, at first, that an index and note-book were required. They are not so much works of art as works of science. To read *The Woman in White,* requires very much the same intellectual effort as to read Motley or Froude. We may say, therefore, that Mr. Collins being to Miss Braddon what Richardson is to Miss Austen, we date the novel of domestic mystery from the former lady, for the same reason that we date the novel of domestic tranquility from the latter. Miss Braddon began by a skilful combination of bigamy, arson, murder, and insanity. These phenomena are all represented in the deeds of Lady Audley. The novelty lay in the heroine being, not a picturesque Italian of the fourteenth century, but an English gentlewoman of the current year, familiar

with the use of the railway and the telegraph. The intense probability of the story is constantly reiterated. Modern England—the England of to-day's newspaper—crops up at every step. Of course Lady Audley is a nonentity, without a heart, a soul, a reason. But what we may call the small change for these facts—her eyes, her hair, her mouth, her dresses, her bedroom furniture, her little words and deeds—are so lavishly bestowed that she successfully maintains a kind of half illusion. Lady Audley was diabolically wicked; Aurora Floyd, her successor, was simply foolish, or indiscreet, or indelicate—or anything you please to say of a young lady who runs off with a hostler. But as bigamy had been the cause of Lady Audley's crimes, so it is the cause of Aurora's woes. She marries a second time, on the hypothesis of the death of the hostler. But, to paraphrase a sentence of Thackeray's in a sketch of the projected plot of *Denis Duval,* suppose, after all, it should turn out that the hostler was *not* dead? In **Aurora Floyd** the small change is more abundant than ever. Aurora's hair, in particular, alternately blue-black, purple-black, and dead-black, is made to go a great way. Since **Aurora Floyd,** Miss Braddon has published half-a-dozen more novels; each, as we have intimated, better than the previous one, and running through more editions; but each fundamentally a repetition of **Aurora Floyd.** These works are censured and ridiculed, but they are extensively read. The author has a hold upon the public. It is, assuredly, worth our while to enquire more particularly how she has obtained it.

The great public, in the first place, is made up of a vast number of little publics, very much as our Union is made up of States, and it is necessary to consider which of these publics is Miss Braddon's. We can best define it with the half of a negative. It is that public which reads nothing but novels, and yet which reads neither George Eliot, George Sand, Thackeray, nor Hawthorne. People who read nothing but novels are very poor critics of human nature. Their foremost desire is for something new. Now, we all know that human nature is very nearly as old as the hills. But *society* is for ever renewing itself. To society, accordingly, and not to life, Miss Braddon turns, and produces, not stories of passion, but stories of action. Society is a vast magazine of crime and suffering, of enormities, mysteries, and miseries of every description, of incidents, in a word. In proportion as an incident is exceptional, it is interesting to persons in search of novelty. Bigamy, murder, and arson are exceptional. Miss Braddon distributes these materials with a generous hand, and attracts the attention of her public. The next step is to hold its attention. There have been plenty of tales of crime which have not made their authors famous, nor put money in their purses. The reason can have been only that they were not well executed. Miss Braddon, accordingly, goes to work like an artist. Let not the curious public take for granted that, from a literary point of view, her works are contemptible. Miss Braddon writes neither fine English nor slovenly English; not she. She writes what we may call very knowing English. If her readers have not read George Eliot and Thackeray and all the great authorities, she assuredly has, and, like every one else, she is the better for it. With a telling subject and a knowing style she proceeds to get up her photograph. These require shrewd observation and wide experience; Miss Braddon has both. Like all women, she has a turn for color; she knows how to paint. She overloads her canvas with detail. It is the peculiar character of these details that constitute her chief force. They betray an intimate acquaintance with that disorderly half of society which becomes every day a greater object of interest to the orderly half. They intimate that, to use an irresistible vulgarism, Miss Braddon "has been there." The novelist who interprets the illegitimate world to the legitimate world, commands from the nature of his position a certain popularity. Miss Braddon deals familiarly with gamblers, and bettingmen, and flashy reprobates of every description. She knows much that ladies are not accustomed to know, but that they are apparently very glad to learn. The names of drinks, the technicalities of the faro-table, the lingo of the turf, the talk natural to a crowd of fast men at supper, when there are no ladies present but Miss Braddon, the way one gentleman knocks another down—all these things—the exact local coloring of Bohemia—our sisters and daughters may learn from these works. These things are the incidents of vice; and vice, as is well known, even modern, civilized, elegant, prosaic vice, has its romance. Of this romance Miss Braddon has taken advantage, and the secret of her success is, simply, that she has done her work better than her predecessors. That is, she has done it with a woman's *finesse* and a strict regard to morality. If one of her heroines elopes with a handsome stable-boy, she saves the proprieties by marrying him. This may be indecent if you like, but it is not immoral. If another of her heroines is ever tempted, she resists. With people who are not particular, therefore, as to the moral delicacy of their author, or as to their intellectual strength, Miss Braddon is very naturally a favorite.

Norman Donaldson (essay date 1974)

SOURCE: An introduction by Norman Donaldson, in *Lady Audley's Secret,* Dover Publications, Inc., 1974, pp. v-xiv.

[*In the following introduction to the 1974 edition of* Lady Audley's Secret, *Donaldson provides an overview of critical comment on the novel through the twentieth century.*]

A rare treat is in store for any reader who encounters *Lady Audley's Secret* for the first time. The book has been strangely neglected in recent decades, but for half a century after its appearance in 1862 it was one of the most popular mystery stories in the English-speaking world. It made an instant reputation for its mysterious young author, Miss Braddon, who was later to number some of the greatest names of English letters among her admirers. Thackeray once walked to the local railroad station three times in a single day to enquire whether his copy of her latest novel had arrived. Tennyson declared himself "steeped in Miss Braddon" and engaged in reading every word she had ever written. R. L. Stevenson wrote to her from Sa-

moa that "it is something to be greater than Scott, Shakespeare, Homer, in the South Seas, and to that you have attained."

It is all the more remarkable, then, that a readable copy of her most popular work, *Lady Audley's Secret,* is nowadays a rarity even in large libraries. Many knowledgeable mystery devotees are unacquainted with it, even by repute. Coming upon the story unexpectedly in 1949, Anthony Boucher did not disguise his delight. The tale's 150,000 words, he was willing to swear, were less padded than the 60,000 words of most contemporary novels, and he found it remarkably fresh and undated. "Imagine my astonishment," he wrote to Vincent Starrett, "to realize that I was reading precisely the same plot and motivations as were contained in a mystery tale I'd read [in a slick magazine] the day before!" Jacques Barzun and Wendell H. Taylor, in their *Catalogue of Crime* (1971), comment with approval that Miss Braddon's story contains "much mystery and more detection than is found in many a modern thriller."

The great attraction of the book—its sheer readability—makes its eclipse in recent years quite unaccountable. It was never out of print during its author's long life. Well over a million copies must have been produced, of which remarkably few have survived. Even the short-lived omnibus in which Boucher encountered it—Edward Wagenknecht's *Murder by Gaslight* (1949)—is hard to find. Wagenknecht may be right: perhaps every available copy was read and reread until the binding gave way and the pages crumbled to dust.

Mary Elizabeth Braddon produced the novel at short notice to help her lover out of a business difficulty. In the early summer of 1861, John Maxwell, a big, broad-shouldered Irishman—an orphan from Limerick—was fast making his mark in the competitive world of London magazine publishing. The first weekly issue of his new fiction magazine, *Robin Goodfellow,* which had been extensively advertised, would be delayed unless he could lay his hands on at least the first few chapters of a serial by the following day. It was Miss Braddon who came to his aid. She was a diminutive, square-chinned woman with great strength of character who, as we shall see, had thrown in her lot with Maxwell a year or so earlier, and would secretly bear their first child about this time. Expanding an idea she had first used in an unpublished short story, she set furiously to work all night and by morning had somehow produced the first instalment of *Lady Audley's Secret.* It is disappointing to record that, despite this valiant effort, *Robin Goodfellow* failed in September, 1861, after only twelve issues. An actor of the day, J. B. Buxton, wrote to the author begging its continuation and, thus encouraged, she took up the manuscript again. Publication began afresh in the *Sixpenny Magazine* in March, 1862. It attracted the attention of the Tinsley Brothers, a new book-publishing house, who brought it out in the fashionable—and profitable—three-volume format. The story had to be completed quickly, so that the book could come out before the denouement was reached in the magazine.

"I wrote some part of the second and [the whole of] the third vol. of *Lady Audley* in less than a fortnight," the author told her friend and mentor, Bulwer-Lytton. Let the modern reader marvel, then, at the superior quality of the chapters scribbled in such haste.

Miss Braddon owed the idea of the book, she told an interviewer years later, to Wilkie Collins' recently published mystery *The Woman in White* (1860), and many instructive comparisons can be drawn between the two works, especially in the contrasted means used to tell the stories. Her signal device of a self-appointed detective in the person of the admirably drawn young lawyer, Robert Audley, is a marked extension of the role filled by the drawing master, Walter Hartright, in Collins' fine tale, and foreshadows that played by Franklin Blake in *The Moonstone* (1868). It seems likely the two authors, who were social acquaintances, learned from one another.

The story's construction betrays a master's hand—"If I could plot like Miss Braddon," said Thackeray, "I should be the greatest novelist that ever lived." The secret thoughts of the wicked Lady Audley cannot be shared with the reader in the early parts of Miss Braddon's book without dissipation of the mystery, but in the later chapters the author makes a brave attempt to render the golden-haired villainess understandable, though never by any means sympathetic. Previous commentators have confused the secret of Lady Audley with her crimes, but this is to misunderstand the title. Her earliest crime, the nature of which is evident almost from the first page, was committed as an adult, but she has carried the burden of her secret throughout her life, and it is only hinted at when the story is well advanced.

Miss Braddon's taste is almost, though not quite, faultless. Only in the early descriptions of George Talboys, who swoons on hearing of his wife's death and betrays petulance in his bereavement, is there a melodramatic taint. After these first few pages, though, there is scarcely a dull page. Mary Elizabeth's grasp is sure, her tempo steady; we feel ourselves to be in excellent hands. Adding to the sense of freshness remarked by Boucher and other modern readers is the lack of moral fervor, even a touch of self-satire that became more evident in her later works and earned her, perhaps, some of the endless reproval and vilification to which she was subjected by the more conservative literary critics. She was linked with Collins, Charles Reade and Mrs. Henry Wood as one of the "sensation novelists." "Excitement, and excitement alone, seems to be the great end at which they aim—an end which must be accomplished at any cost," wrote an anonymous hand in the *Quarterly Review*. Of *Lady Audley* in particular he concludes (after revealing the entire plot):

> Yet, not withstanding all the horrors of the story—and there are enough of them to furnish a full supper for Macbeth—not withstanding the glaring improbabilities of the incidents, the superhuman wickedness of the principal character and the incongruity of others, not withstanding the transparent nature of the secret [he fell into the usual error] from the very beginning, the author has succeeded in constructing a narrative the interest of which is sustained to the end.

When condemnation is so enticingly declaimed, what need of praise? It was doubtless a descendant of this reviewer who begged his colleagues on the board of film censors; "Let's run this movie just once more before we ban it."

Mary Elizabeth Braddon was born in London on October 4, 1837. Her father, Henry, was the black sheep of a well-connected Cornish family. His mother had put up the capital to enable him to join a firm of London solicitors, but the money was soon returned and Henry was invited to depart. His wife, born Fanny White, was Irish. The couple collaborated on some pieces for the *Sporting Magazine,* Henry jotting down rough notes of his exploits, Fanny rewriting them in more acceptable prose. But again Henry was guilty of an irregularity, this time connected with a certain "unlucky bill transaction," and again he was shown the door. When his sexual misdemeanors became too outrageous to pardon, the couple separated. "Papa vanished from our lives," wrote Mary Elizabeth long afterwards; "I know that Mamma went through the rest of her years without an evil feeling about the husband she had never loved."

Miss Braddon wrote prolifically even in the nursery. As a teenager she strayed into the awesome British Museum Reading Room, where, she recollected, "much kindness was shown my inexperience of the book world." Her various enterprises during the following years are still obscure, despite the efforts in this century of Michael Sadleir, Montague Summers and others. An obituary notice in *The Times* of London describes an event not otherwise recorded:

> She early showed a turn for writing, and by the time she was 18 she appears to have been a fairly regular contributor to a Brighton newspaper, helped thereto by a lad of her own age, one William Sawyer, employed on the paper. It is on record that the curious but purely literary friendship between the two went so far that they came to London together, determined to try their fortune, and that they made a compact to divide the profit of whatever work either of them should first produce with any success. Sawyer remained a journalist, but Mary Braddon worked hard at plays and stories, and in 1860 her comedietta, *The Loves of Arcadia* was produced at the Strand Theatre.

This account, while consistent with what we know of Miss Braddon's character, glides too quickly over the intervening years. Her son Willie (the novelist W. B. Maxwell) tells us in his autobiography *Time Gathered* (1937) that Mary Elizabeth, adamant in her plan to support her mother, at about the age of nineteen announced her intention of going on the stage. This at a period when only teaching and nursing were considered respectable careers for young ladies. All the protestations of outraged aunts failing to deflect her, our heroine adopted the stage name "Mary Seaton" and trod the boards for two years with the likes of Charles Kean and even, perhaps, the great Macready. She traveled, always with her mother, to theaters in every part of the kingdom.

A little later, while staying in Beverley, Yorkshire, she embarked on a double literary project: a local printer commissioned a sensational serial, *Three Times Dead,* and a wealthy patron of the arts requested a book of poems about Garibaldi. It was during this happy half-year spent in writing and riding an old farm horse that she probably visited Withernsea nearby and noted the details the reader will find in this volume.

Lady Audley's Secret was published in three volumes by Tinsley Brothers on October 1, 1862 and went through eight editions before the end of the year. The excitement already engendered by the serial grew to a climax, and the presses could not keep pace with the insatiable demand.

The first of many stage versions was put on in London before the end of the year and ran for months. Dramatizations by Colin Hazlewood and William Suter were published. In New York, the well-known Philadelphia actress-manager, Mrs. D. P. Bowers, scored a success with a dramatization—at first titled *The Mystery of Audley Court*—by John Brougham. In deference to current fads, it introduced a "celebrated ghost effect in the form of apparitions." The dramatic versions are but pale shadows of the book. Hazlewood's, for example, makes no attempt at mystery at all, but seems to parody the Braddon text. A five-reel movie was copyrighted in 1915. As recently as 1971 a musical adaptation by Douglas Seale was given fifty-four performances at Chicago's Goodman Theatre. Though it was hailed by one reviewer as a "tender and charming delight," the mood and purpose of the original story had undergone astonishing changes in the lyricist's hands. Here, for example, is the villagers' serenade to the squire, the dignified Sir Michael Audley:

> "Here's to the landlord. Here's to the rent.
> Here's to the honor of an English country gent."

With her fortune apparently assured by *Lady Audley's* success and her mother's future provided for, Miss Braddon's troubles would seem to have been behind her. On the contrary, they were only just beginning.

Sadleir, in a centenary article in the *Times Literary Supplement* in 1937 outlines the financial troubles in which she became embroiled. Maxwell was in debt to his competitors, Ward, Lock and Tyler, and Miss Braddon's future novels were mortgaged to them. She wrote to Bulwer-Lytton in January, 1866, that she was "worried by the attempt of a rich firm (having lent money to the proprietor of a magazine published in the name of Maxwell and Co.) to withhold from me £1,000." She published several books pseudonymously in an attempt to conceal some of her income. Much of her work in the late 1860s was written anonymously and at great speed for halfpenny and penny journals. "It is the most piratical stuff," she wrote to Bulwer-Lytton, "and would make your hair stand on end if

you were to see it. The amount of crime, tragedy, murder, slow poisoning and general infamy required by the halfpenny reader is something terrible. I am just going to do a little parricide for this week's supply."

Added to literary pressures and financial problems was an awesome social and domestic burden. Sadleir hints in his 1937 article of secrets in the young writer's life which he was unwilling, and to some extent probably unable, to reveal. When he revised the article for his *Things Past* (1944) he raised a corner of the veil:

> The development of her friendship with John Maxwell was a subject about which she always maintained the utmost reticence. Consequently, behind the publishing history of her early works there has lain—and must continue to lie—a curious vacuum of personal life. This much may permissibly be said—that Maxwell, when he and Miss Braddon met, was a married man with a wife in a mental home. Not until after her death in 1874 could he face the world as the husband of the "Author of *Lady Audley's Secret.*"

A recent study of the relevant certificates for the purpose of this introduction indicates that Miss Braddon lived with Maxwell for about fourteen years before their union could be regularized. The birth of her first child, Gerald Maxwell, was kept secret. It was apparently never registered, but probably occurred in 1861. Francis was born in Chelsea in 1863, William at 26 Mecklenburgh Square on June 4, 1866, his parents being reported by the father as John Maxwell and Mary Elizabeth Maxwell, formerly Braddon. By selling government securities, Miss Braddon was able to purchase Lichfield House in Richmond, ten miles up the Thames from London, late in 1866, and it was there early in 1871 that Edward was born. The last of her five children, Rose, also seems to have been born before the wedding could take place.

Her predicament during this extended period can scarcely be imagined today. Beset by Maxwell's creditors, socially ostracized, attacked on all sides as a sensation novelist, working long hours at her desk when, often pregnant, her services were needed elsewhere—in addition to her own children, she was bringing up five earlier Maxwells from the lawful marriage—it is small wonder that even her indomitable spirit shuddered in later years to contemplate this bitter servitude. If she had transgressed society's code, she had done so with the steadfast deliberation she had brought to earlier decisions; she had confronted the likely penalties and over the years paid them in full measure.

And there were a few bright spots. *The Times* praised *Lady Audley's Secret* as

> a good galoping novel, and, like a good galop, to be enjoyed rather than criticised. It is well put together. Indeed it is seldom one sees a novel so well balanced in display of power, showing such even excellence of plot, of passion, of character, and of diction.

If her social life were under a cloud, there was always correspondence with those who knew nothing of her personal situation. Bulwer-Lytton and Charles Reade were constant supports, and there is reason to believe that the Reverend Charles Tickell Procter, who became vicar of Richmond in 1867, understood and sympathized with her predicament. When the first Mrs. Maxwell died, Miss Braddon leased Lichfield House and the family moved to Cheyne Walk, Chelsea for several months in a bid to cover their traces.

It was on October 2, 1874, that the Rev. Mr. Procter quietly slipped up to London and, just off bustling Fleet Street, married them at St. Bride's Church. Then they returned to the children in Cheyne Walk. When Willie wrote his autobiography just before his death, he professed to be still ignorant of the reason for the family's temporary move to Chelsea.

After her long-awaited wedding, Mary Elizabeth's life became more tranquil. Her literary bondage came to an end in 1871 when, after Ward, Lock had issued six or seven of her novels, Maxwell became her publisher once more and filled this role until succeeded by Simpkin, Marshall in 1888. Attacks on her in the press gradually gave way to respect and admiration.

She seems to have borne no grudges. Her son describes her as having been "of a happy disposition. She rejoiced in laughter, and taught us young children to love innocent mirth. She used to read to us, walk with us, take us out on drives." Her powers of concentration and her capacity for work were astounding, even in the age of Dickens and Trollope. "Everyone went into her library, we children, the servants, importunate visitors." Always she was ready to drop her work when the children or her husband needed her. Yet she wrote about eighty books under her own name, half-a-dozen pseudonymously. She edited her husband's magazine *Belgravia* for many years and, for varying periods, other publications. She turned out numerous articles and poems, even a novel in French for *Le Figaro*. Unique among her contemporaries, she acted as her own publisher. "She bought the paper," her son tells us, "gave orders to printers and binders, and finally sent the bound and wrappered books to Simpkin, Marshall and Company for distribution."

In addition to Lichfield House, the Maxwells had a summer place in the New Forest, and they traveled widely in Europe. Miss Braddon loved riding but renounced the pleasure after John Maxwell's death. Visitors at Richmond included such well-remembered names as Oscar Wilde, Conan Doyle, E. W. Hornung and Arthur Morrison.

After 1870, Miss Braddon largely deserted books with criminal plots in favor of novels of character and manners, and historical tales. She died at Lichfield House on February 4, 1915, aged seventy-seven years, busy to the last. Her novel *Mary,* published posthumously, is as good as anything she ever wrote.

Benjamin M. Nyberg deserves the gratitude of all Braddon students for his painstaking classification and evaluation of as many of her works as he could lay his hands on—more than sixty in all. In his doctoral dissertation (University of Colorado, 1965) he emphasizes the nonsensational character of most Braddon novels after the first decade, and the many nonsensational elements in *Lady Audley's Secret* and other early novels, including the deep analyses of character. In particular he praises two novels of manners, *The Doctor's Wife* (1864) and *Strangers and Pilgrims* (1873), and her striking character study, *The Rose of Life* (1905).

But readers who turn to *Lady Audley's Secret* for its mystery and detective elements, for the qualities it shares with *Uncle Silas* and *The Moonstone,* will be eager to know what other Braddon titles can compare to it. For them, Nyberg lists *Aurora Floyd* (1863) and *John Marchmont's Legacy* (1863), together with *Birds of Prey* (1867) and its sequel, *Charlotte's Inheritance* (1868). These, with *Lady Audley's Secret* (1862), he considers the best of the sensation novels. Sadleir and W. B. Maxwell would add *Henry Dunbar* (1864) to this list.

If *Lady Audley's Secret* was the archetypal Braddon thrilled to generations of readers (and a favorite of readers who had an entire library shelf of Braddon works to choose from), it was by design of the author herself, who cited it on the title pages of most of her later works. Among those of her works rightly or wrongly labeled sensation novels, it was also the author's own favorite to the end of her life.

Winifred Hughes (essay date 1980)

SOURCE: "The Wickedness of Woman: M. E. Braddon and Mrs. Henry Wood," in *The Maniac in the Cellar: Sensation Novels of the 1860s,* Princeton University Press, 1980, pp. 106-36.

[*In the following essay, Hughes discusses the role of the sinful woman in the works of Braddon and her contemporary, Mrs. Henry Wood.*]

I.

"My own Edgardo!—and you still love me? You still would marry me in spite of this dark mystery which surrounds me? In spite of the fatal history of my race? In spite of the ominous predictions of my aged nurse?"

"I would, Selina"; and the young man passed his arm around her yielding waist. The two lovers gazed at each other's faces in unspeakable bliss. Suddenly Selina started.

"Leave me, Edgardo! leave me! A mysterious something—a fatal misgiving—a dark ambiguity—an equivocal mistrust oppresses me. I would be alone!"

"Ah!—what if he should know that I have another husband living? Dare I reveal to him that I have two legitimate and three natural children? Dare I repeat to him the history of my youth? Dare I confess that at the age of seven I poisoned my sister, by putting verdigris in her cream-tarts,—that I threw my cousin from a swing at the age of twelve? That the lady's-maid who incurred the displeasure of my girlhood now lies at the bottom of the horse-pond? No! no! he is too pure,—too good,—too innocent, to hear such improper conversation!" and her whole body writhed as she rocked to and fro in a paroxysm of grief.

Edgardo galloped rapidly towards Sloperton. . . . "Yet if . . . she knew that I were a disgraced and ruined man,—a felon and an outcast. If she knew that at the age of fourteen I murdered my Latin tutor and forged my uncle's will. If she knew that I had three wives already, and that the fourth victim of misplaced confidence and my unfortunate peculiarity is expected to be at Sloperton by to-night's train with her baby. But no; she must not know it. Constance must not arrive. Burke the Slogger must attend to that."

A nameless terror seemed to have taken possession of Clarissa, Lady Selina's maid, as she rushed into the presence of her mistress. . . . "An accident has happened on the railway, and a man has been killed."

"What—not Edgardo!" almost screamed Selina.

"No, Burke the Slogger! your ladyship."

"My first husband!" said Lady Selina, sinking on her knees. "Just Heaven, I thank thee."

Bret Harte, *Condensed Novels*

These stirring vignettes from "Selina Sedilia, by Miss M. E. B-dd-n and Mrs. H-n-y W-d"[1] represent a kind of distilled essence of sensationalism, a Platonic ideal of the sensation novel. Bret Harte's composite, unfolded in a dozen pages instead of the usual three volumes, manages to include all of the essential devices in their essential multiplications: passion, secrets, murder, bigamy (not to mention trigamy), dark misgivings, and a family curse. There is the wicked and tortured heroine, a titled lady burdened with an inconvenient lower-class husband, the disgracefully ungrammatical Burke the Slogger; there is her dashing lover, the disguised criminal-hero, practiced in seduction and the forging of wills. There is even a railway accident, a crucial occurrence in such novels as *No Name, East Lynne,* and **John Marchmont's Legacy.** On the whole, the parody is inspired, the best of a spirited outpouring, which became "itself a part of the lighter reading of the time."[2] But even "Selina Sedilia" encourages a misleading tendency, common enough in the 1860s and more pronounced since then, to lump the two best-selling authoresses together unceremoniously, without inquiring into any particular differences between them.

Perhaps inevitably, Braddon and Wood were reviewed together, sometimes in the midst of a crowd of the anonymous and forgettable, who busily produced such titles as *Nobly False, Recommended to Mercy, The Law of Divorce, The Weird of the Wentworths,* and *Passages in the Life of a Fast Young Lady.* Because they were women, writing about the sins of women, both of them were subject to reproof in reference to that susceptible organ, "the cheek of the young person." In her extended campaign in

Blackwood's against the author of **Lady Audley's Secret,** the indefatigable Mrs. Oliphant accords similar, often identical, treatment to the author of *East Lynne*: "This is [a] dangerous and foolish work, as well as false, both to Art and Nature. Nothing can be more wrong and fatal than to represent the flames of vice as a purifying fiery ordeal, through which the penitent is to come elevated and sublimed."[3] As Mrs. Oliphant and other critics point out, both Miss Braddon and Mrs. Wood demand sympathy for their fallen heroines, their bigamists or adulteresses, by making them suffer tremendously at the hands of fate and their own remorse. Both write about marriage as an unsatisfactory or illusory state instead of relegating it to the happy ending. Both rely heavily on "involuntary" motivation—destiny, insanity, circumstance. The *Christian Remembrancer* brackets their novels under the single nefarious category of "animalistic" fiction, which is found to register an alarming "drop from the empire of reason and self-control, . . . a consistent appeal to the animal part of our nature." For both Wood and Braddon, with little to choose between them, it appears to be this very quality of abandon and unrestraint, this lack of civilized decorum, that constitutes the irresistible fascination and charm of the ideal heroine.[4] Under the influence of righteous indignation, these reviewers understandably lose sight of any trivial distinctions in their effort to counteract the "perverted and vitiated taste"[5] for sensationalism.

The reviewers who undertake to distinguish between the leading female sensation novelists, do so on two grounds: grammar and morals. While a Henry James may remark of Miss Braddon, with fastidious precision, that she "writes neither fine English nor slovenly English; not she. She writes what we may call very knowing English,"[6] even the average hack reviewer is likely to mention Mrs. Wood's noticeable weakness in the matter of relative clauses, sentence fragments, use of "like" for "as," and general vulgarity of expression. These lapses are accompanied by an incongruous delight in high-sounding phrases and long words as well as a running commentary on the grammatical practice of her characters. In this case, however, style and morality diverge; for those moralists who see any difference at all between the two writers, it is invariably the ungainly prose of Mrs. Wood that receives the imprimatur. The *Examiner,* which comes out with the strongest statement of this position, finds that with the publication of *Verner's Pride* (1863) Mrs. Wood has already begun to "[fall] behind in the race," precisely because she "bases her fiction on a womanly notion of right, and shows a sense of delicacy that restrains her from the coarser imaginings of the sensation novelist."[7] The rationale for this apparently depends on the fact that in *Verner's Pride* supposed bigamy and murder turn out to have been mere seduction and suicide. *Fraser's,* on the other hand, tries to have it both ways, by castigating the system of literary terrorism patronized by Miss Braddon and at the same time criticizing Mrs. Wood for her "temperance tincture" and her ambition to write with-a-purpose. For *Fraser's,* indeed, her less sensational works, *The Channings* and *Mrs. Halliburton's Troubles,* are *too* tame, "wanting in force, in plot, in love-making, in almost everything which goes to make up a novel."[8]

Behind this diversity of opinion, there are crucial indications of what is happening to popular melodrama during the second half of the nineteenth century. In many ways Braddon and Wood had parallel careers: they were chiefly responsible, together with Wilkie Collins, for initiating the craze for sensationalism; they both achieved their most stunning hits with early novels, *Lady Audley's Secret* and *East Lynne,* published within a year of each other; they proved astonishingly prolific afterwards, Wood living to complete more than fifty novels, Braddon more than eighty, both successfully holding on to their loyal public well after the end of the sensation decade. On the surface, their novels deal with the same concerns, fitting them into the same venerable melodramatic molds and exploiting the same sensational turns of plot. But those critics who saw M. E. Braddon as "coarser," more dangerous, more subversive, were right. Mrs. Henry Wood, for all her dalliance with seduction and unexplained drownings and the dead alive, preserves the conventional meanings of stage melodrama, while herself doing much to foster the "increasing tendency of the heroine to die of sin,"[9] through the numerous dramatized versions of *East Lynne.* M. E. Braddon, however, deliberately undermines the traditional moral assumptions. If Wood's novels show a new emphasis on the repentant sinner within the compass of authentic melodrama, Braddon's show the beginning of a change in substance that will eventually make melodrama itself an empty and outdated form.

II.

> "Nothing disagreeable should ever be looked at. Apart from such a habit standing in the way of that graceful equanimity of surface which is so expressive of good breeding, it hardly seems compatible with refinement of mind. A truly refined mind will seem to be ignorant of the existence of anything that is not perfectly proper, placid, and pleasant."
>
> Mrs. General in Dickens' *Little Dorrit*

Mrs. Henry Wood (1814-1887) lived an entirely unremarkable life. She was born Ellen Price, daughter of a Worcester glove manufacturer, and was a semi-invalid from girlhood, suffering from curvature of the spine. At the age of twenty-two, she married *Mr.* Henry Wood, of whom nothing else is known except that he supplied her pen name and himself possessed "a mind a little wanting in ballast."[10] This unfortunate lack finally cost him his job as foreign agent for a banking and shipping firm and sent his family back to England in straitened circumstances after twenty years' affluent residence in France. In this crisis, Ellen Wood hurriedly transformed her hobby of writing short sketches for Harrison Ainsworth's magazines into a paying career. Her first full-length novel was *Danesbury House* (1860), which won her £100 in a contest sponsored by the Scottish Temperance League. Her second—amazingly—was *East Lynne* (1860-61), which took off after a seasonable puff in the *Times* and sold unremittingly for the

rest of the century. Widowed in 1866, she continued to grind out popular fiction, both three-volume snifflers and the "Johnny Ludlow" series of short stories, while at the same time taking over as the editor of *Argosy,* which she single-handedly rescued from the debacle caused by its serialization of *Griffith Gaunt.* She lived quietly and respectably, the only one of the major sensation novelists without scandals and irregularities in private life. She had no literary pretensions and avoided anything like literary circles; Mrs. E. M. Ward found her "a very nice woman, but hopelessly prosaic. Calling upon her one day when she was alone I hoped that perhaps she would reveal some hidden depth yet unseen. But alas! the topics she clung to and thoroughly explored were her servants' shortcomings, and a full account of the cold she had caught."[11] This same quality pervades her fictional world, which is founded on gossip and trivia, much occupied with servants and the lower classes, filled with explicit details of dress, furnishings, and the color schemes of fashionable carriages.

Mrs. Henry Wood seems an unlikely sensation novelist, in her work as well as her life. Her most highly developed talent is for the wringing out of emotion, the calculated and relentless assault on the tear ducts of the average reader. Her books are pure soap opera, loaded down with pathos, disaster, tortures of guilt and repentance, interminable deathbed interviews. One of her favorite situations involves the hero who loves or is loved by two heroines; she focuses, lingeringly, on the anguish of the outsider, forced to contemplate the wedded bliss of her more fortunate rival. All of her novels, in spite of the wild occurrences, have a domestic slant, an air of housekeeping and family relations. It is hardly surprising that the ultimate in ambivalent titles belongs to Mrs. Wood: *The Mystery; A Story of Domestic Life.* Although this touches on the central paradox of the sensation genre, Mrs. Wood remains an extreme case; any of her colleagues would have written "A Romance in Real Life," or "A Matter-of-Fact Romance." The *Saturday Review* describes her novels as a battleground, a scene of competition between two unassimilated modes, sensationalism and domesticity.[12] The sensational incidents exist less for their own sake than for their emotional repercussions, the frequently hysterical encounters between people who have betrayed or persecuted or jilted one another, between people who ought not to reveal their hopeless passions. The murders take place offstage, but the deaths from remorse or consumption are vividly dramatized. What holds it all together is the rule of propriety, in its most rigid and conventional sense. The fact that this rule is continually broken only serves to strengthen it; the offenders are fully aware of the terms of their offenses, either regretting the mad folly that has cut them off from decent society or, if they happen to be villains, striving vainly to keep up appearances. With Mrs. Henry Wood, there is no room for a divergence between morality and propriety. What other novelist could have envisioned this response by an older member of the landed gentry to a possible suicide on his estate? "A well-conducted girl like Rachel Frost throw herself wilfully into a pond for the purpose of drowning! . . . She would be one of the last to do it."[13]

Mrs. Wood's *East Lynne,* having survived an early rejection in manuscript by George Meredith, then a reader for Chapman and Hall, went on to become, with **Lady Audley's Secret,** one of the two top English best sellers of the nineteenth century. If nothing else, it reflects the popular taste of an era. The unbeatable combination of sin and sentiment, the unrestrained emotional wallowing, ultimately depends on an unquestioning acceptance of conventional morality and conventional standards of behavior. It may seem daring, as it was certainly unusual in Victorian fiction, to make the central character an adulteress, and a sympathetic one at that. But the narrator's sympathy, as in stage melodrama, is contingent upon the heroine's remorse, upon the heroine's own total acceptance of the law that she has transgressed. Her greatest punishment, apart from the internal gnawings of shame and guilt, comes from her irrevocable position as a social outcast. From the moment of her elopement with the villain, she has put herself beyond the pale; she may be forgiven, piously and tearfully, by the husband she has wronged, but she can never be taken back. An unmarried and fallen heroine might eventually have made amends by a legal marriage with her repentant seducer, as frequently happened on the nineteenth-century stage.[14] For the adulteress, however, there is only one permissible cure, morally as well as dramatically: an early and contrite death.

The seduction of Lady Isabel Carlyle, scandalous as it might appear in potential, is never permitted to become anything more than an object lesson for erring wives. Like all writers of moral tales, from St. Augustine on, Mrs. Wood is open to the charge of portraying the sin as well as the penance it entails. In *East Lynne,* however, the emphasis actually does fall on the punishment, on the exquisite agony of the penitent adulteress, rather than on the original temptation. Although it is clear enough that Lady Isabel is sexually attracted to Sir Francis Levison, both before and after her marriage to Mr. Carlyle, infatuation alone is not intended to be her "moving motive"; it is not sufficiently powerful to overcome her conventional terror, her sense of duty and propriety. "Oh, reader!" interjects the narrator, "never doubt the principles of poor Lady Isabel, her rectitude of mind, her wish and endeavour to do right, her abhorrence of wrong; her spirit was earnest and true, her intentions were pure."[15] The first time Levison declares his passion, Lady Isabel takes refuge in shocked hauteur and effectively removes herself from his company. But when he reappears at East Lynne, as her husband's guest, he finds an ally in her jealousy of Barbara Hare, a family friend with whom Mr. Carlyle has frequent, unexplained meetings. Apparently Wood cannot bring herself to let her heroine knowingly violate a perfect home and a perfect marriage. In any case, Lady Isabel is given plenty of reason to think that it has already been violated: "She was most assuredly out of her senses that night, or she never would have listened. A jealous woman is mad; an outraged woman is doubly mad; and the ill-fated Lady Isa-

bel truly believed that every sacred feeling which ought to exist between man and wife, was betrayed by Mr. Carlyle."

Following this "moment of wild passion," retribution sets in promptly. The wretched Lady Isabel is not even permitted to enjoy any "fleeting moments of abandonment" unaccompanied by the "adder stings" of conscience. Indeed, from "the very hour of her departure, . . . a lively remorse, a never-dying anguish, took possession of her soul for ever." This supplies the occasion for another direct homily, courtesy of Mrs. Wood:

> Oh, reader, believe me! Lady—wife—mother! should you ever be tempted to abandon your home, so will you awake. Whatever trials may be the lot of your married life, though they may magnify themselves to your crushed spirit as beyond the endurance of woman to bear, *resolve* to bear them; fall down upon your knees and pray to be enabled to bear them: pray for patience; pray for strength to resist the demon that would urge you so to escape; bear unto death, rather than forfeit your fair name and your good conscience; for be assured that the alternative, if you rush on to it, will be found far worse than death.

Although there are ample doses of conventional religious sentiment administered throughout, it is no accident that "fair name" precedes "good conscience" in this central exhortation to the reader. For Mrs. Wood never really addresses the question of morality, or does so only on the most superficial level; "conscience" is mentioned, certainly, but the social punishments are far more graphic and harrowing. In *East Lynne,* the moral sense is bound up in social status; it is equivalent to breeding, to the "feeling of an English gentlewoman":

> It is possible remorse does not come to all erring wives so immediately as it came to Lady Isabel Carlyle—you need not be reminded that we speak of women in the better positions of life. Lady Isabel was endowed with sensitively refined delicacy, with an innate, lively consciousness of right and wrong: a nature, such as hers, is one of the last that may be expected to err; and but for that most fatal misapprehension regarding her husband, . . . she would never have forgotten herself.

Where moral right is so completely identified with genteel conduct, there is no chance of criticism or subversion of conventional values. By "forgetting herself," in Wood's phrase, the adulteress has forfeited her identity as an English lady, becoming "a poor outcast; one of those whom men pity, and whom women shrink from," even before she is reported dead in a French railway accident and assumes the name and occupation of Madame Vine, the widowed governess.

The unique "sensation" of *East Lynne,* undoubtedly the source of its enormous popular appeal, is the return of Lady Isabel, disguised and disfigured, as the hired governess to her own children. For a good third of the novel, Mrs. Wood indulges her heroine (and readers) in a prolonged, luxurious orgy of self-torture, as the miserable governess, in going about her humble duties, must watch the repeated caresses of her former husband showered upon his second wife, the hated Barbara Hare.[16] At every turn Lady Isabel is subjected to agonizing torments: she is reminded, in low tones, of the story of her own disgrace; she suffers through the death of her son William, unrecognized as his mother; she realizes the depths of her own shame when Francis Levison is convicted of murder. In the end it kills her: this is clearly the only proper response for someone in her situation, remorseful but socially irretrievable. If the author admitted any possibility of her being reinstated as a wife and mother, her plight would lose its terrible poignancy. As it is, Mrs. Wood milks the last bitter drops of emotion from the deathbed scene between Lady Isabel and Mr. Carlyle, in which he nobly forgives her and they bid each other farewell, "until eternity." Lady Isabel herself fully expects to go to heaven. That is evidently much easier to achieve than any kind of social redemption: "My own sin I have surely expiated: I cannot expiate the shame I entailed upon you, and upon our children." The novel leaves her figuratively in the same place as the popular stage versions, with their final tableau of Lady Isabel and little Willie enthroned together on a golden cloud.[17]

The narrow focus on emotional states, while effective in its way, deprives *East Lynne* of much of the violence and excitement that enliven more typical sensation novels. Although she invokes the darker elements of evil and crime, so that at least her plot outlines look recognizably sensational, Wood makes no attempt to portray them in any depth or to explain her criminal characters. Sir Francis Levison is a convenience for the plot—he gets final credit for everything from the seduction of Lady Isabel to the impulsive murder of George Hallijohn—but he is a colorless and perfunctory villain, distinguished only by the requisite black whiskers. Although Mrs. Wood has her unlimited reserves of ineptness, to which this failure may easily be attributed, it is also apparent that she intends Levison to be commonplace, a coward and a cad, who receives his most fitting punishment when the mob treats him to a ducking in Justice Hare's horse-pond. On a popular level, this is again symptomatic of the banality of evil as the Victorians perceived it—the "decay of murder" in Leslie Stephen's terms. By the 1860s the primitive vitality of the stage villain has receded even in an unsophisticated melodrama like *East Lynne,* leaving behind only his established physical traits.

In *Verner's Pride,* the case of the diminished villain becomes rapidly more acute. Frederick Massingbird, who seduces and abandons a respectable lower-class girl, is singled out from the beginning by a strange black mark on his cheek, "quite as large as a pigeon's egg, with what looked like radii shooting from it on all sides." In spite of this mark (a dead giveaway to the reader), his guilt remains officially unproven until near the final reckoning. What is most remarkable, however, is the fact that Massingbird is killed off before the end of the first of the three

volumes. Although the supposed appearance of his ghost casts a shadow over the subsequent action, for most of *Verner's Pride* the villain is irrelevant enough to be safely dead and buried in Australia. He is far removed from the center of dramatic conflict—he is never even introduced to the heroine—and the good characters, oppressed mainly by the results of various misunderstandings and misplaced codicils, are left with nothing very tangible to fight against.

Verner's Pride, Mrs. Wood's second attempt at out-and-out sensationalism, lacks the intense urgency of situation that saves *East Lynne* from the cumbersome paraphernalia of its own plot. Here the rule of propriety has tightened its grip, emerging, quite explicitly, as the central issue. What little tension there is results from the spectacle, obviously titillating to Mrs. Wood, of men and women of refined delicacy thrust by circumstance into extremely indelicate positions. The whole plot, reduced to essentials, becomes a series of trials of Lionel Verner's sense of propriety, as he is alternately shunted in and out of his inheritance through the confusion over his uncle's will. The dilemma of his personal life is created by a youthful infatuation with the shallow coquette Sibylla West and failure to recognize his own deeper passion for the heroine, Lucy Tempest. When Sibylla suddenly returns from Australia, already the widow of Fred Massingbird, Lionel proposes to her on impulse, almost immediately regretting it, as he later explains to Lucy's father: "I engaged myself to my first wife in an unguarded moment. . . . I might have retracted: but the retraction would have left a stain on my honour that could never be effaced." For this initial mistake, Lionel condemns himself to "years of penitence" and "expiation" on the principle that "a man who has come to the years I had, should hold his feelings under his own control." Although Sibylla plagues him with her extravagance and her uncertain temper, Lionel resolves never to quarrel with her or complain of her, only reminding her, again and again, "If you have no care for what may be due to me and to yourself, you will do well to bear in mind that something is due to others." Out of chagrin over the loss of Verner's Pride and out of jealousy over Lucy Tempest, Sibylla constantly embarrasses her husband in front of his family, finally accusing him and Lucy of having an affair: "All the courtesies of life were lost sight of—its social usages were as nothing. . . . Sibylla, lost in that moment to all sense of the respect due to herself, to her husband, to Lucy, allowed her wild fancies, her passion, to overmaster everything." All this is unutterably painful to someone of "Lionel's refinement of mind," but even worse is the period of suspense caused by reports of Fred Massingbird's resurrection, which would make Sibylla a bigamist. Although Sibylla herself is indifferent, as long as she remains mistress of Verner's Pride, Lionel stays awake nights pondering his "great anxiety for his wife" in these terms: "To what conflict might she not be about to be exposed! to what unseemly violence of struggle, outwardly and inwardly, might she not expose herself!" In each new instance Mrs. Wood hastens to apply what may be called the "seemliness" test, and the occasions for it become more and more frequent, as though she is in the process of discovering her own true subject in the novel.

Lionel's greatest temptation comes in the stolen interviews with Lucy Tempest, in which he contrives to reveal his passion without gratifying it, generally by patting her on the head "reverently as any old grandfather might have done," for "Lionel Verner was not one to lose his self-control where there was real necessity for his retaining it." Even after Sibylla has conveniently died, he carries on with his romance in the same backhanded way: "There are moments when I am tempted to forget my position, to forget honour, and speak words that—that—I ought not to speak. Even now, as I look down upon you, my heart is throbbing, my veins are tingling; but I must not touch you with my finger, or tell you of my impassioned love. All I can do is to carry it away with me, and battle with it alone." This time the impediment is overwhelming debt, which according to the narrator's solemn pronouncement "placed him beyond the reach of social ties," but which is instantly dissolved by the accidental discovery of the lost codicil. The strained sufferings of the principal characters are based on entirely artificial predicaments, growing out of their own exaggerated notions of honor and delicacy. The minor subplot of Decima Verner's romance is emblematic of the whole: she is arbitrarily separated from her lover, Edmund Hautley, when his father disapproves of their engagement for no other reason than "self-will," merely for the sake of opposing his son's free choice. The lovers are too strictly honorable to elope, or to correspond secretly during the ten years or so of their separation, or even to break their promises to each other. All they can do is wait for the old man's death, while Decima's youth fades and she is taunted as an old maid. This same sort of thing happens in *A Life's Secret* (1867), in which the secret, after ruining a man's life, turns out to have been a lie, told by the villainess for implausibly oblique motives of revenge.

In *Verner's Pride* Mrs. Wood seems almost desperate to avoid vulgarity, which is obviously her element; she betrays herself as the outsider, the glove manufacturer's daughter, imagining the incredible refinement of the upper-middle and gentry classes to which she does not belong. She plays off propriety and impropriety, weaker counterparts of the conventional melodramatic principles of good and evil, but there is no question of which is to be the ultimate standard. The taste of "kitchen literature," though palpable to the discerning reader, is unwitting and unwilling on the author's part; if she imports lower-class fantasies and preoccupations into her respectable drawing rooms, it is out of ignorance, rather than an impulse toward rebellion or an exposure of nasty middle-class secrets. Quite simply, she transfers popular melodrama intact into a more exalted setting, none too convincingly, but in total innocence of ulterior designs. In Mrs. Henry Wood, wicked or unseemly conduct is always identified as such; it is never excused on the basis of circumstance or given the protection of law—this is why she consistently avoids

bigamy, which is a much more equivocal proposition than outright adultery. In all three novels—*East Lynne, Verner's Pride,* and *A Life's Secret*—she provides apparent bigamy, but ultimate legal vindication, for her virtuous heroes. With M. E. Braddon, Mrs. Wood's chief rival and originator of the Bigamy Novel, the lines are never so clearly drawn and the implications are far more revolutionary.

III.

The Forger, the Murderer, the Upholsterer—where is he?

Punch, 1868

Although her son W. B. Maxwell speaks primly of her "entirely sheltered life," Mary Elizabeth Braddon (1835-1915) boldly disregarded, from a very early age, the restrictions and conventionalities that normally shackled Victorian women of her upper-middle-class background. It was her own experience, and not some magical gift of "creative imagination which seems so like the record of reality,"[18] that gave her novels their characteristic flavor of worldliness, or what Henry James would call "the exact local coloring of Bohemia."[19] At the age of twenty-two, determined to support her mother after her father's disappearance, Mary Elizabeth launched her career by taking to the stage under an assumed name,[20] like any typical sensation heroine. By 1860 she was on her own in London, serving her apprenticeship in fiction while turning out blood-thirsty serials for the *Halfpenny Journal* and *Reynolds' Miscellany*. It was around this time that she met John Maxwell, a rising magazine publisher with a wife in a mental institution. For the next fourteen years, the period of her greatest fame, Miss Braddon's well-kept secret was her domestic life with Maxwell, which eventually included five illegitimate children. In spite of the early triumph with *Lady Audley,* she continued to write furiously, even desperately, producing an average of three triple-deckers a year as well as founding the monthly *Belgravia* and keeping up her anonymous connection with the penny dreadfuls. Most of the time she worked under intense pressure, as she explains in more than one letter to Bulwer-Lytton, her literary mentor: "I know that my writing teems with errors, absurdities, contradictions, and inconsistencies; but I have never written a line that has not been written against time—sometimes with the printer waiting outside the door."[21] Incredibly, she came up with the first installment of *Lady Audley* overnight, in a futile attempt to salvage one of Maxwell's publishing ventures, and she later knocked off part of the second and the entire third volume in "less than a fortnight."[22]

For M. E. Braddon, no genteel lady amateur, writing was primarily a way of making money. She lends something of her own experience in the subculture of hack journalism to her young hero in *Birds of Prey* (1867) and its sequel *Charlotte's Inheritance* (1868). His attitude is defined in terms that apply equally to Braddon herself: "He had been brought up among people who treated literature as a trade as well as an art; and what art is not more or less a trade?

He knew the state of the market and what kind of goods were likely to go off briskly, and it was for the market he worked. When gray shirtings were in active demand, he set his loom for gray shirtings; and when the buyers clamored for fancy goods, he made haste to produce that class of fabrics." Here, as well as on questions of morality, she had her chronic difficulties with the reviewers: "The critics were not slow to remark that he worked at a white-hot haste, and must needs be a shallow pretender, because he was laborious and indefatigable."[23] For the most part, however, Miss Braddon approaches her craft with zest and good humor, remarkable under the circumstances, maintaining an ironic perspective on her own stock-in-trade, which some of her more solemn critics would have done well to imitate. To her editor at *Temple Bar* she confides:

> The Balzac-morbid-anatomy school is my especial delight, but it seems you want the right-down sensational; floppings at the end of chapters, and bits of paper hidden in secret drawers, bank-notes, and title-deeds under the carpet, and a part of the body putrefying in the coal scuttle. . . . I will give the kaleidoscope . . . another turn, and will do my very best with the old bits of glass and pins and rubbish . . . the young lady who has married a burglar, and who does not want to introduce him to her friends; . . . the two brothers who are perpetually taken for one another; . . . the high-bred and conscientious banker, who has made away with everybody's title-deeds.[24]

The author of *Lady Audley's Secret* obviously enjoys an inside joke at her own expense. In *Birds of Prey* the hero collects novels for his half-witted mother-in-law; among those "adapted to Georgy's capacity" are some "deeply interesting romances of the sensational school, with at least nine deaths in the three volumes." In *The Doctor's Wife* (1864) one minor character is actually a sensation novelist, who thoroughly enjoys his occupation while slyly admitting that "there's only one objection to the style—it's apt to give an author a tendency towards bodies. . . . And when you've once had recourse to the stimulant of bodies, you're like a man who's accustomed to strong liquors, and to whose vitiated palate simple drinks seem flat and wishy-washy."[25] This cheerful detachment, to which even Bulwer-Lytton objected as "flippancy of tone,"[26] colors all of her fiction; where Wood is mawkish and moralizing, Braddon is jaunty, cynical, and tough. She knows exactly what she is doing; she has no exalted opinion of her material or her mission; she is quite willing and capable of playing around with her chosen conventions and making her own ironic compromises with the sticklish requirements of Victorian taste.

The critical reactions range from amusement to outrage, sometimes both at once, as in the *Examiner*'s intended critique, during the course of which the reviewer gets carried away with his own sensational tale of "Medea Blenkinsop, or the Octogamist":

> But think of the shifts and perplexities of a wife with eight husbands, being not only mysteriously married like Aurora Floyd to her noble husband's horse-trainer,

but . . . also to the Emperor of China, who writes compromising letters by each mail, the more compromising as she is also secretly married to the postman, who is of a suspicious temper . . . ; also, under peculiar circumstances, to the giant of a show that is coming to be set up at a fair in the neighborhood; also to a maniac whom she keeps in the cellar. . . .[27]

In passing the harshest judgment on "Miss Braddon and her class," the *Contemporary* brands them as practitioners of "artistic atheism in its lowest phase," a heresy in which "the existence of any law beyond the caprice of the individual is implicitly denied" and "savage gratification of sense and of personal desire is the supreme good." The *Contemporary* is quite accurate in diagnosing this as a case of "spirit . . . opposed to form";[28] Braddon and Collins, in particular, delight in exposing the arbitrary nature of the letter of the law.

Oddly enough, it is the disapproving critic in the *Christian Remembrancer* who offers the most penetrating analysis. Miss Braddon, he submits, consistently deals with "human nature . . . in a scrape. . . . And it is with people in a scrape, or ready at any moment to fall into one, that she sympathizes." Her heroines possess what might be called "expansive natures," impetuous and undisciplined, while their villainous counterparts, from Lady Audley to Olivia Marchmont, ominously fulfill the role of "the ordinary feminine ideal." The Braddon ethos is compared, unfavorably, with that of the long-forgotten author of *Lost and Saved,* in which a titled murderess is left in "unabated prosperity" at the end:

> If Mrs. Norton attacks apparent and recognized respectability, professes to unmask false pretences, and shows that the worst people are those most in the world's good graces, Miss Braddon, the first and, at present, pre-eminent sensation writer, sets herself to defy and expose the real thing. Her bad people don't pretend only to be good: they *are* respectable; they really work, nay slave, in the performance of domestic duties and the most accredited of all good works. . . . Her odious females are all remarkable for conformity to the respectable type.[29]

Here, of course, the *Christian Remembrancer* falls into the same confusion of goodness with respectability, of virtue with domesticity, that Braddon deliberately combats in the best of her fiction. The feminine ideal, as she portrays it, is potentially treacherous, for both the women who conform and the men who worship them; the standard feminine qualities—childishness, self-suppression, the talent for pleasing—inherently contain the seeds of their own destruction. By reversing conventional expectations, within the safe and familiar framework of stage melodrama, Miss Braddon redefines the heroine and relocates the traditional conflict of good and evil firmly within the boundaries of middle-class domesticity. Instead of abandoning the popular conventions, she circumvents them, using them against themselves, investing them with a new ironic significance.

Lady Audley's Secret (1862), denounced on all sides as "one of the most noxious books of modern times,"[30] is also credited with the introduction of a new type of villain-ess—the frail, fair-haired child-woman with murder and bigamy in her heart. Lady Audley's beauty and charm, de-scribed without editorial comment at the start of the novel, exactly suits the Victorian style: "The innocence and can-dor of an infant beamed in Lady Audley's fair face, and shone out of her large and liquid blue eyes. The rosy lips, the delicate nose, the profusion of fair ringlets, all contrib-uted to preserve to her beauty the character of extreme youth and freshness"; "It was so natural to Lucy Audley to be childish, that no one would have wished to see her oth-erwise."[31] She is irresistibly merry and playful, tripping about the garden, "warbling long cadences for very happi-ness of heart, and looking as fresh and radiant as the flow-ers in her hands." Not only that, she is benevolent, in ac-cordance with the persistent Victorian cliché for the truly virtuous heroine: "Wherever she went she seemed to take joy and brightness with her. In the cottages of the poor her fair face shone like a sunbeam. She would sit for a quarter of an hour talking to some old woman, and apparently as pleased with the admiration of a toothless crone as if she had been listening to the compliments of a marquis."

Her general reward is that "everyone loved, admired, and praised her . . . everybody, high and low, united in declar-ing that Lucy Graham [her alias] was the sweetest girl that ever lived"; her more particular reward is the "pure" and generous love of Sir Michael Audley, a rich and elderly baronet. After her marriage to Sir Michael, which of course is bigamous, Lady Audley successfully performs all the duties of a conventional well-to-do wife, whether engaged in displaying her domestic graces at the tea table or anx-iously nursing her husband, with "the beautiful blue eyes watching Sir Michael's slumbers; the soft, white hands tending on his waking moments; the low musical voice soothing his loneliness, cheering and consoling his declin-ing years." In spite of the initial bigamy, there is not even any question of her chastity, usually all-sufficient for Vic-torian womanly virtue; she is too cold and calculating to be subject to sexual passion: "The common temptations that assail and shipwreck some women had no terror for me. I would have been your true and pure wife to the end of time, though I had been surrounded by a legion of tempters." She is to all appearances the embodiment of the feminine ideal; no one, not even her husband, can tell the difference under ordinary circumstances. Although her nephew, Robert Audley, comes to think of her as an "arch trickster . . . an all-accomplished deceiver," there is no need for deception in her performance as Sir Michael's wife; as long as she can keep her secrets and her position, she is perfectly happy in the conventional mold. This is what she still clings to after she has finally been unmasked:

> I was very happy in the first triumph and grandeur of my new position, very grateful to the hand that had lifted me to it. In the sunshine of my own happiness I felt, for the first time in my life, for the miseries of others. . . . I took pleasure in acts of kindness and be-nevolence. . . . I dispensed happiness on every side. I saw myself loved as well as admired, and I think I might have been a good woman for the rest of my life, if fate would have allowed me to be so.

In sketching the portrait of her "beautiful fiend," Braddon insists upon all the most impeccable of feminine attributes, which themselves lead to bigamy and murder. Lucy Aud-ley may claim, with justice, that she is only doing what is expected of her as a Victorian lady. Like Rosamond Vincy in Eliot's *Middlemarch,* she has an instinct for pleasing, for "mak[ing] herself agreeable to everyone," especially men; when her stepdaughter remonstrates with her, she an-swers, "I suppose you mean to infer by all that, that I'm deceitful. Why, I can't help smiling at people, and speak-ing prettily to them. I know I'm no *better* than the rest of the world; but I can't help it if I'm *pleasanter*. It's consti-tutional." She traces her crimes, again with some justice, to the universal and absolute necessity of finding a hus-band: "I had learnt that which in some indefinite manner or other every school-girl learns sooner or later—I learned that my ultimate fate in life depended upon my marriage, and I concluded that if I was indeed prettier than my schoolfellows, I ought to marry better than any one of them." When the governess Lucy Graham, apparently de-serted by her first husband and teaching under an assumed name, is offered the dazzling opportunity of marrying a baronet, her employer, Mrs. Dawson, impresses on her, in much the same terms, the advantages of the match; in-deed, the Dawsons "would have thought it something more than madness in a penniless girl to reject such an offer." Braddon herself, in the narrator's voice, charts the begin-ning of Lady Audley's history in the "frivolous, feminine sins" of her unthinking youth, in the "petty cruelties" en-couraged by the "right divine" of her good looks. The un-derside of the feminine image, as Braddon exposes it, is anything but pretty: beneath her "innocent frivolity" is shallowness and greed; beneath her childishness is selfish-ness; beneath "the virtue of constancy" is "the vice of heartlessness"; beneath the smiles are deceit and "petty woman's tyranny." Because people believe in the myth, which she so closely approximates, Lady Audley nearly gets away with her masquerade. When she refuses to heed Robert's final warning, it is because she is still supremely confident of her dominion over her indulgent husband; as she boasts to her stepdaughter: "he will believe anything that I tell him."

In *Lady Audley's Secret,* the threat of crime and insanity has penetrated not only into respectable society, but into the family circle itself and into the heart of that circle, the wifely paragon. Lady Audley is completely natural, com-pletely satisfied, in the feminine role. She is childlike and passionless, in the approved Victorian manner, exploiting her charms efficiently to manipulate others but unencum-bered by any active sexuality of her own. She certainly has no objection to the conventional middle-class values of domesticity and respectability; in fact, she commits bigamy in order to get them and murder in order to keep them. Although Lucy Audley is a social climber, originally marrying both husbands for money and position, she em-bodies an internal threat to the respectable classes because she identifies with them; she wants what they value and brilliantly parodies their ideal. It is the validity of this ideal that Braddon repeatedly calls into question, exploring its latent dangers and possibilities in the character of Lady Audley, this "childish, helpless, babyfied little creature," whom even her accuser pities on that account. The import of Lady Audley's crime of bigamy is that the conventional marriage, which remains at the center of so much of Victorian fiction, becomes an illusion. But it is a persuasive illusion, one that only the special knowledge of the amateur detective is sufficient to dispel. During the progress of his investigation after his friend George Talboys, the inconvenient first husband, has been pushed down a well, Robert Audley begins to view the domestic scene at Audley Court with new insight: "What a pleasant picture it might have been, had he been able to look upon it ignorantly, seeing no more than others saw, looking no further than a stranger could look. But with the black cloud which he saw brooding over it, what an arch mockery, what a diabolical delusion it seemed." After the impostor's secrets have finally been revealed, we are left with the image of Robert Audley "brooding over the desolate hearth" with a "sense of strange bewilderment," wondering at "the change in that old house which, until the day of his friend's disappearance, had been so pleasant a home for all who sheltered beneath its hospitable roof." Sir Michael Audley's domestic idyll is discovered to be founded on lies and crime; the unsettling implication is that it could happen under any such "hospitable roof," that the reality of the middle-class dream is not automatically assured. At the end of the novel, as many marriages have been destroyed as have been newly created.

If Lady Audley represents the feminine ideal as would-be murderer, Aurora Floyd, in the novel of that name, represents the *femme fatale* as heroine. For this second smash hit in a row (1863), Miss Braddon exploits the melodramatic stereotype of the villainess, again slyly reversing its accumulated connotations. Aurora Floyd, the banker's daughter, is an imperious, tempestuous, dark-haired beauty, who exerts a powerful fascination over her unwilling admirer, the fastidious gentleman Talbot Bulstrode: she seems "barbarous, intoxicating, dangerous, and maddening"; "she is like everything that is beautiful, and strange, and wicked, and unwomanly, and bewitching."[32] At the same time, there is "a certain gloomy shade [that] would sometimes steal over her countenance," the sign of a "horrible fatality," a "frightful curse," that pursues her. In spite of his misgivings, Bulstrode proposes marriage and is accepted, only to find out about the scandalous rumors connected with her attendance at a French boarding school, from which she once ran away. When he demands an explanation as a prelude to withdrawing his proposal, she demands that he trust her, while hinting mysteriously at her own guilt: "I am only nineteen; but within the last two years of my life I have done enough to break my father's heart." It turns out that Braddon has impishly duplicated the plot of her previous novel in all its memorable details: Aurora, like Lady Audley, has a secret; she commits bigamy; she attempts to bribe her former husband and ends up suspected of murdering him. The surprise is not that she becomes a bigamist but, as *Temple Bar* observes, "that she is an amiable one."[33] Once again, Braddon mixes up the approved

categories, to the reviewers' dismay: "So far as real life sees, or ever has seen anything like this, it is among the Cleopatras and other witch-like charmers who have misled mankind; not among wives and daughters of repute in Christian or even in heathen times."[34]

The essential difference between Aurora Floyd and her lovely predecessor is passion, which Lady Audley lacks and Aurora has in abundance. She is given to sudden rages, of the kind which expend themselves "in sharply cruel words, and convulsive rendings of lace and ribbon, or coroner's juries might have to sit even oftener than they do." On one such occasion, "sublime in her passion," she horse-whips an imbecilic stablehand who has mistreated her dog; on another, she enters into incriminating dialogue, overheard by an eavesdropper, with her legal husband: "'You'd like to stab me, or shoot me, or strangle me, as I stand here; wouldn't you, now?' asked the trainer mockingly. 'Yes,' cried Aurora, 'I would!'" In the course of the novel, she loves three different men and marries two of them, including her father's groom. The nature of her attraction to this James Conyers is evident: "You give him credit for thoughts to match with his dark, violet-hued eyes, and the exquisite modelling of his mouth and chin; you give him a mind as aesthetically perfect as his face and figure, and you recoil on discovering what a vulgar, every-day sword may lurk under that beautiful scabbard." Even though she elopes with him as a schoolgirl, pays him to leave her alone, and lies to her father about his supposed death, Aurora is excused as a "wretched girl, whose worst sin had been to mistake a bad man for a good one; the ignorant trustfulness of a child who is ready to accept any shabby pilgrim for an exiled nobleman or a prince in disguise!" While the narrator admits that "there is much need of apology for her," Aurora Floyd is ultimately vindicated and established in the role of heroine.

Like all English sensation novelists, Braddon is hampered by the code of Grundyism, which makes bigamy an acceptable subterfuge as long as the various ceremonies are duly performed. It has been argued that her compliance with this code leads to a kind of "thwarted sensationalism which did not at bottom make sense," because "she would falsify her own realism by explaining everything away."[35] Actually, Braddon takes full advantage of the prevailing hypocrisy to indulge her heroine in such questionable escapades as running away with a horse trainer before settling down into conventional domesticity. Because of the erroneous obituary in the sporting news, Aurora Floyd is technically in the right; her worst mistake is in concealing her past instead of suing for a divorce from the faithless Conyers. Her second, and bigamous, marriage to the Yorkshire squire John Mellish is ironically more genuine than her legal one. Although she decamps temporarily after the murder of Conyers ("Good-bye, dear home, in which I was an impostor and a cheat"), the narrator obviously approves of the instinct that tells her, "There is no wrong you can do him so bitter as to desert him. There is no unhappiness you can bring upon him equal to the unhappiness of losing you." John Mellish, unlike the retired suitor

Talbot Bulstrode, is tolerant of anything that is Aurora's doing because he is unconditionally in love with her. Not only does he take her back, privately remarrying her, he is willing to do so even while he still thinks she is involved in the murder. The "cruel expiation" for her youthful folly, which causes her to carry on like Bret Harte's Selina Sedilia, is certainly moderate by melodramatic standards. In spite of that unfortunate interlude when Conyers has reappeared and she offers to send him to Australia, thus deliberately continuing the bigamy committed in good faith, Aurora Floyd is granted her happy ending: "So we leave Aurora, a little changed, a shade less defiantly bright, perhaps, but unspeakably beautiful and tender, bending over the cradle of her first-born." This would be inconceivable in popular melodrama, or in Mrs. Henry Wood; it subverts the essential meaning of the heroine, whose absolute purity or sacrificial death true melodrama unequivocally demands.

In *John Marchmont's Legacy* (1863), Braddon proposes a curious amalgam of the darkly passionate heroine (Aurora Floyd) and the conventionally respectable villainess (Lady Audley). The character of Olivia Marchmont is wildly overdrawn but interesting in concept. The strained histrionics, borrowed from the axiomatic tragedy queen of the popular stage, are employed in a new way, not to identify the typical sexually threatening villainess, but to approach a study in sexual repression. Endowed with the "raging fire" of a passionate nature, with "the ambition of a Semiramis, the courage of a Boadicea, the resolution of a Lady MacBeth,"[36] Olivia Marchmont might seem cut out to be one of Miss Braddon's favorites, in the tempestuous mold of Aurora Floyd. Her explosive passions, however, are held rigidly in check by her "sense of duty," which her clergyman father describes as "more powerful than any other sentiment." No wonder the *Christian Remembrancer* bridles at the terms in which Braddon introduces her villainess: "Yes, the life of this woman is told in these few words: she did her duty. . . . She was a good woman. The bishop of the diocese had specially complimented her for her active devotion to that holy work which falls somewhat heavily upon the only daughter of a widowed rector." In fact, she is rather too perfect, with "no blemish of mortal weakness upon the good deeds she performed"; and unlike Lady Audley, she is not loved by "the recipients of her bounties," who, "seeing her so far off, grew afraid of her, even by reason of her goodness." She is "Church-of-England charity personified; meting out all mercies by line and rule; doing good with a note-book and a pencil in her hand." At the same time, there is something obsessive and masochistic in her charity. Even in her girlhood, "her life was one perpetual sacrifice to her father's parishioners. There was no natural womanly vanity, no simple girlish fancy, which this woman had not trodden under foot." And later, in her struggle against serious temptation, "she made a routine of penance for herself . . . going long distances on foot to visit her poor, when she might have ridden in her carriage; courting exposure to rain and foul weather; wearing herself out with unnecessary fatigue, and returning footsore to her desolate home to fall fainting into the strong arms of her grim attendant." Religion becomes an indirect outlet for her passion, an instrument of self-suppression and self-torture for this "woman who was for ever fighting against her nature; . . . for ever measuring herself by the standard she had set up for her self-abasement." Whenever she feels particularly restive, she finds relief in writing sermons—"fierce denunciatory protests against the inherent wickedness of the human heart."

Although it is reiterated that she "tried, and tried unceasingly, to do her duty, and to be good," Olivia's secret is that "she was weary of her life," and further, that she is infatuated with the hero, her boyish cousin Edward Arundel. Because of her "narrow," rigorous existence, because she scorns to "fling myself upon my knees at his feet," this unexpressed and unrequited love becomes the single focus of her "volcanic forces," "until that which should have been a sentiment became a madness." As in other Victorian fiction, female sexuality is connected with insanity—here not in itself or in its unbridled state, as in Reade's novels, but in its systematic repression. The evil is in the thwarting of impulse, which causes Olivia's mysterious illness and leads to her mistreatment of her stepdaughter Mary Marchmont, the ill-fated object of Edward Arundel's affection. For Olivia, love is "a dark and terrible passion, a thing to be concealed, as monomaniacs have sometimes contrived to keep the secret of their mania, until it burst forth at last, fatal and irrepressible, in some direful work of wreck and ruin." Impulse, indeed, is the greatest virtue in Braddon's fictional characters; she suggests that in the case of sexual desire, abandonment, like that of Aurora Floyd, is less destructive than obsessive control: "Better to have been sorrowful Magdalene, forgiven for her love and tears, than this cold, haughty, stainless woman, who had never been able to learn the sublime lessons which so many sinners have taken meekly to heart."

In her despairing jealousy, Olivia Marchmont consigns herself to her attendant devils, giving free reign to "the spirit of a murderess raging in her breast." Twice she drives her stepdaughter to flee from home, and afterward participates in the villainous Paul Marchmont's conspiracy to keep Mary and her child hidden away while he usurps the inheritance of Marchmont Towers. Olivia finally reveals the plot on the day of Edward's second marriage, only because she is jealous of his second bride. In spite of the fatal adherence to duty, Braddon seems to admire this strange villainess, who "had all the elements of greatness" and more passionate energy than the pallid hero and heroine; in fact, the author seems to warm to her own creation once Olivia has lost all control. In the end, the childish, weak-minded Mary Marchmont, briefly restored to her husband, is killed off by consumption, and the other good characters are sparingly provided with "that modified happiness which is chastened by the memory of sorrow." Olivia Marchmont, never exposed or punished, simply "burnt out" at last, is left to her everlasting rounds of charity. Although subject to fits of mental abstraction, she is looked upon by the local villagers "with considerable respect, as a heroine by whose exertions Paul Marchmont's villainy had been discovered." This is not quite the sort of poetic justice to which Victorian readers had become accustomed.

With her revolting combination of "nasty sentiments and equivocal heroines,"[37] M. E. Braddon brashly challenges the two most cherished myths of her middle-class Victorian audience: respectability and the feminine ideal. In her novels, the worst sort of criminality—passionless and calculating—is always associated with a concern for appearances and a high standing in the world's estimation. Philip Sheldon, the murderer in **Birds of Prey** and **Charlotte's Inheritance,** is an "eminently respectable" dentist who later becomes a stockbroker with his ill-gotten gains. These are prosaic occupations, and Mr. Sheldon is a prosaic man, totally absorbed in the business of making money. In the midst of his early financial difficulties, he keeps up a spotless establishment, distinguished by a neat display case of "glistening white teeth and impossibly red gums," causing his neighbors to reflect that "a householder with such a doorstep and such muslin curtains could not be other than the most correct of mankind." The "irreproachable neatness" of his person is complemented by his well-regulated behavior; he gets away with the murder of his wife's first husband, simply because he seems such an unlikely candidate for committing it, even to the servant who has unwittingly helped him to administer the poison: "Day by day she saw the man whom she had suspected, going about the common business of his life, coldly serene of aspect, untroubled of manner, confronting fortune with his head erect, . . . haunted by no dismal shadows, subject to no dark hours of remorse, no sudden access of despair, always equable, business-like, and untroubled; and she told herself that such a man could not be guilty of the unutterable horror she had imagined." This view of him is entirely accurate, except in the conclusion drawn from it; even when he takes the second risk of slowly poisoning his stepdaughter, Sheldon's dreams are troubled only by the mundane images of financial ruin: "a blackboard fixed against the wall of a place of public resort, a blackboard on which appeared his own name"; the sound of the "three deliberate strokes" of the hammer at the Stock Exchange, which precedes the announcement of default. It is the peculiar danger of the modern murderer that he is no different from anyone else, that he inhabits the most ordinary dwellings and executes his crimes in the most scientific and businesslike fashion. "And this is our modern civilization!" exclaims the hero, "Give me the desert or the jungle. The sons of Bowanee are no worse than Mr. Sheldon, and one might be on one's guard against them."

Murder of course has its entertaining aspects, and there is no suggestion that it has the power to dismantle the mechanism of a whole society. That power is reserved to female sexuality, which in the Victorian theory necessarily invites illicit expression. Mrs. Oliphant is not alone in drawing parallels between the sensation novel and the fall of the Roman Empire. "There can be no possible doubt," she fulminates in the pages of *Blackwood's*, "that the wickedness of man is less ruinous, less disastrous to the world in general, than the wickedness of woman. That is the climax of

all misfortunes to the race."[38] Within the limits ordained by Mudie's Circulating Library, Braddon endeavors to counteract this most firmly entrenched of Victorian dogmas. In popular melodrama she finds the perfect vehicle: the heroine's purity, under attack by the villain, is already the central issue; she needs only to reverse, or rather to qualify, the final outcome.

According to the *Examiner,* Miss Braddon's "style and matter" are "perfectly well suited" to *Reynolds' Miscellany* but ought not to be given "currency . . . among educated readers."[39] It is true that she supplies a direct link between the sensation novel and the "kitchen literature" of the penny journals, but it is also true that she succeeded in capturing the mainstream market as G. W. M. Reynolds never did. In spite of her slapdash methods of composition, she is a novelist of genuine talent and vitality; even Dean Mansel is forced to admit that "the skill of the builder deserves to be employed on better materials."[40] This "comet of literature,"[41] in the *Contemporary's* hopeful phrase, had remarkable staying power. Although she never quite lived down her reputation as the author of **Lady Audley's Secret,**[42] she later moved on to other genres besides the sensation novel and outlasted the initial opprobrium through sheer longevity. At the end of the century, she receives affectionate tribute in the *Academy* as "part of England; she has woven herself into it; without her it would be different. . . . She is in the encyclopaedias; she ought to be in the dictionaries."[43] It is ironic to find a mellowed Mrs. Oliphant, thirty years after the series of articles in *Blackwood's,* crediting Miss Braddon's novels with "some sense of life as a whole, and some reflection of the honest sentiments of humanity, amid the froth of flirtation and folly which has lately invaded, like a destroying flood, the realms of fiction."[44] By the time of Miss Braddon's death during World War I, her novels seemed old-fashioned and pleasantly cosy, objects of a wistful nostalgia in an uncertain age.

Notes

1. Bret Harte, *Condensed Novels* (Boston: Osgood, 1871), pp. 61-62; pp. 64-65; p. 68.

2. Kathleen Tillotson, "The Lighter Reading of the Eighteen-Sixties," Introduction to Wilkie Collins, *The Woman In White* (Boston: Houghton Mifflin, 1969), p. xiii.

3. [Margaret Oliphant], "Sensation Novels," *Blackwood's* XCI (May 1862), p. 567.

4. "Our Female Sensation Novelists," from *Christian Remembrancer,* reprinted in Littell's *Living Age* LXXVIII (August 22, 1863), p. 354.

5. "The Popular Novels of the Year," *Fraser's* LXVIII (August 1863), p. 262.

6. Henry James, "Miss Braddon," in *Notes and Reviews* (Cambridge, Mass.: Dunster House, 1921), p. 115.

7. "Mrs. Wood and Miss Braddon," from *Examiner,* reprinted in Littell's *Living Age* LXXVII (April 18, 1863), p. 99.

8. "Popular Novels," *Fraser's*, pp. 255-56, 255.

9. Michael R. Booth, *English Melodrama* (London: Herbert Jenkins, 1965), p. 153.

10. The tactful description of his son, Charles W. Wood, in *Memorials of Mrs. Henry Wood,* quoted in Malcolm Elwin, *Victorian Wallflowers* (London: J. Cape, 1934), p. 235. Elwin is the only readily available source of biographical data.

11. Quoted in ibid., p. 245.

12. J. D. Jump, "Weekly Reviewing in the Eighteen-Sixties," *Review of English Studies* III (July 1952), p. 261.

13. Mrs. Henry Wood, *Verner's Pride* (Leipzig: Tauchnitz, 1863), I, 68. All quotations from this edition.

14. See Booth, *English Melodrama,* pp. 153-54.

15. Mrs. Henry Wood, *East Lynne* (London and Glasgow: Collins, n.d.), pp. 291, 225. All quotations from this edition.

16. For the connections between *East Lynne* and the Divorce Law of 1857, which provided "legal punishment" for the adulteress in the form of a second wife, see Margaret M. Maison, "Adulteresses in Agony," *Listener* LXV (January 19, 1961), pp. 133-34. In the novel, Mr. Carlyle sues for divorce but does not think it right to remarry until after the reported death of his former wife. Because of the divorce, however, he is not legally a bigamist.

17. See Booth, *English Melodrama,* p. 79.

18. W. B. Maxwell, *Time Gathered* (New York and London: Appleton-Century, 1938), p. 269.

19. Henry James, "Miss Braddon," p. 116.

20. For biographical details, see Michael Sadleir, *Things Past* (London: Constable, 1944); Norman Donaldson, Introduction to M. E. Braddon, *Lady Audley's Secret* (New York: Dover, 1974); and Robert Lee Wolff, *Sensational Victorian: The Life and Fiction of Mary Elizabeth Braddon* (New York: Garland, 1979).

21. Letter to Bulwer-Lytton, in Robert Lee Wolff, "Devoted Disciple: The Letters of Mary Elizabeth Braddon to Sir Edward Bulwer-Lytton, 1862-1873," *Harvard Library Bulletin* XXII (January and April, 1974), p. 10.

22. Letter to Bulwer-Lytton, in ibid., p. 12.

23. M. E. Braddon, *Birds of Prey* (New York: Harper, 1867), p. 139; *Charlotte's Inheritance* (New York: Harper, 1868), p. 84. All quotations from these editions.

24. Quoted in Edmund Yates, *Fifty Years of London Life* (New York: Harper, 1885), pp. 336-37.

25. M. E. Braddon, *The Doctor's Wife* (London: Simpkin, 1890), p. 42.

26. See Sadleir, *Things Past,* p. 70.

27. "Mrs. Wood and Miss Braddon," *Living Age,* p. 100.

28. H. A. Page [A. H. Japp], "The Morality of Literary Art," *Contemporary* V (June 1867), p. 178.

29. "Our Female Sensation Novelists," *Living Age,* pp. 367, 366, 364-66.

30. "Sensation Novelists: Miss Braddon," *North British Review* XLIII (September 1865), p. 96. For a feminist interpretation of *Lady Audley* and other sensation novels, see Elaine Showalter, *A Literature of Their Own* (Princeton: Princeton University Press, 1977), pp. 153-81.

31. M. E. Braddon, *Lady Audley's Secret,* pp. 35, 186. All quotations from the Dover edition.

32. M. E. Braddon, *Aurora Floyd* (New York: Frank Leslie, n.d.), pp. 25, 36. All quotations from this edition.

33. "Our Novels. The Sensational School," *Temple Bar* XXIX (July 1870), p. 415.

34. "Our Female Sensation Novelists," *Living Age,* p. 368.

35. Sadleir, *Things Past,* p. 79.

36. M. E. Braddon, *John Marchmont's Legacy* (Leipzig: Tauchnitz, 1864), I, 176, 181. All quotations from this edition.

37. [Margaret Oliphant], "Novels," *Blackwood's* CII (September 1867), p. 280.

38. Ibid., p. 275.

39. "Mrs. Wood and Miss Braddon," *Living Age,* p. 99.

40. [H. L. Mansel], "Sensation Novels," *Quarterly* CXIII (April 1863), p. 491.

41. Page, *Contemporary,* p. 178.

42. Sadleir in *Things Past* offers the opinion that "for forty years at least it [*Lady Audley's Secret*] so dominated its author's life that she had persistently to write more or less to its pattern" (p. 74); the opposite opinion—that she deserted the sensation novel after 1873—is argued in Benjamin M. Nyberg, "The Novels of Mary Elizabeth Braddon: A Reappraisal of the Author of *Lady Audley's Secret*" (unpublished doctoral dissertation, University of Colorado, 1965).

43. "Miss Braddon: An Enquiry," *Academy* LVIII (October 14, 1899), p. 431.

44. Margaret Oliphant, *The Victorian Age of English Literature* (New York: Tait, 1892), pp. 494-95. Although Mrs. Oliphant has mellowed, her style has not improved.

Jeanne F. Bedell (essay date 1983)

SOURCE: "Amateur and Professional Detectives in the Fiction of Mary Elizabeth Braddon," in *Clues: A Journal of Detection,* Vol. 4, No. 1, Spring/Summer, 1983, pp. 19-34.

[*In the following essay, Bedell examines the role of detectives in Braddon's fiction.*]

Unlike Wilkie Collins, her chief rival as a writer of sensation novels, Mary Elizabeth Braddon (1835-1915) is now little known, even to students of mystery and detective fiction. Yet from her first great success, the notorious ***Lady Audley's Secret*** (1862), to her skillful and subdued portraits of Edwardian and Georgian society, Braddon was one of the best known and most popular authors of her time. A youthful and exuberant Henry James began his discussion of "Miss Braddon," as she was always known to her readers, by saying that "Miss Aurora Floyd, as half the world knows, was a young lady who got into no end of trouble by marrying her father's groom."[1] James credited Braddon with creation of the sensation novel and attributed her popularity to "a grim determination to succeed" he called "pluck" and defined as a "strictly respectful" attitude toward her audience and an ability to "keep up" with "delicate fluctuations of the public taste."[2]

James was correct in his appraisal of Braddon's deliberate attention to public taste. Both her humorous portrayal of sensation novelist Sigismund Smith in ***The Doctor's Wife*** (1864) and her letters to Sir Edward Bulwer-Lytton indicate an unusual, if somewhat chagrined, appreciation of public demands. Smith says that his readers ask for "plot, and plenty of it; surprises, and plenty of 'em; mystery thick as a November fog" (p. 40), and Braddon told Bulwer-Lytton that "the amount of crime, treachery, murder, slow poisoning, & general infamy required by the Half penny reader is something terrible."[3] When ***The Doctor's Wife,*** her first attempt at a serious novel of character, did not sell so well as the sensation books, she complained that her audience liked "strong meat" and that "the public shilling can only be extracted with strong measures."[4] During her long career Braddon continued to expand and refine her approaches to fiction, but she could, as she said, "write about villains and villainesses by the mile,"[5] and she exercised this talent to provide Victorian readers with a thrill-a-chapter novels and modern critics with insight into the development of suspense fiction and changing attitudes toward detectives and the art of detection. In particular, analysis of her novels reveals that many conventions, situations, and plot devices we tend to think of as modern were commonplace in the suspense fiction of Victorian England.

Braddon did not, of course, either early in her career, or later in the century when the genre had become established, write detective stories as such. Like Wilkie Collins, whom she once called her "literary father,"[6] Braddon wrote what reviewers of the 1860s christened sensation fiction, a literary form that emphasized secrecy, deceit, crime and mystery in ordinary middle-class domestic settings. In archetypal form, the "novel-with-a-secret," as Kathleen Tillotson has aptly described it,[7] is set in stately country houses or sedate suburban villas where "a taint of mystery and suspense . . . poisoned the atmosphere" (***Strange World,*** p. 86). Within the three-volume format, which typically included one or more subplots and leisurely descriptions of manners, furniture, and clothing (for the female readers who were the sub-genre's most ardent supporters), as well as a strong love interest, there were, however, a number of approaches to detection and a varied cast of amateur and professional detectives. Amateurs predominate; professional or official detectives are often incompetent, unimaginative or greedy, their efficiency impaired by excessive interest in the reward offered for capture of the culprit. But the amateurs, motivated by friendship, family ties or romantic devotion, display intelligence and ingenuity in identifying criminals and discovering the secrets in the past which underlie the crimes of the present. Lawyers, whose professional experience has accustomed them to careful examination of evidence, are most common; literary men, who provided Braddon with opportunity to comment on methods of composition and publication and the literary scene, appear frequently in a cast of detectives which also includes a clergyman, a member of Parliament, a bank clerk and an ex-army officer turned confidence man. Women are usually the victims, not the pursuers of criminals, but Mildred Griswold in ***The Fatal Three*** (1888) successfully uncovers the secrets in her husband's past which have destroyed their marriage, and Kathleen Mortemar in ***Under the Red Flag*** (1886) determinedly and systematically searches Paris in the confusing and dangerous period following the fall of the Commune for the murderer of her husband.

Clever crime and its skillful detection were significant elements in Braddon's first success, ***Lady Audley's Secret,*** whose heroine, outwardly the sweet-tempered, contented "blonde angel" beloved by Victorian authors, is actually a bigamist, arsonist and would-be murderess who eradicates her past by a falsified tombstone and a carefully constructed new identity. His suspicions aroused by the abrupt disappearance of his friend George Tallboys, Robert Audley follows a well-devised set of clues which leads to his discovery of Lady Audley's real identity, her bigamous marriage to his uncle, and her attempted murder of Tallboys, her first husband. Concealment of the past is also a focal point in ***The Day Will Come*** (1889), where James Dalbrook investigates the murder of his cousin's husband and in the process finds in her father's past a secret double life which reveals both murderer and motive for murder.

Wyllard's Weird (1885) is similar and serves well to illustrate Braddon's approach to the creation of suspense and to detection. Like many Victorian writers, she used the double life theme to expose hypocrisy among the seemingly respectable and to comment on the frequent confusion of appearance with truth. When a young French-woman is pushed from a Cornish train as it crosses a gorge, Bothwell Grahame, cousin of Julian Wyllard's wife Dora, is suspected of the crime because he refuses to discuss the reasons for his presence on the train or his visit to Plymouth. At first the novel focuses on the effects of suspicion on the innocent; Grahame is shunned by acquaintances, and even the girl who loves him begins to wonder if life does not resemble fiction:

She had read of darkest deaths, of strange contradictions in human nature, mysterious workings of the human heart. Hitherto she had considered these lurid lights, these black shadows as the figments of the romancer's fancy. Now she began to ask herself if they might not find their counterparts in fact.

She had read of gentlemanlike murderers—assassins of good bearing and polished manners—Eugene Aram, Count Fosco, and many more of the same school. What if Bothwell Grahame were such as these, hiding behind his frank and easy manner the violent passions of the criminal?

(pp. 66-67)

Like numerous subsequent murder suspects, Grahame had refused to account for his whereabouts in order to protect a woman's reputation: "As a man of honour . . . I could not do more or less than I did" (p. 69). Distressed by her cousin's situation, upset by her husband's indifference to it, and convinced that "Nothing but the discovery of the real murderer can ever set Bothwell right with his fellow men" (p. 78), Dora asks her former fiancé, local magistrate Edward Heathcote, to clear his name.

Once Heathcote begins his investigations, the emphasis in the novel shifts to the process of detection and reveals two dissimilar but typical attitudes toward detectives. Dora disapproves of her husband's old friend, criminal lawyer Joseph Distin, because he reminds her of "police agents in French novels. A man of low birth and education, with nothing but native instinct to recommend him; a man whose chief talent is for disguises, and who passes his life in a false beard and eyebrows, in the company of thieves and murderers, whom it is his business to make friends with and then betray" (p. 31). Dora's view of the detective as spy and betrayer, commonplace in early mystery fiction, seems obsolete within the context of the novel as it was in fact by 1885. Braddon's portrait of French detective Félix Drubarde and Heathcote's own consuming detective fever present a positive attitude toward the profession, and the plight of Bothwell Grahame, as Dora's request testifies, necessitates detective activity. Drubarde is elderly and charming; dressed in white linen, he entertains Heathcote in his rooftop garden where he grows nasturtiums, honeysuckle, geraniums and mignonette and sits placidly smoking cigars. Heathcote, who possesses "The detective instinct, which is a characteristic of every well-trained lawyer's mind," finds his desire to solve the crime has "suddenly developed into almost a passion" (p. 125). The distinction between amateur and professional detectives is essentially that established by Poe: "Professional acumen . . . is apt to run in grooves—to be too intent upon following the practical and the possible, to shut out the romantic element, to strangle the imagination, and to forget that it is very often by following the apparently impossible that we arrive at the truth" (p. 126).

Heathcote's methods are, however, essentially practical and inductive, not intuitive. Recognizing immediately that he cannot discover the identity of the murderer without

first knowing that of the victim, he uses an inscription in the dead girl's locket to trace her to a convent in Britany where he comments that only by "working backwards" will he be able to find a solution to the crime. With Drubarde's help he reconstructs the brutal murder of the girl's aunt, actress Marie Prevol, and her lover in the forest of St. Germain ten years earlier. Marie had been the mistress of a mysterious Englishman known only as M. Georges, and since he was both jealous and inclined to violence, there was little doubt that he had committed the crime. The real mystery lay in his identity; he had visited Marie only at night when he led a Bohemian life with artists and journalists, and no one knew his real name or the source of his income. Told that it will be impossible to discover Georges' identity so long after the crime, Heathcote responds by saying that immediately after its commission Georges would have been alert, all his thoughts concentrated on escaping detection, but that now he will have "grown careless." Heathcote conducts a series of interviews, in themselves vignettes of Parisian life and character, with a starving seamstress, a lady's maid turned concierge, and a boulevard gossip columnist; their information gives him a clear picture of the personality and tastes of Georges. This perseverance is, of course, rewarded. Aided by chance, which Braddon, like Collins, refers to as the workings of Providence, Heathcote discovers a secret door in the chambers occupied by Julian Wyllard during the years in which he made his fortune in the Bourse. Heathcote's suspicions of Wyllard prove correct when, through information supplied by the journalist, he visits an artist who had been an intimate friend of Georges and purchases a drawing of the man, "a perfect likeness of Wyllard, so steeped in hypocrisy that he could defy suspicion" (p. 315), and proves that he had killed Marie's niece to gain possession of letters he had written the actress.

A few of the clues which point to Wyllard are typically Victorian: he had proposed to another man's fiancée; he is insensitive to his wife's worries about her cousin. But most would be familiar to modern readers of detective stories: immediately after the murder he shuts himself in his study to attend to correspondence and is surprised by his wife while burning a lock of hair; he makes a sudden trip to Paris while Heathcote is carrying on his investigations there; he mocks Heathcote's efforts and refers to his "detective temper—the genius of the heaven-born police officer" (p. 185).

Deceit, hypocrisy and the deceptive nature of appearance are also central to *Rough Justice* (1898), where the villain, like Godfrey Ablewhite in *The Moonstone* (1868), is a smooth-tongued ladies' man who serves on numerous charity committees. But the most thorough and sustained treatment of these themes occurs in the six-volume *tour de force Birds of Prey* (1867) and *Charlotte's Inheritance* (1868), a double sensation novel in which Braddon uses Balzac's descriptive techniques ironically to portray her villain, Philip Sheldon, an unsuccessful dentist turned stockbroker via marriage to the rich widow of a man he had poisoned. Just as the freshly starched curtains and well scrubbed doorstep of his Bloomsbury house concealed penury, so his fashionable Bayswater villa hides impending bankruptcy and serves as the seemingly respectable background against which he plots to save his faltering fortune by killing his stepdaughter and inheriting the fortune to which he thinks her heiress. These novels offer not one but four characters who function as detectives and simultaneously gather evidence about possible heirs to the fortune of an intestate clergyman and spy upon each other. A combination of interviews in both England and France, old letters, Bible entries, church records, tombstone inscriptions and paintings leads three of the men to a plausible but erroneous conclusion and one, a clever scoundrel described by Braddon as "that free-booter of civilisation, the man who lives by his wits" (*Inheritance,* p. 52), to the correct solution. Captain Horatio Paget resents his position and complains that he has been forced to "employ the services of a hired spy and to degrade myself to the level of a private inquirer" (p. 59), but he performs his tasks with verve and exults in stealing letters from a rival investigator and bribing a greedy Methodist parson. He manages not only to locate the rightful heir in France but to marry him off to his daughter and spend his declining days in comfort on the proceeds of the heir's wealth.

Seeming respectability preserves Philip Sheldon from suspicion of murder for years; in *Henry Dunbar* (1864) wealth provides a similar buffer. Ex-convict Joseph Wilmot is strangled while in the company of Dunbar, a wealthy banker returned to England after thirty-five years' absence in India. The two men had been seen to walk into a grove of trees together; only one emerged. Although Dunbar is arrested, he is released almost immediately because, as one of the policemen says, "Was it likely that a millionaire would commit a murder?" (p. 78). Wilmot's daughter, Margaret, asks her fiancé, Clement Austin, to prove that Dunbar murdered her father. In this endeavor he seeks the aid of Scotland Yard detective Henry Carter, who is astute and skillful. Carter first warns Austin that it is dangerous to begin an investigation with a conviction of a man's guilt because "you'll go hunting up evidence to bolster that conviction" (p. 259) and then, like numerous subsequent detectives, reminds his client of the need for trust between them:

> When you employ a detective officer . . . don't employ a man you can't put entire confidence in . . . if he isn't to be trusted with the dearest family secret that ever was kept sacred by an honest man, why, he's a scoundrel and you're much better off without his help. But when you've got a man that has been recommended to you by those who know him, don't confide in him by halves; don't tell him one part of your story, and keep the other half hidden from him; because, you see, working in the twilight isn't much more profitable than working in the dark
>
> (p. 264).

Carter understands that "helpful" witnesses often elaborate the evidence out of a desire to aid the police and has perfected interviewing techniques by which he gains informa-

tion without the witnesses being aware that he is really interested in the subject, Carter uncovers Wilmot's impersonation of Dunbar, a secret the reader has known from the beginning of the novel, but fails to capture the murderer because his desire to keep the reward money for himself leads him to neglect or refuse help from the local police: "Do you think I'm going to tell him my secret or let him share my gains?" (p. 282). In other ways, however, Carter is much like a modern policeman: he is "used to taking his sleep in railway carriages, and his meals at unusual hours" (p. 323), and when Margaret outwits him and enables her father to escape, he says that it's "humiliating" to have been "sold" by a young woman.

Despite these failings, surely the result of the reward system itself, Carter is both competent and honest, and Clement Austin's acknowledgment of his need for professional expertise provides a direct contrast to the solitary investigations of Maurice Clissold in *A Strange World* (1875). Here Clissold's love for actress Justina Elgood distracts him from his original purpose, to discover the murderer of his friend James Penwyn. Enlivened by Braddon's knowledge of provincial and London stages and the habits of third-rate touring companies, *A Strange World* takes Clissold to Cornwall where meeting a mentally disturbed woman who had had a "disappointment in Love" many years before, sets him on the trail of a secret in the past which proves more enthralling than the murder of his friend. The reader is aware, almost from the beginning of the novel, of the murderer's identity, but Clissold does not ever discover it—a situation almost unique in sensation fiction.

Braddon's amateur detectives are usually more successful and her one important professional, John Faunce, who is featured in two novels, *Rough Justice* and *His Darling Sin* (1899), is eminently so. Chief Inspector Faunce, who retires midway through *Rough Justice,* is an obvious descendant of Sergeant Cuff, intelligent and amiable, but he is first shown as a policeman on active service, which enhances his characterization. He lived in his district, knew its inhabitants well, and was concerned about their problems. When we first meet him, he is making enquiries about a missing child; interrupted by news of a murder, he goes to the scene of the crime and makes a thorough examination of the premises. He finds a fruiterer's bag that had once held grapes, "a valuable item in the sum of evidence" because "Crimes have been brought home to the guilty upon indications as trivial" (pp. 92-3). This careful attention to detail plus his knowledge of the area enables him to reconstruct the victim's last hours and arrest a man who had bought her the grapes, taken her to dinner and quarreled with her. He is the wrong man, but once Faunce has retired from the force, he reenters the investigation and determines the real culprit. In the second novel he is presented as an established private detective who has given "most valuable services in family matters of exceeding delicacy" (p. 101).

Faunce contributes to the narratives of both novels in which he appears and tells the reader about his background, solidly middle class, and, more interestingly, about his reading habits. He finds "a good deal of education to be got out of a respectable newspaper" (*Justice*, p. 105) and is a "devourer of novels," especially those of Balzac, Dumas, Scott and Dickens. He calls Balzac "a born detective" and is "not ashamed to confess a liking for those novels in which some mystery of guilt is woven and unraveled by the romancer" (pp. 106-07). He has read all the "criminal stories" of Collins, Gaboriau and Boisgobey but points out that when comparing his own cases to the "complications, passions and counter-passions of love, jealousy, hatred, and revenge which the novelist can elaborate," he feels "the limitations of a writer who recounts actual experiences, and those often of a most sordid kind" (p. 107). This contrast between "fact" and fiction has long been a staple of the detective story, a device used ironically to highlight the resemblance of the two. Braddon not only anticipates the tendency of modern detective fiction to use itself as a point of reference; she also emphasizes the role of fiction in creating interest in "real" sleuthing. In *His Darling Sin* one of the characters tells Faunce that "ever since I read the 'Moonstone' . . . I have been longing to meet a detective—a real detective" (p. 112). The questions put to Faunce reflect a wide knowledge of detection, a knowledge obviously derived from fiction. Faunce's easy acceptance by socially prominent clients illustrates the impact of fiction in another way, as, of course, it reflects changed attitudes toward detectives in nineteenth-century England. Arthur Haldane is surprised "to find a detective who talked like an educated man" (p. 186), but by the end of the century such terms as "paid spy" or "informer" were obsolete. In *Henry Dunbar,* published in 1864, Braddon felt compelled to apologize for her detective:

> if there is anything degrading in the office, that degradation had in no way affected him. . . . If, in the course of his duty, he had unpleasant things to do; if he had to affect friendly acquaintance with the same man whom he was haunting to the gallows; if he was called upon to worm-out chance clues to guilty secrets in the careless confidence that grows out of a friendly glass; if at times he had to stoop to acts which, in other men, would be branded as shameful and treacherous, he knew that he did his duty, and that society could not hold together unless some such men as himself . . . were willing to act as watch-dogs for the protection of the general fold . . .
>
> (p. 260).

Almost forty years later Faunce's profession is seen as admirable and his methods completely acceptable.

Faunce knows that not all members of his profession are honest and warns a client that "When a detective tells you he has to offer large bribes to get information, you may take it from me that he is either a fool or a cheat" (*Sin,* p. 197), but his own integrity is unquestionable.

In fact, only one of Braddon's detectives, the sinister Dumont in *Ishmael* (1885), is intentionally dishonest. Dumont is a member of "that semi-professional fraternity which ferrets out domestic secrets—the police of private life" (p. 249), an ex-gentleman and an ardent revolutionary. Hired by a successful builder to discover the whereabouts of his wife, or, failing that, evidence of her death, Dumont first accepts money to travel to Valparaiso, where she was last seen. He arranges for a letter to be sent from that city while he remains in Paris and squanders the travel funds on cafe life. Then, in order to claim the large reward offered for information, he presents false evidence of the wife's death and in a cleverly staged scene in which a supposedly dying sailor (he is actually an opium addict) tells Ishmael that she was drowned during a shipwreck.

Missing wives and shady detectives are as up to date as the latest best seller and a striking indication of the continuity between Braddon's mysteries and those of the present. True, her novels are lengthy, their structure less taut than that of the modern detective novel; but her penchant for description deepens characterization and enables us to see the actors in her drama against their own background and to understand their mores and values. Satirical social commentary, varied settings, a cast of characters which ranges from laundresses to duchesses and stable grooms to members of the Royal Academy, and informed discussions of such professions as medicine, stockbroking, and the theatre recreate for the modern reader the world of Victorian England.

Basically, however, Braddon's world is a familiar one to aficionados of detective fiction. Amateur detectives are usually, though not invariably, gentlemen of private means; the professional and police detectives are soundly middle class, and those from Scotland Yard are considerably sharper than "simple rural" officers. Local police call in the Yard only in difficult cases, especially when a "gentleman of property" has been attacked or killed. Policemen rely on information from the public, plodding perseverance, and common sense to track down criminals. Speculation about motives was dangerous; if twenty people had motives and the twenty-first had none, said John Mellish in *Aurora Floyd,* the twenty-first might have been the culprit: "That species of argument which builds up any hypothesis out of a series of probabilities may, after all, lead to false conclusions" (III, 4). Factual evidence is the cornerstone of good detection, and Braddon's detectives "watch people" and "ferret out facts," maintain networks of contacts, and rely on friends in advantageous positions for help. Like their modern counterparts, the detectives are not infallible; they follow false clues, misread evidence or suspect the wrong man.

Criminals display a variety of motives: they kill out of jealousy or greed, for revenge, to conceal their pasts, or to remove impediments to marriage and fortune. Money, then as now, is the most common motive. Many crimes stem from a secret hidden in the past, often illegitimacy, bigamous or unsuitable marriage, or a concealed liaison, whose discovery could have disastrous social or financial implication. This emphasis, while typically Victorian, should come as no surprise to readers of Ross Macdonald, whose interest in family sins and sexual irregularities is as compulsive as Braddon's. Crimes occur not only in metropolitan areas but in the depths of the country; long before Agatha Christie created St. Mary Mead Braddon wrote, "No species of crime has ever been committed in the worst rookeries of Seven Dials that has not been also done in the face of that rustic calm which, in spite of all, we look on with a tender, half-mournful yearning, and associate with—peace" (*Lady Audley's Secret,* p. 36), and John Faunce, like Jane Marple, is not shocked by evil: "After five and twenty years' experience of human nature's dark side, I can believe in anybody's wickedness" (*Justice,* pp. 211-212).

Both detectives and criminals resort to disguise: Melnotte in *Like and Unlike* (1887) stalks a murderer while posing as an African traveller; Carter in *Henry Dunbar* visits the inn where Dunbar stayed after the murder in the guise of a fisherman; and Captain Prodder in *Aurora Floyd* conceals his military bearing under the clothing of an "aristocratic tourist." Two murderers, M. Georges in *Wyllard's Weird* and Churchill Penwyn in *Rough Justice,* wear glasses with tinted lenses; and most conceal their inclinations beneath a facade of respectability. Jasper Dane in the short story "His Secret" stages a burglary to throw suspicion on outsiders when his wealthy employer is murdered, and John Treverton in *The Cloven Foot* (1879) is surely the predecessor of hundreds of murder suspects: he has no alibi because he was taking a walk!

Readers today who share with their Victorian counterparts a delight in "plot" and plenty of it; surprises, and plenty of 'em; "mystery thick as a November fog" will find these in abundance in Braddon's little known but fascinating novels. They will find, too, thoughtful and often revealing portraits of Victorian society and gain valuable insight into the taste of her large and varied public and into the ancestry of modern suspense fiction. Those who sample *Aurora Floyd, Charlotte's Inheritance* or *Taken at the Flood* and observe how skillfully she handles incident and detail, interweaves character and action, and makes the exceptional not only plausible but realistic may come to share Henry James' view that "the novel of domestic mystery"[8] dates from the appearance of *Lady Audley's Secret* in 1862.

The editions of Braddon's works used for this study are listed below, preceded by the original date of publication. All quotations will be cited in the text, followed, when necessary, by a shortened form of the title.

1862 *Lady Audley's Secret.* New York: Dover, 1974.

1863 *Aurora Floyd.* New York: Garland, 1979. 3 vols.

1864 *The Doctor's Wife.* London: John and Robert Maxwell, n.d.

1864 *Henry Dunbar.* London: John and Robert Maxwell, n.d.

1865 *Sir Jasper's Tenant.* London: John and Robert Maxwell, n.d.

1867 *Birds of Prey.* London: Ward, Lock & Tyler, n.d. 3 vols.

1868 *Charlotte's Inheritance.* London: Simpkin, Marshall, Hamilton, n.d.

1874 *Taken at the Flood.* London: John and Robert Maxwell, n.d.

1875 *A Strange World.* London: John and Robert Maxwell, n.d.

1879 *The Cloven Foot.* London: John and Robert Maxwell, n.d.

1884 *Flower and Weed* (and other stories). London: John and Robert Maxwell, n.d.

1884 *Ishmael.* Chicago: Belford, Clark & Co., n.d.

1885 *Wyllard's Weird.* London: John and Robert Maxwell, n.d.

1886 *Under the Red Flag* (and other stories). London: John and Robert Maxwell, n.d.

1887 *Like and Unlike.* London: Spencer, Blackett, n.d. 3 vols.

1889 *The Day Will Come* London: Simpkin, Marshall, n.d. 3 vols.

1898 *Rough Justice.* London: Simpkin, Marshall, Hamilton, 1898.

1899 *His Darling Sin.* London: Simpkin, Marshall, Hamilton, 1899.

Notes

1. "Miss Braddon," *The Nation,* 9 Nov. 1865; rpt. in *Notes and Reviews,* ed. Pierre De Chaignon La Rose (Freeport, N.Y.: Books for Libraries Press, 1968), p. 108.

2. James, p. 109.

3. Robert Lee Wolff, ed., "Devoted Disciple: The Letters of Mary Elizabeth Braddon to Sir Edward Bulwer-Lytton, 1862-1873," *Harvard Library Bulletin,* no. 1, 22 (Jan. 1974), 11.

4. Wolff, "Devoted Disciple," Part II, *Harvard Library Bulletin,* no. 2, 22 (April 1974), 139.

5. Wolff, Part I, p. 34.

6. As quoted by Robert Lee Wolff, *Sensational Victorian: The Life & Fiction of Mary Elizabeth Braddon* (New York: Garland, 1979), p. 324.

7. Kathleen Tillotson, "The Lighter Fiction of the Eighteen-Sixties," Intro., *The Woman in White* (Boston: Houghton Mifflin, 1969), p. xv.

8. James, p. 112.

Ellen Miller Casey (essay date 1984)

SOURCE: "'Other People's Prudery': Mary Elizabeth Braddon," in *Tennessee Studies in Literature*, Vol. 27, 1984, pp. 72-82.

[*In the following essay, Casey examines Braddon's handling of Victorian moral conventions in her works, noting that Braddon tended to be far more conservative in her writing than in her life.*]

In a seminal article on minor Victorian fiction, Louis James suggested that "the most penetrating and imaginative writers transform social reality in their art. . . . The 'bad' writer on the other hand cannot either apprehend or express the social reality."[1] In James's sense, Mary Elizabeth Braddon is neither good nor bad. She apprehends social reality clearly, but does not transform it. As a result she reveals much about the fears of the Victorians and the devices of their novelists. Braddon is one of those novelists who fit well into Richard Altick's category of minor novelists who can be examined "with profit to our understanding both of the nature of popular literature itself and of the frustrations and conflicts that were at work in the ordinary Victorian's subconscious."[2]

A. O. J. Cockshut suggests that if we wish to investigate Victorian standards of moral sensibility and decency we must examine their "half-hearted and unwilling adherent . . . since the willing adherents of the prevailing ethos will be slow to give us any idea of what they are concealing."[3] In her life Braddon absolutely refused to accept Victorian sexual conventions. She lived with publisher John Maxwell for fourteen years, bearing him five illegitimate children. In her novels, however, Braddon was more half-hearted. Although both Victorian and contemporary critics have recognized that Braddon perceived the secrets which underlay respectable Victorian society, she never fully succeeded in transforming that recognition into great art. In her early sensation novels such as *Lady Audley's Secret* (1862) and *Aurora Floyd* (1863) and in her later domestic ones such as *Vixen* (1879), Braddon stopped short of accepting the implications of what she saw, pulling back to a more conventional posture. Nonetheless, her work is worth investigating, for her struggles with the restraints of conventional morality reveal much about both the Victorians and their novels.

Recently, feminist critics have been adding much to our understanding of Braddon's method of operating within the constraints of popular morality. Elaine Showalter, for example, argues that *Lady Audley's Secret* is "a carefully controlled female fantasy of rebellion and power."[4] In her recent book on the sensation novel, Winifred Hughes argues similarly that Braddon deliberately undermines the traditional moral assumptions: "Instead of abandoning the popular conventions, she circumvents them, using them against themselves, investing them with a new ironic significance."[5] Certainly it is true that Braddon is one of those novelists who express what U. G. Knoepflmacher calls the asocial and amoral "counterworld" of Victorian society, who "repudiate yet indulge rebellious attitudes at odds with the dictates of accepted behavior."[6]

Despite her struggle with the restraints which society placed on the expression of such subversive sub-texts, Braddon never totally succeeded in transforming social reality. Her chafing under the constraints of popular morality was evident to critics of her early, sensation novels. The *Reader*, for example, recognized the difficulties of writing a novel such as *Aurora Floyd* in England rather than in France, for an English author was forced to preserve her heroine's "nominal purity," no matter how unrealistic that purity might be.[7] The reviewer of *The Lady's Mile* (1866) in the *Christian Remembrancer* made a similar point: "In comparing themselves with French novelists, our writers must feel at a cruel disadvantage, and must often be ashamed of the clumsy expedients they are driven to by punctilio, the necessities of the publisher, or whoever else feels the pulse of popular morality."[8]

Braddon first excited that pulse with her sensation novels. In these she defied convention by writing of murders and bigamies committed by beautiful women who were regarded semi-sympathetically. Despite the outrage of some readers, Victorian critics recognized that Braddon's sensation novels were responding to their readers' desires rather than defying them. In a review of *Aurora Floyd*, for instance, Henry James suggested that Braddon's popularity was a result of "observing a strictly respectful attention to her readers" and keeping up with the "delicate fluctuations of the public taste."[9]

Braddon kept up with these "delicate fluctuations" by carefully limiting what she wrote. Her subjects were shocking, but she maintained the proprieties by limiting the amount of detail which she provided, by legitimatizing passion with marriage, even if a bigamous one, and by taking care that at the end of the novel the good were rewarded and the evil punished. In other words, she provided a stimulus to Victorian imaginations with a wink for the knowing and a carefully proper surface for the censors.

Limiting detail is an obvious way to maintain the proprieties. It is one thing to assert that Aurora Floyd has eloped with her father's groom; it is quite another to detail the subsequent events. It is one thing to present Lady Audley pushing her husband into a well to prevent the detection of her bigamy; it is quite another to depict in graphic detail the process of drowning. The difference between Victorian and modern novels often lies less in the situations depicted than in the amount of detail provided to flesh out those situations. As A. H. Japp noted in 1867, one could write of immorality so long as one did it objectively, without passion.[10]

To legitimatize passion with marriage is perhaps a less obvious way to placate the moralists. Henry James pointed to this technique in his 1865 essay on Braddon when he attributed her success to her strict morality: "If one of her heroines elopes with a handsome stable-boy, she saves the proprieties by marrying him. This may be indecent if you like, but it is not immoral."[11] As Margaret Oliphant recognized, the English Victorians had a preference for crime over vice and preferred bigamy—an indictable crime—to something plainer.[12] Braddon clearly perceived this national preference. Indeed, Oliphant declared that Braddon began "the reign of bigamy as an interesting and fashionable crime."[13] There is no simple, enjoyable fornication in Braddon's novels. Always the appearances are preserved.

Rewarding the good and punishing the evil is, of course, the most common way to satisfy Victorian sensibilities. In this context it is important to note that poetic justice served social more than religious ends. True, such justice affirmed the providence of God, but more importantly it justified society's values and compensated for earlier impropriety in a novel. Elizabeth Gaskell's *Ruth* and Charles Reade's *Griffith Gaunt* were regarded as much more shocking than anything by Braddon because in both novels those who violated the sexual mores were accorded understanding and sympathy and ended less than tragically. Braddon was occasionally accused of making her readers sympathize with criminals,[14] but she made no mistakes at the ends of her novels. Her villainesses were always punished, thus satisfying the code that is well represented by Robert Buchanan's comment in the *Fortnightly Review*: "Where there is sin in literature and no suffering, the description is false, because in life the moral implication of sin is suffering. . . ."[15]

After 1870, Braddon moved in accordance with popular taste from the sensation novel to the domestic one. One of the best of these later novels is *Vixen,* which appeared in weekly installments in *All the Year Round* from 5 October 1878 to 14 June 1879, and in standard three-volume form in February 1879.[16] With its wealth of detail about the manners and mores of the time, *Vixen* is probably more representative of Braddon's natural taste than the earlier sensation works. (James perceptively compared her to Jane Austen, for example.)[17] In any case *Vixen* was one of Braddon's favorite novels.[18]

In *Vixen,* Braddon abandoned the sensation mode and her attempts to use what Showalter describes as her subversive sub-texts of feminine rebellion. She did not, however, abandon subversion, though as in her earlier novels she did not pass the barrier from expression to transformation of social reality. For understanding the sexual ethos of the Victorian Age, however, and the constraints which it placed on its novelists, *Vixen* is at least as valuable as the earlier novels. Braddon is here writing of ordinary life, not of crime, but her awareness of passion and its possible effects is still present, all the more intriguing because it is repressed, not breaking out in criminal actions. *Vixen* is a nice, quiet, domestic romance whose very real power comes from sexual energy and whose very real failure comes from an inability or unwillingness to acknowledge that energy forthrightly.

Vixen unfortunately confirms Michael Sadleir's judgment that Braddon would have written better novels in an atmosphere of greater freedom in which she would not have had to submit to "other people's prudery."[19] Sadleir and Lionel Stevenson both recognize that although Braddon did not share her readers' "moral prejudices," she nonetheless avoided impropriety by "an unconvincing twist . . . to the story" and "implausible manipulation of the plot."[20]

Certainly the plot of *Vixen* is a contrived one. Two lovers are separated by a variety of incidents including their own misapprehensions. Needless to say, all is resolved happily at the end. At the opening of the novel Violet Tempest, called Vixen by her beloved, fox-hunting father because of her red hair, is just shy of fifteen. She is infatuated with her neighbor Roderick (Rorie) Vawdrey, nineteen, who is resisting his mother's pressure to marry his sophisticated cousin Lady Mabel Ashbourne. Two years later, Vixen's father dies of a sudden heart attack on Rorie's twenty-first birthday, and Vixen is comforted by Rorie's assurance that, contrary to rumor, he is not engaged to Mabel.

Another two years pass. Vixen is "out" and courted by Captain Conrad Carmichael. She spurns him, and he vows that "it shall be measure for measure." Vixen returns home to learn that Rorie's mother has died and that Rorie and Mabel have become engaged to satisfy her dying wish. Carmichael visits and successfully woos Vixen's mother. Despite his threats, Carmichael's only action against Vixen after the marriage is to institute a strict system of economy so that he need not suffer when she inherits the estate on her twenty-fifth birthday.

When Vixen refuses the proposal of Carmichael's friend Lord Mallow, Carmichael is infuriated. During the course of berating Vixen for her improper conduct in spending her time riding with Rorie, Carmichael reveals that she is the only woman he has ever loved. In the course of the subsequent argument, Vixen drops a lamp which sets the house on fire but does not destroy it. Carmichael then banishes Vixen to the desolate house of his eccentric aunt, Miss Skipwith. On the day when Rorie and Mabel are to marry, Rorie suddenly appears there, freed by Mabel's elopement with Lord Mallow. Rorie proposes to Vixen, who immediately accepts him. Vixen's mother dies; Carmichael leaves; Rorie rents his house to Lord and Lady Mallow; and Rorie and Vixen live happily ever after in her old and much beloved home.

Victorian reviewers found *Vixen* slight, readable, and respectable. The *Athenaeum* included *Vixen* among its "Novels of the Week," commenting that the novel had ingenuity of description but a slight plot. "The interest consists in marking how a writer who thoroughly understands her business can make a respectable three-volume novel out of so little material."[21] The *Academy* also had a short notice of *Vixen* in its "New Novels." It described the novel as "in Miss Braddon's later and better manner, put together with but a small stock of incidents, and yet vivid and readable."[22] The *Saturday Review*, Braddon's long-standing opponent, was rather snide, expressing amazement that there was no crime from Miss Braddon this time and asking rhetorically how she managed to fill her pages. It added ironically, "Let Miss Braddon only go on in this most respectable course, and we shall yet have the pleasure of seeing her books given away as prizes in a school for young ladies."[23] Clearly *Vixen* aroused no storms of opposition or approbation.

One must agree with these reviews; *Vixen,* while readable, is no great work of art. Yet this judgment of the novel isn't totally satisfactory, for *Vixen* has a power that is not encompassed by the tepid approbation of the reviewers. This power does not come from clever characterization or vivid description, though both are present. Rather *Vixen*'s power comes from the underlying sexual passions which the novel acknowledges but doesn't develop.

In *Vixen,* the refusal to accept Victorian propriety takes several forms. As in most of her novels, Braddon uses irony extensively.[24] She maintains an ironic stance toward the whole notion of romantic passion without sexual involvement, largely by repeated allusions to great lovers of literature. An ironic contrast to the novel's respectability is provided by frequent references to Shakespeare's *Hamlet* and *Antony and Cleopatra*, Tennyson's *Idylls of the King,* and Dante's story of Paolo and Francesca. We laugh, as Braddon surely intends that we should, at Vixen's overblown language when she thinks of *Antony and Cleopatra*: "that story of a wild undisciplined love grand in its lawless passion—its awful doom. To have loved thus, and died thus, seemed a higher destiny than to do right, and patiently conquer sorrow, and live on somehow to the dismal end of the dull blameless chapter" (p. 308). We also laugh when Mrs. Carmichael, in rebuking Vixen for riding with Rorie, utters one of the greatest lines of Victorian respectability: "it is worse than a crime, Violet; it is an impropriety" (p. 216). No further evidence should be needed to prove Braddon an unwilling adherent to the prevailing sexual ethos.

Despite her irony, however, Braddon does adhere to that ethos. This is most evident in her use of the common Victorian ploy of setting up suggestive situations that prove to be innocent.[25] This ploy is akin to Anne Radcliffe's treatment of the supernatural—after scaring, prove things rational. For the Victorians the motto might well have been—after shocking, prove things innocent.

Braddon begins this pattern of suggesting shocking things with the character of Vixen herself. By a number of hints Vixen is presented as a woman capable of any daring; as a result we expect her to break out in violence. Decorum prevails, but we are always aware of the suppressed violence in Vixen's character. Braddon repeatedly stressed Vixen's tempestuousness. Her name—Violet (Vixen) Tempest—is part of this pattern, as are her red hair and the description of her as a "pretty horsebreaker," a common euphemism for a prostitute. Captain Carmichael describes Vixen as "this fair devil of a daughter, who looks capable, if offended, of anything in the way of revenge, from a horse whip to slow poison" (p. 89). Despite the hints, however, Vixen is not a sensation heroine, though Braddon is clearly exploiting the convention which she helped to establish.

Another situation which is presented and then evaded is the relationship between Vixen and Rorie. He is engaged to Lady Mabel and yet spends his time riding in the forest with Vixen. Mrs. Carmichael reprimands Vixen for her companionship with Rorie: "Violet, you must know that all talk about brother and sister is sheer nonsense" (p. 216). Captain Carmichael is even more direct: "I will come between you and your lover, Roderick Vawdrey. Your secret meetings, your clandestine love-making, shall be stopped" (p. 229). In point of fact there has been no lovemaking, and when Rorie breaks through their reserve to propose to Vixen she rejects him because he is engaged, reminding him of his duty and honor. The words with which she does so are stilted and unbelievable, especially when set in the context of the heightened descriptions of their idyllic ride: "You and I must part, Rorie. This night ride in the forest must be our last. Never any more, by sun or moon, must you and I ride together. It is all over, Rorie, the old childish friendship. I mean to do my duty, and you must do yours" (p. 225). It may be that Braddon intends by this stilted language to indicate that she too finds Vixen's renunciation of Rorie improbable; unfortunately the inappropriate clichés falsify the entire situation and create a sense that art has been sacrificed to propriety.

The most interesting relationship in *Vixen* is that between Vixen and her stepfather. Again, however, Braddon evades the logical consequences of the situation she creates. Captain Carmichael proposes to Vixen and, after she rejects him, marries Vixen's mother. He becomes a tyrannical husband and father, insisting that he will "tame" Vixen. The situation verges on the incestuous. As Carmichael explains to Vixen: "You are the girl I would have periled my soul to win—the girl who rejected me with careless scorn. . . . If you had been my wife, Violet, I would have been your slave. You forced me to make myself your stepfather, and I will be master instead of slave" (p. 229). Despite this melodramatic language, nothing happens. Carmichael does not rape Vixen, does not beat her mother. He only keeps a tight watch on the budget, tries to marry Vixen to his friend Lord Mallow, and sends Vixen off to stay with his aunt. The discrepancy between the potential and the actual is so immense that it is unbelievable. Braddon succumbs to decorum and plays herself false.

Besides creating irregular situations which are never carried to their logical ends, Braddon uses another common Victorian technique for suggesting passion without offending the proprieties. She employs alternative expressions, metaphors, for the passion which she cannot express directly. Although the conventionality of its plot and the weakness and implausibility of Rorie and Captain Carmichael move **Vixen** firmly in the direction of tepid propriety, the sexual metaphors, like the hints about Vixen's character and situation, create a sense of genuine passion. An examination of the central metaphors of Vixen—horseback riding and fire—is valuable for what these metaphors suggest about Victorian fiction in general.

Braddon's metaphors of riding and fire are not, of course, original, having been used by other authors as metaphors for sexual passion in a number of earlier works. For example, riding is used in Browning's "The Last Ride Together" (1855), Reade's *Griffith Gaunt* (1866), and Eliot's *Daniel Deronda* (1876),[26] while fire appears in Collins's *The Woman in White* (1860), Dickens's *Great Expectations* (1862), and Reade's *Hard Cash* (1863). Though Braddon may be drawing on these precedents, she makes the metaphors her own by adding significant symbolic details.

Horseback riding becomes in **Vixen** virtually the synonym for passion. Lord Mallow, for example, falls in love with Vixen while she leads him on a day-long ride. More important, riding substitutes for the words that Vixen and Rorie cannot say. This is perhaps clearest in their ride home after Rorie has proposed and Vixen has refused him:

> It was a long grassy ride, safe only for those who knew the country well, for it was bordered on each side by treacherous bogs. Violet knew every inch of the way. Arion scented his stable afar off, and went like the wind; Blue Peter stretched his muscular limbs in pursuit. It was a wild ride along the grassy track, beside watery marshes and reedy pools that gleamed in the dim light of a new moon. The distant woods showed black against the sky. There was no light to mark a human habitation within ken. There was nothing but night and loneliness, and the solemn beauty of an unpeopled waste. A forest pony stood here and there—pastern-deep in the sedges—and gazed at these two wild riders, grave and gay, like a ghost. A silvery snake glided across the track, a water-rat plunged, with a heavy splash, into a black pool as the horses galloped by. It was a glorious ride. Miserable as both riders were, they could not but enjoy that wild rush through the sweet soft air, under the silent stars.

> (p. 226)

One doesn't need to be a Freudian to recognize the symbolic nature of this landscape. The watery marshes and reedy pools through which the horses with muscular limbs rush on a grassy track describe an archetypal sexual landscape. If that is not enough, one also has the silvery snake and the water-rat plunging into a black pool. The ride is the substitute for a direct expression of the passion the propriety prohibits. One might even suggest that it is more effective in its suggestiveness than a more explicit love scene. In any case, the passage makes clear why Braddon was so frequently praised for her power of description and suggests what she might have been able to accomplish in a

more permissive situation which would have allowed her to bring events to a climax.

Horses play their part in another metaphor for passion. Captain Carmichael repeatedly compares Vixen to a horse which he will tame and ride. Before he has given up the ideal of marrying Vixen, Carmichael thinks: "She is like that chestnut mare that threw me six times before I got the better of her. . . . There are two conquests a man can make over a woman—one to make her love him, the other—" (p. 86). The thought is never completed, unless implicitly a page later: "But I conquered the chestnut, and I'll conquer Miss Tempest—or make her smart for it" (p. 87). After he decides to marry Vixen's mother, Carmichael still uses the metaphor. Mrs. Tempest complains to him how much Vixen opposes the wedding. Carmichael anwers, "Your daughter has a noble nature, but she has been spoiled by too much indulgence: Even a racehorse—the noblest thing in creation—has to be broken in, not always without severe punishment. Miss Tempest and I will come to understand each other perfectly by and by" (p. 129).

The slang use of *ride* for the act of intercourse is at the root of the double-entendres in these passages. Braddon here raises the spectre of sexual cruelty, one which her readers probably perceived, as in an 1867 review in which Mrs. Oliphant identified "horsey" novels as "akin to immoral."[27] Nonetheless, the need for evasion ultimately creates a false and vaguely preposterous situation, for despite all his threats Carmichael does nothing except cut off Vixen's allowance and close her mother's account with her dressmaker.

Fire is another metaphor for sexual passion in **Vixen,** notably in its climactic scene. Confronted by Carmichael after her refusal of Rorie's proposal, told by him that he hates her because she rejected his love, attacked for her "shameful" conduct with Rorie, Vixen is "beside herself with anger."

> She grasped the lamp with both her hands, as if she would have hurled it at her foe. It was a large moon-shaped globe upon a bronze pedestal—a fearful thing to fling at one's adversary. A great wave of blood surged up into the girl's brain. What she was going to do she knew not; but her whole being was convulsed by the passion of that moment. The room reeled before her eyes, the heavy pedestal swayed in her hands, and then she saw the big moon-like globe roll on to the carpet, and after it, and darting beyond it, a stream of liquid fire that ran, and ran quicker than thought toward the open window.

> Before she could speak or move the flame had run up the lace curtain like a living thing, swift as the flight of a bird or the gliding motion of a lizard. The wide casement was wreathed with light. They two—Vixen and her foe—seemed to be standing in an atmosphere of fire.

> (p. 229)

The next day Carmichael refers to this fire when he tells Vixen that she is to be sent to Miss Skipwith:

"Go and pack your boxes!" cried the captain, angrily. "Do you want to raise the devil that was raised last night? Do you want another conflagration? It might be a worse one this time. I have had a night of fever and unrest."

"Am I to blame for that?"

"Yes, you beautiful fury. It was your image kept me awake. I shall sleep sounder when you are out of this house."

(p. 236)

Taken together these two passages illustrate the strengths and weaknesses of Braddon's presentation of sexual passion. Clearly she recognizes sexual obsession and is willing to depict it. Phrase after phrase in the description of the fire scene evokes sexual intercourse, from the symbolic "moon-shaped globe upon a bronze pedestal" to the physical "great wave of blood." Vixen's blood "surge[s]" and her being is "convulsed by the passion of that moment." Carmichael's speech the next day is also suggestive, with its talk of raising the devil and "a night of fever and unrest." Braddon's perception of sexual passion is undercut by conventionality and reticence, but the fire scene succeeds in evoking the passion which it describes despite the conventionality of much of its language. Braddon makes up for the waves of blood and the reeling room with the flame like a lizard and the iconographic quality of the close of the scene when Carmichael and Vixen stand surrounded by the wreath of flame around the casement. There is, however, nothing to compensate for the coyness and artificiality of Carmichael's language the next day. Overwritten though it is, the fire scene is imaginable. What is not imaginable is that anyone in the heat of anger would ask about "conflagrations" or call a woman a "beautiful fury."

The Carmichael/Vixen relationship is alive with the threat of sexual violence which is expressed only in elliptical terms. That relationship also raises questions about the relationship which it replaces, that of Vixen and her father. Vixen's adoration of her father and his fondness of her is succeeded by Vixen's repulsion for Captain Carmichael and his passion for her. *Vixen* presents a dark countervision of the Victorian home. Unfortunately, Braddon retreats from the implications of the Carmichael/Vixen relationship into unbelievable propriety. The threat of rape becomes the cutting off of an allowance.

The falseness of Carmichael's response is epitomized by a passage late in the novel when he sits beside his dying wife "with anger and envy gnawing his heart." He wishes to kill Violet and Rorie but "happily the captain was too cautious a man to be guilty of any overt act of rage or hatred. His rancorous feelings were decently hidden under a gentlemanly iciness of manner, to which no one could take objection" (p. 333). Braddon also hides rancorous feelings under iciness of manner; readers of *Vixen* can object, however, and wish that she had been truer to her own perceptions.

In her sensation novels, Braddon sees through Victorian propriety to a counterworld of feminine rebellion; in *Vixen* she recognizes one of sexual violence and incestuous passion. She dilutes this vision, however, by setting it in a plot of fortuitous errors, weak male characters, and a decorous happy ending. The *Christian Remembrancer*'s reviewer of *The Lady's Mile* had regretted the necessity of "outward illogical attention to the decencies of society; a requirement which must exceedingly bore and embarrass any writer who cares for philosophical correctness and the dependence of effects on causes."[28] One wonders to what extent Braddon was bored and embarrassed by *Vixen,* a novel which succumbed to the pressure of other people's prudery and which is therefore less interesting as a finished work of art than for what it reveals about its age.

Notes

1. Louis James, "The Rational Amusement: 'Minor' Fiction and Victorian Studies," *Victorian Studies,* 14 (1970), 195.

2. Richard Altick, "The Literature of an Imminent Democracy," in *1859: Entering an Age of Crisis,* ed. Philip Appleman et al. (Bloomington: Indiana Univ. Press, 1959), p. 223.

3. A. O. J. Cockshut, *Truth to Life* (London: Collins, 1974), p. 36.

4. Elaine Showalter, *A Literature of Their Own* (Princeton: Princeton Univ. Press, 1977), pp. 163-68.

5. Winifred Hughes, *The Maniac in the Cellar* (Princeton: Princeton Univ. Press, 1980), pp. 120-36.

6. U. G. Knoepflmacher, "The Counterworld of Victorian Fiction and *The Woman in White,*" in *The Worlds of Victorian Fiction,* ed. Jerome H. Buckley (Cambridge, Mass.: Harvard Univ. Press, 1975), pp. 351-69.

7. Quoted in Michael Sadleir, *Things Past* (London: Constable, 1944), p. 80.

8. "Youth as Depicted in Modern Fiction," *Christian Remembrancer,* 52 (July 1866), 185.

9. Henry James, "Miss Braddon," *The Nation,* 1 (9 Nov. 1865), 593.

10. H. A. Page [A.H. Japp], "The Morality of Literary Art," *Contemporary Review,* 5 (June 1867), 187.

11. James, "Miss Braddon," p. 594.

12. Mrs. Oliphant, "Novels," *Blackwood's,* 94 (Aug. 1863), 168-69.

13. Ibid., 102 (Sept. 1867), 263.

14. See, for example, [W. Fraser Rae], "Sensation Novelists: Miss Braddon," *North British Review,* 43 (Sept. 1865), 202, and Page [Japp], "Morality of Literary Art," p. 178.

15. Robert Buchanan, "Immorality in Authorship." *Fortnightly Review,* 6 (15 Sept. 1866), 296.

16. All citations of *Vixen* are from Mary Elizabeth Braddon, *Vixen* (New York: Lovel, Coryell, n.d.); with the exception of the change of Captain Winstanley's name to Carmichael and some consolidation of chapters, this edition is identical to the serialized version which appeared in *All the Year Round.*

17. Henry James, "Miss Braddon," p. 593.

18. Clive Holland, "Miss Braddon," *The Bookman,* 42 (July 1912), 157.

19. Michael Sadleir, *Things Past,* p. 80.

20. Michael Sadleir, "Mary Elizabeth Braddon," *Times Literary Supplement* (2 Oct. 1937), p. 711, and *Things Past,* pp. 78-80; Lionel Stevenson, *The English Novel* (Boston: Houghton Mifflin, 1960), p. 355.

21. *Athenaeum,* 73 (1 March 1879), 275.

22. R. F. Littledale, *Academy,* 15 (15 March 1879), 233.

23. *Saturday Review,* 47 (1 March 1879), 280-82.

24. This irony is not limited to sexual matters. For example, the many satiric comments in *Vixen* on class and money are discussed by Robert Lee Wolff, *Sensational Victorian* (New York: Garland, 1979), pp. 278-81.

25. See Wayne Burns, *Charles Reade* (New York: Bookman, 1961), pp. 266-67.

26. See Russell M. Goldfarb, *Sexual Repression and Victorian Literature* (Lewisburg: Bucknell Univ. Press, 1970), pp. 66-81, for some suggestive comments about riding as a metaphor and for an overextended discussion of Browning's poem.

27. Mrs. Oliphant, "Novels," *Blackwood's,* 102 (Sept. 1867), 272.

28. "Youth as Depicted in Modern Fiction," p. 185.

Natalie Schroeder (essay date 1988)

SOURCE: "Feminine Sensationalism, Eroticism, and Self-Assertion: M. E. Braddon and Ouida," in *Tulsa Studies in Women's Literature,* Vol. 7, No. 1, Spring, 1988, pp. 87-103.

[*In the following essay, Schroeder analyzes the ways in which sensationalist writers like Braddon encouraged Victorian women to subvert repressive social conventions.*]

Twentieth-century critics have recently affirmed the historical, social, and literary importance of popular Victorian fiction.[1] Mary Elizabeth Braddon's and Ouida's (Marie Louise de la Ramee) sensational novels are especially significant today for what they reveal about Victorian women's resistance to conventionally prescribed social roles. By rejecting the prudish moral tone that characterized popular fiction of the 1850s and by devouring novels filled with crime, passion, and sensuality, Victorian women readers began in the 1860s to rebel against the establishment. Monica Fryckstedt attributes the success of sensation novels to the fact that "they touched upon one of the hidden ills of Victorian society: the repressed and unfulfilled lives of women. Middle-class women, pent up in the Victorian home with few outlets for their energies and perhaps entrapped in loveless marriages, dreamed about passionate lovers, capable of arousing their slumbering emotions."[2] That sensation novels indirectly voiced women's ambitions for individuality and power (and not just "passionate lovers") is an even more compelling explanation for their popularity. According to Elaine Showalter, "the sensationalists and their women readers were less preoccupied with sexuality than with self-assertion and independence from the tedium and injustice of the feminine role in marriage and the family."[3]

The undercurrents of feminism in women's fiction, in fact, were a major concern of contemporary Victorian critics. They considered self-assertive or "masculine" female behavior as much a threat to Victorian society as unchastity. Margaret Oliphant, for example, who called Braddon "the leader of her school," stated that the present influx of female sensationalists had "reinstated the injured creature Man in something like his natural character, but unfortunately it has gone to extremes, and moulded its women on the model of men."[4] E. S. Dallas raised similar objections. He considered feminine aggression as unnatural. The feminine influence in literature should, he believed, bring with it "an evident access of refinement."[5] Instead, he complained, the very opposite was occurring:

> The first object of the novelist is to get personages in whom we can be interested; the next is to put them in action. But when women are the chief characters, how are you to set them in motion? The life of women cannot well be described as a life of action. When women are thus put forward to lead the action of a plot, they must be urged into a false position. To get vigorous action they are described as rushing into crime, and doing masculine deeds. Thus they come forward in the worst light, and the novelist finds that to make an effect he has to give up his heroine to bigamy, to murder, . . . and to all sorts of adventures which can only signify her fall. The very prominence of the position which women occupy in recent fiction leads by a natural process to their appearance in a light which is not good. This is what is called sensation. It is not wrong to make a sensation; but if the novelist depends for his sensation upon the action of a woman, the chances are that he will attain his end by unnatural means.[6]

A second major objection to sensation fiction was the potential danger it posed to female readers who might accept what they were reading "as something like the truth."[7] And this danger was perceived as a serious threat since the audience for popular fiction was not limited to the middle-class married women referred to above. In an essay in *Victoria Magazine,* "Ella" defined Ouida's readers as "those experienced in the world's ways" and those "tender blossoms of the school-room, maidens in their earliest teens."[8]

Because Ouida painted "men and manners, not always as they should be, but as they often are; she describes what had better be left undescribed." Her work was "instructive, but not edifying" and ultimately "unhealthy" to the adolescent reader, "Ella" concluded.[9] Thomas Wright, on the other hand, pinpointed both Braddon's and Ouida's main audience as "The Unknown Public," which was mainly composed of easily influenced women of working-class origins. He called them "the 'young lady' classes—the young ladies of the counters, of the more genteel female handicrafts generally and the dressmaking and millinery professions in particular."[10] Also included in Wright's group were young ladies who considered themselves too genteel to work, and wives of clerks, shopkeepers, and well-to-do artisans. Wright estimated the "army" of these readers at five million.[11]

Finally that the authors of such fiction were women was a third objection. It is "less repulsive," Oliphant stated, for example, when male writers used erotic descriptions than when female writers did, for by writing about sexuality, Victorian women were behaving in an unnatural manner:

> The peculiarity of it in England is, that it [an erotic scene] is oftenest made from the woman's side—that it is women who describe those sensuous raptures—that this intense appreciation of flesh and blood, this eagerness of physical sensation, is represented as the natural sentiment of English girls, and is offered to them not only as the portrait of their own state of mind, but as their amusement and mental food. . . .
>
> It may be possible to laugh at the notion that books so entirely worthless, so far as literary merit is concerned, should affect any reader injuriously, though even of this we are a little doubtful; but the fact that this new and disgusting picture of what professes to be the female heart, comes from the hands of women, and is tacitly accepted by them as real, is not in any way to be laughed at.[12]

Indeed women's sensational fiction should not be laughed at. Braddon's and Ouida's novels reflect Victorian women's attempts to rebel against the conventional feminine ideal. Often the authors disguise these feminist struggles in the erotic elements of the novel. Eroticism in Braddon's *Lady Audley's Secret* (1862) and *Aurora Floyd* (1863) and in Ouida's *Strathmore* (1865) and *Folle-Farine* (1871) is directed both inwardly (self-love and masochism) and outwardly (aggression and cruelty). Sexuality becomes a key element in determining feminine power and self-assertion. Through these channels, Victorian women readers got a taste of independence or self-authenticity. Though the authors were forced to bow to convention and punish aggression and self-assertiveness, the predominantly female reading audience was regaled with woman's potential for power, a power that ironically flourishes in a patriarchal society.

Feminine self-love emerges in sensation fiction as an outgrowth of the essentially artificial, supposedly passionless age that encouraged women to worship their youthful beauty and to become passive, angelic child-wives, perfectly innocent and sexless. Ironically, vanity, which increases self-confidence, becomes one way for a woman to assert power in her limited social sphere. Lucy Audley, Marion Vavasour, and Folle-Farine are cases in point. Their self-acceptance underlies the veneer of eroticism and violence.

Showalter and Hughes mention Lady Audley's masculine assertiveness, her cold, calculating behavior, and her lack of sexual passion,[13] but fail to make note of her self-love. All Lady Audley's instinctual sexual desires appear to be sublimated into her self-adoration and the aggressive behavior that eventually results from it. As Lady Audley broods over Robert Audley's threats to unmask her late in the novel, for example, Braddon indicates that vanity is the source of her heroine's unfeminine strength:

> she recalled that early time in which she had first looked in the glass and discovered that she was beautiful; that fatal early time in which she had first begun to look upon her loveliness as a right divine, a boundless possession which was to be a set-off against all girlish shortcomings, a counterbalance of every youthful sin. Did she remember the day in which that fairy dower of beauty had first taught her to be selfish and cruel, indifferent to the joys and sorrows of others, cold-hearted and capricious, greedy of admiration, exacting and tyrannical with that petty woman's tyranny which is the worst of despotism?[14]

Furthermore, to Sir Michael and Robert Audley, Lady Audley admits that unlike other women she is not sexually attracted to men: "The common temptations that assail and shipwreck some women had no terror for me. I would have been your true and pure wife to the end of time, though I had been surrounded by a legion of tempters. The mad folly that the world calls love had never had any part in my madness, and here at least extremes met, and the vice of heartlessness became the virtue of constancy" (*Lady Audley's Secret* [hereafter abbreviated as *LAS,*] p. 233). She loves Sir Michael (just as she loved her first husband, George Talboys) as much as she is capable of loving any man for freeing her from dependence, drudgery, and humiliation, but sexual passion is not involved; she loves him for admiring her and for providing luxuries for her. By marrying the fifty-six-year-old Sir Michael, Lady Audley becomes a child again, a very powerful child who easily manipulates her distinguished husband:

> Lucy was better loved and more admired than the baronet's daughter. That very childishness had a charm which few could resist. The innocence and candor of an infant beamed in Lady Audley's fair face, and shone out of her large and liquid blue eyes. The rosy lips, the delicate nose, the profusion of fair ringlets, all contributed to preserve to her beauty the character of extreme youth and freshness.
>
> (*LAS,* p. 35)

Homoeroticism is a component of Lady Audley's childishness; thus it is not surprising that the cold, selfish Lucy

Audley forms an attachment to her lady's maid, Phoebe Marks, an adolescent who so closely resembles her mistress that in a certain light one could be mistaken for the other. Lady Audley is like a child who has just left the nursery, Braddon says, who "hated reading, or study of any kind, and loved society. Rather than be alone, she would admit Phoebe Marks into her confidence, and loll on one of the sofas in her luxurious dressing-room, discussing a costume for some coming dinner-party; or sit chattering to the girl with her jewel-box beside her, upon the satin cushions" (*LAS,* p. 35).

In a novel where the heroine is not interested in men, Braddon is unable to titillate the reader with veiled suggestions of heterosexual love. In one particularly sensual scene, though, she provides instead an erotic description of the two women together. After Lady Audley enlists Phoebe's aid as her accomplice, she "retired into her bed-room, and curled herself up cozily under the eiderdown quilt. She was a chilly creature, and loved to bury herself in soft wrappings of satin and fur. 'Kiss me, Phoebe,' she said, as the girl arranged the curtains" (*LAS,* p. 39). Lady Audley's self-indulgent manner of attaining warmth—by wrapping herself in luxurious covers and by demanding a caress from Phoebe—suggests both masturbation and lesbianism.[15] The scene is also significant because Phoebe has become Lady Audley's accomplice in the plot against George Talboys. Since Lady Audley's self-love is not sufficient to realize her ambitions in a male-dominated society, she enlists the help of another woman, who, like her, is "selfish, and cold, and cruel, eager for her own advancement, . . . angry with the lot that has been cast her, and weary of dull dependence" (*LAS,* p. 198).

Undercurrents of homoeroticism also account for Lady Audley's strong objections to Phoebe's marriage. As the two women sit together before the fire in Lady Audley's dressing-room, the mistress jealously complains about her maid's approaching wedding: "'You surely are not in love with the awkward, ugly creature are you, Phoebe?' asked my lady sharply" (*LAS,* p. 72). It appears that in his position of groom, Luke had "contrived to attend her in her ride"; he discovered that she was a "timid horsewoman, utterly unable to manage the animal she rode" (*LAS,* p. 72). Lady Audley also objects to Luke's dominion over Phoebe, who fears his violence and vengeance. When she learns that Phoebe has betrayed her secret, she appears more concerned that her maid had shared it with a man than with the betrayal: "Phoebe Marks, you have told *this man!*" (*LAS,* p. 74).

The eroticism in Ouida's fiction is far less subtle than in Braddon's, and feminine rebellion is more openly determined through overt sexuality. Like Lady Audley, Marion Vavasour of Ouida's *Strathmore* is an accomplished actress who worships her own beauty and the power she gleans from it. She too has a secret: she reigns as "Queen of Society," when in actuality she is Lord Vavasour's mistress, not his wife.

"The Vavasour's" beauty is awesome, but her vanity is the source of her power. Like Lady Audley all her love is self-directed: "Love she had never known, save for her own beauty, her own guilty power."[16] Ouida repeatedly describes Marion erotically posing before her mirror, worshiping her beautiful image and contemplating the conquests and powers it grants her:

> ". . . no man living could defy *me*—not even Lord Cecil Strathmore!" And as she thought this last vainglorious but fully warranted thought, Marion, Lady Vavasour, lying back in her fauteuil, with her head resting negligently on her arm, that in its turn rested on the satin cushions, with that grace which was her peculiar charm, as the firelight shone on her loosened hair and the rose-leaf flush of her delicate cheeks, glanced at her own reflection in a mirror standing near, on whose surface the whole matchless tableau was reproduced with its dainty and brilliant coloring, and smiled—a smile of calm security, of superb triumph. Could she not vanquish, whom and when and where she would?
>
> (*S,* p. 64)[17]

Marion Vavasour differs from Lady Audley in that she exploits a mature sexuality rather than childishness to secure power over men. She successfully vanquishes Strathmore, who, until he met her, had been proudly cold and indifferent to all women. Power is Marion Vavasour's idol and religion, and as Strathmore's mistress, she exercises it "capriciously and mercilessly" over him (*S,* p. 154). For a brief time she loves him because of "the mad devotion" that he lavishes on her and for the "imperious force which wakes the heart of women in their own despite" (*S,* p. 435). His devotion feeds her own self-love and strengthens her.

Ouida's Folle-Farine of the novel by that name is yet another female who wants power and who achieves it as an extension of self-love. In her grandfather's home, the orphaned, friendless heroine is scantily fed and forced to perform hard labor. She prays for "strength and power" to escape from her sordid life.[18] When she becomes aware of her own beauty, Folle-Farine learns she already has power. After she sees her own image in one of the young artist Arslan's paintings, a "vain passion" creeps "with all its poison into her veins" (*FF,* p. 604). At first her beauty frightens her, but at the same time it fills her with ecstasy. This self-love results in a new strength, which differs from her physical prowess and ability to endure, the qualities that have kept her mentally free from her grandfather's tyranny. When he next tries to whip her, for example, she threatens to kill him should he touch her again: "Her body had grown sacred to her because a stranger had called her beautiful, and . . . her life for the first time had acquired a worth and dignity in her sight because one man had deemed it fair" (*FF,* p. 610). Her rebellion paralyzes her grandfather for a moment. She continues to work for him, but she remains free, physically and mentally.

Unlike Lucy Audley and Marion Vavasour, Folle-Farine has no mirror in which to worship her beauty; and unlike them, she finds the birth of her self-love oppressive. As Folle-Farine examines her newly discovered beauty under the light of the moon, her erotic self-adulation gives her a pessimistic awareness of her inferior role as a woman rather than a vision of her potential for power:

> The moonbeams fell about her where she stood; and she looked down on her smooth skin, her glistening shoulders, her lustrous and abundant hair, on which the wavering light played and undulated. The most delicious gladness that a woman's life can know was in tumult in her, conflicting with the new and deadly sense of shame and ignorance. She learned that she was beautiful, at the same time that she awoke to knowledge of her dumb, lifeless inferiority to all other human beings.
>
> And her heart was heavy, even amidst all its pleasure and triumph, heavy with a sense of utter ignorance and utter worthlessness.
>
> (*FF*, pp. 612-13)

She thus has a sense of what beauty and sensuality meant in the 1870s—ultimately subjugation.

A second way women exercise power in sensation fiction is through overt aggression. This type of struggle for self-assertion is also integrally connected to eroticism. In *Lady Audley's Secret,* for example, determined to foil Robert Audley even should the struggle "be a duel to the death" (*LAS*, p. 208), Lady Audley becomes more independent, aggressive, and cruel. Braddon's description of her defiantly setting fire to the Castle Inn illustrates the intricate involvement between her heroine's self-love and aggression. Ironically, Lucy's aggressive determination enhances her beauty; even Luke Marks is awed to silence by its "unearthly glitter." And the childlike heroine appears sensual; her windblown hair surrounds her forehead "like a yellow flame" and her eyes flash green flame "as might flash from the changing-hued orbs of an angry mermaid" (*LAS,* p. 211). Entering Phoebe's bedroom, Lady Audley "went to the dressing-table and smoothed her wet hair before the looking-glass, and then put on her bonnet. She was obliged to place the flaming tallow candle very close to the lace furbelows about the glass; so close that the starched muslin seemed to draw the flame toward it by some power of attraction in its fragile tissue" (*LAS,* p. 213). Particularly striking are the erotic implications of the candle's and the muslin's union, following Lady Audley's glance at "her fairy dower of beauty."[19]

The erotic and aggressive undercurrents in Braddon's *Aurora Floyd* [hereafter abbreviated as *AF*] are somewhat different. The vitally beautiful, restless, impatient, passionate, modest Aurora Floyd is the antithesis of the cold Lucy Audley. Her childishness is more natural than Lady Audley's, and she is not vain:

> the secret of her power of charm must have been the wonderful vitality of her nature, by virtue of which she carried life and animal spirits about with her as an atmosphere, . . . or perhaps the true charm of her manner was that childlike exquisite unconsciousness of self which made her for ever a new creature; for ever impulsive and sympathetic, acutely sensible of all sorrow in others, though of a nature originally joyous in the extreme.[20]

Aurora Floyd nevertheless asserts herself and thus shows signs of aggression. At the age of six she rejects a doll for a rocking-horse, and as an adolescent she develops an intense passion for horses.[21] By rebelling, abandoning her doting father, and marrying Conyers, the groom who wooed her with his startlingly handsome features and a romantic lie about his birth, Aurora Floyd faces dangerous repercussions. A year later Aurora returns to her father, subdued and submissive but with a shadow that occasionally falls upon her beauty.

After she marries John Mellish, though, Aurora's former aggressiveness resurfaces. She takes up riding again, and her passion is sublimated into her love for the racehorse named after her. Rather than being submissive, she tyrannizes over her big, blustering husband. He nevertheless has "a mother's weak pride" in his wife; and whenever she is complimented, he simpers "like a school-girl who blushes at a handsome man's first flatteries" (*AF* I, p. 284). By resisting conventionally prescribed social roles, Aurora almost regains the self-authenticity and independent identity she had in her childhood and adolescence. She goes too far, however.

Aurora Floyd is at first repulsed by and terrified of the halfwit Steeve Hargraves, whose "muscular palm" is like "the hand of a gladiator, with horny flesh and sinews of iron" (*AF* I, p. 268). She overcomes her fear, however, after the stable-man kicks her lame dog; then, "convulsed by passion," she whips Hargraves. That scene and a later one, in which Hargraves refers to his fantasies of Aurora, are particularly erotic: "She springs upon him like a beautiful tigress . . . her eyes flashing fury, her hat fallen off, and her black hair tumbling about her shoulders" (*AF* I, p. 273). More powerful than her adversary,

> She disengaged her right hand from his collar and rained a shower of blows upon his clumsy shoulders with her slender whip; a mere toy, with emeralds set in its golden head, but stinging like a rod of flexible steel in that little hand.
>
> "How dared you!" she repeated again and again, her cheeks changing from white to scarlet in the effort to hold the man with one hand. Her tangled hair had fallen to her waist by this time, and the whip was broken in half a dozen places.
>
> (*AF* I, pp. 273-74)

Like Lucy Audley, aggressive violence makes Aurora appear more sensual, but her "beautiful fury" turns Mellish "white with horror." Embarrassed, not aroused by his wife's unfeminine manner, he treats her like an "agitated child," rather than a woman "sublime in her passion," and ultimately she is punished for her sadistic behavior.[22]

Aurora continues to exercise her power over the brutal stable-man, but it is different from the power she has over her husband. Hargraves grows to hate Aurora, but he fears being near her because of his recurrent dreams of her with "her beautiful white throat laid open, and streaming oceans of blood." Even in Hargraves's violent fantasies, Aurora appears sadistic and aggressive, "never . . . dead or quiet," and never "without the whip" (*AF* II, p. 79).

Similarly in *Strathmore,* as Marion Vavasour directs her eroticism outwardly her aggression turns to cruelty, and she too becomes more sensual and more beautiful. Fearing that the force of Strathmore's passion for her "might one day menace her" (*S,* p. 166), she goads her lover to kill his best friend in a duel. Just as Lady Audley's beauty intensifies when she decides to kill Robert Audley, and as Aurora's does when she whips Hargraves, Marion Vavasour acquires a new "dazzling loveliness." She fascinates Strathmore, "luring and tempting him" to kill Erroll (*S,* p. 176), and she promises Strathmore a "reward" (*S,* p. 177) when he returns from the duel. The imminent violence, which will be the proof of her power, is unmistakably derived from her sexuality:

> She pressed his hand to her heart, where it beat warm and quick beneath its costly lace. As she bent over him her voice sank to all its wooing softness, but thrilling with a new and fiercer meaning, which fostered every darker passion in him, as tropic heat fosters the poison-plants to seed and blossom, tempting and goading him to crime. . . . These were the passions that she loved to rouse in men, and see run riot in their deadly course; when a whisper, a caress from her, might have slaked them, her lips only fanned the flame. And here an eager thirst for revenge craved its food in her as in him; here this soft and radiant creature was *cruel* as any panther that ever crouched, any snake that ever reared its brilliant painted crest.
>
> (*S,* p. 177)

Ouida's Folle-Farine, on the other hand, ironically achieves power in yet another way—by masochistically submitting to men. Her submission, like female aggression, is also erotically rendered. Folle-Farine remains throughout the novel an innocent victim; she is both uneducated and naive, but as we have seen, she has a clearer feminist consciousness than Lady Audley, Aurora Floyd, or Marion Vavasour.

From early childhood, Folle-Farine submits to her grandfather's floggings, punishment for her mother's elopement with her gypsy father. Folle-Farine accepts these beatings as a "law of life" (*FF,* p. 436), but she rebels by refusing to cry; she sings instead with "reckless indifference" (*FF,* p. 414). Although she submits, she maintains a kind of freedom and integrity: "There was a liberty in her that escaped his thraldom; there was a soul in her that resisted the deadening influence of her existence" (*FF,* p. 494).

The floggings become more erotically suggestive when, as a beautiful adolescent unaware of her developing body, Folle-Farine must strip and endure the painful blows of her grandfather's whip. Ouida's description of the naked female's submitting to her grandfather's sadistic violence becomes a veiled metaphor for incestuous violation, and it echoes flagellation scenes in Victorian pornographic literature.[23] The scene also depicts an interesting reversal of Aurora Floyd's power and eroticism as flogger. Sensual in her role of victim, Folle-Farine remains stronger than the aged aggressor:

> The white folds fell from off the perfect curves of her brown arms, and left bare her shining shoulders beautiful as any sculptured Psyche's.
>
> She was not conscious of degradation in her punishment; she had been bidden to bow her head and endure the lash from the earliest years she could remember. According to the only creed she knew, silence and fortitude and strength were the greatest of all the virtues. She stood now . . . as she had stood when a little child, erect, unquailing, and ready to suffer, insensible of humiliation because unconscious of sin, and because so tutored by severity and exposure that she had as yet none of the shy shame and the fugitive shrinking of her sex.
>
> He took, as he had in an earlier time, a thick rope which lay coiled upon the turf ready for the binding of some straying boughs; and struck her with it, slowly. His arm had lost somewhat of its strength, and his power was unequal to his will. Still rage . . . lent force to his feebleness; as the scourge whistled through the air and descended on her shoulders it left bruised swollen marks to stamp its passage, and curling, adder-like, bit and drew blood.
>
> (*FF,* p. 492)

I do not think it is straining the point to note the metaphorical significance of the adder-like rope that bites the pubescent girl and causes her to bleed. But more important, once again sexuality is a key element in a female's bid for independence; her grandfather's violation of her body, his cruelty, and his oppression prod Folle-Farine to yearn for escape from her sordid existence: "The desire to be free grew on her with all the force and fury inherited from her father's tameless and ever wandering race. If a crime could have made her free she would have seized it" (*FF,* p. 536).

For a short time after the discovery of her beauty, Folle-Farine maintains a kind of freedom, but like Aurora Floyd she falls in love and loses some of her independence. Her feelings of inferiority and worthlessness lead to masochistic self-abasement. She views Arslan as her superior and worships him because of his artistic genius. She is merely beautiful; he can create beauty. She is also sexually attracted to him. When she first finds him:

> She bent above him her dark rich face, with a soft compassion on it; she stroked the pale heavy gold of his hair, with fingers brown and lithe, but infinitely gentle; she fanned the cold pain of his forehead, with the breath of her roselike mouth; she touched him and stroked him and gazed on him, as she would have caressed and looked on the velvet hide of the stag, the dappled plumage of the white leaf of the lily.
>
> A subtle vague pleasure stole on her, a sharp sweet sorrow moved her,—for he was beautiful, and he was dead.
>
> (*FF,* p. 542)

Here Ouida's eroticism clearly shows a woman acting on impulse rather than by society's rules. Folle-Farine's dark face and fingers also ally her to her dark-skinned predecessors, social outsiders like Scott's Rebecca and Thackeray's Becky Sharp.[24]

Eventually Folle-Farine learns how to get around the rules. Arslan resents her strength; and when she gives him gold so he can paint, he reacts with disgust, loathing, and horror. He teaches her that "Gifts of gold from man to man are bitter, and sap the strength of the receiver; but of a woman to the man they are—to the man shameful" (*FF,* p. 687). From that time on she protects him secretly; continuing to reverse conventionally prescribed sexual roles, she saves his life a second time and provides him with money and fame. She does all this despite his indifference and almost sadistic cruelty: "He liked to make her smile; he liked to make her suffer; he liked to inflame, to wound, to charm, to tame her; he liked all these without passion, rather with curiosity than with interest" (*FF,* p. 636).

Folle-Farine endures hardship, prison, madness, and finally sexual slavery so that the unworthy man she loves and worships can become famous. She learns that she can have power only by giving up her rights to her own body. The lecherous Prince Sartorian offers her the power to save Arslan's life and ensure his fame if she will become his mistress. Her escape from Sartorian and her death are her final rebellion against a society that confines women to an inferior position.

Folle-Farine's submission and self-abasement make her stronger than the three males who exploit and profit from her strength, but her death at the end of the novel confirms her earlier realization of the futility of women's self-assertion in a male-dominated society. She dies keeping Arslan from knowing that she saved his life twice and that she agreed to become Prince Sartorian's mistress when the latter promised to make Arslan famous. Arslan's debt to her would have been an intolerable shame to him in a world in which it "is for the man to give to the woman" (*FF,* p. 687).

But even though she dies, Folle-Farine comes closer to realizing an independent identity than Lucy Audley, Aurora Floyd, or Marion Vavasour do. She remains free, Ouida states at the end of the novel, "even in basest bondage, pure though every hand had cast defilement on it, incorrupt through all corruption—*for love's sake*" (*FF,* p. 801, italics mine). Ironically, she maintains her own identity because she loves an indifferent man who denies her love; thus, she escapes the inevitable loss of self through marriage.

Folle-Farine's relatively successful rebellion is an exception. For the most part sensation novelists bow to convention, and they punish feminine bids for power.[25] Thus Braddon's and Ouida's self-assertive females are in effect emasculated.[26] Even through these punishments, however, the authors communicate a subversive message.

Robert Audley, for example, finally defeats his female adversary, but Lady Audley clearly perceives that she is a victim of a sexual battle: "'You have brought me to my grave, Mr. Audley,' she cried; 'You have used your power basely and cruelly, and have brought me to a living grave'" (*LAS,* p. 256). With the incarceration and subsequent demise of Lady Audley, Braddon makes a pessimistic statement about marriage and the fate of women who try to exercise their strength for their own ends rather than their husbands'.

Aurora Floyd is also punished for her masculine behavior. After the secret of her first marriage is revealed and she is subsequently suspected of murder, a number of protective males rally to relieve the rebellious young woman of all the difficulties that stemmed from her unfeminine behavior. In exchange she must be quiet, submissive, and give up her whip. The passionate heroine becomes subdued, tamed, and feminine. The novel concludes with a description of Aurora: "a shade less defiantly bright, perhaps, but unspeakably beautiful and tender, bending over the cradle of her first-born; . . . I doubt if my heroine will care so much for horse-flesh, or take quite so keen an interest in weight-for-age races as compared to handicaps, as she has done in the days that are gone" (*AF* III, pp. 318-19). Aurora ultimately learns she must accept the conventions of society that she first rejected as a child and later as a young married woman. She replaces the rocking-horse with the doll. Aurora comes close to realizing her own identity, but because of her self-assertion and bids for independence, paternalistic Victorian society robs the heroine of her vital energy and uniqueness.

Ouida's attitude towards the fate of aggressive, self-adoring women is more ambivalent. Ouida at times seems more anti-feminist than feminist, more allied with than ranged against the critics who chastised female writers. She repeatedly points to the futility of overriding vanity in light of human mortality. The Vavasour's power is short-lived, far from the omnipotence she had contemplated before her mirror. Fifteen years after the height of her success, for example, Marion Vavasour, now the owner of a gambling establishment, mourns the loss of her youth:

> "O, my lost beauty! my lost beauty!" since none who remembered what Marion Vavasour once had been, and despised the wreck, remembered and despised as utterly as she; for this woman, who was without remorse for her work or conscience for her crimes, had ceaseless misery for the social degradation which denied her Pride, and for the encroaching years which left her without Power, since these had been her gods, omnipotent and beloved, and were now drifted from her reach forever, never again to be recovered.
>
> (*S,* p. 301)

On the other hand, Ouida treats Marion sympathetically as she sinks lower and lower, simply because Marion is a female; and Ouida maintains a somewhat ironic attitude toward Strathmore's success. As he ages, he becomes proud, dominant, famous, and powerful. Strathmore's marriage to a passive, young bride, in fact, augments his virility. Marion ultimately becomes a repentant nun in the order of St. Vincent de Paul. She is not defeated by her sexual "crimes" but by a patriarchal society in which a woman's beauty and strength fade with her youth, while males reach the fullest vigor of manhood with age.

As I noted above, Victorian reviewers specifically objected to the undercurrents of feminism in women's fiction; but with the exception of Margaret Oliphant, reviewers failed to perceive the more subversive feminism disguised in the erotic elements of the novels. Most of Braddon's and Ouida's reviewers judged their novels in terms of how the female characters measured up to conventional standards of femininity. If a female was aggressive, she was demonic or unrealistic; if her aggressiveness was countered by redeeming feminine weakness, she was forgiven.

H. L. Mansel, for example, stated:

> Lady Audley is meant to be detested, while Aurora Floyd is meant to be admired. The one ends her days in a madhouse; the other becomes the wife of an honest man, and the curtain falls upon her "bending over the cradle of her first-born." . . . Though the moral teaching of the story [**Aurora Floyd**] is more questionable than that of its predecessor, and the interest, on the whole, less sustained, the individual characters are drawn with greater skill. Aurora, with all her faults, is a woman and not a fiend.[27]

Similarly another reviewer compared Braddon's two heroines and noted that a woman "so depraved and devilish as Lady Audley" is an impossibility. While he found Aurora Floyd's behavior at times "revolting" and thus unreal, her charm made her believable and acceptable.[28] Geraldine Jewsbury had similar objections to Marion Vavasour: "The heroine, Marion Vavasour, is a wicked coquette—a beautiful demon—a mixture of Cleopatra, Potiphar's wife, and any other bad heroine of ancient or modern times the reader may please to fancy. As a human being she is utterly impossible."[29]

Over a century later, we are able to laugh at fears voiced by prudish Victorian reviewers that sensation fiction "will breed a pestilence so foul as to poison the very life-blood of our nation"[30] and beliefs that such novels "are not literature at all."[31] Sensation fiction, in fact, had a major impact on canonical Victorian fiction. Dickens, Thackeray, Trollope, and George Eliot influenced sensation novels and took much from them as well. One of the reviewers cited above stated that "Since *Adam Bede,* perhaps no book has made so sudden and decided 'a sensation' as **Lady Audley.**"[32] Furthermore, even though Hardy's first sensation novel, *Desperate Remedies,* was a failure, the positive impact of the sub-genre is clearly evident in his major novels.

Sensational novelists like Braddon and Ouida cannot be facilely dismissed today as dangerous second-rate hacks. Showalter states that although female sensationalists were "thwarted in a full exploration of their imaginative world by Victorian convention and stereotypes, . . . they did move well beyond the code of renunciation and submission that informed earlier fiction."[33] And even more recently, Sally Mitchell says, "Escape reading gives us a clue about what is being escaped from; it may reflect a reverse image of the tone of the times."[34]

Both Mary Elizabeth Braddon and Ouida depict women who are attempting to escape from their limited social spheres. Although the struggles end in defeat, the powerful, erotic, self-assertive females live on in the pages of these and other novels of the period. As a reviewer for the *London Quarterly* (1866) stated, "however it may be said, that in these tales the nemesis rarely fails to overtake the guilty, and that the retribution exacted is sometimes very terrible, it must be felt that even this is insufficient to remove the impression produced by the continued reproduction of such characters."[35] Furthermore, the novelists undercut the defeats by the energy and daring of their female characters, who emerge as far more interesting than and superior to their male adversaries.

Notes

1. See Elaine Showalter, *A Literature of Their Own: British Women Novelists From Brontë to Lessing* (Princeton, N.J.: Princeton University Press, 1977); Winifred Hughes, *The Maniac in the Cellar: Sensation Novels of the 1860s* (Princeton, N.J.: Princeton University Press, 1980); Sally Mitchell, *The Fallen Angel: Chastity, Class and Women's Reading, 1835-1880* (Bowling Green, Ohio: Bowling Green University Popular Press, 1981); Ellen Miller Casey, "Other People's Prudery: Mary Elizabeth Braddon," in *Sexuality and Victorian Literature,* ed. Don Richard Cox, Tennessee Studies in Literature, 27 (Knoxville: University of Tennessee Press, 1984), 72-74.

2. Monica Fryckstedt, *Geraldine Jewsbury's Athenaeum Reviews: A Mirror of Mid-Victorian Attitudes to Fiction* (Stockholm: Almqvist and Wiksell Int., 1986), p. 42.

3. Showalter, p. 161.

4. Margaret Oliphant, "Novels," *Blackwood's Edinburgh Magazine,* 102 (1867), 265.

5. E. S. Dallas, *The Gay Science,* 2 vols. (London: Chapman and Hall, 1866), II, 296.

6. Dallas, II, 298.

7. Oliphant, p. 260.

8. "Ella," "Ouida," *Victoria Magazine,* 28 (1877), 370.

9. "Ella," p. 371.

10. Thomas Wright, "Concerning the Unknown Public," *The Nineteenth Century,* 13 (1883), 282.

11. Wright, p. 279.

12. Oliphant, pp. 259-60; see also, "False Morality of Lady Novelists," *National Review,* 8 (1859), 144-50

and Fryckstedt, p. 38; note also that some reviewers, prejudiced against sensation fiction in general, often failed to perceive subversive feminist undercurrents in the fiction. Fryckstedt points out, for example, that neither Geraldine Jewsbury, in her *Athenaeum* review of Braddon's *The Lady's Mile,* nor the *Saturday* reviewer recognized that the novel "not only presents a grave criticism of matrimony, but even argues for women's freedom from male dominance" (p. 81).

13. Showalter, pp. 163-67; see also Hughes, pp. 125-27. Hughes states that Lady Audley's lack of passion and childishness is a brilliant parody of the Victorian ideal of marriage. The passive angelic child-wife was subject to parody, however, long before *Lady Audley's Secret* in, for example, *Vanity Fair, Jane Eyre,* and *David Copperfield.*

14. Mary Elizabeth Braddon, *Lady Audley's Secret* (1862; rpt. New York: Dover, 1974), p. 196. Subsequent references to this work are cited in the text.

15. See Sara Putzell-Korab, "Passion between Women in the Victorian Novel," in *Sexuality and Victorian Literature,* pp. 180-86.

16. Ouida (Marie Louise de la Ramee), *Strathmore* (1865; rpt. New York: P. F. Collier, 1889), pp. 412-13. Subsequent references to this work are cited in the text.

17. Margaret Oliphant was troubled by the subversive undercurrents she perceived in Ouida's erotic descriptions. Oliphant connected the "luscious" sensual descriptions of Marion's hair, for example, to her struggle to gain power. Note also the descriptions of Aurora Floyd's and Folle-Farine's hair. "Hair," Oliphant stated, "has become one of the leading properties in fiction. The facility with which it flows over the shoulders and bosoms in its owner's vicinity is quite extraordinary. In every emergency it is ready for use. Its quantity and colour, and the reflections in it, and even the 'fuzz,' which is its modern peculiarity, take the place of all those pretty qualities with which heroines used to be endowed. Whad [sic] need has a woman for a soul when she has upon her head a mass of wavy ivory? . . . Power, strength, a rich nature, a novel mind, are all to be found embodied in this great attribute" (p. 269).

18. Ouida (Marie Louise de la Ramee), *Folle-Farine* (1871; rpt. New York: P. F. Collier, 1893), p. 419. Subsequent references to this work are cited in the text.

19. For a discussion of fire and sexuality, see Casey, pp. 78-81.

20. Mary Elizabeth Braddon, *Aurora Floyd,* 3 vols. (1863; rpt. New York and London: Garland, 1979), I, 261. Subsequent references to this work are cited in the text.

21. Mitchell notes that women who rode horses were particularly threatening to men in sensation fiction,

p. 77; see also Casey for a discussion of horses and sexuality, pp. 78-80.

22. See Hughes, pp. 128-31.

23. Showalter notes that "whipping girls to subdue the unruly flesh and the rebellious spirit was a routine punishment for the Victorians, as well as a potent sexual fantasy" (p. 116); see also Steven Marcus's discussion of flagellation in *The Other Victorians* (New York: Basic Books, 1966), pp. 255-68, and Ronald Pearsall's, in *The Worm in the Bud: The World of Victorian Sexuality* (Middlesex, Eng.: Penguin Books, 1983), pp. 404-21.

24. See U. C. Knoepflmacher, "The Counterworld of Victorian Fiction," in *The Worlds of Victorian Fiction,* ed. Jerome H. Buckley (Cambridge: Harvard University Press, 1975), pp. 351-69. After tracing the roles of dark-haired outsiders, Knoepflmacher focuses on Collins's Marian Halcombe, another predecessor of Folle-Farine, who is "led to adopt the lawless tactics of the outsider" (p. 364).

25. According to Fryckstedt, "the necessity of rewarding virtue and punishing vice sprang from their [i.e., mid-Victorian critics] unchangeable principles of Christian morality and became even more important as the sensation novel of the 1860s depicted wicked heroines who held the public spellbound with their crimes. That adultery, bigamy, murder, elopement and attempted arson were tolerated at all by the middlebrow public must be ascribed to the fact that at the end of the novels . . . vice was duly punished" (p. 37).

26. This is a curious inversion of Charlotte Brontë's punishments of her passionate, paternalistic characters, Rochester and M. Paul.

27. H. L. Mansel, "Sensation Novels," *Quarterly Review,* 113 (1863), 492-93.

28. "The Popular Novels of the Year," *Fraser's Magazine,* 68 (1863), 259-60, 262.

29. Geraldine Jewsbury, Review of *Strathmore,* by Ouida, *The Athenaeum,* 29 July 1865, p. 142.

30. Vincent E. H. Murray, "Ouida's Novels," *The Contemporary Review,* 22 (1878), 935.

31. Oliphant, p. 261.

32. "The Popular Novels of the Year," p. 257.

33. Showalter, p. 162.

34. Mitchell, p. 92.

35. "Recent Novels: Their Moral and Religious Teaching," *The London Quarterly Review* (1886); rpt. in *Victorian Fiction: A Collection of Critical Essays,* ed. Ira Bruce Nadel (New York: Garland, 1986), p. 108.

Virginia B. Morris (essay date 1990)

SOURCE: "Mary Elizabeth Braddon: The Most Despicable of Her Sex," in *Double Jeopardy,* The University Press of Kentucky, 1990, pp. 88-104.

[*In the following essay, Morris discusses the ways in which* Lady Audley's Secret *fits into the pattern of criminal women in Victorian fiction.*]

The women who shoot, poison, stab, steal, and blackmail their way through the sensation novels of the 1800s changed the nature of crime and criminals in Victorian fiction. These women are more ambitiously independent and less sexually repressed than traditional heroines, and their criminality is pervasive, violent, and even bizarre. Like comparable characters in other Victorian literature, they reaffirm the nineteenth-century precept that female sexuality and criminality are inextricably intertwined. But they also introduce the revolutionary idea that women are capable of committing almost any crime to achieve their personal goals. Ironically, those goals are almost always highly conventional: romantic happiness and financial security through marriage.

While the criminal women in sensation fiction are assertive and aggressive, they are rarely monstrous, although Margaret Oliphant and her contemporary literary critics persistently labeled them as bestial and inhuman.[1] They do not kill (or try to kill) children or old ladies; instead they kill able-bodied men and women who threaten their plans or their well-being. Nor despite their overtly aggressive behavior, are many women in sensation fiction "masculine" in the pejorative sense that the term is applied to unconventional women. Rather, they are charming and beautiful—and sometimes quite sexy. This combination of apparent loveliness and masked threat was the most radical feature of the genre not only because it confronted the fantasy of the "angel in the house" directly but because it confirmed the worst fears of a society reluctant to admit that women were not adequately protected by the legal system and equally reluctant to change the status quo.

The audience for sensation fiction was predominantly middle class or aspiring middle class and overwhelmingly female. The unparalleled success of the genre strongly suggests that these readers clearly enjoyed being shocked and appalled—within certain well-defined parameters, of course. They relished details of the exotic, the daring, the bizarre—excitement often supplied by accusations against women in widely reported criminal trials of the 1840s, 1850s and 1860s as well as in the fiction. But the readers also came to recognize, if they had not already known, that spouse abuse or the threat of public disgrace could make a woman desperate enough to consider murder.

Partly new novels of manners and partly tales of terror, the sensation novels provided a unique blend of realism and melodrama at a time when the pervasive extent of crime in Victorian society was being explicitly reported in the press.[2] Despite their conventional, if often hollow, romantic endings, most sensation novels accurately depicted the details of Victorian society, including the overwhelming extent to which women were dependent on the authority of men and the rage which women's attempts to gain legal and economic rights evoked. Yet they shifted criminal activity from the working and indigent classes where much of it occurred to the middle and upper classes. There was no particular shock, and not much interest, generated by a housemaid killing her illegitimate baby; that was commonplace and comprehensible. And it was easy for readers to maintain a self-satisfied distance from these girls whom they expelled from their employment and ignored on the streets. In contrast, the machinations of the rich and well-born added a savory touch to violence. When a lady killed her husband, a rich girl horsewhipped a stable boy, or a clergyman's adoring daughter incited her father to murder her unfaithful lover, that was simultaneously a source of titillation and admiration.

Yet even as they described crime among the affluent and the socially prominent, the novelists deftly avoided highly sensitive issues as well as the sexual candor characteristic of contemporary French fiction. I have uncovered no novels, for example, in which middle- or upper-class women murder their illegitimate children and none with explicit incest. Such shocking crimes were too direct an assault on the Victorian obsession with family for the novelists to risk. Furthermore, few unmarried women kill. Because one underlying assumption in these novels was that passion motivated violent crime, women who were presumed sexually inexperienced could not feel passion intense enough to drive them to murder. A similar lack of candor linked married women's violent crimes to unsatiated lust or unintentional bigamy more frequently than to actual adultery or illegitimate children.

Nor were the sensation novelists any more inclined than the authors of more traditional fiction to have their guilty women end up in a courtroom. It was perfectly all right to ask readers to believe that women murdered; many were apparently happy to have their worst fears confirmed. It was quite another to flout what the fiction's audience knew, that middle- and upper-class women were rarely caught up in the criminal justice machinery, seldom convicted, and never executed. But the novelists also avoided court trials because they preferred extrajudicial resolutions where fictional women inevitably suffered stringent, sometimes self-inflicted punishment, often in marked contrast to male characters of comparable guilt.

For instance, Philip Sheldon, the grasping and murderous antagonist of Mary Elizabeth Braddon's ***Birds of Prey*** and ***Charlotte's Inheritance,*** literally gets away with murder as he grows enormously rich at others' expense. He pays no penalty for his crimes because he is never caught and has no conscience to bother him. But women characters are destroyed for a single crime: Sylvia Perriam in Braddon's ***Taken at the Flood*** dies a miserable, lonely death for committing her aged husband to an insane asylum and pretending he was dead so she could bigamously marry her lover, and Honora Grace in A. M. Meadows's *The Eye of Fate* is incarcerated in an insane asylum for killing the man who had rejected her. While neither woman is sympathetic, neither is more culpable than Sheldon. And although Braddon makes Sheldon's success a clear and damning miscarriage of justice, she does not permit any of her guilty women to escape punishment as she does him. This curious inversion of real life—where men were more apt to be imprisoned or executed than women—underlines the highly conventional moral tone of a genre widely condemned as disreputable and immoral.

Finally, there is a striking disparity in the motives of the privileged women who commit crimes in sensation fiction—except in response to physical abuse—and the motives of less affluent women who in real life were more apt to be violent, or at least to be arrested for violence. Repeatedly, in fiction, the urgency to maintain her reputation and the security that reputation provides drive an otherwise conventional woman to crime more often than need or greed. Nowhere is that better illustrated than in *Lady Audley's Secret,* the archetypal sensation novel, where maintaining the secrets of the past are Lucy Audley's motive for murder: The men she attacks know or suspect the truth about her and threaten to expose her. The same motive holds true in novels and stories where women are set up as suspects in murder cases and ultimately cleared—like Aurora Floyd in Braddon's eponymous novel, or Kate Gaunt in Charles Reade's *Griffith Gaunt,* or Grace Dunbar in Conan Doyle's "The Adventure of Thor Bridge." The presumptive motive is fear that their extramarital liaisons will be exposed.

In some sensation novels, a woman's ambition for money, power, or a particular man makes her turn to the efficiency of murder rather than relying on the more insidious, but more ladylike, psychological emasculation characteristic of more conventionally destructive women. In A. M. Meadows's *Ticket of Leave Girl,* Wilkie Collins's *The Legacy of Cain,* and several of Braddon's later novels, women commit murder without the slightest qualm and acknowledge their guilt only when confronted with incontrovertible evidence. Should someone else be punished in their place, their only response, we are led to believe, would be a sigh of relief. Unsympathetic and ultimately unsuccessful, these women nonetheless demonstrate one of the cardinal principles of the sensation fiction genre: women are capable of calculated and violent action when it serves their purpose.

The other direct assault sensation fiction made on its chauvinistic and xenophobic readers was that the guilty women were clearly and undeniably English. Unlike Dickens, whose killers were Europeans, or Conan Doyle, who was partial to Americans, Australians, Russians, or almost anyone "foreign," Braddon, Reade, Collins, and their colleagues had no reservations about hiding a criminal mind behind a pretty English face. Blonde curls and large blue eyes do not necessarily signal placidity and compliance any more than an elevated social position guarantees compassion and tolerance. In fact, after reading a few Braddon novels, the reader grows very wary of beautiful rich women.

No novel about female violence made a more dramatic impact than Braddon's first best-seller, *Lady Audley's Secret* (1862). Lucy Audley's violations of Victorian moral and legal codes in her quest for emotional and financial security are monumental: when her first husband, George Talboys, disappears, leaving no word of his plans or whereabouts, she abandons her child, assumes a false identity, gets a job, and marries Sir Michael Audley bigamously. When Talboys returns, she fakes an obituary, stages her own funeral, attempts murder, and commits arson. The reader must marvel at her energy and ingenuity.

Elaine Showalter suggests that Lucy nearly gets away with her treachery because her innocent looks place her above suspicion.[3] Yet her skills at dissembling learned as woman/wife make her capable not only of deception but of putting her own happiness and success above all other considerations, legal or moral. In addition, Lucy Audley combines classically feminine assets—a beautiful face and an outwardly gentle manner—with a distinctly unfeminine one—her resourceful mind. To be sure that no reader misses the point that Lucy is guilty, Braddon uses the admittedly cliched but extremely effective device of describing her portrait, stressing the strange, almost demonic, quality of her beauty while hinting at a sinister aspect of its loveliness: "Her crimson dress, exaggerated like all the rest in this strange picture, hung about her in folds that looked like flames, her fair head peeping out of the lurid mass of color as if out of a raging furnace. Indeed the crimson dress, the sunshine on the face, the red gold gleaming in the yellow hair, the ripe scarlet of the pouting lips, the glowing colors of each accessory of the minutely painted background, all combined to render the first effect of the painting by no means an agreeable one" (chap. 8).[4]

Robert Audley, a dilettante obsessed with his uncle's wife and his friend Talboys's second disappearance, has the most visceral reaction. For him, the portrait stirs subconscious images of Lucy as a predator and helps convince him she is guilty of some horrible if undefined evil. It also strengthens his resolve to make her pay for her sins—if only he can find out what they are. He dreams of her as a mermaid, "beckoning his uncle to destruction" (chap. 27) and as a Medusa, whose golden ringlets change into snakes and crawl down her neck, threatening the dreamer himself (chap. 13). These conventional Victorian images of feminine power and masculine dread tell the reader as much about Robert Audley as they do about the woman he sees as the personification of evil. But in this context, the golden web of Lucy's hair evokes not only the insidious destructive power that her nephew fears but also the obsession with being rich that has motivated her dishonest marriage.[5]

Lucy Audley's crimes are of two kinds: the careful, crafted deceits which create her new persona and bury her past, and the spontaneous, violent actions to get rid of the two men—George Talboys and Robert Audley—who can destroy her. She pushes Talboys down an abandoned well and leaves him to die. To cover up that crime, she sets fire to the inn where Audley is staying while he investigates her past. Her motive each time is self-defense, but what she is protecting is not her life but her reputation. That reputation as an innocent, helpless, and virtuous woman is what insures her social position and her hard-won security. She threatens, she uses physical force in wanton disregard for human life, and she believes she has committed murder but feels no remorse. As a killer, however, she is a failure; neither man dies. So why does Braddon punish her? Why does Lucy Audley die in an insane asylum? And why, for many readers, does she get what she deserves?

The answer lies in Lucy's refusal to accept her plight as a poor daughter, an abandoned wife, or a penniless governess, when everything she has learned teaches her that a woman's success is measured by an affluent marriage. The bigamy (with its overtones of sexual excess) which is her undoing enables her to marry well and achieve the financial security that neither her father nor Talboys provided. The luxury she craves is guaranteed by being a rich man's wife: having expensive clothes, sumptuous surroundings, a life of ease. She has no objection to marriage, no ambitions for a career, no wish to be independent. She relishes her new position and swears that her strongest desire is to be Sir Michael's faithful and devoted wife.

Robert Audley, as he tightens the web of evidence in which he plans to trap her, is frightened by her violence but absolutely repelled by her resourcefulness in deceiving all of them for so long. Putting her at the end of a long line of deceitful women, he recalls "the horrible things that have been done by women since that day upon which Eve was created" and shudders at Lucy Audley's "hellish power of dissimulation" (chap. 29). Not content with comparing Lucy's behavior to the mythic evil of Eve and the legendary crimes of Lucrezia Borgia, Catherine de Médicis, and the Marquise de Pompadour, Robert Audley also invokes the contemporary personification of feminine deceit, Maria Manning, who had been Dickens's source for the murderous lady's maid in *Bleak House*.

Audley's reaction echoes both the general Victorian dread of women's demonic powers and the inescapable seductive appeal of a woman like Lucy.[6] Young Audley's growing revulsion at and vindictiveness toward his aunt's behavior are fueled by his initial attraction to her, and the intensity of his hatred is set against the adoration he would have felt had she been as sweet and docile as she seemed. It is very much to the point that the once-assertive woman he ends up marrying meekly abandons her independence for domestic bliss, exactly as everyone thinks Lucy has done.

Lucy, after all, is correct in her assessment that a woman's security is determined by how well she marries, but ironically neither of Lucy's husbands defends or protects her when she is in need and neither assumes responsibility for the events which precipitate her self-protecting violence. Talboys abandons her and their child, penniless, without warning or explanation. He sends no word for three years.

Yet it never occurs to him that he has done anything wrong or that she will not be waiting patiently when he returns. Later, Sir Michael walks away from her when her bigamy is revealed, all his "love" gone. The anguish he feels is for himself, not for her, though her plea for forgiveness makes clear that she anticipates the grim fate which awaits her.

The other men in the novel are no more protective. Lucy's father is an incompetent drunk; Robert Audley is a vindictive meddler who can never keep his motives straight; and Luke Marks is a shiftless, ruthless blackmailer who knows no murder has been committed and yet profits from Lady Audley's dread of discovery. No one forces her, of course, to use violence to cover her deceits, as no one had forced her to measure success in materialistic terms. The reason she is punished so cruelly is that she has somehow bested men—or so they believe. Braddon implies that they do not want justice as much as they want revenge.

When Robert Audley confronts Lucy with the results of his investigations, he calls her "an artful woman . . . a bold woman . . . a wicked woman." He concludes this diatribe with an accusation that would be ludicrous if he were not so serious: "If this woman of whom I speak had never been guilty of any blacker sin that the publication of that lying announcement [of her own death] in the *Times* newspaper, I should still hold her as the most detestable and despicable of her sex—the most pitiless and calculating of creatures. That cruel lie was a base and cowardly blow in the dark, it was the treacherous daggerthrust of an infamous assassin" (chap. 29).

And he is not finished: "Do you think the gifts which you have played against fortune are to hold you exempt from retribution? No, my lady, your youth and beauty, your grace and refinement, only make the horrible secret of your life more horrible" (chap. 29). After Lucy's confession of bigamy and hereditary insanity (purportedly the real secret she is trying to hide), Audley finds a convenient Victorian way to punish her without involving the judicial system, and without exposing her—and more importantly, his family—to the scandal of a trial.[7]

The doctor he engages insists that Lucy is not mad, yet he warns that she is dangerous. Convinced that no court in the country would convict her of either George Talboys's or Luke Marks's murder on the basis of the available evidence, he nonetheless arranges for her to be confined in a madhouse for the rest of her life. His reason? He believes—because she does not take the trouble to hide her animosity toward him, as a true lady would—that she poses a threat to society at large, the *one* charge that the narrator never makes and that none of Lucy's actions support. Elaine Showalter thinks that Braddon introduces madness to prevent Lucy from being tried, convicted, and executed for murder. In that way, Braddon could "spare her women readers the guilt of identifying with a cold-blooded killer."[8] That reading ignores the fact that Lucy could not have been brought to trial without some conclusive proof of her guilt in Talboys's second disappearance. Further,

Victorian judicial history suggests that even though Lucy was responsible for Luke Marks's death, she probably would not have been tried, even more probably would not have been convicted, and certainly would not have been executed for killing a man of his class and reputation. Had she been found guilty of either arson or bigamy, the court in all probability would have committed her to an insane asylum just as Audley does.

Rather, Braddon used the insanity device because it allows Lucy Audley to be locked up—not for murder or bigamy or arson but for daring to assert some control over her own life. Her punishment enabled Robert Audley to demonstrate the authority over women that he believes men should have. By labeling Lucy "insane," he can reaffirm that sane women are dependent and need his help in dealing with the problems in their lives. There is, as well, an inescapable connection between Audley's telling himself that Lucy is insane and his letting her step-daughter believe that Lucy has been guilty of some outrageous but unspecified sexual indiscretion. Insane women and promiscuous women fit his, and his society's, perception of deviant female behavior. Women who throw men down wells, set fire to hotels, and try to strangle people with their bare hands do not fit any comfortable Victorian's idea of how a woman would behave.

Braddon's most serious limitation in depicting Lucy Audley as a criminal is that her perspective is not consistent. Not only does she switch the protagonist of the novel from Lucy to Robert Audley partway through the story, but also her narrator's original sympathy for Lucy gives way to open antagonism. As a result, the narrator's comments are ruthless and sometimes incredible in their criticism; yet Braddon surely intended the final scene between Lucy and her "judge and jailer," Robert Audley, to rouse the reader to profound pity for the woman. Lucy's description of George Talboys's goading and tormenting makes her violent response to him perfectly understandable, perhaps even forgivable. The disproportion between the harm she has actually caused and the punishment she suffers is enormous. The gravest injustice of all is that Robert Audley makes no attempt to have her released from the asylum when he discovers that George Talboys is not dead. He is instead confident that "it may be some comfort to her to hear that her husband did not perish in his youth by her wicked hand" (chap. 38).

Lady Audley was Braddon's first big success, but it was not her last. Prolific and inventive, she changed her themes and her characters to keep pace with the demands of popular fiction while continuing to create women who were violent or incited violent actions in others. Whether those books were formulaic tales like *Taken at the Flood* (1874) or powerful analyses of destructive emotions like *Joshua Haggard's Daughter* (1876), Braddon used the serious social and moral issues implicit in crime to produce a radical if circumspect attack on Victorian self-esteem. In the latter novel, a clergyman, his daughter, and his much-younger bride are caught in a web of jealousy, wife abuse, and subliminal incest which results in the murder of the daughter's fiancé and the consequent deaths of Haggard and his wife. Naomi Haggard, whose jealous fury provokes her father to murder, single-mindedly devotes herself to sustaining her father's saintly reputation, although she is fully aware of his guilt and her own complicity. Braddon makes clear that appearance and reality are not the same, that corruption can flourish beneath a respectable facade.

The growing frankness with which Braddon and her contemporaries describe sexual feelings (though not actions) demonstrates the liberating effect of a decade of sensation novels on English fiction. Though still far more discreet than Zola in *Thérèse Racquin* (1869) or Nikolai Leskov in "Madame Macbeth of Mzinsk" (1865) in acknowledging the power of love and hate to beget violence, Victorian novelists were increasingly candid in pointing out the consequences of frustrated emotions in otherwise quite ordinary women (and men).

Oliver Madox Brown is a case in point. In *The Black Swan,* he describes Gabriel Denver's infidelity and his wife's murderous rage as the direct consequences of sexual and emotional frustration.[9] Early in the novel Brown uses conventional imagery to describe the outraged and threatening Dorothy Denver: her teeth glisten in a dark-complected face, her deep-set eyes, "glittering with the revengeful reckless light of madness," make her look diabolical, and the overall impression is that of "an enraged venomous snake" (chap. 1). As the novel unfolds, though, Dorothy becomes less a symbol of evil and more an obsessed woman determined to punish the lovers for her private agony and public embarrassment.

Denver himself recognizes the legitimacy of Dorothy's rage, not only in feeling guilty about the passion he cannot control but also about the hollow emptiness in the life they had shared as man and wife. He freely admits that he married Dorothy for her money and held her at arm's length until she abandoned any attempts to please him or to break through his reserve. "What psychologist," Denver muses, "can fathom . . . the soul of a neglected woman, hardened into strange formations of dull, callous feeling?" (chap. 4). As a result, the more Denver's active hatred for his wife becomes apparent, the more ambivalent the reader becomes about his motives for loving Laura and about Dorothy's justification for wanting to punish them. It is enough, in James Ashcroft Noble's words "to leave a sense of jarring discord between our judgment and our emotions."[10]

An abandoned woman, far from home, without the comfort of children, family, or friends might, in a more conventional novel, have taken to her bed with an attack of brain fever. But not Dorothy Denver. Before she finally sets fire to the ship on which they are traveling and precipitates all their deaths, she threatens to murder both her husband and his beloved Laura. "I could have struck a knife into your hearts!" she shouts at him. "I'll strangle you in your sleep!" (chap. 1).

Dorothy's rage does not make her a heroine, even in an unconventional sense. Physically and morally unattractive, she is a cold-blooded killer, outraged that she does not live long enough to see her enemy die. Indeed she becomes nearly hysterical as the weakened and dehydrated Laura goes on breathing: "Not dead yet? is she always to live on and make my eyesight a curse to me? What have I done to kill and destroy her, that she still lingers there like a starved snake? Oh God! if it's useless after all, and I've given my soul to hell and my body to death only to be cheated! I'll strangle her sooner myself" (chap. 8). This otherwise ordinary Englishwoman commits a crime of such magnitude, of such reckless disregard for the lives of innocent sailors, of such total destruction, that the reader is jolted by the import of her dying words: "I told you you should learn what a woman's love turned to hatred could do" (chap. 8).

Brown is morally conventional in having the guilty Dorothy die a miserable death: the "burning" triggered by the madness of drinking sea water is a none too subtle reflection of her burning hate and the burning ship. It suited Victorian sensibility that she destroys herself by the violence she uses against others. But the novel's jarring power comes from the explosion of emotions which escape from her tightly reined control, a control which Dickens feared because it was so vulnerable to stress, and Eliot advocated because women without it were destructive. Brown's novel is not a plea for more liberal divorce laws nor a moral judgment on loveless marriages and infidelity, but an examination of the internal and external forces which can unite to drive usually conventional, even ordinary, women to gruesome crimes.

Helen Mathers, another popular late-Victorian novelist who regularly cast women criminals as major characters, is the author of a particularly sympathetic and sensitive examination of intertwined passion and guilt: *Murder or Manslaughter* (1885). The novel, which foreshadows the tragedy of Thomas Hardy's *Tess of the d'Urbervilles,* tells the story of the hapless Beryl Booth. Charged with murdering her husband because of the rumor that she was having an illicit love affair at the time of his death, Beryl initially confesses. Lacking the will to defend herself in court because she believes herself responsible for his death, she only reluctantly agrees to allow Hugo Holt, the man she loves, to mount a daring refutation of the charges. Then, when he seems to have convinced the court that the death was a suicide, she cries out that the defense is a lie, that she did meet her lover in the garden, that she meant "to take a human life," and that she deserves to die. The jury, taking her at her word, convicts her and she is sentenced to hang.

She holds herself at fault on two counts: before her husband's death she had confessed to him her passionate attraction to the brilliant attorney, and she had bought the poison her husband drank, intending to take it herself because she could think of no other escape. In her own mind she is as guilty as if she had stabbed him through the heart, although she knows perfectly well that Holt's suicide defense is sound. The underlying issue, as it so often is in novels with women killers, is the guilt attached to extramarital love, even when that love is unconsummated. On that subject Mathers is brilliant, both in evoking the lovers' awakening mutual passion and in dissecting Beryl's obsessive self-denial, initially resisting the truth about her feelings and then rejecting the physical and emotional fulfillment of a love affair because she has internalized the moral values of her time and place.

Like the most perceptive novelists of the period, Mathers is candid about women's craving for satisfying emotional (and romantic) relationships, men's profound chauvinism, and the trap a hollow marriage becomes for women who crave more than financial security and social position. What is more unusual is that moral rectitude is not the only reason Beryl Booth resists adultery; if it were, the modern reader would be less touched by her struggle. Rather, as a woman who has established her own persona through popular success as a painter, she refuses to become any man's mistress. She knows all too well that Holt has no intention of creating a scandal or risking his own reputation by leaving his wife to live openly with her. In fact he says as much. Yet he begs her to do what he will not, to move into the demimonde. And she resents it.

Other evidence of the novelist's serious purpose is found in Mathers's creative use of standard sensation novel devices. For instance, the painting in *Lady Audley's Secret* which suggested some sinister force behind a benign facade is hard to take seriously as character development. But when Beryl Booth, desperately unhappy, paints a domestic scene labeled "Deserted," with her husband hovering between sleep and death while she herself watches impassively from the doorway, there is little doubt that the work echoes the turmoil in her own mind. And when the painting is used during her trial as evidence that the murder was premeditated, the reader can quarrel only with the interpretation. That it reveals something about the psychological state of its creator is never in doubt.

Similarly, the recurrent references to physical abuse are not used for shock effect; in fact, violence never actually occurs. Instead the threats of violence comment on the dynamic of a romantic relationship in which a man (in this case Hugo Holt) expects to have his own way and is denied. On two different occasions he threatens to beat Beryl for resisting his advances. The suggestion, of course, is that he could force her to bend to his will. And though he never strikes her, there is an element of real menace in his words, a threat that grows out of his frustration, that seems to him within the limits of tolerance, and is kept in check only by his own force of will.

Finally, the opposition between a virtuous woman and a shameless adventuress, which is so often the centerpiece of nineteenth-century fiction, is given an ironic twist in *Murder or Manslaughter.* The "guilty" woman is not temptress but tempted. Her husband is so obsessed with his scientific investigations that he has little time for her, though she is eager to be a good wife. Her lover importunes her to no avail. She believes her friends when they insist that men have all the pleasures in love and women all the penalties. And Holt's wife is dull and shallow by comparison with the object of his desire: "Serenely unconscious of rivalry, but fully aware of her advantages, which included her house, her diamonds, her gaieties, her children, and, last of all, her husband, Mrs. Holt looked exactly like what she was—a handsome, well-meaning, good sort of second rate woman" (chap. 37).

But Mathers, like her heroine, was finally a woman of her time, and, in the crunch, virtue, not independence, was the theme she chose to stress. Nowhere is this clearer than after Edmund Booth's death when betrayal is no longer a bar to Beryl's liaison with Holt. Yet Beryl craves punishment, either overtly, for murder, or more ineluctably by running away after she is cleared. Who, the frustrated reader wonders, could have blamed her for staying and taking her chances at happiness with Holt? Yet for all its moralizing, the denouement is more intellectually satisfying than the resolution of Eliot's *Middlemarch,* wherein Dorothea's second marriage reduces her to conventional wifehood. Beryl Booth refuses to yield either body or soul, so although she is lonesome, she is free.

The excesses of sensation fiction had been unfairly maligned and its contributions correspondingly ignored until renewed interest in popular literature, specifically what Victorian women read and wrote, prompted reexamination of the texts.[11] It remains a valid criticism that the frequency with which women are guilty of violent crime stretches the truth, as does the emphasis on the criminality of the middle class. Yet only a hypocrite or a fool would deny that crime was omnipresent in the Victorian world or that it was often engendered by the moral and legal rigidity on which that society prided itself. In the interest of either good taste or good sales, the novelists avoided Kate Webster and her crime (chopping up her employer and cooking the pieces) and the more horrible aspects of baby-farming and infanticide which were all too frequent in working-class and impoverished environments and which contemporary journalists described in gory detail. Similarly, they ignored incest and other sexual "perversions" like homosexuality and sadomasochism. Rather, the crimes the novels describe addressed timely issues. For instance, some of the women killers are truly evil, and their crimes show a malevolence that goes far beyond the bounds of rational behavior. Yet because they maintain an aura of gentility and decorum, they are protected, if only temporarily, from suspicion. Just as emphatically as the novelists wanted to show women capable of anything including murder, they wanted to expose the hypocrisy of equating conventionality with moral virtue.

As a result of its candor and boldness, the sensation genre exerted a strong influence on Victorian fiction at large, although many contemporary novelists declared themselves appalled and shocked by its style and subjects. George Eliot, for instance, believed her own account of the situations which provoked women to violence, and the cultural imperatives that kept them from it, was more honest than what Braddon or Collins had to say. But between Hetty Sorrel (in 1859 before the sensation era began) and Gwendolen Harleth (after it had begun to wane in 1876) an enormous change occurred in Eliot's—and in society's—conception of the kind of woman who could commit murder.[12]

Notes

1. Margaret Oliphant, "Novels," *Blackwood's Edinburgh Magazine* 102 (September 1967): 257-80. See also Leslie Stephen, "The Decay of Murder," *Cornhill Magazine* 20 (December 1869): 722-33, and A. Innes Shand, "Crime in Fiction," *Blackwood's Edinburgh Magazine* 148 (August 1890): 172-89.

2. See Thomas Boyle, *Black Swine in the Sewers of Hampstead* (New York: Viking Books, 1989) for a discussion of the influence of mid-century crime reporting on the plots and language of the emerging sensation novel.

3. Showalter, *Literature of Their Own,* 165ff.

4. Despite the fact that later in the novel Braddon refers to William Holman Hunt, an artist who often used doubling images on his paintings, to reassert the portrait's depiction of Lucy's dual personality, there is no Hunt work as evocative of the sense of feminine evil that Braddon is trying to create as either Rosetti's painting of Lucrezia Borgia (1860-61) or Burne-Jones's of Sidonia von Bork (1860).

5. Gitter, "Power of Women's Hair," 943.

6. For a Victorian reaction to Lady Audley, see Shand, "Crime in Fiction," 188. Audley is labelled a "moral monstrosity," but Braddon is praised for her readability and credibility. "We are inclined to accept all she writes as gospel. If it is not true it ought to be, so great is the air of *vraisemblance.*"

7. The novel reflects the ability of families with the financial or social resources to block or manipulate police investigations and "spare" their women the public disgrace of judicial proceedings. Constance Kent's case provides an interesting illustration. Whatever his motive, Kent's father kept the local police from investigating the scene of the crime for several hours, joined them in their examination of the physical evidence, and was made privy to their findings and suspicions (see Hartman, *Victorian Murderesses,* 118 and *passim,* for discussion of the details of the case). When Constance was not indicted—although she was the prime suspect—he promptly sent her to a convent school in France where she was kept, under a false name, for three years. His machinations put Robert Audley's behavior in Braddon's novel in perspective.

8. Showalter, *Literature of Their Own,* 166, argues persuasively that Audley was not insane and that her

guilty "secret" was that she was a highly competent and assertive woman clever enough to hide her brains behind her physical charms.

9. *The Black Swan,* in Brown, *The Dwale Bluth,* vol. 2 (London: Tinsley Brothers, 1876). To get the novel published the first time (as *Gabriel Denver* in 1873), Brown mitigated Denver's guilt by changing the vengeful wife to an unloved fiancée and added a happy ending, but retained his candid description of the powerful physical attraction between Denver and Laura Conway and the destructive fury of the abandoned woman.

10. James Aschcroft Noble, *Morality in English Fiction* (Liverpool: W and J Arnold, 1887), 53.

11. See Winifred Hughes, *The Maniac in the Cellar: Sensation Novels of the 1860*'s (Princeton: Princeton Univ. Press, 1980), and Sally Mitchell, *The Fallen Angel,* for perceptive reassessments. In this context it is interesting to read George Eliot's "Silly Novels by Lady Novelists," *Westminster Review* 66 (1856): 442-61.

12. The puzzle that women criminals posed for nineteenth-century novelists and their audiences is encapsulated by E. S. Dallas's *The Gay Science* (1866), an exposition and critique of the science of criticism. Before he tackles the way women are described in contemporary novels, Dallas defends sensation fiction as legitimate literature, observing that it differs from respectable literature "solely in the relation of the characters pourtrayed [sic] to the actions described," and insisting that neither the serious novel's emphasis on the control a character exerts on his circumstances nor the sensation novel's suggestion that character is controlled by event is wholly true or wholly false. He attacks the grounds on which sensation fiction is damned: "To show man as the sport of circumstance may be a depressing view of human nature; but it is not fair to regard it as immoral nor to denounce it as utterly untrue" (xvii).

When he turns to a discussion of the feminine influence which "pervades" literature, he forgets his own observations about veracity and the mirroring of society. Novelists "deny truth" if they make women central to the action because that is not the way things are, he says. He sees no irony in his own observation that the first appearance of a woman in literature—Eve in the Garden of Eden—is also the first instance of unfeminine behavior. His eventual point, however, is a reluctant acknowledgment that by concentrating on women, especially women of action, the novelists became increasingly interested in the private individual rather than a larger-than-life character, not only as hero(ine) but also as villain(ess).

Chiara Briganti (essay date 1991)

SOURCE: "Gothic Maidens and Sensation Women: Lady Audley's Journey from the Ruined Mansion to the Mad-house"[1] in *Victorian Literature and Culture,* Vol. 19, AMS Press, 1991, pp. 189-211.

[*In the following essay, Briganti discusses the ways in which Lady Audley is and is not a typical sensation novel villainess and Braddon's ambivalence toward her character.*]

> And I also have no name, and that is my name. And because I depersonalize to the point of not having a name, I shall answer everytime someone says: me.
>
> (Clarice Lispector, *The Passion According to G.H.*)

On the surface, Mary Braddon's **Lady Audley's Secret** seems to endorse Patrick Brantlinger's thesis that paradoxically "sensation novels—and mystery novels after them—conclude in ways that liquidate mystery: they are not finally mysterious at all" (21). The plot is deceptively simple: Robert Audley suspects that his uncle's child-bride is not the angel she seems to be and may in fact be involved in the disappearance of George Talboys, Robert's best friend. Events will prove him right: the former governess Lucy Graham, now Lady Audley, has indeed committed bigamy in marrying the elderly Sir Michael Audley and, to prevent discovery of her crime, has attempted to murder George, her first husband. Later, she attempts to murder Robert too, and when this fails, she claims to be suffering from hereditary insanity. To protect the family from scandal, Robert takes her to an insane asylum in Belgium and leaves her there. The last chapter briefly mentions the death of the woman, announced by the arrival of a black-edged letter, and describes the peaceful life of the "good" characters in a cottage away from Audley Court, the mansion where the events of the novel have taken place.

And yet, even though the mystery of George's disappearance has been solved, in **Lady Audley's Secret** the mystery continues to circulate. Reduced to no more than a black-edged letter, the ghost of Lady Audley comes back to question the sanity of the world that has excluded her. We cannot confidently say that at the end of the novel we have discovered Lady Audley's secret. Her secret may be one of many: it may very well be related to the mother's legacy, but it may also be, as Elaine Showalter has indicated, that she is not insane (114). Her secret cannot be discovered, for secrecy, the inescapable condition for a successful seizure of power/discourse, is the condition under which Lady Audley operates. It is, in fact, the very origin of her being, for the centerpiece of the novel is Lady Audley's secret name.

Seizing on that which is after all a common expectation regarding women's willingness to change names, Helen Maldon, the daughter of a drunk and ineffectual father and of an insane, nameless mother, becomes Helen Talboys, and with this name signs her own death on the gravestone at Ventnor. Having died in 1857 as Helen Talboys, aged 22, she is reborn as Lucy Graham, a self-given name that functions as the working title of the story she is determined to author. It is perhaps a sign of Braddon's ambivalence toward her heroine/villainess that she allows the novel to bear the title that Helen, alias Lucy, has so fiercely struggled to retain. Braddon, whose own lifetime secret was her quasi bigamous liaison with John Maxwell, complied with the conventions of the sensation novel and felt that her duty was to dispose of the villainess. But it is interesting that, like Helen Maldon, she was born in 1835 and like her she was reborn in 1857 with a self-given name, Mary Seyton—to become an actress of pantomimes.

Lady Audley, consummate actress, witch, and enchantress, not only finds her ancestresses in the Cleopatras and Semiramides of history (Uglow xix) but can impersonate her mad mother when madness proves useful and can cast her shadow on the other women in the narrative. She refuses the fixative, unifying power of the name, and thus her identity literally proliferates as though the narrative were driven by the compulsion to repeat: "[Robert Audley] paused upon the threshold of that chamber in which he had left Lucy, Lady Audley; otherwise Helen Talboys, the wife of his lost friend" (309). One of the strongest circumstantial pieces of evidence against her has been the label with the name of Helen Talboys buried under that of Lucy Graham which Robert has carefully peeled from the luggage that she had left with her previous employer. Thus her journey through a series of identities can appear as a journey in search of her own spectral name. That she finds it at the end in the *maison de santé*;—a made-up, improvised name—opens up the disquieting possibility that the madwoman may in fact be any woman.

NUNS AND OTHER REDUNDANT WOMEN

In Audley Court, time has stopped and cannot be told, since the "stupid, bewildering clock" in the clocktower has only one hand (1). Audley Court used to be a convent, and in fact the first human presence in this desolate place overgrown with moss, reminiscent of the ruined mansions dear to the authors of Gothic tales, is that of the quiet nuns who have walked there hand in hand. These women, surrounded by ancient walls, are the first female icon in the text, the first of a series of versions of femininity that is offered, and their presence suggests the possibility that in spite of apparent differences, *Lady Audley's Secret* may still be struggling with the legacy of the Gothic tradition.

Echoes of the Gothic come as a surprise: after all *Lady Audley's Secret* is the story of a strong-minded, self-willed woman, whereas the Gothic, as Michelle Massé has said, imbeds "the refusal of the heroine's existence as subject" (681). In fact, traditionally, in spite of Robert Heilman's claim that "it was the function of Gothic to open horizons beyond social patterns, rational decisions, and institutionally approved emotions . . . to enlarge the sense of reality and its impact on the human being" (108), the Gothic does not expand the horizons of its female characters. The heroine is usually the selfless victim of deceit and scheming, trapped by a villain and rescued by a hero, but never empowered to effect her own self-rescue. To be sure, a sig-

nificant reversal has occurred: in the Gothic "the narrative is shaped by the mystery the male presents and not by the drama of the supposed protagonist, the Gothic heroine" (Massé 679), and, I would like to add, the mystery of the male is often figured in the mysterious mansions that are the common setting of these novels. Here instead the mystery is female, and it is the heroine/villainess, not the hero/villain that is associated with the mystery of the house. And yet, in spite of this ostensible difference, the novel demonstrates that in Audley Court time has indeed stopped and cannot be told. At the end, at least at the level of the plot, the heroine's autonomy is condemned here too; and, significantly, when Lady Audley is removed to the Belgian *maison de santé*, the figure of the nun returns as Robert tells his unfortunate charge that she is after all not worse off than a king's daughter—or even a nobleman's daughter such as Manzoni's *monaca di Monza*—who has joined a convent: "The solitude of your existence in this place," Robert tells Lady Audley, "will be no greater than that of a king's daughter, who, flying from the evil of the time, was glad to take shelter in a house as tranquil as this" (331).

In spite of Robert's embellishments, the women he evokes do not necessarily take vows to fly the evil of the world, or to pursue their religious vocation, but rather because they are redundant. The social system cannot accommodate them without being disrupted and thus finds an "asylum" for them. Probably the most evident sign of Lady Audley's defeat is that all her scheming only serves to replace the asylum of the convent with the insane asylum. The chain of silent women still haunts the novel. The "flaming necklace, or ring, or starry circle of some kind," a bit of specifically feminine jewelry that appears in Esther Summerson's vision in *Bleak House* (432; ch. 35) can also appear in the shape of a black ribbon, the hangman's rope, or the chain of circumstantial evidence that will close around Lady Audley. But while in *Bleak House* the chain in its various figurations bespeaks sexual guilt, here it speaks of the threat of claustration that attends female autonomy.

Massé observes that "the Gothic plot is . . . not an escape from the real world but a repetition and exploration of the traumatic denial of identity found there" (688), concluding that the Gothic "does not in fact function well as 'escape' literature" (689, 24n). I would like to elaborate on this point and argue that the replacement of the quiet nuns with Lady Audley, an attempt to go beyond repetition, marks the passage from the Gothic novel to the sensational novel. Whereas the nuns cannot escape Audley Court and still pace on the gravelled walk, Lady Audley devises her escape and is determined not to let the past strangle her (9). True, the outcome is not substantially different: Lady Audley is strangled by her past, which becomes one with the past of women, of her mad, girlish mother, and of the nuns of Gothic fiction. And she too is buried alive; but at least in her case female subjectivity is allowed some play.

BEHIND CLOSED DOORS

Audley Court, Jennifer Uglow has noticed, is "infected by a sense of probing and questioning (the very cows have inquisitive eyes)" (XIV). Besides being old and bewildered, as if it could not make sense of its own present—and this inability to figure out the present may indicate a failure to understand the past—Audley Court is also bewildering. Visitors will easily lose their way in it, for the building is "very irregular and rambling" (1). The chimneys are "so broken down by age and long service" that they seem to be supported only by the straggling ivy that has wound itself around them. While the parasitic ivy feeds on the building to survive, the structure that provides support for it, although decaying, struggles against destruction and remains impenetrable. The most conspicuous sign of its impenetrability is a door "so thick that the iron knocker struck upon it with a muffled sound, the visitor was fain to ring a clanging bell . . . lest the noise of the knocking sound should never penetrate the stronghold" (2).

Because age seems to be the only claim the house has to nobility and because the structure has not worn well, nobility becomes ambiguously associated with decay. The stagnant well has "a lazy rope so rotten that the bucket had broken away from it, and had fallen into the water" (2). Time has added a room one year, knocking down a room another year, in random sequence. Thus what we have is a rather rambling proliferation of surfaces, which, however, are capable of hiding secret passages. In this respect, Audley Court is a suitable objective correlative of Lady Audley herself who, because of the necessity of rejecting her past, appears to be all surface, but who, like the house, hides secrets. We learn very soon that she wears a locket hidden in her bodice, attached to a black ribbon that she clutches at "as if it had been strangling her" (9). The first of a series of links in the chain that will finally wind itself around her, this black ribbon is the first clue that alerts the reader that Lucy Graham is not who she seems to be. Moreover, it will soon become part of "that invisible rope which is woven out of straws collected at every point of the compass, and which is yet strong enough to hang a man" (104)—not a woman, though, since a more appropriate punishment for her is live burial, a fate that, while sealing her place among the ghostly nuns, by its very nature suggests the impossibility of obliterating her presence effectively.

While the nuns quietly haunt the broad gravelled walk, Lady Audley makes her first appearance in the text sauntering at her husband's side in the shrubbery at the end of a shaded avenue that "seemed a chosen place for secret meetings" (3). And in the avenue we will see her again, no longer sauntering, but "singing as she came" (67)—a scene that acquires a retrospective sinister quality once we discover that she has just attempted murder and, for all she knows, has succeeded. That first motion, her sauntering, rather than walking quietly, separates her from the nuns only apparently. If the nuns are figures of female victim-

ization and repressed desire, figures of redundance even, Lady Audley's childish sauntering is equally a sign of repression, of what is required of a woman to become an image of acceptable femininity. Her sauntering followed by singing after attempting murder casts a shadow on the child-bride figure so dear to the Victorians. This shadow is deepened by Lucy's later account of her encounter with her mother in the mad-house. She expected to see a "raving, straitwaistcoated maniac, guarded by zealous gaolers." But what she encounters is "a golden-haired, blue-eyed, girlish creature, who seemed as frivolous as a butterfly, and who skipped towards us, with her yellow curls decorated with natural flowers, and saluted us with radiant smiles, and gay, ceaseless chatter" (296). Not only does this picture insist on the resemblance between mother and daughter, it also suggests the disquieting possibility that the alternative consequences of female autonomy are crime or insanity, and that enclosure in the insane asylum may be the proper destination for the Angel in the House.

Having started her career as a governess, Lucy Graham has however refused to fit the reassuring stereotype of the ideal governess, "a homely, severe, unfeminine type of woman" (Peterson 19), and has managed to fashion a suitable, unalarming girlish appearance as vessel for her feminine charms. She has almost literally acquired Alice in Wonderland's power of self-miniaturization, which allows her to bewitch without threatening and in fact to support (very much like the ivy that has wound itself around the decaying chimney) Sir Michael's patriarchal stance. We hear much about her charming childishness. She is described as a "childish, helpless, babyfied little creature" (119), with a "feeble hand" (123). How deceptive this feebleness is we will discover when we realize that this is the hand that attempts to murder George Talboys and Robert Audley, not by putting arsenic into their tea (a much more common expedient), but by shoving George down a well.

In her well-known attack against sensation fiction, Mrs. Oliphant remarked how "[h]air, indeed, in general, has become one of the leading properties in fiction. . . . Power, strength, a rich nature, a noble mind, are all to be found embodied in this great attribute" (269). Like these sensational heroines, to whom Mrs. Oliphant so fiercely objected, Lucy too is blessed with an abundance of ringlets. But while their hair is clearly a sexual attribute, hair like Lady Audley's is not only of the wrong color ("[r]ed and gold," Mrs. Oliphant reminds us "in all its shades, are compatible with virtue" 269) but is "rarely seen except upon the head of a child" (132). She can play the role of child-bride to the elderly baronet perfectly well since she has had time to rehearse it with George Talboys, who remembers her as his "gentle, innocent, loving, little wife" (15). We wonder if perhaps Lucy's witchcraft has not effected some actual shrinkage, when in one scene we see her stand "on tip-toe to kiss [Sir Michael] and was then only tall enough to reach his white beard" (65). The closer she comes to being found out, the smaller, younger, and more feminine she manages to appear. Winifred Hughes is right when she claims that by endowing her "beautiful fiend" with "all the most impeccable of feminine attributes, which themselves lead to bigamy and murder," Braddon chastizes the Victorian ideal of femininity. In Hughes's words, "Lucy Audley may claim, with justice, that she is only doing what is expected of her as a Victorian lady" (126). We know that she cannot legitimately aspire to such a position, but what is even more disturbing about her is that she is "completely natural, completely satisfied, in the feminine role" (Hughes 127). Alice, with all the freedom from the constraints of the above-ground reality that her dream-world affords her, still needs a mysterious bottle and a small cake to change her size. All Lady Audley needs to do to appear in the guise of a girl is to feed the Victorian ideal of femininity, thus becoming in the process almost a caricature of domesticity and exposing such an ideal as being unavoidably fraught with dangers.

GOVERNESSES AND THE SEAMLESS FABRIC OF LIFE

As mentioned earlier, before her fortunate (second) marriage, Lucy Graham, like innumerable other Victorian heroines, was a governess. M. Jeanne Peterson has observed that the abundance of discussions centering on the figure of the governess, literary or real, in Victorian England cannot be explained on the basis of numbers alone: "There were about 25,000 governesses in England in 1851, but there were 750,000 female domestic servants, not to mention women employed in industry" (8). Such disparity in numbers, Peterson concludes, as well as the governess's irrelevant social position and lack of political importance, suggests that her seeming ubiquitousness in literature must be the result of her incongruous situation. Peterson elaborates on this status incongruity by indicating how the governess, while becoming a sign of genteel status for the family that hires her, also reveals the anxiety felt by the family as to whether she will know what her place is. For the family does not. It was an apparently well-known fact that the situation of any servant was "'infinitely preferable to that of a governess' . . . [for] there was apparently no small comfort in 'knowing one's place'" (Peterson 16).

Knowing one's own place is as important in narrative plots—what position does Lady Audley occupy? Is she the heroine or the villainess?—as in Victorian households in England and in the rest of Europe. We know, for instance, how deeply troubled Freud was by the tendency to disregard the fixity of her place in his own governess ("his teacher in sexual matters" Gay 7), in Dora's governess, and later in Lucy R.,[2] an English governess employed in the home of a Viennese factory manager, about whom she soon started to entertain nuptial fantasies. Susan Katz has noticed that Freud "is able to cure Lucy, and persuade his readers of the cure's success, by representing reality—in this case, life as a spinster—as being a natural order to which Lucy must acquiesce" (Katz 304). Lucy Graham would not have acquiesced so easily: acquiescence is the result of a failure of beauty, of whose power Lucy Graham is keenly aware. Her beauty would certainly have assisted her in resisting Freud's attempt to constrain her into the

straitjacket of a seamless narrative in the same way that she has resisted Sir Michael's, Robert's, and George's attempts to constrain her within the unchangeable bounds of a fairytale plot. In fact, she would not have needed Freud to cure her; she would have needed no help from men. She would have surely bewitched the factory manager. Lucy R., decidedly a victim of Freud's desire to resist her upstart social mobility, is haunted by a smell of burnt pudding. In contrast, Lucy Graham will not be haunted by the smell of a whole burnt public house. However, she does share the other Lucy's humble origins, and, significantly, the suspicions of the person who hounds her down, Robert Audley, are triggered precisely by his awareness of the advantages that marriage has bestowed on her. Robert Audley has no desire for self-advancement, but he is aware of that dream of upward mobility in which, although a chimera in reality, any Victorian governess was suspected of indulging. Thus, when Lady Audley recalls her past as a governess at Mr. Dawson's, he responds: "It *is* a change. . . . Some women would do a great deal to accomplish such a change as that" (102). Indeed, one way of dispelling such anxiety was to import foreign governesses and to export English gentlewomen to foreign countries.

We encounter one of these exported assets right at the beginning of the novel: Miss Morley, the thirty-five-year-old maiden governess George Talboys encounters on the Argus, has spent fifteen years in Australia (a place to which the Victorians were inclined to dispatch many social aberrations); now, past her prime, her bloom faded, she returns to England to face an uncertain future. Ostensibly a version of acceptable femininity—she is "very quiet and reserved . . . and speak[s] very little" (13)—she is in fact a woman who carries the indelible marks of "unfeminine" intellectual strain.[3] Her melancholy eyes "seemed to have faded with poring over closely-printed books and difficult needlework" and "had faded a little, perhaps, by reason of tears secretly shed in the dead hours of the lonely night" (13). Braddon indicates very clearly that her poor face cannot command George's attention beyond civility and thus suggests that her hope of marriage may have been ruined by her strong adherence to desirable Victorian virtues, by her very patience and acquiescence. Her faded presence serves only to emphasize by contrast George's memories of his child-bride. He launches into a string of praises and, in ironic foreshadowing of things to come, confesses that Helen's unhappiness had made him so desperate that he had felt "a strong inclination to throw myself into the sea, so as to leave my poor girl free to make a better match" (17)—a possibility that Lady Audley will very soon consider when she takes into her hands the task of revising the male plot of rescue (in which she would appear as the innocent recipient of the hero's generosity) and resolves to author her own plot of self-rescue.

SEMIRAMIDES, CLEOPATRAS, JOAN OF ARCS AND CO.

Uglow observes how all the main female characters in the novel (Alicia Audley, Clara Talboys, and Lady Audley) "blend into each other, just as the maid Phoebe resembles Lady Audley in looks and in her approach to life, or the dying Matilda Poyson [notice the name!] looks like the vanishing Helen Talboys" (xviii). Phoebe, who marries because words die in her throat, is literally a paler version of Lady Audley. The narrator tells us that she has "something of the grace and carriage of a gentlewoman," and that when she is chosen by Lady Audley to become her maid she is "quite as much the object of envy amongst her particular friends as my lady in her higher circles" (21). Her possessing the grace of a gentlewoman suggests the possibility that what are usually thought to be qualities bestowed only by birth may in fact be acquired, as becomes clear when Lady Audley remarks on their resemblance and suggests that with the help of a bit of artifice—a bottle of hair dye and a pot of rouge—Phoebe would be "as good-looking as I any day" (49). Modern Cinderellas, as Braddon suggests in a digression devoted to the secret that any lady's maid knows, can set out to conquer their prince without the assistance of a fairy:

> Amongst all privileged spies, a lady's maid has the highest privileges . . . she knows when the ivory complexion is bought and paid for—when the pearly teeth are foreign substances fashioned by the dentist—when the glossy plaits of auburn hair are the relics of the dead, rather than the property of the living. . . . When the lovely fairy of the ball-room re-enters her dressing-room after the night's long revelry, and throws aside her voluminous burnous and her faded bouquet and drops her mask—when all the glittering splendours of the modern Cinderella fade and dwindle into the kitchen-wench's dirty rags, the lady's-maid is by to see the transformation.
>
> (285)

We are reminded here of another governess, the protagonist of Louisa May Alcott's *Behind a Mask, or A Woman's Power.* Jeanne Muir, Alcott's nightmarish permutation of Jane Eyre, suitably donning a name that is a mixture of French and English, proceeds to shed her youthful appearance alone in her garret: "Still sitting on the floor she unbound and removed the long abundant braids from her head, wiped the pink from her face, took out several pearly teeth, and slipping off her dress appeared herself indeed, a haggard, worn, and moody woman of thirty at least" (11-12). Imposture, explicitly explored in Alcott, is obliquely addressed and given ambiguous endorsement in Braddon: by having Phoebe marry a boorish drunkard, Braddon shows the limited range of alternatives available to women and thus implicitly makes allowances for Lady Audley's near-murder to an extent that she could not have afforded to do explicitly.

Phoebe resembles her mistress not just in physical appearance but also in her quickness to glimpse and seize opportunities. But she lacks her courage and eventually she must marry Luke because words fail her:

> There have been times when I've made up the very sentence I meant to say to him, telling him that I couldn't keep my faith with him; but the words have died upon my lips, and I've sat looking at him, with a choking sensation in my throat that wouldn't let me speak. I daren't refuse to marry him.
>
> (93)

Thus, unable to bring herself to speak, she marries him, and on a foggy November morning "a superstitious stranger might have mistaken the bride for the ghost of some other bride, dead and buried in the vaults below the church" (95). By marrying Luke she becomes buried alive in a decaying public house; thus, metaphorically, she joins both the heroines of Gothic tales and the ghostly nuns walking hand in hand around Audley Court.

Phoebe, the white woman if not woman in white, finally falls victim to marital Gothic; nevertheless, she displays "a power of repression and self-control" (21) which, although "not common in a woman of nineteen or twenty" (21), is shared by both Lady Audley and Clara Talboys. If Lady Audley exerts self-control to conceal her crimes, Clara has repressed her passionate nature to adapt herself to a squarely regimented life in her father's prim and square mansion, which stands "in the center of prim, square grounds" (154). Emotionally suffocated by Squire Talboys, a man "tall, straight, bony, and angular, with a square, pale face," she goes through life with her hands clasped to hide her face (164). But passion still fires up and transforms her into a "flying female" (167)—an image which, given the cluster of mythological references Robert Audley has conjured around her, points uncomfortably to the Harpies, originally conceived as winged maidens and later as noisome birds with maidens' heads, and to the Furies, the avenging goddesses of guilt; he thus incorporates the bestial iconography that is typical of male perceptions of female madness.[4] Robert Audley is impressed by her "stoicism" when he witnesses her intense suffering and realizes that it is not indifference that prompts her behavior: "'Oh, let me speak to you,' she cried—'let me speak to you, or I shall go mad! I heard it all. I believe what you believe; and I shall go mad unless I can do something—something towards avenging his death!'" (168). Such passion bewilders him, although he chooses to attribute her shivering to a chill. Clara has grown up "in an atmosphere of suppression," (171), and, like Phoebe, she has known the necessity of repressing her feelings.

It is precisely her ability to repress her feelings that conquers Robert and makes her worthy of becoming the guardian spirit of the fairy cottage where the "good people" find refuge at the end. While "[h]is cousin was pretty [and] his uncle's wife was lovely" (171), Clara is made beautiful by her repressed passion and is elevated by her beauty "into sublimity (171). But, even if repressed, the passion is there. That it scares Robert becomes clearer when after their first encounter he launches himself into a tirade against women. In an interesting crescendo expressed in urgent tones, somewhat of a virtuoso performance for such a lethargic individual, Robert goes from condemning "petticoat government" at the hands of wives guilty of pushing their husbands about, to conjuring up the "Semiramides, and Cleopatras, and Joan of Arcs, Queen Elizabeths, and Catherine the Seconds," who "riot in battle, and murder, and clamor, and desperation" (177). He finally concludes by expressing his hatred against all women in general, resenting Clara's fervent pleas as vehemently as Alicia's "bouncing" and Lady Audley's scheming. But unlike Phoebe and Lucy Graham, Clara is rich and her own mistress; thus she can afford to let Robert have a few glimpses of her real nature. Significantly, she manages to persuade him to carry on the investigation by offering (threatening) to carry it on herself. His acquiescence is motivated by his attempt to keep her as the desired calm angel, that is, by his determination to insist upon sexual difference as a condition for sexual desire, which any violation, even Alicia's innocent bouncing, would destroy.

Clara, grief-stricken Niobe and Pallas Athené, offspring of male parturition untainted by dubious maternal legacy, becomes that hand that has been beckoning to him to go on. Upon their chance encounter in Essex, she in fact becomes associated in his mind with the image that drives him to pursue Lady Audley: "'A hand that is stronger than my own is beckoning me onward on the dark road which leads to my lost friend's unknown grave'" (220). Thus she both represents the law that demands retribution for Lady Audley's deeds and provides the exit for Robert Audley from a detective plot to a providential plot, from physiology to metaphysics. In the process, however, she cannot be allowed to remain a grief-stricken woman of statuesque beauty. She prepares herself for her role as guardian angel of the fairy cottage by undergoing miniaturization. Robert Audley will finally propose to her after she appears to him suitably adorned by "a broad-leaved straw hat and flapping blue ribbons" (367). The marble pallor is gone, and the hand Robert finds "half-hidden among the folds of a silken dress" is now a "soft little hand" (371). Thus miniaturized and rejuvenated, she is ready to assume her proper role at his side, while her difference from the other women in the novel is blurred further. Significantly, Braddon's second bigamy novel, *Aurora Floyd,* will feature a heroine who combines the characteristics of Clara Talboys and Alicia Audley with the bigamy and murderous impulses of Lady Audley.

"OH THE MUTE PROPRIETY OF CHAIRS AND TABLES!"

The thought of women's strength, perseverance, and self-assertiveness dissipates the smugness of Robert's bachelor life. London becomes increasingly inhospitable, as Robert slides into a despondency that even he cannot attribute to smoking the wrong kind of cigars. This thought conjures up the idea of the madness of life, which, suitably modified by giving it gender-specific attributes, will come in handy when he is faced with the necessity of disposing of Lady Audley. Michel Foucault once said that madness "provokes a breach without reconciliation where the world is forced to question itself" (288). Indeed madness, whether real or assumed, has provided a breach in the

world of Audley Court, which already appeared bewildered and questioning at the very beginning of the novel. This world, which has borne many additions, has not been able to assimilate them, least of all the improvements, which have been made since Sir Michael's marriage to Lucy Graham and which have remained limited to her apartments without affecting the rest of the house.

Nancy Armstrong has written that by the early nineteenth-century "the household ceased to display the value of the man's income and instead took on the innermost human qualities of the woman who regulated the domestic economy" (86). Armstrong argues that the logical development of this object language was the creation of "a totally fetishized world" in which "objects enter into a demonic exchange with their owners whereby things acquire human qualities and the people who live in a relationship with such things become as objects regulated by the very things they have endowed with human value" (87-88). In *Lady Audley's Secret* we have, on the one hand, the discontented and civilized world in which Robert Audley feels more and more constrained, and, on the other, Lady Audley's sumptuous apartments. Both are highly fetishized and inhabited by objects that speak—but do not speak to each other. In a telling passage, which comes from the narrator but may very well reflect Robert's musings, Braddon tells of the cramped existence to which human beings must subject themselves:

> Who has not felt, in the first madness of sorrow, an unreasoning rage against the mute propriety of chairs and tables, the stiff squareness of Turkey carpets, the unbending obstinacy of the outward apparatus of existence? We want to root up gigantic trees in a primeval forest, and to tear their huge branches asunder in our convulsive grasp; but the utmost that we can do for the relief of our passion is to knock over an easy-chair, or smash a few shillings' worth of crockery.
>
> (175)

It is in the discontent of civilization, in the thwarting and silencing of the heroic desires of all the characters, that the causes of madness are to be found:

> Madhouses are large and only too numerous; yet surely it is strange they are not larger, when we think of how many helpless wretches must beat their brains against this hopeless persistency of the orderly outward world, as compared with the storm and the tempest, the riot and confusion within;—when we remember how many minds must tremble upon the narrow boundary between reason and unreason.
>
> (175-76)

And it is because Robert has been receptive to this tension between an orderly outward existence and the riot within, because he has felt that madness may lurk even in the most controlled of human beings, because he has caught a glimpse of it even under Clara's self-control and has felt himself become prey to the destructive impulses that threaten civilization, because he has felt the boundary between reason and unreason become narrower and narrower (175-76) that he commits himself to pursuing Lady Audley. The fact that his mind is in sympathy with the mind of the criminal, while terrifying him, allows him to become an efficient detective. In fact, his mind is so much in sympathy with Lady Audley's that he feels threatened by Clara. He feels himself slip from the comfortable active role of reader to the vulnerable role of a text subject to scrutiny. Clara, he broods, "knows half my secret" and "she will soon possess herself of the rest" (175). Thus he commits himself to assume this role, despite his misgivings concerning the figure of the "detective police officer, stained with vile associations, and unfit company for honest gentlemen" (340).

Robert Audley has come closer to madness than he will ever realize, for his aunt has seriously attempted to cast doubt on his sanity. But he is a man of means who, in spite of feeling occasionally constrained, has no fierce quarrel with the world he inhabits. Thus, the possibility of going mad, or of being locked away because he is considered mad, does not constitute a serious threat for him. Indeed it comes as no surprise that the only inmate we encounter in the Belgian *maison de santé;* is a woman—in fact, not a woman in flesh and blood, but the silhouette of a woman seen against the light, significantly stylized to fit more than one figure. The *maison de santé,* while ruled by a male doctor, is, it appears, a household of females.

Before following Lady Audley's entrance into this "asylum" I would like to turn my attention to the totally fetishized world of her luxurious apartments within Audley Court. Entrance to these apartments is gained through an octagonal ante-room, which with its many sides seems a suitable icon for Lady Audley's multiple identities and multiple reflections in the novel, and which sharply contrasts with the dullness of the rest of the house even in the eyes of the boorish Luke. The ante-room leads to a "fairy-like boudoir" and from there to a dressing-room where the centerpiece is a brass-inlaid casket that offers to the astonished Luke the sight of diamonds, rubies, emeralds, and, in a secret drawer, a baby shoe and a lock of silky yellow hair (25-26). These rooms are the receptacles of secrets, and it is here that Braddon, who places great emphasis on Lady Audley's physical situation in the house, most often shows her heroine. When Lady Audley is outside she is usually shown in the avenue, but, if inside, she is likely to be found in her apartments, absorbed, like a child, in playing with her trinkets.[5] However, on the two occasions when this space is subjected to the gaze of others, she is absent. If, ostensibly, Alicia's elaborate directions to Robert and George to enter Lady Audley's apartments echo the instructions given to fairy-tale heroes, what the heroes finally confront is an absence. Even her portrait is misleading: the abundance of crimson, its pre-raphaelite pouting lips, bespeak of a passionate nature, of burning sexuality, but, as Hughes has remarked, Lady Audley is "unencumbered by any active sexuality of her own" (127). Whereas the sensation heroine "waits now for flesh and muscles, for strong arms that seize her, and warm breath

that thrills her through" (Oliphant 259), Lady Audley has no use for flesh and muscles. The beautiful sexual fiend in the portrait is not Lady Audley's exposed self, but yet another disguise.

Indeed, the folds of the dress, resembling flames, and the head, "rising out of the lurid mass of color, as if out of a raging furnace" (60), both grimly foreshadow Lady Audley's subsequent crime of arson and at the same time evoke the figure of the sorceress for which the recurring remarks about Lady Audley's bewitching powers have prepared us all along. She herself has conjured up this image. In an intriguing passage that describes her as indulging "in a species of intellectual tarantella, in which her tongue went mad" (90), Lady Audley recalls the story, read in one of those French novels of which Robert and Alicia are also fond, of a beautiful woman who committed some crime and in old age was tried, found guilty, and condemned to be burnt alive (91). As a witch, she is presented when occupied in the most domestic of English rituals, tea-making, which, because of her presiding over it, becomes a revision of a witches' ritual:

> The most feminine and most domestic of all occupations imparts a magic harmony to her every moment, a witchery to her every glance. The floating mists from the boiling liquid in which she infuses the soothing herbs, whose secrets are known to her alone, envelope in a cloud of scented vapour, through which she seems a social fairy, weaving potent spells with Gunpowder and Bohea. At the tea-table she reigns omnipotent, unapproachable. What do men know of the mysterious beverage? . . . How clumsily the wretched creatures attempt to assist the witch president of the tea-tray. . . . To do away with the tea-table is to rob woman of her legitimate empire.
>
> (190)

As Beth Newman has observed in another context, "*Fascinating,* derived from *fascinum* 'witchcraft,' resonates with the now obsolete meaning of *fascinate*—'to bewitch,' which itself survives in a still current definition: 'to transfix and hold spellbound by an irresistible power.'" And, continues Newman, "We have not far to travel . . . to Freud's 'Medusa's Head,' the direct sight of which evokes the terror of castration in the male spectator, a terror that turns him to stone" (1030-31). Loss of power, fear of castration, may very well be at the root of Robert Audley's languid state when visiting at Mrs. Barkamb's: "'I should like to live here,' Robert thought, 'and watch the grey sea slowly rolling over the grey sand under the still grey sky. I should like to live here, and tell the beads upon my rosary, and repent and rest'" (212)—which is what he will urge Lady Audley to do in the *maison de santé.* The man who has complained of the restrictions that civilization imposes on the desire for action is starting to suffer from that *maladie de langueur* by which Lady Audley, transformed into Madame Taylor, will die.

When Robert Audley and Lady Audley arrive in Belgium, Braddon so describes the madhouse: "The gaunt gateway was lighted by an enormous lamp; a great structure of iron and glass, in which one poor little shivering flame struggled with the March wind" (326). This little shivering flame is then replaced by the image of "a dark shadow, the shadow of a woman with a fantastic head-dress, the shadow of a restless creature, who paced perpetually backwards and forwards before the window" (327). Ostensibly a narrator's description, the image of the shadow may very well be filtered through Robert's consciousness, which would not be too surprising, given his often-voiced uneasiness concerning the restlessness of women. Later, the image of the flame returns, when Lady Audley, after an interval during which she has been nameless, and thus, as it were, robbed of her existence,[6] reappears under yet another identity. Robert Audley seems to share Albrecht Dieterich's belief that "to speak the name may be equal to calling a person into being . . . a name is feared because it is a real power" (Cassirer 53), and he thus reminds Alicia that from now on she is not to utter her name. In the rooms of Lady Audley, now a nameless woman, we are told,

> [t]his solitary flame, pale and ghostlike in itself, was multiplied by paler phantoms of its ghostliness, which glimmered everywhere about the rooms . . . in those glimmering surfaces . . . which my lady mistook for costly mirrors, but which were in reality wretched mockeries made of burnished tin.
>
> (329)

This solitary flame is metaphorically associated with Lady Audley herself not just because it resonates with memories of her crimson portrait and her crime of arson; because of its ability to replicate itself, it reminds us of Lady Audley, whose image can be found in the other women in the novel—in the burnished tin of Phoebe's lower rank existence as well as in the more expensive stuff of which Clara, another woman haunted by the phantasm of madness, is made.

Now her name, devised by Robert Audley who "remembered, for the first time, that he had been recommended to introduce his wretched charge under a feigned name" (328), is Madame Taylor, an interesting mixture of English and French that underscores her foreignness. As Madame Taylor, Lucy Graham/Lady Audley (like Lucy Snowe, another governess who speaks French to express her anger, and like the hysterics, who speak in tongues) switches to French, whose sibilant syllables "seem better fitted to her mood and to herself than the familiar English she has spoken hitherto" (330). By speaking French, she confirms her alterity and seals her exile from England and sanity; by renouncing her native language, the language of her fathers, she challenges the patrilinear law that governs its construction and claims immunity to its laws.

But even the suppressed and repressed Clara, who remains faithful to English and sanity, can prove equally menacing to Robert. If Lady Audley's business-like attitude about marriage has disquieted Sir Michael and reduced his hopes of marital happiness to "a corpse in his bosom" (10), intimations of the passion of Pallas Athené, as Robert Audley perceives Clara, disquiet the young barrister: "She reads my pitiful . . . mind, and plucks the thoughts out of my brain with the magic of her solemn brown eyes" (222). Reading, as this passage indicates, is an act of violence in this novel. It involves plucking the thoughts out of one's brain but also unveiling, peeling off the cover that protects Lady Audley, finding clues, articulating *and* censoring meaning. Robert Audley thinks that he can fathom Lady Audley's personality with the help of her handwriting:

> "It is the prettiest, most coquettish little hand I ever saw. Do you know, Alicia, I never believed in those fellows who ask you for thirteen postage stamps, and offer to tell you what you have never been able to find out yourself; but, upon my word, I think that if I had never seen your aunt [sic], I should know what she was like by this slip of paper. Yes, here it all is—the feathery, gold-shot, flaxen curls, the pencilled eyebrows, the tiny straight nose, the winning smile, all to be guessed in these few graceful up-strokes and down-strokes. George, look here!"
>
> (55)

Robert's confidence in the unproblematic interchangeability of text and body is misplaced and amusing. But eventually such interchangeability becomes sinister as Robert recognizes the same graceful strokes in Helen Maldon's handwriting (135). Lady Audley becomes for him "a slip of paper," all surface, and he declares, "I will read her as I have read her before" (185). This act is continuous with the exposure of Lady Audley, which he tellingly describes in violent language: ". . . and [I] will tear away the beautiful veil under which she hides her wickedness, and will wring from her the secret of my friend's fate, and banish her for ever from the house which her presence has polluted" (217).

Robert's lymphatic imagination is now excited. For much of the novel he has displayed a tendency to reduce psychology to physiology, explaining George's fits of depression as a consequence of smoking the wrong kind of cigars and people's nocturnal visions as the result of indigestion and sleeping under damp sheets (53-54, 57). But now the lethargic barrister becomes an active reader of signs. We should remember that Robert, like Alicia, who has seen through Lady Audley's portrait (61) although she too has misread her as "irretrievably childish and silly" (41), is a reader of French novels.[7] Now not only does he read more insightfully, he even has a spell of inventiveness—for a while he becomes almost imaginative, a sort of storyteller. While Robert had started with a strong inclination toward physiology and had mistrusted psychology and metaphysics, now he indulges in fantasies of storytelling and goes as far as slipping on the mask of a mysterious and vaguely disreputable individual:

> "Nobody ever saw a ghost in a hansom cab," Robert thought, "and even Dumas hasn't done *that* yet. Not but that he's capable of doing it if the idea occurred to

him. *Un revenant en fiacre.* Upon my word, the title doesn't sound bad. The story would be something about a dismal gentleman in black, who took the vehicle by the hour, and was contumacious upon the subject of fares, and beguiled the driver into lonely neighbourhoods, beyond the barriers, and made himself otherwise unpleasant."

(342)

But this impulse is soon checked, and the last paragraph of the novel informs us that the French novels that have sparked it "have been presented to a young Templar, with whom Robert Audley had been friendly in his bachelor days" (376). Curiously, this is the last thing we learn, and physiology comes back into play: Lady Audley's imprisonment in the *maison de santé*; is a defeat of the imagination by physiology and rationalism.

Robert Audley's passage from physiology to psychology and metaphysics, begun with his first question. "What does it all mean," and continued through his speculation as to the nature of life, has carried him very close to madness and shown him the necessity of making a quick retreat into his former self. But madness has made its breach into the narrative. And if the madwoman has been locked away, latent insanity, by its very nature, remains a possibility. She is in the "Asylum" for the same reason that the daughters of kings find "asylum" in a convent. As for them it matters not whether they have a religious vocation, so Lady Audley's secret may very well be not that she is a madwoman, "but rather that, *whether she is one or not, she must be treated as such*" (Miller 121). However, as fairy tales are not impervious to revisions and can find themselves telling the story of a heroine determined to exchange the "wandering prince" George Talboys (297) for an elderly but reliable baronet, so even in fairy cottages one cannot ignore that the boundary "between reason and unreason" (176) is only a narrow one, and one cannot find effectual protection against "the storm and tempest, the riot and confusion" (175) of the mind. Thus the fairy-cottage in this novel is as unable to dispel the threat of Lucy Graham's existence as Esther Summerson's diminutive cottage in *Bleak House* is unable to dispel the misery and squalor of the world of Tom-All-Alone.

A BLACK-EDGED LETTER

Robert attempts to neutralize Lady Audley's womanhood by seeing her as "the demoniac incarnation of some evil principle" (292), but it is madness, which Lady Audley invokes as shield, that finally allows him to see her as "no longer a woman" (292). The diagnosis of insanity ends up erasing the individual woman to protect the myth of femininity, of woman as the Angel in the House, as gentle consoler. In fact, as Shoshana Felman has observed, "'madness' is the very 'absence of womanhood,' what makes a woman not a woman" ("Woman and Madness" 8). As "not a woman" Lady Audley is described by Dr. Mosgrave: "'If she could have sprung at my throat and strangled me with her little hands . . . she would have done it" (322).

The first step toward the disclosure of Lady Audley's secret occurs when Robert and George penetrate her octagonal room and unveil the portrait, thus suggesting that order must be insured by a gesture close to a rape. In this portrait, Lady Audley appears suitably fiendish, exposed, revealing what her girlish appearance had managed to disguise. The portrait also crystallizes her identity into that of Helen Talboys and reduces her to mere surface, initiating a process that continues throughout the novel in increasingly sinister tones and culminates at the end, when she becomes "a black-edged letter, written upon foreign paper" (375). Lady Audley's transformation into Madame Taylor has been accompanied by her switch to French. Her discourse, expressed in sibilant French sounds (did Braddon have in mind the serpentine Hortense of *Bleak House*?), is incorporated into a closed structure. As the funereal Dr. Mosgrave tells Robert, the family need worry no longer about her:

> "From the moment in which Lady Audley enters that house," he said, "her life, so far as life is made up of action and variety, will be finished. Whatever secrets she may have will be secrets for ever! . . . If you were to dig a grave for her in the nearest churchyard and bury her alive in it, you could not more safely shut her from the world and all worldly associations. But as a physiologist and as an honest man, I believe you could do no better service to society than by doing this; for physiology is a lie if the woman I saw ten minutes ago is a woman to be trusted at large."

(322)

Dr. Mosgrave believes that she cannot be trusted, but Robert Audley cannot prevail on him to declare her mad ("There is no evidence of madess in anything she has done," the doctor insists). His diagnosis is "latent insanity" (321), which simply means that because she will not submit she must choose marginalization and madness, although there is no evidence of such madness.

Lady Audley is buried alive. And indeed this is the title of the chapter where she makes her last appearance. Buried alive are of course also those impulses which must be repressed—the unconscious. And Lady Audley, whose silence insists on being heard, becomes the unconscious of the text, the "discourse of the Other," the novel's "censored chapter." She comes back, not just as the dead Madame Taylor, but also as "the pretty, fair-haired woman who died abroad" (376). Lady Audley's ascendancy over the household, as Nancy Armstrong would say, has produced "discontinuities that are never quite resolved through a traditional sexual exchange despite a novelist's gesture toward closure" (54). Blackness has been moved to the edges, to the margins of this newly-found fairy world, haunted by the ghost of Audley Court, now shut up, where "a grim old housekeeper reigns paramount in the mansion which my lady's ringing laughter once made musical." Covers are still necessary—"[a] curtain hangs before the pre-Raphaelite portrait"—and secrets are still kept: "The house is often shown to inquisitive visitors, though the owner is not informed of that fact, and people admire my lady's rooms, and ask many questions about the pretty, fair-haired woman who died abroad" (376). Her place has been restored: as a pretty, fair-haired woman, she is the angel of Audley Court. On the one hand, this passage suggests the hollowness of the ideal of the Angel in the House: this ideal is so close to an easily assumed mask that in spite of all that has passed a criminal can still be taken for an Angel. On the other hand, and this is more disturbing, it also shows that Audley Court has appropriated Lucy Graham—has, in fact, framed her—by ignoring the complexities of her being and reducing her to a painted face. As Sandra Gilbert and Susan Gubar have said apropos of Snow White who, "dead and self-less in her glass coffin" (41), awaits the arrival of the prince, Lady Audley too has been reduced to "the eternally beautiful, inanimate *objet d' art* patriarchal aesthetics want a girl to be" (40). Like Snow White, rigid in her glass coffin, she too has become "an idealized image of herself" (41) even though our knowledge of her present whereabouts is an ironic commentary on the falseness of this ideal.

Notice that the title of the chapter that describes the idyllic arrangements at the end of the narrative—"At Peace"—echoes an earlier passage, where the narrative persona makes an abrupt intervention to comment on the discrepancy between appearance and reality, on the horror *à la Blue Velvet* that lurks under the most innocent surface. This passage, a "microcosm of the sensation novel" (Brantlinger 14), resonates more deeply once it is set against the ending:

> We hear everyday of murders committed in the country. Brutal and treacherous murders; slow, protracted agonies from poisons administered by some kindred hand; sudden and violent deaths by cruel blows, inflicted with a stake cut from some spreading oak, whose very shadow promised—*peace*. In this very county of Essex there is a meadow in which, on a quiet summer Sunday evening, a young farmer murdered the girl who had loved and trusted him; and yet even now, with the stain of that foul deed upon it, the aspect of the spot is—*peace*. No crime has ever been committed in the worst rookeries about Seven Dials that has not had its parallel amidst that sweet rustic calm which, still, in spite of all, we look on with a tender, half-mournful yearning, and associate with—*peace*.
>
> (46, italics mine)

These echoes are strengthened by a certain wondering quality (reminiscent of the sense of probing that infects Audley Court) that remains in the ostensibly certain world of the fairy-cottage and that is again shown through the interplay of surface and depth: "Here, amongst the lilies and the rushes on the sloping bank, a brave boy of eight years old plays with a baby who peeps wonderingly from his nurse's arms at that other baby in the purple depth of the quiet water" (375).

The image of the shut up mansion (where my lady's rooms are the only thing that excites the curiosity of the visitors) together with these echoes calls into question and is ap-

propriate to the claustrophobic ending. Not only is Lady Audley incorporated into a closed system, but the world from which she has been expelled closes upon itself and can survive only by sealing her out. The last chapter is the shortest one—merely two pages—and illustrates the aftermath of Lady Audley's expulsion: a rigid network of kinship shapes the world where George Talboys lives with his sister, her husband Robert, and their baby. Master Georgey comes to visit as do Sir Michael and Alicia, who has been restored to her place at her father's side and will remain there despite the impending marriage (given the silliness of the bridegroom, this marriage is a punishment of sorts for her lack of restraint) that will bestow on her, suitably enough, the title of Lady Towers. "No trespassers," reads the invisible sign on the gate. The only outsider who, although not yet present, will soon be allowed to visit, is the foolish Harry Towers, a harmless and, we may be sure, unquestioning upholder of patriarchy. The survivors of the shipwreck all sit together on the lawn, eating strawberries and cream like so many Curly-locks. In this novel closure firmly coincides with enclosure, ensured by two agencies of claustration—marriage and the madhouse. We can stand reassured that Robert will keep his earlier promise that, if he ever has daughters,

> they shall be educated in Paper Buildings, take their exercise in the Temple Gardens, and they shall never go beyond the gates till they are marriageable, when I will take them straight across Fleet Street to St. Dunstan's Church, and deliver them into the hands of their husbands.
>
> (101)

Should a suitable husband fail to appear (but, of course, in this highly inbred world little Georgey will be the most obvious candidate), the convent could provide a viable alternative.

Neither likable nor simply dismissable, Lucy Graham does not command our allegiance. Her individualism is by no means appealing. Her petty greed is distasteful even to sympathetic readers willing to make allowances for her social disadvantages. She is far from eliciting the kind of sympathy we feel for Austen's sanitized heroines, for Marianne Dashwood, for instance, who has paid for her gestures of trespassing with a near-fatal illness and marriage to a Colonel much given to wearing flannel waistcoats. And yet, for all this, Lucy's death brings no relief. The language of the last chapter undermines the comic ending which the novel strives to make desirable. The hurry with which Braddon concludes her story casts doubt on the judgments that the novel seems to make, and her additions to the 1887 American edition, although partly a reflection of some of Braddon's concern in response to the criticism her novel had received when originally published in 1862, also reinforce our impression that something is amiss:

> I hope no one will take objection to my story because the end of it leaves the good people all happy and *at peace*. If my experience of life has not been very long, it has at least been manifold; and I can safely subscribe

to that which a mighty king and a great philosopher declared, when he said, that neither the experience of his youth nor of his age had ever shown him "the righteous forsaken, nor his seed begging their bread."

(286, American edition, italics mine)

If the return of the figure of the king, with its echo of Robert's reference to those king's daughters who choose conventual life, is not sufficient to dispel the smugness of the ending, the recurrence of "at peace" adds ambiguity to it. This last paragraph indeed operates as an extra padlock on a door that we had been asked to view as already firmly secured and thus shakes our faith in the efficacy of the original lock. Indeed, it makes us wonder: is that door really locked against the madness and folly that threatens it? Why so much agitation? Why so much worry? Rather than putting our minds at rest it alerts us to the fact that the novel is the vehicle of collective anxiety and makes us more sensitive to the tension between the ethical construct that Braddon asks us to accept and the daemonic, destructive element embodied in the "beautiful fiend." This daemonic element demands to be heard through the repetition compulsion of the narrative and through Lucy Graham's silenced rage, a rage last voiced in a foreign tongue, incomprehensible to healthy English ears. The powerlessness of the fairy cottage to shut out this foreign rage betrays the difficulty to master the painful legacy of the Gothic and the inability to understand the past. This rage indicts a social system in which only resilience to change and age are proper claims to nobility. It insists that the "stupid, bewildering clock" in the clocktower be fixed so that time can be told. It is, finally, the "reserve of silence" (Felman, "Turning" 193), the silence of the parasitic and inextirpable ivy, the silence that supports and underlies the text, the silence *out of which* the text speaks.

Notes

1. I would like to thank Susan Jaret McKinstry, Sylvia Tomasch, Robert Tisdale, and the reader for *Victorian Literature and Culture* for their perceptive comments and suggestions, and my students in the seminar on sensation fiction (Winter 1991) for their inspiration.

2. Freud's switch in his case-histories from the "'standard' nineteenth-century narrative" mode to modernist plots is well documented by Peter Brooks, among others (268). However, while Brooks sees this passage as part of Freud's intellectual evolution, Susan Katz has persuasively argued that the shift actually occurred when Freud went from "documenting the cases of women to documenting the treatment of men" (Katz 300). In other words, while Freud was comfortable with a seamless narrative, with "univocal, conventionally 'Victorian' narratives" (Katz 300), when the protagonist was a woman, he was willing to allow his male characters/patients the greater freedom of modernist plots.

3. And we know how harmful intellectual strain can be to "feminine delicacy"; see, for instance, Gorhom (101-18).

4. See, for instance, the description of Hortense in *Bleak House,* and the description of Bertha in *Jane Eyre,* a female-authored character shaped by a desire to conform to male expectations.

5. When she leaves, she will take all her portable property with her—and she might as well, since these trinkets have nothing to do with the rest of the house.

6. As Ernst Cassirer has noted, "the unity and uniqueness of the name is not only a mark of the unity and uniqueness of the person, but actually constitutes it; the name is what first makes man an individual" (51).

7. In view of Alicia's role in the novel as dutiful daughter and the mouthpiece of patriarchy, it is significant that she is the first one to put Lady Audley down on paper, describing her step-mother as "a wax-dollish young person, no older than Alicia herself, with flaxen ringlets and a perpetual giggle" (28).

Works Cited

Alcott, Louisa May. "Behind a Mask or A Woman's Power." *Behind a Mask: The Unknown Thrillers of Louisa May Alcott.* Ed. Madeleine Stern. New York: William Morrow, 1975. 1-104.

Armstrong, Nancy. *Desire in Domestic Fiction: A Political History of the Novel.* New York: Oxford UP, 1987.

Braddon, Mary E. *Lady Audley's Secret.* New York: Penguin, 1985 (Tinsley Bros. 1862 edition) and New York: Dover, 1974 (Robert B. Davis 1887 New York edition).

Brantlinger, Patrick. "What is 'Sensational' about the 'Sensation Novel'?" *Nineteenth-Century Fiction* 37 (1982): 1-28.

Brooks, Peter. *Reading for the Plot: Design and Intention in Narrative.* New Haven: Yale UP, 1984.

Cassirer, Ernst. *Language and Myth.* Trans. Susanne K. Langer. New York: Dover, 1953.

Dickens, Charles. *Bleak House.* New York: Norton, 1977.

Felman, Shoshana. "Turning the Screw of Interpretation." *Yale French Studies* 55/56 (1977): 94-207.

———. "Women and Madness: The Critical Phallacy." *Diacritics* 5 (Winter 1975): 2-10.

Foucault, Michel. *Madness and Civilization.* Trans. Richard Howard. New York: Pantheon, 1965.

Gay, Peter. *Freud: A Life for Our Time.* New York: Norton, 1988.

Gilbert, Sandra M. and Susan Gubar. *The Madwoman in the Attic: The Woman Writer and the Nineteenth-Century Literary Imagination.* New Haven: Yale UP, 1979.

Gorham, Deborah. *The Victorian Girl and the Feminine Ideal.* Bloomington: Indiana UP, 1982.

Heilman, Robert B. "Charlotte Brontë's 'New' Gothic." *The Brontës: A Collection of Critical Essays.* Ed. Ian Gregor. Englewood Cliffs, N.J.: Prentice-Hall, 1870. 96-109.

Hughes, Winifred. *The Maniac in the Cellar: Sensation Novels of the 1960s.* Princeton: Princeton UP, 1980.

Katz, Susan. "Speaking Out Against the 'Talking Cure': Unmarried Women in Freud's Early Case Studies." *Women's Studies* 13 (1987): 297-324.

Lispector, Clarice. *The Passion According to G. H.* Trans. Ronald W. Sousa. Minneapolis: U of Minnesota P, 1988.

Massé, Michelle A. "Gothic Repetition: Husbands, Horrors, and Things That Go Bump in the Night." *Signs* 15.4 (Summer 1990): 679-709.

Miller, D. A. "*Cage aux folles*: Sensation and Gender in Wilkie Collins's *The Woman in White.*" *Representations* 14 (Spring 1986): 107-36.

Newman, Beth. "'The Situation of the Looker-On': Gender, Narration and Gaze in *Wuthering Heights.*" *PMLA* 105. (October 1990): 1029-41.

Oliphant, Margaret. "Novels." *Blackwood's Edinburgh Magazine* 102 (1867): 257-80.

Peterson, M. Jeanne. "The Victorian Governess: Status Incongruence in Family and Society." *Victorian Studies* 14.1 (1970): 6-26.

Showalter, Elaine. "Family Secrets and Domestic Subversion: Rebellion in the Novels of the 1860s." *The Victorian Family: Structure and Stresses.* Ed. Anthony S. Wohl. London: Croom Helm, 1978. 101-16.

Uglow, Jennifer. Introduction. *Lady Audley's Secret.* Harmondsworth: Penguin, 1985. ix-xix.

Solveig C. Robinson (essay date 1991)

SOURCE: "Editing *Belgravia*: M. E. Braddon's Defense of 'Light Literature'," in *Victorian Periodicals Review,* Vol. 28, No. 2, Summer, 1995, pp. 109-22.

[*In the following essay, Robinson discusses Braddon's attempts to influence the critical discussion of "light literature" through the publication of her journal* Belgravia.]

In August 1866, the popular sensation novelist M. E. Braddon wrote to her mentor Edward Bulwer-Lytton: "You will wonder after this—if indeed you honour so insignificant a person with yr wonder—to see my name blazoned anon on hoardings & railway stations in connexion with a new Magazine" (Wolff, "Devoted Disciple" 136). When the first issue of *Belgravia: A London Magazine* appeared the following November, its title page, like the "hoardings & railway stations," declared in bold type that it was "Conducted by M. E. Braddon." By "blazoning" her name in connection with a relatively upscale publication, Braddon hoped to do for her own career what George Augustus Sala had done for his through *Temple Bar*: to achieve a degree of personal and professional respectability that had hitherto eluded her. As editor of *Belgravia,* Braddon was

able to create a critical forum that was friendly to such low-status popular literary forms as sensation fiction, and thus to reshape the critical discourse surrounding those forms. In addition, the editorship of *Belgravia* also provided Braddon with a "ladylike" platform for campaigning *against* contemporary critical practices that she disliked and *for* an alternative, less venomous and more inclusive, form of literary criticism. *Belgravia* thus represented an important opportunity for Braddon: it was a chance for her to elevate herself from the relatively lowly literary status of sensation novelist to the more exalted status of a woman of letters.

By 1866 Braddon was already a successful novelist with a well-established literary career. Her best-known works, **Lady Audley's Secret** (1862) and **Aurora Floyd** (1863), had already made her fortune; she also had seven other novels and a ream of shorter fiction and minor poetry behind her. In addition, she already had more than five years' experience as contributor and assistant editor on at least three other periodicals owned by her publisher-companion John Maxwell: in addition to contributing to the *Welcome Guest,* Braddon did most of the editorial work and wrote most of the fiction for the *Halfpenny Journal,*[1] and she worked for nearly four years under Anna Maria (Mrs. S. C.) Hall as part-time assistant editor of *St. James's.* (She also may have assisted in some capacity with *Temple Bar.*) This literary apprenticeship prepared Braddon to manage a magazine of her own.

Belgravia was conceived as a middle-class literary magazine in the style of *St. James's* or *Temple Bar.* As Braddon frankly admitted to Bulwer-Lytton, *Belgravia*'s posh-sounding name was chosen for its snob appeal—it was "the best bait for the shillings of Brixton & Bow" ("Devoted Disciple" 138)—and the target audience was middle-class circulating library subscribers.[2] Like the magazines of other novelist-editors, *Belgravia* featured its editor's own work; numbers also included other illustrated works of fiction (some serialized) and poetry, and a mix of travel sketches, biographical sketches, literary criticism, reviews of theatre and other events, and essays (serious or satiric) on sports and popular science.[3] Regular contributors also wrote for other popular middle-class magazines, such as *Cornhill, Bentley's Miscellany, New Monthly Magazine, Fraser's, Dublin University Magazine,* and *Temple Bar,* and included Sala, Walter Besant, and T. H. S. Escott.[4] Circulation figures suggest that Braddon's formula for *Belgravia* was relatively successful: from 1866 to 1876, the magazine maintained an average circulation of about 15,000 copies, peaking at about 18,000 copies in 1868 (Sullivan 3:31).

Although at these circulation levels the "shillings of Brixton & Bow" probably represented a comfortable level for *Belgravia*'s editor of what Robert Colby delicately characterizes as "security during periods of lagging creativity" (204), since Braddon was already financially secure, the shillings were not the most important consideration.[5] What mattered more was that *Belgravia* provided Braddon with a respectable literary persona and a voice in Victorian critical discourse. As Colby notes, periodical journalism offered novelists "outlets for the justification of their calling in an age when fiction was widely associated with 'the diffusion of useless knowledge'" (207). Like the male novelist-editors Colby discusses, Braddon, too, sought an outlet to "justify her calling." While as a female sensation novelist, Braddon's literary status—despite her popular success—was relatively low, as the "conductress" of her own magazine, Braddon commanded much more literary authority—and the option of employing other (male) critics to "justify her calling" for her. As editor, she could step in or out of critical arguments as circumstances dictated, thus allowing her to preserve her personal respectability at the same time that she sought to legitimize her own creative work by elevating "light literature" to genuine literary endeavor.

Elevating light literature, especially sensation fiction—indeed, simply *defending* it—was no easy task. As Winifred Hughes, Patrick Brantlinger, and others have discussed,[6] sensation fiction was the focus of a great deal of mid-century critical discourse, compelling critics who wished to account for (or at least grapple with) its unprecedented popularity to rethink "their own most basic assumptions about the role of fiction" (Hughes 47). Perhaps more so than for any other genre, Victorian criticism of sensation fiction foregrounded the intersection of economic, gender, and aesthetic concerns. From Henry Mansel in the *Quarterly Review* to Margaret Oliphant in *Blackwood's,* critics in the high-culture periodicals decried the commodification of literature that appeared to accompany the emergence of sensation fiction; the danger sensation novels posed for women, who were exposed not only to expressly criminal behavior but also to more subversive "unfeminine" behavior; and sensation's danger to both writers and readers, whose talents and tastes would be compromised and degraded by a steady diet of "unwholesome" literary fare. As editor of *Belgravia,* Braddon chose to meet these criticisms head-on. The key to *Belgravia*'s critical position under Braddon was the belief that readers' tastes could be educated or uplifted, so that in pleasing them, authors wouldn't necessarily be guilty of pandering. Through the criticism published in *Belgravia,* Braddon drove home the point that *popular* taste didn't necessarily have to mean *bad* taste.

Braddon established *Belgravia*'s critical position within the first few years of her editorship, by employing two primary strategies. First, she published a number of critical essays that unapologetically presented popular literature as a distinct and worthy literary field, complete with its own standards, goals, and canons. Second, she published essays that exposed the failings of so-called "high-culture" criticism to adequately address the concerns of light literature. This two-pronged critical approach allowed Braddon a great deal of flexibility. As editor of *Belgravia,* she could maintain an ironic detachment from her own most commercially generated fiction at the same time that she defended the benefits of reading that fiction. More important,

she could pick and choose which battles to fight *in propria persona* and which to leave to her troops. In *The "Improper" Feminine,* Lyn Pykett notes that women sensation novelists participated in the "destabilisation" of Victorian gender categories, engaging in a "general struggle about the definition of woman, and also about the nature, power and function of the feminine within the culture" (10). Braddon was participating in this struggle not only as a novelist, but also as an editor-critic, a position that carried much more potential threat to Victorian gender ideology.[7] Her ability as editor of *Belgravia* to marshal critics to speak for her thus enabled her to engage (often fiercely) in critical debates without being seen to do so directly, and thus without necessarily (further) compromising her status as *woman.*

Braddon's first critical strategy, that of presenting popular literature as a legitimate literary field, required that she dismiss the charges that such literature was written solely "for the market"—for money. Braddon herself was acutely aware of the difficulty of reconciling literary values with market demands; as she had admitted to Bulwer-Lytton shortly after the success of **Lady Audley** and **Aurora Floyd**:

> The "behind the scenes" of literature has in a manner demoralised me. I have learnt to look at everything in a mercantile sense, & to write solely for the circulating library reader, whose palette [sic] requires strong meat, & is not very particular as to the quality thereof. . . . I want to serve two masters. I want to be artistic & to please *you.* I want to be sensational, & to please Mudie's subscribers.
>
> Are these two things possible, or is the stern dictum not to be got over, "Thou canst not serve God & Mammon."
>
>   (May 1863; "Devoted Disciple" 14)

In her position "behind the scenes" as editor of *Belgravia,* Braddon could help redefine the debate about the commercialization of literature so that the two masters could in fact be served. The most successful strategy was to recast the problem in terms of professionalism, so that earning money from writing was no longer part of the opposition between sensation/Mudie's subscribers and art/discerning readers; instead earning money was reconceived as appropriate remuneration for the knowledge and exercise of particular literary skills. In such essays as "Literature of the Line," "Writing for Money," and "Literary Bagmanship" (by Sidney L. Blanchard, G. H. Guest, and T. H. S. Escott, respectively),[8] *Belgravia*'s critics stress the difference between a hack and a literary professional, suggesting that the latter—even if a writer of popular works—writes out of genuine love and respect for the craft; the money is secondary. Within *Belgravia*'s critical ethos, earning money is both acceptable and respectable: it is the legitimate outcome of knowing the demands of the craft and meeting them.

In addition to dismissing charges that to write commercially successful works was necessarily to write bad works,

Braddon also attempted to defend light literature by defining it as a distinct and legitimate literary field, one that had its own intentions and rules, and that therefore needed to be evaluated differently from more "serious" or "high-culture" literature. Throughout Braddon's editorship, *Belgravia*'s critical essays stress that popular literature's primary purpose is to amuse and entertain, and that therefore it should only be evaluated on the basis of how well it achieves this purpose. For example, in "Vers de Société," J. Francis Hitchman steadfastly defends "occasional" verse as a legitimate form of poetic expression, precisely because it is *not* high art; rather, it is relaxing, light reading, appropriate for idling away one's leisure time (*Belgravia* 2 [May 1867]: 338-42). Similarly, in an essay entitled "The Value of Fiction," Walter Besant argues that novels are intended to provide a healthy escape from introspection, boredom, and overwork, and that as such they offer readers a refreshment of mind and spirit that "no sermons ever preached" were likely to do (*Belgravia* 16 [Feb. 1872]: 48-49).

As might be expected, *Belgravia* spoke out most strongly in defense of Braddon's own literary domain, the sensation novel. The key to *Belgravia*'s critical position is that it resituates sensation fiction (like other popular literary forms) from the margins to the center of contemporary literary practice, and also asserts the genre's legitimacy by showing that it derives from a long literary tradition that includes many of the nineteenth century's most important authors. It is two early articles by Sala that go furthest towards relocating sensation novels at the center of Victorian fiction. In the first, "The Cant of Modern Criticism," Sala refutes a central claim of Margaret Oliphant's, in her 1867 *Blackwood's* article "Novels," that English novels from the time of Scott to the emergence of sensation fiction were characterized by "sanity, wholesomeness, and cleanliness."[9] Sala rather sternly notes the sensation, crime, and coarse language present in the works of such authors as Bulwer-Lytton, Benjamin Disraeli, and Frances Trollope, and while the main purpose of this essay (as discussed below) certainly is to debunk Oliphant's article, the essay also has the effect of tracing a long and rather respectable list of literary antecedents for sensation fiction (*Belgravia* 4 [Nov. 1867]: 45-55). In the second article, "On the 'Sensational' in Literature and Art," Sala more overtly positions the sensation novel as central to nineteenth-century literature, by providing a list of "sensational" writers and artists that is a virtual "who's who" of the mid-nineteenth century: a list that includes Dickens, Millais, Ruskin, Darwin, Newman, Napoleon, Bismarck, Ulysses S. Grant—and Braddon, of course (*Belgravia* 4 [Feb. 1868]: 457). In both of these essays, Sala not only establishes a kind of "counter-canon" of sensation, but he also stakes out a claim for sensation fiction that is clearly within "mainstream" realist fiction's territory. In "The Cant of Modern Criticism," for example, he specifically links Braddon's novels to *Jane Eyre* and *Adam Bede*, describing Braddon's, Brontë's, and Eliot's works as powerful representatives of "the modern, the contemporary novel of life and character and adventure—the outspoken, realis-

tic, moving, breathing fiction, which mirrors the passions of the age for which it is written" (52).

This specific defense of Braddon's novels may seem like mere gallantry—or, worse, critical brown-nosing—but Braddon's correspondence makes it clear that Sala's essays were the result of her own careful behind-the-scenes work as editor. The consistency of tone—and of contributors—throughout Braddon's editorship of *Belgravia* suggests that the critics presented in its pages represented Braddon's own critical opinions. Direct evidence of this is available in the case of Sala's "Cant of Modern Criticism": writing to Bulwer-Lytton shortly before the article appeared in print, Braddon remarked that she had solicited the article from Sala because she had been sure he "would at once sieze [sic] *my* idea of the subject, and defend the right of the imaginative writer to choose his subjects from that field whence all the great writers of the past derived their fables—that is to say, the tragic, criminal, & exceptional situations of life" (10 Oct. 1867; "Devoted Disciple" 144). Braddon's position as editor, employing writers who shared her critical perspective, enabled her to be—in a neat reversal of ideal ladylike behavior—heard but not seen.

As editor of *Belgravia*, Braddon did not simply defend light literature as a worthy literary field. She went further, publishing articles that exposed the critical shortcomings of those high-culture periodicals that were most dismissive of popular literature. Braddon's second critical strategy in defense of light literature was to expose the failings of high-culture criticism to adequately judge popular literature. The critical position that emerges in *Belgravia*'s pages is that the prevalent anonymous reviewing system has been undermined by institutional pressures that encourage reviewers to write criticism at least as "sensational" as the works being reviewed. *Belgravia*'s critics also take the position that such "sensational" criticism, grounded in the very same market concerns for which it belittles popular literature, fails in its avowed mission to educate the public about literature.

Belgravia's counterattacks against high-culture periodicals began in 1867, after Braddon came under sharp criticism from both *Blackwood's* and the *Pall Mall Gazette*. While Braddon and her work had been subject to criticism from the first, the attacks in *Blackwood's* and the *Gazette* were the first significant ones after she had assumed the editorship of *Belgravia* in search of literary upward mobility. The most stinging of the two attacks was Oliphant's previously mentioned "Novels" essay, in which Braddon and fellow novelist Rhoda Broughton were more-or-less accused of revealing through their fiction that they didn't know how "nice" young women behaved; the essay also accused popular novelists generally of corrupting both the daughters and the literature of Britain. The second attack, launched by the *Pall Mall Gazette*, essentially accused Braddon of plagiarism, pointing out that she had recycled her own and others' novels as "new" works of fiction. While there may have been grounds for some of the *Ga-*

zette's charges (even allowing for the mid-nineteenth century's looser standards regarding plagiarism and text recycling), Braddon believed that both *Blackwood's* and the *Gazette* had crossed the line between literary and personal attack.[10] And, unlike the case with previous critical assaults, Braddon was now positioned to return fire.

Privately, Braddon was furious about the attacks, especially from *Blackwood's*. Writing to Bulwer-Lytton she fumed: "can anything exceed the covert insolence of this? Who is this writer who dares to tell me that I do not know how a virtuous or well-bred woman feels. Does he [sic] judge by the evidence of my books. I say boldly—No" ("Devoted Disciple" 142-43). Braddon had been "stung to the quick" by the *Blackwood's* article, and she mobilized her forces to refute the charges. *Belgravia*'s critical counterattacks were intended, in the first place, to publicly refute the specific charges against Braddon. However, Braddon never allowed her personal battles to overwhelm her second, ultimately more important purpose. The critical counterattacks in *Belgravia* also exposed and repudiated the *kind* of criticism published in the high-culture periodicals, a kind of criticism at least as "sensational" as the works it attacked.

Addressing the issues of how criticism in high-culture periodicals both misunderstood popular literature and resorted to ad hominem—or ad feminam—attacks, Sala's "Cant of Modern Criticism" was the first volley in *Belgravia*'s critical counterattack, and it virtually demolished Oliphant's *Blackwood's* essay. Sala first dismisses the premise that fiction since Scott had been characterized by "sanity, wholesomeness, and cleanliness," by offering a counter-canon that includes much insanity, unwholesomeness, and anything but "cleanliness"—all penned by the finest authors. However, Sala's article goes further, repudiating Oliphant's premise that fiction is necessarily the province of young female readers whose sensibilities must be protected. Countering this idealized notion of readership, and probably more accurately naming the real audience for Victorian fiction, Sala asserts that "novels are written for grown people and not for babes and sucklings" and that, furthermore, those adult readers

> want novels about That which Is, and not about That which never Was and never Will be. We don't want pap, or spoon-meat, or milk-and-water, or curds-and-whey, or Robb's biscuits, or boiled whiting, or cold boiled veal without salt. We want meat; and this is a strong age, and we can digest it.
>
> (54)

Sala argues that *Blackwood's* standards are old-fashioned and do not obtain; in any event, if there is any doubt about a particular work's suitability for a particular Young Person, then private, not public, censorship (the "domestic Index Expurgatorius") should be enacted. Acknowledging that private and public reading standards might not be the same, Sala admits that even his own "phantom daughter" might be restricted from certain literature during her youth.

However, he insists that once his "phantom daughter" reached maturity, her own judgment would prevail: "When she came to be one-and-twenty, or got married, I should no more think of dictating to her as to what kinds of books she should read, than as to what kind of stays she should wear—if she wore any at all. *Cela serait son affaire*" (54). Sala's use of the stays analogy clearly positions *Belgravia* in a progressive critical camp: just as the rational dress advocates took the position that women should be empowered through education to make choices about their clothing, *Belgravia* took the critical position that readers—both women and men—should be empowered to make choices about their leisure reading materials.

While Braddon had been concerned about the critical grounds for the attacks on her work, her letters reveal that what bothered her most about the anonymous reviews was that they were the product of a reviewing system that allowed (if not encouraged) personal rather than literary attacks: as she complained to Bulwer-Lytton, such "little carping criticisms . . . *teach* me nothing, & indeed seem intended only to wound & annoy" ("Devoted Disciple" 145). The critical essays in *Belgravia* take an uncompromising stand against such "carping criticism," not just against individual essays or critics themselves, but against the editorial practices that support them. For example, in "The Cant of Modern Criticism," Sala soundly scolds the *institution* of *Blackwood's*, not just its anonymous critic: "I consider the paper in question . . . to be eminently unjust, mischievous, and disingenuous, and that it exemplifies in a remarkably offensive degree the prevalence of the worst kind of cant, hypocrisy, and sophistry, as applied to literary criticism" (*Belgravia* 4:47-48). And Braddon herself took on the *Pall Mall Gazette*, by assuming the voice of the fictional Captain Shandon in *Pendennis*, who had founded the *Gazette* as "A journal written by gentlemen for gentlemen." In "A Remonstrance," Braddon-as-Shandon sternly takes the contemporary editors to task for straying from that original ideal, describing the latter-day, realized, *Gazette* as

> A bundle of cuttings from other papers, garnished with flippant, frivolous comment; and little carping, spiteful paragraphs; and prurient harpings upon subjects that decency best reprobates by decent avoidance; and sham letters from sham correspondents, all breathing the same malignant feeling against some one or something respected by other people; and, to give spice to the whole, an occasional forgery.
>
> (*Belgravia* 4 [Nov. 1867]: 81)

Braddon-as-Shandon especially criticizes the contemporary *Gazette* for departing from the standards of the great editors and reviewers—such as Addison, Steele, Jeffrey, and Brougham—who had (in her/his opinion) "banished from their minds all party spirit and all personal feeling while engaged in the performance of their self-assumed [critical] function."

Braddon's impersonation of a respected editor and evocation of other great editors suggest what she felt her professional stakes were in editing *Belgravia.* Braddon always managed to maintain an ironic distance from her more market-oriented fiction. She admitted to Bulwer-Lytton that the rapid, market-driven production of her work was not particularly good for it: "It has been my good or bad fortune to be flung into a very rapid market, & to have every thing printed & published almost before the ink with which it was written was dry" (13 April 1863; "Devoted Disciple" 12); and she described the process of writing a new sensation story as simply rearranging a fixed set of components: "I will give the kaleidoscope . . . another turn, and will do my best with the old bits of glass and pins and rubbish" (letter to Edmund Yates, cited in Maxwell 150). Yet despite her ironic treatment of her work, Braddon was eager to improve, and she actively sought constructive criticism. What disturbed her was criticism that was *not* intended to be constructive, such as that launched by *Blackwood's* and the *Pall Mall Gazette.* Such criticism not only failed to educate authors about how to improve their writing, but it also failed to educate readers about the useful value of criticism.

Belgravia's critical essays throughout Braddon's editorship suggest that Braddon hoped to continue the didactic traditions of the great literary editors—if not on the same grand scale, then at least by enabling her own middle-class readers to become more educated consumers of literary criticism. Thus, a number of essays in *Belgravia* address the question of what criticism should seek to accomplish. For example, in "Literary Criticism," J. Campbell Smith describes the ideal critic:

> As he occupies the position of a judge, he should ever be calm and unbiased, permitting no prejudices to obscure his vision and affect his judgment. True criticism cannot exist where there is passion and prejudice . . . a display of temper on the part of a critic is a sure sign that, however competent he otherwise would be to form an authoritative opinion, he is not a person fitted to express that opinion in the pages of a journal which is looked up to as a guide in literary matters.
>
> (*Belgravia* 2 [April 1867]: 225-34)

An essay by Edward R. Russell, "'Thorough' in Criticism," suggests that the reason why many high-culture reviewers fail to live up to this critical ideal is because the editorial policies of these periodicals are as grounded in market concerns as the literature they criticized. Noting that many particularly venomous critical attacks spring "from the deliberate critical policy of certain journals," Russell asserts that such attacks are motivated by the desire to sell copies, rather than to educate either readers or writers:

> The pleasure of "slating" is one that wears off. The less malignant satisfaction of producing criticisms as sensational in motive as the most sensational novel is more enduring. And it pays. Articles of this kind are in demand; and as they can only be produced by repressing all the scruples of natural fairness, the "thick and thin" of literary justice is not allowed to interfere with the supply.
>
> (*Belgravia* 7 [Nov. 1868]: 39-40)

Russell concludes that readers of "sensational criticism" have to become educated consumers, who can recognize the difference between light literature masquerading as criticism and true literary criticism: "one may hope to induce readers to regard as merely entertaining articles which have hitherto been for a great proportion of the middle classes absolute canons of literary judgment" (43).

According to *Belgravia*'s critics, it is this occasional problem of entertainment masquerading as "absolute canons of literary judgment" that seems to be the most damning failure of the high-culture reviewing system. To point up this failure, Braddon satirically describes this style of criticism in one of her own essays, published near the end of her editorship. "Revelations of a Critic" is a sketch of the career of a London critic, whose sole qualification is that he has thoroughly mastered the *jargon* of criticism. The critic offers his own set of rules for the criticism "trade," revealing how to pen a review without actually seeing a play, reading a novel, or viewing a work of art, and he notes that the veracity of a review doesn't really matter because "Nobody cares *what* you say except the author, actor, or producer of a play, the writer or publisher of a book, or the painter of a picture; and these people are really of no consequence" (*Belgravia* 27 [Oct. 1875]: 530). The critic laments the lack of a formalized critical apprenticeship, not because such an apprenticeship would ensure the quality of criticism, but because it represents an unrealized commercial opportunity: "I regret that it is not in my power to make something by teaching the art of criticism, as the memorable Rarey taught horse-training" (529).

Braddon-as-narrator appears briefly at the end of the essay to comment on the critic's confessions:

> If his revelations may be trusted—and I believe they may—"criticism" is neither a bad business nor an arduous one. His profits have, I know, been considerable; his reputation is high, and established on a fair basis. Play-writers, authors, and artists tremble at his name. . . . What he says about "no apprenticeship" being necessary for the business of a "critic" is probably in pure spite and jealousy. *Of course* there is no apprenticeship for criticism. What is there to learn? And if there was anything, who could teach it?
>
> (532)

Braddon's rhetorical questions—"What is there to learn?" "who could teach it?"—sum up her response to the unprofessional, "canting" style of literary criticism found in so many of her competitors' periodicals. Unsubstantial, illogical, and motivated by vanity or greed, canting criticism fails to educate either readers or writers about the art and craft of writing.

In *Belgravia,* Braddon does offer her readers an alternative to this style of "trade" criticism, an alternative model of criticism directed towards the tastes and understanding of a middle-class, general audience but still dedicated to high literary ideals. *Belgravia*'s criticism appears to have had the goal of educating readers, not just about the works and authors at hand, but about the larger fields and ideas within which the works exist, and it sets about that goal not by delivering dry sermons on literary matters, but by offering lighter essays—essays that, like the "light literature" which they often address, would themselves amuse and entertain. About one-fourth of the essays on literary subjects take biographical approaches, from William Stigand's "Byron and the Countess Guiccioli" to Escott's "Concerning the Centenary of Scott" to Braddon's "Lord Lytton,"[11] while another fourth trace themes and images in various works. (For example, Francis Jacox's four articles are all of this kind,[12] as are a number of Sala's.) Even longer, more in-depth articles, such as the four studies that make up Kenningale Cook's "American Novelists" series or Escott's retrospective on Sydney Dobell and the Spasmodic School, are structured so as to be comfortable leisure reading even while they impart useful information about the works and reputations of the authors involved.[13] Even when the articles are less than flattering—as in the case of Escott's essay on Dobell, tellingly titled "Hysteria on Parnassus"—they do not descend into ad hominem attacks. And—countering the editorial practice that seemed most to foster "carping criticism"—all literary essays in *Belgravia* are signed.

Although the critical stance taken in *Belgravia* certainly served to protect Braddon's self-interest as a popular novelist, it also served a larger purpose, educating readers of light literature about literary and critical standards and thereby encouraging them to accept responsibility for their role in determining which voices in literature and criticism would prevail. According to the standards as expressed in *Belgravia* under Braddon's editorship, the ideal criticism, like the ideal fiction Besant describes in "The Value of Fiction," "teaches us tolerance, by showing us the different ways in which our fellows live; and it perpetually, under a thousand new forms, impresses the good old maxim, that the 'only way to be happy is by the narrow road'" (*Belgravia* 16 [Nov. 1871]: 51). This criticism of inclusion, tolerant of "the different ways in which our fellows live," is one that embraces both high-culture and popular literature, evaluating each according to its kind and educating even while it respects both writers' and readers' tastes and inclinations. By espousing and attempting to uphold such critical ideals, Braddon aligned herself with the critical traditions of the great editors and reviewers, and asserted her right to a place among the legitimate literary figures of the day. *Belgravia,* then, was a vehicle for Braddon to establish herself as something more than a "mere" sensation novelist, to define herself as a "woman of letters."

Notes

1. Much of this labor was "subliterary hackwork"—Braddon briefly adopted the pseudonym "Lady Caroline Lascelles" to cover her tracks (*Sensational Victorian* 119). Wolff suggests that Maxwell may have promised Braddon the editorship of the *Welcome Guest* in 1860, but the editorship went to Frederic Charles Lascelles Wraxall instead.

2. While Robert Lee Wolff dismisses *Belgravia* as a "lower-middle-class" magazine, Alvin Sullivan treats it a little more kindly, assessing *Belgravia*'s readership as a "genteel, middle-class, lady public," though "of low to fair educational standard" (3:31).

3. Essays and sketches on literary subjects appeared regularly throughout Braddon's editorship: one or two such articles appear in each of the first 28 volumes, and some volumes contain as many as six. Out of the 60 or so essays on literary subjects, about 12 directly address the standards and canons of popular literature; 11 discuss the professionalism of authors and critics; and 10 discuss various aspects of journalism and the press. The remaining articles range from biographical memoirs to overviews of foreign literature to essays on particular themes and images. The most pointed critical essays seem to cluster in the first 5 volumes, when Braddon was still shaping her magazine.

4. Few of *Belgravia*'s contributors are likely to be familiar to non-Victorian specialists. Other contributors under Braddon's editorship included: Sidney Blanchard, Mortimer Collins, Dutton Cook, John Scoffern, William Blanchard Jerrold, J. Francis Hitchman, Walter Thornbury, Robert Folkestone, Kenningale Cook, W. S. Gilbert, and Percy Fitzgerald. The fact that most of *Belgravia*'s contributors also wrote for *Temple Bar* suggests that Braddon recruited writers she knew through Maxwell's other publishing ventures.

5. As early as 1863 the phenomenal sales of Braddon's fiction meant that she had nearly "earned enough money to keep me and mother for the rest of our lives" (13 April 1863; "Devoted Disciple" 13). In addition, Maxwell's publishing income was sufficient to support her and Maxwell's growing family (Maxwell 163).

6. See, especially, the analyses offered by Winifred Hughes, Patrick Brantlinger, Ann Cvetkovich, and Lyn Pykett, as well as by Sally Mitchell.

7. In *Uneven Developments* (U of Chicago P, 1988), Mary Poovey discusses women novelists and describes the threat to the Victorian social fabric when the categories of "literary man" and "woman" overlapped (125). In my dissertation, I suggest that because their work necessarily identified them with the masculine world of the publishing industry and also required them to assume a critical gaze, women journalists, editors, and critics posed a far greater threat than women novelists.

8. See *Belgravia* 5 (June 1868): 499-504; 8 (June 1869): 573-75; and 13 (Feb. 1871): 508-12.

9. See *Blackwood's* 102 (Sept. 1867): 257-80.

10. Wolff provides very detailed background information and discusses at length the personal impact of these attacks. See *Sensational Victorian* 200ff.

11. See *Belgravia* 7 (Feb. 1869): 491-512; 15 (Sept. 1871): 382-88; and 20 (March 1873): 73-88.

12. See *Belgravia* 9 (Aug. 1869): 250-55; 10 (Nov. 1869): 69-74; and 24 (Aug. 1874): 157-64.

13. See *Belgravia* 18 (Sept. 1872): 379-87; 18 (Oct. 1872): 506-16; 19 (Nov. 1872): 72-79; 20 (April 1873): 222-32; and 26 (June 1875): 485-96.

Selected Bibliography

Belgravia: A London Magazine. Conducted by M. E. Braddon. Vols. 1-29. Nov. 1866-June 1876.

Brantlinger, Patrick. "What Is 'Sensational' about the 'Sensation Novel'?" *Nineteenth Century Fiction* 37.1 (June 1982): 1-28.

Colby, Robert A. "Goose Quill and Blue Pencil: The Victorian Novelist as Editor." In Wiener, Joel H., ed. *Innovators and Preachers: The Role of the Editor in Victorian England.* Contributions to the Study of Mass Media and Communications. Westport, CT: Greenwood, 1985.

Cvetkovich, Ann. *Mixed Feelings: Feminism, Mass Culture, and Victorian Sensationalism.* New Brunswick: Rutgers UP, 1992.

Edwards, P. D., I. G. Sibley, and Margaret Versteeg. *Indexes to Fiction in Belgravia (1867-1899).* Victorian Fiction Research Guides 14. St. Lucia, Austral.: Univ. of Queensland, [1988].

Griest, Guinivere. *Mudie's Circulating Library and the Victorian Novel.* Bloomington: Indiana UP, 1970.

Hughes, Winifred. *The Maniac in the Cellar: Sensation Novels of the 1860s.* Princeton: Princeton UP, 1980.

Maxwell, W. B. *Time Gathered: Autobiography.* New York: Appleton-Century, 1938.

Mitchell, Sally. *The Fallen Angel: Chastity, Class and Women's Reading, 1835-1880.* Bowling Green, OH: Bowling Green U Popular P, 1981.

Pykett, Lyn. *The "Improper" Feminine: The Women's Sensation Novel and the New Woman Writing.* London: Routledge, 1992.

Straus, Ralph. *Sala: The Portrait of an Eminent Victorian.* London: Constable, 1942.

Sullivan, Alvin, ed. *British Literary Magazines.* 4 vols. Westport, CT: Greenwood, 1983-1986.

Wolff, R[obert]. L[ee]. "Devoted Disciple: The Letters of Mary Elizabeth Braddon to Sir Edward Bulwer-Lytton, 1862-1873." *Harvard Library Bulletin* 22.1 (1974): 1-35; 22.2 (1974): 129-61.

———. *Sensational Victorian: The Life and Fiction of Mary Elizabeth Braddon.* New York: Garland, 1979.

Ann Cvetkovich (essay date 1992)

SOURCE: "Detective in the House: Subversion and Containment in *Lady Audley's Secret*," in *Mixed Feelings: Feminism, Mass Culture, and Victorian Sensationalism,* Rutgers University Press, 1992, pp. 45-70.

[*In the following essay, Cvetkovich examines the subversive implications of the sensational novels' upper-class settings, particularly in* Lady Audley's Secret.]

Although it has received little attention from literary critics until recently, **Lady Audley's Secret** by Mary Elizabeth Braddon was one of the best-selling novels, not only of the 1860s but of the entire latter half of the nineteenth century. It is one of the most important novels of the sensation genre, which emerged as a successor to and composite of forms such as the gothic novel, the Newgate novel, and the stage melodrama.[1] The sensation novel is distinct as a genre from its precursors because its crimes and mysteries occur, not in foreign countries or wild landscapes, not among the lower classes or the inhabitants of monasteries and convents, but in the stately homes of the aristocracy, whose lives are depicted in realistic detail. Rather than relegating terror to the exotic fringes of society, the sensation novel exploits the disparity between apparently stable families and marriages and the horrifying secrets and extremes of passion that disrupt them, in recognition (in the words of Henry James) that the "most mysterious of mysteries" are "at our own doors."[2] This constitutive principle of the genre is elaborated in **Lady Audley's Secret** itself:

> What do we know of the mysteries that may hang about the houses we enter? Foul deeds have been done under the most hospitable roofs; terrible crimes have been committed amid the fairest scenes, and have left no trace upon the spot where they were done. I do not believe in mandrake, or in bloodstains that no time can efface. I believe rather that we may walk unconsciously in an atmosphere of crime, and breathe none the less freely. I believe that we may look into the smiling face of a murderer, and admire its tranquil beauty.[3]

As the last sentence suggests, the genre's concern with the deceptiveness of domestic tranquillity is linked to its representation of women. Lady Audley, whose defining characteristics are her golden-haired beauty and her capacity to commit murder, represents the genre in microcosm; the impossibility of recognizing her wickedness from her appearance adds to her power both to fascinate and to threaten others. Only the special skill of the detective can reveal her character. Whereas gothic novels depict the trials of courtship and threats to the purity of virgin heroines, sensation novels are more likely to represent marriage and to show women who produce evil rather than suffer from it. Plots revolve around the legal status of marriage, and the conflicts created by property and inheritance laws. The crime most peculiar to the sensation novel is bigamy, an offense in which a sexual relation or romance is directly under the jurisdiction of the law, and in which illicit passion infects marriage from within, rather than, as with adultery, from without.[4] The genre creates sensationalism by locating crime where one would least expect it—not only in the home but in the actions of a woman—and in the process violates the separation of the private and public spheres crucial to Victorian culture. According to both Victorian and contemporary critics, the affective power of the sensation novel's transgressive heroines has subversive tendencies.

THE SENSATIONAL PORTRAIT OF A LADY

The Victorian critics, for example, were especially vehement about the sensation novel's dangerous portrayal of women whose sexuality and affects are uncontrolled: The figure of the criminal and sexualized woman, by violating the standards of feminine propriety, also threatened the social order. One critic remarked:

> There is nothing more violently opposed to our moral sense, in all the contradictions to custom which they present to us, than the utter unrestraint in which the heroines of this order are allowed to expatiate and develop their impulsive, stormy, passionate characters. We believe it is one chief among their many dangers to youthful readers that they open out a picture of life free from all the perhaps irksome checks that confine their own existence. . . . The heroine of this class of novel is charming because she is undisciplined, and the victim of impulse; because she has never known restraint or has cast it aside, because in all these respects she is below the thoroughly trained and tried woman.[5]

The emphasis here on the danger of "impulse" that is "undisciplined" or without "restraint" reveals the link made between the unleashing of affect, especially in women, and threats to the social order. Psychic discipline becomes the prerequisite to moral and social stability, and women in particular bear the burden of representing virtue as the control of desire. In addition to gender difference, class difference is also implicitly represented in terms of the control of affect; although lower- or working-class women might not be sufficiently refined to manage their impulses, the sign of the middle-class woman's status is her ability to do so. As another critic's remarks about Lady Audley suggest, the woman who does not behave appropriately is unthinkable because femininity is so closely attached to sexual propriety:

> Lady Audley is at once the heroine and the monstrosity of the novel. In drawing her, the authoress may have intended to portray a female Mephistopheles; but, if so, she should have known that a woman cannot fill such a part. The nerves with which Lady Audley could meet unmoved the friend of the man she had murdered, are the nerves of a Lady Macbeth who is half unsexed, and not those of the timid, gentle, innocent creature Lady Audley is represented as being. . . . All this is very exciting; but is also very unnatural. The artistic faults of this novel are as grave as the ethical ones. Combined, they render it one of the most noxious books of modern times.[6]

According to this critic, the novel violates the natural relation between femininity and affect; Lady Audley's crime is that she lacks the affect appropriate to her sex, facing her enemies cold-bloodedly with "the nerves of a Lady Mac-

beth who is half unsexed." Uncomfortable with the discrepancy between Lady Audley's innocent appearance and her behavior, the critic declares her to be an aesthetic and ethical abomination. The claim that the sensation novel produces an "unnatural" excitement is thus grounded in assumptions about the naturalness of gender roles.

It is precisely this threat to gender difference that contemporary feminist critics have seized upon as the source of the sensation novel's appeal and subversiveness. Responding to criticism that sees the sensation novel as a minor and inferior genre, either blandly conventional or irrelevant to cultural and literary analysis, Elaine Showalter argues that the sensation novel gives expression to the violent passions and frustrations of women whose lives are occupied exclusively by romance and the home. She writes: "The sensationalists made crime and violence domestic, modern, and suburban; but their secrets were not simply solutions to mysteries and crimes; they were the secrets of women's dislike of their roles as daughters, wives, and mothers. These women novelists made a powerful appeal to the female audience by subverting the traditions of feminine fiction to suit their own imaginative impulses, by expressing a wide range of suppressed female emotions, and by tapping and satisfying fantasies of protest and escape."[7] Whereas the Victorian critics deplored women's expression of feeling, the contemporary feminist critic celebrates it; both, however, have assumed the repressive hypothesis, equating the unleashing of suppressed feelings with rebellion against social convention. Showalter's discussion of *Lady Audley's Secret* focuses on Lady Audley as the figure who defies conventional expectations by appearing to be demure and innocent when in fact she is capable of the "unfeminine assertiveness" required to commit bigamy, murder, and arson. She argues that the female reader identifies with "a new kind of heroine, one who could put her hostility toward men into violent action."[8] The secret that lies behind the novel's sensational mystery is that Lady Audley is neither insane nor criminal, but instead acts out of rational self-interest to protect her livelihood. Abandoned by her first husband, George Talboys, she commits bigamy because marriage is her only means to economic security. When he returns, she manages to take control of events and get rid of him; murder stands in for divorce, which was only beginning to be an imaginable solution to unhappy marriages and was still very difficult to obtain. Thus, Showalter argues that "as every woman reader must have sensed, Lady Audley's real secret is that she is *sane* and, moreover, representative."[9]

At the same time as Lady Audley's crimes satisfy female readers' fantasies of rebellion and affective expression, her sensational appeal within the narrative is also the product of a masculine fantasy about women's hidden powers. The story is largely told from the perspective of Robert Audley, the nephew who becomes a detective to investigate his aunt's mysterious past. The narrative rarely provides access to Lady Audley's inner life or point of view; instead its sensationalism emerges from descriptions of the haunting beauty that belies the heroine's criminal behavior. The power of Lady Audley's image is evident in one of the novel's more sensational scenes, in which Robert Audley and his friend George sneak into Lady Audley's private chambers, which have been locked in her absence. As if entering the womb that will reveal the mysteries of femininity, they creep along a "secret passage" to find a series of rooms cluttered with "womanly luxuries" (46). They discover not the woman herself, but an excess of the accessories that signify her femininity. "The atmosphere of the room was almost oppressive for the rich odors of perfumes . . . handsome dresses lay in a heap upon the ground . . . jewelry, ivory-backed hair-brushes, and exquisite china were scattered here and there" (46). Their quest culminates in the opportunity to examine the pre-Raphaelite portrait of Lady Audley, which hangs in the antechamber. Rather than confront Lady Audley herself, they seek the safety of a representation to satisfy their curiosity about the mysterious lady of the house; Robert explains, "I would give anything to see it, for I have only an imperfect notion of her face" (45).

The portrait shows Lady Audley as a "beautiful fiend" not because she in unfeminine but because the marks of her femininity are exaggerated:

> No one but a pre-Raphaelite would have so exaggerated every attribute of that delicate face as to give a lurid brightness to the blonde complexion, and a strange, sinister light to the deep blue eyes. . . . It was so like, and yet so unlike. It was as if you had burned strange-colored fires before my lady's face, and by their influence brought out new lines and new expressions never seen before. The perfection of feature, the brilliancy of coloring, were there; but I suppose the painter had copied quaint mediaeval monstrosities until his brain had grown bewildered, for my lady, in his portrait of her, had something of the aspect of a beautiful fiend. Her crimson dress, exaggerated like all the rest in this strange picture, hung about her in folds that looked like flames, her fair head peeping out of the lurid mass of color as if out of a raging furnace.
>
> (47)

Sensational representation is as much the domain of the male artist as of the female novelist. The lurid exaggeration of Lady Audley's beauty makes her frightening but also fascinating as she becomes the object of the male viewer's voyeurism. Once accentuated, the signs of her femininity—her blue eyes, her crimson dress, her fair hair—reveal her capacity to be a demon, confirming male suspicions of her dangerous powers. The fantasy of the beautiful woman as evil has its dividends for men as well as women. By the end of the novel Lady Audley's rebellion is diagnosed as madness and she is exiled to an institution in Belgium to die of "maladie de langueur," while Robert Audley reestablishes the ideal of family life in "a dream of a fairy cottage" (285). By casting Lady Audley as a beautiful fiend, just as the pre-Raphaelite painter does, Robert Audley exorcises the threat she is taken to represent and consolidates the patriarchal family.

The portrait's fascinating allure, both for the men in the novel and for the readers of Braddon's description, lies in the ambiguities of its portrayal of Lady Audley's beauty. It at once reveals and obscures her "true" nature and identity. The portrait is an emblem of how sensational representations work more generally; Braddon's insistent focus on her heroine's appearance seduces the reader with both the possibility *and* the impossibility of making visible the contradictions that mark Lady Audley's identity. I have suggested that sensationalism derives its power from rendering concrete or visible what would otherwise be hidden; the image of the beautiful and transgressive woman becomes sensational when we know that she is evil and we both see and don't see her criminality in her appearance. If Lady Audley looked as evil as she supposedly is, she would be less sensational. (Her mother's insanity, for example, is more rather than less unsettling when it turns out that she has the appearance of a golden-haired child rather than a madwoman.) The sensation of repulsion produced by Lady Audley's criminality is indistinguishable from the fascination produced by her beauty; sensationalism consists in the indistinguishability of the two feelings. The *meaning* of the sensation or affect is thus constructed rather than natural, and the representation that produces it can signify both female transgression and its containment. The fact that neither sensational representations nor the feelings they produce have natural meanings is frequently obscured, however. Representations of beautiful and mysterious women seem naturally sensational, for example, because they engage the apparently natural erotic appeal of female beauty.

SUBVERSION AND THE CRITICS

If the sensational paradox of the beautiful but evil woman can be used both to reinforce and to challenge ideologies of gender and affect, the critic's task is a difficult one. In particular, politically engaged critics, such as Marxists or feminists, who have an investment in literature's potential to subvert or resist dominant ideologies have to contend with the fact that the figure of the mysterious or criminal woman has just as often been mobilized in order to control femininity as to undermine it.[10] More skeptical of literature's oppositional functions, Foucauldian critics have provided useful challenges to claims that transgressive or outlaw figures are subversive. D. A. Miller's work has been one of the more prominent instances of a Foucauldian approach to the nineteenth-century novel, and his discussion of *Bleak House*, for example, offers a theory of the detective novel, one of the genres *Lady Audley's Secret* draws on, that implicitly challenges Showalter's feminist assessment of the sensation novel. Working from the view that literature contributes to rather than critiques dominant ideology and existing structures of power, Miller suggests that the detective plot functions to simplify complex social issues, an argument that implies that popular genres displace and efface real problems:

> The detective story gives obscurity a name and a local habitation: in that highly specific "mystery" whose ultimate uncovering motivates an equally specific program of detection. . . . In relation to an organization so complex that it often tempts its subjects to misunderstand it

as chaos, the detective story realizes the possibility of an easily comprehensible version of order. And in the face—or facelessness—of a system where it is generally impossible to assign responsibility for its workings to any single person or group of persons, where even the process of victimization seems capricious, the detective story performs a drastic simplification of power as well. For unlike Chancery, the detective story is fully prepared to affirm the efficacy and priority of personal agency, be it that of the criminal figures who do the work of concealment or that of the detective figures who undo it.[11]

Miller suggests that the detective plot "solves" complex social problems by rewriting them in simpler terms; once good and evil become readily identifiable entities, evil can be exorcized.

In *Lady Audley's Secret,* for example, Lady Audley is the interloper whose insane behavior threatens the family; by uncovering the secret of her past and consigning her to the madhouse, the novel renders the family safe. Negotiating the tensions between marriage as an economic contract and marriage as an affective bond, the novel scapegoats her for the threat posed to the stability of marriage and the family when either impulse (economic gain or sexual desire) operates to exclude the other. A woman like Lady Audley can take advantage of a man and marry for money rather than love. And blindly infatuated men like Sir Michael and George can choose inappropriate objects of desire. Their desires (implicitly sexual) are figured as madness, "this fever, this longing, this restless, uncertain miserable hesitation, . . . this frenzied wish to be young again" (5). Such desire threatens social divisions when it leads men to choose women, such as Helen Talboys or Lucy Graham, who are outside their class. Yet, ultimately the blame for this error falls upon Lady Audley, whose beauty bewitches and tempts the helpless men. The novel is obsessed with the dangers of excessive passion and sexual madness, but it rewrites this dilemma as the problem of an individual woman's murderous instincts and inherited madness.

The construction of Lady Audley as the repository of dangerous secrets and impulses mobilizes Robert Audley's detective work, which controls the intrusions of this deceptive woman; he has the power to discover truth and administer the law. In an age before psychoanalysis, the detective, the new professional required by the law's intrusion into the family, sought out the family's tensions, its sexual undercurrents, its madwoman (the hysteric's precursor).[12] As the doctor with whom Audley consults in order to diagnose Lady Audley as insane remarks, "Physicians and lawyers are the confessors of this prosaic nineteenth century" (246). Just as the confessional function of the doctor culminates in the production of the psychoanalyst, so the conversion of lawyers into detectives disguises a new form of social control, allowing for a deinstitutionalized, private, and resolvable inquiry into the family. Read according to Miller's model, the detective plot in *Lady Audley's Secret* operates to explore and defuse domestic anxieties.

At the same time, however, detection and the family intersect differently in *Lady Audley's Secret* than they do in *Bleak House.* Miller argues that *Bleak House* uses the detective plot to create an alternative to the interminable processes of Chancery. The detective police represent an institution of power that, unlike Chancery, is containable and that guarantees the possibility of a sphere outside of the jurisdiction of the law, such as the family. Ultimately, *Bleak House* attempts to dissociate itself from this model too, using the dichotomy it establishes between Chancery and the police, which is aligned with the distinction between an unclosed narrative and the detective plot, to claim that its own narrative system is different from either alternative. In contrast, *Lady Audley's Secret,* for all its simplifications, doesn't separate detection from the family, producing no thematic or formal difference between public and private realms, or between realist and detective narratives. Because detection occurs in its midst, the family can no longer serve as a refuge and instead becomes the scene of conflict and anxiety. And rather than being a figure with untroubled authority, like Inspector Bucket, Robert Audley, the detective, doubts his knowledge, efficacy, and motives. Even as it attempts to rewrite the tensions of domestic life in manageable terms, *Lady Audley's Secret* has a far from utopian view of the family, revealing it as a site of relations of power that involve both gender and class.[13] The novel's happy ending, in which the mystery is solved and the family is reconstructed, is less convincing than *Bleak House*'s domestic finale. In *Lady Audley's Secret,* the family is not a refuge from problems that occur elsewhere, but a suddenly healed instance of an institution that has been riddled by conflict throughout the narrative.

Lady Audley's Secret might also seem more subversive than *Bleak House* because Braddon dares to represent her heroine as an unrepentant criminal. Lady Dedlock's story in Dickens's novel could easily provide the material for a sensation novel, but rather than killing the man who threatens to expose her shady past, she becomes the suffering heroine of a maternal melodrama and dies in a lurid episode that resembles the climax of Mrs. Henry Wood's *East Lynne.* Unwillingly separated from her illegitimate daughter Esther, Lady Dedlock must pay for her moral redemption as a mother by being killed off in the narrative. And as the suffering mother, not only does she hide her pain under a carefully wrought demeanor of coldness, but she is kept silent even by the narrator. Her cries of anguish, when they finally do break through, remain trapped and unheard deep within the chambers of Chesney Wold:

> As Sir Leicester basks in his library, and dozes over his newspaper, is there no influence in the house to startle him; not to say, to make the very trees at Chesney Wold fling up their knotted arms, the very portraits frown, the very armour stir?
>
> No. Words, sobs, and cries, are but air; and air is so shut in and shut out throughout the house in town, that sounds need be uttered trumpet-tongued indeed by my Lady in her chamber, to carry any faint vibration to Sir Leicester's ears; and yet this cry is in the house, going upward from a wild figure on its knees.

"O my child, my child! Not dead in the first hours of her life, as my cruel sister told me; but sternly nurtured by her, after she had renounced me and told my name! O my child, O my child!"[14]

The chapter ends there, with the narrator providing the secret spectacle of Lady Dedlock's unheard cries for the reader but refraining from moving in more closely to represent her psychic state. Lady Dedlock remains for Dickens a figure; her secret past and deadened exterior represent the dead soul of the aristocracy. He is unwilling to disrupt that exterior to speak from her point of view, as he does, for example, in the case of Jo. Instead, Lady Dedlock's closely guarded secret becomes a vehicle for the reader's sensational thrills. Most evident in the sadomasochistic relation of surveillance between her and Tulkinghorn, Lady Dedlock's ability to mask her feelings makes her a fascinating mystery. This power is, however, a minimal form of resistance, ultimately one that she cannot maintain and one whose psychic cost is so high it destroys her:

> In truth she is not a hard lady naturally. . . . But so long accustomed to suppress emotion, and keep down reality; so long schooled for her own purposes, in that destructive school which shuts up the natural feelings of the heart, like flies in amber, and spreads one uniform and dreary gloss over the good and bad, the feeling and the unfeeling, the sensible and the senseless; she had subdued even her wonder until now.[15]

Dickens uses Lady Dedlock to promote a politics of affect, suggesting that the aristocracy's suppression of "the natural feelings of the heart" can only lead to destruction. This equation of the repression of feeling with moral and social decay is central to the nineteenth-century novel, and to the sensation novel in particular, and it frequently finds its particular expression in the figure of the silenced woman. Installed within a framework in which a male observer, whether narrator or detective, watches a woman, the spectacle of the suffering woman also makes possible the sensational thrill of uncovering a secret. Suppressed affect provides a vehicle for surveillance, and this apparatus remains hidden behind the lure of that which incites it.

Despite his interest in the sensational power of the woman with a secret, Dickens does not go as far as Braddon and make his heroine a murderer. Within Dickens's narrative, it is unthinkable that Lady Dedlock should be Tulkinghorn's murderer—that job is left to her double, Hortense, who despite her uncanny resemblance to Lady Dedlock, is differentiated from her employer by being a foreigner and a member of the working class. A similar strategy is evident in that other canonical precursor to the sensation novel, Charlotte Brontë's *Jane Eyre*, in which the middle-class heroine's more aggressive tendencies are projected onto the insane and racially other Bertha. Braddon's representation of the blond, feminine, and upper-class Lady Audley as capable of attempting murder does constitute a departure from the narrative conventions of mainstream Victorian fiction. Of the three sensation novels to be dis-cussed in this book, *Lady Audley's Secret* seems the most subversive *if* the sensation novel's subversiveness is a function of its heroine's transgressiveness.

The figure of the mysterious and criminal woman is not, however, intrinsically subversive; it can be deployed both to challenge and to reinforce ideologies of gender and affect. Claims about *Lady Audley's Secret*'s subversiveness might best be understood as strategic responses to other critics and readers. The feminist and Foucauldian approaches exemplified by Showalter and by Miller are not necessarily mutually exclusive, especially since both critics challenge traditional conceptions of literary and aesthetic value. Showalter argues for the subversiveness of the sensation novel in order to foreground the potential value of popular works by women, whereas Miller attacks the assumption that canonical novels criticize their social milieu or processes of representation. Miller's Foucauldian analysis shows how a canonical novel with an ostensibly critical perspective on Victorian society is in many ways implicated in the processes from which it tries to distance itself and less subversive than it might like to be. However, in the analysis of a popular and noncanonical novel such as *Lady Audley's Secret,* exactly the kind of narrative whose limits and blindnesses *Bleak House* might be assumed to transcend, it might be more urgent to see how the text, despite expectations to the contrary, contains subversive elements.[16] The availability of both readings is testimony to the impossibility of separating the mechanisms of subversion and recuperation or designating a particular literary text intrinsically liberatory or reactionary.

Emphasis on subversion or containment in the novel coincides with emphasis on the female criminal or the male detective in *Lady Audley's Secret.* One can read the novel from the detective or masculine point of view as a fantasy of control, surveillance, and power, in which threats to the family can be identified and contained. One can also read it from Lady Audley's or the woman's point of view as a fantasy of rebellion, in which women can take their revenge on a patriarchy that restrains them, and in which madness is a sign of resistance. The latter reading seems to be subsumed to the former by the end of the novel, however, when Lady Audley's rebellion ultimately fails. Less obvious is how Robert Audley's position of power as detective is undercut. Given that his perspective controls the narrative, it seems important not only to show how Braddon's female protagonist subverts traditional roles, but to question the female author's investment in her male protagonist. In doing so, I hope to resolve the apparent conflict between the feminist and Foucauldian paradigms.

AFFECT AND MASCULINE POWER

Criticism of the novel tends to focus almost exclusively on the "beautiful fiend," Lady Audley, thus repeating the text's fascination with the paradoxical character and lurid history of its mysterious heroine. Lady Audley becomes the fetishistic object even in feminist readings, her peculiar combination of beauty, madness, sanity, evil, and calculation serving as the figurative locus to explore the operations of Victorian ideologies of gender. The problem with such interpretations is that they imply that the detective's work is neutral, that he investigates the secrets of the female criminal while himself remaining an object of no particular interest. Yet the novel is sensational not just because crime occurs in the family, but because it occurs in the detective's own family; Robert Audley's best friend seems to have been murdered on his family estate and his aunt appears to be the murderer. This incestuous intermingling of familial relations and detection makes Robert Audley's role peculiar. Like the analyst, he is subject to countertransference; his investigations into a family drama reveal his own desires and blindnesses. He is caught up in an Oedipal drama with his uncle, sexually tied to both George and Clara Talboys, and afraid of his own madness, so that his investment in Lady Audley's secret is far from simple. The novel is not just about how the crime and its detection affect his family, but about how they affect him, as he finds his power both constituted and threatened by his simultaneous roles as detective and family member.

Read as Robert Audley's story, *Lady Audley's Secret* narrates his development from aimless son of the aristocracy, "an idle flaneur upon the smooth pathways that have no particular goal" (281), to a full-fledged member of the patriarchy—husband, father, homeowner, and active professional. The detective case is the means to both professional and sexual maturity. Prior to it, his professional status is ambiguous:

> Robert Audley was supposed to be a barrister. As a barrister was his name inscribed in the law-list; as a barrister he had chambers in Figtree Court, Temple; as a barrister he had eaten the allotted number of dinners, which form the sublime ordeal through which the forensic aspirant wades on to fame and fortune. If these things can make a man a barrister, Robert Audley decidedly was one. But he had never either had a brief, or tried to get a brief, or even wished to have a brief in all those five years, during which his name had been painted upon one of the doors in Figtree Court.
>
> (21)

Supported by an inheritance, Robert Audley can remain a member of the ruling class without having to do any work. Despite its mockery of his laziness, the passage suggests that even if the name on the door doesn't accurately describe the nature of his labor, it does designate his position of power as a member of an important social institution. Ostensibly he is unconventional, but his idleness comes from a class privilege that places him squarely within existing social structures. The novel emphasizes his marginality, suggesting that his reclusive habits and ample leisure time make him the ideal solitary investigator. Ultimately, however, he enforces the dominant social values and upholds the work ethic by finding purpose in his investigation. Once he becomes a detective, he administers the law by actively working, traveling from one end of the country to the other in search of evidence, and by doing so privately, without institutional support. The law turns into detection without declaring itself as such; Robert Audley looks like a family member or a curious gentleman asking after his friend. Detection exists in an odd no man's land between the legal, professional world and the family. Its ambiguous status keeps the boundary between family and professional life fluid, leaving open the question of whether Robert's new maturity is a result of professional discipline or changed familial relations.

As detection, professionalism, and the law infiltrate the family, the family in turn transforms detective work into romance. The incitement to detection for Robert Audley is not a crime but the arousal of affect. Prior to his engagement in George Talboy's life, his "listless, dawdling, indifferent, irresolute manner" and "lymphatic nature" indicate a lack, not only of professional ambition, but of romantic or sexual desire. He is a somewhat eccentric bachelor, even slightly effeminate in his tastes, preferring French novels to hunting. He is indifferent to women as sexual objects and to marriage as an economic benefit (as evidenced by his lack of attachment to his cousin Alicia, who is not only the obvious choice economically, but the most engaging woman in the novel). The moment that marks his change is not the need to find his friend George (itself replaced by the investigation of Lady Audley/Helen Talboys), but his meeting with George and their homoerotic attraction to one another. He first greets him "with an emphasis by no means usual to him." As he plays nurse to his newly widowed friend and then tries to solve the mystery of his disappearance, he finds new passion and direction in life. "The big dragoon was as helpless as a baby; and Robert Audley, the most vacillating and unenergetic of men, found himself called upon to act for another. He rose superior to himself, and equal to the occasion" (26). Suddenly, the passive and boyish Audley is in a position of power and responsibility and he acts accordingly. The language of the passage is distinctly sexualized; "vacillating" and "unenergetic" behavior implies impotence, "rising superior" its opposite. Robert's new professional demeanor is indistinguishable from the signs of attraction to George: "If any one had ventured to tell Mr. Robert Audley that he could possibly feel a strong attachment to any creature breathing, that cynical gentleman would have elevated his eyebrows in supreme contempt at the preposterous notion. Yet here he was, flurried and anxious, bewildering his brain by all manner of conjectures about his missing friend; and false to every attribute of his nature, walking fast" (55). The novel continually conflates the language of affect and the language of work. Their connection suggests that desire is not a natural drive, but is instead constructed in relation to social processes and institutions. Furthermore, the play of desire is integral to the workplace, rather than exorcised to the realm of leisure in the interests of efficiency. Romance and work are not causally related, such that one is more fundamental than the other, nor are they separate domains; this novel continually collapses distinctions between private and public realms, between the domestic and the professional spheres.

The sexualization of nonsexual domains is further underscored by the fact that the object of Robert Audley's desire is a man. Eve Sedgwick, arguing for the connections between the homosexual, the homoerotic, and the homosocial, has suggested that the link, as well as the distinction, between homosexuality and patriarchal power functions to define other relations of power besides those immediately connected to sex and gender:

> Psychoanalysis, the recent work of Foucault, and feminist historical scholarship all suggest that the place of drawing the boundary between the sexual and the not-sexual, like the place of drawing the boundary between the realms of the two genders, *is* variable, but is *not* arbitrary. That is . . . the placement of the boundaries in a particular society affects not merely the definitions of those terms themselves—sexual/nonsexual, masculine/feminine—but also the apportionment of forms of power that are not obviously sexual. . . . In any male-dominated society, there is a special relationship between male homosocial (*including* homosexual) desire and the structures for maintaining and transmitting patriarchal power: a relationship founded on an inherent and potentially active structural congruence.[17]

At the beginning of the novel, Robert's behavior, both sexual and professional, is gendered as nonmasculine; he is more like a boy, a woman, or a homosexual. Sexual manhood would seem to require his insertion into a set of relations with a woman, as husband or suitor, yet professional maturity demands that he relate to other men as colleagues. The two processes converge in his attraction to George Talboys, so that a man is the means by which he comes to work and to love. Furthermore, the distinction between home and work would seem to correspond to the boundary between the sexual and the nonsexual. Yet, detection starts to blur the boundaries by turning the home into a place of work, professionalizing the activity of identifying sexual deviance. At the same time, work becomes sexualized, motivated by desire. This mutual imbrication of the sexual and the nonsexual realms means that the structure of relations in the professional sphere—relations between men—carries over into the sexual domain, as evidenced by the homoerotic bond between George and Robert. Women in the novel merely serve as stand-ins for this homoerotic bond; Lady Audley becomes the ostensible object of detection, and Clara Talboys becomes the ostensible object of affection. The novel ends with the traditional closure of marriage supplemented by the reunion of the two male friends, George having returned from Australia because he "yearned for the strong grasp of [Bob's] hand" (285). Clara seems only to be the medium of exchange that allows for the culmination of the relation between the men. Lady Audley also serves as a means to this end, as the duplicitous woman whose seduction of Michael Audley and George Talboys must be exposed in order to rid the family of female evil and safeguard it for male bonding. The detective story whose focus is the crimes of Lady Audley masks the narrative of Robert Audley's accession to the world of male power by means of his affective ties to a male friend. Patriarchal culture privileges relations between men in every arena; rather than making him deviant, Robert's homoeroticism seems to fit him all the better to be the bearer of social values. The novel's homoerotic subtext not only reveals his investments, but intensifies the links between sexuality and work that the novel brings into play.

AFFECT AND MASCULINE WEAKNESS

Rather than acting as the police for desire, Robert Audley polices by virtue of his own desire, which is never completely dissociated from the domain he investigates. Thus, affect and power are linked rather than intrinsically opposed. It remains unclear, however, whether Audley's affective investment in the case strengthens or weakens his skills as a detective. Although the tie between Helen Talboys and Lady Audley is obvious at a very early stage, Robert continues to collect evidence because he is terrified by the effects of his knowledge. If his investigation of Lady Audley is bound up with his attraction to George, then his reluctance to divulge the secret of her identity reveals the other locus of his investments—his relation to his uncle. The closer he gets to the secret of George's disappearance, the more he resists conclusions that implicate and threaten his own family. His detective work produces an Oedipal family drama: as he shows signs of maturity, forming attachments outside his immediate family and acquiring professional responsibilities, he becomes enmeshed in an Oedipal rivalry with his uncle (explicitly described as his second father), whom he will eventually "kill" and replace as head of the family by revealing Lady Audley's secrets. His search constantly reflects back on himself: "Is the radius to grow narrower day by day until it draws a dark circle around the home of those I love?" (100). Because his work forces him back to his home and his relatives, his professional development depends on resolving family tensions, which increasingly seem to retard his investigations.

Thus the novel foregrounds the detective's role, making him less innocent or neutral than he first appears to be. Audley's sense of his own involvement produces guilt and self-loathing. He is implicated in the events that he uncovers in ways that he hesitates to acknowledge, desperately afraid of his new role: "His generous nature revolted at the office into which he had found himself drawn—the office of spy, the collector of damning facts that led on to horrible deductions" (128). Suddenly the guilt attaches to him rather than to the criminal. Ostensibly the innocent observer of events, he becomes an active participant in the drama he unfolds. He seems to produce the crime in the process of investigating it, making trouble where previously there was none. Surveillance is the problem, not Lady Audley: "He was forever haunted by the vision of his uncle's anguish, forever tortured by the thought of that ruin and desolation which, being brought about by his instrumentality, would seem in a manner his handiwork" (166). Afraid to disturb the patriarch's happiness with his young wife, he sees his work in terms of its effect on his uncle, not Lady Audley. The focus of the investigation shifts away from Lady Audley's history to the underlying relations of power between the son and his father-figure. Because of this relation, Robert and Lady Audley become rivals for Sir Michael's affection; the family romance sub-sumes the detective/criminal relation so that Robert shares the guilt with Lady Audley.

For Robert Audley, detection alternates between private nightmare, exposing horrifying and personal secrets, and neutral science, rationally revealing the truth, with the latter often a defense against the former. This distinction is explicitly elaborated in the chapter in which, pondering the information he has gathered, Robert first has the following dream about the case and then tries to codify his knowledge of the facts:

> In another dream he saw the grave of Helen Talboys open, and while he waited, with the cold horror lifting up his hair, to see the dead woman rise and stand before him with her stiff, charnel-house drapery clinging about her rigid limbs, his uncle's wife tripped gaily out of the open grave, dressed in the crimson velvet robes in which the artist had painted her, and with her ringlets flashing like red gold in the unearthly light that shone about her.
>
> (64)

George has only just disappeared, and Robert has uncovered only one of the many documents that will provide evidence for his discoveries, but his unconscious already knows the solution to the mystery. Not only does his dream reveal the connection between Helen Talboys and Lady Audley, but Lady Audley appears here in her "true" form, that is, endowed with all the power and ambiguity that her portrait reveals.

Unable to trust his dream's revelations, however, Robert gropes his way toward a more scientific method of detection:

> He drew up this record in short, detached sentences, which he numbered as he wrote. It ran thus: "Journal of Facts connected with the Disappearance of George Talboys, inclusive of Facts which have no apparent Relation to that Circumstance." . . . When Robert Audley had completed this brief record, which he drew up with great deliberation, and with frequent pauses for reflection, alterations and erasures, he sat for a long time contemplating the written page.
>
> (67-68)

In producing a record that is complete, neutral, quantitative, and epistemologically reliable, Robert Audley hopes to absolve himself of any personal responsibility for his discoveries. He can infinitely elaborate his work, painstakingly filling in the blanks in a list of facts that have nothing to do with him. His epistemological power, his capacity to note every detail, becomes a juridical power, the capacity to uncover criminals and bring them to justice. He intimidates Lady Audley with the claim that he can collect "a thousand circumstances so slight as to be forgotten by the criminal, but links of iron in the wonderful chain forged by the science of the detective officer" (81). The metaphor of the "chain" translates the wholeness of the evidence directly into the power of the law to capture criminals. He becomes the custodian of social justice, bolstered by the unassailable power of scientific evidence.

Yet, like Freud's appeals to the scientificity of his method, Robert Audley's claims for detection look like a defense against doubts and investments that his dream reveals. The dream work is immediate, subjective, and emotionally powerful, leaving him less in control of his knowledge. In addition to revealing Lady Audley's secret identity, it makes him a central figure in the unfolding drama, as his own unconscious comes into play:

> But into all these dreams the places he had last been in, and the people with whom he had last been concerned, were dimly interwoven—sometimes his uncle, sometimes Alicia; oftenest of all my lady; the trout stream in Essex; the lime-walk at the Court. Once he was walking in the black shadows of this long avenue, with Lady Audley hanging on his arm, when suddenly they heard a great knocking in the distance, and his uncle's wife wound her slender arms around him, crying out that it was the day of judgment, and that all wicked secrets must now be told. Looking at her as she shrieked this in his ear, he saw that her face had grown ghastly white, and that her beautiful golden ringlets were changing into serpents, and slowly creeping down her fair neck.
>
> (64-65)

At first he dreams about the people and places of his investigations, but as in life, he is inexorably led back to Audley Court and to his own family relations. At the moment of revelation he is caught with Lady Audley, whose position as "his uncle's wife" is explicitly emphasized and whose intimate embrace seems to indicate an illicit union. The unveiling of the truth is figured as the last judgment, a horrifying and apocalyptic moment. In this context, the "wicked secrets" seem likely to be Robert's desires rather than Lady Audley's past. Lady Audley is transformed into Medusa, revealing the threatening power that her appearance normally hides. Her "golden ringlets" are constantly used as a synecdoche for her beauty, which in turn constitutes her identity; their mutation dramatically signifies her complete duplicity. Yet, this vision of Lady Audley's evil may reveal more about the beholder than the beheld. Freud's remarks on the Medusa's head are helpful in this context, explaining, as they do, how a representation of the threat posed by a woman can also be reassuring: "The hair upon the Medusa's head is frequently represented in works of art in the form of snakes, and these once again are derived from the castration complex. It is a remarkable fact that, however frightening they may be in themselves, they nevertheless serve actually as a mitigation of the horror, for they replace the penis, the absence of which is the cause of the horror."[18] This logic applies to how the novel functions in general. By fixing a particular danger or anxiety in the person of Lady Audley, it can then control and ultimately exorcise it. Robert's sexualized dream reveals how he will be able to restore the family to peace by first convincing himself that his aunt is evil. The dream thus reveals as much about the process of detection as it does about the secret to be detected.

The dream also transforms Robert's detection into an Oedipal scene. Both Alicia and Sir Michael misrecognize Robert's suspicion of Lady Audley as desire for her, taking the obsession of the detective for the obsession of the lover. The attention he pays to her, the emotions his discoveries produce, the threat those discoveries pose to his uncle—all of these phenomena are seen as the behavior of an infatuated son. Detection begins to resemble incest and brings with it all the guilt and anxiety that might attach to a forbidden desire. Once again work and romance are indistinguishable, the one masking as the other. Robert's dream reveals the complexity of his position, whereas the rational labor of making lists represses it.

Uncomfortable with the disruption his power creates, Robert must find a way to absolve himself of responsibility for his discoveries. He can only bring himself to pursue his case by setting the two families, the Talboys and the Audleys, against one another. He must choose between his love for his uncle and his love for George Talboys, between his position as dutiful son and his position as lover: "I've a comfortable little fortune in the three per cents; I'm heir presumptive to my uncle's title; and I know of a certain dear little girl who, as I think, would do her best to make me happy; but I declare that I would freely give up all, and stand penniless in the world tomorrow, if this mystery could be satisfactorily cleared away, and George Talboys could stand by my side" (105). His affection for George Talboys is directly opposed to the future he would have by remaining within his own family. His uncle represents the law of the father; loyalty and obedience to him installs Robert in a social position that includes income, position, and a wife. Detection and homoerotic affection are transgressive. Rather than simply being anarchic, Robert searches for an outside authority to guide his actions. He goes to George's father, hoping to pit one patriarch against another. When Mr. Talboys refuses this role, he inserts Clara, George's sister, in his place: "I accept the dominion of that pale girl, with the statuesque features and the calm brown eyes. I recognize the power of a mind superior to my own, and I yield to it, and bow down to it. I've been acting for myself, and thinking for myself, for the last few months, and I'm tired of the unnatural business" (136). Robert must have his work authorized by an outside source who functions as a substitute for his uncle. He resists the development his detection demands of him, seeking to remain the submissive boy.

The transfer of authority to a woman is crucial. Clara also functions as a repository for Robert's desire, standing in for George Talboys as well as for his father.[19] This conveniently resolves the problem of homoerotic love; he can have the woman who looks like George and who herself transfers onto him her love for her brother, the only man she has loved. The change in gender of the love object and the authority figure also enables Robert, under the guise of misogyny, to play out his ambivalent relation to sexual involvement and patriarchal power:

> I hate women. They're bold, brazen, abominable creatures, invented for the annoyance and destruction of their superiors. Look at this business of poor George's! It's all woman's work from one end to the other. He marries a woman, and his father casts him off penniless and professionless. He hears of the woman's death and he breaks his heart—his good, honest manly heart, worth a million of the treacherous lumps of self-interest and mercenary calculation which beats in women's breasts. He goes to a woman's house and he is never seen alive again. And now I find myself driven into a corner by another woman, of whose existence I had never thought until this day.
>
> (137)

Robert compares Clara's effect on him to Lady Audley's effect on George, and thus raises the possibility that his infatuation with her is no less misguided or illusory. Like Lady Audley, Clara functions for Robert by means of his image of her physical appearance; "her brown eyes" guide him in his search. At the same time, this female object of desire is constantly denigrated in part because Robert's affection for her is seen as a power she holds over him. The hostility for a father and the affection for a man that could never be expressed directly can be manifested toward a woman.

The novel's use of women as means of exchange for relations between men and then as scapegoats for their anxieties points to the difficulty of locating the text's subversiveness in its representation of a female criminal or madwoman. One can't specify the novel's effect as either subversion or recuperation because both processes occur simultaneously. The passages that are most misogynist can also be read as covert expressions of female power and aggression. Robert's speech about "petticoat government," for example, prompted by his simultaneous resentment of and relief about Clara's effect on him, both elevates and denigrates women:

> What a wonderful solution to life's enigma there is in petticoat government! . . . Who ever heard of a woman taking life as it ought to be taken? . . . It is because women are never lazy. They don't know what it is to be quiet. They are Semiramides, and Cleopatras, and Joans of Arc, Queen Elizabeths, and Catharines the Second, and they riot in battle, and murder, and clamor and desperation. . . . To call them the weaker sex is to utter a hideous mockery. They are the stronger sex, the noisier, the more persevering, the most self-assertive sex. They want freedom of opinion, variety of occupation, do they? Let them have it.
>
> (136-137)

Having articulated the nature of female power, Robert Audley goes on to say, "I hate women." Although the passage can be read as a sign of the novel's subversive tendencies, its context must also be accounted for. Robert Audley views women as powerful and rebellious in order to contain them. The production of Lady Audley's secret, of her madness, crime, and deviance, is how the novel can then convert marginality into something that can be brought under control, ridding the family of that which threatens it. The representation of Lady Audley as a villain is as much the product of a reactionary conservatism as of a covert feminism, and the appeal to her as a figure of resistance is accordingly problematic.

MALE MADNESS

Yet the novel has also worked to question the detective's authority, by revealing how women are used to stabilize the complex forces of desire and investment that inform Robert Audley's work. If the novel has policed illicit female behavior (by first producing it as deviant), it has also subverted its own processes of containment by showing the weaknesses of its detective. The novel's oppositions—between madness and sanity, desire and work, detective and criminal—converge in the figure of Robert Audley, who becomes simultaneously the representative of dominant ideology and the isolated madman, the new patriarch and the homosexual who dodges traditional masculine roles. The interpenetration of family and law, and of desire and discipline, in his work corresponds to a confusion between processes of containment and subversion. The following passage, for example, depicts him as a social outcast, whose detective work undermines his sanity and thus links him to Lady Audley:

> He had dropped away from his old friends. He had shrunk from those men as if he had, indeed, been a detective police officer, stained with vile associations and unfit company for honest gentlemen. He had drawn himself away from all familiar haunts, and shut himself in his lonely rooms with the perpetual trouble of his mind for his sole companion, until he had grown as nervous as habitual solitude will eventually make the strongest and the wisest man, however he may vaunt himself of his strength and wisdom.
>
> (264)

Madness becomes a term to apply not merely to a scapegoat but to anyone. The novel is extremely sensitive to the normalcy of madness, to how excesses of emotion can be produced by constraints that impinge on all individuals. In one of *Lady Audley's Secret*'s more remarkable passages, for example, the narrator meditates on a rather more mundane, but no less severe, form of madness than Lady Audley's, a madness produced by the effects of mid-Victorian capitalism on everyday life:

> Who has not felt, in the first madness of sorrow, an unreasoning rage against the mute propriety of chairs and tables, the stiff squareness of Turkey carpets, the unbending obstinacy of the outward apparatus of existence? We want to root up gigantic trees in a primeval forest, and to tear their huge branches asunder in our convulsive grasp; and the utmost that we can do for the relief of our passion is to knock over an easy-chair, or smash a few shillings' worth of Mr. Copeland's manufacture.
>
> Madhouses are large and only too numerous; yet surely it is strange they are not larger, when we think of how many helpless wretches must beat their brains against this hopeless persistency of the orderly outward world, as compared with the storm and tempest, the riot and

confusion within—when we remember how many minds must tremble upon the narrow boundary between reason and unreason, mad to-day and sane tomorrow, mad yesterday and sane to-day.

> (135)

The protest here seems to be against the commodification and regulation of experience, against how "carpets," "easy chairs," and "Mr. Copeland's manufacture" suppress not only forbidden desires but all desires. The cathartic possibility of unleashing emotion by "root[ing] up gigantic trees in a primeval forest" has been rendered impossible in the face of the "mute propriety" of the commodities now manufactured from the raw materials provided by the forest. Despite the implicit utopianism of the fantasy that in some prior age affect could be more readily expressed, the narrator's complaint does suggest an important discrepancy between psychic life and commodification. What Marx, for example, calls "alienation" is here expressed as the inadequate relation between the "hopeless persistency of the orderly outward world" and the "storm and tempest, the riot and confusion within." If madness is not just a female problem, the sensation novel can be considered a means for expressing the feelings and experiences for which capitalist culture provides no other outlet. The passage reveals what may be a less manageable problem than Lady Audley's madness, which can be attributed to her femininity. Ventriloquizing Robert Audley's position in this passage, Braddon inhabits the position of her male protagonist in a way that challenges the gendering of the distinction between sanity and insanity. She feminizes Robert Audley and empowers Lady Audley by granting them both emotional lives. Robert Audley becomes more sympathetic and less authoritative when his power as detective and patriarch appears unstable.

At the same time, however, Robert Audley's marginality, like Lady Audley's subversiveness, is converted into an operation of the law; his desire, his homoeroticism, and his asociality are all mobilized for the policing of the family. The aristocratic son who refuses to join the mainstream has posed a threat to conservative values. The eccentricity that makes him a good detective ultimately brings him back to the fold, and he emerges as a guardian of the status quo. The class whose very prosperity seems to be producing deviants holds its own. By the end of the novel Robert can return to being a lawyer, and his profession is now revealed to be as thoroughly enmeshed in the world of the family and romance as detection was: "Mr. Audley is a rising man upon the home circuit by this time, and has distinguished himself in the great breach of promise case of Hobbs v. Nobbs, and has convulsed the court by his deliciously comic rendering of the faithless Nobb's [sic] amatory correspondence" (285). Labor and romance interpenetrate again; master of a legal system that presides over courtship and the family, Robert Audley not only uses his knowledge of love professionally, but is ironically superior about it.

Yet, although the sensation novel refuses the family as a refuge, anxiously subjecting it to scrutiny and the law, it also makes it the only place where resistance could occur, since it must come, not from some readily identifiable space outside of power, but from places that, because saturated by both the law and desire, serve as regions within which to change the economy of their relations. Jameson's articulation of the utopian possibilities of mass culture, his claim that "even the most degraded works . . . have as their underlying impulse—albeit in what is often distorted and repressed, unconscious form—our deepest fantasies about the nature of social life, both as we live it now, and as we feel in our bones it ought rather to be lived" resembles Foucault's caution against seeing sites of resistance as distinct from the systems of power that produce them.[20] Both would agree that one cannot find a text somehow outside ideology or unequivocally critical in its relation to society. *Lady Audley's Secret* prevents one from looking to the family, desire, madness, or affect as guarantees of resistance or intrinsically disruptive forces. The novel relentlessly erases the boundaries between sexuality and work, the family and the law, and the private and the public spheres to reveal that one confronts rather than escapes each domain through the other. The fact that subversive forces can be recuperated or that anxieties can be contained doesn't mean that utopian prospects are impossible. Instead, they must be glimpsed from within conservative ideologies as the possibility of another way in which Lady Audley's madness or Robert Audley's disaffectedness might find their expression.

The Sensational Portrait of a Commodity

If Lady Audley is finally neither criminal nor insane, then the sensational and compelling portrait of her might be said to posit a secret where in fact there is none. The apparent discrepancy between her feminine appearance and her unfeminine behavior can be resolved by rejecting the ideology of femininity upon which it is based or by redefining femininity to include Lady Audley's bid for power. The pre-Raphaelite portrait might then be said not to hide but to reveal the power of femininity. Like her "insane" mother, who is not an ugly demon, but a childlike blond beauty, Lady Audley invites the viewer to "see" madness and femininity differently. Yet the portrait's sensational power does not disappear with the demystification of its secret; the secret that it has no secret becomes the source of its continued affective power. It consolidates a more pervasive, albeit socially constructed, form of madness, produced by consumer culture and contemporary urban life, rather than a madness that can be attributed to crime, heredity, or femininity.

The pre-Raphaelite portrait that captures Lady Audley's ambiguous power so well might be juxtaposed against another portrait of a woman whose appearance is deceiving. In *Bleak House*, Lady Dedlock's image appears among a group of pin-up portraits, known as the Galaxy Gallery of British Beauty, with which Mr. Weevle lovingly decorates his humble lodgings:

> But what Mr. Weevle prizes most, of all his few possessions . . . is a choice collection of copper-plate impressions from that truly national work, The Divinities of Albion, or Galaxy Gallery of British Beauty, representing ladies of title and fashion in every variety of smirk that art, combined with capital, is capable of producing. With these magnificent portraits . . . he decorates his apartment; and as the Galaxy Gallery of British Beauty wears every variety of fancy dress, plays every variety of musical instrument, fondles every variety of dog, ogles every variety of prospect, and is backed up by every variety of flower-pot and balustrade, the result is very imposing.[21]

The portrait of Lady Dedlock, deemed by Guppy to be a "speaking likeness," seems to be particularly compelling, but its appeal derives as much from the commodities it displays as from the woman whom they adorn: "She is represented on a terrace, with a pedestal upon the terrace, and a vase upon the pedestal, and her shawl upon the vase, and a prodigious piece of fur upon the shawl, and her arm on the prodigious piece of fur, and a bracelet on her arm."[22] Lady Dedlock almost disappears beneath the catalogue of the objects that surround her, but in fact they are both figuratively, as metonyms, and literally, as the commodities purchased with her wealth, signs of her power. The portrait reveals mass culture's power to sensationalize capitalism by using female display as a vehicle for representing consumer culture. Erotic fetishism is set in motion to produce commodity fetishism. A prototype of advertisements, and such cultural traditions as the gossip magazine and the star system, the Galaxy Gallery of British Beauty demonstrates mass culture's power to combine "art and capital," selling products by selling the life-styles with which they are associated.[23] Mr. Weevle's "weakness" for "fashion" finds its satisfaction in the gossip columns of the newspapers: "To . . . read about the brilliant and distinguished meteors that are shooting across the fashionable sky in every direction, is unspeakable consolation to him. . . . Mr. Weevle reverts from this intelligence, to the Galaxy portraits implicated; and seems to know the originals, and to be known of them."[24] Like mass culture in general, the portraits offer up the life-styles of the rich and famous in order to provide the "unspeakable consolation" of making the powerful classes accessible and knowable. Rendered visible in the sensational and iconic portraits of beautiful women, capitalism's power literally acquires a body and a face. The sensation novel's quest to uncover the secrets of beautiful women satisfies the craving to know and to see consumer culture. The fascination that women like Lady Dedlock and Lady Audley hold for audiences is thus not simply an erotic one, nor can it be demystified or dispelled by analyzing or revising the ideologies of gender upon which it is based. Providing a body for capitalism, a picture of the luxuries it can provide, these women exhibit the power not just of sex but of money. Thus, the sensation novel is not simply a vehicle for repressed female desire, and the liberation of the impulses it represents as criminal or insane would not alone suffice to render it unnecessary. In *Lady Audley's Secret*'s politics of affect, it is not just sexual desire, whether repressed or liberated, that is at stake; the novel sets into motion the relation between affect and capitalism by displaying the beautiful and rebellious woman as the figure for the desiring consumer and the desired commodity. Whether the sensationalized woman provides a deceptive face for capitalism remains to be seen in the chapters that follow [in *Mixed Feelings: Feminism, Mass Culture, and Victorian Sensationalism*].

Notes

1. For the most comprehensive description of the genre, see Hughes, *The Maniac in the Cellar*. Other discussions include Patrick Brantlinger, "What is Sensational about the 'Sensation Novel'?" *Nineteenth-Century Fiction* 37, no. 1 (June 1982): 1-28; Martha Vicinus, "'Helpless and Unfriended': Nineteenth-Century Domestic Melodrama," *New Literary History* 13, no. 1 (Autumn 1981): 127-143; Showalter, *A Literature of Their Own*, 153-181; Jonathan Loesberg, "The Ideology of Narrative Form in Sensation Fiction," *Representations* 13 (Winter 1986): 115-138.

2. Henry James, "Miss Braddon," in *Notes and Reviews* (Cambridge, Mass.: Dunster House, 1921), 110.

3. Mary Elizabeth Braddon, *Lady Audley's Secret* (New York: Dover, 1974), 94. All further references in the text are to this edition.

4. See Jeanne Fahnestock, "Bigamy: The Rise and Fall of a Convention," *Nineteenth-Century Fiction* 36, no. 1 (June 1981): 47-71. In 1857, divorce laws were liberalized somewhat, creating a great deal of public interest in the issue. Fahnestock explains, "These more liberal divorce laws weakened the sanctified, indissoluble state of marriage, and the absence of its former permanence left something of a vacuum, a need for a new definition or basis for marriage" (66). Novels about bigamy present second marriages as both attractive and threatening, thus making it possible to explore ambivalence about divorce.

5. "Our Female Sensation Novelists," *The Living Age* 78 (22 August 1863): 353-354.

6. "Sensation Novelists: Miss Braddon," 186-187.

7. Showalter, *A Literature of Their Own*, 158-159.

8. Ibid., 160.

9. Ibid., 167.

10. For Marxist approaches to the novel that stress its capacity to reveal social contradictions, see Pierre Macherey, *A Theory of Literary Production*, trans. Geoffrey Wall (London: Routledge and Kegan Paul, 1978); Terry Eagleton, *Criticism and Ideology* (London: Verso, 1976); and Jameson, *The Political Unconscious*.

11. D. A. Miller, *The Novel and the Police* (Berkeley and Los Angeles: University of California Press, 1988), 69.

12. See Jacques Donzelot, *The Policing of Families*, trans. Robert Hurley (New York: Random House,

1979), for a discussion of how the institution of psychoanalysis acts as a masked form of social control and discipline. The detective, when investigating the family, performs a similar function.

13. There are, for example, no models of the nuclear family in the novel because mothers are conspicuously absent. Robert Audley, Alicia Audley, George and Clara Talboys, and Helen Maldon have all lost their mothers in early childhood. This fact calls into question the ideal of family life and also allows the novel to reveal more clearly the relations that really seem to matter in the family—those between fathers (all of whom wield their patriarchal authority firmly) and their children.

14. Charles Dickens, *Bleak House* (Harmondsworth: Penguin, 1971), 466.

15. Ibid., 812.

16. The problem, as Dominick LaCapra puts it in a critique of Miller's reading, is to see "how symptomatic, critical, and possibly transformative forces interact in relating a text to its various contexts (or subtexts)." Defending a poststructuralist criticism, and drawing on theorists such as Bakhtin and Derrida, LaCapra argues that narrative or literary representations always contain contestatory moments. See his "Ideology and Critique in *Bleak House*," *Representations* 6 (Spring 1984): 117.

17. Eve Kosofsky Sedgwick, *Between Men: English Literature and Male Homosocial Desire* (New York: Columbia University Press, 1985), 22, 25. Sedgwick is interested in the mutual interaction of questions of class and sexuality in the portrayal of homosexuality in the novel. She has also argued for the centrality of homosexuality in the gothic novel (in a review of *The Literature of Terror*, by David Punter, in *Studies in Romanticism* 21 [Summer 1982]: 243-253), a claim that, given the ties between the sensation novel and the gothic, suggests that the sensation novel might figure importantly in a general theory of the role of homosexuality in nineteenth-century culture.

18. Sigmund Freud, "Medusa's Head," in *Sexuality and the Psychology of Love*, ed. Philip Rieff (New York: Collier, 1963), 212. In the same piece, Freud connects homosexuality and images of the Medusa's head: "Since the Greeks were in the main strongly homosexual, it was inevitable that we should find among them a representation of woman as a being who frightens and repels because she is castrated" (213). I am arguing that Robert Audley's homoerotic tendencies make him a particularly appropriate agent of patriarchal values, which are sustained by projecting responsibility for conflict onto women.

19. Clara's vestigial function in the plot is demonstrated by the adaptations of the novel for the stage, in which her character is left out entirely. See, for example, Brian J. Burton, *Lady Audley's Secret or Death in*

Lime Tree Walk (Birmingham: C. Combridge, 1966), based on the several Victorian dramatizations of the novel that appeared in the 1860s. A narrative that focuses on Lady Audley, as the plays do, doesn't need Clara; she is crucial, however, if one reads for Robert Audley's psychological drama and his relation to Lady Audley and her secret.

20. Jameson, "Reification and Utopia in Mass Culture," 148, 147. For Foucault on power and resistance, see *The History of Sexuality, Volume 1,* 92-96. For example, "where there is power, there is resistance, and yet, or rather consequently, this resistance is never in a position of exteriority in relation to power" (95).

21. Dickens, *Bleak House,* 340.

22. Ibid., 503.

23. For a discussion of the relations between the novel (and Dickens's work in particular) and the developing institutions of advertising and consumer culture, see Jennifer Wicke, *Advertising Fictions* (New York: Columbia University Press, 1988).

24. Dickens, *Bleak House,* 340.

Jill L. Matus (essay date 1993)

SOURCE: "Disclosure as 'Cover-up': The Discourse of Madness in *Lady Audley's Secret,*" in *University of Toronto Quarterly,* Vol. 62, No. 3, Spring, 1993, pp. 334-55.

[*In the following essay, Matus argues that the conclusion of madness in* Lady Audley's Secret *serves as a distraction from the gender and class issues raised throughout the novel.*]

For a work that addresses itself in many ways to the question of madness, *Lady Audley's Secret* broaches the topic only as it nears its conclusion. In terms of the mechanics of this sensation novel, madness is the most melodramatic of a series of scandalous disclosures. Other revelations may have been anticipated, but this one, conventional as it is, startles even the canniest reader, since Lady Audley appears throughout the novel to be perfectly sane. This last secret is also the means by which the novel effects closure. After she has been certified, Lady Audley can be handily dispatched to a homelike asylum. On the face of it, madness is the secret now told, but it functions in significant ways more as 'cover-up' than disclosure.[1]

While we are asked to associate the disclosure of madness with a 'coming out'—the latent hereditary taint is made patent to explain the heroine's conduct—I want to argue that the final focus on madness serves to displace the economic and class issues already raised in the novel and to deflect their uncomfortable implications. This obfuscation is managed through the discourse of madness, because it allows historically specific issues of class and power to be represented instead as timeless and universal matters of fe-

male biology. If gender is understood as a historical and politicized construct, it has to be thought of in relation to the formation of cultural groups, ethnicities, and classes. More than a 'cultural use of the body,' gender participates in the production of culture- and class-specific norms, which are then represented as natural—the uncovered workings of human nature.[2] Victorian constructions of the feminine ideal enshrined certain standards that defined a class of women superior to the women of other social and cultural groups, and helped therefore to support middle-class claims to moral and social superiority. Yet even while social, medical, and biological sciences investigated and produced a gendered body that distinguished the middle class from all other groups, Anita Levy observes that they also provided ways 'of removing individuals of competing classes from their place in history and culture' and drawing them together according to a set of universals which everyone seemed to possess in common. The universalization functioned to forestall any recognition that differences might be produced historically, and to erase the class and economic interests that were at stake in a representation of the 'improperly gendered.'[3] Applying these insights about the work of gender in relation to class to *Lady Audley's Secret* not only raises questions about the functions of medical discourse in Victorian culture, but also allows one to focus on the cogent ironies of Mary Elizabeth Braddon's fictional art.

The novel reveals how Victorian notions of morality and constructions of maternal madness coalesce in defining the 'right' woman by representing her 'other' in terms of a specifically gendered pathology. What makes *Lady Audley's Secret* a fascinating text is that it slyly signals its awareness of the work that notions of madness perform, and in so doing apprehends social and medical discourses in the act of enunciating the nature of an aberrant 'other' in order to shape a healthy, middle-class self. Until madness is pulled out of the hat as a solution and the means of plot resolution, the narrative has dwelt on the attempt by the 'wrong' woman who looks 'right' to usurp a place to which she is not entitled. What seems primarily to be the matter with Lady Audley is that she threatens to violate class boundaries and exclusions, and to get away with appropriating social power beyond her entitlement. Having married Sir Michael, she has made an immense shift from powerlessness to a position of considerable influence. It does not escape the notice of his household that, having been little better than a servant as the governess in the doctor's house, she now controls Audley Court's household keys, an important signifier of domestic and class power.[4] The text draws considerable attention to the keys as a way of representing Lady Audley's new role in managing the 'lower' orders rather than being one of their number.

The events of Lady Audley's life, which are gradually revealed as the novel progresses towards her final confession, emphasize her bid for a life of greater power and comfort, which the keys of Audley Court now symbolize. She first refuses to accept her position as the daughter of a mad and impoverished mother, just as later she refuses to be crushed when her attempt to marry money fails because the wealthy father of the oafish dragoon, George Talboys, has cut him off. Instead of capitulating, she sets about making a new life for herself after George deserts her to seek his fortune in Australia. Male susceptibility to female beauty being what it is, the narrator acknowledges, the lovely Lucy has a golden opportunity to remake her life when Sir Michael falls in love with her. It may seem implausible that Sir Michael would readily accept the story of her background—an orphanage and a quiet secluded convent school life. But the way in which Sir Michael dupes himself is exactly the shocking point. When connections are made on the basis of inappropriate attraction rather than blood, or class alliance, disaster can be expected to follow. An adequate background check is dispensed with, quality control fails and social ranks open to the wrong kind. Playing on current fears about the wrong kinds of women passing themselves off as governesses, Braddon thrills and horrifies her readers with the proposition that the usurper may look right, but who knows what tainted depths her beauty conceals?

When Sir Michael proposes, Lucy briefly hints at her mother's problems in terms of poverty and deprivation, but does not mention madness: 'My mother—But do not let me speak of her. Poverty, poverty, trials, vexations, humiliations, deprivations! You cannot tell; you, who are amongst those for whom life is so smooth and easy; you can never guess what is endured by such as we.'[5] Lucy Audley's difference ('you' as opposed to 'we') is signalled here in terms of economics and social position. In the course of the novel, the representation of that difference as a matter of class, or a set of specific material conditions, shifts to the representation of difference as badness or moral degeneracy, which is in turn symbolically represented as madness inherited from the mother. What is outside, a matter of economic stress and social need, is inscribed and represented as inside, a deviant and disruptive force within the unacceptable woman that wreaks havoc on traditional stabilities and pieties. While madness receives most attention as the sensational secret, social position and poverty are really the issues at stake. Indeed, the desire to change the latter is what leads to the actions that symptomize the former.

Although her biographer Robert Wolff claims that only in later novels did Mary Elizabeth Braddon learn to satirize Victorian social life 'so skilfully that her readers need not see her doing it,' *Lady Audley's Secret* offers strong evidence that her skills are already finely honed.[6] She writes with an eye on the circulating libraries as custodians of middle-class morality, and with deference to those readers who would be happy to see Lady Audley put away, punished discreetly and without public scandal for her wickedness. Taking care not to offend, she closes her story hoping that 'no one will take objection to my story because the end of it leaves the good people all happy and at peace' (447). The 'bad' heroine, whose allure may have fooled us as it initially captivated her step-nephew, Robert

Audley, is punished and her badness rationalized through its representation as madness. But the emerging picture of Lady Audley's life history and sense of abandonment does elicit sympathy, even though the narrator never fails to comment censoriously and sanctimoniously on her heroine's thoughts and behaviour. Then again, the narrator often undermines sanctimoniousness, or teases a complacent reader, trustful of appearances, hinting at what dire thoughts and dangerous motivations might be going on under the superficial calm of gracious, socially approved behaviour. At times the narrator seems to favour Robert Audley and appears to look upon his final marriage and assumption of career with approval, but the narrative tone also encourages us to see him as misogynistic and self-righteous.

While the narrator overtly endorses and blesses Robert's union with Clara, the domestic idyll she presents of Robert, Clara, and her brother George is a mocking parody of respectable upper-middle-class aspirations. For though Robert Audley comes from a family of landed gentry, his development through the novel from a lethargic and purposelessness drifter to a model husband, father, and provider is a parable of solid middle-class virtue. He proceeds from upper-class dissolution and the idle pursuit of pleasure, to respectable health, work, and duty. Only the task of exposing and expelling Lady Audley and winning Clara Talboys prompts him to put away his Meerschaum pipes and relinquish his main occupation of reading French novels. We note, however, that while these French novels may sap his energy, they leave his morals intact. He is less susceptible therefore than Lady Audley, who is an avid and clearly corrupted reader of romances and yellow-papered novels, thought by their more vituperative critics to be dangerous to feminine health and moral well-being. But Robert's responses to reading are not the only grounds on which he invites comparison with Lady Audley. They couple in a number of oppositions, the most obvious of which are sleuth/villain and virtuous hero/vicious heroine. Robert begins the novel aimless and undirected; Lady Audley spends it trying desperately to maintain direction, and to keep the social place and name she has struggled to achieve. Whereas he comes to symbolize the stable future of respectable English society, she represents what threatens it. Most tellingly, Robert marries for love; Lucy Audley for position and money. We remember that Sir Michael dismisses his first marriage as a 'dull jog-trot bargain made to keep some estate or other in the family' and deludes himself that with Lucy he has found love at last (6). But Sir Michael's second marriage is shown to be a grotesque parody of love over class alliance. It contrasts with Robert's choice of Clara, supposedly the right and natural dictation of the heart, since he could have made a more fiscally minded alliance with his receptive cousin, Alicia Audley. What is right about Clara, we suspect, is that she is a proper civilizer of men. She is the conduct book's exemplary wife, whose function was to regulate and socialize from within the domestic space. She therefore urges Robert to use his 'talents and opportunities' and to undertake a life of 'serious work,' in which 'he should strive to be useful to his fellow creatures, and win a reputation for himself' (437). The last we hear of Robert is that he makes his name and his fortune as a barrister. Suggesting that he now profitably rubs shoulders with the members of an exclusive class from which his clientele is drawn, the narrator tells us that Robert comes to fame in a breach-of-promise case—Hobbs vs Nobbs.

In order to see how the novel redistributes questions of power, privation, and survival as matters of biological inheritance and gendered pathology, I want to focus now on the text's engagement with conceptions of moral, hereditary, and maternal madness in constructions of female insanity. The notion of moral insanity has a significant place in the history of the discursive formations of insanity in the nineteenth century, preoccupied as Victorians were with the distinction between physical and moral causes and their relative importance.[7] The term 'moral insanity' referred to madness as the experience of inappropriate emotions rather than the result of defective reasoning or cognitive impairment. It is not difficult to understand the Victorian attention to moral issues: 'In a society as concerned with morality as was Victorian England, a theory which seemed to ascribe moral perversity to insanity was bound to have a strong appeal.'[8] If insanity can be understood as the consequence of defective moral agency, behaviour judged deviant then becomes a symptom of moral insanity.

James Cowles Prichard, physician and ethnologist, introduced the term 'moral insanity' in 1833, defining it as follows: 'This form of mental disease . . . consists of a morbid perversion of the feelings, affections, habits, without any hallucination or erroneous conviction impressed upon the understanding; it sometimes coexists with an apparently unimpaired state of the intellectual faculties.'[9] The definition drew attention to antisocial or deviant behaviour, that is, emotional and ethical confusion resulting from the immoderate, excessive, and undisciplined passions.[10] Moral lunatics were especially interesting because they represented the coincidence of madness and badness, and brought the problematic crime-insanity boundary into focus.[11] 'Persons so affected present great difficulties to the medical man,' wrote L. S. Winslow in his *Manual of Lunacy.* 'The line of demarcation between vice and insanity is most difficult to perceive or define.'[12] By mid-century, moral insanity was an extremely controversial notion in medical and legal discourse, considered by many to be a subversive and mischievous doctrine, and associated with the evasion of criminal responsibility and accountability. An essay in *Fraser's Magazine* observed that since the publication of Prichard's book, moral insanity 'has figured so remarkably, and as we think, so dangerously in our courts of justice, paralysing her arm, and securing impunity to those who have indulged their "homicidal orgasm" as is the fashion to call a propensity to murder.'[13] Those who asserted the usefulness of moral insanity as a category felt they needed to defend themselves against being apologists for vice.[14] While some doctors thought that the insane should be punished for criminal conduct, others

wished to 'extend medicine to criminals,' and looked forward to a society in which doctors isolated and cared for 'degenerate elements.'[15]

Prichard's ideas about moral insanity did not exclude hereditarian assumptions, for he writes about the predisposing causes that may be inferred to have existed in every instance of the disease. But after 1850 and increasingly towards the end of the century, an interest in biological heredity and physical legacy led doctors to the exploration of the physical rather than moral causes of insanity. Insanity came to be seen as part of one's inheritance, and the impossibility of avoiding one's hereditary lot had to be faced. Henry Maudsley, for example, writes about the inescapability and tyranny of what is innate—the determinism of inheritance. Giving psychological disturbance a somatic basis, he subsumes the moral cause in the physical. 'Moral peculiarities' he says are 'constitutional'; they are signs, as it were, of 'the insane temperament.'[16]

In discussions of female insanity, especially, moral and physical causes are not only confusingly intertwined, but often synonymous with hereditary factors. Two factors account, I think, for the overlap or blurring of moral and hereditary causes. The first is the old commonplace about the defective moral capacity of female subjects. Medical discourse appropriates what philosophy has long established—women cannot be considered truly rational, reasonable beings, and therefore moral subjects. The second, closely related, is an assumption that the functioning of the female body renders a woman unstable and liable to madness and moral perversion. An example of this reasoning is to be seen in descriptions of the hysterical patient suffering from 'a perverted moral state,' which is 'somehow connected with the action of the reproductive organs in an unstable nervous system.'[17]

I want to turn for a moment to Charlotte Brontë's representation of Bertha in *Jane Eyre,* which aptly illustrates the virtual synonymity or substitutability of moral and hereditary madness in the representation of female insanity. Much is made of the fact that Rochester is duped into marrying the heiress Bertha Mason, whose mother was a lunatic and who herself turns out to be the 'true daughter of an infamous mother.' Bertha's madness, like that of her mother, is linked to excess and immoderation. Dark and brutish, Bertha is a horrifying vision of the nineteenth-century association of madness with ungovernable appetite, bestiality, and sexuality.[18] Though clearly hereditary, the nature of maternal insanity that Brontë represents is also illuminated by the notion of moral madness, which is the notion that Brontë specifically invokes in a letter to W. S. Williams on her representation of Bertha:

> There is a phase of insanity which may be called moral madness . . . in which all that is good or even human seems to disappear from the mind, and a fiend-nature replaces it. The sole aim and desire of the being thus possessed is to exasperate, to molest, to destroy, and preternatural ingenuity and energy are often exercised to that dreadful end. The aspect, in such cases, assimi-

lates with the disposition—all seem demonised. It is true that profound pity ought to be the only sentiment elicited by the view of such degradation, and equally true is it that I have not sufficiently dwelt on that feeling. I have erred in making horror too predominant. Mrs. Rochester, indeed, lived a sinful life before she was insane, but sin is itself a species of insanity—the truly good behold and compassionate it as such.[19]

Brontë's depiction of Bertha in *Jane Eyre* suggests that madness is intimately related to moral dissolution, itself figured as gross, sensual indulgence. Bertha's indulgent appetite and exotic Creole carnality are made to signify the lack of control that eventually breeds the bloated lunatic in Rochester's attic. But is Bertha mad because she is undisciplined and intemperate, or vice versa? Does her intemperate behaviour activate the inherited seeds of madness, or is that tendency to immoderation itself part of her maternal legacy? We are told that her 'excesses' have nurtured the 'germs' of insanity within her, which suggests that had she been more disciplined and regulated, she would have kept her maternal legacy at bay. Rochester himself has been rather excessive, we may note, but presumably he didn't have any seeds of madness to germinate.

Brontë's Bertha is not contained by Prichard's definition of moral insanity cited above; she exceeds it because she does have insane illusions and she does display remarkable disorder of the intellect (even though it was, according to Rochester, a pygmy intellect to start with). As Brontë herself admits, she is playing up the horror of the demonized lunatic. Moral madness may be a *phase* of insanity in which the will falters, but it is always clear that Bertha's propensity for dissolution is inherited from her mother.

What is interesting is Brontë's debate about how to see Mrs Rochester's sin. On the face of it, the sinful woman may not deserve compassion, but if bad behaviour is really madness, it ought to elicit pity and compassion. Later in the novel, therefore, Jane herself observes that the madwoman cannot help being mad. However, the proposition that sin is itself a species of insanity offers a way of diagnosing insanity through the symptoms of deviant behaviour. The useful thing about this means of diagnosis is that madness is rendered knowable and capable of being policed. Detectable in the early stages as sinful behaviour and progressing to full-blown degeneracy, moral madness, here, results from a defective moral disposition to which Bertha is predisposed through maternal inheritance.

Brontë uses the notion that sinful behaviour is a species of insanity for the purposes of horror, whereas George Eliot invokes similar views for our wry amusement when she writes of the tendency among Middlemarchers to see nonconformity as equivalent to lunacy: 'Sane people did what their neighbours did, so that if any lunatics were at large, one might know and avoid them.'[20] The statement itself seems a humorous exaggeration, but the implied corollary is altogether serious—if you didn't do what your neigh-

bours did, that is, if your behaviour was considered deviant, they were quite justified in calling you a lunatic. Mrs Cadwallader exemplifies this view by insinuating that Dorothea Brooke's unconventional attitudes to life and her choice of Casaubon as a husband provide evidence of 'a little crack in the Brooke family,' and that Dorothea is suffering from a 'deeper and more constitutional disease' than she (Mrs Cadwallader) had been willing to believe. Had Dorothea married Sir James, Mrs Cadwallader opines, there was a chance 'of her becoming a sane, sensible woman.'[21] In the same vein, the narrator of ***Lady Audley's Secret*** observes innocently that had Lucy Graham refused Sir Michael, everyone would have thought it 'something more than madness in a penniless girl to reject such an offer' (9).

The cool Lady Audley illustrates better than the deranged Bertha what moral insanity was thought to be: a morbid perversion of the moral disposition and natural impulses that did not seem to come from any remarkable disorder or defect of the intellect, and that did not result in delusions or hallucinations. As one patient described it, 'I have my reason, but I have not the command of my feelings. Circumstances in life create feelings and prejudices which prevent my passing through life smoothly. My intellect is not insane; it is my *feelings* I cannot control.'[22] Lady Audley herself muses: 'Have I ever been really *wicked*, I wonder? . . . My worst wickednesses have been the result of wild impulses, and not of deeply-laid plots. I am not like the women I have read of, who have lain night after night in the horrible dark and stillness, planning out treacherous deeds, and arranging every circumstance of an appointed crime' (297).

If Brontë's 'clothed hyena' is a stereotype of the brutish and demonic lunatic, Lady Audley is the antithesis, equally sensational in its own way. Braddon is careful to distinguish her supposedly mad heroine from the stereotype: 'All mental distress is, with some show of reason, associated in our minds with loose disordered garments, and dishevelled hair, and an appearance in every way the reverse of my lady's' (397). Lady Audley herself has imagined her own mad mother as a maniacal demon. Helen Maldon (who becomes Helen Talboys, then changes her name to Lucy Graham and then Lady Audley) is a child when she learns the secret that her mother is mad. Her abusive foster mother, a woman whom her father pays (irregularly) to care for her, one day taunts her with the information. Thereafter, the girl lives with the tormenting image of her lunatic mother 'in a cell with a hideous garment that bound her tortured limbs,' who would fall on her and kill her if she came near. She has dreamed of her mother's 'icy grasp around her throat and heard her ravings in her ear' (348-9). But lo, when Lucy does actually visit her mother one day—and why her father would take her is a plot mystery rationalized only by the novel's concern to exploit yet dislodge the stereotype of the demonic madwoman—her mother is a charming, pretty, girlish, blue-eyed creature. She 'skipped towards us with her yellow curls decorated with natural flowers, and saluted us with radiant smiles, and gay, ceaseless chatter' (350). This madwoman does not look mad. She has no lurid visage, swollen lips, matted hair, and so on. She looks like Victorian patriarchy's idealized other—a blue-eyed, curly-headed, infantilized angel. Her fictional predecessor is not so much mad Bertha in *Jane Eyre,* the deranged animal, of giant propensities, but rather someone like Dora Spenlow, the angel who (had she lived to become a mother) might have had the same balancing trouble with her mind as she has with the household accounts.

Like Brontë's Bertha, Lady Audley is presented as mad morally and mad by maternal inheritance. To have argued, however, that the heartless and emotionally depraved Lady Audley was merely morally insane would not have been sensational enough. Her insanity is surely overdetermined, but the most important component of it is that it is hereditary. Lady Audley describes the work of hereditary predisposition in her own experience of becoming a mother: 'My baby was born, and the crisis which had been fatal to my mother arose for me' (352). At one moment, it seems, one may be a conforming, dependent, and ornamental girlish wife; the next, a mother and mad.[23] It should not surprise anyone, therefore, that Lucy's mother was 'sane up to the hour of my birth; but from that hour her intellect had decayed, until she became what I saw her' (350). In case we may have missed the point about the tyranny of maternal inheritance, Lucy Audley throws in her grandmother, who was also mad. Her mother's madness 'was an hereditary disease transmitted to her from her mother, who had died mad' (350).

If Lady Audley is mad because she has a mad mother, she is also mad by virtue of becoming a mother. The representation of Lady Audley draws, therefore, on maternal insanity in the sense of puerperal mania, which accounted for about ten per cent of asylum inmates, and could range from anything like mild melancholia to incurable psychosis.[24] The majority of sufferers recovered, however, within six months. Although it could cover insanity of pregnancy or lactation, by mid-century puerperal insanity was taken to mean mental disorder occurring within four weeks of giving birth, a time during which a woman's mind was thought to be especially weak. The propensity of the female body towards instability, and the moral derangement that is associated with that instability, were therefore most forcibly expressed in ideas about puerperal insanity. Medical opinion held that one of the most dangerous states of excitement and turbulence was the puerperal state, which either predisposed a woman to insanity, or brought it out when there was hereditary disposition or a 'peculiar preaptitude.'[25] Since postpartum women were highly susceptible to both moral and hereditary factors, puerperal insanity could be induced by any powerful influence of 'fright, surprise, or other strong emotions . . . acting on a mind already disposed to mania by some hereditary influence.' 'Sympathy of the brain' for the disordered state of uterine function could account for many cases, but the increased 'nervous excitability' and the influence of moral causes led some physicians to argue that cases arising from *moral*

causes were four times as many as those produced by *physical.* Considering that the 'physical and moral causes of disturbance' were so rife during pregnancy and labour, Dr James Reid thought it surprising that there were not more cases of such insanity.[26]

Since a woman could not exert the usual and necessary control over her impulses and urges at this time, the 'religious and moral principles' which alone give 'strength to the female mind' collapsed, allowing the 'subterranean fires' to smoulder and flame.[27] Not unexpectedly, the sudden moral decline of a hitherto respectable woman constituted evidence of madness. Shrieking obscenities at the doctor and her husband, demonstrating a dislike for her new-born baby, refusing to carry out household duties, and exhibiting other inappropriate behaviour were symptoms of the malaise. Considering the sexual aetiology of much female insanity, and the notion that women were specialized for reproduction, times of change or crisis in a woman's reproductive life were held to be especially dangerous. The onset of menses and the process of menopause were equally high-risk periods in which minds were likely to become unhinged.[28] This meant that the condition of being female was inherently pathological, and the line between biological function and disease blurred. As E. J. Tilt put it: 'It is generally admitted that pathology and physiology are inseparable, and the female organs of generation afford, perhaps, the best illustration of the axiom.'[29]

Inscribing cultural assumptions, medical discourse has represented the emotional fluctuations attendant on changing bodily states as threatening deviations from a norm that underwrites consistency or stability, instead of understanding or interpreting them in ways that might look less fearfully on change and fluctuation. 'With all these episodic exclusions from moral life resulting from one's healthy embodiment as a woman,' a feminist philosopher has recently observed, 'we are left with approximately three to five days a month during which we can act and be held fully morally responsible.' Since various ordinary experiences in the lives of women lead to moral derangement, women are 'necessarily crazy' despite, or rather because of, the healthy functioning of their bodies.[30]

When we look at the maternal madness that Lady Audley claims is responsible for her behaviour, we must see that madness finally deflects attention from distressing material conditions and the opportunities Lady Audley seizes to escape them. Indeed, Braddon takes care not to omit from Lady Audley's confession an account of her legacy of poverty, privation, and fear. After her child is born, Lucy says that her mother's disease rose up in her. Although she escaped, she was left 'much more irritable perhaps after my recovery; less inclined to fight the hard battle of the world; more disposed to complain of poverty and neglect' (352). Her husband then deserts her to seek his fortune in Australia, leaving a note that she will not see his face again till he has made good. Since he could not find a job in England, this development does not fill her with optimism or a sense of security. 'The hereditary taint that was in my blood had never till this time showed itself by any one sign or token; but at this time I became subject to fits of violence and despair' (353). Although this characterization fits very well with the emphasis in medical discourse on the moral susceptibility of women who succumb to puerperal insanity, Braddon suggests to the reader that Lucy is not deranged, but desperate; not mad (insane) but mad (angry). Working within a rigid model of ideal motherhood that emphasized woman's dependency, selflessness, and virtuous influence, Victorian medical constructions represented defiance or nonconformity as derangement.

Not surprisingly, her fits of desperation are calmed when Lucy determines to run away from her wretched situation. Her steps to remedy an unpleasant situation are not very different from those taken by her husband, except that his abandonment of his wife and child to find gold 'down under' is condoned, whereas her departure from her child and her married name is demonic and unwomanly, a crime against nature. Knowing that poverty, labouring for a pittance, and frustrated hope for the return of a husband who has deserted her are likely to wear her down, Lucy seeks to protect and rely on herself. In this way she recalls Jane Eyre, who, when Brocklehurst questioned her about what to do to avoid going to hell, replied that she should stay healthy and not die. This generally unpopular, but frankly self-preservatory answer is similar to the solution that Lucy derives to protect her sanity. She must avoid poverty and privation, which the head of the female department at Colney Hatch admitted were factors in producing moral insanity:

> The unceasing, and in too many cases, the hopeless struggles of the poorer and middle classes for a bare existence necessarily predispose the brain to a diseased action. . . . No wonder then that . . . some addition to the bitter cup of sorrow . . . should wholly unbalance the tottering mind.[31]

Poverty is a dreaded state for Lucy Audley and avoidance of it a primary motivation. Avoiding poverty was also a very real issue for Braddon, who went onto the stage to support her mother and herself. She confessed unabashedly that she wrote the way she did (sensationally and prolifically) to earn a living. When the spectre of poverty was banished, she told Edward Bulwer-Lytton, she would be able to write deeper and more worthwhile fiction—now her books had to sell. Unlike the heroines whose thwarted energies and constraints form the subject of much of her fiction, Mary Elizabeth Braddon triumphs over adversity. As Henry James's review of *Aurora Floyd* notes, the author is aggressive, clever, and familiar with the ways of the world, the antithesis of an ideal of innocent and unchallenging womanhood.[32]

As Robert Audley closes in on her, Lady Audley considers running away. 'But where could I go? I must go back to the old, hard, cruel, wretched life—the life of poverty, and humiliation, and vexation, and discontent. I should have to go back and wear myself out in that long struggle, and die—as my mother died, perhaps' (316). From the time

she was a young woman, the fear of turning into her mother has made her alert to opportunities of avoiding such a fate: 'My ultimate fate in life depended upon my marriage, and I concluded that if I was indeed prettier than my schoolfellows, I ought to marry better than any of them' (350). Her installation at Audley Court means that, like her portrait, painted splendidly in the Pre-Raphaelite manner, she becomes one of Sir Michael's prized possessions. The very specific inventory of lavish, material treasures in her bedroom titillates the reader with a feast of conspicuous consumption as it suggests that Lady Audley's beauty, ornamentality, and apparent conformity are purchased and rewarded by such prizes as Marie Antoinette cabinets, Gobelin tapestries, Pompadour china, Benvenuto Cellini glasses, Leroy and Benson ormolu clocks (302). As if to emphasize that Lady Audley's crimes are linked to her efforts to maintain the luxuries that signify her altered station, she is shown (post-confession) mourning the loss of the precious things in her luxurious apartment and thinking of how much—literally, not morally— they have cost (373).

While a great deal of medical attention was paid to the dangerous flux in which women's bodies found themselves and which therefore rendered their minds unstable, the contradictory imperatives of different aspects of approved feminine behaviour were not so well scrutinized. Through Lady Audley's attempts to capitalize on her appearance, and her rise to comfort and safety, Braddon scrutinizes the sort of behaviour that is valued in a desirable woman and considers how this system of valuation breeds contradictions and presents the female subject thus constructed with divisive choices. Since dependency and innocence are charming feminine qualities, Lucy Audley is frequently represented in terms of her infantilization. She is her husband's 'babyfied' wife, his little darling: 'I left my little girl asleep, with her baby in her arms and with nothing but a few blotted lines to tell her why her faithful husband had deserted her' (18). George's letter informs his sister that he wishes she could see 'his childish little wife,' who is watching him as he writes. 'Her eyes are as blue and as clear as the skies . . . and her hair falls about her face like the pale golden halo you see round the head of a Madonna in an Italian picture' (261).

But, Braddon implies, such delightful dependency does not stand penniless, abandoned mothers in very good stead, nor does the valuation of dependency encourage determination, self-assertiveness, and self-preservation. Since Helen Maldon has had to summon stores of suppressed cunning and self-interest in order to become Lucy Audley, there must be more to her than meets the eye. Frequent references to the deceptiveness of surfaces alert us to the evil that may lurk within her. At the same time as George paints her as the picture of childish innocence, he also presents her as siren to his friend Robert: 'She's for all the world like one of those what's-its-names, who got poor old Ulysses into trouble' (35). Further hints are to be found in the fact that dogs don't like her—a sure sign of moral turpitude—while her step-daughter Alicia testifies to her misleading appearance: 'You think her sensitive because she has soft little white hands, and big blue eyes with long lashes, and all manner of affected, fantastical ways, which you stupid men call fascinating. Sensitive! Why I've seen her do cruel things with those slender white fingers, and laugh at the pain she inflicted' (103). The fine, Pre-Raphaelite portrait of Lady Lucy is a powerful visual symbol, both of her status as Sir Michael's wife and of her covert wickedness. Its strange distortions give a 'lurid' glow to the blonde complexion and a 'strange sinister light' to the deep blue eyes. The pretty, pouting mouth looks almost wicked and hard. Alicia, of course, thinks that the painter is inspired and has seen Lady Audley truly.

Hints such as these about the subterranean depths of cruelty and treachery not only suggest the deceptiveness of appearances, but also raise the issue of manipulative power, the resort of those who are least powerful and who must be covert in the way they try to manage things.[33] Indeed, Braddon teases the reader with a vision of the distortions and contradictions bred by contemporary domestic ideology, which constrains female energy and exertion, relegating it to decorous ornamentality. Though Lady Audley 'looks very pretty and innocent' seated behind the 'graceful group of delicate opal china and glittering silver,' the narrator implies that, for all we know, she might be poisoning her husband's tea:

> Surely a pretty woman never looks prettier than when making tea. The most feminine and most domestic of all occupations imparts a magic harmony to her every movement, a witchery to her every glance. . . . She seems a social fairy, weaving potent spells with Gunpowder and Bohea. . . . Better the pretty influence of the tea-cups and saucers gracefully wielded in a woman's hand, than all the inappropriate power snatched at the point of the pen from the unwilling sterner sex. Imagine all the women of England elevated to the high level of masculine intellectuality; superior to crinoline . . . above making themselves agreeable; above tea-tables . . . and what a dreary, utilitarian, ugly life the sterner sex must lead.
>
> (223)

The passage suggests that if the domestic sphere is the only arena in which women find power, and if they are always supposed to present an agreeable and pleasant prospect, then they may be forced to engage in deceptive and manipulative practices. Shortly before this moment, when Robert is feeling anxious about his growing attraction to Clara, he expostulates: 'If they [women] can't agitate the universe and play at ball with hemispheres, they'll make mountains of warfare and vexation out of domestic mole-hills; and social storms in household teacups' (207). His lengthy diatribe, invoking Catherine the Second, Cleopatra, and other powerful women, articulates an age-old terror of female will-to-power and thirst for influence: 'They are the stronger sex, the noisier, the more persevering, the most self-assertive sex' (207). Lucy Audley does not appear to be strong, noisy, persevering, or self-assertive, but she does become adept at the most effective ways to exercise manipulative power—feigning weakness, and resorting to 'feminine prevarication' and 'womanly trickery'—not as the result of a thirst for dominance and control, but in order to avoid poverty and drudgery (268). Her story gives the beloved Victorian self-help narrative an interesting spin. But since such a narrative should emphasize industry, thrift, and prudence, and offer itself as an example of the opportunities for betterment available to all, hers is not the kind of self-help story that would elicit conventional approval.

I turn now to Braddon's treatment of the topical question of wrongful incarceration and how she uses it to dispatch the wicked heroine at the same time as drawing attention to the reinscription of badness as madness. *Lady Audley's Secret* was written shortly after a period of 'lunacy panic' in England, during which the horrifying possibilities of involuntary and wrongful incarceration were frequently and dramatically brought to public attention in the law courts and the press. In 1858, just a few years before Braddon began the novel, Edward Bulwer-Lytton (to whom *Lady Audley's Secret* is gratefully dedicated) had his wife committed to Inverness Lodge, Brentford. There was a public outcry about the fact that Lady Lytton was made to endure a month at a rather exclusive homelike establishment, but an asylum nonetheless, before she was able to arrange for her release. It is intimated that those in charge tried to conceal from her the kind of place to which she was being taken. Her indignant biographer relates that when Lady Lytton asked the woman in charge whether the unfortunates roaming in the grounds were incarcerated there, that person replied evasively, 'Those . . . are our ladies. They are out gathering strawberries.' Much like the 'Monty Python' character who insists that a clearly dead parrot is not dead, the male head of the establishment is said to have assured her: 'Madhouse! madhouse! nonsense, Lady Lytton! this is no madhouse, and those are my children.'[34] Similarly, when it dawns on Lady Audley that her place of exile is a madhouse, she asks the woman in charge to verify this. '"Ah, but no, Madame," the woman answered, with a shrill scream of protest. "It is an establishment of the most agreeable, where one amuses oneself—"' (387). Lady Audley is furious (as was Lady Lytton), and accuses Robert Audley of using power basely and of bringing her to a living grave. In the case of Lady Lytton, newspapers such as the *Somerset County Gazette* and the *Daily Telegraph* made much of the affair, defending her sanity, and decrying the infringement of the rights and liberties of the subject.

> It is a question of deep importance whether it is not utterly wrong, and most dangerous to the liberties of individuals, that upon the word of two medical men persons may be taken to a madhouse, when, if not already insane, they are undoubtedly placed in circumstances in every way calculated, by their horrible and frightful character, to destroy reason and produce insanity.[35]

The *Gazette* then went on to call for a public inquiry if anyone were to be committed: 'Society in general demands this; helpless women require it. . . . It is true that investigation into cases like that of Lady Lytton is compelled when demanded by friends of the incarcerated person; but the system is altogether contrary to the general equity of British laws and customs.'[36]

On the matter of the 'realism' of her asylum in *Lady Audley's Secret,* Braddon wrote a rather cryptic and tantalizing letter to Bulwer-Lytton, her literary mentor and correspondent, in which she mentions that she would have done better to place her *maison de santé*; at home rather than abroad:

> I wrote the third & some part of the second vol of 'Lady A.' in less than a fortnight, & had the printer at me all the time. I had no one to consult about '*Maisons de Santé*;' & it was only when the book was printed that I heard from a lady whose husband was an inmate of such a house, that what I had done abroad was more impossible than it would have been at home.[37]

What, we may wonder, was 'more impossible abroad'?[38] Possibly she is saying that only in England were such corrupt practices possible, or does she imagine the availability of a homelike institution as a typically English practice? Elaine Showalter comments that the most significant innovation of psychiatric Victorianism was the domestication of insanity, about which many Victorians were proud and patriotic. Even the public asylums were organized on the family model, with the resident medical superintendent and his wife acting as father and mother, the attendants as brothers and sisters, and the patients as children.[39] Especially among the well-to-do, the private 'rest-home' asylum offered a solution to care-giving at home, as well as a way of muffling social shame and stigma.

We do not have Bulwer-Lytton's response to Braddon's letter, in which he may have given her the benefit of his knowledge of English lodges for the wealthy insane. And indeed, we do not know whether she knew how well he was in a position to know about them. While it is remarkable how closely the confinement of Lady Audley parallels accounts of the occasion on which Lady Rosina Lytton was committed, there is no evidence that Braddon bases her representation on circulated accounts of Lady Rosina's confinement. Both Braddon's novel and Lady Rosina Lytton's manuscript autobiography (used later in Louisa Devey's biography) are highly conscious of the 'genre' of wrongful incarceration, which contemporary sensation novels and case histories are helping to form.

In exploiting the topicality of wrongful confinement, *Lady Audley's Secret* operates as any self-respecting sensation novel would. But if sensation novels (like Charles Reade's *Hard Cash* and Wilkie Collins's *The Woman in White*) set out to play on the horror of a conspiracy to incarcerate, they must present protagonists who are clearly sane, or the question of wrongfulness is muddied, and the reader will not thrill to the horrible possibility that a sane person might be unjustly committed. If *Lady Audley's Secret* is examined in these terms, problems immediately arise. Whether we think of her committal as wrongful depends

on whether we believe her confession of madness, and how we understand the doctor's initial and then reconsidered verdict after he has examined her. What also distinguishes the question of wrongful confinement in this novel is that it marks Lady Audley's end, instead of being a starting point or a complicating factor provoking a rescue narrative. The chapter that describes Lady Audley's incarceration is entitled 'Buried Alive,' a particularly grisly title because no chapter of rescue follows it. From the conventional point of view which the narrator officially adopts, the ending functions on the principle of 'just deserts,' for who can deny that Lady Audley has been very wicked and deserves punishing? Yet the ending also shows the extent of her powerlessness. For someone who has been so devious and clever, she hardly puts up a good fight, though it seems for a short time as if her strategy of accusing Robert of madness may provide a match worth watching.

> 'Robert Audley is mad,' she said decisively. 'What is one of the strongest diagnostics of madness—what is the first appalling sign of mental aberration? The mind becomes stationary; the brain stagnates; the even current of the mind is interrupted; the thinking power of the brain resolves itself into a monotone. As the waters of a tideless pool putrefy by reason of their stagnation, the mind becomes turbid and corrupt through lack of action; and perpetual reflection upon one subject resolves itself into monomania. Robert Audley is a monomaniac.'
>
> (287)

She uses the fact that Robert's father was a known eccentric to apply the received wisdom about maternal madness and daughters to fathers and sons: 'Do you know, Alicia, that madness is more often transmitted from father to son, than from father to daughter, and from mother to daughter than from mother to son?' (278). But Lady Audley does not add that 'the tendency of the mother to transmit her mental disease is, however, in all cases stronger than the father's; some physicians have, indeed, insisted that it is twice as strong.'[40] Her attempt to empower herself through a medical discourse that has already positioned her as powerless is therefore futile. Robert Audley's father may have been eccentric, but his son was more likely to inherit income, position, and privilege than madness.

Cornered after trying unsuccessfully to murder Robert by setting fire to the inn where he is lodging, Lady Audley melodramatically discloses her hereditary taint, and Robert briskly makes arrangements with a *maison de santé*; and procures the documents for his step-aunt's certification. When Robert tells the most grave Dr Mosgrave the facts of the case, omitting his suspicions of murder and arson, the doctor's expert medical opinion is that she is not mad. He reasonably points out that she ran away because her life was unpleasant, and committed bigamy to obtain fortune and position. When she found herself in a desperate position, she did not grow desperate but carried out a conspiracy by intelligent means. She is sane but immoral, which is not, he implies, the same as morally insane. Even though her mother was insane, he asserts, that does not necessarily mean that she is insane. But Robert wants her to be certified so he can legitimately incarcerate her and muffle the shame on his uncle's house. He reluctantly confides his suspicions that she may have murdered her first husband, George Talboys. Dr Mosgrave now interviews Lady Audley, reconsiders his diagnosis, and confirms that there is latent insanity, which might arise under 'extreme mental pressure.' The lady is not mad, he says, but she has the hereditary taint in her blood. She has the 'cunning of madness with the prudence of intelligence' (379). We do not know what Lady Audley revealed in the interview, but the doctor is now able to pronounce, darkly, that she is dangerous, and to advise that there should not be any *esclandre*. Whereas he first announced that no jury would entertain an insanity plea on the evidence that Robert disclosed, he now says that there is not enough evidence to link her to the supposed death of her husband. No jury would find her guilty of murder, but, he agrees, she had better be put away. However, he does not wish to appear persuaded by Robert's needs, or seem to be circumventing the processes of the law. He warns Robert that he will not be party to any hugger-mugger smuggling of her out of the reaches of justice, but insists that he does not (unlike the reader) see any reason to suspect that she has murdered her missing first husband. Since Robert's suspicions on this score were what prompted him to revise his initial diagnosis, the doctor's collusion in her incarceration, under a mask of cool, medical impartiality and objectivity, is hardly ambiguous.

Although Lady Audley resists incarceration, she presumably anticipated something like it, since her confession of madness was made to forestall prosecution. She played this card knowing that the family would not wish a scandal and knowing that hereditary madness would be likely to win her clemency in the courts. "'They'll put me away somewhere, I suppose," my lady thought. "That is the worst they can do for me'" (372).

The asylum functions in the novel as a final and effective closet into which to push the family skeleton. Robert, however, presents it to Lady Audley as a penitentiary, a convent, where confinement itself will bring about remorse, contrition, and purification. Robert sanctimoniously assures his deviant aunt (to whom in the course of the novel he has found himself dismayingly attracted) that her fate is not so bad: 'You will live a quiet and peaceful life, my lady, such a life as many a good and holy woman in this Catholic country freely takes upon herself, and happily endures unto the end' (391). If you were a pure and religious woman, he seems to say, you would willingly take on a life of seclusion in a convent, so my sending you here is nothing terrible. The demonstrated function of the asylum—to bury Lady Audley alive—together with Robert's sanctimonious attitude to her incarceration, underscores the text's interest in the relationship between transgressive behaviour and definitions of madness. The ending exposes rather than resolves the confusion created by defining madness in terms of immoral behaviour, and punishing deviant behaviour by means of the institutions set up to deal with madness. It points to that confusion, however, as a screen for issues that bear on class interests and boundaries.

Critics have seen Braddon's novel as subversive because it shows that deviance from a norm of womanly submission and obedience is likely to be labelled madness.[41] But Braddon's sensation novel goes further than that as it puts a finger on the work done by discourses of morality and madness in establishing gender and class boundaries, and contributing to middle-class hegemony. The novel begins with the representation of a woman seeking to avoid 'dependence, drudgery and humiliation' through the best means available. Emphasizing the three-term equation of moral susceptibility, madness, and femaleness, the text directs us to think of maternal heritage in terms of positionality and social power rather than physicality and embodiment. Wrongful confinement and inheritance take on, then, a metaphorical quality, if one thinks of them in terms of relegation to a category entailing privation and impotence. Lady Audley's final words are poignant and pathetic: she says that all she has ever been is afraid of her mother's horrible inheritance, afraid of poverty, and afraid of the men around her with power over her. We remember that, as a child, she went away after seeing her mother, knowing that 'the only inheritance I had to expect from my mother was—insanity' (350). If she has been motivated by the fear of becoming her mother, there is the final irony that she dies, like her mother, in a madhouse, not mad, we believe, but trapped in her efforts to avoid her mother's fate. The time of her greatest vulnerability is that when she becomes a mother, that is, becomes most like her own mother. The act of becoming a mother emphasizes therefore the completed transmission of her own maternal legacy, and threatens her with her own mother's fate, making her confront the fulfilment of a social destiny, represented in the discourse of madness as a biological destiny.

The question 'If I am not my mother, then who am I?' is one that concerns many a nineteenth-century heroine from Fanny Price to Maggie Tulliver. Fear of becoming one's mother, a fear of identification, is often coupled with the fear of leaving mother, of daring to differ and be separate. The problem is intensified, of course, where the mother is mad. The representation of the mad mother or the notion of maternal insanity allows, therefore, a particularly emphatic scrutiny of the problem of inheritance, whether we call it inheritance of a gendered body, or of a class-inflected subject position defined by thwarting and determining notions of moral agency. Such scrutiny urges us to think about the wider problem of identification and inheritance among different classes of women at different historical moments, to the extent perhaps of what it means to be identified within the category 'woman' as social and discursive practices define it.

Notes

1. See D. A. Miller, 'Sensation and Gender in *The Woman in White*,' in *The Making of the Modern Body: Sexuality and Society in the Nineteenth Cen-*

tury, ed Catherine Gallagher and Thomas Laqueur (Berkeley: University of California Press 1987), 110-22. Miller draws attention to the way *Lady Audley's Secret* 'blows the cover' on desires that are socially deviant. He says the secret is not whether Lady Audley is a madwoman, but whether she is or not, she must be treated as one (121).

2. Anita Levy, *Other Women: The Writing of Class, Race, and Gender, 1832-1898* (Princeton: Princeton University Press 1991), 12; see also Ornella Moscucci, *The Science of Woman: Gynaecology and Gender in England, 1800-1929* (Cambridge: Cambridge University Press 1990), 4-5.

3. Levy, 13, 12.

4. See Elizabeth Langland, 'Nobody's Angels: Domestic Ideology in the Victorian Novel,' *PMLA* 107:2 (1992), 290-304.

5. Mary Elizabeth Braddon, *Lady Audley's Secret* (1862; repr New York: Oxford 1987), 10-11; references are hereafter made parenthetically in the text.

6. See Robert Wolff, *Sensational Victorian: The Life and Fiction of Mary Elizabeth Braddon* (New York: Garland 1979), 8.

7. For a fuller discussion of these ideas, see Vieda Skultans, *Madness and Morals: Ideas on Insanity in the Nineteenth-Century* (London and Boston: Routledge 1975), 2.

8. Peter McCandless, 'Liberty and Lunacy,' in *Madhouses, Mad-Doctors, and Madmen: The Social History of Psychiatry in the Victorian Era,* ed Andrew Scull (Philadelphia: University of Pennsylvania Press 1981), 355.

9. James Cowles Prichard, *A Treatise on Insanity* (London: Marchant 1833), 14; for a discussion of Prichard's views see Eric Carlson and Norman Dain, 'The Meaning of Moral Insanity,' *Bulletin of the History of Medicine* 36 (1962), 131; Vieda Skultans, *English Madness: Ideas on Insanity 1580-1890* (London: Routledge 1979), 65-8; and Skultans, *Madness and Morals,* who explains that this account of moral insanity should be understood in relation to a particular psychology: the idea that 'each faculty of the mind is anchored to a particular locality in the brain. If the relevant portion of the brain is damaged or unsound then the corresponding faculty will be defective or absent' (6).

10. See McCandless, 355, who says that modern psychiatrists have found Prichard's definition to be a muddling and confusing 'catch-all,' and that his case studies describe patients who today would be classified as manic depressives, alcoholics, schizophrenics, and obsessionals.

11. See Roger Smith, *Trial by Medicine: Insanity and Responsibility in Victorian Trials* (Edinburgh: Edinburgh University Press 1981), 116.

12. Lyttleton S. Winslow, *Manual of Lunacy: A Handbook* (London: Smith, Elder 1874), 74.

13. 'Moral Insanity—Dr. Mayo's Croonian Lectures,' *Fraser's Magazine* 51 (1855), 246.

14. See J. B. Harrison, 'The Human Mind Considered in Some of its Medical Aspects,' *Journal of Psychological Medicine* 3 (1850), 258-9.

15. See Smith, 56, who is discussing Mayo and Maudsley.

16. Henry Maudsley, *Body and Mind;* quoted in 'Liberty and Lunacy,' 354.

17. Quoted in Anne Digby, 'Women's Biological Straitjacket,' in *Sexuality and Subordination: Interdisciplinary Studies of Gender in the Nineteenth Century,* ed Susan Mendus and Jane Rendall (London: Routledge 1989), 203. See also Levy, 124-7, who argues that emphasis shifts from biological to psychological causes towards the end of the century.

18. Sander Gilman, *Difference and Pathology: Stereotypes of Sexuality, Race and Madness* (Ithaca: Cornell University Press 1985), 99.

19. Clement Shorter, *The Brontës: Life and Letters* (London: Hodder 1908), 383-4.

20. George Eliot, *Middlemarch* (Boston: Riverside 1956), 7.

21. *Middlemarch,* 45.

22. See J. C. Bucknill and D. H. Tuke, *A Manual of Psychological Medicine* (1858; facsimile New York: Hafner 1968), 188.

23. Biographies of Mary Elizabeth Braddon reveal that the subject of puerperal madness must have been of some interest to her. John Maxwell, the man with whom she lived, had a wife who had, he said, become mentally 'defunct' after the birth of their children, and had been confined to an institution for many years. Braddon took over the care of his five children and produced a further six, the eldest of whom appeared during the writing of *Lady Audley's Secret.* In 1867, she herself experienced 'puerperal fever' followed by a breakdown that interrupted her prolific novelistic output for a time.

24. See Elaine Showalter, *The Female Malady: Women, Madness and English Culture 1830-1980* (Harmondsworth: Penguin 1985), 58-9.

25. See Alexander Morison, *Outlines of Mental Diseases;* quoted in *Skultans,* 32; and Reid, 'On the Causes, Symptoms, and Treatment of Puerperal Insanity,' *Journal of Psychological Medicine* 1 (1848), 136.

26. Reid, 128, 143; see also the continuation of this article in *Journal of Psychological Medicine* 1 (1848), 284-93.

27. Bucknill and Tuke, 273.

28. See Kathryn Pauly Morgan, 'Women and Moral Madness,' in *Feminist Perspectives: Philosophical Essays on Method and Morals,* ed Code, Mullett, and Overall (Toronto: University of Toronto Press 1988), 146-67, who suggests that moral madness should be understood as a state of genuine confusion that the experience of lived gender in contemporary Western society can produce. Such experience can distort and even destroy a woman's moral voice and her sense of moral integrity.

29. E. J. Tilt, *On Diseases of Women and Ovarian Inflammation* (London: Churchill 1853), 1.

30. Morgan, 154.

31. Richard Hunter and Ida Macalpine, *Psychiatry for the Poor: 1851 Colney Hatch Asylum—Friern Hospital 1973* (London: Dawsons 1974), 199.

32. See 'Miss Braddon,' review of *Aurora Floyd,* in *Notes and Reviews* (Cambridge, Mass: Dunster House 1921), 108-16; originally published in the *Nation* (9 Nov 1865), 593-4. James also observes that Braddon's fiction, while sensational, does deal with 'intense probability. . . . Modern England—the England of today's newspaper—crops up at every step' (112-13); on the topicality of sensation novels see also Thomas Boyle, *Black Swine in the Sewers of Hampstead: Beneath the Surface of Victorian Sensationalism* (Harmondsworth: Penguin 1989).

33. See Morgan's discussion of manipulative power in 'Women and Moral Madness,' 158.

34. Louisa Devey, *Life of Rosina, Lady Lytton* (London: Swan 1887), 299.

35. *Somerset Country Gazette,* 13 July 1858; quoted in Devey, 317.

36. Devey, 318.

37. 'Devoted Disciple: The Letters of Mary Elizabeth Braddon to Sir Edward Bulwer-Lytton, 1862-1873,' *Harvard Library Bulletin* 22 (1974), 5-35; 129-61.

38. David Skilton, ed, *Lady Audley's Secret* (New York: Oxford 1987), 454, suggests Braddon is referring to the ease with which Lady Audley is confined.

39. Showalter, 28; on the state of Belgian licensed houses, see Winslow, 216-19.

40. Andrew Wynter, *The Borderlands of Insanity* (London: Strand 1877), 48; see also Henry Maudsley, *The Physiology and Pathology of the Mind* (London: Macmillan 1867), 216, who remarks that insanity descends more frequently from the mother than the father, and from mother to daughter more often than to son.

41. Elaine Showalter, *A Literature of Their Own: Women Novelists from Brontë to Lessing* (London: Virago 1978).

Richard Nemesvari (essay date 1995)

SOURCE: "Robert Audley's Secret: Male Homosocial Desire in *Lady Audley's Secret,*" in *Studies in the Novel,* Vol. 27, No. 4, Winter, 1995, pp. 515-28.

[*In the following essay, Nemesvari argues that Lady Audley poses a threat to "male homosocial bonds."*]

Elaine Showalter has characterized Victorian sensation novels of the 1860s as "a genre in which everything that was not forbidden was compulsory."[1] Thus, much to the chagrin of many contemporary reviewers, these works focused on murder, attempted murder, bigamy, adultery, and a series of "lesser" transgressions which shocked and titillated their audience. As well, sensation fiction tended to present sexual irregularities as motivating the crimes which drove its plots, something which played no small role in reinforcing its popularity.

There was, however, one "forbidden" sexual topic which could not be addressed directly, even within the risqué confines of these novels, and that was homosexuality. Nonetheless, even though homosexuality remained, in Lord Alfred Douglas' famous phrase, "the Love that dare not speak its name," the origins and themes of sensation novels allowed them to explore this taboo subject in ways unavailable to most other forms of "mainstream" mid-nineteenth-century literature. In *The History of Sexuality* Foucault asserts that, as far as the categorization of homosexuality is concerned, "Westphal's famous article of 1870 on 'contrary sexual sensations' can stand as its date of birth."[2] The concept of the "homosexual," therefore, as it has come to be understood in the twentieth century, was being formulated at almost the exact historical moment sensation fiction first achieved notoriety. It is perhaps not surprising that sensation authors found ways to work this newly-arisen "category" into their texts, which after all were intended to startle, if not appall, their audience.

Thus in **Lady Audley's Secret** (1862), one of the earliest and most successful examples of sensation fiction, Mary Elizabeth Braddon explicitly presents the threat posed by her central female character as a challenge to male homosocial bonds. Eve Kosofsky Sedgwick's hypothesis of "the potential unbrokenness of a continuum between homosocial and homosexual—a continuum whose visibility, for men, in our society, is radically disrupted"[3] becomes particularly evocative for this novel. By portraying her putative hero, Robert Audley, as driven by repressed homoerotic desires, Braddon exposes the self-interested and self-protective denial which underlies Victorian patriarchal society. The subtextual revelation of the "unspeakable" secret of male homosocial desire is essential to Braddon's feminist critique of the roles and behaviors forced upon women by men who are unwilling to acknowledge their own motives and insecurities.

It has become something of a critical commonplace to describe sensation novels as "domesticated Gothic," since one of their most effective devices is the transferral of Gothic events and emotions from exotic and romantic locales into the heart of respectable, nineteenth-century Britain. While discussing Gothic fiction Sedgwick makes the following observations:

> The ties of the Gothic novel to an emergent female authorship and readership have been a constant for two centuries, and there has been a history of useful critical attempts to look to the Gothic for explorations of the position of women in relation to the changing shapes of patriarchal domination. A less obvious point has to do with the reputation for "decadence": the Gothic was the first novelistic form in England to have close, relatively visible links to male homosexuality.[4]

The critical furor that surrounded the Victorian manifestation of this older genre, and which led it to be judged as "more pernicious than its gothic and romantic ancestors,"[5] was generated by sensation fiction's insistence that even the sanctified realm of Victorian domesticity provided no real barrier to the "deviant" criminal/sexual urges that seemed waiting to overwhelm it. By tapping directly into a series of Victorian anxieties about gender roles and sexual identification, anxieties which became increasingly difficult to repress as the century proceeded, these novels provided an expression of the "desperation and dissent"[6] underlying middle-class assumptions and values. For a writer like Braddon, then, this neo-Gothic form holds obvious attractions: as part of its literary inheritance it already possesses the potentially subversive elements outlined by Sedgwick, while at the same time it provides an opportunity to bring them, both literally and figuratively, "home." Thus the conflict presented in *Lady Audley's Secret* between its two main characters, as Robert Audley struggles to discover and expose his aunt-by-marriage's various secrets, enacts Braddon's own discovery and exposure of the equivocal social "secret" which empowers him to do so.

Most of the critical commentary on Braddon's novel, understandably enough, focuses on its titular heroine/villainess, and in order to present my own analysis of Robert Audley I must necessarily reiterate some of the ideas developed more fully elsewhere. To begin, the disruptive threat posed by Lady Audley is founded on her physical appearance and assumed personality, which so closely match the Victorian ideal of the "angel in the house" that they effectively cloak a willful character ready to dare bigamy and attempted murder to get what she wants. Along with a seemingly "amiable and gentle nature always . . . light-hearted, happy, and contented under any circumstances,"[7] she possesses "soft blue eyes" (p. 6) and "the most wonderful curls in the world—soft and feathery, always floating away from her face, and making a pale halo round her head when the sunlight shone through them" (p. 8). When Sir Michael Audley encounters his future wife, in her guise of the governess Lucy Graham, the narrator's comments make it clear that he is all but helpless to withstand her culturally-defined allure.

> That one quiet evening sealed Sir Michael's fate. He could no more resist the tender fascination of those soft and melting blue eyes; the graceful beauty of that slender throat and drooping head, with its wealth of showering flaxen curls; the low music of that gentle voice; the perfect harmony which pervaded every charm . . . than he could resist his destiny. Destiny! Why, she was his destiny!

> (P. 6)

Braddon undercuts gender stereotypes by demonstrating that "the dangerous woman is not the rebel or the intellectual, but the pretty little girl whose indoctrination in the feminine role has taught her deceitfulness almost as a secondary sex characteristic."[8] Interestingly enough, however, the voluntary adoption and manipulation of this rigid cultural ideal by "Lucy Graham" illustrates a perhaps even more threatening characteristic: her elastic ability to define and re-define herself.

The string of names by which Braddon's female lead is identified throughout the text indicates a protean talent for escaping the constraints of a society which attempts to restrict women's social movement and definition. As Helen Maldon, daughter of an impoverished, half-pay naval officer, she quickly learns that if her situation is to improve she must use her looks to achieve an advantageous marriage. When, as Helen Talboys, her new husband has his income cut off by his disapproving father, and then abandons her for the gold-fields of Australia, she reinvents herself as the governess Lucy Graham, and takes the post which brings her into contact with Sir Michael. When he proposes to her she hesitates only momentarily at the prospect of bigamy, and then accepts him and her next identity as Lucy, Lady Audley. Word reaching her that her first husband has returned, she fakes the death of "Helen Talboys" to prevent the discovery of her crime and ensure the security of her new status; and when that first husband confronts her after accidently discovering her fraud, she tries to kill him by pushing him down a well. Her final "incarnation," as Madame Taylor, is imposed on her by Robert Audley after he exposes her and expels her from England, locking her into an identity just as he locks her into a French *maison de santé*. This act thus symbolizes both his victory over her and his neutralization of the dangerous potential for unrestrained female autonomy she represents.

On an abstract level, therefore, Lady Audley's refusal to accept the limited roles of impoverished daughter, deserted wife, and toiling governess acts as a covert critique of the narrow, unfulfilling roles available to women in general. More concretely, however, Lady Audley's fluid identity, her masculine insistence on self-determination, threatens a patriarchal class hierarchy dependent on the assurance that women remain *passive* objects of exchange through which men determine and create their own status. As Winifred Hughes notes, "[a]lthough Lucy Audley is a social climber, originally marrying both husbands for money and position, she embodies an internal threat to the respectable classes because she identifies with them; she wants what they value and brilliantly parodies their ideal."[9] By aggressively attempting to advance her own social standing, and indeed succeeding in that attempt, Lady Audley challenges her society's assumption that "the power relationships between men and women [are] dependent on the power relationships between men and men."[10] It is Robert Audley's task to meet and beat back the threat posed by Lady Audley by re-establishing the "proper" homosocial bonds she has disrupted. But, in doing so, Braddon has him reveal more about himself and the society he represents than he is willing to recognize.

When the reader is introduced to Robert he seems an unlikely candidate for the role of social guardian. Braddon goes out of her way to provide a description which would have been problematic to a Victorian audience, and problematic in some very specific ways.

> Robert Audley was supposed to be a barrister. . . . But he had never either had a brief, or tried to get a brief, or even wished to have a brief in all those five years, during which his name had been painted upon one of the doors in Fig-tree Court. He was a handsome, lazy, care-for-nothing fellow, of about seven-and-twenty; the only son of a younger brother of Sir Michael Audley. . . . Sometimes, when the weather was very hot, and he had exhausted himself with the exertion of smoking his German pipe, and reading French novels, he would stroll into the Temple Gardens, and lying in some shady spot, pale and cool, with his shirt collar turned down and a blue silk handkerchief tied loosely about his neck, would tell grave benchers that he had knocked himself up with overwork.
>
> (P. 32)

Clearly Robert has no real reason to work for a living, and his aristocratic background, even if he is not in its direct lineage, allows him to indulge in a leisured existence. Nonetheless, as a barrister he is an official caretaker and defender of his society's laws. His "development" throughout the text will be measured by a growing awareness of his social responsibility to ensure their authority is maintained, but his position before that realization takes hold is more interesting. David Skilton suggests that in *Lady Audley's Secret* "the use of French fiction is suggestive of a certain moral and intellectual atmosphere. . . . Audley's failing according to Victorian standards is a quite 'Continental' lack of moral concern and energy in relation to the serious issues of life. . . . But this lack of English moral fibre is vague and his amoral outlook quite unfocused."[11] Thus on one level Braddon begins her text by providing a hero who is in need of some kind of moral reform. However, the question of just how much his "English fibre" has been shaped by "Continental" influences needs to be explored futher.

While Skilton is right to note that Robert's "amorality" never finds an explicit expression within the text, I think he has missed the implied significance of Robert's style of dress, his mannerisms, and his attachment not only to French fiction and German pipes but also, we are later told, to "Turkish tobacco" (p. 113). Robert's tendency to-

wards a laconic, drawling irony in his speech, and his complete lack of skill and interest in fox hunting on his uncle's estate, foreshadow Wilde's quip about the unspeakable in full pursuit of the uneatable, and this anachronistic connection between the two is not completely strained. At the very least a Victorian audience would have associated Robert's habits with the kind of Romantic decadence against which the period defined itself. But by the time Braddon comes to write her novel the very word "decadence" has taken on a more specific connotation, as Sedgwick's earlier-quoted statement about Gothic fiction indicates. In outlining her exploration of potential reader responses to evocations of homosexuality Sedgwick is careful to make clear how tentative any conclusions drawn from such generalizations must be, and I can only echo her cautions here. Still, her observations are helpful in this context:

> With respect to homosocial/homosexual style, it seems to be possible to divide Victorian men among three rough categories according to class. The first includes aristocratic men and small groups of their friends and dependents, including bohemians and prostitutes; for these people, by 1865, a distinct homosexual role and culture seem already to have been in existence in England . . . It seems to have constituted a genuine subculture, facilitated in the face of an ideologically hostile dominant culture by money, privilege, internationalism, and for the most part, the ability to command secrecy . . . This role is closely related to—is in fact, through Oscar Wilde, the antecedent of—the particular stereotype that at least until recently has characterized American middle-class gay homosexuality; its strongest associations, as we have noted, are with effeminacy, transvestitism, promiscuity, prostitution, continental European culture, and the arts.[12]

Now clearly Robert does not fit all the characteristics presented here, or even perhaps most of them, but then I am not arguing anything so simplistic as that he "is" homosexual. Rather, Braddon has associated him with a recognizable aristocratic type possessed of, by this historical moment, clear homosocial/homosexual overtones. His equivocal social status, as a member of an aristocratic family fulfilling the middle-class role of a barrister, makes that association even more provocative in that it hints at the possible transference of this "style" from one class to another. From his first introduction into the text, therefore, Braddon subtly implies that her hero's most intense bonds will be between himself and other men, something which the novel's events bear out.

In particular this view of Robert helps explain his reaction to the plot development which initiates the conflict in the text: George Talboys' return to England from Australia. When the two accidently encounter each other, Robert is momentarily startled out of his air of supercilious detachment.

> "Be so good as to look where you're going, my friend!" Robert remonstrated, mildly, to the impetuous passenger; "you might give a man warning before you throw him down and trample upon him."

The stranger stopped suddenly, looked very hard at the speaker, and then gasped for breath.

"Bob!" he cried, in a tone expressive of the most intense astonishment; "I only touched British ground after dark last night, and to think that I should meet you this morning!"

"I've seen you somewhere before, my bearded friend," said Mr. Audley, calmly scrutinising the animated face of the other, "but I'll be hanged if I can remember when or where."

"What!" exclaimed the stranger, reproachfully, "you don't mean to say that you've forgotten George Talboys?"

"*No I have not!*" said Robert, with an emphasis by no means usual to him; and then hooking his arm into that of his friend, he led him into the shady court, saying with his old indifference, "and now, George, tell us all about it."

(Pp. 34-35)

That Robert reacts "with an emphasis by no means usual to him," before his affected persona reasserts itself, demonstrates an attachment to George that has been elicited by no other character thus far in the book. The description which follows, however, is equally significant.

Robert Audley was for starting off immediately for the Crown and Sceptre, or the Castle, Richmond, where they could have a bit of dinner, and talk over those good old times when they were together at Eton. But George told his friend that before he went anywhere, before he shaved, or broke his fast, or in any way refreshed himself after a night journey from Liverpool by express train, he must call at a certain coffee-house in Bridge Street, Westminster, where he expected to find a letter from his wife.

(P. 35)

This is the first, but certainly not the last, time in which George's wife is going to come between Robert and his friend, and his response to the information that George is married is more than a little revealing: "'The idea of you having a wife, George; what a preposterous joke'" (p. 35). The text's passing reference to Eton provides the clue to Robert's reaction, for the attachments formed there were often more than platonic, and "[c]andid accounts agree that in most of the public schools, the whirlwinds of the soul were often acted out in the flesh."[13] It is also, of course, such elite male schools, which by definition exclude female participation, that form the homosocial bonds at the heart of British patriarchal power.

It is hardly surprising, therefore, that when George receives the devastating news that his wife is dead, and misses the boat which would have returned him to Australia, he "once more threw himself upon Robert Audley's hospitality" and "[t]he barrister received him with open arms" (p. 46). The potential disruption posed by George's "preposterous" wife is momentarily nullified, and the homosocial relationship Robert so clearly craves is re-

established when the two end up sharing his rooms. However, with George's mysterious disappearance Robert is forced into the role of reluctant detective, and into a confrontation not only with Lady Audley but also with his own suppressed feelings.

Throughout much of the rest of the novel, until the mystery is seemingly re/solved, Robert finds himself both wanting and not wanting to pursue the various clues which present themselves. This ambivalence is paradigmatic of sensation fiction, for it "is a characteristic of Robert Audley's hunt . . . as of Walter Hartright's in *The Woman in White* and Pip's in *Great Expectations,* that revelation of the truth will overwhelm the world of the hunter and of those he loves."[14] But in **Lady Audley's Secret** the protagonist's revaluation of self is more potentially threatening than in the novels by Collins and Dickens because it entails questions of sexual identity. Braddon describes Robert's reaction to George's disappearance in the following passage:

If any one had ventured to tell Mr. Robert Audley that he could possibly feel a strong attachment to any creature breathing, that cynical gentleman would have elevated his eyebrows in supreme contempt at the preposterous notion. Yet here he was, flurried and anxious, bewildering his brain by all manner of conjectures about his missing friend, and, false to every attribute of his nature, walking fast.

"I haven't walked fast since I was at Eton," he murmured, as he hurried across one of Sir Michael's meadows in the direction of the village; "and the worst of it is that I haven't the most remote idea of where I am going."

(P. 82)

This second reference to Eton again hints at the reason for Robert's intensity of response, and his perplexity about both why he is acting this way and about "where [he is] going" suggests that on some level he does not *want* to analyze too closely the motives which are driving him. If it is in Robert's own interest to avoid the kind of sexual self-knowledge which seems poised to overwhelm him, at least one character in the novel possesses enough insight to make the most overt statement on this topic in the entire text. Alicia Audley, Robert's cousin, has the distinction, along with her dog, of being the only character to dislike and distrust Lady Audley from the beginning. Her description of her new step-mother as a "wax-doll" (p. 56) indicates an awareness of Lady Audley's calculated artificiality, as well as a rejection of the angel-in-the-house stereotype which she wields so effectively. More significantly, Alicia's unrequited love for Robert apparently gives her a deeper perception of his passions than even he possesses.

As Robert's uneasiness about George increases, and as he becomes more and more fixated on his friend's unexplained departure, Alicia sarcastically exclaims "'What a dreadful catastrophe! . . . since Pythias, in the person of Mr. Robert Audley, cannot exist for half an hour without

Damon, commonly known as George Talboys'" (p. 84). An illustration from Cicero's *De Officiis,* the story of Damon and Pythias, in which Damon stands as a hostage for Pythias, with his life forfeit if his companion does not return in time for his own execution, was for the Victorians, as for the Romans, representative of trust, devotion, and perfect friendship. Yet given the original setting of the tale, the Greek court and culture of Dionysius I of Syracuse, the association of Robert and George with Pythias and Damon has additional implications. An interesting parallel reference occurs in a letter which Arthur Henry Hallam sent to fellow "Apostle" Richard Milnes in 1831:

> Whether it may not be better for you to take me on these terms, and to give up cheerfully the theory to which you have been visibly labouring to accommodate me, and which depends on the pleasant postulate that Arthur Hallam was once an enthusiast, and worthy to be the Pythias of that new Damon, Richard Milnes, but that all of a sudden the said AH became a reprobate, and is now grovelling on some "Alcian field," afar from everything ideal, beautiful and true, and consequently from the aforesaid Richard, this I leave you to consider.[15]

Richard Dellamora interprets this passage as Hallam taking "the opportunity to deny for the record that his earlier confidences may have included the fact that he 'was once an enthusiast': a term that Shelley, Hallam's father, and later Pater use to denote a male committed to sexual and emotional relations with other males," and further suggests that "in referring to Damon and Pythias, two heroic Greek lovers . . . Hallam specifies the context of Milne's investments in male relationships."[16] Clearly at least a portion of Braddon's Victorian audience might be expected to understand the story in this way and recognize what it suggests.

By alluding to a historical moment in which the homosocial bond between men was often initiated and confirmed by sexual relations, and then directly connecting this allusion to her central male characters, Braddon briefly exposes the foundational "secret" of masculine desire which both Robert and his society attempt to elide. Alicia's accurate evaluation of Lady Audley lends credence to her "revelation" about Robert, and although the primary text never explicitly confirms her apparently passing remark, subsequent events in the plot certainly suggest its subtextual aptness. What Alicia has perceived, quite rightly, is that George is her *rival,* and eventually she will indeed lose Robert to "him," although in a way which leaves the homoerotic nature of their relationship safely unspoken.

The further Robert proceeds in his investigation of George's disappearance, the more agitated he becomes. He experiences a series of disturbing dreams and is given to the kind of self-questioning which might lead him to abandon his role as detective: "'Why do I go on with this,' he said, 'when I know that it is leading me, step by step, day by day, hour by hour, nearer to that conclusion which of all others I should avoid? Am I tied to a wheel, and must I

go with its every revolution, let it take me where it will?'" (p. 157). Although Robert tends to couch his reluctance in terms of the effect his disclosures may have on his uncle, it is not difficult to see in quotations such as this a personal fear of self-exposure. In her more recent study, *Epistemology of the Closet,* Sedgwick notes that

> [b]ecause the paths of male entitlement, especially in the nineteenth century, required certain intense bonds that were not readily distinguishable from the most reprobated bonds, an endemic and ineradicable state of what I am calling homosexual panic became the normal condition of male heterosexual entitlement.[17]

This nicely describes the situation Robert finds himself in, for as he proceeds, he becomes increasingly panicked about what he may uncover. Braddon's text therefore reveals the way in which a growing awareness of the homosocial may incite homophobia, as Robert desperately, and at times angrily, struggles to deny the significance of his reactions. Finally, having reached such a psychological impasse that he is ready to abandon his search for the "truth," he decides that he will approach George's family for guidance. And it is here that he finds the resolution to his dilemma in the figure of George's sister, Clara.

Robert's interview with Mr. Talboys does not go very well, for George's father sees his son's disappearance as a ploy to create alarm and worry, thus forcing an eventual reconciliation with his rich and estranged parent. Further, George's sister remains silent during the exchange between Robert and Mr. Talboys, and therefore seems to accept her father's cold response to the suggestion that her brother has been murdered. Robert takes their supposed indifference as a warrant for dropping his role as detective:

> "Thank God!" thought Robert Audley—"thank God! it is over . . . I shall not be the means of bringing disgrace upon those I love. It will come, perhaps, sooner or later, but it will not come through me. The crisis is past, and I am free."
>
> He felt an unutterable relief in this thought. His generous nature revolted at the office into which he had found himself drawn—the office of spy, the collector of damning facts that led on to horrible deductions.
>
> He drew a long breath—a sigh of relief at his release. It was all over now.
>
> (P. 196)

Once again the extremity of Robert's reaction suggests that the "disgrace" he has been saved from deducing is more personal than he might like to admit, but as it turns out he is given the opportunity to pursue the external element of his search while leaving its internal motives securely unexamined. Clara Talboys, following Robert's departure, runs after his carriage: "'Oh, let me speak to you,' she cried—'let me speak to you, or I shall go mad. I heard it all. I believe what you believe; and I shall go mad unless I can do something—something towards avenging his death'" (p. 197). From this point on it is Clara whom Robert will perceive as the driving force behind his investigation; she all but literally becomes the hand of fate "beckon[ing] him onwards to her brother's unknown grave" (p. 253). The key point for my purposes, however, is Robert's perception, and the text's constant declaration, that Clara is exactly like her brother.

Robert's first perception of Clara is "that she was young, and that she was like George Talboys" (p. 187). After this opening statement we are told "she is like George" (p. 189), that she has "brown eyes, like George's" (p. 197), that "she was so like the friend whom he had loved and lost, that it was impossible for him to think of her as a stranger" (p. 202), that her handwriting possesses a "feminine resemblance to poor George's hand; neater than his, and more decided than his, but very like, very like" (p. 209), and that she has his "lost friend's face" (p. 258). Clara provides Robert with the perfect object of transference and offers him the opportunity to turn his "illicit" homosocial desire for George in a socially acceptable direction. Indeed, Braddon goes out of her way to portray almost the exact moment of that transference; sitting alone in his rooms Robert ponders his situation: "'It's comfortable, but it seems so d——d lonely tonight. If poor George were sitting opposite to me, or—or even George's sister—she's very like him—existence might be a little more endurable'" (p. 208).

From here on Robert's pursuit of Lady Audley receives an increased impetus, because the possibility of being forced to confront his own homoerotic responses is safely evaded. Clara becomes the mediating point in a triangulated relationship "in which the true *partner* is a man,"[18] and she thus serves to cement the homosocial bond between Robert and George even as she camouflages its potentially homosexual nature.

Further, although Clara declares that she is willing to hunt down her brother's supposed murderer herself, she never actually does so. Content to remain passive as Robert continues his pursuit, she is the exact opposite of Lady Audley who, when she feels hounded too closely by Robert's investigations, does not hesitate to personally burn down the inn in which he is staying in an attempt to murder him. Robert's eventual destruction of Lady Audley and her marriage(s), and his growing attachment to Clara, therefore re-establish "proper" gender roles by nullifying Lady Audley's dangerous female aggression and the criminally-established relationships which are its result, and by replacing those relationships with the kinds of male-dominated links which ensure patriarchal order.

Indeed, although I have been emphasizing Robert's homosocial link with George, his connection with his uncle, Sir Michael Audley, seems almost as strong. The novel's narrator states that

> Sir Michael had been a second father to the young man, a generous and noble friend, a grave and earnest adviser; and perhaps the strongest sentiment of Robert's heart was his love for the grey-bearded baronet.

> But the grateful affection was so much a part of himself, that it seldom found an outlet in words; and a stranger would never have fathomed the strength of feeling which lay, a deep and powerful current, beneath the stagnant surface of the barrister's character.

> (P. 213)

As already mentioned, Robert's main excuse throughout much of the text for not wanting to discover the truth about George's disappearance is the impact that revelation will have on his uncle. Yet this external reluctance covers a potentially devastating psychological truth, which is that whatever pain unmasking Lady Audley may provide for both George and Sir Michael, the result will profit Robert himself. Robert's self-interest takes two forms, neither of which he consciously wants to recognize, because to do so would destroy his valorizing posture as an "embodiment of justice" (p. 271). As his uncle's heir-presumptive, exposing Lady Audley's crimes prevents the possibility of her bearing a child to come between himself and his uncle's title, thus ensuring the "legitimate" transferral of property and rank so important to patriarchy. Perhaps even more significantly, as the (bigamous) wife of *both* the men for whom Robert feels the strongest homosocial bonds, Lady Audley is his rival for their love in something of the same way that George is Alicia's rival. By expelling her from their lives Robert restores the attachments she has disrupted, with the additional gain of Clara Talboys who allows him to further repress whatever dangerous moments of sexual self-awareness his conflict with Lady Audley might have encouraged.

It is hardly surprising, therefore, that Robert's eventual (and inevitable) proposal to Clara is more than a little conflicted. Having banished Lady Audley to France, and having discovered that her attempt to murder George failed, Robert offers to search for him in Australia:

> "You are very good and generous, Mr. Audley," [Clara] said, at last, "and I feel this offer too much to be able to thank you for it. But—what you speak of could never be. By what right could I accept such a sacrifice?"

> "By the right which makes me your bounden slave for ever and ever, whether you will or no. By the right of the love I bear you, Clara," cried Mr. Audley, dropping on his knees—rather awkwardly it must be confessed— and covering a soft little hand, that he had found half-hidden among the folds of a silken dress, with passionate kisses.

> "I love you, Clara," he said, "I love you . . . and I shall love you for ever and ever, whether you will or no . . . Clara, Clara!" he murmured, in a low pleading voice, "shall I go to Australia to look for your brother? . . . Shall we both go, dearest? Shall we go as man and wife? Shall we go together, my dear love, and bring our brother back between us?"

> (Pp. 440-441)

The conflation here of Clara with George, of marrying the sister with searching for the brother, might leave even the most conventionally romantic of readers feeling a little uncomfortable. And Braddon drives home her point by never showing Clara actually consenting to Robert's proposal, or indeed saying another word for what remains of the novel. Instead there is a break in the text, followed by an interview between Robert and Mr. Talboys which concludes with this statement by George's father: "'You are going to look for my son. . . . Bring me back my boy, and I will freely forgive you for having robbed me of my daughter'" (p. 441). With Lady Audley gone women are securely back in their place as passive and silent objects of exchange, while the men are free to work out the homosocial relationships which determine society's structures.

The final chapter of **Lady Audley's Secret,** which describes events two years after the main action, is so overdetermined that it can only be read as an ironic statement on what the novel has "revealed." George, who as it turns out went to New York instead of Australia after surviving Lady Audley's murderous attack, returns in time to prevent Robert and Clara from setting out on what would have been a fruitless search. Robert, a "rising man upon the home circuit" (p. 445), has established a "fairy cottage . . . between Teddington Lock and Hampton Bridge" (p. 445) for his new family, which now includes a baby, and George "lives there with his sister and his sister's husband" (p. 445). Robert has, as it were, the best of both worlds. "Madame Taylor" dies of a *"maladie de langueur"* (p. 446), and Audley Court, the scene of Lady Audley's sphere of influence, is shut up. The other main characters, while proceeding with their lives, are apparently centered on the blissful domesticity established by Robert, in which "the gentlemen sit and smoke in the summer evenings . . . [until] they are summoned by Clara and Alicia to drink tea, and eat strawberries and cream upon the lawn" (p. 446). But this idyllic scene is undercut by the subtextual secrets which remain unaddressed. The nature of Robert's detections, which uncover just enough to banish the threatening female presence while concealing the male desire which cannot be named, has been "outed" sufficiently that the novel destabilizes the patriarchal/heterosexual norm of its closure. Braddon's presentation of her protagonist subverts his pose as reformed protector of what is right and proper by exposing the illicit foundation upon which his status rests.

Victorian sensation fiction became popular at a time when there was a growing perception "that knowledge meant sexual knowledge and secrets sexual secrets, [and when] there had in fact developed one particular sexuality that was distinctively constituted as secrecy."[19] Thus *both* of the main characters in **Lady Audley's Secret** have guilty secrets which are revealed, but within the text only one is called upon to pay for her transgressions. Because Lady Audley's criminal activities of bigamy and attempted murder embody challenges to a male-constructed social order, they are "spoken" into existence by a male detective who, having done so, is empowered to expose, punish, and therefore nullify her female aggression. Lady Audley has no reciprocal power to speak Robert Audley's secret into existence, but Mary Elizabeth Braddon does. By forcing him to a near-recognition of his homosocial desire, Braddon also forces the reader to recognize the way in which a patriarchal society depends on repression and denial for its very existence. In doing so she reinforces her feminist attack on the *status quo* by calling into question male self-awareness, exposing the profound sexual ambivalence at the core of masculine power, and emphasizing that it is women who pay the price for preserving the secret upon which male privilege rests. As Showalter notes, the "innermost secrets of sensationalism, indeed, deal with unlawful passion,"[20] and in **Lady Audley's Secret** "unlawful passion" is as much, if not more, the defining characteristic of Robert Audley as it is of the woman he pursues and destroys.

Notes

1. Elaine Showalter, *A Literature of Their Own: British Women Novelists from Brontë to Lessing* (Princeton: Princeton Univ. Press, 1977), p. 158.

2. Michel Foucault, *The History of Sexuality: Volume 1: An Introduction* (New York: Random House, 1980), p. 43.

3. Eve Kosofsky Sedgwick, *Between Men: English Literature and Male Homosocial Desire* (New York: Columbia Univ. Press, 1985), pp. 1-2.

4. Sedgwick, *Between Men,* p. 91.

5. Winifred Hughes, *The Maniac in the Cellar: Sensation Novels of the 1860s* (Princeton: Princeton Univ. Press, 1980), p. 5.

6. Hughes, *Maniac in the Cellar,* p. 36.

7. Mary Elizabeth Braddon, *Lady Audley's Secret* (Oxford: Oxford Univ. Press, 1987), p. 5. References in the text will be to this edition.

8. Elaine Showalter, "Desperate Remedies: Sensation Novels of the 1860s," *Victorian Newsletter* 49 (Spring 1976), p. 3.

9. Hughes, *Maniac in the Cellar,* p. 127.

10. Sedgwick, *Between Men,* p. 25.

11. David Skilton, Introduction, *Lady Audley's Secret* (Oxford: Oxford Univ. Press, 1987), pp. xiii-xiv.

12. Sedgwick, *Between Men,* pp. 172-73.

13. *Ibid.,* p. 176.

14. Skilton, Introduction, pp. xx-xxi.

15. Quoted in Richard Dellamora, *Masculine Desire: The Sexual Politics of Victorian Aestheticism* (Chapel Hill: Univ. of North Carolina Press, 1990), pp. 26-27.

16. Dellamora, *Masculine Desire,* p. 27.

17. Eve Kosofsky Sedgwick, *Epistemology of the Closet* (Berkeley: Univ. of California Press, 1990), p. 185.

18. Sedgwick, *Between Men*, p. 26.

19. Sedgwick, *Epistemology*, p. 73.

20. Showalter, "Desperate Remedies," p. 2.

Pamela K. Gilbert (essay date 1996)

SOURCE: "Madness and Civilization: Generic Opposition in Mary Elizabeth Braddon's *Lady Audley's Secret*," in *Essays in Literature,* Vol. 23, No. 2, Fall, 1996, pp. 218-33.

[*In the following essay, Gilbert maintains that Braddon's narrative structure in* Lady Audley's Secret *supports a feminist reading of the novel.*]

Much has been written in the last few decades rereading Lady Audley as a victim of patriarchy, beginning with Elaine Showalter's famous statement that "Lady Audley's real secret is that she is sane, and, moreover, representative" (167). Attempts to recast the novel, however, have paid little attention to the narrative structure which has supported what feminist critics today see as an egregious misreading sustained for the first century of the novel's existence. Moreover, little has been said of the narrative structure that would support their own reading of the novel. In fact, both supporting structures do exist in **Lady Audley's Secret**; their coexistence comments not only on the position of women in mid-Victorian society, but on the analogous position of popular fiction and its relation to "high culture" narrative.

The text contains two primary narratives, and a secondary narrative which mediates between them. Through them, the novel simultaneously presents and validates two contradictory points of view, in two complementary storylines: the coming-of-age and social integration of Robert Audley, a traditional high-culture theme, and the decline and fall of the scheming adventuress, a popular culture melodrama. Together, these two narratives create a dramatic tension born of the ideological contradictions in their mutually exclusive portrayals of feminine evil, a third rhetorical space in which the coherence of the oppositions which drive either of the first two narratives unravel into incoherence, the madness which is finally located and at least superficially contained in the imprisoned bodies of the Maldon women. This third rhetorical space is structured by its own narrative, that of detection, which mediates between the two genres, just as thematically, (male) sexual desire operates to pull Robert Audley's and the Lady's stories together. Thematically and structurally, then, the two narratives are mediated by male desire to know the Other, an Other which is metaphorically represented throughout the text as a desirable female body which is a threat to the masculine social body.

Within the emerging structure of the mid-Victorian popular fiction market, the sensation novel represented the

Other of Belles Lettres. Reviewers for the large middle class quarterlies and weeklies in mid-Victorian Britain, coping with the developing legitimation of the novel as a literary form, often distinguished between the "high" culture novel[1] and "trashy" genres (not coincidentally, those most often defined as "women's" or "lower class" genres) in terms of healthfulness.[2] The sensation novel of the 1860s garnered a great deal of hostile attention from contemporary critics.[3] Much of the opprobrium levelled at sensational fiction was couched in specifically physical terms: infection, addiction, etc. Indeed, the whole notion of a sensation is a physical one, and the effects of sensation fiction are generally defined in physical terms. The *Quarterly Review* defines sensation novels as novels which produce "excitement, and excitement alone" by "preaching to the nerves" ("Sensation Novels" 481), that abound in "action, action, action!" The effects of this action upon the reader are physical:

> A great philosopher has enumerated in a list of sensations "the feelings from heat, electricity, galvanism, &c." together with "titillation, sneezing, horripilation, shuddering, the feeling of setting the teeth on edge, &c.;" and our novels might be classified in like manner, according to what sensation they are calculated to produce. There are novels of the warming pan, and others of the galvanic battery type—some which gently stimulate a particular feeling, and others which carry the whole nervous system by steam.
>
> (487)

The tone here is satiric, of course, but the treatment is fairly consistent across a number of reviews; the core of the sensation novel is the activity of the text in producing a physical sensation (an activity which is complementary to the feminine passivity of the reader in whom the sensation is "produced.")[4] The text is defined as a substance that enters the body of the reader, making him or her passive and dependent on something outside the self—in Bakhtin's terms, grotesque.[5] The grotesque body is constructed in opposition to the controlled, "closed," self-sufficient body of the imperial modern subject; what transforms the closed, self-sufficient body into the open, needy one is desire. In short, discussions of reading were couched in the terms of *desire* and fiction designated as legitimate or illegitimate in terms of *healthfulness*—a healthy object being one which would tend to confirm and complete (close) middle-class masculine imperial identity.

The duel of narratives within **Lady Audley's Secret,** then, replicates the struggle occurring in the popular fiction market between the healthful "taste" for more elevated reading material (biographies, histories, and, to a lesser extent, the novels of what Frye termed the "high mimetic" mode) and the debasing addiction to "low" fictions like the sensational novel. The integrity of high culture as a representation of society depends on the obliteration of the Other—either that narrative must be made to conform to the ideal (in Bakhtin's term, epic) narratives of high culture, or it must be suppressed.[6] Not surprisingly, then, this conflict is played out in metaphors of the body and health (both in the text and in its criticism). The novel's most sensational subversion is not the Lady's violation of gender roles, but its definition of the task of the high-culture hero as the enforcement of a demonstrably false epic narrative at the expense of the narratives—and bodies—of the Other.

Lady Audley's Secret, often credited with (or accused of) laying the foundation for the sensation novel, contains many elements outside of and even contraindicating the sensation genre. Lady Audley, her secret, and her deeds form the sensational story that has traditionally been read as marking the novel's genre, yet the forced growth of Robert Audley and the masculinization of his character constitute an equal and complementary counternarrative to Lady Audley's tale, which itself subverts the "return to order" which marks the sensation story and relocates the source of sensation from the disordered and alien individual female body to the male social body of patriarchal sociolegal institutions. These elements coexist in the text, yet only the former structure was "selected" by readers as a generic property; contemporary critics expressed outrage over the portrayal of the alienated woman and missed the much more subversive portrait of alienated patriarchy. Robert Audley, the Temple Bar lawyer who has never submitted a brief; Lieutenant Maldon, who sells his daughter to the highest bidder and drinks the proceeds; Heavy Dragoon George Talboys, who abandons his wife and baby son; and even Sir Michael Audley, whose love-"fever" drives him to take a wife who admittedly does not love him—these are the aristocratic and generally privileged men who set the events of the story in motion. Robert Audley finally rouses himself from his habitual lethargy to pursue the "madwoman" and himself becomes mad in the process. This madness is "healed" when he takes as a wife Clara, George's sister. The mad wife is replaced by the mad husband, whose madness is more acceptable to society, but it is made perfectly clear that the social order is both artificial and a mere mask for the chaos or "madness" beneath. Thus the story is not merely one of Lady Audley's disguised madness—as Dr. Mosgrave says, "There is no madness in anything she has done" (377)—but of Robert Audley's recognition of his own insanity and of the mad nature of his society, and of his subsequent informed choice to remain complicit in that madness and to become active in supporting it.

If we set aside the Lady Audley storyline and consider only the Robert Audley storyline, the pattern of the coming-of-age story appears clear. A young male character on the brink of manhood has not yet accepted adult responsibilities. Although he is called a barrister, he has never submitted a brief. He prefers the company of his male schoolfriends to women, and he regards marriage with consternation. He is content to "play" and let others manage the serious business of life. Conflict arises when a woman disrupts the homosocial relationship between him and his closest friend. The boy must take adult responsibilities, must act and make decisions. As Lyn Pykett points out, "In his pursuit of Lady Audley, Robert discovers manhood and his vocation. . . . He embarks on a chivalric

quest . . . [which] is transformed into bourgeois epic" (103).[7] Braddon refers to the heroic ur-text of *The Odyssey,* first referring to Odysseus explicitly to set the stage, then combining Telemachus's character with Odysseus's journey. Robert's journey includes many Circean temptations, largely in the person of Lucy, and, of course, a Penelope in the person of Clara (whom Robert first encounters in the act of dropping and unravelling her reels of cotton). The hero's descent into hell is represented (as it often is in modern literature) by a crisis of values, an episode of madness. At the story's end he has withstood the temptations of the mermaid, come through the journey to the underworld, rescued the patriarch of his family, and returned home to take his own place as husband, father, and powerful leader of the community (distinguished by his successful prosecution of a breach of promise case—a typical bit of Braddon irony). In short, Robert Audley is a Telemachus of recognizable form, if diminutive proportions, faithful himself to the social order and ready to punish those who stray from the code.

Braddon makes the Odyssey comparison early in the story. George Talboys's first description of his wife to Robert describes her playing a guitar and singing: "She's for all the world like one of those what's-its-names, who got poor old Ulysses in trouble" (35). Throughout the novel, Lady Audley is associated with the ocean, and we are informed that George first met her at the end of a pier (247). It is perhaps not coincidental that she pushes him into a well, which he survives largely because there is no water in it. Robert dreams of Audley Court "threatened by the rapid rising of a boisterous sea . . . the sleeper saw a pale, starry face looking out of the silvery foam, and knew that it was my lady, transformed into a mermaid, beckoning his uncle to destruction" (246). Although mermaids are not unique to *The Odyssey,* the initial comparison recalls their function specifically as impediments to the hero's journey.[8]

However, Robert Audley's story does not stand alone; it runs alongside the story of the "syren" he must overcome. Braddon's radical departure from tradition is not in presenting the evil mermaid, but in giving her a voice which not only sings sweet lies for men but tells them unpleasant truths. Lady Audley's secret is that evil does not originate in the mermaids or the Clytemnestras, but in the system of representation which makes mermaids and Clytemnestras out of the Melanthos who are pretty enough to attract male attention and unfortunate enough to have no other source of security.

When women like Lucy Audley are not singing and amusing men, however, they speak truths that destroy the idyllic representations of rural feminine beauty and domestic tranquillity as surely as does Braddon's murder in a quiet meadow. When Lady Audley is exposed, she speaks of her childhood:

> "I was not happy, for the woman who had charge of me was a disagreeable woman . . . who was irregu-

larly paid; and who vented her rage upon me when my father was behindhand in remitting her money . . . at a very early age I found out what it was to be poor" . . . He [Sir Michael] sat silent . . . he . . . had believed . . . as he had believed in the Gospel . . . a very brief story of an early orphanage, and a long quiet, colourless youth spent in the conventual seclusion of an English boarding school.

(349)

Her story is most horrifying because it violates a previous narrative which is consonant with the ideal of the unsullied woman. Lady Audley goes on to discuss her fear of poverty and understanding of "what every schoolgirl knows" but none discusses—that her future will depend on a good marriage. In another scene, Phoebe is frank with Lady Audley about her own motivations for marrying: "I daren't refuse to marry him. . . . When he was a boy he was always violent and revengeful. I saw him once take up that very knife in a quarrel with his mother. I tell you, my lady, I must marry him" (107).

Throughout the novel, women express a clear understanding of the relations of power which underlie cultural representations while male characters prefer the "pretty stories" themselves. The contrast is neatly set up in the second chapter of the novel, "On Board the Argus." George and a "pale governess" are discussing their reasons for returning to England, and the governess explains that she has worked for fifteen years in Australia to save up enough money for her marriage to her English fiancé, who has not done well financially. She fears, however, that he may have died, or that his feelings might have changed, or even that he may marry her only for her savings. George is horrified, because, although he had abandoned his wife and never written her, these possibilities had never occurred to him. With great pride, he explains to the governess that he has worked for three and a half years to make his fortune, and finally struck gold. "How brave you were!" she responds (22). Although Braddon presents the governess as sincere in her admiration, surely the reader must sense a rich irony in the disparity between the woman's fifteen years of toil and realistic assessment of the possibility of change in her fiancé, whom she recognizes as a subjectivity distinct from her own, and George's blithely unconscious self-aggrandizement and conflation of his wife's subjectivity with his two-dimensional image of her. The male's "coming of age," therefore, is based on his ability not only to assume the masculine role of hero in the epic narrative that patriarchy approves, but to enforce the subordination of other voices and other subjectivities to their supporting roles in that same narrative. If Melantho's had been the narrative voice of *The Odyssey*, how differently might the story have been told!

Sexual attraction brings the two storylines together: first, Sir Michael's attraction to Lucy and later his nephew's. Peter Brooks points out that sexual desire operates in narrative as an expression of the "epistemophilic urge" or desire to know (xiii). However, for Sir Michael and Robert,

sexual attraction initially fosters the desire not to know— or, more precisely, to "know" a falsehood—the epic representation of Lady Audley as the angel in the house. Desire has its price, though; as Brooks also points out, the desire to know results finally in the unthinkable confrontation with the terrifying spectacle of the female genitals—the end of narrative. In the Audleys' case, sexual mystery is succeeded by the murder mystery, and the angel is unmasked as the devouring syren. Characteristically, sexual passion is defined as a "fever," and in Lady Audley's case, great care is taken to distinguish this diseased attraction from a more ordinary, healthy love:

> What had been his [Michael Audley's] love for his first wife but a poor, pitiful, smouldering spark, too dull to be extinguished, too feeble to burn? But *this* was love— this fever, this longing, this restless, uncertain, miserable hesitation; this sick hatred of his white beard; this frenzied wish to be young again. . . . Sir Michael Audley had fallen ill of the terrible fever called love.

(7)

Lucy, source and object of this affliction, lives as the governess to the local surgeon's children. In the governess position, many oppositions meet: family and not-family, lady and working woman, mother-figure and domestic servant. In Lucy Audley's case, the undomesticated woman is naturalized within a domestic setting; thus, her true nature is disguised and she is enabled to make contact with "good society" like Sir Michael. The source of disease is disguised within the surgeon's home, the very hearth of health. This disease is infectious; Sir Michael

> wondered why Robert failed to take the fever from the first breath of contagion that blew towards him. He forgot that there are men who go their ways unscathed amidst legions of lovely and generous women, to succumb at last before some harsh-featured virago, who knows the secret of that only philter which can intoxicate him and bewitch him. . . . He forgot that love, which is a madness, and a scourge, and a fever, and a delusion, and a snare, is also a mystery, and very imperfectly understood by everyone except the individual sufferer who writhes under its tortures . . . who lies awake at night until he loathes his comfortable pillow and tumbles his sheets into two twisted rags of linen in his agonies, as if he were a prisoner and wanted to wind them into impromptu ropes. . . . He ignored all those infinitesimal differences in nature which make the wholesome food of one man the deadly poison of another.

(332)

In this interesting series of images, we move from the disease metaphor, to a food-consumption image (the philter, the "wholesome food") to a more specifically sexual image of nocturnal crisis. Material is taken into the body, initiating an illness that cannot be healed without releasing it from the body, in this case a desire for sexual fulfillment that can only be "healed" by ejaculation into the body of the Other. Despite Sir Michael's bemusement, however, Robert has indeed been "infected" by desire for Lady Audley; Lady Audley, as the object of his desire, "opens" him, posing a threat to the closed, epic discourses of the social body.

The early sexual attraction that once led Robert to violate the privacy of Lady Audley's locked rooms, burglarizing her suite in order to gaze upon her portrait and personal effects transforms into the desire to know the "truth," leading him to continue violating the privacy of her past in order to expose her "secret." It is significant that this obsessive pursuit generates symptomatic behaviors of such a nature that the other lawyers in Robert's environment speculate that he is in love (211). It is the forced "penetration" of Lady Audley's identity, prefigured in the invasion of her rooms and bonnet box, which will signify mastery over the feminine elements in Robert's own nature. Perhaps even more significantly, at the terminus of this penetrating journey lies not a woman, but a man. In marrying George's substitute, Robert is able to acceptably release the fever that has contaminated his body, restoring his own health and the health of the social body. Fortunately for Robert's fragile mental health, he is not confronted with the final horror of pursuing George down into the well, the womblike opening half-hidden on the Audley estate into which the mermaid has propelled her tiresome first husband. George has, in fact, birthed himself, ably midwived by Luke, who brings home this "gentleman . . . wet through to the skin, and . . . covered with . . . slime . . . like a child . . . and helpless as any baby" (419-24). Robert and Clara, newly married, spend their honeymoon recovering his newborn body, very much alive, from abroad. At the novel's end, George lives on, unmarried, with Robert and his own sister in a rather peculiar *menage a trois.*

Interestingly, although Robert's unhealthy attraction to the Lady is replaced by an ostensibly healthier desire for Clara/ George, this transition from indifference to women at the beginning of the novel to marriage at the end is marked by an increasing dislike for women. As Robert Audley journeys toward knowledge, he comes both to denounce women and to associate them with evil:

> The Eastern potentate who declared that women were at the bottom of all mischief should have gone a little further and seen why it is so. It is because women are *never lazy.* They are Semiramides, and Cleopatras, and Joan of Arcs, Queen Elizabeths, and Catherine the Seconds, and they riot in battle, and murder, and clamour, and desperation. . . . To call them the weaker sex is to utter a hideous mockery . . . I hate women.
>
> (207)

One irony in his growing animosity for women is that it is his own femininity that he is rejecting, and must reject, in order to take on the active masculine role as judge of Lady Audley, head of household, husband, etc. To become a fit husband, he must come to associate femininity in an active state with evil, since women are to be passive, and let men act out social ambitions. Thus, it is through Clara Talboys's strength that Robert pursues Lady Audley; her strength is precisely that she can drive a man to do what

she wants to do while she remains ostensibly passive under the rule of a dictatorial father. For Robert, women are evil when they have masculine ambitions and take on masculine roles; paradoxically, it is precisely because he does not have these characteristics that he finds them hateful. Yet the women who really do evil in *Lady Audley's Secret*—Lady Audley and Phoebe—do not do so out of a desire for leadership, but out of a desire to avoid the pain inflicted by an active masculine element (e.g., Captain Maldon, Luke) and to seek passive comfort in the socially and financially secure role of wife. Thus, contrary to Robert's perception, Lady Audley's story shows that women are most evil when they conform to social expectations—a lesson which Robert must deny if he is to take his place as an active member of the ruling class.

Like the relationship between Lucy's body and that of Sir Michael, the intersection of the two narratives is defined by disease. It is the "fever" of sexual passion that brings the patriarch and the Lady together; wherever difference exists between the two interacting stories that cannot be hidden, there is the disease of madness. As Jacques Sarano argues, disease defines our bodies as both part of the self and alienated from it through the experience of pain (53-54). Robert Audley discovers himself as a member of the patriarchal social body through the pain of contact with one alienated from it. If a healthy body is a body all of whose component parts are telling the same story, without dissonance then the healthy body is a body largely unconscious of that story as a story—it seems a truth that requires no telling. The healthy body is unconscious of its components because it experiences itself as a unity. That unity is violated when one component of the body tells a different story than the whole. (Cancer, for example, is a kind of counternarrative to the narrative of the healthy body.) On the social level, Lady Audley's story must be absorbed into the overall narrative of the healthy social body, if unity is to be maintained. If her story cannot be "absorbed" or healed in this manner, then it must be excised or expelled from the body in order to maintain its unity and health. Robert becomes the sanitary policeman whose task it is to escort the seductive vector of disease to the appropriate lock hospital, risking infection by the contact (and in fact becoming infected with a mild case of madness), excising the Lady neatly from the afflicted area.[9] Sir Michael does his part by refusing to speak of "that person" again, or to know what has been done with her (399), refusing the possibility of any further contamination by her separate story. Every effort is made to restore the unity of the body, the integrity of the epic narrative, to reduce Lady Audley to a representation having no subjectivity, no story of her own. But in any surgery, there is bound to be a scar, a mute testimonial to the vulnerability of the body and the possibility of other stories, just as the epic ending of *Lady Audley's Secret* does not and cannot negate the subversive insistence of the Lady's voice.

Just as desire mediates thematically between the two narratives, the detective plot mediates structurally. The detective story, with its emphasis on the production of knowledge and the rules which govern that production, is particularly appropriate in a novel that dramatizes the slippery nature of truth and its dependence on point of view. We might expect that the detective plot, by emphasizing how knowledge is to be gained and evaluated, would help us to choose between the two principal narratives' arguments. However, if we look past the constant references to the "chain of evidence" and Robert's activities, we find that, in fact, most of Robert's deductions are wrong, his actions yield little knowledge, and, in fact, most of what he is able to use comes to him by chance or through the intervention of other women (e.g., Clara, Miss Tonks). In fact, what he is able to deduce is as likely to be false as true—such as the "death" of George.

There are also important distinctions between Robert and the traditional detective. The detective is usually an outsider, who represents an objective principle of justice and is unwavering in his quest. Perhaps because of this quality, the detective is often a static character, who does not change or learn in the process of his pursuit, and to the extent that he does, such growth is subordinated to the reader's interest in the unfolding of the mystery which is the object of his detection. He uses his will and his reason to pursue his cause. In *Lady Audley's Secret,* however, the reader knows almost from the beginning the general solution to the mystery, if not the details, and Robert Audley changes and grows considerably in the course of the novel; in fact, Robert's growth is one of its primary foci. He is motivated by a personal interest and often questions both the means and the ends of his detecting. Finally, again, his detection is based on chance and what he calls "Providence" and what Braddon frankly labels monomania.

The detective plot is, in fact, an anti-detective story.[10] Robert Audley is (literally) invested in not-knowing. He is perhaps the only detective in fiction who consistently enjoins his informants *not* to tell him the truth; he declines to take advantage of the drunkenness of Maldon or the innocence of Georgey, and he begs Luke Marks not to reveal his secret, under the mistaken impression that Marks will simply repeat the details of the "murder," when in fact what Marks is able to tell him (after some difficulty in overcoming Robert's reluctance to hear it) is that George is still alive. Robert Audley regrets that "a hand that is stronger than my own is beckoning me onward upon the dark road" and implores Clara to let him drop the investigation: "If you knew what misery to me may be involved in discovering the truth . . . you would scarcely ask me to pursue this business any further" (199). His role as a gentleman and member of the ruling class dictates that truth be subordinated to the appropriateness of the means of producing knowledge, even if that means creating falsehood. Thus, Robert's detection takes place in spite of, rather than as a result of, his methods. Given these deviations from the generic norm, Braddon's detective plot dramatizes less the process of producing knowledge than it does the inability to know.

The complementarity of the two principal narratives is underscored by the similarity of the two protagonists. Robert Audley, indolent and comfort loving, presented as something of an exquisite, is first presented as largely unmoved by women, especially his pretty cousin, Alicia, who annoys him with her exuberant energy and strong affections. Robert affects foppish "turn-down collars," surrounds himself in his rooms with flowers, songbirds, and stray dogs, and rides the fringes of the hunt to avoid being in at the death. This portrait borders on what Freud would later call "inversion" and is certainly at the very least laced with feminine characteristics, as many critics have observed.[11] In fact, the person Robert Audley resembles most is not any of his blood relatives, but his relative by marriage, Lady Audley, vain, comfort-loving, lazy, and an avid reader of French novels, as is Robert. The first person for whom we see Robert Audley having strong feelings is a male, his old Eton schoolmate, George Talboys. When George discovers that his wife is "dead," Robert takes him into his home and nurses him, and they become constant companions. Although Robert twice claims that he is falling in love with his aunt, and compares himself to the hero of a French novel in so doing, all his concern is for George:

> If anyone had ventured to tell Mr. Robert Audley that he could possibly feel a strong attachment to any creature breathing, that cynical gentleman would have elevated his eyebrows. . . . Yet here he was, flurried and anxious, bewildering his brain by all manner of conjectures about his missing friend, and, false to every attribute of his nature, walking fast.
>
> "I haven't walked fast since I was at Eton," he murmured.
>
> (82)

Robert marvels at the strength of his emotions—"To think that it is possible to care so much for a fellow!" (89)—and determines to go to "the very end of the world," if he must, to find him. It seems evident that Robert does not so much love Lady Audley as he *is like* Lady Audley—even the object of his affection was once the object of Lady Audley's similar care as her first husband.

Braddon is clearly on dangerous ground here; she can allow Robert to pursue romantically neither his aunt nor his childhood pal. However, instead of taking the ready-made alternative and matching him to his cousin, as foreshadowed throughout the novel, she introduces another character in the second volume: Clara Talboys, George's look-alike sister. This woman acts as a substitute for George, as Robert muses, "It's comfortable, but it seems so d—d lonely tonight. If poor George were sitting opposite to me, or—or even George's sister—she's very like him—existence might be a little more endurable" (208).

Ultimately, Robert will marry this acceptable substitute, and George, found again, will live with the couple. In all ways, Robert replaces Lady Audley—as George's companion, and as the ostensibly normal center of a normal family group, whose mind has yet "trembled on the balance" between sanity and insanity. In short, Braddon takes great pains to show the similarity of Lady and Robert Audley's natures and tendencies; it is the circumstances, not the individuals, which are different. Robert, a privileged male brought up with a great deal of freedom and luxury, is tolerated as a likeable eccentric, and never faces any circumstances which would make him liable to unacceptable behavior. Lady Audley, on the other hand, has little freedom and faces great hardship, and, had the crisis of George's unexpected return never occurred, would probably, as she says to Sir Michael, have been "a good woman for the rest of my life" (354). She does exactly as she is supposed to do, marry well, and as a result is abandoned, penniless, with a young child. She attempts to work to support her family, and her drunken father gambles her earnings away. Desperate, she leaves the child with her father, runs away to earn her living independently under a different name, and sends money back to support her child. These might be read as the actions of a hero, not a villain. (It is, in fact, quite parallel to George's abandonment of her and their child in the "heroic quest" for success in the gold fields of Australia.) Believing herself widowed, she marries again without disclosing her true identity, which is her first crime, and one which is at least explicable within the mores of middle class society, if not morally justifiable. It is not until her new identity is threatened that she becomes a true villain, and resorts to attempted murder. Between the law as represented in the person of Robert Audley and the chaotic madness of Lady Audley lies only a difference of circumstance; their natures are the same.

Braddon's purpose in drawing the characters so identically becomes clear in light of her references to the role of the artist. Several times, Braddon refers to the Pre-Raphaelites and their paintings in characterizing Lady Audley's appearance; the most pointed of these is her description of the full-length portrait by which George first recognizes her. The portrait is a perfect likeness, and yet seems very unlike the Lady in its hard, cruel, almost demonic expression. Alicia suggests that

> sometimes a painter is in a manner inspired, and is able to see, through a normal expression of the face, another expression that is equally a part of it, though not to be perceived by common eyes. *We* have never seen my Lady look as she does in that picture; but I think she *could* look so.
>
> (72)

Robert responds with a plea not to be so "German. . . . The picture is—the picture and my Lady is—my Lady. That's my way of taking things, and I'm not metaphysical; don't unsettle me" (72). The unsettling truth here is that the artist is indeed exposing a hidden reality; underneath the "normal" face of society and its laws is another visage, one normally hidden from the gaze of people like the Audleys, but one that the poverty-stricken and the dispossessed know only too well. In Lucy Audley/Helen Maldon, the two faces really do coexist; in Robert Audley, the potential lies just below the surface, unrealized because of his masculine and class entitlements to security and luxury. It is this coexistence that cannot be tolerated. Braddon's

portrait shows not only that the Lady "*could* look so," but that, from an (im)proper perspective, so could Robert. Yet in his separation of the real Lady Audley and the degenerate popular ("Pre-Raphaelite") representation, he gets it all wrong; it is the epic performance of identity, "My Lady," which is false, while the "odd" portrait he dislikes (71) is the truer one.

Insanity, Braddon implies, is the result of the denial of exactly the coexistence of Other narratives with the dominant ones—of violence and suppression inherent in the creation of the idyll. Although she gives the reader current scientific information about madness through the voice of Lady Audley, throughout the novel she reserves comments regarding the ubiquitous nature of madness to her own narrative voice, linking madness and violence specifically to calm, placid surfaces and idealized images:

> We hear every day of murders committed in the country. Brutal and treacherous murders; slow, protracted agonies from poisons administered by some kindred hand; sudden and violent deaths by cruel blows, inflicted with a stake cut from some spreading oak, whose very shadow promised—peace. In the country of which I write, I have been shown a meadow in which, on a quiet summer Sunday evening, a young farmer had murdered the girl who loved and trusted him; and yet even now, with the stain of that foul deed upon it, the aspect of the spot is—peace. No crime has ever been committed in the worst rookeries about Seven Dials that has not been also done in the face of that sweet rustic calm which still, in spite of all, we look on with a tender, half-mournful yearning, and associate with—peace.
>
> (54)

Here is clearly one characteristic of sensational literature—the location of crime and intrigue in the idealized domestic setting.[12] The explosion of distinctions between the "degenerate" urban and "idyllic" rural landscape, however, and explicit association of evil with male violence against women are not as often remarked, yet Braddon repeatedly refers to them, as when Phoebe explains that she must marry Luke because she is afraid that he will kill her otherwise (107). In short, the source of danger is precisely in the willingness of the reader to accept the idealized, "epic" representation: the artist's job (specifically, the popular novelist's) is to expose the transgression latent in the narratives of the ideal.

Robert's recognition of a reality which contradicts the ideal leads him dangerously near madness. First Harcourt Talboys accuses him of madness (192), then Lady Audley (278), and finally Sir Michael (285). When Robert Audley begins to have hallucinations, immediately after incarcerating Lady Audley, Braddon speaks directly:

> Do not laugh at poor Robert. . . . There is nothing so delicate, so fragile, as that invisible balance upon which the mind is always trembling. Mad today and sane tomorrow. . . . Who has not been, or is not to be, mad in some lonely hour of life? Who is quite safe from the trembling of the balance?
>
> (404)

At the very point at which the madness is contained, the Lady locked away forever (in France, amusingly enough, surgically excised from the "clean and proper" body of England), Braddon speaks directly to shatter that containment, reminding us that not only is madness ubiquitous, but that the very man who judges Lady Audley is himself mad, placing him and the reader and the Lady in the same category, "trembling on the balance."

Lady Audley's secret, of course, is not her prior marriage, alcoholic father, hidden child, or even her series of attempted murders; it is her madness that she so carefully conceals. However, recent critical consensus has dismissed this "insanity," seeing in it merely a convenient device for explaining away perfectly rational behavior unacceptable in a female protagonist. Braddon's ironic references to the madness that lives in all of us certainly undercut the definition of Lucy as mad. As early as Chapter One, she stresses the socially constructed nature of "mad" behavior and shows Lucy's decision to wed Michael Audley as very sane behavior:

> It was a tacitly understood thing in the surgeon's family that whenever Sir Michael proposed, the governess would quietly accept him; and, indeed, the simple Dawsons would have thought it something more than madness in a penniless girl to reject such an offer.
>
> (9)

From the perspective of the lower middle class, marriage is a largely financial arrangement into which love enters as a happy afterthought. Sir Michael, on the other hand, is "disappointed . . . as if he carried a corpse in his bosom" when Lucy tells him plainly both that she does not love him and that she "cannot be disinterested" in the financial aspects of his proposal. Nonetheless, he demonstrates a remarkable flexibility; having said a few moments before Lucy's announcement that he thinks it is the greatest possible "sin" for a woman to marry a man she does not love, he states immediately afterward that he sees no reason, so long as she loves no one else, "why we should not make a very happy couple. Is it a bargain, Lucy?" (11). Later, however, Braddon speculates that he had never really trusted her since that moment. Where Michael Audley fails is in his inability to enforce the representation of the pure woman as marrying for affection, and as ignorant and unconcerned with crassly material issues like wealth. The problem here is not so much that Lucy does think the way she does; it is that he allows her to think this way, knowingly collaborating in her violation of socially approved representations of bridehood by using a term like "bargain" to refer to their marriage. He endangers himself by using language that recasts his own role as a character in her narrative, rather than insisting on preserving the integrity of her representation within his narrative. The epic narrative rights itself by re-representing Lucy as the deceptive and dangerous syren—the only representation which can contain a woman like Lucy when she steps out of her role as the adoring wife.

However, when the Lady speaks, instead of preserving a well-bred silence, we see a woman who has tried to be principled—working as a governess, sending money for her son, attempting to be honest with Sir Michael about her motives for marrying him. She feels guilt, and wonders if she is "*really* wicked," or merely thoughtless (297). Braddon writes not of a "mermaid" who is innately evil, but of a person raised to have certain ambitions without the means of satisfying them, a person who has been driven to desperation by adversity and the betrayals of comparatively powerful males who failed to meet their obligations to her. Through the stories of Lady Audley and Phoebe, the reader is given details about life in the lower classes, the vicissitudes of poverty and legal powerlessness and the practical consequences of hunger which are unknown to the male characters in the novel. In short, Braddon gives Lady Audley what no syren has ever had: a history, out of which a complex character with complex motivations may be constructed by the reader—if she or he chooses to do so.

"My secrets are every body's secrets" says Lucy bitterly (300). Although she is referring to her own lack of privacy, another meaning is suggested as well—Lady Audley's Secret is society's dirty little secret, and Robert's epic narrative depends on how well he can keep this secret once he had discovered it. His "sanity," the coherence of his epic identity, depends on how well he can resist the urge to read Lady Audley on her own terms, as a character in her own story, one who has a history, who has tried to play by the rules and implicitly critiques those rules merely both by articulating them so baldly (and thus calling attention to their arbitrary and artificial nature) and by citing their failure to work. He must read her only as a mermaid, a representation who has no existence separate from her relation to the epic text. To the extent that he fails to do this, he is mad. He regains his sanity by locking her away and her secret with her, protecting the Audley identity from scandal and the epic narrative from the intrusion of the voice of the Other. Victorian readers, presented with a choice of narratives, which is also a choice of tasks, chose Robert's and cried out against the possibility of choosing the other, which would entail formulating a critique of a social narrative which creates Lady Audleys and then refuses to grant them recognition. Yet the existence of Lady Audley's narrative demands that the novel itself be classified as sensational, subversive and unhealthy. Even after being locked away, Lady Audley exerts her fascination; the reader cannot quite walk away from the text with the feeling that justice has been done. Like Robert, the reader leaves Lady Audley in her *maison de sante* too late to escape the taint of madness, the essential fascination of sensational literature—the possibility that there is another reality to know.

Notes

1. Novels designated as "high(er)" culture in this period can largely be described as what Frye would later call the "high mimetic mode."

2. It is important to remember that the novel itself was seen as a "low" cultural form until the advent of

modernism. However, as critics came to realize that the novel was, however vulgar, the dominant literary form of their period, some began to distinguish between novels that either elevated taste or were harmless, and those that were actively harmful. Cf. "English Realism and Romance," "Literary Exhaustion," and Harrison's "On the Choice of Books" for some examples.

3. As has been extensively discussed. See Loesberg; Boyle; and Hughes for analysis. The following are some good examples of such criticism: "Contemporary Literature"; "Literary Voluptuaries"; "On the Reading of Books"; "Penny Fiction"; "The Literature of the Streets"; "The Vice of Reading"; Humphery's "The Reading of the Working Class"; and the infamous review by Margaret Oliphant.

4. The metaphoric linkages of reading and eating have been explored in some detail by Ross and more broadly by Kilgour.

5. The frame I am using here is a critical reinterpretation of Bakhtin in the light of work done by Foucault and other, later, theorists of the body. Bakhtin makes the case in *The Dialogic Imagination* that the difference between the "epic" and the "novel" is that epic (monovocal) narrative tends to confirm the status quo and that the novel, by virtue of its polyvocality, tends to challenge it. In *Rabelais and His World* he argues that the grotesque or open body celebrated in carnival challenges the "closed," controlled body which represents power. Both of these ideas have been critiqued for offering a naive vision of resistance. See, for example, Todorov and also Stallybrass and White. However, the epic and "novelistic" as defined by Bakhtin can indeed be seen as *properties* of texts (rather than types), some texts (and genres) being more readily assimilable to the epic *purpose*. In so far as this epic purpose—that of confirmation of the existing power structure—can be identified with the regulation (disciplining) of the body as Foucault has defined it in *Discipline and Punish,* we can identify the epic with closure of the body, and subversive (carnivalesque) popular form with the grotesque or open body. The openness of the body emphasizes its dependence on Others and on context—in short, its vulnerability. The tendency to identify the independent, closed, invulnerable body with the project of self-discipline demanded by the privileged discourses of modernism has been extensively discussed and historicized by theorists of the body; see, for example, Elias and also Falk.

6. This, of course, despite the fact that the Other provides the necessary basis for the definition of the Self—just as *Lady Audley's Secret,* a sensational novel, dramatizes the suppression of sensation.

7. Pykett does not follow up on this observation with an enquiry into the structure or referents of this epic, as her argument leads elsewhere. However, her suggestion that the quest is "knightly" and "chivalric," although interesting, tends to obscure and ignore the deliberately classical referents of the Ulysses story, which, like Braddon's, rewards Clara/Penelope with her unraveling basket of yarn and kills Lucy/Melantho—whereas the death of the enchantress is generally proscribed in the logic of chivalric romance.

8. For more on literary and artistic manifestations of the mermaid in Victorian and fin-de-siecle culture, see Dijkstra.

9. This metaphor is slightly anachronistic. The earliest of the Contagious Diseases Acts which deals with the regulation of prostitutes will not be passed until 1864, two years after the publication of *Lady Audley's Secret.* However, I wish here to suggest that the Contagious Diseases Acts are the legal expression of precisely the same anxieties traceable in the novel.

10. It is for this reason that I disagree with Cvetovich's critique of Showalter's reading. Cvetovich argues that the subversiveness of Braddon's portrayal of Lady Audley's cannot overcome the work of the detective plot (as Miller argues of the detective plot in *Bleak House*) to "contribute to . . . dominant ideology . . . [by its tendency to solve] complex social problems by rewriting them in simpler terms" (50-51). Miller's excellent analysis is inapplicable here, precisely because this is not a conventional detective plot.

11. Cf. Showalter; Cvetkovich, for examples.

12. See Hughes; Boyle.

Works Cited

Bakhtin, M. M. *The Dialogic Imagination: Four Essays.* Trans. C. Emerson and Michael Holquist. Ed. Michael Holquist. Austin: U of Texas P, 1981.

———. *Rabelais and His World.* Trans. Helene Iswolsky. Bloomington: Indiana UP, 1984.

Boyle, Thomas. *Black Swine in the Sewers of Hampstead: Beneath the Surface of Victorian Sensationalism.* New York: Viking, 1989.

Braddon, Mary Elizabeth. *Lady Audley's Secret.* Ed. David Skilton. New York: Oxford UP, 1987.

Brooks, Peter. *Body Work.* London: Harvard UP, 1983.

"Contemporary Literature." *Blackwood's* 125 (1879): 322-44.

Cvetovitch, Ann. *Mixed Feelings: Feminism, Mass Culture and Victorian Sensationalism.* New Brunswick, NJ: Rutgers UP, 1992.

Dijkstra, Bram. *Idols of Perversity: Fantasies of Feminine Evil in Fin de Siecle Culture.* New York: Oxford UP, 1986.

Elias, Norbert. *Power and Civility: The Civilizing Process.* 1939. Oxford: Blackwell, 1982. "English Realism and Romance." *Quarterly Review* 173 (1891): 468-94.

Falk, Pasi. *The Consuming Body.* London: Sage, 1995.

Frye, Northrop. *The Anatomy of Criticism.* Princeton, NJ: Princeton UP, 1957.

Harrison, Frederic. "On the Choice of Books." *Fortnightly Review* 31 (1879): 491-512.

Hughes, Winifred. *The Maniac in the Cellar: Sensational Novels in the 1860s.* Princeton, NJ: Princeton UP, 1980.

Humphery, George R. "The Reading of the Working Classes." *The Nineteenth Century* 33 (1893): 690-701.

"Literary Exhaustion." *Cornhill Magazine* 22 (1870): 285-96.

"Literary Voluptuaries." *Blackwood's* 142 (1887): 805-17.

"The Literature of the Streets." *Edinburgh Review* 165 (1887): 40-65.

Kilgour, Maggie. *From Communion to Cannibalism: An Anatomy of Metaphors of Incorporation.* Princeton, NJ: Princeton UP, 1990.

Miller, D. A. *The Novel and the Police.* Berkeley: U of California P, 1988.

Oliphant, Margaret. "Novels." *Blackwood's* 102 (1867): 257-80.

"On the Reading of Books." *Temple Bar* 72 (1884): 178-86.

"Penny Fiction." *Quarterly Review* 171 (1890): 149-71.

Pykett, Lyn. "'The Improper' Feminine: The Women's Sensation Novel and the New Woman Motif." London: Routledge, 1992.

Ross, Catherine Sheldrick. "Metaphors of Reading." *Journal of Library History, Philosophy, and Comparative Librarianship* 22 (1987): 147-63.

Sarano, Jacques. *The Meaning of the Body.* Trans. James H. Farley. Philadelphia: Westminster P, 1966.

"Sensation Novels." *Quarterly Review* 113 (1863): 481-515.

Showalter, Elaine. *A Literature of Their Own: British Women Novelists from Brontë to Lessing.* Princeton, NJ: Princeton UP, 1977.

Stallybrass, Peter and Allon White. *The Politics of Poetics and Transgression.* Ithaca: Cornell UP, 1986.

Todorov, Tzvetan. *Mikhail Bakhtin: The Dialogical Principle.* Trans. Wlad Godzich. *Theory and History of Literature* 13. Minneapolis: U of Minnesota P, 1984.

"The Vice of Reading." *Temple Bar* 42 (1874): 251-57.

Pamela K. Gilbert (essay date 1997)

SOURCE: "M. E. Braddon: Sensational Realism," in *Disease, Desire, and the Body in Victorian Women's Popular Novels,* Cambridge University Press, 1997, pp. 92-112.

[*In the following essay, Gilbert examines the ways in which Braddon molded her public image through her use of various literary genres and tropes.*]

M. E. Braddon (1835-1915), certainly one of the most prolific authors and editors of the period, is central to any understanding of the Victorian novel. Although she came to the middle-class public's attention with **Lady Audley's Secret** and **Aurora Floyd** in 1862, in fact she had been writing for six years. Braddon's production encompasses over seventy novels, many short stories, plays, essays, and the editorship of several journals, most notably *Belgravia* and *The Mistletoe Bough.*

Braddon's understanding of the book trade in which and by which she lived is clear-eyed, canny, and comprehensive. Unlike Rhoda Broughton, who had a comfortable social position independent of her literary earnings, Braddon supported herself, her family, and her lover's family by her literary activities. After being "typecast" as The Sensation Novelist after her early two bestsellers—a designation which itself is open to inquiry—Braddon found herself in active competition with the public and critical construction of her and her early work for control of the generic designation and market placement of her many other novels. In the sensation novel, the woman's body is clearly foregrounded. However, in her later novels of any genre, Braddon's constant rewriting of her own position in the marketplace and use of multiple genres to manipulate her placement brings her inevitably back to the woman's body as a site of reading and generic designation. Her reading of the place of the woman's body, as reader, author, and text, forms the substance of her rewriting of *Madame Bovary,* **The Doctor's Wife,** in which she comments on the place of literature, literary genres, the market, and reading practices.

In fact, Braddon produced in many genres, most deliberately in sensation/melodrama (especially after **Lady Audley's Secret** and **Aurora Floyd** were so successful under that designation) and in the realist tradition, which Braddon viewed as the "high" culture novel, in common with the critical view emerging at that time. (She also wrote ghost stories, which are beginning to garner a fair amount of attention now, as the Victorian short story and gothic both receive the attention due them.) Realism comes to be understood as a genre which constructs itself on the basis of difference from the popular, and thus, as a genre which relies on framing the body in more careful, more nuanced and less spec(tac)ular ways.

Braddon, like Charles Dickens, is less interested in character *per se* than in social situations, although she comes to have more interest in character and interiority in her later works. Her work is carefully plotted, and plot, rather than character, tends to motivate the action and support the story. Braddon's exploitation of the trope of woman's body as text and text as body within her novels as part of an ongoing dialogue with the critical commentary surrounding popular fiction blurs, while seeming to reinforce, the boundaries between commodity, artistic statement and critical policing. The epic task is always closure of the woman's body, whose openness creates danger for those around her and, if she is a "good" character, for her as well. Contradicting, reinforcing, or subverting that narrative line run other tales, other genres embedded in the same text, sometimes the same flesh: Lady Audley's body is contained, but the social circumstances which produce her are not controlled—rather the opposite. Protean, Braddon as editor, critic, artist, and purveyor of highly successful commodities vanishes behind and manipulates her various personae in public life and their spokescharacters within her texts to create and maintain a space in which she attempts to direct reading practices.

LADY AUDLEY'S SECRET[1]

Lady Audley's Secret is often accused of or credited with laying the foundation for the sensation novel, and yet the text undermines that foundation at the same moment. Lady Audley, her secret, and her deeds form the sensational story that mark the novel's genre, yet the forced growth of Robert Audley and the masculinization of his character constitute an equal and complementary counter-narrative to Lady Audley's tale, which itself subverts the "return to order" which marks the sensation genre and relocates the source of sensation from the disordered and alien individual female body to the male social body of the patriarchal socio-legal institutions. These elements coexist in the text, yet only the former structure was "selected" by readers as a generic property; critics expressed outrage over the portrayal of the alienated woman and entirely missed the much more subversive portrait of alienated patriarchy. Robert Audley, the Temple Bar lawyer who has never submitted a brief, Lieutenant Maldon, who sells his daughter to the highest bidder and drinks the proceeds, George Talboys, who abandons his wife and baby son, and even Sir Michael Audley, whose love-"fever" drives him to take a wife who admittedly does not love him—these are the aristocratic and generally privileged men who set the events of the story in motion. Robert Audley finally rouses himself from his habitual lethargy to pursue the "madwoman" and himself becomes mad in the process. This madness is "healed" when he takes as a wife Clara, George's sister. The mad wife is replaced by the mad husband, whose madness is more acceptable to society, but it is made perfectly clear that the social order is both artificial and a mere mask for the chaos or "madness" beneath. Thus the story is less one of Lady Audley's disguised madness (as Dr. Mosgrave says, "There is no madness in anything she has done" [***Lady Audley's Secret,*** p. 377]), than one of Robert Audley's recognition of his own insanity and of the mad nature of his society, and of his subsequent informed choice to remain complicit in that madness and to become active in supporting it.

Throughout the novel, Braddon offers observations on the nature of insanity. Although she gives the reader current medical and scientific information about madness through the voice of Lady Audley, she reserves comments regarding the ubiquitous nature of madness to her own narrative voice, linking madness and violence specifically to calm, placid surfaces and idealized images:

> We hear every day of murders committed in the country. Brutal and treacherous murders; slow, protracted agonies from poisons administered by some kindred hand; sudden and violent deaths by cruel blows, inflicted with a stake cut from some spreading oak, whose very shadow promised—peace. In the county of which I write, I have been shown a meadow in which, on a quiet summer Sunday evening, a young farmer had murdered the girl who loved and trusted him; and yet even now, with the stain of that foul deed upon it, the aspect of the spot is—peace. No crime has ever been committed in the worst rookeries about Seven Dials that has not been also done in the face of that sweet rustic calm which still, in spite of all, we look on with a tender, half-mournful yearning, and associate with—peace.

> (p. 54)

Here is clearly one characteristic of sensation literature—the location of crime and intrigue in the idealized domestic setting. The explosion of distinctions between the "degenerate" urban and "idyllic" rural landscape, however, and explicit association of evil with male violence against women are not as often remarked, yet Braddon repeatedly refers to them, as when Phoebe explains that she must marry Luke because she is afraid that he will kill her otherwise (p. 107).

When Robert Audley begins to have hallucinations, immediately after incarcerating Lady Audley, Braddon speaks directly again: "Do not laugh at poor Robert. . . . There is nothing so delicate, so fragile, as that invisible balance upon which the mind is always trembling. Mad today and sane tomorrow. . . . Who has not been, or is not to be, mad in some lonely hour of life? Who is quite safe from the trembling of the balance?" (p. 404). At the very point at which the madness is contained, the Lady locked away forever (in "France", amusingly enough, surgically excised from the "clean and proper" body of England), Braddon speaks directly to shatter that containment, reminding us that not only is madness ubiquitous, but that the very man who judges Lady Audley is himself mad, placing him and the reader and the Lady in the same category, "trembling on the balance."

As Robert Audley journeys toward knowledge, and suspects that the aunt with whom he has fallen in love is a murderess, like Hamlet he comes both to denounce women and to associate them with evil:

> The Eastern potentate who declared that women were at the bottom of all mischief should have gone a little further and seen why it is so. It is because women are *never lazy.* They are Semiramides, and Cleopatras, and Joan of Arcs, Queen Elizabeths, and Catherine the Seconds, and they riot in battle, and murder, and clamour, and desperation. . . . To call them the weaker sex is to utter a hideous mockery . . . I hate women.

> (p. 207)

The more he misses George, and is attracted to George's lookalike sister Clara, the more he rails against women in general. One irony in his growing animosity toward women is that it is his own femininity that he is rejecting, and must reject, in order to take on the active masculine role as judge of Lady Audley, head of household, husband, etc. To become a fit husband, he must come to associate femininity in an active state with evil, since women are to be passive and let men act out social ambitions. Thus, it is through Clara Talboys' strength that Robert pursues Lady Audley; her strength is precisely that she can drive a man to do what she wants to do while she remains ostensibly passive under the rule of a dictatorial father. For Robert, women are evil when they have masculine ambitions and take on masculine roles; paradoxically, it is precisely because he does not have these characteristics that he finds them hateful. Yet the women who really do evil in *Lady Audley's Secret*—Lady Audley and Phoebe—do not do so out of a desire for leadership, but out of a desire to avoid the pain inflicted by an active masculine element (Lieutenant Maldon, Luke) and to seek passive comfort in the socially and financially secure role of wife. Thus, contrary to Robert's perception, Lady Audley's story shows that women are most evil when they conform to social expectations—a lesson which Robert must deny if he is to take his place as an active male member of the ruling class. By the end of the novel, he has successfully done both.

Thus, the novel simultaneously presents and validates two contradictory points of view, in two complementary storylines: the coming of age and social integration of Robert Audley, a traditional high-culture theme, and the decline and fall of the scheming adventuress, a popular culture melodrama. This second plot exceeds the bounds of the usual "adventuress" narrative in that the lady speaks for herself, and in that she does not present herself wholly as a villainess. Together, these two narratives create a dramatic tension born of the ideological contradictions in their mutually exclusive portrayals of feminine evil, a third rhetorical space in which the coherence of the oppositions which drive either of the first two narratives unravel into incoherence, the madness which is finally located and at least superficially contained in the imprisoned bodies of the Maldon women.

Critics have often noted the detective plot in *Lady Audley's Secret,* setting up the opposition between Robert and the Lady as detective and arch-criminal. There are, however, important distinctions between Robert and the traditional detective. The detective is usually an outsider, who represents an objective principle of justice and is unwavering in his quest. Perhaps because of this quality, he is usually a static character, who does not change or learn in the process of his pursuit, and to the extent that he does, such growth is subordinated to the reader's interest in the unfolding of the mystery which is the object of his detection. He uses his will and his reason to pursue his cause. In *Lady Audley's Secret,* however, the reader knows almost from the beginning the general solution to the mystery, if

not the details, and Robert Audley changes and grows considerably in the course of the novel; in fact, Robert's growth is one of its primary foci. He is motivated by a personal interest and often questions both the means and the ends of his detecting. Finally, his detection is based on chance and what he calls "Providence" and what Braddon frankly labels monomania.

If we ignore the Lady Audley storyline momentarily, and consider only the Robert Audley storyline, the pattern of the coming-of-age story appears clear. Braddon uses the traditional model of *The Odyssey,* first referring to Odysseus explicitly to set the stage, and then interpreting the story loosely to fit her needs, combining Telemachus' character with Odysseus' journey. A young male character on the brink of manhood has not yet accepted adult responsibilities. He is called a barrister, yet has never submitted a brief. He prefers the company of his male schoolfriends to women, and regards marriage with consternation. He is content to "play" and let others manage the serious business of life. Into this Edenic peace comes conflict. The boy must take adult responsibilities, must act and make decisions. The hero's descent into hell is represented, as it often is in modern literature, by a crisis of values, an episode of madness. At the story's end he has withstood the temptations of the mermaid, come through the dark night of the soul, rescued the patriarch of his family, and returned home to take his own place as husband, father, and powerful leader of the community (distinguished by his successful prosecution of a breach of promise case—a typical bit of Braddon irony). In short, Robert Audley is a Telemachus of recognizable form, if diminutive proportions, faithful himself to the social order and ready to punish those who stray from the code.

Braddon makes the Odyssey comparison early in the story. George Talboys' first description of his wife to Robert describes her playing a guitar and singing: "She's for all the world like one of those what's-its-names, who got poor old Ulysses in trouble" (p. 35). Throughout the novel, Lady Audley is associated with the ocean, and we are informed that George first met her at the end of a pier (p. 247). It is perhaps not coincidental that she pushes him into a well (a pocket-version of the ocean which he crosses to find her), which he survives largely because there is no water in it. Robert dreams of Audley Court "threatened by the rapid rising of a boisterous sea . . . the sleeper saw a pale, starry face looking out of the silvery foam, and knew that it was my lady, transformed into a mermaid, beckoning his uncle to destruction" (p. 246). Although mermaids are not unique to *The Odyssey,* the initial comparison recalls their function specifically as impediments to the hero's journey. (For more on literary and artistic manifestations of the mermaid in Victorian and *fin-de-siècle* culture, see Bram Dijkstra's *Idols of Perversity.*)

However, Robert Audley's story does not stand alone; it runs alongside the story of the "syren" he must overcome. Braddon's radical departure from tradition is not in presenting the evil mermaid, but in giving her a voice which does not only sing sweet lies for men but tells them unpleasant truths. Lady Audley's secret is that evil does not originate in the mermaids or the Clytemnestras, but in the system of representation which makes mermaids and Clytemnestras out of the Melanthos who are pretty enough to attract male attention and unfortunate enough to have no other source of security. (It is worth noting that Braddon's rereading of *The Odyssey* occurs in the context of other Victorian rereadings, most notably Tennyson's 1842 poem. While most readers note Tennyson's construction of Ulysses as imperial hero, it is often forgotten that this Ulysses is Dante's, not Homer's, and is speaking in the moment of his damnation, that is, specifically, the moment of his betrayal of divinely ordained domestic responsibility in favor of the heroic role.)

When women like Lucy Audley are not singing and amusing men, however, they speak truths that destroy the idyllic representations of rural feminine beauty and domestic tranquillity as surely as Braddon's murder in a quiet meadow does. When Lady Audley is exposed, she speaks of her childhood:

> 'I was not happy, for the woman who had charge of me was a disagreeable woman . . . who was irregularly paid; and who vented her rage upon me when my father was behindhand in remitting her money . . . at a very early age I found out what it was to be poor' . . . He [Sir Michael] sat silent . . . he . . . had believed . . . as he had believed in the Gospel . . . a very brief story of an early orphanage, and a long quiet, colourless youth spent in the conventual seclusion of an English boarding school.
>
> (*Lady Audley's Secret*, p. 349)

Her story is most horrifying because it violates a previous narrative which is consonant with the ideal of the unsullied woman. Lady Audley goes on to discuss her fear of poverty and understanding of "what every schoolgirl knows" but none discusses—that her future will depend on a good marriage. The institution of marriage is exposed as founded on the helplessness and fear of women, rather than on love. In another scene, Phoebe is frank with Lady Audley about her own motivations for marrying: "I daren't refuse to marry him. . . . When he was a boy he was always violent and revengeful. I saw him once take up that very knife in a quarrel with his mother. I tell you, my lady, I must marry him" (p. 107). Throughout the novel, women express a clear understanding of the relations of power which underlie cultural representations while male characters prefer the "pretty stories" themselves. The contrast is neatly set up in the second chapter of the novel, "On Board the Argus." George and a "pale governess" are discussing their reasons for returning to England, and the governess explains that she has worked for fifteen years in Australia to save up enough money for her marriage to her English fiancé, who has not done well financially. She fears, however, that he may have died, or that his feelings might have changed, or even that he may marry her only for her savings. George is horrified, because, although he had abandoned his wife and never written her, these possibilities had never occurred to him. With great pride, he explains to the governess that he has worked for three and a half years to make his fortune, and finally struck gold. "How brave you were!" she responds (p. 22). Although Braddon presents the governess as sincere in her admiration, surely the reader must sense a rich irony in the disparity between the woman's fifteen years of toil and realistic assessment of the possibility of change in her fiancé, whom she recognizes as a subjectivity distinct from her own, and George's blithely unconscious self-aggrandizement and conflation of his wife's subjectivity with his two dimensional image of her. The male's "coming of age" therefore, is based on his ability not only to assume the masculine role of hero in the epic narrative that patriarchy approves, but to enforce the subordination of other voices and other subjectivities to their supporting roles in that same narrative. If Melantho's had been the narrative voice of *The Odyssey,* how differently might the story have been told!

It is, of course, sexual attraction which brings the two storylines together; first, Sir Michael's attraction to Lucy and later his nephew's. Characteristically, sexual passion is defined as a "fever," and in Lady Audley's case, great care is taken to distinguish this diseased attraction from a more ordinary, healthy love:

> What had been his (Michael Audley's) love for his first wife but a poor, pitiful, smouldering spark, too dull to be extinguished, too feeble to burn? But *this* was love— this fever, this longing, this restless, uncertain, miserable hesitation; this sick hatred of his white beard; this frenzied wish to be young again . . . Sir Michael Audley had fallen ill of the terrible fever called love.
>
> (p. 7)

Lucy, source and object of this affliction, lives as the governess to the local surgeon's children. In the governess position many oppositions meet: family and not-family, lady and working woman, mother-figure and domestic servant. In Lucy's case, the undomesticated woman is naturalized within a domestic setting; thus, her true nature is disguised and she is enabled to make contact with "good society" like Sir Michael. The source of disease is disguised within the surgeon's home, the very hearth of health. This disease is infectious; Sir Michael

> wondered why Robert failed to take the fever from the first breath of contagion that blew towards him. He forgot that there are men who go their ways unscathed amidst legions of lovely and generous women, to succumb at last before some harsh-featured virago, who knows the secret of that only philter which can intoxicate him and bewitch him. . . . He forgot that love, which is a madness, and a scourge, and a fever, and a delusion, and a snare, is also a mystery, and very imperfectly understood by everyone except the individual sufferer who writhes under its tortures . . . who lies awake at night until he loathes his comfortable pillow and tumbles his sheets into two twisted rags of linen in his agonies, as if he were a prisoner and wanted to wind them into impromptu ropes. . . . He ignored all

those infinitesimal differences in nature which make the wholesome food of one man the deadly poison of another.

(p. 332)

In this interesting series of images, we move from the disease metaphor, to a food-consumption image (the philter, the "wholesome food") to a more specifically sexual image of nocturnal crisis. Material is taken into the body, initiating an illness that cannot be healed without releasing it from the body, in this case a desire for sexual fulfillment that can only be "healed" by ejaculation into the body of the Other. Despite Sir Michael's bemusement, however, Robert has indeed been "infected."

The progress of this infection is a most curious one. Robert Audley, indolent and comfort-loving, presented as something of an exquisite, is first presented as largely unmoved by women, especially his pretty cousin, Alicia, who annoys him with her exuberant energy and strong affections. Robert affects foppish "turn-down collars," surrounds himself in his rooms with flowers, songbirds, and stray dogs, and rides the fringes of the hunt to avoid being in at the death. This portrait borders on what Freud would later call "inversion," and is certainly at the very least laced with feminine characteristics. In fact, the person Robert Audley resembles most is not any of his blood relatives, but his relative by marriage, Lady Audley, vain, comfort-loving, lazy, and an avid reader of French novels, as is Robert. The first person for whom we see Robert Audley having real feelings is a male, his old Eton schoolmate, George Talboys. When George discovers that his wife is dead, Robert takes him into his home and nurses him, and they become constant companions. Although Robert twice claims that he is falling in love with his aunt, and compares himself to the hero of a French novel in so doing, all his concern is for George:

> If anyone had ventured to tell Mr. Robert Audley that he could possibly feel a strong attachment to any creature breathing, that cynical gentleman would have elevated his eyebrows. . . . Yet here he was, flurried and anxious, bewildering his brain by all manner of conjectures about his missing friend, and, false to every attribute of his nature, walking fast.
>
> "I haven't walked fast since I was at Eton," he murmured.

(p. 82)

Robert marvels on the strength of his emotions—"To think that it is possible to care so much for a fellow!" (p. 89) and determines to go to "the very end of the world" if he must, to find him. It seems evident that Robert does not so much love Lady Audley as he *is like* Lady Audley—even the object of his "affection" was once the object of Lady Audley's similar care as her first husband.

Braddon is clearly on dangerous ground here; she can allow Robert, as a "good" character, to pursue neither his aunt nor his childhood pal. Oddly, however, instead of taking the ready-made alternative and matching him to his cousin, as foreshadowed throughout the text, she introduces another character in the second volume: Clara Talboys, George's lookalike sister. This woman acts as a substitute for George, as Robert muses, "It's comfortable, but it seems so d—d lonely tonight. If poor George were sitting opposite to me, or—or even George's sister—she's very like him—existence might be a little more endurable" (p. 208).

Ultimately, Robert will marry this acceptable substitute, and George, found again, will live with the couple. In all ways, Robert replaces Lady Audley—as George's companion, and as the ostensibly normal center of a normal family group whose mind has yet "trembled on the balance" between sanity and insanity. In fact, Braddon takes great pains to show the similarity of Lady and Robert Audley's natures and tendencies; it is the circumstances, not the individuals, which are different. Robert, a privileged male brought up with a great deal of freedom and luxury, is tolerated as a likeable eccentric, and never faces any circumstances which would make him liable to unacceptable behavior. Lady Audley, on the other hand, has little freedom and faces great hardship, and, had the crisis of George's unexpected return never occurred, would probably, as she says to Sir Michael, have been "a good woman for the rest of my life" (p. 354). She does exactly as she is supposed to do, marry well, and for this she is abandoned, penniless, with a young child. She attempts to work to support her family, and her drunken father gambles her earnings away. Desperate, she leaves the child with her father, runs away to earn her living independently under a different name, and sends money back to support her child. These might be read as the actions of a hero, not a villain. (It is, in fact, quite parallel to George's abandonment of family in the "heroic quest" for success.) Believing herself widowed, she marries again without disclosing her true identity, which is her first crime, and one which is at least explicable within the mores of middle class society, if not entirely morally justifiable. It is not until her new identity is threatened that she becomes a true villain, and resorts to attempted murder. Between the law as represented in the person of Robert Audley and the chaotic madness of Lady Audley lies only a difference of circumstance; their natures are the same.

Braddon's purpose in drawing the characters so identically becomes clear in light of her references to the role of the artist. Several times, Braddon refers to the Pre-Raphaelites and their paintings in characterizing Lady Audley's appearance; the most pointed of these is her description of the full-length portrait by which George first recognizes her. The portrait is a perfect likeness, and yet seems very unlike the Lady in its hard, cruel, almost demonic expression. Alicia suggests that, "sometimes a painter is in a manner inspired, and is able to see, through a normal expression of the face, another expression that is equally a part of it, though not to be perceived by common eyes. *We* have never seen my Lady look as she does in that picture; but I think she *could* look so" (p. 72). Robert responds with a plea not to be so "German . . . I'm not metaphysical; don't unsettle me" (p. 72). The upsetting metaphysical truth here is that the artist is indeed exposing a hidden reality; underneath the "normal" face of society and its laws is another visage, one normally hidden from the gaze of people like the Audleys, but one that the poverty-stricken and the dispossessed know only too well. In Lucy Audley/ Helen Maldon, the two faces really do coexist; in Robert Audley, the potential lies just below the surface, unrealized because of his masculine and class entitlements to security and luxury.

It is this coexistence that cannot be tolerated. If one reads **Lady Audley's Secret** as a coming-of-age novel the hero of which is Robert Audley, one may clearly see that Robert's task is to transfer his affections from unsuitable objects and turn that attraction, which is really an attraction to the unacceptable elements in his own personality, to denial. The attraction that once led Robert to violate the privacy of Lady Audley's locked rooms, burglarizing her suite in order to gaze upon her portrait and personal effects leads him to continue violating the privacy of her past in order to expose her "secret." It is significant that this obsessive pursuit generates symptomatic behavior of such a nature that the other lawyers in Robert's environment speculate that he is in love (p. 211). It is the forced "penetration" of Lady Audley's identity, prefigured in the invasion of her rooms and bonnet box, which will signify mastery over the feminine elements in Robert's own nature. Perhaps even more significantly, at the terminus of this penetrating journey lies not a woman, but a man. In marrying George's substitute, Robert is able to acceptably release the fever that has contaminated his body, restoring his own health and the health of the social body. Fortunately for Robert's fragile mental health, he is not confronted with the final horror of pursuing George down into the well, the womblike opening half-hidden on the Audley estate into which the mermaid has propelled her tiresome first husband. George has, in fact, birthed himself, ably midwived by Luke, who brings home this "gentleman as was wet through to the skin, and was covered with . . . slime . . . [who was] like a child in my hands, and helpless as any baby" (pp. 419-424). Robert and Clara, newly married, spend their honeymoon recovering his body, very much alive, from abroad.

Lady Audley's secret, of course, is not her prior marriage, alcoholic father, hidden child, or even her series of attempted murders; it is her madness that she so carefully conceals. However, many critics have questioned this "insanity," seeing in it merely a convenient device for explaining away perfectly rational behavior unacceptable in a female protagonist.[2] Braddon's ironic references to the madness that lives in all of us certainly undercut the definition of Lucy as mad. As early as Chapter One, she stresses the socially constructed nature of "mad" behavior and shows Lucy's decision to wed Michael Audley as very sane behavior: "It was a tacitly understood thing in the surgeon's family that whenever Sir Michael proposed, the governess would quietly accept him; and, indeed, the simple Dawsons would have thought it something more than madness in a penniless girl to reject such an offer" (**Lady Audley's Secret,** p. 9). From the perspective of the lower middle class, marriage is a largely financial arrangement into which love enters as a happy afterthought. Sir Michael, on the other hand, is "disappointed . . . as if he carried a corpse in his bosom" when Lucy tells him plainly both that she does not love him and that she "cannot be disinterested" in the financial aspects of his proposal. Nonetheless, he demonstrates a remarkable flexibility; having said a few moments before Lucy's announcement that he thinks it is the greatest possible "sin" for a woman to marry a man she does not love, he states immediately afterward that he sees no reason, so long as she loves no one else, "why we should not make a very happy couple. Is it a bargain, Lucy?" (p. 11). Later, however, Braddon speculates that he had never really trusted her since that moment. Where Michael Audley fails is in his inability to enforce the representation of the pure woman as marrying for affection, and as ignorant and unconcerned with crassly material issues like wealth. The problem here is not so much that Lucy does think the way she does; it is that he allows her to think this way, knowingly collaborating in her violation of socially approved representations of bridehood by using a term like "bargain" to refer to their marriage. He endangers himself by using language that recasts his own role as a character in her narrative, rather than insisting on preserving the integrity of her representation within his narrative. The epic narrative rights itself by re-representing Lucy as the deceptive and dangerous siren— the only representation which can contain a woman like Lucy when she steps out of her role as the adoring wife.

However, when the Lady speaks, instead of preserving a well-bred silence, we see a woman who has tried to be principled—working as a governess, sending money for her son, attempting to be honest with Sir Michael about her motives for marrying him. She feels guilt, and wonders if she is "*really* wicked," or merely thoughtless (p. 297). Braddon writes, not of a "mermaid" who is innately wicked, but of a person raised to have certain ambitions without the means of satisfying them, a person who has been driven to desperation by adversity and the betrayal of comparatively powerful males who failed to meet their obligations to her. In short, Braddon gives Lady Audley what no siren has ever had: a history, out of which a complex character with complex motivations may be constructed by the reader—if she or he chooses to do so.

"My secrets are every body's secrets" says Lucy bitterly (p. 300). Although she is referring to her own lack of privacy, another meaning is suggested as well—Lady Audley's Secret is patriarchy's dirty little secret, and Robert's epic narrative depends on how well he can keep this secret once he has discovered it. His "sanity," the coherence of his epic identity, depends on how well he can resist the urge to read Lady Audley on her own terms, as a character in her own story, one who has a history, who has tried to play by the rules and implicitly critiques those rules merely both by articulating them so baldly (and thus calling attention to their arbitrary and artificial nature) and by citing their failure to work. He must read her only as a mermaid, a representation who has no existence separate from her relation to the epic text. To the extent that he fails to do this, he is mad. He regains his sanity by locking her away and her secret with her, protecting the Audley identity from scandal and the epic narrative from the intrusion of the voice of the Other. Victorian critics, presented with a choice of narratives, which is also a choice of tasks, chose Robert's and cried out against the possibility of choosing the other, which would entail formulating a critique of a social narrative which creates Lady Audleys and then refuses to grant them recognition.

Like the relationship between Lucy's body and that of Sir Michael, the intersection of the two narratives is defined by disease. It is the "fever" of sexual passion that brings the patriarch and the Lady together; wherever difference exists between the two interacting stories that cannot be hidden, there is the disease of madness. As Jacques Sarano tells us (see chapter 2, above), disease defines our bodies as both part of the self and alienated from it through the experience of pain. Robert Audley discovers himself as a member of the patriarchal social body through the pain of contact with one alienated from it. If a healthy body is a body all of whose component parts are telling the same story, without dissonance, then the healthy body is a body largely unconscious of that story as a story—it seems a truth that requires no telling. The healthy body is unconscious of its components because it experiences itself as a unity. That unity is violated when one component of the body tells a different story from the whole. (Cancer, for example, is a kind of counter-narrative to the narrative of the healthy body.) On the social level, Lady Audley's story must be absorbed into the overall narrative of the healthy social body, if unity is to be maintained. If her story cannot be "absorbed" or healed in this manner, then it must be excised or expelled from the body in order to maintain its unity and health. Robert becomes the sanitary policeman whose task it is to escort the seductive vector of disease to the appropriate lock hospital, risking infection by the contact (and in fact becoming infected with a mild case of madness), excising the Lady neatly from the afflicted area. Sir Michael does his part by refusing to speak of "that person" again, or to know what has been done with her (p. 399), refusing the possibility of any further contamination by her separate story. Every effort is made to restore the unity of the body, the integrity of the epic narrative, to reduce Lady Audley to a representation having no subjectivity, no story of her own. But in any surgery, there is bound to be a scar, a mute testimonial to the vulnerability of the body and the possibility of other stories, just as the epic ending of *Lady Audley's Secret* does not and cannot negate the subversive insistence of the Lady's voice.

The Doctor's Wife[3]

In 1864, Mary Elizabeth Braddon attempted a decided break with the sensation genre, and decided to write, as she called it, "a novel of character." Always an admirer of the French realists, Braddon was "very much struck" by the premise of *Madame Bovary* (then less than a decade old), and set out to adapt the idea to her own purposes. Many consider the result, *The Doctor's Wife,* to be one of Braddon's finest novels, even if it is derivative of Flaubert's. Braddon's letters to Edward Bulwer Lytton repeatedly refer to her desire to write something "better" than her other bestsellers. Of *The Doctor's Wife* in particular, she writes: "[I am] especially anxious about this novel; as it seems to me a kind of turning point in my life, on the issue of which it must depend whether I sink or swim . . . I am always divided between a noble desire to attain something like excellence—and a very ignoble wish to earn plenty of money.[4] Braddon clearly accepts the distinction here between money-making, "popular" novels and the more privileged realist novel that is aligned with non-commercial motives. In line with her intention to create a realist novel, she attempts to reposition the novel internally; knowing that critics will place the novel in the sensation category by default, she includes many internal references to anticipate and forestall possible undesirable readings. Kate Flint has noted that Braddon tends to be understandably critical of the tendency to blame novels for the irresponsibilities of their readers;[5] though this is generally true, the attitudes expressed in Braddon's writing are more complex and vary more over time than such a categorical statement would imply. (Flint also uncritically categorizes *The Doctor's Wife* as a sensation novel.) Since the novel hinges on a love interest, Braddon anathematizes popular love stories, blaming her heroine's "addiction" to them for her lack of maturity and susceptibility to adulterous romance, signaling that, although she is a woman writing about love, this is not a love story *per se*. The heroine does not, in fact, read sensation—but she does read Byron. More significantly, her key supporting character is himself a sensation novelist in penny numbers who provides a constant and very droll commentary on the way in which sensation is constructed and defined, providing also, in the process, a defense of sensation itself by throwing the blame for the corruption attributed to sensation on the love story instead. This character, Sigismund Smith (he has changed his first name, which used to be Sam, for professional reasons), provides a key thread of contrast between the characteristics of the sensational and the "real life" story in which he plays a minor role. Braddon found this *alter ego* so invaluable that she continued his career in another novel (*The Lady's Mile*), again in a supporting role—something she never did with any of her hugely popular heroines. Early in the novel, Sigismund articulates the dilemma of the penny-a-liner:

> If a man can't have a niche in the Walhalla, isn't it something to have his name in big letters on the play-bills on the boulevard? . . . Do you think I wouldn't rather be the author of "The Vicar of Wakefield" than of "Colonel Montefiasco?" I *could* write "The Vicar of Wakefield" too, but . . . I should do the Vicar in the detective pre-Raphaelite style. . . . There wouldn't be much in it, you know; but the story would be pervaded by Moses's body lying murdered in a ditch half a mile

from the vicarage, and Burchell's ubiquitous eye. I dare say some people would cry out upon it, and declare that it was wicked and immoral, and that the young man who could write about a murder would be ready to commit the deed at the earliest convenient opportunity. But I don't suppose the clergy would take to murdering their sons by reason of my fiction, in which the rules of poetical justice would be firmly adhered to, and Nemesis, in the shape of Burchell, perpetually before the reader.

(*The Doctor's Wife,* pp. 43-44)

The dangerous lure of sensationalism is not, then, in the tendency of readers to imitate the actions they read about; the danger is simply in its addictive quality:

I like writing for them [the penny public]. There's only one objection to the style—it's apt to give an author a tendency towards bodies . . . the penny public require (*sic*) excitement . . . and in order to get the excitement up to a strong point, you're obliged to have recourse to bodies. Say your hero murders his father, and buries him in the coal cellar in No. 1. What's the consequence? There's an undercurrent of the body in the coal-cellar running through every chapter, like the subject in a fugue or a symphony. . . . And when you've once had recourse to the stimulant of bodies, you're like a man who's accustomed to strong liquors, and to whose vitiated palate simple drinks seem flat and wishy-washy. I think there ought to be a literary temperance pledge by which the votaries of the ghastly and melodramatic school might bind themselves to the renunciation of the bowl and dagger, the midnight rendezvous, the secret grave dug by lanternlight under a black grove of cypress, the white robed figure gliding in the grey gloaming athwart a lonely churchyard, and all the alcoholic elements of fiction. But, you see, George, it isn't so easy to turn teetotaller . . . and I scarcely know that it is so very wise to make the experiment. Are not reformed drunkards the dullest and most miserable of mankind? . . . I would rather . . . hear my audience screaming with laughter . . . than write a dull five act tragedy, in the unities of which Aristotle himself could find no flaw, but from whose performance panic stricken spectators should slink away or ere the second act came to its dreary close . . . the father and prince of melodrama . . . was never a great man; he was only popular.

(pp. 42-43)

There is both defiance and capitulation in these lines: Smith offers a spirited defense of his craft while yet accepting the distinction between the great and the popular; he seems to accept the critics' charge that sensationalism is like liquor, and yet equates its absence with the absence of pleasure and the substitution of a sterile critical pedantry for art. Yet Braddon assures the reader of *The Doctor's Wife,* "This is *not* a sensation novel. I write here what I know to be the truth" (p. 309). Braddon does want to write Goldsmith's *Vicar* (or Flaubert's *Bovary*), and sternly denies herself recourse to bodies, ghostly figures, or even Ghastly Secrets—until the ending, which she depreciated as "rushed."

Here also is the common equation between sensation and alcohol addiction, and more importantly, the equation of both with "bodies." Bodies are what sensation has in common with the love story. In the first, a corpse is offered to the reader, whereas in the second it is the sexualized body of the heroine, but in both it is the hidden, the secret quality of the body, its tendency to transform, whether through decay or sexual excitement—to get out of control and to betray or embarrass. In each case the body does indeed run like an "undercurrent" throughout the story, and the question is indeed one of accessibility. Will the corpse be found? Will the woman be seduced? Anxiety over the permeability of the body creates a center stage for the body itself as the chief protagonist, and sexuality, addiction, disease, and decay are the chief expression of that "grotesque" permeability.

Yet sensation fiction's dead bodies, we are shown, are relatively harmless compared to the live bodies found in love stories and novels of high life. The narrator continually repeats that Isabel Sleaford, the heroine of *The Doctor's Wife,* reads novels constantly, imagines herself the heroine in a novel, and is unfitted for real life because of this. She is first introduced to both the reader and her future husband reading in a garden, and when she rises to make acquaintance, she holds the book open so that she may return to it as rapidly as possible. She is described as "addicted," and addiction, like any other passion, represents the dependency of the body on something outside itself, and thus its connectedness to the Other, its nonclosure. Within the world of *The Doctor's Wife,* novels are extensions of Isabel's body—or her body is an extension of the body of popular fiction and its disruptive intrusion into realist "high" culture. Symbolically, Isabel is rarely in the "real world" of *The Doctor's Wife,* but often in the fictional world of other narratives, which is the only framework that she is able to use to interpret her experiences in the "real world," and so she forms a sort of conduit between the fictive world of the popular and the "real" or "realist" world she "lives" in. Through her, the realist world and the privileged fictive form are invaded by elements of the popular—the squire falls in love with the country wife, a murderer and his victim are incidentally brought together, etc. If the popular is the "lower strata" of the body of culture, something to be acknowledged only with amused embarrassment, then Isabel Sleaford represents the carnivalesque collision of romantic idealism with its sordid underpinning—a banal sexual transgression.

Sigismund says of Isabel that, "She reads too many novels. . . . No wise man or woman was ever the worse for reading novels. Novels are only dangerous for those poor foolish girls who read nothing else, and think that their lives are to be paraphrases of their favourite books" (p. 27). Not only does popular fiction make such girls potential victims of seduction by the aristocracy, it also makes them more directly revolutionary. Part of the problem stems from the edict that the middle-class domestic heroine must be passive, yet passivity and melodrama are not always complementary. Braddon's narrative voice explains:

> She was so eager to be *something* . . . I think Isabel Sleaford was just in that frame of mind in which a respectable, and otherwise harmless, young person aims a bullet at some virtuous sovereign, in a paroxysm of insensate yearning for distinction. Miss Sleaford wanted to be famous. She wanted the drama of her life to begin, and the hero to appear . . . [but] Beauty must wait, and wait patiently, for her fate.

Isabel does not become a regicide; however, what she does do is marry George, a good-hearted but prosaic young doctor whom she does not love. The murder of a king and the foreshadowed sexual betrayal of the domestic patriarch are thus equated. Isabel's openness to the fictive, her willingness to collapse the borders between the real and the fictive, are a betrayal of the real—the social order, the family, the empire itself. Braddon says of George that he "had those homely, healthy good looks which the novelist or poet in search of a hero would recoil from in actual horror" (p. 6); he is a "model youth of Graybridge," the backbone of middle-class England, a foundation for an empire which is the opposite and natural enemy of the fictive elements that Isabel seditiously introduces into his home.

The effects of Isabel's passion are manifested in the two male protagonists in terms of disease. Roland Lansdell refers to his passion for Isabel as a "fever" and compares it to delirium tremens as well (p. 204). Isabel is thus both a contagion and a drug. Isabel herself is an addict, and Braddon frequently compares her novels to opium: "[They are] Dangerously beautiful . . . sweetmeats with opium inside the sugar [says Smith, and when he asks if they make her happy, Isabel responds] 'No, they make me unhappy; but'—she hesitated a little and then blushed as she said—'I like that sort of unhappiness. It's better than eating and drinking and sleeping and being happy that way'" (p. 22). The blush, the unhappiness, the indifference for the material needs of the body—all are classic fictional signs of passionate love. She later loves Lansdell as a romantic ideal, as an element of popular fiction, and is confused and horrified when he suggests that she become his mistress. What Isabel really loves are her fictions; the novels are the true object of desire and source of contagion, and through them, the men in Isabel's life become infected—in Lansdell's case, by sexual desire for her which will eventually lead him to take steps which will cause his death. In fact, Isabel is particularly fictive herself; not only is she constantly compared to the heroine of a novel, but Lansdell's jealous cousin warns her that Roland's fancy for her is nothing more than the craving for "a new sensation" (p. 225). Since Roland has come into her life, Isabel sees that her life is indeed like a novel and that it has been "altogether like one long fever since Roland Lansdell's advent" (p. 229). In Isabel's unsuspecting husband, the disease manifests itself as a literal fever. As Lansdell is consumed by a "feverish" love for Isabel, his tenants experience a

minor epidemic of typhus; George attends the families, and himself succumbs to typhus. The two men die within twenty-four hours of each other.

As in many of the other novels discussed here, the principal character inhabits a borderland. Isabel Gilbert lives between the popular and the realist novel for the reader, and for the other characters, between the fictive and the real. Coming from an indeterminate background, raised as a lower-middle-class woman yet really the daughter of a petty con-artist, she breaches class boundaries both by marrying into the solidly respectable middle-class and by her liaison with her aristocratic would-be seducer. Isabel is iconically aligned with boundary transgression as well. George first proposes to Isabel on a bridge, and she later frequently meets Lansdell at another bridge; on this second bridge he will ask her to run away with him. All of this takes place within the domain of the town of Graybridge itself. Isabel is a creature of crossings, of misty indeterminate midway points. If the vampire is only limited by the inability to cross running water, Isabel seems only to exist in that transitional space, in which all her major decisions are made and actions taken. With her pale face, black hair and huge yellow-black eyes, Isabel's resemblance to the type of the Victorian vampire is not accidental—both are transitional creatures, not wholly alive, and both possess sexual attractions that spell doom to the unwary.

As in Broughton's *Not Wisely But Too Well*, Braddon's novel manifests as a storyline the critics' indictments of popular fiction. Through it, a middle-class woman is unfitted for domesticity, and rendered ripe for a seduction which will be the ruin not only of her own home, but of the aristocracy which is infiltrated by the sexually active woman of a lower class. Her desire—which is really the transformation of the fictive desire which drives the popular book market—is murderous and destroys the relatively virtuous men in her life. As in *Not Wisely*, the adulterous passion is manifested as a fever which destroys the men who love her and, following the established pattern of Greek tragedy, extends to affect the lower classes of the surrounding area, representing the failure of the moral stewardship of the upper classes. By turning critical concerns about the novel into a novel itself, Braddon both naturalizes and neutralizes their commentary: "You are precisely right—novels are terribly dangerous," she says, and uses the novel as a cautionary tale to prove that point, thus collapsing the distinction between the "moral" critical discourse and the "immoral" fictive one—a preemptive strike in every sense.

Ironically, although Braddon denies that **The Doctor's Wife** is a sensation novel, it is in large measure Sigismund Smith the sensation novelist who creates a context for the story. He introduces Isabel and George; it is through him that they continue their courtship and that Isabel finds the employment with the family friend of Roland Lansdell, the man whom she will come to love. Smith is presented as a minor character who provides comic relief and incisive commentary from an outside point of view, yet he has an integral function as the very nexus of action, out of which the entire story is generated. In that sense, Smith acts out Braddon's intention to write a non-sensation novel while protectively retaining his own identity as a sensationalist; perhaps by placing Smith in the text, Braddon was exerting control over her public persona as a sensationalist, and placing herself as an author above and outside of that fictive identity. Smith becomes one of many layers of buffers between Braddon as a well-known sensation author and *The Doctor's Wife* as a realist novel which yet situates its "real world" among multiple referents of the landscape of popular fiction. The novel defines itself by references to the thing that it is supposedly not, in fact is created out of webs of those referents, perhaps precisely because the concept of a privileged realist fiction can only exist positioned opposite the popular, mirrored rather than absorbed by its multiple reflective surfaces. The novel uses the fictive to repudiate fiction, references to the popular to repudiate the popular, the theme of passion to repudiate passion—in short, it is a text built entirely on the denial of its textuality. In response, *The Spectator* granted Braddon its first favorable review of her work.

Thus, in *The Doctor's Wife,* we see a number of familiar tropes: reading as a kind of foreplay; reading as a drug; novels as seducers who undermine the middle-class family through the wife; and the sexuality of female readers as diseased. The use of these themes implies an agreement with critics' denunciations of the sensation novel, yet does not so much oppose the concerns of Braddon's own sensation novels as it transforms them. The dangerous sensuality of the female is still the driving force of the narrative, although the heroine of *The Doctor's Wife* is traditionally passive rather than sensationally active—and ironically, it is in her passivity that the danger lies. This mocking bow to the conventions is later highlighted by Smith's (now Smythe—as a three-volume novelist, he has upgraded his name yet again) cynical comments about the differences between middle-class and lower-class fiction in *The Lady's Mile*; his three-volume bestseller is *The Mystery of Mowbray Manor*, a "legitimate three-volume romance, with all the interest concentrated on one body."[6] The difference, Braddon suggests, between the penny public and Mudie's public is simply a matter of quantity, of how many bodies it takes to sate their appetites. It is the same mocking intelligence that transforms a sensation heroine from an active but basically virtuous girl who makes an unfortunate early marriage (Aurora) to a passive, idealistic "heroine" (Isabel) whose near adultery wreaks havoc on the community; the acceptable Victorian three-volume heroine is by far the more dangerous of the two.

Notes

1. M. E. (Mary Elizabeth) Braddon, *Lady Audley's Secret,* ed. David Skilton (New York: Oxford University Press, 1987). All further references will be included parenthetically in the text.

2. See especially Elaine Showalter, *A Literature of Their Own: British Women Novelists from Brontë to Lessing* (Princeton, NJ: Princeton University Press, 1977).

3. M. E. Braddon, *The Doctor's Wife* (London: Ward, Lock and Tyler [no date, 1864?]). All further references will be included parenthetically in the text.

4. Quoted in Robert Lee Wolff, *Sensational Victorian: The Life and Fiction of Mary Elizabeth Braddon* (New York: Garland Publishing, 1979), p. 165.

5. Kate Flint, *The Woman Reader, 1837-1914* (Oxford: Clarendon Press, 1993), pp. 181, 291.

6. M. E. Braddon, *The Lady's Mile* (London: Simpkin, Marshalls, Hamilton and Kent, 1900).

FURTHER READING

Biography

Wolff, Robert Lee. *Sensational Victorian: The Life and Fiction of Mary Elizabeth Braddon.* New York and London: Garland Publishing, Inc., 1979, 529 p.

Biography that focuses on Braddon's writing career.

Criticism

Boyle, Thomas. "The Fishy Extremities of *Lady Audley's Secret.*" In *Black Swine in the Sewers of Hampstead: Beneath the Surface of Victorian Sensationalism*, pp. 145-58. New York: Viking Penguin, 1989.

Examines crime, madness, and social upheaval in *Lady Audley's Secret*.

Brantlinger, Patrick. "What Is 'Sensational' about the 'Sensation Novel'?" *Nineteenth Century Fiction* 37, No. 1 (June 1982): 1-28.

Discusses the roots and major characteristics of the sensation novel, including those written by Braddon.

Casey, Ellen Miller. "'Other People's Prudery': Mary Elizabeth Braddon." In *Sexuality and Victorian Literature,* pp. 72-82. Knoxville: University of Tennessee Press, 1984.

Examines the ways in which Braddon succumbed to Victorian social and literary standards in her novel *Vixen*.

Hart, Lynda. "The Victorian Villainess and the Patriarchal Unconscious." *Literature and Psychology* 40, No. 3 (1994): 1-25.

Explores the psychoanalytic implications of the villainess figure in Victorian literature, using Lady Audley as an example.

Michie, Helena. "'Another Woman in Your Shape': Sexual and Class Duplicity in Sensation Fiction." In *Sororopho-*

bia: *Differences among Women in Literature and Culture,* pp. 58-88. New York and Oxford: Oxford University Press, 1992.

Examines the inability of women in sensation fiction to properly adapt to and transform themselves after marriage.

Showalter, Elaine. "Subverting the Feminine Novel: Sensationalism and Feminine Protest." In *A Literature of Their Own: British Women Novelists from Brontë to Lessing,* pp. 153-81. Princeton: Princeton University Press, 1977.

Discusses the ways in which the sensation novel, and *Lady Audley's Secret* in particular, exploited the boom in publishing in the 1860s, along with the new opportunities offered to women.

Additional coverage of Braddon's life and career is contained in the following sources published by the Gale Group: *Contemporary Authors,* Vol. 108, 179; *Dictionary of Literary Biography,* Vols. 18, 70, 156; *St. James Guide to Crime & Mystery Writers; St. James Guide to Horror, Ghost & Gothic Writers.*

Ross Lockridge
1914-1948

American novelist.

INTRODUCTION

Lockridge published only one novel in his lifetime: the epic, thousand-page *Raintree County* (1948). With a plot that takes place on a single day in a fictional town in Raintree County, Indiana, the book met with instant popular success and was hailed as the greatest American novel of its generation. But shortly after its publication, *Raintree County* began to receive increasingly negative reviews. Struggling with immediate fame and the pressure to write a second work of equal stature, Lockridge committed suicide in 1948.

BIOGRAPHICAL INFORMATION

Lockridge was born in Bloomington, Indiana, in 1914, to highly ambitious parents who were determined that at least one of their children would achieve nationwide admiration. Lockridge graduated summa cum laude from Indiana University in Bloomington in 1935 and did postgraduate study at Harvard University in Cambridge, Massachusetts. In 1937 he married Vernice Baker, with whom he eventually had four children. As an English instructor at Indiana University, Lockridge began planning to write a novel about an Indiana family that would encompass the twentieth-century Midwestern experience. But he became discouraged and abandoned the project around 1938. Instead, Lockridge spent the next three years writing a massive epic poem on the same subject. In 1941 he submitted it—at more than four hundred pages—to the Houghton Mifflin publishing company, who immediately rejected it. Undaunted, Lockridge turned back to writing his novel. Six years later, he sent the finished book to Houghton Mifflin, who this time accepted his work for publication. *Raintree County* received phenomenal publicity from its publisher, was chosen immediately as a selection by the Book-of-the-Month Club, and was granted the MGM Award of $150,000, with the understanding that the film studio would have the rights to make the novel into a movie. Lockridge was delighted and immediately purchased a new house for himself and his family in Bloomington, but he soon began to suffer from emotional instability, experiencing extreme highs of grandiosity and extreme lows of insecurity. Diagnosed as paranoid, he endured a series of shock treatments that he hoped would allow him to begin work on another novel. But in March of 1948, two months after the publication of his only novel, Lockridge committed suicide.

MAJOR WORKS

The main plot of *Raintree County* takes place on 4 July 1892, a single day in the life of its middle-aged protagonist, John Wickliff Shawnessy. Additionally, there are fifty-two scenes of flashbacks to events in Shawnessy's earlier life as well as to events in the development of the United States. Shawnessy is treated as a poetic American pioneer figure in search of a lifestyle to fit his high ideals, as he explores his various options in other cities and has romantic experiences with several women who represent aspects of his youthful exploration. He finally, however, returns to Raintree County to settle with an Indiana girl in his hometown, where he becomes a much-loved husband and father and a highly respected citizen despite having never finished the novel he set out to write. Shawnessy's experiences are presented against a backdrop of major historical events occurring in the United States during his lifetime: the steady replacement of Native Americans by whites in the Midwest, the bitter debate over slavery, the Civil War, the assassination of Abraham Lincoln, political and social corruption during the period of Reconstruction after the Civil War, and the atmosphere of hope and optimism throughout the country as the new century dawned. Throughout the novel, Shawnessy is contrasted with his contemporaries, most of whom leave Raintree County to seek their fortunes elsewhere and never return, becoming cynical and greedy in the process, while Shawnessy returns home and achieves personal integrity and community admiration, realizing that his quest was of more importance than the fulfillment of his ultimate goals.

CRITICAL RECEPTION

Few twentieth-century American novels received the same level of critical and popular attention that *Raintree County* did in its first months of publication. As a Book-of-the-Month Club selection and an MGM Award winner, it attained immediate success with the American reading public. And many critics did offer high praise for the epic scope of the novel and its mythic American themes. Adding to its notoriety was condemnation from religious groups of its sexual content. But some critics found *Raintree County* to be an overly ambitious jumble too derivative of the work of James Joyce and Thomas Wolfe to have any meaningful literary value of its own. By the late 1950s critical discussion of the novel tapered off as many scholars argued that the book's strong popular readership was evidence of its pedestrian worth. *Raintree County* remains an elusive text, resurrected occasionally in critical analysis, that is still considered by some to be one of the most important post-World War II novels written in the United States.

PRINCIPAL WORKS

Raintree County (novel) 1948

CRITICISM

Elizabeth Johnson (review date 1948)

SOURCE: A review of *Raintree County,* in *Commonweal,* Vol. 47, February 13, 1948, p. 450.

[*In the following review, Johnson finds* Raintree County *verbose, overrated, and "sophomoric."*]

Accolades of hysterical praise have greeted *Raintree County* since its publication. There have been boomings from some sagacious critics proclaiming it the turning point in American fiction, the renaissance of the American

novel. True, the savants have more than once accused Mr. Lockridge of crying "Wolfe!" too often, not to mention the author's being hypnotized by Joyce and Faulkner. But that apparently does not detract from the broad panorama bulging with the humans and historical events that Mr. Lockridge has re-created.

By this time, the American reading public knows that *Raintree County* is the story of one day in the life of its Indiana hero, John Wickliff Shawnessy; that through a series of flash-backs, we learn of Shawnessy's boyhood, manhood, his physical as well as mental growth; that en route we are tossed a great chunk of American history, the 1839-1892 span. Interlarded amongst all this to-and-froing is a plethora of "epic fragments" from newspapers, diaries and dreams. All this is executed with much patriotism and gusto on Mr. Lockridge's part. He has done handsomely by Johnny Shawnessy; the Raintree County boy holds one's interest and sympathy in a three-dimensional fashion. The author has done well with most of his other characters, too. His mob scenes, bloody and pastoral, are lively. Raintree County, for all its wenching and revival meetings, seems like the blessed isle of Avalon. That Ross Lockridge writes with pulsing, if misdirected sincerity cannot be greatly questioned.

The only trouble, and considering the 1,066 pages, it is quite a piece of trouble, is that Mr. Lockridge in his fervor to put across his encyclopaedia Americana, has bludgeoned and blasted the reader with *everything* that happened to his Raintree inhabitants and to the nation for fifty-three years! He has no discrimination; the poetic "deepthighed" passages are in excruciatingly sophomoric taste; his river nymphs splash about in endless frenzies; the golden Raintree haunts one to the point of violence. In short, the author has dug and piled, dug and piled all his facts, figments and furies upon the reader in a thoughtless, numbing quantity.

The sheer length of *Raintree County* is wondrous to contemplate, but it takes a deal of endurance to beat one's way through the mazes of throbbing verbiage and two-fisted American growing-pains. Mr. Lockridge has figured out some pretty fancy philosophy in the diatribes of one Jerusalem Webster Stiles ("Perffessor" to we yokels), Johnny's high-school teacher. This nineteenth-century Don Quixote supplies the only wit and most of the humor in the book, but his excessively long bursts of witty rhetoric and sparkling deductions sandbagged this reader into a gray stupor.

Just *how* has the American novel "found" itself again in this behemoth of Ross Lockridge's? In its heft and scope? An achievement of stamina more for the reader than the writer. Because it "sings of America"? Ah, Walt, what sins are committed in thy name! For literary style? Amalgam of undigested Wolfe, murky Faulkner and watery Whitman: a poor excuse for creative writing. For its penetrating characterizations and profound "national" philosophy? Yes, the characters in *Raintree* are generally well drawn, if overdrawn, but the philosophy is, by and large, precocious collegiate patter.

Mr. Lockridge's novel, by winning an M.G.M. award and a goodly subsidy to boot, and being exaltingly boomed as a Book-of-the-Month-Club selection, will bring its author wide fame and quite a pocket of cash. Right there is a good, old American tradition. Quantity, showiness and capital letters are the usual criteria for judging the worth of a novel, a political theory or a prize pig. So *Raintree County* is *the* "American novel of 1948!" America, never a literary nation except incidentally, and now mainly for Hollywood, has exploited its protracted adolescence long enough.

Joseph L. Blotner (essay date 1956)

SOURCE: "*Raintree County* Revisted," in *The Western Humanities Review,* Vol. 10, Winter, 1956, pp. 57-64.

[*In the following essay, Blotner reevaluates* Raintree County *and attempts to account for the extreme diversity of critical opinion that the novel provoked.*]

The arrival of one recent attempt to write the Great American Novel was almost as unique as the book itself. In July, 1947, six months before publication, Ross Lockridge, Jr.'s 1066-page *Raintree County* won the $125,000 Metro-Goldwyn-Mayer Novel Award. When the book was published it was made the January selection of the Book-of-the-Month Club, adding $25,000 more. Financial success was assured before a single copy had crossed a bookseller's counter.

The chorus of yeas and nays that followed from the critics seemed to contain enough favorable notes to assure critical success as well. It was called "an achievement of art and purpose, a cosmically brooding book full of significance and beauty."[1] Dissents were just as emphatic: one writer declared that "the total effect is failure."[2] *Raintree County*'s antecedents were scrutinized as closely as its text. It was said to descend, legitimately and illegitimately, from Joyce, Sterne, Twain, Whitman, and Wolfe. Other forebears assigned to the book included the frontier humorists and the American myth-makers. A temperate, perceptive appraisal of the novel was published by William York Tindall in November, 1948.[3] But in December, *Time* magazine, reviewing the year's books *ex cathedra,* delivered its final judgment:

> Nobody harpooned the . . . mythical white whale known as the "Great American Novel." Indiana's Ross Lockridge (who later committed suicide) made a stab at it; he brought home a huge, *Ulysses*-like animal named *Raintree County,* which was hailed by critics as a monumental attempt and then floated away in embarrassed silence.[4]

Now one notices only occasional references to the novel. Sales, which mushroomed to over 400,000 copies by the end of 1948, had dwindled by 1953 to a few hundred. Just how good is this book which to one was "a novel of rare stature for these days"[5] and to another "an amalgam of undigested Wolfe, murky Faulkner and watery Whitman"?[6] What are *Raintree County*'s ancestors and achievements, its myths and meanings? Across the moderate space of eight years it seems time for a reappraisal of what may well be one of the five or six most important novels of this era.

The story of the book is this. The small town of Waycross, in Raintree County, Indiana, holds a special Fourth of July celebration in 1892. The day-long patriotic program is seen through the eyes of John Wickliff Shawnessy, a 53-year-old schoolteacher and prominent citizen of Waycross. Three of his boyhood friends—a newspaper man, a senator, and a financier—return for the day. Through their arguments and reminiscences, and through fifty-two flashbacks, the most important events in John's life are recreated. This chronicle includes the strange courtship and loss of his first and greatest love, his seduction by his first wife and the tragic events which follow it, and his turbulent wooing of his second wife, with whom he finds peace. These flashbacks give the story of one man's life, but they also form a pageant of American history through fifty tumultuous years. The flashbacks are alternated, chronologically for the most part, with the speeches, parades, and fireworks of the Waycross celebration. The novel's denouement, following a climactic mob scene, finds John alone. His friends have departed and Waycross has gone to bed; he is alone with the night and Raintree County. This is more than the story of John Wickliff Shawnessy; through him it is the legend of Raintree County, of America, and of man upon this earth.

Such a book is rarely a literary virgin birth. Lockridge's debt to others includes elements of concept and style, matter and manner. There are so many similarities that the influence of James Joyce's *Ulysses* is unmistakable. Like Joyce, Lockridge used the single-day framework, multiple symbolism, mythology, and the dream-fantasy. Johnny, as the poet-hero, resembles Stephen Dedalus. Like him, trying to "forge in the smithy of my soul the uncreated conscience of my race," Johnny has labored to "become the epic poet of his people,"[7] to be "an image-bearer of the Republic" (p. 977). Consecrated to their tasks, these two are marked by special and ancient names: Stephen is the Celtic "Kinch"; John is the Indian "Shakamak." Shawnessy is contrasted with Jerusalem Webster Stiles as Dedalus is with Leopold Bloom, and as Dedalus has his Buck Mulligan, so Shawnessy has his Garwood B. Jones. A linguist like Joyce, Lockridge too fused words for special effects: "timesmoothed," "homeremembering," "memory-haunted."

Ross Lockridge freely admitted the influence of Thomas Wolfe on his work, but he felt that his own historical background was stronger. A boyish declaimer at American shrines and writer of historical pageants, he had hymned America all his life. In *Raintree County* he wrote

Of mounds beside the river. Of threaded bones of lovers in the earth. Of shards of battles long ago. Of names upon the land, the fragments of forgotten language . . . Of the people . . . of their towns and cities and the weaving millions. Of the earth on which they lived—its blue horizons, east and west, exultant springs, soft autumns, brilliant winters. And of all the summers when the days were long

(p. 1060).

Walt Whitman's name is mentioned twice in *Raintree County,* his poetry is quoted, and his influence is clear. Lockridge sings of all the people who made America,

Of their vast and vulgar laughters, festive days, their competitions, races, lusty games. Of strong men running to a distant string. . . . Of their plantings, buildings, minings, makings, ravagings, explorings. Of how they were always going with the sun, westward to purple mountains, new dawns and new horizons. Of the earth on which they lived

(p. 775).

He writes of the pioneers, endlessly moving west, and speaks of "Young men, my comrades" (p. 669), many of whom, with Johnny Shawnessy, are borne to the hospitals that receive the backwash of the war.

If the frontier humorists left their mark upon the author's mind, so did Mark Twain. Lockridge makes Flash Perkins representative of the frontiersman; his code is that of "the backwoodsman or river man . . . the code of breezy cocky men, who had no fear in heaven or earth they would admit to" (p. 174). The book is shot through with the humor of this Western man, and the battle vaunts of Flash and Johnny could almost be transposed with those of the raftsmen in *Life on the Mississippi.*

The footsoldiers of all wars have much in common, and anyone who writes of the infantryman's lot will necessarily treat elements others write of. But Johnny Shawnessy's ordeal in the slaughter of Chickamaugua and the vicious charge up Missionary Ridge immediately suggest Henry Fleming's baptism of fire at Chancellorsville in Crane's *Red Badge of Courage.* Each experiences the shame of flight, the confused exaltation of victory, and the aging that comes with both.[8]

Besides these various debts, there are episodes which recall Fielding, Smollett, and Sterne. Lockridge learned from all of these writers, and, like most first novels, his book was sometimes imitative. But the imitation was not slavish, not a substitute for original work. It was rather an attempt to use every literary technique he could to help achieve the extraordinarily difficult goal he had set for himself.

For Lockridge, myth was the means by which both past and present are understood. That is, the only true reality is one's personal experience. The multiplication of individual experience, which constitutes life in the aggregate, becomes an understandable approximation of the truth only when its actually fragmentary nature is cast into an arbitrary order through what is agreed upon as history. For example: the Battle of Gettysburg as related in history books and perceived through the plaques on the battle site is myth. Its reality was the multiplicity of shots, sabre strokes, retreats, attacks, barrages, and silences which impinged upon the consciousness of the long-dead soldiers who fought near that town on July 1-3, 1863. Lockridge felt that history, both formal and informal, was a kind of myth quite as much as that in Bulfinch or Frazer. But this latter kind did more to make experience meaningful.

Questioned by his friend and former teacher, "Perfessor" Stiles, Shawnessy says that "A myth is a story that is always true for all men everywhere" (p. 886). From this implied premise that myths represent fundamental patterns in human experience, Lockridge proceeded to his method: the use of as many myths as possible to compress into *Raintree County* as much of human experience as he could. Raintree County is explicitly called a microcosm. Waycross is the crossing of the ways, a crossroads where all things meet. John Wickliff Shawnessy is man, but appropriately he is man as mythic hero. One can identify him in various sections of the novel as Christ, Adam, Aeneas, Apollo, Alexander, Oedipus, Hercules, Actaeon, Siegfried, and Beowulf. He is also William Shakespeare, the Priest of Nemi described by Frazer, and—in the sense of Joyce's H. C. Earwicker—Everyman. But most of all, he is Adam—knowing Paradise, falling, and expiating his sin. He tells the Perfessor and Senator Garwood B. Jones, his boyhood friend and rival, that he has known not several women, but rather "One Eve in several reincarnations" (p. 588). And each of them is marked by a scar or birthmark, which she wears "as a sign of her mortality" (p. 930), a mortality like that of Eve after the fall. Superimposed upon the old myth is that which Shawnessy calls the American myth, "the story of the hero who regains Paradise" (p. 866). This myth is embodied in the experience of the poet-hero, the new Adam who

learned that Raintree County being but a dream must be upheld by dreamers. So he learned that human life's a myth, but that only myths can be eternal. So he learned the gigantic labor by which the earth is rescued again and again from chaos and old night, by which the land is strewn with names, by which the river of human language is traced from summer to distant summer, by which beauty is plucked forever from the river and clothed in a veil of flesh, by which souls are brought from the Great Swamp into the sunlight of Raintree County and educated to its enduring truths

(p. 1021).

Shawnessy's reply to the Perfessor's cynical Darwinian *History of Mankind* is *The Legend of Raintree County,* which he describes as "A little fable with multiple meanings, and a moral for a vestigial tail" (p. 1019). The moral is quoted immediately above; the multiple meanings are found throughout the novel. For example: the Raintree said to grow near Paradise Lake in the heart of the county is a rare Asian species, a planting of Johnny Appleseed, the Tree of Life, the Tree of the Knowledge of Good and Evil, and the familiar tree of genealogy. The myths which relate to each of Johnny's roles are represented by appropriate Raintree County or national events. Each of the major characters is symbolic. Garwood B. Jones is the demagogue; Cassius P. ("Cash") Carney is the financier (turning yellow in maturity he is reminiscent of Midas); Jerusalem Webster Stiles is the cynical intellectual. Nell Gaither (Venus Anadyomene) is called the perfect blend of the spiritual and the erotic. Laura Golden is the spirit of the City in the Gilded Age. Susanna Drake is the ante-bellum South, seen by Johnny as beautiful, guilty, tragic, and tormented. Lockridge invested *Raintree County* with multiple meanings, and he attempted to make them work on many levels: narrative and symbolic, personal and national, particular and universal.

Lockridge's writing sometimes achieves a high degree of technical virtuosity. The book is constructed according to an intricate chronological plan. Events in the morning of the Fourth of July recall incidents in Johnny's childhood and events in the early history of the United States. As the day progresses, these three schedules roughly keep pace with each other. The flashbacks are tied into the day's events by key words which make the transitions. Within episodes, the same sort of junctions are made between the narrative and other material, such as newspaper excerpts, inserted in it. This device was probably used to indicate the continuity of experience and the similarity, in their basic nature, of events separated by time and space.

There is highly effective use of contrast and the contrapuntal method. John's wedding and its consummation go forward with the grim undertone of John Brown's execution. Little Jim Shawnessy is born as Fort Sumter is attacked. Interspersed throughout John's frantic, tragic search for the mad Susanna, who has fled taking the child with her, are fragmentary reports of the confused violence of the colliding armies at Gettysburg. The Great Footrace between Johnny and Flash Perkins has as a foil descriptions of epic competitions between river steamboats, giant locomotives, and Sullivan and Corbett. This device can also be used ironically, as when Johnny first reads Lincoln's Gettysburg Address in a Chattanooga bordello. Very often Lockridge relates one event in several ways. Besides the narration and dialogue, a description may be inserted from one of the local newspapers. Excerpts from two completely fictitious ones, the *Cosmic Enquirer* and the *Mythic Examiner,* supply descriptions which are satirical, humorous, and sometimes ribald. The novel's descriptive passages come vividly alive, catching the violence of battles and riots, conveying the smoky uproar of conventions, and painting the sweet beauty of the fertile earth. There are only one or two false notes in the hundreds of pages of dialogue which catch the soft nuances of southern speech, the hard nasal tones of the Indiana backcountry drawl, and the clipped accents of city talk. And there are glowing passages, frequently too purple, but all possessing beauty in their song of the land and their lament for things that are lost.

Raintree County presents a panorama of American history, a chronicle of American literature, and a criticism of American society during most of the nineteenth century. Excerpts from the four newspapers mentioned above relate historical events. Many of the most important ones are seen through Johnny Shawnessy's eyes, and none of them, not even Lincoln's assassination or the Pittsburgh strike, seems artificial or contrived to juxtapose the hero and climactic events in the life of his nation.

There are only brief references to Emerson, Poe, and Thoreau, but the effect on Johnny and some of his friends of the work of Whitman, Longfellow, Hawthorne, and Lincoln is shown. One meets in their passing vogue the Horatio Alger stories, *Uncle Tom's Cabin,* Civil War memoirs, and the sentimental novels of the middle and late nineteenth century. The reader sees in all their transience period pieces such as the illustrated gift book, popular elegiac verse, and the Tennysonian imitation. Interwoven with the fabric of the life of which it was a part, this literature gains a special vividness and relevance.

The national problems which deeply concern Johnny Shawnessy parallel the fall from grace and expiation of sin treated on the personal level through the myth of Adam. As the national punishment and atonement for the institution of slavery is the Civil War, so for heedless materialism it is the Gilded Age. The tremendous, onrushing growth of America was to John inevitable, a part of a national destiny. But he felt that the financial titans who flung the iron rails west and reared the smoking factories had done so with ruthless disregard for the human beings who contributed the sweating labor. (The locomotive is presented as the modern equivalent of the Cretan Minotaur.) To John it seemed that the shady manipulation of capital and the exploitation of human and natural resources involved a rejection of the human values implicit in the Declaration of Independence. Equally guilty were the corrupt politicians who swore to represent the people but served only themselves. Communism was anathema to him, but the free-wheeling empire-building of the Gilded Age seemed just as inimical to the spirit of American democracy. Raintree County, and the macrocosm for which it stood, retained archaisms and barbarisms in its moral code. It was a society of Puritan restraints, yet one which said that

> The injured husband may take the life of him who has injured him. . . . Terrible as homicide is, this method must, on the whole, be admitted to be the most effectual, the wisest, and the most natural revenge of an outraged husband

> (p. 216).

Organized religion, as well as that brought by the God-shouting evangelist, is examined closely. The Perfessor attacks the Old Testament Christianity on which it is based as a code springing from the prehistoric past of savage patriarchal Hebrew clans. This is criticism of a culture as well as an institution.

In addition to all its other attributes, **Raintree County** is a comic epic. Jerusalem Webster Stiles is not only an intellectual gadfly and cynical wit; he is also an engaging character in the best picaresque tradition. Like an inverted alter ego, he appears throughout Johnny's life. Living by his wits, goading less agile minds, attempting to run off with the preacher's wife, he is a genuine comic creation of substance and depth. The redoubtable Flash Perkins has a Bunyanesque quality. Ready to outdrink, outrun, or outfight any man in the county, he is fierce and untroubled by intellectual processes, but he is honest and generous. Winning Fourth of July races, capturing Confederate cannon, or joyously challenging a mob in a bawdyhouse, he is an eager spirit living for action and laughter. Garwood B. Jones is successively Johnny's rival for a girl, for journalistic prominence, and for political office. But Johnny knows, and so does Garwood, that he is a charlatan. Completely dominated by self-interest, gifted with spell-binding oratory, he makes his prominent way in the world by cozening the gullible and playing on common wants and fears. And, of course, many of Johnny's amatory adventures are in the comic tradition. There are other touches, such as the medicine show with its phrenologist and seller of guaranteed elixirs. There is the farcical temperance drama climaxed by the burning of the theatre. Accompanying all this is the salty dialogue of farmhands, backwoodsmen, and old soldiers telling outrageous lies about campaigns fought in the long ago.

Why may **Raintree County** be one of the five or six most important novels of this era? Because, despite all its imperfections, it is a sound literary achievement in its technical proficiency, its attempt to interpret a nation and a culture, and its effort to extend this interpretation to life in general. Its faults and virtues are intermixed. The very overcrowding of the book with facts and people and events helps to make it a living panorama of America. Its complex and sometimes cloudy symbolism gives the life of one man and one county relevance to other lives and other places. **Raintree County** is important in yet another way. As Mr. Tindall has suggested, the book has apparently helped to gain popular acceptance for the many-leveled novel.

This novel is also remarkable when it is seen in the perspective of its own time. When other novelists were writing of the desolation of war, of the disillusionment of its aftermath, and of the destruction of old values and orders, Ross Lockridge made an all-consuming effort whose total effect was a reaffirmation of faith in America and the American dream. **Raintree County** is not the Great American Novel, which probably will never be written. But it is a substantial achievement which merits a place in American literature.

Notes

1. Charles Lee, *New York Times Book Review,* January 4, 1948, p. 21.

2. Orville Prescott, *Yale Review,* XXXVII (March, 1948), 574.

3. William York Tindall, "Many-leveled Fiction: Virginia Woolf to Ross Lockridge," *College English,* X (November, 1948), 65-71.

4. *Time,* LII (December 20, 1948), 101.

5. James Hilton, *New York Herald Tribune Book Review,* January 4, 1948, p. 2.

6. Elizabeth Johnson, *The Commonweal,* XLVII (February 13, 1948), 450.

7. Ross Lockridge, Jr., *Raintree County* (Boston: Houghton Mifflin Co., 1948), p. 788. The pages from which further quotations are drawn will be indicated in the text.

8. In this role as in others Johnny is a symbol for a whole group. This is made clear in one dream-fantasy in which he is a Roman centurion.

Gerald C. Nemanic (essay date 1975)

SOURCE: "Ross Lockridge, *Raintree County,* and the Epic of Irony," in *MidAmerica II,* Vol. 2, 1975, pp. 35-46.

[*In the following essay, Nemanic discusses the shocking initial success and ultimate failure of* Raintree County.]

William Carlos Williams may be the only important writer of our time who persisted in believing that an American epic might still be written. His own *Paterson,* an "answer to Greek and Latin with the bare hands," was not to be that work. Williams knew it; indeed, he visualized his efforts as a necessary preliminary, "a gathering up" of raw materials into a foundation on which later poets might build epic structures.

The successful dramatization of American experience would result not from sophisticated commentaries on the nature of the American and his institutions. It would follow from the direct knowledge of objects, a simple apprehension of and generous acceptance of the "beautiful thing." "No ideas but in things" and "beautiful thing" are refrains echoing through *Paterson.* They aid in building a motif central to the meaning of the poem. One reflection of that meaning is the knowledge that any reification of the national experience must begin at the sensuous level, in that world most simple and yet baffling.

Perhaps the implication of Williams' stricture is that the only worthwhile "epic" of American life must of necessity grow from an endearment which might never be associated with "ideas," but only with the destructible world of time and space. If so, how could any one man possibly know enough "things" of this sprawling, chaotic nation to allow for, in his sensibility, the evolution of a metaphorical frame suitable to the demands of an epic vision? Williams thought long on this dilemma and set it before us in his art. He not only believed in the dilemma, he was thoroughly convinced that it could be solved. A quarter century after Book I of *Paterson* issued its challenge to future poets we have not yet seen the fulfillment, nor perhaps even those first halting steps toward the realization of his prophesy. Our best instruction still lies in pondering the import of "pre-epic" poems like *Paterson* or Hart Crane's *The Bridge,* and, in the genre of prose fiction, reflecting on the lessons taught by valiant failures, one of which, **Raintree County,** is the main subject of this essay.

II

Ross Lockridge's mammoth "epic" novel was published, to much fanfare, in 1948. It was the author's first novel, a work more than eight years in the making. Within months of its first printing the obscure English instructor who wrote it had become a wealthy celebrity. A number of prestigious critics had reviewed **Raintree County** with enthusiasm. Howard Mumford Jones went so far as to declare the appearance of this novel as marking the end of a serious slump in American fiction. The motion picture industry, searching everywhere for new filmscripts which might help mine another bonanza like *Gone With the Wind,* provided the author with increased public exposure and a whopping sum for the rights to film his novel.[1] At that moment it seemed quite possible that another youthful and brilliant novelist was coming out of the Midwest, as Dreiser, Lewis, Hemingway, and Fitzgerald had done before him, to reshape the forms of American fiction.

But there were immediate and disturbing side effects resulting from this public display. Lockridge, a highly sensitive and private man, was finding the role of instant celebrity difficult. Despite strong public and critical acclaim for his work, he raged at the minority of nay-sayers who pointed out the shortcomings of his style and formal conceptions.[2] A young man of thirty-three, after eight years of exhausting work on what he believed to be his *magnum opus,* was being churned through the mill of public opinion in a fashion he could hardly have anticipated. With a part of his movie money he purchased a new home in Bloomington, Indiana, his home town. There he brooded and drove his new Kaiser automobile up and down the driveway. Not three months after the first appearance of **Raintree County,** Ross Lockridge had committed suicide. While many groped for reasons his mother said simply that "the boy put his heart's blood into the book, he had nothing left."

III

In the more than twenty-five years since Lockridge's death his novel has steadily lost visibility to the point where, by 1974, it had gone out of print entirely. Lockridge's work has not, it seems, interested many literary critics beyond that initial excitement engendered by its publication. There are some good reasons for this neglect: like many young writers, Lockridge may have attempted to write too much, too soon. His ambition not being matched by his experience, the style and formal qualities of the novel are flawed. The author's romantic conception of the American epic experience, a part of that "Great American Novel" syn-

drome associated with the first half of the twentieth century, has by now lost a good deal of literary caste. And the fact remains that Lockridge wrote only one novel, and this has not been sufficient to establish a literary reputation.

Yet to the student of American cultural life this one novel is arresting—a literary curiosity which exasperates us with its turgidity while as often luring us forward with its beauty. One is tempted to regard it as The Final Experiment with the Great American Novel and to discern, inextricably interwoven through its images, visions and sentiments, the stamp both of its successful vitalism and of its inevitable failures.

IV

Williams' opinion of **Raintree County** has not been recorded, but his stricture, "No ideas but in things," penetrates to what is both good and bad in the novel. For an immediate insight into the methods Lockridge will use to dramatize the essential experience of America, we need look no farther than the title page and dedication. There the author introduces us to Raintree County, Indiana, which has "no boundaries in time and space. . . . You will hunt for it on the map, and it won't be there. . . . For Raintree County is not the country of the perishable fact. It is the country of the enduring fiction." At the outset we are told not to expect the dull, stubborn facts of the real world of rural Indiana but an imaginative vision wherein "ideas" *are* father to the materials they create and not, as Williams would have it, *vice versa.*

In the accompanying dedication we find: "For My Mother / Elsie Shockley Lockridge / This book of lives, loves, and antiquities." Here is revealed the obverse of Lockridge's attitude toward his materials. A "book of . . . antiquities" seems much different than one which has been ascribed "no boundaries in time and space." And this dichotomy informs the entire novel. Much care is taken to recreate the artifacts, tenor, and style of life in nineteenth century Indiana. These "antiquities" are evoked with deep feeling for that fading fabric of life. They delight, and are their own reason for being. And yet, for Lockridge this is hardly enough. He is bent on discovering the principles of American development, the foundation of American character. Raintree County will also have a metaphorical reality, and the author will lead us through interminable Platonic dialogues and prolix theorizings on the nature of history and art in his determination to fully develop that metaphor.

V

In **Raintree County** Lockridge details the life of his epic hero, John Wickliff Shawnessy, from his youth in antebellum Indiana ("that mirror of the ancient republic now lost in time") through the Civil War and into a later life amid the trappings of a "Gilded Age." Mostly we are in Raintree County, the boundaries of which will delimit the existence of Shawnessy, but significant scenes range from the battle of Chickamauga to Ford's Theatre on the night of Lincoln's assassination. Shawnessy's life span has been determined strategically, for into this representative American hero must be woven strands of American experience both old and new. There is the pre-war dream of an Edenic republic; then the chaos of internecine warfare; and finally the increasingly impersonal life of industrial America. "The greatness of Lincoln," says the seasoned Shawnessy of later years, "was the greatness of America in his time."[3] And with this comment Shawnessy passes judgment on himself and his times, for it was that first half of the nineteenth century which was "capable of creating a great man," a man of mythic proportions. The remainder of that century molded the complicated and ambiguous American hero, that prototype of the anti-hero which we may all recognize as contemporary.

VI

Through Shawnessy, Lockridge attempts to mirror the essential American experience. As a Midwesterner, the hero exists at the geographical and cultural middle ground of the nation. The Raintree County culture he absorbs is stable and traditional enough to maintain a strong grip on the hero's moral self. Instinctively vital and curious, young Johnny is fully able to mount a critique of the mixture of puritan and bourgeois values which permeates this society, and yet he is not capable, in the last analysis, of washing them from his conscience.

The isolate purity of the County is lovingly examined in all its "antiquity," and yet it is, at the same time, traversed by the Great National Road, that main artery to the West which carries a steady stream of pioneers past the Shawnessy home. In his earliest recollections Johnny is stirred by the promise of freedom and adventure symbolized by the wagonloads of ebullient emigrants. The young hero is torn by conflicting impulses. He yearns to understand a tribal past and to clarify his own position within the framework of his circumscribed culture.

Thus he clings to that place, Raintree County, which promises answers to his insistent questions. Simultaneously, he is excited by the epic sweep of national experience and dreams of contact with the innocence he associates with westering. A crucial dilemma associated with the production of the American epic is reflected in Shawnessy's quandary. Named "John Wickliff" for that old hero of the race who translated sacred documents into the vernacular, Shawnessy becomes the potential American Homer. The undoing of the pure vision of an American republic, through war and greed, will nullify his efforts to compose the American *Odyssey*. Not only will it be impossible for Shawnessy to absorb the discordant and protean elements of post-war American life, but the maiming experience of his own guilt will sap his resolve to continue.

Raintree County is a novel conceived in paradox, for it is an epic structure which reveals that the artistic realization of the true epic is no longer possible, at least not in America. Shawnessy's epic poem, this epic within the novel, is the work of a lifetime. It is begun in the first en-

thusiasms of youth and carried on doggedly, sporadically, and, finally, perfunctorily, into the last years of the century. As art, this epic poem is fated to remain inchoate and fragmented, a mere literary curiosity. Shawnessy finds that he can hope to succeed ultimately not through his literary efforts but in "the legend of my life, with which I refute all sophistries. By a myth of homecoming and a myth of resurrection." (988) This legend is the fabric of *Raintree County* and it is Lockridge, viewing from the artists's perspective, and not Shawnessy, his creation, who strives to indite the ironical American epic.

VII

Raintree County meanders through more than one thousand pages of flashbacks, dream narratives and philosophical disquisitions, yet the basic outline of the novel is simple, for it is essentially a *bildungsroman*. Here is played out the story of John Shawnessy's education, symbolized by his search for the mythical Rain Tree, the tree of knowledge. He was born in April, 1839, and the novel's literal action takes place on one day, July 4, 1892. From that point in time Shawnessy reflects, through reminiscence and flashbacks, on his life as an American hero.

The hero's first concrete memories are of 1844—pioneers passing his home on their way to Oregon. At that point Johnny first feels a longing for the western star. But youth in rural Indiana is idyllic. In memory, "the clock in the Court House Tower . . . is always fixed at nine o'clock, and it is summer and the days are long." These endless days are spent musing and wandering by the river. John Shawnessy husks corn in the autumn and secretly adores Nell Gaither. He imagines himself a young Adonis and her an airy river nymph. The senior Shawnessys are kindly folk, yet imbued with the implacable moral values of middle America and Scotch Presbyterianism. The father, T. D. Shawnessy, is a doctor, preacher, and mixer of botanical medicines. His wife Ellen is a hardy woman, but softly lyrical as well, the fine fruit of a pioneer heritage. This portrait of the early life of an American hero is one of warmth and security. The occasional vicissitudes are not atypical; indeed the conception is remarkably similar to those of the earlier Indiana masters of sentimental fiction—Booth Tarkington, Maurice Thompson, *et al.*[4]

But troubling undercurrents complicate this idealized picture. Johnny is moved by the restlessness of America in the 1840s and 1850s. Lockridge views these pregnant times as an inevitable climax of two hundred years' history. The westering spirit of a nation catches Shawnessy in its wave; he longs for a free and glorious life which the limits of Raintree County cannot supply. His first fascination with literature stems from a vaguely felt need to rise above the limitations of place. Another shadow is cast over the hero's youth by the building fury of fraternal enmity which will culminate in a civil war. Even before the outbreak of fighting he is caught up in the fate of the South. Seduced by Susanna Drake, an exotic Southern visitor to Raintree County, Johnny is determined to fulfill his responsibilities to the "fallen" girl. They marry and travel South in the troubled days before the firing on Fort Sumter. Susanna, at once incredibly sensual and puritanical, is Lockridge's somewhat stereotyped symbol of the South.[5] She is, finally, a schizophrenic driven to madness by a moral and racial ambiguity. Her derangement results in a desperate flight from her husband and an attempted suicide which brings about the death of their young son. Thus for Lockridge the South represents an American tragedy which destroys both its own and the sons of the Republic.

Once Susanna has been safely institutionalized, Johnny is free to fight for the Republic. He is transformed into the typical American foot soldier: after being wounded in action, he spends weeks in a military hospital near Washington where, among his wounded countrymen, he is visited by President Lincoln and Walt Whitman. Back home in Raintree County, Johnny has been erroneously reported killed in action. Heartbroken sweetheart Nell in turn marries Johnny's boyhood rival, Garwood Jones, and then dies in childbirth.

Having had enough of historical melodrama, Lockridge settles his hero into the life of Raintree County. Except for an ill advised foray into politics and a few minor adventures in the iniquitous East, Shawnessy leads a model life in tranquil obscurity, remarries, rears a family, teaches school, and works fitfully on the epic poem he can never finish. Occasionally former friends return, sons of Raintree County who have moved into the larger world of the postwar Republic. There is the famous journalist, Jerusalem Webster Stiles, who serves as an intellectual mirror image for Shawnessy. Garwood Jones, coward and opportunist, has become a U.S. senator and a candidate for President. Cash Carney was once a local hustler but now, in an age favoring manipulative genius, he has become a financial power and molder of political personalities, a character modeled perhaps on another Midwesterner of obscure roots, Mark Hanna. The "Gilded Age" glitters forth boldly and John Shawnessy, heir of the heroes of old, has in it no place of honor.

VIII

Within the framework of the *bildungsroman* the protagonist becomes life's initiate; he experiences marriage, lost love, death, war, and remorse while his personality slowly ripens. There is a thematic quest—the hero's desire to explore the secrets of the exotic Rain Tree—which is compatible with the growth principle of the novel and helps unify the action.

It would seem that the melodramatic paraphernalia of the plot could be brought forth as evidence of the novel's inherent weakness. And yet Lockridge's melodrama is so self-conscious, so mannered and obviously exaggerated, that we are forced to examine its possible intent. The work, which from one angle seems so romantically earnest, yet from another can be viewed as ironical and satiric. We see that Shawnessy's life story, replete with classic analogues,

describes the development of an heroic American prototype. But the novelist often reminds us of another viewpoint: from it we can see that Shawnessy has evolved into a sententious wind bag who rocks sleepily toward death in an obscure corner of the Midwest backwater. He mutters of a "lost republic" and timorously mollifies the harpies of the local PTA in order to keep his job. In the crucial decisions of his life—marrying Susanna instead of Nell, rejecting the impulse to move West—he has chosen wrongly. His moral earnestness becomes a maddening prudery; his heroic attempt to forge the American epic seems merely the scribbling of an aging schoolmaster who clings pathetically to youthful dreams of glory.

This other, or anti-epic, which coexists with the first is best illuminated in a comparison of the novel's hero and his antagonist, both of whose initials are "J.W.S." John Wickliff Shawnessy is not the exclusive alter ego of Ross Lockridge. As much a part of the author's sensibility is the cynical, bumptious intellectual—Jerusalem Webster Stiles. Shawnessy and Stiles are antagonists, and yet they represent divided segments of that personality which is close to Lockridge's own.

Stiles enters the novel when Shawnessy is an adolescent. The "Perfesser" comes from the East to open an "Academy" in Raintree County, the place of his birth, and it is in Pedee Academy that Shawnessy is introduced to the learning of the ages: English poetry, the classics, philosophy, the new science of Darwin, and the new skepticism in religion. Stiles, the jaded aesthete, exercises a powerful hold on Shawnessy's pliant imagination. Representing the "stile-ish" East, Europe, and modern intellectual taste, Stiles is the primary formal educative force in Shawnessy's youth. It is as if Lockridge splits his own identity in two. The author had, like Shawnessy, grown up to an innocent and powerful idealism in the quietude of pastoral Indiana. We can imagine that Lockridge's father, a college professor, was much like T. D. Shawnessy—earnest, conscientious, kind, and morally upright. The Lockridge family, ensconced in a rambling old house amid the towering elms of a college town, probably lived in much the same warm, wholesome atmosphere as did the Shawnessys of Raintree County.

But for young Lockridge there was also the inevitable move to the state university, and then on to Harvard. We can also imagine some of the disillusionment, the hardening, that most young men suffer when removed from the idyllic life of a small Midwestern community. He was thrust into a competitive, lonely world and was suddenly responsible for a wife and children. Shawnessy also ripens through experience, but his pastoral nineteenth century world still provides enough ballast to maintain him upright. Shawnessy does not sink under the weight of modern life, whereas Stiles, and Lockridge, too, are not so fortunate.

Stiles represents not only the intellectual *avant garde* of the East, but a deeper kind of debilitating knowledge—the finality of death known to young, when psychological defenses have not yet been developed to combat despair. Late in the novel, in a drunken moment, Stiles tells Shawnessy:

> Years ago . . . I was a child in Raintree County. He paused as if the words just said were full of labyrinthine meanings. My father died before I was old enough to remember him. When I was only ten years old, my mother died. In that death, Jerusalem Webster Stiles knew the secret of life—which is death—and never added to his wisdom though he added to his words. And with that act, also, he left Raintree County and went East. . . . He learned early with the bitterness of the homeless child, that the earth cares nothing for our grief, and that even our mother who cared for us in life cares nothing for us in death.
>
> (986, 987)

Stiles, who from one angle appears to be merely the hero's foil, is, in another way, the hero's mirror image, and indeed the two characters, both J.W.S., can be seen as a composite figure which may reflect the complex personality of the author. Accepting this, we could explain the perplexing doubleness of the novel—that tendency to both rhapsodize and satirize, to both *believe* in the epic heroism of John Shawnessy's life and to judge so severely its limitations.

IX

This curious duality, or the depth of Lockridge's irony, if indeed it is conscious irony, brings us inevitably to speculation about the role of the artist's personality in his creation, and, in this case, to consideration of his suicide. It is surely possible that Lockridge's suicide had nothing to do with his literary career, or that the concerns of art played only a minor part in a highly complex situation. Yet in retrospect we can see signs of forboding in the novel itself. The double vision spoken of previously was not necessarily an "enriching ambiguity." Perhaps the doubleness of *Raintree County* is not so much the artistic weaving of an ironic vision as it is the sign of a perilous personal dilemma, one which may have eventually led to the tragic denouement of the author's self-destruction.

In Midwestern fiction we have seen the development of a romantic school—the Hoosiers—and a subsequent reaction toward realism. While neither movement was the exclusive property of Midwestern writers, there were, between about 1870 and 1930, a disproportionate number of writers from the region who took on the key roles in the evolution of literary fashions. Complicated spirits like Theodore Dreiser and Sherwood Anderson showed elements of both romanticism and realism in their fiction. *Winesburg, Ohio* is a fine example of how an ostensibly objective piece of writing can be enriched through an infusion of pathos and human sympathy.

Lockridge, like Anderson, exhibited a complicated relationship to his Midwestern roots. Both writers wished to write the truth about life in the Midwest they had known, and yet the need to confront the facts came into deep conflict with an emotional need to charge that world with significance, whatever these "facts" might show. It is perhaps ironic that Anderson's simpler vision may have benefited him as an artist. He wrote the Winesburg stories much as Twain wrote *Huckleberry Finn,* directly from the heart and with a minimal self-consciousness. The ironies and beauties abiding in those books are inherent in the tangible, dramatic conceptions of their makers.

Lockridge, on the other hand, was an intellectual as well as an artist and his novel is partly conceived in intellectual terms. Although *Raintree County* is brilliant in parts, it fails in its intellectualism—in the abstracted Platonic dialogues which take up too much of its last half. In these debates Shawnessy, the idealist, combats Stiles, the cynic, on subjects ranging from love, marriage and the family to politics, religion, anthropology and myth. We find here a rough analogue to Anderson's conflicting vision of Winesburg. Objectivity clashes with a sense of personal involvement, despair combats hope, elemental hatred strives in no less elemental love. Anderson can present the reader with a moving dramatization of these conflicts; Lockridge too often can only talk about them.

And so we come to face, finally, a clear illustration of art's value, the force of its humanism. The gift of the artist is to be able to confront us with dilemma in a tangible form and through this presentation to reap, for himself and his reader, a spiritual harvest. The imperfect, though valiant, attempts of Lockridge to reach that consolation result in the frustrating ambiguity which is *Raintree County,* a novel which reveals our bewilderment as well as our vitality as a culture.

Notes

1. *Raintree County* was winner of the Metro-Goldwyn-Mayer Semi-Annual Novel Award for fiction suitable for adaptation to the screen. The award provided a minimum of $125,000, with bonus clauses which could bring the total to $275,000. The studio, of course, gained film rights to the novel.

2. Hamilton Basso, writing in *The New Yorker,* simply dismissed Lockridge as a "second-hand Wolfe." *Newsweek* pegged the book as "sprawling, exasperating, tedious."

3. Lockridge, Ross, Jr. *Raintree County.* Boston: Houghton, Mifflin, 1948, 455. All other references in the novel are indicated parenthetically after the quote.

4. Ross Lockridge, Sr., was a scholar of Indiana history and lore while teaching in the Speech Department at Indiana University. He wrote *A. Lincoln* (1930) and *Old Fauntleroy Home* (1939), the latter concerning a well-known house in New Harmony, Ind. His son was probably quite familiar with the Hoosier writers.

5. We discover, partly through some heavy handed symbolism and foreshadowing, that Susanna is a mulatto.

The scar she bears in a particularly delectable location is the result of a fire which killed her father and his black mistress. Note that the surname "Drake" was also used by Faulkner, several years earlier, to designate the neurotic Southern heroine of *Sanctuary.*

Lawrence Jay Dessner (essay date 1976)

SOURCE: "The Case of *Raintree County,*" in *A Question of Quality: Popularity and Value in Modern Creative Writing,* edited by Louis Filler, Bowling Green University Popular Press, 1976, pp. 213-18.

[*In the following essay, Dessner revisits* Raintree County *hoping to find the novel worthy of its initial fanfare, but finds instead very little to praise.*]

Raintree County, a novel of over a thousand pages, was published, with considerable fanfare, some twenty-five years ago. Its author, an obscure young English teacher from Indiana, who had been supporting his wife and their four children on $2,500 a year, had received, six months prior to publication of his first book, the Metro-Goldwyn-Mayer Novel Award and the $125,000 with which MGM asserted their faith in their judgment. The Book-of-the-Month Club had guaranteed another $25,000, and commercial prospects seemed enhanced by early reviews which spoke of "the Great American Novel," and which referred to the book's possibly offensive sexual explicitness.[1] As if in answer to a press agent's prayer, the Reverend Alfred Barrett of Fordham University denounced the novel as "blasphemous." The editors of *Today's Woman* dispatched a writer to Bloomington, Indiana, to do a human-interest story on the great American success story as exemplified by the author, Ross Lockridge, Jr.[2] And to complete this paradigm of the best-seller's progress in our time, the *New Yorker*'s arch and debonair dismissal of the novel, while condescending to discover merit in some aspects of the book, found others to be "swollen," "pretentious," and "absolutely terrible." It was, in sum, "just the sort of plump turkey that they bake to a turn in Hollywood."[3] In its first year, 400,000 copies were sold. By year's end, in the words of America's oracle of popular fashion, *Time Magazine,* it had "floated away in embarrassed silence."[4]

The stage, one might think, is set here for a resurrection, a vindication of this artifact of popular art, and an indictment of those decadent and elitist critics who, blinded by their disdain for the popular, have not judged the novel on its considerable merits. Critical performances of this sort are no longer uncommon, indeed, in some *cul-de-sacs* of the Popular Culture movement, or party, they are the only approved tack. *Raintree County,* however, is not amenable to such treatment. The book's merits, as I have discovered with dismay, and about which I report now with chagrin, are minuscule. Established and establishment critics, for various reasons, about which one may speculate with con-

fidence, have sporadically tried to keep the book alive in this and other cases, with disheartening ease.

The enjoyment of literature, and the study and practice of literary criticism is often, and truly I believe, said to foster the moral virtues of tolerance, sympathy, and compassion. But insofar as the equally moral virtues of clear perception, honest judgment, and painful courage, are concerned, literary criticism may come to seem cruel—although no more cruel than football. We give an E for effort, but no matter how earnest that effort, it is an immaterial factor in our literary evaluation.

In the present case, Ross Lockridge's most earnest effort to write *the* comprehensive American novel is itself at the root of his failure to write one that can be read with pleasure, or even, after a while, with interest. John Shawnessy, and there can be no doubt that this central character of *Raintree County* is another name for Ross Lockridge, wants, furiously, to feel deeply and comprehensively, to ponder the large and capitalized questions of Life, Death, God, Soul, America, and Time. It is a mark of the vastness of his ambition, and of its sublime and self-defeating egotism, that, had *Raintree County* succeeded, it would have been definitive—future novelists and tomorrow's passionate and sensitive young men and women would discover that there was nothing still in need of utterance.

John Shawnessy, for example, contemplates a large rock, older than the civilization that has been built up near it: "The moveless mass of it had been there before the settlers came, had been there when Columbus saw the flowering shores of western islands, had been there when the first man, wandering through the forests of the middle continent discovered a river winding to a lake."[5] The insight, typical of the occasions from which hundreds of such rhapsodies flow, is cerebral and banal. It is not felt. It lacks, precisely, the virtue Coleridge found in Wordsworth, namely "the weight and sanity of thoughts and sentiments, won, not from books, but—from the poet's own meditative observation."[6] Lockridge's thoughts and sentiments, at least the ones he celebrates in *Raintree County,* come from books, and from books poorly written or poorly read. When, or if, the purple prose, extended energetically, succeeds in moving the reader, reaction is sure to follow: the procedure is fraudulent, a manipulation of emotional rhythms and counters which have no basis in experience. It is like a freshman theme on an assigned topic about which the student feels nothing, but over which he knows, or thinks, a bushel of enthusiastic and resounding sentiments should be spread.

The slightest sensation is more deeply felt than the most significant idea, says the English rationalist, and although the dissociation of sensibility his formulation exhibits may, indeed, be undesirable, one does not overcome the liability by an act of will.

It is probable that dinosaurs roamed, in fact that they mated, on the very spot on which I am now standing. John

Shawnessy finds notions like this triggers for the expression, in floods and torrents, of his reverence and special sensitivity to the mysteries of existence. It is the defect Coleridge called "mental bombast,"[7] and when it appears, verbal bombast will not be far behind.

Let me return, almost at random, to the text: John Shawnessy "lay a long time thinking of many things. Around him lay the putrid flower of the City of New Orleans, rankly nodding its head above the magnolia swamp. The languid stream of the river, draining all the water of middle America, found its way here through many changing channels to the sea. Mingled with its yellow tide was the water of a little river far away in Raintree County" (p. 452). He is thinking of many things, we are told, but he is expressing, fervidly, a typical banality. And he continues: "It seemed to him then that she lay there couched in mystery like a sphinx, and that her presence and her musical name meant something tragic and mysterious which was at the heart of all human existence. Surely a strange fate had ferried this scarred, lovely creature up the great river to his arms." Such prose, and the moral, linguistic, and philosophic poverty that underlies it is the basic element of *Raintree County.* There is an egotism, and a pomposity, a churning of emotional waters without first getting one's feet wet, that is embarrassing to see wholeheartedly endorsed by Johnny's creator.

"Think I could fall in love with a girl that was afraid to say her soul's her own! I think of her—and dream! I'd wait a million years and never mind it—for her! The trouble with you is, you don't understand what love means. I love tonight. I love the sand, and the trees, and the grass, and the water and the sky and the moon. . . . It's all in me and I'm in it."[8] That is not John Shawnessy but Richard Miller, Eugene O'Neill's gently comic portrait of a sensitive boy of seventeen. Ross Lockridge, in contrast, intones his "Ah Wilderness" with a straight face.

While there is no irony in the presentation of John Shawnessy, there is a potentially complicating factor to be noticed. John's meditations lead to so many revelations that, whatever a critic might say, John has already proclaimed it his own cosmic and wonderful discovery. The market on truth is cornered, criticism preempted. It is a deeply defensive maneuver and one that cannot succeed. John's practice, not his theorizing, defines him, as in this excerpt: "Sometimes it seemed that in some occult way. . . ." Do not we all beg Freshmen to avoid such empty celebration of vagueness? "Sometimes it seemed that in some occult way John Shawnessy was Willie Shakespeare, and that the plays were still waiting to be written and that everyone was somehow Willie Shakespeare and everyone and everything was Johnny Shawnessy."

To quote a bit of Swinburne's teasing of Tennyson:

> One, who is not, we see; but one, whom we see not, is;
> Surely this is not that; but that is assuredly this.
> 　　　. . . . . .

> God, whom we see not, is; and God, who is not, we see;
> Fiddle, we know, is diddle; and diddle, we take it, is dee.[9]

". . . that life was discovery and not creation—it was permitting oneself to be a great poet and not forcing oneself to be a great poet" (pp. 98-99). Yes, great Art cannot be "forced." Despite the disclaimer, *Raintree County* and Johnny's own work-in-progress are painfully forceful frontal assaults on greatness. This is what follows: "For as he lay on the bank of the Shawmucky, he knew that he too would be a great poet." (Listen to him: "He *knew* that he *too* would be a great poet.") "It seemed to him that he must be a greater poet even than Shakespeare because there was some essence of what he was that Elizabethan England couldn't possibly compose." There is, remarkably, nothing in the text to suggest ironical intent here. Rather, it brings to mind Lockridge's response to a reporter who asked, with not quite a straight face, if he had been influenced by Thomas Wolfe. Lockridge readily acknowledged that influence but added, "I feel that I have a better historical background than Wolfe had."[10] This is the crux of it—the belief, or wish, that Art is made from "historical background," from the reading of many books, and through the exercise of the Will. John Shawnessy entertains the idea that history is myth, a fiction, the product of the collective human sensibility brooding over its condition, that, after all, "feeling comes first." He knows, in fact, all the advanced ideas of his own nineteenth century and of half of ours, and none of them help. There is little perception of feeling in him or in the novel, which is stuffed with the puerilities to which one resorts, in fear and self-defense, from the realities men feel. Human beings can stand very little reality; the Lockridge-Shawnessy amalgam can stand a good deal less than most.

The moral and intellectual and emotional poverty which pervades Lockridge's prose, and which can be demonstrated in short excerpts, also determines the much discussed formal structures of the novel. Its model is the *Ulysses* of James Joyce although there are many other books to which Lockridge's style and structure are obviously indebted. His reading includes, not only primary texts but also modern academic criticism. In turn there has been some academic notice of the complexities of form in *Raintree County.*[11] It is an oddly attractive case, for no matter how far-fetched the analysis gets, *Raintree County*'s text supports it, its allusions and ramifications of imagery and meaning, are printed in red as it were, nuggets of academic gold begging to be discovered. It is as if someone had read Stuart Gilbert's exposition of *Ulysses,* and the files of the *James Joyce Quarterly,* and then confidently set about to write the original novel. But a *Ulysses,* without the richly realized creation of Leopold Bloom, and Molly, and Stephen, and the rest of them, and without the vibrantly keen-eyed and keen-eared verbal presence of Joyce, would be an utterly dead thing.

The last word here I take from the article which most conscientiously discusses "Psychological Symbolism, Archetype, and Myth" in ***Raintree County.*** Jung, and Freud, and Frazer are brought to bear in a most competent analysis whose last sentence gives the charade away: "Through the use of symbolism, Lockridge gives immense meaning and scope to what would otherwise be a banal historical romance."[12] Despite these words, I cannot but believe that their author knows full well that psychological symbolism is not a substitute for psychology, that there can be no meaning on an unpopulated planet, and that "scope" without individual, particularized human sensibilities, is a mouthwash.

"When you called a thing a name, you gave it form" (p. 803). Shawnessy, who says that, shares, with his creator, this central maxim of the modern profession of English literature. But in his hands the flaw in the precept is revealed. Words can give form to things; they can help us understand, and value, and mitigate what we, I hope not pompously refer to as the human condition. But words can also disguise things, blow mist between ourselves and our perceptions of things. They can be man's best means of leading an examined life, or they can be a means of, in the full light of day, refusing to see things as they really are while appearing, courageously, to be doing just that. ***Raintree County*** adopts, with remarkable thoroughness, the second of these courses. The disguise, made by words, succeeds. It is a book all about emotion in which no emotion can be discerned. It is *Everyman* with no man in it.

You can't fool all of the people all of the time. The American reading public is to be congratulated for having only temporarily succumbed to the blandishments of press agentry and to the irresponsibilities of critics who should have known better, and who, if they read the novel through, surely did.

Notes

1. Review of *Raintree County,* Howard Mumford Jones, *Saturday Review,* Jan. 3, 1948; Charles Lee, "Encompassing the American Spirit," *New York Times Book Review,* Jan. 4, 1948; and see *Book Review Digest* (1948). My data derives from these reviews and from the obituary notice, *New York Times,* March 8, 1948, pp. 1, 15.

2. Nanette Kutner, "Ross Lockridge, Jr.—Escape from Main Street," *Saturday Review,* June 12, 1948, pp. 6, 7, 31.

3. Hamilton Basso, Jan. 10, 1948, pp. 72-73.

4. Dec. 20, 1948, p. 101.

5. *Raintree County* (Boston: Houghton Mifflin, 1948), p. 297. Subsequent page numbers, in the text, refer to this edition.

6. *Biographia Literaria,* ch. 22.

7. *Ibid.*

8. Eugene O'Neill, *Ah, Wilderness* (New York: Random House, 1933), conflated from pp. 127, 129, 132.

9. "The Higher Pantheism in a Nutshell," 1880, first and last couplets.

10. Kutner, p. 6.

11. William York Tindall, "Many-leveled Fiction: Virginia Woolf to Ross Lockridge," *College English,* 10 (Nov. 1948), 65-71; Joseph L. Blotner, "*Raintree County* Revisited," *Western Humanities Review,* 10 (Winter, 1955-1956), 57-64; Boyd Litzinger, "Mythmaking in America: 'The Great Stone Face' and *Raintree County,*" *Tennessee Studies in Literature,* 8 (1963), 81-84.

12. Delia Clarke, "*Raintree County*: Psychological Symbolism, Archetype, and Myth," *Thoth,* Fall, 1970, 31-39.

Joel M. Jones (essay date 1977)

SOURCE: "The Presence of the Past in the Heartland: *Raintree County* Revisited," in *MidAmerica IV,* Vol. 4, 1977, pp. 112-21.

[*In the following essay, Jones examines the significance of Lockridge's re-creation of a historical period in* Raintree County.]

> Much care is taken to recreate the artifacts, tenor, and style of life in nineteenth century Indiana. These "antiquities" are evoked with deep feeling for that fading fabric of life. They delight, and are their own reason for being. And yet, for Lockridge this is hardly enough. He is bent on discovering the principles of American development, the foundation of American character.
>
> (Gerald Nemanic, *MidAmerica II,* 1975)

In 1898, Harold Frederic chastized many of his fellow writers by stating that he had once felt a measure of respect for historical fiction, "in the days before the historical novel was a money-making business, and when an author expended all his learning and skill and strength on an historical work for his own credit rather than that of his banking account."[1] In 1900, William Dean Howells, who by both precept and practice gave some indication of the direction historical fiction had to take if it hoped to retain or reclaim any validity as an art form, also objected to the purely commercial nature of the historical romances which were then the craze. Contending that other literary genres had come to be "characterized by the instinct if not the reason of reality," he felt that from historical fiction "nothing of late has been heard but the din of arms, the horrid tumult of the swashbuckler swashing on his buckler." In trying to explain the popular demand for this type of pseudo-historical romance, he conjectured that the American populace at the zenith of the Gilded Age, "having more reason than ever to be ashamed of itself for its lust of gold and blood," was overly "anxious to get away from itself"; therefore it welcomed "the tarradiddles of the historical romancers as a relief from the odious present."

Then he added a most poignant and perceptive comment: that his was a country "which likes a good conscience so much that it prefers unconsciousness to a bad one."[2]

If then, at the turn of the century, most historical fiction was primarily intended and received as escape literature, a significant transformation in the writers' concept of their purpose must have occurred in order to allow Bernard De-Voto to say in 1937 that he and other historical novelists expected their work "to be realistic, to be psychologically valid, and to be socially aware."[3] By the 1930's, then, it was apparent that the nation had a new genre of historical fiction, one of confrontation rather than escape, confrontation of both self and society, of both past and present. The pseudo-historical romance, though by no means extinct, was being countered in large numbers by the true historical novel. Significantly, it was Howells who first posited in 1900—and practiced later in his Midwestern historical novel, *The Leatherwood God* (1916)—several of those principles which would give birth to a form of historical fiction that could truly be called the American historical novel.

One should emphatically note here that not all practitioners of historical fiction turned to a confrontation of historical reality. Most assuredly the twentieth century has delivered its share of histrionic histories and hysterical novels posing as historical fiction; the type Howells objected to so vigorously has not died. But Howells would be pleased, I am sure, with the many works of historical fiction which came to possess inherent value as both literature and history.

Howells objected for several reasons to the historical romances that permeated the literary atmosphere around 1900. He contended that they were "untrue to the complexion of the past" and "to personality in any time," caused largely by the preoccupation of the authors with "bloodshed" and "butchery," and their corresponding inability and lack of desire either to portray character or to capture historical climate. Moreover, he criticized their preoccupation with characters, both fictional and historical, of "titles and ranks," a concern which bore "false witness . . . against the American life of individual worth."[4] Howells' advocacy of the democratization of historical fiction was to become a generally accepted principle among historical novelists several decades later. However, Howells' primary objection to these romances was his belief that "what is despicable, what is lamentable is to have hit the popular fancy and not done anything to change it, but everything to fix it; to flatter it with false dreams of splendor in the past."[5] To Howells the public acceptance of such dreams is the way people come to live on easy terms with themselves. As a literary realist and a philosophical pragmatist, he would have the historical novelist shatter such "false dreams."

Those works of historical fiction of which Howells approved, particularly *War and Peace*, succeed, he says, because "a whole epoch lives again morally, politically, and socially, with such entirety and large inclusion that the reader himself becomes of it." It is by re-creating for us the "motives and feelings" of people in time past—and, therefore, of time present—it is *not* by "taking us out of ourselves, but by taking us into ourselves" that a work of art proves its worth. Acting on the belief of philosophical pragmatism in personal experience as the ultimate source of reality and truth, Howells contends that a novel "convinces us by entering into our experiences and making its events part of that."[6]

In one of his many flashbacks, the protagonist of Ross Lockridge's *Raintree County* (considered by some an American *War and Peace*), John Wickliff Shawnessy, recalls how, while listening to a Centennial Day speech on July 4, 1876, he had "tried to reconstruct the scene of the Founding Fathers founding and fathering the Republic. But it wouldn't come clear and have any meaning. Penetrating into the reality of the Past was an impossible undertaking," he reflects. Then Lockridge proffers the recognition which echoes Howells' prescription for successful historical fiction: "There was . . . only one reality—the reality of someone's experience. What people dealt with when they spoke of the Past was a world of convenient abstractions" (802).[7] These convenient abstractions are the "conventional acceptation by which men live on easy terms with themselves" and which Howells would have the historical novelist disperse. Lockridge, like Howells, tries to go behind those convenient abstraction and conventional acceptations, those illusions of the past, to see the past in terms of that one meaningful reality—the reality of someone's experience.

The particular "someone" in this case is the poet-teacher, John Shawnessy—through whose eyes and mind the reader experiences more than fifty years of life in "an adolescent republic that tried to dream itself to perfection by ignoring the realities of life's remorseless comedy" (162). Though at times Lockridge enters the mind of other characters, most of this massive narrative occurs as the thoughts of one man (Shawnessy) on one day (July 4, 1892) in one place (the imaginary town of Waycross, Raintree County, Indiana). Lockridge chooses for his historical subject matter both the way of life in a small Indiana town in 1892 and the manners and milieu of a larger county and much larger nation from 1839 to 1892.

Raintree County has been described as the most singular of all American historical novels. One should qualify this description by noting that in its singularity *Raintree County* is not simply a historical novel, as I have described that literary phenomenon. A strong case could be made for this work as an example of each one of Northrop Frye's five modes—from the mythical to the ironic. Frye says, for example, the myth "deals with gods," the romance "deals with heroes," and the novel "deals with men."[8] *Raintree County* deals with all three, though significantly, one rarely loses sight of the "men." I think it can be shown that finally the low mimetic mode of literary realism is the controlling one—and though Howells would find it a long trip from Leatherwood Valley to Raintree County, he would find Lockridge's landscape and legends familiar territory. Lockridge's ultimate concern is with all human illusions, and his efforts are directed specifically both to an examination of the illusions of nineteenth-century America—the illusions it had of itself (of its past, present and future) and the illusions the present may have of it—and to a Howellsian revelation of the realities underlying those illusions.

Joseph L. Blotner, writing of **Raintree County** a decade after his appearance, feels this work to be possibly "one of the five to six most important novels of this era," and points out, as did the rest of the contemporary reviewers, that in both narrative technique and structure "the influence of James Joyce's *Ulysses* is unmistakable."[9] Like Joyce, Lockridge needed a method by which to control his materials at all levels; and as William York Tindall remarks, "Lockridge learned many tricks from Joyce."[10] Less esoteric than Joyce, but, considering his intended audience, just as effective, Lockridge's use of the stream-of-consciousness technique dramatically portrays the specious present of a man in the past—and as that individual is a reflector of the social forces and attitudes endemic to his region and nation, his personal experience offers insights into the confluence of complexities and contradictions of the specious present of that historical period in general.

The reader learns at one point that Shawnessy's daughter, Eva, feels that "she, too, like the town of Waycross was a being filled with a becoming" (754). In like manner, the entire novel is filled with the "becoming" of a man and his milieu—and it is through this sense of becoming that the successful historical novelist renders his subject both historical and novel. That is, as Shawnessy, in fifty-two flashbacks, reveals the realities which have constituted a half-century of personal experience—as he attempts to reconstruct his life for himself—the reader also experiences those realities and becomes involved with the emerging of the man and his moment. Shawnessy, with all his dreams and disillusionments comes to life, and so does the nation with its dreams built on illusions. Underlying all the discussion and dramatization of dreams and illusions, though, one finds a never-ending flow of the realistic details necessary for any final understanding of the life of an individual, a region, or a nation.

A contemporary reviewer referred to the effect of Lockridge's technique as being comparable to that of a "time exposure" as opposed to a "snapshot" (represented, he feels, by a work such as *Main Street*).[11] As with a time exposure, Lockridge's technique allows him to capture the transformations, sharp and subtle, which have marked this period in our history. As often happens in a time exposure, there are scenes which become blurred, the reader being unable to discern precisely the physical nature of the setting. One such scene is Johnny's stay in New York. The "city" represents to him obviously the new industrial America juxtaposed to the rural, pastoral milieu from which he comes. One learns through Johnny's thoughts

that "The City was the meeting of the trains in marshalling yards" (817), that the "City was the Great American Newsstory" (818), and that "the City had an insatiable appetite for words and drugged itself with the thin music of a billion cliches" (820). The physical details, though, are missing; the reader gets a sense of the city, and that is all—but perhaps that was all one such as Shawnessy from heartland rural America would personally experience. At other times Lockridge does present the physical realities which are an integral part of the history in question; in his Civil War scenes, for example, one touches and tastes the everyday realities of those, as Johnny calls them, "anonymous architects of History" (601), the privates. The Civil War is just one of several national events which Lockridge transmutes from a conventional abstraction to an emerging reality by presenting it in terms of the personal experience of his protagonist.

Lockridge achieves, finally, what Charles Lee calls "a critical biography of America from the period of its agrarian innocence through the Civil War and into the era of . . . industrial expansion."[12] Shawnessy's biography becomes the region's and the nation's. His is the heart of the heartland. As Lee, Blotner, and Tindall have all pointed out, perhaps Lockridge's most impressive aesthetic achievement is the extensive temporal and structural parallels he establishes between the personal experiences of Shawnessy and public events in the national experience. For example, a long series of important events dealing with the outbreak of the Civil War parallel exactly, in terms of time, the disruptive occurrences in Shawnessy's first marriage. And most significantly, the parallel events on both levels always have the same causal and consequential relationships to preceding and following events. Blotner notes that this constitutes an artistic fusion of private and public levels of meaning accomplished with similar skill by very few historical novelists (or novelists), American or otherwise.[13] The characters and events of **Raintree County** are invested with multiple meanings, and finally function on many levels: the personal and national, the narrative and symbolic, the mundane and mythical, the particular and universal, and the historical and ahistorical.[14]

Always, though, this novel remains the story of an American in Indiana in the nineteenth century; and on just this level, Lockridge renders insights into the American character of that period which later become the theses of scholarly studies. In *The American Adam* (1955) R. W. B. Lewis, in his chapter on Walt Whitman and "the New Adam," writes, "This new Adam is both maker and namer."[15] In **Raintree County** Shawnessy had reflected that Americans "were the new Adams . . . poets of the open road . . . who brought the miracle of names" to the land (887). The thesis of Leo Marx's *The Machine in the Garden: Technology and the Pastoral Ideal in America* (1964)[16] is vividly dramatized in **Raintree County** where one learns that the "sound of this century . . . is the wail of a train whistle at the crossing. In this lone vowel . . . the Nineteenth Century has its perfect poem" (984). Those observations, though obviously the result of hindsight, do not strike the reader as intrusive because the characters personally experience the realities behind the theories. Lockridge has no desire to substitute one "convenient abstraction" for another. Regardless of whatever else Lockridge may have achieved in *Raintree County,* he definitely projects a sense of nineteenth-century America. As Gerald Nemanic points out in his recent perceptive critique (from which the epigraph for this essay comes) of *Raintree County,* Lockridge's projection of person and place is based on a careful familiarity with "the artifacts, tenor, and style of life in nineteenth century Indiana." The ultimate intent of these historical specifics is the discovery, as Nemanic puts it, of "the principles of American development, the foundation of American character."[17] In the fictional mode, then, Lockridge has sought answers to the same questions as those which have motivated American Studies scholars such as Lewis, Smith, and Marx. I would agree with Nemanic that one might regard *Raintree County* as "The Final Experiment with the Great American Novel"—but I also would suggest that it is indubitably "The Great American Studies Novel."

One might even contend that many of the strengths and weaknesses of the novel result from its typically American nature—it is extensively eclectic and markedly experimental. Lockridge, at one time or another, borrows techniques or themes directly from Hawthorne, Tolstoy, Whitman, Twain, Joyce, Dos Passos, Wolfe, and Faulkner. For example, the germ of the novel, if a single one can be identified, must have been Hawthorne's short story "The Great Stone Face"; and Lockridge impressively integrates this motif, as the society he depicts discloses its priorities and value system by hailing the politician, the businessman, and the military leader as its respective heroes—never, significantly, recognizing the poet and hometown philosopher, John Wickliff Shawnessy. His emulation of the Wolfean sprawl and echoing of several Wolfean themes, on the other hand, contributes very little. It is his adaptation of the Joycean stylistic and structural device of the stream of consciousness, of course, which finally enables him to succeed in his multifaceted endeavor. Also in a typically American fashion, he manages to use this traditionally esoteric literary technique in a manner which does not alienate the general reader. Tindall believes that Lockridge "succeeded in narrowing, if not entirely closing, the space that has separated the general reader from the many-leveled novel," doing so "without the loss of value that might be supposed." "Value," says Tindall, "depends not so much upon the amount of reality in a book as the amount of reality under control, and control is a matter of method."[18] Lockridge manages to gain control over a large amount of the historical reality of his region and the nation—and I feel he succeeds in narrowing, if not entirely closing, the space that often separates the general reader from the multileveled reality of the American past.

John Shawnessy's quest for identity in Raintree County embodies the paradoxes and perversities to be experienced by anyone engaged in an authentic realization of what David Anderson calls the "psychological dimension" of a region.[19] To travel to the heart of the heartland—rather with Walter Havighurst or William Gass (to pick two of its more astute contemporary interpreters) as one's guide, makes no difference—is to know the paradoxical symbiosis of the barren and the bountiful, the gray and the green, the oppressive and the liberating, or (to reinforce the metaphor of heart) the arteriosclerotic and aerobic. Ross Lockridge takes us on such a trip to the ever-emerging past of the heartland. His personal response to the psychological dimension of his place and time, suicide, does not preclude the viability of the vision he shares with us in *Raintree County.* Only by returning in thought to the realities of his past does Lockridge's Shawnessy come to recognize that his identity will not be found finally in the simple illusions of innocence he has so long maintained. Only by realizing that "America is the image of human change" (769), that his world has been, is, and will continue to be one of continual change, does he come to know that his "victory is not in consummations but in quests (1059). So must it be for us. And our quest can be immeasurably furthered by the efforts of writers capable of giving to the past a new sense of presence—that sense by which one confronts and comprehends the changing realities of Leatherwood Valley and Raintree County, the sense by which the American past becomes both shadow and illumination, problematic and present.

Notes

1. Harold Frederic, "On Historical Novels Past and Present," *The Bookman,* 8 (December 1898), 333.

2. W. D. Howells, "The New Historical Romances," *North American Review,* 171 (December 1900), 936.

3. Bernard DeVoto, "Fiction Fights the Civil War," *Saturday Review of Literature,* 17 (December 18, 1937), 4.

4. Howells, pp. 939-941.

5. *Ibid.,* p. 943.

6. *Ibid.,* p. 946.

7. Ross Lockridge, Jr., *Raintree County* (Boston, 1948), p. 493. Hereafter the page numbers in parentheses refer to this edition.

8. Northrop Frye, *Anatomy of Criticism, Four Essays* (Princeton, New Jersey, 1957), p. 306.

9. Joseph L. Blotner, "*Raintree County* Revisited," *The Western Humanities Review,* 10 (1956), 58. Also, see John Leggett, *Ross and Tom: Two American Tragedies* (New York, 1974), passim.

10. William York Tindall, "Many-Leveled Fiction: Virginia Woolf to Ross Lockridge," *College English,* 10 (November 1948), 70.

11. James Hilton, "Flashing Vision of America Lost and Found," *New York Herald-Tribune Books,* 24 (January 4, 1948), 1.

12. Charles Lee, "Encompassing the American Spirit," *New York Times Book Review,* January 4, 1948, p. 5.

13. Blotner, pp. 61-65.

14. See Blotner, p. 61, and Tindall, p. 70.

15. R. W. B. Lewis, *The American Adam: Innocence, Tragedy, and Tradition in the Nineteenth Century* (Chicago, 1955), p. 51.

16. Leo Marx, *The Machine in the Garden: Technology and the Pastoral Ideal in America* (New York, 1964).

17. Gerald Nemanic, "Ross Lockridge, *Raintree County,* and the Epic of Irony," *MidAmerica II* (1975), p. 38.

18. Tindall, p. 71.

19. David D. Anderson, "The Dimensions of the Midwest," *MidAmerica I* (1974), p. 10.

Donald J. Greiner (essay date 1978)

SOURCE: "Ross Lockridge and the Tragedy of *Raintree County,*" in *Critique,* Vol. 20, No. 3, 1978, pp. 51-62.

[*In the following essay, Greiner argues that Lockridge's instant success and subsequent suicide are reflected in the experiences of his main character in* Raintree County.]

Although published thirty-one years ago on January 5, 1948, Ross Lockridge's **Raintree County** remains a curio of modern American fiction. Neither taught in the universities nor studied by the specialists, the novel illustrates the old cliche of known but not read. The critical silence is puzzling. Consider these facts: some readers, including me, regard **Raintree County** as one of the ten best American novels published since World War II;[1] it had a widespread pre-publication build-up, including excerpts in *Life*;[2] it won the prestigious MGM award of at least $150,000 and resulting publicity; it was a Book-of-the-Month Club selection; and by March 1948, **Raintree County** was, despite its 1066 pages, the number-one best seller in the country, having earned reviews in most major journals and newspapers. Indeed, according to Lockridge's "unauthorized"[3] biographer, John Leggett, the reviews of **Raintree County** were "of a prominence and profusion that is no longer seen."

Yet by March 1948, Ross Lockridge was a suicide at age 34, and the critical analysis which his fiction invites and rewards never materialized.[4] One can only wonder what happened and hope that the novel will receive the study it deserves. Outlining the high points of Lockridge's life as they pertain to the composition of **Raintree County,** I should like to suggest that the hot flash of success and the sudden plunge to failure which Lockridge suffered are reflected in the characterization of his all-American hero, John Wickliff Shawnessy.

A native of the heart of America, Indiana, and the son of a specialist in local history, Ross Lockridge, Jr., first de-

clared his intent to write a big novel while a college student. He was fascinated by the life of his grandfather, John Wesley Shockley, a man who wrote for his hometown newspaper under the pseudonym "Seth Twigs" which Lockridge later assigned to the fictional John Wickliff Shawnessy. Like Johnny Shawnessy, Lockridge was intrigued by Indiana history, and suspecting, like Shawnessy, that his own forebears were illegitimately descended from Thomas Carlyle, he apparently fulfilled his need for family roots by immersing himself in local myths and traditions. Indeed, his notion of the golden raintree was the result of his research into the history of Robert Owen's nineteenth-century social experiment, New Harmony. He was clearly a bright young boy, praised for his ability to memorize and recite long passages of poetry. Later, graduating from Indiana University with the highest average in the University's history, Lockridge was nevertheless frantic at the thought of failure.

Despite his optimism and a self-confidence which was occasionally misunderstood as conceit and even arrogance, Lockridge forced himself to accomplish more and more for fear of doing less. He was obsessed with being number one, especially when he decided that his way to recognition would be as an author. Leggett reports that Lockridge's original plan was to write a novel about his Indiana family which traced the great changes in twentieth-century America, but this project went nowhere. Putting it aside in 1938, he began an epic poem titled **"The Dream of the Flesh of Iron."**;[5] Clearly the forerunner of **Raintree County,** the poem tells of a sensitive, intelligent young man who, fashioned as an Everyamerican, pursues the meaning of his country and life itself cast in the guise of a beautiful lady. She forever eludes the dreamer, and he discovers that pursuit, the quest alone, has meaning.

Two points are significant here. First, by 1940, Lockridge had written the germ of the unconsummated love affair which gives such poignancy and urgency to **Raintree County,** the story of what would become the courtship of John Shawnessy and Nell Gaither. More importantly, perhaps, Lockridge saw that the American hero would forever fail in his quest. Whether or not Lockridge accepted, however vaguely, inevitable failure for himself at this point in his life is doubtful, but he seems to have understood how the poetic dreams and heroic deeds which he gave his fictional counterpart would remain forever unfulfilled. The contrast between his own confidence and the mood of defeat in the poem is startling. From the vantage point of hindsight, it is also prophetic.

By Christmas 1940, Lockridge, then a graduate student at Harvard, had completed four hundred typed pages of his epic. Uneasy about the poem but unapologetic about his aspirations, he submitted **"The Dream of the Flesh of Iron"**; to Houghton Mifflin in February 1941. It was promptly rejected. Leggett's account of Lockridge's reaction is revealing, for it suggests how the author managed to rationalize failure in favor of his need to protect his confidence: "Houghton Mifflin's reaction bruised Ross's pride and, with what he was to describe as 'a characteristic, grandiose decision,' he shelved the manuscript. But self-certainty was undamaged. He concluded that **'The Dream'**; was sound enough, simply not commercial and he cast off his depression."[6] This description seems accurate, for Lockridge immediately began the novel which would eventually bring him money and fame and which he would not complete until 1947.

Selecting a course at Harvard in contemporary literature, he found Thomas Wolfe's lyrical flow of words, Thomas Mann's shattered culture, and James Joyce's long novel framed by the events of a single day. Just as influential to the structure of what would become **Raintree County** was his appreciation of the cinematic technique of D. W. Griffith's *Intolerance* and Orson Welles's *Citizen Kane,* films which showed him the possibilities of multihistorical layers, flashbacks, and unusual transitions from present focus to past action. From these masters he learned how to set his novel during a single day (July 4, 1892) and still interweave both dream sequences and the literal histories of nineteenth-century America, Indiana, and his mother's family. Leggett quotes his intention: to "express the American myth—give shape to the lasting 'heroic' qualities of the American people." Lockridge believed that he could write the "first real representation of the American culture in fiction."[7] Significantly, his fictional hero has the same goal. Unfortunately, the task devoured his strength. Working on the novel from 1941 to 1946, he earned his living by teaching at Simmons College for $2000 a year. He even scrapped his rough draft and began again after completing 2000 pages of manuscript. The final draft contained 600,000 words which took his wife eighteen months to type. On April 24, 1946, Lockridge submitted *The Riddle of Raintree County* to Houghton Mifflin.

He seemed entirely confident. Yet in less than two years he would kill himself. Although no one knows for certain, the tension between supreme confidence and fear of failure began to stretch tighter following the submission to Houghton Mifflin. Nothing snapped for nearly a year, but in April 1946, Lockridge began a period of unsettling highs and lows. Externally, he radiated confidence. Hearing nothing from Houghton Mifflin, for example, he took the extraordinary step of writing to editor Dorothy Hillyer to tell her that the critics would praise his book and in turn influence the public: "It will be talked about, written about, and read, read, read!" How right he was. He was so convinced that his novel would be discussed as a candidate for the ever elusive Great American Novel that he rejected an offer to serialize in *Ladies Home Journal* despite his need for money. Lockridge wanted **Raintree County** to meet the public in one piece.

The readers' reports from Houghton Mifflin tended to support his high opinion: "the novel Walt Whitman might have written"; "Stephen Benet's sweep of American history, Sinclair Lewis's debunking strain, the symbolism of Hawthorne." Lockridge himself called it the "biggest book ever published in one piece by an American novelist of serious stature,"[8] and immediately following formal acceptance, he flooded the Houghton Mifflin editorial and publicity offices with letter after letter advising the company how to print and publicize his book. One can only marvel at the mixture of confidence, arrogance, and genius, and then point out the irony that at the moment Lockridge was surely not recognized as an American novelist of "serious stature."

Not yet, at any rate. For behind the confidence and genius lurked the shadow of failure which had nagged him all along. Too many years, too much of his spirit had poured into **Raintree County,** and he discovered that he could neither cut it loose without overseeing the entire publication process nor rework the rough edges without giving rein to his doubts. A year after submission to and acceptance by Houghton Mifflin, he was still revising the novel, trying first to omit 50,000 words as a condition for winning the $150,000 MGM award, and then to excise several thousand more for the Book-of-the-Month Club. He had labored on the book for so long that his revising became compulsive. **Raintree County** was more real to him than life itself, and in the end it exhausted him. While awaiting publication, for example, he tried and failed to begin a new novel. Paranoia set in; after recognizing signs of a mental breakdown, he endured a series of electric shock treatments. Pathetically, he even tried to discipline himself with a list of rules of behavior, the foremost of which was to forget **Raintree County**: "I should exclude it from my thoughts or, if I think of it at all, simply pick it up and read one of the optimistic 'sweet' parts."[9] Nothing worked. On March 6, 1948, two months after the publication of his epic novel, now the number-one best seller, and following receipt of a check for $122,500 for royalties and prizes, Ross Lockridge drove his new Kaiser into the garage, locked the door, and turned on the motor to die.

Why? No one knows for certain. Leggett speculates that Lockridge was plagued by the "bitch goddess" of success to which American authors seem especially vulnerable, that Lockridge could not handle the spotlight. He has a point. Equally plausible is the suggestion that Lockridge's confidence in his own genius, a confidence which enables him to endure the long years of work on a first novel he *knew* would be both a critical and popular success, was undermined by the practical decision to change the manuscript in order to win the coveted prizes from MGM and the Book-of-the-Month Club. One of the primary themes of **Raintree County** is the threat of practical action and profits to idealism and art, and it may be that while Lockridge was celebrating John Shawnessy's dreams over Garwood Jones's manipulations, Cash Carney's millions, and Professor Stiles's cynicism, he was also aware that he may have sacrificed the integrity of his novel to the promise of commercial triumph. The point is not that the novel was compromised by the demands of movie studio and book club but that Lockridge thought it was. Finally, I suggest, he recognized in his fictional hero the same process which gnawed at him: well-founded confidence challenged by unexpected doubt.

John Wickliff Shawnessy does not even contemplate suicide; indeed, at the end of the novel he walks home with his dreams and visions intact, having parried verbal thrust after verbal thrust from his attractive yet cynical alter ego, Jerusalem Webster Stiles. But at fifty-three, he has not written the grand epic which has been in the formative stages for thirty years, his tale "of a man's days on the breast of the land,"[10] and we know he never will. Ironically, Ross Lockridge dreamed of writing the legend of America, did so, and killed himself, while John Shawnessy yearns to write the American epic, fails to do so, and lives. At the end of *Raintree County,* Lockridge describes his fictional counterpart: "Make way, make way for the Hero of Raintree County! His victory is not in consummations but in quests!" (1059). Both men fail, but Shawnessy fails with his "great fair dream" still whole. One must wonder if in consummating his own dream Lockridge consumed himself. The quest was all.

Even the reviews of *Raintree County* confirmed for its author his dichotomy of success and failure. Beginning with the premise that "all great literature is of the nature of myth," Lockridge composed a vision of America that is both passionately lyrical and historically accurate. Many of the first reviews celebrated his idealism. James Hilton, for example, wrote that the novel "grips the heart and stirs the mind. By any standard it is a novel of rare stature for these days."[11] Charles Lee called it "an achievement of art and purpose, a cosmically brooding book full of significance and beauty."[12] Elizabeth Johnson praised the "pulsing, if misdirected sincerity" and complained only of the tendency to cram in too much.[13] And Howard Mumford Jones noted that the novel is "everywhere competent and often distinguished"; "the breath of life sweeps through its voluminous pages; and it may be that *Raintree County* marks the end of a long slump in American fiction."[14] These are impressive opinions from important commentators, the kind Ross Lockridge needed to maintain faith in himself and his work, but he shrank from the backlash. *Time*'s complaint that the novel is "an original, spacious, and significant work of the second order" was bested by the *Christian Science Monitor*: "There is, incidentally, a functional lustiness of action and word in Mr. Lockridge which to some readers might be offensive."[15] M. P. Corcoran took up the tone of moral judgment, admitting Lockridge's mastery of style and narration but accusing him of ruining the novel with "eroticism and obscenity."[16] Finally, Hamilton Basso leveled a frontal attack: misspelling Lockridge's name, Basso condescendingly advised that there "is still time for him to learn that bulk is not accomplishment, that fanciness is not literature, and that Thomas Wolfe, while an excellent man in his way, has defects that look absolutely terrible secondhand."[17]

Published while Lockridge was on the verge of a mental collapse, these negative reviews extinguished the glow of those which praised. Especially devastating was the tone of moral censure, for it confirmed his own doubts. Lockridge worried so about his parents' reactions to the descriptions of adolescent love, nude swimming, Nell's na-

kedness, and Susanna's scarred breast that he feared the book's appearance in Bloomington. His fears were justified. Leggett reports that a handful of letters from Indiana readers attacked the novel for lewdness, and in February 1948 Lockridge learned of an article in the *New York Times* which summarized a speech by Father A. J. Barrett in which the Jesuit priest labeled *Raintree County* as "rank obscenity."

Lockridge had already suffered puritan pangs of guilt before they were exacerbated by the public press, and he gave John Wickliff Shawnessy the same moral twinges. Shawnessy seems to be the man Lockridge wished to be, the artist who dreams a masterpiece but never completes it. That situation would also be intolerable, for Lockridge knew that Shawnessy's unfinished epic was a kind of failure. Caught between consummation and quest, between a less than perfect creation and the continuing struggle to create, both men fell short of the mark. Shawnessy holds on while Lockridge tragically dropped out because Shawnessy's guilt can be absorbed in the privacy of his lyrical visions and passionate dreams. Lockridge could not do the same for the obvious reason that his visions became public when he attributed some of them to his fictional hero.

No better illustration exists than the dust jacket and map which Lockridge drew for the novel. Ostensibly a map of Raintree County, the dust jacket depicts a reclining, nude female with hills for breasts and a tributary of the Shawmucky River flowing between her legs toward the genitals. One does not have to read too far with this cover in mind to note that Shawnessy's pursuit of life is somehow wrapped up in sexual intercourse. Just as significant is the map of the County which Lockridge positioned opposite the title page. The metaphorical river of life, the Shawmucky, flows toward both Lake Paradise and the Great Swamp, and the inviting curves around the townships of Mount Pleasant and Summit point toward the town of Climax. One might not make too much of Lockridge's drawings and his apprehensions about moral censure if he had not explicitly identified his hero's quest with the maps. Early in the novel, but chronologically late in his life, John Shawnessy glances at the parchment:

> He was certain that in the pattern of its lines and letters this map contained the answer to the old conundrum of his life in Raintree County. It was all warm and glowing with the secret he had sought for half a century. The words inscribed on the deep paper were dawn-words, each one disclosing the origin and essence of the thing named. But as he sought to read them, they dissolved into the substance of the map. With a feeling suspended between erotic hunger and intellectual curiosity, he looked for the young woman.
>
> (5-6)

The association between the "origin and essence of the thing" and erotic yearning is unmistakable. Surely the map means more to both Lockridge and Shawnessy than merely an indication of local boundaries. For Johnny the parchment looms larger than life, for it holds the essence of all things desirable and mysterious. Later we learn that even as a young boy Johnny Shawnessy patterns his life on the outline of the map: "He had suddenly achieved a world. The dearly bought victory of man over the increate and stubborn earth was his. He had gazed at a map of his own life, the pattern of himself, securely bounded by the four walls of Raintree County. He held the whole great riddle in the focus of his eyes—naked, imminent, perfect" (60-61). And when he finally pursues the secret of Lake Paradise with all of the suggestions of Adam and Eve before the Fall, he tumbles into the Great Swamp and finds himself caught in the solid substance of sexual intercourse, the stuff of life itself: "The creatures of the river swarmed, shrieked, swam, coupled, seeded, bloomed, died, stank around him. He appeared to be in the very source of life, a womblike center. River and shore were one; leaf and flesh, blossom and genitalia, seed and egg were one cruel impulse" (103).

However guiltily, Lockridge uses the sexual allusions consciously. Steeped in Freud's theories, he even suggests that the pagan id propels John Wickliff Shawnessy to connect the secret of America with the mystery of sex: "The two were always colliding with each other as Mr. Shawnessy went his ritual way through conversations and thoroughfares, and mr. shawnessy carried on his eternal vagabondage through a vast reserve of memories and dreams. . . . It was clearly the whim of mr. shawnessy to prepare a naked woman on the stone slab in the Post Office, but it was Mr. Shawnessy who timidly asked for a newspaper, trying his best to adapt himself and his puritan conscience to the bizarre world of his twin" (18).[18] Ross Lockridge could adapt his own puritan conscience to his free flowing visions as long as he gave himself privately to the composition of *Raintree County,* but when he passed the novel on to the world, he feared moral censure from his family in particular and the reading public in general.

One cannot say that John Shawnessy escapes the pangs of conscience but only suggest that, unlike his creator, he does not question the association of sexuality and idealistic visions to the point of desperation. He feels guilty, for example, when he inadvertently sees Nell Gaither swimming nude in the Shawmucky and then makes the mistake of indirectly describing the experience in the local newspaper. Yet he successfully merges his guilt with his idealization of Nell as a goddess and with his acceptance of the lesson from the girl whose "impudent nakedness" stuns him: "Beneath her puritan ways, she was not afraid of life" (108). A similar guilt threatens when he joins Southern belle Susanna Drake for a sexual fling beside the same river, but even though her full yet scar-marred breasts portend her own dissolution and that of the nation in the Civil War, he counters the guilt by marrying her. Later he cautiously accepts an invitation from actress Laura Golden to enter her secret bedroom, only to be spared the experience by the arrival of a telegram announcing his mother's death. Finally, as a middle-aged father and husband, he feels that he must avoid the public eye when perusing a pirated edition of the history of the county in search of nude draw-

ings. The implications are suggestive; his vision of the goddess recedes the older he gets and the more he pursues it. His unobstructed view of Nell, who is unblemished except for a mole on her buttocks, gives way to Susanna's vivid scar. Shawnessy enjoys the nakedness of both, but with Laura Golden he encounters a fully dressed temptress of many masks and names who hides behind a facade of sophistication and experience as Nell would never do. Finally, married to a woman half his age, he finds that he is left with not naked flesh to inspire his dream but only the possibility of nude drawings to satisfy his curiosity.

Professor Jerusalem Webster Stiles nevertheless hints that John Wickliff Shawnessy successfully identifies his life with the sexually suggestive map of Raintree County, and that thus he is a legitimate candidate for the role of creator and preserver of the American dream. At the end of the novel, the Professor traces in smoke the letters JWS which, when buffeted by the wind, assume the shape of the winding Shawmucky River on the map. Ross Lockridge wanted to believe in this identification too. Yet one continues to wonder. We cannot help notice how the Reverend Lloyd G. Jarvey's efforts to label Shawnessy a degenerate fail and yet foreshadow both Lockridge's own reservations about the moral tenor of his book and the forthcoming public accusations of lewdness. More importantly, we question the motive behind the Professor's gesture. That the Professor is Shawnessy's alter ego is suggested by their identical initials. The dark side of Johnny's questing innocence, Stiles serves as a cynical counterweight to his idealism. Shawnessy needs the Professor, for the old mentor forces him to defend his faith in himself and the nation, but Stiles is also associated with the devil. Journalist where Johnny is poet, urban where Johnny is rural, and promiscuous where Johnny is monogamous, the Professor believes as fervently in his cynical view of life as Shawnessy does in his dreams. Note the association with Satan's fire and brimstone when Stiles leaves Johnny for the last time:

> He and Mr. Shawnessy shook hands, and the Professor swung onto the coach behind the coalcar. The glare from the furnace showed a long, thin body in a soiled white suit, a face old and cunning, black eyes shining through pince-nez glasses. Already the engine was beginning to puff. The smoke and the furnace stung Mr. Shawnessy's eyes so that they smarted.
>
> (1056)

The Professor shows his agility by carving the JWS initials backward in the smoke so that they are easily identified by John. Our first thought is that Stiles is celebrating his pupil, but recalling that JWS are also the Professor's initials, we have to wonder if he is playing one more cynical joke, perhaps revealing that Shawnessy's unfinished epic and unfulfilled quest are noble but worth no more in post-Civil War America than initials fading away through smoke.

Lockridge, of course, was aware of these negative implications, just as he knew readers would suspect that Shawnessy's dreams are tarnished by failure. Driving himself for six years to create an ideal American hero who expresses his own aspirations for the nation, Lockridge could not help note the negative reflection upon his own hopefulness when the fictional hero falls short of the goal. On one level, John Shawnessy must leave incomplete the grand epic of America because the country itself fails to fulfill its promise. Fashioning his lyrical reveries in the relative innocence of ante-bellum America, he discovers that his vision no longer touches the reality of a country wracked by slavery, torn by war, and corrupted by urban anonymity. Progress itself and the sickening purge of the national conscience by bloodshed sully both the dreamer and his dream. Johnny's inability to finish his epic, then, symbolizes America's failure to live its potential. When Shawnessy rejects Laura Golden and the city to return home to Indiana, he sees that the land has changed. Instead of Nell beside the river, he finds trains upon the earth: "But listen to the wail of the train at the crossing. O, sound of sorrow and farewell, as we go down the years of life into the gulf together! Lost years. Last years. Stations upon the plain" (988).

On another level, John Wickliff Shawnessy is culpable, as Lockridge undoubtedly knew. Irony dogs his life. Even if Johnny does not understand, we do: he makes the wrong choice time after time. When a young man, he refuses to follow the Great National Road to the virgin West, despite the promise of its lure and the symbolism of its presence through the center of the county. He prefers instead to search for his heritage in the overgrowth of the Great Swamp and Lake Paradise, refusing to leave home. In addition, he never consummates his love for Nell Gaither, the personification of America's potential purity; he marries instead the scarred Susanna, even when he suspects that she is not pregnant, giving himself to a still lovely yet grievously wounded nation. When Susanna collapses in madness and abandons the heart of Indiana to return to the war-ravaged South, Johnny joins the Union Army, losing once again his chance with Nell. Finally, when he returns from the War, reborn from his own mistaken death notice in the newspaper, he marries a country woman half his age. He thus rejects the potential of the city where the new, albeit less glorious America will have to find its future: "Was this the Republic that he and his comrades had been tramping toward in the Great March? Was this the Union they had hammered out ringing on the forge of Battle? Was this the Raintree County of which Johnny Shawnessy had intended to become the hero?" (772). The answer, unfortunately, for both John Shawnessy and Ross Lockridge is yes and no: yes, in the sense that unwise choices soiled the vision and changed the country; no, in the sense that for some the dream still holds out its promise. Shawnessy can accept the paradox; Lockridge could not.

John Shawnessy fails because he declines to grow with the country. Yet his greatness lies in his refusal, for he is a poet-figure who sings not of fulfillment but of quest. Our contradictory opinion of him finds support in the Professor's description of his own early years. Late in the novel we learn that Jerusalem Webster Stiles, like John Wickliff Shawnessy, was also once a child in Raintree County. Unlike Johnny, who goes home when his mother dies, the Professor leaves for the city, returning occasionally to the county but never coming back home. The alter ego tells John that he "learned early, with the bitterness of the homeless child, that the earth cares nothing for our grief, and that even our mother who cared for us in life cares nothing for us in death. . . . She has forgotten us. She doesn't remember our face" (987). We understand that he speaks for both Johnny and himself, for metaphorically they are one character.

If John Shawnessy repudiates the Professor's wisdom, if he insists upon living the legend of his life "by a myth of homecoming and a myth of resurrection," Ross Lockridge was not so sure (988). Wanting to believe while shaping his vision, he could not believe when he finished his novel. Too many of his doubts surfaced in the character of his protagonist, and too much of his guilt seared him when he released his creation to the public. If we censure John Shawnessy even as we praise him, we must wonder if Ross Lockridge deserves the same.

The pathos is that Lockridge apparently tried but could not exorcise during the composition of **Raintree County** the threats to his once supreme confidence. His hero reflects his tensions, and his tensions mirrored an uncertainty which finally consumes him. Unable to finish his epic, John Shawnessy achieves a measure of success—he refuses to abandon his dream. Ross Lockridge was not so lucky. He feared that in completing his masterpiece he had compromised his vision. We can only read **Raintree County** and regret.

Notes

1. For the joy of debate, my other nine choices are: Robert Penn Warren, *All the King's Men*; Ralph Ellison, *Invisible Man*; J. D. Salinger, *The Catcher in the Rye*; Saul Bellow, *Henderson The Rain King*; Joseph Heller, *Catch-22*; John Hawkes, *Second Skin*; William Styron, *The Confessions of Nat Turner*; George Garrett, *Death of the Fox*; and Thomas Pynchon, *Gravity's Rainbow*.

2. The issue of *Life* for 8 September 1947 carried the story of the footrace between Johnny Shawnessy and Flash Perkins.

3. The term "unauthorized" is Leggett's: John Leggett, *Ross and Tom: Two American Tragedies* (New York: Simon and Schuster, 1974), p. 24. Most of the biographical information cited in this essay can be found in Leggett's book.

4. As of this writing, only four critical essays and two notes join Leggett's biographical *Ross and Tom* as the published scholarship on *Raintree County*: Joseph L. Blotner, "*Raintree County* Revisited," *Western Humanities Review,* 10 (1956), 57-64; Boyd Litz-

inger, "Mythmaking in America: 'The Great Stone Face' and *Raintree County*," *Tennessee Studies in English*, 8 (1964), 81-84; Delia Clarke, "*Raintree County*: Psychological, Symbolism, Archetype, and Myth," *Thoth*, 11 (1970), 31-39; Leonard Lutwack, "*Raintree County* and the Epicising Poet in American Fiction," *Ball State University Forum*, 13 (1972), 14-28; Lawrence J. Dessner, "Value in Popular Fiction: The Case of *Raintree County*," *Junction* 1 (1973), 147-52; and Gerald C. Memanic, "Ross Lockridge, *Raintree County*, and the Epic of Iron," *Midamerica*, 2 (1975), 35-46.

5. The poem remains unpublished and apparently unavailable for close analysis.

6. Leggett, p. 68. The reader's report from Houghton Mifflin is telling: "an immensely long narrative poem divided into short lyrics, interspersed with frequent prose passages of exposition. This is all about War and the Machine, human depravity and human aspiration, pretty well tangled up together and expressed through symbols that aren't very fresh."

7. Leggett, p. 79.

8. Leggett, pp. 89, 114.

9. Leggett, p. 178.

10. Ross Lockridge, Jr., *Raintree County* (Boston: Houghton Mifflin, 1948), p. 1058. Subsequent references are to this edition.

11. James Hilton, review of *Raintree County, New York Herald Tribune Book Review*, 4 January 1948, p. 1.

12. Charles Lee, review of *Raintree County, New York Times Book Review*, 4 January 1948, p. 5.

13. Elizabeth Johnson, review of *Raintree County, Commonweal*, 13 February 1948, p. 450.

14. Howard Mumford Jones, review of *Raintree County, Saturday Review of Literature*, 3 January 1948, p. 9.

15. *Time*, 12 January 1948, p. 85; H. M. R., review of *Raintree County, Christian Science Monitor*, 5 January 1948, p. 4.

16. M. P. Corcoran, review of *Raintree County, Catholic World*, 166 (March 1948), 567.

17. Hamilton Basso, review of *Raintree County, The New Yorker*, 10 January 1948, p. 79.

18. See Clarke, pp. 31-39, for an analysis of Lockridge's use of Freud and Jung.

Leonard F. Manheim (essay date 1978)

SOURCE: "An Author Wrecked by Success," in *Studies in Literature*, Vol. 10, No's. 1, 2, 3, 1978, pp. 103-21.

[*In the following essay, Manheim discusses the initial impact of* Raintree County *in popular and literary reading circles and attempts to account for the novel's disappearance into oblivion in subsequent years.*]

The New York Times for 8 March 1948 carried a substantial news article which deals with the suicide which is here being considered:

LOCKRIDGE, AUTHOR, SUICIDE AT 33;
WORN BY WRITING 'RAINTREE COUNTY'
by the United Press

Bloomington, Ind. March 7—Ross F. Lockridge Jr., 33, author of the best-selling novel ***Raintree County,*** was found dead in his locked garage late last night and authorities announced today he was killed by carbon monoxide poisoning.

A verdict of suicide was returned this afternoon. Dr. Robert E. Lyons Jr., Monroe County coroner, who returned the suicide verdict, said he has not been able to determine a motive.

Mr. Lockridge was found unconscious in his car in the gas-filled garage of the new home he built with part of a $150,000 movie studio award for the book. He wrote the novel in seven lean years of trying to break into the writing field.

Dr. Lyons said that relatives told him Mr. Lockridge appeared to be in good spirits yesterday.

Mr. Lockridge's wife, Vernice, mother of four young children, said she knew of no reason for her husband's suicide. Dr. Lyons stated that, according to friends of the writer, he had appeared "nervous and under pressure recently."

Dr. Lyons said Mr. Lockridge left no letters or notes indicating he was despondent or ill and had made no statement to his wife or other relatives that would shed light on a motive for the act.

He added that he had learned Mr. Lockridge has been "not too well" physically recently. Relatives said Mr. Lockridge was exhausted from work on his book and from handling business negotiations in connection with it.

Mrs. Lockridge became alarmed last night when her husband failed to return after a reasonable time from a trip to the post office. She went to the garage shortly before midnight to see if the car was back and found the doors locked and the garage lights on. The car was inside.

She summoned neighbors, who smashed in the doors. They found the car's motor running and Mr. Lockridge sprawled in the driver's seat. The door was open and his legs were hanging over the running board. The garage was filled with carbon monoxide fumes.

Mr. Lockridge was carried outside and city firemen worked over him for an hour in an effort to revive him.

The $150,000 award was from Metro-Goldwyn-Mayer. The book was the only one Mr. Lockridge had written. He had returned only recently from Hollywood, where he worked on a movie adaptation of the book.

Mr. Lockridge was a member of the varsity track team at Indiana University, where he received A. B. and M.

A. degrees. After graduating, he was an instructor in the university's English department and then taught at Simmons College at Boston, where he began work on his novel seven years ago.

Mr. Lockridge is survived by his father, Ross Lockridge, Sr., a historian and lecturer now retired from the Indiana University faculty; his wife, and four small children, Ernest, Jean, Larry, and Ross III.[1]

The novel received many favorable—some highly favorable—reviews. Of these more in a moment. It was the object of an attack by one Father Barrett of Fordham University, who characterized it as "1,066 pages of bombast, rank obscenity, materialistic philosophy and blasphemous impudicity." Houghton Mifflin, the publishers, defended the book, contending that, while some of the characters were irreverent, the novel was not. Rather, its intent was "to give the world a legend of moral and spiritual regeneration in an era when hatred and materialism appear to be enveloping the world—or much of it—in fear and irreligious despair."

Since its original publication the novel has not fared too well. Of course the original shock-appeal of the book did not last long (today its pervasive sexuality would be considered mild indeed). Its selection for accolade by MGM and the Book-of-the-Month Club might have been the kiss of death in academia, but other, to me less valuable literary products have survived that ordeal. There may be other reasons that will help to explain the lapse of the work into oblivion, and it will be some part of the task of this paper to suggest such reasons. For the moment, however, let us consider the impact of the work when it was published.

Howard Mumford Jones found "great narrative and ironic power in about half the book" although characters in the last third "cease to be individuals and become in many cases individualized symbols. . . . But the breath of life sweeps through its voluminous pages. . . . It may be that *Raintree County* marks the end of a slump in American fiction."[2] *The Sunday Times Book Review* critic found it "a critical biography of America from the period of agrarian innocence through the Civil War and into the era of ruthless industrial expansion. And yet on another level it is a brawny poem of man, history, and God." Orville Prescott, in his daily column on books in *The Times* found the book "powerful, poetic, humorous and bursting with life and vigor, and a pagan delight in living." The anonymous review in *Time* for 12 January 1948 proclaims that the book is "the latest and plainest sign that native American and recent European traditions of art and thought can flow together and that this cultural Mississippi . . . may be one of the brightest things moving in the world. *Raintree County* is . . . a philosophical novel (a rare thing in U. S. fiction) and a studied work of art that is striking enough to court comparison, in method at least, with the *Ulysses* of James Joyce." The Joyce influence is certainly marked, although Kelsey Guilfoil, writing in the *Chicago Tribune Magazine of Books* for 4 January 1948, stressed the parallel with Thomas Wolfe, adding, "In many ways it is better than Wolfe. It certainly comes closer to the heart of America, and it is less distorted in its view of life than Wolfe often is."

After a lapse of over 25 years, *Raintree County* reappeared to advantage in a review of Leggett's *Ross and Tom* by Jonathan Yardley (*New York Times Book Review* for 18 August 1974). Mr. Yardley comments on the novel's qualities of endurance:

Read now, a quarter-century after its publication, [*Raintree County*] retains much of its freshness, humor and energy, but it is also shapeless, imitative and rather extraordinarily naive.

It was, however, precisely the right novel for its time, 1947-48 . . . , and it made Lockridge a wealthy and famous man. It also eviscerated him.

(page 1)

In a leading article in *The Saturday Review of Literature* for 12 June 1948, Nanette Kutner reported two visits to Bloomington, Indiana.[3] In January she interviewed the still-living author for a woman's magazine. After his death she paid a second visit to his family.

Miss Kutner's first difficulty was in locating Lockridge. He was said to be still in California, which he had called a "wonderful state in which to rear children." Nonetheless he had left California and he was back in Bloomington where he had bought a house. Miss Kutner's account of her "selling" her assignment to the editors of *Today's Woman* is particularly interesting: "You can't miss. For six years a young English Instructor, married to his childhood sweetheart, supports her and four kids on twenty-five hundred a year. All the while he's writing a book. When it's published he wins a quarter of a million dollars! The important point . . . is that he doesn't go berserk. He and his wife settle down and buy all the things your readers want to buy—the house, the car, the furniture, the electric icebox. What more could a woman's magazine want?" So she made her pilgrimage to Bloomington. She was told that Lockridge was rather vague and yet thought he was the great American genius. But, she comments, if he exhibited such traits, "then he was a schizophrenic personality. He cooperated with me completely, even offering to make hotel reservations for me. To me he seemed wistful, surprisingly boyish, delighted to talk to 'somebody from the outside.'" Her first thought as she drove up to his house was of the "perfect slick magazine-story that [she] was going to write," but she seemed to have altered her viewpoint when she met Lockridge and "his very pretty, blonde wife, Vernice." One of the things that impressed her was that though they had been living in the house a month there were no personal pictures hung on the walls and with the exception of two copies of *Raintree County* and a copy of *Red Plush* standing on the shelves of the secretary there was not a bookcase nor a book in sight.

When they spoke of *Raintree County* and Miss Kutner commented that she thought it was "like a symphony,"

Ross nodded in agreement and his wife added that Lockridge "says that about 'The Magic Mountain'!" Then Mrs. Lockridge added that she never read a thing because she hadn't time. Ross was irritated by the reviews his book had received in *Newsweek* and *The New Yorker.* He didn't think "those fellows had read the book through."

They talked about the years of writing the book, about going out only once a week, about Ross's writing on the back of his discarded papers, about his writing with the children running toy trains under his legs. Lockridge admitted the influence of Wolfe but claimed that he had a better historical background. His comment that "if you read it aloud . . . it scans," is very reminiscent of Thomas Wolfe. Ross referred to his years of writing the book as "like having been eight years pregnant," and Vernice added that "Although we were living in such close quarters—three rooms—Ross never talked to me about the book. . . . Oh, I had a vague idea what it was about. But I didn't really know until I typed it." This is rather remarkable when we recollect that Ross himself had been a prize-winning stenographer and typist, had taken most of the notes for the background of the novel in shorthand, and had typed the original manuscript at the rate, it is said, of a hundred words a minute.

When the talk turned to Lockridge's exemption from military service during the war Vernice expressed her satisfaction that he was rejected when she was in the hospital having her second baby. But Miss Kutner said that she "sensed a feeling of guilt." Perhaps that was the reason why he had scrapped his first two years' work on **Raintree County,** starting all over again so that he could shift the time from the twentieth to the nineteenth century. "Maybe it was easier for him to forget his guilt, writing about the past." There is nothing more to justify this casual intrusion of superficial psychodynamics.

In the course of conversation there was reference to Ross's cousin, Mary Jane Ward, who had written *The Snake Pit.* Ross remarked, "Oh, she made plenty of money out of *The Snake Pit,* but she could have done better with her movie deal."

Later the conversation turned on the marriage of Ross and Vernice, and Vernice admitted that when she was in high school "she was afraid to speak to him 'because he was the smartest boy in my class!'" Ross went on to make it plain that "she's Nell Gaither . . . she definitely influenced Nell." Miss Kutner at this point cogently remarked that Johnny Shawnessy never married Nell.

Comment on Ross's parents included observations that his mother was "proud of her son who had always won things—races, typing championships, scholarships to the Sorbonne, to Yale, to Harvard." Miss Kutner characterizes father as a "sturdy historian . . . , [his academic affiliation had been with the Department of Public Speaking], who other Indiana professors tell me is 'an extreme extrovert.'" Miss Kutner also comments on the fact that although much

of the research Ross did was aided by his father, the book is dedicated "for" his mother, and his father is not mentioned.

She sums up the visit by commenting on the fact that "all the Lockridges were normal, nice, pleasant, kind," typically American and "as smothering as your Aunt Tilly's featherbed."

On the return drive to her hotel, Miss Kutner started to notice some peculiarities in Ross's conduct. He "drove badly, with sudden starts and stops. On the wheel his hands were nervous and unsure." He complained that he had insomnia and had to take sleeping pills. Miss Kutner suggested that perhaps he ought to get drunk, and he replied, "Maybe you've got something there," but he wouldn't join her for a drink, insisting, "*You* grab yourself a couple of good ones before dinner." Later after dinner they said goodbye. "'Now I'll lie awake the whole night,' he declared. 'Vernice, here, she sleeps like a log. I haven't slept since I won those prizes.'" These were the last words he spoke to her.

From then until just before his death they were in communication by letter. In one letter he wrote:

> Things go on much as before here with everything down around our ears more and more. I hope to get out of the woods sometime, though it seems right when I need rest most I get least of it.

In another letter he refers to himself as being "ravaged by illness, additional family responsibilities, etc." And in his last letter he wrote, "Take care. I'm trying to." A few days later he committed suicide.

On her second visit two months later there were the usual flood of post-mortems and horseback diagnoses. There was a neighbor who "never set foot in their living room"—yet said, "He used to drive his car from the garage to the street and back again as many as fifteen times in succession." His wife insisted that Miss Kutner had never seen the real Ross, that "he was sick since October. Sleeping pills strong enough to knock me out for twenty-four hours gave him only two hours. He couldn't eat either. They worked him so hard, rewriting the book for MGM he couldn't do anything after October.[4] *He wanted to go to a sanatorium, but we had put ourselves in the hands of a family doctor who said it would be a disgrace to send Ross to any such place and that he would be all right if he kept to a normal routine*" (Stress is mine!).[5] His mother was proud of the fact that she was the Eva Alice (of whom more in a moment) and also the mother in the book, and she was proud of the dedication not TO her but FOR her. She insisted that he must have met with foul play. The father insisted, "The boy put his heart's blood into the book; he had nothing left. I knew this would happen. A doctor warned me of suicide. So I prayed for him, prayed every day on that porch. He was a good boy, my boy, never drank, swore, or smoked." Miss Kutner adds her own private diagnosis that "he could not find a remedy for the let-down that invariably comes after completing a big job, the let-down Trollope understood so well. He [Trollope] never submitted a novel until he was deep into the next." She feels he should have boarded a ship "for South America, for China, anywhere but Hollywood. No matter where he went, he should never have lugged Bloomington along. But even if he had left it physically, he probably would never have been able to escape it mentally. Like his own Johnny Shawnessy, he knew 'his victory was not in consummations.'

The novel as originally published[6] has a great many devices to guide the reader through its complexities. The end papers represent illustrations that might well have been found in the Atlas of Raintree County which plays such an important part in the story. The frontis piece is a map of Raintree County or that portion of it which is directly involved in the story. As is so often the case in mid-western states, many of the main roads are squarely north and south or east and west. As against this, there is the Shawmucky River which runs in a meandering course through the central portion of the county with a navel point in Lake Paradise and the great swamp which separates the upper from the lower range of the river, and appears to be almost in the center of the map; the actual center is occupied by the main town of Freehaven. The National Road runs east and west almost parallel with the bottom of the map and almost parallels the Pennsylvania Railroad. There are county roads perpendicular to the National Road. The Shawmucky River runs its meandering course from the upper right-hand to the lower left-hand corner. It is not wholly fantastic that at the end of the book there is an identity established between the squiggle that the river makes and the initials J. W. S. (*John Wickliff Shawnessy* and *Jerusalem Webster Stiles*) in mirror-writing (p. 1060).

After page one of the text there is a detailed map of the town of Waycross, showing the National Road running horizontally in the middle, the county road running perpendicular also at about the middle and the railroad making a waving curved line at the bottom of the map.

Between the two maps there is a dedication to Lockridge's mother and an acknowledgement of the assistance of Lockridge's wife. Then follows a chronology of the single day on which the contemporary events of the story take place.

> ***Raintree County*** is the story of a single day in which are embedded a series of flashbacks. The chronologies printed here may assist the reader in understanding the structure of the novel. At the back of the book may be found a chronology of historical events with bearing on the story.
>
> (p. vii)

The first chronology covers events from dawn on the fourth of July, 1892, to midnight of the same day. The flashbacks, given in chronological order, number over fifty. They extend from 1844 to 1890; in fact the last one is headed 1890-1892. Generally speaking the order in which the flashbacks appear in the narrative is chronological, but there are enough exceptions to make the order of events, as one critic complained, a bit difficult to follow.

The method of presenting the flashbacks is unusual and, it seems to me, has a direct bearing on our investigation here. For example, the first 1892 episode (most of which is an erotic dream) ends in the following paragraph:

> It was dawn now on Raintree County, and he would begin with things of the dawn. He would pursue awhile his ancient pastime of looking for the mystic shape of a life upon the land, the legend of a face of stone, a happy valley, an extinct republic, a memory of
>
> (p. 8, bottom)

And here the narrative breaks, but the words which would follow are used as the title of the flashback to

Election day—　　　　　　HOW　　　　　—1844
ON THE MORNING OF ELECTION DAY
THE MOTHER AND THE LITTLE CHILD WERE WAITING
before the cabin.

(p. 9, top)

And the narrative of 1844 continues. All of the bridges from 1892 to former time and from former time to 1892 are carried in the same way except that where the transition is from the flashback to the 1892 narrative there is no caption or title. Still the words run in:

> In the red far light of the star, he saw an immense face of clay, and he and all of the other people were running for President as fast as they could go. So in the still night
> HE DREAMED A FAIR YOUNG
> DREAM OF
> Going (p. 15, bottom)
> WESTWARD, the national road pursued its way, etc.
> (p. 16, top)

This is a device which tends to indicate a fluidity of time in a mechanical, but nonetheless vivid way. Time may flow, at will, forward or backward, and by leaps.

The plot-structure of the novel will probably be sufficiently indicated in the commentary on the pattern hereafter. One facet of the character-structure—which will also be of assistance in allowing the present reader to refer more easily to the names used—is the composition of the characters as multiple projections (psychological decompositions, "doubling"). First, the hero figure is fragmented, represented by several characters. There is the hero in his positive aspects who is called John Wickliff Shawnessy. When his unconscious prototype, the "depth-hero" is referred to, he is called mr. shawnessy. The negative heroes are, to begin with, comrades and peers of Shawnessy. They went to school with him, they grew up with him, they are associated with the town of Waycross, and they continue to the end of the novel. They represent negatives of the hero pattern. Garwood ("Gar") Jones is the smooth-tongued opportunistic boy who rose to be a practical politician, a United States Senator, and a possible presidential candidate. Another aspect of the negative figure is Cassius ("Cash") Carney, whose mind is always fixed on earning a dollar, honestly or otherwise. He appears as a major figure in the steel and railroad industry at the end of the novel. In the final chapters, Shawnessy waits at the railroad at Waycross and meets his old friends. Jones has made a brief stop at Waycross until the train takes him west. Carney makes an even shorter stay there as his train takes him east; he stays only long enough to catch the next train. The fourth figure in this panoply of heroes (Jerusalem Webster Stiles) is unusual in that he is an intermediate figure who is both hero and father. He is only nine years older than Shawnessy, but he has come to Raintree County and set up a school at a semi-college level, the Pedee Academy, where he is administrator and major instructor. In addition to his position as teacher-father, he is also a close friend and companion of the three younger men and continues in that function until the very end of the novel, when he leaves Waycross to make his way back to New York City on a train later than the others. Characteristically, in local parlance he is always referred to as the "perfessor," although Shawnessy, who himself becomes a grade-school teacher, usually uses the correct pronunciation.

The father-images are of differing stature. The father-ideal is the hero's father in the flesh, T. D. Shawnessy, who serves the communities of the story as Methodist preacher and local doctor. There is a statement to the effect that his origins are Scottish, and there is a hint that he is quite possibly the illegitimate son of Thomas Carlyle. The negative father-figure, most interestingly, does not appear until late in the novel. He is the decidedly oedipal father of Esther Root, Shawnessy's second wife, and as such is a rival in every sense of the word for Esther, for Shawnessy at this time is old enough to be Esther's father, and has been her teacher and instructor in pedagogy. Old Root is the avowed enemy of Shawnessy and is implacable in his determination never to recognize Esther's marriage or even her children. His aggression motivates one of the final scenes of violence of the book. Having two such father-figures, it is only necessary to have a rather vague background figure for the third father-paramount, none other than Abraham Lincoln.

The virgin-and-mother figures are even more fragmented. First there is the virtuous but highly desirable heroine, Nell Gaither, whom the hero had known since childhood and who is indigenous to Raintree County. Her truly diabolical major counterpart is Susanna Drake, who invaded Raintree County from the depths of the pre-Civil War South and carried off the hero to her native Louisiana. Shawnessy's marriage to Susanna is truly a descent into the world of the dead, as truly as was Joseph's journey to Egypt, the land of the dead, in Mann's Joseph cycle. Nell, it will be remembered, was the character who Lockridge said was based on his wife, whom Lockridge had known since childhood. But Shawnessy never marries Nell, and

the desirable virgin keeps her sanctity while the dark woman carries off the hero. It would probably be well to anticipate what we want to say about the plot-structure to make some remarks about Nell and Susanna at this point.

Lockridge seems to be deeply involved with physical nakedness. The story opens with a dream sequence in which the Post Office at Waycross is inhabited by a seductive naked female who more or less symbolizes the land itself. Then Johnny swims naked with Nell and later with Susanna. The dip into the Shawmucky River with Nell takes place at the picnic in honor of the graduation festivities of Pedee Academy. It is an innocent swim in the nude, nothing more comes of it because it is interrupted by the startling event of the professor's "elopement" with one of his pupils, the young and beautiful wife of a fanatic preacher. Nell repudiates sexuality and later recants, but finds that her recantation is too late. The dip into the waters with Susanna occurs on the occasion of Shawnessy's victory in an elaborately described footrace in which he is victorious even though he has been tricked into drinking excessively, he who would never touch alcohol at all.

The obsessive wish to find a female nymph-prototype for the personification of Raintree County itself finds itself its outlet in the scene in which Johnny as voyeur lurks naked along the river and sees Nell from a distance as the goddess—all too human indeed—of the countryside. Another interesting variation on this theme is the pattern—that runs throughout the whole book—of the Illustrated Historical Atlas of Raintree County, a single copy of which is traditionally supposed to have been specially designed by the artist so that in that single copy a great many of the ostensibly well-dressed characters in the engravings are actually nude. It was to recover the copy of this atlas in Fairhaven for the delectation of Senator Gar Jones that Shawnessy took his early morning trip on the Fourth of July and made an exchange of his own copy of the atlas for the one that was to be found in the collection at Fairhaven. Old Waldo, its custodian, had always kept it carefully locked up, and suspicions were increased when he fell dead on his way to take the copy and destroy it, leaving it behind instead for a lady relative who had been a pupil of Shawnessy's. Shawnessy's careful examination of the book revealed none of the suspected alterations until at the very end, late in the evening of the Fourth of July there is this colloquoy between Shawnessy and Stiles (let it be remembered that they share the same initials, J. W. S.):

> Wait! Mr. Shawnessy said, trying to remember something. Perhaps that was our mistake. We were *too* subtle. Perhaps the artist hid it by putting it in the most conspicuous place of all. Perhaps old Waldo found it precisely because he wasn't looking for it.

> Like Poe's 'Purloined Letter,' the Professor said, instantly pleased with the idea. The arch-criminal fooled the police by putting the stolen object in front of their noses. It's true, John, only a supersubtle mind detects the supersubtlety of simplicity. Now, following this line of reasoning, what is the most conspicuous location in the whole of Raintree County, children?

The Perfessor thought a moment.

—Obviously the Court House Square, Perfessor, he said, answering his own question.

—And in the Court House Square, children? he asked.

—The Court House, Perfessor, he replied.

—And on the Court House, children?

Mrs. Brown began to laugh, a low, bubbling contralto, as if perhaps the memory of Raintree County Court House with its famous statue of justice over the Main Entrance, spattered with pigeondung, were a delightfully amusing thing, once seen from the proper—or improper—angle.

But Mr. Shawnessy sprang forward, rested the *Atlas* on the shoulder of the fountain, and flapped the leaves to page five where the long form of the Raintree County Court House was couched in darkness like a sphinx. He tried to plunge his eyes into the space above the Main Entrance where in the standard copies the Statue of Justice stood. He saw a pool of shadow there, vaguely alive with sculpture. In his skipping examination of the *Atlas* during the day, he couldn't remember having looked at precisely that spot.

—Give me a light, Perfessor.

The Perfessor struck a match on his sole. He and Mrs. Brown bent over to see.

The flaring match illuminated for a brilliant instant something in the niche above the Main Entrance that left all three speechless.

. . . . .

Etched in flame, the imprint of the tiny group seen slantingly above the Main Entrance to the Raintree County Court House persisted as an after-image. On the instant of seeing it, Mr. Shawnessy had felt that it was just as he had known it would be, and where he had eventually intended to look.

And now that he saw it, it was (in the Raintree County sense) not at all naughty—for what was naughty about the oldest picture in the world, the frontispiece for the first book printed by man—the father and mother of mankind in beautiful nakedness, tasting the Forbidden Fruit! With what an exquisite feeling for paradox, an unknown artist had substituted his symbolic statue of Edenic rebellion for the stern yet necessary lady with the scales, whose upright form had ruled the conscience of Raintree County from the beginning!

. . . . .

So from their infinity of vantage points, in the changing lights and seasons of this mythical Raintree County, they would behold the double figure hewn from the single block of marble, the *E pluribus unum* of the classic coin, the Paradisal pair in the moment of republican and pluviarboreal discovery, trembling nameless on the verge of names.

(pp. 1051-52)

The later sections of the book (that is, chronologically) do not product any virgin-and-mother-figures to compare to Nell and Susanna, but there are some that should be men-

tioned. On the night of Lincoln's assassination Shawnessy is introduced by his friends to a young actress who is said to have understudied Laura Keane in the play performed that night in Ford's Theatre. That actress later becomes a famous figure on the New York stage, Laura Golden. In spite of her wealth of suitors she seems to prefer Johnny Shawnessy, and he has an assignation with her in the innermost chambers of her palatial home when he is summoned by a telegram to return to Raintree County because of the death of his mother.

That mother too has played an interesting role. She is pictured as perennially young and athletic. It is said that she too was a swift-footed runner, and she has been the constant companion and aide of T. D. Shawnessy. The most telling sequence is the one in which Johnny Shawnessy as a small boy waits outside a house where his father and mother are delivering the baby of an itinerant forty-niner, and the men snicker and leer at the screams of the woman and Johnny is initiated into an early experience of the primal scene. Ellen Shawnessy, the mother, is later of course paralleled by Esther Root Shawnessy, the second wife of whom we have commented in connection with her father, and finally by the favorite twelve-year-old Eva Alice of 1892 who, it will be remembered, was the character with whom Lockridge's mother claimed to be identified.

There still remains for our consideration one more aspect of the primal-scene theme. At the very end of the book there is a lynch mob led by "Father" Root and the Fundamentalist Preacher Jarvey intent on tarring and feathering the "atheistic and immoral" John Shawnessy on the porch of Mrs. Brown's home. They are only deflected from their aim when the preacher is accused vaguely by Shawnessy's son (I say "vaguely," because most of this is related as seen but not heard in full by Eva up in her tower room point of vantage overlooking the event) of having had illicit relations with the widow Passiffé (Pasiphae?), and this is corroborated by actual primal-scene evidence given by Wesley Shawnessy and his friend Johnny Jacobs, who says of the preacher that "he didn't even have his glasses on." And on this theme the major incidents of the plot end.

In addition to the symbolic descent to the Land of Blackness, there is one more example—a major one—of the death-and-resurrection theme which is an almost literal return from the dead. Returning to Raintree County from the South in 1863, being about to rejoin Susanna and his young son in Raintree County, Johnny Shawnessy finds his home in flames and is witness to the death of the boy. Susanna disappears and is only discovered much later floating in the river (unclothed, of course), dead, after she had been legally declared dead some time before. Now Johnny has no choice, so he feels, but to enlist in the Union Army, and he does so after an exchange of promises with Nell Gaither. She says that she will wait for his return. He is absent a long time, participates in Sherman's march to the sea, is wounded and near death in a Washington hospital, and is present at the assassination of President Lincoln. Back home, he is reported dead; his obituary is printed in the newspaper for which he had been a writer, and his name seems to have vanished from the rolls of the sons of men. When he does return, he is unrecognized. He finds nobody even to inform him of the things that have taken place but goes into the empty newspaper office and finds in the newspaper file an account of his death and of the marriage of Nell Gaither to Garwood Jones. Again, without any word from other people who ever knew him, he makes his way out to the cemetery, finds a recent grave marked with a stone relating the death of Nell in childbirth only a week before. He also finds a monument erected to his own memory. In an access of rage he uproots this tombstone, sends it rolling down the hill, and then returns to his old home and makes himself known to his father and mother. This return from the grave marks the dividing line in his entire career.

These are, then, the important characters and plot material which, it seems to me, have a direct bearing on the suicide. It would hardly be proper for me to attempt a complete psychiatric diagnosis. Still, a few suggestions may be in order. The first suggestion that comes to mind—and which has been indicated in the title of this paper—is Freud's essay in the general series entitled "Some Character-types Met With in Psychoanalytic Work," particularly the second essay, "Those Wrecked by Success."[7] It will be remembered that the analyses in this essay are based hardly at all upon clinical material but mostly upon literary examples. One example is Lady Macbeth, but although Freud indicates that she is plainly one of those "wrecked by success," he feels that there is insufficient evidence to make a diagnosis of the specific causes of her collapse. The most important literary example is that of Rebecca Gamvik, the so-called Rebecca West, in Ibsen's *Rosmersholm*. Without going into the details of this analysis, it will suffice here to note that when Rebecca finds herself in a position to achieve her goal of marriage to Rosmer, whose wife she has successfully done to death by psychological suggestion, she is rendered impotent to enjoy the fruits of her striving because of her sense of guilt; in this case guilt not only at having had a previous lover in the person of Dr. West but the discovery of the fact that Dr. West was indeed her father and that she therefore was involved in a genuine incestuous relationship.

But while this analysis sheds a great deal of light on the general dynamics of people who are "wrecked by success," there is no grounds for a particular incest-guilt pattern in the case of Ross Lockridge and as far as fantasy-incest is concerned a great many people live through the stress of that variety of guilt without falling into depression and committing suicide. Is there any evidence in the novel that the guilt situation in regard to Lockridge was of a particularly harassing and acute nature? I think it is apparent that there is.

The first thing we ought to do is to make the distinction not specifically made by Freud but fully developed by Erikson in *Childhood and Society*. The Ross Lockridge

pattern is rather one of *shame and doubt* arising from a maladjustment in the period of anal development which would normally in a well-developed personality lead to *autonomy*. This muscular-anal pattern merges imperceptibly into the third, locomotor-genital, pattern of the first oedipal period.

> Shame is an emotion insufficiently studied, because in our civilization it is so early and easily absorbed by guilt. Shame supposes that one is completely exposed and conscious of being looked at: in one word, self-conscious. . . . Shame is early expressed in an impulse to bury one's face, or to sink, right then and there, into the ground. But this, I think, is essentially rage turned against the self. He who is ashamed would like to force the world not to look at him, not to notice his exposure.
>
> . . . . .
>
> Doubt is the brother of shame. Where shame is dependent on the consciousness of being upright and exposed, doubt . . . has much to do with a consciousness of having a front and a back—and especially a "behind." . . . This basic sense of doubt in whatever one has left behind forms a substratum for later and more verbal forms of compulsive doubting. . . .[8]

Shame and doubt, it will be remembered, are the negative aspects of the second (muscular-anal) epigenetic level, as guilt is the negative aspect of the third (locomotor-genital, first oedipal) level.

Let me cite a clinical example from a case history in the practice of a distinguished psychiatrist (not, however, one with an orthodox psychoanalytic approach). The patient complained that at moments of general ease and a sense of successful accomplishment he would be plagued by obsessive-compulsive memories of past events in which he had "lost face," been publicly held up to shame or to actual or potential ridicule. Such events were rarely such as to objectively warrant such a strong emotional tone. But as these memories welled up into conscious awareness, the patient would compulsively utter aloud grunts and groans which he had to use considerable ingenuity to explain away. In its worst manifestation the compulsive utterance would assume the invariable form "I HATE EVERYBODY!" The psychiatrist reassured the patient, telling him that such manifestations were far from abnormal and need not unduly disturb him.

But now consider the case of the "author wrecked by success," Ross Lockridge, Jr. His was no small measure of "successful accomplishment." After a servitude of seven years he had achieved great wealth, potential fame, all that he seemingly could wish for. But how had he achieved this success? Was it not by stripping naked again and again, not only his own inner psyche but also the bodies and minds of those who were closest to him? Had he not exploited every variety of primal scene fantasy, extending from realistic juvenile voyeurism, through the fantasy of the actress-on-the-stage, to the climactic events of the "dirty" spying by the son-and-daughter on the wicked persecutors in the act of intercourse and the "innocent" detection of the scene depicted in the unique copy of the Atlas of Raintree County, in many respects a landscape which, consciously and unconsciously, symbolizes the whole novel? Could any reader fail to comprehend these self-revelations, these shameful self-accusations? And so the Freudian sense of oedipal *guilt* is complicated by regression to the earlier level of *shame*.

And consider for a moment the possible—indeed probable—impact of some of the difficulties with which Lockridge was faced after his monumental novel was accepted for publication and cinema production. We may well understand that a publisher might be unwilling to publish a new author's novel of such gigantic proportions without insisting on some reasonable excisions and abridgements. But to a psyche torn by a sense of unacceptable shame and doubt, could there be any other "explanation" than that there was something "indiscreet," "shameful," about the work, which therefore had to be "expurgated?" (This is, of course, the irrationality of the Unconscious, but that is what we are trying to plumb here.) And certainly the prurient shamelessness of post-WW II Hollywood could not have been reassuring to the shame-ridden author. To be sure, he was spared the final degradation of making **Raintree County** into a movie which would display the already opulent charms of Elizabeth Taylor in the "leading" role of Susanna. But certainly his initial contacts with Hollywood, his naive belief that he could confront the incredibly arrogant Louis B. Mayer man to man, the whole air of unreality which many authors found in the colony of movie-money-makers, could not have failed to increase Lockridge's sense that something was wrong, very wrong; that something must have been going on "behind his back"; that sooner or later he must leave the community toward which he was so markedly ambivalent and retreat with Vernice to the haven of Bloomington. But of course he found, as all those who suffer as he did also found, that he could not run away from his own doubts, fears, and guilt. So the haven of Bloomington had to be inadequate, and a new refuge—this time at the wheel of an automobile in a closed garage—had to be found.

We do not and cannot know the particular complex of memories which drove Lockridge to distraction. They might have been discovered by psychotherapy, but that was made impossible by "shame," not only Lockridge's shame but, even more, by the "shame" of the family physician who thought that admission of a need for local psychotherapy would constitute a family disgrace. But that the sense of guilt and shame must have been most painful will certainly be obvious.

For many writers it can certainly be maintained that "the neurosis leads to the work of art and the art cures the neurosis." But this is probably never wholly true. And Lockridge would never have been certain that he had been fully committed to the creation of a wholly genuine work of art. Had he not given up his cherished epic poem in order to write something that would "sell better"? Had he not

yielded to the urge to avoid a contemporary emphasis by transferring his story from the twentieth to the nineteenth century? Could he have missed his obvious indebtednesses to Thomas Wolfe and James Joyce? No, he might well feel that he had sold something like his "birthright" for a mess of pottage, albeit a gigantic one.

What way out for him? He might, as Miss Kutner suggested, have sought refuge in flight, travel, movement. But, as she also suggested, he would have carried Bloomington with him, and anyhow, his flight to Hollywood had been fruitless, even an exacerbation of his condition. As Menninger suggests,[9] there were other forms of non-acute suicide possible. But the chronic suicide of alcoholism was not for him. His sufferings during the long, long hours of chronic insomnia were not to be endured. And there was no one in whom he could confide, certainly not the family which (in his fantasy) he had "pilloried and defiled." Far better to find his way back to the womb—the womb of a closed auto, in a closed garage, with the blessed stupor of carbon monoxide poisoning.

Here I add a final word of perhaps doubtful speculation. I believe that his suicidal urge encompassed Menninger's first two elements: the wish to kill and the wish to be killed in a propitiatory gesture. But the evidence does not seem to indicate clearly the presence of the third wish, the unmitigated wish to die. That would probably involve regression to something like the oral-sensory level, an irrational urge of an id-directed psyche whose ego-barriers have been broken down, an urge to reverse the birth trauma and return to the period of unconditional prenatal omnipotence. And Lockridge, so far as I can see, was neurotic but now wholly schizophrenic. For him, as for many complete or abortive suicides, there was a fantasy of rescue, the fantasy that leads so many would-be suicides to cooperate with their rescuers and return to life with complete satisfaction.

The evidence indicates that at the last moment he opened the car door, tried to swing his legs out and to step upon the running-board. Two additional points in the newspaper account add to this conclusion. The first is the choice by Lockridge of the postoffice as a "place to go"—perhaps a deeply unconscious indication of an intention to "keep in touch." The second is the fact that he left the garage light on.[10] But all his precautions were futile, and Vernice did not investigate the cause of her husband's long delay in town until after midnight. The medical examiner might will have returned a verdict of "death by misadventure" in an abortive attempt at suicide.

But he was dead at 33 for all that. And I wonder what the state of mind of the "family physician" was when the suicide was reported to him.

Notes

1. In 1974, several years after the present study of Ross Lockridge was written, a biography of Lockridge appeared, bound in with a similar biography of Tom

Heggen, with the subtitle *Two American Tragedies.* The author was John Leggett, who proclaims at the outset:

> I am a novelist and I believe that forceful biography employs all the techniques of the novel; those of setting, narrative, characterization and subjectivity. I believe in the biographer's right, within a limit, to portray his subject's reaction to experience, and the limit is truth, insofar as that can be determined from evidence.

(page 7)

Mr. Leggett's approach has definite advantages, among them being one of decided readability. On the other hand, the absence of documentation makes scholarly use of the material difficult. Not that Leggett did not have a remarkable degree of access to original sources. He expresses gratitude to members of the Lockridge family and to their friends, and he had a decided inside track in having been an editor with Lockridge's publishers (Houghton Mifflin), many years after Lockridge's death, to be sure, but with complete access to the Lockridge files. But the fact still remains that there is no documentation, not even a source given for a letter when it is quoted, possibly but not certainly in full.

I do not consider that the publication of Mr. Leggett's book required any substantial alteration of my conclusions concerning the suicide. My biographical data was taken from newspaper and periodical sources of the time of Lockridge's death. Where these reports are at variance with Leggett's reports I have usually indicated that fact. An important contribution of Leggett's biography is the discussion in some detail of the narrative poem which Lockridge wrote before *Raintree County* (pp. 65-69). *The Dream of the Flesh of Iron* would certainly be material for additional analysis of Lockridge's suicide, but I hardly think that Leggett's summary, with casual Freudian interpretations, could be considered valid source material. Perhaps some day the original text will become available and the present study could be expanded beyond its present scope.

Otherwise Leggett's influence has been limited to occasional silent corrections based on Leggett's revelations; Leggett's dynamic interpretations are not mine; the theories offered here as to Lockridge's suicide are solely my own work.

2. Review in *Saturday Review of Literature* as quoted in *Current Biography* for 1948, p. 29.

3. Pages 6-7 and 31. Page 6 carried a small photograph of Mr. and Mrs. Ross Lockridge and their four children.

4. But see Leggett, pp. 37-38.

5. Leggett reports that Lockridge had indeed had some therapy, but it was through electric-shock treatment and that he had gone to Indianapolis for the "treatment," but had abandoned it before completion, in part because of his long-standing phobia of electric shocks.

6. All page references to *Raintree County* are to my copy of the original edition published in Boston by Houghton Mifflin in 1948.

7. *Collected Papers* (London, 1953, [the essay dates from 1915]), IV, 323-341.

8. *Childhood and Society,* 2nd Edition (New York, 1963), pp. 252-253.

9. See *Man Against Himself* (New York, 1938), *passim.*

10. I am indebted for these last suggestions to Professor Leon Waldoff. He cites "an article [about] a man attempting suicide in a garage, with a light on." (Jensen & Petty, "The Fantasy of Being Rescued in Suicide," *Psychoanalytic Quarterly,* 27 [1958], 327-339). These authors conclude that a fourth element (the wish to be rescued) is almost always present, in addition to Menninger's three.

Fred Erisman (essay date 1979)

SOURCE: "*Raintree County* and the Power of Place," in *Markham Review,* Vol. 8, Winter, 1979, pp. 36-40.

[*In the following essay, Erisman analyzes* Raintree County*'s concern with the influence of geographical location on Americans.*]

Ross Lockridge, Jr.'s novel, ***Raintree County*** (1948) has not lacked critical attention. A Book-of-the-Month Club selection and the winner of a Metro-Goldwyn-Mayer Novel Award before publication, it enjoyed a brief spurt of popular notice. More recently, it has attracted a degree of scholarly consideration. It has been discussed in the context of the epic tradition, has been read through the spectacles of Freudian analysis, has been held up as a good example of many-leveled fiction, and has been variously judged to be a statement of continuing faith in American mythology and a banal, flatulent piece of self-serving hackwork.[1]

That Lockridge intended his novel to be an epic, even mythic account of the American experience is self-evident. As he tells the story of a single day, July 4, 1892, in the lives of his characters, his conscious references to the central themes of American intellectual history, his calculated controlling of time and event, and his careful arrangement of characters speak for themselves. Less evident, but no less significant, is the book's reflection of the importance of space and place as elements in American thought. Whatever else it may be, ***Raintree County*** is a novel of locales and boundaries. Taking its name and its nature from an imaginary place, it incorporates in its story the spatial perceptions and attitudes of its characters as they encounter the American landscape of the nineteenth century. In so doing, the novel provides a notable examination of the influence of spatial attitudes upon human character and in many ways anticipates by a quarter of a century the expansion of those attitudes by the environmental novelists of the 1960s and 1970s.

The simplest view of the world sees it as a series of contrasts. As Yi-Fu Tuan, a cultural geographer, points out,

> A simple two-fold classification might distinguish . . . habitats into the categories 'carpentered' and 'noncarpentered.' The carpentered world is replete with straight lines, angles, and rectangular shapes. Cities are rectangular environment *par excellence*. Nature and the countryside, in contrast, lack rectangularity.

These varying environments, in turn, affect individual perceptions and attitudes. Though the environment is not, Tuan points out, totally determining, it "has an effect on perception. People who live in a 'carpentered' world are susceptible to different kinds of illusion from those who live in an environment lacking in orthogonality."[2] One can, therefore, expect to find different, contrasting locales producing different, contrasting characters.

This is the case with **Raintree County.** The simplest form of spatial contrast, rural versus urban, Lockridge uses many times in the novel. As John Shawnessy, the protagonist, moves through the story, he repeatedly finds himself confronted by the juxtaposition of rural and urban attitudes. Inescapably a child of the country himself, Shawnessy embodies the virtues traditionally associated with rural living; he is, for Lockridge, truly a "child of the sunlight, the corndense earth, the simple beliefs of Raintree County."[3] His rural virtues, however, time and again come up against those of the city. As a newlywed he travels to New Orleans, and finds that the city stinks:

> It stank of fish, tar, rum, cess, garbage, horse dung, human beings. It stank appallingly, and this stink as they neared the docks in the windless night almost choked Johnny. He looked in embarrassment at his wife. . . . Was it possible that she wasn't aware of this stink?
>
> (430-31).

Eighteen years later, he travels to New York only to find it vast and indifferent: "In the late hours, he left the echoing building and stepped out again into the stale valleys and caverns of the City, and the City roared around him, multitudinous, unsubdued, uncaring" (819).

The conflict of rural and urban values, developed piecemeal through Shawnessy's travels, Lockridge makes explicit at the end of the book. There he speaks of the gap between Shawnessy's rural perceptions of life and those extant in the city:

> Go and look at the modern City. How can anyone look at it and believe in love? Or morality? Or the Eternal Ideas? Or the Inalienable Rights? How can anyone believe in the real existence of Raintree County, which you, dear boy and endlessly courageous dreamer, have taken as your image of the enduring values of human life? Yes, go and look at the City, and then look at your little Raintree County, child. Shed a nostalgic tear for

it, because the City's going to eat it up. The God of the City is going to kill the ancient God of Raintree County, who has nothing but a couple of stone tablets and a golden rule for weapons

> (848).

Lockridge's point is obvious. City and country, each inexorably molded by its characteristic outlook, are by nature antagonistic.

More subtle, and more elaborately developed, is Lockridge's attribution of "carpentered" and "uncarpentered" attitudes to specific characters. John Shawnessy, rural man, is plainly the spokesman for the uncarpentered perspective: he runs for Congress on an unabashedly idealistic platform, and he responds to the urban materialism of a financier friend by eloquently pointing out that "there are other republics besides your own and . . . all of them are trying to mingle and become one Republic, which always seems to want to conform to the old pattern envisioned by its creators" (778, 847). Shawnessy's view of America, in sum, is that of the humane idealist, ever hopeful of the future of the diverse American spirit.

Balancing Shawnessy is "Perfessor" Jerusalem Webster Stiles. An educator turned journalist, the Perfessor serves as Shawnessy's gadfly and alter ego, always questioning, always attacking, always embracing whatever outrageous belief opposes the rural values of Raintree County. His is the indifferent view of the city-dweller, and his sense of mankind is influenced accordingly:

> When you stand on a high roof, and look down at the canyons of one of our great modern cities, how can you resist the impression that you are looking into the welter and stench of the Great Swamp itself! The people look like frantic bugs going in and out of holes.

Whereas Shawnessy defends man's independence, the Perfessor denies it: "There aren't trillions of possibilities, as you imply, but only in every case the one thing that happened. Down to the most distant future, everything has to all intents and purposes already happened in the only way it could—through the operation of causality." And, as the book closes, Lockridge spells out the Perfessor's role as Shawnessy's mirror image: "What was in reverse for him had come right for Mr. Shawnessy" (815, 944, 1057). The contrast of carpentered and uncarpentered, expressed in the contrast of urban and rural, cynic and idealist, is one component of American existence.

A more complex statement of socio-spatial relations appears in Lockridge's use of the map. A map, geographers point out, involves personal as well as spatial knowledge; not only does it reflect an individual's ability "to conceptualize spatial relations," but it also involves that person's orienting of himself in space.[4] The individual's perception of himself and his society in relation to the rest of his locale and his world influences how he conceives of his location and the form in which he portrays that location. "Space is historical," says Tuan, "if it has direction or a privileged perspective. Maps are ahistorical, landscape paintings are historical. The map is God's view of the world since its sightlines are parallel and extend to infinity. . . . The landscape picture, with its objects organized around a focal point of converging sightlines, is much closer to the human way of looking at the world. . . . Space and time have gained subjectivity by being oriented to man."[5] Throughout **Raintree County,** Lockridge uses maps as a metaphor for his characters' sense of themselves and the world.

John Shawnessy's first contact with a map comes when, as a small boy, he confronts the map of Raintree County that hangs in the Court House: "It was the first time he had seen a map of his home earth, and he had a Columbian moment of discovery. The earth acquired shape, coherence, meaning. The road traveling before his house joined other roads, was part of an integrated system." Here is God's view of the world, and Shawnessy sees the degree to which he, as a human being, is a part of the specific locale of the County: "He had suddenly achieved a world. The dearly bought victory of man over the increate and stubborn earth was his. He had gazed at a map of his own life, the pattern of himself, securely bounded by the four walls of Raintree County" (60-61). It is, for Shawnessy, a moment of epic discovery.

Two ideas are significant in this account of young Shawnessy's insight. The first is that Shawnessy has for the first time recognized the integrated unity of the County, with its roads, its river, and its lake; here, suddenly, is a coherent world. The second, and more significant, is that this world, though viewed from above in Godlike fashion, is limited by and confined to the borders of the County. The map gives no sense of the continent that lies outside the County, and young Shawnessy has no inkling of that outer world. His world is the County, and his view, Godlike in one respect, is in another finite and limited.

A broader, human perspective enters the novel when, as an adult, Shawnessy encounters the *Illustrated Historical Atlas of Raintree County,* a bulky compendium of the County's architecture, produce, and population. Its vision, combining the map and the landscape painting, is that of a thoroughly humanized, domesticated world extending to infinity, ready for humanity's use:

> Into the faintly golden texture of the great soft sheets, an unknown artist had touched the earth of Raintree County with a sensitive pencil. In the sketches of farm homes, the principal building was seen as from a slight elevation so as to include a generous setting of outbuildings and the land around. Walks, lanes, roads, forests, gardens, pastures, cornfields appeared in accurate perspective. People played croquet on lawns; children skipped ropes, rolled hoops, pulled wagons; families passed in surreys, spring wagons, buggies. . . .
>
> The earth had the effect of being a massy substance continuous under all traces of humanity. Through page after page, this earth of Raintree County appeared in an

> unvaried summer morning, radiant and precise to a depth of miles, until sky touched horizon with a frieze of soft clouds
>
> (36-37).

Unlike the objective map of Shawnessy's youth, the *Atlas* provides a view of the world of mankind, a vision of the limitless America of the pre-Turner years.

The *Atlas* is, to be sure, a map. But it is a map projected from a human rather than Godlike point of view. It is, for example, susceptible to subjective interpretation in a way that the map in the Court House is not. To Shawnessy, the *Atlas* records "the beautiful and secret earth of Raintree County"; the Perfessor, however, sees only "pictures of cows, manure piles, and Raintree County citizens." The *Atlas,* moreover, places the County in context—the human context of the known and surveyed world. In addition to the perspective views of the County are maps detailing the County's townships and communities, the entire State of Indiana, and the all-encompassing United States (275, 36). In short, the *Atlas* portrays the spatial view of the comfortably informed materialist—the person aware of the country and the world outside of his immediate location, but who sees not the earth itself, but only the artifacts of man upon it.

Lockridge's fullest statement of the map motif comes late in the novel, when Shawnessy at last understands that the most profound map is that of the human face. Late in his life, Shawnessy realizes that the individual's self-vision is one with his world-view:

> Raintree County was never contained in its map. Nor, I trust, was a human being ever contained in that semblance made of dust and called a face.
>
> —That's what you meant this morning, John [responds the Perfessor], when you said that a face is a map?
>
> —Yes—a symbol of what is always placeless, being its own place, of what is always wandering, exploring, creating—a human soul. A face—like a map—is the earth imbued with human meanings. And the earth is a Great Stone Face, in which we perceive the profile of our own life
>
> (1024).

The face ties together the finite and the infinite, the tangible and the intangible. Maps and atlases record things; a face records life.

Lockridge's metaphor of the map is a telling one, helping to set the tone and the theme of the novel. Just as his recurring juxtapositions of the carpentered and uncarpentered views help him develop characters and their intellectual stances, so, too, maps help him make a point. A person's initial vision is limited; equally limited is the map of Raintree County in the Court House. As a person grows in experience, he comes to see himself within the context of his society; the *Atlas,* with its manure piles and solid citizens, illustrates that society to the satisfaction of all. And as the person grows older still, coming to understand his place not just in society but in history, his face becomes the symbol and the record of his knowledge. Maps trace the course of civilization; atlases record the coming of society; faces reveal the progress of time.

The last—and most complex—use of spatial perception in *Raintree County* continues the argument established through the metaphor of the map. Lockridge holds that a person's sense of location in space can, perhaps even must, develop into a cosmic sense that situates him not locally, not nationally, but universally. He argues that while individuals are residents of a county and citizens of a nation, they are also members of the human community. As they become aware of their specific locality, they must become aware of their place in the world. By achieving such a dual perception, they gain a new sense of their place and their significance.

This argument, of course, is not new. It builds in general upon the widening of geographical horizons that comes with maturity. The child learns first of his home, then his neighborhood, then his community, and so on. As he becomes older and more mobile, he encounters still more space and experience until, as an adult, he can relate himself and his space through first-hand knowledge.[6] More specifically, the argument builds upon the Transcendental—and ecological—perception of the linkages existing among all life. As Ralph Waldo Emerson wrote in 1837,

> To the young mind, every thing is individual, stands by itself. By and by, it finds how to join two things, and see in them one nature; then three, then three thousand; and so, tyrannized over by its own unifying instinct, it goes on tying things together . . . and goes on forever to animate the last fibre of organization, the outskirts of nature, by instinct.[7]

Intellectual maturity, for geographer or philosopher, brings new knowledge of the cohesiveness of experience.

What is new, however, is the way in which Lockridge applies his belief in cohesiveness to John Shawnessy's life. Shawnessy's initial encounter with the Court House map leads him to see the County as the universe. As he matures, experiencing desire and disappointment, he comes to understand that the County is part of (and one with) the nation: "Raintree County, he felt, lay far beyond the four borders which contained its span of dirt. It was also the Republic, a peerless dream." With this expanded sense of space comes an expanded sense of responsibility; he is responsible to an entity greater than the county of his youth: "He had said good-by to an older, sunnier County. Then the borders of his private little earth had dissolved into something called the Republic, full of duty and the memory of a crime" (489-90, 329-30). Here is as far as most persons come in their self-perception: they acknowledge their responsibility as citizens of a state and a nation.

Shawnessy's perceptions, though, continue to expand. As the novel closes, he returns home, full of a greater sense

of himself and his world, created by his experiences through the day:

> Now, impending in the still night was the world of mystery, the world that hovered forever beyond the borders of the County. What was Raintree County except a Columbian exploration, a few acres of discovery in a jungle of darkness, a few lightyears of investigated space in nebular vastness! That which lay beyond its borders was simply—everything potential. . . .

> The wall between himself and the world dissolved. He seemed suddenly lost from himself, plucked out of time and space, being both time and space himself, an inclusive being in which all other beings had their being

(1057-58).

He has, at last, fully perceived himself. He is a separate individual; he is a citizen of Raintree County, Indiana, and of the United States of America; and he is a representative of the human race, bound to its past and destined for its future.

In Shawnessy's final understanding is Lockridge's message. Though the individual's perceptions are affected by the total environment in which he finds himself and his society,[8] and although those perceptions can sometimes become antithetical, as in the contrast of carpentered and uncarpentered space, the individual must see beyond the appearances. He must realize that the world, though seemingly made up of contradictions and conflicts, is actually a place of complements. Of Shawnessy, Lockridge writes:

> He felt that he had always participated in two worlds. One was the guiltless earth of the river of desire, the earth big with seed, the earth of fruit and flower. The other was the world of memory and sadness, guilt and duty, loyalty and ideas. The two worlds were not antithetical. They were flesh and form, thing and thought, river and map, desire and love

(259).

The conflicts of the world are components of the greater world. The individual, if he is fully to comprehend his role, must perceive them both and understand their parts in the greater unity of all.

After the brief notoriety associated with the publication of *Raintree County* and its author's suicide, the novel dropped from popular view. But after thirty years, the time seems right for its resurrection, for the novel involves itself with themes that more and more are becoming central to American life and thought. The book is unquestionably concerned with the power of place. It speaks of the powerful tug of the homeland and the seductive call of the city. It reflects the ways in which the American individual reacts to the locales from which he springs, and it dramatizes how those reactions color the attitudes that he expresses and the life that he leads. As it does these things, it goes beyond them, calling attention to the extra-personal, extra-national concerns that bind individuals of every region to each other and to the world. Like the environmental novels of the last decade, ***Raintree County*** calls, ultimately, for a perception of space and place that is neither national nor social, but rather is ecological—the perception that person and place, space and time, are interdependent and one.[9] It is an ecological novel written before its time, and its time has finally come.

Notes

1. See, respectively, Leonard Lutwack, "*Raintree County* and the Epicising Poet in American Fiction," *Ball State University Forum,* 13 (Winter, 1972), 14-28; Delia Clarke, "*Raintree County*: Psychological Symbolism, Archetype, and Myth," *Thoth,* 11 (Fall, 1970), 31-39; William York Tindall, "Many-Leveled Fiction: Virginia Woolf to Ross Lockridge," *College English,* 10 (November, 1948), 65-71; Joseph L. Blotner, "Raintree County Revisited," *Western Humanities Review,* 10 (Winter, 1955-56), 57-64; and Lawrence Jay Dessner, "Value in Popular Fiction: the Case of 'Raintree County,'" *Junction,* 1 (1973), 147-152. The fullest available account of Lockridge's life appears in John Leggett, *Ross and Tom: Two American Tragedies* (N.Y.: Simon & Schuster, 1974), but the book should be used with caution.

2. Yi-Fu Tuan, *Topophilia: A Study of Environmental Perception, Attitudes, and Values* (Englewood Cliffs: Prentice-Hall, 1974), pp. 75-76, 246.

3. Ross Lockridge, Jr., *Raintree County* (Boston: Houghton Mifflin, 1948), p. 99. Further references to this edition will appear in the text.

4. Yi-Fu Tuan, *Space and Place: The Perspective of Experience* (Minneapolis: University of Minnesota, 1977), p. 76; Tuan, *Topophilia,* pp. 30-32.

5. Tuan, *Space and Place,* pp. 122-123.

6. Tuan, *Space and Place,* pp. 30-32, 52-53.

7. Ralph Waldo Emerson, "The American Scholar," in *The Collected Works of Ralph Waldo Emerson,* ed. Robert E. Spiller and Alfred R. Ferguson (Cambridge: The Belknap Press of Harvard University Press, 1971), p. 54. For the ecologist's view of interdependence, see Barry Commoner, *The Closing Circle* (N.Y.: Alfred A. Knopf, 1971), p. 33.

8. Tuan, *Topophilia,* p. 79.

9. Typical of these environmental novels are Edward Abbey, *The Monkey Wrench Gang* (1975); A.B. Guthrie, Jr., *Arfive* (1971); and Jack Schaefer, *Mavericks* (1967). For a fuller discussion of the ecological vision in recent fiction, see my "Jack Schaefer: the Writer as Ecologist," *Western American Literature,* 13 (May, 1978), 3-13.

Daniel Aaron (essay date 1991)

SOURCE: "On Ross Lockridge, Jr.'s, *Raintree County,*" in *Classics of Civil War Fiction,* edited by David Madden and Peggy Bach, University Press of Mississippi, 1991, pp. 204-14.

[*In the following essay, Aaron provides an overview of the plot and characters in* Raintree County *as well as a critical assessment.*]

Ross Lockridge, Jr.'s, novel, a mix of history and myth, encloses a single day, July 4, 1892, in legendary Raintree County, Indiana. As the hours tick on from dawn to midnight, flashbacks (some fifty in all) to distant decades gradually fill in the lives of the principal characters who have converged at Waycross Station near the town of Freehaven for the ceremonies. Thus the past is recaptured in the present and the future anticipated in the past. By the end of the day, and 1,060 pages later, all the pieces of what amounts to a giant jigsaw puzzle have fallen into place and the pageant-history of America from the presidency of James K. Polk to Grover Cleveland's brought to a close.

Scrambled chapters don't always mesh smoothy, but the timing of the cutbacks, the abruptness of the scene shifts, and the withholding of essential information until late in the narrative add a degree of suspense to the novel. Its elastic structure seems especially suitable for a writer trying to pour into his single book the history and culture of a people, his own spiritual autobiography, and everything he had ever read, heard, thought, and dreamed.[1]

Raintree County, published in 1948, has no plot to speak of unless it be the unfolding story of John ("Johnny") Wickliff Shawnessy, himself a surrogate of the author, who sets forth like the questing child in Whitman's poem and gathers to himself every object "he looked upon and received with wonder or pity or love or dread." Through the twenty-four hours of the Grand Patriotic Program, Johnny relives more than a half-century of his lifetime. Once again he is initiated into the mysteries of nature and sex, immersed in the affairs of friends and rivals, in the social activities of his time and place, and—his most sustained experience of all—in the Civil War, an event that reverberates through the whole of ***Raintree County.***

The war doesn't seem to have been uppermost in Lockridge's mind when he began to think about writing the Great American Novel. Only later did it become the grand and terrible stage-setting for the hero's and the nation's maturation. In fact, ***Raintree County*** didn't spring apparently from any single historical episode but rather from a Whitmanesque vision the young Lockridge felt obliged to vouchsafe long before he discovered a way to dramatize effectively the "legend called American History, bloody, irrational, and exciting like the Bible."

His first attempt to objectify this vision was "A Pageant of New Harmony" dashed off in 1937 to commemorate the rise and fall of Robert Owen's Utopian community. It ended with an affirmation of beneficent tendency: "the great past still pours its giant strength into the present and our very life is fashioned from the dreams of other days." Two years later he began **"The Dream of the Flesh of Iron,"** a pessimistic and turbid allegorical work, vast in conception but sophomoric and inchoate.[2] "The Dreamer," in pursuit of "The Beautiful One" (signifying elusive Truth and Beauty) is balked by "The Rival" or "The Enemy" (namely lust and gross materialism). The rotten old civilization collapses at the end; a new one is in the making.

Readers of *Raintree County* should have no difficulty detecting the thematic ghosts of these apprentice pieces in the ideas and characters of the finished novel, the shape of which was already taking form in Lockridge's imagination. Some time in 1941—he was then in his late twenties—he set out to write a work about his Indiana homeland at the turn of the century. What he appears to have had in mind was a prose "Song of Myself" written in the manner of Thomas Wolfe's self-absorbed autobiographical fiction that would out-Joyce Joyce by confining the action of the projected novel not to just twenty-four hours but to a series of days.

He labored several years on this plan until the design he had been groping for suddenly materialized before him in a flash of illumination. He would crowd his novel into one synoptic day but push back the time period to the Civil War era (including the years that immediately preceded and followed it) and base the hero on his maternal grandfather, John Wesley Shockley, who had lived through this period and whose life was both real and shadowy enough to provoke his grandson's fancy. Now he had license to range freely across the nineteenth century cultural landscape, blend the national and local, fact and legend. In the guise of John Wickliff Shawnessy—Hoosier shaman, poet, pedagogue, and soldier and author of a remarkable unpublished masterpiece—he could, as he put it, "express the American myth—give shape to the lasting 'heroic' greatness of the American people."

Of all the writers represented in *Classics of Civil War Fiction*, Lockridge probably comes closest to seeing the war from the perspective of a mystical midwesterner, although to be sure from a marked northern bias. For him the Old Northwest was the heartland of the nation, Lincoln country (as it was for his midwestern kindred spirits Francis Grierson, Vachel Lindsay, Sherwood Anderson, Carl Sandburg, and Edgar Lee Masters) and the attempt to pull down the Union an impious act. The gallantry and sufferings of the Confederates may stir his admiration and pity, but the defeat of a recreant South confirms his hero's belief in a providential design.

The war in *Raintree County* is registered, interpreted, and justified by Johnny Shawnessy as he drifts back to the times of "blood and iron." His direct involvement begins in 1863, a low point in his life, when he is estranged from his mad southern wife and mourning his young son, dead through her negligence. Heretofore, the portents and first years of the war have been reported second hand and serve as a kind of mood music. But now it is reenacted in Johnny's meditations. It comes to life in the conversations carried on during the long July 4th day and most graphically in the cutbacks to the war episodes from Johnny's enlistment to the Grand Review in Washington, May 23-24, 1865.

A sizeable chunk of the novel is given over to battle scenes and descriptions of Johnny's soldiering in the Army of the West. Lockridge competently re-tells the familiar and much written about accounts of army experience: how raw recruits were bloodied into veterans and grew accustomed to the "song of the bullets," what it was like to cope with real and fancied terrors, the impulse to panic, the arduous marches through devastated countrysides, the dismal bivouacs, the camaraderie and fierce elations, the fear of dying in "a foreign place." Occasionally his inventions of hand-to-hand conflict and exploits of derring-do ring hollow, as if he had Hollywood already in mind when he composed them, but at his best, he dispenses with heroics and writes with agreeable flatness and directness.

Not surprisingly, given the tone of the writing that followed the recently ended second world war, Lockridge's Civil War is studiedly deprettified, saturated in blood and booze. His novel is occasionally ribald, to the dismay of some of his reviewers, and strains against the proprieties, but it contains none of the expletives thinly disguised in *The Naked and the Dead* (published in the same year) and breaks no taboos. It was enough for Lockridge to explain the "immense profanity" of the soldier as an expression of his "enormous disgust with the inhumanity of his life. What the soldier endured was fit to be described only by verbal excretions. The Civil War soldier cursed fighting, eating, marching. He cursed awake, and he cursed asleep. He was cursing the great insanity of War with the bitter curse of experience." Johnny reads the Gettysburg Address in a Chattanooga whorehouse. He learns to drink, looks benignly on his lustful drunken companions, and grows inured to smashed bodies and sundered arms and legs, to dysentery and suppurating wounds. Certainly *Raintree County* can't be faulted for want of realism or inadequate research. Ross Lockridge read lots of books.

All the same his Civil War is scenic, discussed rather than deeply probed. The progress of the armies from Chickamauga and Missionary Ridge to the investment of Atlanta and the March to the Sea unrolls panoramically, the authorial voice intermittently soliloquizing on America, democracy, history; the action is interpolated with dreams and visions and rhetorical set-pieces. Clearly Lockridge's model wasn't the Melville of *Battle-Pieces* or any of the war obsessed writers like John W. De Forest or Ambrose Bierce or Stephen Crane but Walt Whitman for whom the war was at once a personal and a national crisis and a ratification of *Leaves of Grass*. Johnny, chronicler and seer, ponders the meaning of the "War" without palliating its horrors or plumbing its tragedy. In *Raintree County* it is the *mise en scène* that antedates Fort Sumter and continues after Appomattox; it is also the hinge that links the antebellum republic of the Golden Day with the emerging industrial nation.

Why did it happen? How to interpret its consequences? Did it spell triumph or degradation? These questions, insinuated into the narrative from the beginning, are intimately related to Johnny's speculation about his own destiny, his own success and failure. They are aired in the debates between him and three of his boyhood friends which function as a chorus on the issues that split the Union and which symbolize philosophical positions and social attitudes.

Big florid Garwood P. Jones, Johnny's slightly older classmate at Pedee Academy, is the fictional incarnation of The Rival or The Enemy in Lockridge's already mentioned abortive poetic work. He stands between Johnny and Nell Gaither, Johnny's first and only love (a later version of The Beautiful One) and dooms their union. Doughface, fraud, demagogue, corruptionist, racist, despiser of Lincoln and quintessential cynic, Garwood sits in the United States Senate in 1892 and is angling to become the Republican nominee for the presidency. The Civil War for him is simply an episode in a vast power struggle between two economic systems and a prime opportunity for his own advancement.

Financier Cassius P. Carney, like Senator Jones, has also found Raintree County too small an area to contain his large ambitions. Calculating and prudent and since adolescence impatient of inefficiency, disorder, and waste, he sees no meaning in the war, morally or ideologically; it has only honed his genius for consolidation. He sees it as a training for business. By 1892 he has become a "bloodless abstraction," the cool young clerk of antebellum Freehaven all but obliterated in the unloved money-worshipping older man.

Professor Jerusalem Webster Stiles, the improbable principal of Pedee Academy and the third and most important member of the trio, not without reason shares the initials of Lockridge's hero and grandfather. Although ostensibly Johnny's opposite (for the "perfessor" is a Menckenian type, a pagan, Puritan-basher, scoffer, and iconoclast), he is in reality his alter ego, the only one in Raintree County who discerns and savors his former pupil's wisdom and innocence. Johnny easily counters the sophistries of Garwood and Carney but finds Stiles's dark pronouncements on the War much harder to dispose of.

"How in your theory of history, John," Stiles asks him, "do you encompass this bloody name [Sumter] on which the Republic foundered? Take away the flagwaving and the patriot shrieks, and what do you have?—a few hundred iron balls bounding on brick walls from which a dyed rag fluttered! For this, the Republic resorted to four years of mass murder" (first edition, 475). The issues seem pretty simple to him. He dismisses the cant of Liberty and Union. The South fought to keep the Negro "a slave and productive, the North to keep him from becoming too productive, which meant making him free." War is "neither moral nor immoral." It's just something that happens to vainglorious men, "the clash of forces ruthless and natural." The Civil War gets lost "in a swirl of proper nouns," in the names of battles and battle leaders, but what it comes down to is "the death of a million men in a series of bloody explosions and stinking camps." And what did the dead die for?

"Liberty, Justice? Union? Emancipation? The Flag? Hell, no. They died so that a lot of slick bastards" could exploit the natural and human resources of America and make it possible for "several million poor serfs" to exchange their European slums and ghettos for American ones (767).

Johnny can't shrug off this sardonic declaration and is half-inclined to concede its accuracy. He hadn't foreseen the debacle of Reconstruction, the KKK, the magic growth of the industrial nation, the "tidal glut" of immigrants, the scandals of the Gilded Age, the bitter railroad strikes in 1877, and the "mining and stripping and gutting and draining, and whoring and ravaging and rending the beautiful earth of America" (772). Yet the child of Emerson and Whitman must reject the summation of his teacher and friend as a partial one. The Civil War, he asserts, was fought to preserve the "Republic" or "Union," illusory and unanalyzable concepts but connoting "the denial of tribal boundaries and tribal prejudices." The South fought for freedom to enslave others, the North to keep alive "the last, best hope of earth." The South produced Robert E. Lee, the North Abraham Lincoln. "As a series of physical facts, we know how terrible the War was. As a series of Moral Events, it was necessary and even sublime" (495).

From his transcendental perch, Johnny watches the impious doers of God's work. He is even ready to admit a certain grandeur in the flatulent and crowd-pleasing orations of Senator Garwood and a degree of validity in the cheerful fourflusher's reply to the Professor's diatribes against the crooks and politicians: "you read too much. Go out sometimes, jerk off your specs, and take a look at this nation. This nation is big enough for everyone in it" (767). Of course Garwood, the unregenerate American, mouths words which are merely sounds to him, whereas for Johnny they resonate with historical undertones.

And so do the reminiscences of General Jake Jackson, Johnny's old corps commander and, as it happens, the keynote speaker at the July 4th activities. In 1892 the General is preoccupied with pension bills and the plans for the erection of a huge soldiers' and sailors' monument in Indianapolis. It will consist, he announces, of a peace group ("a great big gal about a hundred sizes bigger than real in the middle holding up a flag" and grouped around her "a farmer, a blacksmith, a veteran, and a dinge at her feet holding up a busted chain") and a war group, the latter a melange of raised sabres, guns, horses' heads, and broken drums. The monument is a cliché in stone and not to be taken seriously, but the General's volumes of military memoirs, sonorously titled and written in the "grand style" of the period, still breathe. His "customed pompous language is steeped in the sadness of the greatest of all wars" (598).

For all its genial and not so genial satire, its somewhat mannered obstreperousness and calculated impiety (echoes of Sinclair Lewis and John Dos Passos here), *Raintree County* is at bottom a reverent and celebratory book. Lockridge-qua-Whitman beheld These States as a Poem and exalted the Poet as one whose educated eye detected patterns in the welter of historical phenomena. To stimulate "the feeling of historic preoccupation," he drew upon any fact or artifact, lofty or low, that would allow his readers to partake of "the sacred communion:" Myths, folklore, and legend, popular songs and poems and novels, Johnny Appleseed, Uncle Tom, John Brown, strikes and prize fights, military and political crises, and especially the words of Abraham Lincoln that illuminated as nothing else the "few hard facts of history."

Passages from Lincoln's speeches resound through the novel. They put the War, and indeed all American history, into the "right context" and, like the words of Jesus, have a "moral gravity" that gives "the feeling of a human life lived in relation to Humanity." Lockridge's Lincoln is a homely made-in-America product, but he is even more a mythic hero ordained for mighty tragedies—America's link with the ages. Shakespeare, Johnny observes, presaged Lincoln's fate in *The Tragedy of Julius Caesar,* "the prelude to another red drama of assassination in a Republic as little known to him as Caesar's Rome" (946). His play steered the hand of John Wilkes Booth.

Sparingly employed, such fancies can be provocative, but Lockridge also celebrated the martyr-President in windy exclamatory prose. ("Where are the days of Abraham Lincoln? They are yours, Republic! They are yours, American earth dense with the roots of prairie grass! They are yours, mythjetting Time. . . . He was a memory and a hundred thousand memories, mostly of the earth. . . . He was a memory of big trees felled for clearings. . . . Lincoln, the seamy, memoryhaunted face, the fabulous flesh of Sangamon County . . ." (477). And not only Lincoln. Lockridge had a fondness for apostrophizing things American, for bardic chants, expostulations and catalogues, for rhetorical questions and rhetorical answers, and for long dream sequences in which he solicitously recorded "the sleeping soul" of a hero. He thought these effusions were artistic and profound and that readers, fed up with the usual pap would think so too. Hence it came as no surprise to him when *Life* magazine, soon to clamor for yea-saying statements commensurate with Henry Luce's "American Century," featured a homespun excerpt from *Raintree County* on the eve of its publication, and when it was made the Book-Of-the-Month Club's January 1948 selection.

Success proved to be his poison. The promotional hoopla and booming sales left him deflated and despondent. Doubts about his accomplishment, enhanced by the barbs of his fault-finders and more so by the reservations of his admirers, soured his triumph. Already beyond the reach of his concerned family and friends, he felt physically and mentally burned out. (His memorialist called it "a case of literary shell shock.") A month after the news that *Raintree County* had topped the *Herald-Tribune*'s national best-seller list, and at a moment when he appeared to be emerging from the swamp of depression, Lockridge went into his garage, shut the doors, and turned on the engine of his new car. He was thirty-four years old.

Raintree County languished after his suicide. Now long out of print, although still plentiful in second-hand bookshops, it is rarely mentioned in surveys of modern American literature. There are plausible reasons to account for its swift eclipse. As many of Lockridge's reviewers complained, his book was awash in talk, self-indulgent, undiscriminating, repetitive, over-ambitious, too complex and intricate for the general audience, too boyishly confessional and intellectually naive for the sophisticated.

One has only to compare it with Margaret Mitchell's *Gone With the Wind,* the well-researched romance by a natural and accomplished storyteller and defiant partisan of the southern view of the War Between the States, to understand why her book became and remained a popular classic and Lockridge's did not. She instinctively divined the taste of her public (especially readers enchanted with Scarlet O'Hara's nineteen inch waist and Rhett Butler's electric kisses) and resorted to time-tested literary formulas and stereotypes without embarrassment: a strong-willed beauty, a dark and insolent lover, a complement of "darkies," "bucks," and "niggers" straight out of Thomas Nelson Page and Thomas Dixon, her friend and correspondent. In Mitchell's Georgia, Yankees are aflame with greed and lust and eyes smolder, glow, gleam, and glitter. Nothing in this tumultuous tale is likely to distract or perplex the reader.

Raintree County, on the other hand, is a man/boy book. Because of its chronological shifts and authorial divagations, what there is of plot line is hard to trace. It is less focused than *Gone With the Wind,* less breathlessly dramatic, more subjective, bookish, meditative, metaphysical. Not that Lockridge can't match Mitchell's sensationalism; if anything he is less squeamish in depicting violence, death, and sex, only his bodice-rippers have white southern hands, not black. But novels that feature idyllic plantation scenes, the lazy grace of booted cavaliers, gallant ragged Confederates, and the Lost Cause, ordinarily catch on better with the public than those that envisage the South as a swamp of prejudice and sensuality, poke fun at John C. Calhoun, and condone the destruction of Atlanta as necessary and just.

Raintree County is hardly the classic Ross Lockridge felt sure he had written but one of those good/bad books difficult to categorize in which the gold and the brummagem are fairly evenly mixed. (Melville's *Mardi* is another example, if on a considerably higher level). It is best in its unpretentious segments—mostly vignettes, asides, impressions—often arresting and shrewd. For instance, he will remark on the War's "epic rhythms, epithets, heroes . . . a newspaper Iliad of seasons, maps, and proper nouns," on the battles whose names "had swum slowly into the columns of the papers, had lain there wallowing bloodily for days, and had swum slowly out again." Or he will passingly reflect on cigar smoke, "incense of the Republic," that pervades his novel from beginning to end and "hovers in the smell of all the pullman cars and diners, and all the lobbies, court rooms, courthouse toilets, all the Senate chambers, hotel rooms, and statehouse corridors. The Republic is rolled up in thin brown leaves and smoked all over the Republic" (293).

Unhappily for Lockridge, the vogue of lusty, folksy, autochthonous American Stuff had already peaked, except in Hollywood, by 1948. To the new crop of literary satirists, all talk of Americans as a "mythic race," all the hymns to "hob-nailed rail-splitters," all the ceremonial clichés of American history were so much "corn," a term that came into popular usage about this time. Even the Civil War was now fair game. In Flannery O'Connor's story, "A Late Encounter with the Enemy," a dotty 92-year-old "general" is loaned out annually on Confederate Memorial Day to the city museum "where he was displayed from one to four in a musty room full of old photographs, old uniforms, old artillery, and historical documents." His fondest memory is the Atlanta premier of a Civil War film when usherettes wearing Confederate caps and short skirts escorted him to the stage where the Hollywood master of ceremonies introduced him to the cheering audience as one "who had fought and bled in the battles they would soon see daringly re-acted to the screen."

Raintree County never got from impatient reviewers the thoughtful reading it needed and deserved. Some of them praised its lyricism, energy, ebullience, its patches of skillful narrative, but came down hard on its egregious flaws. Four decades after its "short echo-walk between the ballyhoo and the hoot" (to quote Vladimir Nabokov out of context), it is now more evident than it once was that Lockridge did manage to recover something valuable from his risky dive into American history. His vulnerable novel, old-fashioned and ingenuous for all its gimmickry, has become in its own right a piece of Americana.

Notes

1. John Leggett's *Ross and Tom. Two American Tragedies* (New York: Simon and Schuster, 1974) is my only source for Ross Lockridge, Jr.'s, life and career, unpublished compositions, and correspondence. As will be seen, I have made extensive use of Leggett's sensitive and even-handed biographical study, but he is not responsible for my hunches and speculations on the material he has provided.

2. Described in a reader's report as "an immensely long narrative poem, divided into short lyrics, interspersed with frequent prose passages of exposition. This is all about War and the Machine, human depravity and human aspiration, pretty well tangled up and expressed through symbols that aren't very fresh" (Quoted in Leggett, 67-68).

Charles Trueheart (essay date 1994)

SOURCE: "The Great American Studies Novel," in *Atlantic Monthly,* Vol. 274, No. 3, September, 1994, pp. 105-11.

[*In the following essay, Trueheart discusses* Raintree County *alongside Lockridge's son Larry's biography of his father,* Shade of the Raintree.]

Fewer and fewer of us can imagine what it was like to be sentient in 1948, and so it behooves us to approach the thousand-piece puzzle of *Raintree County,* by Ross Lockridge Jr., with a certain humility. Such a novel would probably not be published today, let alone be so lavishly received. It is even hard to imagine that it could be written in a time like ours. Yet for a brief moment Lockridge was able to cast himself as an American Homer, whose portrait of an Indiana county sought to remake the American myth. Some critics, and American readers in large numbers, bought his audacious act.

Something was amiss, however, and probably always had been. Eight weeks after the publication of *Raintree County,* on March 6, 1948, the thirty-three-year-old Lockridge furnished a dramatic epilogue to the book. While his long-suffering wife sat inside their house in Bloomington, Indiana, awaiting his return from an evening of errands, and while their four children slept, Lockridge was a few feet away in their garage, asphyxiating himself in the back seat of his Kaiser. The "young hero and endlessly courageous dreamer" of *Raintree County*'s last words had turned out to be the vision of a bleaker sort of fellow.

It is impossible to read *Raintree County* today (some would leave the statement at that) in ignorance of this tragic piece of biographical intelligence. Now that *Raintree County* is being brought back from the dead in a new edition, we have a much richer context to consider, what with all the existential mysteries and traditional verities that surround genius, "success," and suicide. In this relentlessly optimistic novel we can seek clues to the darkness Lockridge seemed unable to face. Dead men do tell tales, but not necessarily the ones they intended.

Briefly in late 1947 and early 1948 Lockridge would have had good reason to believe that his endless dreaming had been providentially fulfilled. *Raintree County* was borne on a river of hype. A thousand-page first novel by a crinkly-eyed Indiana naif who (the legend already went) had brought his bulky manuscript to Houghton Mifflin in a battered suitcase, *Raintree County* was a corn-fed, swaggering, patriotic, highfalutin, and occasionally naughty yarn. "It attempts no less," declared its astonishingly heedless publisher, "than a complete embodiment of the American Myth."

Though Lockridge had settled for—leaped at—a $3,500 advance in mid-1946, *Raintree County* went on sale in the early winter of 1948 a much more valuable property than that. The book was aswarm with industry buzz, such as it was in those innocent days, and bore the Midas touches of the Book-of-the-Month Club and Metro-Goldwyn-Mayer. The studio, in a novel-to-movie promo competition, paid the unknown writer a well-publicized $150,000 for motion-picture rights to this manifestly unfilmable story. He was widely quoted as saying, "Now I guess I can buy that washing machine for my wife."

Lockridge's seven years' work, more important to him than lucre, was rewarded with book-reviewerly encomiums, too. Frank Brookhouser called *Raintree County*'s publication "an event in American letters." Charles Lee, in *The New York Times Book Review,* called it "an achievement of art and purpose, a cosmically brooding book full of significance and beauty." Howard Mumford Jones, in *The Saturday Review of Literature,* said, "it may be that *Raintree County* marks at last the end of a long slump in American fiction." Readers, or at least would-be readers, were responding. On the morning after Lockridge died, as his ebullient publisher had wired him, *Raintree County* became the No. 1 bestseller on the *New York Herald Tribune* fiction list.

"He seems to have gained the whole world and then to have wondered what it profited a man," surmised the Washington *Evening Star* a few days later. This seems right, as far as it goes. Lockridge's ego was both more swollen and more fragile than most. The testimony of Lockridge on Lockridge, which is voluminous, suggests that he experienced the rather familiar deflation and sense of loss that follows any climax—and experienced the unhappy revelation with an intensity to match his elaborate fantasies. Overnight celebrity, the decisive answer to his prayers, had come at a high price—his bitter surrender of hundreds of pages of *Raintree County*'s original immensity.

One so beaten and susceptible found the exposure of publication difficult to bear. A clean-living, seldom-drinking, nonsmoking family man, Lockridge was jolted by attacks from the clergy, directed chiefly at his soft-focus descriptions of carnal relations, most of them only imagined. A Jesuit professor at Fordham University called the novel "1066 pages of bombast, rank obscenity, materialistic philosophy, and blasphemous impudicity," and said, "The devil had a lot to do . . . with the writing of this book." Lockridge seemed to feel the cold stares of reproach on the street in Bloomington.

He also felt wounded, as authors will, by attacks on his masterwork—especially that in *The New Yorker,* which not only called *Raintree County* "the climax of all the swollen, pretentious human chronicles that also include a panorama of the Civil War, life in the corn-and-wheat belt, or whatnot" but also referred to its author throughout, fabled fact-checkers notwithstanding, as "Lockwood." The very detail is poignant to the point of heartbreak.

Lockridge had told his publisher, in language suitable for repetition by publicists, that he had aspired to write "the American *Republic,* in which the relation between the life of the Individual and the life of the State would be studied and interpreted in terms of ideas and by a process of dialectic resembling in some ways that of Plato's *Republic.*"

Lockridge's son Larry, who can be frank as well as filial, says in his new biography that Lockridge was close to a "delusional state of mind" when he wrote his autobiographical notes for Houghton Mifflin. "Grandiosity is a flip side of depression," Larry Lockridge writes. In the months before he died, according to *Shade of the Raintree,* Lockridge suffered from what today we would more quickly treat as a form of clinical depression. In his last months Lockridge clung to his mother's Christian Science before finally seeking treatment and submitting to electroshock therapy—all of this in deepest secret, while the *Raintree County* publicity machine marched forward.

But even the former, supposedly stabler Lockridge had staggered Houghton Mifflin, which had some experience with the stubborn vanity of authors, with his nearly deranged self-regard. During their long struggle over a concluding 356-page "dream section" that the author considered essential to *Raintree County,* Lockridge wrote to his publisher that the decision was "of great importance to me, the book, and possibly the future of American letters." To another editor he wrote, "It is a book that Americans need to read. It will do them good—goddam them." When his publisher, in one of their many contract skirmishes, made a proposal Lockridge considered treacherous, he wrote an enraged letter that must have been widely appreciated in the corridors of Houghton Mifflin:

> This promise—coming from a man who is not aware that he has ever broken a promise so solemnly given to himself or another—is that Houghton Mifflin Company shall *never* have another big book by the author of *Raintree County.* Do not misread your man—do not misread your man.

Lockridge had disclosed his outlandish aspirations in the pages of *Raintree County.* "Perhaps he too was fated to rewrite the great book of God in a new land and in a new tongue," he wrote of his hero and secret sharer, John Wickliff Shawnessy, "budding bard of Raintree County, / Life's eternal young American." There is always peril in conflating fiction and biographical fact, but it is hard to do otherwise when confronted with a passage like this one:

> It seemed to him that he must be a greater poet even than Shakespeare because there was some essence of what he was that Elizabethan England couldn't possibly compose. He, John Wickliff Shawnessy, was perhaps the bearer of the sacred fire of poetic genius that is given from mind to mind like a regenerating torch. It was he, child of the sunlight, the corndense earth, the simple beliefs of Raintree County, who would become the great American poet. Son of his greathearted mother, of his energetic, sanguine father, he was perhaps a chosen seed, brought from far places.

Read to the last page or merely viewed from afar, *Raintree County* is a lot to get one's mind around. Like *Ulysses,* it is the tale of a single day—July 4, 1892, in a fictitious Indiana county. As the day creeps forward in brief installments, the narrative segues repeatedly to key episodes from as far back in time as 1844, both inside and outside the county.

In 1892 Shawnessy is in the early twilight of his life—with *his* epic master-work, incidentally, unfinished. Surrounding this yearning, brooding carrier of the mythic hod are a pageantful of outsized characters. "The Perfessor," Jerusalem Webster Stiles (another J.W.S.), is Shawnessy's cynical tutor and the novel's redeeming if long-winded voice of asperity. Shawnessy's old friend and rival, Senator Garwood B. Jones, silkily captures the tarnish of the Gilded Age. Poor Shawnessy's days are marked by a succession of remarkable women, from Venus to vixen, who provide Shawnessy with a lifetime of fantasy, succor, estrangement, and despair. He has a merry metaphysical twin, lower-case "mr. shawnessy," "a faunlike hero poised on the verge of festive adventures," according to *Raintree County,* in counterpoint to the upper-case "straw man" Shawnessy, "dutiful citizen of the Republic calling for his mail."

Among its other claims to attention, *Raintree County* marked the emergence, Lockridge wrote of his work-in-progress, of "a new form, an art form mingling the characteristics of many previous genres." The narrative appropriates all manner of "text(ure)s," as the academics might type it: doggerel, oratory, song, tribute, journalism, dramatic dialogue, prophecy, pseudoscience, poster, and "epic fragment," a kind of found narrative. Lockridge, youthful in his predilections, is fond of marrying words, German-style: "forestfringe," "dawnsounds," "rivermarge," "streambegotten." The last (periodless) sentences of chapters hook up with the first sentences of ensuing chapters to make new (if awkward) straddling sentences. The book is equipped with two maps and three chronologies, the better to make sense of its sprawl. ("Sprawling" was the descriptive Lockridge most resented.)

Lockridge hated to be mentioned in conjunction with Thomas Wolfe, as he often was, and protested the comparison with such passion as to remind anyone listening of his painfully engorged self-esteem. He could also describe, with less indignation, how his writing differed from Joyce's: Lockridge *wanted* to be understood. Such was the goulash (his fans would say the literary firepower) of *Raintree County* that readers took the name Lockridge in the same vein as Wilder, Dreiser, Whitman, Joyce, Maupassant, Faulkner, Hawthorne, Benet, and Sinclair Lewis. The young first novelist did not seem abashed by the august company. In a letter to one of his editors he wrote, "The BOMC, which missed taking *Grapes of Wrath,* cannot in the long view afford to miss taking books like *Raintree County.*"

The novel was pitched, and is sometimes remembered, as a novel about the Civil War. It is, in part. In his peregrinations outside the county Shawnessy is wounded in Sherman's March to the Sea and happens to be in Washington when John Wilkes Booth does his foul deed at Ford's Theater. He also encounters the brutalities of racism and the mysteries of miscegenation when he follows a nightmarish wife to her ancestral Louisiana. The movie version may have strengthened the impression of what the book was about. When M-G-M finally wrestled *Raintree County* onto celluloid, in 1957, only a fraction—that fraction—of

Lockridge's plot could be squeezed into its interminable three hours and five minutes.

But, as Lockridge would have been—and typically was—the first to say, *Raintree County* has broader shoulders than mere national cataclysm and bloodied social fabric. It sends its innocent, wandering hero on long journeys of battle, temptation, and self-discovery. It plants the mystical raintree of life in the edenic Great Swamp at the center of Raintree County. From its Independence Day vantage, *Raintree County* limns a whole nation throughout much of a century. ("The Union forever! O, beautiful, unanalyzable concept!" goes one piece of verbal bunting I'll always cherish.)

"He deliberately uses many American archetypes," explains the younger Lockridge, a professor of literature at New York University, who has given *Raintree County* an exceedingly close reading: "the New Eden, the Frontier, the Republic, the Fall from Innocence, the Fear of Miscegenation, and character types such as the Innocent American Hero, the Dark Lady and the Light, the Capitalist, the Frontiersman, the Evangelical, the Feminist, the Statesman, the Perfessor." Lockridge quotes approvingly a critic's remark that *Raintree County* was, if not the Great American Novel, then the Great American Studies Novel.

Lockridge was far better when he eschewed unanalyzable concepts and concentrated on Raintree County. The land, the "box" of the county, was a potent piece of imagery for him—more nuanced, more felt, than many of his human portraits. "The formal map of Raintree County had been laid down like a mask on something formless, warm, recumbent, convolved with rivers, undulous with flowering hills, blurred with motion, green with life," Lockridge wrote, as his hero "mused upon this mingling of man's linear dream with the curved earth, couched in mystery like a sphinx." The original cover of *Raintree County*—designed, needless to say, by the author—echoes this conceit. In the green hills of a topographical rendering of the county the accustomed eye can discern the form of a recumbent naked woman: this was the crowning blasphemy to the indignant of 1948.

Lockridge's celebration of Indiana as America's Eden was not merely a creative device. It sprang from his deep attachment to the place where he had first dreamed his dreams, and to which he cleaved in times of doubt and distress—including at the end of his life, a time when he took some of the M-G-M money and exchanged it not for a mortgage on a place in Malibu and a new set of friends but for a house for his wife and children on a pleasant Bloomington street not far from where his parents lived.

More than bedrock family values were at work: Bloomington was a refuge, and a pond small enough for a deeply insecure frog. Though he had studied at Harvard and the Sorbonne after attending Indiana University in his home town, and though he taught English at Simmons College, in Boston, during the composition of *Raintree County,*

Lockridge was the resolutely midwestern character he played. He wanted to belong, and probably did belong, to some rectangular swatch of American soil just like the one on which he wanted to map the American soul.

Larry Lockridge disputes the characterization of his father as a naif. But his portrait only sharpens the impression of fatal innocence left by John Leggett in *Ross and Tom* (1974), a fine dual biography of Lockridge and Tom Heggen, another celebrated young writer (*Mister Roberts*) of the era, and a probable suicide himself. To see the overwrought Lockridge so willingly expose himself to ridicule and disappointment finally elicits in the reader something akin to protectiveness.

Did Lockridge, in his final act, upstage the book he had poured his heart into? Perhaps he did. This may dismay Lockridge sympathizers—and it is impossible not to be one of them in the face of someone so openly tortured. Larry Lockridge believes that *Raintree County* stands on its own as a neglected minor classic, but he acknowledges the rich possibilities for allegory in his father's life and struggle, his dreams and death. They, and not *Raintree County,* give us the story that survives with something still to say. The story isn't pretty, but it has other virtues conspicuously missing from *Raintree County*—among them a haunting conclusion.

Lockridge couldn't bring himself to give his life's work its final punctuation. *Raintree County*'s very last sentence, like the last sentences of the preceding 113 chapters, leaves off without a period—as if it, and Lockridge too, might go on forever.

Gerald Weales (essay date 1996)

SOURCE: "A Return to *Raintree County*," in *The Gettysburg Review,* Vol. 9, No. 1, Winter, 1996, pp. 168-76.

[*In the following essay, Weales recounts the publishing and critical history of* Raintree County.]

Ross Lockridge, Jr. wanted to write a great book, perhaps The Great American Novel, that *ignis fatuus* that used to dance—and perhaps still does—before the eyes of ambitious young novelists. Although he and his publisher avoided the TGAN label when *Raintree County* was published in 1948, Houghton Mifflin marketed the book as a serious work of fiction, if a good read. Both the publisher and the author understandably wanted the novel to be profitable as well as admired. The attention that *Raintree County* got before and at the time of its publication—the MGM Award, a Book-of-the-Month Club selection, an excerpt in *Life* (September 8, 1947)—assured the commercial success of the book. The image of America's newest literary Golden Boy—the poor and unknown writer who left a suitcase full of manuscript in the offices of Houghton Mifflin and went on to fame and fortune—disintegrated two months after the novel was published when

Lockridge committed suicide. Whether because of this startling event or for the book's own sake, the novel sold well in its initial year. After 1948, except for an occasional article in an academic journal, it largely disappeared from sight. It resurfaced in 1957, when MGM finally got around to making a lamentable movie version of one of the dullest sections of the book—Johnny Shawnessy's disastrous marriage to Susanna, the ersatz Southern belle. And again in 1974, when John Leggett published *Ross and Tom,* a double biography of two once celebrated literary suicides (*Two American Tragedies,* as Leggett's subtitle puts it), Lockridge and Thomas Heggen, who did not survive the success of *Mister Roberts.* Now, Ross Lockridge, Jr. and *Raintree County* are back again. In 1994 Penguin issued the monumental novel in one fat paperback volume, almost impossible to read comfortably, and Larry Lockridge published *Shade of the Raintree,* a biography of his father. It seems a good time to reconsider the novelist and his work.

On the surface at least, Ross Lockridge's life was unexceptional. The details of his growing up in Fort Wayne and Bloomington are generically familiar and a bit boring. He went to Indiana University; did his year abroad; came back to marry Vernice Baker, his first and only sweetheart; fathered four children; went to Harvard but did not finish his advanced degree; taught for six years at Simmons College. He was an obviously intelligent young man, a crackerjack student and an impressive teacher, as his professors and his students testify. His friends remember him as a funny, charming, clever fellow, but somehow this figure never really takes shape in *Shade of the Raintree,* except in the few extant letters he wrote home from Europe, which clearly indicate that at eighteen he was already a talented writer.

The remarkable thing about Lockridge was his obsession with becoming a writer. "He said that since he was between seven and eight years of age he had had one settled purpose in life. *He was going to write,*" Ross's mother said after his death. She based her remark on what the adult Ross told her when he was already at work on *Raintree County,* perhaps after he had already written the lines about young Johnny Shawnessy's childhood resolution "that he would someday write the book that would unlock the riddle of the earth of Raintree County, of his mother and father, and himself." Ross wrote at school, in college, and with his father, either as a ghost or under his own name. Ross Lockridge, Sr. was a popular historian, churning out books for special occasions and reveling in oral on-site presentations of Indiana history. In a letter to Miss Mary Emily Fauntleroy, Ross, Sr. insisted that *The Old Fauntleroy Home* (1939) was his book (some of it was Ross, Jr.'s) and rejected her attempts to interfere: "I cannot conceive of myself as an amanuensis. I have had an excellent amanuensis in the person of my son, Ross Jr." This is a serious joke, in the best traditions of both Lockridges, and an indication of an apprenticeship Ross, Jr. needed to escape. Looking for his own voice, he tried all genres and concocted schemes for grand literary projects that would eventuate in *Raintree County.* His first attempt at a grandiose work was **"Dream of the Flesh of Irony,"**; which Larry Lockridge rightly calls "this unreadable 400-page poem." The extant manuscript of the unfinished work, a multilevel allegory, is a mélange of rhymed ("I hid in many a mass / Of odorous, uncut grass") and unrhymed verse, pieced out with prose sections indicating what was to come. When Houghton Mifflin understandably rejected the epic, Lockridge put poetry aside and turned to fiction, beginning *American Lives,* a novel with a protagonist based on his uncle Ernest. He discarded this work as well, switched from his uncle to his grandfather, John Wesley Shockley, and wrote *Raintree County* in three intense years of writing (1943-1946), the pages rolling off his typewriter and passing on to Vernice, the wife as willing typist, who turned them into clean copy.

Once he had finished what he saw as his towering literary work, he and it were ready to breast the dangerous waters of commercial publishing. The initial reaction of the first reader was negative, but Dick Scowcroft, a friend of Lockridge's from Harvard who had published a novel with Houghton Mifflin, persuaded editor Dorothy Hillyer to have a look at it, and she reported to him that "it smells of money." All that was needed presumably was to pare and polish Lockridge's two-thousand-page manuscript into a marketable product. "They are going to try to make a bestseller out of the book," Lockridge wrote to a friend, "although I didn't fabricate a single line with that in mind." By this time he was as eager for a money success as the publisher was and, although he protested most of the editorial suggestions, he acquiesced when the time came for cuts and rewrites. He cut for the MGM Award; he cut for the Book-of-the-Month Club. Late in 1947, after prepublication copies had already gone out, BOMC asked for one more cut, a single possibly blasphemous line, and he agreed without a quarrel.

By this time he had begun to doubt his own book, a reaction that was one of the symptoms of the "flu or something" that he said was plaguing him. Much earlier, even before he began to write *Raintree,* he suffered, as Larry Lockridge put it, from "frequent bouts of 'flu,' as he always called it." Larry chronicles the personality changes that his father underwent in his last months, the lassitude and indifference, the mask of normality that covered the distress he usually showed only to his wife. At the suggestion of his cousin Mary Jane Ward, who was in and out of mental hospitals both before and after the publication of her novel, *The Snake Pit* (1946), he sought psychiatric help. Diagnosed as suffering "reactive depression," a nonpsychotic response to a particular situation, he was hospitalized and underwent electroconvulsive therapy, three treatments before he managed to get himself released. One of the difficulties in treating mental disorder in the 1940s was that it was considered shameful. Lockridge's parents refused to accept the seriousness of their son's illness. He undertook Christian Science counseling at his mother's request and even joined his father in sessions of memorizing and reciting, echoes of their earlier days, in which Ross,

Sr. saw therapeutic value. Writers today are more willing to go public about depression, not only William Styron in *Darkness Visible,* which Larry Lockridge mentions in his notes, but Art Buchwald in *Leaving Home* and Tim O'Brien in *The New York Times Magazine* (October 2, 1994). In this climate, Ross Lockridge might not have felt the need to pretend that things were getting better, might have found the help he needed, might have avoided the death that he chose as the only cure for his "flu."

When a suicide takes place, survivors ask why. When the suicide is a celebrity, there are a great many survivors. When Thomas Heggen died, there was a rumor that he had killed himself for love of the actress Leueen MacGrath, but a woman who was supposed to know the Broadway scene told me, "Nonsense! He was having trouble with his new book." With Lockridge, the assumption was that he, too, was having trouble with his new book, and indeed there was no new book, only hints and promises. But that is too easy a diagnosis, like the assumption that he had simply been overwhelmed by success. Larry Lockridge says, "He wasn't depressed because he couldn't get a second novel going. Rather, he couldn't get a second novel going because he was depressed." Larry declines to fasten "a diagnostic label" on his father, to define the specific nature of his depression, but he gives a wide selection of possible contributive factors—his family history, the exhaustion and distress at reshaping his novel, the negative reviews. Larry suggests that an immediate trigger for the suicide may have been an editorial in a Bloomington paper that was designed to defend Lockridge and his novel, but which in the process quoted extensively from Hamilton Basso's hatchet job in *The New Yorker* (January 10, 1948). Through the thickets of Lockridge's depression, we keep coming back to *Raintree County.* In a smarmy article in *Saturday Review of Literature* (June 12, 1948), Nanette Kutner quoted Ross, Sr., "The boy put his heart's blood into the book; he had nothing left. I knew this would happen." Larry Lockridge, who spends many pages avoiding such a simplistic reading of his father's death, says in the opening chapter (called "Epilogue") that "in a real sense he died for a book" and that "in some ways Ross Lockridge's life is an allegory of the American writer." I am suspicious of turning the novelist into an all-purpose allegory, although it is the kind of thing that Ross Lockridge might have done. Insofar as the novel's protagonist is a self-portrait, disguised as a fictional reading of his grandfather, Lockridge was willing to make a mythic figure of himself.

Raintree County was an unusual novel in 1948. As the 1940s turned into the 1950s, most best-sellers with any claim to literary seriousness dealt with World War II, usually with Americans at war—Norman Mailer's *The Naked and the Dead,* Irwin Shaw's *The Young Lions,* John Hersey's *The Wall,* James Jones's *From Here to Eternity,* Herman Wouk's *The Caine Mutiny,* even Ernest Hemingway's *Across the River and into the Trees.* *Raintree County* was the exception. Although it was set in the nineteenth century, it was not an historical novel in the best-seller tradition of *Gone with the Wind.* It was a complex and ambitious attempt to deal with the themes and dreams of America, using a remarkable bag of literary tricks. It was—it is—both fascinating and exasperating, as it teeters between profundity and foolishness, as it mixes perceptive, often comic observation with windily poetic generalization, as it regularly breaks off a dramatic scene as though its narrative strategy were based on *coitus interruptus.* It is a grand catchall, embracing a mixture of history, myth, and family chronicle replete with dreams, public speeches, private bull sessions, excerpts from John Shawnessy's written and unwritten prose and poetry, newspaper stories, parody newspaper stories, quotations, parody quotations, a flood of the serious and the trivial.

At once a celebration and a warning, the novel uses a single day, July 4, 1892, in the life of John Wickliff Shawnessy, Raintree County, and the United States to present the decline of the American promise through the Civil War and the rise of industrialism (1844 to 1892) and to reassert that promise in the person of Shawnessy. When the book first appeared, Shawnessy was perceived as a bland character, largely because he is more acted upon than acting, an observer not only of life in the county but of major historical events when chance (i.e., Lockridge) puts him—for instance—in Ford's Theatre for the assassination of Lincoln or in Pittsburgh for the railroad strike of 1877. There is charm in the youthful Johnny, who wants to find the raintree, the secret of life, and to become a great poet and a great lover; and there is vigor in such early scenes as "The Great Footrace," which was excerpted in *Life.* As the novel progresses, Johnny becomes more of a device than a character. He takes a wife but loses her to madness and loses their son as well; he fails to win his beloved Nell or the mysterious actress Laura Golden; he fights at Chickamauga, marches with Sherman to the sea, is wounded and reported dead; he loses a race for Congress; he goes to seek and fails to find his fortune as a playwright in the City, New York mythicized into the destructive opposite of Raintree County; he returns to become a schoolteacher and, defying an irate father, takes a former student as his second wife with whom he raises a family. Despite the swirl of drama and melodrama around him, he comes across primarily as the voice for and the embodiment of the American myth. He recognizes himself as mythic man, a recognition that the novelist treats comically by repeating such lines as "He was having one of his epic moments."

Charles Lee, writing in *The New York Times Book Review* (January 4, 1948), was the only critic who, taking Lockridge at his own evaluation, came close to dealing with all the elements that went into the making of the novel. James Hilton, offering **Raintree County** high praise in *The New York Herald Tribune* (January 4), said, "Despite its wealth of practical allusion and realistic detail, it must be diagnosed predominantly as romantic, if that adjective can still have any but a derogatory meaning." Hilton's use of *romantic* may not be what scholars such as Laurence S. Lockridge (Larry Lockridge in his academic guise) mean

when they capitalize the word, as in *The Ethics of Romanticism,* but when Lockridge in that book says that the Romantics "hold to the moral improvement of audience as a primary end of poetry," I am reminded of his father's letter to Dorothy Hillyer, "It is a book that Americans need to read. It will do them good—goddam them."

Larry Lockridge allies his father with the Romantics in the biography when he quotes from a paper on Victor Hugo that Ross wrote during his year at the Sorbonne (1933-1934):

> Let us consider, for example, *Les Miserables,* which contains almost all of Hugo's qualities—the best and the worst—this immense work, full of interminable descriptions, digressions, superfluous episodes, offering us realism, romanticism, sentimentality, artificiality, lyricism, satire—in short, everything—manages even because of this amplitude to give a sensation of epic nobility and diverse genius. . . . The more a genius aspires to the sublime, the more he risks falling heavily into the ridiculous.

Lockridge might have been describing his own novel ten years before he wrote it. When **Raintree County** appeared, however, Hugo was one of the few writers not cited as an influence. The blurb for the book described it as "the novel Walt Whitman might have written of his America," a compliment that annoyed Lockridge who wrote Hillyer that out of "stinking personal vanity" he did not want to be compared to anyone. Thomas Wolfe and James Joyce were the writers most often invoked by reviewers. From Joyce, he obviously borrowed the device of building his novel around the events of a single day and the idea of introducing Greek myth into his native setting. Inevitably, given the excess of high rhetoric in **Raintree County,** reviewers were reminded of Wolfe, that magnificent motor-mouth, but the two voices do not sound alike. The Wolfe comparison was the one that Lockridge most resented, although he had made a marginal note in his copy of *The Web and the Rock:* "Strange how Wolfe anticipates me in many things."

The one work that is central to **Raintree County** is Nathaniel Hawthorne's "The Great Stone Face." Lockridge, describing Johnny's reading as a child, retells, often in Hawthorne's own words, the story by "the great American mythmaker," which contained "the secret Johnny Shawnessy was hunting. . . . Here was the meaning of man's aspiration woven into the very substance of the earth." Ernest's mother, in Hawthorne's work, tells her son the story of the face on the side of the mountain. According to the "old prophecy," a native of their peaceful valley, will grow into "the greatest and noblest personage of his time" and come to "bear an exact resemblance to the Great Stone Face." Ernest hopes to live to see that wonder, but to his eyes the renowned native sons who return—"an exceedingly rich merchant," "an illustrious commander," and a famous orator with presidential ambitions—do not look like the image in stone even though Ernest's fellow townsmen are willing to think they do. Ernest meanwhile grows old and respected, his simplicity and wisdom having gained him a reputation far beyond the valley. When the poet arrives, as much to see Ernest as his old home, Ernest hopes and fails once again to see the long-awaited prophecy fulfilled. It is the poet who finds and declares the resemblance between Ernest and the Great Stone Face. There is a running joke through the early part of the novel in which Johnny's father, or Johnny echoing his father, declares that Henry Clay or Zachary Taylor or John C. Frémont is "the Greatest Living American." If Johnny was haunted by the idea of the Great American, as Ernest in Hawthorne's story longed to see the original of the Great Stone Face, Johnny, like Ernest, was never taken in by public adulation of the celebrated native sons. In Senator Garwood B. Jones, who has been bitten by the presidential bug, Cassius P. Carney, familiarly called Cash, and General Jacob J. Jackson, all of whom return to Raintree County for the 1892 Fourth of July celebration, Lockridge has his own versions of Hawthorne's great statesman, great financier, and great general, although with more than a thousand pages to play with, he can have more satiric fun with them. In both works, these characters reveal themselves as false heroes—not a Great Stone Face in the lot of them.

Although Johnny has literary ambitions and an unfinished epic poem to prove it, he does not function as the great poet does in Hawthorne's story. That role falls to Jerusalem Webster Stiles, who is as unlike Hawthorne's poet as a character can be. Stiles, known as the Perfessor in the county, where he ran the Pedee Academy in the late 1850s, is the novel's resident cynic. He takes a dim if verbally vivid view of sex, religion, politics, government, the family, and the dreams and aspirations of mankind: "drunk or sober [he] was never afraid to be rhetorical." He is cleareyed about Johnny, however, and perhaps a little sentimental in his acid way. At the end of the book, he calls out, "Behold! John Wickliff Shawnessy is himself the Hero of Raintree County!" as the poet in Hawthorne's story, driven "by an irresistible impulse," calls out, "Behold! Behold! Ernest is himself the likeness of the Great Stone Face!"

What are the ingredients that make up the Hero of Raintree County? Toward the end of the novel, the Perfessor boards a train to leave Raintree County, presumably for the last time, and shouts inaudible final words, which he signs with his initials, using his cigar to make a smoky JWS in the air: "Suddenly, [Johnny] realized that the Perfessor with his usual cleverness must have written them backwards, and what was in reverse for him had come right for Mr. Shawnessy." Lockridge even gives us the initials in script at the bottom of the page, and he draws another JWS to form part of the winding Shawmucky River in the map at the front of the book. The novelist, who has a tendency to underline the meaning of his images, wants us to know—as though we had not got the point early on—that Jerusalem Webster Stiles is an aspect of John Wickliff Shawnessy. Their styles are completely different, but they share distress at the materialism that had settled over America in the nineteenth century, and the Perfessor,

who has only an uneasy laugh as a shield, envies Johnny's double role as "father and preserver" and "endlessly courageous dreamer."

As often as not Johnny plays both roles at once, as in a scene in the Waycross Post Office at the beginning of the novel, which is clearly less confusing to him than to readers who may not yet have adjusted to the play of mind of the character and his creator. He has made his mundane way to the post office to pick up his mail, but he seems not at all surprised to find a naked woman stretched out like the Sphinx on the counter—a presence that reminds him of "his plural being," which is often indicated in the novel by the use or the avoidance of capital letters. As Mr. Shawnessy—the name his wife Esther always calls him—he is "a dutiful citizen of the Republic," a husband, a father, a schoolteacher. As mr. shawnessy, he is a "faunlike hero, poised on the verge of festive adventures." Mr. S. is fenced in by social, linguistic, sartorial, and moral conventions and mr. s. is "a fugitive from boundaries," but they are both housed in a single body that belongs in Raintree County, at once a place of boundaries and an Edenic setting for the hidden raintree. "He was annoyed by his affable public self, satirizing it as Mr. Shawnessy," says Larry Lockridge of his father, "and yielding his pen to the lyrical, memory-haunted self within." A reader who is not the author's son may fail to see Mr. S. as a satirical figure; there is a sharp edge to many of his remarks and he is clearly perceived as a subversive presence by the "good" people of Raintree County. And, since one man's lyricism is another's flatulence, one may hope that the novelist was capable of kidding the "self within." A little of "O, blithe days, o, early agrarian days on the breast of the land! O, Eden of bland repose!" goes a long way. Both the domesticated Mr. S. and his interior dreamer, tempered by the sardonic Perfessor, are necessary to the complete character.

The difference between Hawthorne's protagonist and Lockridge's is that while Ernest never saw himself in the Great Stone Face, Mr. Shawnessy is given to musing in a mr. shawnessy vein, as when he drives his family to town for the festivities and lets the sound of the firecrackers and the sight of the flags recall him to his youth: "Make way, make way for the Hero of Raintree County! For he is coming to pluck the golden apples!" He has his Ernest side, of course, an inheritance from his mother, who once explained to him, "A great man, Johnny, is a man who does good for other people." The first of these two quotations is the most appropriate for the ideational thrust of the novel. In the final pages of the novel, Johnny's last long rumination, when the "wall between himself and the world dissolved," he becomes more the generic hero than John Wickliff Shawnessy, a transcendent Johnny Appleseed, always ready to sow "the seeds of words" that will remake the dream of America and "to plant again and yet again the legend of Raintree County." The exclamation returns, as phrases so often do in the novel, but this time "Make way, make way for the Hero of Raintree County!" is followed by "His victory is not in consummations but in quests!"

One of the things that Larry Lockridge hopes to do in *Shade of the Raintree* is to correct—twenty years after the fact—what he sees as the three major misconceptions in Leggett's biography of his father—about Ross as a young man, about his relations with Houghton Mifflin, and about the motivation for his suicide. Since *Ross and Tom* is hardly anyone's daily reading these days, there is something slightly arcane about Lockridge's argumentative tone. Still, *Shade* is more than a Leggett corrective. It is a bonafide biography and—in part, at least—the author's attempt to work his way to and through the confusion that befell the five-year-old Larry when his father died. Despite the extensive research that Larry Lockridge put into the book and the exasperated affection he displays for the father who chose to leave him, Ross Lockridge never quite escapes the net of fact and quotation and memory that Larry has thrown over him, never quite emerges as a recognizable charming or suffering person.

And his novel? Is it a masterpiece or a literary curiosity? At one point in the biography, forgetting for the moment that he is a professional scholar and critic, Larry Lockridge says, "the value judgments of literary offspring are worthless." Since he hedges on this question, I will too. I have just made my nitpicking way through the book, often with pleasure, but then—something of a pack rat myself—I am drawn to curiosities.

David D. Anderson (essay date 1998)

SOURCE: "*Raintree County* and the 'Dark Fields of the Republic,'" in *Myth, Memory, and the American Earth: The Durability of Raintree County,* edited by David D. Anderson, The Midwestern Press, 1998, pp. 9-15.

[*In the following essay, Anderson discusses* Raintree County *as a great chronicle of emerging patterns in twentieth-century Midwestern America.*]

When *Raintree County* by Ross Lockridge, Jr. was published early in 1948, it was subject to a barrage of critical and popular appraisal almost unparalleled up to that time. Whether its 1060 pages, with accompanying chronologies, lists, and maps, were seen as the embodiment of the American myth and the work that was destined to revitalize American fiction or as pretentiously swollen with undigested words and incidents, it could not be ignored, either by critics, by the general public, or, inevitably, by the Book-of-the-Month Club and M.G.M. *Raintree County* was, in those pre-talk-show days, a work of which everyone was aware, many people bought, in one edition or another, and many even read or read at. Ross Lockridge, Jr. became, almost overnight, America's best-known postwar writer, and he might even, had circumstances not prevented, have become an instant celebrity; furthermore, the promised film version was already spoken of as a major event as well as an epic film.

Yet, in spite of the attention, the sales, the Book-of-the-Month distribution, and the eventual appearance of the

film nearly a decade later, starring Elizabeth Taylor and Montgomery Clift, something happened. Perhaps the result of Ross Lockridge's inability or unwillingness to become a celebrity, his suicide on March 6, 1948, widely rumored to be the result of his inability to write anything else or, more likely, the inevitable result of America's short attention span and its eagerness to destroy celebrities as well as to create them, combined with the disdain of Eastern critics caught up in the monosyllabic hairiness of the late Hemingway tradition as interpreted in *Time*-speak, or perhaps simply an inability or unwillingness to respond to the novel's demands, *Raintree County* and Ross Lockridge, Jr. passed out of the American critical and popular consciousness and consequently, unfortunately, never existed for many of the more than two generations of American students, scholars, and readers who have passed since its publication.

Yet for some of us, who had come out of our war and were still trying to extract meaning from random brutal experience, *Raintree County* spoke eloquently upon its appearance and, because we've continued to return to it over the years, sometimes sending perceptive students to it, and increasingly seeing it in the American literary, historical, and mythical context out of which it came and in which it belongs, *Raintree County* has maintained an existence that continues to grow in spite of the vagaries of critical fashion or the transience of celebration.

To me, in 1948, *Raintree County* was an attempt to make sense of a nation that promised human dignity and fulfillment, only to deliver, in my time, a depression and a war that denied both; it was eloquent, compelling, understanding, as it attempted to come to terms with the American promise of the eighteenth century and the reality that had come to dominate the twentieth. And I continue to see *Raintree County,* the novel, the mythical place, the time, and the human experience as the watershed that marks the transition between an American Midwest in which the Jeffersonian dream might have become real but out of which a society dominated by things and machines—and yes, instant celebrities—has come. And I see it, too, as the central document in the attempt by generations of American Midwestern writers to define a time, a place, a complex of human experiences out of which the myth might have become real but somehow did not; it is the work that defines the mythical place to which Americans went in the early nineteenth century to find cheap land and an open society; it is the work and the place, too, out of which a young man named Jay Gatsby came a century later than those seekers and less than a generation after the gala celebration of freedom on July 4, 1892, in the town of Waycross, Raintree County, Indiana.

The people of *Raintree County* of July 4, 1892, are two generations removed from those who had come across the mountains and down—and up—the rivers to make an orderly and prosperous and fulfilling society out of a wilderness. But they were neither American Adams nor their more recently perceived Eves in search of the Eden that had eluded them in the East, nor were they the two-fisted, white-hatted heroes of a more popular empire-building, evil-conquering myth. They were driven not by a search for perfection, either Edenic or moral, but by the curious combination of idealism and practicality with which the eighteenth century had indelibly marked the American psyche. Happiness, they were convinced, could best be pursued on a quarter-section of cleared bottom land planted in corn in "the territory north and west of the River Ohio."

But as the people came—and they came in droves to the Raintree Counties scattered across the Old Northwestern countryside—they were willing to pay the price in hard work, in isolation, in threats, real or imagined, from the creatures that inhabited the virgin forest, and they were aware, too, of the inevitable price and the omnipresent threat of failure. Sherwood Anderson described the source and the impact of that knowledge at the end of the revised version of *Windy McPherson's Son*: "In our father's day," he wrote, "at night in the forests of Michigan, Ohio, Kentucky, and on the wide prairies, wolves howled. There was fear in our fathers and mothers, pushing their way forward, making the new land" (344). And yet they came and stayed and endured.

In little more than half a century, by July 4, 1892, the cheap land was gone and states and cities marked the orderly landscape. The Old West had become the Midwest and had sent its sons to war and to Washington, and that war had been fought and won. Railroads crossed the countryside, and trains roared through the night, one having, at one point and however briefly, attained a speed in excess of 100 miles per hour. Already ended was that brief postwar period that Sherwood Anderson described in *Poor White* as "a time of waiting" (44) in Midwestern America, in which Americans seemed ready to try to understand themselves, the region, and the nation they had created, and the course to which they would commit it. But by July 4, 1892, the course of the future was clear, perhaps even pre-destined, by circumstances, by the aftermath of what was, in retrospect, the first modern war, by the experience of those who had come over the mountains and up and down the rivers and implanted in their children the dream and the fear. "When the land was conquered," Sherwood Anderson wrote, "fear remained, the fear of failure. Deep in our American souls the wolves still howl" (344).

While the solemn, tragic image of Lincoln still brooded over the Midwestern landscape in 1892, steel workers began the ill-fated Homestead strike against Andrew Carnegie, the White House was returned to a Democrat who had sent a substitute to the war, John W. "Bet-a-Million" Gates thrust the nation into panic, and George F. Baer, president of the Reading railroad, piously proclaimed that "The rights and interests of the laboring man will be protected and cared for by the Christian men to whom God has given control of the property rights of the country" (Josephson, 374).

Of all of this John Wickliff Shawnessy, age 53, schoolmaster, of the town of Waycross, Raintree County, Indi-

ana, astride the National Road and the Pennsylvania Railroad, the twin paths of American destiny, was unaware as he awakened on the morning of July 4, 1892. As local chronicler and poet, he was prepared to celebrate the day and to greet the county's authentic home-grown heroes, United States Senator Garwood B. Jones, the illustrious local member of what was already a rich man's club; Mr. Cassius P. Carney, an authentic native multi-millionaire; and an equally authentic native war hero, General Jacob J. Jackson, who will observe the day by waving the blood shirt and demanding more generous pensions. Although John Shawnessy was unaware of it, the time of waiting had been over for more than a decade, the course of American destiny had been marked out, and the nation, the region, the state, and the county were already on the way into an industrial, material, urban future.

In Raintree County in 1892, the railroads all ran East, the new path of American destiny; the National Road, however, still ran, rutted and weedy, to the West. But with all this, John Shawnessy isn't concerned; his reality, human, personal, lost in the mists of memory and of Paradise Lake and the Great Swamp and the county's mythical name-sake, lies somewhere in the complexities of the past, his own and that of the county and of the republic that gave birth to both.

Out of the moment frozen in time and space that is July 4, 1892, in Raintree County, Indiana, out of the assurance that that place is part of the larger dynamic oneness that lies beyond the county's borders, out of the recognition that the county has contributed its share to an age and a country of great men, out of political hatchets and contrary ideals temporarily buried or transcended, Raintree County and John Wickliff Shawnessy, at the threshold of the twentieth century and a continued commitment that will permit no retreat, take time to try to understand themselves, their time, and their place, unaware that it is already too late, that Raintree County is already tied by steel rails to places and purposes that John Shawnessy thought that he had rejected in his youth.

Although the story in the novel takes place on that one significant day in 1892 when the nation and the county paused to celebrate their being, the novel is itself compounded of the complexities of movement, of the search for meaning, for purpose, for fulfillment, for escape that led a people across the mountains and up and down the rivers three generations earlier and that, at day's—and novel's—end takes not only the county's celebrated sons but its chronicler and the nation's back to the City in the East out of which they had come.

Contrary to many assumptions, **Raintree County,** like the vast Midwestern literary tradition, ranging from *The Adventures of Huckleberry Finn* to *Sister Carrie* to *Winesburg, Ohio* to *The Great Gatsby* to *The Adventures of Augie March,* reflects not the stability of place and circumstance or human lives marked by quiet or violent desperation. Instead, in the tradition that had come out of a moribund

East to a promising West and beyond, it reflects the search—for fulfillment, for freedom, for success, for understanding that had taken Huck aimlessly and helplessly down a river and then beckoned from the unattainable territories, that had taken Carrie Meeber to Chicago and then to New York and the success that she pondered from the unstable security of a rocking chair, that had taken George Willard simultaneously West with the setting sun and to the City of a new age and promise, that had taken Jay Gatsby and Nick Carraway to the bright, shining East, and that had taken Augie March out of Chicago to Mexico, to war, and to range aimlessly across the desolated European landscape.

The tradition out of which *Raintree County* comes and in the midst of which Ross Lockridge placed it, at the time in which the nineteenth century becomes the twentieth, urban industrial centers become the new shining places of promise, talent, and the willingness to work, is central not only to the understanding of the novel and its achievement, but to an appreciation of its rightful place at the center of the modernist tradition that had come out of the Midwest to dominate American writing for most of this century.

As the novel opens on that July 4th morning in 1892 John Shawnessy had travelled to the South and the East, had fought and survived a war, had loved and lost and had come home to be the poet and chronicler of his place and people, and at the age of 53, the watershed at which he finds himself parallels that of the nation and the county. While the former moves eagerly on the bright shining rails of progress, he, like his place, seems somehow out of it, old-fashioned, unsuccessful, mired in a morass of unfulfilled promise, tarnished dreams, in a place lost somewhere East of Indianapolis and West of Ohio on the sleepy Shawmucky River.

When the day is over, the celebrities are gone, and Raintree County turns in upon itself again, however, Johnny and Ross Lockridge and the reader have explored the complex intricacies of time, memory, geography, and the depths of the human psyche, all tied together in a complex uniquely American, uniquely Midwestern, uniquely nineteenth century, at once uniquely local and at the same time a clear illustration of Emerson's insistence that the local is the only universal. The novel transcends the limits of its place in time and space even as it defines them more completely than they had been defined before.

Even as the train carrying Professor Jerusalem Webster Stiles out of the county and back to the East disappears in the haze of evening and its own smoke, John Shawnessy muses on the two mysteries and yet one mystery of his place and himself, and he knows that the search has no ending, that goals and achievements are transitory illusions, that life and time and space and meaning are part of an eternal now, and, clutching the Atlas of the record of the County and its secret scandal, he walks home alone, confident that somehow he would keep the faith, that he had found the way and the secret knowledge that, in Lock-

ridge's words, "His victory is not in consummations but in quests" (1059).

Raintree County is at once celebration and denial, celebration of what once was and what might come again, in spirit if not in fact, and denial of an age that deifies things and celebrity. It is a celebration, too, of the ability to rise above the material promise and to seek a fulfillment of the spirit in the places of the memory, the imagination, the dream, where all things are possible in a quest that is itself the human and spiritual goal. Like Whitman's "Song of Myself" it affirms the worth and depth and significance of human life.

And yet, in the shadows that fall over the town of Waycross, Raintree County, Indiana, as John Shawnessy walks home at dusk on July 4, 1892, Johnny and Lockridge and we know that neither Raintree County nor the mythical rain tree of the eternal search for elusive fulfillment, whether permanent or transitory, as goal or as search, has any existence in fact; they are the stuff of dreams, and the nightsounds of trains, steel rails shining in the moonlight, mark the path of American reality into the American future; as John Shawnessy falls asleep on that July evening the quest becomes real in his dreams.

Raintree County is the place of might-have-been, lost "somewhere back in that vast obscurity beyond the city, where the dark fields of the republic rolled on under the night" (Fitzgerald, 137), the place out of which the Jay Gatsbys of this century have come in their conviction that the pursuit of happiness can be concluded successfully, that love, like all the other good things in American life, can be ours, that the green light at the end of Daisy's dock is within reach. But, as Fitzgerald makes clear, and as Lockridge reaffirms, the truth lies behind us, lost in memory and imagination and the lost dreams of what might have been.

For a half century I have remained convinced that *Raintree County* is a major work, that Ross Lockridge, Jr. has come closer than anyone else to defining America and Americans in terms of what might have been and what was and is. I'm well aware of its shortcomings, in terms of sheer bulk if nothing else, but at the same time I remember Faulkner's insistence that we must judge a work not by its achievement but by its attempt, that all works ultimately fail, but that only significant failures endure. *Raintree County* is in his terms and from my perspective a significant, indeed, a magnificent failure.

Works Cited

Anderson, Sherwood. *Poor White.* New York: B. W. Huebsch, 1921.

———. *Windy McPherson's Son,* rev. ed. New York: B. W. Huebsch, 1921.

Fitzgerald, F. Scott. *The Great Gatsby.* New York: Charles Scribner's Sons, 1925.

Jackson, Matthew. *The Robber Barons.* New York: Harcourt, Brace, 1934.

Lockridge, Ross, Jr. *Raintree County.* Boston: Houghton Mifflin, 1948.

Park Dixon Goist (essay date 1998)

SOURCE: "Habits of the Heart in *Raintree County*" in *Myth, Memory, and the American Earth: The Durability of Raintree County,* edited by David D. Anderson, The Midwestern Press, 1998, pp. 56-67.

[*In the following essay, Goist examines the tension between individual and community in* Raintree County.]

Habits of the Heart: Individualism and Commitment in American Life (1985), a widely discussed work by Robert Bellah and a team of social scientists, has once again reiterated the importance and urgency of understanding the tension between individualism and community in America.[1] This provocative work also provides a challenging framework for better understanding our culture, and I would like to use it as a model for analyzing one of the most ambitious novels ever written about life in the Midwest, Ross Lockridge Jr.'s ***Raintree County*** (1948). Lockridge's mammoth novel particularly lends itself to this approach because the tension between individualism and commitment to community forms a major conflict at the very heart of the book.

I

In their study of contemporary American life, Robert Bellah and his colleagues borrow the first part of their title from a phrase used by Alexis de Tocqueville in the 1830s to describe the morés which he felt were helping shape the character of the young republic. Tocqueville found such "habits of the heart" as family life, religious traditions and participation in local politics among Americans as vital elements in helping to create the kind of person who, by maintaining connections to the wider political community, formed the bulwark of free institutions. He warned, however, that another characteristic, which he was one of the first to call "individualism," could potentially isolate Americans one from another, thus ironically undermining the conditions of social institutions based on freedom.

Habits of the Heart is motivated by the same concern that Tocqueville called attention to in the nineteenth century. The individualism which the Frenchman simultaneously admired and feared is, according to Bellah *et al.*, a threat to freedom in the twentieth century. That potentiality was already apparent to Tocqueville, who found that:

> Individualism is a calm and considered feeling which disposes each citizen to isolate himself from the mass of his fellows and withdraw into the circle of family and friends; with this little society formed to his taste, he gladly leaves the greater society to look after itself.

> . . . Such folk owe no man anything and hardly expect anything from anybody. They form the habit of thinking of themselves in isolation and imagine that their whole destiny is in their hands.[2]

Bellah believes that this observation, made about the threat of individualism to community life in the largely agrarian setting of early nineteenth century America, is even more true in the complex and fragmented urban America of the late twentieth century.

According to Bellah and his colleagues, individualism so dominates contemporary American life that we find it difficult to discuss or even talk meaningfully about community. This is due, in part at least, to the fact that we do not have a vocabulary for such a discussion. Further, we have become so individualistic that we find it difficult to think about commitment to anything outside of ourselves and a small circle of family and friends. Bellah and his co-authors want to provide contemporary Americans a means of transforming this largely inner moral debate into public discourse. By so doing they hope it will be possible to develop ways of talking about the relationship between private and public life and of thinking about alternative ways to live.

Habits of the Heart identifies three cultural traditions that can provide a context within which the debate can take place—the biblical, the republican, and the modern individualist. The biblical and republican traditions, embodied in the representative figures of John Winthrop and Thomas Jefferson respectively, represent the major ways in which Americans have thought about and organized community. Winthrop's Puritanism emphasized a utopian community where success was measured in how well an ethical and spiritual life was provided for and where freedom meant a moral freedom—based on a covenant between God and man—to do "that only which is good, just and honest." Jefferson's republicanism sought to found a community of equality and justice among men based on an educated citizen who participated freely in politics and government. Bellah points out that neither the biblical nor the republican tradition of community entertained a notion of freedom which merely allowed people to do whatever they pleased.

It is the third cultural strand, that of the modern individualist, which has emphasized the freedom of the individual to act independently in his own self interest. This individualism exists in two different forms, "utilitarian" and "expressive." The first form of individualism is best exemplified in the life of Benjamin Franklin, whose rise from obscurity to wealth and power emphasizes the notion that what is most important about America is the opportunity of the individual to get ahead and achieve success on his own initiative. Many have found in his example justification for the idea that in a society where everyone freely pursues his own self interest the good of the larger society is best served.

In the second form of individualism, "expressive individualism," devotion is not to the material success valued by the utilitarian, but to a life rich in sensual and intellectual experience, marked by strong feelings and a love of variety. Walt Whitman represents this individualism, which finds true freedom in the cultivation and expression of oneself against social restrictions of any kind.

Habits of the Heart thus suggests a dramatic way of thinking about culture, as a dialogue or conversation among the representatives of opposing values which matter to a particular society. This is an approach which marks the work of such American Studies scholars as R. W. B. Lewis, particularly in his study of *The American Adam* (1955).[3] I have chosen to analyze **Raintree County** within this context partly because it is a way of thinking compatible with my own interests and previous work.[4]

II

Raintree County is a novel which dramatizes the dichotomy and harmony between individualism and commitment. It suggests that there can exist a compatibility between an extreme "expressive individualism," on the one hand, and commitment to a particular place and people on the other. This perspective distinguishes Lockridge's novel from much of American literature which is so often characterized by the flight of main characters from the entanglements of community.

Raintree County tells the story of a single day in the life of John Wickliff Shawnessy, a modest, fifty-three-year-old small town teacher and poet. The day is July 4, 1892 and the town of Waycross, Raintree County, Indiana is holding its annual fourth of July celebration. As John Shawnessy takes part in the various occurrences of the day he also lives in a series of flashbacks which help reconstruct the major events in the fifty years of his life before 1892. We thus learn that throughout his life there has been a constant struggle between two parts of John Shawnessy's personality: the proper upper case Mr. Shawnessy, a staunch member of the community, responsible, involved, upright, committed; and the sensual lower case mr. shawnessy, individualist, heedless, wandering, suspect, often lonely.

A number of dream sequences and the reminiscences of three boyhood friends, who have returned to the county for the day, aid in the recreation of Shawnessy's double life. A stream of consciousness technique connects the flashbacks, dreams and reminiscences. Each scene flows into the next because the last word of one is linked to the first word in the one following with no punctuation marks to interrupt the narrative. The following is an example of how two scenes are thus connected:

> Mr. Shawnessy wondered then if it was still possible to walk through the late afternoon . . . and find strong love and a great wisdom among the faces of

WAYCROSS STATION

Were the words painted on the building by the tracks.[5]

Nor are the fifty-two flashbacks, though each is dated, arranged in chronological order, reflecting the fact that in real life our thoughts are seldom ordered in a logical and linear fashion.

John Shawnessy's life is revealed by these various methods, which also provide a richly detailed portrait of small town life as well as an epic panorama of American history in the nineteenth century. The intertwining of personal experience and historical fact, whereby the occurrences of John's life are often counterpointed in time with major historical events, is one way Lockridge links his protagonist to American culture. Analogies are also drawn between both Shawnessy's life and American history, on the one hand, and a variety of Greek and Judaic-Christian myths of creation and the search for life's meaning on the other. So not only is Johnny meant to reflect the root American experience, but readers are to understand that in his quest he also stands as a universal "everyman." As Delia Clarke has noted, "In his reliance on mythic archetypes and psychological symbolism, Lockridge raises an American story to the mythic level; it becomes a universal portrait, a story in which one man is all men, and one country is all earth and life."[6] This effort makes Lockridge's book unique among American historical romances.

Born in 1839, Johnny Shawnessy is destined to spend his divided days trying to make sense of life, first as he comes to know it in Raintree County and then as it is shaped by the events of his nation's history. In John's first flashback it is election day, 1844, he is five years old and stands beside the National Road waving to a pig-tailed little girl in a covered wagon heading West. He too dreams of going West, to the Lone Star Republic or out to Oregon to help build the future. But he doesn't go; he only dreams of going:

> A small boy had wandered out into the morning of America and down far ways seeking the Lone Star Republic and the Oregon Trail. A small boy had dreamed forever westward, and the dream had drawn a visible mark across the earth. But the boy had never gone that way. He had only dreamed it. He saw the face of a girl fading among the vehicular tangle of the years. All the evenings of a life in the West dyed the sunset peaks with purple—the lost years ebbed with waning voices in the cuts where the little trains passed, crying. Yes, he had been fated to stay after all, chosen for a task that called for more than ordinary strength.

> (21)

This early scene, where Johnny has a strong urge to leave but instead stays, sets the tone and pattern for the rest of his life.

Johnny spends the long summer days of his youth wandering the county and musing by the banks of the Shawmucky River. He ponders the higher meaning of his life and that of his community as they are related to the mythical Asian tree which has given its name to the county. That original tree, symbolic of the divided origins and character of Raintree County, is said to still exist somewhere near where the Shawmucky flows into Paradise Lake, forming the Great Swamp. Johnny dreams of finding that tree and thus solving the mystery of existence:

> Someday, perhaps he would find that tree and thus become the hero of the county, the Alexander who cut the

Gordian knot, the hercules who obtained the Golden Apples of the Hesperides, the Oedipus who solved the Riddle of the Sphinx. The secret of the tree was blended strangely with the whole secret of his life and the mystery from which he had sprung.

(46)

But like so many of his quests, the one time Johnny sets out to actually find the famous Raintree he gets lost, almost drowns in the muck of the Great Swamp, earning for his effort only the laughter of his friends.

Johnny is also a voracious reader, always seeking the connection between the world's great poems to his life in Indiana and the American Republic:

Johnny Shawnessy didn't so much read Shakespeare as he read a vaguely imagined book of himself. In Shakespeare's luxuriant language, strong rhythms, terrific metaphors, Johnny was groping toward a new language of himself, a vocabulary equal to the dramas, characters, ideas, events that only America could produce.

(99)

Like Longfellow and Shakespeare, he would write an epic of his people steeped in the knowledge of the ancient and fruitful land from which they sprang. Here then is the mighty chore to complete by which he is destined to remain in Raintree County.

As he grows older, Johnny enters more fully into the life of his community. County fairs, temperance plays, election campaigns, Fourth of July celebrations, camp meetings, newspaper rivalries—Johnny participates in all of the activities which make up the vibrant life of Raintree County. Johnny also attends and graduates from Pedee Academy, "An Institution Of Higher Learning" founded in the county in 1857, the creation of Jerusalem Webster Stiles, Johnny's close confidant and alter ego. As worldly wise and cynical as Johnny is shy and naive, the "Perfesser" pokes gentle fun at the pretensions of young Shawnessy who, for all his outward shyness, often fancies himself as a young Greek God accomplishing heroic deeds.

Johnny writes a column in the county Republican newspaper under the name of Will Westward who reports on the weekly doings and contemplations of Seth Twigs, a fictitious rustic philosopher and amateur politician known for his earthy wisdom. In this writing venture Johnny faces a friendly rival, Garwood B. Jones, who writes for the Democratic weekly under the name of Dan Populus, another backwoods raconteur creation.

Garwood Jones is also a rival for the attentions of the beautiful Nell Gaither who Johnny, in his shyness, can only admire from afar. One day Johnny sees Nell bathing nude in the Shawmucky, and he forever after envisions her as a Grecian-like river nymph. But in her elusiveness Nell also becomes a symbol, like the mythical Raintree, of the young American Republic. As county maps represent man's effort to impose a linear regularity on the sensuous

and undulating earth of Raintree County, so Johnny sees in Nell a mingling of the area's inherited Puritanism spread thinly over an exciting erotic potentiality. On the brink of realizing the sexual fulfillment of that potentiality on the day of their graduation from Pedee Academy, Nell and Johnny are interrupted by the commotion caused when Perfesser Stiles's indiscretion with a minister's young wife is discovered.

This latter episode, with its threat of violence, takes place in the year prior to the outbreak of the Civil War, and foreshadows external events which are starting to crowd in upon Johnny's existence and upon life in Raintree County. But just before his youthful and innocent days in rural Indiana come to an end, Johnny achieves his greatest individual success; he wins the Glorious Fourth of July foot race in 1859. On the same day, and drunk with the taste of competitive victory (aided by the influence of too much hard cider following the race), he seduces/is seduced by Susanna Drake, a dark haired Southern beauty. Symbolically the seduction takes place in the Great Swamp of Lake Paradise.

Does Johnny's loss of innocence take place under the branches of the long sought Raintree? Johnny is too muddled and excited to be sure. But there is no doubt that this is a crucial turning point in his life, for Susanna soon claims she is pregnant and Johnny dutifully marries her.

One of the most revealing examples of Johnny's desire, but ultimate ambiguity about leaving the county takes place shortly after Susanna Drake tells him she is pregnant. He tries to get away from what seems to him an unjust entrapment (indeed, Susanna later tells him she lied about the pregnancy). Running along the railroad embankment on the night after John Brown's sentencing, Johnny reaches out to grab onto the last car of a train headed for California. He is ready to become "One of that restless, messianic seed," pushing on, leaving the past behind, saying good-bye to the new complications in his life in Raintree County. He will try a new life in the Golden West. But as he takes a last look backward, remembering all that life in the county has meant to him, Johnny slips, becomes entangled in the vines, withering grasses and weeds of the Shawmucky River. He then realizes "that he could no more uproot himself from this memory haunted earth than he could pluck body from soul." (291)

When Johnny becomes involved with Susanna, he is saying good-bye to an older, sunnier, more simple county, the days of his innocence and youth, just as America, in approaching the Civil War, was being forced to abandon its dreams of a united and just republic based on freedom for all men. Like the nation, which had tried to ignore the slave, John realizes that whatever secret there was to learn of Raintree County "was also to learn duty and hot tears." And in leaving Nell, he has also lost his own private republic. "To him, Nell Gaither was an entire republic of beauty and nostalgic memory, which now he had to relinquish." (327) No longer will his identity be defined so completely by the people and concerns of the relative innocence of these early years in Raintree County. He is involved in one of the processes which *Habits of the Heart* has identified as an element in the creation of the self-reliant individual—leaving home.

With his symbolic fall from grace and break with community there begins for Johnny a long exile, marked by a continual leave taking and returning to the county, connected in his mind with the arrival and departure of trains:

> Where had the long days gone? It has seemed that they would be forever. But the train passing behind the land at evening had been calling him all the time, calling him beyond the private square or young illusion. Awaken, it had said. Did you think that you could be a child forever on the breast of the maternal and sustaining earth? . . . Farewell to that more innocent and youthful Raintree County. And to its lost hero. For he is there—he haunts the shape of beauty by the river, ignorant of defeat and death.
>
> (604-605)

First he and his new bride go on a long honeymoon to New Orleans in the days just prior to the firing on Fort Sumter. Johnny is shocked by the treatment of slaves in the South and by the decadence of the Southern aristocrats. They return to Raintree County, where Susanna is soon driven insane by her moral and racial ambiguity, for it is revealed that she is the daughter of her father and his mulatto mistress. In a desperate act of insanity she sets fire to their Raintree home, killing their three year old son, and then disappears, the "lost child of a stained republic."

Devastated by the loss of his son and wife, Johnny leaves the county again, volunteering for duty in the Civil War as a common foot soldier. He fights at Chickamauga and then is wounded while marching with Sherman's troops after the destruction of Atlanta. Recovering in a Washington hospital, Johnny learns that he has been reported killed in action back in Raintree County. When he does return home, it is to discover that Nell has recently died in child birth. Thinking Johnny dead, she had married Garwood Jones.

Johnny's return to the county is a symbolic rebirth. But he is, to an extent, a different person from the youthful dreamer of pre-Civil War America, and he is returning to a rapidly changing world which he only vaguely understands. His personal confusion about the meaning of his life after the war is meant to reflect the social disruptions caused by the emergence of a new, industrialized society. "These post-War years were the saddest and loneliest he would ever have." (772) Both the Republic and Johnny have been transformed by war and industrialization:

> This was the period of awakening into a new age, and a new light was on the land. He thought then of railroads, the newspapers, the speculators, the builders, miners, exploiters of the earth. He thought of the cities crammed with new people. Did they still wait the coming of a young Shakespeare, a hero from the West?

> Was there still a passionate lover waiting for him somewhere, the incarnation of all beauty he had ever seen and coveted?
>
> (772)

Johnny becomes a school teacher, then enters an ill-fated campaign for political office against Garwood Jones, who did not fight in the war but has nonetheless garnered a commission. An example of the self-made political opportunist, Jones has launched a successful political career, resulting in his election to the United States Senate and in becoming a contender for nomination to the Presidency. Johnny's campaign reflects his continued commitment to the community, but his rejection in favor of such an only half honest "utilitarian individualist" leads him to the obvious conclusion that if he has a contribution to make in Raintree County it will surely not be in the realm of elected political office. The compromises with the integrity of self that are required of a politician like Garwood Jones are simply impossible for Johnny to accept in his own life.

Still unsettled by the upheavals in his life, Johnny goes to New York to try his hand as a playwright, seeking in the theatre the meaning of post-war America. Here he meets another of his boyhood friends, Cassius P. "Cash" Carney, a successful but lonely financier. He is also the epitome of the self-made man, the utilitarian individualist who has succeeded largely by his own efforts. In so doing Cash has developed a philosophy that if each individual pursues his own self interest the larger good of society will automatically be served. "Money makes money, not just for the capitalist, but for everybody," he tells Johnny. "That's the American secret as I see it." (828) Looking down on the smoldering yards during the great 1877 railway strike in Pittsburgh, Cash extols the sacred rights of the individual to own property, to invest capital and to use his wealth however he sees fit. Johnny can no more accept this view of life than he can that of Garwood Jones.

In New York Johnny also meets Cash Carney's mistress, Laura Golden, a famous actress who represents the glitter and artificiality of the city. Johnny is attracted to her, but ultimately disillusioned by her city values. Laura, like the city, has something forbidden to teach Johnny, and this makes him uncomfortable. Just as Laura is on the verge of revealing herself and her meaning to him, in the mysterious mirror-lined upstairs room of her elaborate city dwelling, Johnny is called home because of his mother's death. Headed back to Raintree County, his education in the new urban America complete, the questing hero is ready to resume his life among more compatible surroundings.

Back in Raintree County, Johnny meets Esther Root, a former student, now also a teacher, some fourteen years his junior, and after a troubled public courtship, which brings him into conflict with Esther's father, they are married in 1878. They have three children, including Eva who is a reader and dreamer like her father. He becomes principal of the local school and, though the differences between him and his father-in-law are never reconciled, Johnny settles into the rather quiet pattern of life in Raintree County. But the lower case mr. shawnessy still struggles inside of him, and Johnny is still searching for the meaning of life. He resumes work on his American epic, convinced after his stay in New York that he must continue even though he senses it will never be completed because epics such as his may no longer be possible in the new America of industrialism and cities.

Yet Johnny never gives up his dream of understanding the meaning of his life as it is connected to that of his country and his community. He has, through the years, come to know himself. He understands that whatever successes he may have in life, his real "victory is not in consummations but in quests." (1059) The novel ends on midnight of the Fourth of July, 1892, with Johnny much as he has always been, "a dreamer, dreaming dreams in an upstairs bedroom of a little town beside a road in America." (1060) Like Nathaniel Hawthorne's patient hero, Ernest, in the short story "The Great Stone Face," Johnny has achieved a rooted dignity through maintaining his hopes and his commitment to the people and events of his "home place."

Thus Johnny Shawnessy, the forever young hero (even at fifty-three he appears youthful) is engaged throughout the years of his life in a quest for personal identity and meaning. But in contrast to other restless, mobile and lonely figures which dominate American culture, Johnny's search is enmeshed within the lives and events, past and present, of the place in which he lives and the nation of which he and his home are so much a part. As Johnny says at one point, "here where the two roads cross [the County Road and the National Road] I study and study the riddle of the Sphinx, the intersection of my life with the Republic." (273) In this he is unlike such uprooted and isolated figures as Captain Ahab and Jay Gatsby, or Jack Kerouac's Sal Paradise and Dean Moriarty, or any of the lonely movie cowboys and tough T.V. cops. Yet he is in some ways as lonely and at times as isolated as these cultural figures, the difference being that Johnny finally remains rooted in a place, or enters into leave-takings like other ritual questing heroes who return home after their wanderings.

Johnny Shawnessy's life can be seen, then, in terms of the individualism/community dialogue which forms so integral a part of American culture, and which has recently been emphasized by the authors of *Habits of the Heart*. At the core of Shawnessy's being is the struggle of what Bellah and his colleagues call an "expressive" individualist to understand his relationship, and thus maintain his commitment, to both the local community and the larger society. As this dichotomy between modern individualism and a commitment to community is at the center of Bellah's concerns so is it the main source of tension in *Raintree County*. The resolution of that tension in the novel is an uneasy one, for while Mr. Shawnessy is outwardly a respected member of the community, the lower case mr. shawnessy continues to live in a vivid imagination which struggles against all social restrictions.

It is only in an ironic sense that Mr. John Shawnessy, a middle-aged, small town Hoosier school teacher can be considered heroic—an irony not lost on his alter ego, "Perfesser" Jerusalem Webster Stiles. Yet Johnny Shawnessy, whose individualism borders at times on narcissism, is the real hero of Raintree County. Like Ernest in Hawthorne's story, Johnny is a true hero not because he returns as a rich and famous politician (like Garwood Jones) or industrialist (like Cash Carney), but because in rejecting the kinds of successes and utilitarian individualism they represent he finds his commitment and contentment among his own people in his own home place. In Johnny's life, then, the conflict between individualism and commitment, first observed by Tocqueville and recently restated by Robert Bellah and his colleagues, has achieved an uneasy truce. Individualism and commitment are not, finally, at odds in *Raintree County*, but rather exist in a troubled harmony.

Notes

1. Robert N. Bellah, Richard Madsen, William M. Sulivan, Ann Swidler, and Steven M. Tipton, *Habits Of the Heart: Individualism and Commitment in American Life* (Berkeley: University of California Press, 1985).

2. Alexis de Tocqueville, *Democracy in America,* ed. by Richard D. Heffner (New York: New American Library, 1956), p. 193. Cited by Bellah, et al., p. 37.

3. Lewis notes, "Every culture seems, as it advances toward maturity, to produce its own determining debate over the ideas that preoccupy it. . . . The debate, indeed, may said to *be* the culture . . . for a culture achieves identity not so much through the ascendency of one particular set of convictions as through the emergence of its peculiar and distinctive dialogue." R. W. B. Lewis, *The American Adam: Innocence, Tragedy, and Tradition in the Nineteenth Century* (Chicago: University of Chicago Press, 1955), pp. 1-2.

4. Park Dixon Goist, *From Main Street to State Street: Town, City and Community in America* (Port Washington: Kennikat Press, 1977).

5. Ross Lockridge, Jr., *Raintree County* (Boston: Houghton Mifflin, 1948), pp. 752-53. All further citations will be made parenthetically in the text.

6. Delia Clarke, "*Raintree County*: Psychological Symbolism, Archetype, and Myth," *Thoth: Syracuse University Graduate Studies in English*, II, i (1970), p. 38.

Douglas A. Noverr (essay date 1998)

SOURCE: "Memory, the Divided Self, and Revelatory Resolution in Ross Lockridge, Jr.'s *Raintree County*," in *Myth, Memory, and the American Earth: The Durability of Raintree County*, edited by David D. Anderson, The Midwestern Press, 1998, pp. 77-83.

[*In the following essay, Noverr discusses internal tension and the division of self in the protagonist of* Raintree County.]

In her 1988 work titled *Equivocal Endings in Classic American Novels* Joyce A. Rowe finds a fairly consistent and repeated pattern in the endings of classic American novels that enables one to speak of "the American sense of an ending." In this pattern the protagonist of each of the stories is presented as an "idealist" or "visionary" who "in the course of the tale . . . is defeated, as much by his or her own limitations as by society. . . . Yet these endings all adhere to a similar convention: they redeem or rehabilitate the ideal by recasting it in alternative terms. . . . The protagonist refuses to learn anything about self or world from the experiences undergone in the story." Rowe further states that the stories "ratify what they seem to deny, . . . continue to insist, in the face of complex and contradictory evidence, on the redemptive power of the dream." The protagonists avoid or evade self-discovery, fail to come to terms with the conditions of social reality, and are unable to develop a socialized self that is able to interact and connect with significant others. Idealism, the elusive dream, the headiness of autonomy and independent action, transcendence of temporal limitations, integration and wholeness in some other place and circumstances than the one an individual is in, anticipations of beauty, happiness, and perfection in the future—all these exert a pull on the idealist and visionary that dislocates them and disables them from commitment. Visionary hope springs eternal, and this hope assumes a perfection that is not questioned or abandoned, even if it seems crushed due to the material conditions and circumstances of existence.

Part of the problem inherent in the paradigm Joyce Rowe identifies is that the protagonist's conflict is based on or rooted in binary or totalizing oppositions that seem irresolvable or that appear to be resolved only by denying or opposing one in order to realize the other. These binary oppositions include the following: society/nature, natural/rationalized, perfect/imperfect, reality/dream, individual/society, freedom/restriction, ideal/real, male/female, truth/illusion, city/country, along with many others. The problem, then, involves thinking in absolutes or measuring the unsatisfactory, imperfect, and disappointing present with some imagined idyllic past golden age or epic moment or with some anticipated satisfying future. As one can imagine, such a positioning makes the idealist/visionary a conflicted, equivocal, and unhappy individual who yearns for what most likely cannot be had or experienced in an always imperfect and conditional world.

I would like to suggest that John Wickliff Shawnessy in Ross Lockridge Jr.'s *Raintree County* suffers from or struggles with this condition of the divided and seemingly irreconcilable self. However, in and on the day of July 4, 1892, as the past and present intersect, overlap, collide, fuse, and converge in remarkable detail and memory, John W. Shawnessy is able to regain a measure of his lost belief in the value of the quest, to gather strength to face his life beyond his 53rd year, and most importantly to connect himself to his wife and three children as the context and meaning of his life. John Shawnessy experiences a renewal of faith in people and the country as well as a renewal of his love for his remarkable wife on the occasion of their fourteenth wedding anniversary. He realizes that women, including his daughter Eva Alice, are, and have been, crucial to his life and well-being, not as erotic objects or the focus of one's desires or needs but as helpmates, supporters, equals, fellow questers of the ideal beauty, and fellow mortals in need of love, connection, trust and security.

For much of his life, John Shawnessy has been a Grail seeker and a dreamer, and others have realized or been convinced of his probable destiny to be a great man with a "great future," as Professor Horace Gladstone, the phrenologist, had pronounced on July 4, 1854 when Johnny was fifteen years old. With his "holy faith in the printed word," acquired at the little schoolhouse in Danwebster, Johnny desires to become a great poet who "would all at once complete the Great American Epic" (p. 511) and who would live a "lifetime of immortal words, which would one day be treasured by the world in a single volume entitled The Complete Works of John Wycliff Shawnessy." (100) While he does manage to write a series of feature articles for a local newspaper, as well as some verses, John's dreams of literary immortality have failed to materialize in any substantial way. What he has done, however, is to store in his memory and consciousness an incredible history of Raintree County and its people, a knowledge of its remarkable geography and its myths and secret places of beauty and revelations, a sense and awareness of the county's lost past and its constant presence, its personal and communal tragedies as well as its special joys. His memory is individual and collective, and around it swirl and orbit the memories of many others, such as those of his wife Esther and his daughter, Eva Alice. The land, buildings (those gone and those remaining), people, the occasion of the 4th of July at Freehaven, the cemetery, places abandoned, the National Road, photographs, the Old Home Place—all trigger and produce memories that live concurrently with the present and serve to break down the arbitrary dualities of dead/alive, past/present, remembered/forgotten, real/unreal.

While John Shawnessy's epic and his play remain incomplete in 1892, his mind and consciousness are of epic dimensions and capacity, and perhaps this is the greatest work and greatest wonder of existence—that of consciousness and the mind's incredible capacity for recording, registering, and processing experience while filtering it through the memory to be measured, weighed, and evaluated. What he becomes aware of on this remarkable day is the value of the present day and its fleeting moments and sensations. He remembers finding his lost daughter Eva in the woods after she had become lost; his son reveals the true lecherous nature of the revival minister who has publicly accused John Shawnessy of adultery and atheism; he sees his wife in terms of July 4, 1878, when she denied the control of her father over her and ran away with John Shawnessy to get married. Life creates its own epic work, one not fixed in words or on pages but located in the familiar and everyday.

By age 53 John Shawnessy's life as a seeker and a dreamer has been one marked by considerable personal loss: the deaths of his parents and two of his sisters; the death of his first wife, Susanna Drake, and their son's death in a house fire; the death of Nell Gaither in May of 1865; John's own near death in the Civil War and his being reported dead back home; his sense of never having realized his assumed special destiny. In many ways this Fourth of July in 1892, while officially and traditionally the day of the birth of the nation, is also, for John Shawnessy, a day when the dead are remembered. At 7:45 a.m. he visits the grave of Nell Gaither, traces with his finger the hieroglyph of her name in the headstone, puts roses and lilies on the grave, and then goes to the Shawnessy Lot, cutting the grass on the five graves with a sickle and putting the remaining flowers there. (232) Only recently he had inquired about a family burial plot in a cemetery near Roiville that lies between the National Road and the Pennsylvania Railroad tracks. As he tells Perfessor J. W. Stiles shortly before his departure:

> If I should die, the human world dies with me. Nothingness knows no Time or Space. To it ten millions years are like a second. In the very instant of my nothingness, the whole pageant of humanity expires. The faces that leaned over me in the moment of my parting, that sorrowed at my death, they too are gone in the moment of my becoming nothing.
>
> (1026)

This statement reveals the kind of struggle of faith in John Shawnessy, but with the help of the Perfessor's healthy and challenging cynicism he is able to assert that he believes in God and Jesus "In the Raintree County sense." This indicates how one's conceptions of the Deity are localized and personalized, brought down to earth to the time, place, and circumstances by which one forms one's faith. This God takes his place with the local gods of the river and the local symbols of the Tree of Life (the mystical Raintree) and eternity (the Shawmucky River and its Lake Paradise). John Shawnessy has released himself from the fear of death as he realizes the arbitrary divisions of life and death, temporal time and eternity, sacred and mundane. Past and present are totally collapsed in an affirmation of the "sacred and eternal miracle of life." (1029) Existence is perpetual creation, and the hieroglyphics of this miracle are written, inscribed, formed and forming everywhere. Time is stopped; boundaries necessary for fixing places in time and space run to infinity.

It is necessary to look at how the events and structure of the day of July 4, 1892 converge and then break apart and away to produce such a feeling and state of renewal and a sense of human connectedness in John Shawnessy. The past converges on Freehaven, Indiana, with the train arrival of Perfessor Jerusalem Webster Stiles, Senator Garwood B. Jones, and Cassius "Cash" P. Carney, who have all left Raintree County for careers and success elsewhere. Perfessor Stiles has become a nationally known newspaper correspondent; Garwood Jones, the opportunistic politician has survived and ascended to the national level of politics

by shrewdness, accommodation, and his propensity for never letting principles get in the way of expediency; Cash Carney has become caught up in the Wall Street world of wealth, capital, and investment. In their Gilded Age world they must deal with its turbulence and uncertainties stemming from financial panics, labor unrest, the challenge of new politics like Populism. None of the three have children: Perfessor Stiles has never married; Jones lost his wife, Nell Gaither, in childbirth twenty-seven years earlier with Jones forgetting her altogether; Carney is too absorbed in becoming a capitalist and beating back those who assail or challenge the system and has more of a marriage of social convenience than anything. In many ways these three individuals have become "great men" and tasted and enjoyed the fruits of another paradise—the city and the East. In the process they have sacrificed or forgone their origins and roots in Raintree County, except for the Perfessor, who keeps coming back and who knows and understands why John Shawnessy has stayed there and belongs there.

This is, of course, not to say that John Shawnessy's life in Raintree County has been all happiness and contentment. His life has exhibited a restlessness, as he went off to New York in 1876, and earlier, of course, had gone off to New Orleans with Susanna in 1859 and then to the Civil War. Before his marriage to Esther Root (a woman half his age) in 1878, John Shawnessy's life was one of a rush of developments and events seeming to lack continuity or ultimate purpose. Even his life in Raintree County has involved numerous moves and four different places of residence. In this manner he has seen the County from many perspectives, and he has become its mental repository and present consciousness of its history, not in a provincial or insulated sense but in a universal sense. He also exhibits his idealistic belief in a Republic that can be "an Eden of social and economic equality" when, in 1872, as an Independent candidate he opposed Garwood Jones in the election for the U.S. House of Representatives. Even though he lost in his bid to shape and direct a "New Republic," since he is defeated by the political machine that Garwood controls, John Shawnessy does not completely lose his idealism. He becomes the caretaker or representative of a smaller republic—the republic of the classroom as a teacher and the republic of a bounded Raintree County that is limitless and unbounded with its own gods, sacred places, spots of happiness and tragedy. One of these places, of course, is the Shawmucky River and Lake Paradise, where young adolescent Johnny saw Nell Gaither swimming naked and experienced a Venus-like vision of "erotic and spiritual beauty"; where Johnny makes love with Susanna Drake on July 4, 1859, heady and drunk on the glory of beating Flash Perkins in the 300 yard footrace and feeling invincible and immortal like a young god; where John Shawnessy meets young Esther Root on the wild side of the lake in the swamp while he was searching for himself as a "boy twenty years old, a joyous youth. He swam over here eighteen years ago and found his way into this region and never came out again." (404)

All three of these women are, of course, idolized or ideal-ized in various degrees by John as incarnations of beauty. Interestingly, they all have scars, which suggests the im-perfection of any idealization originating from desire and need. The scars of Susanna and Esther are disfiguring scars, and both women have questions about their blood—Susanna's Negro blood and Esther's Indian blood. All three were bonded to John Shawnessy for various periods of time, and all are connected to Lake Paradise, as is Eva, who as a young girl was lost in the swamp until her father found her. The mystery of Raintree County is that when individuals go in search of themselves or some ideal of beauty or mythical/mystical experience they come across others searching for them or seeking to find another who will help them complete the search. As John Shawnessy tells Esther Root,

> No, the tree [the Raintree] is not the secret, but is it-self, like the letters chipped on the stones, part of the secret only. There are secret places in the earth. Every county in America has its secret place and every Ameri-can life its Delphic cave.
>
> (407)

The search for the secret of life, then, leads to others or another, to the opening up or intersection of lives, one to another, so that the oracle can be heard from another cor-responding to the sound of one's own voice and the feel-ings of one's own heart.

On this remarkable day of July 4, 1892, starting at dawn and ending shortly after midnight John Shawnessy sees Raintree County peopled once again with individuals from his past, receives two manuscripts (one from General Ja-cob J. Jackson titled *Fighting for Freedom* and the other from Senator Garwood B. Jones, which is his self-serving autobiography), and discovers with the Perfessor and Mrs. Brown in the *Atlas* "the father and mother of mankind in beautiful nakedness, tasting the Forbidden Fruit!" depicted in the niche "above the Main Entrance of the Raintree County Court House." (1052) As John sees this engraved image and makes this discovery, "now that he saw it, it was (in the Raintree County sense) not at all naughty—for what was naughty about the oldest picture in the world—the frontispiece for the first book printed by man—the fa-ther and mother of mankind in beautiful nakedness, tasting the Forbidden Fruit."

The "Forbidden Fruit" is, of course, that of godlike knowl-edge, a sharing or consuming of the omnipotent and omni-scient mind of the Maker; in other words, a desire to over-come or transcend the status of created and to become like and one with the creator. It is a hieroglyph of the ultimate mystery and beauty of creation, and a depiction of man and woman's desire to live and know in a unified world of fruitful knowledge. This late evening discovery is exciting and exhilarating, as the "symbolic statue of Edenic rebel-lion" causes John Shawnessy to see himself, his wife, and family in a new light.

> Yes, he had overcome the aloneness of the garden. On an unsuspected path he had found her waiting. He had

helped to fashion her, and yet she had lain at the very sources of himself. In her, he had rediscovered Eve. Bearing the name of an old reformer and Bible transla-tor, Mr. John Wickliff Shawnessy had rewritten into the landscape of Raintree County the great book of God in all its beautiful, disarming candor.

> (1053)

The mystery of life then is not discovered in oneness but in the mystery of otherness, of the extensions and connec-tions beyond oneself. While it was the sin that was passed down as a result of the Fall, there was also knowledge passed down. This knowledge was that man and woman are the creators of the world, that God's creation and sa-cred book are rewritten, and thus renewed, that time lives in man, not man in time, that consciousness of creation *is* creation. It is an extraordinary end to an extraordinary day—a day of wonders and revelations. It turns out to be a day when the golden bough is put back in the hands of John Shawnessy, and like a divining rod, it reveals the source and becomes a "map covered with lines and letters, a poem of mute but lovely meanings, a page torn from the first book printed by man, the legend of a life upon the earth and of a river running through the land, a signature of father and preserver, of some young hero and endlessly courageous dreamer." (1060)

Dean Rehberger (essay date 1998)

SOURCE: "Blurred Boundaries and the Desire for Nation-alism in Ross Lockridge's *Raintree County*," in *Myth, Memory, and the American Earth: The Durability of Rain-tree County,* edited by David D. Anderson, The Midwest-ern Press, 1998, pp. 68-76.

[*In the following essay, Rehberger examines nationalism and the possibility of true national union in* Raintree County.]

> What is any nation, after all—and what is a human be-ing—but a struggle between conflicting, paradoxical, opposing elements—and they themselves and their most violent contexts, important part of that One Identity, and of its development?
>
> (Walt Whitman, *Memoranda During the War*)

In *Raintree County,* Ross Lockridge's main character, John Wickliff Shawnessy, quotes the conclusion of Abra-ham Lincoln's "First Inaugural Address." Lincoln's con-clusion is a desperate plea to put off civil war by recalling a deeply embedded nationalism to save the union of states, a nationalism that the narrator of *Raintree County* calls "a mystical covenant" between the "individual and the Re-public":[1]

> I am loath to close. We are not enemies, but friends. We must not be enemies. Though passion may have strained, it must not break the bonds of affection. The mystic chords of memory, stretching from every battle-field and patriot grave to every living heart and hearth-

stone all over this broad land, will yet swell the chorus of the Union when touched, as surely they will be, by the better angels of our nature.[2]

There is perhaps no more lyrical expression of middle-class nationalism in the English language. Lincoln's address both recalls the origins of the nation in the battles of the Revolution and the underlying mystical connection between all the people of the nation, extending from the individual ("every living heart") to the family ("hearthstone"), but his plea could not put off the conflict that had already torn the nation in half by the time of his inauguration. However, Lincoln's "Address" was more than a plea for national reconciliation; it was a move toward preparing the nation for war, or more to the point, a move toward awakening the people's desire to save the Union. For Lincoln, the Union and its Constitution are the only things that save the people from anarchy and chaos.

Similarly, at the end of **Raintree County,** Shawnessy imagines himself falling into chaos and thus losing his identity. As the narrator explains of Shawnessy, "The wall between himself and the world dissolved" (1058). To combat this "immense" sense of "nothingness," Shawnessy desires to find in the documents of the past a way to rebuild a whole and complete image of America. And like Lincoln, Shawnessy believes that it is possible to uncover this wholeness in an underlying mystical bond that connects all Americans and defines "the people." By imagining the boundaries of Raintree County and concomitantly the nation, Shawnessy is able to maintain the boundaries of the self. Yet his identity can only be maintained through his ceaseless desire to give shape and form to the nation by writing the American epic and thus becoming the American poet. That is, identity is maintained only by remaining in a ceaseless state of naivety, a ceaseless state of desire for the whole and perfect Union. This desire is perhaps why the novel sold so well in post-World War II America. As Michael Kammen argues, 1945 was "surely one of the most fateful [years] in modern history" that "brought a pronounced sense of discontinuity between past and present. . . . Lacking an authentic or meaningful sense of continuity, many Americans managed to create one by dramatically increasing their attendance at museums, historic sites, and villages, and by participating in activities that ranged from battle re-enactments to historic preservation at the local level."[3] The post-war citizens, Kammen argues, were particularly nostalgic for the Gay Nineties. Not only did **Raintree County** offer up memories of American history and a version of the small county in the 1890s, but its main character mirrored the desire of many Americans to find continuity in the nation's heritage that seemed increasingly lost in the modern world.

In this paper, I want to argue that Lockridge's **Raintree County** is one of the fullest expressions in novel form of the ideology of nationalism. However, by expressing nationalism, its contradictions and gaps, the novel calls into question the very possibility of imagining the nation as complete and whole. Unlike Lincoln who appealed to na-

tionalism as the only way to save the republic during the Civil War, Lockridge is more ambivalent about American nationalism not only because he wrote the book during an era in which the racist nationalism of fascist states ignited a world war but because the ideology of nationalism with its promise of past and future wholeness negates the possibility of writing *the* American epic in the present. Moreover, by calling into question the ideology of nationalism, Lockridge writes the impossibility of producing *the* American novel.

Lockridge's experiments with the novel form recall Georg Lukacs' premarxist and heavily romantic writings on the theory of the novel. Like Lockridge's narrator, Lukacs imagines that producers of ancient epics were at home in their communities because they could capture the totality of the communities' experiences. This totality, Lukacs argues, expressed a world "where everything is already homogeneous before it has been contained by forms . . . where knowledge is virtue and virtue is happiness, where beauty is the meaning of the world made visible."[4] Lockridge's opening sequence in the novel reflects this longing for national homogeneity and for a literary form that would capture the transcendent qualities of Raintree County. The novel opens with a report about the Semicentennial Edition of Raintree County's newspaper, the *Free Enquirer,* that comes out on July 4, 1892, the day on which the whole action of the novel takes place. Not only is the 4th of July a day of national reflection, but the edition of the *Free Enquirer* is "fifty pages crowded with memories of fifty years" that chronicles "an Era of Progress unexampled in the annals of mankind" (1). The next section shifts to a dream sequence that writes Shawnessy's desire to capture the essence of the community when he sees a naked woman stretched out on a "stone couch." As the narrator explains, "The dream had been vivid with promise of adventure and consummation" (6). But the dream never allows for consummation, never grants him a sense of home, and never allows him to capture the transcendent qualities of Raintree County:

> the dream had left him with an uneasy feeling of being anchorless, adrift on an unknown substance. The formal map of Raintree County had been laid down like a mask on something formless, warm, recumbent, convolved with rivers, undulous with flowering hills, blurred with motion, green with life.

(7)

As Lukacs argues, in contrast to epic, the novel is "an expression of transcendental homelessness" because the novelist can never recapture the perfect wholeness of the community.[5] While the novelist desires to give expression to his/her vision of the world, the very act of giving novelistic form to the vision foregrounds the impossibility of rendering the vision in its totality, or as Lukacs explains "formgiving . . . points eloquently at the sacrifice that has had to be made, at the paradise forever lost, sought and never found."[6]

Timothy Brennan argues that the genre of the novel accompanied the rise of nationalism "by mimicking the structure of the nation, a clearly bordered jumble of languages and styles. . . . [The novel's] manner of presentation allowed people to imagine the special community that was the nation."[7] In Lockridge's novel, Shawnessy imagines Raintree County to be a "special community" that represents both his desires and the desires of the nation. Shawnessy's image of Raintree County in terms of both synecdoche, the single county represents the whole Republic, and metonymy, the physical body of his childhood sweetheart, Nell Gaither, substitutes for the landscape of the county, works to condense into a single image the complex relations figured within the ideology of nationalism. Borrowing terms from Walter Benjamin, Benedict Anderson argues that the idea of a nation—the imagining of a "solid" community moving steadily down (or up) history"—is analogous to imagining an organism "moving calendrically through homogeneous, empty time."[8] Shawnessy's image of Raintree County articulates the special and temporal boundaries figured in Anderson's definition of the nation. The image contains the static figure of a body forever young, forever to be desired, while articulating the sense of continuity between, the body and the ideal, the local and the nation, the individual and the state. As the narrator of *Raintree County* writes, "The Republic is an image that men live by. All life is a self—but in the Republic this self finds a greater self" (273). The image of the county as a woman's body not only figures the county and consequently the nation as an organic whole but it figures the nation in terms of the individual.

The essential connection imagined within the ideology of nationalism between the citizen of the Republic and the national will, the subject and the state, is made painfully clear in the description of Shawnessy's life, particularly during the Civil War period. Shawnessy marries Susanna Drake on the day that John Brown is executed; his baby is born on the day Fort Sumter surrenders; his search for his wife and baby coincides with the battle at Gettysburg. The marriage between Shawnessy and Drake is an all too obvious marriage between North and South that is destined to end in destruction and insanity. Susanna Drake's character is loaded down with all of the stereotypical characteristics of the South: a lustful southern belle whose heritage is either insanity or miscegenation. That is, the marriage points out the impossible union between the products of a slave South and a free North. In the novel, the execution of John Brown symbolizes a moment of no return for the nation by making civil war inevitable. At the same time, Shawnessy's marriage to Drake symbolizes the unbridgeable gap between Shawnessy and his image of Raintree County (he can no longer pursue Nell Gaither). A wedding night dream about his marriage license, like the opening dream sequence, condenses these complex interconnections between the individual and the state, the organic object and the lined map, into a single image of a bleeding map being torn apart:

> The print ran and blurred. The parchment [of the marriage license] was a map of Raintree County. A red gash had been torn in it, the wound was bleeding, staining his hands and covering him with shame and a hid-

eous fear from which he kept trying to awaken with small choked cries.

(353)

Although nationalism takes on the guise of religious dogma, an almost supernatural presence, what must be remembered is that the nation as an organic whole is a continual possibility in the "natural order," a secure part of the secular world. Thus Shawnessy's marriage to the sensual Susanna Drake, which represents the nation's fated union, and the image of the county in terms of Gaither's body, which represents strong images of desire, both emphasize the physical and secular nature of nationalism that requires a libidinal investment by the individual citizen. Nationalism is the desire for consummation, the perfect bond of individual wills. The images of sexual desire for this perfect bond are deeply embedded in the dreams sequences and in the controlling metaphor of the book, the raintree. While Shawnessy imagines the land in terms of the woman's body, the raintree is clearly imagined in terms of a phallus. Shawnessy envisions the "stately trunk of the tree and the clean isolation of it from the other trees" dropping "a rain of yellow pollendust and petals" (45). His attempt to find the raintree in the swamp of the Shawmucky river near Paradise Lake is explicitly described as a journey into "a womblike center" (103). In this way, Shawnessy's personal desires are mapped onto national desires. Moreover, the story that Shawnessy tells about the origins of the raintree—that it originated in Asia and has been moving ever westward—is the same as the story told by nineteenth-century philosophers of nationalism about the origin of nations.

The idea that nationalism requires an awakening of male desire and a libidinal investment by the individual citizen of the Republic was commonplace during and after the Civil War. Within the many novels written about the Civil War during the nineteenth century, the war is figured as a symbolic act of both masculine preservation and masculine regeneration, serving to purify both the national body and the individual body. We could read *Raintree County* within this context as simply another novel that purports to write a national epic about the Civil War, showing how the war rejuvenates the country and fulfills its promise to be a great nation. Indeed, Lockridge is often heavy-handed both in his use of sexual imagery to draw a connection between the individual and the national landscape and in his use of history to draw a connection between Shawnessy's life and the life of the nation.

However, rather than seeing Lockridge's overdrawn use of conventions as a weakness of the novel, we can read the novel as one that attempts to undercut those conventions by exaggerating them and thus exposing their contradictions. Sitting in Ford's Theater on the night that Lincoln is to be assassinated, Shawnessy imagines that "he had assembled here the lost pages of a myth of himself and the Republic, and that he had only to put them together at last into a meaningful pattern. All was promise, excitement, near-fulfillment" (970). Unlike most novels about the Civil

War, the reader is made conscious of Shawnessy's attempt to write a national narrative of the Civil War. In an Emersonian fashion, Shawnessy desires to compose the American epic by reading the signs of nature: "the branch quivered alive in his hands," Shawnessy dreams, "unrolled its bark, became a map covered with lines and letters, a poem of mute but lovely meanings, a page torn from the first book printed by man" (1060). But this belief has profound consequences for the artist, dooming him or her to producing endless copies, endless repetitions of an irretrievable original. As the "Perfessor" explains, "What is all speech, John, but a quotation?" (148). That is to say, the artist is left in a continual state of desire.

Lockridge re-enforces the contradiction between desire and fulfillment in the novel by showing that Shawnessy can produce only fragments of his epic; he is never able to find the "meaningful pattern" (although at the conclusion of the novel he still believes that he can do so). Within the ideology of nationalism, the fulfillment of desire must always be denied. The perfect bond of individual wills is continually deferred, promising—but never fulfilling—that the individual will be self-identical to the national identity. As the narrator explains, "For America was always an education in self denial. And Raintree County was itself the barrier of form imposed upon a stuff of longing, lifejet of the river" (116). The death of Nell Gaither on May 24, 1865, the day Sherman's army marched in Washington D.C. in a victory parade, emphasizes the impossibility of consummating Shawnessy's desires because the past and the image of Raintree County is hopelessly lost and irretrievable. As the "Perfessor" explains, "the War was the end of a rather gentle, rich old life and the beginning of something nobody really wanted" (478). The idea that the origins of the nation are impossible to recover is further emphasized by the inability to locate the raintree as well as the putative illegitimate births in both Shawnessy's family and Lincoln's family, making it impossible to identify the phallic origins and imagine continuity.

In addition to pointing out the contradiction between the promise of nationalism and the possibility of fulfillment, I will only mention a few more ways in which the narrative undercuts the ideology of nationalism. While nationalism focuses on maintaining the boundaries of the autonomous subject, Lockridge writes a double, a reverse image, of his main character: Professor Jerusalem Webster Stiles. Unlike Shawnessy who wants to write the American epic, Stiles is a newspaper man who deals in the daily world of politics. Stiles constantly points out how Shawnessy's dream world ignores the economic and political reality of everyday life so that Shawnessy remains a romantic innocent. The tragic paranoia of Susanna Drake, who believes the United States' government is out to destroy her, becomes rather comic when set against how the novel writes the marriage as the mirror image of the relationship between the North and the South: the South and consequently Susanna Drake will be destroyed by the Union. The image of three old men looking through the *Atlas* for pornographic pictures parodies the idea of awakening national masculine desires

by uncovering the mystical bond embedded in the old documents and epics of the nation. Unlike the convention of Civil War novels, Shawnessy is not regenerated and humanized by the war; rather, he is dehumanized by the war and left after the war an unchanged dreamer.

However, the most consistent way in which Lockridge undercuts nationalism is through the form of the novel. Although the main character of Lockridge's novel imagines Raintree County to be the "special community" that represents the nation, a vision of the nation with hard clean edges and precisely labeled landmarks, the structure of the novel emphasizes the break down and blurring of boundaries. The chapters run into one another without breaking sentences. The time of the novel is compressed into a single day so that the history is told in a series of flashbacks without a steady chronological order. At points in the novel, the narrative completely breaks down into chaotic streams of consciousness. Lockridge even blurs the traditional boundaries of dialogue by removing the quotation marks, and thus undercuts one of the strongest markers of realism, the reporting of direct speech. Without a clear distinction among what is spoken, the narrator's description, and the character's thoughts, the accuracy of the dialogue is undermined. But most important, the boundaries of the novel become permeable to all forms of writing: newspaper stories, editorials, speeches, fragments of epics, sentimental novels, dreams, songs, poems, and plays. Lockridge's inclusion of these different forms coupled with the different perspectives of the characters highlights the heteroglossia of the novel. Mikhail Baktin's term, heteroglossia, is appropriate here since Baktin meant it to describe the "diversity of individual voices" within "the national language," arguing that the novel accompanied the rise of nationalism because the novel works to centralize voices that are in constant conflict. That is to say, novelists would unconsciously mimic the ideology of nationalism by exploring the life of the individual within a larger social setting giving that life a solid boundary and frame. Lockridge takes the novel form one step further by making the reader aware of the process of writing a narrative that attempts to put boundaries around the life of an individual and a nation by foregrounding the tension between the centripetal and centrifugal, the centralizing and decentralizing forces at work in any culture. As Lukacs argues, "the novel is the epic of a world that has been abandoned by God. . . . The objectivity of the novel is the mature man's knowledge that meaning can never quite penetrate reality, but that, without meaning, reality would disintegrate into the nothingness of inessentiality."[9]

At the end of **Raintree County,** we feel sorry for John Shawnessy who still believes that he must

> express, so that it would never die, the legend of his life, which was the legend of his people, the story of the republic in which all men were created equal, the amiable myth of the river and rock, the tree and the letters on the stones, the mounds beside the river,
>
> (1049)

because as readers we know the impossibilities of his task. But perhaps we feel more sorry for the author whose novel writes the impossibility of his desire. We can read the whole novel as a detailed search of Raintree County for the raintree, a symbol that stands in for the phallic origins of the nation, but as the narrator explains in the opening dream sequence, this search is continually doomed to failure. In the dream, Shawnessy is studying a map of the county and

> He was certain that in the pattern of its lines and letters this map contained the answer to the old conundrum of his life in Raintree county. It was all warm and glowing with the secret he had sought for half a century. The words inscribed on the deep paper were dawn-words, each one disclosing the origin and essence of the thing named. But as he sought to read them, they dissolved into the substance of the map.
>
> (5)

Notes

1. Ross Lockridge, *Raintree County,* Boston: Houghton Mifflin, 1948, 23. All subsequent references to the text will be made in parenthetical references.

2. Abraham Lincoln, "First Inaugural Address," *Abraham Lincoln: Speeches and Writings, 1859-1865* (New York: American Library, 1989), 224.

3. Michael Kammen, *Mystic Chords of Memory: Transformations of Tradition in American Culture,* New York: Vintage, 1993.

4. Georg Lukacs, *The Theory of the Novel: A Historico-Philosophical Essay on the Form of Great Epic Literature,* (1920) trans. Anna Bostock, Cambridge: MIT Press, 1987.

5. Lukacs, 41.

6. Lukacs, 85.

7. Timothy Brennan, "The National Longing for Form," *Nation and Narration,* Home Bhabha, Ed. (New York: Routledge, 1990), 49.

8. Benedict Anderson, *Imagined Communities: Reflections on the Origins and Spread of Nationalism* (New York: Verso, 1983), 31.

9. Lukacs, 88.

FURTHER READING

Biographies

Leggett, John. *Ross and Tom: Two American Tragedies.* New York: Simon and Schuster, 1974, 447 p.
> Explores the great successes and sudden tragic deaths of Lockridge and novelist Tom Heggen.

Lockridge, Laurence. *Shade of the Raintree: The Life and Death of Ross Lockridge, Jr.* New York: Viking Penguin, 1994, 500 p.
> Biography by Lockridge's son explores Lockridge's life, suicide, and the impact of his death on his family.

———. "Least Likely Suicide: The Search for My Father, Ross Lockridge, Jr., Author of *Raintree County.*" *Suicide and Life-Threatening Behavior* 25, No. 4 (Winter 1995): 429-35.
> Examination by Lockridge's son of the possible biological and societal reasons for Lockridge's suicide.

Criticism

Basso, Hamilton. "Two Novels: 'Raintree County' and 'The Aunt 's Story.'" *The New Yorker* 23, No. 47 (10 January 1948): 79-80.
> Scathing review in which Hamilton calls *Raintree County* a "swollen and pretentious human chronicle" and misspells Lockridge's name throughout.

Harrington, Alan. "Memorandum." *Chicago Review* 26, No. 3 (1974): 153-64.
> Discusses the biography *Ross and Tom,* finding that the book offers a romanticized picture of the American writer as tragic failure.

Kutner, Nanette. "Ross Lockridge, Jr.—Escape from Main Street." In *The Saturday Review Gallery,* pp. 387-93. New York: Simon and Schuster, 1959.
> Recounts an interview the author did with Lockridge.

White, Ray Lewis. "*Raintree County* and the Critics of '48." *MidAmerica* 11 (1984): 149-70.
> Reprints highlights from reviews of *Raintree County* immediately following its publication.

How to Use This Index

The main references

Calvino, Italo
1923-1985 .... CLC **5, 8, 11, 22, 33, 39,**
73; SSC 3

---

list all author entries in the following Gale Literary Criticism series:

BLC = *Black Literature Criticism*
CLC = *Contemporary Literary Criticism*
CLR = *Children's Literature Review*
CMLC = *Classical and Medieval Literature Criticism*
DA = *DISCovering Authors*
DAB = *DISCovering Authors: British*
DAC = *DISCovering Authors: Canadian*
DAM = *DISCovering Authors: Modules*
      DRAM: *Dramatists Module;* **MST:** *Most-Studied Authors Module;*
      MULT: *Multicultural Authors Module;* **NOV:** *Novelists Module;*
      POET: *Poets Module;* **POP:** *Popular Fiction and Genre Authors Module*
DC = *Drama Criticism*
HLC = *Hispanic Literature Criticism*
LC = *Literature Criticism from 1400 to 1800*
NCLC = *Nineteenth-Century Literature Criticism*
NNAL = *Native North American Literature*
PC = *Poetry Criticism*
SSC = *Short Story Criticism*
TCLC = *Twentieth-Century Literary Criticism*
WLC = *World Literature Criticism, 1500 to the Present*

The cross-references

See also CANR 23; CA 85-88;
obituary CA116

---

list all author entries in the following Gale biographical and literary sources:

AAYA = *Authors & Artists for Young Adults*
AITN = *Authors in the News*
BEST = *Bestsellers*
BW = *Black Writers*
CA = *Contemporary Authors*
CAAS = *Contemporary Authors Autobiography Series*
CABS = *Contemporary Authors Bibliographical Series*
CANR = *Contemporary Authors New Revision Series*
CAP = *Contemporary Authors Permanent Series*
CDALB = *Concise Dictionary of American Literary Biography*
CDBLB = *Concise Dictionary of British Literary Biography*
DLB = *Dictionary of Literary Biography*
DLBD = *Dictionary of Literary Biography Documentary Series*
DLBY = *Dictionary of Literary Biography Yearbook*
HW = *Hispanic Writers*
JRDA = *Junior DISCovering Authors*
MAICYA = *Major Authors and Illustrators for Children and Young Adults*
MTCW = *Major 20th-Century Writers*
SAAS = *Something about the Author Autobiography Series*
SATA = *Something about the Author*
YABC = *Yesterday's Authors of Books for Children*

Literary Criticism Series
Cumulative Author Index

20/1631
See Upward, Allen
A/C Cross
See Lawrence, T(homas) E(dward)
Abasiyanik, Sait Faik 1906-1954
See Sait Faik
See also CA 123
Abbey, Edward 1927-1989 .... **CLC 36, 59**
See also CA 45-48; 128; CANR 2, 41; DA3;
MTCW 2; TCWW 2
Abbott, Lee K(ittredge) 1947- .... **CLC 48**
See also CA 124; CANR 51; DLB 130
Abe, Kōbō 1924-1993 ...... **CLC 8, 22, 53, 81;
DAM NOV**
See also CA 65-68; 140; CANR 24, 60;
DLB 182; MJW; MTCW 1, 2; SFW
Abelard, Peter c. 1079-c. 1142 ...... **CMLC 11**
See also DLB 115, 208
Abell, Kjeld 1901-1961 .... **CLC 15**
See also CA 111; DLB 214
Abish, Walter 1931- .... **CLC 22; SSC 44**
See also CA 101; CANR 37; CN; DLB 130,
227
Abrahams, Peter (Henry) 1919- .... **CLC 4**
See also BW 1; CA 57-60; CANR 26; CN;
DLB 117, 225; MTCW 1, 2
Abrams, M(eyer) H(oward) 1912- ... **CLC 24**
See also CA 57-60; CANR 13, 33; DLB 67
Abse, Dannie 1923- .... **CLC 7, 29; DAB;
DAM POET**
See also CA 53-56; CAAS 1; CANR 4, 46,
74; CBD; CP; DLB 27; MTCW 1
Abutsu 1222(?)-1283 .... **CMLC 46**
Achebe, (Albert) Chinua(lumogu)
1930- ...... **CLC 1, 3, 5, 7, 11, 26, 51, 75,
127; BLC 1; DA; DAB; DAC; DAM
MST, MULT, NOV; WLC**
See also AAYA 15; BW 2, 3; CA 1-4R;
CANR 6, 26, 47; CLR 20; CN; CP;
CWRI; DA3; DLB 117; DNFS 1; MAI-
CYA; MTCW 1, 2; NFS 2; SATA 38, 40;
SATA-Brief 38; SSFS 3
Acker, Kathy 1948-1997 .... **CLC 45, 111**
See also CA 117; 122; 162; CANR 55; CN
Ackroyd, Peter 1949- .... **CLC 34, 52, 140**
See also BRWS 6; CA 123; 127; CANR 51,
74; CN; DLB 155, 231; HGG; INT 127;
MTCW 1; RHW
Acorn, Milton 1923-1986 .... **CLC 15; DAC**
See also CA 103; CCA 1; DLB 53; INT 103
Adamov, Arthur 1908-1970 .... **CLC 4, 25;
DAM DRAM**
See also CA 17-18; 25-28R; CAP 2; GFL
1789 to the Present; MTCW 1; RGWL
Adams, Alice (Boyd) 1926-1999 .. **CLC 6, 13,
46; SSC 24**
See also CA 81-84; 179; CANR 26, 53, 75,
88; CN; CSW; DLB 234; DLBY 86; INT
CANR-26; MTCW 1, 2

Adams, Andy 1859-1935 .... **TCLC 56**
See also TCWW 2; YABC 1
Adams, Brooks 1848-1927 .... **TCLC 80**
See also CA 123; DLB 47
Adams, Douglas (Noel) 1952-2001 .. **CLC 27,
60; DAM POP**
See also AAYA 4, 33; BEST 89:3; CA 106;
CANR 34, 64; CPW; DA3; DLBY 83;
JRDA; MTCW 1; NFS 7; SATA 116;
SFW
Adams, Francis 1862-1893 .... **NCLC 33**
Adams, Henry (Brooks)
1838-1918 .... **TCLC 4, 52; DA; DAB;
DAC; DAM MST**
See also CA 104; 133; CANR 77; DLB 12,
47, 189; MTCW 1; NCFS 1
Adams, Richard (George) 1920- ... **CLC 4, 5,
18; DAM NOV**
See also AAYA 16; AITN 1, 2; CA 49-52;
CANR 3, 35; CLR 20; CN; FANT; JRDA;
MAICYA; MTCW 1, 2; NFS 11; SATA 7,
69; YAW
Adamson, Joy(-Friederike Victoria)
1910-1980 .... **CLC 17**
See also CA 69-72; 93-96; CANR 22;
MTCW 1; SATA 11; SATA-Obit 22
Adcock, Fleur 1934- .... **CLC 41**
See also CA 25-28R, 182; CAAE 182;
CAAS 23; CANR 11, 34, 69; CP; CWP;
DLB 40; FW
Addams, Charles (Samuel)
1912-1988 .... **CLC 30**
See also CA 61-64; 126; CANR 12, 79
Addams, Jane 1860-1945 .... **TCLC 76**
See also AMWS 1; FW
Addison, Joseph 1672-1719 .... **LC 18**
See also CDBLB 1660-1789; DLB 101;
RGEL
Adler, Alfred (F.) 1870-1937 .... **TCLC 61**
See also CA 119; 159
Adler, C(arole) S(chwerdtfeger)
1932- .... **CLC 35**
See also AAYA 4; CA 89-92; CANR 19,
40; JRDA; MAICYA; SAAS 15; SATA
26, 63, 102; YAW
Adler, Renata 1938- .... **CLC 8, 31**
See also CA 49-52; CANR 95; CN; MTCW
1
Adorno, Theodor W(iesengrund)
1903-1969 .... **TCLC 111**
See also CA 89-92; 25-28R; CANR 89;
DLB 242
Ady, Endre 1877-1919 .... **TCLC 11**
See also CA 107
A.E. .... **TCLC 3, 10**
See also Russell, George William
Aelfric c. 955-c. 1010 .... **CMLC 46**
See also DLB 146

Aeschylus 525B.C.- .... **CMLC 11; DA; DAB;
DAC; DAM DRAM, MST; DC 8;
WLCS**
See also DFS 5, 10; DLB 176; RGEL
Aesop 620(?)B.C.-560(?)B.C. .... **CMLC 24**
See also CLR 14; MAICYA; SATA 64
Affable Hawk
See MacCarthy, Sir(Charles Otto) Desmond
Africa, Ben
See Bosman, Herman Charles
Afton, Effie
See Harper, Frances Ellen Watkins
Agapida, Fray Antonio
See Irving, Washington
Agee, James (Rufus) 1909-1955 ...... **TCLC 1,
19; DAM NOV**
See also AITN 1; CA 108; 148; CDALB
1941-1968; DLB 2, 26, 152; MTCW 1
Aghill, Gordon
See Silverberg, Robert
Agnon, S(hmuel) Y(osef Halevi)
1888-1970 .... **CLC 4, 8, 14; SSC 30**
See also CA 17-18; 25-28R; CANR 60;
CAP 2; MTCW 1, 2
Agrippa von Nettesheim, Henry Cornelius
1486-1535 .... **LC 27**
Aguilera Malta, Demetrio 1909-1981
See also CA 111; 124; CANR 87; DAM
MULT, NOV; DLB 145; HLCS 1; HW 1
Agustini, Delmira 1886-1914
See also CA 166; HLCS 1; HW 1, 2
Aherne, Owen
See Cassill, R(onald) V(erlin)
Ai 1947- .... **CLC 4, 14, 69**
See also CA 85-88; CAAS 13; CANR 70;
DLB 120
Aickman, Robert (Fordyce)
1914-1981 .... **CLC 57**
See also CA 5-8R; CANR 3, 72; HGG
Aiken, Conrad (Potter) 1889-1973 .... **CLC 1,
3, 5, 10, 52; DAM NOV, POET; PC 26;
SSC 9**
See also CA 5-8R; 45-48; CANR 4, 60;
CDALB 1929-1941; DLB 9, 45, 102;
HGG; MTCW 1, 2; SATA 3, 30; SSFS 8
Aiken, Joan (Delano) 1924- .... **CLC 35**
See also AAYA 1, 25; CA 9-12R, 182;
CAAE 182; CANR 4, 23, 34, 64; CLR 1,
19; DLB 161; FANT; HGG; JRDA; MAI-
CYA; MTCW 1; RHW; SAAS 1; SATA
2, 30, 73; SATA-Essay 109; YAW
Ainsworth, William Harrison
1805-1882 .... **NCLC 13**
See also DLB 21; HGG; SATA 24
Aitmatov, Chingiz (Torekulovich)
1928- .... **CLC 71**
See also CA 103; CANR 38; MTCW 1;
SATA 56

Amiel, Henri Frederic 1821-1881 .... **NCLC 4**
Amis, Kingsley (William)
  1922-1995 ...... **CLC 1, 2, 3, 5, 8, 13, 40, 44, 129; DA; DAB; DAC; DAM MST, NOV**
    See also AITN 2; BRWS 2; CA 9-12R; 150; CANR 8, 28, 54; CDBLB 1945-1960; CN; CP; DA3; DLB 15, 27, 100, 139; DLBY 96; HGG; INT CANR-8; MTCW 1, 2; SFW
Amis, Martin (Louis) 1949- .... **CLC 4, 9, 38, 62, 101**
    See also BEST 90:3; BRWS 4; CA 65-68; CANR 8, 27, 54, 73, 95; CN; DA3; DLB 14, 194; INT CANR-27; MTCW 1
Ammons, A(rchie) R(andolph)
  1926-2001 ...... **CLC 2, 3, 5, 8, 9, 25, 57, 108; DAM POET; PC 16**
    See also AITN 1; CA 9-12R; CANR 6, 36, 51, 73; CP; CSW; DLB 5, 165; MTCW 1, 2
Amo, Tauraatua i
    See Adams, Henry (Brooks)
Amory, Thomas 1691(?)-1788 .... **LC 48**
Anand, Mulk Raj 1905- .. **CLC 23, 93; DAM NOV**
    See also CA 65-68; CANR 32, 64; CN; MTCW 1, 2; RGSF
Anatol
    See Schnitzler, Arthur
Anaximander c. 611B.C.-c.
  546B.C. .... **CMLC 22**
Anaya, Rudolfo A(lfonso) 1937- ...... **CLC 23; DAM MULT, NOV; HLC 1**
    See also AAYA 20; CA 45-48; CAAS 4; CANR 1, 32, 51; CN; DLB 82, 206; HW 1; MTCW 1, 2; NFS 12
Andersen, Hans Christian
  1805-1875 .... **NCLC 7, 79; DA; DAB; DAC; DAM MST, POP; SSC 6; WLC**
    See also CLR 6; DA3; MAICYA; RGSF; RGWL; SATA 100; YABC 1
Anderson, C. Farley
    See Mencken, H(enry) L(ouis); Nathan, George Jean
Anderson, Jessica (Margaret) Queale
  1916- .... **CLC 37**
    See also CA 9-12R; CANR 4, 62; CN
Anderson, Jon (Victor) 1940- . **CLC 9; DAM POET**
    See also CA 25-28R; CANR 20
Anderson, Lindsay (Gordon)
  1923-1994 .... **CLC 20**
    See also CA 125; 128; 146; CANR 77
Anderson, Maxwell 1888-1959 .... **TCLC 2; DAM DRAM**
    See also CA 105; 152; DLB 7, 228; MTCW 2; RGAL
Anderson, Poul (William)
  1926-2001 .... **CLC 15**
    See also AAYA 5, 34; CA 1-4R, 181; CAAE 181; CAAS 2; CANR 2, 15, 34, 64; CLR 58; DLB 8; FANT; INT CANR-15; MTCW 1, 2; SATA 90; SATA-Brief 39; SATA-Essay 106; SCFW 2; SFW
Anderson, Robert (Woodruff)
  1917- .... **CLC 23; DAM DRAM**
    See also AITN 1; CA 21-24R; CANR 32; DLB 7
Anderson, Sherwood 1876-1941 ..... **TCLC 1, 10, 24; DA; DAB; DAC; DAM MST, NOV; SSC 1, 46; WLC**
    See also AAYA 30; CA 104; 121; CANR 61; CDALB 1917-1929; DA3; DLB 4, 9, 86; DLBD 1; GLL 2; MTCW 1, 2; NFS 4; RGAL; RGSF; SSFS 4,10,11
Andier, Pierre
    See Desnos, Robert
Andouard
    See Giraudoux, Jean(-Hippolyte)

Andrade, Carlos Drummond de ..... **CLC 18**
    See also Drummond de Andrade, Carlos
Andrade, Mário de 1893-1945 .... **TCLC 43**
Andreae, Johann V(alentin)
  1586-1654 .... **LC 32**
    See also DLB 164
Andreas-Salome, Lou 1861-1937 ... **TCLC 56**
    See also CA 178; DLB 66
Andress, Lesley
    See Sanders, Lawrence
Andrewes, Lancelot 1555-1626 .... **LC 5**
    See also DLB 151, 172
Andrews, Cicily Fairfield
    See West, Rebecca
Andrews, Elton V.
    See Pohl, Frederik
Andreyev, Leonid (Nikolaevich)
  1871-1919 .... **TCLC 3**
    See also CA 104; 185
Andrič, Ivo 1892-1975 .... **CLC 8; SSC 36**
    See also CA 81-84; 57-60; CANR 43, 60; DLB 147; MTCW 1
Androvar
    See Prado (Calvo), Pedro
Angelique, Pierre
    See Bataille, Georges
Angell, Roger 1920- .... **CLC 26**
    See also CA 57-60; CANR 13, 44, 70; DLB 171, 185
Angelou, Maya 1928- .... **CLC 12, 35, 64, 77; BLC 1; DA; DAB; DAC; DAM MST, MULT, POET, POP; PC 32; WLCS**
    See also AAYA 7, 20; AMWS 4; BW 2, 3; CA 65-68; CANR 19, 42, 65; CDALBS; CLR 53; CP; CPW; CSW; CWP; DA3; DLB 38; MTCW 1, 2; NCFS 2; NFS 2; PFS 2, 3; RGAL; SATA 49; YAW
Anna Comnena 1083-1153 .... **CMLC 25**
Annensky, Innokenty (Fyodorovich)
  1856-1909 .... **TCLC 14**
    See also CA 110; 155
Annunzio, Gabriele d'
    See D'Annunzio, Gabriele
Anodos
    See Coleridge, Mary E(lizabeth)
Anon, Charles Robert
    See Pessoa, Fernando (Ant
Anouilh, Jean (Marie Lucien Pierre)
  1910-1987 ...... **CLC 1, 3, 8, 13, 40, 50; DAM DRAM; DC 8**
    See also CA 17-20R; 123; CANR 32; DFS 9, 10; EW; GFL 1789 to the Present; MTCW 1, 2; RGWL
Anthony, Florence
    See Ai
Anthony, John
    See Ciardi, John (Anthony)
Anthony, Peter
    See Shaffer, Anthony (Joshua); Shaffer, Peter (Levin)
Anthony, Piers 1934- .... **CLC 35; DAM POP**
    See also AAYA 11; CA 21-24R; CANR 28, 56, 73; CPW; DLB 8; FANT; MTCW 1, 2; SAAS 22; SATA 84; SFW; YAW
Anthony, Susan B(rownell)
  1820-1906 .... **TCLC 84**
    See also FW
Antoine, Marc
    See Proust, (Valentin-Louis-George-Eug
Antoninus, Brother
    See Everson, William (Oliver)
Antoninus, Marcus Aurelius
  121-180 .... **CMLC 45**
Antonioni, Michelangelo 1912- .... **CLC 20, 144**
    See also CA 73-76; CANR 45, 77
Antschel, Paul 1920-1970
    See Celan, Paul

    See also CA 85-88; CANR 33, 61; MTCW 1
Anwar, Chairil 1922-1949 .... **TCLC 22**
    See also CA 121
Anzaldúa, Gloria (Evanjelina) 1942-
    See also CA 175; CSW; CWP; DLB 122; FW; HLCS 1
Apess, William 1798-1839(?) .... **NCLC 73; DAM MULT**
    See also DLB 175; NNAL
Apollinaire, Guillaume 1880-1918 .. **TCLC 3, 8, 51; DAM POET; PC 7**
    See also CA 152; GFL 1789 to the Present; MTCW 1; RGWL; WP
Appelfeld, Aharon 1932- ... **CLC 23, 47; SSC 42**
    See also CA 112; 133; CANR 86; CWW 2; RGSF
Apple, Max (Isaac) 1941- .... **CLC 9, 33**
    See also CA 81-84; CANR 19, 54; DLB 130
Appleman, Philip (Dean) 1926- .... **CLC 51**
    See also CA 13-16R; CAAS 18; CANR 6, 29, 56
Appleton, Lawrence
    See Lovecraft, H(oward) P(hillips)
Apteryx
    See Eliot, T(homas) S(tearns)
Apuleius, (Lucius Madaurensis)
  125(?)-175(?) .... **CMLC 1**
    See also DLB 211
Aquin, Hubert 1929-1977 .... **CLC 15**
    See also CA 105; DLB 53
Aquinas, Thomas 1224(?)-1274 ..... **CMLC 33**
    See also DLB 115
Aragon, Louis 1897-1982 .. **CLC 3, 22; DAM NOV, POET**
    See also CA 69-72; 108; CANR 28, 71; DLB 72; GFL 1789 to the Present; GLL 2; MTCW 1, 2; RGWL
Arany, Janos 1817-1882 .... **NCLC 34**
Aranyos, Kakay 1847-1910
    See Mikszath, Kalman
Arbuthnot, John 1667-1735 .... **LC 1**
    See also DLB 101
Archer, Herbert Winslow
    See Mencken, H(enry) L(ouis)
Archer, Jeffrey (Howard) 1940- ...... **CLC 28; DAM POP**
    See also AAYA 16; BEST 89:3; CA 77-80; CANR 22, 52, 95; CPW; DA3; INT CANR-22
Archer, Jules 1915- .... **CLC 12**
    See also CA 9-12R; CANR 6, 69; SAAS 5; SATA 4, 85
Archer, Lee
    See Ellison, Harlan (Jay)
Archilochus c. 7th cent. B.C.- .... **CMLC 44**
    See also DLB 176
Arden, John 1930- .... **CLC 6, 13, 15; DAM DRAM**
    See also BRWS 2; CA 13-16R; CAAS 4; CANR 31, 65, 67; CBD; CD; DFS 9; DLB 13; MTCW 1
Arenas, Reinaldo 1943-1990 . **CLC 41; DAM MULT; HLC 1**
    See also CA 124; 128; 133; CANR 73; DLB 145; GLL 2; HW 1; MTCW 1; RGSF
Arendt, Hannah 1906-1975 .... **CLC 66, 98**
    See also CA 17-20R; 61-64; CANR 26, 60; DLB 242; MTCW 1, 2
Aretino, Pietro 1492-1556 .... **LC 12**
    See also RGWL
Arghezi, Tudor .... **CLC 80**
    See also Theodorescu, Ion N.
    See also CA 167; DLB 220

Arguedas, José María 1911-1969 .... **CLC 10,
18; HLCS 1**
    See also CA 89-92; CANR 73; DLB 113;
    HW 1
Argueta, Manlio 1936- .... **CLC 31**
    See also CA 131; CANR 73; CWW 2; DLB
    145; HW 1
Arias, Ron(ald Francis) 1941-
    See also CA 131; CANR 81; DAM MULT;
    DLB 82; HLC 1; HW 1, 2; MTCW 2
Ariosto, Ludovico 1474-1533 .... **LC 6**
    See also RGWL
Aristides
    See Epstein, Joseph
Aristophanes 450B.C.- .... **CMLC 4; DA;
    DAB; DAC; DAM DRAM, MST; DC
    2; WLCS**
    See also DA3; DFS 10; DLB 176; RGEL
Aristotle 384B.C.- ...... **CMLC 31; DA; DAB;
    DAC; DAM MST; WLCS**
    See also DA3; DLB 176; RGEL
Arlt, Roberto (Godofredo Christophersen)
    1900-1942 .... **TCLC 29; DAM MULT;
    HLC 1**
    See also CA 123; 131; CANR 67; HW 1, 2
Armah, Ayi Kwei 1939- ...... **CLC 5, 33, 136;
    BLC 1; DAM MULT, POET**
    See also BW 1; CA 61-64; CANR 21, 64;
    CN; DLB 117; MTCW 1
Armatrading, Joan 1950- .... **CLC 17**
    See also CA 114; 186
Arnette, Robert
    See Silverberg, Robert
**Arnim, Achim von (Ludwig Joachim von
    Arnim)** 1781-1831 ..... **NCLC 5; SSC 29**
    See also DLB 90
Arnim, Bettina von 1785-1859 .... **NCLC 38**
    See also DLB 90; RGWL
Arnold, Matthew 1822-1888 ..... **NCLC 6, 29,
    89; DA; DAB; DAC; DAM MST,
    POET; PC 5; WLC**
    See also CDBLB 1832-1890; DLB 32, 57;
    PFS 2
Arnold, Thomas 1795-1842 .... **NCLC 18**
    See also DLB 55
Arnow, Harriette (Louisa) Simpson
    1908-1986 .... **CLC 2, 7, 18**
    See also CA 9-12R; 118; CANR 14; DLB
    6; FW; MTCW 1, 2; RHW; SATA 42;
    SATA-Obit 47
Arouet, François-Marie
    See Voltaire
Arp, Hans
    See Arp, Jean
Arp, Jean 1887-1966 .... **CLC 5**
    See also CA 81-84; 25-28R; CANR 42, 77
Arrabal
    See Arrabal, Fernando
Arrabal, Fernando 1932- ... **CLC 2, 9, 18, 58**
    See also CA 9-12R; CANR 15
Arreola, Juan José 1918- .... **SSC 38; DAM
    MULT; HLC 1**
    See also CA 113; 131; CANR 81; DLB 113;
    DNFS 2; HW 1, 2
Arrian c. 89(?)-c. 155(?) .... **CMLC 43**
    See also DLB 176
Arrick, Fran .... **CLC 30**
    See also Gaberman, Judie Angell
Artaud, Antonin (Marie Joseph)
    1896-1948 . **TCLC 3, 36; DAM DRAM;
    DC 14**
    See also CA 104; 149; DA3; EW; GFL 1789
    to the Present; MTCW 1; RGWL
Arthur, Ruth M(abel) 1905-1979 ..... **CLC 12**
    See also CA 9-12R; 85-88; CANR 4; CWRI;
    SATA 7, 26
Artsybashev, Mikhail (Petrovich)
    1878-1927 .... **TCLC 31**
    See also CA 170

Arundel, Honor (Morfydd)
    1919-1973 .... **CLC 17**
    See also CA 21-22; 41-44R; CAP 2; CLR
    35; CWRI; SATA 4; SATA-Obit 24
Arzner, Dorothy 1900-1979 .... **CLC 98**
Asch, Sholem 1880-1957 .... **TCLC 3**
    See also CA 105; GLL 2
Ash, Shalom
    See Asch, Sholem
Ashbery, John (Lawrence) 1927- .. **CLC 2, 3,
    4, 6, 9, 13, 15, 25, 41, 77, 125; DAM
    POET; PC 26**
    See also Berry, Jonas
    See also AMWS 3; CA 5-8R; CANR 9, 37,
    66; CP; DA3; DLB 5, 165; DLBY 81;
    INT CANR-9; MTCW 1, 2; PFS 11
Ashdown, Clifford
    See Freeman, R(ichard) Austin
Ashe, Gordon
    See Creasey, John
Ashton-Warner, Sylvia (Constance)
    1908-1984 .... **CLC 19**
    See also CA 69-72; 112; CANR 29; MTCW
    1, 2
Asimov, Isaac 1920-1992 ..... **CLC 1, 3, 9, 19,
    26, 76, 92; DAM POP**
    See also AAYA 13; BEST 90:2; CA 1-4R;
    137; CANR 2, 19, 36, 60; CLR 12; CMW;
    CPW; DA3; DLB 8; DLBY 92; INT
    CANR-19; JRDA; MAICYA; MTCW 1,
    2; RGAL; SATA 1, 26, 74; SCFW 2;
    SFW; YAW
Assis, Joaquim Maria Machado de
    See Machado de Assis, Joaquim Maria
Astell, Mary 1666-1731 .... **LC 68**
    See also FW
Astley, Thea (Beatrice May) 1925- .. **CLC 41**
    See also CA 65-68; CANR 11, 43, 78; CN
Aston, James
    See White, T(erence) H(anbury)
Asturias, Miguel Ángel 1899-1974 .... **CLC 3,
    8, 13; DAM MULT, NOV; HLC 1**
    See also CA 25-28; 49-52; CANR 32; CAP
    2; DA3; DLB 113; HW 1; MTCW 1, 2;
    RGWL
Atares, Carlos Saura
    See Saura (Atares), Carlos
Atheling, William
    See Pound, Ezra (Weston Loomis)
Atheling, William, Jr.
    See Blish, James (Benjamin)
Atherton, Gertrude (Franklin Horn)
    1857-1948 .... **TCLC 2**
    See also CA 104; 155; DLB 9, 78, 186;
    HGG; TCWW 2
Atherton, Lucius
    See Masters, Edgar Lee
Atkins, Jack
    See Harris, Mark
Atkinson, Kate .... **CLC 99**
    See also CA 166
Attaway, William (Alexander)
    1911-1986 .... **CLC 92; BLC 1; DAM
    MULT**
    See also BW 2, 3; CA 143; CANR 82; DLB
    76
Atticus
    See Fleming, Ian (Lancaster); Wilson,
    (Thomas) Woodrow
Atwood, Margaret (Eleanor) 1939- ... **CLC 2,
    3, 4, 8, 13, 15, 25, 44, 84, 135; DA;
    DAB; DAC; DAM MST, NOV, POET;
    PC 8; SSC 2, 46; WLC**
    See also AAYA 12; BEST 89:2; CA 49-52;
    CANR 3, 24, 33, 59, 95; CN; CP; CPW;
    CWP; DA3; DLB 53; FW; INT CANR-
    24; MTCW 1, 2; NFS 4, 12; PFS 7; SATA
    50; SSFS 3; YAW

Aubigny, Pierre d'
    See Mencken, H(enry) L(ouis)
Aubin, Penelope 1685-1731(?) .... **LC 9**
    See also DLB 39
Auchincloss, Louis (Stanton) 1917- .. **CLC 4,
    6, 9, 18, 45; DAM NOV; SSC 22**
    See also AMWS 4; CA 1-4R; CANR 6, 29,
    55, 87; CN; DLB 2; DLBY 80; INT
    CANR-29; MTCW 1
Auden, W(ystan) H(ugh) 1907-1973 . **CLC 1,
    2, 3, 4, 6, 9, 11, 14, 43, 123; DA; DAB;
    DAC; DAM DRAM, MST, POET; PC
    1; WLC**
    See also AAYA 18; AMWS 2; CA 9-12R;
    45-48; CANR 5, 61; CDBLB 1914-1945;
    DA3; DLB 10, 20; MTCW 1, 2; PFS 1, 3,
    4, 10
Audiberti, Jacques 1900-1965 .... **CLC 38;
    DAM DRAM**
    See also CA 25-28R
Audubon, John James 1785-1851 . **NCLC 47**
Auel, Jean M(arie) 1936- .... **CLC 31, 107;
    DAM POP**
    See also AAYA 7; BEST 90:4; CA 103;
    CANR 21, 64; CPW; DA3; INT CANR-
    21; NFS 11; RHW; SATA 91
Auerbach, Erich 1892-1957 .... **TCLC 43**
    See also CA 118; 155
Augier, Emile 1820-1889 .... **NCLC 31**
    See also DLB 192; GFL 1789 to the Present
August, John
    See De Voto, Bernard (Augustine)
Augustine 354-430 .... **CMLC 6; DA; DAB;
    DAC; DAM MST; WLCS**
    See also DA3; DLB 115
Aunt Belinda
    See Braddon, Mary Elizabeth
Aurelius
    See Bourne, Randolph S(illiman)
    See also RGEL
Aurobindo, Sri
    See Ghose, Aurabinda
Austen, Jane 1775-1817 ...... **NCLC 1, 13, 19,
    33, 51, 81, 95; DA; DAB; DAC; DAM
    MST, NOV; WLC**
    See also AAYA 19; CDBLB 1789-1832;
    DA3; DLB 116; NFS 1; WYAS 1
Auster, Paul 1947- .... **CLC 47, 131**
    See also CA 69-72; CANR 23, 52, 75;
    CMW; CN; DA3; DLB 227; MTCW 1
Austin, Frank
    See Faust, Frederick (Schiller)
    See also TCWW 2
Austin, Mary (Hunter) 1868-1934 . **TCLC 25**
    See also Stairs, Gordon
    See also CA 109; 178; DLB 9, 78, 206, 221;
    FW; TCWW 2
Averroes 1126-1198 .... **CMLC 7**
    See also DLB 115
Avicenna 980-1037 .... **CMLC 16**
    See also DLB 115
Avison, Margaret 1918- .... **CLC 2, 4, 97;
    DAC; DAM POET**
    See also CA 17-20R; CP; DLB 53; MTCW
    1
Axton, David
    See Koontz, Dean R(ay)
Ayckbourn, Alan 1939- ...... **CLC 5, 8, 18, 33,
    74; DAB; DAM DRAM; DC 13**
    See also BRWS 5; CA 21-24R; CANR 31,
    59; CBD; CD; DFS 7; DLB 13; MTCW
    1, 2
Aydy, Catherine
    See Tennant, Emma (Christina)
Aymé, Marcel (Andre) 1902-1967 ... **CLC 11;
    SSC 41**
    See also CA 89-92; CANR 67; CLR 25;
    DLB 72; EW; GFL 1789 to the Present;
    RGSF; RGWL; SATA 91

Behan, Brendan 1923-1964 ...... **CLC 1, 8, 11, 15, 79; DAM DRAM**
See also BRWS 2; CA 73-76; CANR 33; CBD; CDBLB 1945-1960; DFS 7; DLB 13, 233; MTCW 1, 2

Behn, Aphra 1640(?)-1689 .... **LC 1, 30, 42; DA; DAB; DAC; DAM DRAM, MST, NOV, POET; DC 4; PC 13; WLC**
See also BRWS 3; DA3; DLB 39, 80, 131; FW

Behrman, S(amuel) N(athaniel)
1893-1973 .... **CLC 40**
See also CA 13-16; 45-48; CAD; CAP 1; DLB 7, 44; RGAL

Belasco, David 1853-1931 .... **TCLC 3**
See also CA 104; 168; DLB 7; RGAL

Belcheva, Elisaveta 1893-1991 .... **CLC 10**
See also Bagryana, Elisaveta

Beldone, Phil "Cheech"
See Ellison, Harlan (Jay)

Beleno
See Azuela, Mariano

Belinski, Vissarion Grigoryevich
1811-1848 .... **NCLC 5**
See also DLB 198

Belitt, Ben 1911- .... **CLC 22**
See also CA 13-16R; CAAS 4; CANR 7, 77; CP; DLB 5

Bell, Gertrude (Margaret Lowthian)
1868-1926 .... **TCLC 67**
See also CA 167; DLB 174

Bell, J. Freeman
See Zangwill, Israel

Bell, James Madison 1826-1902 ... **TCLC 43; BLC 1; DAM MULT**
See also BW 1; CA 122; 124; DLB 50

Bell, Madison Smartt 1957- ...... **CLC 41, 102**
See also CA 111, 183; CAAE 183; CANR 28, 54, 73; CN; CSW; MTCW 1

Bell, Marvin (Hartley) 1937- ...... **CLC 8, 31; DAM POET**
See also CA 21-24R; CAAS 14; CANR 59; CP; DLB 5; MTCW 1

Bell, W. L. D.
See Mencken, H(enry) L(ouis)

Bellamy, Atwood C.
See Mencken, H(enry) L(ouis)

Bellamy, Edward 1850-1898 ...... **NCLC 4, 86**
See also DLB 12; RGAL; SFW

Belli, Gioconda 1949-
See also CA 152; CWW 2; HLCS 1

Bellin, Edward J.
See Kuttner, Henry

Belloc, (Joseph) Hilaire (Pierre Sebastien Rene Swanton) 1870-1953 ...... **TCLC 7, 18; DAM POET; PC 24**
See also CA 106; 152; CWRI; DLB 19, 100, 141, 174; MTCW 1; SATA 112; YABC 1

Belloc, Joseph Peter Rene Hilaire
See Belloc, (Joseph) Hilaire (Pierre Sebastien Rene Swanton)

Belloc, Joseph Pierre Hilaire
See Belloc, (Joseph) Hilaire (Pierre Sebastien Rene Swanton)

Belloc, M. A.
See Lowndes, Marie Adelaide (Belloc)

Bellow, Saul 1915- . **CLC 1, 2, 3, 6, 8, 10, 13, 15, 25, 33, 34, 63, 79; DA; DAB; DAC; DAM MST, NOV, POP; SSC 14; WLC**
See also AITN 2; BEST 89:3; CA 5-8R; CABS 1; CANR 29, 53, 95; CDALB 1941-1968; CN; DA3; DLB 2, 28; DLBD 3; DLBY 82; MTCW 1, 2; NFS 4; RGAL; RGSF; SSFS 12

Belser, Reimond Karel Maria de 1929-
See Ruyslinck, Ward
See also CA 152

Bely, Andrey .... **TCLC 7; PC 11**
See also Bugayev, Boris Nikolayevich
See also MTCW 1

Belyi, Andrei
See Bugayev, Boris Nikolayevich
See also RGWL

Benary, Margot
See Benary-Isbert, Margot

Benary-Isbert, Margot 1889-1979 .... **CLC 12**
See also CA 5-8R; 89-92; CANR 4, 72; CLR 12; MAICYA; SATA 2; SATA-Obit 21

Benavente (y Martinez), Jacinto
1866-1954 .... **TCLC 3; DAM DRAM, MULT; HLCS 1**
See also CA 106; 131; CANR 81; GLL 2; HW 1, 2; MTCW 1, 2

Benchley, Peter (Bradford) 1940- . **CLC 4, 8; DAM NOV, POP**
See also AAYA 14; AITN 2; CA 17-20R; CANR 12, 35, 66; CPW; HGG; MTCW 1, 2; SATA 3, 89

Benchley, Robert (Charles)
1889-1945 .... **TCLC 1, 55**
See also CA 105; 153; DLB 11

Benda, Julien 1867-1956 .... **TCLC 60**
See also CA 120; 154; GFL 1789 to the Present

Benedict, Ruth (Fulton)
1887-1948 .... **TCLC 60**
See also CA 158

Benedict, Saint c. 480-c. 547 .... **CMLC 29**

Benedikt, Michael 1935- .... **CLC 4, 14**
See also CA 13-16R; CANR 7; CP; DLB 5

Benet, Juan 1927-1993 .... **CLC 28**
See also CA 143

Benét, Stephen Vincent 1898-1943 . **TCLC 7; DAM POET; SSC 10**
See also CA 104; 152; DA3; DLB 4, 48, 102; DLBY 97; HGG; MTCW 1; RGAL; RGSF; YABC 1

Benét, William Rose 1886-1950 .... **TCLC 28; DAM POET**
See also CA 118; 152; DLB 45

Benford, Gregory (Albert) 1941- ..... **CLC 52**
See also CA 69-72, 175; CAAE 175; CAAS 27; CANR 12, 24, 49, 95; CSW; DLBY 82; SCFW 2; SFW

Bengtsson, Frans (Gunnar)
1894-1954 .... **TCLC 48**
See also CA 170

Benjamin, David
See Slavitt, David R(ytman)

Benjamin, Lois
See Gould, Lois

Benjamin, Walter 1892-1940 .... **TCLC 39**
See also CA 164; DLB 242

Benn, Gottfried 1886-1956 .. **TCLC 3; PC 35**
See also CA 106; 153; DLB 56; RGWL

Bennett, Alan 1934- .... **CLC 45, 77; DAB; DAM MST**
See also CA 103; CANR 35, 55; CBD; CD; MTCW 1, 2

Bennett, (Enoch) Arnold
1867-1931 .... **TCLC 5, 20**
See also CA 106; 155; CDBLB 1890-1914; DLB 10, 34, 98, 135; MTCW 2

Bennett, Elizabeth
See Mitchell, Margaret (Munnerlyn)

Bennett, George Harold 1930-
See Bennett, Hal
See also BW 1; CA 97-100; CANR 87

Bennett, Hal .... **CLC 5**
See also Bennett, George Harold
See also DLB 33

Bennett, Jay 1912- .... **CLC 35**
See also AAYA 10; CA 69-72; CANR 11, 42, 79; JRDA; SAAS 4; SATA 41, 87; SATA-Brief 27; YAW

Bennett, Louise (Simone) 1919- ...... **CLC 28; BLC 1; DAM MULT**
See also BW 2, 3; CA 151; DLB 117

Benson, E(dward) F(rederic)
1867-1940 .... **TCLC 27**
See also CA 114; 157; DLB 135, 153; HGG

Benson, Jackson J. 1930- .... **CLC 34**
See also CA 25-28R; DLB 111

Benson, Sally 1900-1972 .... **CLC 17**
See also CA 19-20; 37-40R; CAP 1; SATA 1, 35; SATA-Obit 27

Benson, Stella 1892-1933 .... **TCLC 17**
See also CA 117; 155; DLB 36, 162; FANT

Bentham, Jeremy 1748-1832 .... **NCLC 38**
See also DLB 107, 158

Bentley, E(dmund) C(lerihew)
1875-1956 .... **TCLC 12**
See also CA 108; DLB 70

Bentley, Eric (Russell) 1916- .... **CLC 24**
See also CA 5-8R; CAD; CANR 6, 67; CBD; CD; INT CANR-6

Beranger, Pierre Jean de
1780-1857 .... **NCLC 34**

Berdyaev, Nicolas
See Berdyaev, Nikolai (Aleksandrovich)

Berdyaev, Nikolai (Aleksandrovich)
1874-1948 .... **TCLC 67**
See also CA 120; 157

Berdyaev, Nikolai (Aleksandrovich)
See Berdyaev, Nikolai (Aleksandrovich)

Berendt, John (Lawrence) 1939- ...... **CLC 86**
See also CA 146; CANR 75, 93; DA3; MTCW 1

Beresford, J(ohn) D(avys)
1873-1947 .... **TCLC 81**
See also CA 112; 155; DLB 162, 178, 197; SFW

Bergelson, David 1884-1952 .... **TCLC 81**

Berger, Colonel
See Malraux, (Georges-)Andr

Berger, John (Peter) 1926- .... **CLC 2, 19**
See also BRWS 4; CA 81-84; CANR 51, 78; CN; DLB 14, 207

Berger, Melvin H. 1927- .... **CLC 12**
See also CA 5-8R; CANR 4; CLR 32; SAAS 2; SATA 5, 88

Berger, Thomas (Louis) 1924- .. **CLC 3, 5, 8, 11, 18, 38; DAM NOV**
See also CA 1-4R; CANR 5, 28, 51; CN; DLB 2; DLBY 80; FANT; INT CANR-28; MTCW 1, 2; RHW; TCWW 2

Bergman, (Ernst) Ingmar
1918-1997 .... **CLC 16, 72**
See also CA 81-84; CANR 33, 70; MTCW 2

Bergson, Henri(-Louis) 1859-1941 . **TCLC 32**
See also CA 164; EW; GFL 1789 to the Present

Bergstein, Eleanor 1938- .... **CLC 4**
See also CA 53-56; CANR 5

Berkeley, George 1685-1753 .... **LC 65**
See also DLB 101

Berkoff, Steven 1937- .... **CLC 56**
See also CA 104; CANR 72; CBD; CD

Berlin, Isaiah 1909-1997 .... **TCLC 105**
See also CA 85-88; 162

Bermant, Chaim (Icyk) 1929-1998 ... **CLC 40**
See also CA 57-60; CANR 6, 31, 57; CN

Bern, Victoria
See Fisher, M(ary) F(rances) K(ennedy)

Bernanos, (Paul Louis) Georges
1888-1948 .... **TCLC 3**
See also CA 104; 130; CANR 94; DLB 72; GFL 1789 to the Present; RGWL

Bernard, April 1956- .... **CLC 59**
See also CA 131

Berne, Victoria
See Fisher, M(ary) F(rances) K(ennedy)

Bernhard, Thomas 1931-1989 ..... **CLC 3, 32, 61; DC 14**
See also CA 85-88; 127; CANR 32, 57; DLB 85, 124; MTCW 1; RGWL

Bernhardt, Sarah (Henriette Rosine) 1844-1923 .... **TCLC 75**
See also CA 157

Bernstein, Charles 1950- .... **CLC 142,**
See also CA 129; CAAS 24; CANR 90; CP; DLB 169

Berriault, Gina 1926-1999 .... **CLC 54, 109; SSC 30**
See also CA 116; 129; 185; CANR 66; DLB 130; SSFS 7,11

Berrigan, Daniel 1921- .... **CLC 4**
See also CA 33-36R; CAAE 187; CAAS 1; CANR 11, 43, 78; CP; DLB 5

Berrigan, Edmund Joseph Michael, Jr. 1934-1983
See Berrigan, Ted
See also CA 61-64; 110; CANR 14

Berrigan, Ted .... **CLC 37**
See also Berrigan, Edmund Joseph Michael, Jr.
See also DLB 5, 169

Berry, Charles Edward Anderson 1931-
See Berry, Chuck
See also CA 115

Berry, Chuck .... **CLC 17**
See also Berry, Charles Edward Anderson

Berry, Jonas
See Ashbery, John (Lawrence)
See also GLL 1

Berry, Wendell (Erdman) 1934- ... **CLC 4, 6, 8, 27, 46; DAM POET; PC 28**
See also AITN 1; CA 73-76; CANR 50, 73; CP; CSW; DLB 5, 6, 234; MTCW 1

Berryman, John 1914-1972 ... **CLC 1, 2, 3, 4, 6, 8, 10, 13, 25, 62; DAM POET**
See also CA 13-16; 33-36R; CABS 2; CANR 35; CAP 1; CDALB 1941-1968; DLB 48; MTCW 1, 2; RGAL

Bertolucci, Bernardo 1940- .... **CLC 16**
See also CA 106

Berton, Pierre (Francis Demarigny) 1920- .... **CLC 104**
See also CA 1-4R; CANR 2, 56; CPW; DLB 68; SATA 99

Bertrand, Aloysius 1807-1841 .... **NCLC 31**

Bertran de Born c. 1140-1215 .... **CMLC 5**

Besant, Annie (Wood) 1847-1933 ..... **TCLC 9**
See also CA 105; 185

Bessie, Alvah 1904-1985 .... **CLC 23**
See also CA 5-8R; 116; CANR 2, 80; DLB 26

Bethlen, T. D.
See Silverberg, Robert

Beti, Mongo .... **CLC 27; BLC 1; DAM MULT**
See also Biyidi, Alexandre
See also CANR 79

Betjeman, John 1906-1984 ...... **CLC 2, 6, 10, 34, 43; DAB; DAM MST, POET**
See also CA 9-12R; 112; CANR 33, 56; CDBLB 1945-1960; DA3; DLB 20; DLBY 84; MTCW 1, 2

Bettelheim, Bruno 1903-1990 .... **CLC 79**
See also CA 81-84; 131; CANR 23, 61; DA3; MTCW 1, 2

Betti, Ugo 1892-1953 .... **TCLC 5**
See also CA 104; 155; RGWL

Betts, Doris (Waugh) 1932- ..... **CLC 3, 6, 28; SSC 45**
See also CA 13-16R; CANR 9, 66, 77; CN; CSW; DLBY 82; INT CANR-9

Bevan, Alistair
See Roberts, Keith (John Kingston)

Bey, Pilaff
See Douglas, (George) Norman

Bialik, Chaim Nachman 1873-1934 .... **TCLC 25**
See also CA 170

Bickerstaff, Isaac
See Swift, Jonathan

Bidart, Frank 1939- .... **CLC 33**
See also CA 140; CP

Bienek, Horst 1930- .... **CLC 7, 11**
See also CA 73-76; DLB 75

Bierce, Ambrose (Gwinett) 1842-1914(?) .... **TCLC 1, 7, 44; DA; DAC; DAM MST; SSC 9; WLC**
See also CA 104; 139; CANR 78; CDALB 1865-1917; DA3; DLB 11, 12, 23, 71, 74, 186; HGG; SSFS 9

Biggers, Earl Derr 1884-1933 .... **TCLC 65**
See also CA 108; 153

Billings, Josh
See Shaw, Henry Wheeler

Billington, (Lady) Rachel (Mary) 1942- .... **CLC 43**
See also AITN 2; CA 33-36R; CANR 44; CN

Binyon, T(imothy) J(ohn) 1936- .... **CLC 34**
See also CA 111; CANR 28

Bion 335B.C.-245B.C. .... **CMLC 39**

Bioy Casares, Adolfo 1914-1999 .... **CLC 4, 8, 13, 88; DAM MULT; HLC 1; SSC 17**
See also Casares, Adolfo Bioy; Miranda, Javier; Sacastru, Martin
See also CA 29-32R; 177; CANR 19, 43, 66; DLB 113; HW 1, 2; MTCW 1, 2

Birch, Allison .... **CLC 65**

Bird, Cordwainer
See Ellison, Harlan (Jay)

Bird, Robert Montgomery 1806-1854 .... **NCLC 1**
See also DLB 202; RGAL

Birkerts, Sven 1951- .... **CLC 116**
See also CA 128; 133; 176; CAAE 176; CAAS 29; INT 133

Birney, (Alfred) Earle 1904-1995 .. **CLC 1, 4, 6, 11; DAC; DAM MST, POET**
See also CA 1-4R; CANR 5, 20; CP; DLB 88; MTCW 1; PFS 8

Biruni, al 973-1048(?) .... **CMLC 28**

Bishop, Elizabeth 1911-1979 .. **CLC 1, 4, 9, 13, 15, 32; DA; DAC; DAM MST, POET; PC 3, 34**
See also AMWS 1; CA 5-8R; 89-92; CABS 2; CANR 26, 61; CDALB 1968-1988; DA3; DLB 5, 169; GLL 2; MTCW 1, 2; PFS 6; 12; RGAL; SATA-Obit 24

Bishop, John 1935- .... **CLC 10**
See also CA 105

Bishop, John Peale 1892-1944 ..... **TCLC 103**
See also CA 107; 155; DLB 4, 9, 45; RGAL

Bissett, Bill 1939- .... **CLC 18; PC 14**
See also CA 69-72; CAAS 19; CANR 15; CCA 1; CP; DLB 53; MTCW 1

Bissoondath, Neil (Devindra) 1955- .... **CLC 120; DAC**
See also CA 136; CN

Bitov, Andrei (Georgievich) 1937- ... **CLC 57**
See also CA 142

Biyidi, Alexandre 1932-
See Beti, Mongo
See also BW 1, 3; CA 114; 124; CANR 81; DA3; MTCW 1, 2

Bjarme, Brynjolf
See Ibsen, Henrik (Johan)

Bjoernson, Bjoernstjerne (Martinius) 1832-1910 .... **TCLC 7, 37**
See also CA 104

Black, Robert
See Holdstock, Robert P.

Blackburn, Paul 1926-1971 .... **CLC 9, 43**
See also CA 81-84; 33-36R; CANR 34; DLB 16; DLBY 81

Black Elk 1863-1950 .... **TCLC 33; DAM MULT**
See also CA 144; MTCW 1; NNAL

Black Hobart
See Sanders, (James) Ed(ward)

Blacklin, Malcolm
See Chambers, Aidan

Blackmore, R(ichard) D(oddridge) 1825-1900 .... **TCLC 27**
See also CA 120; DLB 18

Blackmur, R(ichard) P(almer) 1904-1965 .... **CLC 2, 24**
See also AMWS 2; CA 11-12; 25-28R; CANR 71; CAP 1; DLB 63

Black Tarantula
See Acker, Kathy

Blackwood, Algernon (Henry) 1869-1951 .... **TCLC 5**
See also CA 105; 150; DLB 153, 156, 178; HGG

Blackwood, Caroline 1931-1996 .... **CLC 6, 9, 100**
See also CA 85-88; 151; CANR 32, 61, 65; CN; DLB 14, 207; HGG; MTCW 1

Blade, Alexander
See Hamilton, Edmond; Silverberg, Robert

Blaga, Lucian 1895-1961 .... **CLC 75**
See also CA 157; DLB 220

Blair, Eric (Arthur) 1903-1950
See Orwell, George
See also CA 104; 132; DA; DAB; DAC; DAM MST, NOV; DA3; MTCW 1, 2; SATA 29

Blair, Hugh 1718-1800 .... **NCLC 75**

Blais, Marie-Claire 1939- .... **CLC 2, 4, 6, 13, 22; DAC; DAM MST**
See also CA 21-24R; CAAS 4; CANR 38, 75, 93; DLB 53; FW; MTCW 1, 2

Blaise, Clark 1940- .... **CLC 29**
See also AITN 2; CA 53-56; CAAS 3; CANR 5, 66; CN; DLB 53; RGSF

Blake, Fairley
See De Voto, Bernard (Augustine)

Blake, Nicholas
See Day Lewis, C(ecil)
See also DLB 77

Blake, William 1757-1827 .... **NCLC 13, 37, 57; DA; DAB; DAC; DAM MST, POET; PC 12; WLC**
See also CDBLB 1789-1832; CLR 52; DA3; DLB 93, 163; MAICYA; PFS 2; 12; SATA 30

Blanchot, Maurice 1907- .... **CLC 135**
See also CA 117; 144; DLB 72

Blasco Ibañez, Vicente 1867-1928 .... **TCLC 12; DAM NOV**
See also CA 110; 131; CANR 81; DA3; HW 1, 2; MTCW 1

Blatty, William Peter 1928- .... **CLC 2; DAM POP**
See also CA 5-8R; CANR 9; HGG

Bleeck, Oliver
See Thomas, Ross (Elmore)

Blessing, Lee 1949- .... **CLC 54**
See also CAD; CD

Blight, Rose
See Greer, Germaine

Blish, James (Benjamin) 1921-1975 . **CLC 14**
See also CA 1-4R; 57-60; CANR 3; DLB 8; MTCW 1; SATA 66; SCFW 2; SFW

Bliss, Reginald
See Wells, H(erbert) G(eorge)

Blixen, Karen (Christentze Dinesen) 1885-1962
See Dinesen, Isak
See also CA 25-28; CANR 22, 50; CAP 2; DA3; MTCW 1, 2; NCFS 2; SATA 44

Chaucer, Daniel
See Ford, Ford Madox
See also RHW

Chaucer, Geoffrey 1340(?)-1400 .. **LC 17, 56;
DA; DAB; DAC; DAM MST, POET;
PC 19; WLCS**
See also CDBLB Before 1660; DA3; DLB
146; RGEL

Chavez, Denise (Elia) 1948-
See also CA 131; CANR 56, 81; DAM
MULT; DLB 122; FW; HLC 1; HW 1, 2;
MTCW 2

Chaviaras, Strates 1935-
See Haviaras, Stratis
See also CA 105

Chayefsky, Paddy .... **CLC 23**
See also Chayefsky, Sidney
See also CAD; DLB 7, 44; DLBY 81;
RGAL

Chayefsky, Sidney 1923-1981
See Chayefsky, Paddy
See also CA 9-12R; 104; CANR 18; DAM
DRAM

Chedid, Andree 1920- .... **CLC 47**
See also CA 145; CANR 95

Cheever, John 1912-1982 ..... **CLC 3, 7, 8, 11,
15, 25, 64; DA; DAB; DAC; DAM
MST, NOV, POP; SSC 1, 38; WLC**
See also AMWS 1; CA 5-8R; 106; CABS
1; CANR 5, 27, 76; CDALB 1941-1968;
CPW; DA3; DLB 2, 102, 227; DLBY 80,
82; INT CANR-5; MTCW 1, 2; RGAL;
RGSF; SSFS 2

Cheever, Susan 1943- .... **CLC 18, 48**
See also CA 103; CANR 27, 51, 92; DLBY
82; INT CANR-27

Chekhonte, Antosha
See Chekhov, Anton (Pavlovich)

Chekhov, Anton (Pavlovich)
1860-1904 .... **TCLC 3, 10, 31, 55, 96;
DA; DAB; DAC; DAM DRAM, MST;
DC 9; SSC 2, 28, 41; WLC**
See also CA 104; 124; DA3; DFS 1, 5, 10,
12; SATA 90; SSFS 5

Cheney, Lynne V. 1941- .... **CLC 70**
See also CA 89-92; CANR 58

Chernyshevsky, Nikolay Gavrilovich
1828-1889 .... **NCLC 1**
See also DLB 238

Cherry, Carolyn Janice 1942-
See Cherryh, C. J.
See also CA 65-68; CANR 10; FANT; SFW;
YAW

Cherryh, C. J. .... **CLC 35**
See also Cherry, Carolyn Janice
See also AAYA 24; DLBY 80; SATA 93

Chesnutt, Charles W(addell)
1858-1932 .. **TCLC 5, 39; BLC 1; DAM
MULT; SSC 7**
See also AFAW 1, 2; BW 1, 3; CA 106;
125; CANR 76; DLB 12, 50, 78; MTCW
1, 2; SSFS 11

Chester, Alfred 1929(?)-1971 .... **CLC 49**
See also CA 33-36R; DLB 130

Chesterton, G(ilbert) K(eith)
1874-1936 . **TCLC 1, 6, 64; DAM NOV,
POET; PC 28; SSC 1, 46**
See also CA 104; 132; CANR 73; CDBLB
1914-1945; CMW; DLB 10, 19, 34, 70,
98, 149, 178; FANT; MTCW 1, 2; SATA
27

Chiang, Pin-chin 1904-1986
See Ding Ling
See also CA 118

Ch'ien Chung-shu 1910- .... **CLC 22**
See also CA 130; CANR 73; MTCW 1, 2

Chikamatsu Monzaemon 1653-1724 ... **LC 66**

Child, L. Maria
See Child, Lydia Maria

Child, Lydia Maria 1802-1880 .. **NCLC 6, 73**
See also DLB 1, 74; RGAL; SATA 67

Child, Mrs.
See Child, Lydia Maria

Child, Philip 1898-1978 .... **CLC 19, 68**
See also CA 13-14; CAP 1; RHW; SATA
47

Childers, (Robert) Erskine
1870-1922 .... **TCLC 65**
See also CA 113; 153; DLB 70

Childress, Alice 1920-1994 .. **CLC 12, 15, 86,
96; BLC 1; DAM DRAM, MULT,
NOV; DC 4**
See also AAYA 8; BW 2, 3; CA 45-48; 146;
CAD; CANR 3, 27, 50, 74; CLR 14;
CWD; DA3; DFS 2,8; DLB 7, 38; JRDA;
MAICYA; MTCW 1, 2; RGAL; SATA 7,
48, 81; YAW

Chin, Frank (Chew, Jr.) 1940- ...... **CLC 135;
DAM MULT; DC 7**
See also CA 33-36R; CANR 71; CD; DLB
206

Chislett, (Margaret) Anne 1943- ...... **CLC 34**
See also CA 151

Chitty, Thomas Willes 1926- .... **CLC 11**
See also Hinde, Thomas
See also CA 5-8R; CN

Chivers, Thomas Holley
1809-1858 .... **NCLC 49**
See also DLB 3; RGAL

Choi, Susan .... **CLC 119**

Chomette, Rene Lucien 1898-1981
See Clair, Rene
See also CA 103

Chomsky, (Avram) Noam 1928- ..... **CLC 132**
See also CA 17-20R; CANR 28, 62; DA3;
MTCW 1, 2

Chopin, Kate . **TCLC 5, 14; DA; DAB; SSC
8; WLCS**
See also Chopin, Katherine
See also AAYA 33; AMWS 1; CDALB
1865-1917; DLB 12, 78; NFS 3; RGAL;
RGSF; SSFS 2

Chopin, Katherine 1851-1904
See Chopin, Kate
See also CA 104; 122; DAC; DAM MST,
NOV; DA3; FW

Chrétien de Troyes c. 12th cent. - . **CMLC 10**
See also DLB 208

Christie
See Ichikawa, Kon

Christie, Agatha (Mary Clarissa)
1890-1976 ... **CLC 1, 6, 8, 12, 39, 48,
110; DAB; DAC; DAM NOV**
See also AAYA 9; AITN 1, 2; BRWS 2; CA
17-20R; 61-64; CANR 10, 37; CDBLB
1914-1945; CMW; CPW; DA3; DFS 2;
DLB 13, 77; MTCW 1, 2; NFS 8; RHW;
SATA 36; YAW

Christie, (Ann) Philippa
See Pearce, Philippa
See also CA 5-8R; CANR 4; CWRI; FANT

Christine de Pizan 1365(?)-1431(?) .... **LC 9**
See also DLB 208; RGWL

Chubb, Elmer
See Masters, Edgar Lee

Chulkov, Mikhail Dmitrievich
1743-1792 .... **LC 2**
See also DLB 150

Churchill, Caryl 1938- .... **CLC 31, 55; DC 5**
See also BRWS 4; CA 102; CANR 22, 46;
CBD; CWD; DFS 12; DLB 13; FW;
MTCW 1; RGEL

Churchill, Charles 1731-1764 .... **LC 3**
See also DLB 109; RGEL

Chute, Carolyn 1947- .... **CLC 39**
See also CA 123

Ciardi, John (Anthony) 1916-1986 . **CLC 10,
40, 44, 129; DAM POET**
See also CA 5-8R; 118; CAAS 2; CANR 5,
33; CLR 19; CWRI; DLB 5; DLBY 86;
INT CANR-5; MAICYA; MTCW 1, 2;
SAAS 26; SATA 1, 65; SATA-Obit 46

Cibber, Colley 1671-1757 .... **LC 66**
See also DLB 84; RGEL

Cicero, Marcus Tullius
106B.C.-43B.C. .... **CMLC 3**
See also DLB 211

Cimino, Michael 1943- .... **CLC 16**
See also CA 105

Cioran, E(mil) M. 1911-1995 .... **CLC 64**
See also CA 25-28R; 149; CANR 91; DLB
220

Cisneros, Sandra 1954- . **CLC 69, 118; DAM
MULT; HLC 1; SSC 32**
See also AAYA 9; AMWS 7; CA 131;
CANR 64; CWP; DA3; DLB 122, 152;
FW; HW 1, 2; MTCW 2; NFS 2; RGAL;
RGSF; SSFS 3; YAW

Cixous, Hélène 1937- .... **CLC 92**
See also CA 126; CANR 55; CWW 2; DLB
83, 242; FW; MTCW 1, 2

Clair, Rene .... **CLC 20**
See also Chomette, Rene Lucien

Clampitt, Amy 1920-1994 .... **CLC 32; PC 19**
See also CA 110; 146; CANR 29, 79; DLB
105

Clancy, Thomas L., Jr. 1947-
See Clancy, Tom
See also CA 125; 131; CANR 62; CPW;
DA3; DLB 227; INT 131; MTCW 1, 2

Clancy, Tom .... **CLC 45, 112; DAM NOV,
POP**
See also Clancy, Thomas L., Jr.
See also AAYA 9; BEST 89:1, 90:1; CMW;
MTCW 2

Clare, John 1793-1864 ... **NCLC 9, 86; DAB;
DAM POET; PC 23**
See also DLB 55, 96; RGEL

Clarin
See Alas (y Urena), Leopoldo (Enrique
Garcia)

Clark, Al C.
See Goines, Donald

Clark, (Robert) Brian 1932- .... **CLC 29**
See also CA 41-44R; CANR 67; CBD; CD

Clark, Curt
See Westlake, Donald E(dwin)

Clark, Eleanor 1913-1996 .... **CLC 5, 19**
See also CA 9-12R; 151; CANR 41; CN;
DLB 6

Clark, J. P.
See Clark Bekedermo, J(ohnson) P(epper)
See also DLB 117

Clark, John Pepper
See Clark Bekedermo, J(ohnson) P(epper)
See also CD; CP

Clark, M. R.
See Clark, Mavis Thorpe

Clark, Mavis Thorpe 1909- .... **CLC 12**
See also CA 57-60; CANR 8, 37; CLR 30;
CWRI; MAICYA; SAAS 5; SATA 8, 74

Clark, Walter Van Tilburg
1909-1971 .... **CLC 28**
See also CA 9-12R; 33-36R; CANR 63;
DLB 9, 206; SATA 8

Clark Bekedermo, J(ohnson) P(epper)
1935- .. **CLC 38; BLC 1; DAM DRAM,
MULT; DC 5**
See also Clark, J. P.; Clark, John Pepper
See also BW 1; CA 65-68; CANR 16, 72;
DFS 13; MTCW 1

Compton-Burnett, I(vy)
1892(?)-1969 .... **CLC 1, 3, 10, 15, 34;
DAM NOV**
See also CA 1-4R; 25-28R; CANR 4; DLB
36; MTCW 1

Comstock, Anthony 1844-1915 ...... **TCLC 13**
See also CA 110; 169

Comte, Auguste 1798-1857 .... **NCLC 54**

Conan Doyle, Arthur
See Doyle, Arthur Conan

Conde (Abellan), Carmen 1901-
See also CA 177; DLB 108; HLCS 1; HW
2

Condé, Maryse 1937- .... **CLC 52, 92; BLCS;
DAM MULT**
See also BW 2, 3; CA 110; CAAE 190;
CANR 30, 53, 76; CWW 2; MTCW 1

Condillac, Etienne Bonnot de
1714-1780 .... **LC 26**

Condon, Richard (Thomas)
1915-1996 ...... **CLC 4, 6, 8, 10, 45, 100;
DAM NOV**
See also BEST 90:3; CA 1-4R; 151; CAAS
1; CANR 2, 23; CMW; CN; INT CANR-
23; MTCW 1, 2

Confucius 551B.C.-479B.C. ... **CMLC 19; DA;
DAB; DAC; DAM MST; WLCS**
See also DA3

Congreve, William 1670-1729 .... **LC 5, 21;
DA; DAB; DAC; DAM DRAM, MST,
POET; DC 2; WLC**
See also CDBLB 1660-1789; DLB 39, 84;
RGEL

Connell, Evan S(helby), Jr. 1924- . **CLC 4, 6,
45; DAM NOV**
See also AAYA 7; CA 1-4R; CAAS 2;
CANR 2, 39, 76, 97; CN; DLB 2; DLBY
81; MTCW 1, 2

Connelly, Marc(us Cook) 1890-1980 . **CLC 7**
See also CA 85-88; 102; CANR 30; DFS
12; DLB 7; DLBY 80; SATA-Obit 25

Connor, Ralph .... **TCLC 31**
See also Gordon, Charles William
See also DLB 92; TCWW 2

Conrad, Joseph 1857-1924 .... **TCLC 1, 6, 13,
25, 43, 57; DA; DAB; DAC; DAM
MST, NOV; SSC 9; WLC**
See also AAYA 26; CA 104; 131; CANR
60; CDBLB 1890-1914; DA3; DLB 10,
34, 98, 156; MTCW 1, 2; NFS 2; RGEL;
RGSF; SATA 27; SSFS 1, 12

Conrad, Robert Arnold
See Hart, Moss

Conroy, Pat
See Conroy, (Donald) Pat(rick)
See also MTCW 2

Conroy, (Donald) Pat(rick) 1945- ... **CLC 30,
74; DAM NOV, POP**
See also Conroy, Pat
See also AAYA 8; AITN 1; CA 85-88;
CANR 24, 53; CPW; CSW; DA3; DLB 6;
MTCW 1

Constant (de Rebecque), (Henri) Benjamin
1767-1830 .... **NCLC 6**
See also DLB 119; EW; GFL 1789 to the
Present

Conybeare, Charles Augustus
See Eliot, T(homas) S(tearns)

Cook, Michael 1933-1994 .... **CLC 58**
See also CA 93-96; CANR 68; DLB 53

Cook, Robin 1940- .... **CLC 14; DAM POP**
See also AAYA 32; BEST 90:2; CA 108;
111; CANR 41, 90; CPW; DA3; HGG;
INT 111

Cook, Roy
See Silverberg, Robert

Cooke, Elizabeth 1948- .... **CLC 55**
See also CA 129

Cooke, John Esten 1830-1886 .... **NCLC 5**
See also DLB 3; RGAL

Cooke, John Estes
See Baum, L(yman) Frank

Cooke, M. E.
See Creasey, John

Cooke, Margaret
See Creasey, John

Cook-Lynn, Elizabeth 1930- . **CLC 93; DAM
MULT**
See also CA 133; DLB 175; NNAL

Cooney, Ray .... **CLC 62**
See also CBD

Cooper, Douglas 1960- .... **CLC 86**

Cooper, Henry St. John
See Creasey, John

Cooper, J(oan) California (?)- .... **CLC 56;
DAM MULT**
See also AAYA 12; BW 1; CA 125; CANR
55; DLB 212

Cooper, James Fenimore
1789-1851 .... **NCLC 1, 27, 54**
See also AAYA 22; CDALB 1640-1865;
DA3; DLB 3; NFS 9; RGAL; SATA 19

Coover, Robert (Lowell) 1932- ...... **CLC 3, 7,
15, 32, 46, 87; DAM NOV; SSC 15**
See also AMWS 5; CA 45-48; CANR 3,
37, 58; CN; DLB 2, 227; DLBY 81;
MTCW 1, 2

Copeland, Stewart (Armstrong)
1952- .... **CLC 26**

Copernicus, Nicolaus 1473-1543 .... **LC 45**

Coppard, A(lfred) E(dgar)
1878-1957 .... **TCLC 5; SSC 21**
See also CA 114; 167; DLB 162; HGG;
YABC 1

Coppee, Francois 1842-1908 .... **TCLC 25**
See also CA 170

Coppola, Francis Ford 1939- ... **CLC 16, 126**
See also AAYA 39; CA 77-80; CANR 40,
78; DLB 44

Corbière, Tristan 1845-1875 .... **NCLC 43**
See also GFL 1789 to the Present

Corcoran, Barbara 1911- .... **CLC 17**
See also AAYA 14; CA 21-24R; CAAS 2;
CANR 11, 28, 48; CLR 50; DLB 52;
JRDA; RHW; SAAS 20; SATA 3, 77

Cordelier, Maurice
See Giraudoux, Jean(-Hippolyte)

Corelli, Marie .... **TCLC 51**
See also Mackay, Mary
See also DLB 34, 156; RGEL

Corman, Cid .... **CLC 9**
See also Corman, Sidney
See also CAAS 2; DLB 5, 193

Corman, Sidney 1924-
See Corman, Cid
See also CA 85-88; CANR 44; CP; DAM
POET

Cormier, Robert (Edmund)
1925-2000 .... **CLC 12, 30; DA; DAB;
DAC; DAM MST, NOV**
See also AAYA 3, 19; CA 1-4R; CANR 5,
23, 76, 93; CDALB 1968-1988; CLR 12,
55; DLB 52; INT CANR-23; JRDA; MAI-
CYA; MTCW 1, 2; NFS 2; SATA 10, 45,
83; SATA-Obit 122; YAW

Corn, Alfred (DeWitt III) 1943- .... **CLC 33**
See also CA 179; CAAE 179; CAAS 25;
CANR 44; CP; CSW; DLB 120; DLBY
80

Corneille, Pierre 1606-1684 ..... **LC 28; DAB;
DAM MST**
See also GFL Beginnings to 1789; RGWL

Cornwell, David (John Moore)
1931- .... **CLC 9, 15; DAM POP**
See also le Carré, John
See also CA 5-8R; CANR 13, 33, 59; DA3;
MTCW 1, 2

Corso, (Nunzio) Gregory 1930-2001 . **CLC 1,
11; PC 33**
See also CA 5-8R; CANR 41, 76; CP; DA3;
DLB 5, 16; MTCW 1, 2

Cortázar, Julio 1914-1984 ... **CLC 2, 3, 5, 10,
13, 15, 33, 34, 92; DAM MULT, NOV;
HLC 1; SSC 7**
See also CA 21-24R; CANR 12, 32, 81;
DA3; DLB 113; HW 1, 2; MTCW 1, 2;
SSFS 3

Cortes, Hernan 1485-1547 .... **LC 31**

Corvinus, Jakob
See Raabe, Wilhelm (Karl)

Corvo, Baron
See Rolfe, Frederick (William Serafino Aus-
tin Lewis Mary)
See also GLL 1

Corwin, Cecil
See Kornbluth, C(yril) M.

Cosic, Dobrica 1921- .... **CLC 14**
See also CA 122; 138; CWW 2; DLB 181

Costain, Thomas B(ertram)
1885-1965 .... **CLC 30**
See also CA 5-8R; 25-28R; DLB 9; RHW

Costantini, Humberto 1924(?)-1987 . **CLC 49**
See also CA 131; 122; HW 1

Costello, Elvis 1955- .... **CLC 21**

Costenoble, Philostene 1898-1962
See Ghelderode, Michel de

Costenoble, Philostene 1898-1962
See Ghelderode, Michel de

Cotes, Cecil V.
See Duncan, Sara Jeannette

Cotter, Joseph Seamon Sr.
1861-1949 ...... **TCLC 28; BLC 1; DAM
MULT**
See also BW 1; CA 124; DLB 50

Couch, Arthur Thomas Quiller
See Quiller-Couch, SirArthur (Thomas)

Coulton, James
See Hansen, Joseph

Couperus, Louis (Marie Anne)
1863-1923 .... **TCLC 15**
See also CA 115

Coupland, Douglas 1961- .... **CLC 85, 133;
DAC; DAM POP**
See also AAYA 34; CA 142; CANR 57, 90;
CCA 1; CPW

Court, Wesli
See Turco, Lewis (Putnam)

Courtenay, Bryce 1933- .... **CLC 59**
See also CA 138; CPW

Courtney, Robert
See Ellison, Harlan (Jay)

Cousteau, Jacques-Yves 1910-1997 .. **CLC 30**
See also CA 65-68; 159; CANR 15, 67;
MTCW 1; SATA 38, 98

Coventry, Francis 1725-1754 .... **LC 46**

Cowan, Peter (Walkinshaw) 1914- .... **SSC 28**
See also CA 21-24R; CANR 9, 25, 50, 83;
CN

Coward, Noël (Peirce) 1899-1973 . **CLC 1, 9,
29, 51; DAM DRAM**
See also AITN 1; BRWS 2; CA 17-18; 41-
44R; CANR 35; CAP 2; CDBLB 1914-
1945; DA3; DFS 3, 6; DLB 10; IDFW 3,
4; MTCW 1, 2

Cowley, Abraham 1618-1667 .... **LC 43**
See also DLB 131, 151; RGEL

Cowley, Malcolm 1898-1989 .... **CLC 39**
See also AMWS 2; CA 5-8R; 128; CANR
3, 55; DLB 4, 48; DLBY 81, 89; MTCW
1, 2

Cowper, William 1731-1800 ..... **NCLC 8, 94;
DAM POET**
See also DA3; DLB 104, 109; RGEL

Cox, William Trevor 1928- ... **CLC 9, 14, 71;
DAM NOV**
See also Trevor, William

Didion, Joan 1934- .... **CLC 1, 3, 8, 14, 32, 129; DAM NOV**
See also AITN 1; AMWS 4; CA 5-8R; CANR 14, 52, 76; CDALB 1968-1988; CN; DA3; DLB 2, 173, 185; DLBY 81, 86; MTCW 1, 2; NFS 3; RGAL; TCWW 2

Dietrich, Robert
See Hunt, E(verette) Howard, (Jr.)

Difusa, Pati
See Almodovar, Pedro

Dillard, Annie 1945- .. **CLC 9, 60, 115; DAM NOV**
See also AAYA 6; AMWS 6; CA 49-52; CANR 3, 43, 62, 90; DA3; DLBY 80; MTCW 1, 2; NCFS 1; RGAL; SATA 10

Dillard, R(ichard) H(enry) W(ilde)
1937- .... **CLC 5**
See also CA 21-24R; CAAS 7; CANR 10; CP; CSW; DLB 5

Dillon, Eilis 1920-1994 .... **CLC 17**
See also CA 9-12R, 182; 147; CAAE 182; CAAS 3; CANR 4, 38, 78; CLR 26; MAICYA; SATA 2, 74; SATA-Essay 105; SATA-Obit 83; YAW

Dimont, Penelope
See Mortimer, Penelope (Ruth)

Dinesen, Isak .... **CLC 10, 29, 95; SSC 7**
See also Blixen, Karen (Christentze Dinesen)
See also FW; HGG; MTCW 1; NFS 9; RGSF; RGWL; SSFS 6

Ding Ling .... **CLC 68**
See also Chiang, Pin-chin

Diphusa, Patty
See Almodovar, Pedro

Disch, Thomas M(ichael) 1940- ... **CLC 7, 36**
See also AAYA 17; CA 21-24R; CAAS 4; CANR 17, 36, 54, 89; CLR 18; CP; DA3; DLB 8; HGG; MAICYA; MTCW 1, 2; SAAS 15; SATA 92; SFW

Disch, Tom
See Disch, Thomas M(ichael)

d'Isly, Georges
See Simenon, Georges (Jacques Christian)

Disraeli, Benjamin 1804-1881 ... **NCLC 2, 39, 79**
See also DLB 21, 55

Ditcum, Steve
See Crumb, R(obert)

Dixon, Paige
See Corcoran, Barbara

Dixon, Stephen 1936- .... **CLC 52; SSC 16**
See also CA 89-92; CANR 17, 40, 54, 91; CN; DLB 130

Doak, Annie
See Dillard, Annie

Dobell, Sydney Thompson
1824-1874 .... **NCLC 43**
See also DLB 32

Döblin, Alfred .... **TCLC 13**
See also Doeblin, Alfred

Dobrolyubov, Nikolai Alexandrovich
1836-1861 .... **NCLC 5**

Dobson, Austin 1840-1921 .... **TCLC 79**
See also DLB 35; 144

Dobyns, Stephen 1941- .... **CLC 37**
See also CA 45-48; CANR 2, 18; CMW; CP

Doctorow, E(dgar) L(aurence)
1931- .... **CLC 6, 11, 15, 18, 37, 44, 65, 113; DAM NOV, POP**
See also AAYA 22; AITN 2; AMWS 4; BEST 89:3; CA 45-48; CANR 2, 33, 51, 76, 97; CDALB 1968-1988; CN; CPW; DA3; DLB 2, 28, 173; DLBY 80; MTCW 1, 2; NFS 6; RHW

Dodgson, Charles Lutwidge 1832-1898
See Carroll, Lewis

See also CLR 2; DA; DAB; DAC; DAM MST, NOV, POET; DA3; MAICYA; SATA 100; YABC 2

Dodson, Owen (Vincent)
1914-1983 .... **CLC 79; BLC 1; DAM MULT**
See also BW 1; CA 65-68; 110; CANR 24; DLB 76

Doeblin, Alfred 1878-1957 .... **TCLC 13**
See also Döblin, Alfred
See also CA 110; 141; DLB 66

Doerr, Harriet 1910- .... **CLC 34**
See also CA 117; 122; CANR 47; INT 122

Domecq, H(onorio Bustos)
See Bioy Casares, Adolfo

Domecq, H(onorio) Bustos
See Bioy Casares, Adolfo; Borges, Jorge Luis

Domini, Rey
See Lorde, Audre (Geraldine)
See also GLL 1

Dominique
See Proust, (Valentin-Louis-George-Eug

Don, A
See Stephen, SirLeslie

Donaldson, Stephen R(eeder)
1947- .... **CLC 46, 138; DAM POP**
See also AAYA 36; CA 89-92; CANR 13, 55; CPW; FANT; INT CANR-13; SATA 121; SFW

Donleavy, J(ames) P(atrick) 1926- .... **CLC 1, 4, 6, 10, 45**
See also AITN 2; CA 9-12R; CANR 24, 49, 62, 80; CD; CN; DLB 6, 173; INT CANR-24; MTCW 1, 2

Donne, John 1572-1631 .... **LC 10, 24; DA; DAB; DAC; DAM MST, POET; PC 1; WLC**
See also CDBLB Before 1660; DLB 121, 151; PFS 2,11; RGEL

Donnell, David 1939(?)- .... **CLC 34**

Donoghue, P. S.
See Hunt, E(verette) Howard, (Jr.)

Donoso (Yañez), José 1924-1996 ... **CLC 4, 8, 11, 32, 99; DAM MULT; HLC 1; SSC 34**
See also CA 81-84; 155; CANR 32, 73; DLB 113; HW 1, 2; MTCW 1, 2

Donovan, John 1928-1992 .... **CLC 35**
See also AAYA 20; CA 97-100; 137; CLR 3; MAICYA; SATA 72; SATA-Brief 29; YAW

Don Roberto
See Cunninghame Graham, Robert (Gallnigad) Bontine

Doolittle, Hilda 1886-1961 . **CLC 3, 8, 14, 31, 34, 73; DA; DAC; DAM MST, POET; PC 5; WLC**
See also H. D.
See also AMWS 1; CA 97-100; CANR 35; DLB 4, 45; FW; GLL 1; MTCW 1, 2; PFS 6; RGAL

Dorfman, Ariel 1942- ...... **CLC 48, 77; DAM MULT; HLC 1**
See also CA 124; 130; CANR 67, 70; CWW 2; DFS 4; HW 1, 2; INT 130

Dorn, Edward (Merton)
1929-1999 .... **CLC 10, 18**
See also CA 93-96; 187; CANR 42, 79; CP; DLB 5; INT 93-96

Dor-Ner, Zvi .... **CLC 70**

Dorris, Michael (Anthony)
1945-1997 .... **CLC 109; DAM MULT, NOV**
See also AAYA 20; BEST 90:1; CA 102; 157; CANR 19, 46, 75; CLR 58; DA3; DLB 175; MTCW 2; NFS 3; NNAL; SATA 75; SATA-Obit 94; TCWW 2; YAW

Dorris, Michael A.
See Dorris, Michael (Anthony)

Dorsan, Luc
See Simenon, Georges (Jacques Christian)

Dorsange, Jean
See Simenon, Georges (Jacques Christian)

Dos Passos, John (Roderigo)
1896-1970 ... **CLC 1, 4, 8, 11, 15, 25, 34, 82; DA; DAB; DAC; DAM MST, NOV; WLC**
See also AMW; CA 1-4R; 29-32R; CANR 3; CDALB 1929-1941; DA3; DLB 4, 9; DLBD 1, 15; DLBY 96; MTCW 1, 2; RGAL

Dossage, Jean
See Simenon, Georges (Jacques Christian)

Dostoevsky, Fedor Mikhailovich
1821-1881 . **NCLC 2, 7, 21, 33, 43; DA; DAB; DAC; DAM MST, NOV; SSC 2, 33, 44; WLC**
See also AAYA 40; DA3; DLB 238; NFS 3, 8; SSFS 8

Doughty, Charles M(ontagu)
1843-1926 .... **TCLC 27**
See also CA 115; 178; DLB 19, 57, 174

Douglas, Ellen .... **CLC 73**
See also Haxton, Josephine Ayres; Williamson, Ellen Douglas
See also CN; CSW

Douglas, Gavin 1475(?)-1522 .... **LC 20**
See also DLB 132; RGEL

Douglas, George
See Brown, George Douglas
See also RGEL

Douglas, Keith (Castellain)
1920-1944 .... **TCLC 40**
See also CA 160; DLB 27

Douglas, Leonard
See Bradbury, Ray (Douglas)

Douglas, Michael
See Crichton, (John) Michael

Douglas, (George) Norman
1868-1952 .... **TCLC 68**
See also CA 119; 157; DLB 34, 195

Douglas, William
See Brown, George Douglas

Douglass, Frederick 1817(?)-1895 .. **NCLC 7, 55; BLC 1; DA; DAC; DAM MST, MULT; WLC**
See also AMWS 3; CDALB 1640-1865; DA3; DLB 1, 43, 50, 79; FW; NCFS 2; RGAL; SATA 29

Dourado, (Waldomiro Freitas) Autran
1926- .... **CLC 23, 60**
See also CA 25-28R; 179; CANR 34, 81; DLB 145; HW 2

Dourado, Waldomiro Autran
See Dourado, (Waldomiro Freitas) Autran
See also CA 179

Dove, Rita (Frances) 1952- .... **CLC 50, 81; BLCS; DAM MULT, POET; PC 6**
See also AMWS 4; BW 2; CA 109; CAAS 19; CANR 27, 42, 68, 76, 97; CDALBS; CP; CSW; CWP; DA3; DLB 120; MTCW 1; PFS 1

Doveglion
See Villa, Jose Garcia

Dowell, Coleman 1925-1985 .... **CLC 60**
See also CA 25-28R; 117; CANR 10; DLB 130; GLL 2

Dowson, Ernest (Christopher)
1867-1900 .... **TCLC 4**
See also CA 105; 150; DLB 19, 135

Doyle, A. Conan
See Doyle, Arthur Conan

Doyle, Arthur Conan 1859-1930 .... **TCLC 7; DA; DAB; DAC; DAM MST, NOV; SSC 12; WLC**
See also Doyle, Sir Arthur Conan

Dwight, Timothy 1752-1817 .... NCLC 13
    See also DLB 37; RGAL
Dworkin, Andrea 1946- .... CLC 43, 123
    See also CA 77-80; CAAS 21; CANR 16,
    39, 76, 96; FW; GLL 1; INT CANR-16;
    MTCW 1, 2
Dwyer, Deanna
    See Koontz, Dean R(ay)
Dwyer, K. R.
    See Koontz, Dean R(ay)
Dwyer, Thomas A. 1923- .... CLC 114
    See also CA 115
Dybek, Stuart 1942- .... CLC 114
    See also CA 97-100; CANR 39; DLB 130
Dye, Richard
    See De Voto, Bernard (Augustine)
Dylan, Bob 1941- .... CLC 3, 4, 6, 12, 77
    See also CA 41-44R; CP; DLB 16
Dyson, John 1943- .... CLC 70
    See also CA 144
E. V. L.
    See Lucas, E(dward) V(errall)
Eagleton, Terence (Francis) 1943- .. CLC 63,
    132
    See also CA 57-60; CANR 7, 23, 68; DLB
    242; MTCW 1, 2
Eagleton, Terry
    See Eagleton, Terence (Francis)
Early, Jack
    See Scoppettone, Sandra
    See also GLL 1
East, Michael
    See West, Morris L(anglo)
Eastaway, Edward
    See Thomas, (Philip) Edward
Eastlake, William (Derry)
    1917-1997 .... CLC 8
    See also CA 5-8R; 158; CAAS 1; CANR 5,
    63; CN; DLB 6, 206; INT CANR-5;
    TCWW 2
Eastman, Charles A(lexander)
    1858-1939 .... TCLC 55; DAM MULT
    See also CA 179; CANR 91; DLB 175;
    NNAL; YABC 1
Eberhart, Richard (Ghormley)
    1904- .. CLC 3, 11, 19, 56; DAM POET
    See also CA 1-4R; CANR 2; CDALB 1941-
    1968; CP; DLB 48; MTCW 1
Eberstadt, Fernanda 1960- .... CLC 39
    See also CA 136; CANR 69
Echegaray (y Eizaguirre), Jose (Maria
    Waldo) 1832-1916 .... TCLC 4; HLCS 1
    See also CA 104; CANR 32; HW 1; MTCW
    1
Echeverria, (Jose) Esteban (Antonino)
    1805-1851 .... NCLC 18
Echo
    See Proust, (Valentin-Louis-George-Eug
Eckert, Allan W. 1931- .... CLC 17
    See also AAYA 18; CA 13-16R; CANR 14,
    45; INT CANR-14; SAAS 21; SATA 29,
    91; SATA-Brief 27
Eckhart, Meister 1260(?)-1327(?) ... CMLC 9
    See also DLB 115
Eckmar, F. R.
    See de Hartog, Jan
Eco, Umberto 1932- .... CLC 28, 60, 142;
    DAM NOV, POP
    See also BEST 90:1; CA 77-80; CANR 12,
    33, 55; CPW; CWW 2; DA3; DLB 196,
    242; MTCW 1, 2
Eddison, E(ric) R(ucker)
    1882-1945 .... TCLC 15
    See also CA 109; 156; FANT; SFW
Eddy, Mary (Ann Morse) Baker
    1821-1910 .... TCLC 71
    See also CA 113; 174

Edel, (Joseph) Leon 1907-1997 .. CLC 29, 34
    See also CA 1-4R; 161; CANR 1, 22; DLB
    103; INT CANR-22
Eden, Emily 1797-1869 .... NCLC 10
Edgar, David 1948- .. CLC 42; DAM DRAM
    See also CA 57-60; CANR 12, 61; CBD;
    CD; DLB 13, 233; MTCW 1
Edgerton, Clyde (Carlyle) 1944- ...... CLC 39
    See also AAYA 17; CA 118; 134; CANR
    64; CSW; INT 134; YAW
Edgeworth, Maria 1768-1849 .... NCLC 1, 51
    See also BRWS 3; DLB 116, 159, 163; FW;
    RGEL; SATA 21
Edmonds, Paul
    See Kuttner, Henry
Edmonds, Walter D(umaux)
    1903-1998 .... CLC 35
    See also CA 5-8R; CANR 2; CWRI; DLB
    9; MAICYA; RHW; SAAS 4; SATA 1, 27;
    SATA-Obit 99
Edmondson, Wallace
    See Ellison, Harlan (Jay)
Edson, Russell .... CLC 13
    See also CA 33-36R
Edwards, Bronwen Elizabeth
    See Rose, Wendy
Edwards, G(erald) B(asil)
    1899-1976 .... CLC 25
    See also CA 110
Edwards, Gus 1939- .... CLC 43
    See also CA 108; INT 108
Edwards, Jonathan 1703-1758 .... LC 7, 54;
    DA; DAC; DAM MST
    See also DLB 24; RGAL
Efron, Marina Ivanovna Tsvetaeva
    See Tsve.aeva (Efron), Marina (Ivanovna)
Ehle, John (Marsden, Jr.) 1925- ...... CLC 27
    See also CA 9-12R; CSW
Ehrenbourg, Ilya (Grigoryevich)
    See Ehrenburg, Ilya (Grigoryevich)
Ehrenburg, Ilya (Grigoryevich)
    1891-1967 .... CLC 18, 34, 62
    See also CA 102; 25-28R
Ehrenburg, Ilyo (Grigoryevich)
    See Ehrenburg, Ilya (Grigoryevich)
Ehrenreich, Barbara 1941- .... CLC 110
    See also BEST 90:4; CA 73-76; CANR 16,
    37, 62; FW; MTCW 1, 2
Eich, Guenter 1907-1972 .... CLC 15
    See also Eich, Günter
    See also CA 111; 93-96; DLB 69, 124
Eich, Günter
    See Eich, Guenter
    See also RGWL
Eichendorff, Joseph 1788-1857 .... NCLC 8
    See also DLB 90
Eigner, Larry .... CLC 9
    See also Eigner, Laurence (Joel)
    See also CAAS 23; DLB 5
Eigner, Laurence (Joel) 1927-1996
    See Eigner, Larry
    See also CA 9-12R; 151; CANR 6, 84; CP;
    DLB 193
Einstein, Albert 1879-1955 .... TCLC 65
    See also CA 121; 133; MTCW 1, 2
Eiseley, Loren Corey 1907-1977 .... CLC 7
    See also AAYA 5; CA 1-4R; 73-76; CANR
    6; DLBD 17
Eisenstadt, Jill 1963- .... CLC 50
    See also CA 140
Eisenstein, Sergei (Mikhailovich)
    1898-1948 .... TCLC 57
    See also CA 114; 149
Eisner, Simon
    See Kornbluth, C(yril) M.

Ekeloef, (Bengt) Gunnar
    1907-1968 ... CLC 27; DAM POET; PC
    23
    See also CA 123; 25-28R
Ekelöf, (Bengt) Gunnar
    See Ekeloef, (Bengt) Gunnar
Ekelund, Vilhelm 1880-1949 .... TCLC 75
    See also CA 189
Ekwensi, C. O. D.
    See Ekwensi, Cyprian (Odiatu Duaka)
Ekwensi, Cyprian (Odiatu Duaka)
    1921- ...... CLC 4; BLC 1; DAM MULT
    See also BW 2, 3; CA 29-32R; CANR 18,
    42, 74; CN; CWRI; DLB 117; MTCW 1,
    2; SATA 66
Elaine .... TCLC 18
    See also Leverson, Ada
El Crummo
    See Crumb, R(obert)
Elder, Lonne III 1931-1996 .... DC 8
    See also BLC 1; BW 1, 3; CA 81-84; 152;
    CAD; CANR 25; DAM MULT; DLB 7,
    38, 44
Eleanor of Aquitaine 1122-1204 ... CMLC 39
Elia
    See Lamb, Charles
Eliade, Mircea 1907-1986 .... CLC 19
    See also CA 65-68; 119; CANR 30, 62;
    DLB 220; MTCW 1; SFW
Eliot, A. D.
    See Jewett, (Theodora) Sarah Orne
Eliot, Alice
    See Jewett, (Theodora) Sarah Orne
Eliot, Dan
    See Silverberg, Robert
Eliot, George 1819-1880 ...... NCLC 4, 13, 23,
    41, 49, 89; DA; DAB; DAC; DAM
    MST, NOV; PC 20; WLC
    See also CDBLB 1832-1890; CN; CPW;
    DA3; DLB 21, 35, 55; RGEL; RGSF;
    SSFS 8
Eliot, John 1604-1690 .... LC 5
    See also DLB 24
Eliot, T(homas) S(tearns)
    1888-1965 ...... CLC 1, 2, 3, 6, 9, 10, 13,
    15, 24, 34, 41, 55, 57, 113; DA; DAB;
    DAC; DAM DRAM, MST, POET; PC
    5, 31; WLC
    See also AAYA 28; CA 5-8R; 25-28R;
    CANR 41; CDALB 1929-1941; DA3;
    DFS 4, 13; DLB 7, 10, 45, 63; DLBY 88;
    MTCW 1, 2; PFS 1, 7
Elizabeth 1866-1941 .... TCLC 41
Elkin, Stanley L(awrence)
    1930-1995 .. CLC 4, 6, 9, 14, 27, 51, 91;
    DAM NOV, POP; SSC 12
    See also AMWS 6; CA 9-12R; 148; CANR
    8, 46; CN; CPW; DLB 2, 28; DLBY 80;
    INT CANR-8; MTCW 1, 2
Elledge, Scott .... CLC 34
Elliot, Don
    See Silverberg, Robert
Elliott, Don
    See Silverberg, Robert
Elliott, George P(aul) 1918-1980 .... CLC 2
    See also CA 1-4R; 97-100; CANR 2
Elliott, Janice 1931-1995 .... CLC 47
    See also CA 13-16R; CANR 8, 29, 84; CN;
    DLB 14; SATA 119
Elliott, Sumner Locke 1917-1991 ..... CLC 38
    See also CA 5-8R; 134; CANR 2, 21
Elliott, William
    See Bradbury, Ray (Douglas)
Ellis, A. E. .... CLC 7
Ellis, Alice Thomas .... CLC 40
    See also Haycraft, Anna (Margaret)
    See also DLB 194; MTCW 1

Fair, Ronald L. 1932- .... **CLC 18**
  See also BW 1; CA 69-72; CANR 25; DLB 33

Fairbairn, Roger
  See Carr, John Dickson

Fairbairns, Zoe (Ann) 1948- .... **CLC 32**
  See also CA 103; CANR 21, 85; CN

Fairman, Paul W. 1916-1977
  See Queen, Ellery
  See also CA 114; SFW

Falco, Gian
  See Papini, Giovanni

Falconer, James
  See Kirkup, James

Falconer, Kenneth
  See Kornbluth, C(yril) M.

Falkland, Samuel
  See Heijermans, Herman

Fallaci, Oriana 1930- .... **CLC 11, 110**
  See also CA 77-80; CANR 15, 58; FW; MTCW 1

Faludi, Susan 1959- .... **CLC 140**
  See also CA 138; FW; MTCW 1

Faludy, George 1913- .... **CLC 42**
  See also CA 21-24R

Faludy, Gyoergy
  See Faludy, George

Fanon, Frantz 1925-1961 ... **CLC 74; BLC 2; DAM MULT**
  See also BW 1; CA 116; 89-92

Fanshawe, Ann 1625-1680 .... **LC 11**

Fante, John (Thomas) 1911-1983 ..... **CLC 60**
  See also CA 69-72; 109; CANR 23; DLB 130; DLBY 83

Farah, Nuruddin 1945- .. **CLC 53, 137; BLC 2; DAM MULT**
  See also BW 2, 3; CA 106; CANR 81; CN; DLB 125

Fargue, Leon-Paul 1876(?)-1947 .... **TCLC 11**
  See also CA 109

Farigoule, Louis
  See Romains, Jules

Farina, Richard 1936(?)-1966 .... **CLC 9**
  See also CA 81-84; 25-28R

Farley, Walter (Lorimer)
  1915-1989 .... **CLC 17**
  See also CA 17-20R; CANR 8, 29, 84; DLB 22; JRDA; MAICYA; SATA 2, 43; YAW

Farmer, Philip Jose 1918- .... **CLC 1, 19**
  See also AAYA 28; CA 1-4R; CANR 4, 35; DLB 8; MTCW 1; SATA 93; SFW

Farquhar, George 1677-1707 ... **LC 21; DAM DRAM**
  See also DLB 84; RGEL

Farrell, J(ames) G(ordon)
  1935-1979 .... **CLC 6**
  See also CA 73-76; 89-92; CANR 36; DLB 14; MTCW 1; RHW

Farrell, James T(homas) 1904-1979 . **CLC 1, 4, 8, 11, 66; SSC 28**
  See also CA 5-8R; 89-92; CANR 9, 61; DLB 4, 9, 86; DLBD 2; MTCW 1, 2

Farrell, Warren (Thomas) 1943- ...... **CLC 70**
  See also CA 146

Farren, Richard J.
  See Betjeman, John

Farren, Richard M.
  See Betjeman, John

Fassbinder, Rainer Werner
  1946-1982 .... **CLC 20**
  See also CA 93-96; 106; CANR 31

Fast, Howard (Melvin) 1914- .. **CLC 23, 131; DAM NOV**
  See also AAYA 16; CA 1-4R, 181; CAAE 181; CAAS 18; CANR 1, 33, 54, 75, 98; CMW; CN; CPW; DLB 9; INT CANR-33; MTCW 1; RHW; SATA 7; SATA-Essay 107; TCWW 2; YAW

Faulcon, Robert
  See Holdstock, Robert P.

Faulkner, William (Cuthbert)
  1897-1962 .... **CLC 1, 3, 6, 8, 9, 11, 14, 18, 28, 52, 68; DA; DAB; DAC; DAM MST, NOV; SSC 1, 35, 42; WLC**
  See also AAYA 7; CA 81-84; CANR 33; CDALB 1929-1941; DA3; DLB 9, 11, 44, 102; DLBD 2; DLBY 86, 97; MTCW 1, 2; NFS 4, 8; SSFS 2, 5, 6, 12

Fauset, Jessie Redmon
  1882(?)-1961 .... **CLC 19, 54; BLC 2; DAM MULT**
  See also AFAW 2; BW 1; CA 109; CANR 83; DLB 51; FW

Faust, Frederick (Schiller)
  1892-1944(?) .... **TCLC 49; DAM POP**
  See also Austin, Frank; Brand, Max; Challis, George; Dawson, Peter; Dexter, Martin; Evans, Evan; Frederick, John; Frost, Frederick; Manning, David; Silver, Nicholas
  See also CA 108; 152

Faust, Irvin 1924- .... **CLC 8**
  See also CA 33-36R; CANR 28, 67; CN; DLB 2, 28; DLBY 80

Fawkes, Guy
  See Benchley, Robert (Charles)

Fearing, Kenneth (Flexner)
  1902-1961 .... **CLC 51**
  See also CA 93-96; CANR 59; CMW; DLB 9

Fecamps, Elise
  See Creasey, John

Federman, Raymond 1928- .... **CLC 6, 47**
  See also CA 17-20R; CAAS 8; CANR 10, 43, 83; CN; DLBY 80

Federspiel, J(uerg) F. 1931- .... **CLC 42**
  See also CA 146

Feiffer, Jules (Ralph) 1929- ..... **CLC 2, 8, 64; DAM DRAM**
  See also AAYA 3; CA 17-20R; CAD; CANR 30, 59; CD; DLB 7, 44; INT CANR-30; MTCW 1; SATA 8, 61, 111

Feige, Hermann Albert Otto Maximilian
  See Traven, B.

Feinberg, David B. 1956-1994 .... **CLC 59**
  See also CA 135; 147

Feinstein, Elaine 1930- .... **CLC 36**
  See also CA 69-72; CAAS 1; CANR 31, 68; CN; CP; CWP; DLB 14, 40; MTCW 1

Feke, Gilbert David .... **CLC 65**

Feldman, Irving (Mordecai) 1928- ..... **CLC 7**
  See also CA 1-4R; CANR 1; CP; DLB 169

Felix-Tchicaya, Gerald
  See Tchicaya, Gerald Felix

Fellini, Federico 1920-1993 .... **CLC 16, 85**
  See also CA 65-68; 143; CANR 33

Felsen, Henry Gregor 1916-1995 ..... **CLC 17**
  See also CA 1-4R; 180; CANR 1; SAAS 2; SATA 1

Felski, Rita .... **CLC 65**

Fenno, Jack
  See Calisher, Hortense

Fenollosa, Ernest (Francisco)
  1853-1908 .... **TCLC 91**

Fenton, James Martin 1949- .... **CLC 32**
  See also CA 102; CP; DLB 40; PFS 11

Ferber, Edna 1887-1968 .... **CLC 18, 93**
  See also AITN 1; CA 5-8R; 25-28R; CANR 68; DLB 9, 28, 86; MTCW 1, 2; RGAL; RHW; SATA 7; TCWW 2

Ferdowsi, Abu'l Qāsem 940-1020 . **CMLC 43**

Ferguson, Helen
  See Kavan, Anna

Ferguson, Niall 1964- .... **CLC 134**
  See also CA 190

Ferguson, Samuel 1810-1886 .... **NCLC 33**
  See also DLB 32

Fergusson, Robert 1750-1774 .... **LC 29**
  See also DLB 109; RGEL

Ferling, Lawrence
  See Ferlinghetti, Lawrence (Monsanto)

Ferlinghetti, Lawrence (Monsanto)
  1919(?)- .... **CLC 2, 6, 10, 27, 111; DAM POET; PC 1**
  See also CA 5-8R; CANR 3, 41, 73; CDALB 1941-1968; CP; DA3; DLB 5, 16; MTCW 1, 2

Fern, Fanny
  See Parton, Sara Payson Willis

Fernandez, Vicente Garcia Huidobro
  See Huidobro Fernandez, Vicente Garcia

Fernandez-Armesto, Felipe .... **CLC 70**

Fernandez de Lizardi, Jose Joaquin
  See Lizardi, Jose Joaquin Fernandez de

Ferre, Rosario 1942- ...... **CLC 139; HLCS 1; SSC 36**
  See also CA 131; CANR 55, 81; CWW 2; DLB 145; HW 1, 2; MTCW 1

Ferrer, Gabriel (Francisco Victor) Miro
  See Miro (Ferrer), Gabriel (Francisco Victor)

Ferrier, Susan (Edmonstone)
  1782-1854 .... **NCLC 8**
  See also DLB 116

Ferrigno, Robert 1948(?)- .... **CLC 65**
  See also CA 140

Ferron, Jacques 1921-1985 .... **CLC 94; DAC**
  See also CA 117; 129; CCA 1; DLB 60

Feuchtwanger, Lion 1884-1958 .... **TCLC 3**
  See also CA 104; 187; DLB 66

Feuillet, Octave 1821-1890 .... **NCLC 45**
  See also DLB 192

Feydeau, Georges (Léon Jules Marie)
  1862-1921 .... **TCLC 22; DAM DRAM**
  See also CA 113; 152; CANR 84; DLB 192; EW; GFL 1789 to the Present; RGWL

Fichte, Johann Gottlieb
  1762-1814 .... **NCLC 62**
  See also DLB 90

Ficino, Marsilio 1433-1499 .... **LC 12**

Fiedeler, Hans
  See Doeblin, Alfred

Fiedler, Leslie A(aron) 1917- .. **CLC 4, 13, 24**
  See also CA 9-12R; CANR 7, 63; CN; DLB 28, 67; MTCW 1, 2

Field, Andrew 1938- .... **CLC 44**
  See also CA 97-100; CANR 25

Field, Eugene 1850-1895 .... **NCLC 3**
  See also DLB 23, 42, 140; DLBD 13; MAICYA; RGAL; SATA 16

Field, Gans T.
  See Wellman, Manly Wade

Field, Michael 1915-1971 .... **TCLC 43**
  See also CA 29-32R

Field, Peter
  See Hobson, Laura Z(ametkin)
  See also TCWW 2

Fielding, Helen 1959(?)- .... **CLC 146**
  See also CA 172; DLB 231

Fielding, Henry 1707-1754 ..... **LC 1, 46; DA; DAB; DAC; DAM DRAM, MST, NOV; WLC**
  See also CDBLB 1660-1789; DA3; DLB 39, 84, 101; RGEL

Fielding, Sarah 1710-1768 .... **LC 1, 44**
  See also DLB 39; RGEL

Fields, W. C. 1880-1946 .... **TCLC 80**
  See also DLB 44

Fierstein, Harvey (Forbes) 1954- .... **CLC 33; DAM DRAM, POP**
  See also CA 123; 129; CAD; CD; CPW; DA3; DFS 6; GLL

Genet, Jean 1910-1986 .. **CLC 1, 2, 5, 10, 14, 44, 46; DAM DRAM**
See also CA 13-16R; CANR 18; DA3; DFS 10; DLB 72; DLBY 86; GFL 1789 to the Present; GLL 1; MTCW 1, 2; RGWL

Gent, Peter 1942- .... **CLC 29**
See also AITN 1; CA 89-92; DLBY 82

Gentile, Giovanni 1875-1944 .... **TCLC 96**
See also CA 119

Gentlewoman in New England, A
See Bradstreet, Anne

Gentlewoman in Those Parts, A
See Bradstreet, Anne

Geoffrey of Monmouth c. 1100-1155 .... **CMLC 44**
See also DLB 146

George, Jean Craighead 1919- .... **CLC 35**
See also AAYA 8; CA 5-8R; CANR 25; CLR 1; DLB 52; JRDA; MAICYA; SATA 2, 68; YAW

George, Stefan (Anton) 1868-1933 . **TCLC 2, 14**
See also CA 104

Georges, Georges Martin
See Simenon, Georges (Jacques Christian)

Gerhardi, William Alexander
See Gerhardie, William Alexander

Gerhardie, William Alexander 1895-1977 .... **CLC 5**
See also CA 25-28R; 73-76; CANR 18; DLB 36

Gerstler, Amy 1956- .... **CLC 70**
See also CA 146

Gertler, T. .... **CLC 134**
See also CA 116; 121

Ghalib .... **NCLC 39, 78**
See also Ghālib, Asadullāh Khān

Ghālib, Asadullāh Khān 1797-1869
See Ghalib
See also DAM POET

Ghelderode, Michel de 1898-1962 ..... **CLC 6, 11; DAM DRAM; DC 15**
See also CA 85-88; CANR 40, 77

Ghiselin, Brewster 1903- .... **CLC 23**
See also CA 13-16R; CAAS 10; CANR 13; CP

Ghose, Aurabinda 1872-1950 .... **TCLC 63**
See also CA 163

Ghose, Zulfikar 1935- .... **CLC 42**
See also CA 65-68; CANR 67; CN; CP

Ghosh, Amitav 1956- .... **CLC 44**
See also CA 147; CANR 80; CN

Giacosa, Giuseppe 1847-1906 .... **TCLC 7**
See also CA 104

Gibb, Lee
See Waterhouse, Keith (Spencer)

Gibbon, Lewis Grassic .... **TCLC 4**
See also Mitchell, James Leslie

Gibbons, Kaye 1960- .... **CLC 50, 88, 145; DAM POP**
See also AAYA 34; CA 151; CANR 75; CSW; DA3; MTCW 1; NFS 3; RGAL; SATA 117

Gibran, Kahlil 1883-1931 .... **TCLC 1, 9; DAM POET, POP; PC 9**
See also CA 104; 150; DA3; MTCW 2

Gibran, Khalil
See Gibran, Kahlil

Gibson, William 1914- .. **CLC 23; DA; DAB; DAC; DAM DRAM, MST**
See also CA 9-12R; CAD; CANR 9, 42, 75; CD; CN; CPW; DFS 2; DLB 7; MTCW 1; SATA 66; SCFW 2; SFW; YAW

Gibson, William (Ford) 1948- ... **CLC 39, 63; DAM POP**
See also AAYA 12; CA 126; 133; CANR 52, 90; DA3; MTCW 1

Gide, André (Paul Guillaume) 1869-1951 . **TCLC 5, 12, 36; DA; DAB; DAC; DAM MST, NOV; SSC 13; WLC**
See also CA 104; 124; DA3; DLB 65; EW; GFL 1789 to the Present; MTCW 1, 2; RGSF; RGWL

Gifford, Barry (Colby) 1946- .... **CLC 34**
See also CA 65-68; CANR 9, 30, 40, 90

Gilbert, Frank
See De Voto, Bernard (Augustine)

Gilbert, W(illiam) S(chwenck) 1836-1911 ...., **TCLC 3; DAM DRAM, POET**
See also CA 104; 173; SATA 36

Gilbreth, Frank B., Jr. 1911-2001 .... **CLC 17**
See also CA 9-12R; SATA 2

Gilchrist, Ellen 1935- .... **CLC 34, 48, 143; DAM POP; SSC 14**
See also CA 113; 116; CANR 41, 61; CN; CPW; CSW; DLB 130; MTCW 1, 2; RGAL; RGSF; SSFS 9

Giles, Molly 1942- .... **CLC 39**
See also CA 126; CANR 98

Gill, Eric 1882-1940 .... **TCLC 85**

Gill, Patrick
See Creasey, John

Gillette, Douglas .... **CLC 70**

Gilliam, Terry (Vance) 1940- .... **CLC 21, 141**
See also Monty Python
See also AAYA 19; CA 108; 113; CANR 35; INT 113

Gillian, Jerry
See Gilliam, Terry (Vance)

Gilliatt, Penelope (Ann Douglass) 1932-1993 .... **CLC 2, 10, 13, 53**
See also AITN 2; CA 13-16R; 141; CANR 49; DLB 14

Gilman, Charlotte (Anna) Perkins (Stetson) 1860-1935 .... **TCLC 9, 37; SSC 13**
See also CA 106; 150; DLB 221; FW; HGG; MTCW 1; SFW; SSFS 1

Gilmour, David 1949- .... **CLC 35**
See also CA 138, 147

Gilpin, William 1724-1804 .... **NCLC 30**

Gilray, J. D.
See Mencken, H(enry) L(ouis)

Gilroy, Frank D(aniel) 1925- .... **CLC 2**
See also CA 81-84; CAD; CANR 32, 64, 86; CD; DLB 7

Gilstrap, John 1957(?)- .... **CLC 99**
See also CA 160

Ginsberg, Allen 1926-1997 .... **CLC 1, 2, 3, 4, 6, 13, 36, 69, 109; DA; DAB; DAC; DAM MST, POET; PC 4; WLC**
See also AAYA 33; AITN 1; AMWS 2; CA 1-4R; 157; CANR 2, 41, 63, 95; CDALB 1941-1968; CP; DA3; DLB 5, 16, 169; GLL 1; MTCW 1, 2; PFS 5; RGAL

Ginzburg, Eugenia .... **CLC 59**

Ginzburg, Natalia 1916-1991 .... **CLC 5, 11, 54, 70**
See also CA 85-88; 135; CANR 33; DLB 177; MTCW 1, 2; RGWL

Giono, Jean 1895-1970 .... **CLC 4, 11**
See also CA 45-48; 29-32R; CANR 2, 35; DLB 72; GFL 1789 to the Present; MTCW 1; RGWL

Giovanni, Nikki 1943- .... **CLC 2, 4, 19, 64, 117; BLC 2; DA; DAB; DAC; DAM MST, MULT, POET; PC 19; WLCS**
See also AAYA 22; AITN 1; BW 2, 3; CA 29-32R; CAAS 6; CANR 18, 41, 60, 91; CDALBS; CLR 6; CP; CSW; CWP; CWRI; DA3; DLB 5, 41; INT CANR-18; MAICYA; MTCW 1, 2; RGAL; SATA 24, 107; YAW

Giovene, Andrea 1904- .... **CLC 7**
See also CA 85-88

Gippius, Zinaida (Nikolayevna) 1869-1945
See Hippius, Zinaida
See also CA 106

Giraudoux, Jean(-Hippolyte) 1882-1944 .... **TCLC 2, 7; DAM DRAM**
See also CA 104; DLB 65; EW; GFL 1789 to the Present; RGWL

Gironella, José María 1917-1991 ..... **CLC 11**
See also CA 101

Gissing, George (Robert) 1857-1903 .... **TCLC 3, 24, 47; SSC 37**
See also CA 105; 167; DLB 18, 135, 184

Giurlani, Aldo
See Palazzeschi, Aldo

Gladkov, Fyodor (Vasilyevich) 1883-1958 .... **TCLC 27**
See also CA 170

Glanville, Brian (Lester) 1931- .... **CLC 6**
See also CA 5-8R; CAAS 9; CANR 3, 70; CN; DLB 15, 139; SATA 42

Glasgow, Ellen (Anderson Gholson) 1873-1945 .... **TCLC 2, 7; SSC 34**
See also CA 104; 164; DLB 9, 12; MTCW 2; RHW; SSFS 9

Glaspell, Susan 1882(?)-1948 . **TCLC 55; DC 10; SSC 41**
See also AMWS 3; CA 110; 154; DFS 8; DLB 7, 9, 78, 228; RGAL; SSFS 3; TCWW 2; YABC 2

Glassco, John 1909-1981 .... **CLC 9**
See also CA 13-16R; 102; CANR 15; DLB 68

Glasscock, Amnesia
See Steinbeck, John (Ernst)

Glasser, Ronald J. 1940(?)- .... **CLC 37**

Glassman, Joyce
See Johnson, Joyce

Glendinning, Victoria 1937- .... **CLC 50**
See also CA 120; 127; CANR 59, 89; DLB 155

Glissant, Edouard 1928- . **CLC 10, 68; DAM MULT**
See also CA 153; CWW 2

Gloag, Julian 1930- .... **CLC 40**
See also AITN 1; CA 65-68; CANR 10, 70; CN

Glowacki, Aleksander
See Prus, Boleslaw

Glück, Louise (Elisabeth) 1943- .. **CLC 7, 22, 44, 81; DAM POET; PC 16**
See also AMWS 5; CA 33-36R; CANR 40, 69; CP; CWP; DA3; DLB 5; MTCW 2; PFS 5

Glyn, Elinor 1864-1943 .... **TCLC 72**
See also DLB 153; RHW

Gobineau, Joseph-Arthur 1816-1882 .... **NCLC 17**
See also DLB 123; GFL 1789 to the Present

Godard, Jean-Luc 1930- .... **CLC 20**
See also CA 93-96

Godden, (Margaret) Rumer 1907-1998 .... **CLC 53**
See also AAYA 6; CA 5-8R; 172; CANR 4, 27, 36, 55, 80; CLR 20; CN; CWRI; DLB 161; MAICYA; RHW; SAAS 12; SATA 3, 36; SATA-Obit 109

Godoy Alcayaga, Lucila 1899-1957 .... **TCLC 2; DAM MULT; HLC 2; PC 32**
See also Mistral, Gabriela
See also BW 2; CA 104; 131; CANR 81; DNFS 1; HW 1, 2; MTCW 1, 2

Godwin, Gail (Kathleen) 1937- ..... **CLC 5, 8, 22, 31, 69, 125; DAM POP**
See also CA 29-32R; CANR 15, 43, 69; CN; CPW; CSW; DA3; DLB 6, 234; INT CANR-15; MTCW 1, 2

Godwin, William 1756-1836 .... **NCLC 14**
See also CDBLB 1789-1832; CMW; DLB
39, 104, 142, 158, 163; HGG; RGEL
Goebbels, Josef
See Goebbels, (Paul) Joseph
Goebbels, (Paul) Joseph
1897-1945 .... **TCLC 68**
See also CA 115; 148
Goebbels, Joseph Paul
See Goebbels, (Paul) Joseph
Goethe, Johann Wolfgang von
1749-1832 ...... **NCLC 4, 22, 34, 90; DA;**
DAB; DAC; DAM DRAM, MST,
POET; PC 5; SSC 38; WLC
See also DA3; DLB 94
Gogarty, Oliver St. John
1878-1957 .... **TCLC 15**
See also CA 109; 150; DLB 15, 19
Gogol, Nikolai (Vasilyevich)
1809-1852 . **NCLC 5, 15, 31; DA; DAB;**
DAC; DAM DRAM, MST; DC 1; SSC
4, 29; WLC
See also DFS 12; DLB 198; SSFS 7
Goines, Donald 1937(?)-1974 . **CLC 80; BLC**
2; DAM MULT, POP
See also AITN 1; BW 1, 3; CA 124; 114;
CANR 82; CMW; DA3; DLB 33
Gold, Herbert 1924- .... **CLC 4, 7, 14, 42**
See also CA 9-12R; CANR 17, 45; CN;
DLB 2; DLBY 81
Goldbarth, Albert 1948- .... **CLC 5, 38**
See also CA 53-56; CANR 6, 40; CP; DLB
120
Goldberg, Anatol 1910-1982 .... **CLC 34**
See also CA 131; 117
Goldemberg, Isaac 1945- .... **CLC 52**
See also CA 69-72; CAAS 12; CANR 11,
32; HW 1
Golding, William (Gerald)
1911-1993 ..... **CLC 1, 2, 3, 8, 10, 17, 27,**
58, 81; DA; DAB; DAC; DAM MST,
NOV; WLC
See also AAYA 5; BRWS 1; CA 5-8R; 141;
CANR 13, 33, 54; CDBLB 1945-1960;
DA3; DLB 15, 100; HGG; MTCW 1, 2;
NFS 2; RHW; SFW; YAW
Goldman, Emma 1869-1940 .... **TCLC 13**
See also CA 110; 150; DLB 221; FW;
RGAL
Goldman, Francisco 1954- .... **CLC 76**
See also CA 162
Goldman, William (W.) 1931- ...... **CLC 1, 48**
See also CA 9-12R; CANR 29, 69; CN;
DLB 44; FANT; IDFW 3
Goldmann, Lucien 1913-1970 .... **CLC 24**
See also CA 25-28; CAP 2
Goldoni, Carlo 1707-1793 .... **LC 4; DAM**
DRAM
See also RGWL
Goldsberry, Steven 1949- .... **CLC 34**
See also CA 131
Goldsmith, Oliver 1730-1774 . **LC 2, 48; DA;**
DAB; DAC; DAM DRAM, MST, NOV,
POET; DC 8; WLC
See also CDBLB 1660-1789; DFS 1; DLB
39, 89, 104, 109, 142; SATA 26
Goldsmith, Peter
See Priestley, J(ohn) B(oynton)
Gombrowicz, Witold 1904-1969 .... **CLC 4, 7,**
11, 49; DAM DRAM
See also CA 19-20; 25-28R; CAP 2; RGWL
Gomez de la Serna, Ramon
1888-1963 .... **CLC 9**
See also CA 153; 116; CANR 79; HW 1, 2
Goncharov, Ivan Alexandrovich
1812-1891 .... **NCLC 1, 63**
See also DLB 238

Goncourt, Edmond (Louis Antoine Huot) de
1822-1896 .... **NCLC 7**
See also DLB 123; EW; GFL 1789 to the
Present; RGWL
Goncourt, Jules (Alfred Huot) de
1830-1870 .... **NCLC 7**
See also DLB 123; EW; GFL 1789 to the
Present; RGWL
Gontier, Fernande 19(?)- .... **CLC 50**
Gonzalez Martinez, Enrique
1871-1952 .... **TCLC 72**
See also CA 166; CANR 81; HW 1, 2
Goodman, Paul 1911-1972 ..... **CLC 1, 2, 4, 7**
See also CA 19-20; 37-40R; CAD; CANR
34; CAP 2; DLB 130; MTCW 1; RGAL
Gordimer, Nadine 1923- ...... **CLC 3, 5, 7, 10,**
18, 33, 51, 70, 123; DA; DAB; DAC;
DAM MST, NOV; SSC 17; WLCS
See also AAYA 39; BRWS 2; CA 5-8R;
CANR 3, 28, 56, 88; CN; DA3; DLB 225;
INT CANR-28; MTCW 1, 2; NFS 4;
RGEL; RGSF; SSFS 2; YAW
Gordon, Adam Lindsay
1833-1870 .... **NCLC 21**
See also DLB 230
Gordon, Caroline 1895-1981 . **CLC 6, 13, 29,**
83; SSC 15
See also CA 11-12; 103; CANR 36; CAP 1;
DLB 4, 9, 102; DLBD 17; DLBY 81;
MTCW 1, 2; RGAL; RGSF
Gordon, Charles William 1860-1937
See Connor, Ralph
See also CA 109
Gordon, Mary (Catherine) 1949- .... **CLC 13,**
22, 128
See also AMWS 4; CA 102; CANR 44, 92;
CN; DLB 6; DLBY 81; FW; INT 102;
MTCW 1
Gordon, N. J.
See Bosman, Herman Charles
Gordon, Sol 1923- .... **CLC 26**
See also CA 53-56; CANR 4; SATA 11
Gordone, Charles 1925-1995 .... **CLC 1, 4;**
DAM DRAM; DC 8
See also BW 1, 3; CA 93-96; 180; 150;
CAAE 180; CAD; CANR 55; DLB 7; INT
93-96; MTCW 1
Gore, Catherine 1800-1861 .... **NCLC 65**
See also DLB 116
Gorenko, Anna Andreevna
See Akhmatova, Anna
Gorky, Maxim .... **TCLC 8; DAB; SSC 28;**
WLC
See also Peshkov, Alexei Maximovich
See also DFS 9; MTCW 2
Goryan, Sirak
See Saroyan, William
Gosse, Edmund (William)
1849-1928 .... **TCLC 28**
See also CA 117; DLB 57, 144, 184
Gotlieb, Phyllis Fay (Bloom) 1926- .. **CLC 18**
See also CA 13-16R; CANR 7; DLB 88;
SFW
Gottesman, S. D.
See Kornbluth, C(yril) M.; Pohl, Frederik
Gottfried von Strassburg fl. c.
1170-1215 .... **CMLC 10**
See also DLB 138
Gould, Lois .... **CLC 4, 10**
See also CA 77-80; CANR 29; MTCW 1
Gourmont, Remy(-Marie-Charles) de
1858-1915 .... **TCLC 17**
See also CA 109; 150; GFL 1789 to the
Present; MTCW 2
Govier, Katherine 1948- .... **CLC 51**
See also CA 101; CANR 18, 40; CCA 1

Goyen, (Charles) William
1915-1983 .... **CLC 5, 8, 14, 40**
See also AITN 2; CA 5-8R; 110; CANR 6,
71; DLB 2; DLBY 83; INT CANR-6
Goytisolo, Juan 1931- .... **CLC 5, 10, 23, 133;**
DAM MULT; HLC 1
See also CA 85-88; CANR 32, 61; CWW
2; GLL 2; HW 1, 2; MTCW 1, 2
Gozzano, Guido 1883-1916 .... **PC 10**
See also CA 154; DLB 114
Gozzi, (Conte) Carlo 1720-1806 .... **NCLC 23**
Grabbe, Christian Dietrich
1801-1836 .... **NCLC 2**
See also DLB 133; RGWL
Grace, Patricia Frances 1937- .... **CLC 56**
See also CA 176; CN
Gracian y Morales, Baltasar
1601-1658 .... **LC 15**
Gracq, Julien .... **CLC 11, 48**
See also Poirier, Louis
See also CWW 2; DLB 83; GFL 1789 to
the Present
Grade, Chaim 1910-1982 .... **CLC 10**
See also CA 93-96; 107
Graduate of Oxford, A
See Ruskin, John
Grafton, Garth
See Duncan, Sara Jeannette
Graham, John
See Phillips, David Graham
Graham, Jorie 1951- .... **CLC 48, 118**
See also CA 111; CANR 63; CP; CWP;
DLB 120; PFS 10
Graham, R(obert) B(ontine) Cunninghame
See Cunninghame Graham, Robert
(Gallnigad) Bontine
See also DLB 98, 135, 174
Graham, Robert
See Haldeman, Joe (William)
Graham, Tom
See Lewis, (Harry) Sinclair
Graham, W(illiam) S(idney)
1918-1986 .... **CLC 29**
See also CA 73-76; 118; DLB 20
Graham, Winston (Mawdsley)
1910- .... **CLC 23**
See also CA 49-52; CANR 2, 22, 45, 66;
CMW; CN; DLB 77; RHW
Grahame, Kenneth 1859-1932 ...... **TCLC 64;**
DAB
See also CA 108; 136; CANR 80; CLR 5;
CWRI; DA3; DLB 34, 141, 178; FANT;
MAICYA; MTCW 2; RGEL; SATA 100;
YABC 1
Granger, Darius John
See Marlowe, Stephen
Granin, Daniil .... **CLC 59**
Granovsky, Timofei Nikolaevich
1813-1855 .... **NCLC 75**
See also DLB 198
Grant, Skeeter
See Spiegelman, Art
Granville-Barker, Harley
1877-1946 .... **TCLC 2; DAM DRAM**
See also Barker, Harley Granville
See also CA 104
Granzotto, Gianni
See Granzotto, Giovanni Battista
Granzotto, Giovanni Battista
1914-1985 .... **CLC 70**
See also CA 166
Grass, Guenter (Wilhelm) 1927- ... **CLC 1, 2,**
4, 6, 11, 15, 22, 32, 49, 88; DA; DAB;
DAC; DAM MST, NOV; WLC
See also CA 13-16R; CANR 20, 75, 93;
DA3; DLB 75, 124; MTCW 1, 2
Gratton, Thomas
See Hulme, T(homas) E(rnest)

Hammett, (Samuel) Dashiell
1894-1961 .... **CLC 3, 5, 10, 19, 47; SSC 17**
See also AITN 1; AMWS 4; CA 81-84; CANR 42; CDALB 1929-1941; CMW; DA3; DLB 226; DLBD 6; DLBY 96; MTCW 1, 2

Hammon, Jupiter 1720(?)-1800(?) . **NCLC 5; BLC 2; DAM MULT, POET; PC 16**
See also DLB 31, 50

Hammond, Keith
See Kuttner, Henry

Hamner, Earl (Henry), Jr. 1923- ...... **CLC 12**
See also AITN 2; CA 73-76; DLB 6

Hampton, Christopher (James)
1946- .... **CLC 4**
See also CA 25-28R; CD; DLB 13; MTCW 1

Hamsun, Knut .... **TCLC 2, 14, 49**
See also Pedersen, Knut
See also RGWL

Handke, Peter 1942- .... **CLC 5, 8, 10, 15, 38, 134; DAM DRAM, NOV**
See also CA 77-80; CANR 33, 75; CWW 2; DLB 85, 124; MTCW 1, 2

Handy, W(illiam) C(hristopher)
1873-1958 .... **TCLC 97**
See also BW 3; CA 121; 167

Hanley, James 1901-1985 ..... **CLC 3, 5, 8, 13**
See also CA 73-76; 117; CANR 36; CBD; DLB 191; MTCW 1; RGEL

Hannah, Barry 1942- .... **CLC 23, 38, 90**
See also CA 108; 110; CANR 43, 68; CN; CSW; DLB 6, 234; INT CA-110; MTCW 1; RGSF

Hannon, Ezra
See Hunter, Evan

Hansberry, Lorraine (Vivian)
1930-1965 ..... **CLC 17, 62; BLC 2; DA; DAB; DAC; DAM DRAM, MST, MULT; DC 2**
See also AAYA 25; AFAW 1, 2; AMWS 4; BW 1, 3; CA 109; 25-28R; CABS 3; CANR 58; CDALB 1941-1968; DA3; DFS 2; DLB 7, 38; FW; MTCW 1, 2

Hansen, Joseph 1923- .... **CLC 38**
See also Brock, Rose; Colton, James
See also CA 29-32R; CAAS 17; CANR 16, 44, 66; CMW; DLB 226; GLL 1; INT CANR-16

Hansen, Martin A(lfred)
1909-1955 .... **TCLC 32**
See also CA 167; DLB 214

Hansen and Philipson eds. .... **CLC 65**

Hanson, Kenneth O(stlin) 1922- .... **CLC 13**
See also CA 53-56; CANR 7

Hardwick, Elizabeth (Bruce)
1916- .... **CLC 13; DAM NOV**
See also AMWS 3; CA 5-8R; CANR 3, 32, 70; CN; CSW; DA3; DLB 6; MTCW 1, 2

Hardy, Thomas 1840-1928 .. **TCLC 4, 10, 18, 32, 48, 53, 72; DA; DAB; DAC; DAM MST, NOV, POET; PC 8; SSC 2; WLC**
See also CA 104; 123; CDBLB 1890-1914; DA3; DLB 18, 19, 135; MTCW 1, 2; NFS 3, 11; PFS 3, 4; RGEL; RGSF

Hare, David 1947- .... **CLC 29, 58, 136**
See also BRWS 4; CA 97-100; CANR 39, 91; CBD; CD; DFS 4, 7; DLB 13; MTCW 1

Harewood, John
See Van Druten, John (William)

Harford, Henry
See Hudson, W(illiam) H(enry)

Hargrave, Leonie
See Disch, Thomas M(ichael)

Harjo, Joy 1951- ...... **CLC 83; DAM MULT; PC 27**
See also CA 114; CANR 35, 67, 91; CP; CWP; DLB 120, 175; MTCW 2; NNAL; RGAL

Harlan, Louis R(udolph) 1922- .... **CLC 34**
See also CA 21-24R; CANR 25, 55, 80

Harling, Robert 1951(?)- .... **CLC 53**
See also CA 147

Harmon, William (Ruth) 1938- .... **CLC 38**
See also CA 33-36R; CANR 14, 32, 35; SATA 65

Harper, F. E. W.
See Harper, Frances Ellen Watkins

Harper, Frances E. W.
See Harper, Frances Ellen Watkins

Harper, Frances E. Watkins
See Harper, Frances Ellen Watkins

Harper, Frances Ellen
See Harper, Frances Ellen Watkins

Harper, Frances Ellen Watkins
1825-1911 ...... **TCLC 14; BLC 2; DAM MULT, POET; PC 21**
See also AFAW 1, 2; BW 1, 3; CA 111; 125; CANR 79; DLB 50, 221

Harper, Michael S(teven) 1938- ... **CLC 7, 22**
See also AFAW 2; BW 1; CA 33-36R; CANR 24; CP; DLB 41

Harper, Mrs. F. E. W.
See Harper, Frances Ellen Watkins

Harris, Christie (Lucy) Irwin
1907- .... **CLC 12**
See also CA 5-8R; CANR 6, 83; CLR 47; DLB 88; JRDA; MAICYA; SAAS 10; SATA 6, 74; SATA-Essay 116

Harris, Frank 1856-1931 .... **TCLC 24**
See also CA 109; 150; CANR 80; DLB 156, 197; RGEL

Harris, George Washington
1814-1869 .... **NCLC 23**
See also DLB 3, 11; RGAL

Harris, Joel Chandler 1848-1908 ... **TCLC 2; SSC 19**
See also CA 104; 137; CANR 80; CLR 49; DLB 11, 23, 42, 78, 91; MAICYA; RGSF; SATA 100; YABC 1

Harris, John (Wyndham Parkes Lucas) Beynon 1903-1969
See Wyndham, John
See also CA 102; 89-92; CANR 84; SATA 118; SFW

Harris, MacDonald .... **CLC 9**
See also Heiney, Donald (William)

Harris, Mark 1922- .... **CLC 19**
See also CA 5-8R; CAAS 3; CANR 2, 55, 83; CN; DLB 2; DLBY 80

Harris, Norman .... **CLC 65**

Harris, (Theodore) Wilson 1921- ..... **CLC 25**
See also BW 2, 3; CA 65-68; CAAS 16; CANR 11, 27, 69; CN; CP; DLB 117; MTCW 1

Harrison, Barbara Grizzuti 1934- . **CLC 144**
See also CA 77-80; CANR 15, 48; INT CANR-15

Harrison, Elizabeth Cavanna 1909-
See Cavanna, Betty
See also CA 9-12R; CANR 6, 27, 85; YAW

Harrison, Harry (Max) 1925- .... **CLC 42**
See also CA 1-4R; CANR 5, 21, 84; DLB 8; SATA 4; SCFW 2; SFW

Harrison, James (Thomas) 1937- ...... **CLC 6, 14, 33, 66, 143; SSC 19**
See also Harrison, Jim
See also CA 13-16R; CANR 8, 51, 79; CN; CP; DLBY 82; INT CANR-8

Harrison, Jim
See Harrison, James (Thomas)
See also AMWS 8; RGAL; TCWW 2

Harrison, Kathryn 1961- .... **CLC 70**
See also CA 144; CANR 68

Harrison, Tony 1937- .... **CLC 43, 129**
See also BRWS 5; CA 65-68; CANR 44, 98; CBD; CD; CP; DLB 40; MTCW 1; RGEL

Harriss, Will(ard Irvin) 1922- .... **CLC 34**
See also CA 111

Harson, Sley
See Ellison, Harlan (Jay)

Hart, Ellis
See Ellison, Harlan (Jay)

Hart, Josephine 1942(?)- .... **CLC 70; DAM POP**
See also CA 138; CANR 70; CPW

Hart, Moss 1904-1961 .... **CLC 66; DAM DRAM**
See also CA 109; 89-92; CANR 84; DFS 1; DLB 7; RGAL

Harte, (Francis) Bret(t)
1836(?)-1902 ... **TCLC 1, 25; DA; DAC; DAM MST; SSC 8; WLC**
See also AMWS 2; CA 104; 140; CANR 80; CDALB 1865-1917; DA3; DLB 12, 64, 74, 79, 186; SATA 26; SSFS 3

Hartley, L(eslie) P(oles) 1895-1972 ... **CLC 2, 22**
See also CA 45-48; 37-40R; CANR 33; DLB 15, 139; HGG; MTCW 1, 2

Hartman, Geoffrey H. 1929- .... **CLC 27**
See also CA 117; 125; CANR 79; DLB 67

Hartmann, Sadakichi 1869-1944 ... **TCLC 73**
See also CA 157; DLB 54

Hartmann von Aue c. 1170-c.
1210 .... **CMLC 15**
See also DLB 138

Haruf, Kent 1943- .... **CLC 34**
See also CA 149; CANR 91

Harwood, Ronald 1934- .... **CLC 32; DAM DRAM, MST**
See also CA 1-4R; CANR 4, 55; CBD; CD; DLB 13

Hasegawa Tatsunosuke
See Futabatei, Shimei

Hašek, Jaroslav (Matej Frantisek)
1883-1923 .... **TCLC 4**
See also CA 104; 129; MTCW 1, 2

Hass, Robert 1941- ... **CLC 18, 39, 99; PC 16**
See also AMWS 6; CA 111; CANR 30, 50, 71; CP; DLB 105, 206; RGAL; SATA 94

Hastings, Hudson
See Kuttner, Henry

Hastings, Selina .... **CLC 44**

Hathorne, John 1641-1717 .... **LC 38**

Hatteras, Amelia
See Mencken, H(enry) L(ouis)

Hatteras, Owen .... **TCLC 18**
See also Mencken, H(enry) L(ouis); Nathan, George Jean

Hauptmann, Gerhart (Johann Robert)
1862-1946 .... **TCLC 4; DAM DRAM; SSC 37**
See also CA 104; 153; DLB 66, 118

Havel, Václav 1936- ..... **CLC 25, 58, 65, 123; DAM DRAM; DC 6**
See also CA 104; CANR 36, 63; CWW 2; DA3; DFS 10; DLB 232; MTCW 1, 2

Haviaras, Stratis .... **CLC 33**
See also Chaviaras, Strates

Hawes, Stephen 1475(?)-1529(?) .... **LC 17**
See also DLB 132; RGEL

Hawkes, John (Clendennin Burne, Jr.)
1925-1998 .. **CLC 1, 2, 3, 4, 7, 9, 14, 15, 27, 49**
See also CA 1-4R; 167; CANR 2, 47, 64; CN; DLB 2, 7, 227; DLBY 80, 98; MTCW 1, 2

Hawking, S. W.
See Hawking, Stephen W(illiam)

Hoffman, William 1925- .... **CLC 141**
See also CA 21-24R; CANR 9; CSW; DLB
234

Hoffman, William M(oses) 1939- ..... **CLC 40**
See also CA 57-60; CANR 11, 71

Hoffmann, E(rnst) T(heodor) A(madeus)
1776-1822 .... **NCLC 2; SSC 13**
See also DLB 90; SATA 27

Hofmann, Gert 1931- .... **CLC 54**
See also CA 128

Hofmannsthal, Hugo von
1874-1929 ...... **TCLC 11; DAM DRAM;**
DC 4
See also von Hofmannsthal, Hugo
See also CA 106; 153; DFS 12; DLB 81,
118; RGWL

Hogan, Linda 1947- . **CLC 73; DAM MULT;**
PC 35
See also AMWS 4; CA 120; CANR 45, 73;
CWP; DLB 175; NNAL; TCWW 2

Hogarth, Charles
See Creasey, John

Hogarth, Emmett
See Polonsky, Abraham (Lincoln)

Hogg, James 1770-1835 .... **NCLC 4**
See also DLB 93, 116, 159; HGG; RGEL

Holbach, Paul Henri Thiry Baron
1723-1789 .... **LC 14**

Holberg, Ludvig 1684-1754 .... **LC 6**
See also RGWL

Holcroft, Thomas 1745-1809 .... **NCLC 85**
See also DLB 39, 89, 158; RGEL

Holden, Ursula 1921- .... **CLC 18**
See also CA 101; CAAS 8; CANR 22

Hölderlin, (Johann Christian) Friedrich
1770-1843 .... **NCLC 16; PC 4**

Holdstock, Robert
See Holdstock, Robert P.

Holdstock, Robert P. 1948- .... **CLC 39**
See also CA 131; CANR 81; FANT; HGG;
SFW

Holland, Isabelle 1920- .... **CLC 21**
See also AAYA 11; CA 21-24R; 181; CAAE
181; CANR 10, 25, 47; CLR 57; CWRI;
JRDA; MAICYA; SATA 8, 70; SATA-
Essay 103

Holland, Marcus
See Caldwell, (Janet Miriam) Taylor
(Holland)

Hollander, John 1929- .... **CLC 2, 5, 8, 14**
See also CA 1-4R; CANR 1, 52; CP; DLB
5; SATA 13

Hollander, Paul
See Silverberg, Robert

Holleran, Andrew 1943(?)- .... **CLC 38**
See also Garber, Eric
See also CA 144; GLL 1

Holley, Marietta 1836(?)-1926 .... **TCLC 99**
See also CA 118; DLB 11

Hollinghurst, Alan 1954- .... **CLC 55, 91**
See also CA 114; CN; DLB 207; GLL 1

Hollis, Jim
See Summers, Hollis (Spurgeon, Jr.)

Holly, Buddy 1936-1959 .... **TCLC 65**

Holmes, Gordon
See Shiel, M(atthew) P(hipps)

Holmes, John
See Souster, (Holmes) Raymond

Holmes, John Clellon 1926-1988 ...... **CLC 56**
See also CA 9-12R; 125; CANR 4; DLB 16

Holmes, Oliver Wendell, Jr.
1841-1935 .... **TCLC 77**
See also CA 114; 186

Holmes, Oliver Wendell
1809-1894 .... **NCLC 14, 81**
See also AMWS 1; CDALB 1640-1865;
DLB 1, 189, 235; RGAL; SATA 34

Holmes, Raymond
See Souster, (Holmes) Raymond

Holt, Victoria
See Hibbert, Eleanor Alice Burford

Holub, Miroslav 1923-1998 .... **CLC 4**
See also CA 21-24R; 169; CANR 10; CWW
2; DLB 232

Homer c. 8th cent. B.C.- .. **CMLC 1, 16; DA;**
DAB; DAC; DAM MST, POET; PC
23; WLCS
See also DA3; DLB 176; EFS 1; RGEL

Hongo, Garrett Kaoru 1951- .... **PC 23**
See also CA 133; CAAS 22; CP; DLB 120;
RGAL

Honig, Edwin 1919- .... **CLC 33**
See also CA 5-8R; CAAS 8; CANR 4, 45;
CP; DLB 5

Hood, Hugh (John Blagdon) 1928- . **CLC 15,**
28; SSC 42
See also CA 49-52; CAAS 17; CANR 1,
33, 87; CN; DLB 53

Hood, Thomas 1799-1845 .... **NCLC 16**
See also DLB 96; RGEL

Hooker, (Peter) Jeremy 1941- .... **CLC 43**
See also CA 77-80; CANR 22; CP; DLB 40

hooks, bell .... **CLC 94; BLCS**
See also Watkins, Gloria Jean
See also FW; MTCW 2

Hope, A(lec) D(erwent) 1907-2000 .... **CLC 3,**
51
See also CA 21-24R; 188; CANR 33, 74;
MTCW 1, 2; PFS 8

Hope, Anthony 1863-1933 .... **TCLC 83**
See also CA 157; DLB 153, 156; RGEL;
RHW

Hope, Brian
See Creasey, John

Hope, Christopher (David Tully)
1944- .... **CLC 52**
See also CA 106; CANR 47; CN; DLB 225;
SATA 62

Hopkins, Gerard Manley
1844-1889 .... **NCLC 17; DA; DAB;**
DAC; DAM MST, POET; PC 15; WLC
See also CDBLB 1890-1914; DA3; DLB
35, 57

Hopkins, John (Richard) 1931-1998 .. **CLC 4**
See also CA 85-88; 169; CBD; CD

Hopkins, Pauline Elizabeth
1859-1930 ...... **TCLC 28; BLC 2; DAM**
MULT
See also AFAW 2; BW 2, 3; CA 141; CANR
82; DLB 50

Hopkinson, Francis 1737-1791 .... **LC 25**
See also DLB 31; RGAL

Hopley-Woolrich, Cornell George 1903-1968
See Woolrich, Cornell
See also CA 13-14; CANR 58; CAP 1;
CMW; DLB 226; MTCW 2

Horace 65B.C.-8B.C. .... **CMLC 39**
See also DLB 211; RGWL

Horatio
See Proust, (Valentin-Louis-George-Eug

Horgan, Paul (George Vincent
O'Shaughnessy) 1903-1995 . **CLC 9, 53;**
DAM NOV
See also CA 13-16R; 147; CANR 9, 35;
DLB 212; DLBY 85; INT CANR-9;
MTCW 1, 2; SATA 13; SATA-Obit 84;
TCWW 2

Horn, Peter
See Kuttner, Henry

Hornem, Horace Esq.
See Byron, George Gordon (Noel)

Horney, Karen (Clementine Theodore
Danielsen) 1885-1952 .... **TCLC 71**
See also CA 114; 165; FW

Hornung, E(rnest) W(illiam)
1866-1921 .... **TCLC 59**
See also CA 108; 160; CMW; DLB 70

Horovitz, Israel (Arthur) 1939- ...... **CLC 56;**
DAM DRAM
See also CA 33-36R; CAD; CANR 46, 59;
CD; DLB 7

Horton, George Moses
1797(?)-1883(?) .... **NCLC 87**
See also DLB 50

Horváth, Ödön von
See Horvath, Oedoen von
See also DLB 85, 124

Horvath, Oedoen von 1901-1938 ... **TCLC 45**
See also Horváth, Ödön von; von Horvath,
Oedoen
See also CA 118

Horwitz, Julius 1920-1986 .... **CLC 14**
See also CA 9-12R; 119; CANR 12

Hospital, Janette Turner 1942- .... **CLC 42,**
145
See also CA 108; CANR 48; CN; RGSF

Hostos, E. M. de
See Hostos (y Bonilla), Eugenio Maria de

Hostos, Eugenio M. de
See Hostos (y Bonilla), Eugenio Maria de

Hostos, Eugenio Maria
See Hostos (y Bonilla), Eugenio Maria de

Hostos (y Bonilla), Eugenio Maria de
1839-1903 .... **TCLC 24**
See also CA 123; 131; HW 1

Houdini
See Lovecraft, H(oward) P(hillips)

Hougan, Carolyn 1943- .... **CLC 34**
See also CA 139

Household, Geoffrey (Edward West)
1900-1988 .... **CLC 11**
See also CA 77-80; 126; CANR 58; CMW;
DLB 87; SATA 14; SATA-Obit 59

Housman, A(lfred) E(dward)
1859-1936 .... **TCLC 1, 10; DA; DAB;**
DAC; DAM MST, POET; PC 2;
WLCS
See also CA 104; 125; DA3; DLB 19;
MTCW 1, 2; PFS 4, 7

Housman, Laurence 1865-1959 .... **TCLC 7**
See also CA 106; 155; DLB 10; FANT;
RGEL; SATA 25

Howard, Elizabeth Jane 1923- ..... **CLC 7, 29**
See also CA 5-8R; CANR 8, 62; CN

Howard, Maureen 1930- .... **CLC 5, 14, 46**
See also CA 53-56; CANR 31, 75; CN;
DLBY 83; INT CANR-31; MTCW 1, 2

Howard, Richard 1929- .... **CLC 7, 10, 47**
See also AITN 1; CA 85-88; CANR 25, 80;
CP; DLB 5; INT CANR-25

Howard, Robert E(rvin)
1906-1936 .... **TCLC 8**
See also CA 105; 157; FANT

Howard, Warren F.
See Pohl, Frederik

Howe, Fanny (Quincy) 1940- .... **CLC 47**
See also CA 117; CAAE 187; CAAS 27;
CANR 70; CP; CWP; SATA-Brief 52

Howe, Irving 1920-1993 .... **CLC 85**
See also AMWS 6; CA 9-12R; 141; CANR
21, 50; DLB 67; MTCW 1, 2

Howe, Julia Ward 1819-1910 .... **TCLC 21**
See also CA 117; DLB 1, 189, 235; FW

Howe, Susan 1937- .... **CLC 72**
See also AMWS 4; CA 160; CP; CWP;
DLB 120; FW; RGAL

Howe, Tina 1937- .... **CLC 48**
See also CA 109; CAD; CD; CWD

Howell, James 1594(?)-1666 .... **LC 13**
See also DLB 151

Howells, W. D.
See Howells, William Dean

Jeffrey, Francis 1773-1850 .... **NCLC 33**
See also DLB 107
Jelakowitch, Ivan
See Heijermans, Herman
Jellicoe, (Patricia) Ann 1927- .... **CLC 27**
See also CA 85-88; CBD; CD; CWD;
CWRI; DLB 13, 233; FW
Jemyma
See Holley, Marietta
Jen, Gish .... **CLC 70**
See also Jen, Lillian
Jen, Lillian 1956(?)-
See Jen, Gish
See also CA 135; CANR 89
Jenkins, (John) Robin 1912- .... **CLC 52**
See also CA 1-4R; CANR 1; CN; DLB 14
Jennings, Elizabeth (Joan) 1926- ...... **CLC 5,
14, 131**
See also BRWS 5; CA 61-64; CAAS 5;
CANR 8, 39, 66; CP; CWP; DLB 27;
MTCW 1; SATA 66
Jennings, Waylon 1937- .... **CLC 21**
Jensen, Johannes V. 1873-1950 ...... **TCLC 41**
See also CA 170; DLB 214
Jensen, Laura (Linnea) 1948- .... **CLC 37**
See also CA 103
Jerome, Jerome K(lapka)
1859-1927 .... **TCLC 23**
See also CA 119; 177; DLB 10, 34, 135
Jerome, Saint 345-420 .... **CMLC 30**
Jerrold, Douglas William
1803-1857 .... **NCLC 2**
See also DLB 158, 159
Jewett, (Theodora) Sarah Orne
1849-1909 .... **TCLC 1, 22; SSC 6, 44**
See also CA 108; 127; CANR 71; DLB 12,
74, 221; FW; SATA 15; SSFS 4
Jewsbury, Geraldine (Endsor)
1812-1880 .... **NCLC 22**
See also DLB 21
Jhabvala, Ruth Prawer 1927- . **CLC 4, 8, 29,
94, 138; DAB; DAM NOV**
See also CA 1-4R; CANR 2, 29, 51, 74, 91;
CN; DLB 139, 194; IDFW 4; INT CANR-
29; MTCW 1, 2; RGSF; RGWL; RHW
Jibran, Kahlil
See Gibran, Kahlil
Jibran, Khalil
See Gibran, Kahlil
Jiles, Paulette 1943- .... **CLC 13, 58**
See also CA 101; CANR 70; CWP
Jiménez (Mantecón), Juan Ramón
1881-1958 .... **TCLC 4; DAM MULT,
POET; HLC 1; PC 7**
See also CA 104; 131; CANR 74; DLB 134;
HW 1; MTCW 1, 2
Jimenez, Ramon
See Jim
Jimenez Mantecon, Juan
See Jim
Jin, Ha
See Jin, Xuefei
Jin, Xuefei 1956- .... **CLC 109**
See also CA 152; CANR 91
Joel, Billy .... **CLC 26**
See also Joel, William Martin
Joel, William Martin 1949-
See Joel, Billy
See also CA 108
John, Saint 107th cent. -100 .... **CMLC 27**
John of the Cross, St. 1542-1591 .... **LC 18**
John Paul II, Pope 1920- .... **CLC 128**
See also CA 106; 133
Johnson, B(ryan) S(tanley William)
1933-1973 .... **CLC 6, 9**
See also CA 9-12R; 53-56; CANR 9; DLB
14, 40

Johnson, Benj. F. of Boo
See Riley, James Whitcomb
Johnson, Benjamin F. of Boo
See Riley, James Whitcomb
Johnson, Charles (Richard) 1948- .... **CLC 7,
51, 65; BLC 2; DAM MULT**
See also AFAW 2; AMWS 6; BW 2, 3; CA
116; CAAS 18; CANR 42, 66, 82; CN 7;
DLB 33; MTCW 2; RGAL
Johnson, Denis 1949- .... **CLC 52**
See also CA 117; 121; CANR 71; CN; DLB
120
Johnson, Diane 1934- .... **CLC 5, 13, 48**
See also CA 41-44R; CANR 17, 40, 62, 95;
CN; DLBY 80; INT CANR-17; MTCW 1
Johnson, Eyvind (Olof Verner)
1900-1976 .... **CLC 14**
See also CA 73-76; 69-72; CANR 34
Johnson, J. R.
See James, C(yril) L(ionel) R(obert)
Johnson, James Weldon
1871-1938 .. **TCLC 3, 19; BLC 2; DAM
MULT, POET; PC 24**
See also AFAW 1, 2; BW 1, 3; CA 104;
125; CANR 82; CDALB 1917-1929; CLR
32; DA3; DLB 51; MTCW 1, 2; PFS 1;
RGAL; SATA 31
Johnson, Joyce 1935- .... **CLC 58**
See also CA 125; 129
Johnson, Judith (Emlyn) 1936- .... **CLC 7, 15**
See also Sherwin, Judith Johnson
See also CA 25-28R, 153; CANR 34
Johnson, Lionel (Pigot)
1867-1902 .... **TCLC 19**
See also CA 117; DLB 19
Johnson, Marguerite (Annie)
See Angelou, Maya
Johnson, Mel
See Malzberg, Barry N(athaniel)
Johnson, Pamela Hansford
1912-1981 .... **CLC 1, 7, 27**
See also CA 1-4R; 104; CANR 2, 28; DLB
15; MTCW 1, 2
Johnson, Robert .... **CLC 70**
Johnson, Robert 1911(?)-1938 .... **TCLC 69**
See also BW 3; CA 174
Johnson, Samuel 1709-1784 . **LC 15, 52; DA;
DAB; DAC; DAM MST; WLC**
See also CDBLB 1660-1789; DLB 39, 95,
104, 142
Johnson, Uwe 1934-1984 .. **CLC 5, 10, 15, 40**
See also CA 1-4R; 112; CANR 1, 39; DLB
75; MTCW 1; RGWL
Johnston, George (Benson) 1913- .... **CLC 51**
See also CA 1-4R; CANR 5, 20; CP; DLB
88
Johnston, Jennifer (Prudence) 1930- . **CLC 7**
See also CA 85-88; CANR 92; CN; DLB
14
Joinville, Jean de 1224(?)-1317 ..... **CMLC 38**
Jolley, (Monica) Elizabeth 1923- ..... **CLC 46;
SSC 19**
See also CA 127; CAAS 13; CANR 59; CN
Jones, Arthur Llewellyn 1863-1947
See Machen, Arthur
See also CA 104; 179; HGG
Jones, D(ouglas) G(ordon) 1929- ..... **CLC 10**
See also CA 29-32R; CANR 13, 90; CP;
DLB 53
Jones, David (Michael) 1895-1974 .... **CLC 2,
4, 7, 13, 42**
See also CA 9-12R; 53-56; CANR 28; CD-
BLB 1945-1960; DLB 20, 100; MTCW 1
Jones, David Robert 1947-
See Bowie, David
See also CA 103

Jones, Diana Wynne 1934- .... **CLC 26**
See also AAYA 12; CA 49-52; CANR 4,
26, 56; CLR 23; DLB 161; FANT; JRDA;
MAICYA; SAAS 7; SATA 9, 70, 108;
SFW; YAW
Jones, Edward P. 1950- .... **CLC 76**
See also BW 2, 3; CA 142; CANR 79; CSW
Jones, Gayl 1949- ..... **CLC 6, 9, 131; BLC 2;
DAM MULT**
See also AFAW 1, 2; BW 2, 3; CA 77-80;
CANR 27, 66; CN; CSW; DA3; DLB 33;
MTCW 1, 2; RGAL
Jones, James 1931-1978 ...... **CLC 1, 3, 10, 39**
See also AITN 1, 2; CA 1-4R; 69-72;
CANR 6; DLB 2, 143; DLBD 17; DLBY
98; MTCW 1; RGAL
Jones, John J.
See Lovecraft, H(oward) P(hillips)
Jones, LeRoi .... **CLC 1, 2, 3, 5, 10, 14**
See also Baraka, Amiri
See also MTCW 2
Jones, Louis B. 1953- .... **CLC 65**
See also CA 141; CANR 73
Jones, Madison (Percy, Jr.) 1925- ...... **CLC 4**
See also CA 13-16R; CAAS 11; CANR 7,
54, 83; CN; CSW; DLB 152
Jones, Mervyn 1922- .... **CLC 10, 52**
See also CA 45-48; CAAS 5; CANR 1, 91;
CN; MTCW 1
Jones, Mick 1956(?)- .... **CLC 30**
Jones, Nettie (Pearl) 1941- .... **CLC 34**
See also BW 2; CA 137; CAAS 20; CANR
88
Jones, Preston 1936-1979 .... **CLC 10**
See also CA 73-76; 89-92; DLB 7
Jones, Robert F(rancis) 1934- .... **CLC 7**
See also CA 49-52; CANR 2, 61
Jones, Rod 1953- .... **CLC 50**
See also CA 128
Jones, Terence Graham Parry
1942- .... **CLC 21**
See also Jones, Terry; Monty Python
See also CA 112; 116; CANR 35, 93; INT
116
Jones, Terry
See Jones, Terence Graham Parry
See also SATA 67; SATA-Brief 51
Jones, Thom (Douglas) 1945(?)- .... **CLC 81**
See also CA 157; CANR 88
Jong, Erica 1942- .... **CLC 4, 6, 8, 18, 83;
DAM NOV, POP**
See also AITN 1; AMWS 5; BEST 90:2;
CA 73-76; CANR 26, 52, 75; CN; CP;
CPW; DA3; DLB 2, 5, 28, 152; FW; INT
CANR-26; MTCW 1, 2
Jonson, Ben(jamin) 1572(?)-1637 .. **LC 6, 33;
DA; DAB; DAC; DAM DRAM, MST,
POET; DC 4; PC 17; WLC**
See also CDBLB Before 1660; DFS 4, 10;
DLB 62, 121; RGEL
Jordan, June 1936- .... **CLC 5, 11, 23, 114;
BLCS; DAM MULT, POET**
See also Meyer, June
See also AAYA 2; AFAW 1, 2; BW 2, 3;
CA 33-36R; CANR 25, 70; CLR 10; CP;
CWP; DLB 38; GLL 2; MAICYA; MTCW
1; SATA 4; YAW
Jordan, Neil (Patrick) 1950- .... **CLC 110**
See also CA 124; 130; CANR 54; CN; GLL
2; INT 130
Jordan, Pat(rick M.) 1941- .... **CLC 37**
See also CA 33-36R
Jorgensen, Ivar
See Ellison, Harlan (Jay)
Jorgenson, Ivar
See Silverberg, Robert
Joseph, George Ghevarughese .... **CLC 70**
Josephus, Flavius c. 37-100 .... **CMLC 13**
See also DLB 176

Kumin, Maxine (Winokur) 1925- ..... **CLC 5, 13, 28; DAM POET; PC 15**
See also AITN 2; AMWS 4; CA 1-4R; CAAS 8; CANR 1, 21, 69; CP; CWP; DA3; DLB 5; MTCW 1, 2; SATA 12

Kundera, Milan 1929- . **CLC 4, 9, 19, 32, 68, 115, 135; DAM NOV; SSC 24**
See also AAYA 2; CA 85-88; CANR 19, 52, 74; CWW 2; DA3; DLB 232; MTCW 1, 2; RGSF; SSFS 10

Kunene, Mazisi (Raymond) 1930- ... **CLC 85**
See also BW 1, 3; CA 125; CANR 81; DLB 117

Kung, Hans .... **CLC 130**
See also Kueng, Hans

Kunikida, Doppo 1869(?)-1908 ...... **TCLC 99**
See also DLB 180

Kunitz, Stanley (Jasspon) 1905- .. **CLC 6, 11, 14; PC 19**
See also AMWS 3; CA 41-44R; CANR 26, 57, 98; CP; DA3; DLB 48; INT CANR-26; MTCW 1, 2; PFS 11

Kunze, Reiner 1933- .... **CLC 10**
See also CA 93-96; CWW 2; DLB 75

Kuprin, Aleksander Ivanovich
1870-1938 .... **TCLC 5**
See also CA 104; 182

Kureishi, Hanif 1954(?)- .... **CLC 64, 135**
See also CA 139; CBD; CD; CN; DLB 194; GLL 2; IDFW 4

Kurosawa, Akira 1910-1998 .... **CLC 16, 119; DAM MULT**
See also AAYA 11; CA 101; 170; CANR 46

Kushner, Tony 1957(?)- .... **CLC 81; DAM DRAM; DC 10**
See also CA 144; CAD; CANR 74; CD; DA3; DFS 5; DLB 228; GLL 1; MTCW 2; RGAL

Kuttner, Henry 1915-1958 .... **TCLC 10**
See also CA 107; 157; DLB 8; FANT; SFW

Kuzma, Greg 1944- .... **CLC 7**
See also CA 33-36R; CANR 70

Kuzmin, Mikhail 1872(?)-1936 ...... **TCLC 40**
See also CA 170

Kyd, Thomas 1558-1594 .... **LC 22; DAM DRAM; DC 3**
See also DLB 62

Kyprianos, Iossif
See Samarakis, Antonis

La Bruyère, Jean de 1645-1696 .... **LC 17**
See also GFL Beginnings to 1789

Lacan, Jacques (Marie Emile)
1901-1981 .... **CLC 75**
See also CA 121; 104

Laclos, Pierre Ambroise François
1741-1803 .... **NCLC 4, 87**
See also EW; GFL Beginnings to 1789; RGWL

Lacolere, Francois
See Aragon, Louis

La Colere, Francois
See Aragon, Louis

La Deshabilleuse
See Simenon, Georges (Jacques Christian)

Lady Gregory
See Gregory, Isabella Augusta (Persse)

Lady of Quality, A
See Bagnold, Enid

La Fayette, Marie-(Madelaine Pioche de la Vergne) 1634-1693 .... **LC 2**
See also GFL Beginnings to 1789; RGWL

Lafayette, Rene
See Hubbard, L(afayette) Ron(ald)

La Fontaine, Jean de 1621-1695 ...... **LC 50**
See also GFL Beginnings to 1789; MAICYA; RGWL; SATA 18

Laforgue, Jules 1860-1887 . **NCLC 5, 53; PC 14; SSC 20**
See also GFL 1789 to the Present; RGWL

Lagerkvist, Paer (Fabian)
1891-1974 ...... **CLC 7, 10, 13, 54; DAM DRAM, NOV**
See also Lagerkvist, Pär
See also CA 85-88; 49-52; DA3; MTCW 1, 2

Lagerkvist, Pär .... **SSC 12**
See also Lagerkvist, Paer (Fabian)
See also MTCW 2

Lagerloef, Selma (Ottiliana Lovisa)
1858-1940 .... **TCLC 4, 36**
See also Lagerlof, Selma (Ottiliana Lovisa)
See also CA 108; MTCW 2; SATA 15

Lagerlof, Selma (Ottiliana Lovisa)
See Lagerloef, Selma (Ottiliana Lovisa)
See also CLR 7; SATA 15

La Guma, (Justin) Alex(ander)
1925-1985 .... **CLC 19; BLCS; DAM NOV**
See also BW 1, 3; CA 49-52; 118; CANR 25, 81; DLB 117, 225; MTCW 1, 2

Laidlaw, A. K.
See Grieve, C(hristopher) M(urray)

Lainez, Manuel Mujica
See Mujica Lainez, Manuel
See also HW 1

Laing, R(onald) D(avid) 1927-1989 . **CLC 95**
See also CA 107; 129; CANR 34; MTCW 1

Lamartine, Alphonse (Marie Louis Prat) de 1790-1869 . **NCLC 11; DAM POET; PC 16**
See also GFL 1789 to the Present; RGWL

Lamb, Charles 1775-1834 ..... **NCLC 10; DA; DAB; DAC; DAM MST; WLC**
See also CDBLB 1789-1832; DLB 93, 107, 163; RGEL; SATA 17

Lamb, Lady Caroline 1785-1828 ... **NCLC 38**
See also DLB 116

Lamming, George (William) 1927- ... **CLC 2, 4, 66, 144; BLC 2; DAM MULT**
See also BW 2, 3; CA 85-88; CANR 26, 76; DLB 125; MTCW 1, 2

L'Amour, Louis (Dearborn)
1908-1988 ...... **CLC 25, 55; DAM NOV, POP**
See also Burns, Tex; Mayo, Jim
See also AAYA 16; AITN 2; BEST 89:2; CA 1-4R; 125; CANR 3, 25, 40; CPW; DA3; DLB 206; DLBY 80; MTCW 1, 2

Lampedusa, Giuseppe (Tomasi) di
.... **TCLC 13**
See also Tomasi di Lampedusa, Giuseppe
See also CA 164; DLB 177; MTCW 2

Lampman, Archibald 1861-1899 ... **NCLC 25**
See also DLB 92; RGEL

Lancaster, Bruce 1896-1963 .... **CLC 36**
See also CA 9-10; CANR 70; CAP 1; SATA 9

Lanchester, John .... **CLC 99**

Landau, Mark Alexandrovich
See Aldanov, Mark (Alexandrovich)

Landau-Aldanov, Mark Alexandrovich
See Aldanov, Mark (Alexandrovich)

Landis, Jerry
See Simon, Paul (Frederick)

Landis, John 1950- .... **CLC 26**
See also CA 112; 122

Landolfi, Tommaso 1908-1979 .... **CLC 11, 49**
See also CA 127; 117; DLB 177

Landon, Letitia Elizabeth
1802-1838 .... **NCLC 15**
See also DLB 96

Landor, Walter Savage
1775-1864 .... **NCLC 14**
See also DLB 93, 107

Landwirth, Heinz 1927-
See Lind, Jakov
See also CA 9-12R; CANR 7

Lane, Patrick 1939- ... **CLC 25; DAM POET**
See also CA 97-100; CANR 54; CP; DLB 53; INT 97-100

Lang, Andrew 1844-1912 .... **TCLC 16**
See also CA 114; 137; CANR 85; DLB 98, 141, 184; FANT; MAICYA; RGEL; SATA 16

Lang, Fritz 1890-1976 .... **CLC 20, 103**
See also CA 77-80; 69-72; CANR 30

Lange, John
See Crichton, (John) Michael

Langer, Elinor 1939- .... **CLC 34**
See also CA 121

Langland, William 1332(?)-1400(?) ... **LC 19; DA; DAB; DAC; DAM MST, POET**
See also DLB 146; RGEL

Langstaff, Launcelot
See Irving, Washington

Lanier, Sidney 1842-1881 ..... **NCLC 6; DAM POET**
See also AMWS 1; DLB 64; DLBD 13; MAICYA; RGAL; SATA 18

Lanyer, Aemilia 1569-1645 .... **LC 10, 30**
See also DLB 121

Lao-Tzu
See Lao Tzu

Lao Tzu fl. 6046th cent. B.C.-490 ... **CMLC 7**

Lapine, James (Elliot) 1949- .... **CLC 39**
See also CA 123; 130; CANR 54; INT 130

Larbaud, Valery (Nicolas)
1881-1957 .... **TCLC 9**
See also CA 106; 152; GFL 1789 to the Present

Lardner, Ring
See Lardner, Ring(gold) W(ilmer)
See also RGAL; RGSF

Lardner, Ring W., Jr.
See Lardner, Ring(gold) W(ilmer)

Lardner, Ring(gold) W(ilmer)
1885-1933 .... **TCLC 2, 14; SSC 32**
See also Lardner, Ring
See also CA 104; 131; CDALB 1917-1929; DLB 11, 25, 86, 171; DLBD 16; MTCW 1, 2

Laredo, Betty
See Codrescu, Andrei

Larkin, Maia
See Wojciechowska, Maia (Teresa)

Larkin, Philip (Arthur) 1922-1985 ... **CLC 3, 5, 8, 9, 13, 18, 33, 39, 64; DAB; DAM MST, POET; PC 21**
See also BRWS 1; CA 5-8R; 117; CANR 24, 62; CDBLB 1960 to Present; DA3; DLB 27; MTCW 1, 2; PFS 3, 4, 12

Larra (y Sanchez de Castro), Mariano Jose de 1809-1837 .... **NCLC 17**

Larsen, Eric 1941- .... **CLC 55**
See also CA 132

Larsen, Nella 1893-1963 .... **CLC 37; BLC 2; DAM MULT**
See also AFAW 1, 2; BW 1; CA 125; CANR 83; DLB 51; FW

Larson, Charles R(aymond) 1938- ... **CLC 31**
See also CA 53-56; CANR 4

Larson, Jonathan 1961-1996 .... **CLC 99**
See also AAYA 28; CA 156

Las Casas, Bartolome de 1474-1566 ... **LC 31**

Lasch, Christopher 1932-1994 .... **CLC 102**
See also CA 73-76; 144; CANR 25; MTCW 1, 2

Lasker-Schueler, Else 1869-1945 ... **TCLC 57**
See also CA 183; DLB 66, 124

Laski, Harold J(oseph) 1893-1950 . **TCLC 79**
See also CA 188'

Latham, Jean Lee 1902-1995 .... **CLC 12**
See also AITN 1; CA 5-8R; CANR 7, 84; CLR 50; MAICYA; SATA 2, 68; YAW

Marguerite de Navarre
See de Navarre, Marguerite
See also RGWL

Margulies, Donald .... **CLC 76**
See also DFS 13; DLB 228

Marie de France c. 12th cent. - ..... **CMLC 8; PC 22**
See also DLB 208; FW

Marie de l'Incarnation 1599-1672 ...... **LC 10**

Marier, Captain Victor
See Griffith, D(avid Lewelyn) W(ark)

Mariner, Scott
See Pohl, Frederik

Marinetti, Filippo Tommaso
1876-1944 .... **TCLC 10**
See also CA 107; DLB 114

Marivaux, Pierre Carlet de Chamblain de
1688-1763 .... **LC 4; DC 7**
See also GFL Beginnings to 1789; RGWL

Markandaya, Kamala .... **CLC 8, 38**
See also Taylor, Kamala (Purnaiya)

Markfield, Wallace 1926- .... **CLC 8**
See also CA 69-72; CAAS 3; CN; DLB 2, 28

Markham, Edwin 1852-1940 .... **TCLC 47**
See also CA 160; DLB 54, 186; RGAL

Markham, Robert
See Amis, Kingsley (William)

Marks, J
See Highwater, Jamake (Mamake)

Marks-Highwater, J
See Highwater, Jamake (Mamake)

Markson, David M(errill) 1927- .... **CLC 67**
See also CA 49-52; CANR 1, 91; CN

Marley, Bob .... **CLC 17**
See also Marley, Robert Nesta

Marley, Robert Nesta 1945-1981
See Marley, Bob
See also CA 107; 103

Marlowe, Christopher 1564-1593 ...... **LC 22, 47; DA; DAB; DAC; DAM DRAM, MST; DC 1; WLC**
See also CDBLB Before 1660; DA3; DFS 1,5, 13; DLB 62; RGEL

Marlowe, Stephen 1928- .... **CLC 70**
See also Queen, Ellery
See also CA 13-16R; CANR 6, 55; CMW; SFW

Marmontel, Jean-Francois 1723-1799 .. **LC 2**

Marquand, John P(hillips)
1893-1960 .... **CLC 2, 10**
See also CA 85-88; CANR 73; CMW; DLB 9, 102; MTCW 2

Marqués, René 1919-1979 ..... **CLC 96; DAM MULT; HLC 2**
See also CA 97-100; 85-88; CANR 78; DLB 113; HW 1, 2

Marquez, Gabriel (Jose) Garcia
See Garc

Marquis, Don(ald Robert Perry)
1878-1937 .... **TCLC 7**
See also CA 104; 166; DLB 11, 25

Marric, J. J.
See Creasey, John

Marryat, Frederick 1792-1848 .... **NCLC 3**
See also DLB 21, 163; RGEL

Marsden, James
See Creasey, John

Marsh, Edward 1872-1953 .... **TCLC 99**

Marsh, (Edith) Ngaio 1899-1982 .... **CLC 7, 53; DAM POP**
See also CA 9-12R; CANR 6, 58; CMW; CPW; DLB 77; MTCW 1, 2

Marshall, Garry 1934- .... **CLC 17**
See also AAYA 3; CA 111; SATA 60

Marshall, Paule 1929- .. **CLC 27, 72; BLC 3; DAM MULT; SSC 3**
See also AFAW 1, 2; BW 2, 3; CA 77-80; CANR 25, 73; CN; DA3; DLB 33, 157, 227; MTCW 1, 2; RGAL

Marshallik
See Zangwill, Israel

Marsten, Richard
See Hunter, Evan

Marston, John 1576-1634 .... **LC 33; DAM DRAM**
See also DLB 58, 172; RGEL

Martha, Henry
See Harris, Mark

Martí (y Pérez), José (Julian)
1853-1895 ...... **NCLC 63; DAM MULT; HLC 2**
See also HW 2

Martial c. 40- .... **CMLC 35; PC 10**
See also DLB 211; RGEL

Martin, Ken
See Hubbard, L(afayette) Ron(ald)

Martin, Richard
See Creasey, John

Martin, Steve 1945- .... **CLC 30**
See also CA 97-100; CANR 30; MTCW 1

Martin, Valerie 1948- .... **CLC 89**
See also BEST 90:2; CA 85-88; CANR 49, 89

Martin, Violet Florence
1862-1915 .... **TCLC 51**

Martin, Webber
See Silverberg, Robert

Martindale, Patrick Victor
See White, Patrick (Victor Martindale)

Martin du Gard, Roger
1881-1958 .... **TCLC 24**
See also CA 118; CANR 94; DLB 65; GFL 1789 to the Present

Martineau, Harriet 1802-1876 .... **NCLC 26**
See also DLB 21, 55, 159, 163, 166, 190; FW; RGEL; YABC 2

Martines, Julia
See O'Faolain, Julia

Martinez, Enrique Gonzalez
See Gonzalez Martinez, Enrique

Martinez, Jacinto Benavente y
See Benavente (y Martinez), Jacinto

Martinez Ruiz, Jose 1873-1967
See Azorin; Ruiz, Jose Martinez
See also CA 93-96; HW 1

Martinez Sierra, Gregorio
1881-1947 .... **TCLC 6**
See also CA 115

Martinez Sierra, Maria (de la O'LeJarraga)
1874-1974 .... **TCLC 6**
See also CA 115

Martinsen, Martin
See Follett, Ken(neth Martin)

Martinson, Harry (Edmund)
1904-1978 .... **CLC 14**
See also CA 77-80; CANR 34

Marut, Ret
See Traven, B.

Marut, Robert
See Traven, B.

Marvell, Andrew 1621-1678 .. **LC 4, 43; DA; DAB; DAC; DAM MST, POET; PC 10; WLC**
See also CDBLB 1660-1789; DLB 131; PFS 5; RGEL

Marx, Karl (Heinrich) 1818-1883 . **NCLC 17**
See also DLB 129

Masaoka, Shiki .... **TCLC 18**
See also Masaoka Tsunenori

Masaoka Tsunenori 1867-1902
See Masaoka, Shiki
See also CA 117

Masefield, John (Edward)
1878-1967 ..... **CLC 11, 47; DAM POET**
See also CA 19-20; 25-28R; CANR 33; CAP 2; CDBLB 1890-1914; DLB 10, 19, 153, 160; FANT; MTCW 1, 2; PFS 5; SATA 19

Maso, Carole 19(?)- .... **CLC 44**
See also CA 170; GLL 2; RGAL

Mason, Bobbie Ann 1940- ... **CLC 28, 43, 82; SSC 4**
See also AAYA 5; AMWS 8; CA 53-56; CANR 11, 31, 58, 83; CDALBS; CN; CSW; DA3; DLB 173; DLBY 87; INT CANR-31; MTCW 1, 2; NFS 4; RGAL; RGSF; SSFS 3,8; YAW

Mason, Ernst
See Pohl, Frederik

Mason, Hunni B.
See Sternheim, (William Adolf) Carl

Mason, Lee W.
See Malzberg, Barry N(athaniel)

Mason, Nick 1945- .... **CLC 35**

Mason, Tally
See Derleth, August (William)

Mass, Anna .... **CLC 59**

Mass, William
See Gibson, William

Master Lao
See Lao Tzu

Masters, Edgar Lee 1868-1950 .... **TCLC 2, 25; DA; DAC; DAM MST, POET; PC 1; WLCS**
See also AMWS 1; CA 104; 133; CDALB 1865-1917; DLB 54; MTCW 1, 2; RGAL

Masters, Hilary 1928- .... **CLC 48**
See also CA 25-28R; CANR 13, 47, 97; CN

Mastrosimone, William 19(?)- .... **CLC 36**
See also CA 186; CAD; CD

Mathe, Albert
See Camus, Albert

Mather, Cotton 1663-1728 .... **LC 38**
See also AMWS 2; CDALB 1640-1865; DLB 24, 30, 140; RGAL

Mather, Increase 1639-1723 .... **LC 38**
See also DLB 24

Matheson, Richard Burton 1926- .... **CLC 37**
See also AAYA 31; CA 97-100; CANR 88; DLB 8, 44; HGG; INT 97-100; SCFW 2; SFW

Mathews, Harry 1930- .... **CLC 6, 52**
See also CA 21-24R; CAAS 6; CANR 18, 40, 98; CN

Mathews, John Joseph 1894-1979 .. **CLC 84; DAM MULT**
See also CA 19-20; 142; CANR 45; CAP 2; DLB 175; NNAL

Mathias, Roland (Glyn) 1915- .... **CLC 45**
See also CA 97-100; CANR 19, 41; CP; DLB 27

Matsuo Bashō 1644-1694 .... **LC 62; DAM POET; PC 3**
See also Bashō, Matsuo
See also PFS 2, 7

Matthesson, Rodney
See Creasey, John

Matthews, (James) Brander
1852-1929 .... **TCLC 95**
See also DLB 71, 78; DLBD 13

Matthews, Greg 1949- .... **CLC 45**
See also CA 135

Matthews, William (Procter, III)
1942-1997 .... **CLC 40**
See also CA 29-32R; 162; CAAS 18; CANR 12, 57; CP; DLB 5

Matthias, John (Edward) 1941- .... **CLC 9**
See also CA 33-36R; CANR 56; CP

Matthiessen, F(rancis) O(tto)
1902-1950 .... **TCLC 100**
See also CA 185; DLB 63

See also BW 1, 3; CA 104; 124; CANR 73;
DA; DAC; DAM MST, MULT, NOV,
POET; MTCW 1, 2; WLC

McKuen, Rod 1933- .... **CLC 1, 3**
See also AITN 1; CA 41-44R; CANR 40

McLoughlin, R. B.
See Mencken, H(enry) L(ouis)

McLuhan, (Herbert) Marshall
1911-1980 .... **CLC 37, 83**
See also CA 9-12R; 102; CANR 12, 34, 61;
DLB 88; INT CANR-12; MTCW 1, 2

McMillan, Terry (L.) 1951- .... **CLC 50, 61,
112; BLCS; DAM MULT, NOV, POP**
See also AAYA 21; BW 2, 3; CA 140;
CANR 60; CPW; DA3; MTCW 2; YAW

McMurtry, Larry (Jeff) 1936- .. **CLC 2, 3, 7,
11, 27, 44, 127; DAM NOV, POP**
See also AAYA 15; AITN 2; AMWS 5;
BEST 89:2; CA 5-8R; CANR 19, 43, 64;
CDALB 1968-1988; CN; CPW; CSW;
DA3; DLB 2, 143; DLBY 80, 87; MTCW
1, 2; TCWW 2

McNally, T. M. 1961- .... **CLC 82**

McNally, Terrence 1939- ... **CLC 4, 7, 41, 91;
DAM DRAM**
See also CA 45-48; CAD; CANR 2, 56; CD;
DA3; DLB 7; GLL 1; MTCW 2

McNamer, Deirdre 1950- .... **CLC 70**

McNeal, Tom .... **CLC 119**

McNeile, Herman Cyril 1888-1937
See Sapper
See also CA 184; CMW; DLB 77

McNickle, (William) D'Arcy
1904-1977 .... **CLC 89; DAM MULT**
See also CA 9-12R; 85-88; CANR 5, 45;
DLB 175, 212; NNAL; SATA-Obit 22

McPhee, John (Angus) 1931- .... **CLC 36**
See also AMWS 3; BEST 90:1; CA 65-68;
CANR 20, 46, 64, 69; CPW; DLB 185;
MTCW 1, 2

McPherson, James Alan 1943- .. **CLC 19, 77;
BLCS**
See also BW 1, 3; CA 25-28R; CAAS 17;
CANR 24, 74; CN; CSW; DLB 38;
MTCW 1, 2; RGAL; RGSF

McPherson, William (Alexander)
1933- .... **CLC 34**
See also CA 69-72; CANR 28; INT
CANR-28

McTaggart, J. McT. Ellis
See McTaggart, John McTaggart Ellis

McTaggart, John McTaggart Ellis
1866-1925 .... **TCLC 105**
See also CA 120

Mead, George Herbert 1873-1958 . **TCLC 89**

Mead, Margaret 1901-1978 .... **CLC 37**
See also AITN 1; CA 1-4R; 81-84; CANR
4; DA3; FW; MTCW 1, 2; SATA-Obit 20

Meaker, Marijane (Agnes) 1927-
See Kerr, M. E.
See also CA 107; CANR 37, 63; INT 107;
JRDA; MAICYA; MTCW 1; SATA 20,
61, 99; SATA-Essay 111; YAW

Medoff, Mark (Howard) 1940- ... **CLC 6, 23;
DAM DRAM**
See also AITN 1; CA 53-56; CAD; CANR
5; CD; DFS 4; DLB 7; INT CANR-5

Medvedev, P. N.
See Bakhtin, Mikhail Mikhailovich

Meged, Aharon
See Megged, Aharon

Meged, Aron
See Megged, Aharon

Megged, Aharon 1920- .... **CLC 9**
See also CA 49-52; CAAS 13; CANR 1

Mehta, Ved (Parkash) 1934- .... **CLC 37**
See also CA 1-4R; CANR 2, 23, 69; MTCW
1

Melanter
See Blackmore, R(ichard) D(oddridge)

Melies, Georges 1861-1938 .... **TCLC 81**

Melikow, Loris
See Hofmannsthal, Hugo von

Melmoth, Sebastian
See Wilde, Oscar (Fingal O'Flahertie Wills)

Meltzer, Milton 1915- .... **CLC 26**
See also AAYA 8; CA 13-16R; CANR 38,
92; CLR 13; DLB 61; JRDA; MAICYA;
SAAS 1; SATA 1, 50, 80; YAW

Melville, Herman 1819-1891 ..... **NCLC 3, 12,
29, 45, 49, 91, 93; DA; DAB; DAC;
DAM MST, NOV; SSC 1, 17, 46; WLC**
See also AAYA 25; CDALB 1640-1865;
DA3; DLB 3, 74; NFS 7, 9; RGAL;
RGSF; SATA 59; SSFS 3

Membreno, Alejandro .... **CLC 59**

Menander c. 342B.C.- .... **CMLC 9; DAM
DRAM; DC 3**
See also DLB 176; RGEL

Menchú, Rigoberta 1959-
See also CA 175; DNFS 1; HLCS 2

Mencken, H(enry) L(ouis)
1880-1956 .... **TCLC 13**
See also CA 105; 125; CDALB 1917-1929;
DLB 11, 29, 63, 137, 222; MTCW 1, 2

Mendelsohn, Jane 1965- .... **CLC 99**
See also CA 154; CANR 94

Mercer, David 1928-1980 .... **CLC 5; DAM
DRAM**
See also CA 9-12R; 102; CANR 23; CBD;
DLB 13; MTCW 1; RGEL

Merchant, Paul
See Ellison, Harlan (Jay)

Meredith, George 1828-1909 .. **TCLC 17, 43;
DAM POET**
See also CA 117; 153; CANR 80; CDBLB
1832-1890; DLB 18, 35, 57, 159; RGEL

Meredith, William (Morris) 1919- .... **CLC 4,
13, 22, 55; DAM POET; PC 28**
See also CA 9-12R; CAAS 14; CANR 6,
40; CP; DLB 5

Merezhkovsky, Dmitry Sergeyevich
1865-1941 .... **TCLC 29**
See also CA 169

Mérimée, Prosper 1803-1870 ... **NCLC 6, 65;
SSC 7**
See also DLB 119, 192; GFL 1789 to the
Present; RGSF; RGWL; SSFS 8

Merkin, Daphne 1954- .... **CLC 44**
See also CA 123

Merlin, Arthur
See Blish, James (Benjamin)

Merrill, James (Ingram) 1926-1995 .. **CLC 2,
3, 6, 8, 13, 18, 34, 91; DAM POET; PC
28**
See also AMWS 3; CA 13-16R; 147; CANR
10, 49, 63; DA3; DLB 5, 165; DLBY 85;
INT CANR-10; MTCW 1, 2

Merriman, Alex
See Silverberg, Robert

Merriman, Brian 1747-1805 .... **NCLC 70**

Merritt, E. B.
See Waddington, Miriam

Merton, Thomas 1915-1968 ..... **CLC 1, 3, 11,
34, 83; PC 10**
See also AMWS 8; CA 5-8R; 25-28R;
CANR 22, 53; DA3; DLB 48; DLBY 81;
MTCW 1, 2

Merwin, W(illiam) S(tanley) 1927- ... **CLC 1,
2, 3, 5, 8, 13, 18, 45, 88; DAM POET**
See also AMWS 3; CA 13-16R; CANR 15,
51; CP; DA3; DLB 5, 169; INT CANR-
15; MTCW 1, 2; PFS 5

Metcalf, John 1938- .... **CLC 37; SSC 43**
See also CA 113; CN; DLB 60; RGSF

Metcalf, Suzanne
See Baum, L(yman) Frank

Mew, Charlotte (Mary) 1870-1928 .. **TCLC 8**
See also CA 105; 189; DLB 19, 135

Mewshaw, Michael 1943- .... **CLC 9**
See also CA 53-56; CANR 7, 47; DLBY 80

Meyer, Conrad Ferdinand
1825-1905 .... **NCLC 81**
See also DLB 129; RGWL

Meyer, Gustav 1868-1932
See Meyrink, Gustav
See also CA 117; 190

Meyer, June
See Jordan, June
See also GLL 2

Meyer, Lynn
See Slavitt, David R(ytman)

Meyers, Jeffrey 1939- .... **CLC 39**
See also CA 73-76; CAAE 186; CANR 54;
DLB 111

**Meynell, Alice (Christina Gertrude
Thompson)** 1847-1922 .... **TCLC 6**
See also CA 104; 177; DLB 19, 98

Meyrink, Gustav .... **TCLC 21**
See also Meyer, Gustav
See also DLB 81

Michaels, Leonard 1933- .... **CLC 6, 25; SSC
16**
See also CA 61-64; CANR 21, 62; CN;
DLB 130; MTCW 1

Michaux, Henri 1899-1984 .... **CLC 8, 19**
See also CA 85-88; 114; GFL 1789 to the
Present; RGWL

Micheaux, Oscar (Devereaux)
1884-1951 .... **TCLC 76**
See also BW 3; CA 174; DLB 50; TCWW
2

Michelangelo 1475-1564 .... **LC 12**

Michelet, Jules 1798-1874 .... **NCLC 31**
See also GFL 1789 to the Present

Michels, Robert 1876-1936 .... **TCLC 88**

Michener, James A(lbert)
1907(?)-1997 .... **CLC 1, 5, 11, 29, 60,
109; DAM NOV, POP**
See also AAYA 27; AITN 1; BEST 90:1;
CA 5-8R; 161; CANR 21, 45, 68; CN;
CPW; DA3; DLB 6; MTCW 1, 2; RHW

Mickiewicz, Adam 1798-1855 .. **NCLC 3, 101**
See also RGWL

Middleton, Christopher 1926- .... **CLC 13**
See also CA 13-16R; CANR 29, 54; DLB
40

Middleton, Richard (Barham)
1882-1911 .... **TCLC 56**
See also CA 187; DLB 156; HGG

Middleton, Stanley 1919- .... **CLC 7, 38**
See also CA 25-28R; CAAS 23; CANR 21,
46, 81; CN; DLB 14

Middleton, Thomas 1580-1627 .... **LC 33;
DAM DRAM, MST; DC 5**
See also DLB 58; RGEL

Migueis, Jose Rodrigues 1901- .... **CLC 10**

Mikszath, Kalman 1847-1910 .... **TCLC 31**
See also CA 170

Miles, Jack .... **CLC 100**

Miles, Josephine (Louise)
1911-1985 .. **CLC 1, 2, 14, 34, 39; DAM
POET**
See also CA 1-4R; 116; CANR 2, 55; DLB
48

Militant
See Sandburg, Carl (August)

Mill, John Stuart 1806-1873 .... **NCLC 11, 58**
See also CDBLB 1832-1890; DLB 55, 190;
FW 1

Millar, Kenneth 1915-1983 ... **CLC 14; DAM
POP**
See also Macdonald, Ross
See also CA 9-12R; 110; CANR 16, 63;
CMW; CPW; DA3; DLB 2, 226; DLBD
6; DLBY 83; MTCW 1, 2

Montherlant, Henry (Milon) de
1896-1972 ..... **CLC 8, 19; DAM DRAM**
See also CA 85-88; 37-40R; DLB 72; EW;
GFL 1789 to the Present; MTCW 1
Monty Python
See Chapman, Graham; Cleese, John
(Marwood); Gilliam, Terry (Vance); Idle,
Eric; Jones, Terence Graham Parry; Palin,
Michael (Edward)
See also AAYA 7
Moodie, Susanna (Strickland)
1803-1885 .... **NCLC 14**
See also DLB 99
Moody, William Vaughan
1869-1910 .... **TCLC 105**
See also CA 110; 178; DLB 7, 54
Mooney, Edward 1951-
See Mooney, Ted
See also CA 130
Mooney, Ted .... **CLC 25**
See also Mooney, Edward
Moorcock, Michael (John) 1939- ...... **CLC 5,
27, 58**
See also Bradbury, Edward P.
See also AAYA 26; CA 45-48; CAAS 5;
CANR 2, 17, 38, 64; CN; DLB 14, 231;
FANT; MTCW 1, 2; SATA 93; SFW
Moore, Brian 1921-1999 ... **CLC 1, 3, 5, 7, 8,
19, 32, 90; DAB; DAC; DAM MST**
See also Bryan, Michael
See also CA 1-4R; 174; CANR 1, 25, 42,
63; CCA 1; CN; FANT; MTCW 1, 2;
RGEL
Moore, Edward
See Muir, Edwin
See also RGEL
Moore, G. E. 1873-1958 .... **TCLC 89**
Moore, George Augustus
1852-1933 .... **TCLC 7; SSC 19**
See also CA 104; 177; DLB 10, 18, 57, 135
Moore, Lorrie .... **CLC 39, 45, 68**
See also Moore, Marie Lorena
See also DLB 234
Moore, Marianne (Craig)
1887-1972 .... **CLC 1, 2, 4, 8, 10, 13, 19,
47; DA; DAB; DAC; DAM MST,
POET; PC 4; WLCS**
See also CA 1-4R; 33-36R; CANR 3, 61;
CDALB 1929-1941; DA3; DLB 45;
DLBD 7; MTCW 1, 2; SATA 20
Moore, Marie Lorena 1957-
See Moore, Lorrie
See also CA 116; CANR 39, 83; CN; DLB
234
Moore, Thomas 1779-1852 .... **NCLC 6**
See also DLB 96, 144; RGEL
Moorhouse, Frank 1938- .... **SSC 40**
See also CA 118; CANR 92; CN; RGSF
Mora, Pat(ricia) 1942-
See also CA 129; CANR 57, 81; CLR 58;
DAM MULT; DLB 209; HLC 2; HW 1,
2; SATA 92
Moraga, Cherrie 1952- .... **CLC 126; DAM
MULT**
See also CA 131; CANR 66; DLB 82; FW;
GLL 1; HW 1, 2
Morand, Paul 1888-1976 .... **CLC 41; SSC 22**
See also CA 184; 69-72; DLB 65
Morante, Elsa 1918-1985 .... **CLC 8, 47**
See also CA 85-88; 117; CANR 35; DLB
177; MTCW 1, 2; RGWL
Moravia, Alberto .... **CLC 2, 7, 11, 27, 46;
SSC 26**
See also Pincherle, Alberto
See also DLB 177; MTCW 2; RGSF;
RGWL
More, Hannah 1745-1833 .... **NCLC 27**
See also DLB 107, 109, 116, 158; RGEL

More, Henry 1614-1687 .... **LC 9**
See also DLB 126
More, Sir Thomas 1478-1535 .... **LC 10, 32**
Moréas, Jean .... **TCLC 18**
See also Papadiamantopoulos, Johannes
See also GFL 1789 to the Present
Morgan, Berry 1919- .... **CLC 6**
See also CA 49-52; DLB 6
Morgan, Claire
See Highsmith, (Mary) Patricia
See also GLL 1
Morgan, Edwin (George) 1920- .... **CLC 31**
See also CA 5-8R; CANR 3, 43, 90; CP;
DLB 27
Morgan, (George) Frederick 1922- .. **CLC 23**
See also CA 17-20R; CANR 21; CP
Morgan, Harriet
See Mencken, H(enry) L(ouis)
Morgan, Jane
See Cooper, James Fenimore
Morgan, Janet 1945- .... **CLC 39**
See also CA 65-68
Morgan, Lady 1776(?)-1859 .... **NCLC 29**
See also DLB 116, 158; RGEL
Morgan, Robin (Evonne) 1941- .... **CLC 2**
See also CA 69-72; CANR 29, 68; FW;
MTCW 1; SATA 80
Morgan, Scott
See Kuttner, Henry
Morgan, Seth 1949(?)-1990 .... **CLC 65**
See also CA 185; 132
**Morgenstern, Christian (Otto Josef
Wolfgang)** 1871-1914 .... **TCLC 8**
See also CA 105
Morgenstern, S.
See Goldman, William (W.)
Mori, Rintaro
See Mori Ogai
See also CA 110
Moricz, Zsigmond 1879-1942 .... **TCLC 33**
See also CA 165
Mörike, Eduard (Friedrich)
1804-1875 .... **NCLC 10**
See also DLB 133
Mori Ogai 1862-1922 .... **TCLC 14**
See also CA 164; DLB 180
Moritz, Karl Philipp 1756-1793 .... **LC 2**
See also DLB 94
Morland, Peter Henry
See Faust, Frederick (Schiller)
Morley, Christopher (Darlington)
1890-1957 .... **TCLC 87**
See also CA 112; DLB 9
Morren, Theophil
See Hofmannsthal, Hugo von
Morris, Bill 1952- .... **CLC 76**
Morris, Julian
See West, Morris L(anglo)
Morris, Steveland Judkins 1950(?)-
See Wonder, Stevie
See also CA 111
Morris, William 1834-1896 .... **NCLC 4**
See also CDBLB 1832-1890; DLB 18, 35,
57, 156, 178, 184; FANT; SFW
Morris, Wright 1910-1998 .. **CLC 1, 3, 7, 18,
37**
See also CA 9-12R; 167; CANR 21, 81;
CN; DLB 2, 206; DLBY 81; MTCW 1, 2;
RGAL; TCLC 107; TCWW 2
Morrison, Arthur 1863-1945 .... **TCLC 72;
SSC 40**
See also CA 120; 157; CMW; DLB 70, 135,
197; RGEL
Morrison, Chloe Anthony Wofford
See Morrison, Toni
Morrison, James Douglas 1943-1971
See Morrison, Jim
See also CA 73-76; CANR 40

Morrison, Jim .... **CLC 17**
See also Morrison, James Douglas
Morrison, Toni 1931- . **CLC 4, 10, 22, 55, 81,
87; BLC 3; DA; DAB; DAC; DAM
MST, MULT, NOV, POP**
See also AAYA 1, 22; AFAW 1, 2; AMWS
3; BW 2, 3; CA 29-32R; CANR 27, 42,
67; CDALB 1968-1988; CN; CPW; DA3;
DLB 6, 33, 143; DLBY 81; FW; MTCW
1, 2; NFS 1, 6, 8; RGAL; RHW; SATA
57; SSFS 5; YAW
Morrison, Van 1945- .... **CLC 21**
See also CA 116; 168
Morrissy, Mary 1958- .... **CLC 99**
Mortimer, John (Clifford) 1923- ..... **CLC 28,
43; DAM DRAM, POP**
See also CA 13-16R; CANR 21, 69; CD;
CDBLB 1960 to Present; CMW; CN;
CPW; DA3; DLB 13; INT CANR-21;
MTCW 1, 2
Mortimer, Penelope (Ruth)
1918-1999 .... **CLC 5**
See also CA 57-60; 187; CANR 45, 88; CN
Morton, Anthony
See Creasey, John
Mosca, Gaetano 1858-1941 .... **TCLC 75**
Mosher, Howard Frank 1943- .... **CLC 62**
See also CA 139; CANR 65
Mosley, Nicholas 1923- .... **CLC 43, 70**
See also CA 69-72; CANR 41, 60; CN;
DLB 14, 207
Mosley, Walter 1952- .... **CLC 97; BLCS;
DAM MULT, POP**
See also AAYA 17; BW 2; CA 142; CANR
57, 92; CMW; CPW; DA3; MTCW 2
Moss, Howard 1922-1987 ...... **CLC 7, 14, 45,
50; DAM POET**
See also CA 1-4R; 123; CANR 1, 44; DLB
5
Mossgiel, Rab
See Burns, Robert
Motion, Andrew (Peter) 1952- .... **CLC 47**
See also CA 146; CANR 90; CP; DLB 40
Motley, Willard (Francis)
1912-1965 .... **CLC 18**
See also BW 1; CA 117; 106; CANR 88;
DLB 76, 143
Motoori, Norinaga 1730-1801 .... **NCLC 45**
Mott, Michael (Charles Alston)
1930- .... **CLC 15, 34**
See also CA 5-8R; CAAS 7; CANR 7, 29
Mountain Wolf Woman 1884-1960 .. **CLC 92**
See also CA 144; CANR 90; NNAL
Moure, Erin 1955- .... **CLC 88**
See also CA 113; CP; CWP; DLB 60
Mowat, Farley (McGill) 1921- .... **CLC 26;
DAC; DAM MST**
See also AAYA 1; CA 1-4R; CANR 4, 24,
42, 68; CLR 20; CPW; DLB 68; INT
CANR-24; JRDA; MAICYA; MTCW 1,
2; SATA 3, 55; YAW
Mowatt, Anna Cora 1819-1870 ..... **NCLC 74**
See also RGAL
Moyers, Bill 1934- .... **CLC 74**
See also AITN 2; CA 61-64; CANR 31, 52
Mphahlele, Es'kia
See Mphahlele, Ezekiel
See also DLB 125, 225; RGSF; SSFS 11
Mphahlele, Ezekiel 1919- .... **CLC 25, 133;
BLC 3; DAM MULT**
See also Mphahlele, Es'kia
See also BW 2, 3; CA 81-84; CANR 26,
76; CN; DA3; DLB 225; MTCW 2; SATA
119
Mqhayi, S(amuel) E(dward) K(rune Loliwe)
1875-1945 ...... **TCLC 25; BLC 3; DAM
MULT**
See also CA 153; CANR 87

Ovid 43B.C.- .. **CMLC 7; DAM POET; PC 2**
See also DA3; DLB 211; RGEL

Owen, Hugh
See Faust, Frederick (Schiller)

Owen, Wilfred (Edward Salter)
1893-1918 .... **TCLC 5, 27; DA; DAB; DAC; DAM MST, POET; PC 19; WLC**
See also CA 104; 141; CDBLB 1914-1945; DLB 20; MTCW 2; PFS 10

Owens, Rochelle 1936- .... **CLC 8**
See also CA 17-20R; CAAS 2; CAD; CANR 39; CD; CP; CWD; CWP

Oz, Amos 1939- ...... **CLC 5, 8, 11, 27, 33, 54; DAM NOV**
See also CA 53-56; CANR 27, 47, 65; CWW 2; MTCW 1, 2; RGSF

Ozick, Cynthia 1928- ...... **CLC 3, 7, 28, 62; DAM NOV, POP; SSC 15**
See also AMWS 5; BEST 90:1; CA 17-20R; CANR 23, 58; CN; CPW; DA3; DLB 28, 152; DLBY 82; INT CANR-23; MTCW 1, 2; RGAL; RGSF; SSFS 3, 12

Ozu, Yasujiro 1903-1963 .... **CLC 16**
See also CA 112

Pacheco, C.
See Pessoa, Fernando (Ant

Pacheco, José Emilio 1939-
See also CA 111; 131; CANR 65; DAM MULT; HLC 2; HW 1, 2

Pa Chin .... **CLC 18**
See also Li Fei-kan

Pack, Robert 1929- .... **CLC 13**
See also CA 1-4R; CANR 3, 44, 82; CP; DLB 5; SATA 118

Padgett, Lewis
See Kuttner, Henry

Padilla (Lorenzo), Heberto
1932-2000 .... **CLC 38**
See also AITN 1; CA 123; 131; 189; HW 1

Page, Jimmy 1944- .... **CLC 12**

Page, Louise 1955- .... **CLC 40**
See also CA 140; CANR 76; CBD; CD; CWD; DLB 233

Page, P(atricia) K(athleen) 1916- ...... **CLC 7, 18; DAC; DAM MST; PC 12**
See also Cape, Judith
See also CA 53-56; CANR 4, 22, 65; CP; DLB 68; MTCW 1

Page, Stanton
See Fuller, Henry Blake

Page, Stanton
See Fuller, Henry Blake

Page, Thomas Nelson 1853-1922 .... **SSC 23**
See also CA 118; 177; DLB 12, 78; DLBD 13; RGAL

Pagels, Elaine Hiesey 1943- .... **CLC 104**
See also CA 45-48; CANR 2, 24, 51; FW

Paget, Violet 1856-1935
See Lee, Vernon
See also CA 104; 166; GLL 1; HGG

Paget-Lowe, Henry
See Lovecraft, H(oward) P(hillips)

Paglia, Camille (Anna) 1947- .... **CLC 68**
See also CA 140; CANR 72; CPW; FW; GLL 2; MTCW 2

Paige, Richard
See Koontz, Dean R(ay)

Paine, Thomas 1737-1809 .... **NCLC 62**
See also AMWS 1; CDALB 1640-1865; DLB 31, 43, 73, 158; RGAL; RGEL

Pakenham, Antonia
See Fraser, (Lady)Antonia (Pakenham)

Palamas, Kostes 1859-1943 .... **TCLC 5**
See also CA 105; 190; RGWL

Palazzeschi, Aldo 1885-1974 .... **CLC 11**
See also CA 89-92; 53-56; DLB 114

Pales Matos, Luis 1898-1959
See also HLCS 2; HW 1

Paley, Grace 1922- .... **CLC 4, 6, 37, 140; DAM POP; SSC 8**
See also AMWS 6; CA 25-28R; CANR 13, 46, 74; CN; CPW; DA3; DLB 28; FW; INT CANR-13; MTCW 1, 2; RGAL; RGSF; SSFS 3

Palin, Michael (Edward) 1943- .... **CLC 21**
See also Monty Python
See also CA 107; CANR 35; SATA 67

Palliser, Charles 1947- .... **CLC 65**
See also CA 136; CANR 76; CN

Palma, Ricardo 1833-1919 .... **TCLC 29**
See also CA 168

Pancake, Breece Dexter 1952-1979
See Pancake, Breece D'J
See also CA 123; 109

Pancake, Breece D'J .... **CLC 29**
See also Pancake, Breece Dexter
See also DLB 130

Panchenko, Nikolai .... **CLC 59**

Pankhurst, Emmeline (Goulden)
1858-1928 .... **TCLC 100**
See also CA 116; FW

Panko, Rudy
See Gogol, Nikolai (Vasilyevich)

Papadiamantis, Alexandros
1851-1911 .... **TCLC 29**
See also CA 168

Papadiamantopoulos, Johannes 1856-1910
See Mor
See also CA 117

Papini, Giovanni 1881-1956 .... **TCLC 22**
See also CA 121; 180

Paracelsus 1493-1541 .... **LC 14**
See also DLB 179

Parasol, Peter
See Stevens, Wallace

Pardo Bazán, Emilia 1851-1921 .... **SSC 30**
See also FW

Pareto, Vilfredo 1848-1923 .... **TCLC 69**
See also CA 175

Paretsky, Sara 1947- .. **CLC 135; DAM POP**
See also AAYA 30; BEST 90:3; CA 125; 129; CANR 59, 95; CMW; CPW; DA3; INT 129; RGAL

Parfenie, Maria
See Codrescu, Andrei

Parini, Jay (Lee) 1948- .... **CLC 54, 133**
See also CA 97-100; CAAS 16; CANR 32, 87

Park, Jordan
See Kornbluth, C(yril) M.; Pohl, Frederik

Park, Robert E(zra) 1864-1944 ..... **TCLC 73**
See also CA 122; 165

Parker, Bert
See Ellison, Harlan (Jay)

Parker, Dorothy (Rothschild)
1893-1967 .... **CLC 15, 68; DAM POET; PC 28; SSC 2**
See also CA 19-20; 25-28R; CAP 2; DA3; DLB 11, 45, 86; MTCW 1, 2

Parker, Robert B(rown) 1932- .... **CLC 27; DAM NOV, POP**
See also AAYA 28; BEST 89:4; CA 49-52; CANR 1, 26, 52, 89; CMW; CPW; INT CANR-26; MTCW 1

Parkin, Frank 1940- .... **CLC 43**
See also CA 147

Parkman, Francis, Jr. 1823-1893 .. **NCLC 12**
See also AMWS 2; DLB 1, 30, 186, 235

Parks, Gordon (Alexander Buchanan)
1912- .... **CLC 1, 16; BLC 3; DAM MULT**
See also AAYA 36; AITN 2; BW 2, 3; CA 41-44R; CANR 26, 66; DA3; DLB 33; MTCW 2; SATA 8, 108

Parmenides c. 515B.C.-c.
450B.C. .... **CMLC 22**
See also DLB 176

Parnell, Thomas 1679-1718 .... **LC 3**
See also DLB 94; RGEL

Parra, Nicanor 1914- ...... **CLC 2, 102; DAM MULT; HLC 2**
See also CA 85-88; CANR 32; CWW 2; HW 1; MTCW 1

Parra Sanojo, Ana Teresa de la 1890-1936
See also HLCS 2

Parrish, Mary Frances
See Fisher, M(ary) F(rances) K(ennedy)

Parshchikov, Aleksei .... **CLC 59**

Parson
See Coleridge, Samuel Taylor

Parson Lot
See Kingsley, Charles

Parton, Sara Payson Willis
1811-1872 .... **NCLC 86**
See also DLB 43, 74, 239

Partridge, Anthony
See Oppenheim, E(dward) Phillips

Pascal, Blaise 1623-1662 .... **LC 35**
See also GFL Beginnings to 1789; RGWL

Pascoli, Giovanni 1855-1912 .... **TCLC 45**
See also CA 170

Pasolini, Pier Paolo 1922-1975 .. **CLC 20, 37, 106; PC 17**
See also CA 93-96; 61-64; CANR 63; DLB 128, 177; MTCW 1; RGWL

Pasquini
See Silone, Ignazio

Pastan, Linda (Olenik) 1932- .... **CLC 27; DAM POET**
See also CA 61-64; CANR 18, 40, 61; CP; CSW; CWP; DLB 5; PFS 8

Pasternak, Boris (Leonidovich)
1890-1960 .... **CLC 7, 10, 18, 63; DA; DAB; DAC; DAM MST, NOV, POET; PC 6; SSC 31; WLC**
See also CA 127; 116; DA3; MTCW 1, 2

Patchen, Kenneth 1911-1972 .. **CLC 1, 2, 18; DAM POET**
See also CA 1-4R; 33-36R; CANR 3, 35; DLB 16, 48; MTCW 1; RGAL

Pater, Walter (Horatio) 1839-1894 . **NCLC 7, 90**
See also CDBLB 1832-1890; DLB 57, 156

Paterson, A(ndrew) B(arton)
1864-1941 .... **TCLC 32**
See also CA 155; DLB 230; SATA 97

Paterson, Katherine (Womeldorf)
1932- .... **CLC 12, 30**
See also AAYA 1, 31; CA 21-24R; CANR 28, 59; CLR 7, 50; CWRI; DLB 52; JRDA; MAICYA; MTCW 1; SATA 13, 53, 92; YAW

Patmore, Coventry Kersey Dighton
1823-1896 .... **NCLC 9**
See also DLB 35, 98

Paton, Alan (Stewart) 1903-1988 ...... **CLC 4, 10, 25, 55, 106; DA; DAB; DAC; DAM MST, NOV; WLC**
See also AAYA 26; BRWS 2; CA 13-16; 125; CANR 22; CAP 1; DA3; DLB 225; DLBD 17; MTCW 1, 2; NFS 3, 12; SATA 11; SATA-Obit 56

Paton Walsh, Gillian 1937- .... **CLC 35**
See also Walsh, Jill Paton
See also AAYA 11; CANR 38, 83; CLR 2, 65; DLB 161; JRDA; MAICYA; SAAS 3; SATA 4, 72, 109; YAW

Paton Walsh, Jill
See Paton Walsh, Gillian

Patton, George S(mith), Jr.
1885-1945 .... **TCLC 79**
See also CA 189

Paulding, James Kirke 1778-1860 ... **NCLC 2**
See also DLB 3, 59, 74; RGAL

Ross, (James) Sinclair 1908-1996 ... **CLC 13;**
DAC; DAM MST; SSC 24
See also CA 73-76; CANR 81; CN; DLB
88; TCWW 2

Rossetti, Christina (Georgina)
1830-1894 . **NCLC 2, 50, 66; DA; DAB;**
DAC; DAM MST, POET; PC 7; WLC
See also BRW; DA3; DLB 35, 163, 240;
MAICYA; PFS 10; RGEL; SATA 20;
WCH

Rossetti, Dante Gabriel 1828-1882 . **NCLC 4,**
77; DA; DAB; DAC; DAM MST,
POET; WLC
See also CDBLB 1832-1890; DLB 35;
RGEL

Rossner, Judith (Perelman) 1935- . **CLC 6, 9,**
29
See also AITN 2; BEST 90:3; CA 17-20R;
CANR 18, 51, 73; CN; DLB 6; INT
CANR-18; MTCW 1, 2

Rostand, Edmond (Eugene Alexis)
1868-1918 .... **TCLC 6, 37; DA; DAB;**
DAC; DAM DRAM, MST; DC 10
See also CA 104; 126; DA3; DFS 1; DLB
192; MTCW 1

Roth, Henry 1906-1995 ..... **CLC 2, 6, 11, 104**
See also CA 11-12; 149; CANR 38, 63;
CAP 1; CN; DA3; DLB 28; MTCW 1, 2;
RGAL

Roth, (Moses) Joseph 1894-1939 ... **TCLC 33**
See also CA 160; DLB 85

Roth, Philip (Milton) 1933- ... **CLC 1, 2, 3, 4,**
6, 9, 15, 22, 31, 47, 66, 86, 119; DA;
DAB; DAC; DAM MST, NOV, POP;
SSC 26; WLC
See also AMWS 3; BEST 90:3; CA 1-4R;
CANR 1, 22, 36, 55, 89; CDALB 1968-
1988; CN; CPW 1; DA3; DLB 2, 28, 173;
DLBY 82; MTCW 1, 2; SSFS 12

Rothenberg, Jerome 1931- .... **CLC 6, 57**
See also CA 45-48; CANR 1; CP; DLB 5,
193

Rotter, Pat ed. .... **CLC 65**

Roumain, Jacques (Jean Baptiste)
1907-1944 ...... **TCLC 19; BLC 3; DAM**
MULT
See also BW 1; CA 117; 125

Rourke, Constance (Mayfield)
1885-1941 .... **TCLC 12**
See also CA 107; YABC 1

Rousseau, Jean-Baptiste 1671-1741 ...... **LC 9**

Rousseau, Jean-Jacques 1712-1778 .... **LC 14,**
36; DA; DAB; DAC; DAM MST; WLC
See also DA3; EW; GFL Beginnings to
1789; RGWL

Roussel, Raymond 1877-1933 .... **TCLC 20**
See also CA 117; GFL 1789 to the Present

Rovit, Earl (Herbert) 1927- .... **CLC 7**
See also CA 5-8R; CANR 12

Rowe, Elizabeth Singer 1674-1737 ..... **LC 44**
See also DLB 39, 95

Rowe, Nicholas 1674-1718 .... **LC 8**
See also DLB 84; RGEL

Rowlandson, Mary 1637(?)-1678 .... **LC 66**
See also DLB 24, 200; RGAL

Rowley, Ames Dorrance
See Lovecraft, H(oward) P(hillips)

Rowling, J(oanne) K. 1966(?)- .... **CLC 137**
See also AAYA 34; CA 173; CLR 66; SATA
109

Rowson, Susanna Haswell
1762(?)-1824 .... **NCLC 5, 69**
See also DLB 37, 200

Roy, Arundhati 1960(?)- .... **CLC 109**
See also CA 163; CANR 90; DLBY 97

Roy, Gabrielle 1909-1983 .... **CLC 10, 14;**
DAB; DAC; DAM MST
See also CA 53-56; 110; CANR 5, 61; CCA
1; DLB 68; MTCW 1; RGWL; SATA 104

Royko, Mike 1932-1997 .... **CLC 109**
See also CA 89-92; 157; CANR 26; CPW

Rozanov, Vassili 1856-1919 .... **TCLC 104**

Rozewicz, Tadeusz 1921- ..... **CLC 9, 23, 139;**
DAM POET
See also CA 108; CANR 36, 66; CWW 2;
DA3; DLB 232; MTCW 1, 2

Ruark, Gibbons 1941- .... **CLC 3**
See also CA 33-36R; CAAS 23; CANR 14,
31, 57; DLB 120

Rubens, Bernice (Ruth) 1923- .... **CLC 19, 31**
See also CA 25-28R; CANR 33, 65; CN;
DLB 14, 207; MTCW 1

Rubin, Harold
See Robbins, Harold

Rudkin, (James) David 1936- .... **CLC 14**
See also CA 89-92; CBD; CD; DLB 13

Rudnik, Raphael 1933- .... **CLC 7**
See also CA 29-32R

Ruffian, M.
See Ha

Ruiz, Jose Martinez .... **CLC 11**
See also Martinez Ruiz, Jose

Rukeyser, Muriel 1913-1980 . **CLC 6, 10, 15,**
27; DAM POET; PC 12
See also AMWS 6; CA 5-8R; 93-96; CANR
26, 60; DA3; DLB 48; FW; GLL 2;
MTCW 1, 2; PFS 10; RGAL; SATA-Obit
22

Rule, Jane (Vance) 1931- .... **CLC 27**
See also CA 25-28R; CAAS 18; CANR 12,
87; CN; DLB 60; FW

Rulfo, Juan 1918-1986 ...... **CLC 8, 80; DAM**
MULT; HLC 2; SSC 25
See also CA 85-88; 118; CANR 26; DLB
113; HW 1, 2; MTCW 1, 2; RGSF;
RGWL

Rumi, Jalal al-Din 1207-1273 .... **CMLC 20**

Runeberg, Johan 1804-1877 .... **NCLC 41**

Runyon, (Alfred) Damon
1884(?)-1946 .... **TCLC 10**
See also CA 107; 165; DLB 11, 86, 171;
MTCW 2

Rush, Norman 1933- .... **CLC 44**
See also CA 121; 126; INT 126

Rushdie, (Ahmed) Salman 1947- .... **CLC 23,**
31, 55, 100; DAB; DAC; DAM MST,
NOV, POP; WLCS
See also BEST 89:3; BRWS 4; CA 108;
111; CANR 33, 56; CN; CPW 1; DA3;
DLB 194; FANT; INT CA-111; MTCW 1,
2

Rushforth, Peter (Scott) 1945- .... **CLC 19**
See also CA 101

Ruskin, John 1819-1900 .... **TCLC 63**
See also CA 114; 129; CDBLB 1832-1890;
DLB 55, 163, 190; RGEL; SATA 24

Russ, Joanna 1937- .... **CLC 15**
See also CA 5-28R; CANR 11, 31, 65; CN;
DLB 8; FW; GLL 1; MTCW 1; SCFW 2;
SFW

Russell, George William 1867-1935
See Baker, Jean H.
See also CA 104; 153; CDBLB 1890-1914;
DAM POET; RGEL

Russell, Jeffrey Burton 1934- .... **CLC 70**
See also CA 25-28R; CANR 11, 28, 52

Russell, (Henry) Ken(neth Alfred)
1927- .... **CLC 16**
See also CA 105

Russell, William Martin 1947- .... **CLC 60**
See also CA 164; DLB 233

Rutherford, Mark .... **TCLC 25**
See also White, William Hale
See also DLB 18; RGEL

Ruyslinck, Ward .... **CLC 14**
See also Belser, Reimond Karel Maria de

Ryan, Cornelius (John) 1920-1974 ..... **CLC 7**
See also CA 69-72; 53-56; CANR 38

Ryan, Michael 1946- .... **CLC 65**
See also CA 49-52; DLBY 82

Ryan, Tim
See Dent, Lester

Rybakov, Anatoli (Naumovich)
1911-1998 .... **CLC 23, 53**
See also CA 126; 135; 172; SATA 79;
SATA-Obit 108

Ryder, Jonathan
See Ludlum, Robert

Ryga, George 1932-1987 .... **CLC 14; DAC;**
DAM MST
See also CA 101; 124; CANR 43, 90; CCA
1; DLB 60

S. H.
See Hartmann, Sadakichi

S. S.
See Sassoon, Siegfried (Lorraine)

Saba, Umberto 1883-1957 .... **TCLC 33**
See also CA 144; CANR 79; DLB 114;
RGWL

Sabatini, Rafael 1875-1950 .... **TCLC 47**
See also CA 162; RHW

Sabato, Ernesto (R.) 1911- .... **CLC 10, 23;**
DAM MULT; HLC 2
See also CA 97-100; CANR 32, 65; DLB
145; HW 1, 2; MTCW 1, 2

Sa-Carniero, Mario de 1890-1916 . **TCLC 83**

Sacastru, Martin
See Bioy Casares, Adolfo
See also CWW 2

Sacastru, Martin
See Bioy Casares, Adolfo

Sacher-Masoch, Leopold von
1836(?)-1895 .... **NCLC 31**

Sachs, Marilyn (Stickle) 1927- .... **CLC 35**
See also AAYA 2; CA 17-20R; CANR 13,
47; CLR 2; JRDA; MAICYA; SAAS 2;
SATA 3, 68; SATA-Essay 110; YAW

Sachs, Nelly 1891-1970 .... **CLC 14, 98**
See also CA 17-18; 25-28R; CANR 87;
CAP 2; MTCW 2; RGWL

Sackler, Howard (Oliver)
1929-1982 .... **CLC 14**
See also CA 61-64; 108; CAD; CANR 30;
DLB 7

Sacks, Oliver (Wolf) 1933- .... **CLC 67**
See also CA 53-56; CANR 28, 50, 76;
CPW; DA3; INT CANR-28; MTCW 1, 2

Sadakichi
See Hartmann, Sadakichi

Sade, Donatien Alphonse François
1740-1814 .... **NCLC 3, 47**
See also EW; GFL Beginnings to 1789;
RGWL

Sadoff, Ira 1945- .... **CLC 9**
See also CA 53-56; CANR 5, 21; DLB 120

Saetone
See Camus, Albert

Safire, William 1929- .... **CLC 10**
See also CA 17-20R; CANR 31, 54, 91

Sagan, Carl (Edward) 1934-1996 .... **CLC 30,**
112
See also AAYA 2; CA 25-28R; 155; CANR
11, 36, 74; CPW; DA3; MTCW 1, 2;
SATA 58; SATA-Obit 94

Sagan, Françoise .... **CLC 3, 6, 9, 17, 36**
See also Quoirez, Francoise
See also CWW 2; DLB 83; GFL 1789 to
the Present; MTCW 2

Sahgal, Nayantara (Pandit) 1927- .... **CLC 41**
See also CA 9-12R; CANR 11, 88; CN

Said, Edward W. 1935- .... **CLC 123**
See also CA 21-24R; CANR 45, 74; DLB
67; MTCW 2

Saint, H(arry) F. 1941- .... **CLC 50**
See also CA 127

St. Aubin de Teran, Lisa 1953-
See Teran, Lisa St. Aubin de
See also CA 118; 126; CN; INT 126

Saint Birgitta of Sweden c.
1303-1373 .... **CMLC 24**

Sainte-Beuve, Charles Augustin
1804-1869 .... **NCLC 5**
See also EW; GFL 1789 to the Present

Saint-Exupéry, Antoine (Jean Baptiste Marie Roger) de 1900-1944 .... **TCLC 2, 56; DAM NOV; WLC**
See also CA 108; 132; CLR 10; DA3; DLB 72; EW; GFL 1789 to the Present; MAICYA; MTCW 1, 2; RGWL; SATA 20

St. John, David
See Hunt, E(verette) Howard, (Jr.)

Saint-John Perse
See Leger, (Marie-Rene Auguste) Alexis Saint-Leger
See also GFL 1789 to the Present; RGWL

Saintsbury, George (Edward Bateman)
1845-1933 .... **TCLC 31**
See also CA 160; DLB 57, 149

Sait Faik .... **TCLC 23**
See also Abasiyanik, Sait Faik

Saki .... **TCLC 3; SSC 12**
See also Munro, H(ector) H(ugh)
See also BRWS 6; MTCW 2; RGEL; SSFS 1

Sala, George Augustus 1828-1895 . **NCLC 46**

Saladin 1138-1193 .... **CMLC 38**

Salama, Hannu 1936- .... **CLC 18**

Salamanca, J(ack) R(ichard) 1922- .. **CLC 4, 15**
See also CA 25-28R

Salas, Floyd Francis 1931-
See also CA 119; CAAS 27; CANR 44, 75, 93; DAM MULT; DLB 82; HLC 2; HW 1, 2; MTCW 2

Sale, J. Kirkpatrick
See Sale, Kirkpatrick

Sale, Kirkpatrick 1937- .... **CLC 68**
See also CA 13-16R; CANR 10

Salinas, Luis Omar 1937- ..... **CLC 90; DAM MULT; HLC 2**
See also CA 131; CANR 81; DLB 82; HW 1, 2

Salinas (y Serrano), Pedro
1891(?)-1951 .... **TCLC 17**
See also CA 117; DLB 134

Salinger, J(erome) D(avid) 1919- .. **CLC 1, 3, 8, 12, 55, 56, 138; DA; DAB; DAC; DAM MST, NOV, POP; SSC 2, 28; WLC**
See also AAYA 2, 36; CA 5-8R; CANR 39; CDALB 1941-1968; CLR 18; CN; CPW 1; DA3; DLB 2, 102, 173; MAICYA; MTCW 1, 2; NFS 1; SATA 67; YAW

Salisbury, John
See Caute, (John) David

Salter, James 1925- .... **CLC 7, 52, 59**
See also CA 73-76; DLB 130

Saltus, Edgar (Everton) 1855-1921 . **TCLC 8**
See also CA 105; DLB 202

Saltykov, Mikhail Evgrafovich
1826-1889 .... **NCLC 16**
See also DLB 238:

Samarakis, Antonis 1919- .... **CLC 5**
See also CA 25-28R; CAAS 16; CANR 36

Sanchez, Florencio 1875-1910 .... **TCLC 37**
See also CA 153; HW 1

Sanchez, Luis Rafael 1936- .... **CLC 23**
See also CA 128; DLB 145; HW 1

Sanchez, Sonia 1934- .... **CLC 5, 116; BLC 3; DAM MULT; PC 9**
See also BW 2, 3; CA 33-36R; CANR 24, 49, 74; CLR 18; CP; CSW; CWP; DA3; DLB 41; DLBD 8; MAICYA; MTCW 1, 2; SATA 22

Sand, George 1804-1876 ..... **NCLC 2, 42, 57; DA; DAB; DAC; DAM MST, NOV; WLC**
See also DA3; DLB 119, 192; FW; GFL 1789 to the Present; RGWL

Sandburg, Carl (August) 1878-1967 . **CLC 1, 4, 10, 15, 35; DA; DAB; DAC; DAM MST, POET; PC 2; WLC**
See also AAYA 24; CA 5-8R; 25-28R; CANR 35; CDALB 1865-1917; CLR 67; DA3; DLB 17, 54; MAICYA; MTCW 1, 2; PFS 3, 6, 12; SATA 8

Sandburg, Charles
See Sandburg, Carl (August)

Sandburg, Charles A.
See Sandburg, Carl (August)

Sanders, (James) Ed(ward) 1939- ... **CLC 53; DAM POET**
See also CA 13-16R; CAAS 21; CANR 13, 44, 78; CP; DLB 16

Sanders, Lawrence 1920-1998 .... **CLC 41; DAM POP**
See also BEST 89:4; CA 81-84; 165; CANR 33, 62; CMW; CPW; DA3; MTCW 1

Sanders, Noah
See Blount, Roy (Alton), Jr.

Sanders, Winston P.
See Anderson, Poul (William)

Sandoz, Mari(e Susette) 1900-1966 .. **CLC 28**
See also CA 1-4R; 25-28R; CANR 17, 64; DLB 9, 212; MTCW 1, 2; SATA 5; TCWW 2

Saner, Reg(inald Anthony) 1931- .... **CLC 9**
See also CA 65-68; CP

Sankara 788-820 .... **CMLC 32**

Sannazaro, Jacopo 1456(?)-1530 .... **LC 8**
See also RGWL

Sansom, William 1912-1976 .... **CLC 2, 6; DAM NOV; SSC 21**
See also CA 5-8R; 65-68; CANR 42; DLB 139; MTCW 1; RGEL; RGSF

Santayana, George 1863-1952 .... **TCLC 40**
See also CA 115; DLB 54, 71; DLBD 13; RGAL

Santiago, Danny .... **CLC 33**
See also James, Daniel (Lewis)
See also DLB 122

Santmyer, Helen Hooven
1895-1986 .... **CLC 33**
See also CA 1-4R; 118; CANR 15, 33; DLBY 84; MTCW 1; RHW

Santoka, Taneda 1882-1940 .... **TCLC 72**

Santos, Bienvenido N(uqui)
1911-1996 .... **CLC 22; DAM MULT**
See also CA 101; 151; CANR 19, 46

Sapir, Edward 1884-1939 .... **TCLC 108**
See also DLB 92

Sapper .... **TCLC 44**
See also McNeile, Herman Cyril

Sapphire
See Sapphire, Brenda

Sapphire, Brenda 1950- .... **CLC 99**

Sappho fl. 6256th cent. B.C.- .... **CMLC 3; DAM POET; PC 5**
See also DA3; DLB 176; RGEL

Saramago, José 1922- ..... **CLC 119; HLCS 1**
See also CA 153; CANR 96

Sarduy, Severo 1937-1993 .... **CLC 6, 97; HLCS 1**
See also CA 89-92; 142; CANR 58, 81; CWW 2; DLB 113; HW 1, 2

Sargeson, Frank 1903-1982 .... **CLC 31**
See also CA 25-28R; 106; CANR 38, 79; GLL 2; RGEL; RGSF

Sarmiento, Domingo Faustino 1811-1888
See also HLCS 2

Sarmiento, Felix Ruben Garcia
See Dar

Saro-Wiwa, Ken(ule Beeson)
1941-1995 .... **CLC 114**
See also BW 2; CA 142; 150; CANR 60; DLB 157

Saroyan, William 1908-1981 ... **CLC 1, 8, 10, 29, 34, 56; DA; DAB; DAC; DAM DRAM, MST, NOV; SSC 21; WLC**
See also CA 5-8R; 103; CAD; CANR 30; CDALBS; DA3; DLB 7, 9, 86; DLBY 81; MTCW 1, 2; RGAL; RGSF; SATA 23; SATA-Obit 24

Sarraute, Nathalie 1900-1999 .... **CLC 1, 2, 4, 8, 10, 31, 80**
See also CA 9-12R; 187; CANR 23, 66; CWW 2; DLB 83; GFL 1789 to the Present; MTCW 1, 2; RGWL

Sarton, (Eleanor) May 1912-1995 ..... **CLC 4, 14, 49, 91; DAM POET**
See also AMWS 8; CA 1-4R; 149; CANR 1, 34, 55; CN; CP; DLB 48; DLBY 81; FW; INT CANR-34; MTCW 1, 2; SATA 36; SATA-Obit 86

Sartre, Jean-Paul 1905-1980 . **CLC 1, 4, 7, 9, 13, 18, 24, 44, 50, 52; DA; DAB; DAC; DAM DRAM, MST, NOV; DC 3; SSC 32; WLC**
See also CA 9-12R; 97-100; CANR 21; DA3; DFS 5; DLB 72; GFL 1789 to the Present; MTCW 1, 2; RGSF; RGWL; SSFS 9

Sassoon, Siegfried (Lorraine)
1886-1967 .... **CLC 36, 130; DAB; DAM MST, NOV, POET; PC 12**
See also BRW; CA 104; 25-28R; CANR 36; DLB 20, 191; DLBD 18; MTCW 1, 2; PAB; RGEL

Satterfield, Charles
See Pohl, Frederik

Satyremont
See P

Saul, John (W. III) 1942- ...... **CLC 46; DAM NOV, POP**
See also AAYA 10; BEST 90:4; CA 81-84; CANR 16, 40, 81; CPW; HGG; SATA 98

Saunders, Caleb
See Heinlein, Robert A(nson)

Saura (Atares), Carlos 1932-1998 .... **CLC 20**
See also CA 114; 131; CANR 79; HW 1

Sauser-Hall, Frederic 1887-1961 ...... **CLC 18**
See also Cendrars, Blaise
See also CA 102; 93-96; CANR 36, 62; MTCW 1

Saussure, Ferdinand de
1857-1913 .... **TCLC 49**

Savage, Catharine
See Brosman, Catharine Savage

Savage, Thomas 1915- .... **CLC 40**
See also CA 126; 132; CAAS 15; CN; INT 132; TCWW 2

Savan, Glenn (?)- .... **CLC 50**

Sayers, Dorothy L(eigh)
1893-1957 .... **TCLC 2, 15; DAM POP**
See also BRWS 3; CA 104; 119; CANR 60; CDBLB 1914-1945; CMW; DLB 10, 36, 77, 100; MTCW 1, 2; RGEL; SSFS 12

Sayers, Valerie 1952- .... **CLC 50, 122**
See also CA 134; CANR 61; CSW

Sayles, John (Thomas) 1950- . **CLC 7, 10, 14**
See also CA 57-60; CANR 41, 84; DLB 44

Scammell, Michael 1935- .... **CLC 34**
See also CA 156

Scannell, Vernon 1922- .... **CLC 49**
See also CA 5-8R; CANR 8, 24, 57; CP; CWRI; DLB 27; SATA 59

Scarlett, Susan
See Streatfeild, (Mary) Noel

Scarron 1847-1910
See Mikszath, Kalman

Stevens, Mark 1951- .... **CLC 34**
See also CA 122

Stevens, Wallace 1879-1955 ...... **TCLC 3, 12, 45; DA; DAB; DAC; DAM MST, POET; PC 6; WLC**
See also CA 104; 124; CDALB 1929-1941; DA3; DLB 54; MTCW 1, 2; RGAL

Stevenson, Anne (Katharine) 1933- .. **CLC 7, 33**
See also BRWS 6; CA 17-20R; CAAS 9; CANR 9, 33; CP; CWP; DLB 40; MTCW 1; RHW

Stevenson, Robert Louis (Balfour) 1850-1894 . **NCLC 5, 14, 63; DA; DAB; DAC; DAM MST, NOV; SSC 11; WLC**
See also AAYA 24; CDBLB 1890-1914; CLR 10, 11; DA3; DLB 18, 57, 141, 156, 174; DLBD 13; HGG; JRDA; MAICYA; NFS 11; SATA 100; YABC 2; YAW

Stewart, J(ohn) I(nnes) M(ackintosh) 1906-1994 .... **CLC 7, 14, 32**
See also CA 85-88; 147; CAAS 3; CANR 47; CMW; MTCW 1, 2

Stewart, Mary (Florence Elinor) 1916- .... **CLC 7, 35, 117; DAB**
See also AAYA 29; CA 1-4R; CANR 1, 59; CMW; CPW; FANT; RHW; SATA 12; YAW

Stewart, Mary Rainbow
See Stewart, Mary (Florence Elinor)

Stifle, June
See Campbell, Maria

Stifter, Adalbert 1805-1868 .. **NCLC 41; SSC 28**
See also DLB 133; RGSF; RGWL

Still, James 1906-2001 .... **CLC 49**
See also CA 65-68; CAAS 17; CANR 10, 26; CSW; DLB 9; SATA 29

Sting 1951-
See Sumner, Gordon Matthew
See also CA 167

Stirling, Arthur
See Sinclair, Upton (Beall)

Stitt, Milan 1941- .... **CLC 29**
See also CA 69-72

Stockton, Francis Richard 1834-1902
See Stockton, Frank R.
See also CA 108; 137; MAICYA; SATA 44; SFW

Stockton, Frank R. .... **TCLC 47**
See also Stockton, Francis Richard
See also DLB 42, 74; DLBD 13; SATA-Brief 32; SSFS 3

Stoddard, Charles
See Kuttner, Henry

Stoker, Abraham 1847-1912
See Stoker, Bram
See also CA 105; 150; DA; DAC; DAM MST, NOV; DA3; HGG; SATA 29

Stoker, Bram .... **TCLC 8; DAB; WLC**
See also Stoker, Abraham
See also AAYA 23; BRWS 3; CDBLB 1890-1914; DLB 36, 70, 178; RGEL

Stolz, Mary (Slattery) 1920- .... **CLC 12**
See also AAYA 8; AITN 1; CA 5-8R; CANR 13, 41; JRDA; MAICYA; SAAS 3; SATA 10, 71; YAW

Stone, Irving 1903-1989 . **CLC 7; DAM POP**
See also AITN 1; CA 1-4R; 129; CAAS 3; CANR 1, 23; CPW; DA3; INT CANR-23; MTCW 1, 2; RHW; SATA 3; SATA-Obit 64

Stone, Oliver (William) 1946- .... **CLC 73**
See also AAYA 15; CA 110; CANR 55

Stone, Robert (Anthony) 1937- ... **CLC 5, 23, 42**
See also AMWS 5; CA 85-88; CANR 23, 66, 95; CN; DLB 152; INT CANR-23; MTCW 1

Stone, Zachary
See Follett, Ken(neth Martin)

Stoppard, Tom 1937- ... **CLC 1, 3, 4, 5, 8, 15, 29, 34, 63, 91; DA; DAB; DAC; DAM DRAM, MST; DC 6; WLC**
See also BRWS 1; CA 81-84; CANR 39, 67; CBD; CD; CDBLB 1960 to Present; DA3; DFS 2,5,8,11, 13; DLB 13, 233; DLBY 85; MTCW 1, 2; RGEL

Storey, David (Malcolm) 1933- . **CLC 2, 4, 5, 8; DAM DRAM**
See also BRWS 1; CA 81-84; CANR 36; CBD; CD; CN; DLB 13, 14, 207; MTCW 1; RGEL

Storm, Hyemeyohsts 1935- ..... **CLC 3; DAM MULT**
See also CA 81-84; CANR 45; NNAL

Storm, Theodor 1817-1888 .... **SSC 27**
See also RGSF; RGWL

Storm, (Hans) Theodor (Woldsen) 1817-1888 .... **NCLC 1; SSC 27**
See also DLB 129

Storni, Alfonsina 1892-1938 . **TCLC 5; DAM MULT; HLC 2; PC 33**
See also CA 104; 131; HW 1

Stoughton, William 1631-1701 .... **LC 38**
See also DLB 24

Stout, Rex (Todhunter) 1886-1975 ..... **CLC 3**
See also AITN 2; CA 61-64; CANR 71; CMW

Stow, (Julian) Randolph 1935- ... **CLC 23, 48**
See also CA 13-16R; CANR 33; CN; MTCW 1; RGEL

Stowe, Harriet (Elizabeth) Beecher 1811-1896 .... **NCLC 3, 50; DA; DAB; DAC; DAM MST, NOV; WLC**
See also AMWS 1; CDALB 1865-1917; DA3; DLB 1, 12, 42, 74, 189, 239; JRDA; MAICYA; NFS 6; YABC 1

Strabo c. 64B.C.-c. 25 .... **CMLC 37**
See also DLB 176

Strachey, (Giles) Lytton 1880-1932 .... **TCLC 12**
See also BRWS 2; CA 110; 178; DLB 149; DLBD 10; MTCW 2

Strand, Mark 1934- .... **CLC 6, 18, 41, 71; DAM POET**
See also AMWS 4; CA 21-24R; CANR 40, 65; CP; DLB 5; PFS 9; RGAL; SATA 41

Stratton-Porter, Gene(va Grace) 1863-1924
See Porter, Gene(va Grace) Stratton
See also CA 137; DLB 221; DLBD 14; MAICYA; SATA 15

Straub, Peter (Francis) 1943- . **CLC 28, 107; DAM POP**
See also BEST 89:1; CA 85-88; CANR 28, 65; CPW; DLBY 84; HGG; MTCW 1, 2

Strauss, Botho 1944- .... **CLC 22**
See also CA 157; CWW 2; DLB 124

Streatfeild, (Mary) Noel 1897(?)-1986 .... **CLC 21**
See also CA 81-84; 120; CANR 31; CLR 17; CWRI; DLB 160; MAICYA; SATA 20; SATA-Obit 48

Stribling, T(homas) S(igismund) 1881-1965 .... **CLC 23**
See also CA 189; 107; CMW; DLB 9

Strindberg, (Johan) August 1849-1912 .... **TCLC 1, 8, 21, 47; DA; DAB; DAC; DAM DRAM, MST; WLC**
See also CA 104; 135; DA3; DFS 4, 9; MTCW 2

Stringer, Arthur 1874-1950 .... **TCLC 37**
See also CA 161; DLB 92

Stringer, David
See Roberts, Keith (John Kingston)

Stroheim, Erich von 1885-1957 ..... **TCLC 71**

Strugatskii, Arkadii (Natanovich) 1925-1991 .... **CLC 27**
See also CA 106; 135; SFW

Strugatskii, Boris (Natanovich) 1933- .... **CLC 27**
See also CA 106; SFW

Strummer, Joe 1953(?)- .... **CLC 30**

Strunk, William, Jr. 1869-1946 ...... **TCLC 92**
See also CA 118; 164

Stryk, Lucien 1924- .... **PC 27**
See also CA 13-16R; CANR 10, 28, 55; CP

Stuart, Don A.
See Campbell, John W(ood, Jr.)

Stuart, Ian
See MacLean, Alistair (Stuart)

Stuart, Jesse (Hilton) 1906-1984 ... **CLC 1, 8, 11, 14, 34; SSC 31**
See also CA 5-8R; 112; CANR 31; DLB 9, 48, 102; DLBY 84; SATA 2; SATA-Obit 36

Sturgeon, Theodore (Hamilton) 1918-1985 .... **CLC 22, 39**
See also Queen, Ellery
See also CA 81-84; 116; CANR 32; DLB 8; DLBY 85; HGG; MTCW 1, 2; SFW

Sturges, Preston 1898-1959 .... **TCLC 48**
See also CA 114; 149; DLB 26

Styron, William 1925- .... **CLC 1, 3, 5, 11, 15, 60; DAM NOV, POP; SSC 25**
See also BEST 90:4; CA 5-8R; CANR 6, 33, 74; CDALB 1968-1988; CN; CPW; CSW; DA3; DLB 2, 143; DLBY 80; INT CANR-6; MTCW 1, 2; NCFS 1; RGAL; RHW

Su, Chien 1884-1918
See Su Man-shu
See also CA 123

Suarez Lynch, B.
See Bioy Casares, Adolfo; Borges, Jorge Luis

Suassuna, Ariano Vilar 1927-
See also CA 178; HLCS 1; HW 2

Suckling, SirJohn 1609-1642 .... **PC 30**
See also BRW; DAM POET; DLB 58, 126; PAB; RGEL

Suckow, Ruth 1892-1960 .... **SSC 18**
See also CA 113; DLB 9, 102; RGAL; TCWW 2

Sudermann, Hermann 1857-1928 .. **TCLC 15**
See also CA 107; DLB 118

Sue, Eugene 1804-1857 .... **NCLC 1**
See also DLB 119

Sueskind, Patrick 1949- .... **CLC 44**
See also Suskind, Patrick

Sukenick, Ronald 1932- .... **CLC 3, 4, 6, 48**
See also CA 25-28R; CAAS 8; CANR 32, 89; CN; DLB 173; DLBY 81

Suknaski, Andrew 1942- .... **CLC 19**
See also CA 101; CP; DLB 53

Sullivan, Vernon
See Vian, Boris

Sully Prudhomme, René-François-Armand 1839-1907 .... **TCLC 31**
See also GFL 1789 to the Present

Su Man-shu .... **TCLC 24**
See also Su, Chien

Summerforest, Ivy B.
See Kirkup, James

Summers, Andrew James 1942- .... **CLC 26**

Summers, Andy
See Summers, Andrew James

Summers, Hollis (Spurgeon, Jr.) 1916- .... **CLC 10**
See also CA 5-8R; CANR 3; DLB 6

Temple, Ann
  See Mortimer, Penelope (Ruth)
Tennant, Emma (Christina) 1937- .. **CLC 13, 52**
  See also CA 65-68; CAAS 9; CANR 10, 38, 59, 88; CN; DLB 14; SFW
Tenneshaw, S. M.
  See Silverberg, Robert
Tennyson, Alfred 1809-1892 ... **NCLC 30, 65; DA; DAB; DAC; DAM MST, POET; PC 6; WLC**
  See also BRW; CDBLB 1832-1890; DA3; DLB 32; PAB; PFS 1, 2, 4, 11; RGEL; WP
Teran, Lisa St. Aubin de .... **CLC 36**
  See also St. Aubin de Teran, Lisa
Terence c. 195B.C.- .... **CMLC 14; DC 7**
  See also DLB 211; RGEL
Teresa de Jesus, St. 1515-1582 .... **LC 18**
Terkel, Louis 1912-
  See Terkel, Studs
  See also CA 57-60; CANR 18, 45, 67; DA3; MTCW 1, 2
Terkel, Studs .... **CLC 38**
  See also Terkel, Louis
  See also AAYA 32; AITN 1; MTCW 2
Terry, C. V.
  See Slaughter, Frank G(ill)
Terry, Megan 1932- .... **CLC 19; DC 13**
  See also CA 77-80; CABS 3; CAD; CANR 43; CD; CWD; DLB 7; GLL 2
Tertullian c. 155-c. 245 .... **CMLC 29**
Tertz, Abram
  See Sinyavsky, Andrei (Donatevich)
  See also CWW 2; RGSF
Tesich, Steve 1943(?)-1996 .... **CLC 40, 69**
  See also CA 105; 152; CAD; DLBY 83
Tesla, Nikola 1856-1943 .... **TCLC 88**
Teternikov, Fyodor Kuzmich 1863-1927
  See Sologub, Fyodor
  See also CA 104
Tevis, Walter 1928-1984 .... **CLC 42**
  See also CA 113; SFW
Tey, Josephine .... **TCLC 14**
  See also Mackintosh, Elizabeth
  See also DLB 77
Thackeray, William Makepeace
  1811-1863 ...... **NCLC 5, 14, 22, 43; DA; DAB; DAC; DAM MST, NOV; WLC**
  See also CDBLB 1832-1890; DA3; DLB 21, 55, 159, 163; RGEL; SATA 23
Thakura, Ravindranatha
  See Tagore, Rabindranath
Thames, C. H.
  See Marlowe, Stephen
Tharoor, Shashi 1956- .... **CLC 70**
  See also CA 141; CANR 91; CN
Thelwell, Michael Miles 1939- .... **CLC 22**
  See also BW 2; CA 101
Theobald, Lewis, Jr.
  See Lovecraft, H(oward) P(hillips)
Theocritus c. 310B.C.- .... **CMLC 45**
  See also DLB 176; RGEL
Theodorescu, Ion N. 1880-1967
  See Arghezi, Tudor
  See also CA 116; DLB 220
Theriault, Yves 1915-1983 .... **CLC 79; DAC; DAM MST**
  See also CA 102; CCA 1; DLB 88
Theroux, Alexander (Louis) 1939- .... **CLC 2, 25**
  See also CA 85-88; CANR 20, 63; CN
Theroux, Paul (Edward) 1941- ..... **CLC 5, 8, 11, 15, 28, 46; DAM POP**
  See also AAYA 28; AMWS 8; BEST 89:4; CA 33-36R; CANR 20, 45, 74; CDALBS; CN; CPW 1; DA3; DLB 2; HGG; MTCW 1, 2; SATA 44, 109

Thesen, Sharon 1946- .... **CLC 56**
  See also CA 163; CP; CWP
Thevenin, Denis
  See Duhamel, Georges
Thibault, Jacques Anatole François
  1844-1924
  See France, Anatole
  See also CA 106; 127; DAM NOV; DA3; MTCW 1, 2
Thiele, Colin (Milton) 1920- .... **CLC 17**
  See also CA 29-32R; CANR 12, 28, 53; CLR 27; MAICYA; SAAS 2; SATA 14, 72; YAW
Thomas, Audrey (Callahan) 1935- .... **CLC 7, 13, 37, 107; SSC 20**
  See also AITN 2; CA 21-24R; CAAS 19; CANR 36, 58; CN; DLB 60; MTCW 1
Thomas, Augustus 1857-1934 .... **TCLC 97**
Thomas, D(onald) M(ichael) 1935- . **CLC 13, 22, 31, 132**
  See also BRWS 4; CA 61-64; CAAS 11; CANR 17, 45, 75; CDBLB 1960 to Present; CN; CP; DA3; DLB 40, 207; HGG; INT CANR-17; MTCW 1, 2; SFW
Thomas, Dylan (Marlais)
  1914-1953 ...... **TCLC 1, 8, 45, 105; DA; DAB; DAC; DAM DRAM, MST, POET; PC 2; SSC 3, 44; WLC**
  See also BRWS 1; CA 104; 120; CANR 65; CDBLB 1945-1960; DA3; DLB 13, 20, 139; MTCW 1, 2; PFS 1, 3, 8; SATA 60
Thomas, (Philip) Edward
  1878-1917 .... **TCLC 10; DAM POET**
  See also CA 106; 153; DLB 98; RGEL
Thomas, Joyce Carol 1938- .... **CLC 35**
  See also AAYA 12; BW 2, 3; CA 113; 116; CANR 48; CLR 19; DLB 33; INT 116; JRDA; MAICYA; MTCW 1, 2; SAAS 7; SATA 40, 78, 123; YAW
Thomas, Lewis 1913-1993 .... **CLC 35**
  See also CA 85-88; 143; CANR 38, 60; MTCW 1, 2
Thomas, M. Carey 1857-1935 .... **TCLC 89**
  See also FW
Thomas, Paul
  See Mann, (Paul) Thomas
Thomas, Piri 1928- .... **CLC 17; HLCS 2**
  See also CA 73-76; HW 1
Thomas, R(onald) S(tuart)
  1913-2000 . **CLC 6, 13, 48; DAB; DAM POET**
  See also CA 89-92; 189; CAAS 4; CANR 30; CDBLB 1960 to Present; CP; DLB 27; MTCW 1; RGEL
Thomas, Ross (Elmore) 1926-1995 .. **CLC 39**
  See also CA 33-36R; 150; CANR 22, 63; CMW
Thompson, Francis (Joseph)
  1859-1907 .... **TCLC 4**
  See also BRW; CA 104; 189; CDBLB 1890-1914; DLB 19; RGEL; TEA
Thompson, Francis Clegg
  See Mencken, H(enry) L(ouis)
Thompson, Hunter S(tockton)
  1939- ... **CLC 9, 17, 40, 104; DAM POP**
  See also BEST 89:1; CA 17-20R; CANR 23, 46, 74, 77; CPW; CSW; DA3; DLB 185; MTCW 1, 2
Thompson, James Myers
  See Thompson, Jim (Myers)
Thompson, Jim (Myers)
  1906-1977(?) .... **CLC 69**
  See also CA 140; CMW; CPW; DLB 226
Thompson, Judith .... **CLC 39**
  See also CWD
Thomson, James 1700-1748 ... **LC 16, 29, 40; DAM POET**
  See also BRWS 3; DLB 95; RGEL

Thomson, James 1834-1882 .... **NCLC 18; DAM POET**
  See also DLB 35; RGEL
Thoreau, Henry David 1817-1862 .. **NCLC 7, 21, 61; DA; DAB; DAC; DAM MST; PC 30; WLC**
  See also CDALB 1640-1865; DA3; DLB 1, 223; RGAL
Thorndike, E. L.
  See Thorndike, Edward L(ee)
Thorndike, Edward L(ee)
  1874-1949 .... **TCLC 107**
  See also CA 121
Thornton, Hall
  See Silverberg, Robert
Thucydides c. 460B.C.- .... **CMLC 17**
  See also DLB 176; RGEL
Thumboo, Edwin 1933- .... **PC 30**
Thurber, James (Grover)
  1894-1961 .... **CLC 5, 11, 25, 125; DA; DAB; DAC; DAM DRAM, MST, NOV; SSC 1**
  See also AMWS 1; CA 73-76; CANR 17, 39; CDALB 1929-1941; CWRI; DA3; DLB 4, 11, 22, 102; FANT; MAICYA; MTCW 1, 2; SATA 13; SSFS 1, 10
Thurman, Wallace (Henry)
  1902-1934 .... **TCLC 6; BLC 3; DAM MULT**
  See also BW 1, 3; CA 104; 124; CANR 81; DLB 51
Tibullus c. 54B.C.-c. 18B.C. .... **CMLC 36**
  See also DLB 211
Ticheburn, Cheviot
  See Ainsworth, William Harrison
Tieck, (Johann) Ludwig
  1773-1853 .... **NCLC 5, 46; SSC 31**
  See also DLB 90
Tiger, Derry
  See Ellison, Harlan (Jay)
Tilghman, Christopher 1948(?)- .... **CLC 65**
  See also CA 159; CSW
Tillich, Paul (Johannes)
  1886-1965 .... **CLC 131**
  See also CA 5-8R; 25-28R; CANR 33; MTCW 1, 2
Tillinghast, Richard (Williford)
  1940- .... **CLC 29**
  See also CA 29-32R; CAAS 23; CANR 26, 51, 96; CP; CSW
Timrod, Henry 1828-1867 .... **NCLC 25**
  See also DLB 3; RGAL
Tindall, Gillian (Elizabeth) 1938- ...... **CLC 7**
  See also CA 21-24R; CANR 11, 65; CN
Tiptree, James, Jr. .... **CLC 48, 50**
  See also Sheldon, Alice Hastings Bradley
  See also DLB 8; SFW
Tirso de Molina
  See Molina, Tirso de
  See also RGWL
Titmarsh, Michael Angelo
  See Thackeray, William Makepeace
Tocqueville, Alexis (Charles Henri Maurice Clérel) 1805-1859 .... **NCLC 7, 63**
  See also EW; GFL 1789 to the Present
Tolkien, J(ohn) R(onald) R(euel)
  1892-1973 .. **CLC 1, 2, 3, 8, 12, 38; DA; DAB; DAC; DAM MST, NOV, POP; WLC**
  See also AAYA 10; AITN 1; BRWS 2; CA 17-18; 45-48; CANR 36; CAP 2; CDBLB 1914-1945; CLR 56; CPW 1; CWRI; DA3; DLB 15, 160; EFS 2; FANT; JRDA; MAICYA; MTCW 1, 2; NFS 8; RGEL; SATA 2, 32, 100; SATA-Obit 24; SFW; SUFW; WCH; WYA; YAW
Toller, Ernst 1893-1939 .... **TCLC 10**
  See also CA 107; 186; DLB 124; RGWL

Tolson, M. B.
See Tolson, Melvin B(eaunorus)

Tolson, Melvin B(eaunorus)
1898(?)-1966 .... **CLC 36, 105; BLC 3; DAM MULT, POET**
See also AFAW 1, 2; BW 1, 3; CA 124; 89-92; CANR 80; DLB 48, 76

Tolstoi, Aleksei Nikolaevich
See Tolstoy, Alexey Nikolaevich

Tolstoi, Lev
See Tolstoy, Leo (Nikolaevich)
See also RGSF; RGWL

Tolstoy, Alexey Nikolaevich
1882-1945 .... **TCLC 18**
See also CA 107; 158; SFW

Tolstoy, Count Leo
See Tolstoy, Leo (Nikolaevich)

Tolstoy, Leo (Nikolaevich)
1828-1910 .. **TCLC 4, 11, 17, 28, 44, 79; DA; DAB; DAC; DAM MST, NOV; SSC 9, 30, 45; WLC**
See also Tolstoi, Lev
See also CA 104; 123; DA3; DLB 238; EFS 2; NFS 10; SATA 26; SSFS 5

Tomasi di Lampedusa, Giuseppe 1896-1957
See Lampedusa, Giuseppe (Tomasi) di
See also CA 111

Tomlin, Lily .... **CLC 17**
See also Tomlin, Mary Jean

Tomlin, Mary Jean 1939(?)-
See Tomlin, Lily
See also CA 117

Tomlinson, (Alfred) Charles 1927- .... **CLC 2, 4, 6, 13, 45; DAM POET; PC 17**
See also CA 5-8R; CANR 33; CP; DLB 40

Tomlinson, H(enry) M(ajor)
1873-1958 .... **TCLC 71**
See also CA 118; 161; DLB 36, 100, 195

Tonson, Jacob
See Bennett, (Enoch) Arnold

Toole, John Kennedy 1937-1969 ..... **CLC 19, 64**
See also CA 104; DLBY 81; MTCW 2

Toomer, Jean 1892-1967 .... **CLC 1, 4, 13, 22; BLC 3; DAM MULT; PC 7; SSC 1, 45; WLCS**
See also Pinchback, Eugene; Toomer, Eugene; Toomer, Eugene Pinchback; Toomer, Nathan Jean; Toomer, Nathan Pinchback
See also AFAW 1, 2; AMWS 3; BW 1; CA 85-88; CDALB 1917-1929; DA3; DLB 45, 51; MTCW 1, 2; NFS 11; RGAL; RGSF; SSFS 5

Torley, Luke
See Blish, James (Benjamin)

Tornimparte, Alessandra
See Ginzburg, Natalia

Torre, Raoul della
See Mencken, H(enry) L(ouis)

Torrence, Ridgely 1874-1950 .... **TCLC 97**
See also DLB 54

Torrey, E(dwin) Fuller 1937- .... **CLC 34**
See also CA 119; CANR 71

Torsvan, Ben Traven
See Traven, B.

Torsvan, Benno Traven
See Traven, B.

Torsvan, Berick Traven
See Traven, B.

Torsvan, Berwick Traven
See Traven, B.

Torsvan, Bruno Traven
See Traven, B.

Torsvan, Traven
See Traven, B.

Tourneur, Cyril 1575(?)-1626 .. **LC 66; DAM DRAM**
See also DLB 58; RGEL

Tournier, Michel (Édouard) 1924- .... **CLC 6, 23, 36, 95**
See also CA 49-52; CANR 3, 36, 74; DLB 83; GFL 1789 to the Present; MTCW 1, 2; SATA 23

Tournimparte, Alessandra
See Ginzburg, Natalia

Towers, Ivar
See Kornbluth, C(yril) M.

Towne, Robert (Burton) 1936(?)- ..... **CLC 87**
See also CA 108; DLB 44; IDFW 3

Townsend, Sue .... **CLC 61**
See also Townsend, Susan Elaine
See also AAYA 28; CBD; CWD; SATA 55, 93; SATA-Brief 48

Townsend, Susan Elaine 1946-
See Townsend, Sue
See also CA 119; 127; CANR 65; CD; CPW; DAB; DAC; DAM MST; INT 127; YAW

Townshend, Peter (Dennis Blandford)
1945- .... **CLC 17, 42**
See also CA 107

Tozzi, Federigo 1883-1920 .... **TCLC 31**
See also CA 160

Tracy, Don(ald Fiske) 1905-1970(?)
See Queen, Ellery
See also CA 1-4R; 176; CANR 2

Traill, Catharine Parr 1802-1899 .. **NCLC 31**
See also DLB 99

Trakl, Georg 1887-1914 .... **TCLC 5; PC 20**
See also CA 104; 165; MTCW 2; RGWL

Transtroemer, Tomas (Goesta)
1931- .... **CLC 52, 65; DAM POET**
See also CA 117; 129; CAAS 17

Transtromer, Tomas Gosta
See Transtroemer, Tomas (Goesta)

Traven, B. 1882(?)-1969 .... **CLC 8, 11**
See also CA 19-20; 25-28R; CAP 2; DLB 9, 56; MTCW 1; RGAL

Trediakovsky, Vasilii Kirillovich
1703-1769 .... **LC 68**
See also DLB 150

Treitel, Jonathan 1959- .... **CLC 70**

Trelawny, Edward John
1792-1881 .... **NCLC 85**
See also DLB 110, 116, 144

Tremain, Rose 1943- .... **CLC 42**
See also CA 97-100; CANR 44, 95; CN; DLB 14; RGSF; RHW

Tremblay, Michel 1942- .... **CLC 29, 102; DAC; DAM MST**
See also CA 116; 128; CCA 1; CWW 2; DLB 60; GLL 1; MTCW 1, 2

Trevanian .... **CLC 29**
See also Whitaker, Rod(ney)

Trevor, Glen
See Hilton, James

Trevor, William .. **CLC 7, 9, 14, 25, 71, 116; SSC 21**
See also Cox, William Trevor
See also BRWS 4; CBD; DLB 14, 139; MTCW 2; RGEL; RGSF; SSFS 10

Trifonov, Iurii (Valentinovich)
See Trifonov, Yuri (Valentinovich)
See also RGWL

Trifonov, Yuri (Valentinovich)
1925-1981 .... **CLC 45**
See also Trifonov, Iurii (Valentinovich)
See also CA 126; 103; MTCW 1

Trilling, Diana (Rubin) 1905-1996 . **CLC 129**
See also CA 5-8R; 154; CANR 10, 46; INT CANR-10; MTCW 1, 2

Trilling, Lionel 1905-1975 .... **CLC 9, 11, 24**
See also AMWS 3; CA 9-12R; 61-64; CANR 10; DLB 28, 63; INT CANR-10; MTCW 1, 2; RGAL

Trimball, W. H.
See Mencken, H(enry) L(ouis)

Tristan
See Gomez de la Serna, Ramon

Tristram
See Housman, A(lfred) E(dward)

Trogdon, William (Lewis) 1939-
See Heat-Moon, William Least
See also CA 115; 119; CANR 47, 89; CPW; INT 119

Trollope, Anthony 1815-1882 .... **NCLC 6, 33, 101; DA; DAB; DAC; DAM MST, NOV; SSC 28; WLC**
See also CDBLB 1832-1890; DA3; DLB 21, 57, 159; RGEL; RGSF; SATA 22

Trollope, Frances 1779-1863 .... **NCLC 30**
See also DLB 21, 166

Trotsky, Leon 1879-1940 .... **TCLC 22**
See also CA 118; 167

Trotter (Cockburn), Catharine
1679-1749 .... **LC 8**
See also DLB 84

Trotter, Wilfred 1872-1939 .... **TCLC 97**

Trout, Kilgore
See Farmer, Philip Jose

Trow, George W. S. 1943- .... **CLC 52**
See also CA 126; CANR 91

Troyat, Henri 1911- .... **CLC 23**
See also CA 45-48; CANR 2, 33, 67; GFL 1789 to the Present; MTCW 1

Trudeau, G(arretson) B(eekman) 1948-
See Trudeau, Garry B.
See also CA 81-84; CANR 31; SATA 35

Trudeau, Garry B. .... **CLC 12**
See also Trudeau, G(arretson) B(eekman)
See also AAYA 10; AITN 2

Truffaut, Francois 1932-1984 ... **CLC 20, 101**
See also CA 81-84; 113; CANR 34

Trumbo, Dalton 1905-1976 .... **CLC 19**
See also Rich, Robert
See also CA 21-24R; 69-72; CANR 10; DLB 26; IDFW 3, 4; YAW

Trumbull, John 1750-1831 .... **NCLC 30**
See also DLB 31; RGAL

Trundlett, Helen B.
See Eliot, T(homas) S(tearns)

Truth, Sojourner 1797(?)-1883 ...... **NCLC 94**
See also DLB 239; FW

Tryon, Thomas 1926-1991 .... **CLC 3, 11; DAM POP**
See also AITN 1; CA 29-32R; 135; CANR 32, 77; CPW; DA3; HGG; MTCW 1

Tryon, Tom
See Tryon, Thomas

Ts'ao Hsueh-ch'in 1715(?)-1763 .... **LC 1**

Tsushima, Shuji 1909-1948
See Dazai Osamu
See also CA 107

Tsvetaeva (Efron), Marina (Ivanovna)
1892-1941 .... **TCLC 7, 35; PC 14**
See also CA 104; 128; CANR 73; MTCW 1, 2

Tuck, Lily 1938- .... **CLC 70**
See also CA 139; CANR 90

Tu Fu 712-770 .... **PC 9**
See also Du Fu
See also DAM MULT

Tunis, John R(oberts) 1889-1975 ..... **CLC 12**
See also CA 61-64; CANR 62; DLB 22, 171; JRDA; MAICYA; SATA 37; SATA-Brief 30; YAW

Tuohy, Frank .... **CLC 37**
See also Tuohy, John Francis
See also DLB 14, 139

Tuohy, John Francis 1925-
See Tuohy, Frank
See also CA 5-8R; 178; CANR 3, 47; CN

Turco, Lewis (Putnam) 1934- .... **CLC 11, 63**
See also CA 13-16R; CAAS 22; CANR 24, 51; CP; DLBY 84

Turgenev, Ivan 1818-1883 .... NCLC 21, 37;
   DA; DAB; DAC; DAM MST, NOV;
   DC 7; SSC 7; WLC
    See also DFS 6; DLB 238; RGSF; RGWL

Turgot, Anne-Robert-Jacques
   1727-1781 .... LC 26

Turner, Frederick 1943- .... CLC 48
    See also CA 73-76; CAAS 10; CANR 12,
    30, 56; DLB 40

Tutu, Desmond M(pilo) 1931- .... CLC 80;
   BLC 3; DAM MULT
    See also BW 1, 3; CA 125; CANR 67, 81

Tutuola, Amos 1920-1997 ...... CLC 5, 14, 29;
   BLC 3; DAM MULT
    See also BW 2, 3; CA 9-12R; 159; CANR
    27, 66; CN; DA3; DLB 125; DNFS 2;
    MTCW 1, 2; RGEL

Twain, Mark .... TCLC 6, 12, 19, 36, 48, 59;
   SSC 34; WLC
    See also Clemens, Samuel Langhorne
    See also AAYA 20; CLR 58, 60, 66; DLB
    11, 12, 23, 64, 74; FANT; NFS 1, 6;
    RGAL; RGSF; SFW; SSFS 1, 7; YAW

Tyler, Anne 1941- . CLC 7, 11, 18, 28, 44, 59,
   103; DAM NOV, POP
    See also AAYA 18; AMWS 4; BEST 89:1;
    CA 9-12R; CANR 11, 33, 53; CDALBS;
    CN; CPW; CSW; DLB 6, 143; DLBY 82;
    MTCW 1, 2; NFS 2, 7, 10; RGAL; SATA
    7, 90; YAW

Tyler, Royall 1757-1826 .... NCLC 3
    See also DLB 37; RGAL

Tynan, Katharine 1861-1931 .... TCLC 3
    See also CA 104; 167; DLB 153, 240; FW

Tyutchev, Fyodor 1803-1873 .... NCLC 34

Tzara, Tristan 1896-1963 ...... CLC 47; DAM
   POET; PC 27
    See also CA 153; 89-92; MTCW 2

Uhry, Alfred 1936- .. CLC 55; DAM DRAM,
   POP
    See also CA 127; 133; CAD; CD; CSW;
    DA3; DFS 11; INT 133

Ulf, Haerved
    See Strindberg, (Johan) August

Ulf, Harved
    See Strindberg, (Johan) August

Ulibarrí, Sabine R(eyes) 1919- .... CLC 83;
   DAM MULT; HLCS 2
    See also CA 131; CANR 81; DLB 82; HW
    1, 2

Unamuno (y Jugo), Miguel de
   1864-1936 ...... TCLC 2, 9; DAM MULT,
   NOV; HLC 2; SSC 11
    See also CA 104; 131; CANR 81; DLB 108;
    HW 1, 2; MTCW 1, 2

Undercliffe, Errol
    See Campbell, (John) Ramsey

Underwood, Miles
    See Glassco, John

Undset, Sigrid 1882-1949 .... TCLC 3; DA;
   DAB; DAC; DAM MST, NOV; WLC
    See also CA 104; 129; DA3; FW; MTCW
    1, 2; RGWL

Ungaretti, Giuseppe 1888-1970 ... CLC 7, 11,
   15
    See also CA 19-20; 25-28R; CAP 2; DLB
    114; RGWL

Unger, Douglas 1952- .... CLC 34
    See also CA 130; CANR 94

Unsworth, Barry (Forster) 1930- .... CLC 76,
   127
    See also CA 25-28R; CANR 30, 54; CN;
    DLB 194

Updike, John (Hoyer) 1932- . CLC 1, 2, 3, 5,
   7, 9, 13, 15, 23, 34, 43, 70, 139; DA;
   DAB; DAC; DAM MST, NOV, POET,
   POP; SSC 13, 27; WLC
    See also AAYA 36; CA 1-4R; CABS 1;
    CANR 4, 33, 51, 94; CDALB 1968-1988;

CN; CP; CPW 1; DA3; DLB 2, 5, 143,
   227; DLBD 3; DLBY 80, 82, 97; HGG;
   MTCW 1, 2; NFS 12; SSFS 3

Upshaw, Margaret Mitchell
    See Mitchell, Margaret (Munnerlyn)

Upton, Mark
    See Sanders, Lawrence

Upward, Allen 1863-1926 .... TCLC 85
    See also CA 117; 187; DLB 36

Urdang, Constance (Henriette)
   1922-1996 .... CLC 47
    See also CA 21-24R; CANR 9, 24; CP;
    CWP

Uriel, Henry
    See Faust, Frederick (Schiller)

Uris, Leon (Marcus) 1924- .... CLC 7, 32;
   DAM NOV, POP
    See also AITN 1, 2; BEST 89:2; CA 1-4R;
    CANR 1, 40, 65; CN; CPW 1; DA3;
    MTCW 1, 2; SATA 49

Urista, Alberto H. 1947- .... PC 34
    See also Alurista
    See also CA 45-48, 182; CANR 2, 32;
    HLCS 1; HW 1

Urmuz
    See Codrescu, Andrei

Urquhart, Guy
    See McAlmon, Robert (Menzies)

Urquhart, Jane 1949- .... CLC 90; DAC
    See also CA 113; CANR 32, 68; CCA 1

Usigli, Rodolfo 1905-1979
    See also CA 131; HLCS 1; HW 1

Ustinov, Peter (Alexander) 1921- .... CLC 1
    See also AITN 1; CA 13-16R; CANR 25,
    51; CBD; CD; DLB 13; MTCW 2

U Tam'si, Gerald Felix Tchicaya
    See Tchicaya, Gerald Felix

U Tam'si, Tchicaya
    See Tchicaya, Gerald Felix

Vachss, Andrew (Henry) 1942- .... CLC 106
    See also CA 118; CANR 44, 95; CMW

Vachss, Andrew H.
    See Vachss, Andrew (Henry)

Vaculik, Ludvik 1926- .... CLC 7
    See also CA 53-56; CANR 72; CWW 2;
    DLB 232

Vaihinger, Hans 1852-1933 .... TCLC 71
    See also CA 116; 166

Valdez, Luis (Miguel) 1940- .. CLC 84; DAM
   MULT; DC 10; HLC 2
    See also CA 101; CAD; CANR 32, 81; CD;
    DFS 5; DLB 122; HW 1

Valenzuela, Luisa 1938- .... CLC 31, 104;
   DAM MULT; HLCS 2; SSC 14
    See also CA 101; CANR 32, 65; CWW 2;
    DLB 113; FW; HW 1, 2; RGSF

Valera y Alcala-Galiano, Juan
   1824-1905 .... TCLC 10
    See also CA 106

Valéry, (Ambroise) Paul (Toussaint Jules)
   1871-1945 ... TCLC 4, 15; DAM POET;
   PC 9
    See also CA 104; 122; DA3; EW; GFL 1789
    to the Present; MTCW 1, 2; RGWL

Valle-Inclán, Ramón (Maria) del
   1866-1936 .... TCLC 5; DAM MULT;
   HLC 2
    See also CA 106; 153; CANR 80; DLB 134;
    HW 2

Vallejo, Antonio Buero
    See Buero Vallejo, Antonio

Vallejo, César (Abraham)
   1892-1938 .. TCLC 3, 56; DAM MULT;
   HLC 2
    See also CA 105; 153; HW 1

Vallès, Jules 1832-1885 .... NCLC 71
    See also DLB 123; GFL 1789 to the Present

Vallette, Marguerite Eymery
   1860-1953 .... TCLC 67
    See also CA 182; DLB 123, 192

Valle Y Pena, Ramon del
    See Valle-Incl

Van Ash, Cay 1918- .... CLC 34

Vanbrugh, SirJohn 1664-1726 . LC 21; DAM
   DRAM
    See also DLB 80; IDTP; RGEL

Van Campen, Karl
    See Campbell, John W(ood, Jr.)

Vance, Gerald
    See Silverberg, Robert

Vance, Jack .... CLC 35
    See also Vance, John Holbrook
    See also DLB 8; SCFW 2

Vance, John Holbrook 1916-
    See Queen, Ellery; Vance, Jack
    See also CA 29-32R; CANR 17, 65; CMW;
    FANT; MTCW 1; SFW

Van Den Bogarde, Derek Jules Gaspard
   Ulric Niven 1921-1999 .... CLC 14
    See also CA 77-80; 179; DLB 19

Vandenburgh, Jane .... CLC 59
    See also CA 168

Vanderhaeghe, Guy 1951- .... CLC 41
    See also CA 113; CANR 72

van der Post, Laurens (Jan)
   1906-1996 .... CLC 5
    See also AFW; CA 5-8R; 155; CANR 35;
    CN; DLB 204; RGEL

van de Wetering, Janwillem 1931- ... CLC 47
    See also CA 49-52; CANR 4, 62, 90; CMW

Van Dine, S. S. .... TCLC 23
    See also Wright, Willard Huntington

Van Doren, Carl (Clinton)
   1885-1950 .... TCLC 18
    See also CA 111; 168

Van Doren, Mark 1894-1972 .... CLC 6, 10
    See also CA 1-4R; 37-40R; CANR 3; DLB
    45; MTCW 1, 2

Van Druten, John (William)
   1901-1957 .... TCLC 2
    See also CA 104; 161; DLB 10

Van Duyn, Mona (Jane) 1921- ...... CLC 3, 7,
   63, 116; DAM POET
    See also CA 9-12R; CANR 7, 38, 60; CP;
    CWP; DLB 5

Van Dyne, Edith
    See Baum, L(yman) Frank

van Itallie, Jean-Claude 1936- .... CLC 3
    See also CA 45-48; CAAS 2; CAD; CANR
    1, 48; CD; DLB 7

van Ostaijen, Paul 1896-1928 .... TCLC 33
    See also CA 163

Van Peebles, Melvin 1932- .... CLC 2, 20;
   DAM MULT
    See also BW 2, 3; CA 85-88; CANR 27,
    67, 82

van Schendel, Arthur(-Francois-Émile)
   1874-1946 .... TCLC 56

Vansittart, Peter 1920- .... CLC 42
    See also CA 1-4R; CANR 3, 49, 90; CN;
    RHW

Van Vechten, Carl 1880-1964 .... CLC 33
    See also AMWS 2; CA 183; 89-92; DLB 4,
    9, 51

van Vogt, A(lfred) E(lton) 1912-2000 . CLC 1
    See also CA 21-24R; 190; CANR 28; DLB
    8; SATA 14; SFW

Varda, Agnes 1928- .... CLC 16
    See also CA 116; 122

Vargas Llosa, (Jorge) Mario (Pedro)
   1936- .... CLC 3, 6, 9, 10, 15, 31, 42, 85;
   DA; DAB; DAC; DAM MST, MULT,
   NOV; HLC 2
    See also CA 73-76; CANR 18, 32, 42, 67;
    DA3; DLB 145; DNFS 2; HW 1, 2;
    MTCW 1, 2

Wain, John (Barrington) 1925-1994 . **CLC 2, 11, 15, 46**
See also CA 5-8R; 145; CAAS 4; CANR 23, 54; CDBLB 1960 to Present; DLB 15, 27, 139, 155; MTCW 1, 2

Wajda, Andrzej 1926- .... **CLC 16**
See also CA 102

Wakefield, Dan 1932- .... **CLC 7**
See also CA 21-24R; CAAS 7; CN

Wakoski, Diane 1937- ...... **CLC 2, 4, 7, 9, 11, 40; DAM POET; PC 15**
See also CA 13-16R; CAAS 1; CANR 9, 60; CP; CWP; DLB 5; INT CANR-9; MTCW 2

Wakoski-Sherbell, Diane
See Wakoski, Diane

Walcott, Derek (Alton) 1930- .... **CLC 2, 4, 9, 14, 25, 42, 67, 76; BLC 3; DAB; DAC; DAM MST, MULT, POET; DC 7**
See also BW 2; CA 89-92; CANR 26, 47, 75, 80; CBD; CD; CP; DA3; DLB 117; DLBY 81; DNFS 1; EFS 1; MTCW 1, 2; PFS 6; RGEL

Waldman, Anne (Lesley) 1945- .... **CLC 7**
See also CA 37-40R; CAAS 17; CANR 34, 69; CP; CWP; DLB 16

Waldo, E. Hunter
See Sturgeon, Theodore (Hamilton)

Waldo, Edward Hamilton
See Sturgeon, Theodore (Hamilton)

Walker, Alice (Malsenior) 1944- ... **CLC 5, 6, 9, 19, 27, 46, 58, 103; BLC 3; DA; DAB; DAC; DAM MST, MULT, NOV, POET, POP; PC 30; SSC 5; WLCS**
See also AAYA 3, 33; AFAW 1, 2; AMWS 3; BEST 89:4; BW 2, 3; CA 37-40R; CANR 9, 27, 49, 66, 82; CDALB 1968-1988; CN; CPW; CSW; DA3; DLB 6, 33, 143; FW; INT CANR-27; MTCW 1, 2; NFS 5; SATA 31; SSFS 2, 11; YAW

Walker, David Harry 1911-1992 ...... **CLC 14**
See also CA 1-4R; 137; CANR 1; CWRI; SATA 8; SATA-Obit 71

Walker, Edward Joseph 1934-
See Walker, Ted
See also CA 21-24R; CANR 12, 28, 53; CP

Walker, George F. 1947- . **CLC 44, 61; DAB; DAC; DAM MST**
See also CA 103; CANR 21, 43, 59; CD; DLB 60

Walker, Joseph A. 1935- .... **CLC 19; DAM DRAM, MST**
See also BW 1, 3; CA 89-92; CAD; CANR 26; CD; DFS 12; DLB 38

Walker, Margaret (Abigail) 1915-1998 .... **CLC 1, 6; BLC; DAM MULT; PC 20**
See also AFAW 1, 2; BW 2, 3; CA 73-76; 172; CANR 26, 54, 76; CN; CP; CSW; DLB 76, 152; FW; MTCW 1, 2; RHW

Walker, Ted .... **CLC 13**
See also Walker, Edward Joseph
See also DLB 40

Wallace, David Foster 1962- ..... **CLC 50, 114**
See also CA 132; CANR 59; DA3; MTCW 2

Wallace, Dexter
See Masters, Edgar Lee

Wallace, (Richard Horatio) Edgar 1875-1932 .... **TCLC 57**
See also CA 115; CMW; DLB 70; RGEL

Wallace, Irving 1916-1990 .... **CLC 7, 13; DAM NOV, POP**
See also AITN 1; CA 1-4R; 132; CAAS 1; CANR 1, 27; CPW; INT CANR-27; MTCW 1, 2

Wallant, Edward Lewis 1926-1962 ... **CLC 5, 10**
See also CA 1-4R; CANR 22; DLB 2, 28, 143; MTCW 1, 2; RGAL

Wallas, Graham 1858-1932 .... **TCLC 91**

Walley, Byron
See Card, Orson Scott

Walpole, Horace 1717-1797 .... **LC 49**
See also DLB 39, 104; HGG; RGEL

Walpole, Hugh (Seymour) 1884-1941 .... **TCLC 5**
See also CA 104; 165; DLB 34; HGG; MTCW 2; RGEL; RHW

Walser, Martin 1927- .... **CLC 27**
See also CA 57-60; CANR 8, 46; CWW 2; DLB 75, 124

Walser, Robert 1878-1956 .... **TCLC 18; SSC 20**
See also CA 118; 165; DLB 66

Walsh, Gillian Paton
See Paton Walsh, Gillian

Walsh, Jill Paton .... **CLC 35**
See Paton Walsh, Gillian
See also CLR 2, 65

Walter, Villiam Christian
See Andersen, Hans Christian

Wambaugh, Joseph (Aloysius, Jr.) 1937- .... **CLC 3, 18; DAM NOV, POP**
See also AITN 1; BEST 89:3; CA 33-36R; CANR 42, 65; CMW; CPW 1; DA3; DLB 6; DLBY 83; MTCW 1, 2

Wang Wei 699(?)-761(?) .... **PC 18**

Ward, Arthur Henry Sarsfield 1883-1959
See Rohmer, Sax
See also CA 108; 173; CMW; HGG

Ward, Douglas Turner 1930- .... **CLC 19**
See also BW 1; CA 81-84; CAD; CANR 27; CD; DLB 7, 38

Ward, E. D.
See Lucas, E(dward) V(errall)

Ward, Mrs.Humphry 1851-1920
See Ward, Mary Augusta
See also RGEL

Ward, Mary Augusta 1851-1920 ... **TCLC 55**
See also Ward, Mrs.Humphry
See also DLB 18

Ward, Peter
See Faust, Frederick (Schiller)

Warhol, Andy 1928(?)-1987 .... **CLC 20**
See also AAYA 12; BEST 89:4; CA 89-92; 121; CANR 34

Warner, Francis (Robert le Plastrier) 1937- .... **CLC 14**
See also CA 53-56; CANR 11

Warner, Marina 1946- .... **CLC 59**
See also CA 65-68; CANR 21, 55; CN; DLB 194

Warner, Rex (Ernest) 1905-1986 ...... **CLC 45**
See also CA 89-92; 119; DLB 15; RGEL; RHW

Warner, Susan (Bogert) 1819-1885 .... **NCLC 31**
See also DLB 3, 42, 239

Warner, Sylvia (Constance) Ashton
See Ashton-Warner, Sylvia (Constance)

Warner, Sylvia Townsend 1893-1978 .... **CLC 7, 19; SSC 23**
See also CA 61-64; 77-80; CANR 16, 60; DLB 34, 139; FANT; FW; MTCW 1, 2; RGEL; RGSF; RHW

Warren, Mercy Otis 1728-1814 ..... **NCLC 13**
See also DLB 31, 200

Warren, Robert Penn 1905-1989 .. **CLC 1, 4, 6, 8, 10, 13, 18, 39, 53, 59; DA; DAB; DAC; DAM MST, NOV, POET; SSC 4; WLC**
See also AITN 1; CA 13-16R; 129; CANR 10, 47; CDALB 1968-1988; DA3; DLB 2, 48, 152; DLBY 80, 89; INT CANR-10; MTCW 1, 2; RGAL; RGSF; RHW; SATA 46; SATA-Obit 63; SSFS 8

Warshofsky, Isaac
See Singer, Isaac Bashevis

Warton, Thomas 1728-1790 ..... **LC 15; DAM POET**
See also DLB 104, 109; RGEL

Waruk, Kona
See Harris, (Theodore) Wilson

Warung, Price .... **TCLC 45**
See also Astley, William
See also RGEL

Warwick, Jarvis
See Garner, Hugh
See also CCA 1

Washington, Alex
See Harris, Mark

Washington, Booker T(aliaferro) 1856-1915 ...... **TCLC 10; BLC 3; DAM MULT**
See also BW 1; CA 114; 125; DA3; SATA 28

Washington, George 1732-1799 .... **LC 25**
See also DLB 31

Wassermann, (Karl) Jakob 1873-1934 .... **TCLC 6**
See also CA 104; 163; DLB 66

Wasserstein, Wendy 1950- .. **CLC 32, 59, 90; DAM DRAM; DC 4**
See also CA 121; 129; CABS 3; CAD; CANR 53, 75; CD; CWD; DA3; DFS 5; DLB 228; FW; INT 129; MTCW 2; SATA 94

Waterhouse, Keith (Spencer) 1929- . **CLC 47**
See also CA 5-8R; CANR 38, 67; CBD; CN; DLB 13, 15; MTCW 1, 2

Waters, Frank (Joseph) 1902-1995 .. **CLC 88**
See also CA 5-8R; 149; CAAS 13; CANR 3, 18, 63; DLB 212; DLBY 86; TCWW 2

Waters, Mary C. .... **CLC 70**

Waters, Roger 1944- .... **CLC 35**

Watkins, Frances Ellen
See Harper, Frances Ellen Watkins

Watkins, Gerrold
See Malzberg, Barry N(athaniel)

Watkins, Gloria Jean 1952(?)-
See hooks, bell
See also BW 2; CA 143; CANR 87; MTCW 2; SATA 115

Watkins, Paul 1964- .... **CLC 55**
See also CA 132; CANR 62, 98

Watkins, Vernon Phillips 1906-1967 .... **CLC 43**
See also CA 9-10; 25-28R; CAP 1; DLB 20; RGEL

Watson, Irving S.
See Mencken, H(enry) L(ouis)

Watson, John H.
See Farmer, Philip Jose

Watson, Richard F.
See Silverberg, Robert

Waugh, Auberon (Alexander) 1939-2001 .... **CLC 7**
See also CA 45-48; CANR 6, 22, 92; DLB 14, 194

Waugh, Evelyn (Arthur St. John) 1903-1966 .. **CLC 1, 3, 8, 13, 19, 27, 44, 107; DA; DAB; DAC; DAM MST, NOV, POP; SSC 41; WLC**
See also CA 85-88; 25-28R; CANR 22; CD-BLB 1914-1945; DA3; DLB 15, 162, 195; MTCW 1, 2

Waugh, Harriet 1944- .... **CLC 6**
See also CA 85-88; CANR 22

Ways, C. R.
See Blount, Roy (Alton), Jr.

Waystaff, Simon
See Swift, Jonathan

Webb, Beatrice (Martha Potter) 1858-1943 .... **TCLC 22**
See also CA 117; 162; DLB 190; FW

Webb, Charles (Richard) 1939- .... **CLC 7**
See also CA 25-28R

White, Edmund (Valentine III)
1940- .... **CLC 27, 110; DAM POP**
See also AAYA 7; CA 45-48; CANR 3, 19, 36, 62; CN; DA3; DLB 227; MTCW 1, 2

White, Patrick (Victor Martindale)
1912-1990 ...... **CLC 3, 4, 5, 7, 9, 18, 65, 69; SSC 39**
See also BRWS 1; CA 81-84; 132; CANR 43; MTCW 1; RHW

White, Phyllis Dorothy James 1920-
See James, P. D.
See also CA 21-24R; CANR 17, 43, 65; CMW; CN; CPW; DAM POP; DA3; MTCW 1, 2

White, T(erence) H(anbury)
1906-1964 .... **CLC 30**
See also AAYA 22; CA 73-76; CANR 37; DLB 160; FANT; JRDA; MAICYA; RGEL; SATA 12; SUFW; YAW

White, Terence de Vere 1912-1994 ... **CLC 49**
See also CA 49-52; 145; CANR 3

White, Walter
See White, Walter F(rancis)
See also BLC; DAM MULT

White, Walter F(rancis)
1893-1955 .... **TCLC 15**
See also White, Walter
See also BW 1; CA 115; 124; DLB 51

White, William Hale 1831-1913
See Rutherford, Mark
See also CA 121; 189

Whitehead, Alfred North
1861-1947 .... **TCLC 97**
See also CA 117; 165; DLB 100

Whitehead, E(dward) A(nthony)
1933- .... **CLC 5**
See also CA 65-68; CANR 58; CD

Whitemore, Hugh (John) 1936- .... **CLC 37**
See also CA 132; CANR 77; CBD; CD; INT CA-132

Whitman, Sarah Helen (Power)
1803-1878 .... **NCLC 19**
See also DLB 1

Whitman, Walt(er) 1819-1892 .. **NCLC 4, 31, 81; DA; DAB; DAC; DAM MST, POET; PC 3; WLC**
See also CDALB 1640-1865; DA3; DLB 3, 64, 224; PFS 2, 3; SATA 20; WYAS 1

Whitney, Phyllis A(yame) 1903- ...... **CLC 42; DAM POP**
See also AAYA 36; AITN 2; BEST 90:3; CA 1-4R; CANR 3, 25, 38, 60; CLR 59; CMW; CPW; DA3; JRDA; MAICYA; MTCW 2; RHW; SATA 1, 30; YAW

Whittemore, (Edward) Reed (Jr.)
1919- .... **CLC 4**
See also CA 9-12R; CAAS 8; CANR 4; CP; DLB 5

Whittier, John Greenleaf
1807-1892 .... **NCLC 8, 59**
See also AMWS 1; DLB 1; RGAL

Whittlebot, Hernia
See Coward, No

Wicker, Thomas Grey 1926-
See Wicker, Tom
See also CA 65-68; CANR 21, 46

Wicker, Tom .... **CLC 7**
See also Wicker, Thomas Grey

Wideman, John Edgar 1941- ...... **CLC 5, 34, 36, 67, 122; BLC 3; DAM MULT**
See also AFAW 1, 2; BW 2, 3; CA 85-88; CANR 14, 42, 67; CN; DLB 33, 143; MTCW 2; RGAL; RGSF; SSFS 6, 12

Wiebe, Rudy (Henry) 1934- .. **CLC 6, 11, 14, 138; DAC; DAM MST**
See also CA 37-40R; CANR 42, 67; CN; DLB 60; RHW

Wieland, Christoph Martin
1733-1813 .... **NCLC 17**
See also DLB 97; RGWL

Wiene, Robert 1881-1938 .... **TCLC 56**

Wieners, John 1934- .... **CLC 7**
See also CA 13-16R; CP; DLB 16

Wiesel, Elie(zer) 1928- .... **CLC 3, 5, 11, 37; DA; DAB; DAC; DAM MST, NOV; WLCS**
See also AAYA 7; AITN 1; CA 5-8R; CAAS 4; CANR 8, 40, 65; CDALBS; DA3; DLB 83; DLBY 87; INT CANR-8; MTCW 1, 2; NFS 4; SATA 56; YAW

Wiggins, Marianne 1947- .... **CLC 57**
See also BEST 89:3; CA 130; CANR 60

Wiggs, Susan .... **CLC 70**

Wight, James Alfred 1916-1995
See Herriot, James
See also CA 77-80; CPW; SATA 55; SATA-Brief 44; YAW

Wilbur, Richard (Purdy) 1921- ..... **CLC 3, 6, 9, 14, 53, 110; DA; DAB; DAC; DAM MST, POET**
See also AMWS 3; CA 1-4R; CABS 2; CANR 2, 29, 76, 93; CDALBS; CP; DLB 5, 169; INT CANR-29; MTCW 1, 2; PFS 11, 12; SATA 9, 108

Wild, Peter 1940- .... **CLC 14**
See also CA 37-40R; CP; DLB 5

Wilde, Oscar (Fingal O'Flahertie Wills)
1854(?)-1900 .... **TCLC 1, 8, 23, 41; DA; DAB; DAC; DAM DRAM, MST, NOV; SSC 11; WLC**
See also CA 104; 119; CDBLB 1890-1914; DA3; DFS 4, 8, 9; DLB 10, 19, 34, 57, 141, 156, 190; FANT; SATA 24; SSFS 7

Wilder, Billy .... **CLC 20**
See also Wilder, Samuel
See also DLB 26

Wilder, Samuel 1906-
See Wilder, Billy
See also CA 89-92

Wilder, Stephen
See Marlowe, Stephen

Wilder, Thornton (Niven)
1897-1975 .. **CLC 1, 5, 6, 10, 15, 35, 82; DA; DAB; DAC; DAM DRAM, MST, NOV; DC 1; WLC**
See also AAYA 29; AITN 2; CA 13-16R; 61-64; CANR 40; CDALBS; DA3; DFS 1, 4; DLB 4, 7, 9, 228; DLBY 97; MTCW 1, 2; RHW; WYAS 1

Wilding, Michael 1942- .... **CLC 73**
See also CA 104; CANR 24, 49; CN; RGSF

Wiley, Richard 1944- .... **CLC 44**
See also CA 121; 129; CANR 71

Wilhelm, Kate .... **CLC 7**
See also Wilhelm, Katie (Gertrude)
See also AAYA 20; CAAS 5; DLB 8; INT CANR-17; SCFW 2

Wilhelm, Katie (Gertrude) 1928-
See Wilhelm, Kate
See also CA 37-40R; CANR 17, 36, 60, 94; MTCW 1; SFW

Wilkins, Mary
See Freeman, Mary E(leanor) Wilkins

Willard, Nancy 1936- .... **CLC 7, 37**
See also CA 89-92; CANR 10, 39, 68; CLR 5; CWP; CWRI; DLB 5, 52; FANT; MAICYA; MTCW 1; SATA 37, 71; SATA-Brief 30

William of Ockham 1290-1349 ..... **CMLC 32**

Williams, Ben Ames 1889-1953 ..... **TCLC 89**
See also CA 183; DLB 102

Williams, C(harles) K(enneth)
1936- .... **CLC 33, 56; DAM POET**
See also CA 37-40R; CAAS 26; CANR 57; CP; DLB 5

Williams, Charles
See Collier, James L(incoln)

Williams, Charles (Walter Stansby)
1886-1945 .... **TCLC 1, 11**
See also CA 104; 163; DLB 100, 153; FANT; RGEL; SUFW

Williams, (George) Emlyn
1905-1987 .... **CLC 15; DAM DRAM**
See also CA 104; 123; CANR 36; DLB 10, 77; MTCW 1

Williams, Hank 1923-1953 .... **TCLC 81**

Williams, Hugo 1942- .... **CLC 42**
See also CA 17-20R; CANR 45; CP; DLB 40

Williams, J. Walker
See Wodehouse, P(elham) G(renville)

Williams, John A(lfred) 1925- ..... **CLC 5, 13; BLC 3; DAM MULT**
See also AFAW 2; BW 2, 3; CA 53-56; CAAS 3; CANR 6, 26, 51; CN; CSW; DLB 2, 33; INT CANR-6; SFW

Williams, Jonathan (Chamberlain)
1929- .... **CLC 13**
See also CA 9-12R; CAAS 12; CANR 8; CP; DLB 5

Williams, Joy 1944- .... **CLC 31**
See also CA 41-44R; CANR 22, 48, 97

Williams, Norman 1952- .... **CLC 39**
See also CA 118

Williams, Sherley Anne 1944-1999 . **CLC 89; BLC 3; DAM MULT, POET**
See also AFAW 2; BW 2, 3; CA 73-76; 185; CANR 25, 82; DLB 41; INT CANR-25; SATA 78; SATA-Obit 116

Williams, Shirley
See Williams, Sherley Anne

Williams, Tennessee 1914-1983 . **CLC 1, 2, 5, 7, 8, 11, 15, 19, 30, 39, 45, 71, 111; DA; DAB; DAC; DAM DRAM, MST; DC 4; WLC**
See also AAYA 31; AITN 1, 2; CA 5-8R; 108; CABS 3; CAD; CANR 31; CDALB 1941-1968; DA3; DFS 1,3,7,12; DLB 7; DLBD 4; DLBY 83; GLL 1; MTCW 1, 2; RGAL

Williams, Thomas (Alonzo)
1926-1990 .... **CLC 14**
See also CA 1-4R; 132; CANR 2

Williams, William C.
See Williams, William Carlos

Williams, William Carlos
1883-1963 .... **CLC 1, 2, 5, 9, 13, 22, 42, 67; DA; DAB; DAC; DAM MST, POET; PC 7; SSC 31**
See also CA 89-92; CANR 34; CDALB 1917-1929; DA3; DLB 4, 16, 54, 86; MTCW 1, 2; PFS 1, 6, 11; RGAL; RGSF

Williamson, David (Keith) 1942- ..... **CLC 56**
See also CA 103; CANR 41; CD

Williamson, Ellen Douglas 1905-1984
See Douglas, Ellen
See also CA 17-20R; 114; CANR 39

Williamson, Jack .... **CLC 29**
See also Williamson, John Stewart
See also CAAS 8; DLB 8; SCFW 2

Williamson, John Stewart 1908-
See Williamson, Jack
See also CA 17-20R; CANR 23, 70; SFW

Willie, Frederick
See Lovecraft, H(oward) P(hillips)

Willingham, Calder (Baynard, Jr.)
1922-1995 .... **CLC 5, 51**
See also CA 5-8R; 147; CANR 3; CSW; DLB 2, 44; IDFW 3; MTCW 1

Willis, Charles
See Clarke, Arthur C(harles)

Willy
See Colette, (Sidonie-Gabrielle)

Zuk, Georges
  See Skelton, Robin
  See also CCA 1
Zukofsky, Louis 1904-1978 ... **CLC 1, 2, 4, 7, 11, 18; DAM POET; PC 11**

  See also AMWS 3; CA 9-12R; 77-80; CANR 39; DLB 5, 165; MTCW 1; RGAL
Zweig, Paul 1935-1984 .... **CLC 34, 42**
  See also CA 85-88; 113
Zweig, Stefan 1881-1942 .... **TCLC 17**

  See also CA 112; 170; DLB 81, 118
Zwingli, Huldreich 1484-1531 .... **LC 37**
  See also DLB 179

Literary Criticism Series
Cumulative Topic Index

This index lists all topic entries in Gale's *Classical and Medieval Literature Criticism, Contemporary Literary Criticism, Literature Criticism from 1400 to 1800, Nineteenth-Century Literature Criticism,* and *Twentieth-Century Literary Criticism.*

TCLC Cumulative Nationality Index

AMERICAN

Hippius, Zinaida **9**
Ilf, Ilya **21**
Ivanov, Vyacheslav Ivanovich **33**
Kandinsky, Wassily **92**
Khlebnikov, Velimir **20**
Khodasevich, Vladislav (Felitsianovich) **15**
Klimentov, Andrei Platonovich **14**
Korolenko, Vladimir Galaktionovich **22**
Kropotkin, Peter (Aleksieevich) **36**
Kuprin, Aleksander Ivanovich **5**
Kuzmin, Mikhail **40**
Lenin, V. I. **67**
Mandelstam, Osip (Emilievich) **2, 6**
Mayakovski, Vladimir (Vladimirovich) **4, 18**
Merezhkovsky, Dmitry Sergeyevich **29**
Nabokov, Vladimir (Vladimirovich) **108**
Pavlov, Ivan Petrovich **91**
Petrov, Evgeny **21**
Prishvin, Mikhail **75**
Remizov, Aleksei (Mikhailovich) **27**
Rozanov, Vassili **104**
Shestov, Lev **56**
Sologub, Fyodor **9**
Stalin, Joseph **92**
Tolstoy, Alexey Nikolaevich **18**
Tolstoy, Leo (Nikolaevich) **4, 11, 17, 28, 44, 79**
Trotsky, Leon **22**
Tsvetaeva (Efron), Marina (Ivanovna) **7, 35**
Zabolotsky, Nikolai Alekseevich **52**
Zamyatin, Evgeny Ivanovich **8, 37**
Zhdanov, Andrei Alexandrovich **18**
Zoshchenko, Mikhail (Mikhailovich) **15**

SCOTTISH

Barrie, J(ames) M(atthew) **2**
Bridie, James **3**
Brown, George Douglas **28**
Buchan, John **41**
Cunninghame Graham, Robert (Gallnigad) Bontine **19**
Davidson, John **24**

Doyle, Arthur Conan **7**
Frazer, J(ames) G(eorge) **32**
Lang, Andrew **16**
MacDonald, George **9**
Muir, Edwin **2, 87**
Sharp, William **39**
Tey, Josephine **14**

SLOVENIAN

Cankar, Ivan **105**

SOUTH AFRICAN

Bosman, Herman Charles **49**
Campbell, (Ignatius) Roy (Dunnachie) **5**
Mqhayi, S(amuel) E(dward) K(rune Loliwe) **25**
Plaatje, Sol(omon) T(shekisho) **73**
Schreiner, Olive (Emilie Albertina) **9**
Smith, Pauline (Urmson) **25**
Vilakazi, Benedict Wallet **37**

SPANISH

Alas (y Urena), Leopoldo (Enrique Garcia) **29**
Barea, Arturo **14**
Baroja (y Nessi), Pio **8**
Benavente (y Martinez), Jacinto **3**
Blasco Ibañez, Vicente **12**
Echegaray (y Eizaguirre), Jose (Maria Waldo) **4**
García Lorca, Federico **1, 7, 49**
Jiménez (Mantecón), Juan Ramo´ **4**
Machado (y Ruiz), Antonio **3**
Martinez Sierra, Gregorio **6**
Martinez Sierra, Maria (de la O'LeJarraga) **6**
Miro (Ferrer), Gabriel (Francisco Victor) **5**
Ortega y Gasset, Jose **9**
Pereda (y Sanchez de Porrua), Jose Maria de **16**
Pérez Galdós, Benito **27**
Ramoacn y Cajal, Santiago **93**

Salinas (y Serrano), Pedro **17**
Unamuno (y Jugo), Miguel de **2, 9**
Valera y Alcala-Galiano, Juan **10**
Valle-Inclán, Ramón (Maria) del **5**

SWEDISH

Bengtsson, Frans (Gunnar) **48**
Dagerman, Stig (Halvard) **17**
Ekelund, Vilhelm **75**
Heidenstam, (Carl Gustaf) Verner von **5**
Key, Ellen (Karolina Sofia) **65**
Lagerloef, Selma (Ottiliana Lovisa) **4, 36**
Söderberg, Hjalmar **39**
Strindberg, (Johan) August **1, 8, 21, 47**

SWISS

Ramuz, Charles-Ferdinand **33**
Rod, Edouard **52**
Saussure, Ferdinand de **49**
Spitteler, Carl (Friedrich Georg) **12**
Walser, Robert **18**

SYRIAN

Gibran, Kahlil **1, 9**

TURKISH

Sait Faik **23**

UKRAINIAN

Aleichem, Sholom **1, 35**
Bialik, Chaim Nachman **25**

URUGUAYAN

Quiroga, Horacio (Sylvestre) **20**
Sanchez, Florencio **37**

WELSH

Davies, William Henry **5**
Evans, Caradoc **85**
Lewis, Alun **3**
Thomas, Dylan (Marlais) **1, 8, 45, 105**

TCLC-111 Title Index

ISBN 0-7876-5227-X

90000

9 780787 652272